A History of American Life

REVISED AND ABRIDGED

General Editor
MARK C. CARNES

Consulting Editor
ARTHUR M. SCHLESINGER, JR.

Based on the Series Edited by
ARTHUR M. SCHLESINGER, SR.
DIXON RYAN FOX
CARL BECKER

SCRIBNER

SCRIBNER
1230 Avenue of the Americas
New York, NY 10020

SCRIBNER and design are
trademarks of Simon & Schuster Inc.

Manufactured in the United States of America

1   3   5   7   9   10   8   6   4   2

Library of Congress Cataloging-in-Publication Data is available.

ISBN 0-684-80723-8

This is an abridged version of Macmillan's classic thirteen
volume set, *A History of American Life,* published in 1948.

Contents

Introduction

I know histhry isn't thrue, Hinnissy, because it ain't like what I see ivry day in Halsted Sthreet. If any wan comes along with a histhry iv Greece or Rome that'll show me th' people fightin', gettin' dhrunk, gettin' married, owin' th' grocery man an' bein' without hard-coal, I'll believe they was a Greece or Rome, but not befure. . . . Histhry is a postmortem examination. It tells ye what a counthry died iv. But I'd like to know what it lived iv.[1]

—FINLEY PETER DUNNE, 1902

IT WAS IN MR. DOOLEY'S SPIRIT that Arthur M. Schlesinger and Dixon Ryan Fox decided in the early 1920s that the time had come for American historians to move beyond politics and war and produce a comprehensive *social* history of the American people. Schlesinger and Fox thereupon conceived and edited *A History of American Life,* published in thirteen volumes from 1927 to 1948. Half a century later, a splendid distillation by Mark C. Carnes makes this pioneer adventure in social history available to new generations of scholars, students, and general readers.

A myth has arisen among younger historians that social history is a daring invention of their own generation. Thus we read: "Before the 1960s, most historians focused on the thought and action of white male elites" (George M. Frederickson); and "The content of 'American history' broadened—in monographs in the 1970s and college textbooks by the mid-1980s—to include women, minorities, and working people" (David Thelen); and "The social history research of the past twenty years has lifted from obscurity the lives of those who had been swept to the sidelines in the metahistory of progress" (Joyce Appleby, Lynn Hunt, Margaret Jacob); and "In 1960 this encyclopedia would have been inconceivable" (the editors of the *Encyclopedia of American Social History*); and "Those of us fortunate enough to have practiced history during these decades have been free as never before to move into neighborhoods once blocked to scholars" (Lawrence W. Levine).[2]

It is true that contemporary social history is more systematic and quantitative in its approach than *A History of American Life,* more sophisticated in its use of statistics, more addicted to interdisciplinary jargon, more aggressive in its "from the bottom up" ideology, more euphoric in its claims; but its aspirations—and, as we shall see, its frustrations—are those of the older social history from which it has evolved.

For social history has been around for a long time. In the year 1900, Edward Eggleston, ex-minister, novelist *(The Hoosier Schoolmaster),* and cultural historian *(The Transit of Civilization from England to America in the Seventeenth Century),* delivered a presidential address to the American Historical Association under the truculent title "The New History." "Never was a falser thing said," Eggleston declared, "than that history is dead politics." History without "the people, their manners and customs" was "history hung in the air." Anticipating the year 2000, Eggleston predicted, "I do not say that drum and trumpet history will have gone out; but when the American Historical Association shall assemble in the closing week a hundred years hence, there will be, do not doubt it, gifted writers *of the history of the people.* ... We shall have the history of culture, the real history of men and women."[3]

The New History was one more by-product of the Progressive era. Even historians are prisoners of their own experience, and the history they write embodies the action and passion of their own times. The turn to social history was driven by such contemporaneous developments as the movement to give ordinary citizens a larger role in politics, the spread of social settlement houses and trade union halls, the expanding lives of women, the turmoil of the city, the assimilation of immigrants, the reverence for experts. Nineteen twelve, the year of Theodore Roosevelt's New Nationalism and of Woodrow Wilson's New Freedom, was also the year of James Harvey Robinson's *The New History.*

"History," Robinson began, "includes every trace and vestige of everything man has done or thought since he appeared on the earth. ... Its sources of information extend from the rude flint hatchets of Chelles to this morning's newspaper." To write the New History properly, he added, historians must draw on "the new allies of history"—anthropology, economics, sociology, political science, geography, psychology. All this struck foreigners as a peculiarly American project. "The New History, which comes to us from the United States of course," wrote Albert Mathiez, the Marxist historian of the French Revolution, "declares with pride that to attain its aims its followers must be at once economists, sociologists, philosophers and journalists; altogether omniscient, in short American."[4] Mathiez said this a long time before the 1960s, when a new American generation rediscovered social history and the interdisciplinary gospel.

My father was a natural for the New History. Born in 1888, son of a German Jewish father and an Austrian Catholic mother, raised in the German Reformed Church, he grew up in a small Ohio town that contained large and visible contingents of Germans, Irish, and blacks. Yet his school textbooks portrayed Great Britain as the one and only mother country. When he wondered about this, his father said, "Apparently the only Germans worth mentioning were the Hessians who had fought on the wrong side in the War for Independence."[5] At Ohio State University, where my father went in 1906, the emphasis was the same. American history was strictly Anglo-Saxon. History's domain was politics, war, and diplomacy.

After graduating from Ohio State in 1910, my father went on to Columbia in 1912 and was stirred both by the progressive political enthusiasms of the day and by the young Turks of academe—James Harvey Robinson, Charles A. Beard, James T. Shotwell, Edwin R. A. Seligman—and their New History.[6] In 1914 he married Elizabeth Bancroft, an ardent suffragette who raised his consciousness about the poor deal women received in the conventional histories. Appointed to the Ohio State faculty, he hoped to bring in the New History, but a traditionalist department made him wait seven years before letting him lecture on social history, and then only in summer school. When he moved on to the University of Iowa in 1919 as head of the history department, he could do as he wished, and he immediately introduced a course entitled "New Viewpoints in American History." In 1922 he turned "New Viewpoints" into a book and initiated a new course on the "Social and Cultural History of the United States"—the first such course to be given in any college or university.

New Viewpoints argued that history should be as inclusive as life itself and that American historians must at last recognize the historic function of peoples and forces they had long ignored—women; immigrants; the labor movement; geographic, economic, and humanitarian factors. Two further approaches to American history, Schlesinger noted in a foreword, were "certain to receive more careful attention in the future, that of religious and sectarian influences on American development, and the point of view represented by the psychoanalysts."[7] In later years, he wrote an influential essay on "A Critical Period in American Religion" as well as essays calling on historians to attend to science, technology, manners, voluntary associations, political mobs, even diet and prophecy.[8]

His advocacy of that half of the American people deleted from the conventional historical record resulted in the establishment at Radcliffe College of the Women's Archives, now the Arthur and Elizabeth Schlesinger Library on the History of Women in America. He edited those wonderfully suggestive writings on immigration left by his late friend Marcus Lee Hansen; and, while he wrote little himself about black and red Americans, he encouraged young black historians like John Hope Franklin and Alrutheus A. Taylor and served on the board of editors of the *Journal of Negro History* as well as on the Fund for the Republic's Commission on the Rights, Liberties and Responsibilities of the American Indian.

Social history, he wrote in a note I found in his papers after his death, assumes "that politics has seldom or for long been the major concern of society. Other goals—bread-winning, mating, personal immortality, self-improvement, the betterment of the community, the love of beauty—these and like interests have day in and day out absorbed man's energies and thought. An understanding of the molding forces should go far to answer the question: why we behave like Americans." But while he rejected the conception of history as *only* past politics, Schlesinger never for a moment succumbed to the opposite fallacy: the delusion that it is a virtue for history to neglect the state and public policy. Half the essays in *New Viewpoints* and in his 1949 collection *Paths to the Present* deal with political and constitutional issues.

His determination to recast the shape of American history led him in the spring of 1922 to raise with Allen S. Wilber and Richard R. Smith of Macmillan the idea of a cooperative history of the American people, each volume treating the interests and activities of the people not "separately and independently of one another but as an integral and integrated part" of American life. He proposed 1926, the sesquicentennial of American independence, as a target date and Max Farrand of Yale or W. E. Dodd of Chicago as editors. Macmillan favored Carl Becker of Cornell, who declined but agreed to become a consulting editor.

Macmillan then asked Schlesinger himself to edit the series with Dixon Ryan Fox of Columbia, an able historian (*The Decline of Aristocracy in the Politics of New York*) and a friend of Schlesinger's from graduate school, and the literary critic Carl Van Doren, also at Columbia. Van Doren turned out not to be available, nor was Stuart Pratt Sherman of the University of Illinois; so Ashley H. Thorndike of Columbia became literary adviser. The contract, signed on February 23, 1923, gave the editors $1,500 each for three years and a slice of the royalties. Each author was to be paid $1,000 in lieu of royalties. Lest this sound like slave labor, $1,000 in 1923 would be nearly $20,000 seventy years later.

"Fox and I in planning this work," Schlesinger later wrote, "aimed to free American history from its traditional servitude to party struggles, war and diplomacy and to show that it properly included all the varied interests of the people. Our theme was the growth of American civilization." They drafted guidelines for the authors. The series was to stress "the social, economic, intellectual and cultural development of the American people." "Civilization," the editors emphasized, covered not just the highest intellectual and spiritual achievement but also the interests and tastes of plain people. "The *Saturday Evening Post* has as real a place in this HISTORY as the *Atlantic Monthly,* 'rag time' as choral music, the chautauqua as the great university. . . . Our concerns are those of the common man, the things that touched his every-day life." American social and cultural history, they believed, fell into periods "at least as logical as those of American political and constitutional history. Each of these periods is conceived as possessing a central theme or motif."[9] The editors drew up detailed and rather imaginative checklists of topics to be covered in each volume.

By October 1923 they had recruited authors for the first eleven volumes. Five of the final fourteen authors (one volume had two) were born in the Midwest, four in the mid-Atlantic states, two in the South, and one each in New England, the mountain states, and Japan. At the time of writing, six lived in New York, four in the Midwest, two in New England, and one each in Virginia and California. All save three were of Anglo-Saxon or Scotch-Irish stock, thereby qualifying the proposition advanced in recent years that social history was the peculiar creation of children and grandchildren of immigrants.[10]

Most of the authors were so dilatory that the plan of bringing out the series in 1926 rapidly collapsed. Only James Truslow Adams, a practiced professional, handed in his manuscript in time for the sesquicentennial. The Adams volume was held over until three others could appear with it in 1927; a fifth came in 1929; five in the 1930s; three in the 1940s. Schlesinger and Fox used to marvel at Albert Bushnell Hart's editorial virtuosity in bringing out the twenty-seven volumes of the *American Nation* series in four years.

The series commanded immediate attention. Vernon L. Parrington, whose now forgotten *Main Currents of American Thought* had only recently electrified the younger generation of historians, wrote a front-page review of the first four volumes for the *New York Herald Tribune Books*. The series, Parrington said, demonstrates that "our historians have arrived at intellectual maturity and can view the American past with sober realistic vision." Traditionalists might find the selection of materials "strange if not wilful," but the business of the series was "not how men talked and voted in America, but how they lived and worked and played." While Parrington would have devoted more attention to ideas and to literature, he said that "the reader who does not feel his interest quicken as he turns over the deftly written pages is hard to please."[11]

The *New York Times Book Review* also gave the debut front-page treatment. These fresh young social historians, wrote Allen Sinclair Will, a professor of journalism, were setting the traditionalists aghast, and he couched part of his review as a colloquy between "traditional historian" and "social historian." "I abhor your ways. You are the bad boy of the profession," he had the traditionalist say to the upstart. "In this series," Will concluded, "the new social history of the American people ceases to be an experiment."[12]

The favorable reception was in great part a tribute to the hard work of the editors. Schlesinger and Fox were not only historiographical allies but close personal friends. "Probably no partnership ever worked more harmoniously," Schlesinger said later, though Fox, after he left Columbia in 1934 to become president of Union College, had less time for his editorial duties.

They were keen and conscientious editors, and their correspondence shows the time and care they expended in improving the manuscripts.[13]

Carl Becker read the manuscripts in the final editing stage, but his comments ordinarily dealt with literary form rather than historical substance. His attitude toward the series, Schlesinger later said, "was that of an interested if somewhat skeptical bystander," but he appreciated the labors of the editors.

> What the hell's the matter with American historians anyway? You select twelve of the best you can find who are willing to write short books on the subject they know most about; and it seems that two thirds of them don't know how to organize a book into parts, or parts into chapters, or chapters into paragraphs, or paragraphs into sentences. I should like to have the series published in a new edition. The only change would be in the title page, which would run as follows:

History of American Life
In twelve volumes
Ghosted by
Arthur M. Schlesinger
and
Dixon Ryan Fox
for
the following eminent American historians.[14]

Becker repeatedly and sensibly told Schlesinger and Fox that they should be writing their own books instead of investing time and energy rewriting other people's books. "I swear, my dear Arthur," he wrote Schlesinger in 1943, "if you don't from now on become entirely selfish (professionally) and devote yourself and your talents to the writing of the three or four books which you might have written if you hadn't spent the time correcting other people's grammar and literary construction—why I will condemn you to the lowest depths of hell." My father evidently agreed, for he used to warn me in somber terms against ever assuming any large-scale editorial responsibility.

The editors did indeed have to spend an inordinate amount of time editing. Thus they found Herbert I. Priestley's first draft for *The Coming of the White Man, 1492–1848* "so bombastic, Hegelian, awkward, and in some places trite" (Fox) that they decided to make it easy for the author to withdraw from the series. A typical Priestley sentence went: "Reading was the predilection of an infinitesimal proportion of the population." Schlesinger changed it to: "Few people read books." Priestley took the editorial strictures to heart, and the second draft struck Fox as "an almost entirely new work."

Critics praised the book for its emphasis on Spanish, Dutch, French, and

Swedish colonization as against, in the words of the *Times* reviewer, "the lordly Anglo-Saxon. The Anglo-Saxon does not [even] figure in the beginning chapters." [15]

Volume II, Thomas J. Wertenbaker's *The First Americans, 1607-90,* was another initial disappointment. "Hastily thrown together and ill-digested," Schlesinger said. Fox added, "His facility for misquotation amounts to genius. . . . Think what it would have been if his first draft had gone to the printer!" But both editors labored hard. "Between us," Fox said, "we have done repair work on twenty or twenty-five percent of the book. There is nothing *shameful* about it [now], and some people may like it."

Many did. The historian Ralph H. Gabriel praised it in the *American Historical Review* as "a highly useful study full of new points of view and fresh interpretation. His simple and restrained style has a distinct charm." [16] The polymathic sociologist Harry Elmer Barnes in the *New Republic* commended "the forceful portrayal of American origins against the European background." [17]

Volume III, James Truslow Adams's *Provincial Society, 1690-1763,* came as a great relief. Adams, a stockbroker turned gentleman historian, was a skilled and fluent writer. "I think," Fox wrote, "he has set a standard which we will find it very difficult to live up to in the other volumes." Schlesinger heartily concurred. But Adams disdained footnotes, and in the end the editors had to supply them. "You must excuse him," Becker sarcastically wrote Fox. "He has to write for money, and can't be bothered with footnotes." [18]

Critics were full of praise. Claude Bowers was typical in saying *Provincial Society* was "written with the charm with which Mr. Adams imbues all he touches, with the firm grasp and comprehension of realities that have made him one of the most brilliant and authoritative of American historians." [19]

Volume IV, Evarts B. Greene's *The Revolutionary Generation, 1763-90* was not published till 1943. Both Becker and Samuel Eliot Morison had declined to do this volume, and Clarence W. Alvord, after agreeing, begged off on the plea of ill health. The assignment then fell to Greene. "The reason this volume took so long to complete," Schlesinger recalled, "probably lies in the realm of psychology." When after many years Greene submitted a draft, it was far too long and required, Schlesinger said, "a major surgical operation" to bring it down to the series size. Moreover, the style was "wooden," the narrative "strangely static," and Schlesinger in the end went through it line by line, "tightening the narrative, changing passive sentences to active ones, eliminating repetitive words." He wondered how Greene would take the alterations, but Fox assured him that Greene's "principal concern was to avoid having to go into re-writing himself."

Despite these editorial tribulations, the book did fairly well with the critics. "Greene has unearthed a large amount of new material," the historian Carl Bridenbaugh wrote in the *New York Times Book Review,* "and skillfully fused it with known facts to produce an interesting and informing record."[20]

Volume V, *The Completion of Independence, 1790–1830* was Fox's own, but his new duties at Union College held up his writing. So deeply involved was he both intellectually and emotionally in the series that, as Schlesinger recalled, he was "loath to admit to himself or to me that he would be unable to turn out the book within a reasonable period of time." Finally Fox decided that he would have to take on a collaborator and passed on five chapters in rough draft, four articles, and a stack of fairly indecipherable notes to John A. Krout of Columbia. Krout did such a good job that Schlesinger thought it "one of the best volumes in the series" and Fox confessed to the fear that "I am sailing under false colors in having my name on the back at all." The manuscript was too long, but Krout said of Schlesinger's editing, "You did a great deal more than merely cut down the length, and I appreciate it."

The reviews were admiring. "Not only do the authors analyze with apt and telling phrase the ferment of these forty American years," Bridenbaugh wrote for the *New York Times,* "they also clearly show that notwithstanding some remarkable achievements a truly national culture was still largely an aspiration in the rural Republic of 1830."[21]

Volume VI, Carl Russell Fish's *The Rise of the Common Man, 1830–50,* was the single case in which the editors encountered a refractory author. After reading the first draft, Schlesinger sent Fish a courteous but cogent and detailed critique, to which Fish replied testily that if the letter "is to be taken seriously, you must count my volume out of the series. I am too busy to rewrite it." He was prevailed upon to try again, but the second draft was only a marginal improvement. "He seems utterly irresponsible," Schlesinger told Fox, "as regards dates and other specific data." Fish filed another angry objection to "editorial tinkering," but the editors tinkered nevertheless, and, following Ashley Thorndike's sage advice, sent Fish not the corrected typescript but a clean copy of the edited manuscript—which the author at once accepted as his own.

Again, despite the editorial tribulations, the book impressed the reviewers. "An interesting and valuable piece of work," C. S. Boucher said in the *American Historical Review,*[22] and N. W. Stephenson commended Fish as "a severely analytical historian" in the *Political Science Quarterly.*[23]

Volume VII, Arthur C. Cole's *The Irrepressible Conflict, 1850–65,* was another headache. The editors encouraged him to "bring out more sharply the author's basic point of view, namely, that the Civil War was a product of a contest between antagonistic civilizations"—a point they specifically made because they doubted whether Cole had any clear-cut interpretation at all. "After working steadily for two months [on a second draft]," Schlesinger wrote, ". . . by dint of editorial effort we may be able to turn a fourth-rate piece of work into a second-rate one." Carl Becker said, "With your improvements, I think the MS. is about as good as many of the others."

Avery Craven, a revisionist committed to the theory of the Civil War as needless, denounced the book in the *American Historical Review* for missing most of the significant things in the abolition movement and for leaving "as uncertain as before the 'irrepressible' character of the War between the States." [24] But Bessie L. Pierce in the *American Journal of Sociology* thought the book "fully measures up to the high standard set by other published volumes of this series," [25] and William MacDonald in the *New York Times Book Review* found Cole's outlines clear, his material kept firmly in hand, and the book "as readable as it is instructive." [26]

Volume VIII, Allan Nevins's *The Emergence of Modern America, 1865–78*, was another relief. Nevins, an editorial writer for the *New York World*, was then in transit to a distinguished and productive academic career. The editors were delighted by his first draft. Fox called it "fair, objective, comprehensive in treatment and vivid in style," and Schlesinger praised Nevins's "firm grasp upon the essentials of the social and intellectual life of the period." The only problem was length, but Nevins, a professional, cheerfully cut 45,000 words and granted Schlesinger "absolute authority" to cut 60,000 more and bring it down to the required length. Nevins said, "I am very grateful for what you have done." As Fox commented, "What a gentlemanly letter!"

The reviewers swelled the chorus of praise. "A fascinating story," said Parrington,[27] "masterly . . . incomparable description and analysis," said Harry Elmer Barnes,[28] and Ralph E. Turner wrote in the *American Historical Review,* "In recent biographies the great men have been brought down from the heavens to walk upon the earth. In this book the common men rise from the dust to walk with them. That vacuum . . . is for one period in American history at last filled." [29]

Volume IX, Ida Tarbell's *The Nationalizing of Business, 1878–98* gave the editors particular trouble. The veteran journalist was sixty-six when she signed the contract and nearly seventy-nine when the book was published. Her first draft, Schlesinger observed, was "based upon a minimum of research, loosely and sometimes notionally organized, and rather amateurishly written. . . . I have done some checking of quotations, with somewhat discouraging results." Fox replied, "Very seldom did I find a sentence that I enjoyed reading." The comments, passed on to Tarbell in gentler form, resulted in another draft, which Schlesinger spent nearly four months putting into shape. Fox wrote his coeditor, "I have read your book with admiring attention. Here and there I notice that you have made use of some rough notes furnished by Miss Ida M. Tarbell, the well-known journalist." Tarbell professed herself "very much pleased with the editorial work."

Reviews were mixed. The historian Harry J. Carman wrote in *Social Education* that the book, while not outstanding compared to others in the series, was still "a very commendable piece of work" marked by "ripeness of judgment and a soundness of interpretation."[30] Henry David was less enthusiastic in the *Nation.* "The volume is smoothly written," he said. "Beyond that it has no major virtue, and it is no distinction for the 'A history of American Life' series to have Miss Tarbell's work in it." It sold the least well of any volume in the series.

Volume X, Schlesinger's *The Rise of the City, 1878-98,* set forth an urban interpretation of American development designed to supplement Frederick Jackson Turner's frontier interpretation. The book's theme, as Fox wrote in the foreword, was "the new social force which waxed and throve while driving the pioneer culture before it: the city" or, as Schlesinger put in the text, "the clash between the two cultures: one static, individualistic, agricultural, the other dynamic, collectivistic, urban."[31]

Felix Frankfurter in the *Herald Tribune* and Bernard DeVoto in the *Saturday Review of Literature* hailed the book. But, oddly, since no other volume in the series was so clearly dedicated to a thesis, some reviewers, while praising the book's style and organization, deplored its absence of a guiding philosophy.

Louis M. Hacker, then in his Marxist phase, after noting in the *Nation* that Schlesinger had "retrieved this whole generation from obscurity" and after calling the book "the best example of that [social history] technique thus far afforded us," went on to regret the "monotonous cataloguing of men and events with no effort to point up the significant and dismiss the trivial."[32] Henry Steele Commager was similarly qualified in the *New Republic:* "We cannot admire too much the accuracy, the scholarship, the thoroughness, the catholicity, the impartiality, of Mr. Schlesinger's essay in the new history, but like the life which it describes, it is overwhelming, and demands a philosophy."[33]

Most dismaying of all was the notice in the *American Historical Review* by Schlesinger's old teacher Charles A. Beard. After agreeable words about coverage and presentation, Beard wrote, "Whether this movement and uproar meant anything then or means anything now, whether it had any center of gravity or was merely chaos floating in chaos, whether it had any direction, Professor Schlesinger does not venture to say. . . . Apparently he thinks interpretations are wrong, that none is possible, and that impressionistic eclecticism is the only resort of contemporary scholarship."[34]

It all depends on what one means by interpretation. Sixty years later, in a reevaluation for *Reviews in American History,* Terrence J. McDonald argued that *The Rise of the City* not only showed "breadth of concern, sparkling wit, and prodigious research" but also presented "a theoretical framework that left a lasting impression on the historians of his generation."[35] Why, then, the Beard critique?

The Rise of the City, McDonald perceptively observed, had the bad luck to come out in the depths of the Great Depression. In the despair of 1933, critics evidently felt that historians owed the republic something more than an interpretation of the past—more than a mere demonstration that, fifty years earlier, the retreat of rural and agricultural America before urban and industrial America had changed the character of American life. "What some reviewers wanted by way of 'interpretation,' " McDonald surmised, "was more recognition on Schlesinger's part of the deadly parallels between the 1890s and the 1930s."[36] They wanted to know what consolation, what counsel, historians had to give the desperate present about the darkening future.

Beard in particular was in the throes of his murky struggle with the philosophy of history—the struggle that later in the year produced his famous presidential address to the American Historical Association "Written History as an Act of Faith." "Does the world move," Beard wanted to know, "and, if so, in what direction? . . . Does it move backward toward some old arrangement, let us say, of 1928, 1896, 1815, 1789, or 1295? Or does it move forward to some other arrangement which can only be dimly divined —a capitalistic dictatorship, a proletarian dictatorship, or a collectivist democracy? The last of these is my own guess."[37] He had condemned Schlesinger for failing in *The Rise of the City* to offer his guess about these Toynbee-esque riddles.

If Beard really regarded the book as "impressionistic eclecticism," Schlesinger wrote his old teacher, "I have not made clear to the most acute historical mind in America what I am about." Beard replied that he meant nothing invidious by the phrase; "for all I know it may be all that anybody can do in history." As for Schlesinger's social history, "I do not deny its utility or its interest, but I doubt whether it is really illuminating contemporary thought. . . . I do not want the historian to turn moralist and pontificate, but I want him to recognize that at bottom he believes the world is going around in a meaningless circle or is moving toward good or evil." Schlesinger rejected Beard's thesis that historians should let their guesses about the future determine their interpretation of the past. He wrote Beard, "I do not propose consciously to be concerned with whether the 'damned human race' is growing worse or better." The exchange concluded with warm assurances of mutual regard.[38] Most historians today, I suspect, would agree with Schlesinger.

Volume XI, *The Quest for Social Justice, 1898–1914,* had given the editors a hard time. After Walter Lippmann declined, Harry Elmer Barnes agreed to take it on but then became so involved in impassioned controversy over the origins of World War I that he gave way to Harold U. Faulkner. Again there was a disappointing first draft, and again the editors did not pull their punches. Fox told Faulkner that his style was "highly mechanical and lacking in color and interest," and Schlesinger told him that he had "not done justice to the infinite variety of this continent-spanning nation in which we live" and that his narrative lacked "enlightening generalization." Faulkner swallowed, revised, and later wrote Schlesinger, "I have never experienced more thorough and helpful editing than that which you and Fox supplied. Without it the 'Quest for Social Justice' would have been pretty sad."

John D. Hicks in the *American Historical Review* thought the result achieved "a degree of unity that is really remarkable" and contributes to "the clarification of an exceedingly complex period."[39] and Avery Craven called it "an excellent guide to balance the usual political history of the period."[40]

Volume XII, *The Great Crusade and After, 1914–28* involved another search for authors. After Van Doren, Beard, Becker, Herbert Croly, Charles E. Merriam, Stuart P. Sherman, Ray Stannard Baker, and others turned it down, Preston W. Slosson of the University of Michigan accepted the assignment. His first draft was intelligent but sketchy, and the editors called for a rewrite. Slosson replied, "I thought you wanted a sort of 'consomme,' a light, running discussion-narrative without footnotes. Instead I see it is to be a vegetable soup with lots of onions, carrot, peas, etc. in the form of references, instances and the like." Schlesinger felt that the rewrite lacked "the champagne sparkle of the earlier version," but the result, he decided, was "as good a volume as we had any right to hope for."

"Always interesting, always serio-comic," said Avery Craven in the *Herald Tribune*,[41] and Allan Nevins in the *Saturday Review of Literature* found the book "well worth reading and study."[42] But William MacDonald in the *New York Times* thought that, as an interpretation of American life in a momentous period, "it would have been still better if it had been cast in a broader form."[43]

This completed *A History of American Life* (although a supplement covering the New Deal years appeared later) and commentators noted how it had legitimized social history as a field. When Macmillan in 1944 asked the editors about the impact of the series, Schlesinger replied, "A glance at the annual list of doctoral dissertations shows the extent to which cultural themes have now come to occupy the attention of the rising generation of historians. Courses in social and intellectual history have also multiplied in the colleges and universities."[44] Sales figures as of 1956 reported over 5,000 sets and over 90,000 separate volumes—a total of 150,778 volumes sold. The top three sellers were Wecter, Nevins, and Fish. By the mid-century, social history and its offshoots—intellectual history, women's history, labor history, urban history, ethnic history, the history of immigration, the history of science, legal history—were becoming routine in academic curricula; and political and diplomatic history was increasingly presented as expressions of social, economic, psychological, and ideological forces.

The contrast between Allen Sinclair Will's review of the first four volumes on the front page of the *New York Times Book Review* in January 1928 and Carl Bridenbaugh's review of the whole series in the same place in January 1945 illustrates the rise of social history to academic respectability. Will had described social history as a scholarly heresy rejected by traditional historians. Bridenbaugh now wrote, "So secure is the position of social history today that it may seem strange that even historians once met the new history with scorn. . . . Those who came to scoff were soon won over and remained to praise and borrow. Much of the renewed interest in the American past today is directly traceable to the 'History of American Life.' "[45]

Yet from an early point doubts had been raised about the capacity of the kind of social history presented in *A History of American Life* to produce an integrated synthesis. Carl Becker, for all his collaboration with the series and his affection for the editors, wrote Schlesinger, "I have never made any secret of my lack of enthusiasm for the kind of thing these books attempt to do, and do, on the whole, as well as it is likely to be done." Becker's own great skill lay in the brilliant illumination of climates of opinion over longish periods, and he questioned "the possibility of any genuine 'synthesis' with such short chronological limits" as the series provided. An extraordinary historian like Burckhart, Becker wrote, could organize an era like the Italian Renaissance in terms of a few coordinated ideas; "but in a cooperative work like ours it can't be done," especially when each period is so "brief and abruptly truncated."[46]

The problem of synthesis nagged at the editors. "Critics of social history," they wrote in the foreword of Adams's *Provincial Society,* the first manuscript they had received, "complain that too often it presents vast collections of facts, picturesque and entertaining in themselves, but discrete, unrelated and ungeneralized into any service to the great biography of man, or, at the other extreme, a speculative, theorized 'interpretation,' so thinly stocked with evidence as to make doubtful its claim to the name of history at all." Adams, they not surprisingly claimed, had surmounted these extremes, deriving from a "richly furnished narrative" generalizations valuable "not only to students of American history but to those concerned with society as a whole."

But had the series, for all its richness of detail, really achieved this balance between fact and generalization? Had it developed a larger conception of social history? Where were the underlying structures and the deeper dynamics of social change? Where was the analytic synthesis?

In 1936 the American Historical Association devoted a session at the annual convention to a critical appraisal of the series, producing a spirited discussion later reproduced in W. E. Lingelbach's *Approaches to American Social History.* Roy F. Nichols, presenting the viewpoint of a political historian, agreed that the social context had been too often a missing dimension in political analysis but concluded that the series had "a grand sweep and a certain incoherence." It lacked, he thought, a great synthetic principle. John A. Krout as a social historian admired the density of description but also wished, this time in Beardian accents, for more in the way of synthesis. "Will further studies of this general type, if there is more daring in the search for a dynamic principle, finally reveal to us the direction in which we have been travelling?"

Bernard DeVoto as a student of literature praised the series as "not only the best history of America ever published but so far superior to all other general histories that, with them, American history is acceptably written for the first time. . . . The *History of American Life* serves the literary historian by giving him a more complexly integrated and therefore more usable account of America than history has ever given him before." But in a still valuable analysis of the uses of literature for history, DeVoto argued that the series relied too much on popular literature, on literature that is explicitly sociological, and failed to understand how serious literature illuminates the inward life of society. Historians can still benefit from DeVoto's strictures.

Schlesinger responded in "An Editor's Second Thoughts." "It was an ambitious venture," he remarked, "and, in many respects, a pioneer venture. With so much basic research yet to be done, the task was somewhat like trying to write the story of Columbus while he was still sailing westward." As for the search for a synthetic principle, "It is true that the series offers no metaphysical explanation of the evolution of American civilization." But given the present state of knowledge, he continued, such a principle might divert future scholarship from areas of investigation lying outside the confines established by the interpretation. The fashion of the day would be to entrust the quest to a team of historians, psychologists, sociologists, philosophers, religionists, funded by a foundation and assisted by a research staff. Schlesinger doubted that such an approach would yield a coherent, realistic view of our social evolution. "Should the happy time come when their collective wisdom is fused in the intellect of a single person, then perhaps an adequate philosophy of American history will be within reach." [47]

As the old social history had reflected the action and passion of the Progressive era, so a "new" social history emerged in response to the turbulence of the 1960s. Fueled by the raw emotions of a violent decade, energized by the women's rights movement, by the civil rights crusade, by the plight of ethnic and racial minorities, by the protests against a futile and murderous war in Vietnam, excited by the pretensions of the "behavioral sciences" and by the wondrous potentialities of the computer, a militant generation of new social historians now appeared. If the New History of the Progressive era had been essentially the work of liberals, the New History of the 1970s and 1980s was largely the work of radicals spawned by the New Left of the 1960s.

New History II came on with a confident roar about its own historical omnicompetence. Its practitioners saw themselves as both morally righteous and methodologically sophisticated. Unlike bland New History I, they were prepared to tackle the dangerous questions of power, hegemony, race, ethnicity, gender, and class; and in doing so they would draw —for the first time, some among them implied—on the conceptual armory of the social sciences. One finds the erudite literary critic George Steiner reversing Albert Mathiez's comment on the American origins of New History I: "Following the example set by the *Annales* school of 'historians of mentality' in France, the 'new historian' will enlist anthropology, sociology, economics, social psychology . . . in his explorations of the inner anatomy of a past society." [48]

For a season, New History II swept all before it. By Robert Darnton's calculation, the percentage of doctoral dissertations in social history quadrupled between 1958 and 1978.[49] Peter Stearns, editor of the *Journal of Social History*, reported in 1989 that more than a third of all research historians in the United States styled themselves social historians.[50] Intellectual historians in particular felt themselves outclassed, outgunned, and beleaguered in face of the new revelation.[51]

For the New Left of the 1960s, liberals rather than conservatives were the mortal enemy, and the militants of New History II naturally regarded New History I and the pathbreaking work of *A History of American Life* with scorn. Richard Hofstadter, though not at all of this group, summed up the general indictment by calling the series "a still-birth," an attempt "to write a kind of sociological history without having any sociological ideas," covering sociological topics—marriage and the family, religious and social institutions, education, urbanization, and so on—but lacking "a firm conceptual framework upon which to order the whole."[52] "For most social historians trained in the 1970s," Terrence McDonald writes, "an assignment to read a volume of the History of American Life series then was likely to be regarded either as an insult or a joke."[53]

But in time questions arose about New History II as they had about New History I—in fact, exactly the same question. How well did New History II meet the Hofstadter criteria? Where were the large conceptions, the deep structures, the firm conceptual framework, the analytic synthesis? Soon some of the best practitioners of New History II began to charge it with the same faults they had previously charged to New History I.

The new social history, in the words of Peter Stearns, is characterized by "the centrifugal tendencies of social history itself, as it splinters into hosts of difficult-to-relate subjects."[54] Thomas Bender blames "an extreme specialization that has worked mightily against the larger, synthetic view."[55] So, too, Samuel P. Hays: "This indeterminate quality of social history renders it amorphous, undefined, and often incoherent. . . . Social history has failed to develop its promise of bringing order into the subject matter of history as a whole."[56] And David Cannadine: "Social history is in real danger of imminent and unrestrainable fragmentation. . . . The real problem . . . is that it lacks a hard intellectual centre."[57] And Lawrence Veysey: "A curious aspect of the 'new' social history is that it is almost never pursued as such. . . . *The* society, in its overall dimensions as an evolving structure, is hardly ever studied."[58] And Alice Kessler-Harris: "The subject matter carried with it waves of exciting new knowledge, but coherence, purpose, and direction all floundered in the churning waters," with critics deriding "its indifference to theory."[59] In 1985, Olivier Zunz, seeing social history as marked by "fragmentation and a diminished focus," mobilized five social historians to come up with an interpretive consensus on what the new social history is. The responses only compounded the confusion.[60]

In short, New History II, for all its improved analytical weapons, its computer-driven statistics, its diligence in research, its ingenuity in the definition of topics, its pretentious technical vocabulary, and its righteous moral fervor, has been hardly more successful than *A History of American Life* in finding the philosopher's stone that will transmute a chaos of disparate social data into an interlocked structural analysis and a coherent whole. The dream of integrated social history remains a dream, still a faint glimmer in the far distance; most probably, a will-o'-the-wisp. History in all its forms will very likely be forever defiantly pluralistic because life is defiantly pluralistic. Maybe Beard was right in suggesting that "eclectic impressionism" is all that anybody can do in history.

A History of American Life can hardly be blamed too much for having failed to do what later social historians, benefiting from its mistakes, have also failed to do. This pioneer venture, especially as shorn by Mark C. Carnes in this edition of misjudgments and longueurs, must be seen as a milestone in the road toward a better knowledge of our past—and of ourselves. Here you will find a still rich and absorbing portrait of the national experience, a vivid first take on the still compelling problem: How transplanted and diverse peoples seeking in a strange world to achieve a fuller, freer and better life collectively shaped a new society; why, in short, certain human beings come to behave like Americans.

ARTHUR M. SCHLESINGER, JR.

Note by the General Editor

Becoming acquainted with the thirteen volumes of the *History of American Life* has been a pleasure—and an education. The writing was fixed at so high a pitch that to sustain it throughout a single volume nowadays would be noteworthy, and throughout a multiauthored collection virtually unimaginable. Nearly every page contains absorbing revelations, compelling descriptions, and arresting quotations. The *History of American Life* was—is, indisputably—a treasure, and historians, always a piratical breed, have plundered it incessantly, often maintaining a prudent vow of silence as to the provenance of the spoils.

I am delighted to share with general readers the riches of these twelve books, and to do so within the rather distant covers of a single volume. I have necessarily cut slightly more than half the original words and proportionately as many pictures. General editors Schlesinger (senior) and Fox had sought to show what people "lived iv," (in the words of F. P. Dunne's "Mr. Dooley"), but nearly every volume contained substantial sections on political and even diplomatic history. I have greatly trimmed most of these, as well as narrative sections on business and labor union history. Wayward flights of fancy were remorselessly shot down, and tangential points promptly circumscribed. I mostly refrained, however, from making cuts within paragraphs and have nearly always retained the evidence on which assertions were based. I reduced the number and range of observations but not the ways in which they were proven and developed.

Sometimes, to retain a smooth flow of words and ideas, I have been obliged to write transitional phrases or sentences; my own views, I hope, have not intruded inadvertently. On the other hand, I have intentionally deleted some language, usually in reference to Native Americans or African Americans, that however common in progressive circles in the 1920s and 1930s would now offend. The original volumes are available in nearly every major university library; scholars of American historiography must consult them rather than the present revision.

In 1976, whem I embarked on a doctoral program at Columbia University, formerly the citadel of progressive history, the *History of American Life* formed no part of my graduate training. The "new social historians" to whom I was drawn usually dismissed the series as mere description, unimproved by the exciting new tools of the social sciences. But the volumes warrant reconsideration. I think it clear that beyond the usual theses found in any work of history, the *History of American Life* possessed an entire deep structure of historical consciousness, embedded in its choice of subject, evidence, metaphor, and rhetorical strategy. The critics of the

History of American Life, themselves a product of the progressive consciousness the series sought to promote, were thus blind to its workings and imagined it had none. My bibliographical essay at the end of this volume further suggests that historian combatants have recently reoccupied, often unknowingly, many of the redoubts and fortresses that had been erected a half-century ago by the *History of American Life* authors.

Perhaps, as Freud suggested, no generation can rest assured of its sense of self until its progenitors have been buried. But we deceive ourselves by forgetting our origins. Thus, as we survey with satisfaction the many and vast realms of contemporary social history, we would do well to remember and perhaps even to celebrate the pioneering efforts of the *History of American Life* authors, who blazed a trail through thickets of professional prejudice and pointed with absolute conviction to a dazzling panorama in the distance.

Mark C. Carnes
Professor of History
Barnard College, Columbia University

A History
of American
Life

BOOK I

The Coming of the White Man,

1492–1848

THE WESTWARD IMPULSE

IT IS OF PRIME SIGNIFICANCE for the life of America today that the first white men to settle on these western shores were Spaniards and Roman Catholics, representatives of a powerful nation that was the citadel of a united faith. If men from northern Europe had been the first to arrive in America during the Reformation and had discovered the wealth of Montezuma and Atahualpa, the direction of modern history would have been so different from what it has been that the imagination finds no halting place in its contemplation of the possibilities. Happily, it is not the task of the historian to speculate upon these. We shall do well if we seize upon a few of the significant phases of the great Spanish occupation. Almost within a half-century a motley group of men created an empire which strained the resources of the fatherland to organize and govern. Yet precarious as it seemed at first, the civilization which they planted has persisted in full vigor; nearly all the nations south of the United States still retain the language, the customs, and the institutions transmitted from Catholic Spain.

It has often been said that the national development of Spain had brought her, by 1492, to a state of preparedness for expansion. But at the moment of the discovery Spain lacked many of the traditional characteristics of nationality, such as a common tongue, a literature of commanding importance, a unified territory, a common religion, or a social ideal. Nor did she have a military or a naval establishment equal to the strain of overseas adventure.

The general aversion of the Spaniard for the sea was expressed in the popular *refrán* which the Reverend Father Antonio de Guevara, writing in the sixteenth century, used as a text for his *El Arte del Marear*, a proverb which might be freely rendered "Let God give a life on the galleys to him who knows no better." The Mediterranean galleys may have had special terrors of their own, but they could scarcely have been more formidable than those the rolling sea had in store for the transatlantic voyager. Conveniences there were none; the food was unspeakably bad; crews were of the lowest social type; and their skill and devotion to duty seldom impressed the passenger. Eugenio del Salazar, who went from Tenerife to La Española in 1573 as judge of the *audiencia*, wrote letters to his friends vividly describing a sea voyage.

He, his wife, and his children were crowded into a low-ceiled cabin five feet square where, in the midst of their suffering (for no one paid them the slightest attention during their days of seasickness), they could hear the ship's page outside doing official devotions: "Amen; God give us good day; a happy voyage; may the ship make a good passage, sir captain, master, and goodly company. Amen. May it make a good voyage, indeed. God give your lordships good day, my lords, from stern to prow." In the semidarkness inside they could feel swarms of cockroaches and could hear droves of rats ceaselessly active. When the good judge staggered to the deck he could see the "castle" at the prow and the alcazar, or quarterdeck, at the stern, so feebly supported that it seemed likely to be caught up by the next breeze. Between were the artillery, the tables for the attending garrison, and one or two pumps, the water from which made little appeal to tongue or palate —"foaming like hell and stinking like the devil." Above the filthy deck stretched the shrouds endlessly intricate, so that the people below felt like fowls in a coop. When at evening the page sang out: *"Tabla puesta, vianda presta.* Long live the king of Castile on land and sea," the dirty sailors cried amen and scampered to their seats on the floor beside the evil-smelling food. The upper officers dined apart, and also the passengers, who prepared their meals at the same time as the others, else they found a cold stove.[1] It was a sharply graded little society: the pilot in charge of navigation, the captain of defense, the *maestre* of the treasure, the *contramaestre* of stowing the cargo, the barber-leech, the guard whose honesty might be doubted, the caulker, the engineer, and then the sailors—the *chusma*, with its peculiar jargon—waited on by the cabin boys.

Spanish maritime officers were of as fine material and possessed as excellent esprit as those of any rival maritime establishment. In leadership and seamanship, captains like Pedro Fernández de Quirós in the South Seas or Estevan Martínez in the North Pacific have had few superiors in the annals of ocean discovery. The common sailors who went with Columbus were largely of the seafaring type, and not taken from the jails as Columbus had intended before the Pinzón brothers came to his aid.[2] Among the seventy-one names preserved of the ninety who went, one was that of an Irishman, one of an Englishman, one of a Jew, several were Basques, and at least one third were from the interior of Castile; the last were probably not of the seafaring proletariat. It was of course difficult for Spain to maintain the secrecy—heritage of medievalism—with which she tried to surround the discoveries, simply because this *chusma* was international in composition. Despite prohibitions against Lutherans, Moors, Jews, and "New Christians"—in fact, against foreigners in general—as the conquest advanced it was inevitable that some of these world wanderers should find their way into the new Indies as settlers. One Scotchman, Tomás Blaque, for instance, was with Coronado in New Mexico, though whether he was Black or Blackie it is too late to determine.

But it would be far from the truth to think that all the Spanish settlers were sea rovers or the offscourings of society. In the beginning of the colonial enterprise on La Española, when Columbus was in Burgos in 1496, he asked for a number of salaried artisans and farmers and they were given to him. The colonial administration more than once made special arrangements to permit artisans of Catholic faith, even from other nations, to have a home and an opportunity in the New World kingdoms. In the first instance, that of Columbus, criminals not heretics were allowed to expiate their offenses by emigrating to Isabela in La Española. Murderers, smugglers of coin, and those guilty of lèse-majesté were allowed to go at their own expense. The death penalty was to be commuted to two years in Isabela and lesser penalties to one year's service, after which the beneficiaries could return free to Castile.[3]

How numerous or how satisfactory these contingents proved we have little means of knowing; certainly the paid colonists proved unworthy of their hire, for they assisted the rebel alcalde Roldán in his mutinous disturbances against Columbus, and after a brief trial their use was discontinued. Troops of more highly born adventurers who belonged to the entrepreneur class—men of the nobility and warriors released from the Italian and other campaigns—helped to make the Spanish settlements heterogeneous, even fairly international in character; the "common man" as distinguished from the conquistador, of whom we shall hear more, came also, and a sprinkling of the lowest types.

It must be remembered that the driving force of Spain was at the same time going forward in South America and in the Philippines. The North American area used less than half the effort expended; yet even here it was surprisingly large in contrast with the French and English growth during the next cycle. This enormous expansion is explained by the wide distribution of silver mines, the aridity of many areas which made them useless for farming, and by the eagerness of the missionaries for souls to save. The manpower was meager. The entire Spanish possessions in both Americas in the last quarter of the sixteenth century contained not more than 160,000 heads of families in some 200 towns, and in many cases these heads of families (vecinos) were spouses of Indian women. Only about 4,000 of them were encomenderos (feudal lords of estates worked by Indians in practical serfdom)—that is, men of the entrepreneur type. The remainder were small settlers, miners, traders, clericals, and soldiers. It is safe to say that the Spanish achievement in North America during the Great Century of the Conquest was brought about by an active group never numbering more than 75,000 or 80,000, less than 2,000 of whom possessed qualities of leadership.[4]

The sober judgment and idea of permanency with which this great occupation was effected are evidenced by the thoroughness with which the material elements of European life were introduced. These Spanish conquerors are often pictured bloodstained, sword in hand, bent on looting the new country they had entered. We overlook the tools, the plants and seeds, the livestock they carried, and their homelier achievement of establishing the fundamental arts.[5] The important European plants first disseminated throughout Spanish America make a long list. They included wheat, barley, rice, rye, beans (though there were American varieties of these), chickpeas, and lentils. The Spaniards also introduced almonds, mulberries, cherries, walnuts, chestnuts, medlars, tulip trees, linen, flax, alfalfa, alpiste or canary seed, quinces, apples, apricots, and most of the other pitted fruits (certain plums were already here), oranges, limes, lemons, citron trees, cedars, pears, rosemary, willows, broom, roses, lilies, and a multitude of the old-fashioned flowers. From Africa they brought, by way of the Azores or Andalusia, the sugar cane and certain varieties of bananas, and from Asia the cañafistula or Cassia fistularis, tamarinds, the huge orangelike lukban or dry grapefruit of the Philippines and the delectable mango. Virtually all of these transmissions occurred during the sixteenth or Great Century of the Conquest.[6]

In the seventeen ships with which Columbus sailed on his second voyage were many seeds and animals as well as agricultural workers. At old Isabela in La Española, Peter Martyr said, the truck gardens produced vegetables in from sixteen to thirty-six days after planting. Ojeda and Nicuesa took seeds to the mainland in 1509. Cortés reported to the emperor that Spanish plants were bearing well in New Spain and requested that no future ship come without plants and seeds. The most difficult transplantation was that of wheat. The elder Columbus brought some and Diego, when he came as governor, was ordered to try out 200 bushels of wheat seed, but it spoiled on the voyage. "Three months' wheat" was tried in 1511, but probably failed; more was sent three years later, this time to Castilla del Oro in Central America, and again in 1520, with chickpeas, beans, and flax.

Sugar cane was brought from Spain or her Atlantic islands where it had been established shortly before the discovery. Columbus tried to start it, but his plants did not thrive. No sugar was made in the Antilles before the beginning of the sixteenth century, and in 1511 there was not enough made to supply local consumption. Six years later, however, the Geronymite friars sent home a precious casket bearing samples of field cotton, *cañafistula*, and sugar, which they had been promoting. They encouraged sugar mills by a bounty of 500 pesos on each one built, and the king in 1520 removed all duties on machinery needed for them. Experts were sent from the Canaries, and the plantations throve amazingly.

Garden flowers were brought over in the same way as the edible plants. Red carnations, and the white ones splotched with red, grew all over Peru by the middle of the seventeenth century, but, like those of Mexico, they were not so fragrant as in Spain. Roses were plentiful; the first ones came by seed in 1552, and mass was said in Lima, with one of the seeds on the altar, to celebrate the event. But there were varieties native to the soil; the Franciscan fathers who pioneered the California coast were cheered in their marches northward, just as the founder of their order might have been, when they spied in the forests the single pink blossoms which they named *rosas de Castilla*.[7]

In rehearsing the long story of this western transit it must not be forgotten that the economic resources of Europe were enlarged by importation of the flora of the New World. Indian corn had been acclimated in Spain before 1530 and potatoes had been raised in Italy by the middle of the century. The tomato was in general use in Southern Europe long before 1800. Most tropical plants were ill-adapted to the climate of the old country, but their products, previously rare or entirely unknown, like cacao and vanilla, became common articles of trade.

More spectacular was the revolution wrought by Spain in the transmission of European fauna. By 1525 they were shipping cowhides to Spain from the Antilles; cattle were so numerous that the people did not know what to do with them. Father Cobo declared that the spread of Spanish cattle had a great deal to do with ending the cannibalism of the Chiriguana of Los Charcas and of the Carib. Gómara said that the Indians of Mexico took very kindly to the cheese made from cow's milk, marveling that the liquid could be thickened to make it. As for horses and mules, "they blessed the beasts which relieved them from burden-bearing."[8] Horses and asses were taken to La Española by Columbus on his second and third voyages, later by Ovando. Vicente Yáñez Pinzón sent mares with his ships in 1507; Nicuesa and Ojeda took them to the mainland in 1509 and more went to Antigua in 1513. Probably the original stock, coming from Andalusia, was Arabic. How rapidly they spread over Spanish America is shown by the fact that horses were running wild, on the southern plains of Paraguay and Tucumán, and in the hills of New Mexico, by the middle of the seventeenth century.[9] They had become so cheap that they were hunted instead of bred. Mexico got her supply of mules from twelve jennies and three jacks sent in 1531. Bishop Fuenleal asked for 300 jennies to give to the Indians.

The supply of cattle for meat increased more slowly than horses and mules.[10] Hogs showed remarkable reproductive power. By 1508 the people of La Española were given royal permission to hunt for a pastime the droves of wild descendants of the first hogs which had been brought. Soto in Florida was accompanied by a herd of several hundred hogs, and he left many behind; some may have strayed, too, from those which Coronado took with him for food in New Mexico. Sheep were the only imported livestock that did not come to run wild; they were brought to Mexico in 1531 and at a later date to Peru. The good Bishop of Fuenleal, along with his other benefactions, gave flocks to the Indians, who prized them and raised them carefully. But for years the wool was wasted, as there were no mills, but the manufacture of woolen cloth became a leading industry of Peru in after years. The woolens of New Spain were, said Acosta, coarser than those of the home country.[11]

These first Christians brought with them the cross and the sword, it is true, but they also brought all they had of practical civilization. It was the judgment of Father Cobo that America in that early day received in plants and animals as much wealth as she returned in gold and silver;[12] the new land was just ripe for what the Spaniards had to offer. It was their misfortune that the papal bulls gave them broader domains than their strength sufficed for. But they were great in their conception of a New World to be won for Spain and for the faith, and they were notable in the simple practicality with which they undertook to make the wilderness blossom with a European culture by which the Indian was to become a husbandman and Christian.

PIONEERS OF NEW MEXICO AND FLORIDA

NEW MEXICO, projecting northward toward the heart of the continent, several hundred miles beyond the early Chihuahua settlements, lay at the utmost fringe of the white man's civilization.[13] Here a handful of Indians, "half-breeds," and mulattoes, led by a few civilians, missionaries, and soldiers, were engaged in a highly dramatic episode in Spain's long effort to subdue and hold a continent. But the long-drawn disappointment of New Mexico left little that was romantic in the end. Failing to conquer a continent from that direction, Spain turned to fairer valleys in the east, but, drained by the immense cost of new enterprises, faltered and finally resigned them to the English and the French.

The New Mexican effort was the last notable Spanish expansion before that eighteenth-century defensive thrust which added the northern Pacific coast. There were minor activities in the Texan and Gulf areas at the close of the seventeenth century, and a continuous effort to hold the Florida-Carolina frontier, but these were forced reactions to foreign aggression and without the great compelling lure which beckoned into New Mexico. They were intended chiefly to hold, by adding new frontier strips, that which had been already gained—defensive operations instead of bold strokes for empire.

When the advance was made into New Mexico it was by no means conceived of as the last step in the great northward movement. The seventeenth-century governors and missionaries of New Mexico were quite as willing, even as anxious, to press on in the path of expanding empire as were their swashbuckling predecessors of the preceding cycle. They stopped where they did for two cogent reasons: They had exhausted their manpower, and they had come upon a region in which the aspiration for sudden wealth could not be realized. No wonderful silver mines appeared, or fabled treasure stores; the trade in hides and furs was precarious; the distance to the real center of the life of the realm, Mexico City, was not only cruelly long, but hazardous because of the Indians. Moreover, the pueblo Indian was a rebellious thrall of the Spanish exploitative system. In the conflict with distance, aridity, poverty, and rebellion, this far-flung frontier presents all the elements of strength and weakness in the early conception of colonial empire. It was, in that sense, a typical frontier; from its story, sordid or glorious, now presenting meek men patient in Christian suffering, now vengeful, contumacious rebels, may be gleaned an impression of what the process of widening the borders of empire really meant to its active participants.

During the sixteenth century New Mexico lay yet in the lands of northern mystery. It first dawned on the white man's consciousness during the romantic wanderings of Cabeza de Vaca, who learned of it by hearsay while on his pioneer transcontinental journey after the dismal undoing of the Narváez expedition along the shores of the Gulf of Mexico. Then the overwrought imagination of the propagandist Friar Marcos of Nice, picturing the cities of Cíbola with turquoise-studded doors, brought about the spectacular but unhappy quest of Coronado for a new kingdom that should excel in wealth and grandeur the lands conquered by Cortés.

After Coronado's expedition New Mexico was not visited for a generation or more. Then, in 1581, an expedition explored the wide region between the Pecos River and the pueblos of Ácoma and Zuñi, and it was not long before efforts at occupation began. A host of would-be leaders competed for the opportunity, but not until 1597 was Juan de Oñate the successful contestant. In the next year he took possession and initiated several attempts at further expansion, after which the country settled down to the more prosaic pursuits of the missionaries and the exploitation of the pueblo tribes in the Rio Grande Valley.[14] Before the end of the year Oñate had won the general submission of the pueblos, and the Franciscans who went with him were assigned to missionary posts. The governor himself was chiefly interested, as several of his successors continued to be, in plans of wider empire—in the still-dreamed-of Quivira, the eastern country sought by Coronado, which would yield untold treasure, and in the equally mythical easy passage to the great South Sea.

But there were practical achievements within New Mexico. Shortly after Oñate's recall in 1608 the villa of Santa Fé was founded by Governor Peralta, his successor, and the new frontier became one of the "kingdoms" of the viceroyalty. By 1617 the friars had eleven churches built and professed to have converted 14,000 Indians. The new province was headed by a governor appointed by the viceroy. Under the viceroy López Pacheco, duke of Escalona, it was ordered that the defense of the province should be provided by the creation of thirty-five *encomiendas.* The *encomenderos* were to receive the tributes from the Indian towns under their control as a stipend for furnishing men and horses for military campaigns, all at the instant call of the governor. Settlers of lower rank were also thus used as they came in. The hard and almost endless duties of war consumed much of the energy of the frontiersmen. In the intervals of peace they engaged in cattle raising, grain farming, and trading with the Indians of the pueblos and with the unreduced Apache on their outskirts.

In 1621 the missions were organized into a *custodia,* called San Pablo, of the Franciscan province of El Santo Evangelio de México. At its head was the *custodio,* who was presently made commissary of the Inquisition for the region, the first incumbent being that notable friar Alonso de Benavides, the earliest historian of the province. As chief of a well-knit organization of friars with a territorial jurisdiction equal to that of the governor, his influence was really greater than that of the political executive, for he reached the entire converted Indian population through his friars, who were normally of a type superior to the alcaldes and settlers. Many of the latter were half-breeds and mulattoes whose departure from the older regions had been unmourned. When not held close to the friars by self-interest or religious zeal, they were usually of an unruly adventurous spirit, willing partisans of the governor in his traditional conflict with the missionaries.[15]

By 1620 a phase of the frontier situation had developed which was to characterize the whole century. The civil and ecclesiastical officers clashed with regard to the exercise of judicial authority. The governor asserted his right to appoint the petty Indian officials whom the missionaries used in reducing the natives to the Christian polity; the *custodio* refused to admit the governor's authority to do this and excommunicated him for his interference. The nub of the problem lay in the fact that the missions, on the one hand, and the governor, on the other, were competing for the opportunity to exploit the unpaid labor of the Indians. The conflict soon took the form of rivalry for the exercise of the full judicial authority. The *custodio,* under papal bulls and alleged permission by royal decrees, claimed free right to exercise ecclesiastical jurisdiction. This included all cases involving friars, and the usual affairs of life for everyone if they could be construed as arising out of the obligations created by the sacraments of the church. Throughout the century the governors steadfastly contested the pretension, and nearly all the troubles which visited the province rose directly or indirectly from the struggle.[16]

Lacking the local prestige to effect their will, the *custodios,* as commissaries of the Inquisition, used the powerful court of that institution to hold the governor in subjection or to secure his removal and punishment. The power of the commissaries forms a striking, though incomplete, analogy to the powers and policies of the French-Canadian bishops, whose corps of seminary priests gave them great power over the settlers through the confessional and excommunication,[17] as was generally true throughout Spanish America. It is of more than passing interest to find that the Spanish Inquisition, against whose mystery and relentless severity so many American writers of history have inveighed, was, through its Franciscan commissaries, once the most potent political influence in territory now a part of the American Union. We shall see how it exerted its power.[18]

Up to 1630 the province had but one Spanish settlement, the villa of Santa Fé, where lived 250 Spainiards with twice as many half-breeds and Indian dependents.[19] Radiating from Santa Fé were friars in twenty-five missions serving ninety pueblos and claiming 90,000 neophytes. But these alleged converts were resentful of the tributes levied on them, sullen toward their exploiters whether lay or clerical, and anxious to resume their old barbarous life. Churchmen and settlers alike kept alive the hope of finding Quivira and Texas, fabulous kingdoms of riches, through which they might open connections with the eastern inland country and the coast of the Gulf of Mexico. Gradually the western part of Texas, home of the Jumanos Indians, became an outlying goal for New Mexican trade. If only a little rich treasure could have been found, the pueblo region would have become at once a new focus of diffusion of Spanish power throughout the great interior region.

The governors were likely to be men of little education who had seen service as alcaldes mayores, petty governors, or the like. Many of them were frontiersmen of long experience and had acquired small fortunes by barter among the Indian tribes for hides and furs, which they shipped south in the annual caravans known as "the king's wagons." These great freight trains traversed the 2,000 miles of hazardous Indian country between Mexico and Santa Fé with nominal regularity after 1629 under command of a "general" with a military escort. One of the governors, Francisco de la Mora, took office in 1633 with the idea of gaining wealth by enlisting the friars to help him dispose of a large stock of knives which he had brought for barter, persecuting them if they did not consent to further his Indian trade. Soon he began to sow discord by seizing Indian orphans, "like calves and colts," to work on his own farms. He also encouraged the establishment of stock farms on the cornfields of the natives, and forced Spanish soldiers to leave their own small properties to work on his estates. As there seemed to be no curb on his ingenuity at the expense of the Indians, the friars appealed to the "fountain of law and justice" at Mexico City for relief.

In 1659 there came to the province as governor, Bernardo López de Mendizábal, a roistering frontier trader and soldier of wide experience who intended that his term of office should not be unprofitable to himself. He soon set the friars by the ears, not only by his own acts but by those of his alcaldes mayores. Of these the most notorious was a half-breed, Nicolás de Aguilar, who, it was alleged, had murdered his uncle at Parral in Nueva Vizcaya and fled to the farther frontier to escape justice. He was in charge of the *alcaldía* which comprised Tajique, Chililí, and Senecú, east and southeast of the later Albuquerque. It contained large salt deposits worked by the governor and a prosperous *encomendero* named Diego de Guadalajara, deposits especially valuable since that mineral was indispensable to the patio extraction process used by the silver miners in the vicinity of Parral.

The sycophantic Aguilar—"Attila," the friars dubbed him—was the agent through whom Mendizábal delighted to pester the missionaries. The pair took puerile delight in encouraging the natives in their "heathen" rites, especially the dances known then and now as the *Catzinas*[20]—ceremonies to invoke the benign interest of the gods of the crops. Led by medicine men in masks of horrifying aspect, the dances included flagellation and incestuous orgies; of course they were strictly forbidden by the missionaries as demoniacal and superstitious in character. The alcalde mayor, obeying with zest the commands of the governor, insisted that there was no harm here but mere barbarous diversion, and gave the Indians permission to continue the practice. Here was a challenge to be met by no hesitation. At Cuarac, Friar Diego de Parraga tried to stop the rites by whipping the dancers. In Isleta, Father Salvador Guerra went out to meet his disobedient neophytes with a cross upon his back, a crown of thorns upon his brow, and a rope about his neck, lashing his naked flesh as he walked about the town. Thereupon his disciples gave up their celebration, tearfully assuring him that the governor had ordered them to dance.

When the Indians of Cuarac went to Jumanos at the request of the friars to sing high mass on the patron saint's day, they were given fifty lashes each by Aguilar for going into enemy country. He prevented the use of an interpreter to translate the service of the mass at Abo, thus impeding the exercise of the sacred cult. For these sins, committed about 1660, Aguilar was arrested by the commissary and sent to the Inquisition in Mexico, though he claimed the status of a pious Christian.[21]

Aguilar's defense is of chief interest for its intimate picture of seventeenth-century life in New Mexico. He testified that he believed that false witness had been brought against him by his enemies, among them Father Parraga, whom he had accused of libertinage, and Father Freitas, who had once drawn a pistol on him in an altercation. Many of the friars, he said, were immoral and cruel to the Indians. In Moqui they had encouraged flagellations of Indian *penitentes.* They hindered him in his incessant effort to prevent Apache inroads, when these Indians, coming from Siete Rios to trade, stole into the woods near Tajique and carried off Christian captives. They would tie them to huge burning fagots and dance about them, cutting off slices of flesh which they cooked and ate while their victims were perishing. It was to prevent such acts that he had forbidden his charges to go to the woods for fuel. For this, Friar Fernando de Velasco had upbraided him, and in a quarrel tried to kill him with a knife. Though the glib alcalde never admitted an accusation or retracted a charge, he was found guilty of scandalous language and lukewarmness in the faith, and was banished for ten years.

The governors of New Mexico were habitually negligent in their respect for religion. One of them once seized the Holy Sacrament, and taking it to his "palace," there celebrated Holy Week with it. Another carried the Host about with him in a silver snuffbox in his saddlebags. When Diego de Peñalosa, Mendizábal's successor as governor, made an expedition to Moqui, he entered the church at Santa Fé with his hat on and partook of the Sacrament with clanking spurs. Besides arraigning governors, the Inquisition had plenty to do with the common folk. Take, for example, a case of unauthorized supernaturalism. A certain German trader, Bernardo Grüber by name, who went into New Mexico from Sonora with a pack train of merchandise in 1668, was arrested for sorcery. It appears that one day the alcalde mayor of Las Salinas was surprised to see his ten-year-old son demonstrating with a great sliver of wood that he was impervious to wounds. The good alcalde promptly reported this witchcraft to the friars, who set upon Grüber as an alien and a sorcerer. He had, it was found, gone into the choir in the church when mass was being sung and offered the boys some scraps of paper bearing cabalistic characters and crosses. He declared he did this in imitation of a custom he had learned in Germany; that he who ate such paper as the first mass of the Nativity was being sung became so potent that for twenty-four hours no weapon could harm him. Grüber was imprisoned but managed to escape; the thrifty alcalde consoled himself by seizing over forty of the trader's mules and horses. There were numerous other trials for more worldly offenses, especially bigamy, for it was then, as now, a low-caste New Mexican practice to leave one's encumbering mate behind when faring forth to new fields. There was a considerable traffic in charms, albeit they did not always work.

It was not long before the great Indian revolt of 1680 began brewing.

Probably the seizure and sale of Apaches as slaves had a large part in rousing the nomadic tribes to cooperation with the rebellious pueblo Indians. By 1672, Apache raids on the towns and the murder of friars began. In stern reprisal for hostile acts, in 1675 several natives were hanged, nearly fifty whipped, and a large number imprisoned. The natives, however, had a numerical superiority too great for the faction-torn Spanish establishments. In 1676 the crisis was seen to be near and help was called for from Mexico; but the train left there tardily in 1679 and reached the frontier too late to be of aid.

The devastating revolt, led by Popé, a Tewa Indian who managed his campaign from Taos in the extreme north, was inspired by a long succession of abuses, but there can be little doubt that chief among them was the repression of native religious rites, such as the *Catzinas* dances. The uprising had been planned with great secrecy in the underground *estufas,* or council chambers. There, dropping one by one down their rough ladders, the braves gathered around their council fires, which lit their sullen faces as they sat in a circle plotting the resumption of their old cult and a bloody vengeance on their masters. Though the plot was discovered, the blow fell on the Spaniards with blasting fury. Four hundred of them were killed and all the rest, numbering about 2,000, were driven out. The fugitives retired nearly to the southern limits of the present state of New Mexico to pass the winter near the site of the later town of Las Cruces.[22] El Paso del Norte (now Ciudad Juárez) was built by them in 1682, and from that point operations for rewinning the lost kingdom were carried on, more for the sake of Spanish pride than for any gain to be obtained.

On the eastern side of the country expansion was undertaken as a measure against foreign aggression—foreign arms, and, as far as the English were concerned, foreign heresy. The government at Mexico did not forget that Florida was Spanish, but it realized that this was so, as yet, only on the map. When at last the renowned Pedro Menéndez de Avilés planted the cross and the lions of Castile on the Floridian shore in 1565, his little post of San Agustín (the modern St. Augustine) brought to consummation a long series of endeavors, hitherto in vain, to fix the power of Spain in this area. Given a little more manpower, a more inviting shore, a closer contact with the viceroyalty, and a little more strength, the story of Spain's "window on the Atlantic" would have made North American history vastly different.

Always a citadel and little else, San Agustín possessed none of the glamour of the silver country. It interests us here as a little frontier community. We may say in the beginning that this most ancient city of the Black Belt owed much to the labor of black slaves whom the Spaniards employed to establish their stronghold. Black slaves of the Spanish king were sent to Florida in 1581, and a small party of them was engaged for two years in making wooden platforms for the artillery of the fort at old San Agustín. Black hands set up the first smith's forge and there made needed repairs, while two of the best were sent to Santa Elena to help the soldiers saw out boards to be used for covering the fort there. The soldiers, being free and white, received wages for their work; for the blacks, it was only needful to see that they were provided with bread and meat and wine. Nearly a dozen black slaves were used in these fortifications, in building the church at San Agustín, putting up dwellings, and clearing away the forests for planting crops. Some blacks, possibly the earliest importations, remained in the province for forty years serving the white man's needs; at the end of that time they were reported as having died, and a request was sent to Spain for a dozen more men together with three or four black women.

The colonial government had problems in plenty, the morals of the settlers, among other things, requiring attention. In 1635 the monarch sent a new governor to San Agustín "to improve the conduct and manners of the people." Street processions were held for the expiation of the sins of the community, and the king threatened that, if need be, he would punish his vassals severely for their iniquities. Five years later the commissaries of the Inquisition visited San Agustín, with what improvement of popular morals we do not know; apparently, the most important fruit of their visitation was a decision as to the proper order to be observed in outdoor processions.

The truth is that there were never enough soldiers, settlers, or missionaries, for the area Spain had seized was too great for her resources. San Agustín was an illustration of this weakness in all respects. Yet it had to bear attack as frequently as almost any of Spain's citadels. First there was the Huguenot Dominique de Gourgues in 1568; then "El Draco," Drake the terrible, in 1586; later there were Governor Moore of South Carolina in 1702, Oglethorpe in 1732–40, and, finally, all the incidents of the English seizure in 1763 and the retrocession two decades later. With all its weakness, San Agustín had justified its existence for more than 200 years.

The town itself was three quarters of a mile long by half a mile wide, not counting the Indian villages outside its walls. It was built on a little bay at the foot of a wooded hill, with the four well-shaded streets placed at right angles in the traditional fashion legally prescribed for all Spanish-American towns. The well-built houses, three or four churches, fort, hospital, and monastery all gave indication of a definite plan of permanent occupation.[23] The best part was on the north side, in the immediate vicinity of the fort called by the English St. John's, around which was a ditch fringed with a *chevaux de frise* of "Spanish bayonets." The record pictures "a square building of soft stone, with whole bastions, a rampart twenty feet high, with a parapet nine feet high, and it is casemated. The town is fortified with bastions and with cannon."[24]

The traditional *plaza mayor,* as characteristic of all Spanish towns as was the green of the New England villages, closely obeyed the laws made in the sixteenth century by being set facing the harbor. On one side of it was the spacious palace of the governor with its high windows, front balcony, and galleries on the sides. At the back the watch tower commanded the harbor, with its lighthouse on Anastasia Island and its breeze-swept marshes. The houses were commonly built of "free stone," having two rooms on each of two stories and spacious balconies and windows. The entries were usually protected by porticoes with stone arches, and grapevines with excellent fruit grew on arbors before each door. The roofs

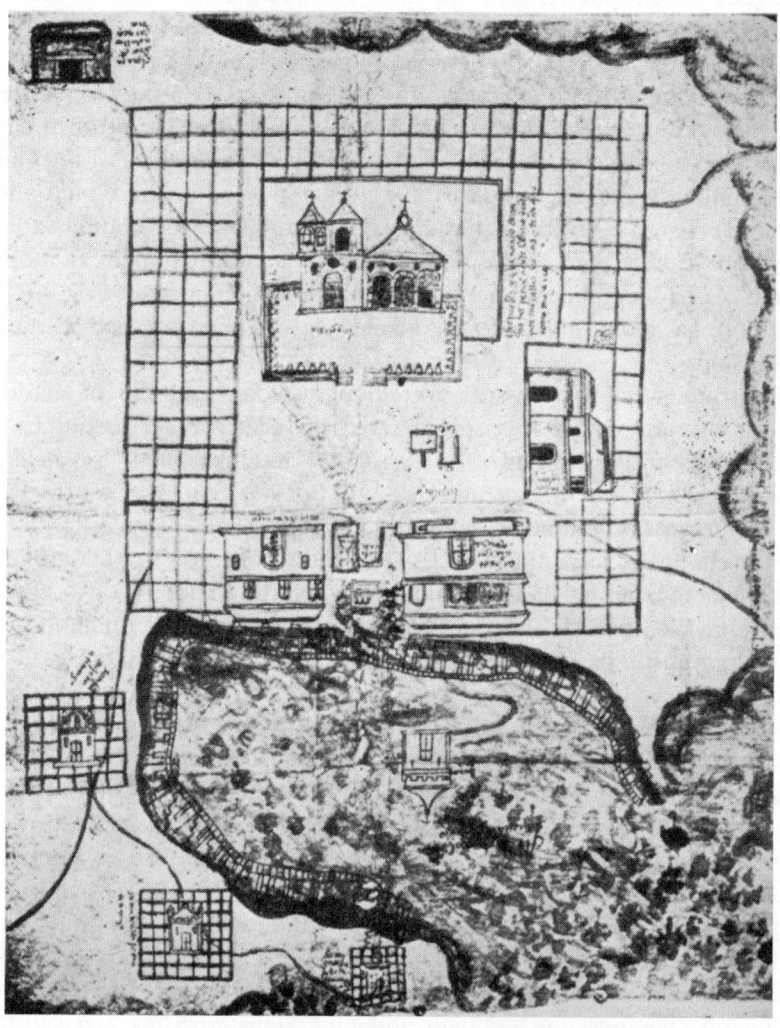

A Specimen Town Plan in New Spain,
centering in the church gate.

were flat in conformity with universal Spanish style; the window-gratings projected into the streets sixteen or eighteen inches. On the west side of the houses the windows were quite small; the north sides had none, but here were placed galleries, with double walls from six to eight feet apart, within whose cool recesses were put the cellars and pantries. In their gardens the first inhabitants had planted the flowers and fruits of the home-land—fig trees, guavas, plantains, pomegranates, lemons, limes, citrons, shaddock, bergamot. The mandarin orange vied with that of Seville, while the familiar pot herbs were sturdy enough to survive cold weather. But the temperature rarely sank too low for comfort. There were no chimneys or fireplaces; on the occasional cold days the people used stone braziers filled with charcoal.

When the English came in 1763 there were a number of centenarians among the departing dons, their many years being considered ample proof of the salubrity of the Florida climate, an advantage which has not gone unmentioned in our own day. The Spaniards, on departing, left as many as 900 houses, but those of the suburbs, being of wood, soon fell into ruins. The population, half of it comprising the military establishment, numbered about 5,000 at the time of the evacuation. Those who remained were of all colors—white, black, and mulatto—with a generous sprinkling of Indians.

When the fortunes of war brought Florida again under Spanish control, the English in turn generally left during 1784. For one generation the Spanish colors flew once more over the fortress, but the centuries-long strain of colonial competition had left no power to extend the province, or even to rehabilitate the ancient citadel.[25]

THE LAST CYCLE OF NEW SPAIN

THE EXTENSION OF New Spain into Alta California was the last great Spanish territorial effort in North America, contemporary with the attempts to oc-cupy western Louisiana. The story of the quest for empire on the western shores of America is too long to detail here, but it may be said to date from the advent of Hernán Cortés in Pacific waters. Ever inspired by fear of competition from the Drakes, the Cavendishes, the Spilbergens, and the Behrings, the Spanish enjoyed the advantage (lost too early on the Atlantic side) of anticipating all rivals and getting a foothold in spite of long odds of distance and attenuated manpower. The climax of the quest came under Charles III, and its success was largely due to the vision and energy of José de Gálvez. A prime purpose was to draw the Indians into their proper place in the grand defensive-offensive which should anticipate Russia or England, then approaching these northern reaches, the one by sea from the north, the other by land from the east.[26]

Santa Barbara, established 1786.

San Luis Rey, established 1798.

San Francisco de Asis, at Dolores, established 1776.

Three Franciscan Missions of Alta California.

One is struck by the meager physical resources which entered into such imperial projects. The great coastline of California was taken for Spain by a joint sea and land expedition from Lower California. The land forces were in two detachments totaling eighty-six men; the sea forces, in two tiny packet boats, numbered ninety. So ill equipped were the vessels that, when they were blown far off their course on the voyage, the food and medicines became exhausted long before the arrival at San Diego, and shortly after their landing two thirds of the expeditionaries were dead. The land parties, on the other hand, succeeded in crossing the 200 miles of desert from Santa María to San Diego without incident or loss of life. From San Diego a land force of sixty-four promptly traversed the 150-odd leagues to occupy Vizcaíno's famous port of Monterey. Of the forty people left behind, half were dead when the commandant Gaspar de Portolá returned from the north in January 1770.

This first white man's march up the coast must have provided thrilling entertainment for the Indians. In advance went a sergeant with six or eight *exploradores* to select the route and fix the next campsite. The main force followed, headed by the plumed and gaitered commandant, his second in command, and his engineer. Beside them jogged Father Junipero Serra and his fellow brown-garbed Franciscan, spiritual conquerors, with an escort of Catalans. Then came the Christian Indians of Lower California, with adzes, mattocks, and other tools to cast up the highway; next, the troops in four squads, each guarding a part of the hundred pack animals. A rear guard convoyed the extra beasts. These *soldados de cuera* were experienced frontier fighters, able to make daily advances of from two to four leagues through unknown country. Clad in leather jackets thick enough to stop an Indian arrow not driven at too close a range, they wore bull-hide shields on their arms to protect themselves and their mount's flank. On their pommels were leather aprons, or *armas,* hung to the stirrups to shield the legs in brush riding. As arms they carried lances, muskets, and broadswords.[27]

The route was in large part over what came soon to be known as the Camino Real, a name usually thought by modern language-fanciers to mean the "King's Highway," but which meant to the actual pioneers merely the "main road." Scattered along it for official convenience and hospitality's sake there quickly appeared, at intervals of a day's march, the twenty-one missions—inviting structures with red tiles and cool adobe walls, shady *portales,* surrounding gardens, Indian quarters, and fields of grain and fruit, with pasturelands farther out. Along the sun-swept reaches of this old road, today smelling perpetually of burned gasoline, trudged or rode the cloaked and sandaled sons of St. Francis on their errand of love and empire. For their protection against possible annoyance by the natives four presidios were erected—San Diego in 1769, Monterey the following year, San Francisco in 1776, and Santa Barbara in 1782. The commander at Monterey was governor.

In the presidios the tedium of garrison life was broken by occasional escort service, now and then a rounding up of renegade neophytes, and a little gardening. As elsewhere on the fringes of civilization, the influence of the troops tended to debase the lives of the none too Edenic Indians. In time, villages grew up about the presidios. Only two other towns were founded in the Spanish period—San José in 1776 and Los Angeles in 1781. Their populations consisted mainly of a mixed assortment of pioneers, often retired presidial soldiers with Indian wives, although members of the ancient sedentary tribes and the mulatto-Indian half-castes of New Spain were by no means missing.

In the presidios and missions, and on the few ranchos—which were set as far as possible away from the missions since the good fathers had keen eyes for the most desirable lands—the Spanish population never exceeded 3,000 persons. In the Mexican period, when outside ships came to the ports more freely and the advance agents of American pioneering, the fur traders, began to slip over the mountain passes, not more than 10,000 white people awaited the day of annexation to the United States.[28] In these later days life continued in the pastoral and agricultural stage undisturbed by the separation from Spain or the faraway control of Mexico City.

The missions, as the paternalistic agencies of civilization, were naturally the chief directors of economic life. The holy fathers had brought the wheat and barley, the fig, olive, pomegranate, orange, lemon, and vine in a long plant-migration from the Moroccan shore, the hills of Andalusia, and the slopes of the Canaries. In the busy mission centers were produced the crops, and also the herds of horses, mules, and cattle, from which were derived the chief articles of commerce, hides and tallow. As everywhere in New Spain the Indian was at the base of society. Though the law knew neither *encomiendas* nor chattel slavery, the Indian was a virtual serf unless he was clever enough to stay in the foothills out of contact with the white man's culture.

California Indians did not inspire the whites with any great respect; there was no Montezuma among them, still less a Philip or a Tecumseh. Their greatest sins were reversion to sexual laxity, desertion of the missions, and a liking for the flavor of stolen horse meat. They drove off the stock in great numbers and received frequent attention from the *juez de campo,* the civil officer whose business it was to harry the Indians from their retreats with such refinements of cruelty as were familiar to the whites everywhere in America in dealing with the natives. Most of the expeditions sent out in the later days to find mission sites were prompted by the desire of the civil arm to occupy strategic positions from which the marauding bands could be better restrained.[29]

The mission neophytes were trained in morning prayers, sent to work with their spiritual fathers in the fields, nurtured again with physical and spiritual pabulum, and locked up at night by sexes safe from the lusts of the flesh and the call of the wild. They learned the rude craftsmanship of the farm, mingling with it some of their native skill. They pined and died, or, escaping, sought again their old haunts whence they sallied forth to forage off the mission cattle unless hauled back by the mission guard. The remnant of their progeny forms a negligible part of California society.

Among the townsmen and rancheros outside the missions and presidios life flowed an uneventful course. Men spent their lives in the saddle, and the horses were good. Women stayed at home; they were often beautiful and almost invariably domestic, religious, and chaste. Social intercourse was an unending round of simple amenities, punctuated with outdoor amusements, such as the hunt and the rodeo, and with church festivals. The gaming table was by no means neglected. California hospitality became proverbial among the traders and voyagers from other parts. Since there were no inns, travelers were everywhere welcome at the table and in the guest chamber, with generous provision in the form of food and mount for their departure.[30]

There were no schools to go to and little to read.[31] The first press, set up at Monterey in 1834, was used to issue governors' orders and little else. When the Hijar colony arrived in the same year, it brought a teacher for the proposed normal school at Monterey and eight others for the primary schools, but education did not prosper. The Californians objected to some of the masters on moral grounds and others returned to Mexico because they did not find conditions in the colony to be as represented to them. Richard Henry Dana's description of the people of Monterey in 1835 would do for many a Spanish-American town of those days and later:

> The officers were dressed in the costume which we found prevailed through the country,—broadbrimmed hat, usually of a black or dark brown color, with a gilt or figured band round the crown . . . a short jacket of silk, or figured calico . . . the shirt open in the neck; rich waistcoat, if any; pantaloons open at the sides below the knee, laced with gilt, usually of velveteen or broadcloth; or else short breeches with white stockings. . . . They have no suspenders, but always wear a sash round the waist, which is generally red. . . . Add to this the never-failing poncho, or serape, and you have the dress of the Californian. . . . The *gente de razon,* or better sort of people, wear cloaks of black or dark blue broadcloth, with as much velvet and trimmings as may be; and from this they go down to the blanket of the Indian, the middle classes wearing a poncho, something like a large square cloth, with a hole in the middle for the head to go through. . . . Among the Mexicans there is no working class (the Indians being practically serfs, and doing all the hard work); and every rich man looks like a grandee, and every poor scamp like a broken-down gentleman.[32]

About the time of Dana's memorable voyage to California there were 30,000 Indians in the missions. Four hundred thousand horned cattle,

60,000 horses, and 300,000 sheeps, goats, and hogs attested to the growth of pastoral interests in sixty short years. Cereals amounted to 120,000 bushels a year, and there was also a considerable production of wine, brandy, soap, leather, oil, cotton, hemp, and tobacco. Two hundred thousand cattle were killed annually for their hides at $10 each, the missions supplying half. The annual wealth of the missions alone was as high as $2 million, even after the initial steps were taken in "secularization," which was carried out to gratify the white man's cupidity under the zealous Mexican plan of putting the Indians into full status as "citizens." With its wealth, its indolent inhabitants, its incomparable climate, and its favorable position for the fur trade, it was small wonder that the path of American empire should shortly include it.[33]

In summing up the merits and demerits of the Spanish occupation of America, it may be said that, given the defects of the society and the handicaps of the field of operation, the result was better than might have been expected. A constant difficulty throughout the 300 years was the political necessity for territorial expansion beyond the strength of the available manpower, a deterrent influence which the English escaped through their advantage of concentration behind the Alleghenies. For the Spaniards, the need was to defend their holdings by interposing great distances, in a scantily cultivable area, between rich treasure mines and the enemy. This policy involved a further necessity for holding territory against the hazard of hostile Indians where the benefits were not commensurate with the outlay of energy. Long seacoasts and a futile attempt at restriction of trade added to the useless expenditure of resources. A century of indolent kings without insight or policy led to the stagnation of the old system, which not even the energy of Charles I or Philip II could make work successfully. The great reformative period of the Bourbons was full of the promise of recuperation until dynastic decay set in again. The principal weakness, after all the notable reforms of Charles III, was his failure to raise up a worthy successor in his son. The growth at the same time of the English system, sharply competitive and everywhere intrusive, roused Bourbon Spain to an energy that would have effected permanent results had society continued on its old basis of the organization of the plunder of dependent peoples.

The worst handicap during the whole period was the immobile character of the colonial population. The Spanish policy of restricted immigration and the liberal importation of black slaves resulted during the sixteenth century in a greater influx of black men than of whites into New Spain. The laws forbade, but could not prevent, the mixing of Indian and black blood. The preservation of the Indian and his general fusion with the Spaniard created a type of society distinguished by the position of social and economic inferiority held by the "castes," the name applied to all persons below the creoles. Such a social system bred incompetency and lack of initiative in the group which grew fastest in numbers. The evil effect of the land system, which was in turn the result of climate, topography, and social organization, completed the vicious circle. It was a natural, tragic denouement. Publicists of constructive vision saw the impending disaster and Charles III battled with it valiantly, but like all the other powers, Spain lacked the imagination to foresee the trend of the Revolutionary epoch. In the colonial era that dawned with the passing of the desire of the European white man to hold in political and economic dependence his white nationals, the ideal of an empire of cooperating nations, as the British Commonwealth, was to rise. Beyond that still lies the empire of the man of other colors. Whether the world is to learn the lesson of the Spaniard or that of the Englishman in its solution of relations with this newer mass of humanity is the problem of today.

THE WARDS OF THE SPANIARDS

TWO BASIC CONSIDERATIONS must be kept constantly in mind in arriving at an understanding of the historical significance of the Spanish neighbors of the English in North America. The first is that the social and political organization which Spain succeeded in planting within the present bounds of the United States was of a transitional frontier type, its spirit but feebly reflecting that greater Spain of which the conquistadores were vaguely conscious. To judge the influence of Spain in North America by the meager results of daring *entradas* or by the social development of Florida or Texas or California is to misinterpret an important phase of the subjection of the New World to European ideals. We must get back of the frontier to the type of life developed in old Mexico. The second consideration is the need to realize the significance of the survival of the Indian masses in Mexico, with all the social, political, and economic implications of that unique factor in American history. Without the survival of Indian blood and tradition, the growth of New Spain would have been quite unlike what it came to be; so, too, the life of the Mexican nation and its relations with the United States.

It requires a considerable effort of the imagination to appreciate the element of surprise experienced by both the Spaniards and the Indians when they first came face-to-face. Europeans had long been familiar with exploitable nonwhite peoples brought from Asia and Africa; the slave ships of Portugal had been bringing home their cargoes of "black ivory" for many years before the voyages of Columbus began. But here was a new, strangely hued race with alien languages and customs, the tribes upon the mainland plateaus living in barbaric splendor with a highly developed social organization. The pugnacious character of the Spaniard, his belief in his divine mission acquired from his seven-century war on the Mohammedan invader,

the freedom of action permitted by distance from Spain and by papal favor
—all these, when brought in contact with the peculiar fatalistic stoicism of
the American Indian, were well adapted to create a unique situation, and
necessitated some kind of a system for regulating the relations of two
widely unlike types of culture. Thanks to his superior organization and his
possession of firearms, the Spaniard could almost everywhere in the New
World assume the role of conqueror and exploiter far more easily than
could the Europeans in the Orient. There were minor variations in the
methods of exploitation he adopted; from its worst forms the Indians won
temporary immunity by ferocious revolts, only sooner or later to become
the subordinate element in the social group.

In the long run perhaps it would have been better for the world, as well
as for the Indian, if the attempt to effect spiritual change had been less
peremptory and exigent. He might have been left to the enjoyments and
consolations of the faith of his fathers until he could himself develop some
volition in the matter of a more complete salvation. As it was, the Indians
never really assimilated the spirit and beauty of the Christian religion; there
was something wrong with it from the Indians' point of view, which is the
one that matters. The essential defect was that it did not, in its historical
development or its philosophy, touch a responsive chord in their own
tradition or experience. In moral precepts the faith of the Aztec touched a
sublimity quite comparable with the teachings of Christ, but its social
tradition and practice were utterly unlike that of the European.[34] Hastily
imposed and imperfectly practiced, Christianity could not, amid the social
destruction of the conquest, become a subjective development in the minds
of the Indians. It could not, first, because it was alien; second, because they
had a thoroughly accepted and well-tried-out set of gods of their own, to
whom their spirits cried in the hour of anguish and to whom they addressed
thanks or petition as occasion demanded.

Christianity unquestionably softened the asperities of the conquest,
bringing the amenities of civilization in the wake of the Spanish swashbuck-
lers. But its spirit was incomprehensible, and its indoctrination, given the
practical social and economic code which in fact it protected, was the most
refined persecution which could have befallen the Indian. The imported
religion would have proved more convincing, and its introduction better
justified, had its exemplars followed the principles they professed with less
lip service and more genuine spirituality.[35] But the world being for the
Spaniard what his experiences had made it, such a theory of society was an
impossibility. The strife with Islam had produced a consciousness of national aim before the New World was reached. Only unity of belief could
be trusted to effect the national safety.

For the Indian, then, the process was a sharp crisis with a sequel of
long-drawn-out tragedy, while for the Spaniards themselves the doctrine
brought abundant trouble. Their great mistake in the colonial adventure

was not so much in their harmful development of a rigid policy of commercial exclusion and governmental monopoly of all activity, or their scheme of social and political privilege; for in those respects Spain was by no means unique among the European colonizers. The chief error lay in the Spanish failure to grasp the fact that humanity was being liberated at last from the idea that social security lay in unity of religious thought.[36] By their policy of transplanting Europe to America under the theocratic formula, the conquerors set up an obscurantist ideal opposed to the current of ideas then newly gaining force, in much the same way as the New England Puritans "reverted to type" in the legal establishment of Calvinism.[37]

Yet the faith of the Spaniard was the best thing he brought with him, and in his own way, according to his own psychology, he bestowed it upon his new and unexpected charges. It was the most unselfish gift, the most beneficent agency at his command, for effecting the elevation of a dependent people to the standards of European culture. Ranking second among his settled ideals was his officially sanctioned program of encouraging the fusion of Spanish and Indian blood. To create in the Indies an entirely new society by amalgamating the races under a unified faith was the spiritual vision of the Catholic Monarchs, duly signalized by one of the earliest laws.[38] The faith was his most generous gift, the transfusion of his blood his most lavish compliment. Unity of spirit and identity of body, these were the basic concepts out of which grew the institutions upon which society rested.

A corollary of these two ideas was that of the physical preservation of the Indian for the double purpose of evangelizing and exploiting him. Indian social and political organization rapidly went the way of Indian religious practice. In one feature only was it preserved, the utilization of the tribal or village organization for providing pressed labor gangs. In this preservation of the natives, Spain's policy was comparable to that of the French in Canada, but in sharp contrast with the English and Dutch policy of expulsion and annihilation. The Anglo-Saxon method was to treat the Indian as an alien and independent political entity with whom treaties of mutual exclusion could be solemnized so one-sided in application that white violation was the normal course of action. This left the aborigine entirely out of reach of the protective influences of the white social structure.

Sixteenth-century colonization, being in the hands of Latin peoples, was free from the racial antipathies which cloud the contacts of dominant and subject peoples of the more modern world. The idea of interracial marriage was not repugnant to the throng of adventurers who overran Middle America, and unions, even of legal status, were normal and frequent. Of still greater influence in the amalgamation of the races were the illicit unions which have placed their stamp upon the Spanish-American peoples.

The preservation and Christianization of the Indian, and his fusion with the Spaniard even though on the exploitative basis, made the Spanish colonial system inherently different from those of the rival nations. Portugal tried it with dismal failure in the Orient, with somewhat better success in Brazil; France tried it in Canada with the same ideal but with a less favorable outcome because of the economic environment and social organization. The path of English expansion was strewn with treaties violated immediately they were signed, but with no set of laws governing interracial relations comparable to that of Spain in the Laws of the Indies. One seeks vainly in English- or French-colonial literature for such a treatise as Solórzano's *Política Indiana,* 1,000 and more pages of which are devoted to laws and commentaries expounding the status of the bondsmen.

In a theocratic scheme of things it was logical that the process of evangelization should be one of the prime functions of the supreme government. It is doubtful whether any other western nation so completely fused church in state and state in church as did the Spanish. The kings all insisted that conquest should be softened by being designated "pacification," and that surrender to the political power should be followed by prompt incorporation into the church. Far from offering any essential obstacle to his complete exploitation, the evangelization of the Indian materially aided it. The church definitely avowed and participated in it and built itself up thereby. Churches, monasteries, convents, hospitals, schools, as well as government palaces and other public works, were built by the taxation of Indians and their unrecompensed labor.

As time went on, the institutions through which race contacts were made took form. On the high plateau the church, the monastery, the school, and the *encomienda* were the chief agencies. As the conquest progressed into the nomadic areas of the mines and the missions, the haciendas and the mines themselves became focal points of interracial fusion. Along with these local agencies went the conception of wardship promulgated by the royal government, out of which sprang the regime adopted for the government of Indian towns, the recognition of native land rights, and the policy of manual and intellectual education. All contributed to the sum of the social forces designed to make the Indian one physically, morally, and spiritually with the Spaniard.

It was a basic conception that the direction of all this should be in the hands of the crown. The royal monopoly was based upon the sovereign rights plus the property rights, both bestowed by the papal grants. The combination of these two rights, the one adverse to the pretensions of rival nations and the other exclusive of the vassals of Spain, was an extension of the royal prerogative beyond its scope in the Peninsula. The kings of Spain possessed legally and actually more power in America, whose soil they never trod, than in their European dominions. It was the pervasive and universal application of this principle that helped give the Spanish colonial institution its unique character. It exerted practical, if not theoretical,

A Spaniard, his Indian wife and their child, a mestizo.

A Spaniard, his wife, an octoroon or albina, *and their child,*
by chance a torna atrás.

Castes in New Spain.

power over the lives and property of all the vassals. Monopoly of land, of industry through license and control, of commerce through exclusion and localization, of religion in that the church was national with the king as its head, monopoly even in thought and feeling through the intrusive attention of the Inquisition—these were the ingrained principles of the first great modern colonial enterprise. Individual enterprise as subordinated and controlled.

It was an undertaking by and for the crown, not the Spanish nation. In no other case save that of Portugal was the system placed so immediately and thoroughly under the care of officers appointed by the crown and responsible directly to it. The absence from the Spanish plan of the joint-stock-company device, the attempted monopoly of all trade as well as of all territory, the almost continual use of a single Spanish port for trade, and the appointment of crown employees not only to supervise but to conduct actual business operations—all these made the king the official head of the greatest business organization in the world.[39] From the day of the conquerors and first settlers there grew up a society of great rigidity, dominated by an official class in both the civil and the spiritual fields. Private individuals performing no administrative duties were few in number among the upper classes; in this aspect society in the colonies became a variant from that of Spain. And however unhappily this system worked in the long run, it possessed marked advantages at the beginning. It was fortunate for the immediate purpose that this rigidly formal officialdom could be organized, though it proved disastrous in the end when it became crystallized and had to meet fierce outside competition.

The Spanish colonial empire, monopolistic, exclusive, endowed by virtue of priority with a vast income from the exploitation of native peoples and great silver-bearing regions, formed the example, the norm, and at the same time the obstacle against which strove the emulative spirit of the rivals. The all-pervasive Spanish institution, which unified the Tagalog, the Argentinian, the Sonoranian, and the Madrileño into a single civilization, was blended in the minds of the Raleighs, the Hudsons, the Cartiers, and their ambitious successors into one great impediment. It was counted in with the hazards of angry seas, strange shores, rebellious Indians, and an inhospitable climate that had to be overcome before the lavish bounty of the New World could be gained. Within a century after Columbus, Spain's loss of seapower relegated her to a minor role in history. The drain of her colonies told on her population and her national life, but always while the Old Regime persisted she was an important American power, if not the most important.

Without a very thorough knowledge of the difficulties involved, the Catholic Monarchs adopted in La Española the policy of considering the natives as free vassals. The Castilians were not to molest their properties or subject them to forced labor, and were to pay them wages. It presently developed, however, that there could be no progress upon this basis, for the Indian had to be compelled to labor. When discontent among the settlers taken out by Columbus caused lands to be allotted to them, groups of Indians were told to work these under the species of serfdom called the *encomienda*. The Indians of the Caribbean islands were rapidly destroyed by the system. Before the continental areas were entered, the island population had to be recruited by slave-catching expeditions to till the farms and work the mines. This quest initiated the series of voyages which led Cortés to the conquest of Mexico. There the emperor Charles V, recognizing the presence of a higher type of culture than the insular one, recommended the adoption of the system of Indian wage-labor which Isabella had vainly tried to establish. But the practical-minded conquerors foresaw no reward for their campaigns in the wage system, and so, in the logic of events, the *encomienda* spread to New Spain and each of the successive conquests. Only in Venezuela, California, and Texas did it fail to become fixed.

The formula for this rural institution was in general as follows. A leader of an expedition pacified an area and obtained the right to govern it. He then granted in the king's name to his followers, according to their merits of service and social position, tracts of land contiguous to Indian villages whose inhabitants were required to work for their overlord with but nominal pay. He was also paid the tithe and the tribute, keeping most of the latter for himself. He was to see that his tributaries were taught the Christian religion, but this obligation was little observed.

The natives were thus held in a tutelage initiated by custom and sanctioned by law. They became the base of the social pyramid, the foundation of the colonial structure upon which the upper parts pressed with relentless force. The system had the advantage of preserving the race, but the disadvantage of preserving it in habitual abjection and misery. The lot of the Indian was mitigated, however, by softening influences as the conquest gave up frenzied expeditions and turned to agriculture, commerce, and mining, and by the refinements of art, literature, and science, which modified society into a semblance of its European prototype.

The spirit of rapine, greed, and cruelty which imbued the *encomienda* system was bitterly censured by Bartolomé de Las Casas before the conquest had passed to the continental stage. His propaganda for the amelioration of the condition of the natives is the best-known incident of the Spanish conquest. In 1542, when the colonial experiment was nearly half a century old, it led to an attempt to remodel its entire economic basis. His "New Laws of the Indies" are always characterized as regulations for the better treatment of the Indians, but the gist of the reform lay in their prohibition of the permanent *encomienda*. It had indeed been the purpose of the original grants that they should endure only through the lifetime of the grantee, the Indians then to become free vassals under the administration of an alcalde mayor or *corregidor* with the right to receive wages for labor and pay tribute to the king. The hostility of the monarch to the *encomienda* was based on its feudal character, which was inimical to the autocratic centralist form of government; he was also anxious to collect the tributes, the chief source of revenue from the Indians.

It was hoped gradually to bring about the elimination of the *encomienda*. A general decree for its abolition was issued in 1720; in 1765, José de Gálvez was instructed to concern himself, in his general visitation of New Spain, with the condition of Indians who were being exploited by the governors and alcaldes who apportioned merchandise to them. Hence it is to be inferred that most of the *encomiendas* had by that time lapsed. Until the promulgation of the ordinance of the intendants in 1786, reorganizing the government of New Spain, the privilege of supplying the Indians with food, supplies, seeds, and animals as advances upon their crops had been in the hands of the alcaldes mayores. This aid was then withdrawn; as a result, the Indians fell under the system of debt peonage which only ended with the revolutions beginning in the time of Porfirio Díaz.[40]

The theory of legal wardship for the natives was exemplified by legislation giving them certain immunities, but at the same time placing them under restrictions which have, because of subsequent developments, seemed to warrant the assumption that the status of legal incapacity was intended to be made permanent. While it did turn out to be so, there is abundant evidence that the social institution was planned to be modified as soon as the native should become morally capable of profiting thereby. The mission system, with its contemplated process of secularization after a ten-year period, and the gradual abolition of the *encomienda* system just described are evidences of the desire to assist the evolutionary process where possible.

The mission system was an example of the quick modification of the machinery of the church to fit the needs of the progressive spiritual conquest. The mission most closely fitted the Indian situation because it embodied the altruistic and beneficent ideals of the conquering nation, and through it the blander side of the Spanish character was exhibited. All those paternalistic solicitudes which today characterize the civil state were then displayed by the church. Regrettable as it came to be in later years when the spirit of the state had developed, the very absorption by the church of the gentler duties of governmental activity served amiably the cause of humanity in the early period.

The mission was the most effective and widespread of the social agencies.[41] It was developed by the regular clergy, notably by the Jesuits and the several branches of the Dominicans, Augustinians, and Franciscans. Each mission was initiated on a frontier, of course, by one or more fathers imbued with apostolic zeal. The beginning depended upon the consent of the Indians, usually obtained by gifts or argument, and the permission of the government. The chief practical essentials were good farm land, irrigating water, and building materials. Each mission became an agricultural school, for self-support was indispensable. After stability in crop production was attained came instruction in building, weaving, sewing, leather work, pottery making, and other practical arts and crafts. These became the surest means through which growth was maintained.

Not much appeal was made to the neophyte's pride in the possession of property or the fruit of his handiwork. This unconscious weakness is easily explained. The fathers observed the rule of individual poverty, though their order might acquire unlimited collective wealth; hence the collectivity was the sole object of solicitude. The friar's pittance from the king was spent for such normal necessities of life as had to be imported to the frontier; the thousand pesos similarly bestowed for robes and vessels made no provision for upkeep and repairs. As a result the missions tried to produce more than they could consume, and disposed of the surplus to pay for costs of maintenance or expansion. In sharp contrast with the history of the secular church little or no evidence remains of the accumulation of ostentatious wealth or the indulgence of physical luxury in the missions, though the Jesuits of Puebla in the early days undoubtedly made large profits in the sugar industry, and by research perhaps such instances might be multiplied. It was a common accusation during the entire colonial period that the religious engaged in smuggling oil, wine, chocolate, and other articles primarily used by them for the support of the cult, and put their merchandise in the avenues of trade, reaping the advantages of their immunity from taxation and duties on such articles. This is vehemently but unconvincingly denied by many stout defenders of the religious orders.

The routine of the Indian in the mission included frequent religious exercises, sacred music, and crude but practical manual training.[42] The actual toil of the estate was shared by the fathers, two of whom were usually attached to each institution. Baptism, at first promiscuous and political in character, was early made contingent upon acceptance by the neophyte of the tenets of Christianity to the best of his understanding. Morality was guarded by insistence upon monogamy under Christian rites. Unmarried neophytes were locked up in separate buildings at night, as were the families, for the added reason of preventing flight. Recently reduced nomadic groups were permitted seasonal excursions to their traditional food-gathering resorts, both for economic and sentimental reasons. Fugitives were persuaded to come back by gentle means, if possible, but in many instances their return required the use of the small escort-guard of soldiers which was usually stationed near enough for protection, usually too near to avoid corruption of Indian morals. Moral lapses by friars were occasionally scandalous, but the mission as an institution was characterized by the integrity of most of the missionaries. The punishment of offenders fell to the ecclesiastical jurisdiction and was not, it must be confessed, remarkable for its frequency or severity. Indians who transgressed were whipped for offenses ranging from absence from mass to adultery. There are no cases on record of executions of mission Indians, though when rebellious they often met death at the hands of punitive expeditions. As in the case of all Indians, the Inquisition was prohibited from interfering in their lapses from the faith.

Theoretically the neophytes were the owners of the lands and buildings they occupied, but none of them seem to have comprehended this, and they had little conception of the idea of private ownership. When missions were secularized—that is, when the Indians were considered civilized and their religious care taken from the missionaries and given to parish priests —the lands belonging to the missions were apportioned to the natives collectively as needed, but almost inevitably the best lands were sooner or later seized by Spaniards. Secularization was the ideal goal of missionary effort, the theory being that the neophytes would be ready to be made free vassals in ten years. The result was seldom realized. The missionaries resisted secularization to the utmost of their ability. The religious history of New Spain is replete with accounts of their clashes with the secular clergy and the state officials over the issue.

The government of the missions, actually in the hands of the priests, was given a fictitious political organization for the sake of civil instruction. The principal Indians were given annual positions as governors and alcaldes and taught to carry with true Castilian pride the gold- or silver-topped canes that were the insignia of their proud consequentiality, as they were of Spanish official positions. But it is not to be supposed that the Indians, official or nonofficial, ever attained anything like a proper conception of town or city government from such a tutelage.

Much has been written about the futility of the mission system by those who are either hostile to the church or skeptical of the capacity of the Indian. The missions did fail to bring him to the cultural stature of the whites, but, on the other hand, they furnished him a refuge from the more selfish exploitation of the lay conquerors. They were the schools in which the native learned more, and enjoyed greater peace and security, than in any other institution devised for his improvement. They measurably advanced his status, and probably would have worked greater permanent benefit had their opportunity been of longer duration, and had the ideal included the development of the notion of personal chattel property and then of individual ownership of land. As a social institution the mission compares favorably indeed with the modern reservation or Indian school. Its disappearance was as much due to the cupidity of its competitors, the lay Spaniards, as to any weakness inherent in its conception. Its accomplishment challenges the result of any other system of control of dependent peoples developed in the field of modern colonization.[43] Yet the attitude of the Spaniard was not unreservedly benign. No Indian might possess a firearm or ride on horseback, the order being reiterated throughout the official documents. No Indian was admitted to any of the 100 or more trade guilds which flourished during the seventeenth and eighteenth centuries. None of them ascended to the priesthood during colonial days or to any other position of trust or public confidence, save that some of their nobility served as leaders to build defensive towns along the frontier.[44]

Christian Doctrine for the Indians.

The evidence is conclusive that the Indians were ruthlessly and promiscuously deprived of their lands by the conquistadores and their heirs. The pre-Spanish towns had definitely allotted plots of ground for each family, with certain areas left untilled for rotation or expansion. These untilled lands were the special objects of Spanish cupidity. Alonzo de Zurita averred in 1582 that there was "no farm nor land which has been given to Spaniards which has not injured the Indians. . . . In some of the towns they are so surrounded by the fields of the Spaniards that they have no place left to sow in."[45]

Though the first onslaught of conquering bands was destructive of the Indian land rights, it was the early and continuous policy of the crown to safeguard native tenure. As most of the new lands conquered were given municipal status, so the Indian towns were protected by a similar form of grant for the benefit of free natives not held in *encomienda*. This was done by royal recognition of the towns or villages in which they lived as communal owners. This practical recognition of the native communal tenure was effected by decrees of Charles V on March 21, 1551.

Indian towns were more numerous than Spanish ones, though individually they were, of course, of very much less importance. Protected from Spanish greed by royal legislation, they were an important agency, possibly not even second to the church, in preserving the native population. The agencies for cultural growth in such groups of huts were of course few. To the benefits of the sedentary life were added the ministrations of the parish priest, either a resident or a visiting minister. His usefulness was limited by his training and interest and by the size of his parish; often it extended little beyond the formal demands of the sacraments. Sometimes the priests were mere tyros in the use of native languages. Parochial schools were limited in number and scope, their purpose being chiefly to train acolytes for the dignified observance of the liturgy. No medical aid was available other than that afforded by native *curanderos;* in large Spanish towns there was usually hospital accommodation where nuns served as nurses but patients did without medical attendance.

It is the opinion of some scholars that the condition of these serfs, for such they were, was superior to that of the English peasantry of their day, and that the exactions upon them were not more oppressive than the French *corvée*. Thomas Gage found in Guatemala artisans, such as smiths, tailors, carpenters, masons, and shoemakers, but as we have seen, they were not members of the corresponding Spanish guilds. Hipólito Villaroel, a sharp critic of Spanish civilization in New Spain, declared in 1786 that the protective laws issued for the Indians had outlasted their utility. He believed that the officers of the *audiencia* were injuring the natives as well as society in general by insisting on the observance of legislation which pauperized the Indians and reduced agricultural production.[46]

The results of Indian policy, after the lapse of nearly 300 years, were anything but consoling to the intelligent officers of the viceroyalty. The expectation of a speedy and general conversion to Christianity and a genuine absorption of the civilization of Spain had been realized in far less degree than had been anticipated. The condition of the Indian towns about the close of the eighteenth century was drawn in somber colors by Villaroel, who, viewing the body politic through jaundiced eyes, found it diseased in all its members. Many of the towns, he said, did not really merit the name, being mere aggregations of families scattered about at random on the plains, in dark ravines, or on riverbanks, connected by trails leading from one miserable hut to another. Often not even a barber was to be found to render the services of leech, while a surplus of physicians resided in the capital. Many priests also refused to leave the capital, pleading that the towns could not support them. As to education in the Indian towns, it was of very indifferent quality since the priests were often college graduates without experience. Naturally the Indians felt little respect for such pastors, and made scant progress as compared with that of the early days of finer apostolic zeal. The agricultural education, dispensed informally by the alcaldes mayores in the pursuit of their official vocation, was little better, for these officers were bent only upon gain, those who showed real interest in their work receiving small encouragement from the central government.

The specific reforms Villaroel suggested throw interesting light on the social life at the base of the pyramid. First of all, he would abolish the law which prevented Spaniards and other castes from living among the Indians, for the isolation of the natives was the greatest hindrance to their development. He would compel them to move their villages out of the mountains and forests, where, hidden away on their little corn patches, they felt free to indulge their customary vices. He would see that all should receive ample land since many towns had been deprived of their holdings by the aggressions of the Spanish farmers. Moreover, the towns, instead of being limited to the customary 1,200 yards square, should have enough land so that half of it might be left fallow in alternate years. He would also do away with the prevalent vagabondage, preventing the natives from wandering from place to place to escape the penalties of their crimes or to avoid payment of the tribute. Enforcement of regulations like these should be entrusted to the priests and alcaldes.

Much was made of the idea that the Indians ought to be subjected to the Inquisition because of their widespread and persistent idolatry. He also warmly recommended that a new code of legislation should be drawn up to fit the actual state of affairs and the well-recognized selfish astuteness of the Indians.

The old legislation was thought necessary when the Indians were tender plants, irrigated by the healthful waters of the doctrine of Jesus Christ. But now, when for lack of a systematic method they have become robust trees in every manner of vice and evil . . . it is necessary to give thought to their conversion, and subject them by punishment to acknowledgment of their social obligations; otherwise they will be lost both to God and to the State. . . . For experience teaches that the more gently and suavely these people are dealt with, the more insolent do they become, the more insubordinate, and the more deeply are they rooted in their abominations, vices, and evil habits.[47]

This attitude of self-righteous impatience is not an aid to happy race relations. The path upward does not lie through sudden compulsion by the stronger nation but, rather, through a patient understanding of the desire of the dependent people to direct its own development. In the case of native peoples of the central plateau, the Spanish system raised up a moderately successful society. In the farther northern reaches, now within the bounds of the United States, the nomad Indians were less amenable. That the mission and the *encomienda*, with a social structure based on the legal wardship of the Indian, did not become the foundation of the life of Florida, Texas, and California is due to the combination of human geography and the inflexibility of the Spanish colonial ideal.

THE BUILDERS OF FRENCH EMPIRE

THE EARLY FRENCH VOYAGES, like those of the English, affected colonization only indirectly. If Jean Cousin, with Pinzón, made a western discovery in 1487, five years before Columbus, the French won nothing by it, the incident having received far less notice than the Norse voyages.[48] Verrazano gave impulse to Cartier and the fisherfolk who followed his seaways, but real French beginnings awaited a new century. When Cartier on his second voyage undertook the first Canadian colonial enterprise, Cortés was on his way to Lower California, New Spain had been made a viceroyalty, and the foundations of Lima were being laid. While Roberval was trying ineffectually to plant a jailbird colony on the frigid Saguenay, Coronado was overrunning New Mexico and marching into eastern Kansas, and Orellano was floating down the Amazon. The fastnesses of two continents were penetrated by the lions of Castile while the English and the French were yet hovering in the coastal stages of empire. The colonial efforts of these two during the sixteenth century ran closely parallel in purpose, inadequacy for their task, and similarity of failure. Their challenge was first to Spain, but with the establishment of Quebec in 1608, the second attempt to colonize on the St. Lawrence began their mutual rivalry for the northward reaches.

The French had been slow to migrate for many reasons. They loved to dwell in peace at home, as they do yet. They dreaded the dreary Canadian winters and the fierce Indians. For the most part they had no need of a haven from religious persecution and would not provide one under the national flag for the Huguenots. Nor were they enticed by the company system to undertake to win fortune in the wilderness. In the West Indies, where settlement began in 1625, success against English pressure and Spanish hostility was greater; for, though the various companies which operated there went successively bankrupt, the French islands, home of tropical products, grew in population to 7,000 by 1642, whereas Canada then had only 250. By 1665, France held fourteen Caribbean islands with a population of over 15,000 whites and almost as many black slaves. Prosperity continued, Guadeloupe being in the eighteenth century the most lucrative colonial holding in the world.

The occupation of the Great Lakes region and the later thrust down the Mississippi was, though tardy, the most brilliant strategical move in the fight for the continent. It was done with the small resources of Canada and despite other impediments to colonization. The St. Lawrence was closed to navigation half the year, and the winter enforced idleness among the inhabitants for the same interval. Moreover, French command of the river was more apparent than real. With the English holding the coast, the isolation of Quebec was a liability which increased as the disparity between the English and French fleets grew. Had the French chosen the Hudson instead of the St. Lawrence, or seized it when the intendant Talon made the proposal in 1665, the problem of access to the backcountry below the lakes, as well as that of coastal control, would have been simplified. The main motives of the French—desire for furs and yearning for Indian souls— were offset by the languid interest of the peasants in the breaking of the wilderness. Yet there was abundant enterprise among the individual soldiers, traders, and priests; their rivalries as well as their common drive give the heroic dispersal over a third of the continent vivid flashes of dramatic coloring which challenge the imagination quite as sharply as do the tremendous spurts of energy of the sixteenth-century Spanish conquistadores.

The colonial mechanism through which French social ideals expressed themselves exhibits interesting variations from the form and spirit of rival organizations. The state policy demanded expansion of commerce, and Cartier and Roberval began their colonizing scheme with state funds.[49] When they failed, tacit permission sufficed to send the Huguenots to Brazil and Florida, but the quest for religious security, which might have made great French colonies, was neglected. Furthermore, the driving individual will, which in England's expansion sought adventure and wealth for personal gratification, was lacking. The expansionist organization, created by governmental initiative, was, then, more like the Spanish in spirit though it had the company form used by the English and the Dutch. The effect of this dependence upon royal favor determined the type of society that grew up in the French and Spanish areas, where feudalism and paternalism fixed the forms of landed proprietorship, the enjoyment of commerce, and the practice of religion.

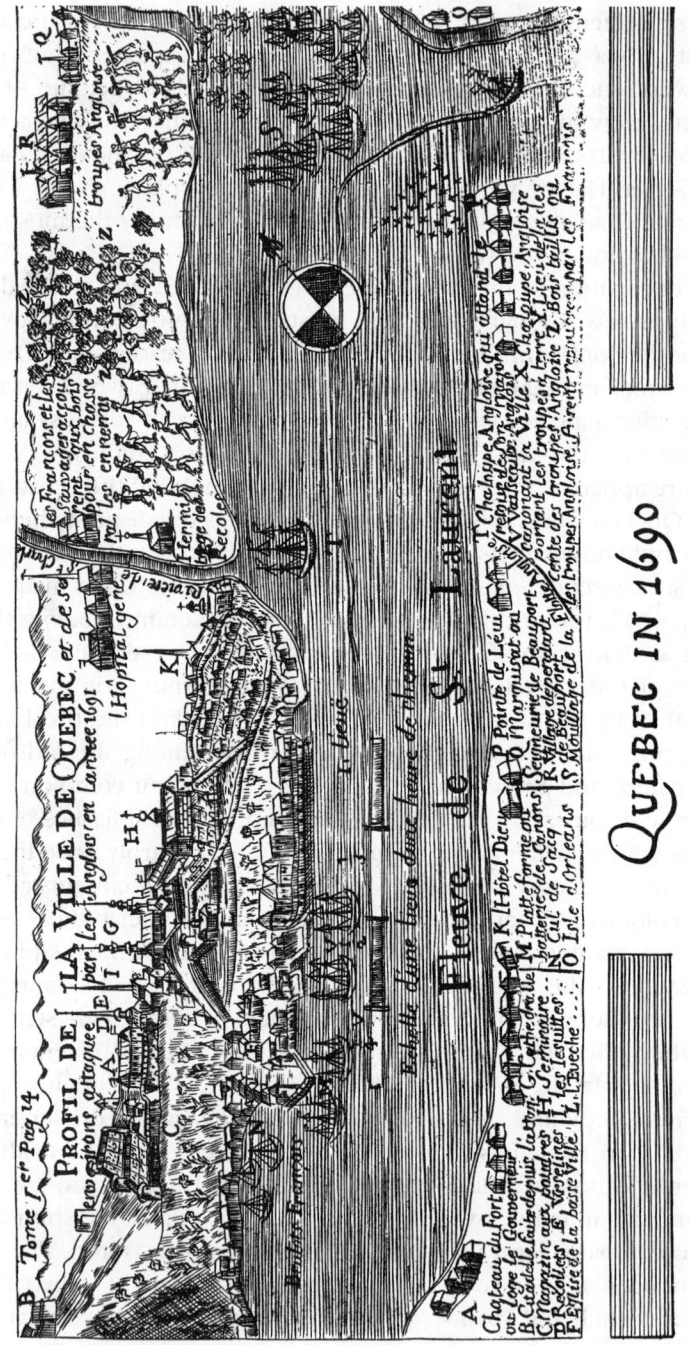

Quebec in 1690

If the differing organization and aims of the colonial societies were determined by home governmental policies, their contrasts in character were nonetheless clearly revealed in the various attitudes of the nations toward the natives. Parkman, epitomizing and contrasting these attitudes, says, "Spanish civilization crushed the Indian, England scorned and neglected him, while France embraced and cherished him.[50] This sweeping comparison overlooks the basic truth that each group of white men used the Indians for its own purposes as best it could, according to the character of the white men, the objects of their enterprise, the economic possibilities of their country, and the kind of Indians they found. It would be truer to say that the Protestant Teutonic nations felt indifferent to the uplift of the natives and thought marriage with them miscegenation, while the Catholic Latin nations tried to convert them to Christianity and their own type of society and, legally or illegally, intermarried widely with them.[51]

But in all cases European contact acted as a withering blast on the tender plant of native culture. Spanish civilization did oppress the Indian, but the mortality among the Huron and Algonquin was as severe as in any Spanish area; neither the Dutch nor the English wars with the Indian were models of civilized practice. The Frenchman "cherished" the Indian with brandy for furs and fighting men, with a spirit of camaraderie natural to the French mind perhaps, but consciously intended to win its purpose; the Spanish land system used and preserved the Indian at the lowest level of subsistence and survival. It was everywhere too easy to kill off the Indians in Spanish territory, if need be, save on the fierce northern frontiers. The French had a trading system in which Indians were useful collaborators on a plane of practical equality—if they could not be bested in barter while drunk. The bond of union rested on the difference between the European and the American valuation of beaver skins. The imputation of vice or virtue to the attitude of any white nation merely overlooks the self-interest under which each worked and seeks to impose secondary psychological reactions as prime factors. In the English labor system the Indian had no place, and so he was "scorned." But the French plan meant his extermination when the expansive life of the trapper should vanish, just as surely as did the English plan a little more promptly.[52]

The effect on colonial expansion was characteristic. The English, feeling no strong missionary impulse, still kept near the coast when the French had reached Georgian Bay. Canadian society developed the métis, cognate with the mestizos of Spanish America, but negligible elements in Dutch and English areas. The métis, though relatively few as compared with the mestizos, made worthy contributions to civilization. The half-breed of the French and Spanish areas marked one of the chief differences between the kind of society evolved in the Latin areas and that of the Teutonic colonies.

The chief social characteristics of French and Spanish colonies were evolved from their land systems, which gave distinctive tone and color to the Latin occupation of America. Both held that the king possessed sovereignty as well as direct dominion over the land. The French applied the basic principles of their land system at home to Canada, in part to the West Indies and even to Louisiana, whereas the trend of Spanish land administration was a continuous effort to get away from the vestiges of feudal form under which colonization began. The warm-hued old-worldliness of the Old Régime in Canada is tied up with this surviving feudalism. The French monarch based his title upon discovery and occupation, the kings of Spain upon these backed by the papal bulls. The French-American area was granted en bloc as a fief to the successive trading companies. Society was made compact by the absence of the high nobility, by the obligations of habitant to seigneur, seigneur to company, and company to king, with the exaction of dues, rents, and symbolic ceremonies.[53]

In the Spanish system the land was granted direct by the king or his agencies, the viceroys, *audiencias*, and municipalities. After 1630, land in New Spain was more often sold directly than bestowed by grants. The patriarchal rather than the feudal tenure of land was strengthened in Spanish America by the law of primogeniture, so that there was always a constant increase in the size of holdings instead of the diminution which occurred in New France under the *droit d'ainesse* of the Custom of Paris.[54] The effect of primogeniture was to withdraw land from circulation, making it impracticable for younger sons or less favored subjects to get it. In New France, on the other hand, the divided inheritance created parcels too small for practical cultivation.

The feudalism of New France, under which the seigneurs worked in the fields with their tenants and married their daughters, was a sort of economic democracy rare in Spanish America, for no hacendado entertained the slightest notion of dismounting from his horse to do a manual task. It is an interesting paradox that the social mold of Mexico, where feudalism was rejected by royal authority, should have become far more feudalistic in its pervasive paternalism than Canada, where feudalism was more prevalent than in France itself at the time the institution was transmitted. It is explained by the caste line of New Spain, which was created by race cleavage and by the growth of vast wealth from mining and agriculture.

The land tenure evolved by the French, excluding as it did any form of freehold save in isolated instances, was ill-adapted for frontier needs and inimical to agricultural expansion and the growth of a prosperous society. The autocrats of the Old Régime were unmoved by the fact that their system added one more handicap to those imposed by nature and the Indian, because there were certain merits in it and it was traditional.

Contemporary opinion as well as later judgment is divided as to whether the French land system was suited to the character of the habitants. It may be safely asserted that, while it no doubt served to promote solidarity and contributed to the French tenacity of occupation, it also tended to stir up litigation.[55] and to drive the most venturesome Canadians into the forest and the fur trade and thus to retard substantial growth. And yet, even with a more generous land policy, the problem of markets would have proved as serious as it often did for tobacco planters in Virginia or for stockbreeders and corn growers in New Spain. A more general agricultural opportunity was really dependent upon the development of American markets by the growth of population, for most farm products not tropical would have made unprofitable ocean freight.[56] Nearly all local communication was by water; the few roads built were quite inadequate to serve as incentive to agricultural expansion. In those goods which did admit of ocean transportation the trammels of mercantilism were effectively set aside by the wholesale smuggling activities of the European colonists of every nationality, activities which contributed to the final downfall of the exclusive system.

The agricultural production of Canada was thus restricted for the most part to supplying the wants of her population, though there was a limited export trade in wheat and flour. In 1716 this was made subject to the governor and the intendant if crops were light. The material aim of the colonists was primarily to support their own lives, and in this task they were often obliged to call upon the homeland for food. The characteristic condition of the inland as well as the coastal settlements was one of almost uniform poverty.

The relation of the church to the land presents in New France broad analogies with that in the older Latin establishments to the south. In each the ecclesiastical bodies, notably the Jesuits, gained control of superior holdings. Usually the type of agriculture maintained by the clerical bodies was of a better grade than that common among lay farmers. The possession of an undue amount of land by the church was characteristic of New France and of New Spain; in some of the English colonies the same economic phenomenon came into existence by action of large landholders of nonclerical status. But the church of New France, for obvious reasons, did not function as banker and mortgagee to the extent that it did in New Spain.[57]

In both French and Spanish areas, perhaps on account of the cheapness of land, grants and purchases were vaguely defined. The French transferred land without any measurements at all or upon mere description by a petitioner, or with metes and bounds based on previous ill-defined contiguous properties. Inevitably litigation over land became as acrimonious as it did in New Spain, or occasionally in English America. The French system enjoyed one very marked superiority in that the title deeds were registered in a public cadastre to which recourse could be had in difficulties, whereas such was not attempted in Mexico until the days of Porfirio Díaz. The Canadians had also, in the *aveu et dénombrement,* or report of the seigneuries, especially in those required every twenty years, a means of preserving agricultural history paralleled most successfully in Spanish America only by church organizations.[58]

Yet we know that New Spain supported its 4 or 5 million inhabitants, in spite of recurrent crop failures, with little food importation, while New France, with less than 80,000 inhabitants, was never entirely free from such aid. The Spaniards regularly exported the tropical agricultural products, cacao, indigo, and sugar, and even at times wheat and flour, as did the Canadians occasionally. Up to 1661, after fifty years, Canada was not self-supporting, even though the rural population around Quebec was three times that of the 547 inhabitants of the city itself.

In stock raising New France should be compared with New Netherland, where animal husbandry was also on the domestic rather than the ranch scale from the beginning. In 1647, when there was but one horse in New France, there were hundreds of thousands of cattle and horses in the valleys of New Spain; Champlain himself had remarked upon their number at an earlier date.[59] Before the seventeenth century was well ushered in, the Indians were driving off the ranches of northern Mexico more animals than the whole of New France ever possessed. In 1683, Canada, with 10,000 settlers, had 7,025 horned cattle, 56 horses, 625 sheep, and 2,320 hogs. New France was spared the Indian use of the horse in warfare because there were forests instead of plains, bitter winters instead of perpetual summer, and because the French had not been brought up in the tradition of grazing which made the cattle industry a great Spanish institution. Yet animal husbandry had moderate success. In 1719 the number of cattle had grown to 18,241, and to 33,179 in 1734; hogs in 1720 numbered 13,823, and 19,815 in 1734; sheep rose from 1,820 in 1706 to 13,823 in 1720, and 19,815 in 1734. Horses numbered about 5,000, causing the authorities much disquietude, for beef would have utilized forage to better advantage.

Uniform poverty, due largely to the land system, did not, in general, mean lack of actual food, clothing, warmth, and shelter—discomforts often bitterly experienced in New Spain—save in the early days when there was too little preparation for the cold Canadian winter. Canada was much like New Netherland in that there was a liberal supply of wild food, and in great diversity, from both forest and stream. Agricultural methods were extremely wasteful, as in other American frontier communities; this was the more surprising since crop rotation and fertilization were skillfully practiced in France. Gédéon de Catalogne, the inspector of ninety-two seigneuries in 1710-12, said that if the methods of the Canadians were to be employed in the home country, three fourths of the people would starve.

The Canadians felt little distinction between American- and European-born, perhaps because there was not time for society to crystallize in this way, and because fur trading as well as seigneurial life had its elements of equality. Not a conspicuously large number of Canadian-born seemed inclined to seek administrative positions, the famous sons of Le Moyne serving to illustrate the exception which emphasizes the rule. Little racial strife entered church circles. In spite of the all-pervasive control over their lives, the habitants developed surprisingly little rancor toward their rulers. The preliminary protests, which led to the organization of the Company of New France for habitant control of the fur trade in 1645, are strikingly mild in tone compared with the *Representation of New Netherland* in 1650. In the rural communities the seigneur and the curé—the estate and the parish being practically coterminous—were the arbiters of life among the habitants, just as *corregidor* and *cura* managed the people of New Spain. But the latter rarely showed mutual helpfulness such as prevailed in New France, because their interests were opposite, each seeking control of the Indians for his own ends.

THE PEOPLE OF THE MIDDLE BORDER

THE FRENCH OCCUPATION of the lower reaches of the Mississippi, brought within the imperial purview by La Salle, took place only after the Peace of Ryswick and under an impulse from New France. The Canadian-born sons of Charles Le Moyne, Pierre Le Moyne d'Iberville and Jean Baptiste Le Moyne de Bienville, took up the task of anticipating the possible Spanish and English seizure of the Gulf region. The English movement was narrowly averted; that of Spain to Pensacola in 1698 was met by the prompt founding of Biloxi, which was moved to Mobile Bay in 1702 and named St. Louis. Eight years later a further removal was made to the site of the present city of Mobile.

The tiny population was more than doubled in 1704 when seventy-five new soldiers arrived with supplies, some artisans, a priest, and twenty-three women—in the charge of two Grey Sisters—for wives. Unlike some of the later shipments to the matrimonial market, these young women were industrious and "respectable."[60] By 1706 the land enclosed within Mobile measured 190 arpents and held nearly ninety settlers; the presence of some 200 soldiers emphasized the character of what was always a military occupation, and the slavery of Indians had begun. In 1712 the Crozat Company, that year superseding crown administration, raised the population to 400. Under Lamothe-Cadillac, who had charge, active efforts were made to establish trade with the Spaniards, Natchitoches being established for this purpose in 1713. Fort Toulouse on the Alabama among the Creek became a fur post the next year, and served later to ward off the English from Georgia, whose Fort Okfuskee on the Talapoosa stood only forty miles away. Fort Rosalie, at the Natchez site, was established in 1716 in a vain attempt to subdue the tribe of that name. Fort de Chartres, built by Boisbriant, a cousin of Bienville—later to become the Quebec of the middle border—was founded in 1718-20 in the Illinois country.[61]

When John Law began in 1717 to make Louisiana the bright flower of his great design of French colonial empire and finance, the peopling of the valley received decided impetus. In that year New Orleans was begun, becoming the capital five years later. The "Law People" were brought out to be settlers on Law's two concessions—one on the Arkansas, the other some twenty-one miles below New Orleans on the Mississippi. They were Rhinelanders and German Swiss, who came out under the influence of "boom" literature portraying the prospective wealth awaiting them after their sufferings in a land that had not yet recovered from the Thirty Years' War. Of the 10,000 who, it has been asserted, were intended for the venture, some 2,000 arrived; the others deserted the enterprise or perished in ports of embarkation, in pest ships on the ocean, or on the miasmatic coast after landing. These people were Catholics. In the time of Bienville, the Huguenots were denied entrance, though there were 400 of them in the Carolinas who had left France after the revocation of the Edict of Nantes and now sought a welcome in Louisiana. By this rebuff to Protestant nationals an industrious element of population was rejected, but it may be that the English conquest was delayed by the same act, for the Huguenots planned close relations with the English pioneers among the Cherokee.

A large installment of settlers numbering 800, arriving in 1718, doubled the French population of the province, but was apparently more impressive in size than in quality. In these times such immigrants were rounded up in France by a regiment of archers at 100 livres per head. Then, too, prisoners were set free if they would marry prostitutes; otherwise, chained together, they were cast aboard ship and hurried off to certain misfortune or death in the wilderness. This kind of recruiting lasted for only two or three years, and the slum element is declared to have proved remarkably sterile, scarcely a score of families of that origin surviving until the Independence epoch.[62] After the bursting of Law's "Bubble," some of his colonists stayed on the Arkansas, while others came down to the settled region near the Gulf. The soldiers who garrisoned the district were released by twos from their companies each year, so that they formed a small but steady accretion to the agricultural element.

There were also Jews among the early arrivals, though they were forbidden in 1724. But the most valuable element was furnished by the Germans, who settled on the "Côte des Allemands," which came to mean both sides of the river for a distance of from twenty-five to forty miles above New Orleans, in what are now St. Charles and St. John the Baptist parishes. This German Coast was described fifty years after its beginning as the best worked and most thickly settled part of the province; with the Acadians who came later, its cultivators formed the backbone of Louisiana colonization.[63] More Germans came in 1754 from Lorraine, and others in 1774 from Frederick County, Maryland. "Dutch Highlands," near Hackett's point, commemorates their advent.

Local conditions made for somewhat the same kind of disposal of arable holdings as existed in Canada.[64] The tillable land ran back some three miles from the alluvial rise at the riverbank to cypress swamps. Single holdings measured an arpent in width (182 feet) on the river and about forty arpents in depth. Levee building and clearing had to be done without animals. The levees, finally some twenty or thirty feet high, grew annually with the danger from floods, but they furnished precarious security from the waters which might break through a crevasse and sweep miles of farm away. The settlers faced danger from spring floods and hurricanes, performed their daily toil on monotonous diet, and cleared forest and jungle in which lurked Indians and wild animals.[65] Another disadvantage of the colony was the yellow fever which appeared in 1701 and again in 1704, possibly from Santo Domingo; in the latter year Tonty of the Iron Hand was one of the victims at Mobile.

Indian troubles, such as the Natchez massacre of 1729, and expeditions like those against the Chickasaws in 1726 and 1740, were recurrent for the greater part of the period of French domination. The Natchez were dispersed in 1742, but hostile tribes frequently cut off communications with the Illinois country northward, and raids on the lower settlers occurred in 1747 and 1748. In early times the farmers tilled their fields while their wives watched from treetops with flintlock in hand to anticipate attacks. During later years the stirring up of the eastern tribes by the English formed an unremitting peril of colonial life.[66]

Black slavery gave impetus to agriculture, as did free trade with France and her colonies. The main crops were rice, tobacco, cotton, and indigo; sugar cultivation began as early as 1751 but was not of prime importance until nearly a half century later when a way was found to accommodate it perfectly to the climate. Cattle were never numerous and horses were brought in from the Spaniards in the west; they were dear, and even the thrifty Germans could obtain them, as well as slaves, only by mortgaging their properties. As land was soon scarce, the governors were denied agricultural grants for themselves, but Bienville evaded the regulation by taking large "vegetable gardens" and fixing his "habitation" upon one of them. He also undertook a system of feudal tenure, the exaction of ground rents, products, and services; but as all large concessions below Manchac were canceled by royal edict on August 10, 1728, for the purpose of redistribution, feudal organization did not become characteristic. As they prospered, the country folk would send their farm produce to New Orleans by rowboat to be sold on Sundays in front of the cathedral. Closer neighbors sent such stuffs on the heads of slaves who vended them from door to door.

Ten years after the British dispersed the Acadian "neutrals" from the shores of the Basin of Minas, these exiles began to appear in Louisiana from Halifax as well as from their temporary homes in New England, Santo Domingo, and France. Though skillful farmers, they came empty-handed, in ill health, and sadly lacking many of those gentle graces attributed to the principals of Longfellow's poem. About 1,000 of them were located in various parts, notably at Opelousas in the country of the Attakapas, and at Cahabanoce or "Attakaban nosse." They were scantily provided with subsistence, in some cases by the king of France while en route; later, when Spain ruled the province, that court took an interest in their needs and aided them to find homes along the lakes and bayous of the region. Known colloquially in later days as "Cajuns," they did not generally enter the upper ranks of society, though some of them intermarried with the French creole element and a few attained political and economic importance. They spread gradually and widely from their original location in what is now St. James Parish.[67] Their coming severely tried the patience of the officials, who resented the expense and trouble they entailed, their complaints about the raids of hostile Indians, and their demands for frequent assistance for their agriculture.[68]

The composite social character of Louisiana under the French was further increased by the large black population. When the Spaniards took over the trans-Mississippi territory in 1769, the population numbered probably between 8,250 and 11,500. Between Pointe Coupé and New Orleans there were more than 7,000 people, but two thirds of them were blacks, who increased much faster than the whites. Black slaves were used in both field and home, where they absorbed many of the characteristics of the whites.

In spite of the obvious danger in the practice and the prohibition against their bearing arms, it soon became a necessity to use blacks in fighting the Indians. Many of them helped defend Louisiana for the French king; still others became renegades among the Indians, where life was easier, and turned their strength against their old masters. The Spaniards from Catalonia mingled on familiar terms with the blacks, causing the French much uneasiness because of the danger to white rule. Fear of insurrections, indeed, led Bienville in 1724 to promulgate the Code Noir. This legislation imposed heavy fines for marriage between blacks and whites and punished illicit relations between masters and black women. Children of mixed unions, with their mothers, were to become the property of the New Orleans hospital.[69]

In the presence of a dominant number of blacks, the black strain soon became a social taint. The institution of marriage among the whites was fortified by the legal requirement of four birth certificates from each high contracting party; yet this did not prevent admixture, though even the remotest tinge continued to place the bearer among the tabooed race. It has often been said that the Code Noir was a cruel system of laws, but it should be remembered that it was for the control not only of blacks but of their white superiors. It provided for the humane treatment of slaves according to the quality of mercy of the times, including a system of manumission, for the exclusion of Jews and Protestants, and for the observance of religion.

The creole society bred in Louisiana claims fairly unmixed descent from the officials who were first in the province. The Canadians did not use the word "creole"; criollo was a habitual designation among the Spaniards for those of full Iberian blood born in America. In this sense it was used by the Louisianans, perhaps as a result of contiguity with the Spanish. By extension, the designation creole was applied to children of European parents born in the colonies; so there came to be in Louisiana French, Spanish, German, Scotch, and Irish creoles.

New Orleans, once made the capital, never lost its ascendancy over the other Gulf settlements. When Charlevoix saw it in 1722, it was a "wild, lovely place," with about 100 huts among trees and underbrush. There were only two or three good houses and a *magasin,* one half of which was used for church services. Forty years later, when it passed into the possession of Spain, the capital had a population of about 3,200 of whom 1,900 were free, including thirty-one blacks. There were sixty-eight persons of "mixed breed"; slaves numbered 1,225, sixty of them Indians. The streets, set at right angles, made blocks around which ditches for drainage were dug, each block being called an "islet." Every block originally provided for four lots and as many residences, but these came to number twelve. The houses, 468 in all, were low, built of cypress logs, with steep, bark-covered roofs sheltering from four to eight rooms. They were set about eight feet above ground level, with galleries all around them; the doors and windows were of solid cypress.

Some of these old houses stood for 150 years, but most of Bienville's old city was wiped out by the destructive fires of 1787 and 1794. The rebuilding was confined by law to brick, in which material the town then assumed much of its present appearance. The yards were surrounded by high, sharp-pointed picket fences; sour-orange trees lined the streets, loading the moist hot air with languorous perfume. Toward the quay was the Place d'Armes, the long low church of St. Louis facing one side, with the cemetery behind. On the other side of this "civic center" stood a prison, a convent, the government buildings with a pillory facing them on the Place, and quarters for the troops. Palisades enclosed the whole, with a ditch to serve as protection against uprisings of plantation blacks or forest Indians.

The tradespeople and artisans lived mostly on Royal and Bourbon Streets; the Jesuit Convent was on Charters, while Bienville Street was the aristocratic section, with the house of the governor among its attractions. The city boasted three surgeons, two of them in private practice. Life for the upper classes was not uncomfortable. Linen, furniture, and glassware were brought from France, while imported laces, jewelry, silk, and satin were among the delights of feminine souls.[70] Some of the men of the upper class wore perukes and queues, silk stockings and silver-buckled shoes. Servants were plentiful and well trained, and the markets, or the slaves who vended wares from nearby plantations, purveyed game, vegetables, and fruits. Imports from Illinois were usually on hand unless Indian hostilities interrupted communications. The practice of depending upon importations was well-nigh constant.[71]

The forced colonization from France tended to create a discontented element in society which refused to look upon the Valley as a real home and taught its children to assume the attitude of exiles. Even officials as a rule looked upon the mother country as home and exerted themselves to acquire a competency and depart in hope of a promotion. Many of the immigrants, disillusioned of their dreams of easily acquired wealth, went home in disgust. On the other hand, many of the best families date back to the earliest settlements at Biloxi, Dauphin Island, and Mobile. They formed the nucleus of the early aristocracy of New Orleans, and their members have left enviable records of service during every period of subsequent history.

During the Spanish domination there was an influx of Spaniards of the official class and also of Mexican troops. Despite the early antipathy created by the policies of Ulloa and O'Reilly, the Spaniards and the French rapidly came to live upon amicable terms and soon began to intermarry. Governor Gálvez later took as his wife a daughter of the Maxent family. Young German women also married freely into the French families; the gallicization of family names served to conceal German identity and to blend these two elements.

Not much can be said of the opportunities for education in the Gulf territory. It began, if we may stretch the meaning of the word a little and ignore for the moment the work of the church, with the efforts of the literary carpenter André Pénicaut, whose *Relation* is one of the earliest, if somewhat romantic, sources of the history of the region. Voyaging to the Natchez in 1706, he spent the winter among them, whiling away its tedium by teaching the chieftain's daughters to dance minuets and speak French. "They nearly made me die with laughter," he says, "with their savage pronunciation, which comes only from the throat."[72] In later days the spread of culture was much in the hands of the Capuchin friars, who managed to hold their own against the bishop of Canada and the Jesuits, and received the clerical effects of the latter when they were expelled in 1764. The Mobile region was under the ministration of the Carmelites; the Ursuline nuns had a school in New Orleans.

Such education as was given by the church was quite elementary. Masters of slaves were supposed to attend to their educational needs, which cannot be imagined as urgent. The official and aristocratic elements possessed such enlightenment as was essential to the performance of duty or the management of plantations worked by slaves. There were two elementary church schools in New Orleans in Spanish days and several insignificant private ones. As in Canada, there was no early newspaper, the *Moniteur de la Louisiane* not being established until 1794 and finding even then but few readers.[73]

Fear of black uprisings was never quite absent, especially after the bloody events in which the blacks of Santo Domingo had expressed their appreciation of *liberté, fraternité,* and *egalité* by the massacres of 1791. It was well known in Louisiana that the blacks were in complete control of the island and were mistreating the survivors of the former planter population; they wanted independence of everything white, even of the French Republic. The governor, Le Baron Carondelet, was much upset over the prospect of a spread of the same spirit to his territory. Many of the planters in March brought their families into New Orleans for safety, which alarmed everyone and was not lost on the slaves. Two or three blacks had been discovered talking about possibilities, but no plot could be unearthed—the mere fact of the superior numbers of blacks made the planters panicky. By May, Carondelet, becoming convinced of this, began to relax the unusual precautions he had been taking.[74]

A more real danger was the epidemic of yellow fever. The people, especially the women, were in abject fear; they took precaution "to wear garlic on their bodies and carry hartshorn; everywhere tar is being burned." The strong, young, and wealthy were succumbing; a captain of the Mexican regiment was seized with the malady. Corpses were found unburied in the Protestant corner of the cemetery, hastily concealed by branches and leaves; no one knew who was guilty, all were afraid to touch the bodies. Though the authorities made efforts to conceal the deaths of from fifteen to seventeen daily victims, those who had country places to go to fled the city. "We are all agreed that it is the yellow fever, which rages nearly every year in Philadelphia, and that the Americans brought it in." The governor would not leave, lest his departure increase the panic. He, Pontalba, and their set made an earnest pretense of enjoying themselves in all sorts of frolics and extravagances, but they were constantly chewing quinine nevertheless. By mid-November, with sharp winds and cold weather, the plague departed.

When news of the treaty of 1795 came down by way of Kentucky, with its promise of free navigation of the river and the right of deposit, there was a stir of new life:

This country is going to become one of the most prosperous in the world. The population will increase in an incredible manner; property will double in value; stores and houses will be rented at exorbitant prices and our city will soon resemble Philadelphia in the diversity of nations that will live here. One of the articles of the Treaty permits liberty of worship, and the Ameri-

cans will be permitted to bring their own lawyers to settle their differences.
. . . I think from all this that I shall be able to sell advantageously all my
built-up lots. . . . The city is building up all with terraced roofs and framework
covered with brick or plaster. . . . I judge that this great rush of building will
make rents fall, and for this reason I feel like not putting the ceilings in the
houses of your aunt and leaving the woodwork very simple . . . for fear she
might not receive the rent I flattered myself she would. I am following the
same course with mine. . . .[75]

The costs of building are shown by the fact that two little houses, thirty-
four by twenty-eight feet in dimension, were to cost a total of $8,000, each
to have one little story and a kitchen. A house Pontalba built on the levee
would bring a rent of $178 a month, and one facing the Place d'Armes
$118. He had finished building eleven stores, though only five were
rented.[76] Then came news by sea that Spain had declared war upon England, and there was an ugly rumor that the king expected within three or
four months to free all the slaves within his dominions; "If that should
happen in so short a time we should all find ourselves ruined.[77]

In the Illinois country the French pioneers, who linked Canada with
Lower Louisiana, led a simpler, harder life. These frontiersmen were in
theory subject to all the whims of faraway imperial control, but their remoteness actually gave them relief from too close supervision. Their rather
indeterminate territory was a strip extending from the Alleghenies to beyond the Mississippi and from the Ohio northward. There was also the
larger area of the commmandery, which included a small post and settlement on the Arkansas, another on the Missouri, and Vincennes on the
Wabash. This great area was subordinate to Louisiana after 1731.[78] Its governing head, the major commandant, not only had charge of the military
establishment, but also promoted agriculture, watched the fur trade, protected religion, and supervised the annual census, all for a stipend of 1,200
livres. His chief post was Fort de Chartres, some sixteen miles above
Kaskaskia on the left bank of the Mississippi. The garrison was never over
300 men, and usually numbered about 100.

The population was always small. In 1723 there were 196 whites in
Kaskaskia, 126 in Chartres village, and twelve in Cahokia, a total of 334 men,
women, and children; in 1732 the population numbered perhaps 600. After
the English had taken the country and many French had gone over for the
time being to the newly founded St. Louis on what was supposedly French
soil, there were 600 people in Kaskaskia, twenty-five families at Prairie du
Rocher, three each at Chartres village and St. Philippe, and six at Cahokia.
The total free population at the height of prosperity was not over 1,500 or
2,000, including soldiers. At the time of the French exodus the remaining
settlers were estimated at 1,200 adults, 600 children, and some 900 blacks.

Lands were laid out on much the same plan as was used in Canada. The

After the fire of 1788 the Cathedral of St. Louis was rebuilt; flanked by the Calaboose and the Cabildo, it still dominates the old Place d'Armes, since called Jackson Square.

New Orleans, the Crescent City, soon after it became a part of the United States.

houses clustered in the village, with the cultivated fields running in long strips with a few rods' frontage and sides many times as long. At Kaskaskia they stretched from the village to the Mississippi. Separate possessions were marked by furrows and contained from 40 to 183 acres, the latter being the size of the Jesuit farm. Along the front of the fields nearest the village a common fence was kept up by the owners of the strips to keep the cattle out of the crops, but the livestock grazed at will in the commons, each animal bearing its owner's brand. As these pioneers were not expert farmers, the returns were always disappointing; where large estates depended upon Indian or black slave labor, it was least satisfactory. Fertilization was little used and, as in the English colonies along the Atlantic, the tools were crude. The wooden plow, with iron point tied in place with a leather thong, scratched the virgin soil as it did in Canada, New Spain, and New England.[79] Two-wheeled carts, drawn by oxen with a bar fastened across their horns instead of a yoke, as in present-day Mexico, or horses driven tandem by voice and whip but no reins, animated the rural picture.

The common-fields system limited initiative; everyone must plow, plant, cultivate, and harvest at the same time and in the same way. All this was determined by the village assembly whose voice, expressed in churchyard meetings presided over either by syndics or *marguilliers,* was decisive. Spring wheat, introduced by the Jesuits, was the chief crop, the surplus being exported to New Orleans. Two thousand hundredweight went in 1732 and 6,000 in 1740; in 1745, Louisiana was saved from threatened famine after a hurricane by Illinois wheat. Oats, hemp, hops, and some tobacco were raised. The French used little corn and that only for their livestock. Melons, potatoes, and squashes grew in their gardens, and their fruits were apples, pears, and peaches; European grapes could not be acclimated, though wine was made from the wild ones. Small sturdy cattle, driven down from Canada, mingled on the common with horses often wild, brought in from the Spanish to the southwest. A little butter was made by shaking cream in bottles. Bear meat and grease, venison, hides, and buffalo wool were obtained in sufficient surplus to export regularly to New Orleans.[80]

The fur trade rivaled agriculture. The attempt of Talon by ordinance of 1672 to forbid it to the inhabitants of Canada, and the order of 1680 prohibiting the issue of trade permits by the governor, served only to spread the *coureurs de bois* over the west and divert their peltries to the British at Albany. In 1681, issue of *congés,* or permits, twenty-five in number, had like effects. The order of 1696, recalling all these proscribed forest traders under pain of sentence to the galleys, was equally ineffectual. In 1700 the king took in charge the entire beaver trade and the service was leased at various posts. This method rendered collection easy from the French point of view but worked hardship upon the Indians, who had become accustomed to receiving in their villages such European artifacts as they required. After the failure of Crozat the usual method was to leave the trade of the southern province free, though prices were fixed. Inasmuch as furs shipped to New Orleans spoiled in the heat, the trade went regularly north by way of Detroit or Mackinac, but most of the imports into Illinois came from the south at a price of perhaps 100 percent above their cost in France.[81] The circulating medium consisted of beaver skins, Spanish coins smuggled through in large quantities, and paper tokens of various kinds carefully marked in a vain attempt to prevent forgery.

Communication was largely by canoe, pirogue, or bateau over the rivers and portages to the north and down the Mississippi to New Orleans. Pirogues—hollowed tree trunks—had no keels and were guided by oars fastened at the stern, or even plank rudders; they were used as convoys but, like canoes, were easily capsized or captured. *Cajens,* or sets of canoes fastened together, were used in the lower country. In 1732 began the use of large bateaux of from sixteen to twenty tons' burden, propelled by sails and oars; and numerous other craft with sails came into use in time. The royal convoy usually left New Orleans in late winter or early spring, a second one setting out in August. The upstream voyage consumed from seventy days to three months, but in the spring fast bateaux went downstream to the capital in twelve or thirteen days. Private boats were constantly plying up and down, merchants often combining forces for sociable cooperation in landing for the nights on the high bluffs, for protection from accidents of travel, such as snags and shoals, and Indian hostility. Voyages to Canada consumed several weeks. A wagon road connecting Kaskaskia with Cahokia was built at an early date, and other roads in many directions followed old Indian and buffalo trails; one of these ran from Cahokia to Peoria and Galena, another to the mouth of the Tennessee, and there was a well-worn road between Peoria and Detroit.[82]

Kaskaskia was typical in many ways of other French villages. At its center was a large grass-covered square with narrow streets leading at right angles from it; facing it stood the church and the picketed fort. The blocks were some 300 feet square and each contained four lots. Because of its many stone houses, this peaceful village had an air of permanence unusual for the frontier. The wooden houses were of upright timbers hewn with concave sides, the spaces between filled with clay, straw, and stone, no iron being used in their construction. The pointed roofs, covered with thatch or bark, extended over the front, making a porch or gallery such as may still be seen in parts of the South. Most of the houses were of one story and a half, though some boasted two; chimneys stood at one end, sometimes at both. Set in friendly fashion close to the street, the homes were surrounded by whitewashed picket fences enclosing the flower garden, fruit trees, vegetables, the slaves' cabins, and barns.

In a home of comparative wealth one would find a hall running from the front gallery to the back, flanked by the various rooms—not an unusual feature of Southern houses today. The important furniture was good; there was even some silver plate; usually religious pictures hung beside French mirrors in gilt frames; and sometimes there was a billiard table. The homes of the habitants possessed little decoration and had only homemade furniture. One of the finest establishments was that of the Jesuits. The house was 120 feet long; another building was divided into many low apartments; there were also slave cabins, cowsheds, a barn, a stable, a weaving room, a horse-mill, and a dovecote. Sixty-eight black slaves served as farmers, blacksmiths, carpenters, brewers, and masons. Several private farms were developed on a similar scale.[83]

The highest social caste was represented by the military officers, who belonged to the gentry at home or even to noble families. Their bright uniforms of long coats, embroidered vests, and knee breeches set them in sharp contrast to the enlisted men, whose ragged poverty and underfed condition made them caricatures of soldiers. The latter came from the slums of France and often cheerfully deserted to the Spanish or English settlements, knowing their lot could be no worse. Fur traders, following Paris styles tardily through New Orleans, wore lavish costumes with richly trimmed hats, embroidered waistcoats with "diamond" buttons, silk hose, and silver buckles. The habitants wore *capots* of Mackinaw blankets, a blue hood for winter, deerskin trousers and moccasins. A short clay pipe blackened with much communion, a shirt of colored cotton, and trousers held up by a broad beaded sash tied outside the coat often figured in the costume; over the head was the invariable colored handkerchief. The vivacious and turbulent voyageurs affected leather-ruffled shirts and bright caps with tassels hanging on one side. As the women did not spin or weave, their clothing included imported fabrics. Those of the lower class were clad in short skirts reaching to the knees, underneath them long petticoats; their heads they covered with straw hats or, in winter, with fur hats or bonnets. On their feet they wore the habitual moccasin.

Illiteracy was general among the habitants, while education among the gentry was comparable with that of France. In 1796 two thirds of the population of Vincennes could not read or write. A certain social charm these western Frenchmen retained, it is true, but they slowly lost all traces of the mental alertness of their race.[84] As to their morals, these were, if court records mean much, as good as those of the traditional frontier, in spite of the accusations of priests and officers who confessed their lack of influence by blaming the people with low habits. Certainly they were thrifty, even niggardly, and as crafty as one need be to fight the battle of the wilderness. Lighthearted and easygoing, they all danced on Sunday evenings; even the priest dropped in for a chat at the home of the well-to-do farmer where the party was held. Mixture with the native race was chiefly at the lowest level; the *coureurs de bois* married squaws freely, celebrating the ceremony when the priests could compel them. Kaskaskia was for two decades mostly of such origin. In 1735 the commandant's consent was required for mixed unions, the Jesuits submitting with forced grace. The number of illegitimate children was always high.

The Illinois country had a democratic institution, the village meeting, not used in Canada. The people elected syndics to represent them in lawsuits, and the church congregations elected *marguilliers,* or wardens, at Kaskaskia, Cahokia, and perhaps at Chartres. These local officers functioned with some regularity, reporting to their constituents after mass at the church doors, where auctions and other public meetings were held; the priest presided in case of church affairs, but the syndics at civil convocations. Here the people, including boys over fourteen and perhaps widows, elected officers, chose the times for farm operations, church repairing, and road building, and decided other community interests.

Farther to the north and more within the area of Canadian than Louisiana influence, the French trappers and woodsmen left their impress upon Wisconsin society in remnants of imperial design now surviving in vestiges of the fur trade at occasional posts, where memories linger on the path of enterprise now trod by more vigorous feet. The wide middle border of French-American empire was to become in time the real heart of the continent, where the races of men were to mingle in an actual conquest dreamed of by Versailles and Quebec, but unrealized until American colonization of the Middle West supplanted the overseas efforts of men of mixed minds and interests.[85]

OUR DUTCH HERITAGE

NEW NETHERLAND, partly because of defects in policy, failed to establish itself as a strong well-based community. But ineptitude in politics was not the only shortcoming. It must be confessed that the Dutch, like the French, made no notable contribution to the transmission of the higher forms of European culture to America during their period of colonization. At a time when Amsterdam surpassed London in wealth and commercial importance, and the University of Leyden enjoyed better repute than Oxford, the Dutch colony on the Hudson produced little to compare even with the cultural achievements on Massachusetts Bay.[86]

There were good reasons why Dutch intellectuality and prosperity found feeble echo in early New Netherland. It was a small colony of less than 10,000 even at the end. Few if any of the immigrants were superior to those who were the original settlers of New France, New Spain, or New England. As has been observed, life was sufficiently attractive in the old country to prevent a rush of talent to the new. Most of those who came could neither read nor write. Among the peasants who settled Rensselaerswyck, hardly one possessed a patronymic. Van Rensselaer said in 1642 that they were extravagant, licentious, and wanton. During Kieft's war the colonists committed horrible murders and other excesses on the Indians. "They were a rough lot," writes a descendant, ". . . they cheated the savages . . . and most cruelly oppressed them. Also on occasion they cheated one another; out of which habit, as is shown by the verbose records of their little courts, arose much petty litigation of a snarling sort among themselves. . . . They consistently cheated the revenue laws . . . and . . . any other laws which happened to get in their way. . . . But also they had certain virtues. . . . With all their shortcomings they were tough and they were sturdy and they were as plucky as men could be."[87]

The fact is that the European character in the wilderness environment worked much the same in New Netherland as elsewhere in American colonization. The settlers there were unusually happy in their choice of a habitat, for the country was favorable both in climate and natural resources. Domestic cattle alone were lacking, but these were more plentifully imported than in New France, though never lavishly. The sowing of European seeds amply rewarded effort, so that there was little reason why a good agricultural colony should not have developed. The natives, though thieving and treacherous, were fearful and timid and were amenable to kind treatment. It was said that they were willing to work for pay, especially for carrying burdens on long journeys. It did not help the relations of the races, however, that the white employers sometimes dismissed their Indians without paying them their wages.[88] If the Dutch patroons and farmers could have succeeded in developing a system of forced labor, milder and more domestic than the Spanish one, they might have created a temperate-zone plantation colony and preserved the native race. But they found that the Indians would not endure the exaction of tributes, and hence achieved no greater success than the French and English in the way of developing the human resources of the continent.

They did attempt the slavery of both Indians and blacks, but the institution did not flourish. Indian slavery was almost casual in New Netherland; the colonists did not object, but the authorities feared that it would give the French a text upon which to urge the Iroquois to treat the Dutch as enemies. In 1679 the Indian slaves were declared free. The first blacks were brought over in 1625 or 1626, several years after the familiar Virginia episode. Their numbers were few until 1646, when a cargo from a slave ship was purchased with pork and peas. From them much was expected, "but they just dripped through the fingers." Inasmuch as agriculture suffered from lack of markets, the colonists were in 1648 allowed to export fish, flour, and other produce to Brazil, for which they might accept in payment slaves, among other things. Since this expansion of trade did not encourage agriculture as had been expected, the demand for blacks remained slight. However, the burghers of the capital petitioned in 1660 to be allowed to enter the West African slave trade, and on the eve of the surrender to the English in 1664 a delayed shipload of 300 blacks arrived.

That slavery was fostered for its effect on trade rather than on industrial development is shown by the fact that the blacks were brought over by merchants licensed by the company, largely in the hope that they could be sold to the neighboring English. Most of the blacks were used in domestic service, and when employed as farm hands were in a true domestic relation, often working side by side with their masters in the fields. The happy relations existing between masters and slaves near Albany during the eighteenth century were probably characteristic of other localities as well. Black children were attached to young members of their own sex in their master's family and grew up with them in intimate friendship.[89]

The most terrible punishment for occasional malefactors among the blacks, short of death, was to be sold to the island of Jamaica. As late as 1703 there were but 1,300 blacks to 7,767 whites in five counties about New York city. Indians, mulattoes, and *mustees* (mestizos) might also be found among the slave population as a result of voluntary sale, sentence for crime, or natural increase; children of slave mothers inherited the status.[90] Evidently the number of half-breeds was fairly large, for they received legislative attention, but references to them are relatively few in the documents on New Netherland. Slaves might be beaten or sent to the house of correction, but masters might not kill them. They could testify in court against each other, though not against a freeman. When on trial, they were denied benefit of counsel, nor could they hold property or engage in trade.

Fear of servile insurrections led to repressive laws. Not more than four slaves—after 1702, three—might congregate anywhere off their master's estate. On Sunday, their day of rest, they were closely watched. The corporation of New York forbade them to ride horseback on the streets or common; they might not go over to Brooklyn without permission. Negro plots in 1712 proved that the fear had some basis in fact, though no such trouble had arisen under the Dutch regime. In this case the blacks killed nine men and wounded six before they were dispersed by the troops. Twenty who were captured were hanged, burned, or broken on the wheel; six who escaped found refuge in committing suicide. In the second or Great Plot of 1741, newcomers from Africa probably incited incendiarism and thievery. There were then 2,000 black slaves, representing about one fifth of the total population of the city of New York. A servant woman, Mary Barton, accused certain blacks who had met on the estate of her master. Upon these the whites fell, the victims of their own terror. They cast 154 slaves into jail, burned fourteen, hanged eighteen, and arrested twenty-four whites, of whom four were executed. When Mary became so pleased at her success that she began to accuse people of the upper classes, society came to its senses.[91] But by this time the colony was losing its Dutch character.

In agriculture the settlers in New Netherland had much to learn from the Indians.[92] In the fields about the Fresh Water Pond, or Collect, the Manhatoes cultivated peas, beans, corn, and pumpkins. To these simple farmers the whites were debtors for the delights of succotash. No dikes were required for tillage as in the fatherland; post and rail fences sufficed for enclosures, such materials being usually made available in clearing the land. Land grubbed and plowed twice was ready for winter grain; for summer grain one plowing was enough. The summer stubble was plowed in, but in the 1650s no fertilizer was used. Though peas were often sown to soften the soil, it was too rich to yield good ones, and probably the farmers did not know the nitrogenous effect of this crop, but two harvests of it could be taken in a year. Indian corn, then often called Turkish wheat, grew well in almost any soil; it was followed by winter grain. Rye grew taller than a man's head, as did barley, and both produced lavishly. Wheat could be sown as many as eleven years in the same soil without alternation, and thus became the agricultural staple of the province. Father Isaac Jogues, visiting New Amsterdam in 1643, found that 300 ships had been there to load wheat for the West India trade.[93] But much of the wheat was kept at home and ground into flour in the various mills driven by wind, water, or horses.[94]

The cultivation of tobacco was engaged in by most of the farmers, the leaf being considered second in value only to that of Virginia. The wealth of the latter colony from this source had been one of the incentives to Dutch emulation of English colonization, and by the middle of the thirties tobacco was being exported to Holland in substantial quantities. Nevertheless, it was not allowed to supersede the food crops; when a famine seemed imminent in 1653, tobacco planters were ordered to plant as many hills of maize, peas, or grain as they did of their commercial crop.[95] Flax and hemp would do well, but as the Dutch women did not spin much during the first two decades, and since the Indians used their own wild hemp for making ropes and nets, little attention was given these crops. All things considered it was hardly to be expected that the colony would sustain itself, yet shortly after 1630 that became the ideal. "If agriculture were promoted a little," wrote Governor Van Twiller, "we could arrange to have enough of everything with the exception of salt, oil and vinegar."[96]

In one of its bursts of generosity the company offered free sea passage for farmers and their families and, on their arrival, a grant of land partly cleared, a house, barn, tools, and animals. The grantee was to have the usufruct of these advantages for six years, then return the number of cattle originally placed at his disposal after retaining the increase. Under this plan six *bouweries* were laid out between Wall Street and 14th Street early in the time of Kieft. Each was a little farmstead; the record shows one to have consisted of a dwelling house thirty by eighteen feet in area with two transom windows and two round windows, a tobacco barn sixty feet long and a separate kitchen building twenty feet by sixteen.[97] By 1635 there were eight of them above the town, reached by Bouwerie Lane, but despite their log palisades and their short distance from the main defenses, these farms were hazardous places of abode during Indian troubles. Emanuel de Groot, a freed black, took ten heads of colored families and founded an agricultural settlement at Werpoes. It became known later as the Bowery and was the first extensive clearing outside the original settlement. Peter Stuyvesant's pear orchard, planted about 1664, had in later years one sole surviving tree which long stood as a city landmark.[98]

In spite of the ideals of Usselinx and the efforts of men like Van Rensselaer and De Vries, agriculture remained of less importance than fur trading until about 1660. Van Rensselaer had begun farm operations thirty years before; his superintendent received from 150 to 180 guilders a year, and his laborers from forty to ninety, pledging themselves to four years' service. Mechanics earned as much as the superintendent, but were obliged to turn in half of all they received for outside work. Though the first harvests would not feed the people and provide seed, and though the cattle and hogs could not be eaten, the game hunted or bought from the Indians sufficed. Roelof Jans of Janssen, the superintendent at Rensselaerswyck, moved to Manhattan when he finished his service and began the farm known later by his wife's name, Annetje, and also as the Domine's Bouwerie. This piece of property, which brought no revenue for five years, was about sixty-two acres in size and of irregular shape. It finally became the property of Trinity Church.

Field husbandry was generally the task of the men with their blacks and bound servants. But everyone in town or country in the Albany region of the eighteenth century had in addition a house garden whose plants received the skillful and loving attention of the women. There, kidney beans, asparagus, celery, and many sweet herbs no longer known to average gardens grew in the closely planted rows and helped to vary the diet of the family. Red and white roses, eglantine, violets, marigolds, and many other flowers were also found in the gardens. By Van der Donck's time many homes had fruit trees—peaches, apricots, cherries, figs, almonds, persimmons, plums, gooseberries, and quinces from England.[99]

The relations of the Dutch with the Indians varied little from the experiences of the other European nations. Oft-repeated legislation proves that liquor and firearms were shamelessly sold to the natives for furs. The use of *seawant* (wampum) and beaver skins as media of exchange indicates the degree of dependence of the whites upon the Indians.[100] But there was little that was unique in these mutual manifestations of dependence; the Indian wars of New Netherland merely ring the changes on the continentwide experience of Europeans. With but few exceptions, like that of Crol, they would not try to learn Indian languages, but developed a rude jargon suitable for the elementary needs of trading.

Contact with the Indians had the same demoralizing effect upon Dutchmen as it did upon the Spaniards, Swedes, and French. They did not adopt the practice common among the French and Spanish of taking Indian women, with or without marriage ties, as heads of their households. Nevertheless, there was a continuous illicit intercourse which, as it did on the English frontiers, affected the formation of society. The price of a Mohawk squaw's virtue, wrote Domine Megapolensis, was from one to three shillings, "and our Dutchmen run after them very much." [101] It is thus evident that the moral reaction of the Dutch pioneers to New World influences was like that of the English, and less idealistic than that of the French or the Spanish who professed the principle of race amalgamation and the universal acceptance of Christianity.

There were indeed several attempts to Christianize the Indians. Megapolensis tried to learn the Mohawk language for that purpose, but found its construction mystifying. One must smile at the solemn perplexity of the reverend domine when he asked his Indian teachers by what names things were called. "One tells me the word in the infinitive mood, another in the indicative; one in the first, another in the second person; one in the present, another in the preterite. So I stand oftentimes and look, but do not know how to put it down." He reports of one Indian who had been considered redeemed, having learned Dutch prayers, catechism, and scripture, but "he took to drinking brandy, he pawned the Bible, and turned into a regular beast, doing more harm than good among the Indians." [102]

At all events the Indians took little stock in the Dutch exemplification of religion. "When we pray they laugh at us. . . . Some, when we tell them what we do when we pray, stand astonished." So, too, they found it hard to reconcile Dutch actions with their spiritual admonitions and decided after prolonged experience that the French "were better Christians than the men of New Netherland." Doubtless the dramatic features of Roman Catholic worship had something, though not everything, to do with this appreciation.

Public education began in New Amsterdam in 1638, shortly after its inception in New England. The first teacher, Adam Roelantsen, was a sorry scapegrace; Jan Cornelissen, who taught ten years, was a seasoned tippler. Six other schoolmasters, of general good repute, taught during the Dutch period, but the profession was apparently not always thought a high one. Everyone was ordered, when Evert Pietersen taught in the governor's *bouwerie,* not to molest or ridicule him, but "deliver him from every painful sensation." Teachers were licensed by the Classis of Amsterdam and engaged by the company, being considered servants of the church.

Generally, in the city and throughout the ten or eleven villages which by the middle of the century were supporting schools, the public teacher was also the reader, the chorister, and the sexton of the church. The domine and wardens of the parish along with the magistrate supervised his work in the classroom. The latter was in most cases the schoolmaster's own house or at least a house built by the village for his lodging as well as for the school. Here, from eight in the morning, except on Sundays and the five general holidays, he taught boys and girls reading and writing, the elements of arithmetic if local commerce had advanced enough to make it necessary, and perhaps now and then even a little modern history; provision was made for girls to learn needlework at school as well as at home.

"The knowledge and fear of the Lord" was always stressed as a subject of teaching. Domine John Backerus, writing to Holland for a teacher in 1647, asked particularly for piety. "We must begin with the children," he said, "for many of the older people are so far depraved, that they are now ashamed to learn anything good." For his services the teacher collected a small salary, eked out by tuition fees paid in beaver or bearskins or the like, save from pupils who were poor and needy enough to ask free tuition "for God's sake." [103]

The clergyman, as everywhere in early America, had been the first professional man, the schoolmaster developing as an inferior functionary under his control; the specialized medical doctor and the lawyer were more slowly needed. Amateur prescription for the soul, apparently, seemed less adequate than amateur prescription for the body. Yet certain professionals emerged in this department before the first two decades had passed. In 1638 a small house was built at public expense in New Amsterdam for the town midwife,[104] and a university-bred physician was to be found as well. Several other practitioners came, though generally they combined their healing function with other duties, as in the case of Dr. Curtius. By the middle of the century, certainly, they could sue in the courts for their fees, as is revealed in an interesting case at Fort Orange. Master Jacob de Hince, the surgeon, sued for compensation for treating a wound of Mrs. Thomas Pouwelsen, claiming that his yearly contract with the defendant covered only accidents, whereas this injury, he alleges mysteriously, had been deliberately inflicted.[105]

In spite of its autocratic organization and the arbitrary spirit of its governors, New Netherland provided an unfavorable soil for social and economic inequality. By the composition of the company the colony was in fact a bourgeois enterprise, and while the colonists improved in quality and worldly substance as time went on, particularly as agriculture superseded the fur interest, it was not a rich or aristocratic Dutch dependency. An attempt was made in 1657 in New Amsterdam to create a privileged class of "great" burghers: first, those who had been members of the supreme government; second, municipal officers past and present; third, ministers of the gospel; fourth, military officers. "Small" burghers were to be those who were bona fide residents, citizens in fact. When the ordinance was proclaimed only twenty persons presented claims for, or purchased, great-burgher rights, while 200 became small burghers, the list later increasing.

But these distinctions soon broke down, perhaps because the ranks were purchasable. In 1668 any householder might receive all the burgher privileges for fifty guilders. The right persisted in New York until 1815.

Under the English, social gradations were really more marked than among the Dutch. During the eighteenth century the official group and the large landholders dominated politics and society. The country dwellers, many of whom had developed estates of considerable importance, formed a rural gentry of sturdy integrity, esteemed for their hospitality and public spirit. Besides abundant food and little intellectual stimulus, there must have been among the Dutch country folk some of that quaint phlegmatism, naive philosophy, or apparent inability to see the humor in their own odd quirks of indecision, which is suggested in more than one writing on the period—in J. K. Paulding's *Dutchman's Fireside,* for example. The homely virtues of the provincials contrasted sharply with the sophistication of the city dwellers, who admired the airs of English officialdom and aped imported social practices.[106]

New Netherland architecture went through the same phases of development as did the modifications of society, and had a lasting influence. Though the house in the fort on Manhattan built by Peter Minuit was of stone, it was thatched with reeds, as was the nearby treasury building. The original thirty bark huts of the first settlers along the eastern riverbank were the work of quick necessity; indeed, some of the first comers were obliged to live in pits in the ground or in caves. The "mean barn" built within the fort for the first church, with a dwelling and stable for the use of Domine Bogardus, marked more deliberate attention. In 1642 the contract for the first schoolmaster's house showed further advance. This dwelling was to be thirty feet long by eighteen wide and eight in height, with the beams square-hewed, the sides tightly clapboarded, the roof reed-thatched, and the floor boarded. Two doors, an entry, a pantry, a bed, and a stairway to the garret added to the refinements of this early home, which was to cost about $140.[107]

When the houses became more elaborate they had brick gable ends set facing the street, with sides of planks; sometimes the bricks were of various colors, arranged checkerboard fashion. In Albany white-pine shingles or Holland tiles were often used on the roofs, the use of such tiles spreading to New England by the early eighteenth century. Roof gutters projected into the middle of the streets, dripping rain on passersby. Single-story houses had high roofs, making lofts used for storage of food, as in old Holland today, and for other traditional purposes. As they rarely had eaves, the metes and bounds in old deeds often contained provisions for "free drip." Front doors had top and bottom halves, and opened with latches. They had benches beside them on which the people sat and visited in good weather, receiving the merry greetings of their neighbors. Windows were quite small, frequently being of one or two panes of glass only, or simple apertures protected at option by wood shutters. The stairways were often white-tiled, the material being cheap. Bedsteads were frequently built in, and the people slept between two feather beds; there seem to have been no fire-heated beds. Early chimneys were of wood, lined with a coat of plaster, but as the congestion increased and with it the fire risk, an ordinance was passed in 1653 ordering all such chimneys as well as thatched roofs and hayricks to be removed from New Amsterdam, a regulation but indifferently enforced.[108]

The farmhouses built about early New Amsterdam had the pleasing concave roof curve which has so strongly influenced modern architecture. Its extension over the front has become the typical American front porch, supported by the columns which its wide overhang made necessary. The gambrel roof, which had such wide vogue in New England, was likewise adapted from the Dutch. The high stoops of New York, derived from the Netherlands idea of having the main entrance on the second floor, led into the best rooms, which were set high so as to be dry when the ground floor might be damp.[109] Venerable houses, such as the Van Cortlandt mansion at Croton, illustrate the old design today.

New Netherland was the first American scene of sleighing, skating, and coasting. The burghers skated to market. "It is admirable," wrote a visiting English clergyman in 1678, "to see Men and Women, as it were, flying upon their Skates from place to place with Markets [market baskets] on their Heads and Backs."[110] The children of Albany had to be restrained by law from endangering elderly limbs with their sleds. Ice carnivals, once unique on the Collect Pond, find their modern counterparts in many American municipal parks. Hockey and skate racing were popular, players and watchers fortifying themselves against the cold by heartening nips of liquors sold at booths on the ice. Sleighing gave opportunity for colonial speed-limit breakers, who rode several miles out to the Bowery to feast at the resorts there.

Calvinism in the Netherlands, old or new, was never an enemy to innocent amusement as it was sometimes among the English Puritans. Certainly there was no lack of fun in those communities along the Hudson River and on the nearby islands. The maypole, of immemorial antiquity, came with the baggage of European civilization nearly everywhere; here it was set up without encountering the suspicions which it met at Merry Mount in Massachusetts Bay. At Shrovetide, the old feast of Bacchus, the Dutch farm boys pulled the goose; this was "a pagan and a popish feast . . . looked at through the fingers" in the Netherlands, and, because of its accompanying dissipation, at last rigorously forbidden by Stuyvesant. The boys greased a live goose thoroughly and suspended it between two poles; the test was to catch and hold it while riding by at full tilt.[111] There were contests in marksmanship here as elsewhere, particularly the shooting at the popinjay, a bird hung by the feet to a pole. A keen shot that severed the head from the body was, it seems, rewarded with the first prize while one which merely splintered off a feather got the least.[112]

Other sports had no such element of cruelty. Golf, the name of which is said to have been derived from *kolf,* the Dutch word for club, was an importation from the old country. Clumsy the implements doubtless were, but the ball must have been driven with dangerous force, for the principal towns forbade the game within the closely settled areas.[113] Bowling, we are bound to believe, whiled away the time of Rip Van Winkle's elves, and the great popularity of the game extended later into the English period. There was not as much card playing as in the other American colonies excepting New England. A favorite evening game was a species of backgammon called tick-tack; if one touched his man he must complete his game, hence the name, which meant touch and take. Trock, the name of which came from the Spanish *troco,* to exchange, was played at a table by driving an ivory ball under a wicket with a cue. It was also played upon the lawn, thus joining in the ancestry of the modern game of croquet.

Reading did not figure largely among the diversions as far as the record goes; we know little of the importation of books, and there was, of course, no printing in the little province. The writing of the citizens themselves was confined to a few political letters, some histories and descriptions of the province, and a very few adventures into belles-lettres. Jacob Steendam, clerk of the company and sea-wanderer, lived some years in the colony, writing verses of rather middling merit, but fresh with the aspirations of New World life.

There were festival customs, too, which entered permanently into the round of American life. Our use of Easter eggs is as Dutch as our Santa Claus; indeed, St. Nicholas was the patron saint of New Amsterdam, and the children set out their shoes in true Latin fashion on December 6 to receive his gifts, gradually shifting the observance to Christmas Eve. New Year's calls, now fallen into disuse, began, as far as America is concerned, in these settlements of New Netherland. The celebration was as vivacious, noisy, and alcoholic as our modern Saturnalia on the same occasion, though nowadays we frown on the firing of guns in the public street.[114]

The slaves' own frolic was "Pinkster" (Pentecost) Day on Whitsunday. Its most famous celebrations were at Albany on Capitol (then called Pinkster) Hill where criminals were hanged. The blacks kept up the fun for a week—dancing, eating gingerbread, and drinking in honor of their legendary "Old King Charley." They used cast-off finery to bedeck themselves and consumed so much liquor that the bacchanalia had finally to be suppressed. On Long Island the festival was observed by whites as well as blacks, in parts of Pennsylvania and Maryland usually by the blacks only. It was perhaps a corruption of some African land-distribution ceremonial; from its description it seems to have analogies to certain American Indian festivals. Vestiges of the tradition subsisted among rural New Yorkers long after the name of the feast and the custom had been forgotten.[115]

The trading privileges conceded by the company helped to spread Dutch influences along the Atlantic coast despite the official resistance of the English. This influence, for instance, was shown by the distribution of furniture and household effects. Card tables, Dutch folding tables, Spanish tables, and leather-covered brass-nailed chairs, called "Cromwell chairs," were imported into Virginia, either directly or through England. The Southern Atlantic colonies imported darnick or "silk dornex," a coarse table damask, from their thrifty neighbors. Francis Daniel Pastorius, founder of Germantown, Pennsylvania, had Dutch books worth £11, and Governor Gordon of that colony, fond of Dutch paintings, prided himself on *landskips* of Low Country origin.[116] Flanders bedticks and Ghentish sheeting were gifts of Benjamin Franklin to his wife. Leyden and New Amsterdam provided New England with rush-bottomed green chairs such as the Pilgrims had brought from the place of their Dutch sojourn.

The period after 1656 showed the evolution of luxury among well-to-do merchants of New Amsterdam, their lists of household effects making evident the changes which society underwent. By 1674, when Fort Orange finally became English,[117] ninety-four citizens were worth over 1,000 guilders, and twenty-two had between 5,000 and 10,000 guilders each. In 1686, Cornelis Steenwyck, opulent when New Netherland fell, died worth £15,930. Visitors like the famous Labadist voyagers, Danckaerts and Sluyter, could be received in a kermis bed built like a huge box, ceiling high, in the corner "alongside of a good fire." Warming pans of copper or brass, Spanish leather stools, Turkey-work, and Oriental goods found their places with pictures and the inevitable *kas* or *kos,* a huge wardrobe of plain but substantial build, oftentimes decorated with brightly painted flowers.

In 1695, New York contained 3,000 families, half of whom were Dutch, with many English and some French inhabitants. The Reverend John Miller said that they were divided in religion, a few of them intelligent and sincere, but the most part ignorant, conceited, and fickle. The Dutch were "rich and sparing," the English "neither very rich nor too great husbands," while the French were "poor, and therefore penurious."

New Netherland as a Dutch enterprise was out of the reckoning before the real English battle with France began. The Peace of Westphalia, concluding the Dutch struggle against Spain, also closed the chief fields of enterprise to the West India Company. It was even then in turbulent financial waters and, after the adjustment with Spain, was never able to recuperate its financial status. Thus, when the need of an effectual colonization policy had finally been driven home by the New Netherland settlers, it had no funds for expansion. A new danger now appeared. With Spain reduced to impotence on the sea there arose the vital matter of English trade ambitions. While England was weak on the seas the Dutch and the French had had their opportunity, but when English merchants saw the long lines of Dutch ships anchored on the Thames for the English carrying trade, it was time to pass navigation acts, measures which forgot old alliances and ties

NEW AMSTERDAM

Left and right: Costumes in New Netherland.

Below: "New Amsterdam lately called New York, and now retaken by the Netherlanders on August 24, 1673," showing the skyline (a little idealized) in the times of Peter Stuyvesant.

of blood, religion, and politics. Only four short years after her success against Spain, Holland had to take up a struggle with England which ended in colonial disaster.

By 1650, thirty English villages lay between Cape Cod and Stamford, half of the area claimed by New Netherland then having been occupied. The same process had gone on elsewhere, on the Delaware and on Long Island. In September 1663, Stuyvesant tried, as he had in 1650, to obtain a firm boundary agreement with the commissioners of the United Colonies of New England; his envoys tried again in October before the general assembly of Connecticut. Meantime discontent had been shaking the company's rule; possibly the fall of the colony in 1664 had Dutch support from within, though conclusive proof is not available.[118]

The two peoples had, indeed, preserved mutual amenities during their close contacts. There were plenty of Dutch wives of Englishmen. It was Captain Underhill who brought to a decisive end Kieft's unrighteous Indian war. Stuyvesant favored admitting the English to responsible government positions, and the company welcomed them, so that the Dutch had not much complaint against the logic of events whatever they may have thought of the policies of the fatherland.

Finally, in reviewing the Dutch episode in America, we must ask ourselves what were its real and lasting values. Some forty years of effective occupation by not more than 10,000 people at the maximum would seem but a tiny eddy in the current of human endeavor sweeping on to the conquest of the continent. In the matter of territorial expansion and the subjugation of the forces of nature the Dutch performance was meager and progressively restricted. In the transmission of governmental institutions they were on the losing side as society swung from autocracy to democracy.[119] In the art and literature of colonial times or the present day their contribution has not been significant; with a few notable exceptions even their history has been written by persons in whom other blood predominated. In disseminating the artifacts of European civilization they performed the carrier's part, initiating little and establishing no widely spread permanent adoptions. In education and religion they left a creditable tradition and an admirable, though conservative, institution.

In social customs they made their most profound impression because their practices elicited interest and sympathy as those of a closely related people. In our internal life their value lies in those traits which gave this country a stable, conservative element which, however much imbued with the "feeling of kind" almost to clannishness, was yet so tolerant of other men. Their city harbored, with eighteen languages spoken and many sects present, a most cosmopolitan society in an age when the bigotry of Old World religiosity was still the binding tie in most New World transplantations. That spirit of tolerance and world-mindedness has yielded rich results in welding the nation into unity.[120] The genuine sons of New York are, in much the same spirit as Californians and Texans, prone to indulge themselves in what may be smiled at as egocentric interpretations of history. There are even other parts of the United States, where the present inhabitants share little in the blood, language, or traditions of the first alien settlers, in which the people are obsessed with the old Hebraic idea that a perfect society is one in which the chosen few hold fast all that is good against a great outer darkness. That is the great American illusion, the sure mark of immanent provincialism. When we rid ourselves of the fatuous notion of a providence, divine or otherwise, which bestows special favors on any race or people, we attain a dignified, self-reliant realization that there is no guarantee or promise of grandeur or permanence for any nation or its institutions save in its own creative force.

BOOK II

The First Americans,

1607–90

A NEW WORLD MAKES NEW MEN

WHEN THE ENGLISH PEOPLE first planted themselves in the New World, they had very definite ideas as to the character of the industrial and social life they were to establish there. The settlements at Jamestown and Plymouth were not, as is so often supposed, isolated enterprises, carried out in the one case solely for private gain and the other for religion's sake. It is well to remember that neither the London Company nor the Pilgrim Fathers could have succeeded in their perilous ventures without the consent and support of the crown, and the crown acquiesced in each case because of the benefits which were expected to accrue to England. In fact, the founding of colonies in America was but the fruition of hopes and plans nourished for a full half century before Captain Christopher Newport set sail in late 1606 upon his first memorable voyage to Virginia. These plans envisaged the creation of industrial communities to supply England with various commodities which she herself could not produce, to create a market for English manufactures, and to provide a stimulus for English shipping.

But in attempting to devise in advance a workable social and industrial scheme for far-off colonies, Sir Humphrey Gilbert, Captain Christopher Carleill, the indefatigable Richard Hakluyt, and other able publicists had set themselves an impossible task. They might propose what they would, but in the end the character of their colonies would be determined largely by geographic conditions, the location of their settlements, the configuration of the country, and its climate and soil. To understand the history of the English in America, one must study those great natural features which the mother country could neither change nor fully reconcile with what became her fixed colonial policies.

The determining factors in the life of the English colonies were the Atlantic Ocean, the character of the coastline from Maine to Florida, the great coastal plain, and the Appalachian range. All-important was it to the Englishmen who settled on the banks of the James or the shores of Massachusetts Bay that 3,000 miles of water lay between them and Europe.

A Seventeenth Century Home

The Whitman House
Farmington, Connecticut

1664

Despite their sentiments of loyalty this made it impossible for them to remain Englishmen; slowly, but inevitably, it transformed them into Americans. Before the seventeenth century had drawn to a close Virginia and New England had developed types of men distinctly their own, with occupations, manners, dialect, interests, and outlook upon life different from those of Englishmen. The government at London awoke gradually to the fact that England after all had not been extended to the shores of the New World, but that her settlements there were things apart, with separate economic and, therefore, with separate political and social interests.

Even in the most homogeneous nations various sections, because of different geographic conditions, often develop divergent economic interests which lead to bitter political strife, if not to civil war. But if these differences are not too profound, if they are not racial, for instance, it is often possible to remove them and so to restore unity. The freeing of the slaves in the United States and the resulting collapse of the peculiar economic and social structure of the South has eliminated, perhaps forever, the only deep-rooted cause of hostility between that section and the rest of the country. But the separateness of Britain and her colonies was based upon conditions beyond the power of man to change, upon the broad expanse of the Atlantic, upon soil, climate, and geography.

It was this fact which made the American Revolution inevitable. Edmund Burke well understood this at the time and explained it in simple terms which should have given pause to the government of George III. "The last cause of this disobedient spirit in the colonies is . . . deep in the natural constitution of things. Three thousand miles of ocean lie between you and them. No contrivance can prevent the effect of this distance in weakening government. . . . Nothing worse happens to you than does to all nations who have extensive empire; and it happens in all the forms into which empire can be thrown."[1]

The only means of communication was the crude sailing vessel of the day. Not only did it require from four to eight weeks to make the voyage from England, but one might have to wait for months before finding a ship bound for his place of destination. The merchantmen trading to the Chesapeake Bay colonies usually made one trip a year, sailing from England in September or October, and returning after they had taken on their cargoes of tobacco. So general was this custom that an impression prevailed that a voyage of six or eight months was required to reach America.

Correspondence was carried on with great difficulty. If a dispatch was too late to go out with the fleet, it might not reach its destination for a full year. When charges were brought against Sir Francis Nicholson by members of the Virginia council of state, so many months elapsed before his answers could be received by the board of trade that they became tired of waiting and removed him unheard. It was the custom for officials in the colonies to write to the board concerning important events as they occurred, so that their letters would be ready for the first sailing. Often a large number of communications would pile up in this way. In the meantime, the British government would remain in ignorance of what was taking place in the colony. Months passed after the outbreak of Bacon's Rebellion before any official report reached England, and Charles II did not know the extent of the uprising or whether it would be necessary to send troops.

As the years passed, England and her colonies drifted apart. The American community grew as family after family was established. Despite the common heritage of blood, language, political institutions, and traditions, the line of development for each led in different directions. After the lapse of a century and a half England awoke to the realization that she was trying to govern a foreign people, that the British child had grown into the American man.

It must be remembered, however, that though the Atlantic separated mother country and colony, it also served as the only highway between them, the highway over which passed immigrants and merchandise and all communications of whatever character. It was vital, then, that the settlements should be made upon or near its shores. For decades after Jamestown was founded the colonies were but infants, requiring the support of the Old World for nourishment and protection.

It was fortunate that the eastern shore of North America from the Gulf of Mexico to the Gulf of St. Lawrence should be so admirably suited for a seafaring people. At every point its lines are broken by sounds, bays, and wide river mouths, large enough to harbor the greatest fleets. Massachusetts Bay, Narragansett Bay, Long Island Sound, New York Bay, Raritan Bay, Delaware Bay, Chesapeake Bay, and Albemarle Sound afford natural shipping points for transatlantic traffic. Had it not been for this fact, it is probable that the English would have failed in their attempt to colonize this region. It is noteworthy that the character of the shores of Palestine, which contain not one harbor worthy of the name, has shaped the history of that land by turning the faces of the people away from the sea, and making of them an Asiatic rather than a Mediterranean folk. In sharp contrast to the course of events in the Holy Land, the inviting doors of the northern Atlantic Coast of America beckon always outward and thus made it possible for the struggling colonies to keep their saving contacts with the Old World. Virginia and Maryland sent out their tobacco fleet each year, and received in return the manufactured products of England; New York sold her furs in the European market; and New England found her prosperity in the carrying trade, shipbuilding, and fishing.

The navigators of that day did not always cast anchor at the coast ports, for the rivers with which the country abounds gave them ready access to the interior. The Connecticut, the Hudson, the Raritan, the Delaware, the Susquehanna, the Potomac, the Rappahannock, the York, the James, the Roanoke, the Santee were all navigable for many miles for the oceangoing vessels of the day. The Dutch masters often took on their cargoes of furs at Fort Orange, where Albany now stands, while the tobacco traders ascended the great tributaries of Chesapeake Bay and tied up at the private wharves of the planters. And above the fall line were long stretches of river, deep enough for the shallop or the canoe, which served as avenues of approach to deep water. Had man himself planned this system of waterways, it could hardly have been better suited for the needs of foreign trade.

It was inevitable that the settlements should first group themselves around the bays and push up the river valleys. In 1665 the colonies could be divided into six distinct geographic units, all shaped by considerations of transportation: The Massachusetts Bay group; the Narragansett Bay group; the Long Island Sound and Connecticut River group; the New York Bay and Hudson River group; the Delaware Bay and Delaware River group; and the Chesapeake Bay, Potomac, Rappahannock, York, and James group. At this date hardly a settler had planted his home more than a dozen miles from deep water, and many could step directly from their own wharves upon the vessel which conveyed their produce to Europe.

By the end of the century two new groups had been formed, one around Albemarle Sound and the other around Charleston Harbor, while in the older communities the settlements had in a few cases extended some distance inland. All central New Jersey had filled up, Penn's Quaker colonists were pushing northward and westward from Philadelphia, and the Virginians were seeking new lands above the falls of the Rappahannock, the Matapony, and the Pamunkey. But even at this late date, nearly a century after the establishing of Jamestown, most of the colonists were still clinging to the coastal waterways, and their settlements formed a narrow fringe along the shore of the great body of water which connected them with the Old World. In the eighteenth century came a remarkable growth of population and wealth, which made it possible for them to break in part this dependence on Europe and for the first time to turn their faces westward. In another 150 years they were destined to push out 3,000 miles until they had covered the central parts of the continent and had reached the Pacific Ocean.

It is misleading to say that the colonists, during this first century, were prevented from spreading into the interior by the great mountain chain which extended from Maine to Alabama. Except in New York and New England, their settlements in no place approached the mountains, while in the South they were still hundreds of miles away. The colonists did not move westward in this their formative period, because there were no great rivers leading in that direction which they could follow without getting out of touch with the Old World. It was the mountain barrier, of course, which shaped the rivers, making them short and swift, but we must not lose sight of the fact that the all-important consideration with the settlers was the question of foreign communication. A great plain would have blocked their expansion as effectively as the mountains, had it been destitute of navigable rivers.

Not any less important than the Atlantic and the river systems in shaping the destinies of the English colonies in America was the great coastal plain which stretches from northern New England to the Gulf of Mexico. Here the settlers, their children, and their children's children were to remain and make their homes. This plain presents in its different portions wide divergences in configuration, soil, and climate. In New England the belt of lowland is narrow, varying in width from fifty to eighty miles; in new Jersey, Delaware, and Pennsylvania it widens to 100 miles or more; while in the Carolinas the mountains recede a full 200 miles from the shore.

The New England soil is largely of glacial origin, most of it boulder clay, not infertile but difficult to cultivate. In the southeastern part is a wide strip of sandy land which is almost useless for agriculture. The summers are comparatively short and the period of cultivation restricted; the winters are long and severe. With a small agricultural area, a stubborn soil, and a harsh climate, the region is not well adapted to farming. To hard labor and intelligent management the land will yield a fair return, but for extensive agriculture, for great staple crops produced with cheap labor, it will not do. Although the Puritan settlers succeeded in producing food in abundance, New England was not intended to be a great agricultural region, and their utmost efforts could not make it so. For commerce, however, there were splendid opportunities. Harbors abounded. In the extreme north, it is true, the lack of fertile backcountry and the extremely high tides offered serious obstacles to trade, and Maine and New Hampshire were slow in filling up. But Massachusetts, Connecticut, and Rhode Island, because of their great protected bays, had every facility for commerce.

The settlers found the forests growing to the very edge of the shore, and the combination of cheap timber and excellent harbors offered an inviting outlook for shipbuilding. This industry gained an early start in New England. During the reign of Charles II, under the protection of the navigation acts, it became of prime importance. It has been said that in the history of the region, "one seems never to get away from the sound of the shipbuilder's hammer, and the rush of the launching vessel." Labor in New England, as in all the colonies, was much dearer than in Europe, but the readiness with which masts, timber, and pitch could be had made it possible for the shipwrights of Ipswich and Salem to undersell their rivals of the mother country.

In the Middle colonies the wider plain presented a more inviting prospect for agriculture than in New England. The area of arable land was larger, there were fewer stones, and the fertility was greater. In certain parts of south Jersey the soil was sterile, and this region remains today almost a wilderness, but elsewhere intelligent cultivation yielded an excellent return. The Middle colonies found no staple comparable to tobacco or sugar, but they produced wheat, rye, barley, and oats in considerable quantities. Fruit trees bore well, while cattle and sheep throve on the native grasses.

The rivers, although less numerous, were wider and deeper, and led farther inland. The Hudson was navigable to Albany, the Raritan to New Brunswick, the Delaware to Trenton, while small boats could use the upper reaches miles above the fall line. For western Pennsylvania, the Susquehanna, despite its shallow waters and its rapids, was a commercial highway of prime importance. On the other hand, the long unbroken expanse of the Jersey coast from Sandy Hook to Cape May, in contrast to the jagged New England shore, tended to keep the people of the region from turning to the sea. The Middle colonies were destined in the main to become an agricultural rather than a commercial section.

South of Pennsylvania, where the coastal plain widens, the summers are hot, and the period of cultivation long, it was inevitable that extensive farming should absorb the attention of the settlers. The region around Chesapeake Bay proved especially suited to the cultivation of tobacco, and this plant became the staple, almost the only, product. Natural facilities for other things were not lacking. Wheat, barley, oats, Indian corn, and many kinds of fruits grew in abundance; the timber was suitable both for shipbuilding and for smelting; and the harbors afforded ample facilities for commerce. But in all these concerns Maryland and Virginia would have faced the sharpest competition, whereas in tobacco they could undersell the world. For a century and a half the history of the tidewater region from the mouth of the Susquehanna to Albemarle Sound was shaped by the needs of the Indian plant.

Since tobacco was a product which sought, almost demanded, a world market, it was fortunate that facilities for transportation were excellent. Chesapeake Bay stretched north and south like a vast natural boulevard, while to the westward were a number of connecting rivers that served as cross streets. Each river in turn was fed by many navigable creeks, so that the entire region assumed the aspect of a "sylvan Venice." Until the growing population pushed the settlements far inland above the fall line, almost every planter shipped his crop from his own wharf.

England, when she secured a foothold in America, was far from understanding the irresistible force exercised by geography and climate upon the life of the inhabitants. She was intent on securing one great natural resource —the resource which she herself lacked and which she considered vital to her industrial life. This was wood. Three centuries ago the forests played a role in industrial life comparable with that of iron and coal today. For England, wood was necessary for three great industries: shipbuilding, smelting, and the manufacture of woolens. The first it supplied not only with timber for frames, planking, and masts but with the pitch, tar, and resin essential for making vessels watertight; for the second it served as fuel for the iron, copper, and glass furnaces; for the third it yielded potash and dyes. Wood was a considerable element in the early cargoes sent back to England. A London poet wrote of the *Blessing* and the *Hercules* in 1610: in these

> Two ships, are these commodities, furres, sturgeon, caviare,
> Black walnut-tree, and some deale boards, with such they laden are;
> Some pearle, some wainscot and clapbords, with some sassafras wood,
> And iron promist, for tis true their mynes are very good.[2]

With the growth of population in England and the consequent encroachment upon the forests, prosperity declined and unemployment became widespread. By the end of the Tudor period the country was face-to-face with the alternative of securing new territory in which woodland abounded or of sinking into a position of economic dependence. "When therefore our mils of Iron, and excesse of building, have already turned our greatest woods into pasture and champion, within those few years," says one writer, "neither the scattered Forrests of England, nor the diminished Groves of Ireland will supply the defect of our Navy."[3]

No wonder farsighted Englishmen began to cast longing eyes upon America. Many navigators of the time of Queen Elizabeth had already crossed the Atlantic, returning with stories of the amazing expanse of forest land which lined every shore and extended far into the interior. In some regions, long before the sailors sighted land, they could detect the odor of the pine trees wafted out by the wind. In 1584, Hakluyt pointed out that America could produce ship stores and potash enough for all England, while Carleill pleaded with the Muscovy Company to divert at least a part of its energies from Russia to the northwest Atlantic. Thus, years before the London Company received its charter from James I, Englishmen had learned to regard America as the land of promise which was to put new vigor into their drooping industrial life.

The settlements of Virginia and New England were mere incidents in the story of English expansion, an expansion impelled chiefly by economic necessity. The London Company, among whose stockholders were some of the greatest noblemen and richest merchants of the kingdom, was national in its character and its aims; the Pilgrim Fathers and those who followed them would never have gained permission to found their Bible commonwealths had it not been anticipated that they would produce the raw stuffs needed at home. There were other motives in the English settlement of America—the desire to check the power of the king of Spain, the prospect of discovering a new route to the Orient, the hope of converting the Indians. But one need only read the letters and broadsides of the statesmen and economists of the day to realize that their minds dwelt long and hopefully upon the economic phases of the great undertaking. "The staple and certain commodities we have are Soap-ashes, pitch, tar, dyes of sundry sorts and rich values," wrote the council of the London Company, in February 1608, "timber for all uses, fishing for sturgeon and divers other sorts . . . making of Glass and iron, and no improbable hope of richer mines."[4]

The same expectation was an impelling motive in the settlement of New England. "How serviceable this Country must needs be for provisions for shipping, is sufficiently knowne already," said John White in *The Planters Plea*. "At present it may yield Planks, Masts, Oares, Pitch, Tarre and Iron, and hereafter (by the aptnesse of the Soyle for Hempe) if the Colonie increase, Sailes and Cordage." This pamphlet, written in 1630, at the moment when the great Puritan exodus was beginning, suggests that there were other than religious motives for that movement. Two years later Thomas Morton emphasized the benefits to England which should accrue from the forests of New England: "Of these may be made rosin, pitch, and tarre, which are such useful commodities, that if wee had them not from other Countries in Amity with England, our Navigation would decline. Then how great the commodity of it will be to our Nation, to have it our owne, let any man judge."[5]

We are left in no doubt, then, as to what England expected of her colonies. British America was not to be a mercantile country in a general sense, or an agricultural country. It must not compete with England herself, must not duplicate her manufactures—her cloth and clothes, her household utensils, her metalware, her furniture. But it was to produce—indeed, it was founded chiefly for the purpose of producing—the raw materials which the mother country sorely needed. Had the original wishes of England been fulfilled, the Chesapeake Bay colonies would never have been covered with tobacco plantations, and New England would not have turned to farming, shipbuilding, fishing, and trading. She had expected to people the forests of the New World with smelters of iron and copper; with glass makers; with workers in potash, pitch, and tar; with rope makers.

Nor was she lacking in persistence in her attempts to carry out this purpose. No sooner had the settlement at Jamestown been made than the London Company sent over a number of Dutchmen and Poles to begin the production of pitch, tar, turpentine, and potash. Immediately after came machinery for the smelting and manufacture of iron. Later, ironworks were set up at Falling Creek, on the James River, so ambitious in size that the total cost to the company was between £4,000 and £5,000. As early as 1608 a glass furnace was built at Jamestown, while thirteen years later Captain William Norton arrived with skilled Italians to continue the manufacture of glassware. In these first permanent English colonies on the mainland, Virginia and Plymouth, the colonists were regarded as servants of the English traders; for a time they worked under company direction and piled up their products in company storehouses, not their own. The colony existed for the benefit of the mother country, not for the benefit of the colonists.

There is no more interesting experiment in the history of colonization than this attempt by England to establish a prearranged economic system in her new possessions. Had she succeeded and the British America of her plans become the British America of reality, the course of events through succeeding centuries would have been entirely different. Slavery would probably not have been fixed upon the South; there might have been no Civil War. But the experiment was foredoomed to failure. It was the geography of the region selected for settlement which was destined to shape its economic life, not the designs of the London Company, nor even the efforts of the British nation. The glass furnaces at Jamestown proved a failure, the potash workers deserted, the iron furnaces were destroyed by the Indians. Before the end of the third decade of the seventeenth century, Virginia had given up all immediate hopes of producing the commodities England needed and had turned her energies into the cultivation of tobacco.

Hakluyt and his fellow publicists had failed to realize that the infant colonies could not hope to compete with the long-established industries of other countries unless possessed of some outstanding advantage in soil or other resources. Virginia lacked skilled labor, especially such as would work at a reasonable wage. It had been expected that the colony would avail itself of the surplus population of England to supply her needs; in this way idle hands could be set to work producing the raw materials, the lack of which was chiefly responsible for unemployment in England. But the man who was classed as cheap labor in England, the moment he set foot on the soil of Virginia became dear labor. The voyage across the Atlantic was long and expensive, and the colonies at no time were able to secure workers enough for their needs. Virginia found that she could not compete with the Baltic nations in producing ship stores, potash, and iron, and was forced to devote herself almost exclusively to tobacco, for which her soil and climate were so wonderfully suited.

The results in New England were even more disappointing. The Massachusetts Bay Company, especially after the transfer of the charter to America, was less national in character than the Virginia Company. It concerned itself with the prosperity of Massachusetts rather than with that of England. It would have been glad to produce the materials needed by the old country, had it been profitable to do so, but it had no idea of repeating the costly experiments which had been made on the James. The first concern of the Puritan settlers was to ensure an ample food supply, and for a number of years agriculture absorbed much of their interest. In after years, when they actually turned to the production of masts, timber, pitch, and cordage, it was more to supply their own shipbuilders than those of England. New England never assumed the place intended for her in the British colonial system, and so far from supplementing and aiding English industries, to a large degree paralleled and competed with them.

Though the ambition of England to plant colonies in North America was gratified, though the foundations of her empire were securely laid, she failed in her chief end. The colonies eventually proved for her a means to prosperity and wealth—they absorbed her manufactured goods, stimulated her carrying trade, aided the royal revenue, and supplied her with articles for foreign export—but for many decades they failed to furnish the raw stuffs she needed to free her from dependence upon foreign imports. As for the economic and social structures of the various colonies, so far from following the plans mapped out for them in advance of their settlement, they were shaped by their own peculiar conditions of climate, soil, and geography.

LAND AND LABOR IN THE TOBACCO COLONIES

THE SETTLERS IN VIRGINIA, as we have seen, were not long in discovering that their soil was peculiarly suited for the cultivation of tobacco. When Captain Newport first sailed up the James, the English, who were accustomed to the product of the Spanish West Indies, considered the native leaf "poor and weake and not of the best kynde."[6] But in 1612, Captain John Rolfe, the future husband of Pocahontas, by setting out a small crop and curing it according to the best methods, produced tobacco which Ralph Hamor considered as "strong, sweet and pleasant as any under the sun." Immediately the colonists turned to the cultivation of the plant, almost to the exclusion of all else, and at one time tobacco was seen growing in the very streets of Jamestown. The planter calculated he could do six times as well with this crop as with any other.[7] By 1627 the exports of leaf amounted to half a million pounds. The English kings and the board of trade made repeated efforts to turn the colony away from the all-absorbing culture of this one product, but in vain. Throughout the colonial period it remained the staple crop of the region surrounding the Chesapeake Bay and almost its sole export. It was inevitable, then, that tobacco should prove of prime importance in molding the economic and social life of Virginia and Maryland and, to a lesser extent, of North Carolina. The requirements of the plant determined the character of immigration, the labor system, the apportionment of land, the daily life of the planter.

The greatest need of the tobacco colonies was for cheap labor. Tobacco requires not skilled hands but many hands. With land to be had almost for the asking, the only impediment to the rapid accumulation of wealth was the difficulty of securing adequate help in the tobacco fields. Had the English during the early years of the seventeenth century shared in the African slave trade, there can be little doubt that Virginia and Maryland would have been from the first inundated with black workers and the entire region divided up into large estates. But at this time slaves in large numbers were not to be had. The Dutch, the Spaniards, and the Portuguese monopolized the trade, and woe to the English ship which ventured too near their stations on the Guinea Coast. A few enterprising planters succeeded in stocking their estates with slaves, even before the middle of the century, and by so doing laid the foundations of large fortunes; but for 100 years the number of blacks was insignificant. Virginia and Maryland had to solve their labor problem in some other way.

Naturally they turned their eyes to the unemployed of the mother country. At this time England was overflowing with indigent persons who worked for meager wages, if indeed they could find work at all. In 1622 a distinguished minister declared that often the ablest London workers complained to him that though they and their families wore away their flesh with long and excessive labor, they could hardly keep breath in their bodies. In 1610, Rutland County fixed the annual wages of a plowman at fifty shillings, of an ordinary workingman at forty shillings, of a skilled woman worker at twenty-six shillings and eight pence, of a female drudge at sixteen shillings.[8] Had the Virginia planters been able to secure labor at such prices, they would have flooded the world with tobacco and reaped a tremendous profit.

But it was no easy matter to transport thousands of laborers from the farms and towns of England to the planters on the James and the Potomac. The fare was from six to ten pounds sterling, sums so far above the means of the poor English laborer as to make the voyage impossible for him unless some scheme were devised to advance him credit. This scheme took the form of the indenture. The planters and their agents agreed to pay the immigrant's passage to America, and he in turn bound himself to make good the sum by working after reaching the colony. In this way, the indentured—or indented—servant, as he was called, sold his labor in the better market. It would have required a lifetime for him to save enough from his wages in England to pay his fare, but in Virginia the work of four or five years was sufficient. True, he had to surrender for this period the liberty so dear to every Englishman, but the compensations were great. When his service was completed he found himself a freeman in a new country where land was cheap, wages high, and advancement rapid.

This system of immigration was the foundation of the economic life of the tobacco colonies for almost a century. The English manufactured goods, which were the chief imports of Virginia and Maryland, were far less bulky than their exports of tobacco, so that on every vessel which left England for the Chesapeake there was space available for passengers. The indentured servant became a regular part of the cargo, and the incoming fleet never failed to bring its annual supply. Not until the influx of black slaves at the end of the century finally satisfied the need of the planters for cheap labor did this tide of immigration cease. To Virginia alone there came annually from 1,500 to 2,000 in the years from 1635 to 1705, making a total for these seven decades of from 100,000 to 140,000.[9] The men and women who availed themselves of the indenture to better their fortunes in the New World were, for the most part, neither menials nor criminals. A certain proportion of undesirable persons joined the movement, but the bulk were poor laborers who were no longer content to work in misery and rags in England while opportunity beckoned from across the Atlantic.

The fact that the term of service for indentured immigrants was short was of the utmost importance to the economic and social life of the tobacco colonies. If we assume that in both Maryland and Virginia the average was four years (and the records prove that this is approximately correct) and the annual number of newcomers 2,500, there might be working in these two colonies at any one time 10,000 servants.[10] As the mortality was very high, however, and as a certain proportion escaped, the actual number was probably smaller. Sir William Berkeley estimated the number of servants in Virginia in 1671 at 6,000. Since at the same time he placed the number of slaves at 2,000, there were then in Virginia about 8,000 workers, other than freemen, to serve the needs of a population of about 45,000.[11] In other words, more than 82 percent of the people were free, about 13 percent were under indenture, and about 5 percent were slaves.

Under these circumstances, even the cheapness of land and the fertility of the soil were not sufficient to build up a large group of wealthy planters. It would have been easy for the well-to-do to accumulate large tracts of land, but there was no object in doing so when it was impossible to secure the labor to put them under cultivation. A few men, possessed of larger capital or greater business acumen than their neighbors, succeeded in overcoming these difficulties and in laying the foundations of fortunes of considerable size. During the last decades of the century the powerful clique which centered in the council of state was made up chiefly of planters owning several plantations and many servants and slaves. Typical of this group were the elder Nathaniel Bacon, Lewis Burwell, William Fitzhugh, William Byrd II, and Robert Carter. "In every river there are from ten to thirty men who by trade and industry have gotten very competent estates," wrote Colonel Robert Quary in a report to the board of trade in 1703.[12] It must be understood that these large planters were possessed of influence in the colony out of proportion to their number. "The Council have vanity enough to think themselves almost upon equal terms with the House of Lords," it was stated, and more than one governor found himself little better than a puppet in their hands. The poorer planters both respected and feared them.

Nothing can be further from the truth, however, than the common belief that in the tobacco colonies of the seventeenth century the average plantation was 5,000 acres or more in extent. It is true that the proprietor of Maryland, with the purpose of imitating the old manorial system of England, made many large grants in the first years of that colony.[13] In a few cases the holders of these tracts succeeded in getting a certain proportion of tenants and actually established leet courts. But Lord Baltimore soon discovered that it was impracticable to initiate in the wilderness of America a system peculiar to medieval Europe.[14] With land to be had almost for the asking, there was no reason why a man with the ability to shift for himself should voluntarily become a manorial tenant. It became obvious that if Maryland were to attract settlers, land must be granted in fee simple to all comers, and soon after 1640 patents were issued in large numbers to small holders. As for the manors themselves, some of them held together until the influx of slaves made it possible to cultivate them profitably; others began to disintegrate immediately.

Most of the indentured servants who came to Virginia and Maryland did so with the intention of become freeholders upon the expiration of their terms. The prospect of owning land was held up to them as a principal inducement for leaving England, and in certain cases the indentures stipulated that they were to receive fifty or more acres. In 1648 the council of Maryland issued an order that "every man servant of British or Irish descent . . . shall at the Expiration of the Time of their Service . . . be accompted a Planter within the said Province and shall have . . . Land Granted unto him."[15] In Virginia the servant could claim no such right, but this was not a matter of great importance, for a very small sum would purchase all the land he could put under cultivation. George Alsop, who himself came to Maryland under terms of indenture, pictures the life and prospects of the servant in a most favorable light. They are no sooner free, he says, "but they are ready to set up for themselves, and when once entered, they live surprisingly well."[16]

Each year hundreds of men and women graduated from the class of indentured servants and, as freemen, began the work of establishing for themselves a place in colonial life. Despite the heavy mortality among the newcomers it seems certain that not less than 100,000 persons completed their terms and became freedmen in the tobacco colonies in the seventeenth century. The freedman, then, rather than the servant, became the most important factor in the industrial structure of this region.

The tax lists in both Maryland and Virginia give ample confirmation to the size and importance of the yeoman class. In Baltimore County in 1699 there were 647 tithable persons, of whom only 21 were servants and 98 slaves. Timothy Connell, who possessed 12 slaves and 6 servants, was the only planter listed who could possibly have had under cultivation an extensive tract of land. In Surry County, Virginia, the lists for 1675 show 245 taxpayers and 198 persons, whether servants, slaves, or the planters' sons, whose taxes were paid by others. In all Virginia south of the Rappahannock, the tithables, which included free males over sixteen, all servants over fourteen, female servants who worked in the fields, and all slaves over sixteen, amounted in 1702 to 19,715. After deducting all male freeholders listed in the rent roll, there are left only 14,700 persons to make up the total of servants, slaves, wage-earners, professional men, and male minors over sixteen.[17]

As for the distribution of servants and slaves, a study of wills, inventories, and tax lists, both in Virginia and Maryland, shows that by far the larger part of the freeholders owned none, that a fair number had from one to five, and that a few wealthy planters had gathered around them from ten to one hundred. In Surry County, in the years from 1671 to 1686, we find listed the estates of fifty-nine persons. Of these no less than fifty-two are accompanied by no mention of servants or slaves.[18] Other county records yield similar results. A conservative estimate would place the proportion of freeholders who owned no slaves or servants and cultivated their plantations with their own hands at 65 percent.

By no means all the yeomen were recruited from the ranks of the freedmen. Many came from England not bound by indenture, paying their own fare and that of their wives and children. The patent rolls, both of Virginia and Maryland, contain innumerable cases of this kind. Typical of this class of immigrants are John Gresham, of Isle of Kent, who received 100 acres "for transporting himself into the Province" of Maryland, and Roger Symonds who had 100 acres in Charles City County, "due him for the transportation of his wife, Alice, and one servant, Richard Key." It has been estimated that of the 2,675 persons listed on the rolls of Virginia during the years from 1623 to July 14, 1637, 675 came to the colony as freemen.[19]

Thus from these two sources, from the servants who had completed their terms and from the free immigrants of small means, there was built up in Virginia and Maryland a yeomanry which constituted the main strength of those colonies. Almost entirely Anglo-Saxon in blood, they promised for the future a homogeneous community, sound socially, economically, and politically.[20] There exists an essential difference between the seventeenth and eighteenth centuries in Virginia and Maryland. In the seventeenth century the economic system of these colonies was based chiefly upon the labor of free citizens who tilled their own soil with their own hands; that of the eighteenth century was based almost entirely upon the toil of black slaves. The importation of blacks in large numbers did not destroy the class of small farmers, but it transformed their economic and social life by making them slaveholders. The indentured servant, by the nature of his agreement, could not play the role afterward taken by the slave. At no time were there enough to make possible the building up of numerous large estates, while their early translation into freemen constantly swelled the ranks of the small proprietors. Nor was the seventeenth century the eighteenth in embryo. Although an inkling of what was to happen in the latter period is found in the limited number of large estates in the earlier, the two are separated by an important social and economic revolution, caused by the introduction of thousands of African slaves.

The cheapness of land and the unscientific methods of cultivation then in vogue made it advisable for the small planter to secure a much larger tract than he could put under cultivation. Tobacco quickly exhausted the soil, and there were no precautions taken to preserve its fertility by a rotation of crops or by the use of manures. The planter sowed the same crop year after year in the same spot until the diminishing yield warned him that the time had come to clear new fields. A plantation of 500 or 600 acres usually consisted of a goodly expanse of virgin forest, a restricted area of cultivated land, and perhaps one or two abandoned fields. A freehold which in England, or even in the Northern colonies, would have been considered a large estate, in Virginia or Maryland supported but one family of yeomen.[21]

When the planter first settled upon his land, his severest task was the clearing of a space in the woods for his crop. This he did in the crudest way, often cutting down the trees, but usually girdling the trunks and leaving the trees to die, and cultivating between the stumps. Consequently, he found it difficult to make use of the plow and had to break the ground with the spade and hoe. Even in the eighteenth century, we learn from Hugh Jones, cultivation consisted of "hoeing up the ground and throwing seed upon it and harrowing it in."[22] The plow—a clumsy wooden hulk with iron tip and share—was not unknown, but its use in the first half century was very restricted. In 1649 the total number of plows in Virginia was about 150.[23] Even in later years, when references to this implement are more numerous, the yeoman still clung to his spade and his hoe.

The chief crop of every planter, large and small, was tobacco. The plants were set out in the spring in little mounds placed about four feet apart. Care was taken to keep them free of weeds, and when a certain number of leaves had appeared, the stalk at the top was broken off. As the tobacco became ripe it was cut down and carried to the barn to be cured. After this process had been completed the leaves were stripped from the stalk, sorted, and packed in hogsheads for shipment. Some of the small planters possessed private wharves capable of receiving oceangoing vessels, but it was more usual for them to make use of those of their well-to-do neighbors. In return for his tobacco the planter received from the English merchant all the articles which he found it impossible or uneconomic to make for himself—clothing, shoes, farm implements, household furniture, tableware, linen, firearms, tools. His welfare was bound up in foreign trade, and he had little of the economic independence which usually attends frontier life. A decline in the price of tobacco, whether occasioned by legislation in England or by a war in the Baltic, brought him hardship, if not suffering. With business transacted in terms of tobacco, a note of hand given in one year for so many pounds might be worth twice as much or half as much the next year with a turn in the price.

But nothing could deprive even the poorest planter of an adequate supply of food. The abundance of land and the mild climate made the raising

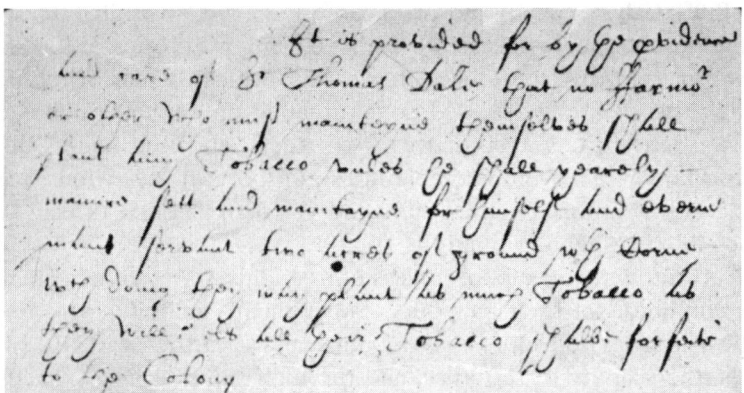

John Rolfe describes the legislation on tobacco, 1616.

Nathaniel Bacon's Castle, Surry County, Virginia, built before 1676.

The Tobacco Country.

of cattle easy and lucrative. In 1649 there were in Virginia alone "of Kine, Oxen, Bulls, Calves, twenty thousand, large and good."[24] while fifteen years later the number had increased to 100,000. The inventories of the smaller estates usually show from one to ten cattle. Typical is that of John Gray. Although this planter possessed goods totaling only 9,340 pounds of tobacco, he left six cows, six calves, two steers, and one heifer. In both Maryland and Virginia innumerable hogs ran loose in the woods, feeding upon acorns and roots. On the other hand, the scarcity of pastureland made it impossible for sheep to multiply.[25]

The inventories of the poorer class of freeholders give an excellent idea of the conditions of their daily life. The yeoman's spinning wheel shows that the making of homsepun was not unusual; the earthenware, the pewter utensils, the scarcity of furniture, and the high value placed on beds and bolsters all picture the crudeness of his domestic economy; the gun reveals him as a hunter; from his pots, pestle, and frying pans we gather the details of his primitive methods of cooking.

Christopher Pearson, who died in 1698, left two feather beds, four blankets, two bolsters, two pillows, a curtain, and valance, in all worth £7; a pair of sheets, some old table linen, valued at 18s.; plates and other pewter worth £1 18s.; an old warming pan and other brass articles, placed at 6s.; woodenware at £4.13.6 comprising three chairs and one table, a couch, four old chests, a cask, two ten-gallon rundlets, a cheese press, a box of drawers, an old table, three pails, a spinning wheel with cards, two sifting trays, a corn barrel, three bedsteads, four sieves, and a funnel; ironware worth £2.1.0, including three pots, two pot rocks, a pestle, a frying pan, a looking glass; three cows appraised at £6.5.0, a yearling at 10s., a colt at £2 sterling. The entire estate was valued at £25.19.6.[26]

The yeoman class of Virginia and Maryland was formed and attained its greatest prosperity in the period preceding the restoration of the Stuarts. During the Civil War and under the Commonwealth, England had no opportunity to perfect her colonial policy. While Cavalier was fighting Roundhead or while Cromwell was busy with his wars, the Chesapeake Bay colonies were enjoying a large degree of freedom from political and economic control. This freedom they made use of to build up their exports of tobacco to foreign markets, which passed chiefly through the hands of Dutch merchants. Before the end of the sixth decade of the century, Virginia and Maryland enjoyed a world market for their staple, the price of tobacco was high, and the margin of profit for every planter excellent.

With the accession of Charles II, Parliament enacted the navigation acts, designed to make the British Empire a compact economic unit. The planters were forbidden to ship their tobacco to foreign countries; the colonial market was reserved in large part for English exports and the colonial carrying trade monopolized by English and colonial masters. At the same time, the government placed a duty upon colonial tobacco consumed in

England varying from 200 percent in 1660 to 600 percent in 1705. To prevent these huge tariffs from stimulating the otherwise unprofitable culture of tobacco in England and so cutting down the revenue, the law forbade anyone to grow it there. Despite this favorable feature, the navigation acts seriously injured the people of the Chesapeake Bay region, for they increased both freight rates and the price of imported goods, and by limiting the market for their staple reduced the price received for it.[27] The small farmer, who formerly had lived in plenty, now found himself living in straitened circumstances. The margin of profit from his little crop was either entirely wiped out or so reduced that he found it difficult to make ends meet.

"Twelve hundred pounds of tobacco is the medium of men's crops," stated Secretary Thomas Ludwell in 1667, "and half a penny per pound is certainly the full medium of the price given for it, which is fifty shillings out of which when the taxes . . . shall be deducted, is very little to a poor man who hath perhaps a wife and children to cloath and other necessities to buy. Truly so much too little that I can attribute it to nothing but the great mercy of God . . . that keeps them from mutiny and confusion."[28] Nine years later, when Bacon's ragged men swept Governor Berkeley from his capital and took possession of all Virginia west of Chesapeake Bay, these fears were fully realized. This long period of hardship did not destroy the yeomanry of Virginia and Maryland, but it greatly retarded its growth. The small proprietor who had bought his plantation prior to the navigation acts usually managed to keep it, even though he and his family were in rags. But the indentured servants who completed their terms after 1660 found it very difficult to establish themselves as independent planters. Consequently, it became usual for them to move away to the frontiers or, in the later years of the century, to Pennsylvania, Delaware, and New Jersey, where there was a better chance for advancement.

This movement was accelerated by the great increase in the importation of slaves which began about 1680. The poor white man, already struggling against adverse economic conditions, now had to face the competition of slave labor. The tobacco which the small planter raised with his own hands he had to sell in the same market with that made by the blacks. It sold, therefore, for a price so low that the white man could hardly live on the returns. For a full half century the tobacco colonies were subjected to a double movement, the influx of African slaves, and the flight before them of poor whites.

The life upon the plantations of the well-to-do differed widely from that of the yeoman. The possession of capital and the employment of servants and slaves made it possible for the large planter to enjoy a degree of economic independence impossible for his smaller neighbor. The case of Captain Samuel Matthews, prominent in the first half of the seventeenth century, is typical. "He hath a fine house," we learn from a contemporary, "and all things answerable to it; he sowes yearly store of Hempe and Flax, and causes it to be spun; he keeps Weavers, and hath a Tan-house, causes Leather to be dressed, hath eight Shoemakers employed in their trade, hath forty negroe servants, brings them up to Trades in his house: He yeerly sowes abundance of Wheat, Barley, &c. The Wheat he selleth at four shillings the bushell, kills store of Beeves, and sells them to victuall the ships when they come thither: hath abundance of Kine, a brave Dairy, Swine great store, and Poltery."[29]

The example of Captain Matthews in instituting plantation manufacture was followed by the large landholders of later decades. The will of Colonel Robert Carter shows that on one of his farms were two house carpenters, a ship carpenter, a glazier, two tailors, a gardener, a blacksmith, two brick-makers and two sailors, all indentured servants. The inventory of Ralph Wormeley, who died in 1691, mentions at the main residence eight English servants, among them a shoemaker, a tailor, and a miller.

Thus the large plantation was a little community to itself, bustling with activity and depending upon its own exertions for many of the necessities of life. One might see at work, in addition to the field hands, carpenters, coopers, sawyers, blacksmiths, tanners, curriers, shoemakers, spinners, weavers, and distillers. The woods furnished plank for the erection of the outhouses and charcoal for the blacksmith; the cattle supplied skins for the tanners and shoemakers; the sheep gave wool and the fields cotton and flax for the weavers; the orchard produced the fruit used by the distillers. The coopers made the hogsheads in which the tobacco was shipped, and the casks for wine and cider. The blacksmith repaired plows, harrows, chains, and hinges; the shoemaker made shoes for the black slaves; the spinners and weavers the cloth for their clothes.

Though the skilled English servant was useful in this system of plantation manufacture, the existence of the large estates themselves was dependent from the first upon slave labor. The indentured worker was too expensive, his term of service too short to permit of a large margin of profit from his work. But when the planter was farsighted enough or fortunate enough to secure a supply of blacks, his fortune was as good as made. An examination of the patent rolls, inventories, and wills shows that the slaves were almost exclusively brought in by wealthy planters, or purchased by them when imported by slave dealers. When we consider that there were but 2,000 slaves in Virginia in 1671 and probably not more than 4,000 in 1690, these figures throw fresh light upon the size of this select group. Had all the slaves in the colony in 1671 been distributed among the large planters in holdings of fifty each, there would have been enough for forty estates only.

With the influx of blacks that followed England's successful intrusion upon the slave trade in the latter part of the seventeenth century, the class of large slaveholders in Virginia and Maryland was widely expanded. It is probable that, at the time of the American Revolution, Dinwiddie County alone could boast of more planters who owned twenty or more slaves than all Virginia 100 years earlier. The study of the history of these colonies in the seventeenth century has proceeded so far that we can no longer accept the small group of wealthy men as typical of all the planters, and ignore the thousands of small freeholders who owned the bulk of all the cultivated land, produced the bulk of the exports, controlled through their votes the lower houses of the assemblies, and struggled manfully to maintain their liberties against the encroachments, on the one hand, of the Stuart monarchs, and, on the other, of the aristocratic clique whose influence centered in the council of state.

THE NEW ENGLAND TOWN AND ITS PEOPLE

THE HOPE OF THE ENGLISH economists that the New England forests would afford the mother country a large measure of economic independence was, as we have seen, destined to disappointment. To a less degree the hopes of the settlers themselves also proved illusory. The Puritans who swarmed into the region in the fourth decade of the seventeenth century came not only with the purpose of working out their religious ideals secure from the dangers and heresies of the Old World, but also with the firm intention of pursuing their hereditary occupation as cultivators of the soil. But these two things they found difficult if not impossible to reconcile. Land they secured in abundance, and though not very fertile, still it yielded to well-directed effort an abundant food supply. Isolation, however, could be had only with economic independence, and for that, agriculture alone was not sufficient. Either the colonists had to produce some staple agricultural product which could be exchanged in the markets of the world for manufactured articles, or develop other forms of industry. Since the soil was not adapted to tobacco, sugar, or indigo, some of the settlers had to lay aside the hoe for the fisherman's net or the shipwright's hammer and saw. Hard work and intelligence did make it possible for the New England farmer to produce a surplus above local needs, and agricultural products constituted an important item in exports, but they were at all times insufficient in quantity to balance the essential imports.

Agriculture in New England, for a new country where land was plentiful, was intensive in character, following somewhat the custom of the English manor, though with no vestige of a manor lord's monarchical control. In fact, the land system of the New England towns affected their life profoundly, the agrarian bond rivaling the ecclesiastical in holding the community together. First, a company of applicants to the legislature, perhaps a fragment of a church congregation, was granted a "plantation right," which authorized a settlement in a designated region just beyond the existing frontier line. If, in the passing of a year or two, the experiment proved successful, they were given a "town right," allowing them not only full representation in the general court but the common proprietorship of the land, which was at this time precisely bounded.

Through selected representatives, the group then assigned the holdings to the individuals, small plots they could till with their own hands: the home lot, varying in size from a little yard to some thirty acres, where the farmer had his dwelling, his cowshed and garden, and the share of long strips scattered through the arable upland where he might plant his Indian corn or rye. These he held in severalty, but the outlying meadows and pastureland, including woods and waste, were held in common and regulated by town ordinances. The allotments were made according to each family's ability or need, and in some towns the "planters," or "commoners," were classified into groups according to their wealth. At any rate, the magistrate and the minister were given larger plots, oftentimes near the meetinghouse and green, and corresponding holdings in the arable land.[30] An industrious man with an unusually large family might find himself similarly favored with more acreage.

Thus, when the division of land was made in Salem in 1634, it was ordered that "the least family shall have 10 acres, but greater families may have more according to their number." In Dorchester every settler received "a great lot" of from sixteen to twenty acres. The first Watertown "dividient," containing about 1,090 acres, was parceled out among thirty-one men in lots ranging from twenty to seventy acres; in both the second and third divisions the average grant was about thirty-five acres, while in the fourth the lots varied from twenty to sixty acres. The typical holdings of one man in this place consisted of "a homestead of six acres, one acre and a half of planting ground, one acre of plowland in the further plain and nine acres of upland beyond the further plain." The holdings at Dorchester may be judged by a purchase made by David Sellecke, a "soape boyler," of William Hutchinson of Aquidneck and Edward Hutchinson of Boston. For the sum of £80 the purchaser received "one Dwelling house situate in Dorchester," and "all outhouses and one garden or home lott thereunto belonging and sixteen acres of wood ground," together with an interest in some three acres of land on Dorchester Neck. The holdings were seldom more than 100 acres in extent and usually much smaller.

The "arable" was generally divided into great fields, at least the north and the south, and the commoners within such limits might carry on their operations jointly, if they could come to an agreement as to what and when to plant. In such cases they were responsible as a group for keeping up the fence. But these attempts at cooperation were so unsatisfactory that in most towns the individual plots were soon enclosed, and the farmer went out each morning over an intricate system of paths and rights of way to till one or another of his little parcels.

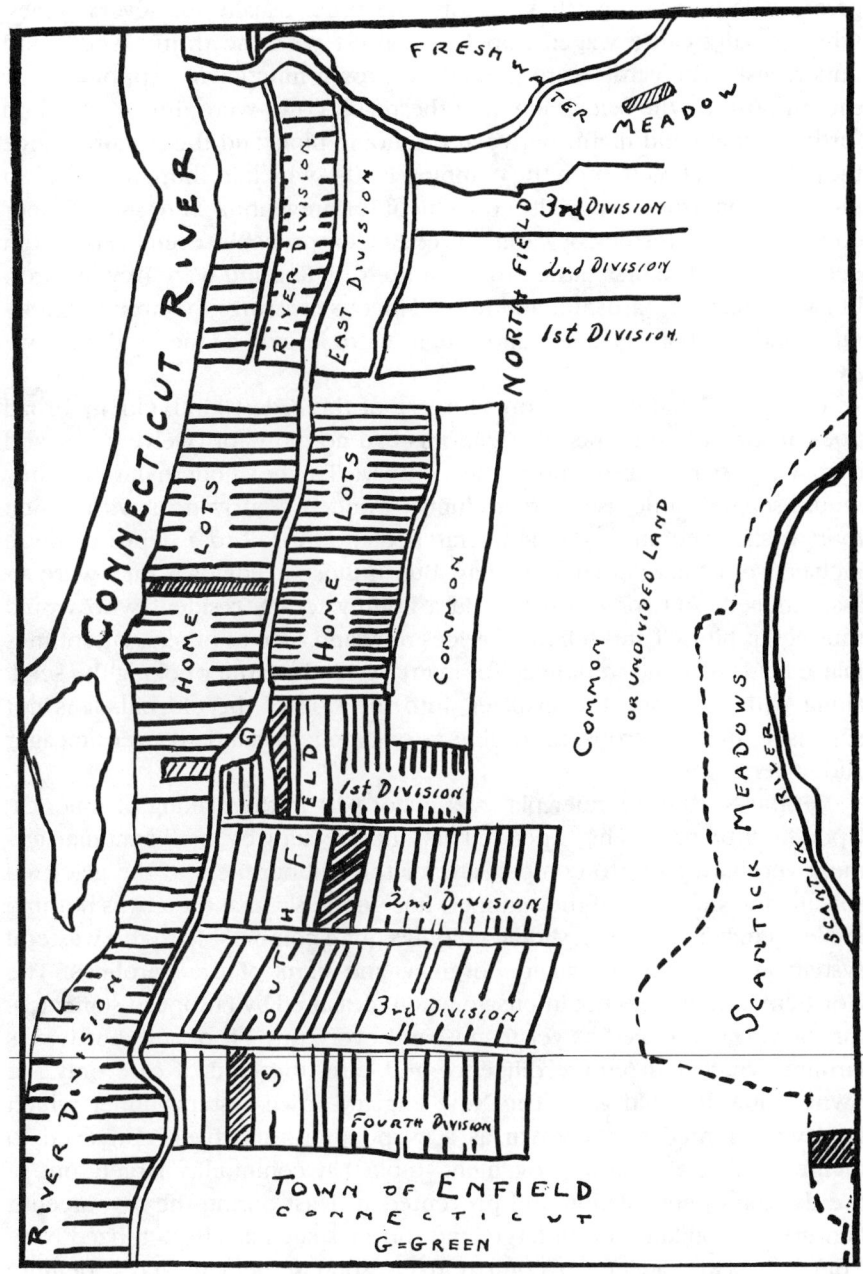

Land Division in a New England Town.

Since little or nothing was known of the rotation of crops, about half the great fields were lying fallow at any one time, usually for several years, while grazing cattle waged hopeless contest with the thrifty weeds and underbrush. The cattle were herded by a town functionary, appointed for the purpose by the selectmen, and the milch cows were driven back and forth, morning and night, between the home plots and the pasture. Since they all ranged together on the common land—which in shore towns often included peninsulas especially convenient for preventing strays—no farmer could improve his stock by careful breeding or, probably, even keep it from deterioration. The first cattle brought into New England were Devonshires, but with neglect, hardship, and miscellaneous crossings the breed deteriorated and, big-boned, rangy, and tough, were known as the "red" or "native" stock.[31]

The tools, handmade of course, were of the rudest kind, chiefly broad hoes, mattocks, and forks. The Pilgrims had no plow for twelve years, and they were scarce throughout the century. To the modern farmer they would seem of little use—great clumsy wooden contrivances with which four or six oxen and two men scratched the topsoil to a depth of three inches over an acre of land in a day. But in those needy days they were an asset indeed, and some towns paid a bounty to any resident who would thus equip himself and sell his services now and then to others. Oftentimes maize fields were not replowed for many years, the farmer poking the seed, along with a herring for fertilizer, into the side of the old hill. It is not surprising that the crops, according to our modern standard, were meager and uncertain.[32]

Yet the Northern farmer played a major part in the making of America. Upon his little parcels he expended his labor, seeking by intelligent management and hard work to compensate for the stubbornness of the glaciated soil and the shortness of the summer. It is safe to say that there was nothing in New England or in the Middle colonies quite comparable to the wasteful system in vogue in Maryland, Virginia, and parts of the Carolinas. The Northern farming was not intensive when measured by European standards, for there was no need as yet to husband every tiny bit of soil; but it was farming which did require diligence and care, the kind of care only the owner himself could give. The New England town system, under which land was granted to the town as a corporation, and by it conveyed to members for personal improvement, took that commodity largely out of the domain of speculation and prevented, at least during the seventeenth century, the building up of large land fortunes such as characterized New York.[33] It also made for a comparatively solid settlement and a definite frontier. Common possession of land and the problems involved in it gave the New England townsman a certain political training that was recognized as important in Revolutionary days. Land was a community concern, which made the records of transfer particularly important; to ensure that it was held by proper citizens, provision was early made that anyone desiring to sell his plots or his "undivided rights" must first offer them to the town and that no stranger should buy without the town's consent.[34]

The New England town strove to attain to some degree of economic independence and imported nothing which it could make for itself. The village shoemaker, the blacksmith, the currier, the carpenter, the cooper, the miller, the tanner, the weaver, the bricklayer, the mason, the wheelwright, the tailor, the glazier—all played important parts in the economy of the little community. It is interesting to note the extent to which the division of labor was carried, the town records disclosing such specialists as the "set work cooper" and the "clapboard-dryver." Many times an artisan was also a farmer, but in most cases, versatile though he might be, he gave most of his attention to his trade. So important to the town were these workers that the authorities often sought them out and offered them special inducements to settle in their midst. In 1658, Haverhill presented a house and land valued at £20 to a blacksmith, John Johnson, in return for his promise to follow his trade there for seven years. In 1655, Windsor, Connecticut, gave a currier a house, land, and "something for a shop, to be to him and his heirs, if he lives and dies with us, and affords us the use of his trade."[35]

The industry of the seventeenth century is remarkable for two things: its diversification and the high type of labor it required. The region never became dependent upon one staple crop or upon one all-important industry. Virginia was the land of tobacco planters, where the bricklayer laid down his trowel and the shipbuilder his saw to devote themselves to the needs of the Indian plant. In New England, living side by side were men of widely divergent occupations—merchants, fishermen, farmers, shipbuilders, artisans, sailors. Upon the Hingham board of selectmen we find Daniel Lincoln, "seaman"; James Hersey, "husbandman"; William Hersey, "farmer"; John Fearing, "weaver"; Matthew Cushing, "wheelwright"; Jeremiah Beal, "blacksmith."[36] New England was by no means cut off from the rest of the world—it did not enjoy complete economic independence, for her ships and her products found their way into many distant lands, but the diversification of industry added strength to the economic system and made for a vigorous, wholesome society.

Even more important was the fact that in all these various industries the fundamental need was for skilled, not unskilled, labor. Massachusetts and Rhode Island had a better opportunity to secure black slaves than the Chesapeake Bay colonies, for their own traders were not slow to take advantage of the opening afforded to independent merchants by the activities of the Royal African Company. As early as 1676 we find them starting out for Guinea and Madagascar with masts and yards and returning with cargoes of slaves. But there were blacks in New England many years prior to this date. Mr. Chester of Hartford died in 1650, leaving "a neager Maide," valued at £25. The inventory of the estate of Robert Keayne, filed in 1675, mentions "2 negros and a negro child" worth £30; while in 1661, John Hanniford left a Negro boy, valued at £20. The farmers failed to turn the blacks into "handy men," and slavery never secured a firm foothold in New England.

Nor could the custom of bringing poor persons from England and binding them to work out their passage supply New England with the needed labor. Indentured servants, although not uncommon, were far less numerous than in Virginia and Maryland. One could kidnap a man at random in the alleys of London and be sure of a ready sale for him in the South, no matter how untrained or whatever his antecedents. But in New England the case was different. The newcomer had to have some experience as a seaman before he could be disposed of to a shipowner; unless he was a skilled ship carpenter, the master builders would not want him; unless a blacksmith or shoemaker or cooper or weaver or bricklayer, he would not be desirable as a helper to any of these artisans.

Skilled men, even in England, were by no means financially helpless. They usually could pay their own fare across the ocean and so start life in the New World as freemen. Despite this fact we know that many youths were brought to New England to become apprentices. Lechford cites a case in which a worker "did retayne one Servant Ambrose Sutton to serve in the trade of Carpentry" for the space of five years. Among the lists of runaway servants we find tailors, clothiers, house carpenters, and other skilled workers. In September 1639, John Bourne offered to bind himself to Nehemiah Bourne "for 6 yeares if he will undertake his coming from England to instruct him in the trade of shipwright." In the same year, Richard Gridley turned over his servant William Boreman to William Townsend of Boston, to be "Apprentice of the crafte of thatcher."

On the other hand, in securing promising apprentices, it was not necessary for artisans to look all the way across the Atlantic. If the weaver, mason, or wheelwright had no son of his own to succeed him in his trade, he could easily secure a youth from among the neighboring families. John Chandler, a Boston shoemaker, placed his son John as "Apprentice unto William Webb, of Roxberry," for seven years, "to be instructed in the trade of Baker and to have meate & cloths, washing and wringing, and in the end of the term double apparell & 20s." We find John Crabtree, a Boston joiner, agreeing to take John Greene, the son of Solomon Greene of Hadley, as his apprentice for seven years, after which he was to become his journeyman for a year at a salary of £8. Samuel Cole of Boston placed his grandchild, John Cole, as apprentice for seven years to John Mylam, a cooper.

It was more usual, however, for the son to follow in his father's steps. There are innumerable cases in colonial New England in which one trade persisted in the same family for generations. When there were several sons in one family, the father, after taking one as his own assistant, usually put the others out as apprentices. Among the sons of Samuel Lincoln of Hingham were Samuel, the carpenter; Daniel, the planter; Mordecai, the blacksmith; and Thomas, the tailor. John Tower, of Hingham, had five sons who attained to maturity, of whom John probably became a farmer, Ibrook and Samuel were coopers, while Jeremiah and Benjamin were weavers. When parents neglected to teach their children to read, public officers bound them out as apprentices so that they might receive the rudiments of an education. The officers also found places for the children of the poor.[37]

The limited scope of the trade between New England and the mother country also retarded the immigration of indentured servants. Moreover, most of the people who came to Massachusetts under terms of indenture seem to have been used as domestics. We know that the early settlers brought household servants with them, and the demand for this kind of labor was constant throughout the period. John Josselyn, in the account of his second voyage to New England, declared that the people were "well accommodated with Servants," of whom some were English, others blacks. On the other hand, a correspondent writing in 1660 advises well-to-do persons who expected to migrate to New England to bring their own servants, as there were few available there and not to be hired for any length of time. The shortness of the term of indenture, together with the prevailing high cost of labor, tends to confirm the latter statement rather than the former. Even so prominent a man as Cotton Mather found the problem of securing domestics a difficult one, and made it "an Article of special Supplications before the Lord, that He would send a good Servant into" his family.[38] John Wheelwright sent all the way to County Glamorgan for a servant, and contracted to pay not only her passage but wages of three pounds sterling a year. John Beal, of Hingham, when he came to New England in 1638, brought two servants with him.

In New England as elsewhere in America, a bright future opened to servants of ambition and industry. Two decades after the founding of Boston, Edward Johnson states that "there are many hundreds of laboring men who had not enough to bring them over, yet now worth scores, and some hundreds of pounds." John Winthrop was much annoyed because his former servant Richard, immediately after securing his freedom, took very high wages in ready money only, and in a little more than a year "had scraped together about £25, and then returned with his prey to England." Most of the freedmen remained to make the most of their opportunities for advancement, many becoming landowners and some winning positions of honor and influence. Although servants who had just finished their terms were excluded from participation in the divisions of land in some towns, in many others they shared equally with those who had come over as freemen. In 1662, Hadley granted three men, at least one of whom had been a servant, home lots and £40 allotments in the meadow.

The indentures usually specified that the master should furnish his servant, at the end of his service, with at least a meager equipment for starting life as a freeman. Clothing, provisions, guns, and even domestic animals were among the articles usually demanded. Dermodt Matthew, a servant of George Strange, stated that his indenture called for wages of four pounds sterling a year, "a pigg to be payd at every years end and in the end of the term to have a Convenient lott," together with "three suits of apparel & six shirts." William Boreman, for serving Richard Gridley of Boston, was to receive "meat, drink, lodging & apparell, & double apparell at the end of the term." Isaac Cullimore agreed to give his apprentice, beside his board and keep, a ewe kid at the end of four years and five at the end of his term, besides "double apperell." Masters, out of a sense of duty or kindliness, would often give assistance to the servant beyond the specifications of the indenture. Benjamin Bates in his will, dated 1678, made especial provision for his "'servant Nathaniel Wilson," while Joshua Beal left property to Ruth Gannett "that was formerly my servant."

Of the so-called criminal class of servants who were swept over to America in the seventeenth-century tide of migration, New England received her share. President Timothy Dwight of Yale went so far as to state that the early settlers brought them "a collection of peasants and servants remarkable for their profligacy." Certain it is that some of the freedmen neglected their opportunities and fell into a life of crime and idleness. In 1657, Boston gave notice that every master must see to it that his servant, upon attaining freedom, secure employment and not, through idleness or other cause, become a burden upon the town. An examination of the criminal records in the various New England colonies reveals the fact that the servant class was responsible for a very large proportion of the worst offenses. A New England historian, after following the lives of many persons of this class, found proof that they provided most of the early criminals. "The fittest seemed to survive," he adds. "Others of the baser sort perished."[39]

The use of indentured labor on farms seems to have been the exception rather than the rule. The cost of servants was too high, the requirements of the task too exacting, the available supply too limited. Upon the few larger estates, on the other hand, labor of some kind had to be secured, or a part of the land would lie idle. We find Edmund James, a planter of Watertown, paying eight pounds sterling for the passage of a servant and agreeing to furnish food, clothing, and lodging, and to give him at the end of seven years of work "double apparell & five pounds in money." It is almost certain that this man acted as a farm laborer. In 1639 a farmer of Piscataqua was in search of Richard Price, his servant, who had escaped while his term still had four years to run. In 1640, Zaccheus Gould of Lynn complained to the governor and assistants, on behalf of himself and other husbandmen, that their servants were often "drawne from their worke to trayne in seed time, hay tyme & harvest," and petitioned that they might be excused from military service during these seasons.[40] On the whole, however, the average New England farmer must have depended entirely upon his own labor or that of his sons.

New England industry, then, in all its various forms was based, not on the work of slaves or servants, but upon free labor. It was this all-important fact, even more than the rigid moral code prescribed by the clergy, which made the social fabric sound; it was this, even more than the inherited ideals of liberty, which rendered it democratic. The small farmer, the skilled artisan, the fisherman, and the sailor were the backbone of the region, and in the end nothing could deprive them of the influence which came from that fact. The magistrates and clergy might extend the franchise to them sparingly, they might withhold certain social privileges, but there is obvious at all times a grudging recognition of their power.

At first the aristocracy were much alarmed at the excessive wages demanded by artisans, or the high prices they charged for their products. If these men could earn a living hardly inferior to that of many gentlemen, there would be a general leveling of society. Over and over again the magistrates tried to set a maximum wage for all kinds of workers. In 1633 a Massachusetts statute limited master carpenters, sawyers, masons, bricklayers, tilers, mowers, and other skilled workers to two shillings a day when "boarding themselves," or fourteen pence when "dyett" was provided. All were to work the whole day, with a reasonable time for "foode and rest," while idleness, so abhorrent to Calvinists, was sternly punished.[41] In 1635 several men were fined for accepting two shillings sixpence per day. But it was obviously impossible to enforce the law. There were too many opportunities for advancement in this new country, and the demand for labor was too great for the artisan to be held down by restrictive legislation. If the blacksmith were limited to two shillings a day, he would desert his bellows to become a farmer in some other town. The law of 1633 was repealed after two years, although individual towns were still permitted to fix wages. During the economic crisis of 1640 the general court attempted to make wages conform to the increased purchasing power of money, but they met with scant success. It was economic law that determined the wages of these workers, and economic law could not be upset by the Massachusetts legislators.

In fact, the New England artisan attained a degree of well-being unheard-of in England and rare in all ages. We find Christopher Stanley, a tailor, purchasing "one house & garden thereto belonging, lying in Boston betweene the houses of Richard Bellingham, Esqr., on the eastparte & the house of Thomas Buttolph on the west, for £50 in hand."[42] Edward Wood, baker, could afford to buy a dwelling house in Charlestown for £39 10s. Andrew Lane, hatter and farmer, left an estate appraised at £235 3s., which included dwelling house, barn, salt meadow and other lands, four oxen, four cows, two yearlings, etc.[43] The property of John Tower, "boatman and weaver," was valued at £171.12.10.[44] In the affairs of the town the farmer and the artisan were alike prominent. We find them serving as selectmen, constables, and as officers in the militia. These men held a social rank next to that of the clergymen, squires, merchants, and men of substance, a rank carrying privileges which they guarded with jealous solicitude.

As for the upper class, in the early days its bounds were narrow and clearly drawn. To it belonged only the ministers and the small group of Puritan gentlemen who had been their backers in the pilgrimage to America and who cooperated with them fully after reaching New England. These men opposed democracy in any form, for they believed that the state should be based upon an aristocracy of God's elect. It was from this class almost exclusively that the early magistrates were drawn. But with the beginnings of trade, merchants began to come to New England, men often not fully in sympathy with the old order, yet whose wealth and influence could not be ignored. That the merchant class was forming even in the first decade after the Massachusetts Bay settlement we gather from Thomas Lechford's "Note-Book." Among the traders were William Tyng,[45] John Cogan, Richard Parker, and John Pollard. Soon after the founding of New Haven a number of wealthy and experienced merchants settled there and erected "fair and stately homes." To Rhode Island came several families of rich Jews from the Netherlands, bringing with them their goods and their unsurpassed mercantile skill. Typical of the early traders was John Holland, who settled at Dorchester. This man, through his various ventures in fitting out vessels for fishing and trading, accumulated a fortune estimated at his death in 1652 at £4,000.

Thus it will be seen that New England society in the seventeenth century was divided into several groups with clearly defined limits.[46] At the top was an ill-assorted aristocracy of religion, wealth, and rank—an aristocracy which included the clergyman, whose power rested upon his moral influence and his control of the franchise; the gentleman, who brought his rank with him from England; and the merchant, who won recognition through the vitally important part he played in the economic upbuilding of the country. Next in rank were the skilled artisan and the freeholder, who did most of the work and were responsible for most of the economic output. Sturdy, intelligent, hard-working folk they were, priding themselves on the title of "Goodman" or "Goodwife" and jealous of the social distinctions due their rank. Constituting the greatest element of strength in New England society, not only did many of them enjoy the franchise but they furnished most of the town officials. Next beneath them was the unskilled laborer—the wage-earner or the journeyman—who not only had no title but who was usually addressed by his Christian name alone. The indentured servants formed a fourth class, and the slaves, whether Indian or black, a fifth. Men of the three lowest classes were often admitted to the church society, but seldom to political citizenship, and the line of social distinction was sharply drawn in each case.

These various ranks by no means existed only as an arbitrary valuation set on men by their neighbors, but carried with them certain well-defined legal privileges. The gentleman was permitted to adorn himself with articles of dress forbidden to the goodman; the goodman wore others, which were withheld from the day laborer or the servant. Lace, silver and gold thread, slashed sleeves, embroidered caps, "bands & rayles," gold and silver girdles, hat bands, belts, ruffs were forbidden to all save the upper class. In 1653 two women were presented at Newbury for wearing silk hoods and scarfs, but they were discharged upon presenting proof that their husbands in each case were worth £200. John Hutchins's wife, in a similar case, was discharged "upon testimony of her being brought up above the ordinary ranke." In 1676, Connecticut passed a law that any person wearing "gold or silver lace, or gold or silver buttons, silk ribbons or other superflous trimmings" was to be taxed as though in possession of property valued at £150. But the families of magistrates and commissioned officers in the militia were excepted, together with "such whose quality and estate have been above the ordinary degree though now decayed." Even before this date we find thirty women of various towns in Connecticut presented as "persons of small estate who used to wear silk." Again in 1676, thirty-eight women and thirty young men were called to account by the magistrates for "wearing silk, some for long hair and other extravagancies."[47]

These class distinctions were also carried into the allotment of pews in the church. In Dedham the elders assigned seats in accordance with the amount of taxes paid by the members, but in most towns it was rank as well as property which determined precedence. In New Haven no seats were assigned to any beneath the rank of goodman, while "four backer seats in the gallery" were set aside for young men.[48] At Saco the people were divided into seven classes and were seated accordingly by a vote of the town. Woburn had a committee of five to assign seats to the congregation in respect to "estate, office and age," while the committeemen themselves were seated by another committee of two. Stamford voted to assign pews to its people according to "dignity, age and estate." Persons who ignored these allotments by intruding upon the pews of their neighbors were often heavily fined.[49]

An interesting illustration of the sentiment in favor of rigid class distinctions is furnished by Swansea. When the town was laid out in 1667 the committee appointed to carry out the work arbitrarily divided the inhabitants into three ranks. Not only did this action receive the sanction of the townsmen, but in later years committees were appointed to perpetuate these distinctions, or to promote and degrade persons from one rank to another.

The same spirit appears in the matter of punishments, it being a fairly well-fixed principle that all gentlemen should be exempt from corporal punishment. In 1631, when Mr. Josias Plaistowe was convicted of stealing corn from the Indians, the court merely imposed a fine and directed that thenceforth he "should be called by the name of Josias, and not Mr. as formerlie." On the other hand, his servants who had assisted in the theft were severely flogged. Though the upper classes usually escaped the whipping post and the pillory, in the matter of fines they suffered more than their humbler neighbors. At Swansea, for certain offenses the first class had to pay £3 12s., the second £2 8s., and the third only £1 4s.

It must not be imagined from these distinctions that colonial New England was essentially aristocratic. The great contrasts in the life of the people, on the one hand a privileged class of wealth and power, on the other a fairly large group of servants, slaves, and unskilled laborers, form but a part and not the most important part of the picture. Overshadowing all else was the great middle class, composed of small freeholders and skilled artisans. Upon this class the economic and social fabric was based. Sooner or later social distinctions disappear when they have no foundation in economic conditions, and colonial New England economically was democratic. Much has been said about the influence upon American life of the New England conscience, much concerning her contributions to political freedom, but her most valuable legacy has been overlooked or minimized —her essentially sound economic and social system, her democracy of labor.

The New Englander, unlike his cousins of Virginia and Maryland, was himself compelled to produce most of the manufactured articles essential to his daily life. The tobacco colonies found it profitable to devote their energies almost exclusively to their one great staple crop, receiving from England in exchange all kinds of fabricated goods. But since New England had little which the mother country desired, the people of that region could not make extensive purchases of English goods. Their export of furs, naval stores, and fish oil gave them but a meager credit in London and Bristol upon which to draw for farm implements, clothing, glass, leather, gunpowder, and other needed articles. And so, with characteristic energy and resourcefulness, they set to work to supply their own wants.

In the earliest days, before mills were constructed, the settlers had ground their corn in primitive mortars, hollowed from a block of wood or the stump of a tree, after the Indian manner. The pestle, which was also of wood, was often fastened to the top of a slender sapling, which aided in lifting it after each blow. These sweep or mortar mills, as they were called, were superseded by hand mills in many localities, which in turn gave way to the more powerful and practical mills run by water, wind, or tide. It is said that the Indians at first had a superstitious dread of the windmills, and looked with wonder at "their long arms and great teeth biting the corn in pieces." The first water mill was erected in 1633 at Dorchester. It was antedated by a windmill, however, for it is stated that in 1632 a mill which had been set up near Boston was taken down and reassembled on a hill in the north part of the town.[50]

The home life of the average New England rural family was wholesome, practical, arduous. With the first streaks of gray in the east the father was out of bed, to strike a light with flint and steel and kindle a fire in the huge stone fireplace. As the others arose, they took their turns at the wooden basin, perhaps breaking the icy surface before washing their faces and hands. The father and older sons then went to the cow yard to milk the cows, while the younger boys fed the hogs. In the meantime, the mother and daughters had been cooking the porridge, and when the reading of the Scriptures and the family prayers had been concluded, breakfast was ready. The family gathered around the long, narrow table-board, perhaps by the light of candles, and reverently gave thanks. After the porridge had been dealt out in small wooden bowls, all sat down to enjoy this early repast.

The father and sons then went forth to the fields for the day's work. If it was spring or early summer, they armed themselves with hoes and brought out the wooden plow, drawn by slow-moving oxen; if late summer or autumn, they carried scythes and two-pronged pitchforks. While they labored, breaking the soil or mowing wheat or stacking corn stalks, the women of the family were busy at home. One cleared the table and washed the dishes, one labored at the cheese press, one busied herself at the washtub, another at the soap kettle,[51] another prepared the midday meal. The cooking was done over the log fire in the huge fireplace. Here the skillful cook boiled her Indian corn and kidney beans, flavored with a slice of salt venison; here she made her pumpkin pie, slicing the ripe fruit, boiling it in a little water, and adding butter, vinegar, and spice.

At noon the table-board was set for dinner—the high salt cellar at the center, then clumsy wooden trenchers, round pewter platters heaped with delicious succotash, a great wooden noggin, several wooden tankards, a number of pewter spoons, but no forks, no glassware, no china, no covered dishes, no saucers. At the summons of the horn the workers hurried in from the fields, and the family seated themselves on long narrow benches on each side of the table to help themselves to the plain but bountiful food.

The midday meal over, the father and the boys returned to the fields for five more hours of labor, while the mother and daughters resumed their separate tasks. As evening approached the hogs and sheep were driven into their enclosures near the barn, where the faithful dog could guard them throughout the night. Supper was simple—for the children milk porridge or hasty pudding, for the father and mother a slice of cold pork, brown bread, and a mug of beer. Once more the Scriptures were read, while the family sat with bowed heads. By eight o'clock all were in bed.

The distinctive feature of New England life was the town, for the family whose daily life we have just been following was closely flanked by neighbors. Had Sir William Berkeley visited the colonies east of the Hudson, he would have been deeply interested in this system of community organization, which differed so greatly from that of the South. He would have thought it strange that men who made agriculture their chief pursuit should live in little villages and not in the midst of the fields they cultivated. The villages themselves would have held his attention, with their boarded houses, some having projecting second stories with turned pendants at the corners, some with steep shingled roofs sloping nearly to the ground in the rear, all fronting on the street; the neat back lots, the outbuildings, the fences, the gardens, the orchards. Here he would have seen the meeting-house, its pointed roof and open belfry standing out above the other houses; here the tavern with its swinging sign; here the dreaded pillories and stocks; here, on the banks of a little stream, the grist mill; here the schoolhouse, with its single chimney in the center and its roof sloping off on all four sides; here, perhaps, the gloomy log blockhouse, to which the people could flee in case of attack by the Indians.

Beyond the village the visitor would have seen the pasture fields where several hundred cattle were grazing under the watchful eyes of two herdsmen; on this side was an expanse of dense woodland where the villagers cut their firewood and at times timber for building; on that, the common meadow; far out to right and left the arable land where workmen were busy amid the patches of golden wheat or Indian corn or waving flax. Here and there, dominating a lovely hillside, was the isolated residence of some farmer who preferred to live apart from the village. A charming, peaceful picture the little community made, a picture which would perhaps have disarmed even the deep-seated prejudice of Sir William for everything that had to do with Puritans.

THE FALL OF THE WILDERNESS ZION

ALTHOUGH THE ENGLISH GOVERNMENT, in permitting the settlement of New England, was actuated by economic considerations, a large proportion of the settlers themselves journeyed into the wilderness chiefly for religion's sake. Not only did they wish to escape persecution in England, but they were determined to establish in America a retreat for all of like faith with themselves, a bulwark against the forces of Antichrist. "All other churches of Europe have been brought under desolations," they said, "and it may be feared that the like judgements are coming upon us; and who knows but God hath provided this place to be a refuge for many, whom he means to save out of the General Destruction." They hoped to better their condition in a new and fertile country, of course, for the decline of industry and the lack of employment made conditions difficult in England. "The whole earth is the Lord's garden, . . . why then should we stand starving here for places of habitation, and in the mean time suffer whole countries . . . to lye waste without any improvement?"

But their minds were fired chiefly with the hope of establishing a Bible commonwealth, sealed against error from without and protected from schism from within. "What can be a better or nobler work, and more worthy of a Christian," they said, "than to erect and support a reformed particular Church in its infancy. . . ."[52] It is incorrect to infer that most of the colonists were not deeply religious merely because it is found that church members were in the minority. Many righteous Puritans were unable to state an overwhelming religious experience which would qualify them for membership, yet they were sympathetic with the church's purpose.

In so large a movement some were unquestionably impelled by one motive, some by another. Of the thousands of men and women who landed on the New England shores in the years from 1629 to 1640, there were many who felt little sympathy with the erection there of a powerful theocracy, some who had come on the representations of the shipping agents as to the opportunities to win a competence in America.[53] But they were forced to conform to the wishes of the leaders, men of the type of John Winthrop, John Cotton, John Norton, and John Wilson. This latter group enjoyed a prestige which was born not only of superior education but of an extraordinary talent for leadership. Schooled in the bitter controversies of the day, hardened in the fires of adversity, they were well fitted to play the role of Moses in the removal of this modern host to the promised land. "Though the reformed church, thus fled into the wilderness, enjoyed not the miraculous pillar," Cotton Mather tell us, "we enjoyed many a person, in whom the good spirit of God gave a conduct unto us, and mercifully dispensed those directing, defending, refreshing influences, which were as necessary for us, as any that the celebrated pillar of cloud and fire could have afforded."

These men were intent on establishing a theocracy in which their tenets and their form of worship should be upheld by the hand of the law. They were not Separatists but Church of England men, and what they designed was an established church in New England. At the very outset they made it clear that "they did not separate from the Church of England, nor from the ordinances of God there, but only from the corruptions and disorders of that Church: that they came away from the Common-Prayer and Ceremonies."[54] On another occasion they called the Anglican church "their dear mother, desiring their friends therein to recommend them unto the mercies of God in their constant prayers, as a Church now springing out of their own bowels, nor did they think that it was their mother who turned them out of doors, but some of their angry brethren, abusing the name of their mother."[55]

The migrating preachers had fought in the old country, not only for the right to worship as they chose in their individual churches but also for control of the Anglican establishment. Had they succeeded, they would have forced the church into complete conformity with their views, driving out those who persisted in opposing them. Failing in their efforts, they removed to America, where there could be no opposition to their plans. Having set up their reformed church, having transplanted what they believed to be the true Anglican church to their new homes, they intended to protect it from innovation by the authority of the civil law. "We came hither because we would have our posterity settled under the pure and full dispensations of the gospel; defended by rulers that should be of ourselves."[56] These words, delivered at one of the notable election sermons, give the keynote of the movement. Their church they intended to buttress by a state especially designed for its protection.

Obviously toleration had no part in such a plan. It is a singular perversion of history which attributes ideals to the prime movers in this great migration that they themselves would have been the first to repudiate. The sermons and published writings of the founders of Massachusetts make it clear that they never entertained the thought of opening the doors of their new Zion to those who differed from them. So far from being champions of toleration, they opposed it bitterly. " 'T is Satan's policy, to plead for an indefinite and boundless toleration," said Thomas Shepard.[57] Urian Oakes denounced religious freedom as the "first born of all Abominations,"[58] while Increase Mather sternly rebuked the "hideous clamours for liberty of Conscience." John Norton denounced liberty of worship as liberty "to answer the dictates of the errors of Conscience in walking contrary to Rule. It is a liberty to blaspheme, a liberty to seduce others from the true God. A liberty to tell lies in the name of the Lord." The Puritan community thought that heretics should have only the liberty to leave. As Nathaniel Ward said, "All Familists, Antinomians, Anabaptists, and other Enthusiasts shall have free liberty to keepe away from us."[59]

We fail to grasp the spirit of these men unless we realize that they considered themselves a chosen people, one to whom God had revealed himself and had led to the promised land far from the sins and corruptions of the Old World. "The ministers and Christians, by whom New England was first planted, were a chosen company of men," says Cotton Mather, "picked out of, perhaps, all the counties in England, and this by no human contrivance, but by a strange work of God upon the spirits of men that were, no ways, acquainted with one another, inspiring them as one man, to secede into a wilderness, they knew not where."[60] William Stoughton expressed the same idea in his famous statement that "God hath sifted a nation, that he might send choice grain into this wilderness." God's concern for the settlement had been lovingly manifested by striking the Indians with a plague a few years before the migration, thus making the waste places safe for his children.[61] Such an attitude does not conduce to toleration. Convinced that he had been selected by God to receive and expound the truth, the Puritan minister could but look upon those who opposed him as minions of Satan.

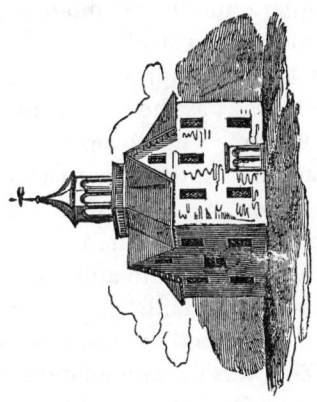

Center: A Sermon in praise of Harvard College, 1655.

Below: The "Old Tunnel" Meetinghouse at Lynn, Massachusetts, 1682–1827.

GODS

MERCY,

SHEWED TO HIS PEOPLE IN GIVING THEM A FAITHFUL MINISTRY AND SCHOOLES OF LEARNING FOR THE CONTINUAL SUPPLYES THEROF.

Delivered in a Sermon preached at Cambridg, the day after the Commencement, by Charles Chauncy, B. D. *President of* HARVARD *Colledg in* New-England.

Published with some additions there-unto, at the request of diverse Honoured, and much Respected friends, For publick benefit, *as they judged.*

1 Thef. 5. 12. *We beseech you brethren to know them that labour among you, &c are over you in the Lord, and esteem them very highly in Love for their work sake.*

Printed by *Samuel Green* at CAMBRIDG in New-England 1 6 5 5.

The Reverend Richard Mather, 1596–1669, the first engraving produced in America, 1670.

As for democracy, the New England fathers dreaded it as a form of government inconsistent with the rule of the best and most pious men. "Democracy I do not conceive that God did ever ordain as a fit government for either church or commonwealth," says John Cotton. "If the people be governors, who shall be governed? As for monarchy and aristocracy, they are both clearly approved and directed in the Scriptures. . . . He setteth up theocracy . . . as the best form of government in the commonwealth as in the church." [62] Winthrop agreed heartily, averring that democracy had no warrant in Scripture and that "among nations it has always been accounted the meanest and worst of all forms of government."

Thus the earnest men who led the Puritan exodus planned their new Bible commonwealth and thus they built it. Composed in large measure of persons of like faith, protected from invasion by its very isolation, guided by the clergy and by magistrates in close sympathy with them, this wilderness Zion was the culmination of their fondest hopes. Yet from the first the theocracy found itself faced by a multitude of difficulties that threatened its supremacy and slowly undermined its strength.

The first of these was that love for self-government so universal among Englishmen. All the reverence, all the love, all the admiration which the people had for their leaders did not reconcile them to the loss of their liberty. In the early days of the colony the outstanding leader was John Cotton. This remarkable man has been spoken of as "the unmitred pope of a pope-hating people." What he advised from the pulpit was usually enacted into law. The chronicler of Christ's wonders in America says that Cotton was the great director, "the father and glory of Boston." [63] Yet even the influence of John Cotton could not prevent a strong faction of the people from demanding that in their new home they should not be deprived of their rights and liberties. According to the charter all important matters of government were left to the discretion of the stockholders, or freemen, in the general court. Only twelve of these freemen had come to Massachusetts in 1630, and all had been made magistrates. Since they were in full sympathy with the leading clergymen, and supported them in all their policies for both church and state, the arrangement constituted the government by the best, which Winthrop and Cotton so earnestly advocated. Democratic it was not. When the first general court convened in October 1630, the magistrates had shrunk in number to eight, and this small group were confronted with a demand from 109 of their fellow settlers to be admitted as freemen. These men were doubtless all Puritans, but they could see in their demand for citizenship nothing inconsistent with the dictates of their religion.

The magistrates postponed action on this petition until the spring. In the meanwhile they decreed that the assistants and not the freemen should make laws and elect the governor, and that the assistants should hold office during good behavior. This left the freemen only the right to select new assistants when vacancies occurred. The applicants agreed to this arrangement although it left them only the husks of real citizenship, and for some months more the little body of magistrates continued to tax and legislate. In 1632, however, when the assistants voted a levy for fortifications, the town of Watertown entered a vigorous protest. Under the leadership of their minister the people passed a resolution "that it was not safe to pay moneys after that sort, for fear of bringing themselves and posterity into bondage."[64] Governor Winthrop, greatly disturbed at this show of insubordination, summoned the Watertown men before him, and after they had made their submission, pardoned them. But the other towns were not less concerned at the limitations set upon their liberty. When the general court met in May, the body of the freemen voted that the governor and his assistants must be elected each year, and that every town should elect two delegates to act with them in levying taxes.

Although this was a long step toward representative government, it still left the deputies without a hand in making laws. In 1634 they assumed this right also. In May, two men from each of the eight towns met in Boston and demanded to view the charter of the colony. Winthrop dared not refuse, and they at once called his attention to the fact that the charter gave the making of laws to the whole body of freemen. When the general court met a few days later, three deputies appeared from each town, ready to demand their rightful share in the government. Against this action the magistrates and leading ministers protested. The very foundations of the newly established theocracy seemed to be crumbling. John Cotton threw the full weight of his influence in favor of upholding the established order, pleading that the Bible clearly showed that the magistrates ought to hold office for life. But the freemen, so far from yielding, refused to reelect Winthrop governor, and actually imposed fines upon some of the magistrates for abuse of power. They then decreed that henceforth the general court, consisting of the governor, the assistants, and deputies elected by the towns, alone should have the right to tax, make laws, and admit freemen.

Thus, four years after the Massachusetts Bay charter was brought to America, the government was changed from a narrow oligarchy to what appeared to be a little republic. Yet even after the establishment of representative government, very little real liberalism existed, and the theocracy still ruled almost supreme. The freemen were only a small part of the population and the law forbidding the admission of non-church-members was rigidly enforced. Moreover, the prestige of the few leading laymen of the colony was such that they were selected as magistrates over and over again. John Cotton insisted "that a magistrate ought not to be turned into the condition of a private man, without just cause, and be publicly convict, no more than the magistrate may not turn a private man out of his freehold, etc., without like public trial." The idea became fixed that every official should be reelected unless convicted of misconduct. Consequently, the governor and his assistants continued to represent only the narrowest aristocratic clique in the colony, and the deputies a comparatively small body of voters, picked by the ministers from church members.

The theocratic form of government not only created internal dissension, but it was a leading cause in weakening Massachusetts by the withdrawal of several congregations to the Connecticut Valley. The liberal views of Thomas Hooker were so greatly at variance with those of Winthrop and Cotton that he could not rest at ease in his Newtown settlement. "There is a great disunion of judgement in matters of religion amongst good ministers and people which caused Mr. Hooker to remove," wrote the Reverend R. Stansby to John Wilson, "and that you are so strict in the admission of members to your church, that more than half are out of your church in all your congregations, and that Mr. Hooker before he went away preached against that." [65]

Although those who favored representative government had won a certain measure of success, schismatics and heretics at first could do nothing. The magistrates and ministers were adamant against attempts to break down the unity of their "City of God on earth." Yet both schism and heresy were prompt in showing themselves. In 1631 the scholarly and liberal Roger Williams arrived, and accepted a pastorate at Salem. An avowed Separatist, he at once attacked the established order for not renouncing fellowship with the Church of England. Besides inveighing against legal oaths and against the validity of titles to land granted by the general court, he also denounced the union of church and state, declaring from the pulpit that the magistrates had no right to punish Sabbath breaking or other violations of the first four commandments.

This open attack upon the theocracy could not be passed over. The ministers rendered their judgment "that he who should obstinately maintain such opinions, whereby a church might run into heresy, apostacy, or tyranny, and yet the civil magistrate could not intermeddle," was too dangerous to be tolerated.[66] Williams was cited to appear before the authorities and, after a trial, was sentenced to banishment. The decree was suspended until spring on condition that he refrain from attempting to spread his opinions. This he was unable to do, and when the magistrates decided to keep him on shipboard pending the next sailing for England, he escaped through the frozen forests to the Narragansett Bay region. The theocracy had won an easy victory, but it was a costly one because it was achieved by appealing to the civil authorities. Schism for the moment had been blocked, but physical force cannot prevent the growth of divergent opinions, and before long heresy reappeared in a far more dangerous form.

Anne Hutchinson, who had been a parishioner of John Cotton in England, is described by Winthrop as a woman of "ready wit and bold spirit." Several years after her arrival in Boston she began the dangerous practice of holding meetings in her house to rehearse and discuss the sermon of the previous Sunday. From this she passed to comparing the teachings of the clergymen, and then to the evolution of a doctrine of her own. The ministers were expounding a covenant of works, she maintained, whereas the Bible showed that salvation was based on a covenant of grace. Although Winthrop wrote that "no man could tell (except some few who knew the bottom of the matter) where any difference was,"[67] he and the other leaders of the theocracy understood clearly enough that her ideas were inconsistent with the established order. The covenant of grace made religion a matter of direct communication between man and his Maker, while the covenant of works required only obedience to a prescribed code of which the minister was the official interpreter. Should the former doctrine secure wide acceptance, not only would unity be lost, but a stunning blow would be struck at the theocracy.

For a time Boston supported Mrs. Hutchinson with something like unanimity. Even the great John Cotton was inclined to embrace her doctrines. The religion of love which she preached was more in keeping with his naturally kindly nature than the established tenets of law and judgment. But he drew back in time. John Wheelwright, Mrs. Hutchinson's brother-in-law, and young Harry Vane bore the brunt of the battle. The former was summoned before the general court, and although he refused to answer questions because the proceedings were held in secret, was found guilty of sedition and contempt. To weaken the influence of Boston, a resolution was passed transferring the next court of elections to Newtown. When the vote was taken, the orthodox party succeeded in restoring Winthrop to the governorship. Boston, however, sent as its deputies Vane, Coddington, and Hoffe, all favorable to Mrs. Hutchinson. The court at first refused to seat them, but when Boston held a new election and returned them again, "the Court not finding how they might reject them, they were admitted." In the following summer the clergy met in synod and condemned as erroneous and blasphemous the Hutchinson heresies. At the November court Wheelwright was disfranchised and banished, while other members of the dissenting faction were severely punished. Mrs. Hutchinson was "banished from out this jurisdiction as being a woman not fit for our society."[68]

In this way was the church purged of heresy, and the theocracy saved from what to its leaders seemed the most deadly peril. It is folly to condemn these men for bigotry and intolerance. They had given up their homes and had fled into the wilderness for the purpose of establishing a society free from error. How natural, then, that they should have combated what they considered error, when to their horror they found that it had followed them across the Atlantic. "Two so opposite parties could not contain in the same body without hazard of ruin to the whole," said Winthrop. Conformity was gained, but only at the cost of a bitter struggle which left scars that were slow to heal. Theocracy was so weakened that another great heresy might shatter it.

Though for some time no such heresy arose from within, the ministers soon found themselves confronted with peril from without. In 1656, Quaker missionaries invaded New England with the avowed purpose of making converts. The democratic leanings of the Quakers, their refusal to accord special respect to magistrates, and their denial of the need of an established clergy combined to make them obnoxious to the Puritan leaders. When Mary Fisher and Ann Austin arrived in Boston the colony was stirred to its foundations. "Why was it that the coming of two women so shook ye, as if a formidable army had invaded your borders?" George Bishop inquired of the magistrates.[69] But the magistrates would undoubtedly have been less dismayed at the invasion of an armed host. Powder and shot could only imperil men's lives; the Quakers were assaulting their souls. We gain an insight into the state of mind of these stern Puritans, not so much from their action in arresting these women, denouncing their doctrines, and burning their books, as from the care they took to board up the windows of their cell so that the prisoners could not preach to the people. After five weeks of imprisonment they were shipped back to Barbados whence they had come.[70]

A few days later eight more Quakers arrived from London. Governor Endicott immediately put them in prison and at the first opportunity sent them out of the country. In October the general court fixed the fine of any master who should bring in a Quaker at £100, and declared that the Quaker himself should be severely whipped. By a later enactment the offender's tongue was to be bored with a hot iron, his ears were to be cut off, he was to be banished, and if he returned, to be executed. New Haven, Plymouth, and Connecticut also passed severe laws against the Quakers, but the death penalty was prescribed by Massachusetts alone. Rhode Island, under the leadership of Roger Williams, would have none of this persecution. A band of Quakers who landed at Newport were received with kindness. But the other colonies, fearing that the missionaries would use Rhode Island as a base of operations, entered a vigorous protest. Pointing out that the "contagion" could easily spread across the borders, they threatened to take strong action "to prevent the aforesaid mischief."[71]

The reply of Williams might well have given pause to the Massachusetts magistrates and ministers. We "finde that in those places where these people, aforesaid, in this colony, are most of all suffered to declare themselves freely, and are only opposed by arguments in discourse, there they least of all desire to come . . . surely we find that they delight to be persecuted by civil powers, and where they are soe, they are like to gain more adherents by the conseyte of their patient sufferings."[72] The Rhode Island assembly answered in similar vein, reiterating their intention to uphold freedom of conscience, which they prized as their greatest happiness.

The Massachusetts magistrates continued their pitiless warfare against the invaders. In September 1659, Mary Dyer, William Robinson, and Marmaduke Stevenson, who had come to Boston courting martyrdom, were all banished. Mrs. Dyer reached Rhode Island, whence she immediately returned, but the two men went only to Salem before facing about. All were sentenced to death. Robinson and Stevenson were hanged, but Mrs. Dyer, after her hands and legs had been bound, her face covered and the rope adjusted about her neck, received word that she had been reprieved. Once more she was sent to Rhode Island, but the efforts of her family to keep her there failed. In the spring she came back to Boston where she, too, was executed. In November 1660 another Quaker, William Leddra, suffered the same fate.

Though the theocracy went to those extremes, the battle was going against them. Endicott and Norton had good reason to realize that Roger Williams had been more farseeing than they, for the sufferings of the Quakers won for them the sympathy of thousands who had only contempt for their doctrines. A few days before the execution of Leddra, Wenlock Christison, another Quaker, strode into the courtroom, and looking into the face of Endicott, said to him, "I came here to warn you that you should shed no more innocent blood, for the blood that you have shed already cries to the Lord for vengeance to come upon you."[73] He was seized and brought to trial. The magistrates debated long as to what should be done, for public sentiment was turning rapidly against them; but for Endicott there was no hesitancy. Pounding the table he shouted out, "You that will not consent, record it. I thank God I am not afraid to give judgement." Christison was condemned to death, but the sentence was never carried out. Partly from fear of interference from the crown, partly because of the evident opposition of the people, the persecution had to take a milder form. There were no more executions.

It was a severe defeat for the theocracy. The ideal of a Puritan commonwealth walled in against heresy had broken down. The suffering Quakers had proved that the New World did not offer so safe a refuge from the "poison of error" as the leaders of the exodus had hoped. Moreover, it had been made apparent that there were limits beyond which the people of Massachusetts would not follow the magistrates and ministers. The sight of a suffering Quaker, stripped to the waist and tied to a cart's tail, his back clotted with blood from frequent whippings, trudging through snow and ice, could but cause revulsion in men's minds against the system which was responsible for it. The Puritan leader in the days of his exile and his sacrifices was an inspiring figure; the Puritan persecutor seemed in contrast unlovely indeed.

In addition, the conflict brought interference from England, and with it the threat of an early termination of the charter upon which the established order was based. Charles II, displeased at the executions, gave orders that the vein of innocent blood opened in his dominions should be closed. The English Quakers actually chartered a ship to carry this message to New

England and in six weeks delivered it into Endicott's hands. Accordingly, the laws against heresy were modified so that many mouths were "opened which were before shutt."

Had Charles confined his attack to the narrow theocratic group in Massachusetts, he would have found powerful support within the colony itself. But he was bent not only upon overthrowing the established order but upon substituting for it the despotic rule of the crown. The people were not to benefit by this transfer of power, and even the forms of representative government which had persisted under the old regime were to be swept away in the new. Edmund Andros, who was made governor-general of all New England despite the guarantees of the Connecticut and Rhode Island charters, trampled ruthlessly upon the rights held most sacred by Englishmen. In conjunction with his council he made laws, gave judicial decisions, and ordered the collection of taxes. The Massachusetts general court was abolished, and every freeholder was made uneasy by the threat to revoke existing land grants.

Fortunately, the tyranny of Charles II and James II in New England proved short-lived. The English nation rose in 1688, drove James into exile, and granted the throne to his daughter Mary and her husband, William of Orange. The Glorious Revolution is a landmark in the history of English liberty, a landmark between the period in which the theory of divine right received widespread acceptance, and the period of parliamentary supremacy. In America, especially in New England, the effects were not less far-reaching. The old Massachusetts theocracy which was demolished to make room for royal absolutism was not fully restored when absolutism in its turn was overthrown. Increase Mather went to England to plead for the renewal of the original charter, but fortunately for Massachusetts he was not successful. Mather claimed to be the representative of the whole people; yet we know that public sentiment, while hoping for the restoration of the former status of semi-independence, by no means favored the old narrow administration in local affairs. In other words, the people wanted both autonomy and political liberty, only one of which they had enjoyed prior to the second Stuart despotism, and neither under the rule of Andros. The resolution passed by Watertown in May 1689, asking that the number of freemen "be inlarged farther than have been the Custom of this Colony formerly," was no doubt representative of opinion throughout Massachusetts.

They had their wish. The new charter, which was issued in 1691, instituted a royal government not unlike that of Virginia. There was to be a representative assembly, while the franchise was based, not on church membership, but on property holdings. The crown appointed the governor, who had the power to veto bills of the assembly, appoint judges and other officials, and put the laws into execution. Members of the council were nominated by the legislature and confirmed by the governor. Religious freedom for Protestants was guaranteed. Thus was established a new order distinctly more liberal than that under which Massachusetts had lived during the past six decades. The power of the clergy was not completely crushed; the social and political structure of the colony was not revolutionized. A full century and more was to pass before Massachusetts became in any real sense democratic. But the old buttressed Bible commonwealth, the Zion which had been the dream of Winthrop and Cotton and for which they had made such sacrifices, was gone forever.[74]

It must be remembered that from the first many persons settled in New England from economic rather than religious motives. Cotton Mather relates that once a Massachusetts minister, who was preaching to a congregation in the northeast region, urged them to continue a "religious people from this consideration that otherwise they would contradict the main end of planting this wilderness; whereupon a well-known person, there in the assembly, cryed out, Sir, you are mistaken, you think you are preaching to the people at the Bay; our main end was to catch fish."[75]

Even at Boston itself there were many who had come to better their fortunes rather than to escape persecution. With the development of trade and industry this group received gradual accessions until a separate merchant class had developed. Between the merchant and the clergyman there was a distinct and growing divergence of interests. The former looked out upon the whole world, his vessels wandered from the West Indies to England, and from Chesapeake Bay to the Mediterranean; he learned to know the Catholic Spaniard, the Anglican Virginian, the Quaker of Pennsylvania, and found good in them all. He had no sympathy with the policy which would make of New England a Zion, walled against the contagions of a sinful world. When Boston made it illegal for townsmen to "entertain any strangers into their houses for above 14 days" without special permission from the authorities, it aroused the merchants to protest.

We find the pious Edward Johnson, as early as 1650, expressing alarm at the growing spirit of commercialism. Merchants and vintners "would willingly have had the Commonwealth tolerate divers kinds of sinful opinions to intice men to come and sit down with us, that their purses might be filled with coyn, the civil Government with contention, and the Church of our Lord Christ with errors."[76] As the century grew older the merchant class increased both in numbers and influence. The prosperity which they brought to New England, the outlet they offered for its products, and the employment they gave to thousands of workers rendered them formidable opponents. The ministers railed at them and warned them that they must not attempt innovations. "New England is originally a plantation of Religion, not a plantation of Trade," thundered Higginson in his election sermon of 1663. "Let Merchants and such as are increasing Cent per Cent remember this."[77] But the merchant class added a leaven to public opinion which the clergy could not ignore and found it difficult to combat. During the Salem witchcraft delusion it was Thomas Brattle and Robert Calef, both merchants, who had the common sense to see the folly of the inquisition and the bravery to denounce the justices and the ministers for their part in it.

The closing years of the seventeenth century witnessed in Massachusetts a far-reaching change. The experiment of a Bible commonwealth had definitely failed; the influence of the clergy in civil government, although by no means entirely eliminated, was greatly restricted; their hold upon the hearts and minds of the people distinctly weakened. From the first the theocracy was doomed to defeat because it set itself against men's natural instincts; and natural instincts cannot permanently be suppressed. During the half century of its supremacy the theocratic establishment had to endure a succession of shocks. The struggle for representative government, the Roger Williams and Anne Hutchinson heresies, the Quaker invasion, the annulling of the old charter, the defeat in the witchcraft prosecutions —each played an important part in the overthrow.

More powerful than any one incident was the slow, almost imperceptible change which was coming over men's minds, the trend toward rationalism, the development of liberalism, the widening of human sympathies. This movement found no corresponding development among the old school of churchmen. So far from attempting to keep in step with the times, to shape their theology in conformity with new ideals and new points of view, they remained rigid and unyielding. Regarding the leaders of the exodus as saints, they sought to perpetuate their tenets and to pattern their lives after them. In this they failed, for the ability of the early fathers to move the hearts of men lay in their creative force. John Winthrop and John Cotton were living actors in the drama of their times; Cotton Mather was little more than a stereotyped imitator. In the last analysis the New England theocracy fell because it tried to crystallize the Puritan spirit of the early seventeenth century, while the tide of a new civilization swept over and past them.

A TRANSPLANTED CHURCH

WE HAVE SEEN HOW CLIMATIC, geographic, and economic conditions affected the life of the European settlers in America—how these factors defeated England's chief purpose in founding the colonies, tended to undermine the theocratic structure in Massachusetts, brought the artisan in Virginia and Maryland to drop the saw or the shuttle for the plow or the hoe, changed the New England farmer into a shipbuilder or a merchant, and made fur traders of the French on the St. Lawrence and the Dutch on the Hudson. We may now turn to the profound changes which they wrought in a typical old-world institution, the Anglican church.

During the seventeenth century, Virginia was the only English colony on the American continent in which the majority of the people adhered to the established faith of the mother country. In Maryland the church was first set up by law in 1692, and prior to that date there were usually three or four Anglican clergymen in the colony. For a generation after the founding of South Carolina the proprietors opened the doors of their settlements to all kinds of dissenters, so that when at last, in 1704, a conformity bill was passed, the Anglicans are said to have constituted but one third of the population. Elsewhere the Church of England had but few adherents and lived only on sufferance. It is in the Old Dominion, then, that one can study to the best advantage the interesting experiment of transplanting into the New World this religious establishment so vigorous and important in the Old.

It was inevitable that in the American branch there should be many changes. The basic doctrines remained the same, but from the first there was divergence in organization, in government, even in the form of worship. In England the church was controlled by a highly developed hierarchy, while in Virginia it was more democratic. In England the clergy as a body enjoyed a certain degree of independence, and exercised a powerful influence upon civil affairs. In Virginia the church was largely controlled by the people through their vestries, while in state matters it was, at most periods, quite devoid of influence. The ecclesiastical establishment began from the very hour of its foundation a separate and peculiar development: It had to mold itself into something suited to the peculiar requirements of a new country.

The Anglican church, unlike English representative institutions, did not flourish in the soil of Virginia. The democratic tendencies of the colonists and their scattered mode of life proved serious obstacles to the development of a truly religious life. Before the end of the century pious men were noting with misgivings that the character of the clergy was bad, that many parishes were vacant, that the liturgy was neglected, and the religious wants of the people imperfectly met. Unless vigorous efforts were made to effect a thorough reform, decay and ruin seemed inevitable.

Thoughtful clergymen in the colony attributed these unfortunate conditions chiefly to the sparseness of the population. The Virginians were a race of plantation dwellers. There were no real towns. Jamestown itself, for a century the capital and the chief entrepôt of the colony, was no more than a straggling hamlet. Since none but the most fertile lands could be cultivated with profit, extensive untouched tracts lay between the various settlements. Vessels navigating the tributary streams of the James, the York, and the Rappahannock frequently had to make their way for miles under the shadows of the virgin forest.

This made it necessary to create parishes of very great size, so great, in fact, that no man could alone minister to any one of them. As time passed and the population became more dense, the parishes changed in size and shape, but they remained to the end too large to be cared for properly. In 1724, St. Paul's Parish in Hanover County was sixty miles long, Bristol and Hungers were each forty, and Westminster and Westover each thirty.[78]

Neglect of religion was inevitable. Regular attendance at worship was difficult, for few had the constancy to make their way ten or fifteen miles to church through the forests or on the rivers. The great distances, moreover, made it difficult for ministers to win the friendship and love of their flocks, for they could not be frequent visitors at homes that were perhaps ten or fifteen miles from the rectory. "The inconvenience and prejudice of such large bounded parishes are very great," wrote the Reverend Alexander Forbes,[79] ". . . for the Word of God can be preached but seldom among them; the use of the Sabbath day is converted by them into some diversion or worldly business; they cannot be catechized so frequently as their need requires; their sick cannot be visited." Some of the Virginia parsons struggled manfully against those unfortunate conditions. It must have been a familiar sight to see them upon their mud-splashed horses, making their way along the narrow forest paths to bring the comforts of the church to the homes of their scattered parishioners. But the fight was a hard one, and many of the clergy were neither earnest enough nor brave enough to make it.

Such was the condition of the Virginia church as the seventeenth century drew to a close. To thoughtful men it seemed that things could not be worse. With the clergy poorly paid, too few in numbers, and of inferior ability and character; with the liturgy frequently disregarded; with the parishes too large, the church government weak and disorganized, unless radical reforms were instituted, ruin was inevitable.

The great churchmen of England were not ignorant of the danger which threatened. The Virginia clergy, in letters and pamphlets, made frequent complaint of their troubles. yet no one in England felt a direct responsibility in the matter, and no reforms were made until the accession to the see of London, in 1675, of Henry Compton. This able man took seriously his duties as diocesan of the colonial church. After a careful investigation, he laid before the board of trade a report on ecclesiastical abuses in the colonies. He complained of the laxness of the Virginia governors in not upholding the right of patronage, of the hiring of ministers by the vestries, the payment of salaries in cheap tobacco, the custom of burying in "gardens, orchards and other places," the use of laymen to perform the marriage ceremony.

Neither Compton nor the board of trade realized that these abuses were rooted deep in the economic and social life of the colony. The board had no remedy to suggest, and simply directed the governors to put an end to each abuse, as though those officers by mere command could revolutionize the colonial church.[80] Having directed them to see that adequate salaries

1656—James Blair—1743.

✠ Old Trinity, Dorchester County, Maryland. ✠

✠ St. Luke's, Isle of Wight County, Virginia. ✠

be paid the clergy, that violations of the liturgy be stopped and that the tenure of the clergy be made secure, they forgot the whole matter, and turned to their accustomed business of regulating the trade of the colonies.

The bishop of London, however, orchestrated a campaign to combat the evil influences which were undermining the Virginia church. Pressure was to be brought upon the parishes to present their ministers for induction, so as to free them from their dependence upon the vestries. Ecclesiastical discipline was to be made a reality. A college was to be founded in which young Virginians could be trained for divine orders. The clergy were to have a representative in the council of state to guard their interests in civil affairs.[81]

Yet the efforts for reformation failed dismally. After years of endeavor, years filled with bitter contests and heartburnings, no permanent good was effected. The movement for the reform of the Virginia colonial church ended in utter failure and the influence of the Anglican church continued to decline until, during the American Revolution, it reached its lowest ebb. Its history throughout the entire colonial period is one long recital of disappointment, of wasted opportunities, and gradually diminishing strength.

THE INVISIBLE WORLD

THE COLONISTS BROUGHT WITH THEM from Europe a vivid consciousness of the supernatural. Any variation, great or small, from the known routine of nature was taken as a "sign." Thus, when a calf was born with six eyes, the pious Winthrop shook his head in solemn apprehension: "What these prodigies portend the Lord only knows, which in due time he will manifest."[82] It was an age of magic and witchcraft, an age which believed that thunderstorms were caused by malignant spirits, that persons in league with the devil could sink ships at sea, ruin crops, strangle infants in the crib, cause sickness and death. The powers of the air were everywhere. Like their forefathers, the colonists regarded comets and other such phenomena as supernatural manifestations, set in the sky to mark some event of special importance, to give warning of God's anger, or to herald the approach of famine or war or pestilence. The wheat blight of 1665 in Massachusetts was preceded by "a great and blazing comet," while the comet of 1680 gave Increase Mather inspiration for a sermon entitled "Heaven's Alarm to the World." When John Cotton died a comet appeared in the heavens as a signal testimony, so it was thought, "that God had removed a bright star, a burning and a shining light out of the heaven of his church here."

That comets great men's deaths do oft forego,
This present comet doth too sadly show.[83]

A spearlike form in the northern lights of 1667 presaged the deaths of three revered clergymen: Samuel Shepherd, Henry Flint, and Jonathan Mitchell.[84] The Dutch settlers on the Hudson trembled at the "dreadful comett starr" of 1680 with its "fyery tail or streemer," and, feeling that God had threatened them, petitioned for "a day of fasting and humiliation." In Virginia the people were warned of the approach of Bacon's Rebellion by a comet "streaming like a horse tail westward."

Increase Mather, in his *Remarkable Providences,* tells how certain holy men were preserved at sea, when all others in the ship's company were lost. Lightning he calls "Heaven's arrow," and relates numerous instances in which men were "smitten with the fire of God." The smell of brimstone, which so often accompanies the thunderbolts, he considered proof positive that they were of supernatural origin. He was not a little perplexed that these dreadful visitations should come so often to pious persons, in some cases when they were assembled for prayers and worship. Meteorites he regarded as missiles hurled from heaven. In fact, every manifestation of nature which science had left unexplained he instantly assigned to the sphere of the supernatural. "There is also," he says, "that which is very mysterious and beyond human capacity to comprehend, in thunder and lightning."[85]

Cotton Mather, having lost the manuscript of three lectures, satisfied himself that "Spectres, or Agents in the invisible World, were the Robbers." When New England was swept by yellow fever, he ascribed his escape to the intervention of a good angel. In 1696 he set out for Salem, undeterred by a threatening storm, whereupon "the storm strangely held off," until his return more than a week later. He constantly prayed to be protected from magic, and ascribed to the work of a demon the death of his infant.[86] The God of seventeenth-century New England was a God of dramatic revelations. In June 1647, when no news had come to New Haven of a great ship which six months before had sailed away with some of the finest manhood of that struggling little settlement, a phantom replica appeared in the harbor and rehearsed the tragic wreck before the eyes of the astonished townsmen. The Reverend John Davenport explained "that God had condescended, for the quieting of their afflicted spirits, this extraordinary account of his sovereign disposal of those for whom so many fervent prayers were made continually."[87]

It was a terrible, mysterious world, this world of the imagination which was so real to the colonists, a world in which devils entered men's bodies and expressed things of which they themselves knew nothing, in which goblins stole infants from the cradle substituting for them hideous elves old in sin, in which Satan's agents took strange forms the better to carry out his evil commands, in which the very air was full of unseen spirits, some good, others ever alert to do harm, in which the powers of darkness could destroy crops, bring on pestilence, cause droughts. Human confederates, peradventure might be enlisted in this hideous work.

Witchcraft as a living force in European life is of comparatively recent origin. During the Dark Ages, when faith was universal and doubt almost unknown, men regarded the devil with something akin to contempt. He was usually depicted as an insignificant imp whose malignity was easily rendered harmless by the repetition of a prayer or by making the sign of the cross. With the first traces of skepticism he became more terrible, and the church began to concern itself with his direct relations with human beings. It was in the thirteenth century that theologians worked out their theory of witchcraft, and in the fourteenth that they drew all witchcraft cases into their own jurisdiction. The end of the sixteenth century and the beginning of the seventeenth, a period noted for religious chaos and conflict, marked the height of the witchcraft prosecutions. The Protestant movement had dignified the Bible into a unique authority, and the Bible commanded, "Thous shalt not suffer a witch to live."[88] Many thought the Roman church had been criminally lenient in this matter.

Such was the age which saw the establishment of the English colonies in America. The settlers, whether they landed on the banks of the James or in Boston Harbor, shared fully the almost universal belief in the constant presence of the supernatural. In fact, the transition from Europe to America tended to stimulate rather than weaken the dread of the unknown. This vast country with its strange wild coast, its mysterious forests, and its savage Indians seemed a place especially suited to magic and witchcraft, a place for centuries set aside by Satan for his own uses. At the mummery of the Indian medicine men the Europeans looked on, not with incredulity or derision, but with mingled fear and indignation. To them it seemed a direct manifestation of the devil's power. Happily there were no witch panics and probably no executions in America outside the confines of New England,[89] but only the boldest and most skeptical dared question the reality of the crime of witchcraft. Witch trials took place in almost every colony.

Several years before the Massachusetts Bay Company received its charter a grand jury in Virginia was considering charges of witchcraft against a certain Goodwife Wright. To the modern mind the evidence presented was trivial and absurd. She was heard to curse Sergeant Booth, after which "he having very fair game to shoot at yet he could never kill anything." She was rejected as midwife for Mrs. Giles Allington, who with her husband and infant immediately after fell ill, the infant finally dying. She had come to the home of a Mr. Moore to purchase some little chickens, and when he would sell her none, not only the chicks died but the hen also.[90] Apparently the grand jury did not consider the case against Goody Wright a strong one, as there is no record of a presentation for trial.

Later came the case of Paul Carter and his wife, Sarah, who were accused of infanticide and brought before the Accomac court in 1680. Both were compelled to stroke the body of the child, it being the popular belief that the wounds would bleed afresh at the touch of the murderer. This Virginia grand jury reported that when Sarah touched the corpse, they "saw no alteration," but when Paul's turn came, "immediately whilst he was stroaking ye childe the black & sotted places about the body of the child grew fresh and red so that blud was redy to come through ye skin. . . ."[91] Equally interesting is a case of witchcraft in Northumberland County, Virginia, in which a certain William Harding was accused by the Reverend David Lindsay. The prisoner was found guilty, and although he escaped the death penalty, he was punished with ten stripes on the bare shoulders and banishment. In 1665, Alice Stephens was brought before the general court on a charge of witchcraft. In 1679, Alice Cartwright was accused in the court of Lower Norfolk and examined for witch marks by a jury of women.[92]

Of special interest was the case of Grace Sherwood of Princess Anne County. In 1689 this woman, together with her husband, James Sherwood, brought action for slander against John Eisburne for declaring that she had bewitched his hogs and crops, and against Anthony Barnes for declaring that she had ridden his wife and then, in the shape of a black cat, had slipped through the keyhole. In both cases the jury decided against Grace, possibly because they considered the accusations established. Yet she was not brought to trial until 1708, when a formal charge of witchcraft was lodged against her by Luke Hill and his wife. After some delay she was subjected to the trial by water and to examination for witch marks, both tests going against her, "she swimming when therein and bound contrary to Custom and Judgement of all the Spectators, and afterward being serched by Five Antient weomen who have all declared on Oath that she is not like them."[93] The final records in this famous case are missing, but it seems certain that she escaped severe punishment, for reference to her occurs several times in later records.

On the whole, however, the Virginia justices weighed with a more critical exactness the witchcraft charges than the magistrates in New England. The accused persons were not driven to confession by judicial pressure, there was no disposition to prejudge their cases, the evidence was not twisted to bring about convictions. Above all, when charges of witchcraft were made, either in moments of anger or out of deliberate conviction, so far from bringing the accused to the gallows, they were apt to result in a lawsuit and a fine for the persons presenting them.[94] This attitude of the courts may have been partly the result of a dawning skepticism among the more enlightened men in this colony, but it is more readily explained by the absence of interference on the part of the clergy. In Scotland, in the Puritan shires of England and in New England, the court which dealt leniently with a suspected witch was certain to incur many a fiery denunciation from the pulpit, but the Anglican ministers who came to Virginia were laggards in this matter. The fear of witchcraft in Virginia seems to have sprung more from folklore than from theology.

Across the Potomac, in Maryland, the strong Puritan element made the charge of witchcraft a more dangerous matter. The justices were instructed "to enquire of all manner of Fellonyes, witchcrafts, inchantments, Sorceries, Magick Arts, etc.," and there is evidence that this order was not neglected.[95] During the reign of Charles II, John Coman, who was accused of "witchcraft, conjuration, sorcery or enchantment upon the body of Elizabeth Goodale," was tried and sentenced to death. In 1675 he petitioned the lower house of the assembly to intercede for him with the governor. The governor, who had a keener appreciation of his own profit than the perils of witchcraft, commuted the sentence on condition that Coman work for him in the capacity of a servant. The sheriff of St. Mary's conducted the culprit to the gallows and placed the rope around his neck before informing him that he was not to be put to death.[96]

In William Penn's settlement upon the banks of the Delaware witchcraft attracted little attention. The Quakers believed in the reality of the crime and George Fox himself exclaimed, "Arise, children of God, and suffer not a Witch to live." But the gentle mysticism of the sect was out of harmony with the vivid consciousness of demonology and the spirit of religious militancy essential to every great witch inquest. Having no clergy, inclined to charity, slow to credit evil of their neighbors, the Quaker colonists escaped almost entirely the witchcraft charges and trials so common elsewhere. The most important case was that of Margaret Mattson, who was accused before the governor and council in 1683 of having bewitched her neighbors' cows. Although she was pronounced not guilty "in manner and forme" as indicted, the court declared her convicted "of haveing the Comon fame of a witch." Eight years later Robert Guard and his wife came before the council complaining that John Richards, a butcher, together with his wife, Ann, had accused them of witchcraft. "The matter was inquired into, and being found trifling, was dismissed."[97]

In the Dutch colony of New Netherland we hear nothing of witches, because Holland, even in the seventeenth century, had largely outgrown the superstition. The country had had its share of witch executions under the Spanish Inquistion, and a wholesome reaction was now in progress. The works of Dutch writers were full of arguments against the reality of demonology and against the use of torture in witch cases. The foes and the victims of the witch prosecutions in other lands were welcomed. So far as is known, there were no trials for witchcraft in Holland after 1610; the Dutch traders who settled on the Hudson were almost entirely free from the current superstition.

In New England, witchcraft in America reached its greatest excesses. The Puritan teaching made it appear that supernatural intervention was a commonplace event. The New Englanders sent witches to the gallows in part to champion the cause of God against the devil, in part out of fear of what the witches might do. Back of every witch epidemic was a strong element of terror, and superstition was the soil from which each sprang.

Nevertheless, the actual growth required a special preparation, usually the broadcasting of books and pamphlets on the subject. At any time in the seventeenth century the contortions of sufferers from epilepsy, the vagaries of the insane, or the tricks of mischievous children might spread alarm, and place many persons in danger of the gallows. But there would be no frantic searching out of witches, no wholesale trials and executions, without some unusual inciting cause.

In New England there were two well-defined epidemics of witch hunting, one in the years from 1647 to 1663, the other from 1688 to 1693. The first seems to have been inspired by the witchcraft frenzy which swept the Puritan counties of England at the time of the Civil War. Many of the settlers in Massachusetts and Connecticut had left these districts but a few years before Hopkins and Stearne began their notorious proceedings, and the details of trials and hangings must have been almost as well known in Boston as in London. Bewitched and bewitchers alike were doubtless personally known to many, while no letter from Suffolk or Norfolk could fail to dwell upon the subject which was uppermost in every mind. Moreover, some of that swarm of books and pamphlets generated by the English trials unquestionably found their way across the Atlantic. Matthew Hopkins's *The Lawes Against Witches* appeared in 1645, followed two years later by his *The Discovery of Witches,* while Stearne's *Confirmation and Discovery of Witchcraft, The True and Exact Relation, Signs and Wonders from Heaven,* and *A True Relation of the Arraignment of Eighteen Witches at St. Edmundsbury,* all were issued in 1645. So profound was the influence of Hopkins and Stearne in Massachusetts that the highest court of the colony in admiration of their achievements was "desireows that the same course which hath been taken in England for the discouery of witches, by watchinge, may also be taken here."[98]

Early in 1647, Governor Winthrop of Massachusetts wrote in his journal, "One of Windsor arraigned and executed for a witch." This short entry long baffled New England historians, for the official records make no mention of the case. The identity of the unhappy victim seems now to be established, however, by the discovery of the following entry in the diary of Matthew Grant of Windsor: "May 26, '47, Achsah Young was hanged."[99] With the details of this, the first execution for witchcraft in any of the colonies, we are still entirely unacquanted.

Massachusetts, as though jealous of Connecticut for having been before her, was quick to follow her example. Margaret Jones of Charlestown was accused because, "after some angry words passing between her and her Neighbours, some mischief befel such Neighbours in their Creatures." Although she was urged on the day of her execution to confess and repent, "she constantly professed herself innocent of that crime."[100]

Trials and executions now followed with monotonous regularity, both in Connecticut and in Massachusetts. In 1648 one Mary Johnson was hanged at Hartford. "Her first familiarity with the Devils came by Discontent, and wishing the Devil to take that and t'other Thing, and, the Devil to do This and That; Whereupon a Devil appeared unto her, tendering her the best service he could do for her." After this he would clear the hearth, and when her master would send her to the field "to drive out the hogs that us'd to break into it, a Devil would scowre them out, and make her laugh to see how he feaz'd em about."[101]

In 1651, John and Joanna Carrington of Wethersfield were executed for having "intertained familiarity with Sathan the Great Enemye of God and Mankinde," while a certain Goody Bassit went to her death in the same year for a like crime. The trials continued in Connecticut for another decade, but prior to 1662 there was no panic, and in some cases the juries actually brought in acquittals. The most notable execution of the period occurred in Boston, where Mrs. Ann Hibbins paid the penalty, as has been said, of "having more wit than her neighbors." This lady was the widow of William Hibbins, who had served twelve years in the council of assistants and at one time had been the agent of Massachusetts in England. The affair aroused fierce excitement, and doubtless was in part responsible for the long lull which followed in the witchcraft prosecutions in that colony.

In Connecticut there was a recurrence of the craze in 1662, which threatened a panic hardly less terrible than that which occurred at Salem three decades later. Ann Cole, daughter of a Hartford carpenter, "was taken with very strange fits, wherein she (or rather the Devill as t'is judged) made use of her lips and held a discourse." Her ravings were taken down and used as evidence of witchcraft against several neighbors, among them Mr. and Mrs. Greensmith. Both were old and ignorant, the wife probably half-crazy. The poor woman confessed her familiarity with Satan, declaring that he had just appeared to her in the image of a deer. The witches had meetings near her house, she testified, in which some assumed one shape, others another. The Greensmiths were both executed, together with Mary Barnes of Farmington, also accused by Ann Cole. Mrs. Elizabeth Seager was tried but acquitted, while William Ayres and his wife, after submitting to the water ordeal, to see if with Satan's aid they would float, saved themselves by flight.[102]

In all, there were, during this period of sixteen years, eight hangings in Connecticut and six in Massachusetts. This was a terrible toll to take from these infant settlements, a toll which makes it evident that the colonial ministers and magistrates were quite as zealous as those of England in searching out Satan's brood. The executions per capita in New England probably outnumbered five to one those of the mother country during this, the greatest witch-hunting period in English history. To what extent torture to wring confessions was used in the early trials cannot be determined. Since the Massachusetts court advocated the adoption of the methods in vogue in England, it is probable that the "watchings" so vividly described by Hopkins and Stearne were practiced in that colony. It was believed that the spirits which attended all witches were accustomed to visit them once in every twenty-four hours, usually in the form of an insect or an animal. If the witch were placed upon a chair in the middle of the room and kept awake, the imps could not approach her. This led to the custom of making the accused person walk in order to prevent sleep, and protracted sleeplessness was productive of confessions.[103] Perhaps more frequent in New England was the pressure brought to bear by "Godly Divines," who pleaded with the witches, "laying the hainousness of their sins to them," and depicting the terrible fate which awaited them in the next world should they refuse to confess.

In the quarter of a century from 1663 to 1688, witchcraft obtruded less upon the New England consciousness. But in the last quarter of the seventeenth century the theocracy was becoming alarmed at the decline of its influence and was trying to buttress its power. It was Increase Mather who conceived the idea of publishing a record of "illustrious providences" or supernatural happenings, an attempt to prove by a sort of scientific induction that God had special concern for New England.[104] At a synod in 1681 it was resolved that "Divine Judgements, Tempests, Floods, Earthquakes, Thunders as are unusual, strange Apparitions, or what ever else shall happen that is Prodigious, Witchcrafts, Diabolical Possessions, Remarkable Judgements upon noted Sinners, eminent Deliverances, and Answers to Prayer, are to be reckoned among Illustrious Providences." In 1684 this project found expression in Increase Mather's *An Essay for the Recording of Illustrious Providences.* The book met with a ready welcome, went through three impressions before the end of the year, and unquestionably did much to prepare the minds of the public for a new witchcraft epidemic.

When the children of a Boston mason named Goodwin became afflicted with fits, complaining that they had been bewitched, the entire community was alarmed. An old half-crazy Irish Catholic laundress was accused of the crime and brought before the court. The finding of several small rag dolls in her house weighed heavily against her, and she was said to have confessed that by wetting her finger and stroking these images she could torment her victims. Her incoherent and wild answers to questions were accepted as evidence of guilt; she was pronounced sane by a board of physicians, and was led forth to execution. The matter might have ended there had not Cotton Mather, in an effort to confute the Sadduceeism of the skeptical, brought the oldest Goodwin girl into his own home for observation. This was a great event in the life of the child, for Mr. Mather was perhaps the most influential man in the colony. The little child of an obscure workman suddenly found herself the object of the great man's interest. Her every movement was closely watched, her every word weighed and duly recorded in a new work on memorable providences. She knew what was expected of her, and, consciously or unconsciously, played her part.

As she went through her antics the famous minister looked gravely on, or actually stimulated her imagination by leading questions. She rode imaginary horses, was pulled hither and thither, was strangled by invisible spirits; this so impressed the eminent observer that he seriously set down: "I shall count that man Ignorant who shall suspect, but I shall count him down-right Impudent if he Assert the Non-existence of things which we have had such palpable Convictions of." His witchcraft clinic, to his own mind, had proved a complete success. His account appeared in 1689. "The old Heresy of the sensual Sadduces, denying the Being of Angels either good or evil died not with them," he wrote. "How much this fond opinion has gotten ground in this debauched age is awfully observable; and what a dangerous stroak it gives to settle men in Atheism, is not hard to discern." [105] This heresy the book was intended to combat, a task it accomplished so successfully that within three years New England was beside itself with the witchcraft terror, hundreds of persons had been accused, scores sentenced to death, and no less than nineteen executed.

In the household of Samuel Parris, minister of the church at Salem Village, were two West Indian slaves, John Indian and Tituba. This pair, themselves steeped in voodoo lore, gathered around them a group of young girls who listened with fascination to their stories of fortune telling and witchcraft. The girls, who came to be known as the "afflicted children," began to show all the symptoms of magical possession, falling on the floor, speaking in a meaningless jargon, screaming as though in agony; whereupon they became objects of supreme interest. Ministers and physicians flocked to see them, watched their antics with close attention, and plied them with questions.

When asked to name their tormentors the girls accused one neighbor after another until it seemed that half the village must have sold themselves to the devil. Terror seized the community. The ministers and the magistrates, triumphant at this manifestation of the supernatural, staunch in their determination to put to rout the forces of evil, proved blind to reason. The accused, some of them persons of blameless life and elevated character, received the mockery of a trial and were hastened to the gallows. The idle gossip of neighbors counted heavily against them, trivial incidents in their lives received the most sinister interpretations, the obvious meaning of their answers was twisted to their undoing. At the trial of the Reverend George Burroughs the afflicted girls fell into such violent fits that for a long while they were unable to testify. "The chief judge asked the prisoner who he thought hindered these witnesses from giving their testimonies? and he answered, He supposed it was the Devil. That Honourable person then reply'd, How comes the Devil so loathe to have any Testimony born against you?" "Which cast him," Cotton Mather tells us, "into great confusion." [106]

Old Giles Corey pleaded not guilty but refused to put himself on trial, whereupon he was pressed to death, the old English *peine forte et dure.* "In pressing his Tongue being prest out of his Mouth, the Sheriff with his Cane forced it in again, when he was dying." [107] When Mr. Burroughs was upon the scaffold he made a speech to the assembled crowd, asserting his innocence with such earnestness as to force conviction. As he was concluding with the Lord's Prayer, many eyes were dim, and there was a movement as though some would hinder the execution. But his accusers explained that he was able to simulate innocence through the devil's promptings, and he was quickly dispatched.

Among those accused was the wife of Mr. Nathaniel Cary, a prominent shipmaster of Charlestown and later a member of the general court. "I having heard some days that my Wife was accused of Witchcraft," wrote Mr. Cary, "we went to Salem-Village to see if the afflicted did know her. . . . They all came in, who began to tumble down like Swine, and then three Women were called in to attend them. We in the room were all at a Stand to see who they would cry out of; but in a short time they cried out, Cary; and immediately after a warrant was sent from the Justices to bring my Wife before them. . . . My Wife declared to the Justices that she never had any knowledge of them before that day; she was forced to stand with her arms stretched out. I did request that I might hold one of her hands, but it was denied me; then she desired me to wipe the Tears from her Eyes, and the Sweat from her face, which I did; then she desired she might lean herself on me, saying she would faint. Justice Hathorn replied, she had strength enough to torment those persons." The poor woman was committed to Boston prison, but Cary succeeded in having her removed to Cambridge, where she was kept in irons. "The Tryals at Salem coming on," he recorded, "I went thither, to see how things were there managed; and finding that the Spectre-Evidence was there received, together with idle, if not malicious Stories against peoples Lives, I did easily perceive which way the rest would go." He then petitioned that his wife's trial might be held in her own county, but receiving word that it would not be granted, he managed to deliver her from prison and the two fled to Rhode Island. Even there she was not safe, and "along with some others that had escaped their cruel hands," they made their way to New York, where they were courteously received by Governor Benjamin Fletcher. [108]

The terrible epidemic wore itself out through its own excesses. When a score of persons had been executed, when eight more were under sentence, when fifty others had confessed themselves to be witches, when 150 were in prison and 200 accused, things came to a sudden halt. People began to reflect that it was most improbable that "so many in so small a compass of Land should so abominably leap into the Devil's lap at once." [109] Nor did any man know when his own turn might come. Eastern Massachusetts became a place of terror, where neighbor looked with suspicion upon neighbor. When the afflicted girls began to accuse prominent persons, the magistrates, seeing that things had gone too far, threw out the indictments and opened the jails. The episode proved a boomerang for the clergy. Skeptics appeared on all sides, and it was soon widely recognized that many, if not all, the persons executed had been innocent. Judge Sewall, five years afterwards, got up in the Old South Church and publicly acknowledged his repentance and shame. Ann Putnam, one of the most active of the afflicted children, later admitted that she had been instrumental in the shedding of innocent blood. So far from striking a blow at Sadduceeism, the affair tended to discredit the men who, by their influence and example, had done so much to stir up the trouble. The Salem witch executions played an important part in undermining the power of the old theocracy.

The gradual decay of the belief in the supernatural, a decay which was marked in the colonies as well as in Europe, was not, however, the result of one incident, but of a subtle and far-reaching mental change. The seventeenth century saw the growth of the spirit of rationalism, which was destined eventually to sweep the civilized world. Superstition is the child of ignorance. The ecclesiastical mind, brought into contract with the forces of nature and completely ignorant of the laws which govern them, saw in them the visible manifestation of the spirit world. The eclipse of the sun was a token of divine anger, the lightning bolt was thought to be the witches' plaything, the hurricane the work of the magician. The normal person of the fifteenth or sixteenth centuries lived in a realm of the supernatural because he found no ready natural explanation for the phenomena which surrounded him. Deformed persons, half-wits, the blind were possessed of devils; disease was produced by magic; drought, hail, and tempests were the work of malignant spirits.

When science began to reveal the true causes of these things the world of the supernatural faded away. The appearance of a comet loses its awful significance when we know just what it is, when we can determine its component elements, estimate its density, measure its velocity, and, if it be periodic in its character, foretell the exact date of its reappearance. It was Copernicus, Galileo, Kepler, Newton, Halley, Walton, Boyle, and hundreds of lesser scientists, working patiently at their separate tasks, who freed the human mind from the chains of the invisible empire. One after another the phenomena of nature were shown to be the result of natural causes, and the conclusion was almost unescapable that all things could be so explained.

The change was not the work of a decade or even of a century; it began in the Middle Ages, and is not yet completed. Before the end of the seventeenth century it had progressed far enough to make many thoughtful men skeptical of the reality of witchcraft. It was the growth of this spirit which the New England ministers noted with apprehension, denounced as Sadduceeism, and combated fiercely in sermon and pamphlet. But they were powerless to sweep back the advancing tide of rationalism. The *Remarkable Providences* and the *Memorable Providences* did indeed for the moment rouse anew the latent fear of the invisible, but they were swept away in the very storm they blew up. There were witchcraft trials in America even in the eighteenth century, the belief in supernatural intervention in human affairs lingered on well into the nineteenth, but the champions of the invisible world had made their last real stand, and had met defeat.[110]

THE PRACTICE OF PHYSIC

EARLY IN THE SEVENTEENTH CENTURY when the English laid the foundations of their empire in America, there was general ignorance of the composition and processes of the human body. This age, the age of Shakespeare and Jonson, of Francis Bacon and Galileo, was also the age of fetish cures and mysterious quack remedies, an age which discouraged anatomical study and looked with contempt upon the surgeon—the barber-surgeon, whose lancet brought him no more prestige than his razor. While all Europe was tingling with the intellectual impulse given by the Renaissance, the Reformation, and the opening of the New World, the science of health remained much as it had been in the days of Charlemagne.

The chief cause of error was the belief, widely accepted for many centuries, that disease is caused by diabolic influence. "It is demons which produce famine, unfruitfulness, corruptions of the air, pestilences," said Origen, and Saint Augustine agreed that "all diseases of Christians should be ascribed to these demons." From this conception to a condemnation of the use of medicines was an inevitable step—it was worse than futile to apply natural remedies to supernatural ills.[111]

These views did not prevent a serious attempt by scholars to learn the secrets of the human body. Giles Firmin, indeed, as early as the 1640s was "reading" to Massachusetts pupils on the basis of an "anatomy," or skeleton, which he had articulated, probably the beginning of clinical instruction in America.[112] Autopsies were sometimes performed, such as that by Dr. Bryan Rossiter in Hartford in 1662 upon the Kelly child; yet this particular demonstration may have advanced science but little, as it proved to the doctor's satisfaction that the girl had died of witchcraft.[113] In southern Europe, where the Saracen influence was strong, medicine was taught in the universities. But it must be said that at the opening of the seventeenth century the science was everywhere still traditional and empirical. There grew up the wildest and most absurd notions concerning remedies. It was reasoned that since the universe was made for man God must have put his sign upon everything designed to serve as specifics for disease—the doctrine of signatures. Eyebright, which is marked with a spot like an eye, was thought to be excellent for diseases of the eye; bugloss, resembling a snake's head, was good for snake bite; celandine, which has a yellow juice, was used in cases of jaundice. "Like by like is to be cured—that is, similar ulcers by similar forms," said Paracelsus.[114]

Amid the general ignorance and superstition, observation and experience had brought to a few men some faint conception of the real causes of disease. It was known that certain maladies were communicated from one person to another and some crude efforts were made to isolate the sufferers. On the vessels which brought immigrants to Virginia in 1610 a number of wretches who developed yellow fever or the plague were promptly thrown overboard. When the *Sarah Constant,* the *Discovery,* and the *Goodspeed* set sail for Virginia in 1606, the council in England gave instructions that in selecting a site for their town; "Neither must you plant in a low or moist place because it will prove unhealthfull."[115] *The Laws Divine and Martial,* published at Jamestown some years later, displayed a certain knowledge of the principles of hygiene. "There shall no man or woman . . . dare to wash any unclean linnen . . . within the Pallizadoes . . . nor rench, and make clean, any kettle, pot or pan . . . within twenty foote of the olde well . . . upon pain of whipping."[116]

The colonists, themselves filled with superstition, valued highly the hocus-pocus of the Indians, and their medical men were pronounced "as able physicians as any in Europe." The Indians used herbs for cathartics and emetics and as remedies for various diseases. These medicines were soon borrowed by the white men, some actually being sent to Europe where they came into wide repute. Tobacco, which was supposed by the Indians to possess extraordinary medicinal powers, was used by the English as a specific for a number of maladies. It was thought to be a sure antidote for all poisons and to have the power of "expelling rheums and sour humours." As for healing wounds, it was better than St. John's wort, hitherto accounted the sovereign remedy. Some persons used it in cases of gout or ague, others to relieve hunger and weariness or to neutralize the effects of drunkenness.[117]

In the colonies, medical practice was not regulated as it was in England, where every accredited doctor belonged to the College of Physicians. The governments seldom concerned themselves with the training of the practitioner; no licenses were required; and anyone who had a superficial knowledge of medicine was at liberty to put up his sign. The extent of his practice would be determined by his success with his patients. If his treatments were ineffectual, he was deserted, but a tolerable degree of skill would ensure him a fair living in the more thickly settled communities.[118]

According to the standards even of the seventeenth century the colonial doctors were usually sadly deficient in skill. There were no facilities for medical training in America, while inducements for able English practitioners to migrate were lacking. Dr. Samuel Fuller, who came over on the *Mayflower,* was typically ignorant of his profession, if we may believe Thomas Morton. "Dr. Noddy did a great cure for Captain Littleworth," he says, "he cured him of a disease called a wife." [119] Dr. John Clark, who died at Boston in 1661 and whose interesting portrait has come down to us, according to tradition was the first regularly educated physician in New England. [120] Quacks appeared on every hand. It was complained that "Shoemakers, Weavers and Almanack makers . . . have laid aside the proper busi-

A Seventeenth Century Physician—Dr. John Clark,
of Newbury and Boston.

ness of their lives to turn Quacks." In 1649 a law was passed in Massachusetts to regulate the practice of medicine by "chirurgeons, Midwives, Physicians and others," but it seems to have accomplished little. In many communities the minister acted as a doctor, and mingled with his prayers for the sick of his parish applications of plasters and doses of "physick." Bleeding was almost universal. It was supposed to free the patient of hostile humors. The infant in the cradle and the tottering octogenarian alike were subjected to this treatment, which often weakened them at the very time when their strength was most needed. The pernicious practice continued even into the nineteenth century. It was the bleedings of a country doctor, seconded by a bad case of laryngitis, which cost George Washington his life.

The medical profession should have been foremost in pointing out the folly of the belief in witchcraft, but unfortunately it often lent its support to the delusion. Many a physician, when his concoctions failed to bring relief, excused himself by complaining that the patient had been bewitched. Few seemed to have had any conception of the real nature of insanity or of epilepsy, and the ancient theory of demoniacal possession was generally accepted. Dr. John Swinterton, of Massachusetts, was a notable exception to the rule, and throughout the Salem witchcraft craze used his influence on behalf of the victims. Other doctors fully concurred with the ministers and the judges in diagnosing the troubles of the Goodman children and the "afflicted" girls of Salem as magic. When on rare occasions physicians ascribed mental disturbances to natural causes, their judgment was still ridiculously at sea. In Massachusetts a case is recorded of a man who sent for a doctor to treat him for hallucinations. The physician was unable to come in person, but "sent word that the vapours ascending from his sore legg had cause a water in his eyes, and disturbance in his braines, by means whereof he was troubled with such Visions; and sending an eye water to wash his eyes with, and a cordial to take inwardly, upon the use of these, this disturbance vanished in half a quarter of an hour." [121]

In the Southern colonies, where the settlements were scattered and the means of communication very poor, it was difficult even for the best of doctors to make a living. Consequently there were few practitioners, and among them many quacks. Alsop, upon his arrival in Maryland, complains that he fell into the hands of "a Galenist with his bag-pipes of physical operations," who could not put him to rights. The London Company, solicitous for the health of the first settlers in Virginia, took pains to send over several able physicians. Among the settlers of 1607 were William Wilkinson and Thomas Wotton, both skilled in medical science. The First Supply, or relief expedition, which arrived in January 1608, brought "Walter Russell, a Doctor of Physic and Post Guinnot, a chirurgeon." Lord Delaware brought with him, in June 1610, Dr. Lawrence Bohun, who had been educated "among the most learned surgeons and physicians in the Netherlands." But

Russell died, Bohun was killed in the West Indies, and some years later Governor Harvey wrote that Dr. John Pott was the only physician in Virginia. The records contain many references to practitioners in the colony during the period from 1635 to 1690, but it is certain that skilled physicians were at all times rare.[122]

It was customary for the planter and his wife to make a superficial study of medicine, so that when a physician could not be had, they themselves could care for the sick of the family. We find in almost every colonial library treatises on the practice of medicine. Among Madam Wormeley's books were "A Chirurgicall old Book," *The Chyrurgan's Mate, Treatis of the Gout*, Galen's *Art of Physick, Universall Body of Physick, The English Physitian*, and Dr. Willis's *Practice of Physick*. In the library of Matthew Hubbard we find Riverius's *Book of Physic, Physician's Library* in folio, Culpeper's *Dispensatory*, Culpeper's *Anatomy* in folio, and the *Institution of Physick*. Unfortunately, what was learned from these books could have done little good, unless to help the patient along to a speedy conclusion of this earthly sufferings.

In the South the care of the sick was entrusted especially to the planter's wife, who was always armed with an assortment of remedies and upon the larger estates made periodic rounds in the slave or servant quarters. Obstetrics everywhere in the colonies was very largely in the hands of women. In 1690 the Reverend Samuel Lee, writing to Dr. Nehemiah Grew from New England, stated that "of midwifes everyone takes whom they please."[123] For this service the compensation varied with the skill and success of the practitioner. In 1634, Agnes Williams, who lived in Virginia, paid the Widow Hollens a dozen hens for attending her in confinement. In the eastern Long Island communities, midwives were elected in town meetings.

All the colonies were subject to epidemics which took a terrible toll in human life. In tidewater Virginia the mosquitoes and the unwholesome drinking water made malaria and dysentery almost universal. Three months after Captain Newport's first landing, sickness and death appeared at Jamestown. "If there were any conscience in men," said Captain George Percy, "it would make their harts to bleed to heare the pitifull murmurings and outcries of our sick men without relief, every night and day for the space of six weeks; in the morning their bodies being trailed out of their cabines like Dogges, to be buried."[124] The settlers who came in succeeding years had a like experience. The Spaniard Molina, writing in 1613, declared that fully 50 percent of the newcomers died before they had been in the colony twelve months. "June, July, and half of August," writes De Vries, "are very unhealthy there for those who have not lived there a year. The English die there at this season very fast."[125] The Company took no adequate precautions to exclude infected persons from the immigrant vessels, with the result that epidemics frequently occurred at sea. One ship is said to have lost 130 persons out of 185. On the fleet which left for Virginia in 1609, both yellow fever and bubonic plague appeared. In this way these diseases were brought to the colony, where they spread rapidly. The Virginia physicians were incapable of coping with the situation. They knew little of the principles of quarantine or of sanitation; their remedies were inadequate. The epidemics, running their course unchecked, threatened to depopulate the country. It is true that Governor Harvey wrote that Dr. John Pott was "skilled in the Epidemicall diseases of the planters," but it is probable that his treatments did little real good to his patients.

The London Company, which saw all of its efforts jeopardized by these epidemics, urged a more careful observance of religious matters, so that God might be induced to withhold his chastening hand. They also sent directions for the erection of four guest houses or hospitals. But all this was to little purpose. In the year ending March 1621, over 1,000 persons died on the way to Virginia or after landing. During the next twelve months 1,200 perished, and George Sandys wrote that the worst fever ever known in Virginia was raging. The epidemic, he thought, had been introduced by the *Abigall,* many of whose passengers had died on the way over. Immigrants who escaped death from the diseases indigenous to Virginia were said to be "seasoned" or immune, and could feel reasonably safe from their recurrence. But they were still susceptible to epidemics from the London plague and yellow fever.

The introduction of cinchona bark proved a great boon to the planters. It is related that the wife of Count Cinchona, Viceroy of Peru, was cured of an intermittent fever by the native physicians through the use of this remedy. In the year 1640 the count's own physician brought the Peruvian bark to Spain, and fourteen years later it found its way to England. Although the price was £8 a pound, it was introduced into the tobacco colonies, and greatly reduced the mortality from malaria. Formerly not one servant in five survived the first year, wrote Berkeley in 1671, but now most of them escape.

The Chesapeake Bay colonies were not the only ones to suffer from epidemics. In New England, smallpox appeared early in the century, and throughout the colonial period continued to exact a heavy toll.[126] In the winter of 1633–34 a smallpox epidemic raged among the Indians, but the white men seem to have escaped. In 1636, however, the general court sat at Roxbury in order to avoid the smallpox at Cambridge. In 1677 the Reverend Thomas Thacher issued a *Brief Rule to Guide the Common People of New England; How to Order Themselves and Theirs in the Small Pocks, or Measels.* This work proved timely, because in 1678 occurred the worst smallpox epidemic of the century. Cotton Mather, then but fifteen years old, wrote to John Cotton, describing the ravages of the disease. "Never was it such a time in Boston," he said. "Boston burying-places never filled so fast. It is easy to tell the time when we did not use to have the bells tolling for burials on a Sabbath day morning by sunrise; to have

7 buried on a Sabbath day night, after Meeting. To have coffins crossing each other as they have been carried in the street;—To have, I know not how many corpses following each other close at their heels,—to have 38 dye in one week,—6, 7, 8 or 9 in a day. Yet thus hath it lately been; and thus it is at this day. Above 340 have died of the Small Pox in Boston since it first assaulted this place. To attempt a Bill of Mortality, and number the very spires of grass in a Burying Place seems to have a parity of difficulty and accomplishment."[127]

Despite all, despite the prevalence of epidemics, the ignorance of hygiene, and the crudeness of medical practice, it was not uncommon for the men and women of the time to attain a ripe old age. Of this fact the genealogical history of the town of Hingham, Massachusetts, supplies interesting evidence. The records of this place, which have been carefully preserved from its first settlement in 1635, give the ages of hundreds of the inhabitants. The family histories have been carefully worked out and published under the direction of the town. Of the 827 persons mentioned as belonging to this period and whose length of life is recorded, 105 reached the age of eighty or over, 19 lived to be ninety or over, and 3—Daniel Stodder, John Beal, and Sarah Gardner—attained the century mark. This is a truly notable record; it would be difficult to find a community in the twentieth century which can match it.

The explanation lies partly in the sturdiness of the stock, partly in the simplicity of the people's lives. Their food was plain and wholesome, their work hard but not enervating; their houses were not overheated; they were free from the nervous strain attendant upon life today. They were prepared to offer a sturdy resistance to organic diseases, and if they escaped epidemics or accidents, were apt to live to a ripe old age. Notwithstanding the fact that a number of Hingham men lost their lives in the unfortunate expedition of Sir William Phips against Quebec in 1690, the expectation of life for persons attaining the age of twenty-one was excellent. For males it seems to have been 41.3 years, for females 39.7 years, as compared with a general average of about 43 in the registration area of the United States in 1920.

This record, especially that of the women, is all the more remarkable because of the large families which were so common during the seventeenth century. For the 153 married graduates of Harvard in the years from 1658 to 1690, the recorded number of children is 808, giving an average family of 5.21. This compares with an average of 3.09 for graduates in the years from 1872 to 1879. Of these men, one had twenty children; one had fifteen; three, fourteen; three, thirteen; two, twelve; seven, eleven; four, ten; and fourteen, nine.

Cotton Mather gives some interesting testimony concerning the size of New England families. Mr. Sherman, he tells us, was twice married, having six children by his first wife and twenty by the second. "Another woman had no less than twenty-three children by one husband, whereof nineteen lived unto men's and women's estate. A third was mother to seven-and-twenty children, and she that was mother to Sir William Phips, the late Governor of New England, had no less than twenty-five children besides him; she had one and twenty sons and five daughters."[128] The Reverend Samuel Willard, the first minister of Groton, had twenty children, and was himself one of seventeen children. The Reverend Abijah Weld of Attleboro had fifteen children, the Reverend Moses Fiske had sixteen, Samuel Green, the Boston printer, was the father of thirty. William Rowson had twenty children by one wife. Of the Hingham matrons Hannah Beal had twelve children; Sarah Cushing, twelve; Christian Dunbar, thirteen; Rebecca Hersey, twelve; Hannah Jacob, twelve; Mary Joy, fifteen; Elizabeth Stodder, ten; and Remember Ward, twelve.

It might be imagined that such large families would result in a heavy mortality among the mothers. Indeed, many cases may be cited in which they succumbed to the cares and dangers of incessant childbearing. The following inscription is one of many to be found upon the seventeenth-century tombstones: "Here lyeth the body of Elizabeth Haynie, daughter of Richard and Jane Bridger. Was born July 16th, 1665, married Richard Haynie Oct 10th 1681, by whom she had 8 children & died his wife 2. . . . 1697." Cotton Mather's first wife was married at the age of sixteen, bore him ten children, and died at the age of thirty-two. "The Women, like Early Fruits, are soon Ripe and soon Rotten," says an unfriendly English critic of the New Englanders. "A Girl there at thirteen," he adds with obvious exaggeration, "thinks herself as well Quallified for a husband, as a forward Miss at a Boarding School does here at Fifteen for a Gallant." Many cases of early death may be found among the Hingham matrons, some of them easily traceable to excessive childbearing. Thus, Elizabeth Lincoln died at forty, having had seven children; Sarah Cushing had twelve children and died at thirty-eight; and Jail Cushing had ten, dying at forty-six.[129]

On the other hand, the cases of those who had very large families and yet lived to old age are even more numerous. Ruth Andrews, who had ten children, lived to be ninety-seven; Hannah Beal, with twelve children, died at ninety-three; Sarah Gardner lived to be 101 despite her nine children; Mary Joy had fifteen children, yet lived to be seventy-seven; Triphary Lane, with nine children, died at ninety-five; Elizabeth Stodder, with ten children, died at eighty-eight. The average life of the married women of Hingham during the seventeenth century seems to have been 61.4 years. There were 105 women, concerning whom we have data, who had five or more children. The combined number of their offspring was 818, giving an average of 7.8 for each family. The average age at death was 65.5 years. These figures apply to one little town only, and cannot be accepted as conclusive for conditions throughout the colonies, yet they permit of the strong presumption that much which has been written concerning the short expectation of life for women of large families is based upon insufficient evidence.

The dangers which surrounded childhood during the seventeenth century were numerous. Ignorant of hygiene, without competent medical assistance, possessing but a hazy conception of infant dietetics, mothers frequently lost their children in rapid succession. The case of Cotton Mather's family as set forth in his *Diary* is typical. This noted clergyman had sixteen children and survived them all except his son Samuel. Abigail I, William, Mary, Joseph, Mehitabel, Samuel I, Nathaniel, Eleazer, and Martha all died in infancy. Jerusha succumbed to measles at the age of two years and seven months. Katherine and Abigail II both lived to be twenty-seven, Hannah twenty-four, Increase twenty-five, Elizabeth twenty-two, and Samuel II seventy-nine. Four of the children contracted smallpox, several had scarlet fever, while most of them had measles and three died of it. The *Diary* contains many references to these misfortunes and to Mather's agonized prayers for the recovery of his children.

Joseph Joy of Hingham had fifteen children and lost eight of them before they were two years old. A Plymouth gravestone tells a significant story: "Here lyeth —— with twenty small children." Cotton Mather himself tells us of the case of a woman who had twenty-two children, "whereof she buried fourteen sons and six daughters."[130] The old family Bibles have preserved many of these stories of blighted hopes. In one case a matron, the mother of many children, lost her first child four days after the birth of the second. Five times she suffered the death of a child with an infant in her arms, and after being married nine years had but one living child. Of Judge Sewall's fourteen children, only three outlived their father.

Of the 808 children of Harvard graduates for the years from 1658 to 1690, 162 died before maturity. This gives a recorded child mortality among this selected group of 20 percent. As it is fairly certain that there were cases of deaths, especially of infants, for which no records have been left, it may be taken for granted that the actual percentage was higher. These were the homes of ministers and magistrates, where fortune and intelligence provided exceptional care, and if their family histories can show so many gloomy pages, it is a safe inference that death was an even more frequent visitor in the households of their humbler neighbors. The child mortality for Hingham was 33.3 percent, 276 of the 827 persons whose ages are known, dying before reaching twenty-one. The mortality among infants accounts for the greater part of these deaths, the percentage of males dying under two being 22.2 and of females 17.8.[131]

Perhaps fewer children would have succumbed had the diseases from which they suffered been left to run their courses. But the suffering child had to encounter the additional peril of the doctor with his bleeding and his physic. It is not hard to imagine the effect upon cases of measles or smallpox of such concoctions as mithridate or Venice treacle. The latter was a compound of vipers, white wine, opium, spices, licorice, red roses, St. John's wort, and some twenty other ingredients. We are left much in the dark concerning the feeding of the colonial baby, but there is reason to believe that its food was not only often unwholesome but administered without regard to regular intervals or stated amounts. Several of Mather's children had convulsions, among them Samuel I, who died in this way. Children suffered often from rickets, and went through life hopeless cripples. The remedies were typical of the age, for example:

> Dip the child in the morning, head foremost in Cold Water, don't dress it Immediately, but let it be made warm in the Cradle & sweat at least half an Hour moderately. Do this 3 mornings going & if one or both feet are Cold while other Parts sweat Let a little blood be taken out of the feet the 2d Morning. . . . Before the dips of the child give it some Snakeroot and Saffern Steep'd in Rum & Water, give this Immediately before Diping and after you have dipt the Child 3 Mornings. Give it several times a Day the following Syrup made of Comfry, Hartshorn, Red Roses, Hog-brake roots, knot-grass, petty-moral [pennyroyal?] roots; sweeten the Syrup with Melosses.

In Europe, the seventeenth century, despite all its backwardness, was marked by certain great figures who were pointing the way to better things in medical science. In 1628, William Harvey published his treatise on the circulation of the blood, which revolutionized modern medicine and gave a death blow to the slavelike adherence to Galen. In 1661, Malpighi, by the use of the compound microscope, was able to exhibit the corpuscles of the blood, while Robert Boyle, in the latter half of the century, was laying the foundations of the science of analytical chemistry. But these things found no reflection in America. Colonial medicine was less efficient in 1690 than in 1640, for the physicians of the second generation had a more imperfect training than those who migrated from England. An apprenticeship with an older doctor and a short course of reading in medical books were probably the extent of the equipment of the native practitioner. If he had ever heard of Harvey, he probably distrusted his conclusions and had no conception of the significance of his discovery. To the end he remained engulfed in the clouds of ignorance and superstition.

MAN'S TREATMENT OF MAN

THE PEOPLE OF THE SEVENTEENTH CENTURY had very crude ideas concerning crime and its prevention. Since it was necessary to protect society by inflicting punishments, they believed that the severer the penalty, the greater would be the measure of protection. At the same time the horizon of their sympathies was too restricted to include the criminal himself. They had no conception of the possibilities of reforming offenders, or of preventing crime by alleviating poverty, drunkenness, and bad social environment. A terrible fate was meted out to them, inflicted usually in public that others might beware.

It has been estimated that at the beginning of the seventeenth century the number of executions annually in England were not less than 800. The number of crimes for which the death penalty could be exacted, long enough in the days of James I and Charles I, continued to grow until well into the nineteenth century.[132] In the years from 1660 to 1820 no less than 187 capital offenses were added to the code, and one could be led to the gallows for picking a pocket or stealing a pewter pot.

In such an age severity would be expected in the colonies, but with the exception of the drastic administrations of Dale, Gates, and Argall in Virginia, and perhaps the persecution of the Quakers in New England, punishments were far milder than in the mother country. In 1610 the London Company, upon receiving information that insubordination was causing trouble at Jamestown, sent Sir Thomas Gates to restore order. Gates brought the "Divine, Moral and Martial Laws," which later, upon the arrival of Dale, were carried out with savage harshness. "The Colony . . . remayned in great want and misery under most severe and Crewell lawes sent over in printe," said the Virginia assembly of 1624,

> and contrary to the expresse Letter of the Kinge in his most gracious Charter, and as mercylessly executed, often times without tryall or Judgement. [Many of the people fled] for reliefe to the Savage Enemy, who being taken againe were putt to sundry deaths as by hanginge, shooting and breakinge uppon the wheele and others were forced by famine to filch for their bellies, of whom one for steelinge of 2 or 3 pints of oatmeal had a bodkinge thrust through his tounge and was tyed with a chaine to a tree untill he starved, if a man through his sicknes had not been able to worke, he had noe allowance at all, and soe consequently perished.[133]

When several men stole a barge and a shallop in the attempt to get back to England, they "were shot to death, hanged and broken upon the wheel." But with the ascendancy of Sir Edwin Sandys in the company, and the establishing of the first representative assembly in America, this cruel regime came to an end.

From this date a noteworthy feature of the administration of law in Virginia and Maryland was the relative leniency of the courts. For crimes which in England would have brought death, the colonial judges would often impose fines, imprisonment, or at most whippings. This wide difference is explained by the fact that crime was more common in the mother country and human life cheaper. The decay of commerce and industry in the first years of the seventeenth century in England, which produced so much poverty, left many the alternative of starvation or a life of crime. The jails were always filled and the hangman was always busy. No wonder it was said, "The land grows weary of her inhabitants, insomuch that man, which is the most precious of all creatures, is here more vile and base than the earth he treads upon."[134] The gallows constituted a poor remedy for unemployment and its results, but the English courts were bent on suppressing crime rather than altering the conditions out of which crime grew.

In America, labor was scarce and there was less incentive to crime. Unemployment was unknown, land cheap, food abundant, wages high. No one had the excuse of desperate poverty for adopting a life of crime. The situation is the more interesting in the light of the attempts of the English authorities to export criminals to the colonies. The belief that America was settled by jailbirds—a belief voiced by Dr. Samuel Johnson when he spoke of the colonists as "a race of convicts"—has no foundation in fact. All save a very small percentage, even of the indentured servants, consisted of honest men who made the trip on their own initiative. On the other hand, we know that from time to time the authorities in England did lighten the expenses of maintaining their prisons by emptying them upon the shores of America.[135] Among these persons, most of whom had been guilty only of petty offenses, were a few hardened criminals. Under such circumstances it might be expected that robbery and murder would be frequent in the colonies. That such was not the case gives interesting confirmation to the contention that usually it is not heredity or naturally depraved instincts which produce the cutthroat, but the environment of poverty and misery. For many a man, whom poverty had driven to petty crimes in England became, in the New World, a substantial, law-abiding citizen. "All villanous Outrages that are committed in other States are not as much as known here," says George Alsop in his *Maryland.* "A man may walk in the open Woods as secure from being externally dissected, as in his own house or dwelling. So hateful is a Robber, that if but once imagin'd to be so, he's kept at a distance and shun'd as the Pestilential noysomness." He adds: "Those whose lives and conversations have had no other gloss nor glory stampt on them in their own Country, but the stigmatization of baseness, were here by the common civilities and deportment of the Inhabitants of this Province, brought to detest and loath their former actions."[136]

In Maryland a severe law was passed in 1638 which fixed the penalty for treason. If the culprit happened to be a woman, she was to be burned at the stake; if a man of ordinary rank, he was to be hanged, drawn, and quartered; if a lord of a manor, he was to be beheaded. Apparently, however, none of these stringent provisions were ever carried out.[137]

In Massachusetts the list of crimes for which the death penalty was inflicted was much larger than in the South. Under the stern Puritan rule persons were hanged for heresy, murder, treason, and unnatural vices as well as for witchcraft. As we have seen, several Quakers paid with their lives for their attempt to gain converts, while many innocent persons were hanged for their supposed contracts with Satan. But when the offense was against the civil code rather than against religion, the New England courts were not overharsh.[138] In 1654, Edward Sanders, convicted of rape in Massachusetts, was sentenced, not to the gallows, but to be whipped and to carry a rope around his neck hanging down two feet. A black woman who murdered her bastard child in 1674 was placed on the gallows with a rope around her neck and then whipped "at the Carts Tayle." On the other hand, James Brittaine and Mary Lothain were both condemned to death for adultery, while there were several executions for "beastiality." Most unusual was the case of Marja and Cheffaleer Jack, blacks who pleaded guilty to arson, the first being burned at the stake, the other first hanged and then burned. In New England, as in other colonies, there were also executions for piracy.

Mutilation was not uncommon in New England in the early years of the century. In 1631, Phillip Ratcliffe, "for uttering mallitious & scandalous speeches against the government & the Church of Salem," was sentenced to "be whipped, have his eares cut of, fyned 40 shillings and banished." Nine years later it was ordered that James Luxford "be bound to the whiping poast," and "have his eares cut of . . . for his forgery, lying & other foule offences." For contempt of court Maurice Brett was to stand in the pillory, to which his ears were to be nailed, "& after an hours standing there to be cut of." In 1684, Joseph Gatchell, convicted of blasphemy, was to stand in the pillory, "have his toung drawne forth out of his mouth, & peirct throyh with a hott iron." During the Quaker persecution, three of the invading missionaries had their ears cut off.

In Virginia and Maryland, mutilation was of less frequent occurrence. In 1624 a certain Edward Sharpless, for betraying the secret correspondence of the Virginia government, was sentenced to "stand in the Pillory and there to have his Ears nailed to it, and cut off." His punishment was modified, however, so that he "lost but a part of one of his eares."[139] In 1630 a man found guilty of perjury was sentenced in Virginia to stand in the pillory and lose his ears. On the whole, however, this punishment for free white men was extremely rare; even Berkeley seems to have refrained from mutilation in taking his revenge on Bacon's followers. But for slaves who had run away, it was not uncommon that the ears should be nailed to the pillory and later cut off. This served the double purpose of warning other blacks not to imitate the offense and of identifying the offender forevermore. Mutilation, though rarely practiced by the Dutch settlers of New Amsterdam, was not infrequent after the English conquest of 1664. The hangman at Fort Albany, himself found guilty of "Divers Thefts and Robbings . . . escaped his neck through want of another Hangman to truss him up, soe that all the punishment he received . . . was only 39 stripes at the Whipping Post, loss of an Ear and banishment."

All through the seventeenth century, whipping, branding, cutting the ear, and other corporal punishments were commonly practiced in all the colonies.[140] In Virginia the whipping post was resorted to on innumerable occasions for offenses ranging from petty larceny to attempted murder or rape. In 1640, Thomas Bates, who had wronged his master by seducing his wife, was sentenced to nothing worse than thirty lashes to be laid on at the fort in Jamestown.[141] In contrast to this was the case of Christopher Bryant, who was whipped for milking Goodwife Powell's cow by stealth. About 1666 a woman was condemned to twenty lashes in Lower Norfolk County for stealing two smocks; in Accomac another was whipped for making off with a handkerchief, a pillowbere, a hood, and a towel. In 1627 the Virginia general court condemned Margaret Partein to "forty stripes" for "concealing the offence of Thomas Hayle lately executed."[142] In the same year Alice Thornburg was given forty lashes "for her offence in fighting with Anne Snoode and beating her, whereby just suspicion may be had that she" caused abortion. A whipping post was erected near every prison and courthouse in the colony.[143] In Maryland, thieves were usually whipped. Forgeries were punished with thirty-nine lashes, while to counterfeit the great seal of the province might entail whipping, the pillory, and banishment.

Imprisonment was far less common in the colonies than in England. In a thinly settled country, especially where there was practically no criminal class, the people were reluctant to vote funds for erecting and maintaining prisons. To give a culprit a sound lashing was quite as effective as keeping him in jail and far less expensive. The Virginia assembly early empowered each county to erect prisons and passed a law making the sheriffs responsible for the escape of prisoners. That this provision was neglected, however, its repeated reenactment makes obvious. In 1658 and again in 1662 the assembly directed the local authorities to construct jails of ample size and strength.[144] In 1684 the law was passed once more, with the added provision that a certain amount of land was to be laid off adjoining the prison to serve as "a place of liberty and privilege" for prisoners held for minor offenses.

The prisons in most cases were merely places of temporary confinement. Often they seem to have been no more than dwellings or rooms leased by the authorities, and were so insecure that it was easy for the inmates to escape unless securely manacled and guarded. Governor Culpeper writes that he could hardly sleep for fear the men under sentence for participation in the plant-cutting riots of 1682 would get away.[145]

The American jails of the day could not duplicate the ghastly conditions existing in many English prisons, "Here's no Newgates for pilfering Felons," says George Alsop, "nor Ludgates for Debtors, nor any Bridewels to lash the soul of Concupiscence into a chast Repentence."[146] The crowding together of prisoners, the immorality, the foul air, and spread of contagion, must have been unknown in a tumble-down country jail. When the prisoners were laden with chains and put in damp cellars, suffering and sickness often followed, but such cases were rare. James Barrow, one of Bacon's followers who was locked up at Governor Berkeley's home, complained "of the extremity of Cold, hunger, lothsomness of Vermin, and other sad occasions." But Barrow would have felt his Virginia prison quite comfortable had he ever seen the inside of Newgate.[147]

Solicitude for the creditor demanded the imprisonment of the man who did not pay his debts; yet the laws of the seventeenth century dealing with this subject were milder than those of the eighteenth. Some, indeed, actually protected the debtor. In the Duke's Laws, proclaimed in New York in 1664, it was provided that "no man shall be longer in prison for debt or fine than he can find sureties." Twenty years later a law was passed which forbade the imprisoning of minors for debt except in cases of indebtedness for food or apparel.[148]

A favorite mode of punishment in the colonies was to fasten the hands and feet of the offender in a wooden frame and put him on public display. During the seventeenth century the pillory and the stocks came into almost universal use in the colonies. Thus, the Virginia assembly passed an act in 1662 requiring the erection in every county of stocks, pillory, and whipping post. The use of the pillory was often accompanied by other and harsher punishments, as we have seen, when the ears were nailed to the post or cut off, or when the tongue was bored.

The problem of social control was complicated in the colonies by the introduction and spread of slavery. The appearance of this institution excited little moral disapprobation in the seventeenth century. It was generally held that any hardships suffered by the African—in the stifling hold of the slaver or later in the service of his master—was more than offset by his fortunate delivery from a life of idolatry and savagery. To be sure, here and there a voice was raised in protest. After the Pequot War, Roger Williams pleaded with the Massachusetts authorities that the remnants of the tribe should not be sold into slavery, while John Eliot many years later declared that "to sell soules for mony seemeth to me a dangerous merchandize."[149] In 1688 some of the Pennsylvania Quakers addressed a memorial to the Philadelphia yearly meeting, protesting against the perpetual bondage of men and women. Twelve years later Judge Sewall atoned for his mistakes in the witchcraft trials by denouncing the slave trade.

These lone voices found little response. Even in New England it was thought that to enslave an African and bring him under Christian influences was an act in every way commendable. The doctrine of election accepted by the Puritans did not incline them to gentleness in their dealings with "inferior" races. The "savage" blacks and the "savage" Indians were accursed peoples whom it was quite proper to destroy or to enslave. "We know not when or how these Indians first became inhabitants of this mighty continent," says Cotton Mather, "yet we may guess that probably the Devil decoyed these miserable savages hither, in hope that the gospel of the Lord Jesus Christ would never come to destroy or disturb his absolute empire over them." Efforts were made to convert the Indians, but with very little success; and in the end they were swept out of the way of the

Puritan state by force of arms. After the Pequot War some of the prisoners were turned over to the Narragansetts for incorporation into that tribe, some were kept by the English, and others were sent to be sold as slaves in the West Indies. Of the captives taken in King Philip's War many were distributed among the whites as servants for a limited period.[150]

The clergy not only sanctioned these acts but took their share of the Indian slaves. "Mr. Endecot and my selfe salute you in the Lord Jesus," wrote a minister to Governor Winthrop after the Pequot War. "Wee haue heard of a diuidence of women and children in the bay and would bee glad of a share viz: a young woman or girle and a boy if you thinke good."[151] When some gentlemen of Cotton Mather's church purchased for him a valuable black slave, it seemed to that noted clergyman "a mighty Smile of Heaven" upon his family. More interesting still as an illustration of the fact that there was no necessary connection between Puritanism and opposition to slavery is the will of John Bacon of Barnstable, which provided that, if his slave Dinah should survive his wife, she should be sold and the money laid out in buying Bibles for his heirs.[152] During the Quaker persecution Daniel Southick and Provided Southick, children of one of the missionaries, were sold into bondage in Virginia and the West Indies to pay the fines levied on their parents.[153] Slavery never became general in New England because the industries of that region required intelligent, skillful labor, not because public sentiment condemned the institution as a moral evil.

In the tobacco colonies the demand for slaves was urgent throughout the seventeenth century, but it was only in the last two decades that they could be secured in quantity, and not until after the Treaty of Utrecht in 1713 that they became cheap. By that time the British had established themselves so firmly in the slave trade that they could supply the needs not only of the sugar colonies but of the Chesapeake Bay region as well. Prior to 1690, however, the number of slaves in Maryland and Virginia together probably did not exceed 5,000. On the whole, their treatment on the tobacco plantations seems to have been better than that of the indentured servants. Since they served for life, there was every incentive for their masters to keep them in good condition. To break the health of a black by brutality or overwork was a costly bit of folly.

It is true, however, that slaves often fled from their masters. The poor wretches while in transit often fancied that they were to be eaten, and so, when once on shore, took the first opportunity to escape. If the new slave happened to find himself upon a plantation with native-born blacks, their influence and assurances tended to allay his fears and reconcile him to his new life. But if he were placed in the company of unruly white servants, their example was apt to increase his natural desire to escape.

The laws concerning runaway slaves were harsh. In case they fled to the wilderness, there to maintain themselves by raiding the nearest plantations, they might be outlawed. In 1672 an act of the Virginia assembly declared that, since "many negroes have lately beene, and now are out in rebellion in sundry parts of this country, and that noe meanes have yet beene found for the apprehension and suppression of them,'' it should be lawful for any person to arrest or, in case of resistance, to kill them.[154] In 1627, Captain Sampson brought to Virginia a number of native West Indians and delivered them into the custody of the council. They made their escape, however, in an attempt to reach the Virginia Indians, and, hiding in the woods, lived by pillaging the planters. The council considered them so great a menace to the colony that they issued an order that they should be taken and hanged. The black was always reckoned a potential adversary, and there were laws forbidding him to carry arms.

The Virginia laws of the seventeenth century gave the master full power to correct his slave. "If any slave resists his master, or other by his master's order correcting him,'' reads the act of 1669, "and by the extremity of the correction should chance to die . . . his death shall not be accompted a ffelony . . . since it cannot be presumed that prepensed malice, which alone makes murder ffelony, should induce any man to destroy his owne estate.''[155] In some instances the records show that the masters took advantage of this provision to treat their slaves with excessive cruelty. The Reverend Samuel Gray, when his runaway boy returned, bound him to a tree and compelled another slave to beat him until he died.[156] In 1662 a woman was tried in the Maryland provincial court for causing the death of a slave. This black, often having been put in chains for misdemeanors refused to work and pretended to be in a fit. For this new offense hot lard was poured on his back, he was tied to a ladder and left in a cold wind. As a result he soon died. In extenuation of this barbarous treatment the overseer testified that the slave had been "an ugly, yelling, beast-like brute,'' who ran away and lived by stealing.[157]

Measured by the standards of the twentieth century it cannot be said that in their treatment of their fellow man the colonists were always inspired by enlightened and humane instincts. Toward those who transgressed there was harshness and even some terrible cruelty. But measured by the contemporaneous European standards, the settlers were notably humane. The translation to the New World, however detrimental in narrowing the intellectual interests of the immigrants, gave them a more advanced conception of the value of human life and the dignity of man.[158] The wretch who in the slums of London inspired only scorn and contempt assumed in the forests of Virginia or the New England hills his rightful place as a man among men.

THE BEGINNINGS OF AN INTELLECTUAL LIFE

IT WAS NOT TO BE EXPECTED that the colonists should display any marked degree of literary or scientific activity. The settlers had to devote their energies to the enormous task of conquering the American wilderness and developing its resources. These first Americans were pioneers in opening to civilization a vast continent, not pioneers in chemistry, anatomy, zoology, engineering, or literature. From Maine to the Carolinas we look in vain for a single figure of note in such matters, one standing out above the level of mediocrity. This does not mean that the New England trader or the Virginia planter was inferior in natural capacity to the men they left behind in England; it means rather that their energies turned to the practical problems of clearing the forests, building homes, planting crops, constructing ships, trading, and fishing; to the subtleties of Indian warfare; to the unceasing political struggle with the crown.

In New England, where the inclination to investigation and study was greatest, the intellectual streams were in large measure dried up in the arid wastes of theological disputation. Of the 157 books put out by the press at Cambridge from its establishment through the year 1670, 63 were upon religious subjects.[159] The really vigorous minds of the period were interested in discussions of the covenant of grace and the covenant of works, or were writing treatises on religious melancholy or the maxims of piety. John Norton devoted himself with burning zeal to writing *The Orthodox Evangelist,* "wherein he handles the abstruse points of the existence and subsistence and the efficience of God"; John Cotton produced his *Ecclesiastes and Canticles*—John Cotton, who, after his daily study of twelve hours, loved "to sweeten his mouth with a piece of Calvin."[160] If there appeared among the laity some person of more than ordinary mental activity, he, too, was almost inevitably drawn into the field of theological discussion.

Nor were the clergy content with guiding the course of intellectual activity through example and leadership, for they exercised a strict censorship over the ideas and reading of the people. The man who showed a "novile disposition" was asked to leave the colony; the church member found with a heretical book in his possession was frowned upon or even severely disciplined. The spirit of the early magistrates is illustrated by the reception accorded a work by the lawyer Thomas Lechford, entitled *Of Prophesie.* He entrusted the manuscript to Thomas Dudley, with the request that he advise him as a "private friend" whether it ought to be published. Dudley was so aroused by what he read that he wrote Winthrop, "I find the scope thereof to be erroneous and dangerous, if not hereticall. I have sent you the book herewith that instead of puttinge it to the presse as he desireth it may rather be putt into the fire as I desire."[161]

The first printing press in Massachusetts—and for a generation the only one in English America[162]—was set up in 1639, and for some years thereafter no legal restrictions were put upon its output. This is explained by the fact that it was so under the influence of the theocracy that there was no fear of its turning out anything of which they did not approve. That little actual freedom of the press existed, however, is shown by the reception in

1650 of a pamphlet entitled *The Meritorious Price of Our Redemption,* written by William Pynchon of Springfield. The general court, finding the work "erronyous and hereticale," ordered it to be burned by the common executioner in the marketplace at Boston.[163] Four years later, when certain books appeared in Massachusetts teaching the tenets of the Quakers, the general court required every inhabitant having copies in his possession to bring them at once to the nearest magistrate upon pain of a fine of £10; "And as many of the said books as can or may be found to be burned by the executioner at Boston." Later it was decreed that any person who "shall knowingly import into any harbor of this jurisdiction any Quaker books or writings concerning their divilish opinions, shall pay for every such booke or writing, being legally prooved against him or them, the some of five pounds." In 1669 the general court, learning that a reprint of *The Imitation of Christ* by Thomas à Kempis was in press, ordered it to be revised before being issued to the public.[164] The loss of the right of censorship, which came with the Andros regime, was bitterly resented by the clergy.

Suppression of opinions and of free discussion[165] was by no means confined to New England. In 1671, Sir William Berkeley boasted that there was no printing press in Virginia, and the Quaker or Puritan who came to that colony with the purpose of making converts found himself outside the pale of the law. But in none of the Middle or Southern provinces was there anything comparable to the rigid control over men's thoughts and opinions exercised by the New England theocracy.[166] Thus circumscribed, the mental activities of the people of this section were marked by neither progressiveness nor breadth of interest. Increase Mather, whose reading may easily be traced through his habit of citing or quoting the writers with whom he was acquainted, seems to have read something of Sir Thomas Browne, Thomas Fuller, and Robert Boyle, but to have known nothing of Shakespeare, Ben Jonson, or Bunyan. Apparently, though Cotton Mather read Milton and quoted from him in his *Magnalia,* and shows a wide acquaintance with ancient and medieval writers, he, too, failed to keep abreast the most progressive thought of his own day.

Some idea of the subjects which held the New England mind at the end of the seventeenth century may be gained from the inventories of books sent to the Boston booksellers. The Volumes delivered by Chiswell of London to John Usher in May 1684 were two Bibles, thirty Greek grammars, three copies of *Bythner on the Psalms,* six copies of *Sincere Converts,* ten copies of *Flavel on the Sacrament,* ten copies of *Cattechise,* two copies of the *Cambridge Concordance,* two of Sellers's *Practice of Navigation,* two of Wilson's *Christian Dictionary,* five of Clark's *Tutor,* four of Burroughs's *Gospel Remission,* and four of the *State of England* in two volumes.[167]

Though the Puritan was not up-to-date in English literature, in amount his reading was nevertheless considerable. The libraries of the leading men, even in the early years of the settlement, not infrequently contained several hundred volumes.[168] William Brewster left, at his death in 1643, nearly 400 books, Miles Standish about fifty; John Winthrop, Jr., possessed in 1640 over 1,000; the volumes left to Harvard College by John Harvard numbered 320. In many cases these private libraries were brought over by the settlers when they migrated from England, but from the first, numerous additions were made by shipment across the Atlantic. New Englanders were prolific writers. The leading ministers were quick to expound their doctrines or to answer their opponents in books, pamphlets, and published sermons. In the years from 1682 to 1689 inclusive, of the 133 works published in Boston, fifty-six were sermons, thirty-nine others were religious in character, while of the remaining thirty-eight, twelve were almanacs and seventeen proclamations or public pamphlets.

It was in New England that the colonial common school found its highest development. Though pioneer conditions obviously are not conductive to an efficient educational system, in New England the compactness of the settlements—which were usually grouped around the church, the meeting-house, and the village school—made it possible to gather in one schoolhouse enough pupils to provide at least a fair living for a capable teacher. Important also was the insistence of the clergy upon education. The need of schools, especially elementary schools, was constantly urged in the sermons of the day. The leaders of the theocracy saw that unless the people were educated it would be impossible to maintain an adequate ministry. The Anglican church in Virginia secured its clergymen from England, but no such course was possible for the New Englanders. Whatever their theory, they had in fact broken with the old establishment, had formed a reformed church of their own, and, before many years, were out of touch and sympathy even with the Puritan group of which they had formerly been a part. Moreover, it was necessary that all serious people should read the Bible in order to learn the tests by which each might be certain of his own election and that of his neighbor.

While the clergy encouraged education, they took pains to control and direct it. The textbooks were carefully selected with a view to inculcating the precepts of the established church, while no appointments of teachers were made without the full approbation of the ministers. The schools in one sense were church schools, supported out of church funds.[169] In Massachusetts a law of 1642 made it compulsory that all children be taught —either by their parents or otherwise—to "read and understand the principles of religion & the capitall lawes of the country." This act did not establish schools nor did it direct the employment of schoolmasters. The results proving unsuccessful in thwarting "the ould deluder Satan," the famous statute of 1647 was passed for expressly establishing a school system and thus preventing knowledge from "being buried in the graves of our fathers in church and commonwealth."

The primary teaching was done partly at home and partly in dame schools, kept perhaps by a busy housewife or a schoolmaster's daughter. Here were taught the alphabet, spelling, primary reading, and the catechism. First came the old hornbook,[170] then the so-called a-b-c's, and finally the primer, containing prayers and religious meditations. Later the primer was made to include the hornbook and the a-b-c's. Reading was taught also from books of verse "full of precepts of civilitie." The pupil was now ready to enter the grammar school, where he was supposed to make a beginning in Latin, which was still the sacred language of religion and learning. The Massachusetts law of 1647 required that every town of fifty householders or more should establish an elementary school, and those of 100 householders a grammar school as well. This provision, although by no means fully enforced, was of far-reaching importance in setting a standard toward which the community must strive. Many of these grammar schools in reality taught but little Latin, and confined their attention largely to the English primer.

To New England belongs the distinction of establishing the first college in British America. The failure of the London Company to complete its design for an Indian school at Henrico in Virginia left the field vacant until 1636 when the Massachusetts general court voted £400 for the erecting of "a schoole or colledge." Two years later, when the project still hung fire for lack of adequate funds, John Harvard, a minister of Charlestown, bequeathed to the institution his entire library and half his estate; and the same year the institution was opened as Harvard College at Cambridge. Other gifts came from time to time, and before the end of the century £6,134 had been received, together with large bequests of land and books. The first teacher, a certain Nathaniel Eaton, had been educated in Holland, and Cotton Mather says that he "marvellously deceived the expectations of good men concerning him, for he was fitter to be master of a Bridewel than a Colledge." He was soon succeeded by Henry Dunster, under whose direction a class of nine graduated in 1642.[171]

From the first the requirements seemed to have been rigid. "When any schollar is able to understand Tully, or such like classical Latine author extempore, and make and speake true Latine in verse and prose . . . and decline . . . the paradigms of noune and verbes in the Greek tongue: Let him then . . . be capable of admission." The course of study included logic, physics, ethics, geometry, astronomy, Greek, Hebrew, rhetoric, and Latin. "The President inspected the manners of the students," wrote Cotton Mather, "and unto his morning and evening prayers in the hall joined an exposition upon the chapters; which they read out of Hebrew into Greek, from the Old Testament in the morning, and out of English into Greek, from the New Testament in the evening; besides what Sermons he saw cause to preach in publick assemblies on the Lord's day at Cambridge where the students have a particular gallery allotted unto them."[172] It is improbable that these high standards were rigidly adhered to, and we know

A Hornbook for little children, about 1675 (left).

A popular catechism by a leading minister (right).

Seventeenth Century Schoolbooks.

that the attempt to compel conversation in Latin among the students failed. About 1670, Copernican astronomy, it appears, was getting a little foothold in Harvard, a century after its promulgation in Europe, but it was not formally taught until much later.[173]

Like the schools of Massachusetts, Harvard was founded primarily to train ministers for the New England churches, and in this it seems to have succeeded admirably. In 1696, of the eighty-seven Massachusetts clergymen seventy-six, and of the thirty-five Connecticut clergymen thirty-one, were graduates of Harvard.

During the last quarter of the century, Harvard became the battleground of the conservative and liberal groups in Massachusetts, and suffered much in consequence. For several years it was without a president, its attendance fell away, and it became little more than a divinity school. The Dutch scholar, Jaspar Danckaerts, who visited the institution in 1680, gives a most unfavorable account of it.

> We found there eight or ten young fellows, sitting around, smoking tobacco. . . . We inquired how many professors there were, and they replied not one, that there was not enough money to support one. We asked how many students there were. They said at first, thirty, and then came down to twenty; I afterwards understood there are probably not ten. They knew hardly a word of Latin, not one of them, so that my comrade could not converse with them. . . . The minister of the place goes over there morning and evening to make prayer, and has charge over them; besides him, the students are under tutors or masters.[174]

However, nothing can be more misleading than the superficial observations of a stranger. Two members of the class who must have been present in the group afterwards became tutors in the institution, and one of them, John Leverett, was elected president. Even though its scope had been greatly restricted, Harvard was unquestionably still doing good work. Possessing the only college in the colonies, with a good-sized reading public and a creditable system of common schools, New England was well in advance in the matter of education. Although illiteracy was by no means uncommon, the percentage of those who could neither read nor write was undoubtedly lower than elsewhere in the colonies. But this superiority was in a measure offset by the close supervision over education and thought exercised by the clergy, and the consequent narrowing of the horizon of intellectual interests.

In the tobacco colonies the prevalence of plantation life made it impossible to establish effective school systems. It proved difficult enough to go ten or fifteen miles to attend church through the forests, or in boats on the rivers and creeks; to send children such distances to school was not to be thought of. Even in the most thickly settled parts, seldom could one find within a reasonable radius enough children to make up a school or provide a living for a competent teacher. The Virginians and Marylanders struggled earnestly with this problem, but found no way out of it.

In 1670, when the board of trade inquired of Sir William Berkeley what course was taken about the instruction of the people in Virginia, he replied, "The same course that is taken in England out of towns, every man according to his ability instructing his children."[175] Unquestionably thousands of planters, especially those of the yeoman class, were forced themselves to act as instructors, or induce some neighbor to do this service for them, paying in tobacco or other farm produce. The wills of the period show that parents and guardians often sought to make sure that the education of their children would be provided for. William Moseley of Princess Anne County, Virginia, left directions that his family should be "brought up in such learning as is most useful and necessary for this country's affairs," while Thomas Whitlock of Rappahannock made provision for placing his son in the care of a teacher.[176]

There were in existence in all parts of this region what were known as Old Field schools. This name originated from the custom of establishing schools in abandoned fields located within walking distance of several plantations. Here the children received instruction in reading, writing, and the catechism. The schools were small and inefficient. In certain cases the parents in the neighborhood were numerous enough or rich enough to secure the entire time of a competent teacher, but it was more usual for the clergyman, the lay reader, or the wife of one of the planters to preside over the school. In cases where there were professional masters, they usually increased their meager stipends by putting out a crop of tobacco.[177]

The Virginia planter who wished his son to receive a college education sent him across the Atlantic to one of the English universities. William and Mary, it is true, was chartered in 1693, but it was not opened until April 1697, and then only as a grammar school. As a matter of fact, few young men actually undertook the journey to England, for the danger and expense of the voyage made many parents hesitate. And for all save a handful, instruction came to an end with the grammar school, and any education beyond that was obtained from private tutors, or from experience, observation, and reading.

Virginia was without a printing press through almost the entire century. In 1680, it is true, the merchant John Buckner brought in a press and received an order from the assembly to print the acts passed that year. Later he was accused of working without a license, summoned before the governor, and forced to close his establishment.[178] So far as is known not a single book was printed in the colony during the century. This circumstance, along with the fact that the energies of the people were turned chiefly to conquering the wilderness, rendered the literary output extremely meager. Robert Beverley's *History of Virginia,* which was written at the end of the century, stands almost alone as a product of a native-born Virginian of the period. But the accounts of the Rebellion of 1676 known as *Bacon's Proceedings* and *Ingram's Proceedings,* together with Mrs. An. Cotton's *Our Late Troubles in Virginia,* are written in a vivid style and with a touch of humor which makes them fascinating reading.[179] The pamphlets descriptive of Virginia and Maryland, intended to attract settlers, are fluent, interesting, and well suited to their purpose.

If the people of Virginia published few books, they read extensively. It is by no means unusual for inventories of the seventeenth century to show, even among planters of the yeoman class, a considerable number of volumes. In Lower Norfolk County alone there have come down to us for the half century from 1640 to 1690 the names of more than 100 persons who possessed from one volume to several hundred.[180] Before the end of the century some of the wealthier planters had collected really extensive libraries. The will of William Fitzhugh refers to a "study of books."[181]

However, neither books nor schools shaped the education of the Virginian or Marylander as much as life upon the plantation. The son of the poor planter was schooled in the arts of the woodsman: he knew how to handle his ax and his gun, how to bring down the wild turkey, the deer, or even the occasional bear; he had to assist his father in clearing away the great trees of the virgin forest, in planting and tending the tobacco crop, in cutting, curing, and packing the ripened leaves, in placing the hogsheads on shipboard; he must know how to repair barns, work in the garden, care for the cattle. It was a free, invigorating school—this practical school of the pioneer life in the woods of America. No wonder George Alsop speaks of the native Marylanders as "conveniently confident, reservedly subtile, quick in apprehending." The author of the *Sot-weed Factor* gives a most unfavorable picture of

> . . . that Shoar, where no good Sense is found,
> But Conversation's lost, and Manners drowned.[182]

As for the wealthy planters, even in the seventeenth century they were being molded by the influences under which they lived into that type of Southern gentleman which in succeeding generations became so distinctive a feature in the nation's history. The boy who was reared upon a plantation of several thousand acres, tilled perhaps by forty or more slaves and servants, was taught the various duties which were to fall to his lot when he grew to be a man. When still quite young he exercised authority over the workmen and directed them at their tasks, so that he might develop the habit of command. He acquired versatility by performing the 101 tasks required in the conduct of the plantation—the raising of stock, the planting and tending of tobacco, the laying out of orchards, the building of fences, the purchasing of goods from the English importers, the care of the sick, the superintendence of plantation manufacture. While his mind was thus trained to business, his body was developed by an active out-of-door life—by hunting, fishing, swimming, and racing. From his father and his guests he became acquainted with the political life of the colony, and no doubt kept fairly well abreast of the chief happenings in England. All in all, the plantation life tended to make him practical, inquiring, robust, and self-reliant, even though it seldom instilled into him the inventive spirit or inspired him to literary effort.

In forming our judgment of the intellectual activities of the colonists we must remember that in the seventeenth century, British America constituted the extreme western frontier of civilization. The narrow fringe of settlements from Maine to Carolina faced on the one hand the vast expanse of the Atlantic Ocean, on the other the trackless wilderness. Despite constant communication with the mother country, a large degree of isolation was inevitable. There could be no personal touch with the great minds which were taking the lead in science and literature, none of the inspiration which comes from companionship and emulation. It is true that the colonists could read the books of such men, but one usually peruses published works with the detached mind of the spectator, while personal acquaintance leads to intellectual stimulus. Even within the limits of the colonies themselves, distances were so great that it was difficult for men of like interests to commune with each other for the exchange of ideas and the quickening of creative ambition. Under the circumstances a literary or scientific circle was well-nigh impossible.

Equally important was the fact that no leisure class existed as yet in British America. The small groups in New England and the tobacco colonies who acquired wealth were composed of active businessmen. The Boston merchant and the Virginia planter were still in the stage of accumulation, and could devote little time to study and investigation. It is true, as we have seen, that these men, in an attempt to keep in touch with the great world of Europe, gathered libraries and read somewhat extensively. But they read not as scholars or creators, but as men whose chief interest lay elsewhere, in the spare moments snatched from the details of purchases and shipments and planting.

PLANTER AND PURITAN AT PLAY

Despite the difference in the motives of their emigration, the early American colonists, North and South, were much more alike in tastes and deportment than has been commonly understood. The seventeenth century was the seventeenth century behind the Accomac Peninsula as well as behind Cape Cod—for instance, the government's concern in private conduct was not confined to either latitude. The first legislature in Virginia took measures which the Pilgrims, had the *Mayflower* brought them to that region the following year, would have cordially approved. There were laws against idleness, drunkenness, and Sabbath breaking; laws placing heavy penalties on those who gamed at dice and cards; and laws against "excesse in apparell," it being provided, as a deterrent, that each subject should be assessed for public contribution according to the degree of luxury in dress shown by himself and his family.[183] Yet the circumstances of life and the course of leadership in the two sections developed on such different lines that by the middle of the century the rules of right and wrong had grown quite different, and the tobacco planters, whatever the statute books might say to the contrary, felt free to follow pleasure as far as might be convenient. In Virginia and Maryland, racing, hunting, dancing, and card playing all found many enthusiastic devotees.

The Southerners were especially fond of horse racing. As soon as they passed through the pioneer stages, regular courses were laid off and matches were frequently held. Horses abounded. In 1649 the *Perfect Description* stated that in Virginia "there are of an excellent raise, about two hundred Horse and Mares,"[184] and before many years the number had multiplied many times over. In the last quarter of the seventeenth century all save the very poorest planters had one or more horses, while the well-to-do possessed all that they could use. Although the breed of horses as a whole tended to deteriorate, on certain farms care was taken to uphold the highest English standards.

The sport of racing was at first indulged in only by the richer planters. In 1674 a tailor was fined by the court of York County, Virginia, for "haveing made a race for his mare to runn with a horse belonging to Mr. Mathew Slader for twoe thousand pounds of tobacco and cask, it being contrary to Law for a Labourer to make a race, being a sport for Gentlemen."[185] But with the breaking down of class distinctions among white freemen, which followed the introduction of slaves in large numbers, such restrictions were ignored. "The Common Planters leading easy lives don't much admire Labour," says the Reverend Hugh Jones, "or any manly exercise except Horse racing. . . . The Saddle-Horses, though not very large, are hardy, strong and fleet; and will pace naturally at a prodigious Rate. They are such lovers of Riding, that almost every ordinary Person keeps a Horse."[186]

Not less popular in the South than horse racing, and even more universal, was the sport of hunting. Every planter had his gun and knew how to use it, for about him was game in great abundance. If he wished the excitement of bringing down really dangerous animals, the presence of wolves, bears, and panthers gave him wide opportunity. If he took delight in hunting smaller game, he could find foxes, rabbits, squirrels, raccoons, and opossums; if he went out in quest of wild fowl, he could make his selection from partridges, turkeys, geese and ducks. Tracking the raccoon or the opossum at night was a favorite sport and seems to have been conducted much as at present in the South. Selecting a bright night, the hunters took their dogs to woods where these animals were known to live, and having located one of them, drove it up a tree. The nimblest member of the party then climbed up and shook the creature down among the yelping hounds. On such nocturnal hunts it was customary to take along a certain number of large dogs to guard against attack by wildcats and wolves.[187]

In the Southern colonies dancing was a common form of diversion. The music was usually provided by a female member of the family, but there were among the servants and slaves some skilled fiddlers who were called in at house parties or formal dances. The Jack Foresters and Tubals of Thomas Nelson Page's stories had their predecessors on the plantations of the seventeenth century. The isolation of the life upon the farms was in part offset by frequent social gatherings at the homes of the planters, and on these occasions gaiety was unrestrained. The guests often remained for several days, dancing, playing cards, and partaking of the ample larder of their host.

The love of the planter for card playing is evidenced by the frequent reference in the records to packs of cards. In 1665, Captain Jeremiah Fisher of York owned nine packs, and a few years later we find Jonathan Newell in possession of eight. In 1678 the grand jury of Henrico presented Joseph Royall for playing cards on the Sabbath. The first assembly which met in Virginia passed an act prohibiting gambling with cards and dice under penalty of fine, but this law of 1619 certainly fell into abeyance in later years, for the courts not only permitted these games but actually enforced the payment of money bet on them. Hardly less popular than cards was ninepins. This game was played usually at taverns where there were specially constructed alleys, but at times also in private residences. Here, too, betting was customary, in some cases resulting in quarrels and appeals to the courts.

An occasion of great festivity in Maryland and Virginia was the wedding. The Anglican church made an effort to have all marriage ceremonies performed in the church building, but this was impracticable. When guests came from many miles around it was necessary to provide food and in many cases lodging for the night. Such accommodations could not be had at the isolated churches and chapels, and so it became the practice to hold the ceremony at the home of the bride, where every preparation was made for the entertainment of a large number of guests. Although the records are singularly silent as to the details of the early wedding festivals, yet it is certain that it was the custom, as it was in other social gatherings, to indulge in dancing, drinking, and feasting.[188]

The people of New York, although not so given to the quest of pleasure as their Southern neighbors, and more frequently kept indoors by the severity of the climate, had an advantage in the enjoyment of winter sports.

Madam Knight, a visitor from Boston, wrote in 1704: "Their diversions in the Winter is Riding Sleys about three or four Miles out of Town, where they have Houses of entertainment at a place called the Bowery, and Some go to friends Houses who handsomely treat them. . . . I believe we mett 50, or 60 slays that day——they fly with great swiftness and some are so furious that they turn out of the path for none except a Loaden Cart."[189] When the tardy northern spring made its appearance the people turned eagerly to the open air for exercise and pleasure. A favorite diversion of young folk was to set out in canoes on rural excursions or picnics. After arriving at some sheltered spot where delicious wild fruits abounded or the fishing was good, they clambered ashore and with merry shouts chose their camping ground. In the forenoon the young men fished and hunted, while their companions busied themselves with their needlework and gathered dried branches for the fire. The ample luncheon basket contained tea, sugar, a little rum, and now and then some cold pastry from the home larder, but the party depended upon the fish they could catch or the game they could bring down for their more solid food. In the cool of the evening the picnickers, tired after their day's pleasure, resumed their canoes for the trip home.[190]

No sooner had the English secured possession of New Netherland than they introduced the typical British sports. Racing had not been popular with the Dutch, but Governor Nicolls announced in 1665 that a horse race would take place at Hempstead. He was interested in this matter not so much for "the divertissement of youth as for the encouraging the bettering of the breed of horses which through great neglect" had been impaired. Four years later Governor Lovelace directed that a race should be run each year in May and that the subscriptions would be received from all who were disposed to run for a crown in silver or the value thereof in wheat. The first course was laid off on Long Island in a level place called Salisbury Plains. Here, wrote Daniel Denton, that indefatigable seventeenth-century advertising man, in 1670, "lieth a plain sixteen miles long and four broad . . . where you shall find neither stick nor stone to hinder the horse-heels, or endanger them in their races." Once a year, horses of the best breed were brought to this course to test their speed and compete for two silver cups.[191] As in the South, the young people amused themselves with horse hunts. "They commonly turned their spare horses into yᵉ woods, where they breed and become wild; and as they have occasion to catch up yᵉ colts, and break them for their use."[192]

In New England, pleasure-seeking was looked upon with something akin to suspicion, and was narrowly watched and circumscribed. Games and sports which in other English communities seemed innocent were here prohibited. "Those infamous Games of Cards and dice," especially condemned "because of the lottery which is in them," were placed under the ban of the law. "Stage-Players and Mixed Dancings" were frowned upon,[193] while even shuffleboard was condemned as an idle game which caused the youth to waste precious time. One of the duties of the tithing man, who had ten families under his care, was to see that no boy went swimming.[194] Toys might sell in New England, wrote the Reverend John Higginson to his merchant brother in England, "if in small quantity."[195]

Yet human nature demands recreation, and even the Puritans were not without their diversions. When the first harvest was gathered in at Plymouth, Governor Bradford sent out four men to kill wild fowl so that he could spread a feast for the members of the little colony. This celebration, the first Thanksgiving Day, was attended by the Indian chief Massasoit and his people, "whom for three days we entertained and feasted."[196] The first Thanksgiving in Boston was held February 22, 1630, as an expression of gratitude for the safe arrival of ships from England bringing supplies of food and additional settlers. The next year Thanksgiving Day was held on November 4, and from that time until 1684 not less than twenty-two public days were appointed in Massachusetts for rendering thanks. But Thanksgiving Day did not become a fixed annual observance until many years later, and in times of deep gloom during the seventeenth century the feast was omitted. The harvesting of an abundant crop was not the only occasion for this celebration, for at various times it was held in gratitude for a victory over the Indians, for the success of the Protestant arms in Germany, the accession of a king, the abatement of epidemics, the "healing of breaches" in church congregations, or the suppression of pirates.[197] Nor was the celebration confined to any one month or any one day of the week. One year it was appointed for a Tuesday, another for a "Wednesday com fortnit," and it was only after years that the custom of holding the feast on Thursdays became fixed.[198]

Training days offered other opportunities to break the monotony of New England life. When the Puritans began pouring into the Massachusetts Bay region in 1630, they came, as did the Israelites to the Promised Land, as an armed host. Cotton Mather tells us in his *Magnalia* that "their arms, ammunition and great artillery cost twenty-two thousand pounds," quite enough to equip several thousand fighting men. The leaders were keenly alive to the possibility that they might have to battle in the New World as their fellow Calvinists were battling in the Old, and they were determined that this last retreat of God's people should not be carried by an enemy without a struggle. In order to keep the men proficient in military exercises, special training days were held at regular intervals. Winthrop says that at the training at Boston in May 1639, 1,000 men took part, with arms of various shapes and sizes, while in the autumn of the same year the number was 1,200. The officers were usually chosen by the men.[199] In the sober life of the Puritan the training days offered an innocent diversion which was eagerly anticipated. Although the exercises were always preceded by prayers and the singing of psalms, the occasion was enlivened by a bountiful dinner on Boston Common.

Election day in New England also early assumed the character of a holiday, and was seized upon by the young as an occasion for gaiety. Urian Oakes complained that it was becoming a time "to meet, to smoke, carouse and swagger and dishonor God with the greater bravery." The soberness of early New England life is further illustrated by the eagerness with which the people grasped at the rather arid bit of amusement afforded by the midweek lecture, at the conclusion of which marriage engagements were announced, public notices posted, and once in a while some seditious or heretical book was burned. The young folks attended in great numbers, and actually went to neighboring towns in order to enjoy several of these "treats" during the same week. This seemed to the magistrates a form of dissipation so undesirable that in 1633 they attempted to limit each minister to one lecture in two weeks. But the law was not enforced, and in 1639 we find John Cotton complaining that the lectures were proving harmful to the people by diverting them from their necessary tasks.

Christmas the New Englanders hated as a "wonton Bacchanallian" feast. Any person who observed the day in Massachusetts not only incurred the disapproval of the clergy but was subject to a fine of five shillings. On Christmas Day, 1621, the newcomers who had arrived at Plymouth on the *Fortune* excused themselves on the ground of conscientious scruples from going to work with the original Pilgrims. When Governor Bradford returned at noontime, he found them "pitching ye barr" and playing "at stoole-ball." Thereupon he ordered them to stop "gameing or revelling in ye streets," declaring that it "was against his conscience that they should play & others worke."[200] With the coming of many Anglicans in the closing decades of the century, the Puritan clergy became even more determined to permit no observance of Christmas. On December 25, 1685, at the time of the new regime instituted after the revoking of the Massachusetts charter, Judge Sewall wrote in his *Diary,* "Carts come to town and shops open as usual. Some somehow observe the day, but are vexed I believe that the Body of the People Profane it, and blessed be God no authority yet to compel them to keep it." A few years later, when the Anglicans observed Christmas under the protection of Governor Andros, Sewall forbade his son to accompany a party of friends to the services. But the temptation to join in the Christmas festivities soon proved too much even for members of some of the most conservative congregations. "I hear a Number of young People of both Sexes, belonging, many of them, to my Flock, have had on the Christmas-night, this last week, a Frolick, a revelling Feast, and a Ball," wrote Cotton Mather, "which discovers their Corruption, and has a Tendency to corrupt them yett more, and provoke the Holy One to give them up unto eternal Hardness of Heart."[201]

It will be seen that the New Englander, although his pleasures were strictly circumscribed by law and custom, was not without amusements. He could not, like his Southern neighbors, dance freely or play cards or race horses without risking punishment, but he had his own holidays and his own recreations, which no doubt he fully enjoyed. After all, pleasures are largely a matter of contrast, and to the Boston youth the weekly lecture or the training day seemed, in comparison with the somber religious cast of his everyday life, occasions of rare pleasure. Human nature was not wholly suppressed; there were some pleasures which were permitted to all and there were some stolen sweets. But the picture as a whole is not bright, and there is something unhealthful in a social life which could make it possible for one of the leaders of public life to amuse himself by arranging the coffins in the family vault, and speak of the task as "an awful yet pleasing Treat."

HOMES AND TAVERNS

THE BITTER STRUGGLE for existence which confronted these first Americans made it impossible for them to construct comfortable and permanent homes. While disease was taking its toll, while the Indian danger was ever present, while the little crop of wheat or corn alone stood between the people and starvation, they were forced to content themselves with the rudest and flimsiest shelters. "In foule weather we shifted into an old rotten tent," says Captain John Smith in his description of conditions at Jamestown, "for we had few better. . . . This was our church, till we built a homely thing, like a barne, set on Cratchets,[202] covered with rafts, sedge and earth, so was also the walls: the best part of our houses of like curiosity; but the most part farre worse workmanship, that could neither well defend wind nor rain."[203] The colonists themselves often spoke of their first abodes as wigwams, although apparently they were modeled after crude English houses rather than the Indian huts. "They burrow themselves in the earth for their first shelter under some Hill side," wrote Edward Johnson, "casting the Earth aloft upon Timber . . . yet in these poor Wigwames they sing Psalms, pray and praise God till they can provide them houses."[204] When Penn's Quakers established themselves on the banks of the Delaware, some of the poor families made similar shelters, with one chamber, half-underground, covered with rushes, bark, and sod.

Captain Nathaniel Butler in his *Unmasked Face of Virginia,* written in 1622, declared that the "Howses are generally the worst that ever I sawe, the meanest Cottages in England being every waye equall (if not superior) with the most of the best."[205] This evidence was corroborated later by the Virginia general assembly. "For our howses and churches in these tymes," they wrote, "they were so meane and poore . . . that they could not stand above one or two yeares." That log cabins of the familiar American type were constructed in any of the English colonies prior to 1660 is open to doubt. Isaac de Rasières declared that the Plymouth houses were of "hewn plank," but he gives no hint as to the way in which the timbers were put together. Some authorities are inclined to believe that the hewn logs were set vertically in the ground, and not horizontally after the manner of the American frontier of later times.[206]

In continued use of thatch for roofing may be seen a remarkable instance of the survival of a practice long after new conditions rendered it uneconomical and unwise. English peasants of this period covered their humble homes with thatch, because the growing scarcity of timber placed the cost of shingles beyond their means. But in the colonies, with the erection of the first sawmills, all kinds of boards became exceedingly cheap. Despite this fact, despite the poor protection from the cold afforded by thatch and its extreme combustibility, many persons persisted in its use until into the next century. Apparently they were reluctant to avail themselves of the cheaper and better material, simply because they and their fathers for generations had been unaccustomed to it.

At Plymouth the first houses were thatched. Governor Bradford relates that during the winter of 1620–21 the common house of the tiny settlement was set on fire "by a spark that flew into the thatch, which instantly burnt it all up." That the practice had not been discarded forty-three years later is shown by one of the incidents described by Increase Mather in his *Remarkable Providences.* "A company of neighbors being met together at the house of Henry Condliff, in North-Hampton . . . ," he says, "there came a ball of lightning in at the roof of the house, which set the thatch on fire. . . ." It was long the custom in New England for the town government to assign certain lots for the growing of thatch.[207] In the actual work of erecting the thatched roof the colonists seemed to have followed closely the established practice in England. The rushes or straw were gathered and made into bundles about six inches in diameter. The bundles were then placed upon the framework of the roof, in even rows, one overlapping the other in the manner of shingles, and securely fastened with short willow sticks. It was customary to lay the thatch six or eight bundles deep.

No sooner had the people of each colony overcome the initial difficulties of settlement than they began building substantial frame houses. "The Towne itself by the care and Providence of Sir Thomas Gates . . . is reduced into a handsome forme," wrote Ralph Hamor concerning Jamestown in 1615, "and hath in it two faire rowes of howses all of framed Timber, (two stories, and an upper garret, or corn loft, high)." At Henrico, Virginia, there were three streets of "well framed houses," besides "a faire framed parsonage house," which was occupied by the Reverend Alexander Whitaker.[208]

Later in the century, with the advent of prosperous times, the construction of comfortable homes became general in the colony. "Pleasant in their building," wrote John Hammond in 1656, "which although for the most part they are but one story besides the loft, and built of wood, yet contrived so delightfully that your ordinary houses in England are not so handsome, for usually the rooms are large, daubed and whitelimed, glazed and flowered, and if not glazed windows, shutters which are made very pritty and convenient." "They have Lime in abundance for their houses," said another writer in 1649, "store of Bricks made, and House and Chimnies built of Brick, and some of Wood high and fair, covered with *Shingell* for *Tyle.*"[209]

The typical residence of the tobacco country in the seventeenth century was a rectangular framed building with shingled roof and a chimney at each end. The small planters, who constituted the bulk of the population, contented themselves with little houses averaging perhaps twenty by sixteen feet, with but one room on the main floor, a loft or attic and no cellar. The "great houses" of the wealthy group, while seldom large or handsome when measured by modern standards, were far more pretentious. The residence of Nathaniel Bacon, the elder, contained seven or eight rooms, that of Ralph Wormeley eight rooms, that of Richard Willis eight, that of Adam Thoroughgood six. Green Spring, the home of Sir William Berkeley, was divided into six rooms, while William Fitzhugh's house had no less than twelve or thirteen.

In New England the lowly hovels which for a time sheltered the newcomers were also soon discarded for more comfortable abodes. Upon his arrival at Charlestown in 1630, John Winthrop ordered his house to be cut and framed, and when the colonists moved to Boston, the "frame of the Governor's house" was carried to that place. In 1636, Samuel Symonds at Ipswich gave directions for the erection of a frame dwelling, with wooden chimneys at each end lined with clay, the stairs to be "close by the door," the windows provided with "draw-shutters," the cellar extending under the entire structure, the sides covered with "very good oake-hart inch board."[210] Men of more moderate means built smaller houses. William Rix, a weaver, signed a contract in 1640 for a frame house, "16 foot long & 14 foote wyde, with a chamber floare finisht, summer & ioysts, a cellar floare with ioysts finist, the roofe and walles Clap boarded on the outsyde, the Chimnay framed without dawbing to be done with hewen timber."[211]

In the South, few frame houses remain which can be positively identified as belonging to the seventeenth century. Less sturdily constructed than the homes of New England, apparently they have succumbed sooner to the ravages of time. Some, no doubt, were converted into slave quarters when the owners built more pretentious residences, and so lost their identity. On the other hand, a number of frame houses now standing in New England are known to have been built in the years from 1650 to 1700. These old houses show that the builders of early colonial times followed the traditions of the Middle Ages in structure, form, and details, but stressed those features well adapted to their situation. All were originally simple rectangular houses, with a steep gable roof to deliver the snow, a single chimney rising through the middle so as to conserve the heat, the main frame of heavy

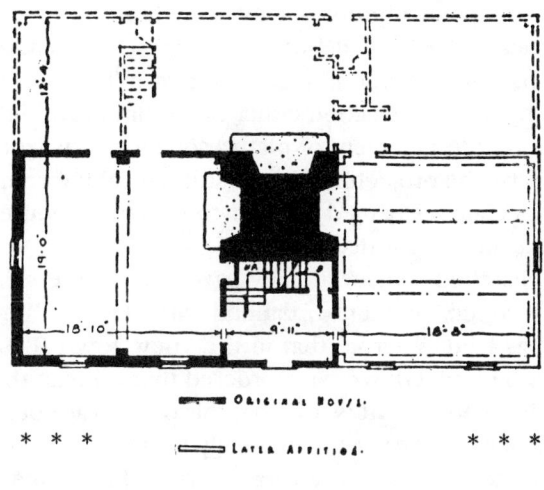

Above: The
Hempsted House,
New London,
1643-.
Center: A
Betty lamp.

Below: The
Kitchen in the
"Old Ordinary"
1649-,
Hingham,
Massachusetts.

timber with elaborate jointing, the walls covered with wooden boards, the roof shingled, the plain interior set off by winding stairs, and the huge fireplace spanned by one great beam. In some cases where the building originally had had but one room in each of two full stories, it was substantially enlarged by the construction either of a room beyond the chimney or a lean-to in the rear. An element of picturesqueness was lent to these New England houses by the projecting second story, recalling cramped medieval streets, but especially esteemed here in the garrison houses as affording better defense against the Indians.

Just as the thatched roof eventually gave way to the shingled roof, so brick and stone superseded timber daubed with clay for chimneys. As early as 1631, Thomas Dudley wrote that in the "new town [Boston] intended this summer to be builded; we have ordered that no man there shall build his chimney with wood."[212] It is true that this order was not always obeyed, yet the ever-present danger of fire gradually brought about the elimination of wooden chimneys, even in the rural districts. Brick chimneys are mentioned in the records of Hartford as early as 1639. In various parts of New England chimneys were built of stone, but in tidewater Maryland and Virginia, where stones were scarce, brick, certainly by 1690, came into almost universal use.

The windows were built small to minimize the cold draft from without. It is probable that the "shutting draw windows" of the first settlers remained in use in the humbler homes throughout the century, but from the first glass was used to some degree. "Be sure to furnish yourselves with . . . glass for windows," wrote Francis Higginson in 1629 to intended immigrants to Massachusetts. The glass casements, which seem to have been universal in the better class of houses in the first part of the century, were hinged sashes, provided with leaded panes, diamond-shaped in some cases, oblong in others. Doors were made of wide boards in two thicknesses, vertical on the outside and horizontal inside. The interior walls and partitions were frequently sheathed with boards, grooved together and molded at the joints. Some however, were plastered with clay or perhaps white-limed. The stairs began with a few steps which wound around the newel post, continued with a short straight run, and ended with another wind at the top.

Although most of the seventeenth-century houses were constructed of wood, brick was not unknown even in the earliest days. Bricklayers were included among the settlers at Jamestown in 1607, and it was stated that the first story of the houses at Henrico, erected in 1611, was of brick. In Massachusetts, brickmaking was in progress in 1629, in Maryland in 1653, and in Pennsylvania in 1684. In Philadelphia the settlers soon learned the advantages of brick residences. "Now as to the Town of Philadelphia," wrote Robert Turner to William Penn in 1685, "it goeth on in Planting and Building to admiration." His own house, the first to be built of brick, he said, he "did design after a good manner to incourage others, . . . and some that built wooden Houses, are sorry for it; Brick Building is said to be as cheap. Brick are exceeding good, and better than when I built." He added that he was engaged in putting up a new house, "three large Stories high, besides a large Brick cellar under it, of two Bricks and a half thickness in the wall, and the next story half under ground, the cellar hath an Arched Door for a Vault to go to the River, and so to bring in goods, or deliver out."[213]

It will be seen that the typical homes of the colonists in the seventeenth century followed closely prevailing types in England and the continent. The early residences, with their steep gables and leaded casements, represent merely a survival of medieval architecture, the Anglican churches adhered to the Gothic style still common in England outside London, while the Puritan meetinghouse imitated the Protestant type of churches so widely diffused in France after the Edict of Nantes. In architecture, as in other arts, the colonists showed little creative power.

Naturally, too, the cabinetmaker's art was imitative. Though but little furniture could be crowded into the tiny ships that brought the early immigrants,[214] the old tastes were a part of their mental outfit, and the home environment was reproduced as nearly as could be. During the seventeenth century the Gothic tradition persisted, though dwindling rapidly toward the end—a tradition of architectural form in oaken furniture, of large and heavy cupboards and paneled solid-back chairs, save where lightened by the use of spindles. The inventories of the time reveal a considerable range in the degrees of comfort. The parlor, or best bedroom, of the affluent pastor of Ipswich, Massachusetts, the Reverend Nathaniel Rogers—with its great chairs, its livery cupboards (having grills for ventilation), its framed pictures, window curtains, clock, and violin—must have astounded some of his parish, even in the 1650s. His neighbor Ensign Whittingham had a canopy bed and gear, which without counting linen was worth £20, exactly twice the sum that represented the entire outfit of William Averill who lived among the humbler houses down toward the river.[215]

In the South there was somewhat more luxury, at least in the last half of the century when the tobacco plantations were fully developed. To transport the bulky crop it was necessary to send good-sized ships from England, whose outward cargoes, valuable as they might be, left space for furniture in part payment for the staple. The home of Nicholas Wyatt in Maryland, whose inventory bears the date of 1676, may stand as an example. In the hall, or dining room, there were seven framed pictures, an oblong table covered with a "carpet," and six joint stools, that is with corners mortised. But though such stools and short forms were still the more common furniture for sitting,[216] Master Wyatt had in this same room a complement of twenty-three chairs, covered with leather and Turkey-work upholstery. The splendid post beds, the looking-glasses, the elaborate hangings, and capacious chests throughout the eight-room house all marked it as typical of the well-to-do planters.[217] It was after 1680, for the most part, that the use of cane and lacquer, and some imported china dishes, showed the influence of European contacts with the East. The advent later of the Jacobean chair with the rudiments of structural curves indicated the beginning of a period of more grace and comfort.

The homes of seventeenth-century Americans, it may be said in summary, were simple but not crude, at least among the well-to-do in the later decades. One qualified authority maintains that in point of design the houses and furnishings between 1670 and 1700 were better than those which followed; going further, he says that the men and women of that time "were better clad, and spoke better English than has been the case at any time since."[218]

In all the colonies the ordinary or tavern was a center of life. In the North it was to be found, not only in almost every village, but also along the more frequented highways. Here the weary traveler secured rest and refreshment; here the villager enjoyed his "beare and cracks" at noontime; here the shivering people thronged from the icy meetinghouse to warm themselves between services; here the jolly good-natured crowd gathered on training days. The water of Plymouth was wholesome, wrote Governor Bradford, though not, of course, as wholesome as good beer and wine; in proper quantities these formed an element of diet whenever they could be had.[219] As for the tavern keeper, he was an important figure in every community.[220] We find him running a ferry near his ordinary, or leading the singing on Sunday, or serving as selectman, or heading the local militia, in addition to regaling his guests with rum and food and tidbits of gossip. Typical of the old New England hosts was Captain Marshall, whose ordinary lay halfway between Boston and Salem. "Here I staid to refresh nature with a pint of sack and a good fowl," says the book dealer, John Dunton. "Capt. Marshall is a hearty old gentlemen, formerly one of Oliver's soldiers, upon which he very much values himself. He had all the history of the civil war at his fingers end, and if we may believe him Oliver did hardly anything that was considerable without his assistance, and if I'd have staid as long as he'd have talked he'd have spoiled my ramble at Salem."[221]

Taverns were established in New England with the first coming of the Massachusetts Bay settlers. We know that the famous Anchor, at Lynn, whose hospitable sign was hailed with joy by travelers for nearly two centuries, was in existence as early as 1630. A few years later taverns were open for business in Boston, Salem, Dorchester, Newbury, Charlestown, Duxbury, Portsmouth, and other places. Some of the inns were small, cheerless places with but two or three rooms and scant furnishings. Such was the house of John Whipple at Providence, which consisted of "ye lower room" and "ye chamber," containing in all little more than one bedstead, three featherbeds, four chairs, and a chest.[222] In the larger towns the taverns were more pretentious. It was a common custom to give each of the rooms a separate name. The King's Arms, at Boston, kept by Hugh Gunnison, boasted of the "Exchange," the "Court Chamber," the "London," and the "Star." The Blue Anchor, also a Boston institution, contained the "Cross Keys," the "Green Dragon," the "Anchor and Castle Chamber," and the "Rose and Sun Low Room."

In the South the eagerness of the planters to entertain guests made taverns less necessary than in the North. Nevertheless, they were often to be found at the county seats and other places where the people were accustomed to assemble. At the time of Bacon's Rebellion, Jamestown is described as a village of "som 16 or 18 howses . . . and in them about a dozen familes getting their liveings by keeping ordnaries at extraordnary rates." [223] In 1668, taverns and tippling houses in Virginia had increased so rapidly that the assembly passed an act strictly limiting the number in each county. In case of urgent need, however, additional taverns were permitted at ports, ferries, or the crossings of important roads. Any person who conducted a tippling house without a license was liable to a fine of 2,000 pounds of tobacco.

The history of architecture and travel during the seventeenth century illustrates admirably the play of forces in the transit of civilization from the Old World to the New. So far as they could, the Pennsylvanians or New Englanders or Virginians clung to the customs and practices of the mother country, but when conditions made this impossible, they adjusted themselves to their new surroundings. Reluctantly they substituted shingles for thatch and weatherboarding for half-timber filled in with clay or bricks; reluctantly they accepted the canoe or the packhorse for inland travel. In these things, as in all others, they were compelled to yield to the forces which were slowly operating to change them from Englishmen to Americans.

THE PROGRESS OF A CENTURY

THE OUTSTANDING ACCOMPLISHMENT of the seventeenth century in American history was the planting of the colonies. When the Virgin Queen passed on the English throne to James of Scotland, the Spaniards and the Portuguese alone had secured a hold upon the New World; a century later Englishmen were firmly planted in the Carolinas, around Chesapeake and Delaware Bays, and in New England; the French had taken possession of the Valley of the St. Lawrence; while the Hudson, as a reminder of its original possessors, was lined with the hamlets and farms of the Dutch.

The typical New Englanders or Virginians of 300 years ago may have contributed little to the advance of science, art, or literature, but they did their part in a work no less important, that of adding a vast continent to the civilized world. While they were founding homes and tightening their grip on the country, they were also steadily advancing the cause of liberty. They were frontiersmen, and frontiersmen are proverbially haters of tyrannical restraint. It was in vain that the English kings sought to crush out the representative system in America, that the Dutch and the founders of Maryland attempted to introduce the manorial system, or the Carolina proprietors to establish Locke's constitutions in the South. Equally futile was the effort of theocratic or aristocratic groups to prevent the growth of democracy. The isolation from Europe, the life in the woods, the contest with the forces of nature, tended to make men impatient of restraint. The seventeenth century brought not only the first representative assembly in America, not only the first American rebellion against despotism, but a long, persistent, and successful struggle for liberalism in government. The vigilance with which the assemblies, in the royal and proprietary colonies, defended their control over taxation is in itself a stirring theme of our early history. The liberty George Washington and Samuel Adams and Thomas Jefferson fought to preserve in the years from 1765 to 1783 in no small degree was won by their ancestors in the colonial legislative halls.

From the womb of this century was also born a new order of men—the first Americans. John Cotton, John Winthrop, Peter Stuyvesant, Sir Thomas Gates, and Sir Thomas Dale were Europeans, and remained Europeans to the day of their death. William Byrd II, Robert Carter, Cotton Mather, and Sir William Phips were Americans. The vast distance between the two continents, the development of distinct interests, the adoption of an imperial policy which subordinated the welfare of the colonies to that of the mother country, the growth of separate customs, points of view, dialects, occupations, and religious organizations—all tended to this end. Thus, while the white settlers were transforming America, America was transforming the settlers. It found them Englishmen and by its irresistible alchemy, it made them Americans.

The transplanting of European culture to North America forms perhaps the most significant chapter in the epic story of the expansion of European influences to the rest of the world, and forms a theme for study by the social historian which has not yet received adequate attention. Men, like plants, cannot be uprooted from their native soil and set again in some distant land without undergoing profound changes.

In none of the colonies was this more marked than in Virginia and Maryland. Here the settlers were brought under the influence of an economic system which had no counterpart in Europe. The culture of tobacco entailed methods of work and conditions of life to which the newcomers were strangers. If they were men of means and purchased or developed considerable estates, they had to take upon themselves the responsibility of controlling, directing, and caring for their servants and slaves. This developed in them a sense of self-reliance, self-respect, and the power of command. The planting, tending, and curing of tobacco made them practical farmers; the marketing of crops and the purchase of merchandise from Europe made them businessmen; the building and repair of houses and barns, the manufacture of beer and wine, the making of clothing for the workers, the care of the horses and cattle, combined to make them efficient managers. The mild climate and out-of-door life gave them a love of sport.

The galaxy of great Virginians who played so important a role in the Revolutionary War was the product of the tobacco plantation. It is futile to argue that these men displayed such remarkable leadership and statesmanship because of qualities inherited from distinguished English ancestors. They were unlike anything England ever produced, whether at the time when their ancestors migrated or, later, in their own day. The widespread belief that during the years from 1645 to 1660 Virginia was the refuge of large numbers of English Cavaliers is entirely without foundation in fact, but had wealthy adherents of the unhappy Charles I flocked thither, the tobacco plantations would in a few generations have transformed them from Cavaliers into Marylanders and Virginians. The small farms which covered their tidewater section had upon their owners an effect no less significant. The English farm laborer who found himself in possession of 200 acres, who raised his own tobacco and sold it to the exporters, who prided himself on his right to vote, who cut his own firewood from his own woods, became a responsible, self-respecting, prosperous man—a free American, no longer a European peasant. He, too, was the product of soil, climate, and geographic conditions.

In like manner the fur trade developed a class of men peculiar to itself. The traders of New York, like the famous *coureurs de bois* of Canada, became creatures of the wilderness, setting their traps in distant places, driving their bargains with the Huron or the Illinois, pushing their slender canoes through lake and river, wandering along the tangled forest trails, enduring hunger, cold, and fatigue. Generous, open-handed, improvident, given to the use of strong liquor, in their dress and manner of life they closely resembled the Indians. As for the merchants of Manhattan, the manor lords along the Hudson, the rice planters of South Carolina, the shipbuilders, traders, and fishermen of New England, they, too, in varying degree, felt the molding influence of the New World of which they had become a part.

These first Americans were deeply affected by the proximity of the frontier. Even in later days, when not a few native-born colonists were rounding their seventh or eighth decade, when Boston, Portsmouth, New York, and Charleston had become thriving towns, when well-to-do merchants and planters were building substantial homes and fitting them out with every comfort of the old country, even then the fresh scent of the forest came strong with every breeze from the west, while the tomahawk and the scalping knife continued menacingly near. In the Virginia house of burgesses, when it assembled in the charming new state house at Williamsburg, were to be seen not only the wealthy planter of Gloucester or Middlesex, impressive in periwig, silk stockings, plush breeches, and broadcloth coat with ruffled cuffs, but also the rude frontiersman of the upper James or the Pamunkey, clad in canvas or buckskin.

As we have seen, the frontier in the seventeenth, as in the eighteenth and nineteenth centuries, was an ever-active school of democracy. The free life of the backwoods, the common struggle to conquer the forest and wring a living from the soil, the common peril from the Indians, tended to break down social distinctions and make all men, in fact, equal. From the first the frontier districts have been prompt to raise a strident voice against privilege, injustice, and the creation of artificial distinctions in government. When Virginia was suffering from the navigation acts, when Sir William Berkeley had so corrupted the assembly as to make it the mockery of a representative body, it was the frontiersmen who raised the standard of rebellion and drove the governor into exile. The aristocratic clique sneered at Bacon's men as "rag, tag and bobtayle," but their rough garb concealed true lovers of liberty, and the laws these men wrung from the reluctant assembly and the still more reluctant governor mark an epoch in the history of liberty in the New World. In its essential features Bacon's Rebellion was a wind of democracy blowing from the west, a wind that was to come again and again as the frontier receded.

The influence of the Indians upon the life and customs of the colonists was profound. In every practical concern the English learned more from the Indians than the Indians learned from them. For centuries the Indians had lived in the forest, and their civilization had been shaped to meet its needs. As long as the Europeans built their homes or hunted, or made war in the shadows of the great trees, they found it necessary to turn to the Indians for instruction. Englishmen and Frenchmen might despise the squalid life of the aborigine, they might abhor his religion, but in woodcraft they became his imitators. In the course of time, as the forests disappeared, the white men abandoned many of the Indian customs, but others remained with them throughout the eighteenth century, a few until the present day.

It required only a few years for the English settlers to discover that in the forest the Indian method of fighting was superior to their own. Before the seventeenth century had run half its course they were pursuing the Indians in the woods in small bands unencumbered with baggage trains, sleeping in the open, bringing down their food with their guns, creeping through the underbrush to catch the foe by surprise, making use of every bit of natural shelter once the battle had begun. In September 1676, when a report reached Virginia that 2,000 redcoats were on their way to restore peace to the distracted colony, Nathaniel Bacon expressed confidence in his ability to beat them with 500 men. Our use of ambushes, our knowledge of the country, our skill in forest fighting, and our marksmanship will render their discipline of no avail, he said. Had the rebel leader been alive at the head of his veteran band when the British troops actually arrived, it is not improbable that he would have driven them into Chesapeake Bay within a month. His estimate of the helplessness of disciplined troops under wilderness conditions was strikingly vindicated three quarters of a century later by Braddock's defeat on the Monongahela.

The white men learned from the Indians not only the art of fighting in the forests, but also the art of living in them. They copied their methods of trapping the beaver and the fox, of hunting the deer and the bear, of blazing a way through the trackless wilds, of building fires, of signaling with smoke columns, of using wild herbs for medicines, of making maple sugar, dressing skins, cooking food, detecting the approach of enemies. Most important of all, they learned from the Indians how to make and use that merchant vessel of primeval America—the canoe. It was the canoe, put together skillfully with birch bark, which made possible the fur trade with the interior, and it was the fur trade which laid the foundation of some of the colonies. "A mocacin's the best cover a man ever had for his feet in the woods," said an old New England peddler, "the easiest to get stuff for, the easiest to make, the easiest to wear. And a birch-bark canoe's the best boat a man can have on the river. It's the easiest to get stuff for, easiest to carry, the fastest to paddle. And a snowshoe's the best help a man can have in the winter. It's the easiest to get stuff for, the easiest to walk on, the easiest to carry." [224]

The white man adopted as his own the maize of the Indian, imitated his method of cultivating it—including the efficacious herring in the seed hill —and accepted his way of preparing it for the table.[225] The Indian words "pone," "succotash," and "hominy" bear testimony to his obligation to the aborigine.[226] The early settler, in imitation of the Indian, often heated water by dropping hot stones in it, he lighted his cabin with the pine-knot torch, caught fish in a fishweir, and solaced his idle hours by smoking the Indian weed, tobacco.

Unfortunately, many of the frontier dwellers copied the Indian's vices as well as his useful arts. At times they repaid treachery with treachery, cruelty with cruelty. The backwoodsman whose wife had been scalped before his eyes or whose children had been carried off into captivity was not slow to take a terrible revenge whenever the opportunity presented itself. From the day when John Pott, the convivial physician of Jamestown, poisoned large numbers of Indians until Chief Logan uttered his famous remonstrance because of the murder of his relatives, the white men were perhaps the equals of their foe in deception and cruelty.

While the settlers were falling under the spell of the frontier, the life and thought of Europe were making upon them an ever fainter impression. As quiet pools often form near the river's bank while the current rushes on, so these dwellers on the outskirts of civilization missed the main trend of progressive thought. In medicine there was deterioration; in literature almost nothing of value was created, while there was little real appreciation of the best contemporaneous English productions. Painting and graphic art were rare indeed, and sculpture was almost unknown.[227]

The America of three centuries ago offered a limitless opportunity for the poet's pen or the painter's brush. But the settlers were too much engrossed with the bitter struggle for existence to revel in the beauty of the scenery or to appreciate the romantic features of wilderness life. Newcomers from Europe, it is true, were wont to give expression to their admiration and wonder as the grandeur of the new continent for the first time broke upon their eyes. Some of the most interesting pictures of the American scene in the seventeenth century came from the pens of those who merely sojourned in this country, like John Smith and John Josselyn, but they devoted more space to nature than to man. It may be said in passing that the writings of such seventeenth-century observers helped to turn the attention of philosophers to the earth itself and its wonders, an interest so elaborately indulged in the *Encyclopedie* of the following century.[228] When the *Sarah Constant,* the *Discovery,* and the *Goodspeed* sailed into Chesapeake Bay in 1607, the adventurers were entranced with the fair meadows, sweet with the smell of spring, with the bits of woodland, the song of birds, the rivulets dappled with sunlight. But the rigors of frontier existence soon robbed the settlers of their aesthetic appreciation. Jeremiah Dummer, silversmith and engraver and a man of standing in the society and politics of Boston, had somewhere and somehow learned to paint by the end of the 1680s; at least, in 1691 he did such creditable portraits of himself and his wife that he may take his place, as far as the record shows, as the first native American painter of competence.[229] He had few rivals.

The vast leafy ocean stretching out as far as the eye could see seemed to the settlers only a tremendous barrier to settlement; the picturesque Indians were a deadly enemy to be subdued and swept aside; the broad rivers were of interest chiefly as obstacles or avenues of transportation. They lived too close to the mighty forces of nature to paint them or sing about them. Their task was to fight, to conquer, to labor, and to build.

In material progress the accomplishment of the seventeenth century was not great; as compared with that of the eighteenth century it was almost insignificant. Despite the continued migration to the various colonies, the growth of population was slow and halting. The census figures for the time are unsatisfactory. The pious New Englanders believed, on the authority of I Chronicles 21, that God's wrath would follow any enumeration. This fear, which they carried to New Jersey and New York, forced Governor Hunter to ingenious shifts to get an estimate. Yet there were reckonings based often upon the tax lists or the strength of the militia.[230] In 1649, forty-two years after the founding of Jamestown, Virginia had but 15,000 people. The

Jeremiah Dummer,
by himself.

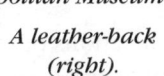

A group from the Metropolitan Museum

| *A high chair* | *A leather-back* |
| *(left).* | *(right).* |

An oak court cupboard.   *A high chest of drawers*

The Touch of Art.

prosperity which attended the economic freedom of the commonwealth period brought about a sudden increase to 40,000 in 1662, but the navigation acts of 1660 and 1663 put a halt to this movement. In 1698, Governor Nicholson placed the number of people in the colony at 58,040; within the century to follow it was to increase nearly twelvefold. The story is similar in the other colonies. In 1643, Massachusetts boasted of a population of about 16,000,[231] in 1658 the number was about 30,000, in 1700, perhaps 60,000. In 1643, Connecticut had possibly 5,500 people; in 1689, from 17,000 to 20,000. New York grew from 7,000 in 1664 to 18,067 in 1698; Maryland, from 8,000 in 1660 to 32,000 in 1701; Rhode Island, from some 1,200 in 1658 to 7,181 in 1708. All in all, the colonies grew from about 25,000 in 1640,[232] to about 80,000 in 1660, to over 200,000 in 1689.[233]

Though the population was still small at the end of the century, though the forest in places stretched unbroken almost to the ocean shore, in social well-being and the comforts of life the advances were impressive. The most successful planters of Virginia and Maryland and the leading merchants of New England and New York had, by the year 1690, acquired a considerable degree of wealth,[234] built substantial homes, bought silver cups and candlesticks, and surrounded themselves with servants. Even the humbler classes — small planters, artisans, shopkeepers — had discarded the huts of the earlier days for larger and better-constructed homes. The life of the settlers of 1620 or 1630 was one of hardship and incessant labor; in 1690 their descendants enjoyed comforts which the well-to-do of England itself might have envied.

Nor were other indications of material progress lacking. The Indian trails which in the early days served as routes of travel were gradually giving way to roads suitable for horse-drawn vehicles; over many of the rivers and creeks bridges were supplementing the primitive ferries; the two-wheel cart was beginning to challenge the ascendancy of the packhorse and the canoe. The tiny rude churches where the first settlers had worshiped were now replaced by larger buildings, solidly constructed. Well-laid-out race courses, handsome state houses, comfortable inns, likewise bore testimony to the transformation which, in the older communities, was taking place. Though the tender plant of European civilization had not yet grown large in American soil, it had taken firm root, was healthy and vigorous. The way had been prepared for the remarkable growth of succeeding decades.

The American of 1690 no doubt often pictured his pioneer grandfather as he went about the work of subduing the wilderness. He could see him, broadax in hand, hewing away at the great oaks or pines or sycamores to make a first clearing in the forest. He pictured him erecting his little cabin, while his wife cared for the baby or cooked the food in the open; or breaking the ground with his spade or clumsy hoe for his crop of maize or tobacco. He could see him alone in the forest bringing down the wild turkey or the deer with his bell-mouthed musket; barricaded in his house, holding off the bloodthirsty Indians; hastening over the forest trail to bring the distant pastor-physician to sick wife or child; wending his way by boat or horse many miles to attend church. He thought of the perils of those early days, of the thousands who succumbed to malaria or the plague; of those who perished of hunger, privation, and cold; of those who fell beneath the tomahawk of the Indian; of the ever-present dread of the hated Spaniard.

Then he turned his vision to the America of his own day, and smiled at the pleasing contrast. If he were a well-to-do planter, he thought of his estate of 1,000 acres, 300 of them cleared and under cultivation; of his comfortable dwelling house, its great hall hung with tapestry, its chambers provided with all kinds of furniture; of his cellars stocked with wines, his crops of tobacco and corn, his servants and slaves, his cattle, horses, and sheep. If he were a prosperous merchant, his mind perhaps dwelt on his swift sloop, beating its way to the West Indies laden with provisions, timber, fish, and rum; his warehouse at the water's edge filled with sugar and molasses; or his commodious dwelling house in Boston or Portsmouth.

All in all, the men of the seventeenth century did well the task which fate assigned them. Their failures, such as they were, are readily explained by the peculiar conditions of their life. When the inventory of their accomplishment is taken, it bulks large in the history of American life. Their arduous labors in conquering the wilderness, their hardships and sufferings, were not in vain, for they planted firmly on the northwestern shores of the Atlantic the standard of European civilization, and laid the broad foundations of nationality upon which future generations were to erect the mighty structure of the United States.

BOOK III

Provincial Society,

1690–1763

THE STRUCTURE OF SOCIETY, 1690-1700

IN 1690, along the entire length of the colonial shore, everywhere sweeping backward from the sea, creeping up the slopes of the mountain barriers and over their untrodden crests, lay the shadow of the virgin forest, illimitable, silent, starless. So thick was this covering in parts that an Indian trader two generations later reported that at times for miles he could find no place the size of his hand where the sunshine penetrated on the clearest day. The innumerable tree trunks, dusky beneath the green covering of summer or bare and gaunt above the winter's snow, formed a trackless maze save for the labyrinth of Indian trails. These were widened and trampled between certain of the more important English settlements into ways fit for the saddle horse or packtrain. For the infrequent wayfarer or trafficking merchant there were no highways of communication other than the sea and its arms, or the rivers which gave access to the interior up to the fall line where rock and cataract blocked further passage.

Two quests had for some years been luring people toward the interior. These were the retreating fur trade and the search for new lands where an untilled soil would reward the wasteful farmer or where meadows lying open to the sun, like green islands in the darker green of the forest, would save the labor of clearing. But whereas the picturesque and dissolute trader penetrated hundreds of miles, the settler went but tens. Although in eastern Massachusetts, and to a slighter extent in the other colonies, single plantations or small villages were being planted in sections not served directly by a waterway, the great bulk of the colonists as yet lived within a few miles of ocean or tidewater stream.

It was a population sparsely scattered over great stretches. South of the Delaware River the unit of settlement was the solitary farm or large plantation, and that section contained not a single town, with the exception of the large village of Charleston which may have numbered 250 families by 1700. Philadelphia, laid out only in 1683, had but a few hundred houses some years later and is said to have had not over 700 at the close of the century. New York was slightly larger, its population being given as 4,900 persons in 1698, but it was the only community in that colony larger than a hamlet, for Albany as yet was scarcely more than a trading post. Newport could count less than 2,000, and Boston, the largest center of population on the continent, not over 7,000 individuals, free and slave. If we accept the figure of 206,000 as the possible population of the twelve colonies in 1689 (exclusive of the Native Americans), it is evident that nearly 200,000 persons must have been living either on isolated farms or in little communities of a few score souls, at most a few score families.

Under such conditions it is evident that the local interest would be the supreme interest and that the average small community would be a fertile field for the development of indifference, jealousy, prejudice, or antipathy regarding the inhabitants of other colonies. Differences in history and in religious, economic, and social conditions also contributed to emphasize and to perpetuate the separatist tendencies in spite of fundamental similarities. Yet there was a greater uniformity in the warp and woof of the social fabric in 1690 along the entire seaboard than at any subsequent time until perhaps our own. We shall have occasion to touch upon this uniformity later in some of its aspects—schools, culture, landholding, labor, morals— here we will merely note its racial one. Heterogeneous as the population of the colonies always was even from the beginning, it was to become far more so in the course of the eighteenth century, and it was less so, perhaps, in 1690 than at any other time before or after.

If the human elements forming colonial society were complex, nevertheless the structure itself was simple. There was no hereditary aristocracy, and the only insurmountable barrier between classes was that between the slave for life and the freeman. There was, indeed, a certain hierarchy of wealth and occupation and discrimination in the voting franchise, but the large amount of free or almost free land, the resources of a virgin continent, the insatiable demand for and limited supply of labor, and the absence of any permanent legal disabilities applying to any class above the slave made for extraordinary opportunity and consequently a very mobile society.

The dominant note in this social life was that of domesticity. In the somewhat romantic atmosphere with which Americans clothe this early period, it is perhaps the peace, simplicity, and unity of family life which contribute the elements of greatest charm. This domesticity afforded the most characteristic and appealing quality in colonial architecture even after passing into the more formal Georgian phase of the eighteenth century, and the most significant arts and crafts were those devoted to fashioning the furniture and utensils of the household. It is noteworthy that although American cultural life was woven of many ethnic strands, all of those which at the end of the seventeenth century were most effective—English, Dutch, French, and German—were of races in which the solidarity of the family was strongly ingrained. To this homemaking instinct, rooted in the inheritance of the settlers, was added the influence of environment. Under the conditions of a frontier existence, the family tended to become greatly strengthened as a social, economic, and even military unit.

The lack of accumulated resources, the scarcity of labor, and other factors in the life of a new country emphasized in a high degree the economic interdependence of all its members, and the family group in some of the colonies, at least, tended to include legally the wards, apprentices, and servants as well as the children. The work of subduing the wilderness and establishing the economic position of the family was of necessity shared by the women and children to an extent that has not been adequately recognized. Indeed, the large number of offspring in the majority of households had a very close connection with the exploitation of child labor. This, of course, was not true of such families as had established themselves near the top of the economic scale, but the rich formed only a small part of the total population. Probably about 90 percent of the colonists were engaged in agriculture. Of these, in 1700, the vast majority, Southern as well as Northern, tilled small farms largely by their own labor and that of the members of their households. There were, everywhere, larger units of agricultural production, and some very large ones, but this does not alter the fact that numerically the great bulk of the people were living near the lower end of the social scale. At that end the necessity of utilizing the physical labor of women and children added its heavy weight to inherited instinct so as greatly to strengthen the position and organization of the family as a social unit.

The family was thus closely connected with another fundamentally important institution, land, which provided its economic base and to a large extent molded its social and legal aspects. The two most essential factors with regard to land were the tenure on which it was held and the ease with which it might be acquired, both of which varied in the different colonies. Throughout all of them the prevailing types of ownership were freehold and leasehold, but with the exceptions of Massachusetts, Connecticut, and Rhode Island, no land anywhere was held under any form of tenure save that from an overlord, either the king or proprietors to whom the crown had granted the lands, which they in turn either sold or leased to the settlers.

The colonial land system was thus mainly feudal in character, but by the end of the seventeenth century the strictly feudal tenures with the personal service exacted from tenant to lord had largely disappeared and the quitrent had come to be the measure and fulfillment of most of the tenant's obligations. Although its payment was acknowledgment that the actual title to the property lay with the overlord and not with the tenant, nevertheless, this did not in the least limit the latter's entire freedom to sell or bequeath his acres provided he had fulfilled his obligations to the overlord. Nor was this obligation, which lasted until the Revolution, a heavy one, for not only was it in many cases merely nominal, as in the example of a red rose sent annually as the quitrent for a "manor" in Pennsylvania, but even when the money payment was exacted the amount did not bear, like ordinary rent, any relation to the value of the land, and was frequently only a fraction of a penny per acre. Moreover, the obligation was not seldom left unenforced, although in some cases, as the lands of the Penns, Baltimores, Fairfax, and Granville, the sums annually raised were considerable.

Land, however, when once acquired by the settler was not heavily burdened, and more important as a factor in his content or discontent was the ease with which it might be obtained. In proportion to the population the supply of land may appear to have been practically unlimited, but if we take certain factors into consideration we find that it was not so even physically. That lying remote from coast or river was as difficult of utilization as that which today is remote from any means of transport. Moreover, the pioneer was deterred from making too far a removal by the danger of isolating himself within the range of the Indian. The unscientific agriculture of the day and the lack of fertilizers quickly wore out much of the acreage used and prevented the use of much more which otherwise might have been brought under profitable cultivation. Not only was much of the richest land of the present then lying under innumerable undrained swamps, but these interfered with transportation and rendered still other lands inaccessible. Owing to the almost continuous forest, open tracts of meadow which could be used without the costly and toilsome work of clearing were comparatively scarce. The available supply of land at the beginning of the new century was thus by no means as ample proportionately as it had been a generation earlier. Another factor even more important and more resented was the increasing tendency to segregate large holdings in the hands of fortunate individuals.

At the close of the seventeenth century all of the institutions of the settlers were yet in the formative stage, each of them being molded by environment and new conditions of life, and in turn acting upon one another. Of none was this truer than of the law. The accepted legal theory that the first settlers brought the English common law with them, using such portions as were applicable to the new conditions, is a view of the case which needs much qualifying. During the seventeenth century there had been scarcely an English-trained lawyer in America. The codes adopted by the several colonies were largely the work of laymen and wholly administered by them. In 1700 the English professional lawyer Atwood became attorney general in New York, but for several decades later the highest legal officers in many of the colonies and almost the entire bench in all of them, as well as the members of the legislative assemblies which constituted courts of appeal, were laymen. In some of the colonies, notably New England, the common law was distinctly repudiated as a subsidiary system and the "law of God," which as one offender truly said admitted of many interpretations, was substituted in its stead. The fact that colonial law was to so great an extent made and interpreted by laymen contributed greatly to its flexibility at this stage of its growth.[1]

The flexibility of colonial institutions was greatly aided by the division of the colonies into a dozen separate governments, which permitted a far greater number of experiments to be made than would have been possible had there been a single administration from Maine to Carolina. Although this political subdividing of the settlers had its obvious disadvantages in fostering a spirit of separatism, and in reducing at times the combined military strength of the colonies almost to a nullity, it had the advantage of permitting experimentation and of assisting the clarification of certain ideas.

Perhaps the most obvious example of the latter is that of the relation of church to state. In New Hampshire, Massachusetts, and Connecticut the Congregational, or town, church was the legal ecclesiastical establishment to which the taxpayers were obliged to contribute support whether members of the congregation or not. In Rhode Island there was no establishment of any sort, and in New York the situation was an anomalous one. The Dutch Reformed Church, as a legal establishment, had fallen with the Dutch government at the time of the English conquest. In 1693 the colonial legislature had finally been induced by English solicitations to pass an act establishing a church, but the act was of intention so vaguely worded as to leave it uncertain what church was established. In spite of efforts, the Church of England was never able to make its claim good and there was much confusion among the conflicting claims of the various sects. A somewhat similar situation prevailed in New Jersey, where the crown had undertaken to establish the Anglican church by means of a royal decree. There were, however, no Anglican congregations, and the provincial legislature never passed an act establishing that or any other church. In Pennsylvania and Delaware, which were separated in 1702, there was no establishment. In Maryland from 1692, and in the Carolinas, the Church of England became the state church, as it had been in Virginia from the beginning.

The most notable feature of the ecclesiastical situation was thus its extreme diversity. In America in 1700 none of the establishments had behind them that long history of achievement or service, the sentimental recognition of which may sustain an institution long after other props have fallen. Nor could the belief in a divinely appointed order fail to be regarded with skepticism in the face of such a heterogeneous jumble achieved by methods with which the colonists were all too familiar. There was still to be a long struggle for complete religious liberty, but at least there were forces at work tending to disintegrate the belief in the necessity or desirability of a union between church and state.

Just as the institutions briefly outlined showed local variety and yet a broad underlying uniformity, so, too, did the political framework into which colonial society was built. The units of local government in all the colonies had naturally developed from those with which the colonists had been familiar in England at the time of the beginning of emigration, but for a variety of reasons they had developed differently in different sections. Thus, whereas in New England the town had gathered to itself functions performed in England by several local organs, so in the South the parish had developed in a similar way, and the town was there a later and always a much less effective division, as was also the county.

At the beginning of the century, the tendency was to broaden the suffrage. Even so, the suffrage was an exceedingly limited one. In 1703, for example, out of a population of about 7,000 in Boston, only 206 voted for representatives. Throughout all the colonies the qualified voters were but a fraction of the adult male population, whole classes such as laborers, artisans, servants, fishermen, the smaller shopkeepers, and others being automatically excluded. Limited as the suffrage was, however, it was a distinct advance over conditions in Europe, and by the end of the seventeenth century, England had recognized the right of popular representation in the legislative branch of the government in all the colonies.

In each of them there was a governor and a legislature consisting of an upper and a lower house. The governor, elected by the people in the corporate colonies of Connecticut and Rhode Island, was in the other colonies appointed either by the proprietary or the crown. In the two colonies just mentioned the upper house of the legislature was elected by the people, in Massachusetts by the lower house with the governor's consent as to each name, and in all the others was appointed in the same manner as the governor. In all of the colonies, however, the lower house was elected by the voters whose qualifications we have just considered. In most of the provinces the executive and judiciary were as yet beyond popular control and represented the external power of the British government.

As it was thus through the legislatures alone that the people could make their wishes felt, the story of the prerevolutionary years was, politically, to be one of persistent encroachment of the legislative upon the other two branches, dramatically shown by the constant struggles between the assemblies and the governors. This drama, played out in every colony with a royal governor, is so obvious that the characteristic political struggle has constantly been considered as one solely against external control. A study of conditions in the two colonies which elected their own governors, as well as a closer examination of the many influences at work in the others, indicate, however, that the struggle was not solely for home rule, but was incidental to a far wider movement designed to bring all power into the hands of the "people," understood in a steadily broadening sense. Not only do we find certain incidents of the contest repeated in the two corporate colonies in which there was no question of external control, but we also find economic grievances at work among certain classes and sections slowly tending toward expression in the form of political demands.

Voluntary organizations have been an increasingly important factor in American society. Of these we find scarcely a trace in the seventeenth century. The old guilds and labor organizations of England had been abandoned and no newer form had developed in their stead. Charity and education were functions either of the local governments or of individuals. Social clubs and artistic or scientific associations begin in a later period. There were no organized, or indeed sharply defined and continuing, political parties. On the one hand, certain social duties or obligations, such as education, were being grafted on to the governmental machinery. On the other, much was left to the individual, which in the England of the day or later in America was assigned to some private corporate body. The great foundations, educational and charitable, of the old country had been left behind. The lack of accumulated wealth at this time in the colonies did not permit of new colonial ones. With the exception of a certain amount of group emigration to New England, the immigrants had all come as individuals or families, and time was required for a new social integration.

At the opening of our period, we thus have to deal with a widely scattered and mainly agricultural population leading a hard-working, narrow, parochial, and sometimes dangerous existence in solitary farms, tiny hamlets, or at most in what would now be considered small villages. Few of these last, except in eastern Massachusetts and around Williamsburg, Virginia, were connected by even the shortest roads fit for wheeled traffic. It was a society in which all the conditions tended greatly to emphasize the solidarity of family life and that of the smaller political units. The collection of provinces with varied governments and religious beliefs was peopled by groups of differing nationalities, yet, speaking broadly, all alike were subject to the similar influences exerted by life in a new country and by fundamental similarities in the relations of the individual to his government. The eighteenth century was to be marked by growing differentiation in social and economic conditions, yet also by an increasing tendency toward intellectual and political unity.

The young American society, or rather the collection of societies, was closely articulated with others overseas. Indeed, these connections with other communities across the water were in many cases closer than those which bound the several continental colonies to one another. Politically, of course, all the colonies, island and continental alike, centered in England, and as there were no intercolonial political bonds, there were no reasons for the New Englander and the South Carolinian, for example, to consider themselves as bound to one another in any closer relationship than each was bound to the Jamaican or Barbadian. Each was but a resident of an English colony, and the closeness of the relationship between any two of them could be based only upon the closeness of their social or economic ties. In fact, there was far more intercourse between Boston and the West Indies, and between the West Indies and Charleston, than there was between Charleston and Boston. The absence of political ties binding a group of any of the colonies served to bring out more clearly the relationship of each to the only political entity of which it formed a part, the British Empire. That term, indeed, as used to include the overseas possessions, makes its first appearance in the decade we are discussing.[2]

With England herself the relations of the colonists were of the closest sort and embraced every field of political, economic, and social life, although the closeness of these relations varied to some extent in the different colonies. She was not merely the source of protection, the seat of power, the center of empire, but was still "home" in the speech of all Americans of English descent. At the opening of the eighteenth century there was no fully differentiated American life, no American people. There was merely a loose group of English colonies in the West Indies and on the American continent. The latter possessed, it is true, certain fundamental institutions in common and were subject to certain common influences, but as yet they were without any common consciousness, common culture, or even a vague premonition of a common destiny.

THE "ARISTOCRATS," 1690-1713

FROM THE VERY BEGINNING of settlement there had been marked social distinctions between the colonists. Yet compared with a later age or even with the England of the later Stuarts, the differences in social classifications were, indeed, slight. Instead of ascending by a multitude of gradations from the plowman or artisan through the yeomanry, several grades of gentry, large county families, and a half dozen ranks of nobility to a duke, one climbed from indented servant to the middle gentry, and there one abruptly stopped. There never was an aristocracy, strictly speaking, in the colonies and perhaps never more than a few score at most of genuine aristocrats permanently domiciled there. Nevertheless, the term in its denatured form is a convenient one to use for colonial social figures of a certain type, for what is frequently, and obviously incorrectly, referred to as the colonial aristocracy was something more than a plutocracy. Breeding, learning, length of residence, political control, and other factors all combined to establish a social position based upon something more than mere wealth. The fact, however, that the entire population of the colonies, English or foreign and practically without a single exception, were from the middle or lower classes was a social fact of great importance.

This abbreviation of the social scale did not prevent such distinctions as there were being taken with extreme seriousness. "Mr." and "Gent." were insisted upon in life and carved upon the tombstone in death. Place at table, position in the college classroom in New England, seating in church, and many other minor matters were regulated with a nicety of regard for social status that was equaled only by the minuteness of the differences upon which it was based. This was probably due to the extreme rarity of the social atmosphere. Frontier existence always tends to obliterate certain aspects of social cleavage. In its simplest form, that of a wilderness which must be subdued by the hand of man and from which a subsistence must somehow be wrung by physical toil, claims of social consideration grounded on conditions existing in the country left behind suffer short shrift. Even the power of money goes under a partial eclipse where money no longer can buy service and where everyone works for himself. The trappings of every sort, which in the complex society of the older settle-ment covered one so comfortably, and perhaps disguised one so conve-niently, tend to fall away or be pulled off, and leave one socially naked to the critical eyes of one's fellow pioneers; and one clings to such shreds as may remain.[3]

In the first two generations of settlement along the coast, this frontier tendency toward social denudation had been operative to a considerable extent, but had also been offset to some degree by the strong inherited sense of social stratification which the settlers had brought with them from Europe. Moreover, many of the leaders of the first settlements had been worthy pioneers as well as socially superior to the bulk of the colonists in their respective settlements. In addition, during the earlier part of the seventeenth century the enforced simplicity of life in America prevented to a large extent that flaunting of the advantages of wealth and privilege which is more irritating to the common man than the mere knowledge of their existence.

In a new country the possibilities of making a fortune are by no means commensurate with those of making a living. It might in a sense be true, as Franklin said a half century later, that any man who could bait a hook or pull a trigger could get food in America, but this brought him no nearer to becoming a mercantile magnate or an opulent planter. For that he needed political influence with the authorities, the luck of inherited capital, or the always rare ability to acquire it rapidly for himself. For the first, he had in some way to gain access to official circles, which was not easy without some money or social position to begin with. For the last, the way then as always was much easier for those who had some capital to start with than for those who had none. This was obviously true of the increasingly mercantile North, and in the change soon to come over the agricultural South the way to wealth lay through the control of slave labor, and slaves cost money. By the first decade of the eighteenth century, therefore, the possession of money in the older seaboard settlements was becoming more effective, and the differences between the man who started with advantages and the man who did not, more definite and more fixed.

The most important social figure in most of the colonies was the royal governor. In closer touch with the home country than the colonists because of his being a mere sojourner, frequently a member of the nobility with the glamour of a title and familiarity with London society, always, owing to his position, the source of political, social, and frequently economic advancement, the governor himself and the "governor's set" naturally occupied the leading place in the social life of the provinces. Occasionally, as in the case of such a bankrupt rake as Lord Cornbury, the influence exerted was unmitigatedly bad. On the other hand, with governors of the better type, such as Spotswood of Virginia or William Burnet of New York, their culture, their close connection with the social or intellectual life at home and their genuine interest in the colonies which they governed, enabled them to bring to a focus in their small circle those ideals of a polished society that are lacking in the life of any new community concerned of necessity mainly with rapid commercial exploitation.[4]

At the opening of the eighteenth century two of the professions were in an interesting transition stage with regard to differentiation and social status. Throughout all the colonies it was customary for litigants to be represented in court by attorneys in fact, but there was a strong feeling against attorneys at law, not seldom leading to statutes inimical to their pursuing their calling. This was true even in Maryland, where they rose to prominence earlier than in any other colony. In 1700, and perhaps down to the Revolution, there was scarcely a single well-educated colonial lawyer in all New England or, with a few brilliant exceptions, in New York. In the period 1690–1713, the Marylander Andrew Hamilton, who became attorney general in Pennsylvania and whose later reputation was to become not only intercolonial but international, was first rising into prominence. The Welshman David Lloyd was also doing much in the Quaker colony to develop its crude legislation into a system of jurisprudence. At the beginning of the century, however, there was neither large fortune nor high fame to be won at the bar. Consequently that absence of specialization which is characteristic of all colonial life at this period is noticeable here as elsewhere. In Connecticut, for example, attorneys at law seem to have been first authorized in 1708, and such men as Roger Wolcott, Thomas

Welles, and Edward Bulkeley were admitted to the bar, but Bulkeley's grist and fulling mills were his primary concern, and the law occupied but little of the time of the others. In Virginia, William Fitzhugh had received a professional training in England and practiced actively after coming to America, but his wealth and social standing were derived rather from his occupations as merchant, shipper, and planter than from his legal work.

The period we are considering was one of transition in the medical profession as in so many other phases of colonial life. In New England it had early been the custom of the clergy to minister to the bodily as well as the spiritual ills of the parish and to apply mustard or hell fire according to the need. To the southward, the owners of large plantations included the care of their slaves, servants, and poorer neighbors in their multifarious duties, and everywhere the women of the households practiced the simpler forms of physic. Nevertheless, physicians who occupied themselves either mainly or wholly with their profession were becoming numerous.

If we can judge from the bills of a certain Dr. John King down in the Albermarle, the physicians in the Carolinas did not do badly, as he seems to have charged ten shillings a visit. In 1702 a resident of Germantown wrote to Germany that a "student of medicine that well understands surgery . . . should find rich rewards of his money as soon as he had mastered the English language," and in the same year a traveler in Virginia reported that "doctors and surgeons are well-to-do and have a large income."[5] A decade earlier a doctor had been referred to in the latter colony as "a considerable dealer here and an able Practitioner in Physick, both laudable and profitable employs."[6] The more eminent men, however, seem to have been less well satisfied. Not long after their respective arrivals in Boston and New York, Dr. William Douglass wrote to Dr. Cadwallader Colden that "you complain of the practice of Physick being undervalued in your parts and with reason; we are not much better in that respect in this place; we abound with Practitioners though no other graduates than myself."[7] "I have here practice," he wrote in another letter, "amongst four sorts of People; some families pay me five pounds per annum each for advice, sick or well, some few fee me as in Britain, but for the Native New Englanders I am obliged to keep a daybook of my consultations, advice and Visits, and bring them in a bill; others the poorer sort I advise and visit without expectation of any fees."[8] Although we still find frequently the combination of the pursuits of clergyman, planter, farmer, lawyer, and various political offices such as sheriff with medicine, nevertheless the physician is clearly beginning to emerge as an independent entity and, at least in the case of men who were particularly successful, to occupy a social position of some eminence due solely to success in his profession.

The clergyman had always done so, though his established position varied much in the different colonies, and had been highest in New England. There, indeed, Cotton Mather was beginning to note mournfully how times had changed since the people used to regard their ministers as "Angels of God" and how reverently they had formerly wished to have them provided for.[9] At the end of the century he was right in believing that conditions were altering and that many things had combined to lower the prestige enjoyed by the clergy. In the South, although there were, of course, many earnest men in the church, nevertheless, it was too often considered in England that an inferior type was good enough to send out to the colonies, and in many a parish the cloth received no more respect than it deserved. In the Puritan colonies of the North, the first fervor of religious enthusiasm had long since evaporated, and the growth of other interests tended to dislodge the ministers from the remarkable position of leadership which they had occupied.

In all the colonies, land and ever more land was the goal of those who wished to advance in the most rapid way possible both their financial and social position. For this, influence in the right quarter was absolutely essential. For the acquisition of a rapid fortune in land merely by standing well with the powers that be, New York, in particular, offered a rich field. Among Governor Fletcher's grants, for example, was one to his favorite and right-hand man, Captain John Evans, of an area of indeterminate extent of between 350,000 and 600,000 acres, at a quitrent of only twenty shillings a year for the whole, for which Evans alleged he was later offered £10,000 in England. Bellomont indeed asserted that nearly three quarters of the available land in the province had been granted to about thirty persons, many of poor character, before Fletcher finished. Lord Cornbury's grants while governor from 1702 to 1708 were equally extravagant but were made to companies of speculators rather than to individuals. They included such grants as that of the "Little Nine Partners" of 90,900 acres, Wawayanda of 356,000, and Great Hardenburgh of 2 million acres, and were so loosely worded that sometimes the original intention as it appeared was so stretched as to result in claims of a hundred times the original acreage. In the Southern colonies, more particularly Maryland and Virginia, political influence resulted in enormous grants to favored individuals, such as 60,000 acres to Charles Carroll, and there were large grants in Carolina, in addition to the "Baronies," of 12,000 acres each. The same influence which secured the grants also resulted in many cases in evading completely the payment of quitrents.

Vast estates and political preferment enabled the aristocrats to lead a life of very considerable charm. In many of its outward and visible trappings, however, it was as yet set off from the life of the somewhat less fortunate members of the community to only a moderate degree, as compared with a generation later. The contrast in size and type of dwellings, for example, was modest as compared with the period after 1720 when the introduction of the Georgian style and the increase of wealth permitted the building of the "great houses" both north and south. The architecture of the well-to-do was still strictly "colonial." It was of the type which had been known to the settlers in their native lands, occupied there by people of similar standing, and modified by the new local conditions.

In New England about 1700 the old type of lean-to, with its long sloping rear roof, tended to give place to one of full two stories. Brick was used to some extent in such towns as Boston where an unsympathetic observer noted that "the Buildings like their Women" are "Neat and Handsome, and their Streets like the Hearts of their Male Inhabitants, are Paved with Pebble." [10] Brick was rarely used in the country, however, and stone practically never, the lack of good lime, as well as the belief that such houses were not suited to the climate, acting as deterrents. The better class houses were clapboarded, with shingle roofs, unpainted and severely plain. In those which did not wander off into little additions and afterthoughts, beauty was a matter of proportion only. In the Dummer house, erected in 1715, we get one of the earliest hints of the coming change to Georgian, just at the close of our period. This house was built for a wealthy family and gives us an idea of what a "modern" mansion for a New Englander of position was at that date. It is perfectly rectangular, two stories and an attic, with five windows in front, two in the gable ends, and three dormers in the attic. There is no porch, a feature rarely met with in this period, but the new elaborateness of the ornamentation of the doorway must have given it distinction in its day. In our own time, it might be the home of a small farmer in comfortable circumstances.

In the Middle colonies, the styles were markedly influenced by the nationalities of the builders, and Dutch, Welsh, Germans, and Swedes have left fascinating traces of their work and national predilections. Stone and colonial-made brick were both much used, and in the little town of New York many of the houses were placed gable end to the narrow streets, some "very stately and high" with bricks of various colors laid in checkers. In the country the use of varied materials and the low sweeping roofs lent a charm and struck a note of appealing domesticity. The larger houses were merely larger, for the most part, and in no way aimed at grandeur or flaunted the superior wealth of their inmates. Such survivals as the Welsh "Wynnestay" in Philadelphia or the German "Wyck" at Germantown, both dating from about 1690, and precursors of what is known as the Pennsylvania colonial farmhouse type, bespeak the excellent craftsmanship of their builders and the solid comfort of their indwellers. There is an utter absence of pretension or of aim at effect which is characteristic of all the architecture of the period. Throughout all the North few of even the largest houses could boast of more than eight rooms.

In the Southern colonies this would also seem to have been true of most of those owned even by the wealthiest planters, although none of the largest houses of authentic date in this period have been preserved. The difference in climate, however, largely influenced the architecture in many minor ways. The chimneys, which in New England were built wholly within the house to keep in as much heat as possible, were placed at the ends in the South, just as the entry hall which in the North was small with the stairway frequently enclosed to prevent drafts, was broad and open in the South, tending to become a feature in the building. William Fitzhugh, speaking of his own house, which he described in 1686 as "furnished with all accommodations for a comfortable and gentile living," said of the rooms that "four of the best of them" were "hung and nine of them plentifully furnished with all things necessary and convenient." [11] The kitchen was in a separate building and there were numerous outhouses of various sorts.

The smaller houses were frequently, if not generally, of wood, but the larger ones after 1700 were almost invariably of brick, usually colonial-made but occasionally imported. In one respect the houses of the aristocrats were no better than the log huts of the pioneers—there was no plumbing. Sanitary arrangements were of the simplest, and baths must have been of the scantiest. Tubs for that purpose were unknown in America for a century and a half after our period, and even large vessels are disconcertingly absent. In the summer, the young men and boys went swimming and the number reported drowned while thus "washing," as it was often called, was not inconsiderable. There is no record of feminine bathing.

Such mansions as those spoken of above marked the very summit attained by wealth in the colonies at this time, and although the contrast was not as striking as that to be noted later, they were beginning to afford one to the houses of the poor and the pioneers which we shall note in the next chapter. This contrast extended to the furnishing with the same qualification. When the first William Byrd was building "Westover" in 1690—not the beautiful "Westover" of thirty years later but the first house which marked his advancing fortunes—he ordered his correspondent in Rotterdam to send him bedsteads, curtains, looking-glasses, tables, some Russian leather chairs, and other furnishings, which he noted with quite a New England spirit of frugality were "to be handsome and neat but cheap." [12] This importing of household gear was characteristic of all those, North and South, who had the wealth to do so, though the furniture was of English rather than of Dutch origin. From the cabinetmakers of London went forth a steady stream of beautiful pieces—desks, highboys, chests, chairs, bedsteads—in oak, walnut, olive wood, lacquer, or marquetry to the houses of the rich in all the colonies. The introduction of mahogany just at this time was to prove of marked influence on the style of eighteenth-century furniture, its strength permitting more delicate, even lacelike, carving, and from 1708 onward we find these new pieces taking their places somewhat slowly in company with the older ones in luxurious homes. With the beginning of the century also, china began to replace pewter on the tables, and as another indication of the refining of manners, forks, which had been laughed at as little instruments "to make hay with our mouths," came at last into general use among the genteel. Self-indulgent comfort was also increasing, and from about 1700 we can date the substitution of the upholstered wing "easy" chair for the somewhat Spartan wood or hard leather seats.

The furnishing of the homes of the rich and even the merely well-to-do at this time was indeed not only comfortable and in excellent taste but even extravagant. On the Tooboodoe Plantation of Joseph Morton in South Carolina, the inventory at the time of his death in 1723 shows the furniture in the "best chamber" as worth £195, that in the dining room as £126, in the parlor as £135, and in the other rooms to correspond. His linen was worth £217 and his silver plate £600. The last, of course, was not merely for ostentation but was generally considered as an investment or, as William Fitzhugh wrote to his London correspondent, it "gives myself the present use and credit, is a sure friend at a dead lift without much loss or is a portion for a child after my decease." [13]

Except in the very greatest houses, the small number of rooms still precluded too rigid a differentiation as to use, and we not infrequently find beds inventoried in halls in the South and in parlors in the North. The bed, indeed, both as to its high massive carved frame and costly hangings, and the feather mattress and pillows, was one of the most valued possessions in the house. Springs for the beds, it may be noted, were unknown until well into the nineteenth century. Carpets had not yet come into use for floor coverings and the "Turkey carpets" so often inventoried were merely table covers. Nor was wallpaper introduced until the next period, but in the houses of the very rich the walls were hung with tapestry, frequently of considerable value.

Perhaps the most striking visible contrast between moneyed and poor was the richness of the costume of the former. As the opulent or well-to-do gentleman walked abroad, his clothes proclaimed aloud his bulging money-bags or broad lands. They were advertised equally by golden-laced hats, powdered wigs, patches on the cheeks of the younger dandies, brilliantly colored coats, velvet or satin waistcoats, silver buckles and buttons, silken hose, and silver- or gold-headed canes. The ladies followed close upon the latest London fashions, which, indeed, were said to reach the colonies sooner than the outlying counties at home, and the deep maroons, brilliant blues, flaming scarlets, silver and golden embroideries, and cascades of creamy lace used by both sexes make our modern assemblies drab by comparison, and this was as true of Puritan New England and Quaker Pennsylvania as of the supposedly more worldly colonies.

Breakfast was usually a light meal, more so in the Southern than in the Northern colonies, and was frequently not taken until nine o'clock, but it was a period of heavy eating and yet more heavy drinking. There were no kitchen ranges, and all the innumerable dishes had to be prepared by the open fire on the enormous hearth. Kettles sometimes held a dozen or more

Elegance in mid-century Virginia.

An early eighteenth century room in Rhode Island; the home of a prosperous merchant.

gallons, and iron pots weighed forty pounds, yet the task of preparing a dinner in a large household was as complicated for the number of dishes on the menu as it was arduous for the mere quantity of food. Sometimes a half-dozen different kinds of meat alone would appear, as the tripe, pork, beef, turkey, mutton, and chickens served to Lord Cornbury, and this seems to have been the rule, at least for a meal of any formality. Most of the vegetables and fruits of the old country were grown here and served on the tables of the rich. Almonds, cloves, cinnamon, currants, figs, ginger, nutmeg, pepper, raisins, and salt were imported, and the herb garden yielded many of the ingredients called for by the recipes of the day. These appeared in printed form but even more frequently in the manuscript volumes kept by careful housewives, such as that of Mary Doggett in which are jumbled together methods of making "cowslip wine," "fine cakes of lemons," "drinks to cause sleep," "Lemon Creame," "orange Biskett," "cheese cakes of oranges," "to candy double marygold, roses, and other flowers," "to perfume gloves after the Spanish manner," and how "to souse a pigg."[14] Desserts and sweets of all sorts were without number in the richer households, but that American favorite, ice cream, seems to have come only with the next generation, when a traveler reports it as being served with strawberries and milk as a novel rarity at the governor's house in Annapolis.[15]

The favorite nonalcoholic beverage was chocolate, though coffee was used, and the first notice of the newly introduced tea appears just at the close of the period in 1714. With the eighteenth century, rum became an increasingly favorite drink in New England, as beer was in the Middle colonies, but wines of several sorts were always on the tables of the rich. Madeira, canary, claret, burgundy, port, brandy, and champagne were all imported, and—more particularly in the Southern colonies—the cherries, peaches, and other fruits were all made into "flings" or "bounces" or brandies. Madeira, however, was the most popular of all and the foundation of a considerable trade. In the matter of drunkeness there was no difference observable between the classes or colonies, and not seldom as much liquor was consumed in the ordination of a minister in New England as at a barbecue in the South, while the velvet-coated dandy slipped under the table no less readily than the leather-jerkined plowman.[16] In smoking there was probably more distinction, for although all men smoked, the use of tobacco by women seems to have been mainly confined to the less aristocratic. Ward said of those in New England that they "smoke in Bed, Smoke as they nead their Bread, Smoke whilst they're Cooking," and although he is not always a trustworthy reporter there is other evidence for the frequent indulgence by women.[17]

In regard to the influence of New World life upon women, we may note that in the case of those of the first generation of immigrants, the transplanting had the effect which change to a new environment with new problems always has in quickening the action of mind to meet them. The conditions of life in a new country also tend to raise woman's position owing to her greater economic service and to the simple arithmetical fact that there are not enough to go round as wives. In a number of ways she attained a somewhat more independent status in America in the eighteenth century. Her property rights were greater in a number of the colonies than in England, as were rights of inheritance in case of intestacy. She was freer to move about without male escort or a chaperon of her own sex.

Yet in many respects, life for a woman changed little. Her work on both sides of the Atlantic was the same—running the household. Of the special trials and work of the poorer and pioneer women we shall speak briefly in the next section, but for all of them, rich and poor, the sphere of duty remained the same, nor was the door of opportunity opened much wider. For the aristocratic woman, the only career was that of wife and mother, which she did not attempt to evade, but performed with consummate grace and skill. Though her servants were frequently numerous, her duties were multifarious, either as the wife of a prosperous businessman of the North or planter in the South. There she often lived an isolated life on a plantation, where not seldom, she looked after herself during widowhood or the absence of her husband. Enough contemporary travelers, particularly in the south, comment upon the superior industry, ability, and attractiveness of the women, especially of the lower classes, to the men to cause us even this early to analyze a phenomenon which many have considered not limited to the eighteenth century. Possibly this is to be connected with what we have said as to the effect of colonial life with reference to strengthening the solidarity of the home, and that in this respect life under colonial conditions tended to bring out a woman's finer characteristics, whereas in many cases the new conditions of men's lives tended to have a contrary effect upon them.

For them the uprooting of their lives in emigrating wrought a far more complete change, and, in the winter particularly, time must have hung rather heavily on the hands of those of the richer class. The small farmer and the pioneer had their innumerable daily chores and, in addition, winter was the time when much of the household manufacture was carried on of tools, furniture, and apparel. But the wealthy town-dwelling merchant, the land speculator, the hanger-on of official circles in the North, or the planter in the South whose overseer looked after many of the details of management, must have suffered not a little boredom with its consequences. As we shall see later, there were not a few men in all sections who loved and possessed books—John Locke, for example, found his way to many library tables—but after all the number who care for the things of the mind are always in the minority in any age and place.

Again, although the ways of life in the old country had been reproduced in many points, there had been nevertheless a break with established custom and hereditary duties. By 1700 the country had been settled in part for three generations but society was still in an inchoate state. Many of the newly rich men had come, as it were, but yesterday. Capital which they had brought with them, a few years of lucky trafficking, privateering or piracy, a grant of an estate due to influence with the governor or in England had founded their fortunes. The relations which the grantee of a tract of 10,000 acres bore to those whom he settled on his land, the relations of a planter to his slaves or of a farmer or a merchant to the servants whose time he bought, the relations of everyone, in fact, to one another had little of that traditional mutual obligation which was one of the morally valuable elements in feudalism and which still to a considerable degree survived in England.

The possibilities of the limitless resources of the new land offered rich prizes to audacity. In spite of the aristocratic tendencies of the older families, the man who suddenly acquired wealth and stood well with the governor could not long be resisted in communities so small that such a man became at once a leading figure. In England not only was wealth accumulated more slowly in most cases, but even its acquisition did not bring to its new possessor the sudden social transformation which it did in America. Thus, on the one hand, the absence of the traditional relationships binding together the various elements in society, and, on the other, the opportunities for exploitation, and the results of economic success, all combined to make of the successful American a businessman rather than a genuine aristocrat and to give a marked individualism to his outlook.

At the time of the signing of the Treaty of Utrecht in 1713, his position was unusually alluring. The colonial population had grown sufficiently to give stability to the older settlements and was increasing so rapidly as to assure markets for goods and lands in the future. The political and social framework had become set enough in form to enable him to count with some certainty upon the lines within which he could work out his plans and career. The routes and methods of commerce were established and the resources of the country had become known. Colonial capital, also, had begun to accumulate. There were not many, perhaps, who had done so well as Robert Carter of Virginia who, when he died in 1722, was said to have left 300,000 acres of land, 1,000 slaves, and £10,000 in money, but fortunes of from £5,000 to £15,000 were not infrequent all along the seaboard. That colonial capital was seeking investment is sufficiently indicated by the fact that by 1720, if not before, South Sea stock, bank stocks, lotteries, and annuities in London were quoted regularly in New York. With the end of the war and the prospect of some years of peace, the outlook offered glowing opportunities to the rich American. His surroundings thus already tended to make him a little more daring than his cousin at home, a little more optimistic, a little more individualistic, a little more preoccupied with the problem, not so much of getting rich as of getting rich with the utmost possible speed.

THE COMMON MAN, 1690-1713

ALTHOUGH THE "ARISTOCRATS" exerted great influence, they were, numerically, small compared with the total population. Economically, societies are
always like a pyramid, and the mass of men at the opening of the eighteenth
century was composed of those who had made only a moderate success or
none at all in the art and practice of living. Outside the select group of the
mercantile and landed "aristocracy" were the smaller merchants, shopkeepers, farmers, planters, artisans, mechanics, pioneers, fishermen, free
day laborers, indented servants, and slaves.

Although the "gentlemen" drew sharp distinctions, not seldom legal,
between these smaller fry and themselves, they could hardly be accused of
snobbishness by the farmers, tradesmen, and others who in turn insisted
just as rigidly upon distinctions among themselves. In fact, perhaps, snobbishness has never been more rampant anywhere in America than it was in
the small Puritan villages of New England, where it received an added and
ugly twist of Pharisaism. This came out most clearly in the meticulous
measurement of the personal and social qualifications of every member of
a congregation before he or she could be assigned a sitting in church. Age,
estate, "place and qualification" were weighed with the utmost care to
determine the conflicting claims to precedence of the various small farmers
who made up the bulk of every rural village. Infinite were the rulings giving
each seat its specific social rank, such as that the "fore seat in the front
gallery shall be equal in dignity with the second seat in the body," the front
seats in the gallery with the fourth seats in the body, and so forth, as was
painstakingly worked out in Deerfield even while facing annihilation by the
Indians. Not infrequently the settlement of such vexed questions, when
disputed, was referred to the town meeting for decision. On the other
hand, within the households of the tradesmen or small farmers there was
little of that distinction between master and man or mistress and maid,
which developed later. Indeed, when crossing Connecticut, Madam Knight
was somewhat scandalized to find the farmers were equally indulgent to
the black slaves, "permitting them to sit at table and eat with them (as they
say to save time), and into the dish goes the black hoof as freely as the
white hand." [18]

Immediately below the "aristocrats" were the richer town merchants or
planters who had not yet fully arrived in a social sense but whose wealth
and general position placed them between those above them and the
smaller people of the descending economic scale. There was nothing essentially characteristic of them as a class, setting them off from others; here
we are concerned with those still lower for whom the New World offered
special opportunities, and with those lower yet for whom it offered none.

Although luxury, of course, was limited to the wealthy, there was ample comfort for those who were able to do moderately well for themselves. The small shopkeeper or tradesman of the towns and the farmer or planter of the rural districts were well housed, clothed, and fed. As was pointed out earlier, their houses differed as yet in little but size from those of the ranks above them. The materials of which they were built were, in most colonies, the same, although from 1700 there tended to be a distinction in the South, as we have noted. Within, of course, there was a noticeable difference. Pictures were naturally absent from the walls of the more modest homes. The several fireplaces of the rich were represented by the one great one in the poor man's kitchen. Although occasionally pieces of furniture might be found that had crossed the ocean, most, when not all, of the furnishing was colonial-made, if not, indeed, made by the owner himself and his family.

In fact, such a household, particularly in the country, was self-sustaining to a remarkable degree. A few things, like the iron pots in the kitchen, the pieces of pewter—if the household boasted of them—the materials for the best clothes, a few of the necessities for the table, such as salt, came from outside but otherwise almost every article consumed or worn was the produce of the farm or the immediate neighborhood. The beef and bacon came from the owner's cows and hogs, slaughtered in the fall and salted down. The former also supplied his leather. The wool, which the women of the household carded and wove and spun, was from the sheep of his own fields. The cider was pressed from his own apples. The winter's fuel was from the woods of his own woodlots or the village commons. The candles were made from tallow, produce of the farm, or from bayberries gathered by the children. The clothes worn by the entire household were frequently made by the women and even sometimes by the men. During the long days of winter, the men and boys fashioned the wooden farm implements, made innumerable utensils for the kitchen, or built and carved and painted the beds, chests, and chairs that slowly filled the rooms and added to comfort.

In the diaries kept by such men at this period we get a vivid impression, even from their extremely brief entries, of varied duties and manifold abilities. For example, in that of Manasseh Minor of Stonington, Connecticut, from 1696 to 1720, we find such entries as "I went a fishin to naraganset," "I mad Els coat," "Thomas begun to mak shoes," "I gelt lambs," "the whole town worked at the highways," "I help make Watson's coat," and others showing him as shearing sheep, hunting wolves, attending town meetings, making different pieces of furniture, training with the militia, carting hay, traveling on one errand or another to Rhode Island, Fisher's Island, New London, and Boston, and on one day, "I went to preson."[19] The diary of another Connecticut man, Joshua Hempstead, which begins in this same period, shows him leading an incredibly active life as farmer, sailor, trader, carpenter, shipbuilder, stonemason, surveyor, and lawyer.

Like Minor, he was continually moving about within a considerable field on his various activities. This multifold life was common to most of the small farmers throughout all the colonies.

The clothing of this class was in marked contrast to that of their wealthy neighbors. With the exception of a better suit for church or other high occasions, it was mostly made of coarse heavy cloths, such as "ozenbrig," which we find constantly in use throughout the whole eighteenth century. The skins of animals, particularly deer, were much used as furs and as tanned leather. Leather breeches, indeed, sometimes adorned even the legs of ministers in New England for their rougher work, and when the Reverend Mr. Buckingham went as chaplain with the expedition against Port Royal in 1710 he took such a pair with him. The stockings were heavy woolens and were worn to the knee as a rule, but in summer both these and shoes were discarded even by men and women throughout the rural sections. In Pennsylvania a writer noted that they could be worn only in the evening, and that by day the only costume of the men was a shirt and "thin long pantaloons which reach down to the feet."[20] In the far South, the black children went naked and the men wore only a loincloth when working in the fields. However, the passing of sumptuary laws prescribing the economic or social position requisite for the wearing of clothes of certain materials or cost shows that there was a constant tendency on the part of the poorer people, particularly in the towns, to adorn themselves more elegantly, and to copy the fashions of those who could better afford them. The love of finery is also indicated by the frequent offering of silk stockings or other articles of dress as prizes at the country fairs.

Food was simple but abundant. The West India sugar of the rich was replaced in the poorer households by that from the maple tree or by honey, and butter seems to have been a luxury only for the wealthy. In New England, for those of moderate means, including the clergy, both breakfast and supper were often composed only of bread and milk. The produce of their own fields, the fish from nearby waters, or game from the forests ensured a plentiful supply, though little variety. There was no ice for preserving food in summer, the spring house taking the place of the ice box, and in winter salted meats or fish had to serve. Cider and rum in the North, beer in the Middle colonies, and homemade drinks of one sort and another in the South replaced the imported wines of the rich, though wine was drunk in America by classes that could not have afforded it in England.

Farther out on the frontier of all the colonies conditions of every sort were, of course, much more primitive, even the costume changed and the use of the Indian hunting shirt was general. Indeed, in the later years of the Indian wars many of the younger pioneers adopted more of the native dress, making the leggings longer so as to reach over the thigh and replacing drawers with the Indian loincloth. On account of their costume the frontiersmen were called "buckskins" and it is a fact of no little significance regarding the relations between tidewater and frontier that the residents of the former used the term as one of obloquy.

The first shelters erected by the frontiersmen were merely temporary and need not be described, but the permanent homes were log cabins, usually about sixteen feet by twenty, and when done by community labor took only two or three days to build. The type scarcely varied either in different localities or decades, and Byrd has described it for us in southern Virginia at the time of surveying the boundary line between that colony and North Carolina in 1728. "Most of the Houses of this Part of the Country" he wrote, "are Log-Houses covered with Pine or Cypress Shingles, 3 feet long and one broad. They are hung upon Laths with Peggs, and their doors too turn upon wooden Hinges, and have wooden Locks to secure them, so that the building is finished without Nails or other Iron-Work." [21] In most places the shingles would have been considered luxurious, the chinks between the logs being filled only with mud and moss and plastered over with clay. The doors and windows were sawed out after the logs were laid, and there was no glass for the latter. When there was any covering at all for the windows, other than solid shutters, it was paper smeared with hog's lard or bear's grease. Light in the evenings came only from the blaze on the hearth or from pine knots which served as candles.

Sometimes there was a small room above the main one below, reached by a few slats fastened against the wall. When one passed from a mere dirt floor to the next stage of luxury it was to broad slabs laid on the ground. The furniture was equally primitive, a section of tree trunk or a slab on three legs for chairs and a longer slab for the table. The bed, fastened against the wall, was a mere bunk or low shelf.

In one place where Byrd stopped, he says that "there was a dirty poor house, with hardly anything in it but children, that wallow'd about like so many pigs," and in another he had to sleep with ten or more people "forct to pig together in a Room . . . troubled with the Squalling of peevish, dirty children into the Bargain." [22] In fact, for a very considerable part of the population conditions must have closely approximated those obtaining today among the first generation of immigrants, such as the "Polacks" who take up abandoned farms in the East, or others whose standards of living we consider so totally "un-American." There was the same fierce and sordid struggle to obtain a foothold so as to secure the means of subsistence, the same squalor and dirt, the same annual addition to the number of children and the same working of women and children at field labor. Of the wife of one frontiersman we read in the contemporary account of a visitor that "she is a very civil woman and shows nothing of ruggedness or Immodesty in her carriage, yett she will carry a gunn in the woods and kill deer, turkeys, etc., shoot doun wild cattle, catch and tye hoggs, knock down beeves with an ax and perform the most manfull Exercises." [23]

How young the children were when set to hard physical toil we do not know, but when Deerfield was threatened by the Indians in 1703 the minister reported that they no longer dared to allow the youngsters under twelve to work in the fields for fear of the Indians. Evidently, therefore, they were set to work earlier than that and a child of twelve was considered not only capable of heavy labor but of performing it in the face of possible Indian attack. When the era of land speculation set in, it was the toils and dangers of such people as these that gave the speculators their profits, and these heroic, if often squalid and uncouth, figures should be traced on the reverse of that tapestry on the other and brilliant side of which are the gay and attractive figures of gentlemen and ladies in satin and brocade in houses where the light of abundant candles set in silver flickered across many a treasured portrait of today.

Still farther beyond this frontier region, which already lay behind the older settlements all the way from New England to the Carolinas, was the shadowy border land of the Indian trader. As we have said earlier, the forest yet covered the entire land and if one could have looked down upon the Atlantic coast from the air, he would have seen an almost unbroken sweep of treetops from the sparkling waves of ocean westward, showing only here and there the glint of river and stream and the clearings of occasional solitary farms or, more seldom, the larger ones of village or town. But this forest, more and more being threaded with trails and narrow roads, was tenanted and known. Beyond the last fringe of settlement, however, the traders plunged into the depths of primeval woods where, except for themselves, there were no inhabitants but the Indians and those wild animals whose skins were the object of their quest. There, far beyond the habitation of the hardiest pioneer, the traders built their "trucking house" or trading post where they stored their guns, ammunition, duffels, blankets, rum, and other articles which they exchanged for beaver and other skins.

To return to the settlements, we have still to consider those who ranked below the shopkeepers and small farmers: that is, indented servants and slaves. Almost every observer agrees as to the scarcity of free white labor. Nevertheless, in the older settled portions of the colonies there must have been a considerable number of those who had to work for wages and yet who did not wish to sell themselves as indented servants for a term of years. In the town of Newbury, Massachusetts, for example, a list of heads of families shows that, out of 269, twenty-seven possessed no land, and of these one had only one cow, one had two cows, and a third had a horse. The remaining twenty-four had no property of any kind. Ten percent of the heads of families in that village must therefore have been wage-earners and to these may be added such younger members of their households as were not serving as apprentices. Mere reference to artisans of various sorts means nothing in this connection, for they may have been either indented servants or free, but other references indicate that however scarce such wage-earners may have been, they, nevertheless, were everywhere present.

It may well have been that such a class was not recruited to any great extent from immigration at the opening of the century, but it must have received more or less constant accretions both from above and below in the colonial population. Contemporary observers agree that there was comparatively little extreme poverty in any of the colonies at this time, but the occasional laws for the relief of debtors, the frequent ones regarding poor relief, and the constantly expressed fear lest the poor become heavy charges on the communities, all indicate that there was more or less poverty in spite of optimistic descriptions. The obstacles thrown in the way of the poor taking up residence in a town, so that they might not become entitled to poor relief, must have tended to sink them lower where they had already begun to fall. Certainly all poverty was not limited to the frontier, and as an example of what might be found even on the Boston Post Road we have a description by Madam Knight of a household near the Pawcatuck River. The building was made "with Clapboards, laid in Lengthways, and so much asunder, that the Light came throu' everywhere; the doors tyed with a cord in the place of hinges; the floar the bear earth; no windows but such as the thin covering afforded, nor any furniture but a Bedd . . . an earthen Cupp, a small pewter Bason, a Bord with sticks to stand on, instead of a table and a block or two in the corner instead of chairs." Yet these were not shiftless people, for she adds that "bothe the Hutt and its Inhabitants were very clean and tydee: to the crossing of the Old Proverb, that bare walls make giddy Howswifes." [24]

In a note that shows one phase of the possibilities attending emigration, a traveler in Pennsylvania writes that "well-to-do people and such as cannot perform manual labor, but have all their work done by paying for it, can easily become poor in a few years—yea even fall into the greatest misery. The reason for this is that the days' wages are so excessively high, and help is occasionally not even to be obtained for money. . . . We have here, as I am told by a trustworthy party, cases where people who came to this country with much money and wanted to establish large plantations, were forced to relinquish them to their day laborers to whom they were indebted, and go away themselves empty handed." [25] Under the conditions of life for those with little accumulated capital, the mere maintaining of a neat and comfortable home required unremitting work, no little ability, and strong character. America was no place for the idle, the weak, or the sick.

If misfortune or lack of ability thus added recruits to the wage-earning class from above, it must also have been receiving constant accretions from below. The great servant-importing provinces were Pennsylvania, Maryland, and Virginia, but the need and desire for such servants in the North were great, and in Massachusetts, in 1710, the legislature passed an act offering a bounty of forty shillings a head to any ship captain who would bring into the colony any male servants from eight to twenty-five years of age. In Maryland, the proportion of indented servants and convict laborers to the entire population seems to have remained fairly constant at about 9 percent, but as the figures for servants include practically no small children, whereas these are included in the population figures, the proportion of servants to all adults in the colony would be much greater, perhaps 25 percent.[26] As the average period of servitude was five years, one fifth of the servant class, or 5 percent of the total adult population, was passing annually from that status to the one of free whites. Of these, some, for one reason or another, reentered upon a new period of servitude and others became landowners, but a very large proportion must have become wage-earners. The fifty acres of land which in many of the colonies were given as a "head-right," that is, fifty acres for every servant brought into the colony, inhered in the person importing the servant and not in the servant himself. It is therefore a mistake to think that on completion of his or her term of service the servant at once and automatically entered upon the status of freeholder. The indenture usually called only for clothes, a little ready money, and an ax or hoe. It was, however, not difficult for the new freedman to acquire the fifty acres upon application if he so desired. The instructions to the governors of North Carolina, for example, from 1667 to 1681, required them to grant to freed servants fifty acres, and this was occasionally done as late as 1737. The same instructions were issued to the governor of Virginia and probably complied with. In Maryland the old system of granting the importer of servants the fifty acres per head was abolished in 1683 and thereafter all land was sold, but there seems to have been no case in which the freed servant did not receive the fifty acres if he demanded them.

In several ways the position of the indented servant was altered during this period. The change in the Maryland law just noted put an end to the connection between the importing of servants and the acquisition of land, and thereafter the servant became a mere article of traffic like the slave, imported by captain or merchant and sold to the planter. This did not alter his condition for the worse perhaps, for merchants and large landowners had thus imported them for some time, and they continued to form part of the stock in trade of such men as Colonel Byrd all through the colonial period. In a number of the colonies several laws, such as those of 1705 in Virginia and of 1715 in Maryland and North Carolina, were passed around this time, tending materially to improve the legal position held by the servant and to ameliorate his social condition. Contemporary descriptions of what that may have been vary widely, and undoubtedly the real position varied just as widely in the individual households or plantations where the servant may have been employed. Examination of court records indicates that his rights were upheld with considerable fairness whenever they came up for judicial decision. This was rendered easier in Virginia by the law of 1705, which gave servants the right to bring complaints against their masters into court on petition only and without formal process of an action. By the same act, any contract for further service between him and his master or any matter relating to his personal liberty could be entered into only in the presence of a county court. Laws were also passed limiting corporal punishment and to some extent placing it under court supervision, although in the early part of the century such punishment tended more and more to be replaced by fines.

Beginning with this period, however, although the servant was gaining in legal rights, he was, speaking broadly, losing in social position. Throughout all the colonies, the increase in wealth and the growing distinctions between those who possessed it and those who did not tended to lower the servant's position as compared with the previous century when all alike were more under the leveling influence of the frontier. In Maryland, the increase in the number of convicts shipped by the British government brought the indented class in general more and more into disrepute, a condition affecting all the colonies to a lesser degree. In those in the south, however, the factor which operated most to lower the position of the white servant, as well as of the white landless wage-earner, was the enormous increase in the number of black slaves in that section which began in this period. Up to about 1700 the great majority of the laboring class had undoubtedly been indented servants with a smaller number of free wage-earners on the one hand and Indian or black slaves on the other. From that time on the slave for life rapidly tended to displace the indented servant and free white wage-earner in the colonies from Maryland southward and to differentiate that section economically and socially from the North.

With regard to enslaving the Indians, New England had early taken the lead and throughout the colonial period held more Indians in slavery than any of the other colonies except South Carolina, where, in 1708, there were 1,400 Indian slaves against 4,100 blacks. As late as 1706, Massachusetts provided for the sale of Indian children under twelve years of age taken in war. With the chartering of the Royal African Company in 1672, however, the traffic in blacks had entered upon a more active stage. The greatest demand came from the sugar islands, where the blacks soon outnumbered the whites several times, and it was probably the very close connection between South Carolina and the West Indies, as well as the nature of its crop, which caused that colony early to become a leader in the use of black slave labor. By 1715, with a white population of 6,200, there were over 10,000 black slaves there, a much more rapid increase than in any other colony. In the same year it is estimated that there were 23,000 blacks in Virginia with a white population of a little more than 72,000, and in Maryland, three years earlier, 8,000 blacks against 38,000 whites. In succeeding years the proportion of blacks rose rapidly and the type of agricultural labor under Southern conditions thus became definitely determined.

In some respects the black slave's position was similar to that of the indented servant. As the colonial system of labor based upon indentures was a development of the apprentice system, so was the system of slavery, in a way, a development of the indenture system, in which servitude was for life instead of for a fixed number of years. Although from one aspect slavery at first differed from white servitude, mainly in the mere extension of its period, the results of this extension were so great as gradually to alter the whole conception of the system and to change fundamentally the legal status and social position of the slave.

Although legislation from 1660 onward tended to define and somewhat to alter the status of blacks, it was only after they became numerous in proportion to the whites that we can trace the beginnings of the American system of slavery, and that was in the first decade of the eighteenth century. Even as late as 1698, although there were many slaves in all the colonies, they were not coming in more rapidly than white servants, and Governor Nicholson of Virginia advised the board of trade that 600 servants had recently been imported and that 400 or 500 blacks only were expected during the summer. The colonists, however, desired slaves, in the North mainly for house servants, and in the South for field labor also.

By 1700 there were many American-born blacks, but those constantly being brought over from Africa were unable to speak English and naturally rebellious at their new condition. As the numbers increased, the possibility of a general uprising against the whites or of the massacre of white families on isolated plantations was a real one. Even by 1712 in three of the southern counties of Virginia blacks outnumbered the white population, and throughout the early eighteenth century there were a number of attempted insurrections in several of the colonies, which kept the whites in terror. Moreover, along the entire border, until the Peace of 1713, there was the menace and often the presence of warfare with the Indians. The various acts passed by one colony and another, in the South as well as the North, during this period, and which were aimed at restricting the importation of additional blacks undoubtedly had their origin in the fear of their increased numbers. All these laws, however, were disallowed in England as interfering with a lucrative trade, the fostering of which was beginning to be one of the prime commercial concerns of the merchants of the mother country.

On the other hand, in spite of his dangers, the black unquestionably filled both an economic and social need of the colonists. The supply of domestic servants, either free or indented, was inadequate. In the South, white labor was not adapted to the cultivation of rice, which was rapidly becoming the leading source of wealth in Carolina. The development of large tobacco plantations depended upon the presence of a correspondingly large labor supply. So long as a planter was limited to tilling the soil himself with the help of only a few others, there was no possibility of rising above the grade of yeoman farmer. Although the economic development of America would have been impossible without the indented servant, nevertheless there were distinct drawbacks to that type. The first year was usually lost to the Southern employer while the newcomer was becoming acclimated. There was also the necessity of an annual turnover of a part of the labor owing to the fulfilling of the term contracted for and the impossibility of replacing the laborers thus lost except by a new importation from England. These conditions made the slave for life appear an attractive asset in spite of his drawbacks. The conflict of opinion on the part of employers is evidenced by the laws to hinder importation, which represented fear, and the continued purchase and demand, which represented economic necessity.

The former motive was also represented by domestic laws regarding blacks. Prior to 1692, for example, in Virginia, slaves accused of capital offenses had been entitled to the same procedure, including a jury, as whites, but by an act passed in that year the accused was to be tried immediately by persons designated by the sheriff, without jury, and the evidence of even one witness was held sufficient to convict. By the law of 1723, any number of blacks over five found guilty of conspiring together for murder were to be punished by death.

In Virginia, by the time of the codification of 1705, slavery had advanced sufficiently far from the conception of mere servitude to create the legal necessity for the fiction of considering the slave in some of his aspects not as a chattel but as real estate. Aside from the purely legal influences of this upon his condition, the mental influence was distinctly inimical to consideration of him as a man. In the earlier decades evidence indicates that although the English always showed more racial consciousness and prejudice than the French or Spanish, nevertheless, neither on that score nor on that of type of labor was there then any such impassable gulf between the races as developed later. Not only in the house but in the fields, white servant and black slave worked side by side, and the law frequently took note of cases where they absconded in company from their master's service. Slavery was not a legal status recognized in England and in its development in the colonies the distinction between those who must be free and those who might be enslaved was based upon that between Christian and heathen. As the seventeenth century drew to a close, however, legislation brought out clearly the new conception of racial inferiority rather than religious difference. By the Virginia act of 1682, Christianity was held not to confer freedom upon blacks, mulattoes, and such Indians as were sold by others as slaves. This was made even more severe, as was punishment for intercourse between the races, in the codification of 1705. That either the race prejudice against the black was becoming much stronger than against the Indian or the economic factor more determining, is indicated by the fact that in 1705 the term "mulatto" was legally held to include not only the children of mixed unions between whites and Indians but also the great-great-grandchildren of such connections with blacks. Miscegenation will be considered again but we may here note, in connection with the developing race prejudice, that it was legislated against in all the colonies, always with severer penalties for the black.

That the disabilities of the black were beginning to be racial and not merely due to his status as a slave in this period is also shown by the laws as to free blacks. In Maryland, for example, in 1717, it was enacted that no Indian, slave, free black, or mulatto servant could testify in cases concerning a white person. In 1705, in Virginia, blacks, mulattoes, and Indians were

Negro slavery in South Carolina made possible such great houses as Drayton Hall early in the century.

A little later, for like reason, the Georgian house appeared in Virginia—such as Mt. Airy (1758), "a composition in five parts."

forbidden to hold any civil, military, or ecclesiastical office, and in 1723 even suffrage was denied to free blacks, mulattoes, and Indians. In North Carolina, in 1715, the same three classes were excluded from voting, and in the same colony, the much later law of 1746 seems merely to have put in statutory form what had been the custom in part in this period of forbidding "negroes, mulattoes, bond and free to the third generation, and Indian servants and slaves" from testifying in cases involving white persons. To have continued to develop the fields of America by the use of white labor would have been a slow process. History is a matter too complex for us to remove one element and to picture what might have been the result. As a consequence, however, of attempting to exploit rapidly the illimitable resources of the American forests by the unlimited labor supply of the African jungles, we find already arising that "little cloud out of the sea, like a man's hand" that was later to overspread the heavens.

Having thus reviewed some of the main groups of colonial society in a rapidly descending scale, we may inquire what were the possibilities open to the colonist starting in any of these ranks to advance himself above it. The most hopeless position, of course, was that occupied by the slave. Following earlier laws passed in Maryland and Virginia, it was enacted by Massachusetts in 1698, Connecticut and New Jersey in 1704, Pennsylvania and New York in 1706, and South Carolina in 1712, that a child of a slave became himself a slave, thus apparently closing the avenue of escape for the future as well as the present. In the same period new laws were also passed which made manumission more difficult. Moreover, the slave could not legally own any property. Although in practice he was allowed to gather together some personal belongings and occasionally given a patch of ground which he might plant for himself, nevertheless, in spite of rare cases in which he made money enough to buy his freedom from a willing master or was manumitted for other reasons, the odds against this new recruit to civilization were too heavy, and there is no case during this period of a free black having achieved anything beyond the position of a wage-earner or the owner of a small farm with, very rarely, a slave of his own.

For the indented servant, the case was very different. He could look forward at the end of a few years to becoming free to work for himself, and practically no social disability seems to have been attached to his former period of servitude, which was merely a contractual relation entered into voluntarily by himself (with the exception of the convicts), usually as a means of defraying the cost of his emigration to America. When his contract time expired, he was therefore in the same position as any other freeman with little or no capital. For such there were ample opportunities depending upon ability and inclination. If he had the luck to have a good master who became interested in him, his progress might be made easy in many ways. In the South, he might often become an overseer and, if industrious and saving, could accumulate enough in a few years to start a small plantation of his own, though an observer in South Carolina said that few did so on account of their shiftlessness. For those with less administrative ability and only their trade or labor to offer, the wages were high and the demand for their services practically unlimited.

Many of the contemporary descriptions must not be taken too literally as they were written for the purpose of inducing immigration and were no more reliable than such literature in our own day. Against such it is well to set the less optimistic utterances of occasional homesick souls. "O these Liars," writes one of these, who says that they described the climate and country only to lure others over. "If I but had wings to fly, I would soon hie myself from hence to Europe, but I dread the tempestuous ocean and the pirates." "Whosoever is well off in Europe better remain there. Here is misery and distress, same as everywhere, and for certain persons and conditions incomparably more than in Europe." The cost of all manufactured articles is high, he says, and the administration of justice speedy and good, "otherwise we have the same old world as in Europe" [27]

On the other hand, wages were three times as high as in England, wrote another, and although this was an exaggeration, the high wages did make the accumulation of a modest property possible for the skillful and industrious.[28] Letters from immigrants to their relatives picture the conditions. "It is a great deal better living here than in England for working people," wrote one. "Poor working people doth live as well here as landed men doth live with you thats worth £20 a year. I live a simple life and hath builded a shop, and doth follow weaving of linen cloth, but I have bought 450 acres of land in the woods." [29] Another, evidently under the influence of the new freedom, wrote that "the farmers or husbandmen live better than lords. If a workman only work for four or five days in a week, he can live grandly. The farmers here pay no tithes or contributions. Whatever they have is free for them alone. They eat the best and sell the worst." [30] Still another wrote that "here is no want of victuals or clothing. Here it is a good Country for you people to come into" and offered to take care of one of his young cousins should he be sent over.[31]

The high wages both for labor and all sorts of craftsmen and artisans, the fishing on shares, the possibilities for the adventurous in the fur trade, positions for the clerically minded in a shop or the office of a merchant, the welcome accorded the country peddler, the small scale on which foreign commerce might be begun—all these and many other ways of beginning modestly with large possibilities made America a land of opportunity for those with energy and industry. It was above all else, however, the chance to secure land that attracted the majority of the immigrants, as it became the ambition of most Americans themselves. This was, perhaps, particularly true of the Germans, and in one list of 2,928 adult males passing through England on their way here in 1709, 1,838 were farmers. In another list there were 1,083 out of 1,593. In this regard, however, in spite of ample land yet available here and there, the land accumulations of the very rich and the desire on the part of the well-to-do to keep as much in their own hands as possible, were beginning to have their effect on the opportunities for the small man. In local struggles against new methods of the rich engrossers or in the diversions of the streams of migration and settlement, we can trace the beginnings of such effects, although in the next period this struggle was to become sharper, more bitter, and more vocal.

As the older portions of the colonies became more crowded and even the wilderness far beyond the range of settlement became preempted by those fortunate or astute enough to secure title, the small man without capital or influence began to feel himself more and more hemmed in and enmeshed in the power of those who had both. Little by little the resentment over the land situation, combined with other factors which one by one came into play as the century advanced, tended to bring classes and sections into sharp alignment, and to create a smoldering fire of resentment on the part of the frontiersmen and frequently the small farmer or landless man of the older settlement against the rich, which was to create a fertile field for propaganda in the days to come.

THE INTELLECTUAL OUTLOOK, 1690-1713

IN THE HISTORY of the American mind, the period from 1690 to 1713 is a notable one. If we estimate it merely by production we may agree with most students who find it to be the nadir of the intellectual life of the colonies, but its most essential feature is that the pause thus indicated was not a mere halting of activity in one direction to be resumed later, but the hesitation which comes when one movement has spent its force and before a wholly different one has got under way. During all the earlier part of the seventeenth century, the culture of America, like most of the settlers themselves, had been merely transplanted from Europe, mainly from England. In 1643, of the eighty ministers in New England, one half had been graduates of Cambridge or Oxford. Fifty years later, however, seventy-six out of eighty-seven in Massachusetts and thirty-one out of thirty-six in Connecticut were graduates of Harvard. "The Country consists now most of Natives, few of which have read much or been abroad in the world," wrote Governor Nicholson of Virginia in 1701, and again he says that the natives "begin to have a sort of aversion to others, calling them strangers."[32] From the days of settlement down to the end of the seventeenth century we have to note the slowing down of a cultural movement imported from the mother countries. From the beginning of the eighteenth onward we have to deal with the rise of a distinctly colonial culture. It is, perhaps, needless to add that this was constantly under the influence of the European.

The university-bred and other cultured men who had come from England and elsewhere had not realized the magnitude and absorptive power of the task of subduing the forest. By degrees they had found their energies diverted into new and more material channels. Many a one must have echoed Pastorius when even he said, in a moment of discouragement in his Philadelphia outpost in the wilderness, that "never have metaphysics and Aristotelian logic . . . earned a loaf of bread." Not only the work to be done but the rewards to be gained must have led many, as we have already noted in speaking of the clergy, to abandon the life of the spirit for that of active business.

If the earlier culture had withered it had by no means died, and the constant importation of books indicate a widespread taste for reading, confined to no one section. In the South, there were no bookshops because there were no towns and consequently no centers for distribution of books any more than of clothes or other articles, but this does not mean there were not constant importations. The rich imported them direct from their English agents, as they did everything else, whereas the smaller people could get them at the stores of the planter-merchants, as they did other things. "You know some of the newest books, if they be ingenious will be mighty acceptable," wrote William Fitzhugh from Virginia to his brother in England in 1690.[33] In Philadelphia, books were probably imported by the general merchants, but by 1714, at least, there seems to have been a shop devoted particularly to them, for Colden wrote in that year that "our Bookseller tells me that there is not one Bible in Town to be sold."[34] At least a dozen years earlier Abraham Delanoy was selling books in New York and at the beginning of the century we know the names of nine booksellers in Boston. In New England the dealers also used the itinerant peddler as a selling agent, and although we do not know what works may have been sold in that way the business thus handled seems to have been considerable. James Gray, for example "that used to go up and down the Country Selling of Books," as his obituary in the *Boston News-Letter* says, left £700 in coin.[35]

In the seventeenth century, the conception of the absolute in America had been dualistic; in the eighteenth it was to become monistic. The intellectual colonist, closely linked as he was with the movement of thought in Europe through practically every book upon his shelves, was to duplicate in the movement of his own thought that rationalizing tendency which was to be characteristic of eighteenth-century Europe. Whatever may have been the comparative numbers of books or their readers in New England and the rest of the colonies, there was a difference in spirit which is evident. The New Englanders, although narrower, were more intense. The Southerner read and pondered. The New Englander wrestled with his ideas. The things of the spirit for him had not simply reality but almost corporeality. He was fairly scorched by the flames of hell — or rather, perhaps, he marveled why his neighbor was not. Whereas in the other colonies, therefore, the transition from the seventeenth-century viewpoint to the rationalism of the eighteenth was gradual, it is not a mere chance that we find the same change in New England marked by a spiritual crisis of the first magnitude.

It is not necessary to rehearse all the well-known details of the Salem witch trials of 1692, during the course of which 150 accused persons were imprisoned, legal evidence being set aside, and twenty victims put to death, one by the horrible torture of being pressed for several days under heavy weights. The story of this blot on the history of Massachusetts has been related at length in the preceding book. Finally the reaction came. Sober sense asserted itself after the irreparable harm had been done. Courageous laymen like Thomas Brattle and Robert Calef exerted themselves to the utmost. In 1700, Mather's *Wonders of the Invisible World,* which had been published in 1684, was mockingly answered by Calef's *More Wonders of the Invisible World,* which was a rationalistic attack, and an effective one, upon the clergyman's attitude toward natural phenomena. After due reflection, Samuel Sewall as well as some minor actors in the tragedy made public acknowledgment of their transgression and asked for forgiveness. Even Cotton Mather confided to his diary doubts as to his own part, and later was on one occasion to do public battle for scientific enlightenment. That a merchant should worst one of the most noted clergymen in all New England and carry the minds of the people with him was surely a portent of coming change.

The change in the intellectual atmosphere is also illustrated in the field of historical writing. In 1702, Mather published his *Magnalia Christi Americana,* an ecclesiastical history of New England from its founding to 1698. As a picture of the ideals of the Puritan ministers as depicted by one of them, it has high value, but it is full of errors and thoroughly uncritical. Five years later young Thomas Prince graduated from Harvard but he had already begun to make his remarkable collection of books, documents, and source material of all sorts on which he was later to base the first critical historical work produced in America, and, although his book was to be long delayed and not to appear until well into the next period, we may note the spirit with which he is already at work, as contrasted with Mather. "I would not take the least iota upon trust," he says. "Some may think me rather too critical. . . . I think a writer of facts cannot be too critical." "In short, I cite my vouchers to every passage; and I have done my utmost, first to find out the truth, and then to relate it in the clearest order."[36] Here indeed is the freshness of a new dawn illumined by the first glow of the rationalizing and scientific spirit.

The founding of the Royal Society in England in 1662 had been of marked influence in fostering scientific interest in America as well as at home, and Americans made many communications to it. In 1713, Cotton Mather, who was a somewhat frequent contributor,[37] sent in his paper "Curiosa Americana" and soon after was elected a Fellow, as was William Brattle the next year, and in the following period a number of colonials, South as well as North, were thus honored. Science, however, was still in its infancy, and even in Europe natural history, for example, was yet in the stage of making collections of objects and discussing "their meaning in terms of the flood of Noah." Here and there colonists were busy in such work, and Paul Dudley, Cotton Mather, and others in New England were sending specimens or accounts of strange phenomena to England. Absurdly unscientific as many of these were, such as Mather's description of a Triton, half man and half fish, which was supposed to have been seen on the shores of Connecticut, they were not considered unworthy of credence by European scientists, and undoubtedly stimulated American scientific interest. In South Carolina in 1705, a Mrs. Hannah Williams was collecting specimens of "some of Our Vipers and several sorts of Snakes, Scorpions and Lizzards in a Bottle" as well as "Other Insex," pressed plants, birds, a wild bees' nest, and native clothing and utensils to send to England, apparently to Sir Hans Sloane.[38] In Philadelphia, a few years later, Christopher Witt, who joined the theosophical colonists upon the Wissahickon, probably founded the first botanical garden in America.

Medicine at this time was far below even the condition of that science in Europe. There was no means of securing a medical education in the colonies except by apprenticeship to some practicing physician. Boys of from fourteen to seventeen might be apprenticed for from four to seven years, and besides picking up such information from their master as they could, were obliged to perform all sorts of menial work, even those who came of good families. What constituted sufficient medical education to permit of being licensed by the legislature at this time may be learned from the petition of Samuel Higley of Connecticut, who was licensed in 1717. He states that he had "more than common education" and that "being employed three years in keeping school, did improve all opportunities in the study of physick and chirurgery," and for two years had studied under Drs. Thomas Hooker and Samuel Mather. The library of the ordinary doctor must have been very scanty, for in the inventories of even successful practitioners we frequently find the books valued at only a pound or two. The centers of medical education of the time were Leyden, under the celebrated Hermann Boerhaave, and Paris for surgery, but in this period not a single American took his medical degree in Europe, the first to do so being William Bull of South Carolina in 1734.[39] As no provision was made for instruction at colonial colleges, the consequence is that no colonist of this period had a right to the use of the title.

Although lectures on the cadaver were being given regularly in Paris and Strassburg, dissections were very seldom performed in the colonies until after 1760, except by stealth.[40] In 1690, owing to the suddenness of the death of Governor Slaughter in New York, an autopsy was performed on his body by six physicians to see if he had been poisoned, but these were not usually permitted unless suspicions of foul play had been aroused. There were no hospitals until later and the apprentice's opportunities of studying diseases were limited to those his master's patients might have the goodness to contract. Midwifery was wholly in the hands of women, obstetrics not usually forming part of the doctor's studies or practice until after the middle of the century. It was not until its later decades that the duties of apothecary and physician were divided, and the more lucrative branch of the doctor's work in our period was still the compounding of his innumerable "potions," "elixirs," "infusions," and "electuaries." What they may have contained, we do not know. Elder, wormwood, anise, nitre, antimony, iron, sulphur, calomel, and sometimes opium in enormous doses were among those mentioned. It is probable that some of the fantastic compounds of the day were not in actual use, though in some of the household books of receipts we find remarkable remedies. Thus in William Penn's "Book of Phisick" he notes that to cure a pain in the eye, a white-shelled snail should be pricked and the liquid dropped into the eye several times daily. To draw out a thorn, a dried snakeskin was to be applied, and for bruises he advised a disgusting concoction of six pounds of butter, a bottle of black snails, rosemary, lavender, elder, "new Cow-dung as much as will go into a great oyster shell and half as much new hen dung," frankincense, and other ingredients.[41] If these were the medical notions of an intelligent man such as Penn, we need not wonder at some of the country remedies then in vogue. The prescriptions were as vague as their contents were varied, and we find as doses "a pretty draught," "the bigth of a walnut," or "take a pretty quantity as often as you please."[42] The general credulity, the lack of any proper system of licensing, and the absence of degrees, all helped to make the field a fertile one for the quack, and in Europe as well as in America, the eighteenth century was quite as much the age of quackery as of common sense. The first American patent medicine seems to date from this period, and from 1711, "Tuscarora Rice" became a favorite remedy for tuberculosis.

In literature, the works which have most retained their vitality for modern readers were almost all written in the South, although published in England. In Maryland, an unknown author, who chose to call himself Ebenezer Cook, produced in 1708 in *The Sot-Weed Factor,* a satiric poem of genuine power. The picture he gives of certain aspects of life in the colony may not be accurate and certainly is not flattering, but there was no poetry produced elsewhere in America at the time which has retained its interest as has this racy and vigorous satire by the unknown Marylander or English visitor. In Philadelphia, it is true, young Aquila Rose was considered a poet, and in Connecticut, Richard Steere, in 1713, was influenced by Milton and in one short poem showed a somewhat unusual appreciation of nature. Sewall and others in Boston handed about both Latin and English verses, but the entire Northern output of the period is negligible except as an indication of misdirected energy and lack of taste.

In 1690 the first attempt to publish a newspaper in America was tried in Boston but suffered from censorial infanticide, and the journal, *Publick Occurrences,* was murdered in its first issue. Five years later, Thomas Maule, a Quaker of Salem, was proceeded against merely for circulating a book which he had had printed in New York; he escaped owing partly to the reaction following the witchcraft excitement.[43] In 1700 an answer to one of Cotton Mather's pamphlets was written by the Reverend Mr. Colman and others, who found it necessary to send it to New York to be printed on account of the control of the Boston press by the clerical clique. For the same reason, Brattle had to send his book against Mather to London, and when it arrived in the colony, Increase Mather, who was then president of Harvard, had it publicly burned in the college yard. The system was beginning to break down somewhat during this period, but the few cases cited show the difficulties, and to some extent the risks, an author ran who wished to publish matter displeasing to the official and clerical censors.

Throughout the whole period, the only journal of any sort published in any of the colonies was the *Boston News-Letter,* a pitifully small and dull weekly which was founded in 1704. It contained belated news from Europe, the clearings and entries at the Custom House, and other bits of one sort and another. It has an importance as the beginning of the periodical press in this country but did not afford the slightest opening for literary talent. An author of a book or pamphlet was thus limited to running the gauntlet of official censorship and religious prejudice attending publication by the few local presses in the North or sending his work to England, a lengthy and costly proceeding. For shorter productions, such as poems or brief essays, the only method of bringing them to the notice of others was the "broadside" or else circulation in manuscript.

Moreover, there was almost no public an author could reach. The population of the colonies was so scattered that, in the absence of a periodical press, the problem of the distribution of ideas was almost as great as that of evolving them at all. The lack of postal facilities was another factor militating against the spread of ideas. With respect to the development of even a local culture, the South, owing to its lack of presses, was particularly handicapped. It is naturally in centers of population, where opportunities for intercourse and discussion are greatest, that the interest in intellectual matters is keenest. In this regard, South Carolina was the best off of the Southern colonies, and in Charleston there did develop an intellectual and artistic life which was equal to that of the Northern towns. At this period, however, even the towns of the North were so small that the difference between that section and the South was less than was to be the case later.

The facilities for education of the people at large from Pennsylvania northward, although somewhat better than in the South, were not notably

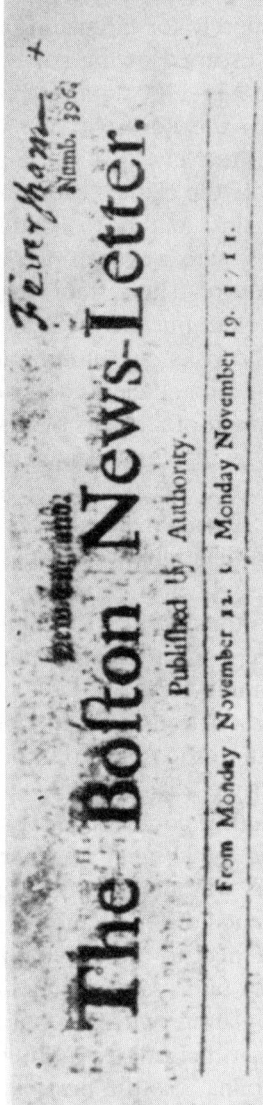

A specimen copy of the first newspaper in America. Despite the failure of the Walker-Hill expedition and the great fire of October 2, 1711 (which destroyed nearly a hundred buildings), there is apparently still cause for Thanksgiving.

so in this period. The halfhearted attempt made by Penn's government to make education a function of the state was soon given up, and the only school in Philadelphia, an excellent one in which Pastorius was teacher, was a religious institution of the Quakers. It was by no means typical, however, in its high standard, of the educational facilities in the rest of the colony. In New York there were few schools and those of poor quality. All accounts agree as to the low intellectual level of the people, both rich and poor. Some of the best families sent their boys to England for schooling or occasionally to Boston, but "the City is so conveniently Situated for Trade and the Genius of the people are so inclined to merchandise, that they generally seek no other Education for their children than writing and Arithmetick. So that letters must be in a manner forced upon them" wrote one observer in 1713.[44] The people objected to any expenditure for educational purposes, and the poorer elements depended much, as everywhere in the colonies, on child labor. In the whole of Westchester County in New York in 1704 there were only six families who were able "to spare their children's time more than to learn to read and write."[45] In the town of New York itself there was considerable illiteracy, and in a petition to the king in 1701, of the 687 who were of sufficient importance to sign such a document, sixty-one, or nearly one in ten, had to sign by mark. Early in the eighteenth century the Society for the Propagation of the Gospel opened a missionary school in the town, but the people generally showed no inclination to help themselves.

New England girls were rarely taught more than reading and writing at most, although there was a girl's boarding school in Boston by 1706 and by 1714 a "finishing school" where various minor arts were taught in addition to arithmetic. In the homes, dame schools, and town schools, boys learned reading, writing, and arithmetic, although a good many learned none of these. A very few comparatively attended the higher grammar grades, and an occasional lad from New York went to England. The population of the colonies from Pennsylvania northward in 1700 may be estimated at about 143,000. Of this total the only boys receiving any education higher than that afforded by the grammar grades of a few schools were the "forty or fifty children" who were studying the narrow ecclesiastical curriculum at Harvard. Such in brief was the educational situation in the North at the opening of the new century.

Turning now to the South, we find different conditions resulting in somewhat different systems but without any great difference in the resultant level of general education in this period. The scattered nature of the population and the absence of towns and villages introduced an element of great difficulty. Facilities were best in Virginia, where we find grammar schools, endowed free elementary schools, the "old Field Schools," (formed by several families in a neighborhood combining to hire a teacher), and private tutoring.

In the South as in the North, the laws governing apprenticeship, both of children learning trades and of poor children without homes, required that the master or guardian should see that the child was taught to read and write. That the law was enforced in Virginia and also that there were facilities for learning is indicated by the records of Surrey County, where we find between 1679 and 1684 fifty instances of guardians giving bonds to have their wards taught in schools.

Probably in the other colonies as in Virginia, the richer planters had their children taught first in the "old Field Schools" or by private tutors. To a much greater extent than in the North, the older lads went to England for their higher education, and in this period, from Virginia, we find among others Bartholomew Yates receiving his B.A. from Oxford in 1698, John Span going there in 1705 as a boy of eighteen, and Mann Page there four years later at seventeen. In Maryland there was the same practice, and young Charles Carroll went to Europe for a number of years' study, returning in 1723. The same was true of the South Carolinians and the educational opportunities thus given to wealthy Southern lads were incomparably greater than those obtainable by New England boys at Harvard, practically none of whom went abroad. For those in the South who could not afford this training the door of opportunity was opened by the fulfillment of a long-cherished scheme in Virginia when William and Mary College was founded in 1693. Virginia seems to have led the South as Massachusetts and Connecticut did the North and, indeed, all the colonies, but if we consider the whole of the two sections there was apparently no startling difference in the level of general culture between them. This is also borne out by a comparative study of signed documents, those in the South showing no larger a percentage of signers by mark than in the North. In the South, among the more highly educated, there were no such men of encyclopedic learning as Mather and some of the other New England clergymen. On the other hand, among the greater number of Southerners who had had an Oxford training and European education there was a more humane attitude toward art and letters, a more cultivated savoring of life.

THE ARTS AND RELIGION, 1690-1713

ONE CANNOT ARBITRARILY DIVIDE man's psychic life into intellectual and spiritual, and it is somewhat arbitrary to discuss literature in one section and the other arts in another. Yet in dealing with arts and crafts, painting, music, morals, and those actions and reactions we designate as humanitarian, we have entered upon a part of human nature which defies sharpness of definition. What, for example, is art? What are the essential qualities which justify us in speaking of a people or of an age as artistic, and in the absence of which we may pronounce them inartistic? It is obvious that such questions cannot be discussed at length here, and yet it is necessary to raise them in order to approach that of the artistic life of the colonies in this period with understanding or at least with modesty. There were certain obvious shortcomings which strike us at once. Although, as we shall see later, there were some painters at work, they did not produce a single canvas of high quality. There were no museums or exhibitions. There was no musician of note and no concert. With one possible exception there was not a poem written which has now any interest other than antiquarian. And yet, although art produced fewer flowers at the top, it is by no means certain that it did not strike its roots deeper in the soil and that America was not then more artistic than now.

Granted that in every department of life it is to the exceptional individual that we must look for the highest achievement, nevertheless we may question the vitality of any movement which has no roots in the life of the common people. Art today, to a considerable extent, is like one of those floating islands of roots and branches bound together and covered with soil and vegetation but which have no foundation and are sustained in insulation above the earth. This was not the case in the earlier colonial period, and in tracing the development of art in America we have to follow two distinct movements—on the one hand, the continuous degradation of the art of the people, and on the other, the temporary disintegration of the artistic life of the upper classes, but which later with the turn of the century entered upon a new period of growth.

In many respects the increasing accumulation and concentration of wealth during the early eighteenth century tended to widen the breach between the rich and poor. This was true of art as well, but it is not altogether easy to see why it should necessarily have been so, for folk art is never dependent upon the possession of wealth. Puritanism partially accounts for it but, although the Puritan spirit was inimical to the artistic spirit, it did not banish all its forms or impulses. Such a Puritan of the Puritans as Samuel Sewall was one of the most constant versifiers of the period, and the sternest of them had their portraits painted, wore rich clothes, and accumulated beautiful furniture and costly plate. Nor can we explain it wholly by the primitive existence of frontier life. One of the most vigorous of all arts is that of the half-naked black of the African jungle, who lives under conditions far more primitive, and with less resources, than any American frontiersman ever had to face.

No explanation of this more rapid degradation of the artistic impulse of the people in America as compared with Europe is wholly adequate. Perhaps we may find one as good as any in the fact that, unlike the native Indian, the colonists in America were trying, each in his own generation, to attain at once to a level of cultural equipment that was a product of many centuries of civilized effort and to do so in a new environment which was, in itself, adapted only to the level of savagery. The task was too great and the instrument—the human spirit itself—broke down and disintegrated. The qualities it lost were those which were least essential to the material struggle with the environment, as those which were strengthened were the ones most essential.

It was not wholly an unconscious process. "The Plow-man that raiseth Grain is more serviceable to Mankind, than the Painter who draws only to please the Eye," wrote a New Englander in 1719. "The Carpenter who builds a good House to defend us from the Wind and Weather, is more serviceable than the curious Carver, who employs his Art to please the Fancy," [46] Food and shelter are indeed the primary requirements. But after securing these, the African and the American Indian had time and energy left for art in the same environment, which was beginning to make it seem a superfluous luxury to the white man. The latter did not have it, because of his insistence upon that higher standard of material living to which he was accustomed and which was beyond the ken of the Indian. Insofar as outward conditions were concerned, it was not the frontier that destroyed such arts as the people practiced, but the effort to maintain the only familiar standard of living, under conditions which made it impossible except by a partial exhaustion of energy. It may be noted that the only parts of the country where the folk songs and folk art continued to live—such as the Carolina mountains—were precisely those where the standard of living remained stationary at a primitive level from the beginning.

The movement of degradation was to be retarded from time to time by the infusion of new blood in streams of fresh immigration from Europe, and in the period from 1690 to 1713 there was still much genuine artistic impulse among the people. We have already spoken of the self-sustaining nature of the ordinary colonial home of the more modest type, and of the multiplicity of household industries. It was in these that the art of the people found its expression. Of the household utensils of one sort and another, a great number were carved by the men in the long winter evenings and were not only made serviceable but were ornamented with designs, though this minor art was found rather more often among the Dutch and Germans than the English. By the opening of the eighteenth century, the latter had already lost much of the love of carving which they had brought with them in the seventeenth, and we do not find later the carved beams, posts, studs, or pendants which the earlier settlers had wrought into their houses. These expressions of the builder-owner's craftsmanship and taste were disappearing under a clapboarded exterior and a lathed and plastered interior. Moreover, although the great mass of the furniture used by the common people was of native and, much of it, household manufacture, the elaborate designs carved upon the flat surfaces were disappearing from the pieces made at home, which were becoming simpler and cruder from the standpoint of craftsmanship, at the same time that the

Glass by Baron Stiegel, of Pennsylvania

Early Eighteenth Century Silver from New England

Stove Plate: Joseph and Potiphar's Wife

Carved Wood in Gloria Dei Church, Philadelphia

furniture being made by the professional colonial cabinetmaker was rapidly improving. By 1713, few rural householders had either the desire or the ability to make such elaborate pieces as their fathers or grandfathers had made in the preceding century. The somewhat easier method of painting was being employed, though this also frequently gave scope for artistic impulse and ability, and was in vogue all through the colonies, the styles varying somewhat with the nationality of the craftsman. The art ran the gamut from a mere outlining of the panels to most elaborate patterns of leaves and flowers, sometimes combined with carving, sometimes replacing it entirely, and giving ample satisfaction to the strong colonial love of color. It must be remembered that we are now speaking of work done by the farmer or artisan for his own use and satisfaction and not by a professional for sale.[47]

In this period, the musical life of the colonies consisted almost wholly of instrumental or vocal music in private houses, taverns, or occasional gatherings out of doors, such as impromptu dances or the country fairs. In New England, the first pipe organ was installed in King's Chapel in Boston in 1713, it having been given to that church by Thomas Brattle after having been refused by the Brattle Street Church. The congregational singing throughout New England was incredibly bad, and the first instruction book was published at Newbury in 1712. Nevertheless, singing was popular even in Puritan Massachusetts, and Cotton Mather complained that the minds of the country people were being much corrupted by the "foolish songs and ballads" which the peddlers were carrying into all parts of the colony. As an "antidote" he proposed to distribute hymns. There were some instruments in New England, such as a virginal in Sewall's house, and by 1716 the organist of King's Chapel advertised that he taught music and dancing, mended virginals and spinets, and offered for sale a recent importation of flageolets, flutes, hautboys, bass viols, and violins.

Evidently there was an increased interest in musical matters becoming apparent, but the influence of New England in colonial musical culture has been much overrated, and the musical life of the Middle and Southern colonies was far richer. Pipe organs had been installed in Philadelphia and in Port Royal, Virginia, by about 1700, and all musical instruments were more numerous than in the North. The Swedes and early Germans had brought their fiddles and flutes with their folk songs,[48] and there were many violins among the English, and an occasional bagpipe wakened Scotch echoes. The spinets and virginals were found only in the richer households.

Nowhere in the colonies in this period, however, was there any organized musical life. The opera and, so far as we have record, concerts do not appear until a few decades later. At this time Charleston, South Carolina, and not Boston, would seem to have been the musical center of the continent. Artistically her citizens were more cultured and the Southern port was that of entry for most of the artists who, in the van of the never ending

European stream, were already beginning to come to "barbarous America" to sell their talent for a better price, oddly, than it would fetch at home. These went first, as a rule, to the rich islands of the West Indies, and thence naturally took the short route to America by way of the South.

In another art, that of the theater, New England influence was not simply negligible but openly hostile, and the development of the drama, one of the notable features in the later decades covered by this book, has to be traced during the whole period in the Middle and Southern colonies only. Even there, however, it was not successful at the opening of the century, although a professional troupe appeared in Charleston in 1703 and in New York the following year.

Of paintings produced in the colonies in this period, we have no records except of portraits. In New England, it is believed that a Tom Child was painting in Boston from 1692 to 1706, Joseph Allen from 1684 to 1728, and a Lawrence Brown was also there in 1701. In New York there was the interesting family of Duyckinck, of whom the first Evert seems to have been still painting portraits until his death in 1702. A grandson was painting on glass, and Evert 3d was also painting in this period, probably being the artist of the Beekman portraits. Gerret Van Randst was another New York artist of the time. John Watson made pencil drawings in Perth Amboy as early as 1715 and was said to have had a collection of European pictures, both originals and copies. In Philadelphia, Christopher Witt painted portraits, at least one of which, that of Johannes Kelpius, has come down to us. In Delaware and Maryland, by 1711, Gustavus Hesselius, the Swede, was beginning his long career. It has been said that there was no painter in Virginia and that all the portraits of this period were done in England, but a letter from William Fitzhugh in 1698 in which he orders six frames, some colors and oils, "with half a doz. 3 quarter clothes to set up a painter," indicates that one was at work there, or at least expected. In Charleston we know that a portrait of Governor Johnson was painted as early as 1705 and a certain Henrietta Johnson was painting pastels there by 1708, at least fifteen examples of her work surviving. Both in the colonies named and others, there may have been more obscure artists at work, and it must always be remembered that our knowledge of all such facts depends upon painstaking local research, much more of which has always been done in New England than in the South. The more that we learn of the life of the latter, the more does the similarity of conditions in the two sections appear, until the great social change brought about by the rapid development of slavery.[49]

This similarity, however, was least marked in the religious life and outlook of the Northern and Southern colonies. The citizens of both sections, speaking generally, were largely under the influence of certain ideas that we are wont to consider as being essentially Puritan in character but in reality were but the outlook on life of the more sober elements of the

English middle class of the period. In 1699, petitions were sent to the house of burgesses from three Virginia counties praying that every citizen should be forced to attend some place of worship, and such a law was passed in that year. The grant of a charter for William and Mary College had been requested by the assembly in words which might have been used for Harvard or Yale. It was desired, so the petition read, "to the end that the Church of Virginia may be furnished with a seminary of ministers of the gospel, and that the youth may be piously educated in good letters and manners, and that the Christian faith may be propagated among the Western Indians."[50] All this is merely to say that the sound elements of the English population of all the colonies were drawn originally from the same reservoir of sober, God-fearing people in the home country. The old belief of the New Englanders, carefully nursed by their later historians, that they alone formed such a strain in the colonial population was based only on prejudice, ignorance, and abounding conceit. The pictures of Virginia and Maryland as settled almost exclusively by gay Cavaliers, so dearly cherished by certain local writers in the nineteenth century, is quite far from fact.

During the early eighteenth century, there were two conflicting tendencies at work, one toward a greater toleration and the other toward the setting up of established churches and even toward persecution. The former of these was most noticeable in the North, and the latter in the South. In Massachusetts a great step forward had been taken under the compulsion of the English government when the new charter of 1691 had done away with the Congregational Church test for the franchise. Moreover, both in that colony and Connecticut, partly owing to the drawing in of the frontier on account of the Indian wars, the population of the older towns had become greater, and just as we have noted how this affected an alteration in the school system, so it also affected the parishes. In many cases the town, in a word, had become too big for the single town church just as it had for the single town school, and the records are full of demands for a division of the church to suit the needs of new neighborhoods. So many exceptions had to be made from the old rule that the church rapidly tended to become divorced from the political town and to become rather an affair of the ecclesiastical parish. This occasioned many quarrels among the congregations, and occasionally that part of one which wished to, split off and reorganized as a different sect.

The numbers of these had been slowly but steadily increasing, and due partly to the general decline in religious zeal and partly to better acquaintance, much of the old spirit of persecution was dying out among the Puritans. By 1700 there were nine Baptist churches in New England, a Baptist had been president of Harvard, and at the ordination of a Baptist minister in Boston in 1717, Cotton Mather preached the ordination sermon and deprecated the earlier persecutions. That the sectarian spirit was still very much alive, however, may be savored in a tart and amusing colloquy which has come down to us. Being in great danger crossing the ferry at Portsmouth, Rhode Island, the Anglican missionary George Keith was rescued by a former Quaker acquaintance who refused to allow his men to receive any pay. "I thanked him very kindly for his help in our great Danger," wrote the Anglican in his journal, "and said to him, John, ye have been a means under God to save our natural Life, suffer me to be a means under God to save your Soul. . . . He replied, George, save thy own Soul, for I have no need of thy help; then said I, I will pray for your conversion; he replyed, the Prayers of the wicked are an abomination." [51] Nevertheless, mutual toleration was growing, although both in Massachusetts and Connecticut all taxpayers had still to contribute to the established Congregational Church, and, thus, if they belonged to some other, had to pay doubly for religious support. Connecticut, originally the more liberal of the two, had become the more narrow, and although in 1708 it passed an act permitting the establishing of Anglican churches, this was mainly due to a fear for the charter in view of the Anglicans' complaints of their treatment. Nevertheless, it was a step forward.

In both North and South Carolina in this period, also, the Anglican Church was established and the payment of tithes made obligatory. It is notable, however, that in South Carolina the law establishing the church provided that the minister should be chosen by the majority of the inhabitants, as had been the custom if not the law in Virginia. To show the conflicting currents of the period, it may be noted that whereas in 1691 the English government had abolished the church test for the franchise in Massachusetts, in the Carolinas in 1704 conformity to the Church of England and receiving of the sacraments according to the rites of that church were made essentials for election to the assembly. Although taxation to maintain an established church was still the law in Connecticut and Massachusetts, early in the next period this was to be greatly modified in favor of the dissenter, the tendency now started in those colonies thus running counter to the new movement inaugurated in the South. The new Southern policy, indeed, was not wholly unopposed, and it is not unlikely that the two "rebellions" in North Carolina in the first decade of the eighteenth century were caused by dislike of the new establishment and by the uneasiness of the dissenters.

And what of a department of moral life based upon human nature rather than religious doctrine? Was sexual immorality greater or less in 1700 than in 1900? Although we have no statistics, we have numerous comments, court records, and, in New England, certain church records which serve to guide us. The increasing number and severity of the laws against miscegenation suggests that the ownership of slaves involved certain temptations, and offers ample evidence of moral laxity in the South, increasing toward the end of the seventeenth century.

Interest, however, centers on the inquiry as to whether the supposedly stricter religious principles inculcated in New England resulted in a morality superior in this respect to that of the other colonies. Evidence indicates that it did not, although the problem is complicated by the fact that a peculiar standard became common, more or less, among New Englanders of all social classes in the early part of the eighteenth century, according to which fornication if followed by marriage, no matter how long delayed, was considered a very venial sin if sin at all. Thus, in 1722, a society of some of the ablest Harvard students of the day, including Oliver Peabody, John Davenport, and Charles Chauncy, debated the question "whether it be Fornication to lye with ones Sweetheart (after contraction) before Marriage?"[52] In 1728 the minister at Longmeadow offered for signing by his congregation a "covenant for reformation" in which among other things they were particularly to express their "abhorrence of that notion advanc'd by some of late" that the practice just named was no breach of the seventh commandment.[53] Jonathan Edwards was, in part, driven from his church because of his strict attitude toward this custom. In New York, in 1695, a traveler reported that antenuptial fornication was not at all considered a sin, and his generally unflattering picture of the morals of that town is borne out by other evidence.

The church records that contain the public acknowledgments of such "faults" show that the practice was extremely prevalent. In one Massachusetts church, for which the record seems to be complete, the practice would seem to have been indulged in before practically every marriage in the congregation, and the fact that, a little later in the century, a church in Connecticut passed a rule that out of charity, seventh-month children should be considered legitimate shows the extent of the laxity. As marriage was entered into very early, usually under twenty for boys and frequently as early as sixteen and even fifteen for girls, the conditions are obvious. Such cases were dealt with very leniently by the churches and as a rule the parties were accepted into good standing immediately after their ordeal of public confession before the congregation.[54]

The main difference between the Southern colonies and the North, therefore, seems to have been that although indulgence may have been equally common in both, what was frankly regarded as a sin in the former was coming to be regarded in the latter very much as a mere peccadillo for young people, provided marriage followed, should there be a child. It is fair to say, however, that we have much fuller records for New England, and that silence may not of necessity mean innocence in the colonies to the south. From Pennsylvania north, "bundling" was a common practice among the lower classes, and although it may have arisen from the primitive sleeping arrangements, as has been suggested, the same custom is by no means uncommon among primitive races, and is practically identical with the *viagagavu* or "bush sleeping" of the Melanesians. In the colonies it seems to have been mainly confined to the Germans, Dutch, and New England Puritans.[55] Divorces were rarely granted in the colonies, the English church not allowing them and the crown refusing to sanction any law permitting them. They were, however, occasionally obtained in the semi-independent Puritan colonies of Massachusetts and Connecticut, which led the way toward a more liberal divorce policy.

Throughout all the colonies drunkenness was a prevailing vice, as it was in England, and nearly every event, such as house raisings, harvestings, christenings, college commencements, funerals, and even the ordinations of New England ministers, was frequently made the occasion of scandalous intemperance. The vices of the period, however, were mainly those incidental to the characteristic coarseness of the times, and crimes of violence are rather notable for their comparative rarity. There were occasional cases of arson, rape, infanticide, and murder, but in general, life and property would seem to have been far safer in the colonies than in England. This was probably due mainly to the better economic condition of the lower classes. In marked contrast to the plague of highwaymen in England, and in spite of the fact that the roads in the colonies led through long lonely stretches of woods, I have found only one case of a colonial traveler being robbed in the whole of the century preceding the Revolution. In the larger towns footpads were more common, notably in New York, and as the century advanced mob violence and disregard of law became more frequent everywhere.

Of the more humanitarian ideas of a later period or of any organized charities, there is as yet but little trace. Punishments for crimes and misdemeanors, if somewhat milder than in contemporary England, were still brutal and severe. In Quaker Philadelphia, for example, both men and women were lashed on the bare back while driven at the cart's tail, and the criminal code of all the colonies was inhumane. As yet imprisonment played only a slight part in the punishment of offenders, and was employed, according to contemporary European practice, rather for vagabonds and debtors. Although the criminal received such punishments as death, mutilation, branding, whipping, and the stocks, the idea still uppermost was restitution to the wronged individual and to society.

The poor were cared for by the local administrative units, town or parish, but there was no special provision for the insane. It was not a period of institutions or organizations, and charity was almost wholly an affair of individual cases. Occasionally churches would take up collections for some particular victim of misfortune, but throughout all the colonies probably the only organized charitable society for the relief of the poor in this period was the Scots' Charitable Society of Boston, first started in 1657 and reorganized in 1684.[56] From time to time, spasmodic efforts were made to do educational or missionary work among the Indians, and Governor Spotswood was particularly interested in such work at the beginning of the eighteenth century, but there was little general interest and only rare efforts on the part of any of the colonial churches.

Slavery and the slave trade aroused few doubts in even the sternest of the Puritans, although Samuel Sewall wrote a tract called *The Selling of Joseph* in 1701, to influence the passage of a law designed to discourage the importation of blacks. The pamphlet was wholly without effect and in fact was by no means as zealous in its advocacy of the cause of the blacks as the earlier protest of the Mennonites of Germantown in 1688 or the *Exhortation and Caution to Friends* published in Philadelphia by George Keith in 1693, although the older New England historians used to give it greater prominence. Both in this and the next period the most powerful advocates of antislavery were all to be found in Pennsylvania, New Jersey, and New York rather than in New England, where the trade in slaves was already taking strong hold.[57] The utilization of slave labor was not generally profitable in New England, but the capture and importing of slaves for use in the other colonies was greatly so, and the leading merchants of Boston and Newport became deeply engaged in it. Complaints, indeed, were heard from the Southerners that the New Englanders were ruining them by forcing so many blacks upon them for the sake of the double profit from slaves and rum.

In Boston, Cotton Mather was interested in alleviating the condition of such slaves as were there, and organized a small society for their betterment. The most zealous worker for the welfare of the slaves in any section at this time, however, was the French merchant Elias Neau of New York, who gave up his business and devoted his entire time to visiting and laboring among both black and Indian slaves in the face of violent opposition.

In the brief survey we have made of some aspects of colonial life at the opening of the eighteenth century, we have also seen that its culture was more or less uniform and evenly spread throughout the entire length of seaboard. This was due to the similarity of the sources of emigration in Europe and of economic and social influences first met in the New World rather than, as yet, to any development of a common consciousness or of intercolonial influences making for uniformity. As this text progresses, we shall note how the increasing richness of colonial life and the complexity of social structure resulted in a greater differentiation between the several sections, and yet, on the other hand, how increased communication, the growth of the press, and the pressure from outer dangers tended to bring the colonists together intellectually as they diverged socially.

The new social structure which was rapidly to be built up in the colonies during the eighteenth century, although drawing heavily upon Europe for its intellectual and artistic sustenance, was to be American in origin. Whether the original settlers had come, as in New England, largely in neighborhood or church groups, or singly or in family groups only, as was the case in the South, they had brought with them a conception of society and of life woven together unconsciously by a thousand subtle threads derived from the culture of the mother lands. Upon this conception, quite as unconsciously, the wilderness had acted as a powerful solvent. The process of disintegration, about which we have spoken in connection with New England, had been increasingly rapid throughout all colonial life as the seventeenth century advanced. In Europe, the immigrant had been surrounded and supported by a thousand influences of which he was but dimly aware if at all—established methods of earning a livelihood and of distribution of goods, endowed institutions, traditional beliefs and customs, political institutions, organized arts, such as the theater, all sorts of social conventions. He did indeed bring the consciousness of these things and was deeply influenced by them in his new environment, but in their tangible forms they had been left far behind, and the new colonial-born generation knew them not at all. The period of disintegration, however, was now drawing to a close. The wilderness was subdued in the older settlements. Wealth was accumulating. A leisured and cultivated class was demanding a fuller and richer life. If the novel and exigent conditions of the wilderness had for a time lowered the interest in things of the mind, the minds themselves had been quickened by the necessity of new adjustments and of building up social life afresh from its foundations. "The youth are very Ingenious, Subtile and of quick Capacities," wrote one observer of the lads of New York, and others comment in similar strain of the other colonies. The time had come for a new integration of colonial life.

THE CHANGING SOUTH, 1713-45

AT THE OPENING of the eighteenth century the main interest of all colonists, North and South, was agriculture. In the North, there were diversified crops and a marked tendency for the inhabitants to settle together in fairly compact groups. In the South, on the other hand, there were the great staple crops of rice and tobacco, and the people were scattered over the country to a far greater extent than their Northern neighbors. In both sections, however, the great mass of the population were small yeoman farmers. The lands were seldom held on lease, and the labor was performed by the farmers themselves or by the help of white labor or a few slaves, the latter only slightly more numerous in the South than in the North. In Maryland, exclusive of a few great landholders, it is probable that the average farm or plantation was from 100 to 200 acres, and in Virginia the large majority of the population tilled lands not much greater in extent. As North Carolina was largely settled by poor immigrants from other colonies, the holdings there must also have been small.

Before the period of an ample labor supply and of a leasehold tenantry, it is interesting to note the sources of income of even such a large landholder as William Fitzhugh of Virginia. Although he was nominally a planter and owned 24,000 acres, he derived a larger net income from his inland trade than from his plantation. Both yielded the same amount of 60,000 pounds of tobacco a year, but in the case of his plantation this was subject to deduction for feeding and clothing his slaves.[58] In those localities or periods in which quitrents were collected, these also tended to disperse large holdings or at least to discourage them. For example, in Maryland in the five years preceding 1733, warrants were taken out at the land office for an average total of over 28,000 acres annually. In that year the quitrent was raised from four shillings to ten a year, and during the next five years the amount of land annually taken up decreased about 90 percent. In the next five years, when the rent was put again at the old figure, the amounts taken out increased fivefold even though the purchase price had been considerably advanced.

Such factors as these, however, were merely brakes retarding here and there a movement which others tended successfully to bring into full play. Probably the most important of these favorable factors was the illimitable labor supply produced by the development of the slave trade, combined with the better position of the tobacco market in Europe following the Peace of Utrecht in 1713. In the seventeenth century there had, of course, been large estates and a difference between rich and poor, but the impetus now given so emphasized certain existing tendencies as to make this difference far more striking and to create a new social structure, differentiated both from that of the preceding century and from that of the North.

Even allowing that slave labor was less efficient than that of the white indentured servants, its cost was perhaps only from one quarter to one half as great, and the supply ample. A white servant cost from £2 to £4 a year for the period of service, at the end of which he could, and usually did, leave his master just when his training had made him most valuable. On the other hand, a slave for life could be bought for from £18 to £30, which would average about £1 a year provided he lived for from eighteen to thirty years. Then, too, unlike the case with servants, the children bred from the slaves added to the master's wealth just as did the increase of his herds. It was obvious therefore that the landowner who had sufficient capital to invest in slaves would be at a greater advantage compared with the farmer who had to till his lands himself or even compared with one who had to depend wholly upon the use of servants.

Thus, when through the rapid increase of slavery the amount of land which the rich man could bring under cultivation was limited only by the number of slaves he could buy, the advantage of capital became overwhelming. Not only was the economic surplus vastly increased by additional acreage and labor but there accrued also all the advantages attending any large-scale production, for the large plantation became nearly self-sustaining through slaves trained for the various tasks. Moreover, the large merchant-planter had advantages both in shipping his crop and in marketing it in England, and in purchasing such goods and supplies as came thence, which in turn he sold at a profit to his poorer neighbor. In addition, by the use of the overseer system, he could multiply the number of his plantations, depending only on the amount of capital at his disposal. By 1749, for example, Richard Bennet had a dozen or fifteen plantations all the way from Accomac in Virginia to Cecil County in Maryland.

It is true that slaves were not owned solely by the rich. Indeed, perhaps the majority of all slaves in Virginia were owned by planters who had five or less.[59] Numerically these small slave owners continued to form the bulk of the population, but as is always the case when there is a field for its profitable employment, large wealth multiplied faster in proportion than the gains of the small man. At the bottom of the economic scale there was the poor man who tilled his few acres with little or no help. During the years of the wars the demoralization in prices had brought him to the brink of destruction, and the soil from which he drew his exhausting crop was yearly wearing out. He had no money with which to buy new lands or slaves, and was fortunate if the year's end did not leave him in debt to the merchant-planters. Above him was the class of small farmers who had the advantages of larger lands and sufficient capital to buy a few slaves, and who thus maintained themselves in moderate comfort but without accumulating fortunes. At the top were those whose credit, capital, or influence sped them rapidly along the new road opened up.

At first the small planter who tilled his own land had been able to raise better tobacco than the newly imported slaves. As late as 1731, Governor Gooch wrote to the lords of trade that "the common people make the best," but as the slaves became more efficient this countervailing weight grew less, and, in any case, as the governor added, "the rich Man's trash will always damp the Market and spoil the poor Man's good Tobacco which has been carefully managed."[60] The margin of profit was small, and although when planted on a large scale, the profits for the large planter were correspondingly great, the small man had a hard time making both ends meet. After 1700 we do not find the freed servant easily accumulating enough surplus to enable him in turn to become a landowner; less than 5 percent of those who arrived in the colony near the end of the seventeenth century, in certain test districts, appeared on the rent roll of later years.

A new social structure, in short, was arising in the Southern colonies, some of the more striking aspects of which are those that have usually been abstracted and mingled together to form the popular picture of the "Old South." The intercourse between the rich Southerner and England was far closer, as we have seen, than was that of the inhabitants of the Northern colonies. Men and women on the large plantations did their shopping not in such shops as those of Philadelphia or Boston but direct from London, and the ships which brought the goods came as it were to their very doors, or at least to the foot of their lawns and gardens, which sloped to the river's edge.

Their ideals of social life were to a great extent those of the English country gentry with whom they mingled when in England, with whom they corresponded, and whom they imitated as far as possible. Both the conditions of the wilderness and the lack of the proper economic base had permitted this only to a very moderate extent during the seventeenth century, but as frontier conditions disappeared in the tidewater sections and as the factors outlined in this chapter permitted the rise of a conspicuously wealthy class, its members began to utilize this new wealth in spacious and comely living. It is from this period that we can date the rise of the great places, such as "Shirley," "Rosewell," and "Westover," though many of the large mansions like "Mt. Airy" date from about the middle of the century. The rapid advance in the scale of living of the upper classes is well exemplified in the case of the Byrds, father and son. The father, who belongs to the period of our earlier sections, was content to dwell in the first "Westover," a large but comparatively modest house. At his death he left about 26,000 acres.[61] His son, who died in 1744, left nearly 180,000 acres and built the beautiful house.

When the newly acquired wealth of the period both permitted and seemed to require new homes befitting its owners, they turned naturally to the new style then beginning to prevail in England, as did the builders in all the colonies. The earlier colonial architecture had been largely medieval in its affinities, informal and picturesque, and had embodied much of the genuine folk spirit of England, Holland, Wales, Sweden, or Germany, depending upon the nationality of the colonists. There had been both diversity and individuality, but the new builders, consciously striving for dignity, spaciousness, and beauty, adopted the new Georgian style which, after about 1720, spread very rapidly throughout the country.

The plan of the new Southern mansions was a composition in five parts, the large central mass and two smaller ones at each end, usually but not always connected with the center by passages.[62] The ceilings were extraordinarily high, and the proportions of the rooms of striking charm and dignity. The great hall frequently ran through the entire building and was sometimes open for two stories in height with the graceful staircase forming a notable feature. The main part of the building contained from eight to a dozen or more rooms, and the placing of the kitchens and other offices in one of the wings added to the total. The treatment of the grounds and gardens also became much more elaborate, the house usually standing far back from the entrance and approached under an avenue of trees, though these shaded approaches, 70 to 100 feet wide, were rather more common in Maryland than in Virginia.

The life lived by the fortunate dwellers on these great estates has often been described, albeit a bit too romantically, and is probably the main feature in the popular view of the South. It was a life, as we have said, as far as might be on the lines of the smaller country gentry of England. "The eleven of Prince George's County" in Maryland, and "the eleven South River Gentlemen" contended at cricket. Where, two generations before, their ancestors carried their guns through the tangled wilderness in fear of the Indians, the young bloods now pursued on horseback the equally wily but distinctly less dangerous fox, and one of the earliest "leading articles" of the newly established *Virginia Gazette* was on hunting to hounds.[63] What some have claimed to be the earliest Jockey Club in the world appears to have been founded at Charleston in 1734, and the Maryland Jockey Club, founded at Annapolis in 1745, included in its membership men from several different colonies. From that time on, although more notable a decade later, began the importation of blooded stallions from England, and racing stables began to be a costly item in a gentleman's estate.

The eighteenth century did not inaugurate the distinction in the South between rich and poor, or even mark the introduction of slavery, but in its earlier decades it did witness the establishment of a class so wealthy, so powerful, its members so bound to one another by marriage and other ties, and so entrenched in influence with the various authorities as to set them apart in quite a different way from that in which the moderate distinctions of wealth had operated earlier. These new leaders, indeed, were true empire builders, and if they were absorbing to themselves princely estates by means and influences denied to the hard-working farmer, nevertheless they were developing the country at a rate which might otherwise not have been possible. Certain stratifications were becoming so fixed as definitely to determine the status of the great majority of the Southern population in a fashion which had not been characteristic of the more mobile society of a few decades earlier.

The great cleavage, of course, was that between bond and free, and it has been claimed that this fundamental distinction tended to obliterate the lesser ones of differing wealth and social position among the free whites. It may be true that the slave owners did form a class which had a certain solidarity of feeling and of interest, but it must not be forgotten that the stigma brought upon physical labor by associating it with slavery became so great, as the number of slaves increased, as to react upon the white laborer, and to create a gulf between the white who owned even one or two slaves to toil for him, and the farmer or mechanic who labored for himself. Aside from its effect upon the black, it was probably this influence upon the whites which was one of the most evil effects of the "peculiar institution."

Out on the frontier the air cleared. From western Maryland to the backlands of the new colony of Georgia, Germans, Swiss, Scotch, new immigrants from Europe, and the poor from the older tidewater regions poured in to hew clearings, till new fields, and build homes. There slavery brought neither wealth to the few nor blight to the many. "When we came to the Bluff," wrote one of the Scotch immigrants who penetrated into South

Carolina in 1734, "my mother and we children were still in expectation that we were coming to an agreeable place. But when we arrived and saw nothing but a wilderness, and instead of a fine timbered house, nothing but a mean dirt house, our spirits quite sank," and here their guide left them unexpectedly. The father encouraged them by manly words, but while they were beginning to make their clearing the fire they had brought with them went out, and with no means of kindling a new one, the father had to try to find his way through the wilderness to another settler's to renew it. "We watched him as far as the trees would let him see, and then returned to our dolorous hut, expecting never to see him or any human being more. . . . Evening coming on, the wolves began to howl on all sides." [64]

It was a lawless life at first, and the endorsements on the Augusta County sheriff's writs of execution in the Shenandoah Valley of Virginia are illuminating. "Not executed by stress of water," we read on one, "and def[en-dan]t swore if I did get across he would shoot me if I touched any of his estates; also he is gone out of the country." A whole cinema drama in three clauses! On others we find endorsed, "not executed by reason there is no road to the place where he lives," "not executed by reason of a gun," "not executed by reason of an axx," and "kept from Miller with a club." [65] There were religious Germans in the valley who had not been able to hear a sermon in five years. Nevertheless, the frontier prospered and as the mountain slopes and valleys to the westward of all the Southern colonies slowly filled up there came into being a new sectional alignment, and tidewater and frontier divided the South into two contrasted types of culture.

This contrast came to exist in all the colonies, North as well as South. In the North also, as we shall see, the rich likewise drew much farther away from the mass of the people in this same period, but there were two points in which the two sections were sharply contrasted. In the North, although slavery was well established, it did not develop sufficiently as to have the effects just noted in the South, and the problems that the increasing complexity of society brought did not include the crucial one of the difference between the white artisan, laborer or farmer, and the slave owner. If to that extent, at least, there may have been a greater solidarity of interest and sentiment among all classes of whites in the North, there was an influence at work in another respect which later tended to divide the wealthiest class in the North from the people at large, as was not the case in the South.

The important relationship of debtor and creditor did not differ very materially between the tidewater and frontier sections or between the rich and poor in the North and the South. In the South, however, the position of the rich was by no means as independent as was that of the same class in the North. The great planter had, indeed, his tens of thousands of acres, his hundreds, possibly, of slaves, and his mortgages on the farms of his poorer neighbors, but there was a flaw in his imposing economic position.

It seems to be the nature of the large planter, and everywhere, to run into debt to his agents. Whether it is due to the extravagance engendered by the traditions of open-handed hospitality on great estates, whether to the fact that a considerable time elapses between the drawing against his bankers for the proceeds of his crop and the sale of it, whether because these drawings are apt to be optimistically large and an unexpected drop in price starts the planter irremediably wrong, or whatever else it may be due to, the fact remains, and was as true of the West Indians as of the continental planters. The Southerner who was growing richer seemed to need ever more and more money to sustain the equally rapidly advancing scale of his living, the need of capital for the development of his plantations, the purchase of slaves, or the vast speculation in frontier lands. In the North, the divorce between the agriculturist and the merchant had become fairly complete, and the mercantile, money-lending speculating class was not involved in large agricultural operations as was the southern merchant-planter. The fact that such a differentiation had not taken place in the South and that there the merchant class and the planter were to a great extent identical is the clue to certain later events.

As the century advanced, the Southern planter and the London merchant exchanged sharp letters over their mutual affairs, and complaints became more bitter on both sides. It was true that the mercantile nabobs of the North were also in debt to their English correspondents, but there was the great difference between the two cases, that whereas the Northerner was in debt for merchandise which could, more or less readily, be liquidated, the Southerner had spent the money represented by his debts either for living expenses or in such ways as did not permit of a speedy realization.[66] There were, of course, some in the South as well as in the North who had handsome free balances, but for the most part the planters seem to have had one subtle bond in common with the poor frontiersman who had borrowed money to set himself up — they both owed that which they could not pay, and the feelings which the poor debtor entertained for his rich creditor of the seaboard, the opulent planter in turn entertained for the still richer London merchant upon whose advances he depended to a large extent for the conspicuous luxury in which he lived.

THE COMMERCIALIZATION OF THE NORTH, 1713 – 45

THE PERIOD IMMEDIATELY FOLLOWING the Peace of Utrecht was one of very considerable expansion in the north, both of trade and of the frontier. As in the South, those with business acumen, capital, and influence took advantage of the new conditions to build fortunes rapidly. Whereas in the

South, however, the new class which came into being was that of wealthy planters, in the North it was made up in the main of merchants and a very few manufacturers, and the new Northern "aristocrats" became sharply differentiated by occupation as well as by wealth, from the tillers of the soil. The development of commerce and the change from an agricultural to a commercial community are well illustrated in Rhode Island. In 1680 it had been reported to the board of trade that there was not a single merchant in the colony, but that the people lived comfortably "by improving the wilderness." In 1708 there were 29 vessels owned by its citizens. By 1739 the little fleet had increased to 100, and by the middle of the century the number even of those over sixty tons had grown to 300. By 1720, Providence had embarked on its career as a seaport, and such families as the Tillinghasts, Powerses, and Browns were turning from farming to trading.

The little trading vessels which sailed from the Northern colonies set out from almost every village on seacoast or navigable stream. In the years immediately following the war, however, a stricter and apparently unnecessarily harsh and nagging enforcement of the laws by port officers made the carrying on of trade from any except the ports of entry very difficult. A memorial issued at Hartford in 1716 states that the surveyor-general was trying to close up all Connecticut ports, save one or two, in an apparent endeavor to force all vessels to clear from New London only.[67] In New York, two years earlier, Samuel Mulford, in a speech to the assembly, called attention to the abuses practiced in that colony by the naval officers even at the port of New York where so annoying were the conditions that, as he said, "not any man was fit to be Master of a Vessel . . . except he were a Lawyer; and then they should not escape, except it was by favour."[68] Among the examples he gave of the pernicious activities of the officials was that of a young man who sailed from the Connecticut shore to Long Island to be married and to carry over his wife's goods. The boat was seized, taken to New York, and confiscated, the unfortunate bridegroom having to pay the owner of £30 damages. To have sailed to New York to get his clearance papers would have added about 150 miles to his 20-mile trip. Although wheat was selling in Boston for nearly twice what it would bring in New York, the people at the east end of Long Island, 100 miles east of New York, were not allowed to carry their produce to Massachusetts unless they took it to New York first and cleared thence.

Commerce, indeed, continued from the smaller places, but such obstructive tactics on the part of royal officials must have helped the natural tendency to concentrate trade in the larger centers. The increasing size of the vessels also forced shipping from creeks and coves into larger harbors. Moreover, in several respects, business was becoming better organized, and shipping could be more advantageously carried on from those places where there was a certain amount of accumulated wealth and more frequent foreign news.

At the opening of the century, Boston was far in advance of any other port on the continent, with New York second. By the beginning of the third decade, although Boston's shipping had increased so that the entries at the customs house numbered 578, that of other ports had been increasing at an even more rapid rate, so that the figures were 173 for Philadelphia, 196 for New York, and about 220 a year for Charleston, South Carolina. By the middle of the century Boston had fallen considerably behind Philadelphia, which became the center of both commerce and culture but which, in turn, was beginning to find a new, though less important, rival in Baltimore. That town developed rapidly because of three factors: first, the ease of floating the produce of the backcountry down the Susquehanna; second, unlike Philadelphia, the access to its wharves in winter; and third, the greater foresight of the Baltimoreans in building good roads to tap the hinterland. In population, the New England metropolis became steadily less important in comparison to the others. Her rivals New York and Philadelphia, originally far behind her, gradually overtook her, and then forged ahead. Later, her commerce was to decline both relatively and actually, but up to the middle of the period covered by this section, she was still the leading town on the continent and the richest commercial port.

This rivalry of towns, however, was a new phase in colonial life, and brought new motives and forces into play. The way to riches in the North did not to any extent lie in agriculture, and mere speculation in land could be carried on quite as advantageously, if not more so, by living in town than in the country. The opportunities for trade and commerce were greater and the amenities of life far pleasanter there than on the frontier or in the rural districts.

The great increase in population and the extension of the frontier and the area under cultivation were irresistible forces steadily increasing the total produce of the colonies, and consequently the need for enlarging markets, swelling the volume of commerce, and the opportunities for profit. As always, there were fluctuations and occasionally crises. One of these began about 1730 and lasted for a number of years. In September 1731, a correspondent wrote to the *Boston News-Letter* from New York that there "is little or no News in this Place, nothing but the melancholy scene of little Business and less Money, the Markets grow very thin."[69] Two years later a versifier inquires:

Pray tell me the Cause of Trade being so dead,
Why Shops are shut up, Goods and Owners are fled,
And industrious Families cannot get Bread?[70]

In a few years the annual tax raised in that town for the poor had to be doubled, and a writer to the papers spoke of "the many Beggarly People daily suffered to wander about the Streets."[71]

In spite of these ups and downs, however, the volume of business grew decade by decade, and capital accumulated. This naturally sought profitable employment, and it is in this period that we have to note the beginning of manufactures on a commercial scale as contrasted with the home industries of an earlier day. In New England the chief manufacturing industry became that of rum, which formed the basis of the slave trade, and, with the decline in the general taste for beer, became the popular drink among the lower classes. Moreover, it was one of the mainstays of the fishing industry which advanced rapidly in the third quarter of the century. Marblehead, which at the opening of the century had scarcely ventured into fishing, was sending out annually 120 schooners by 1732 and owned 160 a decade later.

In the Middle colonies, the capitalists seeking investment in manufactures turned to iron, and many companies, most of them successful, were formed to engage in the industry. Until about 1720, Massachusetts had been the chief manufacturer of iron but from that time forward the center of the industry shifted to Pennsylvania, and was one of the many indications that leadership was passing from the Puritan colony. The number of plants in Massachusetts, Connecticut, New Jersey, and Maryland increased but the primacy in the industry passed to the capitalists of Philadelphia. So far behind did New England fall that by the middle of the century the people of New Hampshire were paying "a most intolerable price" for the iron which they imported chiefly from Pennsylvania, Maryland, and Virginia.[72]

New York distinctly lagged behind both her Southern and Northern neighbors in manufactures as well as commerce, but wealth was accumulating there also. Among the most important of the occupations in its effects was the illicit trade in Indian goods with the French of Canada by way of Albany and devious woodpaths. Governor Burnet, Cadwallader Colden, and other honest officials and colonials realized the extreme danger of this trade in detaching the Indians from the all-important alliance with the English and immensely strengthening the French influence among them. The danger to the colony, and in fact to the entire structure of the English empire in America, weighed nothing with the merchant group who were becoming rich from this easy and lucrative business, and intrigue followed intrigue to outwit the governor and deceive the government in England. In fact, the merchants of New York early in the eighteenth century have the unenviable record of having been allied with the pirates, engaging in the most unsavory land scandals of any of the colonies, and risking the safety of all by the Canadian trade.

One of the notable features of this period was the rise of new men. Such names associated with the wealthy groups of the several colonies, Brown, Faneuil, Waldo, Morris, Rutter, McCall, Potts, and others, mark a distinct break with the seventeenth century. These were not the descendants of the early leaders and founders but men of a new type, and their emergence from obscurity represents both new ideals for the upper classes and new relationships with the lower. Many of them were men of keen business ability, often only slightly troubled by ethical scruples, and bent upon carving out for themselves positions of prominence in the new world. Leadership in the North was becoming essentially a business affair.

As in the South, so in the North, the growing wealth of the few was utilized in a more luxurious mode of living and in the erection of commodious mansions which mark a great advance upon the preceding period, the introduction of the Georgian style everywhere modifying the earlier type of house. Dignified dwellings, of wood in New England, and of brick in New York, New Jersey, and Pennsylvania, replaced the simple homes of the close of the preceding century. As contrasted with the South, however, these were for the most part town houses and must be looked for in Portsmouth, Boston, Newport, New York, Philadelphia, or other towns and their near neighborhoods. Moreover, especially in New England, they were almost without exception the homes of merchants, such as those of Faneuil or Hancock in Boston or that of Captain Godfrey Malbone in Newport, the latter of which, in spite of its bad style, that entertaining and observant traveler from Maryland Alexander Hamilton found to be "the largest and most magnificent dwellinghouse" he had seen in all America.[73]

Let us now contrast this pleasing picture of rapidly accumulating wealth with the land position of some of the less fortunate neighbors of these shrewd colonial magnates, whose figures hitherto have loomed so much larger than those of the poor men at their gates. In 1733 five of these "simple men," who had settled on a largely barren tract of about 1,400 acres in western Massachusetts, petitioned the legislature. They stated that they had "not a foot of land to imploy our selves and families upon, were exposed to idleness and pinching want, and being then unsensible how highly the Court resented such a way of settling, and apprehending that the principle thing they insisted on was that there should be no trading or stock jobbing [biting but unintentional irony, this] but an actual settlement and improvement in husbandry by the Grantees themselves with which we were ready to comply,—wherefore being thus unhappily entangled on said land" they humbly prayed for a grant, based on charity and pity. Charity and pity, however, were not the proper appeals for legislative grants, the prayer was refused, and only after four years did the legislature, which was quite ready to grant fraudulent speculators six miles square gratis, agree to allow these few poor men to remain on the rocky acres they had cleared— that is, after they should have paid an adequate purchase price.

The new method of settling towns by granting them to speculators brought another grievance. In the earlier days most of the grantees of a town became its actual settlers and bore its hardships and burdens in common, all contributing to its upbuilding. Under the new system, however, the men who had the needful influence with the legislatures to receive grants or the necessary amount of capital to be able to buy at auction

*Lieutenant Governor
William Dummer's
house at Byfield,
Massachusetts (1715).
An early example of
New England Georgian.*

*Splendid "Mount Pleasant," Philadelphia (1761), built by John
McPherson, on the profits of privateering in the French Wars.*

*Built at Portsmouth,
New Hampshire (1720),
by Capt. Archibald
Macphaedris from the
proceeds of an iron
furnace and the fur
trade.*

the enormous tracts which the legislatures sold only in single blocks were not pioneers but the capitalists of the settled towns. To them, land was a mere commodity and their shares in the new towns mere counters in the game of moneymaking, as stock certificates are today for the active trader. To the actual pioneer and settler, however, his land was his all. His acres and the sweat and the back-breaking toil which went to their clearing and cultivation were all that lay between his family and starvation. As he and his equally hard-working neighbors felled the forest, laid out roads, built together the rude meetinghouse, and pinched their bellies to pay the minister's salary, the growth of their little town was of more significance to them than the whole of the empire; and the questions of taxation, land tenure, and local government were the most important in the world.[74]

But in case after case that might be cited, they found that although they were doing all the work of establishing the new settlement, a large number, often a majority and occasionally the entire body, of grantees remained behind in the comfortable old towns and from them controlled absolutely all matters of taxation and government, the settlers on the spot not being grantees but mere purchasers without the rights of townsmen. In Westminster, for example, in 1739 the proprietors met in the town itself for the first and last time for many years. With the exception of a very few, who became actual settlers, they were all nonresidents living in towns from forty to fifty miles away and refused to travel through the wilderness that distance to attend meetings. They voted themselves exemption from taxes and declined to assist in building a meetinghouse and making certain needed improvements, while they at the same time voted to themselves some of the taxes for dinners and other expenses. In 1743 the few resident proprietors journeyed to Cambridge, where the meetings were held, but they were ignored and returned to the town, unsuccessful in all their efforts and deeply aggrieved. The next year twenty-four families petitioned the legislature, complaining that the meetings were held fifty miles away from the town, that the clerk and treasurer resided at that distance, and that when the resident proprietors made the arduous journey to cast their vote in the town's affairs, they were "outvoted by a Majority of the Proprietors present who living so far distant from the Spot cannot be supposed to know so well as the Settlers what is necessary to be done." They added that when the nonresident proprietors are prevailed upon to vote any money at all for highways they spend most of it in sending up committees to look them over, and that "they are so free and generous when they assemble together at their meetings that a very great part of what they vote to be raised for the Settlement is generally expended to pay Tavern expenses."[75] The proprietors continued to hold their meetings in the vicinity of Boston and not a single settler was made a member of their standing committee. In 1749 the settlers again appealed to the deaf legislature for relief. After two years more a legislative committee finally appeared at the town, but it was not until 1759, when the maddening situation had already lasted for over twenty years, that their prayer to be incorporated as a town was only so far granted that they were set off as a district without representation in the legislature. This was just what they had begged should not be done.

It is not difficult to realize how, as these very real grievances against the capitalists and the colonial government were borne in upon the poor, hard-working pioneers of Westminster and of many other such communities, their attitude would become one of extreme resentment against those capitalists who were reaping unearned increment upon their landholdings, while at the same time refusing to bear their share of the burdens and treating the settlers very much like a colony of slaves who were to toil for their masters rather than for themselves. When some years later the word "slave" assumed an extreme prominence in the propagandist literature of the Revolutionary period it carried a meaning, though not as related to the British government, to innumerable settlers who had spent the best years of their lives in just such toil, and in embittering contests with the capitalists and with just such vain appeals for justice to the local government, as we have described. We have not as yet made a sufficiently detailed survey of the geographical distribution of radicalism, but it is significant that for a generation at least before the Revolution such districts as the northern frontier, western Massachusetts, or eastern Connecticut where radicalism was much in evidence, were exactly those districts where disputed land titles, difficulties with speculators, absenteeism, and other agrarian troubles were most in evidence.

In New Jersey, in the latter part of the period covered here and for some years thereafter, serious riots occurred owing to disputes between the proprietors of the colony and those landowners who had not acquired titles as legally required. Ejectment suits were brought wholesale, and frequently against those who honestly believed they had valid title by purchase or long possession. Throughout all the colonies, land titles were uncertain and even in Massachusetts, at the time of the Andros administration, there were few titles which could stand a rigid technical investigation. The efforts of the New Jersey proprietors, which became notable after 1743, irritated the people and kept the province in a turmoil for a decade. "Persons who had long holden under the proprietors were forcibly ejected; others compelled to take leases from landlords whom they were not disposed to acknowledge; while those who had courage to stand out, were threatened with, and in many instances received, personal violence."[76]

It is in this period that we note clearly the rising tide of this radicalism, the beginning of a distinct class conflict, the birth of the modern politician as a colonial type, and some of the evolving characteristics of our political machinery. The more than doubling of a population which had been largely confined within its old borders, had naturally greatly increased the keenness of competition between individuals and between social groups. Although this added to the opportunities for those who could avail themselves of them, it at the same time forced into lower economic rank, even if not into abject poverty, large numbers of those who proved less well able to take care of themselves under the harder test.

Local political action became more and more the expression of radical sentiment and in assuming some of its modern aspects proved the seedbed for the growth of the politician. Governor Shirley's description of a Boston town meeting has a singularly modern ring when he says that one of them "may be called together at any time upon the Petition of ten of the meanest Inhabitants, who by their constant attendance there generally are the majority and outvote the Gentlemen, Merchants, Substantial Traders and all the better part of the Inhabitants; to whom it is Irksome to attend at such meetings, except upon very extraordinary occasions."[77]

The change of interests which we have already noted in New England life was thus beginning to bring not only the lawyer, the great merchant, the speculator, and others of the more fortunate or favored economic classes, but the professional politician who based his leadership upon voicing the ills of a common people growing more self-conscious. Popular grievances, the forum of the public meeting and the apathy or self-confidence of the upper classes combined to open his way. The upper economic group, in spite of their numerical inferiority, had hitherto remained in comfortable control partly because of the extremely limited franchise and partly because of the lack of grievances, leaders, and cohesion among the common people. Grievances were now accumulating and leaders, though still obscure, were developing. The strength recently displayed by the "popular party" had seriously alarmed the merchant-capitalist group and they now realized what had apparently escaped them before: that there was danger in the constantly increasing numbers of the assembly, owing to the fact that as each new town was incorporated it became entitled to send two representatives. Already there were eligible 320 assemblymen as against only the permanently fixed number of 28 members of the council. Steps were immediately taken, therefore, by the conservatives to prevent further increase in popular representation, and it was arranged by orders from the lords of trade that thereafter the privilege of sending representatives from newly incorporated towns should depend upon the governor's consent.

Evidence of the growing sectionalism and fear of losing control on the part of the entrenched groups appears just as clearly in Pennsylvania, where the rapid increase in population of the newer counties was threatening the control of the old "East," and the increasing number of citizens in Philadelphia was threatening that of the old municipal ruling class. Efforts therefore were made to prevent the intrusion of these new elements both by suffrage qualifications and the representation of counties. When Lancaster was formed in 1729 it was allowed only four votes in the assembly instead of the eight which were enjoyed by the older ones. For the next twenty years, in spite of great increase in population in the outlying districts, no new counties were erected, and when in 1749 and 1750 two were created, they were allowed but two members each, and two years later two others were given but one vote each.[78]

The social and economic life of the period, in both the South and the North, was marked by a more distinct difference between rich and poor, by the increase and concentration of wealth, and by the resultant growth of economic and social grievances upon the part of considerable sections of the population. There had never been entire equality or harmony but in the comparative simplicity of the earlier periods and under the rigid discipline of unsubdued wilderness, wild beast, hostile foe, and the ever present specter of stark hunger, the differences in both rank and opportunity had been reduced to a minimum. With the change from forest to field, the rapid growth of wealth and the development of a more complex society, there had also come into play forces tending to cleave that society into sections and classes. The poor whites of the South, the foreigners of the Middle colonies, and the depressed agriculturists and befooled frontier settlers of the North were among the groups which developed genuine and special grievances.

Back of all the colonies there was developing a frontier section in which the ideals, ways of living, hopes, and animosities bore a common stamp from the woods of Maine to the mountain valleys of western Carolina. Within the older tidewater sections themselves there was no longer comparative unity of interest in the several localities but growing diversity and conflict, with an increasingly sharp alignment between classes and an increasing self-consciousness on the part of both the upper and lower. We are too apt to picture the life of the eighteenth century from the dignified homes of the rich, the literature found in their libraries, and the dull and stately if withal somewhat boisterous and coarse lives carried on within their walls and scented gardens. Beneath all this there was fermenting a new life among classes largely illiterate, without leadership and with but little voice in legislative halls. As individuals they had been bent upon making their own way in a new world where they found few of the restraints of the old, but when they began to feel that, one by one, hindrances and restraints were again appearing to tangle their way, they began to turn restive, to become conscious of their aims and their common grievances, and to follow those who here and there essayed the role of leaders or of demagogues. The traces of this aspect of colonial life are far harder to disinter than are those of imperial conflict or of high social life. They are, as it were, written in invisible ink, but they cannot be ignored if we wish to understand rather than merely to recount the greater social movements of the later period of which they were the forerunners. That they were far from being ignored by the upper classes in their own day is shown by the various political moves that were made to thwart the awakened consciousness and the frequently crude efforts at self-assertion of the farmers and artisans.

In addition to such cleavages as were common to all the colonies, we have also to note the rise during this period of the two contrasted types of civilization in the North and the South, the one mainly agricultural and based upon slavery, the other becoming commercial and based upon free labor. We have so far been concerned with forces that tended to divide the colonists into classes and sections, to set off the rich against the poor, the exploiters against the exploited, the East against the West. It is now time to examine those other forces which developed from the rise of an indigenous colonial culture and which tended to unite the various colonists by a common intellectual outlook, even as the frontier sections had been united in a common outlook upon the practical life of suffering, work, and effort.

THE GROWTH OF A COLONIAL CULTURE, 1713-45

WE HAVE SPOKEN of the three periods of distinct cultural difference in the colonies. First that characterized by a purely transplanted growth, subject to slow modification and disintegration under the influences of the wilderness. Next the short period of extreme declension and of hesitation succeeding upon the withering of this imported culture, and third the period of development of a native-born one. It is with the beginnings of this last that we have now to deal.

In spite of the many tendencies which were making for cleavages of one sort or another in the provincial society of the several colonies, we have nevertheless already noted several which were of considerable unifying power. So long as the colonies, and the innumerable villages and settlements in them, were separated from one another by long stretches of wilderness, and communication of any sort was scanty, there could be no development of a common consciousness or of a common public opinion. These are essentially growths of common interests and of interchange of ideas. The steadily increasing intercolonial trade was a factor of prime importance in this regard, as, in their narrower range, were the itinerant peddler, shoemaker, candle dipper, and other petty tradesmen or artificers who made their way from neighborhood to neighborhood, weaving from the news and gossip of one and another a web of common thoughts and knowledge. The traveling preacher, and particularly the Quakers who were constantly on the move from one community to another, often with unpleasant encouragement from the citizens, were additional influences in bringing various groups into contact, as were also the intercolonial migrations which we have noted.

Throughout this period, the improvement in the roads and the enlarged size of vessels did much to facilitate traveling and thereby to promote intercourse. It is true that even the main highways were none too good and that once off these the traveler fared badly even on horseback, but well before the end of this period there was a much traveled system of roads connecting the different colonies with one another and the principal places in each. By 1732 there was enough public demand to warrant publishing the first American guidebook, which gave, along with much other useful information, the location and dates of the chief fairs in the Northern colonies and the roads and distances between the more important points.[79] It gave the road from Boston through Providence, New London, New York, and Philadelphia to Jamestown, Virginia, in all 711 miles, and a number of branches from this main artery. This road continued as far south as Charleston, and traveling overland was now becoming frequent both for business and pleasure.

One of the notable social movements of the period, and one which had a marked effect upon the dissemination of news and upon the formation of a public opinion, was the establishment of innumerable and now mostly forgotten organizations for social, intellectual, and other purposes. We have noted how immigration from Europe to the colonies necessarily broke most of the ties uniting individuals in the social structure, which itself thus disintegrated, and how time was required for a new integration. That the time had now come for a coalescing of the individual atoms of society into a new social order is shown by the numerous voluntary organizations which sprang up in all the colonies. The simplest of these was the club, which was also just entering upon its great vogue in England. These colonial clubs, which we find mentioned in surprisingly large numbers from the second decade of the century, were groups of individuals, mostly although not always men only, which met at stated intervals, frequently once or twice a week, at a tavern or private residence for social intercourse, the interchange of ideas, and the generous absorption of liquor. Made up of men of a common trade or profession, of a single racial group, of a special social set, or merely of congenial spirits, they must have been of vast influence in helping to overcome the extreme individualism of society and to form public opinion.

Travelers were welcomed at their gatherings if properly introduced, and it is from such guests that we get many glimpses of clubs that would otherwise be forgotten. Thus, in 1710, John Fontaine, as a visitor in New York, amused himself with frequent evenings at the Irish Club and the French Club; Hamilton on his journey north in 1744 mentions a "drunken club" at a tavern near Joppa, Maryland, the "Governor's Club" and Musick Club at Philadelphia, the Hungarian Club in New York, the Philosophical Club at Newport, and the Physical Club and the "club at Withered's" in Boston; Black, in the same year, speaks of the Beefsteak Club of Philadelphia; and we have also mention of a fishing club of the same town formed in 1732 as the Schuylkill Fishing Company, the Hum Drum Club in New

York in 1734, the Tuesday Club of Annapolis, founded in 1745, the South River Club near that town and already called "antient" in 1747, the Maryland Jockey Club established 1745, the French Club of Charleston, 1737, and many others. In fact they sprang up everywhere and evidently answered to a genuine social need.

The name, whether serious or playful, was often belied, and the main object was usually conviviality and talk. Thus, Black tells us that the "Beef Stake Club" was so called because the members gathered to eat steaks but that when he attended and the dinner came on there were over twenty other dishes. At the Philosophical Club in Newport, Hamilton says that they drank punch and smoked tobacco and that at their meeting he "was surprised to find that no matters of philosophy were brought upon the carpet. They talked of privateering and the building of vessels."[80] This failure to cling to high matters was evidently a common one. In 1747 a club member of Chestertown, Maryland, wrote to the *Gazette* saying that "when Clubs (consisting of Men rightly sorted) meet together, to hear and impart News, communicate Thoughts and improve one another by Conversation, they pass away their spare Hours agreably, and to good Purpose; but the Intention is wholly frustrated by an *Omnium Gatherum,* who are neither capable of improving or being improved."[81]

The fact that the philosophers of Newport preferred to discuss privateering rather than philosophy and that the affairs of the day were the topics at most of such gatherings elsewhere was not a serious drawback. The important thing was that everywhere, from Salem to Savannah, there were coming into existence focal points for the creating and sharpening of a common consciousness and a new social organ for the formation of common views.

In this period we have another instance of the same cohesive forces at work in the establishment of numerous lodges of Freemasons. The first reference to Masonry in America seems to have been a letter from the collector of the port of Philadelphia in 1715 in which he speaks of spending "a few evenings in festivity" with his Masonic brethren. By 1730 there appear to have been several lodges established in Pennsylvania, and in 1735 one was established at Savannah, one at Charleston, one at Portsmouth in 1737, one at Norfolk in 1741, and within this period Masons were meeting regularly in Boston and New York, though there is much uncertainty as to a number of these early dates. That, however, is not essential, our main interest being in the establishment of an order which had ramifications in more than half of the colonies, soon to appear in a number of the others. By the middle of the century, a Mason traveling through America instead of being a lonely stranger would have found himself among an organized band of his brothers in the principal town of every one of the colonies with the exception of North Carolina. Here was another thread in the growing pattern of Americanism.[82]

To what an extent colonial boundaries were disappearing in social and

intellectual relations is shown by the membership of one of the most interesting organizations which was founded within this period. In 1727, Franklin had organized the "Junto," a debating society of young men who met
to read papers and discuss them afterward. This seems to have declined in
interest, and in 1743, Franklin, together with Cadwallader Colden, and
others, formed the first "American Philosophical Society." In the proposal
he put out he suggested that such a society should be "formed of the
virtuosi or ingenious men residing in the several colonies, to be established
in the city of Philadelphia as the most central place.[83] Although the society
at that time languished, and Franklin had to confess that the members were
"very idle gentlemen," nevertheless, the membership included men from
the colonies of New York, New Jersey, Pennsylvania, Maryland, Carolina,
and several from New England, representing the best intellectual elements
in America. Its mere formation indicates that communication, culture, and
common interests had at least progressed sufficiently to make such a combination seem feasible to so practical a man as Franklin. That it was formed
is far more significant of the new conditions than that it failed.

The growth of population in the several colonies which made practically
a continuous line of settlements up and down the coast brought people
together by the mere physical fact of being neighbors. Commerce, travel,
better roads, the post, and other elements we have mentioned were all
adding their share in the formation of a common life and thought for all the
colonies. Another and most important factor was the growth of a periodical
press. Various things combined to make such a growth possible in the
period. There was first the physical problem of distribution and this was
greatly facilitated by the improvement in the roads and the establishment
of many postal riders on local routes about the main centers. By means of
these it became possible to extend the circulation of the journals beyond
the mere house-to-house delivery for the townsmen. There was also essential a public demand for news. Man is a gregarious and conversational
animal. If he talks about what he is interested in, he is also apt to grow
interested in what he talks about. Talking first and learning afterward is
by no means a rare dialectical process. It is probable, therefore, that the
innumerable clubs which came into existence at every crossroads tavern
were by no means negligible in stimulating the demand for the news sheets
which had their rise within the same period.

Although the circulation remained small—as a rule only a few hundred
copies of any of the journals established being printed—this by no means
represented the public which they reached as they were handed about
from one to another and became stained and torn from use in many a
tavern and coffeehouse. In the preceding period only one small journal, the
innocuous *Boston News-Letter,* had represented the entire periodical press
of the colonies, whereas in the one now under review twenty-two weekly
publications were started, of which six were in Massachusetts, one in

Rhode Island, four in New York, six in Pennsylvania, two in Maryland, one in Virginia, and two in South Carolina.[84] A few of these died untimely deaths or merged with more prosperous contemporaries or successors, but by the end of the period the weekly newspaper was firmly established in the six leading colonies of Massachusetts, New York, Pennsylvania, Maryland, Virginia, and South Carolina. Of the six journals noted as having been started in Pennsylvania, three were in German, of which Christopher Sauer's *Der Hoch-Deutsch Pennsylvanische Geschicht-Schreiber,* founded in 1739, was the earliest in the field.

In breadth of interest these new publications marked a great advance upon the bare bones of scanty news purveyed in the *News-Letter*. Beginning with the *New-England Courant,* founded by James Franklin in Boston in 1721, they developed a distinctively literary quality. The *Courant*, indeed, lived only a few stormy years until 1727, but the type had been successfully established, and although much of the literature in which the various journals indulged was either copied from English models such as the *Spectator* or was of frankly inferior native growth, nevertheless it did provide the colonists with reading matter of some literary interest.[85] Young Benjamin Franklin had worked with his older brother on the *Courant,* but the well-known episode of his flight from Boston to Philadelphia resulted in establishing the latter town as the journalistic center of the colonies. Not only did his paper, the *Pennsylvania Gazette* (1729) become the most important and entertaining journal in America, but his influence both directly and indirectly extended to those of other colonies in which he financed many journals. With the *South-Carolina Gazette* his relations were close and his influence is easily detected.

The makeup of these various semiliterary, seminews journals was much the same for all. In its first year, 1736, the *Virginia Gazette,* for example, published mainly brief news dispatches from other colonies, local items, letters from Europe, reprints of English articles or literary productions, original poems, essays, and advertisements. In the latter part of the period the literary interest of the Virginia and South Carolina journals was rather greater than that of any published in New England, and the culture of both those colonies cannot be appreciated without a careful study of the files of their two gazettes. The old tradition of the continuous literary preeminence of New England was largely based upon mere ignorance of conditions and sources in the other colonies. Indeed, in original verse, no other colonial journal can equal the *South-Carolina Gazette,* with the *Virginia Gazette* second, and the prose articles of the latter were quoted throughout all the colonies.

If the literary quality, meager as it was, of the many newspapers of this period was influential in molding public taste, it was to their news columns that the growth of public opinion was most indebted. The failure of the attempt to indict the elder Franklin in Boston for libel on account of certain articles in the *Courant* in 1723 cleared the way in that colony for the complete freedom of the press, as did the case of John Peter Zenger for New York eleven years later. In the latter case, although the whole influence of the governor and court was against the publisher, the brilliant pleading of Andrew Hamilton, the most noted lawyer in America, who had been induced to travel from Philadelphia to appear for the defendant, won a verdict of not guilty from the jury, and Zenger continued to publish the *Journal* until his death. Hamilton's speech showed profound learning, and although some of the propositions which he advanced were not tenable as points in Anglo-American law at that time, they became permanently grafted into our political jurisprudence, and the speech, which was frequently reprinted in England, established his reputation abroad.[86]

Aided by these two victories, the evidently growing interest in intercolonial news, and better communications, the news elements in the journals increased, and when the largely literary *New England Journal* was merged with the *Boston Gazette* in 1741, the new organ was distinctly more of the modern newspaper type than any which had thus far appeared. That the colonists were taking a considerable interest in the affairs, political as well as commercial, of colonies other than their own is shown by the increasing number of items copied from other papers, such as speeches of the governors, acts of legislatures, and brief notes of murders, drownings, cases of arson, infanticide, and other crimes or accidents. The fact that such items from New England found their way into the *Maryland Gazette* or that similar happenings in South Carolina appeared in the Northern papers was itself indicative of a growing solidarity of acquaintance and knowledge.

That the press was already being used as a means of influencing public opinion in other than political matters is shown in some of the entries in the diary of William Seward, who preceded George Whitefield on his revivalistic tour of the colonies in 1741 and who may be called the first press agent in America. For example, we find him recording that he "wrote Paragraphs for the News, where our Brother was to preach and had preached," and again, from New Brunswick, "wrote Paragraphs for the News, of our Brother's Preaching, etc., particularly the following, to be published in New York," it being an article describing the remarkable success of the missionary in Philadelphia.[87] This work he continued, even editing Whitefield's own contributions, and preparing the way for him as he advanced by an adroit manipulation of articles in the press.

The success of the newspapers, which had to a considerable extent filled their columns with literature rather than news, seemed to indicate that there was a public which was ready for that sort of fare and the trend toward a pure news sheet of the modern type, which we have just noticed on the one hand, was balanced on the other by an attempt to segregate the purely literary portion of the papers and to establish magazines of the sort becoming popular in England. The time was not quite ripe for this ambitious effort and although three monthly publications were started none succeeded. The *American Magazine and Historical Chronicle* published in Boston from 1743 to 1746 lasted longest, but it was merely a close imitation of the *London Magazine,* and was largely devoted to the republication of English articles. The most interesting attempt was that of the *General Magazine and Historical Chronicle for all the British Plantations in America,* started by Franklin in Philadelphia in 1741.[88] The advance from the extreme parochialism of earlier days was indicated by the scope of its contents. It was distinctly a production by Anglo-Americans for Anglo-America, including not only the continental colonies but also the West Indies. One department was devoted to the reprinting of essays from colonial papers—instead of from English journals—including selections from publications as far apart as Massachusetts and Virginia. Poems by colonials were also reprinted from the papers of New York, Pennsylvania, Virginia, and South Carolina. In the department called "Accounts of or Extracts from new Books, Pamphlets, &c. published in the Plantations" we have not only the first attempt at systematic book reviewing in the colonies but a reviewing devoted entirely to the products of the colonial presses. It is evident that we are entering upon a period in which there was not only a distinct colonial culture developing but a culture which was becoming self-conscious. The content of this culture calls for a brief examination before considering other unifying forces in operation at the close of this period.

Its beginning was marked by a fierce conflict between science and religion in connection with the introduction of the new method of inoculation for the smallpox, which conflict started in London and spread thence to the colonies. Beginning with 1714 several articles appeared in the *Transactions* of the Royal Society and elsewhere on the results of inoculation as practiced in Turkey. These called forth denunciatory sermons by clergymen who called it "a Diabolical Operation, which usurps an Authority founded neither in the Laws of Nature or Religion, which tends to anticipate and banish Providence out of the World and promotes the Increase of Vice and Immorality."[89] In the course of a serious epidemic of the disease in Boston in 1721 the articles fell into the hands of Cotton Mather who saw their importance and communicated them to the physicians of that town. Dr. William Douglass, who was the only doctor there entitled to the degree, was deeply opposed to the innovation, which was as warmly espoused by the American Zabdiel Boylston, who tried the process. At once the town was in a ferment, and the people were so enraged that his life and Mather's were both threatened, and it was said that if any patient died the doctor should be considered a murderer. In spite of a prolonged and violent opposition, Boylston won the day, backed by the two Mathers and three others of the leading clergy of Boston. The conflict, however, was repeated at intervals in other colonies.

Within this period Cotton Mather, Paul Dudley, and John Winthrop of Massachusetts and Jared Eliot of Connecticut all continued to interest themselves in science, and in 1738, Winthrop was appointed to the new chair of mathematics and natural philosophy at Harvard. There was also evidence of a certain amount of popular interest in such matters. In 1734, Professor Isaac Greenwood gave "astronomical lectures" twice a week in Boston, apparently successfully.

In the arts, we have to note the continuance of the two tendencies mentioned earlier, a decline in the folk art and a gradual advance in that for the rich. The moderate increase in manufactured articles kept pace with a decrease in their home or individual production. Among the comparatively poor, for example, crude manufactured pottery tended to replace the few pieces of treasured pewter. In other articles, cast iron was beginning to be substituted for the hand-wrought work of the smith, and in architecture, carving completely disappeared from the houses of the small farmer or artisan, which were losing their picturesque quality and tending to become the hopeless square boxes with which the countryside is too familiar today. The graceful Windsor chair, which although it may have originated in England became far more characteristic of the colonies, began its vogue about 1725 and was found everywhere, with slight local differences throughout the colonies, but in general there was a distinct decline in the aesthetic quality of the furniture of the people.

On the other hand, the number of painters and of pictures in the houses of the well-to-do increased. In Charleston, B. Roberts, Alexander Gordon, and Jeremiah Theuss were all at work in this period, Theuss being the painter of the Ravenels, Porches, Manigaults, Izards, Allstons, and other social leaders there. In Virginia, Charles Bridges, from 1730 to 1750, was painting many of the portraits—including that of Evelyn Byrd—which have often hopefully been ascribed to Sir Godfrey Kneller. In Maryland, Hesselius, whom we have already mentioned, besides much portrait work, executed in 1721 the first ecclesiastical decoration in North America in a painting of the Last Supper for the Church of St. Barnabas in Queen Anne's Parish. Philadelphia, New York, Boston, and Newport all had their favorite portrait painters; Robert Feke of Newport is now recognized as the best, certainly among those of American training. In Boston, Smibert seems occasionally to have imported and sold pictures as well as painted them. In 1735 he offered for sale a large collection of valuable engravings after Raphael, Michelangelo, Poussin, Rubens, and others, including the principal artists of England, Holland, France, and Italy. The mere fact of naming the artists in this period indicates an increasing interest in art. Sculpture makes its first appearance in the inventory of Smibert's estate in 1752 in which there was included £4 worth of "Bustoes and figures in Paris plaster."

Music and the drama showed a more noteworthy advance than did painting. The execrable church singing in New England was defended against attempted improvement by recalcitrant deacons and other conservative persons who claimed that the suggested new singing by note would grieve good men, exasperate them and cause them to "behave disorderly," that it was popish, that it might—horrible thought!—introduce instruments, that the names of the notes were blasphemous, and for other equally good reasons. Finally the new method won its way, and the change to Watts's psalms in many churches and the doing away with the old system of "lining out" greatly improved the music. New England, however, was not musical, and even in cultivated and wealthy Newport the organist of Trinity Church complained in 1739 that any musician was metaphorically buried alive there.

There may have been a concert in Boston as early as 1732, and a notice in the *Boston News-Letter* of the postponement of one in 1734 indicates that they may have become more or less frequent by that time "in the Consort Room in Wing's Lane." [90] The first recorded one in New York was given in 1733, but we have no notice of any in Philadelphia during this whole period, although there is a trace of a musical society in 1740 and we have already noted Hamilton's attendance at the "Musick Club" four years later. Nevertheless, there was apparently more interest in music in the Middle and Southern colonies than in New England. The best to be heard at this time was undoubtedly that at the Moravian settlement of Bethlehem, founded in 1741, and which was destined to become the center of the Bach cult in America. In addition to the organ, the concerts at Bethlehem employed the violin, viola da braccio, viola da gamba, flutes, and French horns, and the fame of the concerts became so great as to attract as visitors Franklin, Washington, and others of the most prominent men in the colonies.

For the current discussion of music we can turn to the *Virginia Gazette* and there find several of the leading articles devoted to it, one of them being a long disquisition on Italian opera.[91] Charleston, however, probably had the best public musical life in the colonies. Good concerts were frequent there after 1732, the first song recital in America was given there the following year, and in 1735 the first ballad opera.

Sporadic efforts were also made during this period to establish the drama, but the real beginnings of the American theater belong to the decade following 1750. There was certainly a theater in Williamsburg, Virginia, by 1722 and possibly earlier but it was not successful, although occasionally used. In New York, the "New Theater" was used from 1732 to 1734, among other performances given being *The Beaux' Stratagem* and *The Busybody.* It appears to have been opened again in 1739 but there is nothing known of it definitely. In Charleston, the successful concert season to which we have just alluded was followed by the building of a theater, which opened in January 1735, with the performance of Otway's *Orphan.* In 1737 a performance was given by the Freemasons, but no play is heard of again for another dozen years. Philadelphia had puppet shows in 1742 but no dramatic performance during this period, and New England throughout the whole colonial time was negligible in the history of both drama and opera.

Science and the arts, however, affected but a small part of the population. Science was only for the intellectually elite and the arts as they were developing were mainly for the rich. The mental life of the mass of men, outside of the daily routine of living, ran almost wholly in the two channels of politics and religion, which were subtly intermingled. In politics the period witnessed the steady advance in the theory of natural rights and the law of nature. The important work of John Wise, which was published just as the period opened, and the doctrines he had so ably put forth were springing up almost spontaneously throughout the colonies. Thus Samuel Mulford in his speech before the New York assembly in 1714 invoked "the Law of God and Nature," as protection for the rights of the people against the unjust attitude of the customs officials. He added that the law complained of was "settled upon the Subject by Act of Parliament," but as the century advanced, Parliament retreated into the background in the popular theory, which more and more posited natural rights and a natural law superior to any made by man.

Although one of the chief influences in legal development was derived from the legalistic aspects of religious doctrine, we have already several times had to note the decline in religious interest among the people. The original fervor of the New England Puritans had long since passed, and throughout all the colonies the growing variety of life, the economic struggles and opportunities, the encroachments of Deism, Arminianism, and other first fruits of the growing rationalism notable in the period, turned men's thoughts away from the old doctrines. There was everywhere not only a secularizing of interests but a growing coldness and formalism in religious life. During these years, however, the colonists were to be caught up in a movement, the sources of which were in Europe, that was to sweep through America, completely altering the outlook of the people and leaving behind results of the first importance in every department of colonial life.

Long before the coming of George Whitefield in 1739, there had been stirrings here and there which presaged a change in spirit and a deep discontent with the stereotyped and formal religion which had become the type of no one church alone. Among the varied sects of the German immigrants to Pennsylvania there were many Pietists and a deep infusion of the pietistic spirit, and throughout the century these settlers were peculiarly liable to religious excitement. Before the Awakening in its narrower sense, there had been a number of revivals in that colony which had converted to a more zealous religious life many of the Lutherans and Reformed, whose churches had been largely neglected.

In 1726, Theodorus J. Frelinghuysen held a notable revival in New Jersey.

But the leading figure in the Great Awakening was Jonathan Edwards, unquestionably one of the greatest intellects this country has produced. Interpreting the universe solely in logical terms, however, he was led to the seemingly inevitable conclusion that God was the author of evil, that He was a monster of wrath, and that man was utterly helpless in his moral strivings against the incomprehensible predestination of the Deity. In spite of much original sweetness both of mind and character, Edwards deliberately preached the most damnatory doctrine in the name of Christ which it is possible to conceive. Content neither to rest in suspense upon the insoluble problem of the existence of evil, nor to accept as an act of faith the doctrine of God as love, which was preached by the founder of that religion of which Edwards had been ordained a minister, he described God as a being with no more pity than a fiend, holding those who had striven for righteousness, as well as the abandoned, "over the pit of hell, much as one holds a spider, or some loathsome insect, over the fire" and rejoicing, in a manner which would shock the most degenerate human criminal, over the consequences of the evil of which He was himself the author. To this had New England Puritanism come at last. There had been a revival, the most important of which had then occurred, in Enfield under his preaching in 1735, with many of the frenzied physical manifestations which were to become common as the movement continued, and Edwards wrote an account of it which was widely read both in the colonies and England.

All of these, and other scattered manifestations of revival, were destined to be swept up together in the great movement which was initiated by the preaching of Whitefield on his several tours through the colonies, beginning in 1739. Accounts of the marvelous influence of his preaching in England and the astounding size of his audiences had been described in a number of the colonial newspapers, such as the *South-Carolina Gazette,* the *Virginia Gazette,* and the Philadelphia *Mercury,* and when he landed the way had been prepared for similar results here. Wherever he went the people poured out to hear him and the new evangelism swept like a fire across the colonies.

The ascendancy of the old established churches had been shaken, and the people had to a great extent won the right to such a religious life as seemed to them best for themselves. Underneath the purely religious aspects of the movement, there was a deep undercurrent of democracy and individualism. The control of the conservative element was everywhere shattered, and the evangelicals of all denominations felt themselves in far closer sympathy with one another than with the "Old Lights" of their several churches. The intellectual as well as the emotional life of the colonies had been stirred deeply, and the residents of them all had watched the phenomena of the others with rapt attention. It was the first movement which had embraced them all and for the first time they found themselves caught up together in a single wave of emotion. Not only the rigid distinc-

tions between colonial churches but boundary lines and provincial prejudices had been swept aside, and when the movement passed, the new
evangelistic denominations were to a considerable extent no longer provincial but American.[92]

It is also within this period that we begin to find comments upon "Americanisms" in our language making their appearance. For example, a traveler
in 1745 notes the changed meaning in America of the term "ordinary" as
applied to an inn, though the *New Oxford Dictionary* does not trace this
divergence prior to 1774.[93] Similarly the word "branch" in the sense of "a
stream running across the road" is found and defined by the same traveler,
although the dictionary does not trace it before the nineteenth century.
The use of "fall" for "autumn" appears so casually, in letters of William
Logan in 1727 and Eliza Lucas in 1742, as to indicate that it was already an
accepted form. Samuel Johnson in 1756 spoke of the "American dialect,"
and many of the words most familiar in the colonies must have been utterly
strange to ears in the mother country.

*From a contemporary anonymous cartoon probably produced in
Pennsylvania about 1760. Franklin points out that the noncombatant
Quaker (with the sheep's head) is bound to flourish, whether the French
or the English win the war.*

Part of the new American vocabulary came from borrowing from other languages. Skunk, hickory, squash, caribou, porgy, catalpa, raccoon, terrapin, and a host of other names now in common use came from the native Indian, as well as those used to designate the new implements of one sort or another which the colonists adopted, such as canoe, toboggan, moccasin, tomahawk, and wigwam. By the middle of the century such French words as bureau, gopher, bogus, portage, prairie, and chowder had become an integral part of "the American language." The Dutch had contributed cruller, stoop, waffle, scow, boss, cookey, span (of horses), pit (of a peach), and others unknown in England. More important than these borrowings were the new words the colonists coined for themselves, such as bull-frog, egg-plant, snow-plow, cold-snap, trail, pop-corn, shingle, back-log, sophomore, schooner, cat-boat, to mention at random a few from the mass of terms which were beginning to make the common language of Americans sound strange and uncouth to their English cousins. Many new adjectives, such as handy, kinky, chunky, were well established before the Revolution. Many of the terms which were sound old English and which the colonists had brought with them were being retained here, whereas they were falling into disuse in England, so that they came later to be considered "Americanisms" and added to the divergence between the two countries. Among these we may note burly, cater-corner, likely, deft, scant, and ornate. Bub, for a boy, is very old English but has been retained only in America. In sounding the vowels, the colonists retained the flattened *a,* which was then common in England, and did not differ in this respect from the English until the latter began to use the broad *a* in the third quarter of the century.[94] In Maryland, however, traveling Englishmen already noted that, by association with the blacks, the children unconsciously imitated their speech, and that Southern pronunciation was thus beginning to assume its peculiar characteristics.

Among the common people, if there was ample ignorance, bigotry, and prejudice, there was a mental activity which had been much stirred by the experiences of newcomers in their immigration; and for the native-born, by life in the wilderness, the constant shift of many from one locality to another, the military expeditions, changing social conditions, and the great revivals. For the most part, the farmers and artisans and petty tradesmen have left no written record of their thoughts, and it is only now and then that the veil lifts and allows us to see what these may have been. Conversation seems to have been one of the staple products of colonial life, and we have frequent reports of its subjects by the travelers now wandering about.

Hamilton was careful to note many as he rode from Annapolis northward, and helps us to fill in the outlines of a picture of popular thought and preoccupations. In one of the inns at which he stayed, the "learned company consisted of the landlord, his overseer and miller and another greasy thumbed fellow," and the topics of dispute were "politicks, news, and the dreaded French War." Riding along a day or so after, he fell in with a Scotch-Irishman who "had a particular down-hanging look, which made me suspect he was one of our New-light bigots" and who told Hamilton, after a little preliminary religious discourse, that he "was damned without redemption." A little farther along, picking up the proprietor of the Principal Iron Works, the conversation turned from religion to politics. Crossing Elk Ferry, he says that the ferryman plied his tongue much faster than his oar, understood a few scraps of Latin, and had heard of Terence. At the next inn the landlord again discoursed only of religion. On the next stretch he picked up three Pennsylvanians whose topic was "the insignificancy of the neighboring Province of Maryland" as compared to their own. At the inn in Philadelphia there were "several comical grotesque Phizzes . . . which would have afforded variety of hints for a painter of Hogarth's turn," but their possessors talked "upon all subjects, — politics, religion and trade. Some tolerably well, but most of them ignorantly," displaying, however, that curiosity which was one of the characteristics of the American rustics everywhere. At the inn at Trenton, the conversation ranged from politics and religion to physics, and at the next stop he was treated to a discussion between two Irishmen, a Scot, and a French Jew about sacred history. At Saybrook Ferry, in Connecticut, a rabble came in and began to discuss theology, and of the lower classes generally in that colony he says that they talked "so pointedly about justification, sanctification, adoption, regeneration, repentance, free grace, reprobation, original sin, and a thousand other such pretty chimerical knick-knacks, as if they had done nothing but studied divinity all their lifetime, and perused all the lumber of the scholastic divines, and yet the fellows look as much, or rather more like clowns than the very riff-raff of our Maryland planters. To talk in this dialect in our parts would be like Greek, Hebrew or Arabick."[95]

In the constant recurrence of religion as a topic even five years after the main year of the great revival, we can see the influence which that movement was still exerting, and in the frequent reference to politics we can divine that there were many thoughts stirring among the lower classes besides the petty affairs of their households or villages. Wherever we touch the life of the period, we get a sense of change, of restlessness, of commercial, political, and intellectual activity, and yet of growing stability, prosperity, intercolonial acquaintance, unity, and self-confidence. In the next period, a great war, which was to tax colonial resources to their utmost, was to strengthen and bind together many of the strands which we have indicated in this rapidly developing colonial life and culture.

THE MIDCENTURY, 1745-63

ALTHOUGH THE PEACE OF AIX-LA-CHAPELLE in 1748 was supposed to end hostilities, and the Seven Years' War did not officially begin until 1756, nevertheless there was unofficial warfare between the French and English during more than half of the intervening period, just as there had been much of the time between 1713 and 1739. Throughout the midcentury years, the life of the colonists was deeply affected by the military situation. This influence can be traced in the rise in speculation, the growth of radicalism, stimulation of the intellectual life, development of the idea of colonial union, and in other aspects economic and social.

During the wars, practically all the ports in the colonies fitted out their privateers to prey on the enemy's commerce, and the papers of the day are filled with exciting stories of rich captures. Thus in the earlier ones, we read of three New York privateers which took a Dutch ship with $38,000, one from Philadelphia capturing 10,000 pieces of eight, another taking a ship with $30,000 in cash, while ship and cargo were worth $40,000 more. Of two others, one made a haul of 38,000 pieces of eight and another took a boat worth £100,000.[96] In 1745 a letter from St. Kitt's to Annapolis says that "there is hardly anything to be seen now in the West Indies but English Men of War and Privateers."[97] In Rhode Island the number of privateers rose from three in 1739 to twenty-one in 1744, from which there was a decline to five by 1748. In New York, however, the number steadily increased to the end of the war, when that port had sixteen.[98]

In the next war the privateers again swarmed out of every port from Boston to Savannah, and in 1757 the *New York Gazette* was full of stories of rich captures running from £9,000 to £15,000 sterling. On the other hand, it cost much to outfit the vessels engaged in the business, there was trouble from desertions of crews, occasional difficulties with dishonest captains who appropriated prizes to themselves, and more especially was there delay and loss due to the numerous appeals taken. This was particularly true of the Dutch vessels, and these appeals were not seldom sustained by the higher authorities in England. As the prize money had to be distributed to the crews prior to appeal, a reversal usually resulted in heavy loss for the owner of the privateer.

During the whole war, the illicit trade with the French West Indies was carried on with the enemy with an entire disregard of the exigencies of the military situation. This was shared in by the merchants of all the colonies from Pennsylvania northward and to a lesser extent by the Southerners. Increasing as the war continued, it has been estimated that in 1760 between 400 and 500 Northern vessels carried French cargoes from the Spanish "free port" of Monte Cristi, where the trade had centered and where the French secured provisions and military stores and marketed their sugar and molasses.

In 1754, Boston was obviously lagging behind her more prosperous rivals, New York and Philadelphia, through whose customs houses there entered in that year 368 and 476 vessels respectively as compared with only 196 and 173 twenty years previously.[99] The increase in number of vessels, however, tells only part of the story of enlarged commerce. If we examine the cargo lists of the Virginia vessels engaged in the West India trade we find that whereas those we listed for the earlier period carried only about 10,000 staves or shingles in their mixed cargoes, those of 1752 were carrying as much as 48,000 staves and 100,000 shingles.

With every increase in the size of the unit of trade it becomes correspondingly difficult for the small man to compete with the capitalist who possesses ample resources. When we consider, in addition, the heavy expenses incidental to conduct of business in wartime—one of the noteworthy features of the period was a rise in interest rates—and the great risks involved, it becomes evident that what was an incidental loss to be averaged out by the great merchant was ruin for the small trader of the earlier day. In fact, two of the most marked characteristics of the period were the rampant speculation and the rise of "big business" with its attendant ramifications into local politics.

To a certain extent all classes shared in the speculative mania. Lotteries were set on foot for every conceivable purpose, from the founding of churches or schools to the extrication of bankrupts from their personal difficulties. The great speculations of the time, however, were in privateering, commerce, and land, and in all these the scales were heavily weighted in favor of the capitalists and those influential in politics.

In New England, partly because of the mercantile character of the life and partly because the records are more complete, the new tendencies can be more clearly traced than elsewhere, and in that section we note them in many lines of business. Until 1760 the great New England pine belt, which extended southwest from Nova Scotia to the Connecticut River, had been tapped only through New Hampshire, where lived Mark Hunting Wentworth, brother of the all-powerful governor, and himself one of the richest men in America and the "lumber king" of the day. The woods in that colony had been cut so far back from the coast that it was becoming increasingly costly to carry on operations. On the other hand, Connecticut had no staple. It carried on only a coasting trade and one of moderate size to the West Indies, all its European imports coming through the neighboring colonies. The customs house entries for 1775, as recorded in the *Connecticut Gazette,* fail to show the arrival of a single vessel from England. As articles in that journal about the middle of the century abundantly testify, this dependence upon their neighbors was becoming galling to the more ambitious mercantile leaders of the little colony.

A group of these decided to try to compete with New Hampshire by lumbering in the upper Connecticut Valley. However, in order to forestall Wentworth's certain antagonism, it appeared necessary to secure the appointment of a local admiralty judge, who also by virtue of his office would have ample powers in regard to the king's woods. An admiralty judge was one of the most hated of the royal officials in all the colonies, and Connecticut had always been the leader in attempting to maintain absolute independence of the home government. We cannot here develop the whole story of the intrigues which followed, but it is indicative of the growing influence of business over the colonial legislatures that that of Connecticut was finally induced to send an application for the appointment of such an official, whose good offices, if they could be obtained, would be of benefit only to the small group of capitalists interested in the logging scheme, and whose appointment would otherwise be inimical to the interests and deep prejudices of the great majority of the citizens of the colony.

The speculation in lands, which we have had occasion to note several times as influencing the social, or rather antisocial, outlook of the poorer classes, rose to new heights both during and after the wars. The most noteworthy case in New England was that of the Susquehanna Company, organized to exploit wild lands on the river of that name in Pennsylvania, and for which the stockholders had only a flimsy Indian title. Not only did the operations of this company threaten to embroil the colony of Connecticut in a war with that of Pennsylvania, but after a long period of protests and ill will, they did bring on hostilities with the Indians. So important was the persistent action of the stockholders with regard to the colony's relations with its neighbor, with England, and with the natives, that the whole population of Connecticut became split into rival parties, the radicals favoring expansion, and the colony dividing sectionally between a radical east and a conservative west, as it happened to be in this case. In spite of bitter opposition, the company was finally successful in securing the majority of the members of the lower house of the legislature in their favor, and the whole unsavory affair became another evidence of the close connection which was developing between large-scale business and the legislatures.

Speculation in new townships, with all the attendant grievances on the part of actual settlers to which we have already called attention, became rampant toward the end of the war, and among the moneyed men of the old settlements shares in these ventures changed hands as readily as stocks today. Ezra Stiles, for example, who had a 13,000-acre interest in the Susquehanna purchase, was also buying and selling shares in the towns of New Concord, Lempster, New Britain, Killington, Harwinton, Cornwall, North Haven, South Kingston, and others in New Hampshire, Connecticut, and New York. He was careful as far as possible to buy proprietors' rights only, which, as in one recorded case, the speculators declared they intended to retain in as few persons as possible so as to prevent control of taxation and other local matters passing into the hands of the actual settlers.

Such speculation was by no means limited to the North, and in 1749 two large companies, the Loyal and the Ohio, were granted respectively 800,000 and 500,000 acres west of Virginia across the Alleghenies. Quarrels between the two rivals ensued, and although more or less land was disposed of to settlers by both, legal proceedings delayed settlement. Just before the opening of the Seven Years' War another company, the Greenbrier, was granted 100,000 acres by the Virginia legislature but, the war immediately ensuing, no advantage could be taken of the grant and a renewal was later refused owing to the new Western policy based upon the British proclamation of 1763.

The actual military operations of the wars were either at sea or on the frontier, and the older seaboard settlements did not suffer. Indeed, in them, commerce, wealth, and intercolonial travel, both for business and pleasure, all increased. These demanded better means of communication, which rapidly improved in the middle of the century. Many travelers of different sections comment on the excellence of the roads and the frequent advertisements for the sale of carriages indicate that their use was becoming much more general. In 1754 an advertisement in Boston offers "to let at a reasonable rate" a "handsome compleat coach" to go to Piscataqua, Rhode Island, or any other place with two or four horses.[100]

This, however, though better than horseback riding, was still an individualistic mode of travel. A new epoch in intercolonial communication and acquaintance came only with the establishment of stagecoaches and boats, running on regular schedules and carrying passengers at moderate tariffs. In 1753 an advertisement informs us that the Trenton Ferry has been "revived" and that a stage will run from Brunswick to Trenton, and a "Stage Boat" from that point to Philadelphia. The next year James Wells undertook to operate a combined stage and boat line twice a week "load or no load" between New York and Philadelphia. One or two other routes were added, and in 1757, as "the Stage-Boats and Waggons employed between Philadelphia and New York are found considerably advantageous to Travellers," it was announced that the line would be extended to Annapolis.[101] Although these early lines seem to have met with some vicissitudes, the new method of travel persisted on the most important highway in the colonies, and in 1760 another line was advertised between the largest two Eastern towns.[102]

The postal service also reveals the increasing demands of the times, as well as the all-pervading cultural influence of that midcentury American Benjamin Franklin. The service had been declining for some years when he was appointed deputy postmaster general jointly with William Hunter of Virginia in 1753. It had taken six weeks to make the trip between Philadelphia and Boston, and in winter the post set out only fortnightly. The new postmasters established weekly posts and cut the time in half. By 1757, during the summer months, the mails passed between New York and Philadelphia twice a week, and their increasing use is indicated by the fact that 150 letters were advertised at the end of 1756, as held at the New York office, and three years later the number unclaimed in Philadelphia was over 500.[103] With the general increase in communication there was a decided improvement in the character of the inns. The number of "clean, decent houses" increased, and occasionally they became notably good, as one described by that English traveler and chronic fault-finder George Fisher, who found a tavern in Maryland full of fine mahogany furniture and the rooms "so stuft with fine large glaized Copper Plate Prints" that he fancied himself back in one of the best print shops in London.[104]

It would be interesting to trace all the various influences at work to account for the great increase in the demand for reading matter which is notable in this period. That war, as always, stimulated the demand is probably unquestionable, and we may, perhaps, find two more humble contributing causes in the improved facilities for warmth and light. Although stoves of a Dutch type were occasionally used, most colonial households had been obliged to content themselves with the cheerful but not very satisfactory heat from the roaring log fire in one or two rooms. Although from at least as early as 1731 onward coal began to be imported and grates used to some extent,[105] the introduction of the new type of stove invented by Franklin in 1742 fairly revolutionized the heating of the colonial houses of the simple as well as the more expensive sort. The great majority of the early colonists had been without lights except for the flaming pine knot or the open fire. In 1761 the president of Harvard College made some experiments to calculate the cost of the various sorts of candles, including the greatly superior and newly introduced spermaceti. From his table we learn that the "common sale candles" cost one and three-quarter pence per hour, an amount which would have been prohibitive in most households. The spermaceti candles were a great improvement but they cost more than double the ordinary ones based upon light per hour. However, the increase in wealth and luxury, the introduction of several sorts of lamps from about 1750 onward, and the well-heated rooms must have added greatly to the number of winter-evening readers. One no longer had to choose between burning one's face and freezing one's back while hugging the fire in a half-dark room or going to bed, but could sit in a well-warmed apartment by a lighted table.

This increase in reading is evidenced in many ways. We have not only numerous lists of excellent private libraries but also the advertising of books for sale in the news sheets, including those from Maryland southward, becomes more frequent and notable. The *Georgia Gazette* was not founded until 1763, but among its earliest issues are lists of books for sale, including, besides many religious works, a good collection of the Latin classics and such modern writers as Milton, Hume, Shakespeare, Bacon, Congreve, Burnet, Dryden, Pope, Smollett, Gay, and Bunyan as well as Molière, and songs set to music for the violin and flute.[106] Not only were the number of booksellers and that of imported books both rapidly increasing, but new trade methods indicate a widening interest. In 1760, James Rivington, recently arrived in Philadelphia from England, established a new store in that town and at once entered upon an energetic campaign of advertising. The enlarged scale of his operations is characteristic of the change in business methods in general. In December he stated in his first newspaper appearance not only that he had a large stock for retailing in Philadelphia but that "country Shopkeepers may be furnished with a very great variety of such Books as are usually kept for the Supply of their Customers."[107] A few months later we find him making an offer in the papers of the other colonies, for example in the *Maryland Gazette,* to supply all public and private libraries on such reasonable terms "as to prevent the Managers of them sending to England for supplies," and renewing his bid for the trade of the country bookshops.[108] He also established branch shops of his own in some of the other colonies.

The public library movement, now no longer as in Bray's time fostered from without but an indigenous growth from colonial needs, is another indication of the increased taste for reading and of the intellectual stimulation of the period. In the very closing years of the preceding era, five subscription libraries had been started, of which the most important was that organized by Franklin in Philadelphia, but between 1745 and 1763 there were no fewer than seventeen founded, of which one third were in Pennsylvania. These beginnings of a most important popular movement have not yet received the attention they deserve, and further research will undoubtedly add considerably to their number, for their wide distribution is indicated by the fact that a majority of those already known were not in the large centers but in small villages, and were scattered all the way from Portland, Maine, to Savannah, Georgia.[109]

The mental activity of the times is also clearly revealed in the increased circulation and better quality of the periodical press. In 1755 the *Connecticut Gazette* said that "the Utility of a publick News-Paper in an English country is now so universally acknowledged as scarcely to admit of dispute," and during the years of the war the press certainly reflected its growing prosperity.[110] The *Maryland Gazette,* for example, greatly improved with the beginning of hostilities and its news of the conflict was excellent. By 1758 it is noteworthy that the general post office had to issue orders that whereas the newspapers theretofore carried free had "of late years so much increased as to become extremely burthensome to the Riders, who demand additional Salaries," on that account, a charge would have to be made.[111]

The time seemed ripe for attempting a new magazine, and the publishers in Philadelphia were fortunate in securing the Reverend William Smith, provost of the new college, as editor. Arrangements were made to receive subscriptions in Boston, Newport, New Haven, New York, and many other places, and the journal was stated to be of "general use for all the British colonies," correspondents being secured in all of them on the continent and in several of the West Indies. It was also said that it had been brought into existence by the war, and from its first issue the new journal, called the *American Magazine,* had a distinguished literary and financial success. Unfortunately, after a year it had to be suspended because its editor returned temporarily to England. A successor, the *New American Magazine,* published at Woodbridge, New Jersey, lacked editorial ability and proved a failure.

That the demand for literary fare of some sort was by no means confined to the more cultivated circles is evident from the change which was coming over the almanacs. These little annual publications, which came from the presses of every colony and which were thumbed and read by the common people from year's end to year's end, became almost small magazines themselves. Although by far the best known, Franklin's *Poor Richard* was only one of a host, and the *Pennsylvania Town and Country-Man's Almanack,* for example, contained many short stories, essays, and articles on slavery and temperance. West's *Almanack* at Providence had tales, essays, poems, and a little historical writing. Under the influence of the war, Hutchins's *Almanack* in New York became almost a miniature copy of the *Annual Register* in London, and besides the usual stock in trade of funny stories, poems, and essays, contained each year excellent historical reviews of the progress of the war and the colonies, with maps and portraits.

An undertaking which illustrates the mercantile and scientific activity of the times, as well as the close cooperation in which men of different colonies were now acting together, was the attempt made in 1753 to find a northwest passage, and failing that to explore the coast of Labrador. Organized in 1752, mainly as a Philadelphia enterprise, it received subscriptions from merchants in Maryland, Pennsylvania, New York, and Boston, and although unsuccessful as regards the passage, it did accurately map the coast from latitude 56 to 55. Another similar expedition set out from Rhode Island the same year, and in 1754, the Philadelphia vessel *Argo* made a second attempt. The great scientific impulse of the time, however, came from the popular interest in the new developments in electricity. Electrical experimenting became a fad with all people of fashion. Franklin's active mind at once fell under the spell, and his eleven experiments with the jar in 1747 covered all the "essential phenomena of the condenser" and stand almost without need of revision today. He devised a motor which could make fifty revolutions a minute and run half an hour from one discharge. His demonstration that lightning was electrical made the greatest impression upon laymen of any of his discoveries, but, scientifically, his rejection of the theory of action at a distance and his substitution of the theory of an all-penetrating fluid was of more significance. Perhaps even more significant, however, was the discovery both by America and Europe that the colonies had at last produced a scientific mind of nearly the first order, although we ought not to overrate the results of his researches.

In music, the theater, painting, and the other arts, the activity of the period was as marked as in other respects. By 1753, New York and some of the other larger centers, both South and North, were having frequent concerts of the best music of the day, performed by orchestras large enough to render overtures, *concerti grossi*, and symphonies. In 1759 the "Orpheus Club" was formed in Philadelphia and three years later was founded the celebrated "Saint Cecilia Society" at Charleston. With the coming of the professional Murray-Kean theatrical company, probably by way of the West Indies from England, the history of the theater in America entered upon a new phase. The event of greatest importance, however, was the arrival in 1750 of Mr. and Mrs. Lewis Hallam, both of whom were artists of note in London and whose company, joining with a part of the earlier one, remained together for twenty years and gave the residents of the colonies, outside of New England, opportunities to see performed by an excellent company all the plays which were on the stage at that time in London— Shakespeare, Addison, Rowe, Congreve, Farquhar, and Steele. The repertoires of plays given in such towns and villages as New York, Philadelphia, Williamsburg, Annapolis, Norfolk, Hobb's Hole, Port Tobacco, Upper Marlborough, Petersburg, and Fredericksburg would put most theaters of the present day to shame. Playing three days a week in New York, from September 1753 to March 1754, they performed twenty-one plays of the very cream of English dramatic literature, a theatrical season which, in that respect, that town has never equaled since. New theaters were built in several places, but such in New England were still called "Houses of Satan," and that section lay wholly outside the history of the art.

In painting, John Singleton Copley, who began his American period in 1753, was the fashionable painter of the time, and Benjamin West, the only American to become president of the Royal Academy, was just beginning his career in Philadelphia in the same year. Not only were portraits of the colonists being painted, but artists also gave some attention to the landscapes about them.[112] In 1757 we find the first exhibition of colonial paintings being held in New York, and the beginnings of colonial sculpture belong to the same period. These first appear in the form of portrait busts in churches, commemorative of the dead; importation of sculpture now becomes more frequent also. The effect of Washington's interest in the art, evidently influenced by the martial ideals of the war, is seen in an order he sent in 1759 for busts of Caesar, Alexander the Great, the Duke of Marlborough, Charles XII of Sweden, and other generals. Instead of filling the order his London correspondent sent him statues of Bacchus and Flora. Unfortunately, the comments of the not unemphatic Father of his Country have not been preserved.

The impulses following the religious revival, of which we spoke in the last period, found expression in this one in the founding of the College of New Jersey (later Princeton College) in 1746, of Wheelock's Indian School in 1754 (later to develop into Dartmouth College), of King's (later Columbia) College in the same year, and of Rhode Island College (afterwards Brown) in 1764. The nonsectarian institution which was to become the University of Pennsylvania was also established during these same years, in

1751, so that, including the three more ancient colleges, by the middle of the 1760s there were institutions of higher learning established in seven of the ten colonies north of the Carolinas.

As in so many other respects, we can trace in education during these years of the midcentury the distinct turn in tendencies long at work to change the transplanted culture derived from England into one more genuinely colonial. In the North, the grammar school of the traditional English type had been slowly declining, and in this period we mark the first beginnings of that distinctively American type, the academy, which was to have so great and so characteristic an influence later. In the South, the factors we have noted tending to depress the poor white and to develop an aristocratic or, more accurately, plutocratic planter type, were beginning to result in a decline educationally as compared with the North. Among the rich, the use of tutors, combined with a few years of English university training, continued to produce individuals of high cultural attainments, but even among them we note a change, for although the South Carolinians continued to go abroad for their education, both the Virginians and the Marylanders now began to some extent to attend the new colleges in the North. Between 1757 and 1763 we find no less than seventeen rich Maryland lads, including the Pacas, the Dorseys, and the Chews, entered as students at Princeton, and a number of Virginia boys both there and at the new college in New York. It is probable that the risks at sea incidental to the war had much to do with this by no means unimportant change.

Closely connected with education and with the new humanitarian movement following upon the Great Awakening was the new attitude toward children and child life. In the earlier periods, natural affection had of course always been in evidence in spite of Puritan doctrine and economic exploitation, but the difference between the old and the new is exemplified by the writings of the Puritan Jonathan Edwards and the Anglican Samuel Johnson, both of Connecticut. Whereas the former collected and published a selection of the most infamous passages from the Old Testament to show God's wrath against infants, the latter insisted upon the intellectual light to be found in children and asserted that we owed them the utmost reverence — *pueris maxima reverentia debetur.* The increased interest in the youngsters is shown not only by the increasing number of their portraits which were painted but by numerous advertisements in the newspapers of the different colonies, and even in the almanacs, of "English and Dutch Toys," "a large assortment of curious Toys for Children," "a great Variety of Play-Books for Children," or of "lotteries or small prints" for them.[113]

The same humanitarian impulse is found, more particularly among the Quakers, with reference to the blacks, and in the writings of Anthony Benezet and John Woolman, found expression at once sweet and strong. The evils of drunkenness prevalent among all classes, and indeed all ages — for even small children were given raw rum to drink — also began to meet with frequent reprobation in the press. The opening of the Pennsylvania Hospital, which owes its origin to Dr. Thomas Bond, in 1751, inaugurated a new era in the treatment of the insane, who now began to be considered as sufferers whom it was possible to relieve rather than as criminals whom it was necessary to restrain. Throughout the colonies societies sprang up having as their object the alleviation of the distresses or sufferings of the poor, such as "The Society for encouraging Industry and employing the Poor" in Boston, or the "Corporation for the Relief of poor and distressed Presbyterian Ministers, their Widows and Children" in Philadelphia. South Carolina had been an early leader in charitable work, and in 1764 an organization was founded in Savannah to relieve "every poor person without

George Whitefield, the prophet of the "Great Awakening," and Nassau Hall, built at Princeton, 1754, one of its results.

distinction," reference being made to the great good that such societies had accomplished in the other colonies and to an earlier one in Georgia itself.[114] Charity, indeed, was intercolonial in its scope, and at the time of the great Boston fire of 1760, collections among all the counties of Maryland netted £2,004, and Virginia contributed £1,340 sterling for the sufferers.

In one way or another, in the life of the colonists, we have noted the many strands which little by little were being woven into one common fabric. The purely political movements toward governmental union lie outside the limits of our survey, and of the meeting at Albany in 1754 under stress of the common danger from the enemy, we need only say that its vain attempt to frame a political union of all the colonies was indicative at once of the fact that sentiment had advanced sufficiently far to make such an attempt appear feasible but not far enough to make it successful. Had the various intercolonial influences which began mainly to be important toward the middle of the century—such as commerce, the press, better means of travel, improved postal facilities, the education of Southern boys in Northern schools, and all the rest—been in operation longer by the time that the leaders met at Albany the results might have been different. However, the meeting there of twenty-five delegates from seven different colonies, an assemblage, as Hutchinson said, the "most deserving of respect of any which had been convened in America," attracted wide notice and focused attention upon the common interests of all the colonies and tended to familiarize the colonists with the thought of such interests transcending the old boundary lines. The journals in different colonies followed the proceedings, and many articles advocating union appeared up and down the coast, affording, with the military events of the war a little later, subjects which inevitably widened the colonists' visions.

A sign of the times indicating the passing of the old simple conditions may be found in the marked decrease in marriage. Both spinsters and bachelors, so rare in the early days, now became more numerous, and this new situation called forth not a little comment, humorous and serious, in the papers of New York, Maryland, and the other colonies. With the passing of almost universal marriage came an increase in prostitution in the larger towns.

In spite of the bitterness against the French, which on account of their inhuman employment of the Indians against the settlers was growing in all the frontier sections, the inhabitants of the tidewater country seem to have felt little active animosity. Whatever poverty and hardship the war might bring to the frontiersmen and the poorer classes in the older settlements, the merchants in many of the colonies were fattening on profitable war contracts, on illicit trade with the enemy, and on speculation of various sorts. As the war progressed and large bodies of English troops were employed in ever greater numbers, the funds sent over for their maintenance actually turned the customary unfavorable balance of trade into a favorable one for the colonists. Most of the upper classes were in one way or another involved in mercantile affairs, and for them, remote for the most part from the scene of actual operations, the war was far from being an unmixed evil. In fact, it seems to have brought about a marked accenting of French influence both in styles and literature, which was to become even greater in the next period, although it is easy to overrate its importance. Indeed, it may be noted that just before the beginning of the war in 1754 a poem in a New York newspaper ends with

> But mount on French Heels when you go to a Ball,
> Tis the Fashion to totter and shew you can fall;
> Throw Modesty out from your Manners and Face,
> A la Mode de François, you're a Bit for his Grace.[115]

In 1746 the *American Magazine* had had a long article to show that the English had followed French fashion for a half century, but the vogue of the enemy seemed to grow greater with the war.[116] French teachers and even French tutors frequently appear in the advertisements, and the number of French books in the booksellers' notices increase notably. In 1762 and 1763, works by Montesquieu, Voltaire, Rabelais, Racine, and other French authors were offered for sale in the principal journals in the North and South. Of these works the most popular appear to have been Rousseau's *Emile* and *Nouvelle Héloise* and Montesquieu's *Spirit of Laws,* the last usually in the enormously popular two-volume English translation. Rousseau's *Contrat Social* did not appear in the colonies until the very end of 1764 and seems never to have achieved a wide sale or notable influence.[117] On the other hand, Montesquieu was advertised everywhere, from the Massachusetts to the Georgia *Gazettes.*

Although the war was thus stimulating the intellectual life and lining the pockets of certain classes and fortunate individuals, there were others who were beginning to suffer severely before its close. For a while wage-earners benefited greatly owing to the advance in wages. Free labor had always been scarce and this situation was emphasized by the number of men drawn away for military service. High wages, the scarcity of labor and its inefficiency become notes which are heard with increasing frequency in all the colonies. In North Carolina, Governor Arthur Dobbs wrote that labor was so scarce that the workmen would do only about a half-day's real work, yet wages had gone to such high figures that between the two conditions, building and improvements to plantations had to be wholly suspended, except by slave labor. The same story came from Virginia, where it was stated that wages had become so high that for less than a third more than a year's wages of an inefficient, bungling free laborer, one could buy a slave for life, the comparison being made by one who was opposed to slavery and dreaded its increase. In Maryland the numerous advertisements for labor of all sorts offered inducements far above those formerly prevailing, and in one notice we read that the price of the advertiser's goods have had to be vastly increased because workmen are "very difficult to be met with even at the most extravagant wages."[118] In Pennsylvania, employers advertised not only that "high wages" would be paid but liberal tips and cash every week, and the same conditions prevailed farther north. It is evident that labor was temporarily in a position to demand almost anything it wished, and that its great improvement in relative status would make the reaction more bitterly felt when labor should come to suffer in the general collapse incidental to the pricking of the bubble of fictitious wartime prosperity.

On the other hand, heavy taxes and high prices due both to real needs and to profiteering, caused much suffering among those who were not in a position to increase their incomes as rapidly. The war debts of the colonies rose to previously unheard of figures—£818,000 in Massachusetts, £385,000 in Virginia, £313,000 in Pennsylvania, and proportionately large sums in the others.[119] Even early in the war a writer in Connecticut complained that "people groan under heavy Taxes; we have no fixed Medium of Trade; and Poverty rushes in, like an armed Man."[120] It is noteworthy that in this most independent of all the colonies he lays much of the trouble to the unnecessarily large number of public officials. Just after the close of the war Peter Fontaine, in Virginia, wrote that "things wear but a gloomy aspect, for the country is so excessively poor, that even the industrious, frugal man can scarcely live, and the least slip in economy would be fatal."[121]

In many of the colonies a heavily depreciated paper currency with attendant inflation in prices added to the distress of many, and was a fertile source of discontent. In Massachusetts and Connecticut the issues had been redeemed in 1750 under pressure from the British government, with the cash received to reimburse those colonies for the expenses incurred on the Louisburg expedition, and hence they were thereafter on a sound money basis. This change, however, was bitterly opposed by the debtor class and the ignorant, and when Parliament passed an act in 1751 forbidding the further issue of paper money in any of the New England colonies, except in certain cases, it met with violent opposition.

By the end of the war, the farmers were feeling the reaction in general business, and the price of all agricultural produce fell rapidly.[122] In Connecticut, of the 265 lawsuits in the New Haven County court in 1761 most were for debt, and "the general inability of People to make due Payments" became the subject of comments in the broadsides as well as of legislative action.[123] Although the war did not actually end until 1763, operations in the American continental sphere were practically over by 1759, and the opening of new frontier lands to settlement, combined with the poverty of many in the old sections, caused fresh emigration to the outlying regions on an enormous scale. This, in turn, reacted upon prices of lands in the old settlements and caused a severe decline. By 1762 the value of farms in many sections of New England, for example, had fallen one half, and the farmers' equities in their mortgaged properties were practically wiped out. Those who left them and went to seek new homes in the wilderness did so smarting under the sense of economic injustice, only to encounter those other causes of irritation of which we have already spoken in the new speculative towns. In some sections, more particularly in Pennsylvania, the seaboard settlements had shown themselves unable or unwilling to protect the frontiersmen in the earlier stages of the conflict, and to the economic resentment was added a burning anger against the classes or the governments which exploited the frontier while refusing it assistance.

In the two generations we have covered, from 1691 to 1763, the growth of the colonies had been most extraordinary, the population increasing nearly sevenfold. Instead of the scattered settlements in the nearly unbroken forest, separated from one another by leagues of Indian trails, there was now almost continuous settlement from Maine to Georgia, connected by a network of roads over many of which wheeled traffic was constant and on not a few of which stagecoaches plied regularly several times weekly. In most of the colonies, with the increase of communication and papers, there had developed not only a local public opinion but some glimpse of a larger common life and destiny. In all of them, the formation of opinion had largely passed from religious to lay leaders, and politics had freed itself from clerical control. The transplanted culture, which we found slowly dying of inanition in the 1690s, had given place to a vigorous development of native growth, and the content of colonial life had become vastly enriched. In commerce, the imports of manufactured goods from England had risen from approximately £140,000 in 1697 to £1,630,000 in 1763. Even local manufactures had begun to compete with agriculture as a leading factor in at least one section. The frontier, which had been merely at the back door of the tidewater sections at the beginning, had been pushed far across the backcountry, even over the mountains, and in the whole tidewater section there was now a stability and an immunity from danger almost as great as in the mother counry itself.

On the other hand, these very facts had brought into existence new animosities and divisions, and a sectionalism of deeply disruptive tendency. Although the tidewater sections of all the colonies had been brought far closer to one another than had been the case at the opening of the century, almost every colony now had its own problem in the conflict—economic, political, and cultural—between its older portion and its newer frontier. Moreover, with the increased wealth and the fullness of cultural life had come a separation between the rich and poor far more marked than anything which can be observed in the simpler days of the beginnings. Wealth had concentrated, and whereas the capitalist of the older towns was far richer than his grandfather had ever dreamed of becoming, the poor settler was no better, if as well, off as *his* grandfather had been. His house was no better, nor his food, nor his educational facilities, and on the other hand he was apt to be much farther removed from the centers of culture, was more despised by the rich, and was exploited by them in a way the earlier frontiersmen had not been when they planted their homes on free land and but a short distance from tidewater. In the South, the great planter, by the use of slave labor, had enormously increased the productive capacity of his plantation, but his poorer neighbor had gone down in the struggle, or moved away beyond the mountains where the blight of the comparison of slavery with his own free labor did not fall. In the towns, theaters, concerts, and art exhibitions added steadily to the amenities of life for those who dwelt in the ever-enlarging stately Georgian mansions, but in the small houses of the farmer or mechanic the art of the people had deteriorated. New blood, also, had come into colonial life, and with the influx of Germans and Scotch the old racial solidarity and sentimental allegiance of the colonists had to a marked degree been lost. Nevertheless, the disappearance of the French power from Canada and the West by the Treaty of 1763 seemed for the time to offer boundless opportunity for expansion and to open new lands where the discontented and the exploited might find a freer and less hampered life.

BOOK IV

The Revolutionary Generation, 1763–90

SOCIAL RELATIONS

STATISTICS OF POPULATION of the thirteen colonies are only approximations. In 1763 they had perhaps 2 million people; twelve years later the total probably stood between 2.5 and 3 million. The number south of the Mason and Dixon line was about equal to that north of it. Virginia still ranked first; next in order came Massachusetts (including Maine), Pennsylvania, North Carolina, and Maryland. New York, the future "Empire State," and Connecticut competed for sixth place. There were roughly half a million blacks in the colonies in 1775, perhaps a fifth of the whole population. Probably not more than one out of seven lived north of the Mason and Dixon line.[1]

In the decade or so before the war began some important shifts of population took place. Between 1765 and 1775 the interior counties of Massachusetts grew three times as fast as those on the seaboard. Settlement advanced along the Merrimac and thousands of persons followed the Connecticut Valley up into New Hampshire and Vermont. In New York the principal gains occurred in the upper Hudson Valley and in New York City. In Pennsylvania, Philadelphia was growing steadily, but the most striking movement of people was northward in the Delaware Valley and westward along the Maryland boundary. Farther south, Maryland's population was increasing chiefly about the new urban center of Baltimore and in the frontier county of Frederick. Similar changes were occurring in the Virginia piedmont, the Shenandoah Valley, and the Carolina backcountry.

The cities were small by modern standards. Boston remained nearly stationary during these years. Next door, in Rhode Island, Newport and Providence contained hardly a quarter of the whole population. New York City grew faster than the province as a whole; between 1756 and 1771 the population of New York County rose from 13,000 to nearly 22,000. Otherwise the province was almost wholly rural, as were also New Jersey and Delaware. In 1775 some 30,000 Pennsylvanians, or about one in every ten, lived in Philadelphia; next came the inland town of Lancaster. Baltimore and Charleston were the largest urban communities in the South, with approximately 6,000 and 12,000, respectively, in 1775. Though Charleston was gaining, the South Carolina backcountry was increasing much faster. Of the other Southern capitals, neither Annapolis nor Williamsburg numbered more than a few hundred permanent residents.

A major factor in the rapid growth of colonial population was the custom of early marriages and the resulting high birth rate. Families of from six to ten children were usual, while larger ones were not uncommon. Two Virginia Carters possessed, respectively, seventeen and twenty-three. Among Revolutionary leaders, Charles Carroll had seven; Henry Laurens, twelve or more; and William Livingston, thirteen. Chief Justice John Marshall, born in 1755, was the eldest of fifteen children. The high birth rate was to some extent offset by the appalling mortality among infants and young people generally. Of Carroll's seven offspring four died in childhood, of Livingston's thirteen only seven survived him, and of Lauren's children only four reached maturity. Unhealthy climatic conditions in South Carolina and Georgia made for exceptionally high death rates, but eighteenth-century mortality tables indicate that even in Hingham, Massachusetts, more than a third of the youngsters died before the age of five.[2]

Immigrants came, not only from England and Scotland but also from Ireland and Germany. Official lists show, for instance, that in a single week in December 1773, 117 persons, all servants, left London for the colonies, mainly bound for Virginia. During one fortnight in January 1774, 264 persons sailed from London for Maryland, Pennsylvania, or the Carolinas; and the movement continued during the early months of 1775. Though most of these migrants came from English homes, some set forth from Scotland or Ireland.[3] The Scots were largely from the Highlands and the northern islands, but the Lowlands also sent a substantial number. Among their reasons for moving were "racking rents," "arbitrary and oppressive services," failing crops, and the enclosure of commons. The bulk of them landed in New York, Philadelphia, North Carolina, and Virginia. Available lists for 1774 and 1775 show more than 1,000 persons departing for New York from Scotland alone, while others embarked at English ports. Though most of the Scots were poor, they included a few men of means. In 1771 about 500 persons sailed with a "gentleman of wealth and merit" of an old family in their neighborhood.[4]

About three fifths of the whites enumerated in the federal census of 1790 were of English stock, a ratio probably not very different from that of 1775. Most definitely English in origin were the inhabitants of New England and the Chesapeake tidewater. Of the remaining two fifths about half may be credited to other parts of the British Isles: Wales, Scotland, and Ireland. These included some Gaelic-speaking people, but most of them used English with dialectal variations not much greater than in different English counties. In both Scotland and Ireland there had been a mingling of Celtic, Anglo-Saxon, and Scandinavian strains—the Celtic element being strongest in the Scotch Highlands and in the south and west of Ireland. Of the Irish immigrants to America, a majority had come from the north, which had been largely colonized from Scotland in the seventeenth century, and somewhat more than a third from the more Celtic south and west. There was also a religious differentiation between these two groups, the former being preponderantly Protestant, the latter mainly Catholic.[5]

Of the Continental Europeans, the Germans were by far the most numerous, including probably between 8 and 10 percent of the colonial whites. In Pennsylvania, however, they numbered about a third of the total population. They were also strong in the Middle region generally and in the Southern backcountry. New England had very few. More than any other foreign group, the Germans preserved their native language and culture, whether in separate communities or through separate churches in the larger towns.

Unlike the Germans, the early Dutch, Swedish, and French settlers had not been substantially reenforced by later comers and hence formed a steadily diminishing proportion of the inhabitants, often scarcely distinguishable from their English neighbors. Though Swedish was still used in a few churches on the Delaware, it was gradually disappearing. The Dutch element, largely concentrated in New York and New Jersey, maintained their identity more successfully and the language continued to be used in a few communities until long after the Revolution. Some Dutch Reformed churches had to provide English-language services for their young people in order to avoid dwindling congregations. Intermarriage played a large part in hastening assimilation. Dutch blood flowed in the veins of Morrises and Livingstons, while Schuylers and Van Cortlandts had British as well as Dutch ancestors. In the case of the French, the melting-pot process was almost complete. Though a few congregations, as in Charleston and New York, conducted services in French, they were quite exceptional. Such names as those of Bowdoin, Revere, Jay, and Laurens indicate a Gallic origin, but none of these men belonged to a sharply differentiated national group.[6]

The influence of the non-English stocks, especially in politics, was hardly in proportion to their numbers, partly because the social patterns had been largely fixed by earlier English settlers, partly because of the poverty of many of the newcomers, and partly because they were less numerous on the seaboard, where political control was principally centered. Though social discontent among the less fortunate immigrants contributed to the break with Britain, most of the Revolutionary leaders, with their more articulate followers, thought of themselves as transplanted Englishmen demanding English liberties. After the Revolution, however, the immigrant stocks tended to become more influential. It is suggestive that the first speaker of the U.S. House of Representatives was the son of an immigrant German pastor.

Social conventions in the colonies were the product of the interplay of old-world traditions and American conditions. This marriage, in England as in Catholic Europe, was regarded as peculiarly within the jurisdiction of the church and of ecclesiastical courts. Yet even in those colonies where the Anglican Church was established, there were modifications of the English practice. Under Virginia law the established clergy had the exclusive right of performing the marriage ceremony, but the absence of a resident bishop made necessary also governmental action. The provincial assembly regulated the conditions of marriage, the governor issued licenses, and lay judges determined matrimonial cases. In Maryland and North Carolina marriages might be celebrated by civil magistrates. In general, however, the Southern colonies, following Anglican tradition, made no provisions for absolute divorce.[7]

Puritan New England departed radically from English precedents, treating marriage as a civil contract and referring matrimonial questions to secular courts. Though the ceremony was usually conducted by ministers, they acted as agents of the state, and a purely civil marriage was permissible. Secular courts granted not only legal separation but absolute divorce. Between 1760 and 1774 the Massachusetts governor and council, sitting as a court, heard thirty-six cases, and in a majority of them granted absolute divorce. Acceptance of divorce did not, however, imply an indulgent attitude toward marital infidelity, which was severely dealt with by both church and state.[8]

The Middle colonies pursued no uniform practice. In New York, marriages were usually celebrated by ministers. No church, however, had a monopoly, and civil services were legal. The Pennsylvania Friends required their members to marry "in meeting," but made no attempt to impose their ideas on outsiders. The law required registration and due notice, leaving any denomination to set standards for its communicants. Though divorce had been permitted in New Netherland and later in Pennsylvania, British policy was against it, and in 1773 a new royal instruction specifically forbade legislation for that purpose.[9]

Provincial laws prohibited the intermarriage of whites and blacks, but illicit relations between master and slave were evidenced by the large mulatto population of the South. A few references to the legal marriage of slaves occur in Quaker and Anglican records, but for most blacks legal wedlock did not exist. The permanence of any union depended on their masters, and a considerate owner might take pains to keep families together. Even a white servant could not marry without his or her master's consent.[10]

Though court proceedings and church records may suggest a gloomy view of sex morality, most European travelers were impressed by the comparative soundness of colonial society, a condition characterized by freedom and informality before marriage and a fundamental respect for the institution itself. "Gallant adventures" seemed less common than in Europe, and marital infidelity more severely judged, even if the offender were "protected by wealth, position or other advantage." Conversely, Americans abroad commented on the laxity of European manners.[11]

As to the position of women, most eighteenth-century Americans did not differ fundamentally from their European contemporaries. "By the Law of God, as well as that of the English Government," said the Philadelphia lawyer Joseph Galloway, "a wife is enjoined to be Obedient and Subject to her Husband." No less conservative was Oliver Ellsworth, the future chief justice of the United States, who defended the common-law rule that a married woman could not bequeath her estate. Public policy required the maintenance of this principle "because the government" was "not placed in her hands." An example of comparatively liberal action was the Massachusetts law of 1763, which enabled a woman living apart from her husband to convey real estate independently. A similar measure in Virginia was, however, disallowed by the crown since it altered "the Law in so Settled and Known a point."[12]

Large families gave matrons ample opportunity to display managerial capacity, especially when they had to direct numerous slaves. Widows sometimes took over the stores, taverns, or printing shops of their husbands. Others engaged in the familiar feminine occupations of seamstress, nurse, and dame-school teacher. Occasionally women managed large business enterprises. A Mrs. Bowling was reputed to own half the town of Petersburg, Virginia, with tobacco warehouses and an establishment for making millstones and bolting machines; "lively, active, and intelligent," she knew "perfectly well how to manage her immense fortune."[13] In general, however, most provincials would probably have agreed with the following lines in the *American Magazine* for July 1769:

A woman's noblest station is retreat:
Her fairest virtues fly from public sight.

Probably about a third of the people were legally unfree in 1763. For nearly all the blacks, this servile status was permanent and hereditary. Some forty years before the Revolution a Virginia court held that, while for certain purposes slaves were classified as real estate, they could be taken for debt as chattels, "considered no otherwise than Horses or Cattle." Thomas Jefferson, however, reported a decision of 1772 asserting the hereditary and human association of the slave with his master and with the land. Blacks, it said, were "not the subject of perpetual transfer from hand to hand, but live in families with us, are born and die on our lands, and, by their representatives may continue with us as long as the lands themselves." Though slave codes were naturally most severe where blacks were numerous, Massachusetts and Connecticut resembled the South in discouraging manumission and subjecting blacks to special police control. In criminal cases, there was a special procedure for colored defendants, and in South Carolina, where the death penalty might be imposed by two justices and three freeholders, Josiah Quincy was told that "for killing a negroe ever so wantonly —there could be nothing but a fine." In 1775, however, the *Virginia Gazette* approved the capital punishment of a white man for beating a black to death, as a "warning to others to treat their slaves with more moderation." Even in the Lower South, there was some frank criticism of slaveholders. A letter in the *South-Carolina Gazette* in 1772 spoke of "people who boast an attachment to Freedom; yet are mean enough to beget children that must follow the condition of their mothers."[14]

White servitude was most prevalent between the Potomac and the Hudson, and especially in Maryland and Pennsylvania. Broadly speaking, the legal status of the men and women involved was much the same everywhere. The indentured servant, the most familiar type, was commonly an immigrant, though sometimes a poor inhabitant who found in such employment the best cure for his troubles. The length of service usually varied between one and four or five years. One instance of nineteen years is on record. The law required the master to supply food, clothing, and shelter to the servant and at the expiration of the period to make allowances known as "freedom dues."

Besides the redemptioners and other indentured servants, there were transported convicts generally serving for seven years. These "Seven-Year Passengers" or "King's Passengers" were especially numerous in Maryland. Colonial legislation to check their importation by tariff duties was usually, though not always, disallowed. Thus in 1775 a tax of forty shillings a head was held to be in "direct opposition" to the authority of Parliament. Another group of the unfree consisted of defaulting debtors and vagrants sold by court order. On a somewhat higher level were the apprentices and also the indentured workers who received fixed wages and differed only slightly from free wage-earners. Apprenticeship at its best provided vocational education, arranged by parents for their children or by public authority for orphans. White servants enjoyed some protection against ill treatment by their masters. Thus in Maryland a servant might bring his complaints into court, summon witnesses, and demand a jury trial.[15]

Of the many who at one time or another passed through some form of unfree status, a certain number of the less fit became "poor whites" or lawless frontiersmen, but many others graduated into self-supporting artisans or small farmers. Indentured service might thus be a kind of initiation into colonial life. Once established as a landowner, even on a small scale, a former European without political privileges might become a citizen and a voter. Many servants, however, enjoyed the initial advantage of knowing a trade. Some were schoolmasters and one was said to be the pastor of a Lutheran congregation.[16]

Of free wage-earners the number was limited, partly by the ease with which men could become independent farmers or master workmen and partly by the competition of unfree labor, including slaves hired out by their masters. A familiar example of the rural wage-earner is the New England hired man, who supplied the labor largely provided elsewhere by slaves or white servants. On the smaller farms of the Middle colonies conditions resembled those in New England, but on large New York estates hired men worked along with slaves and white servants. Southern plantations also employed wage-earners. Washington paid expert mowers by the day, a joiner for a year's service, and a stonecutter by the month.[17]

In the towns, unskilled persons toiled as carters and boatmen and performed all sorts of rough labor. Higher in the social and economic scale were the skilled workers—weavers, tailors, shoemakers, house carpenters, and cabinetmakers—with no clear line between the capitalist-workman, who had his own shop and tools, and the simple employee of a master workman. The leaders of the Philadelphia Associated Carpenters were not ordinary wage-earners, and the New York Friendly Society of Tradesmen, House Carpenters, was not strictly a labor union. The conflicts in which the latter society engaged were not between employers and workmen but rather between the local industry and competing country carpenters who paid no city taxes. On one occasion the organization also complained of municipal building regulations.[18]

Even when legally free, many wage-earners lacked the suffrage qualifications. Some could vote, as in New York, where certain of them qualified as "freemen," but in Philadelphia the number excluded by property tests was sufficient to make the extension of the franchise a political issue. Radical factions enlisted the workers. Through "mechanics' " tickets at elections, Samuel Adams in Boston and Christopher Gadsden in Charleston furthered patriotic measures. Even nonvoters were useful in popular demonstrations.

As against the ruling classes, the small farmers had something in common with the city workers. In 1765, Governor Colden divided the free inhabitants of New York into four classes, of which the first three were privileged groups: large landowners, well-to-do merchants, and professional men. Below these he put the mechanics and small farmers.[19] By contrast, New England yeomen occupied a more favorable position. Owning small farms and working independently or with one or two hired men, they lived among neighbors much like themselves. Similar conditions prevailed in parts of the Hudson-Delaware country, though certain New York counties were dominated by a few great landlords. The Southern tidewater had many small farmers living close to the margin of decent existence or below it, but also "middle-class" farmers, small slaveholders living in fair comfort.

How some of the humbler Southern freemen felt toward the landed aristocracy may be seen in the autobiography of Devereux Jarratt, the son of a carpenter-farmer in tidewater Virginia. From "gentlemen as beings of a superior order" he kept "a humble distance," and his folk took for granted the distinction between "gentle" and "simple." Politically, the small farmer suffered a disadvantage even though many of them owned enough land to qualify as voters. In New England town meetings their "rude democracy" could assert itself, and in Virginia the number of white persons actually voting in provincial elections seems to have been proportionately larger than in Massachusetts. In Virginia, however, viva voce elections exposed voters to social pressure from the "gentry." [20]

The ruling elements in the pre-Revolutionary era consisted mainly of the great planters, the more substantial merchants, and such predecessors of our later "captains of industry" as the ironmasters, shipbuilders, flour millers, and distillers. Drawn largely from this aristocracy of wealth were the officeholders, provincial and local. The social standing of these classes was commonly shared by the clergymen, lawyers, and physicians. The high status of the clergy dated from early colonial times, but the lawyers and physicians were now gaining in number and influence.

Professional standards were gradually advancing. John Adams's diary throws light on preparation for the Massachusetts bar. After leaving Putnam's office he was sponsored by a leading Boston lawyer who vouched in court for the young man's character and legal knowledge. Adams was then admitted to the status of an "attorney" with the right to practice in the inferior courts, "shook hands with the bar" and invited them to drink punch with him. After three years' further study he became a barrister. The final ceremony was held in 1761 in the superior court, then presided over by Thomas Hutchinson, where the prospective lawyers presented themselves duly garbed with gowns, bands, and tie-wigs. In 1766, Adams noted that the bar, in an effort to stiffen requirements, had "at last introduced a regular progress to the gown" with a seven-year "probation." The New York supreme court in 1767 issued rules requiring candidates, with some exceptions, to show satisfactory service as clerks to a "sworn attorney" — for three years in the case of college graduates and five years for others. In Virginia, applicants appeared before an examining board, but apparently with no prescribed period of study or apprenticeship. Patrick Henry was admitted after a few weeks' study, while Jefferson qualified after several years of serious preparation. In South Carolina, admission to the bar without entry at the Inns was said to be exceptional. [21]

The medical profession also made progress, though it still had to meet much nonprofessional competition. Many people patronized a motley assortment of drug sellers, bonesetters, and plain quacks, while obstetrics fell largely to midwives. Perhaps not one in eight or ten of the 3,000 to 4,000 practitioners in the colonies held a medical degree. Some others, however, had received passable instruction from older physicians. The Ames almanac for 1765 denounced the failure to protect the public against so-called doctors who had "the audacity to practice their Butchery on the human Race."[22] The methods of even the more intelligent physicians left much to be desired. Dr. Theodorick Bland of Virginia, after study at Edinburgh and London, treated a slave for epilepsy by bleeding, purging, and, when these failed, giving the patient an electric shock. Heavy medication was general, and the doctor was usually himself a drug seller. Dr. John Kearsley, a leading Philadelphia practitioner, endorsed "Keyser's Pills" as a "wonderfully efficacious" panacea for rheumatism, "leprosies," "stiff joints," gout, and "dry gripes."[23]

Until 1765 medical instruction in the colonies could be acquired only through apprenticeship. As in the case of legal training, the practitioner-teacher often failed in professional competence or in consideration for his pupils. Dr. John Bard of New York, a pupil of Dr. Kearsley, who prepared many provincial physicians, complained of the menial services, which left little time for study. On the other hand, Dr. John Redman of Philadelphia, who had taken his doctorate in Leyden and also studied in Edinburgh, London, and Paris, was highly praised by his pupils, including Dr. John Morgan and Dr. Benjamin Rush, who became medical professors in Philadelphia College. In Boston, Dr. Joseph Warren gave stimulating and fairly systematic instruction to his students. An important advantage enjoyed by Philadelphia as a medical center was the Pennsylvania Hospital, founded in 1751, which was as yet the only general institution of its kind in British America.[24]

One handicap to professional instruction was the popular opposition to the dissection of human bodies. Though there had been earlier instances of dissection, Shippen was the first American to make systematic use of it in teaching. As a result, his students were charged with grave-robbing and he himself was publicly denounced. He explained that the only corpses were those of suicides and criminals, with an occasional one from the potter's field. While insisting on the great scientific value of the practice, he promised to "preserve the utmost decency with regard to the dead." Shippen also introduced the scientific teaching of obstetrics into this country.[25]

Supplementing the advice of physicians were manuals for laymen. Two popular handbooks were those of the Scotch physician William Buchan and André Tissot, a medical authority of Lausanne. Buchan's *Domestic Medicine* aimed to show people what could be done by "Regimen and Simple Medicines." Tissot's *Avis au Peuple sur la Santé,* which was translated into several languages, was well known in the colonies, partly through extracts in English printed in *Brickerstaff's Boston Almanack* (1768) and in Thomas's *Royal American Magazine* (1774). Other advice—sensible, harmless, or pernicious—appeared in newspapers, periodicals, and almanacs.[26]

Common professional interests were not the only reasons for forming social groups. Urban gregariousness manifested itself in a variety of ways. Among the clubs in Philadelphia was the Junto, of which Franklin wrote affectionately in 1765: " 'Tis now perhaps one of the oldest clubs, as I think it was formerly one of the best in the King's Dominions. . . . We are grown Grey together, and yet it is too early to part." In Charleston, Quincy met with the Friday-night Club, whose members were "substantial gentlemen" of the older set; the Monday-night Club, which entertained itself at a tavern with "cards, feasting, and indifferent wines"; and the Sons of St. Patrick. Boston also had such groups, including the Fire Club to which John Rowe belonged. In New York, William Livingston's wit enlivened a club of gentlemen at Mother Brock's tavern. Societies representing particular British nationalities—St. George's, St. Andrew's, St. Patrick's, and St. David's—combined charitable service with good fellowship.[27]

Many prominent colonists also belonged to Masonic lodges, which sometimes existed in smaller towns as well as in the cities. Some lodges were affiliated with the Grand Lodge of England, others were of Irish or Scotch origins. There were also "Atholl Masons," called "Ancients" to distinguish them from the "Moderns" associated with the English Grand Lodge. Rowe described his installation as grand master at St. John's Lodge in Boston as a "very solemn ceremony," followed by a procession to Trinity church. It is difficult to generalize about the religious and political attitudes of the colonial Freemasons. Their ritualistic language, once distinctly Christian, was now sufficiently general to accommodate Deists and freethinkers, but American Masonry included clerical as well as lay members. Representative Masons also differed politically. Rowe was a cautious Whig while Warren, another Mason, was a radical. Over against such Whigs as Franklin and Washington may be set a strong Loyalist element in the South Carolina lodges. In general, the "Ancients" tended to be more liberal than the "Moderns." In any case, connections formed through Masonry probably facilitated intercolonial acquaintance and that interchange of ideas without which the Revolution could hardly have succeeded.[28]

The most fashionable social institution for both sexes was the dancing assembly. At such a gathering in Annapolis a royal official fresh from England was impressed by the "affability and propriety" of the ladies as well as by their modish appearance. The Philadelphia assembly also enjoyed great prestige. In Boston, John Rowe was apparently a kind of *arbiter elegantiarum,* and when his Cambridge friends gave a "Genteel Ball" at the town house, he was asked to serve as "Master of the Ceremony." Some people, however, had misgivings—not only New England Puritans but also good Presbyterians and Philadelphia Quakers. Abigail Adams's sister and brother-in-law, after seeing a Harvard commencement, concluded that "all such as learned to dance are so taken up with it, that they can't be students." Adams himself said he had never known a good dancer to be good for anything else; some "men of sense and learning . . . could dance . . . but none of them shone that way. . . ."[29]

Taverns and coffeehouses played an important part in urban social life. At Philadelphia's London Coffee House patrons could drink punch and hear of "everything that is done, or to be done." Another Philadelphia resort, later frequented by delegates to the Continental Congress, was the City Tavern. Williamsburg had its Raleigh Tavern with the beautiful Apollo Room, famous for peacetime gaieties and even better known for its Revolutionary associations. In New York one may still lunch at the Fraunces Tavern of colonial days where Washington said farewell to his fellow officers in the Continental army.[30]

In one important respect voluntary associations performed what is today regarded as a governmental function. For fire protection, towns still depended on volunteers, though by 1772, New York City's eleven companies were directed by a municipal fire chief. Fire risks emphasized the need of building regulations. In 1761 the New York assembly enacted a law, to take effect in 1766, making stone or brick, with slate or tile roofs, compulsory for new houses in the business section of Manhattan, but the opposition proved strong enough to prevent enforcement. In Charleston, restrictions on the building of wooden houses were said to be generally ignored. In 1762, however, John Adams noted the prosecution of several Bostonians for using wooden shingles.[31]

Such community services as water supply, sewerage, and lighting were generally primitive. In 1774 the New York common council authorized the young Irish engineer, Christopher Colles, to construct a well with a pumping system and wooden pipes to distribute the water, but the work was not finished before the Revolution. The Moravians at Bethlehem forced water from the Lehigh River to a tower from which it was piped through the town. In the matter of wastes, even so enterprising a town as Philadelphia made a bad showing. Graydon told of walking to school through a street which resembled "a filthy uncovered sewer." On the other hand, one British observer commented on the well-paved Philadelphia streets with footwalks on both sides. He found New York streets irregular and narrow, but so graded as to be "washed by every rain, which makes it clean and wholesome." Public lighting was improving. In 1774, Boston installed a new system of street lamps, and somewhat earlier New York had an imperfect municipal lighting service. In 1772 a citizen complained that no lamp had been lighted for three months, apparently because of an oil shortage. The Charleston system was operated for the city by private contractors.[32]

In contrast to earlier times provincial society was more highly organized. But class distinctions continued to be conspicuous, notably in the case of the numerous unfree persons, black and white, and of those men who lacked property qualifications for voting. A Philadelphia assemblyman complained of inconsiderate treatment because he had once been a "Tradesman." He insisted that "true nobility" could as often be found among "honest Farmers, Mechanics and Tradesmen . . . as among those who affect the character of Gentlemen and Assume the Airs of Quality." Jarratt's youthful experience of the distinction between "gentle" and "simple" was shared by many colonials, and modes of dress were more significant of social status than in later days.[33]

Yet apart from the black slave, New World conditions facilitated the movement of individuals from lower to higher levels and lessened, though they did not destroy, class feeling. A familiar example of antidemocratic prejudice is Gouverneur Morris's remark: "The mob begin to think and to reason. Poor reptiles! . . . they bask in the sunshine, and ere noon they will bite, depend upon it. The gentry begin to fear this." John Adams, later denounced as a partisan of the "well-born," now resented the pretensions of the "first families." Was it not a pity, he asked in 1772, "that a brace of so obscure a breed" as the two Adamses "should be the only ones to defend the household, when the generous mastiffs and best-blooded hounds" were taking the Tory side? Yet there was already a certain fastidiousness in his republicanism. Passing through Connecticut and having to sit at the table with his hostess's carpenter, who "might be smelled from one room to another," he wrote in his diary: "these republicans are not very decent or neat."[34] The elder Charles Francis Adams, who as a youth was familiar with a New England society not far removed from that of his grandfather's time, made this suggestive comment on social relations. There were, he thought, "more of admitted distinctions" in the old days but more "general equality." What most impressed contemporary European observers of the American scene was not the "admitted distinctions," but their lessened importance, comparatively speaking, in colonial life.[35]

These last years of the provincial regime were thus marked not only by steady expansion but also by progress toward a maturer social order and by a social outlook increasingly differentiated from that of the mother country. The rapidly growing population contained a large proportion of non-English elements, a development partially offset, however, by the fusion of earlier migrants. One mark of a maturing society was the improved position of the legal and medical professions. Judged by European standards, the Americans had advanced far toward an equalitarian order, though against that advance must be set the servile status of a substantial minority.

PRE-REVOLUTIONARY RELIGION

THOUGH POLITICAL RELATIONS with England grew more and more strained as the Revolution approached, religion continued to play an important part in colonial life. The toleration of Protestant dissenters was now a fixed principle of British policy. Church-state connections continued in the majority of the colonies, but even where this relationship was approved in principle, uniformity could no longer be effectively enforced.

The Anglican establishment was most powerful in Virginia, where dissenters were taxed for its support. Nonconformity was further hampered by registration and licensing requirements for preachers and meeting places. Though the Presbyterians had lately secured some relief, Baptists were still fined or imprisoned for taking part in unauthorized gatherings. In 1774, James Madison wrote that several "well-meaning men" in his neighborhood were in jail because of their "religious sentiments."[36] Nevertheless, the dissenting churches steadily gained as a result of immigration, the revivalism of "New Light" preachers, and the anticlericalism of many Anglican laymen. When the assembly required the clergy to accept money in place of tobacco at what the clergy considered an unfair ratio, they succeeded in getting the law disallowed by the crown and sued for recovery of their salaries on the old basis. Their attitude was widely resented, however, and the verdict of the jury in the famous "Parson's Cause," in which Patrick Henry skillfully exploited popular feeling, practically defied the royal order.[37] Meantime, Madison returned from President Witherspoon's teaching at Princeton an earnest advocate of religious liberty, and there was an unorthodox circle at Williamsburg of which Jefferson was a junior member.

In Maryland also the Church of England had long been established, but its adherents were in a minority and its position was weakened by the unfortunate character of some of its clergy. In the Carolinas and Georgia the Anglican establishments were similarly confronted by dissenting majorities. North of Maryland, the Church of England had no establishment except a partial and ineffective one in four New York counties. In the province as a whole it faced a majority of hostile and suspicious dissenters. In the North generally the Anglicans, while enjoying a certain social prestige in the large towns, counted as only one of several competing denominations; in New England it was commonly regarded as an intrusive dissenting sect. As a result of this unsympathetic environment, however, the Episcopal clergy tended to be more aggressive than their Southern brethren.[38]

In the North, as in the Carolinas, the missionaries of the Society for the Propagation of the Gospel helped to strengthen the Anglican position, though they were not adequately supported by the authorities in England. The society and its colonial representatives urged the appointment of American bishops, but the opposition of dissenters on both sides of the Atlantic and the indifference of British politicians prevented action.

Though the Puritan establishments had lost ground, they were well rooted, and most of their pastors had behind them several generations of New England ancestry. In Boston, Samuel Mather had a clerical forebear in every generation from the days of John Cotton, while Jonathan Mayhew was the son, grandson, and great-grandson of Congregational ministers. These clergymen had commonly studied at Harvard or Yale, where the curriculum, though not exclusively planned for them, was fairly adapted to their requirements as then understood. For more definitely professional training, aspirants relied mainly on the older ministers. Once installed, a preacher could generally count on a long tenure. Clerical influence, though diminished, was still important, especially in rural communities.[39]

Except in Rhode Island, Congregational ministers were generally supported by public taxation. Both Massachusetts and Connecticut reluctantly exempted from church taxes Baptist and Quaker members of local congregations, and the law provided that those paid by Episcopalians might go to their own ministers. Persons not affiliated with these denominations were still expected to pay such taxes and attend church services. The Baptists were the most vigorous champions of religious equality, but in Connecticut especially, the tax issue was complicated after the Great Awakening by the formation of "New Light" or "Separate" Congregational churches, whose members did not at first receive the concessions made to Baptists and Episcopalians. Soon, however, most of the "Separates" either joined the Baptists or were reunited with the Congregationalists.[40]

Though the New England nonconformists were increasing, they were still, except in Rhode Island, outnumbered by their fellow citizens who, if not members or adherents of the "standing order," at least acquiesced in it. More serious than the competition of the dissenters were the divisions within the established churches, which during this period included three distinct elements. The followers of Jonathan Edwards, commonly known as "Edwardians" or "New Divinity" men, stood for a freshly interpreted Calvinism, touched with a new emotional quality.[41] Though largely engaged in refining and systematizing the "New England theology," they were not wholly occupied with theological subtleties. Among others, Samuel Hopkins and the younger Edwards were ardent antislavery men. A second group, the "Old Calvinists," distrusted the "New Divinity" and the emotionalism of the Edwardian revival. Satisfied with the ancient ways, they took less interest in dogmatic controversies. A third group resembled the "Old Calvinists," in disliking the "New Divinity," but its members were turning away from Calvinist teaching altogether. Some of them, rejecting more or less definitely the historic doctrine of the Trinity, prepared the way for Unitarianism.

In Rhode Island and the Middle colonies the voluntary principle of church support prevailed. In New York and New Jersey most church members belonged to one of the Calvinist denominations. The Dutch Reformed Church was still supported by many families of Dutch descent. Though associated with the state church of Holland, the American branch showed an increasingly independent spirit, but it was weakened by the gradual

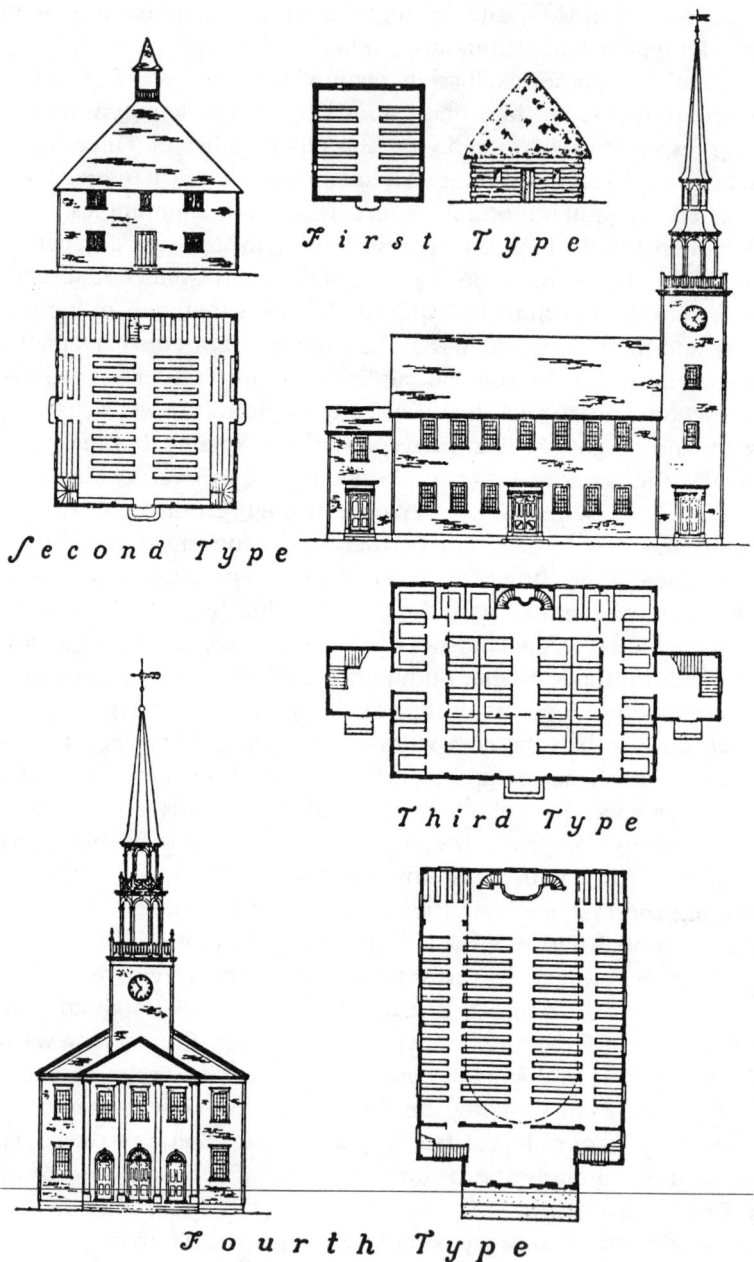

The Development of the New England Meetinghouse

Anglicizing of the Dutch stock. Other Calvinist groups in this region were the German Reformed, a few French Protestants, and the Presbyterians. This last denomination had grown rapidly through the fusion of Puritans from New England with Scotch and Irish Presbyterians, with some recruits from the non-English Reformed churches. Other elements in the ecclesiastical complex were the Anglicans—numerically weak though politically influential—the German Lutherans; smaller groups of Quakers, Moravians, and Baptists; and a Jewish synagogue in New York City.

In southern New Jersey and Pennsylvania the Quakers exerted a strong religious influence and were also an important factor in politics. They had long been embarrassed by imperial opposition to their scruples about oaths and military service. The first of these issues was finally compromised by permitting them to substitute an affirmation for an oath in all cases, though the more conscientious adherents were barred from serving as judges because they were not willing to administer oaths to other persons. Military legislation caused more trouble, especially during the recent French war when Quaker members avoided responsibility by resigning from the assembly. The Pennsylvania Friends were conspicuous in humanitarian activities. Two of them, John Woolman and Anthony Benezet, strove for greater justice for the Indian and the black. Woolman, who died in 1772, was largely responsible for the agitation which in 1776 led the Philadelphia yearly meeting to exclude slaveholders from membership in the Society of Friends. Benezet, through his publications and his correspondence with British sympathizers, crusaded against the slave trade.[42]

In Philadelphia the Church of England, to which the proprietary family now belonged, enjoyed a certain prestige. The old antagonism between Quakers and Anglicans was less intense and the latter tended to be less militant here than in other Northern colonies. The Anglicans were, however, outnumbered by the Presbyterians, who, while strong in Philadelphia, were especially aggressive in the backcountry where, faced by Indian troubles, they naturally disliked Quaker pacifism. Most of the Germans belonged to one or the other of the two Protestant state churches of the fatherland, Lutheran or Calvinist.

Generally speaking, the minor German sects advocated a return to primitive Christianity, and many of them were pacifists. Though usually inactive politically, they could not be ignored by the politicians, and they commonly sided with the Quakers.[43] Especially important among these groups was the Moravian Church or *Unitas Fratrum,* then directed from headquarters in Germany. Their chief colonial center was in and about Bethlehem, Pennsylvania, but they had congregations elsewhere, as at Philadelphia and New York City; they also had a group of villages in North Carolina known as Wachovia. Strongly pietist in religion, they were friendly, tolerant, and practical in their communal enterprises. They were also conspicuous for courageous and humane missionary work among the Indians and for the

high quality of their church music. Mennonites and Dunkers, whose parents or grandparents had come to Penn's colony long before, held their ground in the central counties, particularly Lancaster; still spoke German exclusively; cherished their belief in special revelations; abhorred war, oaths, politics, and for the most part, secular learning.

In the South religious diversity was becoming almost as marked as in the Middle provinces. South Carolina had long had French Protestant, Congregational, Presbyterian, and Lutheran congregations as well as Anglican parishes. Similar conditions existed in Georgia and in the Southern backcountry generally. By 1775, Presbyterianism was an important force throughout the South not only in religion but also in education and politics. Its ministry, at first recruited largely from Scotland and Ireland, was now mainly native-born, with the college at Princeton as a principal source of supply. Though the American presbyteries had no organic connection with those of Scotland and Ireland, they accepted the doctrinal standards of the Scotch Church as "their pattern in general," while seeking to adapt themselves to American conditions.[44]

In the South as well as in the North the Baptists were gaining rapidly, especially among the "plain people." In theology they differed among themselves, some accepting certain Calvinistic tenets, while others emphasized the principle of free will. They agreed, however, in limiting baptism to converted adults and in practicing the rite of immersion. Both these doctrines were well adapted to the psychology of the Great Awakening, which continued longer in the South than in New England. Though Rhode Island had been the first Baptist stronghold, Philadelphia was now the principal base. Accepting the Congregational theory of church government, the Baptists acknowledged no central authority, but their Philadelphia Association was an effective missionary agency, through whose efforts several churches were organized in Virginia and grouped in a new association. Even earlier there had been an association in South Carolina.[45]

More aggressive than the "Regular Baptists" were the "Separate Baptists," an outgrowth of the Great Awakening in New England, where a marked growth of the denomination had occurred. Two of the most successful New England evangelists, Shubal Stearns and Daniel Marshall, carried their preaching into Virginia and North Carolina. Their strenuous revivalism was especially attuned to the common folk, who, according to another Baptist preacher, would often "cry out, fall down, and for a time lose the use of their limbs." In Virginia these itinerant exhorters suffered more than the Presbyterians from the restrictions imposed on dissenting preachers. They and their followers were frequently fined or imprisoned, sometimes on charges of vagrancy or disorderly conduct. As the most active opponents of church establishments wherever found, the Baptists gave a definite impulse to the democratic movement.[46]

To this period also belong the origins of organized Methodism in the colonies. Though American Methodism owed something to George Whitefield, the British evangelist, who was well known all along the seaboard, his permanent influence counted for less than that of John Wesley. The latter, in contrast with Whitefield's Calvinist ideas, emphasized the doctrine of divine grace freely offered to all men for their acceptance or rejection. Though stressing personal religion and the necessity of conversion, the Methodists combined their emotional appeal with a remarkable practicality and organizing power. Their first American societies were formed in New York City, where a chapel was built in 1768, and in Maryland. A picturesque early disciple of Wesley was Thomas Webb, a retired British officer who impressed John Adams by his eloquence.[47]

From these modest beginnings Methodism gradually expanded. Presently Wesley sent out several lieutenants, including the future bishop, Francis Asbury. At the third conference of colonial preachers in 1775 the Methodists claimed over 3,000 members. With "circuits" in New York, New Jersey, and Pennsylvania they had their greatest following in Maryland and Virginia. Notwithstanding that Wesley was a clergyman of the Anglican Church, his adherents were coldly received by most of his fellow churchmen in America. Nevertheless, the Methodists during these years did not establish a distinct church. In general, the crowds who were stirred by these pioneer preachers consisted mainly of comparatively uneducated persons, including many blacks. Among the few upper-class converts was one of Asbury's Maryland supporters, who was said to possess a large fortune.[48]

The Catholics still formed a small minority. Shortly before the Revolution the English vicar apostolic who supervised the colonial clergy estimated the number of Catholics at about 16,000 in Maryland and 6,000 or 7,000 in Pennsylvania, making a total of 22,000 or 23,000. Even after the Revolution, Bishop John Carroll thought there were only about that number in the thirteen states. There were, of course, persons of Catholic sympathies in places without organized congregations, where their public worship was prohibited. Catholic interests were cared for by Jesuit missionary priests. In Maryland they held services in private chapels, but in Pennsylvania they were free to worship publicly. When in 1773 the Jesuit order was dissolved by the pope, its members were seriously embarrassed.[49]

The Maryland Catholics, though subject to serious legal disabilities, included socially important families. The Carrolls, for example, contributed both a signer of the Declaration of Independence and the first Catholic bishop in the United States. Elsewhere the adherents were mainly recent immigrants from Ireland and Germany, often distrusted by their neighbors and likely, according to a Catholic contemporary, to "become in general, poor and dejected." Anti-Catholic feeling stemmed partly from the wars between Protestant England and the Catholic governments of France and Spain, but one important factor was the activity of the Jesuits in extending French influence among the Indians. Few Americans before 1776 knew a

Catholic priest or had seen a Catholic service, but in 1773 and 1774 two representative New Englanders attended services in Philadelphia with mingled feelings of admiration and disapproval. Josiah Quincy noted "the deepest solemnity of worship and musick: the greatest sanctity of countenance and gesture," whereby "reason lost part of her influence." John Adams, similarly impressed, wondered "how Luther ever broke the spell."[50]

No one can say how far in any church personal convictions harmonized with the professed tenets. Even authentic records of individual thought and feeling may not be really typical. For some church members religion meant primarily a means of maintaining social morality and public order, and though many were led by zealous preaching or long usage to emphasize sectarian dogmas, others in the same groups took little interest in such distinctions.

Sophisticated older communities were affected by European attitudes associated with the Age of Enlightenment, and particularly with the rationalistic philosophy of Deism. This in turn was related to the changed outlook on the physical universe resulting from the recent developments in natural science, represented in England by the work of Sir Isaac Newton. Even for men who like Newton desired to harmonize the new theories with the older faith, some readjustment seemed inevitable. Men wondered how far the conception of a universe governed by fixed laws was consistent with supernatural occurrences. The thoroughgoing Deists rejected miracles and such historic dogmas as the Incarnation and the Trinity. They insisted also that truth was to be determined by the human reason rather than by any special divine revelation in the Scriptures. They had, however, their own "natural religion" with its "Supreme Being" or "Supreme Architect of the Universe," and generally believed that in a future state virtue would be rewarded and vice punished. Many of them, indeed, were ready to accept a simplified Christian teaching stripped of "superstitions."

Though British Deism probably reached its high point in the first half of the eighteenth century, it became influential in America somewhat later. John Adams found Deistic literature in the country town of Worcester and reported that his lawyer-teacher was skeptical about the New Testament narratives. Of three outstanding leaders in the Revolution, Franklin and Jefferson may fairly be called Deists, and Adams was certainly far from orthodox, though he valued the social influence of the churches. President Samuel Johnson of King's College considered New England in danger both from the vagaries of religious "enthusiasm" and from "infidelity." As for Philadelphia, Quincy observed that "the more influential, opulent and first characters rarely attended any public worship." It is only fair, however, to note the conservative religious outlook of such Revolutionary leaders as Samuel Adams, Patrick Henry, and Henry Laurens.[51]

The tendency toward a more secular outlook was displayed in various ways: the diminishing proportion of college graduates attracted to the ministry, the large number of academic theses dealing with secular topics, and the shift of interest shown in contemporary publications. Regarding the American scene as a whole, however, it is difficult to generalize. Though in New England the Great Awakening had largely spent its force, elsewhere Presbyterian Calvinism had never been more widespread or vigorous. Significant also was the success of Baptists and Methodists in cultivating neglected areas and social classes. Even in New England the drift of sophisticated persons from traditional orthodoxy was partially offset by the evangelism of "Separates" and Baptists.

Then, as now, churches concerned themselves with problems of social control involving ethical issues. Most obviously related to religious teaching was the governmental regulation of Sabbath observance. In 1764, New York had a pillory for Sabbath-breakers, and in Charleston fines were imposed for walking the streets during Sunday services. Others, however, were not so austere. Franklin observed that the freedom of a Dutch Sunday did not seem to provoke "God's judgment" and concluded that the Deity was less disturbed about such matters than a New England justice. John Adams, riding through Rhode Island, found people there "much more gay and social" on Sunday than in Massachusetts. Young Philip Fithian noted differences in this respect between the Virginia planters and the New Jersey Presbyterians. While being rowed to Sabbath service, he saw the river "alive with boats," some people going to church, others fishing or "sporting." People who came under the influence of dissenting preachers were said to be stricter in such matters. According to Quincy, a Charleston Sunday was "a day of visiting and mirth with the rich, and of license, pastime and frolic for the negroes."[52]

Toward alcoholic beverages the clergy were comparatively indulgent. Few persons advocated total abstinence, though efforts were made to check abuse of liquor on grounds of health and social welfare. John Adams was disturbed by the corrupting effect of the business on local politics and favored reducing the number of licensed houses. The Quakers Woolman and Benezet preached temperance, and among the Baptists and Methodists drunkenness was a frequent cause for penalties. Wesley's *Book of Discipline* condemned the sale of spirituous liquors or their "use unless in cases of extreme necessity." Probably, however, most respectable colonials would have approved these lines in a contemporary almanac:

> The Minister, the Merchant, and Physician,
> The Lawyer, and the deep-schem'd Politician
> Meet round the friendly Board, crown'd with the Bowl
> Which drowns their Cares and recreates each Soul.[53]

Many clergymen were active in promoting education, tutoring boys for college, conducting private schools, and founding academies. The institutions of higher learning were still largely under clerical control and all their heads were ministers. Even at the nondenominational College of Philadelphia, the provost and vice provost were respectively Anglican and Presbyterian divines. It was also the clergy—Baptist, Dutch Reformed, and Congregational—who took the lead in founding the three new colleges of Rhode Island, Queen's, and Dartmouth. The third of these was established in 1769 on the New Hampshire frontier. The intellectual interests of the ministry appeared in other ways as well. In a small New Hampshire parish Jeremy Belknap was beginning to write his excellent history of that colony. Several preachers were members of the American Philosophical Society, and much of Franklin's correspondence was with clergymen, several of whom shared his scientific curiosity. Ezra Stiles, while a Congregational pastor at Newport, showed himself to be one of the most energetic and active-minded Americans of his day. His diary records friendly conversations with a Jewish rabbi and a "romish priest," and though he denounced the Deists, he was ready "to come forth into the open field, and dispute the matter on even footing." One of his special interests was astronomy.[54]

In the field of religion generally there was an obvious continuance of trends apparent in the preceding period, notably the weakening of church establishments and the growing strength of dissent. In matters of thought and feeling there were, as before, clearly defined cross currents. One was the essentially "fundamentalist" emotionalism generated by the Great Awakening, now past its peak in New England but gaining strength in the South. Opposing this trend were the increasing secularism in many circles and a widespread intellectual revolt against orthodoxy, whether Puritan or Anglican.

PRE-REVOLUTIONARY CULTURE

HOW FAR THE AMERICANS of 1775 were literate, in the minimum sense of ability to read and write, is not easily determined. Undoubtedly overoptimistic was John Adams's claim that a native inhabitant who could not read was "as rare as a comet or an earthquake." But equally exaggerated was the comment of the British Lieutenant Thomas Anburey, while a prisoner in Massachusetts, that "very few" of the American sentinels could read. No exact statistics are available except of the most fragmentary sort. These indicate that the number of persons who had to sign their marks instead of their names was probably diminishing.[55]

In systematic provision for publicly supported schools New England was still in the lead, even though the statutory requirements were not always enforced. John Adams considered it one of the chief glories of Massachusetts "that the education of all ranks of people was made the care and expense of the public, and this in a manner unknown to any other people —ancient or modern." Though some of his fellow citizens regarded government support of schools as "an imposition upon the rich in favor of the poor," he insisted that the maintenance of this principle was more important to the community than "all the property of all the rich men in the country." Doubtless this emphasis on public responsibility, however imperfectly the theory may have been applied, fairly represents prevailing opinion among intelligent New Englanders. In Boston an outstanding annual event was the formal inspection of the town schools. In 1766 these exercises were conducted by the selectmen accompanied by clerical and lay dignitaries, who joined in a public dinner afterwards in Faneuil Hall.[56]

Outside New England, education was still considered as primarily the duty of the family or the church. In New York City the Dutch Reformed and Anglican denominations maintained charity schools. In 1765 the Dutch school was in the charge of a master whom the consistory had brought from Holland. Besides teaching the catechism he also served as church clerk and chorister. Among its various activities the Society for the Propagation of the Gospel (S. P. G.) subsidized schoolmasters. In Pennsylvania and New Jersey the Friends displayed a warm interest in elementary education, while the German church schools tried to preserve the cultural traditions of the fatherland. Especially significant for the Middle colonies, though not peculiar to them, were the freelance teachers who advertised their services in the newspapers and were, sometimes at least, men of character and intelligence. Their offerings ranged from the most rudimentary to fairly advanced studies. A substantial number of men and women must have received some part of their education from such teachers.[57]

Though the South generally followed the English tradition of parental rather than public responsibility for education, poor children were partially provided for through apprenticeship or on a charity basis. Rich planters could engage well-trained tutors for their offspring. In Councilor Carter's family the tutor was a young Princeton graduate whose work ranged from teaching the youngest daughter her letters to reading Sallust with an older brother. Near by, in a plantation schoolhouse, an indentured servant from Scotland with a decent, if not extensive, education taught the children of the household and those of neighboring families. The South had occasional school endowments, and in the Carolinas Presbyterian ministers as well as the S. P. G. interested themselves in education. Local societies also raised money for schools. Charleston, like the Northern cities, had numerous freelance teachers.[58]

How many families availed themselves of these various opportunities or gained an elementary education without formal schooling, we cannot say; but the experience of three Southern leaders is suggestive. Patrick Henry went to a "common English school" until he was ten, and though he attended no other school he received further instruction from his father.

Of Washington's teachers we know little, but besides the usual elementary subjects, he learned business forms and enough mathematics for surveying. Charles Carroll, like other wealthy Catholic boys, attended a Maryland Jesuit school before going abroad.[59] By contrast, Devereux Jarratt belonged to a humble family whose expectations did not rise beyond reading, writing and "some knowledge of Arithmetic." At eight or nine he went to a nearby school and continued his education with "great interruptions" until he was twelve or thirteen. Rounding out this instruction by private reading, he became a teacher himself.[60]

Though girls received less formal education than boys, the careers of such distinguished Massachusetts women as Abigail Adams and Mercy Otis Warren show that literary cultivation was not limited to men. Church schools in New York and Pennsylvania provided elementary instruction for both sexes, while tutors on Southern plantations taught girls as well as boys. In addition, advertisements of private teachers—masters and mistresses— offered girls training in "the common branches" and in such "accomplishments" as music and needlework.

On the eve of the Revolution higher education was provided by nine colonial colleges: Harvard, Yale, William and Mary, King's at New York, the College of New Jersey at Princeton, the College of Philadelphia, Rhode Island College, Queen's, and Dartmouth. There were also unrealized projects for new colleges in Massachusetts, Maryland, and South Carolina. The most interesting of these, the proposed "Queen's College" in western Massachusetts, was blocked by Harvard influence in the legislature. The line between secondary and higher education was not, however, always clearly drawn. Jefferson complained that William and Mary was full of "children," and certainly many undergraduates were very young.[61] Among the eight Harvard signers of the Declaration, John Adams left college under twenty and five others at eighteen or less. Of Princeton alumni in the Federal Convention at least three finished their course before they were eighteen.

Perhaps one out of every thousand colonists in 1775 had been to college at some time or other. Information as to the areas from which students were drawn and the distribution of graduates is too fragmentary for exact statistical statement, but certain generalizations are possible. Harvard attracted nearly all of its students from Massachusetts and New Hampshire, and few of its graduates settled outside New England. Similarly, William and Mary College was almost wholly a college for Virginians as King's College was for New Yorkers. Yale students, though drawn chiefly from Connecticut, came also from western Massachusetts, with a fair number from New York, and Yale alumni included several influential leaders in the last province. Philadelphia College because of its central location enjoyed an intercolonial constituency, limited, however, almost wholly to the Delaware Valley and Maryland. From this standpoint the institution at Princeton was the least localized of the older colleges, whether in respect to the territory from which its students came or the spread of its alumni. New England and the Southern colonies were both substantially represented in its student body. Of its alumni, roughly a quarter found careers south of the Mason and Dixon line, and another quarter went to New England. The influence of personal associations, formed in student days, was an important factor in broadening the outlook of men who were to become leaders in widely scattered communities, whether within the same colony or across provincial boundaries.[62] It is highly significant that of the fifty-four signers of the Declaration of Independence at least eighteen had attended college—eight at Harvard, four at Yale, three at William and Mary, two at Princeton, and one at Philadelphia.

Though, in general, the curricula gave central importance to the classics, some interest was displayed in modern subjects. There was a substantial collection of physical apparatus at Harvard, where losses by fire in 1764 were repaired by contributors on both sides of the Atlantic. The most eminent college teacher of science was Harvard's John Winthrop, a member of the American Philosophical Society, a fellow of the Royal Society, and an honorary doctor of the University of Edinburgh. Winthrop taught mathematics, astronomy, and physics with "Philosophic Experiments." Among his students was one destined to become a distinguished scientist, Benjamin Thompson. Shortly before the Revolution, chairs of science were provided at Yale, Princeton, and King's College. The corresponding professorship at William and Mary, established many years earlier, was given in 1773 to James Madison, a kinsman of the better-known statesman of that name. John Adams, on a visit to Princeton in 1774, admired its planetarium, constructed by David Rittenhouse, and also its electrical apparatus.[63] At Philadelphia, Provost William Smith lectured on natural philosophy, but the chief scientific work there was that of the medical faculty, which extended its charge over botany and chemistry.

Contemporary criticism of the colleges found expression in John Trumbull's *Progress of Dulness,* which satirized pedantic teachers who

> Read ancient authors o'er in vain,
> Nor taste one beauty they contain.[64]

Innovators, however, faced difficulties. When William and Mary was urged to follow the example of Princeton under Witherspoon, a defender of the old order scored the New Jersey faculty for attempting too much. "Your Nassaus alone," he wrote, "can boast the truly magic art of forming, in a year or two, the classic, the mathematician, the moral philosopher, and the patriot."[65]

Though college libraries were usually small and apparently not much used by students, the case may be overstated. Harvard in 1773 owned a well-balanced collection, much of it given by Thomas Hollis, the English liberal. The works on theology and philosophy represented various shades of opinion—Anglican, Puritan, and Deistic. Treatises in politics included some by Grotius, Locke, Pufendorf, Vattel, Montesquieu, Burlamaqui, Beccaria, and Blackstone. Along with volumes on British history by Hume and Robertson were such standard treatises of Continental European and Asiatic history as Rollin's *Ancient History;* the Jesuit *Lettres Édifiantes;* histories of France, Spain, Holland, and Poland; and the important works on China and Japan by Duhalde and Kaempfer. There is some interesting information about the books used by Dartmouth students and teachers from 1773 to 1777. In most frequent demand was Rollin's *Ancient History;* Pope stood first in English literature; and Locke's *Essay on the Human Understanding* was apparently more called for than his *Treatises of Civil Government.* Other authors chosen were Jonathan Edwards, Richard Baxter, John Bunyan, and Bishop Butler.[66]

Student discipline was adapted to young boys. At King's College undergraduates who went over the fence to swim were kept in bounds for a time and required to translate four pages of a sermon into Latin. Complaints of food in college commons led to the Harvard "Butter Rebellion" of 1766, and an uprising at Yale precipitated President Thomas Clap's resignation. Deference to superiors was enforced by tradition and sometimes by college rule, and social status was considered in listing Yale and Harvard students, though both colleges abandoned the practice shortly before the Revolution. Extracurricular activities centered in student clubs. Harvard had three new ones in the 1770s, all interested in public speaking. Yale had its Linonian Society and Brothers in Unity, and Princeton its Cliosophic and Whig societies. Undergraduates were also interested in plays. At Harvard in 1765 the "Day of Judgment" was "acted in a very shocking manner," arousing fears in some quarters that the college would suffer unless the "profane wretches" who participated were expelled.[67]

As an instrument of popular education, the newspaper supplemented the schools and colleges and attained a greater importance than ever before known in America.[68] By 1775 there were about thirty newspapers, against twenty in 1763, and before the war there was one in every colony except New Jersey and Delaware. Each of the four principal towns had three or more of these weeklies; Philadelphia had seven. Circulation statistics are scanty. James Rivington's *New-York Gazetteer* was said to have 3,600 subscribers in 1774, but that, if true, was probably exceptional. Rivington's contemporary, Isaiah Thomas, estimated that in 1754 the average circulation of the four Boston papers did not exceed 600 apiece. William Goddard began the publication of his *Pennsylvania Chronicle* in 1767 with 700 subscribers, a figure soon raised to more than 1,000. Most newspapers had readers in other colonies. Goddard employed subscription agents in Delaware, New Jersey, Maryland, and Virginia. Hugh Gaine boasted that his *New-York Mercury* went to all the "Capital Places" and many rural communities in the colonies and to the West Indies as well.[69]

The colonial newspaper was of tabloid size, and usually comprised four closely printed pages without headlines or pictures. A characteristic makeup was that of the *Pennsylvania Gazette* on January 6, 1763. The whole first page was given to a poem and certain legal documents. Of the next page about a third consisted of European items; the remainder, of miscellaneous notes from Boston and Salem, shipping news from New York, and legislative proceedings in Jamaica. The last two pages contained advertisements and two paragraphs of shipping news. Since the sheets appeared once a week and were handicapped by slow communications, the editors found it difficult to provide fresh news. The *Pennsylvania Gazette* of January 3, 1765, carried no English or Irish advices later than September 1764, Jamaica reports were over two months old, all the Charleston items but one had November dates, and Boston notices were at least two months old. The latest European entry in the *South-Carolina Gazette* of September 24, 1772, was dated July 14. The *Gazette* sometimes postponed an issue, awaiting news from an incoming vessel.[70]

Rivaling the newspaper in importance was the almanac. "Our business," wrote one almanac maker, "is looked upon by many as low and vulgar . . . yet there are no Works so essential to the Well-being of the community, so universally beneficial, so constantly purchased as ours. . . . The most accurate Scholar has recourse to us and we are read by Multitudes who read nothing else." Probably the most important of these publications in this period was the one taken over in 1764 by Dr. Nathaniel Ames of Dedham, Massachusetts, from the elder Nathaniel, but it had numerous competitors, German as well as English. Sauer's *Hoch-Deutsch Americanische Kalender* and another issued by John Henry Miller had an intercolonial circulation.[71]

Though colonial readers still depended mainly on British publications, colonial imprints were increasing. Between 1765 and 1774 they rose from fewer than 400 to nearly 700, though many of the issues were newspapers, pamphlets or broadsides, or American reprints of European books.[72] Of the total amount of reading matter, theological works, though less prominent than in earlier years, still bulked large. Among David Hall's book importations at Philadelphia in 1763 were numerous religious titles—Anglican, Calvinist, and Quaker. The Philadelphia Library Company advertised for sale Foxe's *Book of Martyrs,* Bunyan's works, Anglican treatises by Jeremy Taylor and Archbishop Tillotson, and volumes by such Deistic or skeptical writers as Hume, Bolingbroke, Voltaire, and Rousseau.[73]

The classics still ranked high with cultivated readers. In the controversial essays of Charles Carroll Latin authors were freely quoted. Jefferson was apparently influenced by reading Homer and, through Cicero, by Stoic philosophy. George Wythe, writing to Adams, quoted Greek lines from the *Odyssey.* Though Adams made no special claim to classical scholarship, he continued to read Latin authors after leaving college, including Horace, Pliny's letters, Cicero's *De Officiis*, and Ovid. Boston lawyer James Otis was reputed to be "a passionate admirer of the Greek poets." Plutarch's *Lives*, available in English translation, helped to form American notions of ancient personages and ideals. The *Ancient History* of the French scholar Charles Rollin was also well known. There was nevertheless some skepticism about classical training, as in the case of Franklin. Henry Laurens thought the classics had "often been impediments to the success of young men," and another contemporary maintained that English literature offered more than "all the boasted treasures of antiquity."[74]

In English literature, Shakespeare and Bacon were read less than the later seventeenth-century authors such as Milton and Dryden among the poets, and these in turn less than the writers of the "Augustan Age." Interest in the *Spectator* was continuous from the days of Franklin's youth. Some Americans knew Dean Swift and the dramatist Congreve while the favorite poet was Pope. The mid-eighteenth-century novelists — Richardson, Fielding, Smollett — were widely advertised in the press. Richardson was generally considered the most edifying, but in spite of some misgivings about Fielding and Smollett, they were read even in Puritan Boston. Sterne's *Sentimental Journey,* Goldsmith's *Vicar of Wakefield,* and Chesterfield's *Letters* were known, and, among the British historians, Clarendon, Burnet, Hume, and Robertson. Most influential of all was John Locke's *Two Treatises of Civil Government.* Through the "intellectuals" — lawyers, politicians, and clergy — Locke's ideas were passed on to the plain people in pamphlets, newspapers, and sermons. Sydney's seventeenth-century republican *Discourses Concerning Government* was also highly regarded and so was Milton's political writing. Harrington's seventeenth-century account of an ideal commonwealth was still read, and Coke gave Americans an argument for fundamental law as transcending ordinary legislation.[75]

Of the modern literature of Continental Europe, Americans knew less, though some could read French in the original. John Adams, Carroll, Franklin, and Jefferson illustrate varying degrees of proficiency in this respect. A number of standard French books were, of course, also available in translation. Rabelais and Montaigne were probably the best-known sixteenth-century French writers. Rabelais was advertised by the Philadelphia Library Company and was in Bowdoin's private collection. Councilor Carter owned Montaigne's *Essays*. In 1774, William Paterson of New Jersey wrote to his Virginia friend Henry Lee that Montaigne's manner was "Full of himself yet ever agreeable." The plays of Corneille, Molière, and Racine were advertised in a Boston almanac for 1769. Mrs. John Adams sent a copy of Molière's plays to Mercy Warren, though she feared he had "ridiculed vice without engaging us to virtue." Boileau, Bossuet, Pascal, and Fénelon were also known, the last because of his ideas on education.[76]

Notwithstanding Voltaire's unorthodox views he found many readers. *Bickerstaff's Boston Almanack* (1769) listed his works for sale and Bowdoin had them in his library. Josiah Quincy read them, we know, as did Jonathan Mayhew, who without endorsing Voltaire's religious views lingered over him "with high delight." Rousseau was probably best known through the educational philosophy of his *Émile* rather than for his *Contrat Social* (1762), though John Adams quoted the latter in 1765. Adams considered Rousseau "too virtuous for the age and for Europe," but Charles Carroll called him "that restless, fantastical Philosopher." Especially important in influencing American political theory was Montesquieu's *Esprit des Lois.*[77]

But the colonists did not draw all their intellectual sustenance from abroad. To an increasing degree they were striking out for themselves. Political pamphlets by Stephen Hopkins and James Otis were printed on both sides of the Atlantic; Daniel Dulany's argument against the stamp act won the approval of William Pitt; and John Dickinson's *Letters from a Pennsylvania Farmer* were translated into French. The most scholarly product of this period was Governor Thomas Hutchinson's *History of the Colony [and Province]* of Massachusetts Bay. The first two volumes and a collection of documents appeared before the Revolution; the third, dealing with the stormy years 1750–74, was finished while the author was a Loyalist exile. The earlier volumes, based on original sources, were well written and impartial and, in spite of the partisanship in the last volume, Hutchinson is fairly entitled to first place among colonial historians.

Of the fine arts, the most significant during these years were architecture and painting. The former usually followed English models, at least for the more pretentious buildings. These were generally planned by owners or master builders using standard English manuals rather than by professional architects. The governor's mansion at Newbern, North Carolina, completed in 1770, was, however, apparently the work of a British architect. An extremely skillful designer of Maryland and Virginia houses was William Buckland, who built George Mason's Gunston Hall (1758) and the Hammond house in Annapolis (1774). In Philadelphia the Carpenters' Company helped maintain good architectural standards. Probably no public building erected at this time equaled Independence Hall, completed some years earlier. Of special interest, however, is Carpenter's Hall built in 1771 and soon afterwards used by the Continental Congress. Church edifices were represented by St. Paul's Chapel (1766) in New York, constructed in the Italian Renaissance style then popular in England; the Brattle Square Church (1772) in Boston; and the First Baptist Meeting House (1775) of Providence. A good example of a country meetinghouse was that of Wethersfield, Connecticut (1761). Growing interest in the stage was reflected in new theaters at New York, Philadelphia, Annapolis, and Charleston.[78]

More important, on the whole, than public architecture was domestic architecture. The finer private dwellings were still usually in the Georgian style. Notable in New England were the Jewett house (1774) in South Berwick, Maine; the residences at Portsmouth, New Hampshire, which favorably impressed a French visitor; the homes of prosperous shipowners on the North Shore of Massachusetts; and certain country houses in western Connecticut. In the Chesapeake colonies, Annapolis constructed an attractive group of Georgian houses, two owned by signers of the Declaration of Independence. The best examples of Virginia Georgian were built earlier. Significant for the future development of American architecture was Jefferson's house at Monticello, to which he brought his bride in 1771–72 and on which he continued to work for many years, adapting classical ideas to American requirements. Also of this period was the three-story Charleston home of Miles Brewton, said to have been designed by a London architect. Josiah Quincy thought it "most superb."[79]

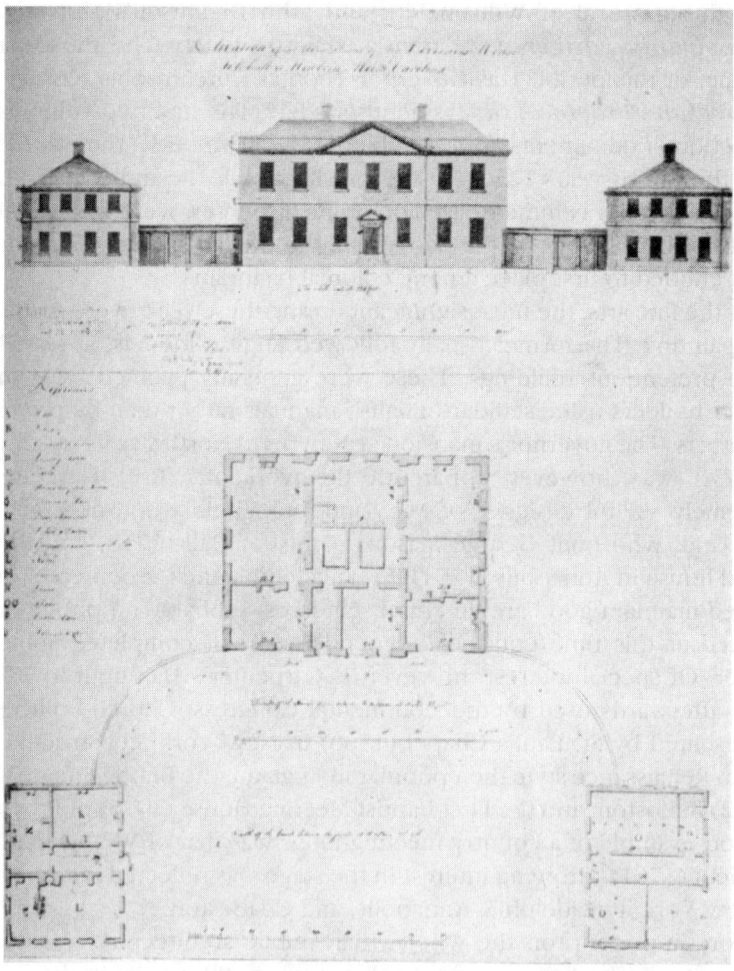

Tryon's Palace

In household furnishings well-to-do provincials tended to follow English styles, depending partly on imported work and partly on native craftsmanship. From abroad came Oriental rugs, Chinese wallpaper, Chinese and English porcelain, and occasional furniture. Yet when Samuel Powel needed furniture for his new Philadelphia house, he was told he could do as well at home as abroad and at less cost. Americans did some excellent work, but they usually followed contemporary English patterns, notably those of the London designer Thomas Chippendale, whose *Gentlemen's and Cabinet Maker's Director* was widely used. The general tendency was toward decorative effects: the curved instead of the straight line, as in the cabriole leg for chairs and tables, and elaborate carving. Americans also did well in silverware. Paul Revere was a successful Boston silversmith several years before his famous ride, and when Harvard's graduating class of 1763 wished to honor a college tutor, they gave him a silver teapot made by Samuel Minot. Similar craftsmen were active in other colonies.[80]

To plain folk the homes of their prosperous fellow citizens seemed magnificent. John Adams thought that Nicholas Boylston's Boston mansion with its Turkish carpets, painted hangings, and "rich beds with crimson damask curtains" was fit for "a prince." Later he saw furniture in New York "as rich and splendid as any at Mr. Boylston's," and he was similarly impressed by Philadelphia houses. At Charleston, Quincy admired the "magnificent plate" of the Brewton home.[81]

In painting, Benjamin West enjoyed the greatest reputation, though, on a whole, he seems rather a British than an American artist. Born in Pennsylvania, he went abroad in 1763 before doing any important pictures, and he never returned. In London he was aided by royal and fashionable patronage, ultimately becoming president of the Royal Academy. Nevertheless, West is significant for American art as the friend and teacher of younger American painters who found their way to England.

The best colonial work was in portraiture. With the accumulation of wealth and the improvement of taste, more families could now recognize competent work and pay good prices. John Singleton Copley, the Boston artist, wrote of his New York patrons, "The Gentry of this place distinguish very well, so I must slight nothing."[82] Philadelphia, being centrally placed, offered special advantages to painters. One of the ablest was Matthew Pratt, a pupil of West's in London, whose picture, "The American School" shows the master teaching a group of his countrymen. Besides being patronized by Pennsylvania notables, Pratt in 1771 painted a likeness of Lieutenant Governor Colden for the New York Chamber of Commerce. Better known than either of these was Charles Willson Peale. Helped by wealthy Maryland friends, he also studied with West in London, where he did a likeness of the Earl of Chatham. Returning to America, Peale became the principal delineator of Virginians, Marylanders, and Pennsylvanians, beginning during these prewar years a series of portraits of Washington.[83]

But the outstanding pre-Revolutionary artist was Copley, a young man still in his thirties when his American career ended. At twenty-seven he painted his much admired "Boy with the Squirrel," which was exhibited in London in 1766, and he was presently chosen a fellow of the Society of Artists. Encouraged by West to go to England, he at first declared that he was doing very well at home. Not until 1774 did he remove to London, where he settled permanently. Notwithstanding Copley's important place among British artists, he performed much of his best work in America, and even among his later portraits were those of Americans, notably John and John Quincy Adams.[84]

American interest in music was marked chiefly by indications of improving taste. The use of church organs was increasing. Trinity Church in New York City imported a new one from England in 1764 and employed a paid organist. Even in New England, where organ music had a doubtful repute among Puritans, a pipe organ was acquired by the First Congregational Church of Providence. Instrumental music was much cultivated by the German sects. The Lutheran Church in Lancaster installed an organ which had been built by a neighboring German craftsman. The Moravians maintained at Bethlehem a *Collegium Musicum,* which under John Frederick Peter's direction performed the work of outstanding European composers as well as of the director himself. The North Carolina Moravians, who used various instruments in their services, obtained a new organ in 1772. John Adams, who heard Catholic music in Philadelphia, described it as "exquisitely soft and sweet."

Performances of secular music could occasionally be heard in Boston, New York, Philadelphia, and Charleston. The St. Cecilia Society of Charleston paid its principal performers and even advertised for musicians in a Boston paper. At one of its concerts Quincy thought a French violinist played "incomparably better" than anyone he had ever heard. Boston, too, had a concert hall, where in 1769 John Rowe found a "large genteel Company." He also attended performances directed by David Propert, organist of Trinity Church, and at a musical evening in Rowe's home Propert played the spinet.[85]

There are glimpses, too, of family music. In Franklin's household Scotch songs were sung to the accompaniment of his daughters on the harpsichord and of his own "armonica." In Virginia the Carters of Nomini Hall were especially musical, using a variety of instruments. Besides playing the "Forte-Piano," the father collected scores and "made great advances in the Theory, and Practice of music." Jefferson, on the eve of his marriage, ordered a clavichord from Hamburg, though later he decided instead on a "forte-piano."[86] Washington played the flute. There were newspaper advertisements of music teachers and of collections of popular songs, some imported and others printed in the colonies. Among them were *The American Mock-Bird* (New York, 1760), *Masque, a New Song Book* (New York, 1767), and the *American syren* (Williamsburg, 1773). Knowledge of the better European composers was spreading. The best known was doubtless Handel.[87]

Interest in the theater was growing also. After peace returned in 1763 the "American Company," then directed by the actor-manager David Douglass and composed of British actors, presented plays in various places. During the winter season of 1763–64 at Charleston this company gave three performances a week for two months to crowded houses, with nightly receipts said to average more than £100 sterling. After a short sojourn in England the troupe began in 1766 a period of almost continuous activity. Washington was an ardent playgoer; during one week in 1770 he attended the theater five times. In the North opposition to the stage still proved strong. No theater was permitted in Boston, while in New York and Philadelphia public opinion was sharply divided. When a benefit performance was given for the New York Hospital in 1773, President Myles Cooper of King's College wrote the prologue, but a writer in the *New-York Journal* protested that theatrical productions were "against the inclinations of all the most sober and respectable inhabitants," and William Livingston forbade his daughters to attend them. Several religious groups in Philadelphia took a similar stand and the provincial assembly in 1767 received a protest against the opening of the Southwark Theater. Both there and in New York, however, the cause of the drama made progress.[88]

Shakespearean plays were frequently given, though often in eighteenth-century adaptations. Six of them marked the first season of the Southwark Theater. Other dramatists represented on the provincial stage were Otway, Addison, Congreve, Farquhar, Rowe, and Gay with his *Beggar's Opera.* Among contemporary English plays promptly reproduced in the colonies were Cumberland's *West Indian,* first given in London in 1771 and performed the same year at Williamsburg, and Goldsmith's *She Stoops to Conquer,* first presented at Covent Garden in 1773 and seen a few months later in New York.[89]

Young Lewis Hallam, son of an earlier actor on the American stage, played leading Shakespearean roles and seems to have been a fair performer. Graydon complained of his "mouthing or ranting" in tragic parts, but thought him a "thorough master of all the tricks and finesse of his trade" with a manner both "graceful and impressive." John Henry, a native of Dublin, began his American career in 1767, though his chief successes were to come later. His Irish characterizations were especially popular. Leading female parts were taken by Margaret Cheer and by her successor, a cousin of Hallam's, who also had ardent admirers. A writer in the *Maryland Gazette* expressed his enthusiasm in verse:

Ye Gods! 'Tis Cytherea's face;
   'Tis Dian's faultless form;
But hers alone the nameless grace
   That every heart can charm[90]

At Annapolis and Williamsburg the players could always count on large and appreciative audiences, and even smaller places in Virginia and Maryland saw occasional performances. Notwithstanding legal prohibitions, New Englanders were not wholly uninterested in the drama. In 1765, John Rowe witnessed Otway's *Orphan* "miserably performed" before a Boston audience. Five years later he heard the reading of a contemporary English farce, *The Mayor of Garratt.* At the Boston Concert Hall the *Beggar's Opera* was read with some of the music. Away from home Quincy visited the New York theater and thought that if he lived there he would attend "every acting night."[91]

This story of pre-Revolutionary culture is mainly one of gradual advance on lines previously indicated. New Schools and colleges were founded, with some reconsideration of educational programs, and the graduates of the colleges were contributing significantly to political leadership. Meantime there was a notable expansion of the newspaper press, which was increasingly active politically. For progress in science, letters, and the arts Americans were almost inevitably dependent on their contacts with Europe. Important in this mediatory service were such men as Winthrop, Garden, and, above all, Franklin, with his Philosophical Society associates. American achievements in literature and art perhaps most nearly achieved distinction in the best of the political pamphlets and in Copley's portraits.

THE OLD WEST AND NEW FRONTIERS

THE PRE-REVOLUTIONARY WEST contained a society less marked by class distinctions than that of the East, but inequalities existed even here. The capitalist-promoter played a part in the process of expansion. New England had its proprietors, absentee or resident, whose interests often clashed with those of the ordinary settler. The interior South possessed landed magnates like Lord Fairfax in Virginia and Lord Granville, the absentee landlord of a great tract in North Carolina. Washington himself had rent-paying tenants in the backcountry. In western Maryland the Dulanys controlled a numerous tenantry, and in New York even Revolutionary leaders like James Duane, Philip Schuyler, and the Livingstons carried the leasehold system into newly settled areas.[92]

Alongside the yeoman farmers, the western edges of the piedmont also had their large plantation owners, including such champions of the backcountry as Jefferson and Madison. It has been estimated that Jefferson during "most of his mature life" owned "approximately ten thousand acres of land and from one to two hundred slaves." Another example was Richard Henderson, the North Carolina judge who planned the proprietary colony of Transylvania. In the 1770s a Moravian preacher noted sharp contrasts of this kind on the Virginia–North Carolina border. One of his hosts owned great tracts, but in the same region he found a poverty-stricken Irish settlement of "robbed and plundered people." Between these extremes were numerous farmers with moderate holdings.[93]

One characteristic of the backcountry was the mobility of its inhabitants. Though some settlers, securing legal rights by purchase or lease, established permanent homes, others, more restless or less industrious, soon shifted to fresh tracts. Even in New England the residents of new towns tended to migrate more freely than those of older communities. The careers of certain Pennsylvania delegates to the state ratifying convention of 1787 are suggestive. Two of the chief leaders of the backcountry anti-Federalists were natives of Ireland while the third was the son of a Scotch-Irish immigrant. All three had tried an older section of the interior country before transferring to newer settlements. Another delegate of Irish birth had lived for a time in Lancaster County, then went west into the Cumberland Valley, and later died in a town on the Juniata River. Daniel Boone, a native of what was then frontier country near Reading, Pennsylvania, went successively to the Shenandoah Valley, the North Carolina piedmont, and Kentucky.[94]

The rural economy of the "Old West" was not all of a kind. In New England its agriculture did not differ radically from that of many older communities. In the Middle region and the Chesapeake provinces, however, the backcountry farmer possessed an important export staple. His wheat and flour went out through Philadelphia, Baltimore, Fredericksburg, and Alexandria. Though upper Carolina had no staples comparable with the rice and indigo of the lowlands, its cattle might be driven to Philadelphia as well as to Southern ports. In all parts of this interior region wagoners transported farm products and skins to storage and market centers on the fall line, whence they could be floated to the seaboard. The result was a marked development of inland towns. Typical examples in Pennsylvania are Lancaster, York, and Carlisle; in Maryland, Frederick and Hagerstown; in Virginia, Richmond, Fredericksburg, Falmouth, and Alexandria on the fall line and also the Valley towns of Winchester and Staunton; and in the Carolinas, Hillsborough, Salisbury, Cross Creek at the head of navigation on the Cape Fear, and Camden. At such points the farmers could exchange produce for manufactured goods.[95]

Outside the towns extremely primitive houses were still usual. In western Maryland, in fairly well-cultivated country, they were described as of "rude construction." A British traveler in Virginia during the Revolution observed that about Charlottesville only the better dwellings were lathed and plastered within. Most of them had wooden chimneys and wooden shutters without glazed windows. More ambitious were the homes of Madison at Montpelier and of Jefferson at Monticello. Comparable with these were some attractive residences in western Connecticut. Backcountry travel, with poor taverns or none at all, was uncomfortable, but there was some simple hospitality in private houses. A Moravian preacher told of a leading citizen in upper North Carolina who built a tavern to relieve his home from "the constant stream of visitors."[96]

Regarding religion on this newer frontier three facts stand out: the weakening of the older churches, the highly emotional evangelism required for unsophisticated folk, and, sometimes, a more tolerant outlook. Among the pioneers there was not so much intellectual dissent from orthodox theology as the disuse of religious habits enforced by public opinion in their old homes.

The religious variety characteristic of the older settlements in the Middle provinces reappeared in the backcountry. The chief difference, in Pennsylvania especially, was in the weakness of the Friends and Anglicans and the comparative strength of the Scotch-Irish Presbyterians with their vigorous hostility to Quaker and Moravian pacifism. In the South the ecclesiastical divergence of tidewater and backcountry was even more striking. Though the Church of England was legally established, its adherents in the inland communities were far outnumbered by nonconformists of various denominations. Even in legally organized parishes vestries might be controlled by dissenters, as in certain Scotch-Irish settlements in Virginia. In Wachovia in 1773 the freeholders of Dobbs Parish actually chose Moravian churchwardens. In much of the interior country no organized churches or settled pastors were to be found. Hence the religious life in these parts depended on itinerant preachers, Moravian, "New Side" Presbyterian, or Baptist. One Baptist preacher had a circuit of four counties, including both slopes of the Blue Ridge.[97]

Education naturally suffered under pioneer conditions, though something may be said on the credit side. In Massachusetts the setting apart of a school lot was a usual condition of grants for towns, and town appropriations for education came early. In 1762 the new Berkshire town of Pittsfield voted for school support, and before the Revolution it had five schoolhouses. Peterborough, New Hampshire, gave £40 for education at its first regular town meeting.[98]

While New England extended to the backcountry a school system already established by law, that was not the case in those colonies where education had been mainly left to churches, private philanthropy, or family initiative. A few schools existed in the freshly settled areas of New York; a Presbyterian minister is credited with founding the first New York grammer school west of Albany. In inland Pennsylvania the Moravians conducted schools at Nazareth and Bethlehem, while others were maintained by clergymen. One of the latter, at Carlisle, offered to teach Greek and Latin "in the most concise and perfect manner." In the Virginia piedmont John Marshall read Horace and Livy with a young Scotch clergyman. There were also the piedmont and Valley academies of Liberty Hall and Hampden-Sydney. The Moravians of Wachovia maintained schools for boys and girls, and in both the Carolinas Presbyterian ministers did their part.[99]

Maladjustments between seaboard and backcountry proved important in the political and social life of these times. In Virginia such tension was not yet troublesome, but obvious differences in outlook existed between slave-owning planters and yeoman farmers, between the aristocratic older families and the more democratic newer settlements, between Anglicans and dissenters. Though Jefferson in 1782 noted the inadequate representation of the interior counties in the legislature, the issue was not pressed until after the Revolution.[100]

In Pennsylvania, on the other hand, the inland counties actively complained of the unfair legislative apportionment. Easterners and Westerners also disagreed about Indian policy. If the people a little west of the Susquehanna had been able to put their true weight into provincial policy, they might have brought protection to the frontier. As it was, the Philadelphia Quakers persisting in their traditional pacifism refused to vote adequate defense, while some Philadelphia merchants were accused of making swollen profits out of selling firearms to the warlike savages. Raids from the Western tribes had penetrated Pennsylvania in 1763, sowing broad destruction. The menace was brought home to Shippensburg, Carlisle, and other settled places by the arrival of hundreds of refugees. Utterly disgusted by Eastern indifference, and madly bent on destroying Indians—any Indians—fifty-seven rangers from the town of Paxton fell upon the peaceful and defenseless Conestoga, living by their handicrafts near Lancaster, and killed twenty in cold blood. Local magistrates were so sympathetic with the rioters that Governor John Penn's command to bring them to trial had no effect. The following year 600 armed "back inhabitants" marched on Philadelphia to enforce redress. In required all the diplomacy of Benjamin Franklin to dissuade them from civil war.[101]

The most violent sectional disturbances, however, took place in the Carolinas. The Regulator movement in North Carolina was mainly a protest against Easterners who controlled the assembly, the revenue system, and the courts. The Western counties complained of unequal taxation, excessive court fees, land administration in the interest of Eastern politicians, and a marriage law discriminating against dissenting ministers. Among other things they demanded freer paper-money issues, the trial of debt cases without lawyers by a jury of freeholders, and the ballot in place of viva voce voting. At the Battle of the Alamance in May 1771, about 2,000 poorly armed Regulators were dispersed by Governor William Tryon and the provincial militia led by several future leaders in the Revolution. A similar but less serious rising in South Carolina was directed against the Charleston government for not providing adequate law enforcement agencies. When the decent elements in the backcountry resorted to lynch law for their protection, they clashed with the provincial authorities. Fortunately, however, the assembly proved conciliatory and established new courts. No such spectacular outbreaks occurred in New England, though there already

existed some of that antagonism between the mercantile seaboard and the
rural interior which later flamed up in the Shays Rebellion.[102]

While new societies were thus growing up between the coastal region
and the mountains, many Americans were looking hopefully toward the
recently acquired trans-Appalachian empire. This land of the "Western
Waters" had long been known to adventurous individuals and plans for its
exploitation had precipitated the last intercolonial war, but its vast resources were hardly realized. Many provincials of 1763 were, however,
attracted by the prospect of an expanding fur trade. Others knew of agricultural resources in the bottom lands of the Ohio and Mississippi, and speculators were planning new colonies.

Nevertheless, the victors over France in the late war had hardly more
than a quitclaim deed to the greater part of this area. Most numerous among
its human occupants were the Indians, perhaps 200,000 in all. Behind the
Northern colonies the principal group was still the Iroquois Confederacy.
Though its base lay in the Mohawk Valley, it had to be reckoned with in
the trade and warfare of the farther West. To the south were the Delaware,
then being pushed back into the Ohio Valley. Unlike the Iroquois, most of
whom had favored the British in the recent war, the Delaware, formerly
allied with the French, were troubled both by colonial frontiersmen and by
Iroquois claims to overlordship. Also in the Ohio Valley were the Shawnee,
whose raids disturbed the frontier settlements of Pennsylvania and Virginia.

In the southern Appalachians, the Gulf Coast, and the lower Mississippi
Valley dwelt four important tribes or confederacies numbering perhaps
15,000 warriors: the Cherokee to the rear of the Carolinas, and the Creek,
Chickasaw, and Choctaw in the present Gulf states. All these had to be
carefully handled and clashes with the settlers resulted from lawlessness on
both sides. Conflicting tribal claims complicated land cessions, and hostilities between Northern and Southern Indians also made trouble for outlying
white settlements. More remote from the English colonists than these bands
were those of the upper Mississippi Valley and the Great Lakes region.
Among them were the Chippewa and the Ottawa whose chief was Pontiac.
Half a century passed before the larger part of the Northwest could be
effectively occupied.[103]

Many of the early trans-Allegheny pioneers were people of the older
frontier who had been prepared for similar undertakings in the newer
West. The actual settlements in these years were chiefly in western Pennsylvania and the present West Virginia, with smaller ones in eastern Kentucky
and Tennessee. By 1765 there were a few permanent residents about Fort
Pitt with the soldiers and traders, and during the next ten years a rush of
pioneers occurred into southwestern Pennsylvania, where two new counties were organized by 1773. Other migrants passed farther down the Ohio
Valley, settling on or near the Ohio, Monongahela, and Kanawha rivers.
From such outposts developed the West Virginia cities of Wheeling, Mor-

gantown, and Charleston. Here was a fighting frontier frequently traversed by Indian war parties. North of the Ohio, except for a few old French communities, lay Indian country.[104]

The Northern migration to the West came largely from Pennsylvania and New Jersey—overland to the upper Ohio and thence downstream. Virginians and Carolinians generally traveled either by the Ohio and its branches or by land through the Cumberland Gap. The volume of this human stream can only be conjectured. In 1770, George Croghan stated that the previous year had seen between 4,000 and 5,000 families settle beyond the mountains, and "all this spring and summer," he added, "the roads have been lined with wagons moving to the Ohio." In 1771 it was estimated, perhaps optimistically, that 10,000 families dwelt along the Ohio and its tributaries. In the words of Governor Dunmore, "the emigrating Spirit of the Americans" could not be controlled. The chief base for Western enterprises—trading, military, or colonizing—was Pittsburgh, with its motley assemblage of soldiers, traders, adventurers, and farmers.[105]

The people in these westward-moving throngs were of many sorts. Judge Henderson and George Washington were promoters rather than settlers: they and their agents surveyed sites for others to live on. Yet no sharp line can be drawn between speculators and settlers. Arthur St. Clair, after resigning from the British army and marrying into a well-to-do Boston family, moved to western Pennsylvania, where he acquired a large estate. A representative promoter-settler in Kentucky was James Harrod who after founding Harrodsburg became a leading citizen of the new commonwealth. The careers of Tennesseans like James Robertson and John Sevier further illustrate the success of frontier leaders with a flair for promotion. Sevier was a particularly active speculator.

Of course, not all settlers were community builders. For some the master interest was hunting and trapping—the "call of the wild." But far more important were the obscure men and women who tilled the farms, founded homes, and built ordered communities. For such people the establishment of secure titles to their homesteads was often difficult. Provincial land offices were generally far from the frontier, adequate surveys were lacking, and land warrants frequently conflicting. A considerable number were squatters without titles, staking out claims by clearing the land, building primitive cabins, and planting crops. As Jefferson later said, many people were "appropriating lands of their own authority, and meditating to hold them by force. . . ." Such folk usually had the sympathy of their neighbors when newcomers with formal titles contested possession. In the end, the Virginia legislature found it necessary to give way to the torrent and accept the principle of preemption, or preference to actual settlers. Other states took similar action during the Revolution. A North Carolina statute gave the occupant the preference "even against a prior certificate of entry." According to Jefferson, a liberal policy would ultimately be more profitable to

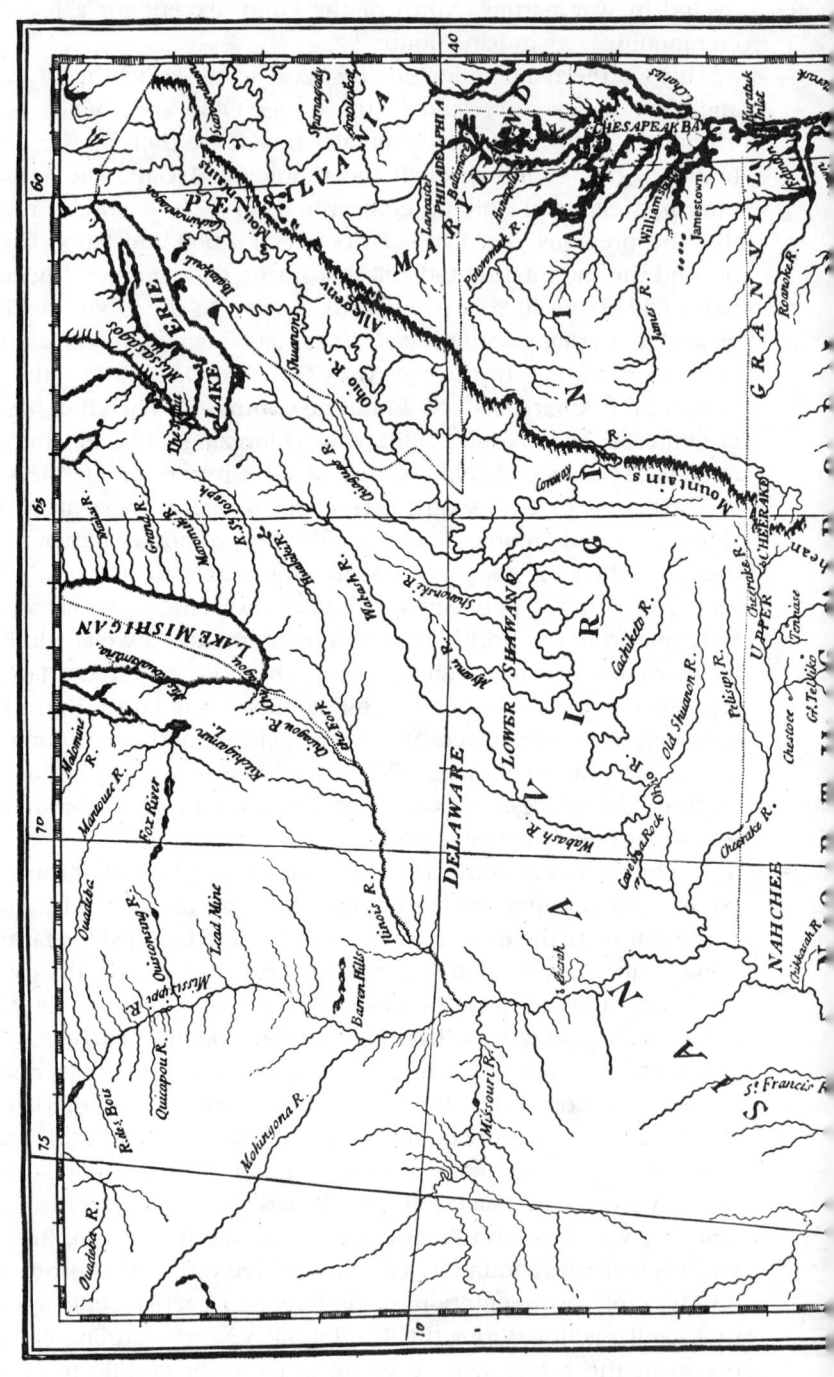

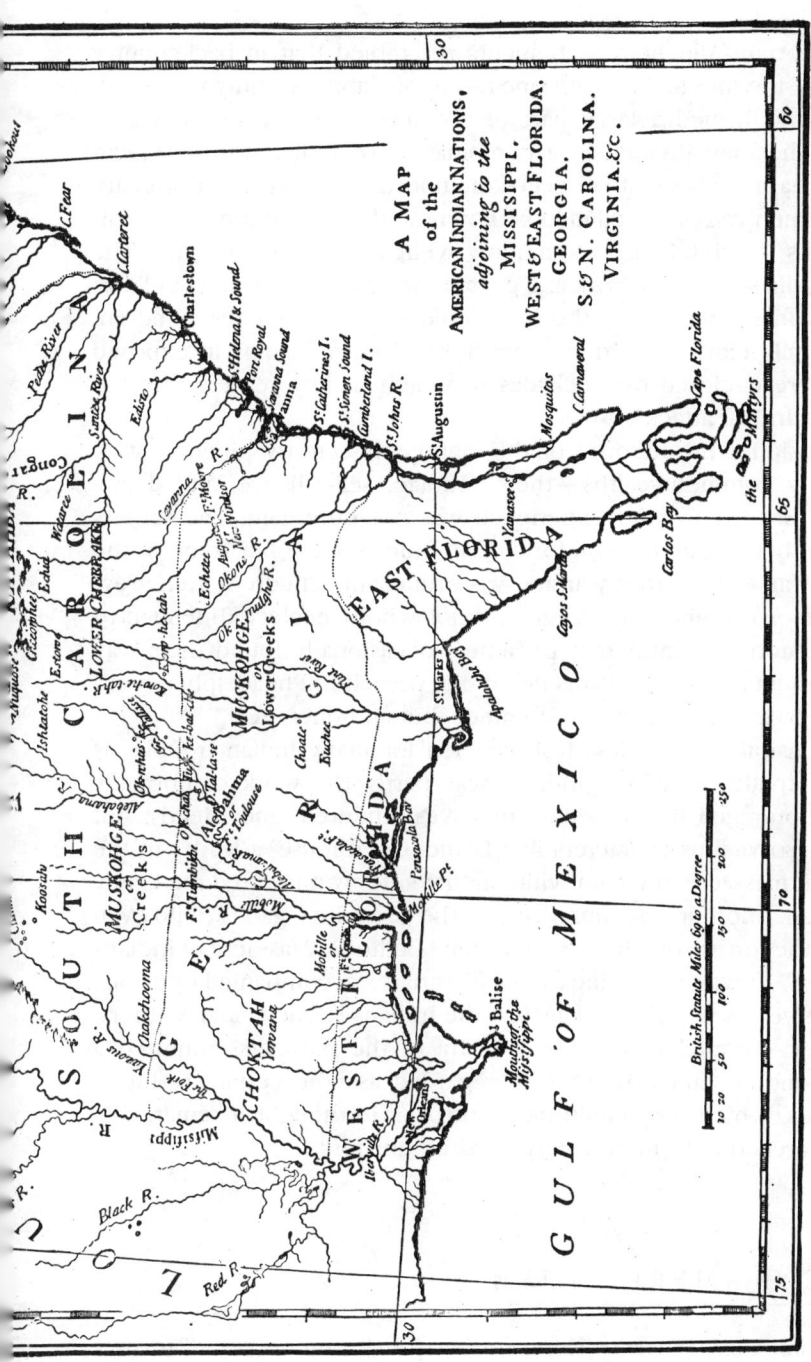

James Adair's Map, 1775

The West

the government since the frontiersmen would "settle the land in spite of everybody."[106]

Life in the trans-Allegheny settlements resembled that in backcountry homes east of the mountains, with one-room log cabins scantily furnished. Corn and pork formed a large part of the diet, varied with game and vegetables. The men dressed in a combination of Indian and European modes, with garments of cloth or deerskin, moccasins, and caps or ordinary hats. The women were clothed in loose gowns and large sunbonnets. Wearing moccasins in winter, they commonly went barefoot in summer. The men hunted, did some farm work and guarded their families against Indians, while the women performed the household tasks, reared the children, made the family clothing, and commonly hoed corn. Cabins in exposed situations were enclosed by stockades to which nearby settlers resorted when fearing Indian attacks.[107]

None can doubt the heroism of the eighteenth-century pioneers who built the new commonwealths—their courage, self-reliance, and democratic spirit. But the frontier experience was not pure gain. The settlers lacked not only the material comforts of an older society but some of the higher values as well. Border warfare was brutalizing; children often grew up with little or no schooling; religion, if not wholly neglected, tended to be crudely emotional. Intinerant preachers occasionally found their way across the mountains. John Adams heard one preach in Philadelphia "with no learning, no grace of action or utterance, but an honest zeal."[108]

The responsibility of lawless frontiersmen for many Indian troubles is clear. Brutal treatment of the Indians was partly the work of normally decent men outraged by the killing of wives, children, and friends; but there were also vicious characters like Daniel Greathouse, a leader in the Yellow Creek massacre in which white men wantonly murdered the family of Chief Logan. Another was Simon Girty, "the Great Renegade," who even encouraged the torture of white captives. The Bulltown Massacre of Indians by whites in 1772 was, according to one historian, "accompanied by atrocities as repulsive" as any charged against the Indians.[109] Alexander Withers, a sympathetic chronicler who knew many of the pioneers, admitted a lowering of moral standards. This he regarded as "the certain result of circumstances, which they could not control." He thought it remarkable that "their dereliction from propriety" was no greater.

EMERGING AMERICANISM

THE FRENCHMAN CRÈVECOEUR, writing during the Revolutionary War after some twenty years' residence in the colonies, recorded his conviction that the people, despite their divergent origins, possessed certain characteristics that differentiated them from Europeans and which might fairly be called American.[110] Many elements of this underlying unity may be easily perceived. The men politically and socially influential were English-speaking and chiefly of British stock. Governmental institutions everywhere rested on such fundamental notions as popular representation, trial by jury, and other common-law safeguards of liberty and property. The eighteenth century brought about a more general acceptance of common-law principles than earlier. This was the natural result of a more settled society, a bench and bar increasingly familiar with English precedents, and imperial insistence on the harmonizing of colonial legislation with English law.[111] The rapid expansion of the newspaper press also promoted unity through intercolonial circulation and exchanges. Nor were religious differences seriously divisive. Except for small Catholic and still smaller Jewish minorities, the British Americans, so far as they were religious at all, were Protestant Christians. Within particular denominations there were some intercolonial associations, as in the Presbyterian synod, the Friends' meetings, and the correspondence or occasional conferences among the Anglican clergy.

In their formal publications Americans expressed themselves in English much like that used across the Atlantic. Even in the colloquial speech the differences were apparently less than might be supposed. Lord Adam Gordon found the language of Bostonians quite like that of the "old country." Visiting Philadelphia, he declared that English was "spoken by all ranks, in a degree of purity and perfection, surpassing any, but the polite part of London." William Eddis, whose experience was chiefly in Maryland, said "the pronunciation of the generality of people" had an "accuracy and elegance" which must gratify "the most judicious ear." Considering the mixed origin of the inhabitants, he thought it remarkable that the spoken language should show so few divergences. The young English traveler Nicholas Cresswell was also surprised to find the speech of colonials as good as it was and the variations no greater. "In general," he believed, they used "better English than the English do."[112]

There were, of course, immigrants from Continental Europe who spoke either their own native tongue or a hybrid speech, and other differences were due to the survival in America of forms which had become archaic in England. There were, besides, minor local divergences. Philip Fithian, for instance, noted that Virginians spoke of a "sale" instead of a "vendue," the New Jersey term, and of an "ordinary" instead of a "tavern." A Virginian would have called a horse "vicious" when the Jerseyman would have said "mischievous." Regarding colonial speech Franklin was probably a better judge than most Americans because of his broader experience. He believed that, on the whole, the colonists spoke well and that informed Englishmen agreed with him. Though the people of different counties in the homeland could be distinguished by dialectal peculiarities, one could not so "distinguish a North American." President of Princeton John Witherspoon thought the common man in the colonies spoke better than an Englishman of the corresponding class, while the language of educated Americans was less correct than that of educated Englishmen. Nevertheless, one hopeful colonial maintained that the "highest perfection" of the English tongue was "reserved for this Land of light and freedom." He proposed, therefore, the choice of "Fellows of the American Society of Language" to "correct, enrich and refine" the speech.[113]

One factor in the rise of Americanism was an increasingly detached and critical attitude toward British society. By 1772, Franklin was emphasizing the imperfections of a social system which depressed "multitudes below the Savage State that a few may be rais'd above it," and a little later he noted the "extream Corruption prevalent among all Orders of Men in this old rotten State." Virtuous America should avoid too close association with so vicious a society. Henry Laurens thought chastity was "out of fashion" in England. Even Loyalists were not always happy there. Samuel Curwen complained of "vicious indulgences of every kind" as well as of "the deplorable venality" in politics. When the Revolutionary War ended, he gladly returned to Massachusetts. Ward Chipman, a Harvard graduate who served in the British army, declared that life in England, even with a full purse, did not offer "half the rational social enjoyments" of colonial society.[114]

As an eighteenth-century interpreter of Americanism perhaps no one surpassed Crèvecoeur. Its chief characteristics, he thought, were a comparatively simple and democratic society and an expansive outlook. In America the European peasant, accustomed to work for princes or nobles and lacking political privileges, might easily become a freeholder and a citizen. There was a change of scale also: "two hundred miles formerly appeared a very great distance, it is now but a trifle." In this bracing atmosphere men were inspired to undertakings which would neverhave occurred to them in Europe: "Thus Europeans become Americans."[115] Crèvecoeur's picture was somewhat idealized, for America, too, had its class distinctions and the colonial franchise was quite undemocratic. In terms of contemporary Europe, however, his analysis was essentially sound.

Emotion as well as reason contributed toward a revolutionary psychology. Evidences of social unrest may be found first in the older countryside. In rural New England existed survivals of the ancient antagonism between town proprietors and nonproprietary inhabitants, and that between country debtors and merchant-creditors who had opposed such agrarian measures as the land bank and the expansion of paper currency. Here the British government was also involved since Parliament had suppressed the land bank and checked the issue of legal-tender paper. Elsewhere quitrents, royal or proprietary, accounted for some discontent, though these payments, irregularly collected, were hardly a major issue. In some provinces, however, efforts to enforce them had led to acrimonious controversies, notably among the tenants of Lord Granville who had inherited extensive proprietary rights in North Carolina. In New York many great landowners paid only nominal quitrents, but their tenants complained of oppressive dues and, during the 1760s, uprisings on Hudson Valley estates were not suppressed without some bloodshed. In the South, parliamentary restraints on tobacco exports to Continental Europe limited the planter's market, but the chief object of complaint was the British creditor and his agents on whom was blamed the accumulating debt burden at a time when the plantation economy was declining through soil exhaustion.[116]

Though rural discontent helped to prepare the way for radical proposals, mercantile grievances were at first more conspicuous. The difficulties of the colonial merchant did not arise wholly from government policies: one factor was the transition from war to peace after 1763. Privateering was over, army contracts were smaller, and the exceptional profits of enemy trade were ended. Governmental action did, however, complicate the situation through stricter enforcement of existing trade regulations, especially those affecting commerce with the foreign West Indies. The navy cooperated with the customs service, seizures of suspected vessels increased, trade fell off, and, as we have seen, an acute depression set in. Then came the new parliamentary measures which further depressed colonial business. Customs officials and admiralty courts received additional powers for the enforcement of commercial regulations. In 1764 and 1765 followed the sugar act, the sweeping prohibition of legal-tender paper, and the stamp act.[117]

Though radicals and conservatives agreed in condemning the obnoxious legislation and, as General Thomas Gage said, "differed only in the means to be pursued," that difference became increasingly important. Radicals were ready for violent resistance, while others, fearing its effect on the masses, favored methods less obviously illegal. Nevertheless, wealthy merchants sat in the Stamp Act Congress, supported the boycott of English goods, and, with more or less misgiving, acquiesced in the riotous proceedings of the Sons of Liberty. The business depression survived the repeal of the stamp tax and the modification of the sugar act, and before long the merchants were again protesting against parliamentary measures.[118]

The Townshend acts of 1767 brought a further tightening of the enforcement machinery directed against illicit trade, while the taxation issue was revived through "external" duties on glass, paper, painters' colors, and tea. Again the merchants responded with nonimportation agreements, but the experience of the stamp act riots and the consequent disturbance of business led to more emphasis on orderly procedures, as in Dickinson's *Letters from a Pennsylvania Farmer.* Intercolonial cooperation proved difficult, however, and it was not until 1769 that the three principal Northern ports were united in nonimportation agreements. In Charleston the merchants acted reluctantly under pressure from the "mechanics and tradesmen."

Even so, the various mercantile communities feared loss of trade and were mutually suspicious. When, therefore, all the Townshend duties except that on tea were repealed, many merchants accepted this as substantial, if not complete, redress, with the result that the nonimportation program broke down. In 1770 business was reviving and there was a tendency to let well enough alone rather than risk the consequences of radical appeals to the masses.[119]

From the standpoint of class feeling, an important group was that commonly known as the "mechanics and tradesmen"—small traders, clerks, artisans, seamen, carters, and common laborers. At the upper levels a fair number of these people could vote, being "freemen" pursuing recognized

EDES & GILL'S
NORTH-AMERICAN
ALMANACK
For the Year of our Lord
1769.

Being the First after BISSEXTILE or LEAP-YEAR.
Calculated for theMeridian of BOSTON, N.E.Latt. 42°25′ North.
CONTAINING,

An Extract from theHistory of *Publius Clodius Britano Americanus*; Judgment of the Weather; Sun and Moon's Rising & Sitting; Time of High Water; Public Roads, with the best Stages or Houses to put up at; Eclipses; Courts in *Massachusetts-Bay*, *New-Hampshire*, *Connecticut*, and *Rhode-Island*; Feasts & Fasts of the Church of England, &c. &c. *To which is added,* The CHARTER of the Province of the *Massachusetts-Bay.*

THERE will be Five ECLIPSES this Year in the following Order, *viz.*—The First of the SUN, *January* 7th invisible. —The Second of the SUN, *June* 4th, invisible.—The Third of the MOON, *June* 19, visible and Total. Beginning, 1h. 45m. 25f. Middle, 3h. 30m. 57f. End, 5h. 17m. 28f. Duration, 3h.32m.3f. Digits eclipsed, 12 19.—TheFourth of the SUN, *November* 28th, invisible.—The Fifth and last of the MOON, *December* 13th, visible. Beginning, 0h. 18m. 8f. Middle, 1h. 41m. 15f. End, 3h. 5m. 10f. Duration, 2h. 47m. 2f. Digits eclipsed, 8 56.

The FRONTISPIECE represents
Two Female Figures. The principal, richly decorated, is seated on a Throne with an Imperial Diadem on her Head, and a Spear in her left Hand. The other Figure exhibits a Virgin with a Civic Crown, in the utmost Agonies of Distress and Horror. The Cap of Liberty falling from the Spear of one, and tottering to fall from the other. The Label of one, isCollidimur; of the other, Frangimur. Two Ships are represented to View in a Tempest in the Instant of dashing to Pieces against one another, and sinking between the Rocks of Sylla and Caribdis. In the Interim are seen two Arch-Angels, flying as "on the Wings of the Wind." The Label of the one is, "Shall not the Lord of all the Earth do "Right." The other is, "The Fool" only "hath said in his "Heart there is no God." Above all, in a Glory, is inscribed these Words, "The Lord GOD Omnipotent reigneth, let the "Earth rejoice!"

BOSTON: Printed and Sold by EDES & GILL, in Queen-Street. [Price Four Shillings per Dozen, and Six Pence single.]

occupations or owners of sufficient property to meet minimum suffrage requirements. Many others, however, could not qualify or, if they could, lacked effective organization. Of employer-labor conflicts comparable with those of later times we hear little, though in 1768 the *New-York Journal* reported a strike of journeymen tailors whose wages had been reduced. More common were such other indications of class consciousness as resentment at social pretensions and demands for a larger share in public affairs.

The latter appeared, for instance, in Philadelphia, where a close corporation directed the city government and the suffrage was so sharply restricted that few even of the taxpayers could vote. In the *Pennsylvania Journal* (1773) "Mechanic" denounced the upper-class "Junto" who might pose as friends of liberty but could not be trusted. Another newspaper communication, from "Citizen," complained that, though the "laborious Farmer and Tradesman" had always been the support of liberty, the ruling class did not wish them to "intermeddle in State affairs." [120]

The urban working class counted heavily in the Revolutionary movement. Public meetings repeatedly occurred in which suffrage requirements did not apply or were not enforced. In New England, royal officials complained of "town meetings," regular or irregular, where "the lowest Mechanics" could discuss "the most important points of government, with the utmost freedom." [121] Conservatives regarded such gatherings, guided by a "few hot and designing men," as a "constant source of sedition." In New York, where mass meetings in the interest of particular candidates had long been familiar, they were used to bring forward mechanics' tickets. When mercantile opposition to British measures seemed too cautious, the mechanics here and elsewhere had their radical spokesmen, not necessarily members of their own class, but commonly skillful politicians like Samuel Adams, Christopher Gadsden, and the New York triumvirate of Lamb, Sears, and McDougall. Adams was a Harvard graduate; Gadsden, a substantial business man; John Lamb, a moderately prosperous wine merchant; Alexander McDougall was fairly well off; and Isaac Sears was an early member of the New York Chamber of Commerce.

In short, the mechanic-tradesman group offered combustible material which might be effectively directed in critical situations. In New York it forced conservatives to accept measures about which they felt misgivings. In Charleston it turned the tide in favor of the nonimportation agreement of 1769. A corresponding group was active in the Boston Tea Party, and in 1776 combined in Pennsylvania with backcountry farmers to overcome the conservativism of the legislature. In the larger capitals especially, urban radicalism could exert pressure on provincial assemblies and officials.

There were also dissatisfied elements in the "Old West," jealous of the overrepresentation of the East in the colonial legislatures. Along the New York border a petty warfare of a dozen years had developed partly out of the territorial claims of Massachusetts and partly from the resentment of native tenants against the Livingston, Van Rensselaer, and Van Cortlandt landlords. The three great manor lords took the Whig side in the Revolution, and that temporarily assuaged the class feeling between landlords and tenants, but apparently the latter felt, and quite rightly that a successful revolution would in some way improve their status.

There were further sources of discontent in the problems of the trans-Allegheny country. Both the frontiersmen themselves and the land speculators or promoters were involved. Each group resented more or less keenly the restrictive policies of the home government in relation to the newly acquired territory. Two of the grievances listed in the Declaration of Independence dealt with this Western situation: the complaint against the new regulations for taking up Western lands and the denunciation of the Quebec act.

To the friction resulting from economic grievances were added less material factors. Efforts to exploit religious feeling may not always have been sincere, but they would hardly have been made if the feeling had not widely existed. In New England the political influence of Puritanism was clearly recognized by Whigs and Tories alike. The inheritors of that tradition had been generally loyal to the Hanoverian dynasty as the symbol of Protestant victory over Jacobites and "papists," but now their attitude gradually changed, partly because of the frequent association of Loyalism with Anglican churchmanship. Though rigid Calvinism had weakened, even unorthodox ministers like Jonathan Mayhew and Charles Chauncy were aggressively Protestant, resembling their Puritan ancestors in repudiating Anglican theories of divine right. No Revolutionary leader appealed more effectively to such sentiments than Samuel Adams. Among the grievances he listed in 1772 for the Boston town meeting and for circulation in the country towns, one dealt at length with the proposed Anglican episcopate, reminding people that their fathers had crossed the sea to preserve religious and political liberties now endangered. Many years later John Adams declared that "the apprehension of Episcopacy" had stimulated "close thinking on the constitutional authority of parliament."[122]

The Puritan conception of the Anglican Church as a "half-way house to Rome" appeared in the discussion of the Quebec act, which established the Roman Catholic Church in Canada. In Isaiah Thomas's *Royal American Magazine* for October 1774, a cartoon entitled "The Mitred Minuet" pictured the supposed alliance of "Popery" and "Prelacy." The famous resolves of Suffolk County, Massachusetts, denounced the Quebec act as a menace to Protestantism and the "civil rights and liberties of all *America*," a sentiment presently echoed by the Continental Congress. The Tory rector, Charles Inglis of New York, regarded the Presbyterians as a subversive influence, insisting that the grand object of the dissenters was "an abolition of the Church of England." The idea that religious as well as political rights were involved in the Revolution appears also in the South. In short, religious grievances contributed to the emotional attitudes which helped to make many men responsive to radical propaganda.[123]

Though the importance of political theories in the Revolution may easily be exaggerated, the slogan "No taxation without representation" was not mere camouflage. Assembly journals long before the Revolution show that the essential doctrine, whatever the various forms in which the issue was raised, was deeply rooted in the colonial mind. It rested on a reasoned belief in the power of the purse as an essential safeguard of self-government and of the right of a community to deal freely with its own problems. Though many, probably most, men fight for specific and immediate interests, some at least of the American leaders had a longer perspective, recognizing that the assertion of principle, even thought the interest directly involved was slight, might in the end prove highly practical. Nor, when all is said, can we ignore that emotional factor called "the spirit of liberty."

THE PARTING OF THE WAYS

SOCIAL DISCONTENT in given groups or areas did not always determine the final choice of individuals between Whigs and Tories. Furthermore, party lines were not definitely drawn once and for all at any stage of the controversy. The alignment of 1774 differed from that of 1765, and other changes followed successively the outbreak of hostilities in 1775, the Declaration of Independence, and the veering fortunes of war. The sequence of events during the five years immediately preceding the appeal to arms sheds considerable light on these shifts of attitude.

The year 1770, marked by the so-called Boston Massacre on the one hand and the partial repeal of the Townshend duties on the other, began a period of rapid recovery from economic depression. The small surviving tax on tea seemed hardly worth fighting. Tea drinking was a popular diversion even among radicals, who did not always ask too curiously whether the obnoxious duty had been paid. Meantime, however, the radical leaders, especially in Boston, refused to let matters rest and, aided by the tactical mistakes of their opponents, continued to remind their fellow citizens that their liberties were still in danger.

Nevertheless, there was still general reluctance to adopt extreme measures until the passage of a new tea act, which, while making tea cheaper for the colonists by removing certain duties in England, kept the tax issue alive by retaining the threepenny duty payable in America. The act also antagonized colonial merchants by authorizing the East India Company to export directly to American agents, thereby enabling them to undersell independent traders. As a result the radicals were reinforced by a considerable body of moderate men. Though the latter group deprecated violence, the radicals in December 1773 took matters into their own hands in the Boston Tea Party, which not only defied Parliament but alienated many colonial adherents of public order and property rights. Though other ports also adopted hostile measures, the Boston resistance was the most destructive affair and the most objectionable to conservatives both in England and America.[124] Even some American Whigs favored compensation to the East India Company.

Just as the Boston proceedings were threatening to divide the colonial opposition, parliamentary action helped to close the broken ranks. The series of measures seemed to Americans not only unfair but revolutionary. Three of them—the act closing the port of Boston, the Massachusetts government act, and the act for the "impartial administration of justice"— aroused sympathy throughout British America because of their extreme severity and the precedents set for arbitrary interference with local self-government.

During the summer and early autumn of 1774 events moved rapidly. General Thomas Gage succeeded Hutchinson as governor of Massachusetts and proceeded to enforce the coercive acts. The port of Boston was closed, "mandamus" councilors replaced those formerly elected, and town meetings were restricted. The people, however, proved recalcitrant. "Mandamus" councilors resigned under the pressure of public opinion, and the house of representatives, having refused to work with the governor, managed to choose delegates to a Continental Congress before being dissolved. Gage's government, supported by the military, controlled Boston and its vicinity, but elsewhere the real power passed rapidly to a de facto government consisting of a provincial congress and of a committee of safety which served as a central executive with the backing of local committees. Taxes were paid to this extralegal government and most of the courts of justice were suspended.

Parallel with this development in Massachusetts was the activity of committees in other colonies in enforcing the tea boycott and collecting supplies for the relief of suffering Boston. Such contributions were partly a natural expression of popular sympathy, but they also helped to bind the colonies more closely together. There was continuous discussion in conventions, committees and the press of appropriate modes of resistance. New nonimportation agreements were adopted, and finally local activities came to a head in the First Continental Congress, to which every colony but Georgia sent delegates.[125]

When the members assembled at Philadelphia on September 5, 1774, they all agreed on the need of uniting in defense of colonial rights, but differed as to the method to be pursued. New England radicalism, though distrusted by men from other sections, was nevertheless supported by such Southerners as Patrick Henry, Richard Henry Lee, and Christopher Gadsden. The conservatives favored the plan proposed by Joseph Galloway, which would have required the concurrent action of Parliament with a general American legislature on measures involving the colonies. Its adoption would have marked a distinct advance in the colonial system. Though supported by some cautious Whigs, this scheme was rejected. The conservatives met a further defeat when Congress approved the revolutionary proceedings in Massachusetts. Congress's declaration of principles was, however, a compromise between those who denied to Parliament any legislative authority in the colonies and those who admitted some parliamentary control outside the field of taxation, especially in the regulation of trade.[126]

Most significant of all was the congressional plan known as the Association, which included nonimportation, nonexportation, and nonconsumption agreements against British trade. To protect the Southern staple-producing planters, the enforcement of nonexportation was postponed until September 1, 1775, but nonimportation was to start within a few weeks. To replace imports, native industry was to be stimulated and sheep conserved for woolen manufactures; and profiteers were to be boycotted. The execution of such measures required not only the support of popular opinion but an adequate organization. For this purpose provincial and local committees were to be further developed to deal with violators of the Association, who were to be publicly denounced as "enemies of American liberty." Here were the elements of a far-flung de facto government whose orders, though not legally enforceable, would nonetheless have the effect of law. As a directing agency for the provincial and local organizations, the Second Continental Congress was to assemble in May 1775.[127]

From now on, party lines were more sharply drawn. The supporters of the Association, who called themselves Whigs, were denounced by their opponents as "republicans," "Cromwellians," and the like, while the conservatives were variously characterized as "friends of government," Loyalists, or Tories. Both parties engaged in various propaganda through public meetings and in the press.

Everywhere committees ordered violators of the Association publicly listed so that they might be cut off from "all commercial intercourse and connection whatsoever." In Maine, tenants of the Loyalist landowner Sir William Pepperell were advised not to renew their leases. A Virginia agent of a Scotch firm was disciplined for refusing to allow inspection of his books without his principal's consent. Profiteers were punished for raising prices unduly or "engrossing" essential commodities. In short, these bodies were exercising governmental functions.[128]

When war began, the royal and proprietary governors in most instances were wielding hardly more than a nominal authority. Virginia public affairs were for the most part controlled by a convention which replaced the house of burgesses and was largely directed by former members of the provincial assembly and county governments. While the royal governor remained at Williamsburg, the convention sat at Richmond and the regular courts were suspended. In North Carolina, also, the old administration was nearly powerless.[129] In Pennsylvania the framework of proprietary government was maintained with a conservative assembly, but the real power was passing to revolutionary committees. The royal governments most nearly held their own in Georgia and New York, both of which had strong Loyalist elements. Neither Rhode Island nor Connecticut needed an extralegal government since their officers were already chosen directly or indirectly by the voters.

So matters stood in April 1775 when a British attempt to seize some Whig military stores at Concord, Massachusetts, precipitated civil war. That this was no mere local incident was soon evident. News of the fight, sent on the nineteenth, reached the New York committee on the twenty-third and was immediately forwarded to Philadelphia. A later message arrived in New York on the twenty-fifth, Philadelphia on the twenty-sixth, Baltimore on the twenty-seventh, and Virginia on the twenty-eighth, though it did not reach Charleston until three weeks after the engagement.[130] During the next two months the Massachusetts troops were expanded into a New England army and Congress provided for an intercolonial force with a Virginian at its head.

Of the subsequent political history up to the Declaration of Independence only the principal steps need be noted. Of prime importance was the gradual elimination of provincial governments. Most of them had disappeared before Congress, in May 1776, formally decreed the end of all authority under the crown. This meant that, except in Rhode Island and Connecticut, a new governmental structure had to be built and a new basis for civil authority laid to replace the old allegiance. Meantime, the normal processes of law protecting life and property were interrupted. For the responsible Whig leaders this proved a source of real anxiety. One argument for independence was the need of a new public law based on the principle of popular rule.

No simple formula explains why particular classes or individuals chose to be Whig, Tory, or neutral. Some students have assumed a clean-cut division between Tory aristocrats and liberty-loving, democratic Whigs who opposed imperial policies in the interest of self-government. Tories have further been conceived of as officeholders or closely related to that class, or else as temperamental conservatives under the spell of old-world traditions. The class-conflict form of economic interpretation had made headway, while still other historians have emphasized religious affiliations. These explanations each contain an element of truth, but no one of them takes sufficiently into account the complexity of human motives.

In general, officeholders tend to support the existing order, and that was usually true of those who held important royal or proprietary commissions. The governors, whether sent from England or American-born, adhered to the home government. Wentworth in New Hampshire, Hutchinson in Massachusetts, and Benjamin Franklin's son William in New Jersey—all members of old colonial families—were strongly Loyalist. Provincial councilors usually took this side, partly no doubt because they frequently held other profitable appointments. Sharper differences distinguished minor officials such as sheriffs, county justices, and militia officers, who had to consider

J. Yeates

COMMON SENSE;

ADDRESSED TO THE

INHABITANTS

O F

AMERICA,

On the following interefting

SUBJECTS.

I. Of the Origin and Defign of Government in general, with concife Remarks on the Englifh Conftitu.ion.

II. Of Monarchy and Hereditary Succeffion.

III Thoughts on the prefent State of American Affairs.

IV. Of the prefent Ability of America, with fome mifcellaneous Reflections.

Man knows no Mafter fave creating HEAVEN,
Or thofe whom choice and common good ordain.

THOMSON.

PHILADELPHIA:
Printed, and Sold, by R. BELL, in Third-Street.
MDCCLXXVI.

not only their official and legal obligations but also local opinion. In Massachusetts the county militia colonels were about evenly divided. Social connections also counted. Officials who were permanent residents usually had business and family ties with many persons whom they could influence.

The professional groups illustrate clearly the disruptive effect of the Revolution on colonial society. In eastern Massachusetts a large proportion of the leading lawyers became Tories. Among them were Jonathan Sewall; Samuel Quincy, who was a marriage connection of John Adams; and Daniel Leonard, author of the "Massachusettensis" essays. Many years later, Adams spoke of these men as having been his "cordial, confidential, and bosom friends." Conspicuous lawyers who took the Whig side included Adams himself and John Lowell, afterwards a U. S. judge.[131]

Of the famous triumvirate of New York lawyers—William Livingston, John Morin Scott, and William Smith—Smith became a Loyalist. A much more strenuous Tory was Judge Thomas Jones. Peter Van Schaack, another outstanding lawyer, though not an active partisan, refused to swear allegiance to the Revolutionary state government. Among the moderate Whig members of the bar were Duane and Jay, both of whom supported the conservative Galloway plan but later rendered good service to the Continental cause. Several prominent Philadelphia lawyers were Loyalists, neutrals, or conservative Whigs. Joseph Galloway and Chief Justice William Allen were Tories, and Benjamin Chew was suspected of Loyalism and temporarily imprisoned. John Dickinson opposed the Declaration as premature, but once the decision was made he acquiesced. On the other hand, two of the ablest practitioners—James Wilson and Joseph Reed—were definitely Whig. Tory lawyers were scarcer in the South, where the profession furnished such conspicuous patriot leaders as George Wythe, Patrick Henry, Thomas Jefferson, James Iredell, and the young Charlestonians: the Rutledges and Pinckneys.

The political attitude of ministers depended partly on their denominational affiliations. In the North most of the Church of England clergy were Tories. Though mainly of colonial ancestry and often graduates of New England colleges, they accepted the church's tradition of loyalty to the crown. Among the Loyalist exiles were the three Anglican rectors in Boston. When the American army occupied New York, Episcopal services had to be suspended because the clergy refused to omit the prayers for the king. But from Pennsylvania southward the alignment of the Anglican preachers was less distinct. Their three principal functionaries in Philadelphia at first supported Congress and preached patriotic sermons even after the war began. One of them, Jacob Duché, was chosen as congressional chaplain. None of these men, however, really favored independence. Two of them subsequently became Loyalists while the third, Provost William Smith, was distrusted by the more ardent Whigs. On the other hand, William White, a future bishop of Pennsylvania, took the American side. In the

Chesapeake provinces many of the clergy joined their Whig parishioners and supported the Revolution, some serving as army chaplains. The church suffered, however, through the Loyalism of some conspicuous representatives, notably the rector at Annapolis and the Tory clergy of William and Mary College. In Charleston also the churchmen were divided. The rector of St. Philips Church was so strenuous a Whig that during the British occupation he was imprisoned and later banished.[132]

For reasons already indicated, most of the Congregational and Presbyterian ministers were Whigs, though even among the New England Congregationalists there were a few exceptions. The conspicuous clerical leaders of the Revolutionary party included Samuel Cooper and Charles Chauncy in Boston and the Presbyterians: President Witherspoon of Princeton, John Rodgers of New York, George Duffield of Philadelphia, and David Caldwell in North Carolina. These two denominations contributed by far the largest number of chaplains in the Continental army.[133]

The Baptist preachers, in spite of the discrimination they suffered at the hands of their colonial neighbors, also generally supported the Revolution. Democratic in their social philosophy, they hoped for fairer treatment under the new governments. With the Methodist preachers, often newcomers from England, Loyalism proved stronger—naturally enough, in view of John Wesley's condemnation of independence. The Dutch and German Protestants were divided in opinion with the younger Muhlenbergs conspicuous among the Lutheran Whigs. Though the few Catholic priests in Maryland and Pennsylvania could hardly exert much political influence, Father John Carroll cooperated with the committee of Congress in the effort to win over the French Canadians.[134]

As for the educators, there is no reason to suppose that their political attitude differed from that of the communities in which they lived or the religious societies with which they might be affiliated. It happens, however, that three well-known schoolteachers were Tories: John Lovell of the Boston Latin School, the Philadelphia Quaker Robert Proud, and the Maryland clerical tutor Jonathan Boucher. On the eve of the Revolution two heads of colleges were also Loyalists—Myles Cooper of King's and John Camm of William and Mary. Cooper fled to England, while Camm was dismissed in favor of a young Whig professor. At Philadelphia the dubious position of Provost Smith almost broke up the college. The New England and New Jersey faculties, however, adhered to the patriot side.

In the political cleavages the position of the merchants is of special importance. Though generally opposed to the revenue measures of 1764–65 and the Townshend acts of 1767, they had become increasingly troubled by the violence of the radicals, the interference of the Continental Association with private business, the taking up of arms against the king's representatives, and the idea of separation from the empire. A representative statement was the address of the "Merchants and Traders" and others of

Boston to Governor Hutchinson as he was leaving for England in 1774. These "addressers" disapproved the harsh provisions of the port bill, but they favored indemnification of the East India Company and denounced the radicals. During the next year the position of the conservatives grew more unhappy, and when Howe evacuated Boston some 200 merchants became refugees, including members of solid old Massachusetts families. Nevertheless, many substantial New England merchants remained. Typical of the cautious Whigs in this group was John Rowe. He called the Tea Party "a Disastrous Affair," but though he believed his fellow citizens had "done amiss" and favored compensation to the East India Company, he considered "the revenge of the Ministry . . . too severe." Staying on in Boston during the siege, he complained of misconduct by the British troops, and after Howe's withdrawal invited Washington to dinner. Though many of his intimates were Tory refugees, Rowe continued active in town affairs.[135]

In New York a majority of the members of the Chamber of Commerce seem to have been Tories, with perhaps a quarter out-and-out Whigs and the rest neutral. Loyalists and neutrals were influenced by family and official connections, profitable business relations with the government, and early British occupation of the city. Conspicuous on the Loyalist side was John Watts, for many years in the official circle. Isaac Low's Toryism may be contrasted with the opposite stand of his brother Nicholas. Other prominent Whig merchants were Philip Livingston and Francis Lewis, both signers of the Declaration of Independence. Many of the Philadelphia merchants were Quakers who, opposed on principle to armed resistance, refused allegiance to the Revolutionary state government. Though not necessarily Tories, they were naturally distrusted by the Whigs, who sent some of them away to Virginia when the British army approached in 1777. Some well-known merchants actively supported the Revolution, including General Thomas Mifflin, who was disciplined by the Quakers for taking up arms, and Robert Morris. Morris voted against independence on July 2, but two days later refrained from voting, making possible Pennsylvania's affirmative action. He subsequently signed the Declaration.[136]

Among the Charleston merchants Loyalism was strong, especially with the agents of British firms, but two of the wealthiest, Henry Laurens and Gabriel Manigault, were ardent patriots. In the other plantation provinces the merchants were usually Tories. In Virginia the Scotch traders formed the backbone of the Tory element; farther south there were strong pro-British groups in and about Wilmington and Savannah. A typical Loyalist of Scotch background was Robert Hogg, member of an important Wilmington firm, who after cooperating for a time with the Whigs drew back as they took control of affairs, and left the province. On the other hand, the chief leader of the local radicals was also an outstanding merchant. In Savannah the Tory merchant Joseph Habersham had a son and a nephew on the American side.[137]

Though the urban working classes were natural allies of the radicals, lists of Loyalists include many mechanics and tradesmen—"shopkeepers," shoemakers, blacksmiths, milliners, "servants," and "laborers." Still others were probably too obscure to be listed. But the great bulk sided with the radicals, making up for the lack of support from the "best people." Loyalists and conservative Whigs alike feared the increasing influence of the masses. The "mobility," to quote Gouverneur Morris, could not always vote, but they could join in popular demonstrations and attend town meetings where votes were not closely scrutinized.[138]

Rural communities exhibited similar contrasts. In New England some conspicuous Loyalists were to be found among the comparatively few "country gentry," but most of the farmers belonged to the Whig camp. Consequently, the division between the two parties caused no serious social cleavage.[139] In New York the proprietors of great landed estates, though naturally conservative and preponderantly Tory, included, on the patriot side, the heads of four important manors: Cortlandt, Rensselaerswyck, Livingston, and Morrisania. Among the owners of large tracts not strictly manorial, Roger Morris and the De Lanceys were Tories, while Philip Schuyler was a Revolutionary general. Several families of this group were divided in allegiance. Thus, of the Morrisania Morrises, two were Whig leaders and one became a British general. Even many tenants on the great estates and some of the yeoman farmers were Tories, but probably a majority of the latter vigorously supported the patriot cause. As a result, rural New York was badly rent, with the situation further complicated by British control of the lower Hudson during most of the war. New Jersey, nearly all rural, had fewer consistent Tories than New York, but the Loyalists were numerous enough to call for constant vigilance on the part of the Revolutionary government. In Pennsylvania, Tory and neutral landowners, many of them connected with Philadelphia mercantile families, were strong in the eastern counties, making up more than two thirds of the attainted Tories in this state outside Philadelphia. The inland farmers tended to be Whigs.[140]

In the Chesapeake tidewater region Loyalism proved weaker than might have been expected in the case of normally conservative landowners, though some among them felt no enthusiasm for the Revolution. The weakness of Toryism here was due to the energy and prompt organization of the Whigs; to Lord Dunmore's inept leadership as governor of Virginia, including his threat of slave insurrections; and to the lack of a strong British force about which Loyalists could rally. The out-and-out Tories among the planter class belonged chiefly to the officeholding group. Of the Virginians who later claimed British compensation for their losses, only eight were planters, the majority being merchants. Among the Virginia Whigs, however, a well-marked line separated radicals and moderates, though the division was not wholly determined by economic status. Many of the extremists stemmed from the large-planter class. A good example is that of the Lee brothers.[141]

The Whiggism of the Virginia landholders may be variously explained. One cause was the old antagonism between the planter-debtor and his British creditor, with the opportunity offered by the war to get rid of burdensome obligations. Early legislation enabled such debtors to discharge their accounts by payments to the state in depreciated paper. Aside from this and other specific grievances, such as the regulations regarding Western lands which had antagonized Virginia promoters, there was the broad issue of self-government, the desire of a community accustomed to a considerable measure of autonomy to defend itself against interference from further external control. On this issue planters and farmers could and did agree. One factor that aided the Loyalist cause in the North was absent in Virginia. In this province there was no large urban community where unprivileged groups directed by radical agitators aroused the anxiety of the property-holding classes. The situation in Maryland resembled that in Virginia, but with some special features, notably the parasitic character of the Baltimore proprietorship. Though the Catholics had legitimate grievances against their Protestant neighbors, most of them apparently followed Charles Carroll's Whig leadership. While no effective pro-British party existed either here or in Virginia, Tory activities in both provinces proved temporarily disturbing. Early in the war Lord Dunmore received aid from the Loyalists, and later Tory risings occurred on the eastern shore of Maryland.[142]

In eastern North Carolina the Whigs of the Edenton district included planters, merchants, lawyers, and even some royal officeholders. One of their leaders was Samuel Johnston, Scotch-born nephew of a former royal governor, himself a substantial landowner with numerous slaves, a lawyer, and royal official. In the Roanoke Valley the outstanding radicals were the well-to-do planters Willie and Allen Jones, while in the Cape Fear Valley, with its commercial outlet at Wilmington, one of the foremost patriots was Robert Howe, a prosperous rice planter. An influential Loyalist element in this neighborhood consisted of the Scotch merchant-planter group. In South Carolina nearly all the conspicuous Whig leaders belonged to the socially and politically dominant class, including some who had held important royal appointments. The Revolutionary government was thus chiefly in the control of a fairly conservative group which disliked government by outsiders but wished to avoid extreme measures.[143]

Though the uprising was mainly directed by seaboard leaders, the back-country people also played a part. In New England the newer country towns seem generally to have taken much the same stand as the farmers of eastern Massachusetts and Connecticut. In New York, however, Whigs and Tories faced each other in the Mohawk Valley as well as on the lower Hudson. The special significance of the inland settlements in relation to the patriot cause is clearest in Pennsylvania, where they had long been refused adequate representation in the assembly by a conservative minority in the

East. The Revolution here combined two distinct but connected objects: the dislodging of a provincial oligarchy, and a more aggressive opposition to British policies than the mercantile and landowning aristocracy of the East liked. A revolutionary organization and an extralegal "provincial conference" gave the interior inhabitants a better representation and forced the assembly into line on the question of independence. The way was now prepared for a more democratic state constitution. Though here as elsewhere the principal Whig leaders were Easterners, their support came largely from the backcountry. In no other province did the conflict between seaboard and interior so nearly parallel that on imperial issues.[144]

In Virginia no such fundamental cleavage divided tidewater and backcountry on the question of independence. As between moderate and radical Whigs, however, the inland counties inclined toward the latter. Henry and Washington lived on the eastern edge of the piedmont, Madison in one of its central counties, and Jefferson among the foothills of the Blue Ridge. Washington had important interests in the Great Valley which gave him his first election to the house of burgesses. Jefferson was to become the most vigorous advocate of political and economic democracy.

In the Lower South the relation of the backcountry to the Revolution exhibited other features. The interior communities of the Carolinas were more isolated from the seaboard, took little part in the war at first, and were much preoccupied with local problems. They also distrusted the tidewater Whig politicians, several of whom had supported the royal governor against the Regulators. Moreover, the remoteness of the new settlements from one another and the variety of their foreign elements interfered with effective organization, while the proximity of this area to enemy-controlled East Florida further strengthened the backcountry Tories. For these reasons the Loyalists of this region were expected in 1776 to support the British sea attack on Charleston. In fact, a number of the prisoners taken by the Whigs after the battle of Moore's Creek Bridge were former Regulators, and though the Tory uprising failed it might have succeeded with better leadership.[145]

In northern and western New York, Loyalists were active and the border fighting compared in bitterness with that of the Carolinas. In the Great Lakes region, where British posts—at Oswego, Niagara, Detroit, and Mackinac—existed throughout the war, most of the prewar traders and Indian agents were Tories. On the upper Ohio, then troubled by disputes between Virginia and Pennsylvania, the Tory Connolly tried to organize an attack on the rear of the Southern colonies, and though this failed, some Loyalists remained in or about Pittsburgh. Not until this post was taken over by Congress did the more important of them withdraw. There were also some Tories among the West Virginia pioneers, but there and in Kentucky Whig sentiment prevailed. From the exposed Kentucky stations George Rogers Clark planned his famous expedition against the British posts in Illinois.

Farther south, the British superintendent of the Southern Indians used his influence on the Tory side, but the Tennessee settlers, though chiefly occupied with frontier problems, occasionally cooperated with the Whigs east of the mountains, notably at the battle of King's Mountain in 1780, when they helped to defeat the British and Tories in upper Carolina.

Though it has been said that the alignment of parties betokened a struggle between affluent and privileged classes as against less fortunate groups, the various local situations show that this was only partly true. The Revolution helped to transfer power from provincial aristocracies to an economic middle class, but the shift may be exaggerated. The personnel of the Continental Congress included a substantial proportion of rich men. New England was represented by such well-to-do persons as John Hancock and the Rhode Islanders, Stephen Hopkins and Samuel Ward. Elbridge Gerry of Massachusetts was an important merchant, and John Adams a leader at the Boston bar. None of the four New York signers could be called poor, and, judged by colonial standards, Robert Morris, Charles Carroll, and Washington and his Virginia colleague Thomas Nelson were all wealthy. John Adams's references to Whig leaders in New York and Philadelphia indicate comfortable and sometimes luxurious living. In the South especially, most of the outstanding patriots were men of social prestige, who lived well and with dignity.

As to the relative strength of Whigs, Tories, and neutrals one cannot go beyond plausible conjectures, especially since questions of definition are involved. Should an opponent of independence in 1776 who thenceforth remained passive be regarded as a Tory? What of the South Carolinians who after being associated with the Revolutionary government accepted protection from the British invader, or of the North Carolina Moravians who submitted to the Revolutionary government while refusing to renounce their old allegiance, or of the former Tories or neutrals who changed their attitude on account of British depredations?

On the basis of incomplete information one historian has estimated the total American enlistments either with the British regulars or in special Loyalist units at about 50,000. Including all the irregular fighters, the number of Tory combatants may well have been much larger. Available figures for civilians are even more fragmentary and uncertain. Lists of Loyalists named in confiscation acts or compensated by the British government for their losses tell something, but there were many other active or passive Tories too obscure to be enumerated. Roughly speaking, possibly a third of the population was Loyalist, a third definitely Whig, and a third not active on either side.[146]

The size of the opposing parties varied in different areas. In New England the Tory stronghold was mainly in eastern Massachusetts, but there were similar though smaller groups in New Hampshire, Rhode Island, and western Connecticut. In New England, however, and also in Virginia the Tories constituted an inconsiderable minority. In the Middle colonies and the Lower South they were more numerous. The Whigs and Tories in New York seem to have been nearly equal in strength. Pennsylvania had fewer avowed Tories than New York, but more pacifists and neutrals. In all the colonies, the success of the radicals in spite of their numerous opponents was due to their positive program, to efficient organization, and to skillful propaganda. Important, too, was their ability to carry with them many moderate persons who, though not desiring independence, had so far cooperated with the radicals that they could not effectively withdraw.

SOLDIER AND CIVILIAN

BETWEEN THE FIGHT ON Lexington common in April 1775 and the formal cessation of hostilities in February 1783, nearly eight years elapsed. Conditions approximating a state of war existed for even a longer time—from the autumn of 1774 until the British evacuation of New York in November 1783. New England's contact with invading forces came early. During the winter of 1774–75 both Gage's royal government and the de facto government of the provincial congress engaged in military preparations. Minutemen were drilled and military stores collected, and, as we have seen, the Massachusetts congress adopted a plan for a provincial army. Meanwhile there were exciting "incidents." As early as September 1774, the seizure of powder by the British led to reports of soldiers and naval vessels firing on Boston. The whole country, wrote Gage, was "in Arms and in Motion" before the rumors were corrected.[147]

The blows of the war fell with different weight on different areas. All the chief seaports except Baltimore experienced British occupation for periods ranging from less than a year in Philadelphia to more than seven in New York. On the other hand, much of the countryside, including that of New England and the great wheat-growing areas of Pennsylvania, Maryland, and Virginia, suffered comparatively little from the contending armies. Quite different, however, was the tragic experience of the rural population in the Lower South.

In the frontier region, as we have seen, the Whigs had to contend mainly with Tories and Indians, who were frequently directed by British agents. Beyond the mountains the Indians were the chief enemies, though some Loyalists were active here also.

Besides being a harsh and sometimes tragic experience, war was a business which had to be learned by both civilians and fighting men. Tory writers had insisted that the colonists could not cope with British armies. "War," said one of them, "is no longer a simple, but an intricate science." Against trained soldiers the Americans could oppose only the "tumultuary rage" of "a militia unused to service, impatient of command, and destitute of resources." Moreover, how would they secure munitions with the British navy patrolling the sea, what would happen to their commerce and fisheries, and how could the war be financed? Meanwhile, the Whigs displayed something of the "valor of ignorance." Their numbers included, said John Adams, hardy countrymen accustomed to Indian warfare.[148]

When Washington assumed command at Cambridge in July 1775, the Massachusetts "army" embraced perhaps 12,000 men. With accessions from other colonies the New England troops numbered roughly 17,000 with fluctuating strength. During the latter half of the year an army, Continental in fact as in name, gradually took shape on the basis of one-year enlistments, observance of the Articles of War, and other conditions which many early volunteers would not accept.

It is impossible to say even approximately how many Americans actually engaged in military service. Of those whose names appear in army and militia lists a large proportion served but a few months. Even in the Continental army most enlistments were for only a year, though bounties and promises of Western lands caused some to be for the duration. Outside the Continental army were many more militiamen, besides irregular fighters who spent only a few weeks or months in the field. Including the American soldiers on both sides and all those who served at all, whether actual combatants or not, there was, perhaps, a fair proportion of participants to the total number of males of military age.

Available statistics of men in service at any given time, however, present a different picture. Washington's army during 1776 ranged roughly from 27,000 to 10,000; in December those actually fit for duty were fewer than 5,000.[149] When Washington prepared to attack Trenton, he had only 2,400 men, "all that were left of the Continental regulars." In the Saratoga campaign in 1777 the entire number of Americans involved was over 20,000, including emergency volunteers who helped to block the British advance, but Horatio Gates's immediate army of regulars and militia comprised perhaps half as many. In November 1779, Washington's summary of state muster rolls, excluding South Carolina and Georgia, showed a paper total of about 27,000, with fewer than 15,000 enlisted for the whole war. At Yorktown in 1781 there were, according to official returns, about 5,500 American regulars, 3,500 militia, and 7,000 Frenchmen, omitting an undetermined number of Virginia militia in the neighborhood who doubtless contributed to the final result.[150]

Relative to the male population of military age the proportion of trained men engaged for any length of time in serious combat service seems small. Comparatively raw troops occasionally fought well, but they proved more useful in irregular fighting, as in operating on the flanks of Burgoyne's army, interrupting communications, and cutting off supplies. Recruiting was stimulated by Continental and state bounties, and when state quotas were not readily filled, drafts were resorted to, though well-to-do persons could hire substitutes. The strain on particular communities sometimes proved severe. In September 1776, Abigail Adams reported a shortage of farm labor, with more than half the men between sixteen and sixty in the army. If more enlisted, she said, the women would have to do the harvesting. That summer there were similar complaints in Connecticut.[151]

As to the quality of the rank and file, contemporary testimony varied. A British ship's surgeon visiting the New England army early in 1775 called it "nothing but a drunken, canting, lying, praying, hypocritical rabble, without order, subjection, discipline, or cleanliness," which would soon "fall to pieces of itself." Another English observer spoke of the Americans as "ragged, dirty, sickly and ill-disciplined." Nor were Washington's early impressions of the army at Cambridge encouraging. Yet after Bunker Hill an enemy "Officer of Rank" admitted that the colonists when "equally well commanded" were "full as good soldiers" as the British. One of Burgoyne's officers later declared that the Americans he had observed were "never contemptible in the eye of a soldier," fighting with "great courage and obstinacy." A German officer who saw Gates's troops when Burgoyne surrendered said that in spite of their nondescript appearance "they stood like soldiers." "The whole nation," he thought, had "much natural talent for war and military life."[152]

Besides the land soldiers, there were the sea fighters in the state and Continental navies and privateers. Eleven states had their own navies, and in addition, Congress early in the war authorized the building of thirteen frigates. The Providence sea captain Esek Hopkins was commissioned as "Commander in chief of the fleet," together with four captains and several first lieutenants, including John Paul Jones, a recently arrived Scotch shipmaster. Hopkins had commanded a privateer in the French war, and one of his captains, Nicholas Biddle, had been a British midshipman. Another officer, not in this first list, was the young Irish shipmaster John Barry, who rivaled Jones in brilliant accomplishment. The total personnel of the Continental navy and marine service at its maximum strength probably did not exceed about 3,000. The most numerous sea fighters were the privateersmen, perhaps 70,000 in all on the American side. The great expansion of privateering under Continental and state commissions sometimes interfered with army and navy recruiting. Yet its special attractions enlisted many adventurous individuals, who inflicted serious damage on British shipping.[153]

During the greater part of the contest the army was badly clothed. Notwithstanding the prevalence of homespun textiles the country was embarrassed by the interruption of shipments from Britain, and some clothing contractors charged exorbitant prices. To a large extent uniforms had to be imported. During the early years many of the Continental troops presented a motley appearance, sometimes lacking even the elementary requirements for health and decency. At Valley Forge, Washington reported nearly 4,000 of his men unfit for duty for this reason. A British agent predicted his defeat if the flow of European woolen goods could be stopped. Uniforms in actual use varied. One New York order called for a coat, deerskin waistcoat and breeches, felt hat, two pairs each of stockings and shoes, and a blanket. A later Continental uniform was blue, with facings differing according to states and branches of service. Toward the end of the war the supply of apparel improved under the new clothier general. Tents of sailcloth or "country linen" sometimes provided shelter. During the winter of Valley Forge, where canvas tents were used at first, the men suffered badly from the cold, but later they were a little better housed in log cabins.[154]

The food supply was hampered by transportation difficulties, poor administration, and fluctuating prices. Subject to the direction of Congress and its committees, the two principal officers in this branch were the quartermaster general and the commissary general. During the first year of the war Washington took occasion to compliment Commissary General Joseph Trumbull of Connecticut. "Few Armies," he wrote, "have been better and more plentifully supplied than the Troops under Mr. Trumbull's care." At Valley Forge, however, the provision services were in bad order, with tragic consequences. The situation temporarily improved later, with General Greene as quartermaster general and Jeremiah Wadsworth in charge of the commissariat. Soon, however, there was more trouble in these offices and the army again suffered. The experiment of asking the states to furnish "specific supplies" having failed, soldiers were for a time reduced to half rations. In 1781, with Superintendent Robert Morris in charge of contracts, the army fared better, but there were still complaints of profiteering and of insufficient and inferior food.[155]

At Valley Forge the army ration consisted of a pound and a half of flour or bread per day; beef, fish, or bacon; sometimes peas or beans; and a gill of spirits. On occasion, however, the men went for days without meat or even bread. Some critics also noted the lack of vegetables. Greene maintained that "putrid fever" resulted from an undue proportion of meat: "vegetables would be much more wholesome." In Congress, Gerry declared that the physical condition of the British troops profited by a suitable allowance of vegetables and vinegar and that the United States would "never have a Healthy and Vigorous Army without them." John Adams added his objections. "Our frying-pans and gridirons," he wrote, "slay more than the sword." The provision of liquor also excited comment. Rum is a normal part of the army ration and Washington once complained of an inadequate supply. Dr. Benjamin Rush, however, favored milder beverages.[156]

The Continental medical corps must not, of course, be judged by twentieth-century standards. Though the British fared better, they, too, had many inexperienced surgeons. The American service made a bad start, with its first director, Dr. Benjamin Church, soon dismissed for treasonable correspondence. Congress then appointed Dr. John Morgan, who stood high in the profession but who was hampered by inadequate equipment and by jealousies complicated by his own defects of temper. The regimental surgeons were often incompetent, and some of them, according to Washington, were "very great rascals." [157]

The suffering of patients through inattention, lack of suitable diet and medicines, and the unsanitary housing proved serious. Without anaesthetics and modern antiseptics the mortality from disease and wounds was often appalling. Epidemics played havoc with the army. The prevalence of smallpox in 1777 caused widespread anxiety. There were, however, occasional comments of a favorable character. A German prisoner described a hospital, in which British soldiers were treated, as "well-equipped," providing even such luxuries as tea, sugar, chocolate, and wine. Some surgeons were capable and conscientious.

Every army has its undesirable characters and the Continental army was no exception. Its regulations, following the British model, penalized drunkenness, profanity, maltreatment of civilians, and other offenses. Looting was punishable by whipping on the bare back, and more serious crimes entailed the death penalty. Nevertheless American as well as British soldiers were guilty of mistreating noncombatants. In one case of robbery two men were sentenced to be hanged, one of whom was "pardoned under the gallows" and the other executed. [158]

In an age when most penal institutions were barbarously managed, the inhumane treatment of military captives was not surprising. Difficulties of housing and shortage of supplies also were factors. Nevertheless, in the enemy prisons and more particularly in the prison ships there was often inexcusable neglect and cruelty. Philip Freneau's poem "The British Prison Ship" reflects the impression made by such conduct on one sensitive personality. British captives had their complaints, too. Stedman quoted Sir Archibald Campbell's protest against his Concord jail, "a dungeon of twelve or thirteen feet square . . . black with the grease and litter of successive criminals." But relations with the captor were sometimes more agreeable. The American captain Alexander Graydon was courteously treated by Britons, whose kindness he was later able to reciprocate. Sterner patriots, however, entertained doubts about such amenities. Governor Livingston feared that as a result Americans might be "humanized" out of their liberties. [159]

ECONOMIC EFFECTS

Even before the outbreak of hostilities the colonial merchant had to make drastic adjustments. The First Continental Congress had forbidden the importation of European and East Indian goods from Britain. Moreover, molasses could no longer be bought in the British West Indies or wine from the Portuguese islands or slaves from Africa. The export trade had more time for adjustment, but when nonexportation finally took effect in September 1775, it closed most of the normal markets to colonial staples. In the meantime, British legislation reinforced congressional prohibitions. The "restraining acts" of March and April 1775 barred the limited commerce previously permitted outside the empire. Especially serious for the New Englanders was the exclusion from the fisheries. When the war began, the commerce of the insurgent colonies became enemy traffic and ships engaged in it were liable to seizure by British warships.

It was soon realized that the Continental Association would have to be modified in order to secure munitions and other necessaries. "We are," said Robert R. Livingston, "puzzling ourselves between the commercial and the warlike opposition." The army, said James Duane, must have powder, and powder could not be had without "breaking the Association." Before the nonexportation agreement went into effect, shipments to Great Britain and the West Indies temporarily increased, those from New York and Philadelphia more than doubling in value. Congress now authorized unconditionally the exchange of American produce for munitions, "the non-exportation agreement notwithstanding." Finally, in April 1776, Congress opened American ports to vessels of all nations other than Great Britain and her possessions.[160]

Business was also affected by enemy occupation of the chief commercial centers. In the case of New York City this interrupted normal trade with the upper Hudson Valley, with other colonies, and, to some extent, with other countries. The city, however, received partial compensation from British army purchases and those of numerous Loyalist refugees. The much shorter British dominance of Philadelphia proved less unsettling. Until 1777 comparatively few businessmen left the city. But when Howe's army took possession, the more active Whig merchants withdrew and newcomers arrived, taking over their shops or establishing new ones. Another shift came when the British army retired, with Tories going out and Whigs returning. Thereafter, Philadelphia, as the seat of Congress, prospered through government business.[161]

Trade was also disturbed by the currency situation. Inflation and depreciation, with varying standards of value, had formerly been checked by imperial restrictions; but with these removed, a combination of circumstances —lack of specie, loss of normal export trade, military expenditures—led to an immense expansion of paper money. By 1779, Continental issues exceeded $200 million and the states had printed almost as much. Meanwhile, attempts were made to increase or maintain the supply of hard money. Early in the war Morris proposed a congressional committee to "bring in Gold and Silver and keep it in the country," reporting later that the treasury had only £6,000. These efforts to halt specie exports were not, however, very successful.[162]

The final collapse of the Continental paper is a familiar story. A Philadelphian had predicted in the summer of 1775 that these bills would at once be "as current as gold," but they were soon being accepted with great reluctance. According to New York and Philadelphia letters, the hoarding of specie began quickly, notwithstanding that guilty persons were threatened with tar and feathers as "the least of their punishment." Robert Treat Paine, a good patriot, declared early in 1777 that the "glut of money" was "horrible" and he feared Rhode Island would "drown New England with paper." Though Massachusetts finance was more conservative, many creditors even there refused to take paper currency in payment of debts.[163]

How far rising prices were due to cheap money as compared with scarcity of goods and profiteering it is hard to say. At any rate there was a staggering increase. In Massachusetts a bushel of corn climbed from five shillings in the spring of 1777 to $80 in paper or $4 in hard money by the summer of 1779, and beef from eight pence a pound to six or eight shillings. In 1780, Governor William Livingston of New Jersey calculated that his salary of £8,000 in currency was worth no more than a £150 in silver.[164]

For many merchants the war proved educational. Government business led to interstate cooperation and also to personal associations which bore fruit later in land speculation, schemes for internal improvements, and banking projects. Similarly, war finance emphasized the need of agencies for mobilizing credit for public and private undertakings. In 1780, Elbridge Gerry suggested an interstate alliance of merchants to support congressional finances. Shortly afterward a merchants' association was formed at Philadelphia, which, though not strictly a bank, was designed to supply war funds. Proposals for a real bank soon followed. In December 1780, Congress, though uncertain of its authority, incorporated the Bank of North America. Thus real banking in the United States originated in wartime necessities.[165]

Educational also were the effects of the collapse of the Continental currency. Though cheap money did not end with that experience, mercantile opposition to currency inflation was strengthened and the way prepared for safeguards against it in the federal constitution. The war also stressed the desirability of a stable and uniform hard-money supply. Robert Morris outlined a plan for a national coinage based on the decimal system and Jefferson was studying the problem as early as 1776.[166] Significant, too, in its long-term effects was the issue of congressional and state certificates of indebtedness which the original holders were commonly forced to sell far below their face value. Even during the struggle a fairly compact group of men acquired such securities on a large scale, and trading in them was publicly advertised. At Philadelphia in 1782 brokers' advertisements were published by Isaac Franks, Haym Salomon, John Macpherson, and Morris

Cohen. Thus the exigencies of war greatly expanded this form of property and the practice of stock speculation.[167]

An educational result of a different kind was the new interest in communications. The imperial postal service had been replaced by a Continental administration, headed first by Franklin and later in succession by his son-in-law, Richard Bache, and Ebenezer Hazard. British occupation of important seaboard towns naturally complicated the mails, so much so that in 1781 a Rhode Island delegate declared that the scheme might well be abolished or suspended. But Congress busied itself with plans to improve the service and lessen its cost. In spite of handicaps the wartime government did establish a Continental system. At the same time tragic experiences like those at Valley Forge, when desperately needed supplies were almost unsalable only a short distance away, emphasized the need of better transportation. Though postwar internal-improvement projects cannot be wholly explained by war experience, it is at least suggestive that George Washington and other prominent Revolutionary leaders were active in such enterprises.[168]

Wartime adjustments proved less difficult for industry than for commerce, partly because most manufactures were of a household character, carried on in rural and sparsely settled communities remote from battle areas. Nevertheless the war inevitably affected the situation. In response to the prewar propaganda for commercial retaliation and economic self-sufficiency, the Revolutionary organizations listed products which should be encouraged by premiums, bounties, or loans, and the Second Continental Congress recommended the formation of societies to promote native industries. There were local efforts also, as, for instance, the Virginia convention's offer of premiums for textiles, textile machinery, nails, and powdermills. Similar action was taken by Virginia counties. To conserve wool the Revolutionary governments discouraged the killing of sheep. Even so, the army had to rely largely on imports for uniforms. Other states also offered bounties for war materials. Daniel Roberdeau, president of a Pennsylvania company to establish textile manufactures, advocated economic independence both as a defense measure and on the ground that money could be saved by using home products. The wearing of homespun at weddings and college commencements became a favorite form of propaganda, and household manufactures expanded to meet the growing popular demand.[169]

By and large, agriculture proceeded more normally than commerce or manufactures. Though rural New England saw few enemy troops, even in peacetime it had imported breadstuffs; during the war it suffered from insufficient supplies, partly due to embargoes elsewhere. For certain farm products the war brought increased demands and rising prices, with Connecticut contributing substantial amounts to the army's food supply. In 1780, when beef was urgently needed, Congress called on New Hampshire,

Massachusetts, and Connecticut for a thousand head of cattle weekly. That year Connecticut's quota of forage grain exceeded any other state's except Pennsylvania's and Maryland's. New England also furnished draft horses. During the middle years of the conflict, the Yankee husbandmen prospered, paying off debts and living more comfortably. The subsequent period of deflation, however, told another story. Massachusetts then turned from paper money to specie, with increasing taxation of a kind that proved especially burdensome to the tiller of the soil. Retrenchment became necessary and, as might be expected, agrarian discontent followed.[170]

In rural New York many farmers lived within the enemy lines or in areas disturbed by armed strife. Though the British occupation of New York City deprived up-state farmers of their normal outlet for produce, they did not always find it easy to maintain a proper food supply. Recruiting, guerrilla warfare, army calls for draft animals, and a shortage of agricultural implements—all these interfered with normal operations.[171]

The New Jersey countryside also suffered seriously at times from military operations, especially during 1776-78. At the end of the latter year John Jay reported that wheat crops in this and neighboring states had fallen far below the usual output. Nevertheless, if the war period be taken as a whole, the Jersey husbandmen, like those of Pennsylvania, plied a good business with the various armies. Two years after hostilities began, John Adams gave glowing accounts of the Pennsylvania and Maryland grain fields. Here, too, farmers were charged with profiteering and with refusing to sell to the American troops at army prices or in depreciated currency while willing to traffic with the enemy. Nevertheless, the Continental army drew its provisions and forage largely from this region. There was some concern about the distilling of liquor from grain when food conservation was important. John Adams heard that it might be "a question whether the people should eat bread or drink whiskey." In 1778 a congressional committee advocated state action to prevent the "converting of that Bread which was meant for the sustenance of Man into a Liquid poison for his Destruction." Insect pests also made trouble.[172]

In Virginia the farmers provided breadstuffs to supply the army or to ship abroad in exchange for war material, but with tobacco the story was different. The British market was now blocked despite some of the crop that slipped in indirectly. Though the government sent shipments abroad to establish credits, exports apparently declined, thanks partly to the increasingly effective blockade. In 1778 a congressional committee reported that large quantities of tobacco shipped to Continental agents had been lost. Later, Chesapeake Bay was said to be controlled by the enemy. A British prisoner in Virginia noted the glutting of the market because of enemy privateers. As a result of such complications Jefferson declared that his tobacco sold for a quarter or less of its normal price. Planters were also troubled about their slaves, some of whom ran away to the enemy. Toward the close of the war thirty of Jefferson's blacks were said to have been carried off by the invading British army. It was estimated that Virginia lost some 30,000 in all. In the last months before Yorktown one of Jefferson's plantations was occupied by the British for ten days. His tobacco barns were burned, his fields wasted, and his livestock killed or carried off.[173]

The South Carolina planters were also deprived of customary markets. Before the nonexportation regulation took effect in November 1775, and in anticipation of the event, rice and indigo exports to Great Britain went up by nearly a half only to drop to negligible proportions. This decline was partially offset by shipments, direct or indirect, made to Continental Europe with the cooperation of Congress. Here, too, slaves were lost and plantations seriously damaged.

In the Southern uplands the experience was somewhat different. Piedmont and Valley farmers in Virginia and Maryland raised wheat and cattle much as usual, selling to the seaboard South, to New England, and to the army. The stock raisers of the Carolina backcountry sent cattle northward in order to feed troops or provide leather, but in the later years of the war this region suffered badly from partisan strife.

In brief, then, agricultural conditions varied according to the fortunes of war and special marketing problems. Rural New England, the Shenandoah Valley, and most of Pennsylvania went almost unscathed, profiting by new demands from the fighting forces, American, British, and French. Other regions, such as the "no-man's-land" in New York, the Jerseys at certain times, and the Lower South during the British invasion, with its accompanying Whig-Tory feuds, suffered severely. Marketing problems proved particularly difficult for the Southern planters, whose oversea exports were reduced, notwithstanding some indirect trade with the enemy and the finding of new customers in Continental Europe.

NEW MODES OF THINKING

THE WAR EXPERIENCE brought "a new mode of thinking" in many ways. Friendships formed in the army and in the Continental Congress and its agencies gave men from widely scattered communities a broader outlook. This was true not only of major figures but also of lesser ones. Thus James Thacher, a young army surgeon who entered the service from Massachusetts, campaigned and shared hardships with New Yorkers on the Hudson and Virginians in New Jersey. Associations with foreign officers, beginning early and increasing after the French alliance, still further enlarged the horizons of many. There was a kind of intellectual shaking up through absence from familiar scenes and the necessary adjustment to novel situations.

One human interest greatly affected by the conflict was religion. Of all the sects the Church of England suffered most in material resources, popularity, and morale. Outside the British lines a considerable number of its clergy closed their places of worship and some became refugees. In Virginia, where the Anglicans were strongest, disestablishment was not completed during the war, but compulsory tithes were abolished and, when peace came, less than a fourth of the ministers were at their posts, even though many of them had supported the Revolution. Deism and anti-clericalism were contributing factors.[174]

The Quakers also lost ground though for different reasons—their pacifism and their official stand against forcible resistance. Young men who enlisted were disowned and membership fell off. Prominent Friends were accused of Toryism, giving intelligence to the British, or trying to discredit the Continental currency. The Moravians were similarly troubled, though some of them rendered noncombatant service, as in caring for wounded Continental soldiers. Methodism, too, experienced a temporary setback because of popular distrust of its leaders. John Wesley and some of his American preachers disapproved of the Revolution, and the future Bishop Francis Asbury refused for a time to swear allegiance to the Revolutionary government. Asbury, however, soon discreetly adjusted himself to the new order and the feeling against his followers diminished sufficiently to make possible a rapid advance of membership when the war ended.[175]

Among the Calvinist denominations the New England Congregationalists maintained their preferred legal status. Many ministers became army chaplains; some even served as combatants. Elsewhere the patriotic activity of such Presbyterian clergymen as John Witherspoon and John Rodgers enhanced the prestige of that church. Partly for this reason, however, the Presbyterians endured much at the hands of the enemy. Dr. Rodgers declared that more than fifty of their churches were destroyed.[176] The Baptists, while suffering somewhat from the general preoccupation with politics and war, profited by the greater tolerance resulting from the need of cooperation in a common cause. During the struggle the Virginia Baptists gained freedom of worship and exemption from church tithes. In New England, however, the old discrimination against them continued, though on one occasion a Baptist, invited to preach an election sermon before the Massachusetts legislature, seized the opportunity to urge equal rights in religion.

The Catholics also gained from the war. The desire of Congress to win over the Catholic Canadians, France's participation in the conflict, and the partial collaboration of Spain all helped to weaken, though they did not end, the traditional anti-Catholic feeling. Catholic chaplains arrived with the diplomatic and military representatives of France and Spain, and Protestant congressmen attended Catholic services on certain public occasions. Though the Tories tried to exploit the popular misgivings on this score—

shared, indeed, by some patriots—most penal legislation against Catholics disappeared.[177]

Much was said, then and later, about the disintegrating effect of war on religion. The Massachusetts authorities early complained that the Sabbath was profaned by improper diversions and unnecessary business. Ecclesiastical historians of Virginia—Anglican, Presbyterian, and Baptist—have noted the general "declension" of Christianity in that state. When the Marquis de Chastellux referred to religion among the inhabitants, he noted "the facility with which they dispense with it." In disturbed areas there and elsewhere places of worship were dismantled and services suspended. In 1778 the Dutch Reformed clergy deplored "the malicious and God-provoking" destruction of churches, scattering of congregations, and the prevailing religious indifference. Army life also interfered with customary observances. Moreover, orthodox theology suffered. Among the American officers Charles Lee and Ethan Allen were hostile critics of traditional Christianity. In New England the reaction against Calvinist theology, apparent before the war, developed further, whether as Deism or as incipient Unitarianism. Timothy Dwight regarded the Revolution as a period when "Infidelity began to obtain in this country an extensive currency and reception."[178]

Puritanical standards of conduct somewhat relaxed. At first, however, there was a natural emphasis on the need of subordinating amusements to patriotic duties. In 1774, Congress discountenanced balls and theatrical entertainments in the interest of economy and concentration of effort. Later it condemned army dramatics as "disagreeable to the sober Inhabitants" of Philadelphia. When pleasure lovers invited Martha Washington to a ball, a local committee objected and she withdrew her acceptance. James Warren felt unhappy about the "Magnificent Ball" given by John Hancock to the French officers in Boston and deplored the conduct of "Genteel People" with their "Assemblies, gameing, and the fashionable Amusements." On such matters Samuel Adams, the Puritan, and Christopher Marshall, the Quaker, agreed. According to Arthur Lee, Philadelphians were forgetting Quaker simplicity and losing "that unostentatious virtue" which should animate the "Infant republic."[179]

In other respects also men were concerned about the effect of the war on public morals. In 1775 the Massachusetts committee of public safety, reporting hard drinking among the soldiers, urged Washington to suppress the retailing of liquor in and about the camps. Notwithstanding complaints that gambling was on the increase, lotteries were still considered a suitable means of raising money and Congress publicly advertised its U.S. lottery office, whose tickets sold rapidly even in Boston.[180] Crime flourished in areas not effectively controlled by either party. There were also allegations of a decline in business morality. In 1779, Samuel Blachley Webb wrote gloomily of paper "money depreciating, public Virtue totally damn'd—

Morals of good men effected." Mercy Warren considered war in many respects "unfriendly to Virtue" and called the deterioration of manners in her neighborhood unprecedented "in the History of Man." In Virginia, Landon Carter expressed a similar opinion. Elbridge Gerry, while agreeing that in this as in other revolutions morals suffered, took a longer view, holding that Americans had enough "Wisdom and Vertue" to save the day.[181]

Probably comments on "licentiousness" often covered dislike of a radicalism which seemed to threaten vested rights. Samuel Adams early in the war found "everywhere" men who feared "a free Government" lest it become "a Cloke for Licentiousness. . . . as if anything were so much to be dreaded by Mankind as Slavery." His more conservative kinsman, John, was one who emphasized the need of "Decency, and Respect and Veneration" for men in authority. Some Southerners, while accepting the new order, felt misgivings about a situation in which "everyone who bore arms, esteemed himself upon a footing with his neighbor." Samuel Johnston of North Carolina complained that gentlemen were overridden by "a set of men without reading, experience, or principle to guide them."[182]

Of humanitarian legislation the war period produced little except as to the black. Congress's suspension of slave importations was a retaliatory measure directed against the British. State action flowed from broader considerations. Between 1774 and 1783, laws against importing slaves were enacted by Vermont, Connecticut, Pennsylvania, Delaware, and Virginia. Only two states, however, at this time adopted emancipation, though the declaration of rights in the Massachusetts constitution (1780) was so interpreted by the courts in 1783. Vermont, which had practically no slaves, declared slavery a violation of natural rights, and Pennsylvania, which had comparatively few, provided for gradual liberation.[183]

Elsewhere, though many people felt that human bondage violated Revolutionary principles, no legislative action followed. In 1774 a Providence town meeting resolved that gradual emancipation followed logically from American ideas of "natural rights" and "personal liberty." Citizens of Danbury, Connecticut, held it "a palpable absurdity to complain of attempts to enslave us while we are actually enslaving others." Even from Darien, Georgia, came a declaration that the retention of slavery would set "that liberty we contend for upon a very wrong foundation." Nevertheless, many men both North and South who, like Jefferson, were conscious of this anomaly shrank from the practical difficulties of manumission. When a Massachusetts emancipation bill was shelved, John Adams hoped it would "sleep for a Time" since there were already "causes enough of Jealousy, Discord, and Division." Similarly, when Governor Livingston asked the New Jersey legislature to "lay the foundation" for emancipation, no action was taken.[184]

From the standpoint of culture the war years brought both losses and gains. The effect upon education has been described as "disastrous." In New England the heavy taxes lessened public support with the result that terms were shortened and some schools were closed. Elsewhere private and church schools were abandoned. Military operations interrupted instruction and destroyed or damaged buildings. Nevertheless many teachers carried on. Freelance schoolmasters continued their advertisements in the press. The Friends' meetings showed an active interest in maintaining and improving their schools, and Robert Proud, the Quaker historian, though a Loyalist, resumed his work as master in the Penn Charter School at Philadelphia. In New York City the charity school of Trinity Church had pupils during the British occupation, and also in upstate New York some teachers were at work. Likewise, the Virginia academies of Liberty Hall and Hampden-Sydney and the Moravian schools in North Carolina went on in spite of the turmoil about them.[185]

Here and there forward steps were taken. The constitutions of Massachusetts, Pennsylvania, North Carolina, Georgia, and Vermont recognized public responsibility for education, thus at least pointing the way to future action. During the war Jefferson drafted his "Bill for the More General Diffusion of Knowledge" to give Virginia a public school system.[186] Though never passed, it showed the importance attached to education by an outstanding Revolutionary statesman. In New England a new type of academy began with those founded by members of the Phillips family at Andover, Massachusetts, and Exeter, New Hampshire, in 1778 and 1781. In 1782 the Andover institution had a pupil from Washington's hometown of Fredericksburg, who was soon followed by some of his young relatives. Another wartime enterprise was Timothy Dwight's popular school for boys and girls at Northampton. In New York, clergymen at Claverack and Salem founded academies.[187] There were also new secondary schools at Chester, Lancaster, and York, Pennsylvania, the first two under Presbyterian auspices and the third conducted by an Episcopal clergyman. Provost William Smith revived an old school in Kent County, Maryland, which by 1782 was said to have 140 pupils. In 1777 a young Princeton graduate opened a classical school in the Northern Neck of Virginia, later incorporated as Warren Academy in memory of the Boston patriot. In North Carolina, James Hall, Princeton graduate and Presbyterian clergyman, opened "Clio's Nursery," which trained some influential laymen and many preachers.

All the colleges suffered in the war. For some it was calamitous. King's College virtually ceased to exist and the new Queen's College barely survived. Partly because Provost Smith was distrusted, the Whigs revoked the Philadelphia College charter and incorporated a new institution: the University of the State of Pennsylvania. William and Mary College continued its work under a young Whig president. The dominant influence in the other colleges was definitely patriotic. In 1775, after the Massachusetts provincial congress ordered Harvard to dismiss members of the faculty who appeared to be "unfriendly to the Liberties and Privileges of the Colonies," the overseers presently reported that they were all politically sound.[188]

Most of the colleges were occupied for longer or shorter periods by armed forces. For about a year Harvard's buildings served as American army barracks. Nassau Hall at Princeton was badly damaged during the Trenton-Princeton campaign and the Americans subsequently used the college for barracks and hospital service. William and Mary College, which escaped enemy occupation until 1781, was temporarily Cornwallis's headquarters and after his surrender became a French military hospital.[189]

College incomes were seriously reduced. Harvard encountered difficulties because of Treasurer John Hancock's mismanagement of its finances, the depreciation of public securities, and a currency inflation resulting "in a fruitless endeavour to overtake . . . the vanishing value of paper currency." According to President Madison, the income of William and Mary was "almost annihilated." Similarly, Princeton lost much of its endowment. The revenue from college fees naturally fell off with reduced enrollments. Undergraduate enlistments seem, however, to have been less than might be supposed and state legislatures commonly exempted professors and students from military service. Of nearly 200 students at Harvard in 1775, very few entered the army before graduation. Apparently William and Mary College and Princeton furnished a larger proportion of recruits. All the colleges were, however, represented by alumni or teachers in war service, civil and military. Notable examples of faculty participation were John Witherspoon of Princeton and John Winthrop of Harvard. Timothy Dwight left a Yale tutorship for an army chaplaincy, three Philadelphia medical professors held important military posts, and Madison of William and Mary served for a time as a militia captain.[190]

But the war helped as well as hurt higher education. The most interesting effort to modernize the curriculum was that of Jefferson at William and Mary, where chairs in modern languages and law were substituted for those in classics and divinity. The new posts were given respectively to Charles Bellini and George Wythe. Medical education, too, had gains as well as losses. The King's College department disappeared and instruction at Philadelphia suffered from the conflict between the old college and the new "University." On the other hand, the Harvard medical faculty was a by-product of the war, and its chief founder, Dr. John Warren, had profited by army contacts with the Philadelphia faculty and with French military surgeons. In 1782, Warren became the first professor in the new school.[191]

For the medical profession the war proved educational also in other respects. As in the case of Warren, young doctors from several states came under the influence of the comparatively advanced group at Philadelphia and of European surgeons—British, German, and French. Just as the war began, Dr. John Jones of the King's College faculty issued his *Remarks on the Treatment of Wounds and Fractures* (new editions, 1776, 1777), based on the teaching of British and French experts—the first American treatise on the subject. Publications by Drs. Morgan and Rush discussed the treatment of smallpox epidemics. Rush also printed an essay on the health of the army. Probably the most important wartime production by a Continental medical officer was Dr. William Brown's pharmacopoeia (1778), the first ever published in the United States—a pamphlet of thirty-two pages in Latin. After the war several doctors wrote articles based on their field experiences.[192]

One step toward higher standards was the setting of examinations for the army medical service. According to Dr. James Thacher, an early test at Cambridge resulted in the rejection of six out of sixteen applicants. Dr. Morgan undertook to arrange state examining boards, a difficult task because of the attitude of the surgeons and the laxity of regimental commanders. Meanwhile a growing professional spirit led to the formation in 1781 of the important Massachusetts Medical Society. Though progress in preventive medicine was slight, there was some serious discussion, from this standpoint, of sanitation, the army ration, and ventilation.[193]

But medicine was not the only branch of science to gain from war experience. Robert Erskine, the Scotch-born engineer and ironmaster who was appointed geographer and surveyor general to the Continental army, made important maps of the Hudson Valley. Better known is the American-born Thomas Hutchins, a former British engineer officer who served in Greene's Carolina campaign and in 1781 became "Geographer to the United States." He had previously published *A Topographical Description of Virginia, Pennsylvania and Carolina* (1778). Jefferson's *Notes on Virginia,* written during the war, shows a systematic interest in American geography, which also owes something to maps by European officers.

The war helped to promote scholarly cooperation. John Adams, who noted the reputation enjoyed by the American Philosophical Society abroad as well as at home, and who attended at least one session of the French Academy of Sciences, was eager to establish a similar organization in his own state. One result was a clause in the Massachusetts constitution of 1780 calling for the encouragement of scientific associations. Shortly afterward the legislature chartered the American Academy of Arts and Sciences at Boston. Founded to "cultivate every art and science which may tend to advance the interest, honor, dignity and happiness of a free, independent and virtuous people," the Academy soon began its still continuing series of publications. The preface of its first volume emphasized its wartime origin, and among its early contributors Surgeon Major Feron of the French navy wrote a survey of the Boston water supply; General Benjamin Lincoln, who had served in the Yorktown campaign, described "strata of earth and shells" in that neighborhood; and there were articles by army surgeons.[194]

Newspapers fared better, for both Whigs and Tories needed them for propaganda and the public demanded war news. Though there were somewhat fewer papers in 1778 than in 1775, in 1783 they had passed the prewar figure. Moreover, some were now issued two or three times a week. In Massachusetts the only colonial journal still published in 1778 was the *Boston Gazette;* the pro-British *News-Letter* ended when the enemy withdrew from Boston. During the first year of the war, with the Whigs in control, New York newspapers had to be on that side or at least be neutral. After the destruction of Rivington's press in November 1775, his *Gazetteer* was suspended. Gaine's *Mercury* showed cautious Whig leanings, while Holt's *Journal* was the patriot organ. When Howe came in, conditions were reversed.[195]

Philadelphia began the war with six newspapers, five English and one German. All but one were definitely Whig, and that one, James Humphreys's *Pennsylvania Ledger,* tried to be neutral. Denounced as a Tory, however, Humphreys was soon forced to quit. When General Howe took over, the Whig printers had to leave, three of their journals were suspended, and John Dunlap transferred his *Pennsylvania Packet* to Lancaster. Humphreys now revived his *Ledger,* and Benjamin Towne, a former Whig printer, also conducted a British organ. When the British withdrew, the tables were again turned. The Whig printers came back and the Tory partisans had to flee, except Towne, who again changed his spots and managed to stay in business. Of three prewar journals in Charleston the Loyalist printer of one departed, leaving the paper to his son. Of the two Whig editors, Peter Timothy published his *South-Carolina Gazette* until the British occupation when he was imprisoned and his sheet suspended.[196]

Wartime journalism, both Whig and Tory, dealt largely in propaganda. Rivington's *Royal Gazette* praised the proposals of the Carlisle peace commission of 1778 as highly magnanimous, while the Whig *Pennsylvania Packet* spoke of their final announcement as illustrating the "contemptible figure which the British king and ministry have cut in the present war." To Holt's *New-York Journal* the reception of the French envoy was a "noble sight," marking America's entry "among the powers of the earth ... in robes of sovereignty," but Rivington suggested that America had been "sold to the French King." After Major John André's execution, Rivington's sheet denounced Washington as a "murderer." More creditable was the comment of the Boston *Independent Chronicle,* which defended André's sentence but spoke of his courage and dignity in the face of death. The *Pennsylvania Packet* of November 14, 1778, contained savage lines about King George, one of which ran, "Go second Cain, true likeness of the first."[197]

Of patriotic songs the Revolution produced few that outlived the times. Perhaps the best known is Timothy Dwight's "Columbia":

> Columbia, Columbia, to glory arise
> The Queen of the world, and the child of the skies.

Military music was usually played with fife and drum. "Yankee Doodle," though not a native production, was, according to Lieutenant Anburey, "a favorite of favorites." One composer whose music proved popular in the camps was the Yankee singing master, William Billings. One of his songs began:

> Let tyrants shake their iron rod,
> And Slavery clank his galling chains;
> We fear them not, we trust in God;
> New England's God forever reigns.[198]

In spite of congressional disapproval of stage plays, the theater, such as it was, also went to war. A few dramatic pieces were primarily for readers. One, entitled *The Fall of British Tyranny; or American Liberty Triumphant,* was said to have been "lately planned at the Royal Theatrum Pandemonium at St. James'." British statesmen, Whig and Tory, were dramatis personae, with American officers in a closing act. Two dramatic poems by Hugh H. Brackenridge, "The Battle of Bunker's Hill" and "The Death of General Montgomery," stressed the tragic element with an appeal to patriotism. In the former the British officers are not wholly odious and Howe is represented as appreciative of American gallantry. There was more bitterness in "The Death of General Montgomery," with Sir Guy Carleton exulting in the sufferings inflicted by his Indian allies.[199]

National sentiment implies not only community of thought and feeling, but also awareness of what is distinctive. The differentiation of Americans from Englishmen was sharpened by Revolutionary propaganda and wartime animosities. After the French alliance a writer in the *Pennsylvania Packet* argued that this new association was safer than sympathetic relations with the mother country since the common inheritance of England and America would tend to perpetuate undesirable influences: the "pomp"of the Anglican Church, British class distinctions, and the British political system "so perfect in theory, but so corrupt in practice." He thought there was a danger also that the Republican simplicity and sound morals would be corrupted. Such contamination by America's connections with France was less likely because of natural barriers of language and religion. Good citizens should therefore keep alive anti-British feeling.[200]

American nationalism was, however, jealous even of France. There were misgivings about association with a "Popish" king and nation, and a Connecticut delegate queried whether it would not have been better to win without such aid. Henry Laurens was also troubled about "our delicate connection with France." The unsuccessful Franco-American operations of 1778 and later complications resulting from France's alliance with Spain emphasized the need of an independent course. Economic nationalism also developed early. "Shall we," asked John Adams, "invite all Nations to come with their Luxuries, as well as Conveniences and Necessaries, or shall We think of confining our trade with them to our own Bottoms, which alone can lay a Foundation for great Wealth and naval Power?" Though foreign shipping was then essential, the concept of nationalist economics was already rooted in men's minds.[201]

If nationalism was developing, there was also some international thinking. So far as Americans were influenced by European liberals, or sought their support, they thought of themselves as helping to realize the ideals of the Age of Enlightenment. The French king was toasted as "the magnanimous protector of the rights of mankind," and the hope was expressed that America's example might excite the oppressed everywhere to resist tyranny and secure their "natural and inalienable rights." America was not only taking her rightful place among the nations but introducing "a new era in the happiness of mankind."[202] Thus the long years of warfare brought intellectual as well as political adjustments. The next decade was to show how the new republican society would repair its losses, consolidate its gains, and apply more effectively "the new mode of thinking."

REPUBLICAN SOCIETY

AT THE CLOSE of the war the United States numbered somewhat over 3 million souls. Phineas Bond, the British consul general, estimated the drain of population from the war at "perhaps little short of 100,000 men"; but no exact statistical evidence is available. Among the reasons for loss were deaths among soldiers and civilians, the large-scale exodus of Tories, and probably some slackening of the birth rate due to the disturbance of normal family life. To some extent, however, these factors were offset by the considerable number of prisoners or deserters from the British and German troops who stayed on in the United States. Of the Germans there may have been as many as 6,000 or 7,000.[203]

The Loyalists migrated chiefly to British North America. The most careful estimate is that for New York, where some 35,000 may have departed, forming a much larger proportion of the population than in any other state. Nevertheless, even here the refugees were far outnumbered by the Tories who remained. Of this latter group, many were obscure persons, while others had been comparatively inactive. Some exiles returned after the war and, notwithstanding popular hostility and severe legislation, old animosities gradually softened.[204] Peter Van Schaack, the lawyer refugee, was restored to citizenship and readmitted to the bar, of which he continued to be a distinguished member. Before he left London he saw John Jay, and they met, wrote Jay, "with all the cordiality of old friends, who had long been absent, without the least retrospect to the cause of that absence." Richard Harison, another returned exile, became a delegate to the New York convention which ratified the Federal Constitution. William Seton, the first cashier of the Bank of New York, was another rehabilitated Tory.[205]

Practical considerations favored the rehabilitation of the Tories. In 1784 the New Haven town meeting voted to allow their return in the interest of business. President Ezra Stiles thought the Tories numerous enough there to count seriously in a local election. New York opponents of harsh legislation argued that it would keep out capital, and in 1787, Jay reported that most of the Loyalists had been reinstated. Stephen Higginson of Massachusetts took a similar stand. Among influential Southerners, Jefferson favored reconciliation with open enemies, but not with those who "remained among us and strove to injure us by their treacheries." Charles Carroll, opposing the exclusion of Loyalists from legal practice, wished to end such "odious distinctions" and unite all citizens "in the pursuit of the common good." Forgetfulness of the past came most slowly in regions where savage fighting had occurred between Whigs and Tories. Love, a South Carolina Tory and a participant in a brutal massacre, was lynched after his discharge by a trial court. Aedanus Burke, the presiding judge, believed that Love's neighbors could forget injuries inflicted in "fair action," but not "wanton acts of barbarity."[206]

By 1789 most states had repealed legislation against the Loyalists conflicting with the peace treaty, though confiscated estates were not restored. Conservative Whigs were glad to have Tory support for strong government and for laws favorable to business. Of sixty conspicuous New York leaders during the "Critical Period," eleven were Loyalists, seven of whom advocated ratification of the federal constitution. Quite naturally John Jay and Alexander Hamilton favored conciliation.[207]

After the war the population of the country grew rapidly, partly through accessions from without. In spite of adverse legislation, slave importations during this period increased the number of blacks by several thousand. More important was the resumption of immigration. Bond reported the arrival of over 25,000 redemptioners and servants in Pennsylvania between 1783 and 1789, including Irish, Scots, and Germans. Public opinion generally favored immigration. The young republic was conceived of as a land of freedom and economic opportunity for unfortunate Europeans. "It is our business," wrote John Adams, "to render our country an Asylum, worthy to receive all who may wish to fly to it." William Grayson of Virginia, hoping for speedy land sales and lower taxes, observed that "the want of inhabitants" was "perhaps our only calamity." Tench Coxe urged the outstanding advantages of Pennsylvania, which offered civil and religious liberty, land on easy terms, voting citizenship after two years' residence, and freedom from old-world restraints on trade and industry. Here, too, he pointed out, newcomers would feel at home among neighbors speaking their own language — English, Dutch, or German. On the other hand, both Bond and Lord Sheffield emphasized the difficulties that the foreign-born faced.[208]

Though law-abiding immigrants were welcomed, Congress, noting recent attempts to send convicts to America, urged the states to stop them. Franklin stressed the need of caution even in the case of other arrivals. He thought office seekers, military men, and persons who relied on aristocratic connections were not needed. In the United States the stranger was asked not *"What is he?"* but *"What can he do?"* Industrious farm workers could, however, earn enough to buy land; the mechanic could practice his craft freely; servants or journeymen, if "sober, industrious and frugal," might hope to become masters, heads of families, and "respectable citizens."[209] Though immigration was much less than in later years, men were already thinking about the problem of assimilation. A German observer commented on the "promiscuous crowd of almost all nations in Europe," adding, "Such a mixture will require a long fermentation before it will contain the spirit, the feelings, and the imprint of a united people." A generation passed, however, before the newcomers materially affected institutional life.[210]

The postwar society lived within a governmental framework that contained elements both old and new. The local governments, which most nearly touched the ordinary citizen, were not radically altered. New England town meetings went on as before, and Virginia counties were administered much as in earlier days and largely by the same kind of people, though the royal governors no longer appointed the justices. Between these local communities and the extremely slight authority of the Confederation stood the states with their new constitutions. In Rhode Island and Connecticut the transition from colony to commonwealth proved simple. Royal collectors and admiralty courts had disappeared, but otherwise the form of government was little changed. A generation passed before these states replaced their colonial charters with constitutions of their own making. But in each of the former royal and proprietary provinces an old edifice was pulled down and a new one built, even though much of the same material was used. The process, begun in 1776, was nearly completed with the adoption of the Massachusetts constitution of 1780.[211]

Naturally, the new governments were formed by supporters of the Revolution, but in their ranks were many who desired only a minimum of internal innovation. Between this conservative group and the more liberal elements compromises had to be effected. Some of the democratic leaders were, like Patrick Henry, "new men," but others, like the Virginia Lees and

Edmund Randolph, belonged to the "first families." Henry, who called himself "a Democrat on the plan of our admired friend, J. Adams," complained of a "bias to Aristocracy" among the opulent.[212] Typical representatives of conservative views in the state conventions were Robert Carter Nicholas and Edmund Pendleton in Virginia, James Duane and John Jay in New York, and Henry Laurens and John Rutledge in South Carolina.

This group included substantial landowners, well-to-do merchants, and successful lawyers. One aggressive republican who gradually moved to the "right" was John Adams, chief architect of the Massachusetts constitution. To many of the Virginia gentry the first clause of the state bill of rights, drafted by George Mason, which declared all men "by nature equally free and independent," seemed to embody subversive doctrine, "the forerunner or pretext of civil convulsion." The conservatives were beaten on this issue as well as on the clause pledging the "free exercise of religion," but the constitution was not strictly democratic. Though it provided for annual elections, property qualifications remained, and the method of apportionment still favored the tidewater planters as against the piedmont and Valley farmers.[213] In the South the radicals were strongest in North Carolina, where they defeated the conservative tidewater planters, lawyers, and merchants. All adult free men could vote for members of the lower house after one year's residence, but there were property qualifications for membership in the legislature.[214]

In Pennsylvania the radicals dominated the convention of 1776 through a combination of backcountry farmers with Philadelphia mechanics and small tradesmen. As a result, the new instrument reduced the representation of the conservative older counties and increased that of Philadelphia and the interior counties. The suffrage was somewhat broadened, no upper house was provided to check the popularly elected assembly, and the plural executive received no veto. Conservative opposition, combined with the need of a stronger executive, led to further constitutional changes in 1790, including provisions for a single executive with a veto on legislation, judicial service during good behavior, and an upper house.[215]

The original constitutions of New York (1777) and Massachusetts (1780), being adopted after a longer war experience, were perhaps partly for that reason comparatively conservative. The presence of the British army in New York called for a strong executive there, and influential members of the convention represented the less democratic wing of the patriot party. Jay's "favorite maxim" was, according to his son, that "those who own the country ought to govern it." Except for city freemen previously admitted to the suffrage, the constitution provided that electors had to be either £20 freeholders or renters of tenements worth forty shillings a year. Voters for governor and senators had to meet higher qualifications, and the governor was to serve for a three-year term. One liberal provision required the legislature to try the experiment of a secret ballot and another guaranteed religious liberty. The freehold qualification for voters did not prevent the yeoman farmers, led by Governor George Clinton, from dominating state politics during the next few years.[216]

The Massachusetts constitution has been called a merchants' and lawyers' instrument designed for "quarterdeck efficiency in government, and the protection of property against democratic pirates." In general, it mirrored the ideas of the commercial seaboard and a conservative reaction against Revolutionary radicalism, a point of view apparent in the manifesto, known as the "Essex Result," which advocated frank recognition of class interests in a bicameral legislature, with one house, chosen by the people, checked by an upper house.[217]

Thus the early constitutions reflected various shades of opinion, from those favoring a comparatively advanced democracy to more conservative attitudes. It must be remembered, however, that property qualifications based on land were at that time more easily met by a preponderantly agricultural population than they would be today. From an eighteenth-century European standpoint, the American states had gone far toward equalitarian democracy.

Aside from constitutional provisions, it is hard to say how far the Revolution affected class distinctions. The confiscation of Loyalist estates and the abolition of primogeniture helped toward a wider distribution of landed property, and some large fortunes were broken up in other ways. Meanwhile, however, "new men" who gained riches during the war acquired social prestige and political power, thus forming a new aristocracy beside the old or in place of it. Dr. J. D. Schoepf, a thoughtful observer of the American scene, remarked that without a nobility or gentry in the strict sense there were men whose exceptional ability or wealth caused them to "think and act precisely as do the nobility in other countries." In Virginia, Devereux Jarratt, in spite of his humble origin, regretted that the "high republican times" had caused "more *levelling* than ought to be, consistent with government." Nevertheless, there was some lessening of traditional deference to superior social status. The will of Thomson Mason, who died in 1785, advised his sons to avoid the tidewater aristocracy lest they "imbibe more exalted notions of their own importance." Jefferson, however, expected the "plebeian Interest" to prevail over "the old aristocratical interest."[218]

Conservatives feared that social disintegration would follow the wartime interference with public order. The agrarian disturbances in New England culminating in Shays's Rebellion increased this sense of instability. Hostile critics abroad, making the most of such disorders, painted a gloomy picture of the United States drifting toward anarchy, and much was said of unruly frontier communities. Franklin and Jefferson insisted, however, that press reports were exaggerated and Jefferson noted the respect for life and property shown in the early stages of the Massachusetts uprising. A fair statement is that of Dr. David Ramsay: "To overset an established government unhinges many of those principles, which bind individuals to each other. A long time, and much prudence, will be necessary to reproduce a spirit of union and that reverence for government, without which society is a rope of sand." [219]

Generally speaking, the older private law survived the Revolution—the English common law, certain acts of Parliament, and colonial statutes and judicial decisions—with some local variations. A Virginia committee of which Jefferson, Pendleton, and Wythe were members recommended some radical changes in the existing laws. According to Jefferson, the alterations would constitute "a system by which every fibre should be eradicated of antient or future aristocracy; and a foundation laid for a government truly republican." A principal result of these proposals was the repeal of primogeniture and entail. [220]

Jefferson also displayed a keen interest in penology and knew the European writings on this subject by Montesquieu and the Italian criminologist Beccaria. His committee agreed to limit capital punishment to treason and murder, though this recommendation did not become law until 1796. In Pennsylvania the constitution directed the legislature to reform the colonial code so that punishments might be "less sanguinary, and in general more proportionate to the crimes." Franklin told an Italian jurist that no branch of law was more in need of reform. Rush not only opposed the death penalty for many crimes, but declared the time "not very distant, when the gallows, the pillory, the stocks, and the whipping post" would be regarded as barbarous. By 1786, Pennsylvania had reduced the number of capital offenses and prohibited the more cruel forms of corporal punishment. The next decade brought further revision, the death penalty being eliminated except for murder in the first degree. [221]

In New York, where sixteen crimes were punishable by death for the first offense and severe flogging might be inflicted on women as well as men, the one substantial advance before 1790 was the constitutional provision securing the right of a defendant to counsel. This was nearly half a century before England established the principle. In New England, some more or less academic discussion of penal reform took place. Yale seniors were set to debate whether American criminal law was not "too rigorous . . . for the present State of Society," and at the commencement of 1788 young Jeremiah Mason based his argument against capital punishment mainly on Beccaria. In general, the New England codes had been more humane than the British. An English visitor in Boston noted with surprise that forgery was not there a capital offense. [222]

Public interest was also being awakened to abuses in the management of prisons. As in England, such places were overcrowded and unsanitary, and the inmates were herded indiscriminately, with little or no regard to sex, age, or degree of guilt. Early American reform efforts derived much inspiration from the work of John Howard, whose recently published *State of the Prisons in England and Wales* reached a third edition in 1784. With the formation at Philadelphia in 1787 of a society "for Alleviating the Miseries of Public Prisons" the influence of this "friend of mankind" was publicly acknowledged. Some of the worst penal abuses were presently remedied and in 1790 a law provided for other reforms. In New England, Isaiah Thomas published two articles commending the Philadelphia society, but its most significant influence appeared some years later in New York, where Thomas Eddy, Quaker migrant from Philadelphia, became the most effective advocate of prison reform.[223]

A special phase of penal reform pertained to the treatment of debtors. In 1785 they constituted half the inmates of Philadelphia prisons. Often dependent on charity even for the necessaries of life, they suffered, like other prisoners, from brutal keepers. Public attention began now to be drawn to these abuses. In 1786, Yale seniors argued the affirmative of the question: "Whether Imprisonment for Debt ought to be abolished in all civilized States." Here and there newspaper articles on the situation excited sympathy, and philanthropic men sought to ameliorate hardships. In 1783 the New York legislature voted to free insolvent persons from prison, but the bill was vetoed by the council of revision, and for nearly half a century the law remained with only minor changes. Partial remedies were all that public opinion would support. Meanwhile, the New York Society for the Relief of Distressed Debtors mitigated some cases of extreme need.[224]

The most successful humanitarian effort of the Revolutionary era concerned slavery. Until 1783 the institution was not finally ended in any of the thirteen states. In that year, as we have seen, it became illegal in Massachusetts through judicial interpretation of its bill of rights. Three years earlier Pennsylvania had begun its program of gradual emancipation. The Quakers continued their efforts after the passage of this law and one of the last acts of devoted Friend Anthony Benezet was a letter to Queen Charlotte on the slave trade. Revolutionary ideas of natural rights, as well as economic factors, contributed to the progress of abolitionism, which was also related to contemporary discussion in England. Granville Sharp, the outstanding British antislavery advocate, corresponded on this subject with Franklin, John Adams, and Jay. Adams declared that Sharp "merited the respect and esteem of all men, amongst whom liberty and humanity are not disregarded." The Pennsylvania society "for Promoting the Abolition of Slavery and the Relief of Free Negroes unlawfully held in Bondage" elected Sharp an honorary member and corresponded with the English Society for the Abolition of the Slave Trade. The New York Society for Promoting the Manumission of Slaves, headed by Jay, had among its foreign associates Sharp, Lafayette, and Brissot de Warville.[225]

The emancipation act of 1780 gradually reduced the number of slaves in

Pennsylvania until by 1800 fewer than 2,000 remained. During the postwar decade local reformers worked to improve the condition of blacks generally and advance the antislavery cause in the country at large. In 1789 a society was formed for "the free instruction of orderly Blacks and People of Color." In the other Middle Atlantic states, where slaves were more numerous, not even gradual emancipation was undertaken during this period. Nevertheless, antislavery sentiment was growing. In New Jersey, where the Quakers were active, Governor William Livingston favored abolition and freed his own slaves, and in 1786 the legislature prohibited further importations. In New York, which had more slaves than any other Northern state, Jay and his associates kept the issue alive. In 1777 he had proposed the constitutional prohibition of slavery, but the convention rejected it two to one. In 1784, when gradual emancipation was voted by both houses of the legislature, it was vetoed by the council of revision. Though some blacks were freed because of army service or through the confiscation of Tory estates, and though voluntary manumission by owners was facilitated, New York in 1790, possessed more than 20,000 slaves.[226]

In New England, which had few slaves, emancipation came more easily. In 1783, New Hampshire, like Massachusetts, excluded human bondage by judicial interpretation, and in 1784, Rhode Island and Connecticut passed gradual-emancipation acts. If the vested interest of New Englanders in domestic slavery was small, both Massachusetts and Rhode Island had been deeply involved in the oversea traffic. Though the importation of slaves into these states had been prohibited, their people could still sell blacks elsewhere. By 1789, however, both these states and Connecticut had made this practice illegal. Nevertheless, some New Englanders continued in the business. In 1789, John Quincy Adams found "remnants" of it in Newport, and even a decade later John Brown of Providence did not see why Americans, as well as Britons, should not engage in that "lucrative traffic." William Bentley's Salem diary noted violations of the law in that neighborhood and a tendency to connive at them. At the Federal Convention some New England delegates voted against prohibition of the slave trade before 1808, but their chief motive was probably to keep the Lower South in the Union and also to prevent more burdensome restraints on Congress's power to regulate commerce.[227]

The status of women excited little attention except in relation to education. Dr. Rush was a promoter of two girls' schools in Philadelphia and set forth his liberal views for a wider public in *Thoughts upon Female Education* (1787). In Boston the selectmen approved a school for young ladies conducted by Caleb Bingham, a recent Dartmouth graduate who published, especially for his pupils, *The Young Ladys Accidence or a Short and Easy Introduction to English Grammar* (1785). Among the representative New Englanders of this period who taught girls either separately or in coeducational academies were Timothy Dwight, the Reverend Jedidiah Morse, author of the *American Geography*, and Noah Webster. Webster prepared a public lecture on the "Importance of Female Education in domestick Life, in Society, and in Government."[228]

Advocacy of female education was not, however, generally associated with advances in the status of the sex. Enos Hitchcock, a Providence clergyman who wrote on the training of girls and who rejected some traditional views of female inferiority, insisted on the subordinate position of the wife. There was, however, more emphasis on the mother's part in training sons for citizenship. A writer in the *Pennsylvania Gazette* in 1787 suggested that women had a peculiar interest in maintaining orderly republican institutions as against either monarchy or radical democracy. In monarchies they were considered primarily as "mothers for soldiers"; only under a free government could they "retain their rank as rational beings." Yale students went so far as to debate "Whether Women ought to be admitted into the Magistracy and Government of Empires and Republics."[229] Abigail Adams considered her American sisters superior to English society women, who seemed to abandon "the softness peculiarly characteristic of our sex for the masculine attire and manners of Amazonians," Jedidiah Morse, an orthodox New England pastor, thought the New England women he knew "genteel, easy and agreeable" as well as good household managers. One British visitor found the Boston ladies too reserved.[230]

Though dancing was no new thing in the New England towns, one is surprised to find Morse calling it "the principal and favorite amusement" in this region. The diary of John Quincy Adams, then a law student in Newburyport, gives a similar impression of gaieties there. Mrs. Adams's letters from abroad show her adjusting herself to European usage in such matters as theatrical and operatic entertainments. Stage dancing she saw at first with "disgust," but later "with pleasure" though not without misgivings. Opposition to the theater was weakening in Massachusetts, but the official ban was not finally removed until the next decade. Not all the foes of the drama lived in New England. When the Old American Company opened its New York season in 1785, 700 persons signed an unsuccessful appeal to the legislature to suppress the performances. In Philadelphia the Southwark Theatre reopened, though the opposition was strong enough to prevent formal repeal of the law against it until 1789.[231]

Organizations for social recreation remained much as in colonial days. Besides such older groups as the societies of St. George, St. Andrew, and St. Patrick, there were more recent German societies. Brissot de Warville was pleased by the politeness and agreeable conversation of a Boston club. The Wednesday Evening Club there, visited by Yale President Stiles in 1787, included clergymen, lawyers, physicians, and merchants. He heard a lawyer tell of his travels and met Charles Bulfinch, then beginning his distinguished architectural career. In New York, convivial groups bore such names as Sub Rosa, Turtle, and Black Friars. Among the craft organizations the Gold and Silver-Smith's Society and the Society of Peruke Makers, Hair Dressers, etc. included social features.[232]

Masonry continued to flourish. The Massachusetts Grand Lodge of Scottish Rite Masons now took occasion to declare itself "free and independent in its government and official authority, of any other Grand Lodge, or Grand Master in the universe." Chancellor Robert R. Livingston headed the New York Grand Lodge of Free and Accepted Masons. President Stiles was told in 1784 that there were 187 organizations in the United States. He thought the fraternity would prosper unless it developed "sinister national & illiberal Views," in which case there might be a "storm." In 1787 the *American Museum* printed a defense of Masonry as helpful to good citizenship and a safeguard against exaggerated nationalism, which "often destroys in warlike republics, the love of general humanity."[233]

In brief, the young republic made some progress toward realizing the Revolutionary ideal of equality. State legislation had restricted the slave trade, and several Northern states had either ended human servitude or provided for gradual emancipation. The abolition of primogeniture and entail favored a wider distribution of landed property; hereditary privileges were constitutionally excluded; and some states had extended the suffrage. Yet the conservative classes were still strong. Though weakened by the emigration of Loyalists and the confiscation of Tory estates, they re-formed their lines with new accessions from the rising capitalist group. Class consciousness was too deeply rooted to be ignored except by doctrinaire reformers. The antislavery efforts of Southern liberals failed save in the prohibition of black importations by the border states. Property qualifications, though sometimes reduced, were still general, and Jefferson's endeavors to equalize educational opportunities came to nil. In the eyes of advanced reformers certain features of the federal constitution, especially its protection of vested interests, seemed likely to interfere with the full realization of democratic ideals. John Quincy Adams considered regretfully that the adoption of the new system would be "a grand point gained in favour of the aristocratic party," and he added, "it is hard to give up a system which I have always been taught to cherish, and to confess that a free government is inconsistent with human nature."[234]

CULTURE IN THE NEW ORDER

THOUGH SUBSTANTIAL PROGRESS had been made during the war toward religious liberty and equality, some forms of discrimination survived. Maryland had limited its constitutional guarantee of equality to Christians, and South Carolina had accorded toleration only to churches and individuals acknowledging one God, a future state of rewards and punishments, and the duty of public worship, reserving the privilege of incorporation to groups professing the Protestant faith. Religious tests for office also remained. In the Carolinas and Georgia certain offices were confined to Protestants. Distrust of ecclesiastical influence is indicated in the constitutional exclusion of clergymen from the legislature, as in the Carolinas and Georgia, and by the Maryland rule limiting the landholdings of ecclesiastical corporations.[235]

After the war some restrictive features of the early constitutions were removed. Georgia legislators no longer had to be Protestants, and South Carolina ended the preferential status of Protestants, granting equal rights of religious profession and worship to "all mankind." Of prime importance was the action of Virginia, where, after the practical disestablishment of the Anglican Church, the precise status of religious societies had not been defined. Such men as Richard Henry Lee and Patrick Henry still believed that the state should, without discriminating in favor of any particular sect, assume some responsibility for the maintenance of the Christian religion. This point of view found expression in two important measures: the legal incorporation of the Episcopal Church, and the proposed "general assessment" bill which would have authorized a tax whose proceeds should be applied, at the option of the taxpayer, either to the denomination of his choice or to education.[236]

The former act, which guaranteed the property rights of that church, was, however, soon repealed, partly because it was thought to give the clergy too much power. The latter failed to pass. In Jefferson's absence abroad the chief spokesman against it was Madison, who, working with the Baptists, most of the Presbyterians, and many liberal Episcopalians, advocated complete separation of church and state. Their success was followed in 1785–86 by the passage of Jefferson's famous "Bill for Establishing Religious Freedom," with its preamble beginning: "Whereas Almighty God hath created the mind free. . . ." Coercion, it said, could only "beget habits of hypocrisy and meanness," whereas without it truth would prevail. No man, therefore, should be forced to attend or support any form of worship, or suffer discrimination of any kind because of his religious opinions. The statute concluded with a formal declaration that its repeal would violate "the natural rights of mankind."[237]

In New York the comparatively weak Anglican establishment was easily disposed of. The state constitution guaranteed liberty of "religious profession and worship . . . without discrimination or preference." Anti-Catholic feeling found expression, however, in a clause requiring applicants for citizenship to renounce allegiance to foreign rulers "in all matters, ecclesiastical as well as civil"; but this provision became nugatory with the adoption of the federal constitution, which transferred control of naturalization to Congress. Though the other Middle states had no establishments to abolish, they retained religious qualifications for office.

In New England outside Rhode Island the colonial association of church and state continued. Even here, however, there was some progress. The Massachusetts constitution acknowledged every man's right to worship God "in the manner and season most agreeable to the Dictates of his own conscience," thus making possible the public worship of the Catholic Church. At the same time, however, Massachusetts asserted the duty of all men "publickly, and at stated seasons to worship the Supreme Being," and required legislation to enforce town provision for "public Protestant teachers of piety, religion, and Morality." There were vigorous protests by the New England dissenters against these discriminatory provisions, but prosecutions for nonpayment of church taxes continued for many years. In Rhode Island, where religious liberty had always enjoyed wide scope, the legislature formally repealed the statute excluding Catholics from citizenship.

Under the Articles of Confederation religion was clearly not a federal matter and Congress expressly disclaimed such jurisdiction. The subject was, however, discussed in Congress and later in the Federal Convention. In the debate on the land ordinance of 1785, Madison objected successfully to a clause allotting one section in each township for the support of religion. Five states, however, voted for it. In the Northwest ordinance of 1787, Article I prohibited interference with anyone "on account of his mode of worship, or religious sentiments," and Article VI merely referred in general terms to religion as one object to be promoted through education.

Shortly afterward the Federal Convention adopted without serious opposition the prohibition of religious qualifications for "Office or public Trust under the United States." There were some objectors, however, in the state ratifying conventions. In Maryland, Luther Martin declared that "in a Christian country, it would be at least decent to hold out some distinction between the professors of Christianity and downright infidelity or paganism." A member of the Massachusetts convention "shuddered at the idea that Roman Catholics, Papists and Pagans might thus be introduced into office," and a North Carolina critic complained of what he called "an invitation to Jews and Pagans of every kind to come among us." Among those who argued effectively against religious qualifications were clergymen. One Massachusetts Congregational minister called such tests "impious encroachments" upon the divine prerogative.[238]

A by-product of the debates on ratification was the enactment of a more general guarantee of religious liberty. Richard Henry Lee had argued that "the free exercise of religion" should be established "as a part of the national compact." Minority denominations also desired more protection and in doubtful states their support was important. As a result, the First Amendment included the familiar clause: "Congress shall make no law respecting the establishment of religion or prohibiting the free exercise thereof." Though neither this provision nor that prohibiting religious tests limited the action of state governments, they did embody liberal opinion in "the supreme law of the land." [239]

The churches also felt the impulse toward greater internal union. In the case of the Catholics, Bishop Carroll actively directed the clergy from Maryland to New England. The Episcopalians, beginning with three independent dioceses, soon set up a national organization governed by a general convention in which the bishops formed an upper house while clerical and lay representatives from each diocese comprised the lower house. The bishops themselves were chosen by diocesan conventions consisting of clerical and lay delegates. The Presbyterians likewise founded a federal organization with a general assembly of ministers and laymen chosen by the presbyteries. Somewhat later, similar bodies were established by the Dutch and German Reformed churches. The American Methodists also organized a general conference for the United States. On the other hand, the Lutherans did not advance beyond regional associations, while the Congregationalists and Baptists held to the principle of loosely grouped, independent local churches. [240]

In the realm of religious thought and feeling certain developments stand out: first, an intellectual revolt against traditional orthodoxy; second, the effect of the Revolution in somewhat weakening accepted sanctions of personal conduct and profession; and third, the influence of emotional appeals on people who were dissatisfied with conventional forms and ready for what they considered a more vital personal religion adapted to the common man. These tendencies, already apparent in the colonies, were variously affected by the Revolution.

Radical opinion expressed itself both in headlong assaults on orthodox Christianity and in "peaceful penetration" within the churches. Ethan Allen's *Reason, the Only Oracle of Man* (1784), illustrates a crude form of frontal attack. Rejecting historic dogmas and declaring that "most of the human race" were "miserable Priest-ridden," he proposed to free them "from this ghostly Tyranny." An article in the *American Museum* spoke of Allen's "contemptible plagiarism of every hackneyed, worn-out half-rotten dogma of the English deistical writers." Some New England ministers were deeply disturbed by this book, and when Allen died in 1789, Yale President Stiles predicted future torments for this "profane and impious Deist." Even to own the book aroused suspicion of "infidel" sympathies. [241]

Stiles complained of increasing indifference to the religious attitudes of public men, observing even a tendency to regard Deists and indifferentists as "the most suitable persons for public office." He maintained, however, that Deism should be opposed only by "argument and truth." Stiles considered that Timothy Dwight's undiscriminating attack on heretical tendencies in his *Triumph of Infidelity* (1788) had "overshot the Mark, and hurt the Cause which he meant to defend." To Philip Mazzei, however, it seemed that his American friends combined tolerance with real respect for religion: atheism was unknown among them while skepticism was rare and usually not publicly avowed. Gibbon's *Decline and Fall of the Roman Empire* was read in New England and his unsympathetic treatment of Christianity noted. John Quincy Adams thought it "equally injurious to the author's character —as a philosopher and as an historian."[242]

Popular discussion of Deism was not confined to New England. Noah Webster's *American Magazine* printed an anonymous article on discrepancies in the New Testament, followed by an anonymous reply. William Livingston and John Dickinson defended orthodoxy against "infidelity," and Livingston's *Thoughts on Deism* was frequently reprinted. Among the Southern gentry skepticism was common. Jefferson advised a young nephew to read the Bible as he read Livy or Tacitus, treating accounts of supernatural occurrences with reserve and relying on his own reason, "the only oracle given you by heaven." Deistic or rationalistic ideas were attributed to George Wythe in Virginia, Willie Jones in North Carolina, and C. C. Pinckney in South Carolina. On the other hand, Patrick Henry was disturbed by "French infidelity" and Bishop William Meade noted the baneful influence of the alliance with "infidel France," nowhere more evident than in Virginia. While Henry valued Hampden-Sydney College as a bulwark of orthodoxy, Jefferson condemned the "religious phrensy" with which it inspired its students.[243]

More important probably than these external attacks on the Christian tradition were the latitudinarian tendencies within the churches, even among the clergy, as represented, for instance, by the Anglican Provost William Smith of Philadelphia. A committee of which he was chairman proposed radical changes in the prayer book, including the omission of the Nicene and Athanasian creeds. In the end, however, the doctrinal statements of the English prayer book were retained with a few exceptions, chiefly those made necessary by the new political order.[244] Meanwhile, in New England, the revolt against Calvinism continued. After the Revolution the conflict between the "liberals" and the conservatives became more sharply defined, partly under the influence of English Unitarianism. In 1785, King's Chapel, the oldest Anglican church in Boston, was transformed under the leadership of young James Freeman into a Unitarian society. Another example of the drift from orthodoxy was William Bentley, pastor of a Congregational church in Salem, who declared that he had abandoned many of his "early prejudices," including the doctrine of the Trinity. Nevertheless he maintained his standing in the church. A young English visitor reported that the Bostonians, from being "perhaps the strictest Calvinists in the world," had gone to the opposite extreme, so that the "revolution of religion" had been "greater than that of politics."[245]

Aside from doctrinal issues, there were widespread complaints of apathy. In 1783, Schoepf noted the ruinous condition of Virginia churches and was told that religion had become "very faint." In New England, too, there was talk of lessened zeal. In 1790 a Connecticut preacher, describing local conditions, complained of the prevailing "profaneness, disregard of the Sabbath, neglect of family religion, unrighteousness, intemperance." The Reverend Jedidiah Morse thought a "more enlarged intercourse with mankind" had bred greater tolerance, a good thing if it did not "liberalize away all true religion." Dr. John Collins Warren of Boston, who spent his boyhood in a churchgoing household during this period, believed that in the community at large the characteristic "religious habits and opinions" of New England had weakened. Sabbath observance, however, was still strict enough to annoy foreign visitors.[246]

Generalizations about sexual morality are precarious, but European observers commonly took a favorable view of conditions. Brissot de Warville thought there was comparatively little prostitution even in the seaboard towns. For what there was he considered foreigners chiefly responsible. According to Schoepf, "Gallant adventures" were "little known and still less practised." He did not overlook, however, the numerous mulatto children born to "gentlemen" by slave mothers, or the evil influence on white children of "ignorant, careless, immoral" slaves. Though divorce legislation in New England had been comparatively liberal, the disuse after 1782 of the scarlet letter to mark persons found guilty of adultery suggests a more humane attitude. There was some discussion of the divorce question. Yale seniors debated, "Whether Christianity permits Divorces in any cases but Fornication or Adultery," and in 1788, Benjamin Trumbull, the clerical historian of Connecticut, published *An Appeal to the Public with Respect to the Unlawfulness of Divorces.*[247]

While the older churches worked their fields with diminishing returns and suffered from the inroads of indifference or "infidelity," the so-called popular churches, notably the Baptists, Methodists, and "New Side" Presbyterians, vigorously cultivated neglected social groups.[248] As for the Baptists, the years between 1785 and 1789 were marked in Virginia by revivals which brought them several thousand new members. They had also to be reckoned with as a democratic force in politics. With increasing prosperity and the winning of some well-to-do converts came a certain change of outlook and more interest in ministerial education. Moreover, progress was made in reconciling differences between "Regular Baptists" and "Separates." Even in New England the Baptist churches gained rapidly, especially in the northern parts.[249]

Although the Methodists, like the Baptists, had been troubled by the war, they recovered quickly under capable leadership. Their revivals resembled those of the Baptists, but they developed a distinctive technique for consolidating their gains: classes for converts, an itinerant ministry, quarterly meetings, regional conferences with presiding elders, and, over all, the general conference and the superintendents or bishops. In particular,

Bishop Asbury proved himself a skillful leader and organizer. The Methodists won their greatest successes in the South. A Virginia revival, at its height while the Federal Convention was sitting, attracted attention throughout the country. According to one Baptist minister, the Methodist preachers in this region surpassed all others in "spreading their books and tenets among the people." Advancing into the Lower South and the Southwest, the Methodists reported in 1789 nearly 7,000 members in the North Carolina conference, including some from beyond the Alleghenies, and over 2,000 in Georgia. In 1787 they claimed for the country as a whole more than 21,000 members, not counting 4,000 blacks.[250]

Another "popular" movement was that of the Universalists. Chiefly active in the North and particularly in New England, they were much less numerous than the Baptists and Methodists, but their doctrine of ultimate salvation for all men, presented by such preachers as John Murray and Elhanon Winchester, probably influenced many outside the fold. Smaller religious groups, mainly in New England and New York, were the Shaker followers of Ann Lee and a few disciples of Jemimah Wilkinson, the "Universal Friend."

The Catholics began a notable progress. For the first time they had an official head for the country as a whole. To the early congregations in Maryland and Pennsylvania were added parishes in states where the Mass had previously been forbidden by law. Formerly isolated members were formed into congregations and reinforced by immigration. Though the recognized Catholic population of the United States was estimated at about 25,000, chiefly in Maryland, Pennsylvania, and New York City, the stage was set for a rapid advance.[251]

In the field of education, clergymen occupied an important place, holding all but one of the college presidencies and a large proportion of the professorships. Perhaps equally significant was the interest of public men in education. In his *Defence of the Constitutions of the United States* (1787), John Adams insisted on instruction for "every class and rank of people, down to the lowest and the poorest." Community schools would "draw together the sons of the rich and the poor."[252] Similarly, Jefferson argued that, since the people were the "only safe depositories of political power," at least a modicum of education should be given free to all children for at least three years in publicly supported schools. The more capable boys should then be selected for free tuition in "grammar schools," and especially promising ones should proceed to college at public expense, though well-to-do parents might pay for the higher education of their sons without this sifting process. This proposal was as nearly democratic as could then and there be reasonably expected. Though Jefferson's plan was not adopted, he did not give up the fight. "Preach," he wrote to Wythe, "a crusade against ignorance. . . ."[253]

Postwar educational legislation in New England tended to follow colonial precedents. The Massachusetts school law of 1789, for instance, was largely a codification of existing arrangements, including the public support of elementary and grammar schools. Enforcement of these latter provisions, however, still depended on community sentiment and the efficiency of local officials. Jedidiah Morse admitted that grand juries were lax in presenting cases of neglect. One result of the division of towns into school districts was to shorten school terms. On the other hand, legislative charters encouraged private schools, though generally without state appropriations. Some academies, however, were helped in other ways, as when Phillips Academy at Andover was partially exempted from taxation.[254]

The Middle states tended to continue their laissez-faire attitude toward education. No general school legislation was adopted in New Jersey or Delaware, and little in Pennsylvania, though some aid was given to particular institutions, including the new colleges at Lancaster and Carlisle. In 1786, Pennsylvania also granted certain unappropriated lands to provide money for public schools. New York did somewhat better, thanks largely to the efforts of Governor George Clinton and his political associate, Ezra L'Hommedieu. In 1782, Clinton urged on the legislature "the peculiar duty of the government of a free state" to support education, pointing out that the war had produced "a chasm in education, extremely injurious to the rising generation." Acts of 1784 and 1787 established a "University of the State of New York" with a board of regents charged with general responsibility for education. The regents presently resolved that elementary instruction "ought not to be left to the discretion of private men, but be promoted by public authority." Otherwise, however, not much was accomplished. Though in 1786 certain lands were set apart for an educational fund, no general school law was passed for many years.[255]

Maryland, Virginia, and South Carolina took no steps whatever toward a public educational system, while North Carolina did nothing more than to authorize in 1789 the setting up of a state university. The institution did not open until 1795. More than any other Southern commonwealth, Georgia, under the leadership of Lyman Hall and Abraham Baldwin, both native New Englanders and Yale graduates, showed a serious interest in educational planning. Following an appeal from Governor Hall, the legislature granted 20,000 acres for "a college or Seminary of learning." A later act "for the more full and complete Establishment of a public School of Learning" was passed in 1785 to inaugurate something like the New York plan of a central educational authority, in which all public schools were to be "parts and members of the University." Baldwin was chosen president of this institution, and discussed with Ezra Stiles his ambitious hopes for a university to "comprehend the whole of the *Res Literaria.*" One academy had then been opened and two others authorized, but the college had to wait.[256]

In secondary education the new academies were especially significant.

In 1786, Stiles reported that "Academy-making" was proceeding rapidly. He listed thirteen in Connecticut, all but two of which had been set up after 1780, but he admitted that some of these schools were meagerly equipped.[257] Of the few New York academies founded after the war, two were promoted by Dutch Reformed clergymen: Erasmus Hall at Flatbush, which still exists, and a school at Schenectady, which became the starting point of Union College. Pennsylvania had its Presbyterian, Episcopal, Quaker, and Moravian schools, some new and some revived after wartime suspension.[258]

There are comments on Virginia academies by James Madison in answer to Jefferson's inquiry about suitable schools for his nephews. Madison spoke well of the "very flourishing" school kept by an Episcopal clergyman and also of the Hampden-Sydney Presbyterian academy. He complained, however, that private schools suffered from frequent changes of masters and methods. Some Southern boys still went abroad. Charles Carroll of Carrollton continued a family tradition by sending his son to a Jesuit school in Liège and later a daughter abroad to a convent school. South Carolina youths were said to return from English schools "little more improved & much more dissipated than they went."[259]

Of the colleges Yale stood first in enrollment, with 270 students in the academic year 1783–84.[260] The annual average of Harvard's graduates during the ten years following the war was somewhat smaller than in the prewar decades.[261] Outside New England the colleges fared less well. Queen's College did not reopen for several years. Columbia had fewer than forty students in 1787. New Jersey College at Princeton survived but also with diminished numbers. At Philadelphia the division between the old college and the new state university continued until 1791. William and Mary, another war casualty, had in the first year of peace about 100 students. By 1789, however, the aggregate attendance at all the older institutions of higher learning was probably not far from the prewar figure.

Changes in the curriculum were comparatively few. Harvard appointed its first salaried teacher of French. Though Silas Deane's plan of a French professorship at Yale was not carried out, President Stiles was sufficiently interested in the subject, at the age of fifty-six, to read Racine's plays with a private tutor. At Columbia one professor was named to teach German along with geography, but the first modern-language chair was that held by Charles Bellini at William and Mary. Though a certain amount of science was taught, no college teacher in this field was quite the equal of John Winthrop, who died during the war. Some scientific instruction in chemistry and natural history was offered by medical professors. Harvard's president Joseph Willard contributed to the publications of the American Academy. At Yale, scientific lectures were given by young Josiah Meigs, later a professor there and subsequently president of the University of Georgia. The college also appropriated money for the purchase of physical apparatus in England. Yale and Princeton classes in politics used Montesquieu's *Spirit of the Laws,* and President Madison chose Adam Smith's *Wealth of Nations* as a William and Mary textbook. Yale disputations dealt with such political issues as the free navigation of the Mississippi and the eligibility of "Infidels and Libertines" for public office.[262]

In Maryland, which had no college before the Revolution, four new institutions had been founded by 1791: Washington College at Chestertown, St. John's at Annapolis, Cokesbury near Baltimore, and Georgetown in what is now the District of Columbia. St. John's grew out of the old King William School at Annapolis, and was associated with Washington College in a somewhat shadowy "University of Maryland." Cokesbury, established primarily to train Methodist preachers, was soon abandoned.[263] In the neighboring state of Virginia, Hampden-Sydney Academy now became Hampden-Sydney College, its ardent Calvinism in marked contrast with the mild Anglicanism of William and Mary.

The colleges did not lack critics. Francis Hopkinson wrote a satire on "Modern Learning Exemplified by a Specimen of a Collegiate Examination." Harrison Gray Otis, the future senator, assured a Harvard classmate that he would be glad to get away from "the sophisticated Jargon of a superstitious Synod of pension'd Bigots." At Yale there was talk of undue clerical control. Certain observers, however, were more friendly. Jefferson, after some reforms for which he was largely responsible, declared optimistically that in most subjects needed by young Americans they could do as well at William and Mary as in Europe. John Quincy Adams, a graduate of Harvard in 1787 after a previous period of study at Leyden, wrote many years later, "My short discipline of fifteen months at Harvard University was the introduction to all the prosperity that has ever befallen me."[264]

Legal education was still acquired chiefly through apprenticeship, and medical training was still handicapped by popular prejudice. The "Medical Institution" at Harvard, founded in 1782, was slow in getting under way, and in 1784 the Harvard professors were refused clinical facilities in the Boston almshouse. Inability to get material for dissection by legitimate methods led to grave robbing. In New York public protests culminated in the "Doctors' Riot" in 1788 when militia were called out. Three persons were killed and others injured, including John Jay, who had tried to pacify the rioters. Jefferson believed that medical students still needed to go abroad. The Pennsylvania Hospital, the most efficient institution of its kind in the country, nevertheless kept insane patients, some of whom were "nearly or quite naked," in cells ten feet square, partly underground.[265]

Of scientific progress in the new nation Franklin took a hopeful view. The first volume of the American Academy of Arts and Sciences asserted the stimulating effect of political freedom upon the diffusion of knowledge, engaging the mind in "noble and generous pursuits." Even "civil wars and commotions," said Dr. Benjamin Waterhouse, were likely to foster intellectual advance. Another optimist was Noah Webster. "The minds of the people," he wrote, "are in a ferment, and consequently disposed to receive improvements."[266] The learned societies at Philadelphia and Boston were now joined by the Connecticut Academy of Arts and Sciences, organized in 1786. An ambitious project was that of Quesnay de Beaurepaire for an Academy of Sciences at Richmond on the French model, with branches in other cities and distinguished foreign intellectuals as nonresident associates. A building was erected and studies were planned, but Jefferson kept aloof and the enterprise failed. Another undertaking of scholarly significance was the Philological Society, founded by Noah Webster in 1788 for "ascertaining and improving the American tongue."[267]

Among native imprints in science, geographical works and travel books bulked large, including Jedidiah Morse's *Geography Made Easy* (1784), followed by his *American Geography* (1789), John Filson's *Kentucky* (1784), Thomas Hutchins's *Narrative and Topographical Description of Louisiana and West Florida* (1784), and Christopher Colles's *Survey of the Roads of the United States* (1789). American interest in Georges Buffon continued. Though Jefferson rejected his theories of animal degeneration in the New World, he considered him "the best informed of any Naturalist who has ever written." American contributions in botany included Humphrey Marshall's description of trees and shrubs in *Arbustrum Americanum, the American Grove* (1785), and Manasseh Cutler's creditable studies of New England flora. Popular interest is suggested by articles in the *Massachusetts Magazine* (1789–90) on "American Natural History." Samuel Latham Mitchill published magazine essays on geology, and there were other articles on paleontology. John Morgan was said to own a large collection of fossils from the Ohio country.[268]

One intellectual interest stimulated by political independence concerned the "American language." Should the speech and writing of the new nation conform to English standards? On this subject opinions differed. Franklin thought the British should encourage emigration to the United States because this would increase the number of people who would read English authors. Otherwise the foreign elements in the population might "drown and stifle the English." He cared little for an "American language" and, though he favored phonetic spelling, was something of a purist in other respects. Another conservative was Princeton President John Witherspoon who, though a staunch Whig, disliked departures from English usage.[269]

The most vigorous advocate of linguistic emancipation was Noah Webster, whose *Spelling Book* gradually displaced Dilworth's English textbook. Webster prefaced his work with a strenuous assertion of nationalism, which appeared also in his *Grammar* and *Reader*. For America to adopt the maxims of the Old World would be to "plant the seeds of decay in a vigorous constitution." Arguing, in his *Dissertations on the English Lan-*

guage (1789), for an "American tongue," he insisted that national honor required "a system of our own, in language as well as government." Dissimilarities in situation and experience would gradually produce a language "as different from the future language of England, as the modern Dutch, Danish, and Swedish are from the German."[270]

Webster desired not only divergence from British English, but also uniformity of American usage, "demolishing those odious distinctions of provincial dialects." After presenting his views in various parts of the Union he believed that such uniformity could be achieved. His textbooks exerted a certain influence in this direction, though his New England standards did not go unchallenged. Webster felt his optimism was justified by existing conditions. Were there, he asked, in the United States a hundred words, other than those of purely local application, which were not "universally intelligible"? There might indeed be difficulties in maintaining this degree of uniformity because of non-English immigration, but education would overcome this obstacle.[271]

One reason for Webster's hopeful attitude was his estimate of the intelligence and literacy of the average rural dweller, whom he considered far superior to the "illiterate peasantry of England." Most of them, he thought, read newspapers and, besides the Bible "found in all families," other substantial books. Even if he overstated the case for the country as a whole, he was doubtless right in believing rural Americans better off in this respect than their English contemporaries. If literacy is defined in a broader sense, many eighteenth-century political leaders compare favorably with their successors in the next century. This was certainly true of such men as John Adams, Jay, Hamilton, Franklin and his Philadelphia friends, and Jefferson's circle of Virginia intimates. George Wythe could guide Jefferson's nephew in the classics, reading with him "Aeschylus and Horace, one day, and Herodotus and Cicero's orations, the next." In Philadelphia, Schoepf found people of all classes using the Library Company's collection. But Franklin, while stating there were more readers than before the Revolution, believed there was less demand for serious works.[272]

Journalism after the war showed some advance over earlier years. The number of newspapers almost doubled between 1783 and 1790, reaching a total of about ninety, though some were short-lived. Besides six Boston papers, Massachusetts had seven more in other towns. Upstate New York had six and there were several in inland Pennsylvania, including one at Pittsburgh. Weekly issues continued to be the rule, though by 1785 Philadelphia, Charleston, and New York had dailies. For the most part they were still limited to four pages. Nor had the contents changed much: shipping notices, scanty news items from other states and from Europe, legislative proceedings, public announcements, political communications, some literary articles, and advertisements.

The public was still reading books mainly by British authors. Fanny

Burney's *Evelina* (1778), which scored a brilliant success in England during the war, quickly interested Americans. Gibbon's *Decline and Fall* (1776–88) was read, and the poets, Burns and Cowper, were just rising above the American horizon. Burns's *Poems Chiefly in the Scottish Dialect* (1783) and Cowper's *Task* (1785) were both soon reprinted in the United States. Sheridan's *School for Scandal,* first played in London in 1777, was published in America shortly after the war. Continued interest in earlier English fiction led to the printing of Richardson's novels and two of Fielding's. The years from 1786 to 1789 also saw four issues of *Robinson Crusoe*. Among British juveniles bookseller and publisher Isaiah Thomas reprinted *Goody Two Shoes* and *The House That Jack Built*. Curiously enough, one of Thomas's most successful ventures was his reprinting of a standard British spelling book—this in spite of the increasing popularity of Webster's speller, which he also issued.[273]

Among books of American authorship those dealing with politics have best stood the test of time. *The Federalist* by Hamilton, Madison, and Jay, which appeared first in the newspapers and then promptly in book form, has become a classic. The controversial essays of anti-Federalist writers are less familiar, though some still deserve study. The most ambitious exposition of political theory was John Adams's *Defence of the Constitutions of the United States,* the first volume of which was printed in time to influence members of the Federal Convention.[274]

The output of historical works was slight. Popular interest in military history is indicated by the reprinting in America, soon after its publication in London, of Sir Henry Clinton's *Narrative,* defending his record against the charges of Cornwallis. Another controversial piece, Joseph Galloway's criticism of Howe, was published in Philadelphia in 1787 as a *Short History of the War in America under the Command of Sir William Howe*. In 1789 appeared the comprehensive accounts of the war by William Gordon and David Ramsay. Though both works relied unduly upon the British *Annual Register,* Gordon's treatise is useful on a few matters falling within his personal experience, and Ramsay's *History of the American Revolution,* in spite of obvious defects, contains some original observations. George R. Minot's *History of the Insurrection* (1788) was a scholarly conservative's account of the Shays Rebellion. Jeremy Belknap's *History of New Hampshire* (1784–92) was also an excellent work of its kind.

As for the fine arts, a writer in the *American Museum* in 1787, eager to "explode the European creed" of America's inferiority in culture, noted the distinguished English careers of the American-born West and Copley and the more recent work of John Trumbull and Gilbert Stuart. Besides Charles Willson Peale, still painting American subjects, there were two other creditable artists: Ralph Earle, a New England pupil of West, and Robert Pine, an Englishman who spent his last years in Philadelphia and is best known for his portraits of the Washington family at Mt. Vernon. Trumbull, after further study abroad, was already becoming the outstanding figure in depicting the Revolution and its leaders. His first war scenes were the "Battle of Bunker's Hill," with the death of Warren, and the "Death of General Montgomery in the Attack on Quebec." On seeing the Bunker Hill picture in London, Abigail Adams wrote, "My whole frame contracted, my blood shivered, and I felt a faintness at my heart. He [Trumbull] is the first painter who has undertaken to immortalize by his pencil those great actions, that gave rise to our nation." Before 1789, Trumbull had begun his notable small canvass of the signers of the Declaration of Independence and, besides, painted three other episodes: the "Surrender of Cornwallis," the "Death of General Mercer," and the "Capture of the Hessians at Trenton."[275]

In architecture the so-called colonial style still prevailed in the better houses. A well-known example and one of the best of its kind was the Providence home of the wealthy merchant John Brown. Other contemporary work in this mode was that of Samuel McIntire in Salem and eastern Massachusetts. Meanwhile, Jefferson's influence in favor of classical forms commenced to be felt. He gave Virginia the designs of the Maison Carré to

An American Artist Shows His Work

Young William Dunlap and His Parents

serve as the model for the state capitol, begun in 1785. Jefferson also encouraged Charles Bulfinch, who after travel abroad returned to Boston and by 1789 was receiving commissions for churches and other buildings. Bulfinch is said to have been influenced by the Adam brothers, then the leading "classical architects" in England.[276]

All in all, life in the "Critical Period" was far from dark, whether from an economic standpoint or from that of cultural progress. The conflict with Britain had brought its setbacks and left difficult problems in its train, but the wartime experience and the freedom it had won contained seeds of new life.

HORIZONS WEST AND EAST

THOUGH BRITISH RECOGNITION of American sovereignty beyond the Alleghenies offered new opportunities to home seekers, much of the westward movement was still into untenanted areas on the eastern side of the mountains. Suggestive in this connection is the removal of Southern state capitals from tidewater locations to the inland towns of Richmond, Raleigh, Columbia, and Augusta. Similar shifts in the North, though not actually made, were discussed. Beyond the mountains the problem of colonization was far from simple. Within the treaty limits of the United States there were British posts throughout the Great Lakes region and as a result thirteen years passed before it was really open to American occupation. South of the Ohio, the Gulf Coast was in Spanish hands, including the mouth of the Mississippi. Even north of the thirty-first parallel Spain refused to accept the boundaries set by the Anglo-American peace treaty and continued to keep a governor at Natchez. Another complication in the Gulf region was the presence of British traders in the Floridas.

The Western Indians, generally allied with the British during the war, had resented the surrender of their country to the Americans. Nevertheless some cessions of Indian land were secured by peaceful means. Except for a few reservations in New York, the native title had by 1790 been extinguished in that state and in western Pennsylvania. By the treaty of Fort Stanwix in 1784 the Iroquois yielded also their claims farther west, and the next year four Western bands did the same for the greater part of the present state of Ohio. Other tribes, however, remained hostile and there were almost continuous border disturbances. In the Southwest the Kentuckians also were menaced by Indians and the Tennessee pioneers suffered severely at the hands of the Cherokee and the Creek, partly because of white encroachments on Indian lands. Though U.S. commissioners negotiated a treaty with the Cherokee, it was practically nullified because a considerable part of the land then reserved to the Indians had already been occupied by Tennessee frontiersmen, and so the warfare went on. The only area beyond the Alleghenies in which white colonization made much progress was in the valleys of the Ohio and its two great tributaries, the Cumberland and the Tennessee.[277]

The frontier attracted lawless as well as law-abiding elements. The former were publicized by unsympathetic critics and blamed for needless conflicts with the Indians. General Josiah Harmar, who commanded U.S. forces on the Ohio, referred to the squatters there as "banditti" whose conduct was "a disgrace to human nature"—a description which hardly applied to all men whom the army removed for lack of proper land titles. Among the better settlers were war veterans who had bought tracts with army scrip. In 1783 one such group, whom Washington considered peculiarly fitted for frontier life, planned a settlement north of the Ohio. War experience sometimes determined the choice of locations, as when Yankees who had engaged in border fighting in western New York later settled there. Unfortunately, a great deal of the army scrip was sold to speculators.[278]

Since migration proceeded northward and southward as well as westward, all the older sections participated. Connecticut folk were active in colonizing Vermont and western New York. Pennsylvanians and Jerseymen went to the upper Ohio and sometimes to Kentucky. Most of the Kentucky and Tennessee pioneers, however, hailed from Maryland, Virginia, and North Carolina. Still other Southerners moved to sparsely populated areas in Georgia. The motives for change varied with the individual. Restless and adventurous persons wanted to avoid the social patterns of a settled community. A New Jersey migrant willing to stop in a region that was partly occupied found others eager to go farther: "It seems as if people were mad to git afloat on the Ohio." One man, complaining of too many neighbors though the nearest was seven miles off, said his hunting was spoiled and he hated to pay taxes. Probably, however, most persons were prompted chiefly by the desire to establish permanent homes. Thus a Virginia planter planned to sell his property to buy land in Kentucky in order to "give each of his children a sufficient portion." Soil exhaustion in the tobacco country sent some younger sons of planter families to Kentucky. Vermont attracted followers of Shays and other Bay Staters escaping from burdensome taxation.[279]

A considerable number of American people were in motion. The exodus of so many—perhaps a quarter of a million in all—from settled areas to "wild lands" affected the communities they left behind. Newspapers in the old states noted the departure of emigrants and the sale of farms to provide funds for acquiring new homes. Slow communications did not prevent Easterners from keeping in touch with Western relatives and friends. From Kentucky, Mrs. James Wilkinson reported to her Philadelphia father her difficulties of adjustment to frontier conditions and the gradual progress in social amenities. Readers of the *Massachusetts Spy* learned of social affairs in Marietta, including a ball at which the ladies were "as well accomplished in the manners of polite circles . . . as any in the old states." Carey's *American Museum* printed many Western items: Indian troubles on the Ohio, a "nest of pirates" at Muscle Shoals on the Tennessee, the "State of Franklin," and the Mississippi question.[280]

Settlers in western New York and the Northwest were much less troubled by the Indians than the pioneers of Kentucky and Tennessee, where raids on exposed "stations" still occurred. A typical station was an enclosure, consisting of one-story or two-story log cabins or block houses, with connecting stockades, where occupants of outlying farms could, if threatened, take refuge. In such places as Lexington and Louisville conditions of living were more normal, but elsewhere field-workers had to carry arms, and the loss of life was heavy. Kentucky and Tennessee, though within the jurisdiction of adjoining Eastern states, could not count on their protection against Indian raiders. The Westerners also faced the problem of maintaining order among themselves. By 1783, Kentucky possessed county courts and a superior court of its own from which, however, appeals had to be taken to Richmond. Meanwhile Tennesseans complained that North Carolina failed to provide them with sufficient agencies for the administration of justice.[281]

In 1790 the postmaster general listed only one regular route across the mountains, that from Philadelphia to Pittsburgh, and at first this mail went only once a fortnight. No post office existed in Kentucky or Tennessee, in New York west of Albany, or in Vermont. In such areas letters must be entrusted to occasional travelers. There was also the problem of marketing products and obtaining supplies. In 1789 a visitor in Vermont reported famine conditions and in that year the New York frontier was likewise suffering, largely because of poor communications. In Tennessee the first real road between Nashville and the Holston Valley settlements was opened in 1788. Peltry was carried to the East on packhorses. Much of this trade went through the Shenandoah Valley to Baltimore and Philadelphia. Kentucky had similar difficulties, though James Wilkinson's voyage down the Mississippi with tobacco and provisions indicated possibilities of trade with New Orleans. Such exchanges were handicapped, however, not only by Spanish regulations but by the need of taking return cargoes upstream.[282]

As a stabler society emerged here and there from primitive conditions, the type of Western settlers tended to change. Representatives of the Virginia gentry who moved to Kentucky with their slaves organized a plantation life similar to that of their old homes. To a considerable extent Western politicians belonged to this class. In the words of a recent student, "political office, even on the frontier, was rarely sought by any but the natural leaders of society," George Nicholas, Kentucky's first attorney general, was the son of a well-known Virginia lawyer and Revolutionary leader and his mother belonged to one of the "first families." Other families which played important roles on both sides of the mountains were the Marshalls and Breckenridges.[283]

At some points urban life was emerging. In 1783, Pittsburgh was the principal settlement on the upper Ohio, although as late as 1790 it numbered fewer than 400 people, largely engaged in "catering" to westbound travelers. The New Englanders possessed a genuine community life at Marietta almost immediately, and though Cincinnati had few inhabitants in 1789, it, too, was regularly laid out as a town. Nashville, with its courthouse, public square, jail, and pillory, was the earliest urban center in Tennessee. In Kentucky, Lexington soon forged to the front as the principal market town and the meeting place of the first state legislature. Gilbert Imlay a contemporary observer, described Kentucky's progress "from dirty stations or forts and smoky huts" to "fertile fields, blushing orchards, pleasant gardens . . . neat and commodious houses, rising villages and trading towns." Kentucky was beginning to export tobacco and to breed better cattle. By 1789 it possessed a commercial distillery and had devised a process for improving whiskey which was presently to establish the reputation of "Kentucky Bourbon." Linen was manufactured from Kentucky flax, some of which went to Eastern markets, and a Kentucky Manufacturing Company was organized for textiles.[284]

In sparsely settled areas it was hard to maintain churches, though this proved less true of the New England migrants. Congregational churches were quickly planted in western New York as well as at Marietta. In the Southwest fewer immigrants came from compact communities with strongly established religious traditions. Episcopalian influence was comparatively weak and the three major groups were the Presbyterians, Baptists, and Methodists.[285] The Presbyterians, who early formed a congregation at Cincinnati, soon had a few ministers in Kentucky. One of them, David Rice, sat in the convention which framed the first state constitution. By 1788 the Kentucky churches had organized the Transylvania presbytery. In Tennessee another Princeton graduate, Samuel Doak, established a presbytery with twenty churches. He, too, was politically influential.[286] The Virginia migrants to Kentucky included a considerable number of Baptists. By 1785 they had formed eighteen churches. A frontier revival increased the membership and soon there were four Baptist associations. Meanwhile the Methodists sent preachers all the way from the upper Ohio to Tennessee, and Bishop Asbury himself traveled widely through the West, where the denomination also maintained "circuit riders" and "local preachers."[287]

Though there were comparatively few Catholics in Kentucky, Bardstown had a resident priest by 1787 and built its first Catholic church in 1790. Many pioneers, however, remained aloof from any faith, whether because of hostility to traditional theology, preoccupation with practical problems, or remoteness from religious services. Some of the Kentucky "gentry" had been affected by Virginia liberalism of the Jeffersonian type and others were "infidels" of a less intellectual sort. By contrast, church members were commonly "fundamentalists."

The frontier attracted a certain number of educated persons. Humphrey Marshall, a pioneer settler, became the earliest formal historian of Kentucky, and Isaac Shelby, its first governor, had a fair schooling and serious intellectual interests. Among the "Franklin" leaders one was a Princeton graduate, another had studied at Liberty Hall and a third at a Presbyterian academy in North Carolina. A list of 113 petitioners from eastern Tennessee to the North Carolina legislature included only two who had to use marks for their signatures.[288]

Local provisions for education varied. Vermont on the northern frontier named a legislative committee in 1789 to prepare plans for a college, and two years later the University of Vermont was established at Burlington, with Ira Allen as one of its chief promoters. In western Pennsylvania, Thaddeus Dod, a young Presbyterian minister, opened in 1782 what has been called "the first classical school west of the Alleghanies." Seven years later he was made principal of an academy which eventually became Washington College. In 1787 the legislature granted $5,000 to endow an academy at Pittsburgh.[289]

Western journalism began with the *Pittsburgh Gazette,* founded by John Scull and Joseph Hall in 1786. To its first issue Hugh H. Brackenridge, then a local lawyer, contributed an idealized picture of the infant community. The second newspaper was the *Kentucke Gazette* at Lexington. In his opening announcement (1787) the editor, John Bradford, promised to deal not only with Western topics but with world affairs and "all the Republic of letters." Bradford also issued the *Kentucke Almanac* (1788) and *Kentucke Miscellany,* the first book printed in the district.[290]

As interest in the unfolding West developed, national feeling in the country as a whole seemed to gain ground. The common experience of having fought for independence was an important factor. When Franklin returned to Philadelphia in 1786, he noted the general rejoicing on the anniversary of the day when he and his associates had "hazarded Lives and Fortunes." In New York that year the city and state governments, Congress, and the Society of the Cincinnati joined in commemorating the occasion, with bells ringing and the thunder of cannon. At a dinner given by the Cincinnati one of the customary thirteen toasts was: "May the powers of Congress be adequate to preserve the General Union." Two years later in far-off Kentucky the celebration reflected patriotism not unmixed with doubts. One toast was: "The Western World—perpetual union, on principles of equality, or amicable separation"; but the last word was more hopeful: "The Commonwealth of Kentucke, the fourteenth luminary in the

American Constellation, may she reflect upon the original States the wisdom she has borrowed from them."[291]

By the time the Confederation gave way to the "more perfect union" of the new Constitution, Americans had gone far in their detachment from old-world dominance. Independent politically, they had progressed in economic self-sufficiency and had done something to apply republican ideals to social reconstruction. A further pull away from Europe resulted from the westward movement and the new problems and vistas that it opened. Yet the ocean which separated the people from their ancestral homes remained an area where their interests and those of Europe inevitably met, in conflict or in mutually profitable exchanges. Even on the frontier, men had to take account of British and Spanish policies, while on the seaboard, escape from the Old World was still less possible. Americans needed foreign markets and looked abroad as well for much that seemed essential to comfortable living. English social conventions influenced the "best people" and scientific advance depended largely on the flow of ideas from Europe. In spite of political independence and the westward extension of their horizon the most respected citizens of the young republic still lived in an Atlantic, rather than a strictly American, world.

Something of this dualism of European tradition and ideas based on American experience appeared in the Constitution of 1787 as that document was rounded out by the first ten amendments. The distribution of functions among legislative, executive, and judicial branches of the government was not a native invention, but followed roughly the British system as interpreted by its French admirer, Montesquieu. The independence of the judiciary, a cardinal maxim of British policy since the Revolution of 1688, figured importantly in the American Constitution, though the precise method of securing it differed somewhat. The idea of a bicameral legislature formed another part of the European inheritance, while the provisions for the protection of parliamentary privilege likewise stemmed from British precedent. So also did the bill of rights and related clauses of the original Constitution, which reasserted doctrines familiar to seventeenth-century Englishmen: security for personal liberty through jury trial, due process of law, and the writ of habeas corpus; the prohibition of excessive bail or cruel and unusual punishments; and the right to petition for relief of grievances.

Though much of the governmental fabric rested on old-world principles and practices, the total result was quite unlike anything to be found in Europe. There had been earlier federations of a sort, from those of ancient Greece to the unions of Swiss cantons and Dutch provinces, but the American Union, with its skillful division of powers between national and state authorities, was unique. Though elective monarchies were not unknown, nothing in Europe resembled the American president, entrusted with large powers but chosen for a limited term. Partly because of the requirements of the federal system, Congress, unlike Parliament, was not given unlimited sovereignty. Whereas the English bill of rights was directed only against abuse of royal authority, the corresponding American provisions aimed to protect the individual against usurpations by the legislative branch. Among other distinctive products of native experience in the Constitution was the prohibition of religious tests, of any "establishment of religion," and of any interference with its free exercise.

In the field of literature a work of art, say a play of Shakespeare, may have borrowed freely from earlier writers and yet be accepted as essentially a new creation. If the same principle be applied to politics, Gladstone's much criticized characterization of the Constitution as the most wonderful work ever struck off at a given time by the brain and purpose of man is not so unreasonable as it has been made to appear.

The new Constitution reflected in many of its provisions the social conditions of the time in which it was written. So far as it dealt with economic matters, it was undeniably influenced by vigorous capitalist groups, formed in part during the war and matured during the years of peace. Interested in promoting internal improvements, the exploitation of Western lands, industrial projects, the organization of investment capital through banks, and the merchandising of public securities, the "big business" of that day wanted a strong central authority for protection and active assistance. In particular, these groups now secured federal regulation of interstate and foreign commerce, together with safeguards against excessive paper-money issues and measures impairing contract obligations. Distrust of the moneyed interests undoubtedly prompted much of the rural opposition to the Constitution.

Yet the conflict over the adoption of the Constitution may easily be misunderstood if considered simply as an alignment between capitalist promoters and democratic agrarians, between conservatives and radicals. If the new system represented a retreat from the equalitarian aspirations of 1776, particularism and the defense of local interests did not always imply strictly democratic principles. On the other hand, the makers and champions of the Constitution were, by and large, the men of wider experience and consequently broader horizons. For some this larger experience had come through legislative and administrative service in the Confederation; for others, through association in the army or in business enterprises with persons from different parts of the Union. Similarly, the more important men who served the Confederation abroad—Franklin, Adams, Jay, and Jefferson—all shared, though in differing degrees, a national point of view.

Important, too, as a factor making possible the "more perfect union" was the gradual development, from pre-Revolutionary years through wartime and postwar experiences, of ideas and emotions associated with what may be called Americanism. It was a state of mind shared by men of divergent local interests and traditions. It was, therefore, a powerful unifying influence, preparing the way for a genuinely national outlook. There is no need here to discuss the nationalist and states rights' theories as to the nature of the Constitution. On that issue, now more academic than practical, men differed then as well as in later years. It is perhaps safest to conclude with Madison that the Philadelphia plan was, "in strictness, neither a national nor a federal Constitution, but a composition of both." [292]

BOOK V

The Completion of

Independence,

1790–1830

REPUBLICAN ARISTOCRATS

THOUGH THE EUROPEAN ARISTOCRATIC TRADITION in American life had been weakened by the philosophy of the Revolution, the rapid accumulation of wealth and the institution of a more vigorous federal government were factors strengthening it again. The state and national constitutions had proclaimed that all men were equal before the law, but not necessarily in political privilege. Whether the new nation should favor or forbid a social stratification was as yet quite undecided.

When it is remembered that in every other country throughout Christendom certain families enjoyed the distinction of honorific titles, it is not surprising that their American counterparts in the reorganized society of 1790 felt a secret envy. But American custom had long opposed such marks of privilege, and most of the constitutions explicitly forbade titles of nobility. The European tradition of aristocracy managed to persist in America, but it was challenged by 1800 and deposed, at least politically, by 1830.[1] Hereditary privilege and the engrossment of opportunity proved impossible in a country where every ambitious man had so many chances to begin life anew. Sometimes it was the lure of a Western farm, more often the possibilities of a new business, that prevented free Americans from falling into a permanently unprivileged class. Foreign visitors who said that money alone counted in the United States spoke with some exaggeration, but money did mature into prestige faster here than in most places.

Rank and birth, as assets, could not be carried to a poorer market than America.[2]

In the cities there were no well-marked "quarters." Usually shopkeepers and even many wealthy wholesalers lived over their stores or behind them, and most professional men received their clients in their homes.[3] Nevertheless, there were some mansions belonging to those generally admitted to be "the quality." From their windows on winter evenings streamed the light of many candles and the sound of flute and violin, and gaily painted carriages, with liveried coachmen, clattered over the cobbles to their doors.

At the top of the social scale were the well-to-do merchant-shipping families, especially those who had taken the right side during the Revolution, together with their lawyers, and at a little economic (and therefore social) distance, their physicians. Next came the rich newcomers who had moved in from the country during the war or afterward, a class of great importance in Boston—the Prescotts, Lees, Cabots, Lowells, and others—who, it was said, had bought the property of exiled Tories at bargain prices.[4] Then followed the self-made businessmen, whose rise from humbler circumstances the community could still remember.

Many of these families had broad-lawned suburban houses for the hot months, especially on Manhattan Island and beside the Schuylkill, which without achieving a baronial dignity compared well with the lesser manor houses of the old country. But by the first years of the nineteenth century such families were discovering the watering place as a summer resort. In 1789, Saratoga Springs consisted of three log cabins hidden in a wilderness; then a dissertation published by a New York doctor in 1793 began the widespread advertisement of the virtues of the waters, and soon a number of hotels were built.[5] By 1809, we are assured, "invalids of fashion and opulence" could find at nearby Ballston every luxury they desired.[6] Originally a resort of the stricken, it had developed facilities for recreation and become a center of elegant leisure. In the phrase of Washington Irving's *Salmagundi Papers,* Southern ladies arrived, each with the annual produce of a rice plantation in her costume, and encountered an occasional competitor from Salem wrapped in the net proceeds of a cargo of whale oil.[7]

Though other springs in the state came into vogue,[8] they were soon rivaled by those in Virginia. Berkeley Springs could show the airs and graces of fashion as well as cure neuralgia, while the White Sulphur Springs were described in 1817 as a backwoods therapeutic resort as yet without a drawing room. Far to the west at Olympia, "the Bath of Kentucky," cards, billiards, and horses supplemented the attractions of the waters.[9] As early as 1790, valetudinarians from the Southern states and the West Indies were being solicited to summer at Rockaway, where sea bathing might cleanse and brace the body against debility. The watering place was the first theater of conspicuous leisure in America.[10] In a land where work was generally praised, idleness could be justified only by the affectation of ill health.

The snobbishness of the fashionable circles in the cities was doubtless a little cruel, though it pales beside the real thing as portrayed by Thackeray. At the Philadelphia dinner parties of the dazzling Mrs. William Bingham one might hear oaths and stories of a more or less delicate naughtiness, echoing the banter of modish tables in Mayfair or in the old Faubourg St. Germain. A Bostonian like H. G. Otis, or a French puritan like Brissot de Warville, might be startled by the generous revelation of the female form in the salons of New York and Philadelphia. But these coteries were useful in conserving the arts of deportment which otherwise might easily have been forgotten.[11] They and their imitators studied Lord Chesterfield, whose writings had been reprinted in America several times before 1790 and formed the central canon of etiquette for more than half a century. Though the polished meanness of the noble earl was plentifully satirized, it was a matter of personal interest to many Americans to learn that eating principally with a knife, using a fork to pick one's teeth, and raking the mouth with a finger, were to be deprecated.[12]

In some particulars, standards of polite behavior differed from those in England, notably in the use of tobacco. "No gentleman in Europe ever smokes except by way of a frolic," the reader was told. William Pinkney, sent across in 1800 on a diplomatic mission, had to puff his cigars furtively behind the closed doors of his London apartment so as not to prejudice his reputation.[13] The Spanish cigar, introduced into the United States shortly before 1790, gained vogue rapidly despite warnings from some physicians. About fifteen years later Americans were annually importing $140,000 worth.[14] No one lost caste, even in the cities, by the public chewing of tobacco, though a writer on *Clerical Manners* questioned the propriety of spitting in church.[15] With cigars, after the ladies had left the dinner table, came the best port, madeira, and brandy the host could furnish. Almost no American at the end of the eighteenth century scrupled a moderate amount of good liquor, even among the "middle class."[16]

The gentleman of 1790 could still evidence his status by his dress. In all the coastal towns he followed the same fashions, imported like his manners. Traveling Frenchmen recognized the Paris modes of two years back slightly modified by a year's sojourn in London.[17] For design the well-dressed found mere pictures insufficient and had dolls sent across to display the latest conceits.[18] People bought imported clothes partly under the impression that goods worth sending 3,000 miles were probably better than home products, and partly because they actually saw superiorities in articles fashioned in the European tradition of highly specialized skill; but to a large degree, especially with respect to style, their purchases reflected mere colonialism. "Many *hats*," said Professor Adam Seybert in 1809, "are annually fabricated in the United States, and *labelled* as of English manufacture, which would not be worn if this harmless deception were not practised. . . ."[19] Such deference aroused the boundless scorn of nationalists like Noah Webster, who wanted to complete our independence.[20]

Though American gentlemen had far less exemption from labor than those whose styles they imitated, they too paraded color as a badge of class. Scarlet coats lined the aisles of the Brattle Street Church in Boston as well as the theater boxes in New York. It was a day when gentlemen, if occasion suited, let themselves into their white, close-fitting doeskin breeches by stepping from a little platform to which the fragile articles were attached by hooks.[21] Swords had disappeared from civil dress but sword canes were popular with the buckish,[22] a transition to the more peaceful walking stick that still advertises the hand without employment. Wigs were giving way except among the clergy, but the gentleman wore his hair long, even if not powdered, and tied it in a queue. Of the fifty-six members of the New York legislature in 1798, all but five were so depicted.[23] That this style was expensive—a hairdresser in Philadelphia cost twenty-two shillings a month[24]—made some cherish it the longer as evidence of their social standing.

Suddenly all this was challenged. Startled into fear by the rise of the workers, the Paris beau monde disguised itself in workmen's pantaloons by way of protective coloring. The new fashion spread, partly by the authority of the place of its origin and partly because it symbolized an equalitarian tendency which was to be widely accepted, with acclaim or with resignation. When the government lists in 1804 revealed that two patents had been granted for galluses to hold up trousers, another step in the history of democracy was registered.[25] Irreconcilable old gentlemen refused to give up the traditional costume even in the thirties, but James Monroe was the last president to wear smallclothes, silk stockings, silver buckles, and a queue.[26]

Women's fashions underwent a like reaction toward simplicity, a reflection of the Romantic movement. The mountainous headdress reared on wire cage and cushions and harnessed together with streamers now gave way as girls clipped their tresses almost to the scalp, heavily pomading the short ends about the face. "At the assembly," wrote a miss of 1798, "I was quite ashamed of my head, for nobody has long hair."[27] New light muslin dresses cut low and sleeveless and draping naturally over the figure aroused criticism as being ridiculous imitations unsuited to winter weather; the consequent exposure to the night air was certain to lead to consumption. A poet admonished the wearers:

Full many a beauty blasted in her bloom,
This stripping mania hurries to the tomb . . .[28]

Moreover, they were shrouded from head to foot in combustibles, a disadvantage in those days of open hearths and candles.[29] Something, though not much, was also said about immodesty.

The new style also had its enthusiastic advocates, who rejoiced to see the old whalebones and heavy petticoats yield to simpler garments, whereby the muscles had free play and beauty could be "ascertained by the unequivocal testimonies of symmetry and nature."[30] But a fashion never survives simply because it is hygienic, cheap, comfortable, or graceful. The conservatives who sighed for the return of silks and stuffs were to see them all again with the passing of a few more years. By the middle of the second decade of the nineteenth century the style was veering back. Soon the doctors were again inveighing against stays, busks, and stomach boards, and a new generation of conservatives spoke pensively of the good old days of muslin.[31]

Perfection in the amenities of urbane society requires study and, by implication, models. Suddenly in the early 1790s the explosions in revolutionary Europe threw the most perfect patterns into American coastal towns. If in times past refugees had fled to escape the exactions of an aristocracy, now came aristocrats fleeing the fury of the mob. The rebellion in Santo Domingo, begun in 1791 by blacks in the interest of liberty, fraternity, and equality, sent thousands of French colonists to American shores. Probably Baltimore was affected most by the coming of 1,500 in a single month, notwithstanding the larger numbers of French who later landed at New York and Philadelphia. Accustomed to luxury and refinement, many of them arrived with scarcely more than the clothes they wore and a meager English word or two to ask for shelter. Hospitality was more severely tested by the shiploads of French royalists who a few years later saved their lives but not their property by emigrating from a homeland enveloped in the Terror. The total number has been estimated all the way from 10,000 to 25,000.[32]

Some gained a livelihood by teaching their culture to any who could pay, instructing in the arts of dancing, music, and French conversation. But much of the French influence was less direct, though not less effective.[33] The nine or ten French newspapers maintained for the émigrés doubtless found some native readers who desired to increase acquaintance with the language.[34] French books were to be had more easily at such establishments as that set up by Moreau de Saint-Méry.[35] The exiles sponsored numerous concerts and the first rendering of opera in a foreign language.[36] Certain merchants, like Stephen Jumel, made fortunes by importing French merchandise, mostly articles of luxury, such as wines, fine fabrics, jewelry, gold watches, and gilt frames for mirrors and pictures.[37] With the refugees also came French cooks. These had been known before, but never a great artist like Brillat-Savarin, who later recorded his American experiences in his *Physiologie du Goût.* Vegetables began to find a larger place on American menus, some, like artichokes and okra, appearing for the first time; yeast commenced to supplant the old dough-leaven previously in general use; and confectioners and caterers wrought miracles in pastry, ices, and blancmange. The word "restaurant" was naturalized. By the early thirties a competent observer could say that "American cookery has somewhat engrafted the French upon the English."[38]

The French Revolution accounted, too, for another group of immigrants, who though small in number were not without influence. Irish nationalist leaders, desperate in discouragement, had emigrated from time to time to the French West Indies or to France itself. But French soil was none too safe when the Terror triumphed, and these "wild geese" now took their flight to the American continent, especially to the Southern towns. The failure of the United Irishmen's final stroke started many more, one ship landing at Norfolk in 1798 with over 400 such passengers, mostly persons of property. Some, like the leading French refugees, returned home when political skies cleared, but others stayed to win high places in their professions.[39] Like the French, too, as a whole they added prestige to the Catholic Church. Unlike them, the Irish found an important function as interpreters between their peasant compatriots, who soon began to arrive in great numbers, and the older Americans.

European émigrés and travelers were surprised to see how generally respectable in the United States was ordinary labor: for example, how many cultivated women did their own work. Americans took pride in the fact. "No country of the same wealth, intelligence and civilization," remarked Tench Coxe, the economist, "has so few *menial* servants (strictly speaking) in the families of persons of the greatest property." This was a result, at least in part, of the dearth of available servants. The competition in America was not for the place, but for the service.[40] It was to meet this condition that the early settlers had introduced black slavery. This, of course, remained the dominant labor system of the South, but it was disappearing elsewhere.

Only one out of fourteen slaves, according to the first census, was held north of Maryland and Delaware. Vermont, Massachusetts, and New Hampshire had forbidden slavery in their constitutions and one by one other Northern states followed with laws for gradual freedom.[41] The institution had been strongest in New York, but there, as elsewhere in the North, the movement for emancipation aroused little controversy and was largely carried through by the slave owners themselves or those connected with them. Most of the blacks, especially the older ones, remained in the households of their former masters, following the family to church and celebrating their old "Pinkster" holiday after the final date of 1827 just as before, hardly conscious that their legal status had changed. In New Jersey the process was likewise slow and peaceful, a few remaining in bondage until after 1860.[42] Pennsylvania was called the paradise of the blacks.[43] Except for an occasional outbreak, such as that at York in 1793, the relations were certainly as friendly as in the states to the east, and the blacks for the most part continued in domestic service.[44]

Older even than slavery as an American means of regimenting labor was the system of indenturing immigrants. This, too, was rapidly passing, but by force of circumstances rather than by law. The reduction of immigration was partly responsible. The Revolutionary philosophy, too, had done its work and made the unfree white man seem an anomaly. The system lingered longest in Pennsylvania, but there the last act to govern such contracts was passed in 1818 and no trace of the practice has been found after 1831. The system had disappeared in Maryland and New Jersey a little before.[45]

Another source of household labor, though in no great quantity, was the bound apprentice, whose origins date back to the days of Queen Elizabeth.

Street Scene, Philadelphia

In the Southern states, where slavery tended to suggest protection for the white, it was usually required that a pauper child apprenticed by the authorities to a master must be taught a trade, but in the North a provision for "other useful employment" legally made a household drudge out of an orphan girl throughout most of the nineteenth century.[46] Philanthropic women, especially in New England, organized "female asylums," where orphans dressed in neat blue uniforms were schooled up to the age of ten, after which they were bound out to pious families for a period of eight years.[47] But the pretentious homes in the Northern towns depended for the most part on free servants, black or, more generally, white.

Large establishments maintained rather imposing retinues. When Washington set up as president in New York he had eighteen house servants, seven of them slaves and the others white. Five of the latter received $7 a month each, besides liveries costing $29 each; three women were content with $5; a housekeeper with eight, a valet with thirteen and a half, and a steward with twenty-five. Jefferson, living more simply as secretary of state in Philadelphia, had six menials.[48] The president's wage scale was about normal, though in New England, where the willing hands of spinster aunts and daughters reduced the need for domestics, a dollar a week was usually considered sufficient.[49] But the servant was coming to demand something besides money—a distinctly higher social status than his class had enjoyed before.

With the passing of the indenture the social chasm narrowed. The first stage in the history of domestic service had closed and the second, a democratic period, opened, to be followed in the fifties by a third, when with new immigration the advent of large numbers of servants speaking English with difficulty, if at all, somewhat restored the distance familiar in the eighteenth century. But the phenomenon of the contented intelligent servant, so constantly encountered in the Old World, was rare indeed. English menials who crossed the sea were lonesome for like-minded company. Few American women and fewer men studied to perfect themselves in domestic service as a permanent calling, because, in contrast with England, there were openings to so many other occupations which led one higher.

The housewife finding help hard to get, and being unable as yet to bring home a dinner half-prepared from the shops, succumbed more and more to the seductions of the boardinghouse. There were said to be 330 such establishments in New York in 1789.[50] The boardinghouse developed into the residence hotel, though in later times a reaction occurred, wholesome as far as it went, to the small housekeeping flat where maids were scarcely needed or, as was the case with larger apartments, cut to a minimum.[51] It may be hazarded that with all the increase in wealth since 1800, the proportion of American families employing domestic service was as great then as it is today.

COUNTRY LIFE

IN THE EARLY DAYS of the republic at least nine Americans out of ten, even in "commercial" New England, dug their living from the land. Self-esteem, if nothing else, led them to glorify country life as the noblest state of man. "Those who labor in the earth," said Jefferson, "are the chosen people of God. . . . They are the most vigorous, the most independent, the most valuable citizens."[52] Rural simplicity and manly self-respect were contrasted with the cunning found in towns, where traders filled their pockets by overreaching other people—sentiments reminiscent of a passage from Plato or Vergil.[53] One may smile who has noted among farmers no deep disgust for an unearned dollar when it chanced to come their way, but there was a core of truth in this praise of American husbandry. When land was parceled out to a great number of independent proprietors enjoying low taxes without ecclesiastical encumbrance or feudal imposition, the average farmer had a sense of liberty and opportunity which most European tillers of the soil might well have envied.[54]

The typical Northern farm comprised from 100 to 200 acres, seemingly a great deal for one family's care in a day of hand tools; but only a small part was planted at one time. On a 100-acre farm in eastern Massachusetts but half-a-dozen acres would be in crops, a little more in meadows, plowed at infrequent intervals, and about the same amount in permanent pasture. The rest, if cleared, usually lay fallow until such time as sheer exhaustion of the tilled soil forced the transfer of crops to these fields, which were supposed to have regained their fertility during the period of idleness or, rather, their devotion to weeds and brush. But generally this remainder was only partly cleared and served as woodland range for swine and cattle. The price of fair farm land, except near cities, averaged between $10 and $15 an acre, figures which seem surprisingly high. Many an Eastern farm must have sold in 1800 at a higher price than it did, with better buildings, in 1900.[55]

On good land as well as bad the farmer's methods were primitive and, by English standards, scandalously wasteful. To the modern scientific age it seems that he practiced agricide, not agriculture. He knew little of the rotation of crops and would have been astonished to learn that certain plants would return to the soil values that others had extracted.[56] Maize was the mainstay of New England—"nearly as valuable to this country," said Timothy Dwight, "as all other kinds of corn united."[57] Wheat was failing in that region, partly because of the blight of parasites harbored in barberry bushes. At the end of the eighteenth century wheat lingered only in the western hills and in Vermont, and white bread largely disappeared from the Yankee's table, giving place to "rye and Injun," a bread made from rye flour and maize meal.

Tillage was chiefly by the strain and sweat of human limbs. The disgusted Richard Parkinson warned any English farmer who might plan to migrate to America that he would have to learn a new trade: "He will have to chop up trees, and cultivate the land by the hoe and pick-axe, instead of the plough and harrows."[58] But plows and harrows were available, such as they were. The common Carey plow was made entirely of wood save for an iron colter to cut the sod and oftentimes a sheathing of odd fragments of saw-plate, tin, or iron sheets. With such an implement an acre was a good day's work. Strong arms were needed to hold it in the ground and twice the modern pulling power was required.[59] Oxen were the favored work animals, for over rough slopes, among the stumps and stones, or in the half-drained swales, the ox alone could hold his footing, and his steady, patient pull was worth infinitely more than the fitful spurts of the less stolid horse. Besides, he could live on grass without grain and stand almost any exposure; and when he closed his service at about the age of ten he furnished beef and boot leather. As the land was smoothed during the early decades of the nineteenth century and harder roads lamed the cattle, horses superseded them in many sections.[60]

The other tools were few. It is said that at the beginning of the nine-teenth century a strong farmer could have carried them all on his shoulder except for his spike-tooth harrow, sledge, and two-wheeled oxcart. Gener-ally he dug with an iron-plated shovel, though, if the metal were more plentiful, he pounded out his spades and two-tined forks upon his own anvil, or had them made at a blacksmith shop.[61] The farmer sowing his seed in the spring gauged his area by what he could cut in the late summer days by the back-breaking labor of the sickle, but a new contrivance was making its appearance, the cradle, with its long scythe blade paralleled by a rack of wooden fingers. Swinging this with strength and skill, the harvester might reap three quarters of an acre in a day. About Thanksgiving time he beat the grain from the straw with his flail upon the barn floor and then held it in a half-moon basket for the wind to drive away the chaff. Ground at the neighborhood mill beside the waterfall, it filled his larder or, binned in his stilted granary, awaited the needs of the cattle — or the rats.[62]

The farmer's livestock in 1800 were lean and rangy, partly by degenera-tion that followed neglect and partly as a result of adaptation to environ-ment. The old "black cattle," compounded by chance out of all sorts of importations, now showed so many colors as to make the old name inap-propriate. "The scimitar-ribbed, flat-sided lubberly big-legged cattle," cried one disgusted farmer, "what are they other than expensive masses of unim-portant bone!"[63] The average farm in eastern Massachusetts could show one or two horses, one or two yoke of oxen, fifteen head of cattle including five dairy cows, and about as many swine, while half the farms had flocks of from ten to twenty sheep.[64] When butchering season came in early winter, there was fresh meat for a few weeks, but most of it had to be cured for future use, smoked, dried, or pickled in the brine barrels which lined every cellar. Sheep were raised for wool, though the longest staple was scarce seven inches, as compared with English records of three times that length. As the farms in the Northern states matured, better barns brought better stock. The natural grasses, which grew lush on the bottom lands, were now less valued, and the "artificial" timothy and clover began to cram the mows for winter feeding.

In the milder climates to the southward intelligent men deplored the custom of letting cattle run and feeding them from stacks in the fields. Wide-ranging cattle were often at the mercy of the forest beasts, and farmers even in the older regions had to keep alert to drive off wolf, lynx, wildcat, and bear.[65] Swine became as fleet as the woodland enemies they eluded; often the owner needed his gun to capture them.

Englishmen traveling in the United States missed the hedgerows that so pleasantly striped their native countryside. Americans often marked the bounds of their fields with stumps, laboriously pulled by ox chain and forming a grotesque *chevaux-de-frise* no animal would care to hazard. In New England and New York stones for walls were all too plentiful, and wood was at hand everywhere in the East. Chestnut or cedar rails were split for fences that were "horse-high, bull-proof and pig-tight," whether zigzagged or more thriftily set into posts.[66]

The systematic application of manure to the soil was rare. Where the cattle roamed wood pastures through the year it was impossible, but even in the North, where they were stabled, the accumulations of the barnyard were oftentimes considered as a nuisance, not an asset. Even after the Civil War a Kentuckian could write that in his youth he never knew of dung being put on land. Along the shores of New England and Long Island menhaden, or whitefish, were spread on the fields, to the olfactory distress of passersby.[67]

The farm was a family unit. Extra hands at from fifteen to eighteen guineas a year, as Dr. Benjamin Rush estimated wages, or at from $6 to $12 a month, as others testified, were beyond the reach of the average husbandman, though he might finance a man or two in harvest at fifty cents a day or an expert cradler at twice that sum.[68] The hired man, where he could be obtained, was generally a youngster waiting his chance to conquer Nature for himself, or a deficient man whom Nature had conquered at the start. With labor difficult to hire, the farmer and his sons tilled and reaped for the most part unaided and, except among the Germans and the Scotch-Irish, called upon the womenfolk for hard field work only in a desperate emergency.[69] In these circumstances it was unfair to compare the agriculture of the New World with that of the Old, where a Yorkshire yeoman, for example, would employ eight or ten laborers on his 150 acres and spread 800 or 900 loads of manure.[70] "Though in America less grain is produced per acre than in England," wrote Dr. Cooper for English readers, "they get more per man. There, land is plentiful and labour scarce. With you, it is the reverse. Hence the accuracy of British, and the carelessness of American cultivation."[71] In farming "carelessly" perhaps the American was farming wisely.

Though the work of the fields and barns absorbed the farmer's energies for much of the year, it was not his sole concern. His happiness often depended upon how he solved the problem of housing. Many of the rural folk along the coastal plain, it is true, had inherited colonial homes, but even for these the early years of the republic were a time of reconstruction. With the passing of the older frontier, primitive log cabins were being abandoned to the pigs and substantial frame houses were rising in front of them. Generally the farmer got out his own lumber from the wood lots, hewed the beams with a bent-handled broadax, and even sawed the boards, though this was less necessary now that makeshift sawmills had been set up on every Eastern river. With the help of neighbors, summoned to his meat and drink, he joined and raised the frame. Then, when the boarding was finished, the simple hardware was attached, all made to order at the blacksmith's shop, and the glass was set in that he had secured for produce at the village store. Homemade shingles had been shaved at the rate of almost 1,000 a day. Thanks to Jacob Perkins's invention of his nail-making machine, nails were no longer rare and costly as they had been when hammered out on small anvils. In 1790 an establishment to make nails was set up at Taunton, Massachusetts.[72]

Nearness to the soil and to domestic stock gave that generation the abundant food which unlimited families and hard outdoor work demanded.[73] "Settin' a good table" meant loading it with plenty, if not variety. Breakfast included boiled fish, beefsteak, ham, and sausages. Count Volney, a dyspeptic Frenchman, writhed under the effects of "hot bread, half baked, soaked in melted butter with the grossest cheese, and salt or hung beef, pickled pork or fish." Many European visitors rebelled at the prevalence of pork and grease. Physicians added their warning that Americans ate too much meat and too little of vegetables.[74] Dinner and supper were merely elaborations of breakfast. Even the farmer's fare was coarse and dull, especially "out of season," and generally ill cooked and ill served.[75] All foreigners observed that Americans ate too rapidly and swallowed almost without attempt at mastication.

For persons who liked vegetables the "sarse patches" furnished most of those we know today except the tomato.[76] Cauliflower, head lettuce, eggplant or "vegetable eggs," salsify, and rhubarb were, however, rare.[77] Cookbook references to such European delicacies as borage, broccoli, and sweet basil merely evidence too slavish copying from foreign sources.[78] Though oranges and lemons had long been known, they were scarcely cheap enough for common folk till after 1832, when Sicilian cargoes were first shipped direct. Pineapples had come in with the expanding commerce since the Revolution and by 1804 bananas were known to a few. These were regarded as dainties to grace a banquet table or to serve as presents of affection, as when friends brought such viands to Aaron Burr awaiting his trial for treason at Richmond.[79] Country people contented themselves with peaches, pears, plums, and berries, usually dried or preserved with sugar, and apples which kept most successfully and furnished the ubiquitous cider. Raisins, prunes, and dried currants had been known at least since 1762. Spices were enumerated in the cookbooks, but most farm women relied, perforce, on garden thyme, summer savory, and sweet marjoram.

Not only in shelter and food, but also in family clothing, the old farmstead had to be largely self-sufficing. In 1791, Hamilton complacently surveyed a "vast scene of household manufacturing" and computed that through it "two-thirds, three-fourths, and even four-fifths of all the clothing of the inhabitants are made by themselves." Twenty years later his great successor in the treasury Albert Gallatin made nearly as generous an estimate.[80] According to his figures, every person in the Union, countrymen as well as townsfolk, averaged $6 worth of cloth or other household goods, Rhode Island leading with $11.70 and New Hampshire, Georgia, and Connecticut showing more than $8.50 each.

Woolens and linens were the chief concern. "The sheep being washed and sheared, the wool must first be picked by hand, and this was generally done by the family in the evening; then it must be . . . broke, as they called it, and afterwards carded into rolls by hand, when it was fit for spinning."[81] The preparation of flax, more laborious than that of wool, was a responsibility of the men and older boys, who with flax brake and swingling knife separated the fibers from the woody portions. The matted fibers were then combed by the women with a spiked instrument called the hatchel, just as bunches of wool were drawn over a wire-studded block in carding. Spinning either flax or wool, being a relatively simple process, often fell to the older girls in the family, some of whom became so proficient as to secure employment as "spinning girls" in the neigborhood.

In Northern farmhouses at the beginning of the nineteenth century the hand loom was less in evidence than the spinning wheel. It was a time of transition even in communities somewhat distant from the centers of trade. If the fabrication of hats had already become a shop industry, the weaving of cloth and the making of shoes were entering the domestic stage, with the craftsmen either working in their own homes or more frequently going from house to house.[82] Whether she wore her own cloth or hired an itinerant artisan, the farmer's wife was generally ingenious in securing variety. Besides the better grades of woolens and linens and the coarser tow cloth, she contrived mixtures of wool and flax, known as linsey-woolsey, then popular on Northern farms and in frontier communities. Fustian was a mixture of cotton and flax, used chiefly in the South, while jeans, containing wool and cotton, figured prominently in men's clothing.[83]

The finishing of the cloth must have taxed the patience and skill of the womenfolk. In order to give their linen a satisfactory whiteness, they soaked the yarn in warm water for three or four days, changing it frequently and rinsing in cold water; then they treated it with ashes or slaked lime and hot water. They next spread the woven fabric on the grass and sprinkled it hour after hour for several days. Thirty or forty bleachings were not uncommon. With woolens the process was less tedious, but strength was required to pound out the product of the hand loom after it had been shrunk in warm water containing strong soap or fuller's earth. Native barks—hickory, walnut, and oak—berries, and nuts usually supplied the dyes.[84] No housewife, however, turned away the indigo peddler, for his commodity more than any other colored the dye pot in its customary place by the kitchen fire. Mixed with native stains, it produced attractive shadings of blue when handled by those expert in its use.

The long and laborious manufacture of textiles was for the farmer's wife and daughters but an additional task in the perennial round of cooking, washing, sewing, and cleaning. These other duties required similar skills. Light, for example, meant more than the cheerful glow from the fireplace. If one wished to read after dark, there must be blazing hemlock knots, or tow-wicked candles molded of bayberry, tallow, or beeswax. Soap was made by combining lye from leached ashes with grease carefully saved for that purpose. Autumn brought the drying of fruits and vegetables against the long weeks of winter, and the butchering season was another busy time in the kitchen. So it was also in the spring, when the sap first began to run in the maples and preparations were made for the sugaring. In 1791 forty families in Oneida County, New York, made 13,000 pounds of sugar, while a few years later eighty families in the town of Cavendish, Vermont, produced 80,000 pounds. It was estimated that the average Vermont household at the end of the century turned out 250 pounds. Tench Coxe reported that in the better sections of the maple country, particularly northern New England and northern New York, it was possible for husband, wife, and a ten-year-old child to make 1,000 pounds on a 100-acre farm.[85]

The Northern farmer at the beginning of the nineteenth century was less self-sufficient than he had been fifty years earlier. He might still be a Jack-of-all-trades, but there was less reason for his being so. Perhaps his experienced eye still picked out the straightest hickory, ash, and white oak to be saved from the capacious maw of the kitchen chimney so that he might deftly fashion cart tongues, oxbows, plow handles, ax helves, and hoes. The heavy work with wood, however, was generally done at a nearby sawmill, and the services of an itinerant carpenter, with some pretension to the name of cabinetmaker, were often available. Hides from the family's cattle supplied numerous needs, but there were experts to do the tanning and to fabricate shoes and boots from the leather. Visits of traveling artisans, now becoming more frequent, brought the skill of the tailor, the weaver, the butcher, and the chandler to lighten household burdens. The extent to which the farmer could rely upon such itinerant craftsmen was measured by the quantity of desirable commodities he could offer in exchange, or by his ability to secure cash in some market center for his small surpluses of grain, meat, and wood.[86]

To the plain folk of the soil the passing seasons brought occasional opportunities to break the laborious cycle of the farm. Rural life in New England and certain sections of New York and New Jersey centered in the village, with its meetinghouse, tavern, and town hall, each of which offered facilities for recreation. In such communities there was no isolation comparable to that of the frontiersmen on the slopes of the Alleghenies and in the Mississippi Valley. One could attend Sunday church services, midweek lectures, or the protracted meetings when some visiting preacher strove to breathe new zeal into a dispirited congregation. There was also the local tavern with its convivial cheer. "Dancing," wrote Jedidiah Morse in an early edition of his famous *Geography,* "is the principal and favourite amusement in New England; and of this the young people of both sexes are extremely fond."[87] But the older generation looked reprovingly upon youth who were drawn too often to public balls.

The farmer still found much of his recreation in close association with his work. "Bees" were organized on the slightest provocation—to get out a supply of logs for future building, to clear a field of stumps, to raise a barn in record time—and the toil was enlivened by gaiety, sometimes spontaneous, more often induced through generous quantities of rum or whiskey. Such gatherings usually culminated in a square dance under the enthusiastic direction of the local fiddler. Many a house "sprung up at the wagging of the fiddle-sticks, as the walls of Thebes sprang up of yore to the sound of the lyre."[88] For the womenfolk there were spinning and quilting bees, the social value of which fluctuated with the conversation, liberally spiced with unpremeditated gossip. But the most popular festivity came when the maize was ready for husking. The young people speeded up the work, well aware of the custom so pleasantly noted by Joel Barlow, the "Hartford Wit":

> The laws of husking every wight can tell
> And sure no laws he ever keeps so well
> For each red ear a general kiss he gains.[89]

After the ears had been stripped, time always remained for foot races, leaping contests, shooting at the mark, and wrestling. These "athletic and healthy diversions" received the approval of the generally censorious Jedidiah Morse, who was pleased to record that "the odious and inhuman practices of duelling, gouging, cock-fighting and horse-racing are scarcely known" in New England.[90]

The farmer could live in modest comfort, or at least security, by a sort of skimming agriculture, and there he stopped. He had little money income since no market demand spurred him to produce a surplus. Without good highways he could not economically haul his commodities to the few cities where he might have found purchasers. The average countryman seemed invincibly conservative. If he did not yoke the same number of oxen to his plow, plant the same number of acres and that, too, "in the old of the moon," and get the crops in on the same day as did his father and grandfather, he was shunned by the neighborhood as a visionary.[91] With little incentive to increase his output, he saw no reason to disturb the old round that insured his comfort. For him, then, husbandry was a way of life and of getting a living. It was subsistence, not enterprise.

American agriculture in 1830 was not sharply different from what it had been in 1790. Farm machinery, which was to effect a revolution in production, had scarcely taken form; the railroad, which was to bring large areas into market contacts, was merely a curiosity. State and federal experiment stations and scientific services and the great university schools of agriculture were in the distant future. Yet new forces were at work, set in motion almost entirely by the precept and example of gentlemen amateurs, who had time to read and discuss and capital to test new methods and materials.

AGRARIAN EXPANSION

SLIGHTLY MORE THAN HALF the people who undertook the task of building a new nation lived south of the Mason and Dixon line in 1790. Numbering approximately 2 million, of whom three out of every eight were blacks, the Southerners occupied a rural domain half again as large as the area of the seven Northern states. Their market centers were few and small, only Baltimore and Charleston having more than 4,000 inhabitants. The latter, with 16,000, still ranked first, but it was soon to be outstripped by the busy Maryland port. In Virginia, Richmond and Petersburg, despite inadequate facilities, were entering a period of unusual commercial activity, while Norfolk, tragic victim of the Revolution, was rising but slowly from its ashes. In all North Carolina no town contained more than 2,000 inhabitants, and Georgia's metropolis, on a bluff above the Savannah River, was only a lively village, where the streets on hot, dry days reminded the traveler of the sands of the Sahara.[92]

The decline in American agriculture, which William Strickland thought he observed at the close of the eighteenth century, was in many districts merely a sign of temporary readjustment rather than of long-term collapse. This was well exemplified in the South with reference to the older staples of indigo, rice, and tobacco. Having thrown off the restrictive, but protective, mantle of British mercantilism, the South Carolina planters had lost their bounty on indigo and, as Great Britain found new supplies in the East Indies, its production almost disappeared from the sandy soils of the Southern river valleys.[93] Though rice was still in considerable demand, especially for the Russian market, its cultivation after the Revolution was marked by a period of confused transition, for at the same time that indigo planters were trying to save themselves by concentrating on this more profitable staple, the rice fields were being shifted from inland swamps to any river bottom where tidal flooding could be advantageously used.[94]

In tidewater Maryland and Virginia, where tobacco had long held undisputed sway, acute distress also prevailed. Many a field, surrendering to the forest, bore silent witness to poor tillage and soil exhaustion, while newly cleared acres produced crops for which there was no market.[95] Maryland tobacco had lost its French customers during the Revolution and it was difficult to regain them. European markets generally were so upset by the wars of the French Revolution, and the trade routes to America were so uncertain in the years of nonintercourse and embargo, that Europeans either imported tobacco from Cuba, Colombia, and Sumatra or tried to produce their own. As a result the American production for a long generation after 1790 declined in the tidewater regions and showed little increase in the piedmont. Chesapeake Bay planters were turning over in their minds the possibility of migrating westward or of sowing their fields with grass and small grain.[96]

Wheat culture, far from being peculiar to Pennsylvania and New York, was, in fact, late in the eighteenth century pushing steadily southward under the impetus of high prices and a broadly speculative market.[97] The Valley of Virginia, despite difficulties of transportation, was hauling its surplus grain into Philadelphia, while planters along the James River were growing corn for local consumption and wheat for export. In the northern piedmont, grain and livestock were replacing tobacco. Travelers reported new gristmills in the North Carolina backcountry, symbols of the expanding domain of wheat and corn.[98]

Though Virginia, largest and wealthiest state in the young republic, ranked for a time among the leading wheat producers, neither its tobacco nor its grain became the economic basis for Southern expansion. In 1790 the planters' great asset, as yet unrealized, lay in the ripening cotton boll. Great Britain's cotton industry, successfully imitating the cloths once imported from the Orient, had been revolutionized during the eighteenth century through the use of power-driven machines. By 1790 its mills and factories were slowed down, waiting for cotton fiber. The supply to meet that need was soon available, from American fields.

A few years after the War of Independence long-staple cotton began to appear on the export lists for England. The large amount of fiber in proportion to seeds made profitable their extraction by hand, pound by pound;

but few pounds could be grown since climatic requirements confined it to a very narrow strip along the Carolina and Georgia shores and to the "sea-islands" nearby. While still colonials, a few planters had tried to make some use of the short-staple boll, which grew so easily farther inland, but the tightly wrapped green seeds took too much labor in the separation to make a crop worthwhile.[99] Extensive cultivation was assured, however, in 1793 when Eli Whitney, the young Yale graduate then serving as tutor on a Georgia plantation, demonstrated both his Yankee ingenuity and his thorough training in his father's machine shop by making a contrivance which separated the seed from the lint cheaply and easily. The speed with which rivals appropriated the basic features of his invention left Whitney with little income beyond the sums necessary to fight infringements on his patents. But his device quickly converted the South to a new staple.[100]

That the cotton gin opened the uplands as well as the tidewater to short-staple cotton is strikingly revealed in the statistics of production. The crop of 1804 proved eight times as large as that of 1794, and almost three quarters of it was picked in the eastern districts of central Georgia and the northern counties of South Carolina.[101] The attractive prices presently whetted the appetite of the Georgia planters for fertile acres still in the hands of the Creek Indians.[102] North Carolina's piedmont, though producing chiefly for domestic consumption, also began to add to the bales which were handled either at Petersburg, Virginia, or at Charleston. In southeastern Virginia, planters readily abandoned tobacco for cotton, just as some of their neighbors had turned to wheat and corn. The new staple was also becoming important across the mountains in central Tennessee and along the Mississippi, where merchants from Vicksburg to Natchez accepted it as a medium of exchange.[103] But it was not yet clear at the turn of the nineteenth century how greatly the cotton gin would give a new direction to economic and social trends in the South.

The organization of agriculture in many Southern regions at this period was not unlike that of the North. Except in the rice districts of Georgia and South Carolina and the tidewater of Virginia and Maryland, the typical unit could be more appropriately called a farm than a plantation. Its 200 or 300 acres, only partially under cultivation, were usually divided into small fields by worm fences made of split rails from the adjacent woodland. Farmers generally followed a three-year rotation, hallowed by English precedent, which permitted each field one year in three to revert to "spontaneous rubbish pasture."[104]

At the close of the eighteenth century most of Maryland and the piedmont and Valley of Virginia, as well as the uplands of the Carolinas and Georgia, were in the hands of farmers and small-scale planters. The more prosperous among them tried to imitate the social amenities of the great plantations and hoped to ally themselves, by marriage or otherwise, with the aristocratic families of the seaboard. But the majority, descendants perhaps of indentured servants or of others who had found life difficult even in the New World, lived simply and independently, tilling their few acres alone or with their sons' help. They possessed few slaves and some had moral scruples against investing in such servants. Without education or leisure for self-improvement they tended to be narrowly provincial and intensely sectarian. Among travelers their hospitality was proverbial, but the accommodations which they had to offer seldom matched their warm generosity.[105] From southeastern Pennsylvania to the Georgia uplands, the low German speech of the "Pennsylvania Dutch" was increasingly heard in communities where many still spoke the English variants peculiar to Ulstermen or Highland Scots.[106] But whatever their national origins, they were inclined to give political allegiance to the agrarian republicanism of Thomas Jefferson and to respond quickly to the preaching of Methodist circuit riders and Baptist or Presbyterian itinerants.

Out of their ranks came many young men who found their first economic opportunity as overseers on plantations. Aspiring to secure land in their own right, they occasionally realized their ambitions and rose above the social limitations of mere servants of the landed aristocracy. But most failed to maintain even its modest standards; they could not hold their own in face of the spreading large-plantation system based on considerable capital. Some, without prospect of inheritance and ill-adjusted to their social environment, found a life more to their liking in the mountains of western Virginia and North Carolina, where farming need not infringe too deeply on time more enjoyably spent in hunting and fishing. Isolated and illiterate, proud of their self-sufficiency, they perpetuated in their highland clearings seventeenth-century superstitions and folkways and preserved a consistent hostility to the nineteenth-century concept of progress.[107]

Poor and lazy though the mountain folk might be, they escaped the curse of that sluggish inexertion which caused the "poor whites" to be regarded with contempt in the older regions. Physicians who visited the Carolinas and Georgia shortly after 1800 attributed to disease and bad diet the spiritual degradation of those whites known as "sand hillers" or "clayeaters." Dr. J. E. White sent an excellent clinical description to the *Medical Repository:*

> The countenance is pale and bloated; . . . the breathing is difficult, and is easily hurried by brisk exercise; the pulse is small and weak, but sometimes tense, and the carotid arteries in the neck beat with unusual force. . . . The person . . . is fond of a life of listless inactivity. The appetite is sometimes voracious, and is often insatiable for eating dirt, which forms the characteristic symptom of the disease.[108]

But the malignant activity of the parasitic hookworm was not yet suspected.[109] "Malacia, or dirt-eating," said the observers, resulted from faulty diet—too much salt meat and greens—which had a more "debilitating" effect in the South than in the North. The prevalence of this habit explained, in Dr. White's opinion, the inertia which held men on unproductive pine barrens, indolently scratching the earth for a bare subsistence, when better lands beckoned in trans-Appalachia.[110]

If Southern agriculture, responsive to the demands of world markets, had not achieved a high general standard of physical comfort and social well-being, it had created, at least in Virginia and South Carolina, an aristocracy at once powerful and intelligent. These landed gentry honored English tradition long after political independence had been won, and some could claim noble lords or country gentlemen among their English forebears. At the close of the eighteenth century, London was still the metropolis for the Virginia tidewater, for young Richmond as well as old Williamsburg transacted business in terms of bills of exchange originating in mercantile offices on the Thames. Though the planters found it increasingly difficult to finance elaborate country houses such as Nomini Hall, Mount Airy, Shirley, and Westover, these colonial mansions and many others like them continued to serve as symbols of a standard of living which their owners were striving to maintain. Within the great houses there still was insistence on that courtly hospitality and social grace which superficially marked the landed aristocracy.[111] Far more vital in the Virginia tradition was the ancient custom of combining with plantation management some training in law and a career, however casual, in politics. Though Virginia was the most populous of the thirteen states in 1790, that fact alone does not explain the preeminence of her sons in public service during the early years of the republic. They were now playing on a larger stage the roles to which generations of provincial leadership had accustomed them.

In South Carolina the tidewater gentry wore their social prestige with an urbanity scarcely equaled by the Virginians. Charleston provided a focus for their interests and activities. Here the aristocracy of the rice and indigo fields had joined with that of the wharf and countinghouse to create, in a semitropical setting, a graceful reminder of the variant groups whose customs and traditions were determining the pattern of American life. If London was still the mirror of fashion for South Carolinians, their own little metropolis possessed a distinctive flavor, a rare blending of influences emanating from the West Indies, France, and Holland as well as Great Britain. No other city in English America was quite so "Continental."[112]

According to the 1790 census, Charleston was almost as large as Boston and ranked fourth in the nation, containing more than 16,000 inhabitants of whom 6,000 were blacks.[113] Its rapid recovery after the Revolution was attested by the brigs, scows, and schooners in the harbor and by the new houses of brick and stone replacing the wooden ones which had been burned during the conflict. In adopting fire-resistant materials Charlestonians managed to escape the monotonous uniformity, so oppressive in the residential sections of Baltimore and Philadelphia, by covering the brick with stucco in delicate shades of blue, green, yellow, and pink. Shingles likewise gave way to colored tiles rather than to drab slate, an additional symbol of the city's individuality. In most dwellings the Georgian style, with its balanced facade and ornate classical doorway, had supplanted the French and West Indian influences. Householders, reluctant to give up the two- or three-tiered piazzas which helped ward off the heat, sometimes compromised by placing a pediment above the piazza and then constructing a partition with a false door on the street end. Such a facade, however skillfully designed, illustrated the willingness of Americans to sanction minor violations of European canons of taste in order to secure greater utility. If the effect was not always pleasing, it was at least distinctive; and it represented no revolt from Georgian dominance.[114]

The city was run by a planter oligarchy whose leaders, unlike their colonial predecessors, generally shunned trade just as the wealthy merchants ignored politics. The planters thought of themselves as agrarian republicans and their principles were often expressed in the vibrant phrases of the rights of man, but the manner and tone of their society would have shocked the Republicans who were joining Jefferson's party in Kentucky, western Pennsylvania, northern New York, and the towns of Vermont. An observant Yankee called Charleston, despite its ostensible Jacobinism, "the most aristocratic city in the Union."[115] The ruling class may have admired certain philosophers of the Enlightenment and have sympathized for a time with French revolutionaries, but such sentiments, even when reinforced by resentment against British creditors, furnished no solid foundation or democratic institutions. The framers of the state constitution had made sure that no one with less than a fifty-acre freehold could vote and that only the well-to-do could hold office.

Charleston society suited its plans to the convenience of the wealthy planter. He liked to visit his estate—sometimes fifty or sixty miles from the city—as soon as the November frosts had removed the danger of malaria or "country fever."[116] After the festivities of Christmas week in the plantation mansion, he brought his family back to town for the "season" from January to March. During the early spring, when the routine of rice culture was most demanding, he returned to the country, where he usually stayed until the ponds began to "green over." The enervating summer months might find him in the seclusion of his darkened town house, or in his summer cottage on Sullivan's Island or at such favored resorts as Virginia Hot Springs, Newport, and, a little later, Saratoga.[117]

The "season" in Charleston was filled with concerts and balls of the St. Cecilia Society, supplemented by private dinner parties at which the raconteur was even more honored than the epicure. So general was the spirit of gaiety that the Duke de La Rochefoucauld-Liancourt, probably in exaggeration, remarked that from four in the afternoon the people rarely thought of anything but pleasure and amusement.[118] Race week in February, followed by the Jockey Club ball, marked the climax. Upcountry planters joined heartily with those of the tidewater in supporting the Jockey Club, and numerous coaches, richly ornamented and bearing family crests, brought hundreds of spectators to the grandstand.

Because of their frequent dueling, reckless gambling, and excessive drinking, the Southerners whose social activities focused in Charleston were often judged to be indolent and self-indulgent, if not dissolute.[119] Yet the Duke de La Rochefoucauld-Liancourt, who knew the capitals of Europe, found in Charleston better company and livelier entertainment than he had expected, while that devout Calvinist, Jedidiah Morse, declared that in no part of America were "the social blessings enjoyed more rationally and liberally."[120] Life in plantation mansions and spacious town houses would have been less pleasant had the aristocracy not possessed an army of servants unable to "give notice" at will, who kept the routine of the household functioning smoothly. While Northern communities were making the adjustments necessitated by the rapid decline of indentured servitude and the gradual emancipation of slaves, Southern families, especially in the tidewater, were enjoying the tradition of personal service which had slowly been created among the slaves and was now exemplified by blacks several generations removed from their African origins.[121]

Throughout the South, slaves were growing more important as a base for the whole social structure. This was notably so in South Carolina where the lowland counties in 1790 reported almost three times as many blacks as whites.[122] The black resisted the malaria of the moist rice fields and swamps much better than the white man, and he could be sacrificed, if need be, when yellow fever struck with epidemic force. As cotton spread into the uplands, the market for servile labor became wider and stronger. In 1790 only a fifth of the population of the South Carolina piedmont was black; twenty years later the ratio had risen to a third. The retreat of the farmer who used only free white labor had already begun.[123] It was the Carolina rice planters who had blocked prohibition of the African slave trade in the federal constitution, and in 1803 the Carolina cotton planters took the lead in securing state legislation reopening the traffic.[124]

From the day the first blacks were brought into Virginia there was persistent doubt, despite the hardening of custom into law, concerning the moral justification of hereditary bondage; and probably at no time were the slave owners themselves more deeply troubled than in the half-century after the Revolution. The system seemed peculiarly offensive in communities where liberty poles had but recently been raised and the "rights of man" were still much discussed at tavern and courthouse.[125] North of Maryland this anomaly was slowly disappearing as gradual emancipation was written into state laws. Though the Southern states, as well as the Northern, had eloquent opponents of slavery, the institution could not easily be modified in regions where climate, the routine production of staples, and large numbers of blacks provided utilitarian arguments for its perpetutation.

Southern liberals at the close of the eighteenth century were deeply impressed by the European philosophers of the Enlightenment and desired to make their rationalistic philosophy a force for social reform.[126] Yet their humanitarian program concerning slavery far outran their actual achievements. Most of Virginia's great political leaders agreed with George Mason, aristocratic owner of Gunston Hall and 300 blacks, who had written the state's bill of rights, that slavery was a slow poison infecting the body politic. Jefferson rejoiced that Chancellor George Wythe and St. George Tucker were indoctrinating youthful abolitionists in the College of William and Mary; he could not foresee that some thirty years later Thomas R. Dew, from a professorial chair in that same faculty, would formulate the historical and theological justification of slavery.[127] The influential liberals found strong supporters among the patrician planters—many in Maryland and Virginia and a few in South Carolina and Georgia—and for the generation before 1800 they gave the stamp of social approval to manumission, but in no Southern state were they able to repeal those statutes without which slavery could not long have survived.

The relation between master and man was not, in the long run, to be determined by the libertarian doctrines of patrician planters or by the high ideas of humanitarian Quakers and other religious folk. More influential was the achievement of those pioneers who went out and possessed the fertile river valleys between the Alleghenies and the Mississippi. This agricultural conquest of the West meant not the decline but the expansion of slavery—expansion into the pennyroyal districts of Kentucky, into the limestone basins of Tennessee, and along the streams that watered the broad coastal plain as they flowed toward the Gulf of Mexico. Men of property were not numerous among these pioneers who first defied the menace of hostile Indians in order to seek new homes in the wilderness, and such property as they owned seldom included slaves. Yet the census of 1790 revealed that a sixth of the Kentuckians were blacks. Already the tobacco planter had pushed his way through the mountain passes to escape the declining production of worn-out acres, and within a decade the cotton grower would start that steady advance into the fertile alluvial strips south of Tennessee, where the plantation system with slave labor was to dwarf all other forms of agriculture.[128]

Some Americans, observing the rapidity with which new states were admitted into the Union of the original thirteen, tried to analyze and describe this westward migration. Timothy Flint thought he could distinguish successive waves of settlers: first, the man with the gun, beating down old trails and blazing new ones in search of food and furs; second, the man with the ax, a descendant of those forest-farmers who had learned to cultivate their crops wherever the sun shone through the bare branches of

Fig. 1. A Birch Canoe poled by an Indian.
   2. A Birch Canoe paddled by Squaws.
   3. A Baboose, or Indian Child.
   4. A Log Fence.
   5. Worm Fences.
   6. Post and Rail Fence.
   7. Virginia Rail Fence.
   8. Dwelling House and Wings.

Mc Intyre

Plan OF AN **AMERICA**

EW CLEARED *FARM.*

9. *Barracks or Dutch Barn.*
10. *Barns rooffed with Singles.*
11. *Shade for Cattle to ly in Winter.*
12. *Shade for winning Indian Corn.*
13. *Fold for confining Cattle at night, &*
    in which they are milked.
14. *A dwelling Log House covered with Bark.*
15. *An Indian Dog.*

girdled trees; then the man with the plow, eager to acquire tracts partly cleared, so that he might get forward more quickly with the routine of farming. To him, much more appropriately than to his predecessors, the term "settler" could be applied. Finally came the man with the dollar. In a society where all were speculating on the rise in values which increased population would bring, he was peculiarly sensitive to opportunities for investing his capital, however small. Merchandising was usually the entering wedge, but it merely pried open the door to an undifferentiated activity in transportation, banking, and manufacturing. Occasionally these variant types seemed to represent chronological stages in the process of settlement. More often migration was so rapid that their commingling became a distinctive aspect of frontier communities.[129]

The universal symbol of the pioneer's first victory in his struggle against the encompassing forest was the erection of his cabin. West of the coastal towns the great majority of houses in 1790 were built of logs crudely notched and laid horizontally. Such a dwelling could easily be finished by half-a-dozen men in three or four days, and the cost was negligible, for the "raising" became a neighborhood enterprise enlivened by music, dancing, and a tub of whiskey. The cabins which Thomas Cooper saw in interior Pennsylvania in 1790 would accommodate a family, he thought, quite as well as the better cottages of England. He admired those that were sheathed with pine slabs and finished off inside with plain wainscoting, panel doors, and glazed windows. They could be duplicated for £150 sterling, if one could get one's timber to a sawmill.[130]

But it was an exceptional frontiersman who spent much time on details within his cabin. If space permitted there were two low-ceilinged rooms, one always dominated by the large fireplace, a sort of dictator of household routine. Chairs and tables revealed what could be done by inexpert hands with simple tools. A rough-hewn ladder gave access to the sleeping quarters where there was sometimes space under the sloping roof for bed frames with rawhide or rope bottoms. Highly prized in every such household was that piece of furniture, perhaps a desk or a chest of drawers or a bedstead, which had been carried at great effort into the new country. It might be the only tangible link with that older community which had but lately been called "home." The simple furnishings of the frontier cabins indicate that in the westward migration the skilled artisans invariably sought the more populous towns.

A river, the first highway in every new area of settlement, was usually the dominant factor in the growth of towns. Along its banks appeared the initial commercial activities, housed at first in wood, but moving soon into buildings of brick and stone. Pittsburgh, where the colorful Conestoga wagon trains reached the headwaters of the Ohio, had fewer than 400 inhabitants in 1790, but a decade later its population had increased fourfold. One visitor from the East was so impressed that he described the town as "a reflex of New York, the same earnest bustle in its business, and that same national variety in its thickly thronging strangers."[131] Among them were skilled artisans—cabinetmakers, cobblers, tailors, hatters, watchmakers, and silversmiths—as well as purposeful businessmen looking for investment opportunities. There was nothing fortuitous about their coming. They had calculated the potential profits in manufacturing enterprises which could utilize Western materials to supply Western settlements at prices considerably below those charged for Eastern imports. During the first decade of the nineteenth century they established glassworks, iron foundries, ropewalks, and textile mills. Shipwrights were busy at the shipyards, and carpenters along the principal streets.[132]

Optimism was strong in the early years of the nineteenth century, but it represented the enthusiasm of prospectors in a new country rather than sound financial calculation. As the shifting sand bars and turbulent rapids took a heavy toll of Western-built ships, so profitable markets were lost to the unpredictable ambition of Napoleon Bonaparte and to Great Britain's determination to maintain a balance of power in Europe. Many an Ohio River capitalist, long before the steamboat gained supremacy, came to the conclusion that building oceangoing vessels was of minor economic importance in comparison with handling cargoes which kept barge, keel, and flatboat busy on the Mississippi and its navigable tributaries.[133]

It was this traffic, linking the frontier from western Pennsylvania to Louisiana and, in turn, binding it to the older part of the nation, which enabled the river towns to build steadily upon the production of the expanding agricultural districts. In 1800 no port between Pittsburgh and Natchez had as many as 1,000 inhabitants, but the next decade brought rapid growth.[134] Over all these communities was the lingering mood of the backwoodsman, confident of the future and keen for any speculative enterprise. There was much that was coarse in the towns as well as throughout the countryside. Travelers commented on the incivility, boorishness, fighting, and heavy drinking which they encountered, but the more discerning realized that in the settlement of any new country the rough would become rougher and that standards generally would decline.

The initial result of physical hardships wherever civilization met the wilderness was manifest in widespread social leveling. Professional competence and craft skills were less highly esteemed when men were literally engaged in struggling for a living. For a brief period frontier society, as compared with the older communities from which its members had come, seemed to be singularly homogeneous. Men were equal, or nearly so, in challenging the natural forces which encompassed them. A sense of equality permeated their thinking about social relationships and was translated, somewhat imperfectly, into legal codes and political forms.[135]

On successive frontiers this phase of the transit of civilization seldom endured long. Social maturity, or at least the semblance of it, came quickly in crude settlements where pioneers were determined to conserve the best that they had known.[136] They had lost much but not all in the process of moving. Fortescue Cuming, commenting on life along the Ohio in 1807, found evidence on every side that the homogeneous frontier society was beginning to break up. Economic and political leadership was being assumed by men who had risen above their fellows, thanks largely to advantages which they had enjoyed in the communities whence they migrated. There were sons of Eastern land speculators, realizing profits from the unearned increment of town lots; Revolutionary officers whose recompense for former services had been commuted into Western acres; planters who had exchanged farms in the tidewater for a chance to work new and fertile soil with their slaves; merchants sent out by Eastern houses, now able to establish independent stores; lawyers, well read in some preceptor's office, advancing more rapidly than would have been possible in any Eastern county.

The gap between the most prosperous and the least fortunate seemed to be steadily widening. Alexander Wilson, the ornithologist, noticed this during his travels in 1810. The privations, which initially had been "the offspring of necessity," became familiar habit with many a squatter. While boasting loudly of the fertility of his land, he was content to throw his seed into the ground, neglect its cultivation, turn his hogs loose in the woods, and live on "pork, cabbages, and hoe-cakes." His cabin was often worse than a pigsty and his person ill-clothed, dirty, and diseased. "What a contrast," remarked Wilson, "to the neat farm and snug cleanly habitation of the industrious settler[s] that opens their green fields, their stately barns, gardens and orchards to the gladdened eye of the delighted stranger!"[137]

Evidence of a rapidly maturing society was more impressive in the towns than in the rural districts. Lexington, though far from typical, stood as a symbol of what could be accomplished within a single generation. Situated in the heart of the Kentucky Blue Grass country, Lexington in 1783 was little more than a military stockade. A quarter-century later it had become the "Athens of the West," with broad streets and substantial brick houses, the seat of Transylvania University. Its 3,000 inhabitants supported a circulating library, two newspapers and publishing houses, three boarding schools for girls, and five churches. The foreign merchandise handled annually by its twenty-two retail stores was valued at over $300,000. More than 100 small factories and artisans' shops produced cordage, sailcloth, cotton thread, nails, shoes, hats, and furniture. Since this was much more than the local market could use, the surplus, together with the agricultural products of the countryside, supplied the Lower South or flowed out by way of the Mississippi into the channels of transatlantic trade.[138]

As commercial and industrial statistics revealed the growth of river ports and inland towns throughout the West, the opportunities for professional competence grew apace. More districts were able to furnish the support necessary for the specialized knowledge of the doctor or the lawyer. In 1790, Pittsburgh had two physicians; nine years later the number had risen to seven, two of whom had been trained in the Western country. Yet the degree of risk was still high for those who had the courage to carry to the frontier the elements of civilization. Faith played a mighty part in the westward transit of newspapers. In 1786 a Conestoga-wagon team had brought to the forks of the Ohio the press, type, ink, and paper that were to make up John Scull's *Pittsburgh Gazette.* Here Fielding Bradford, who planned to assist his brother John in establishing a paper in Kentucky, learned something of the art of printing. Within a year John Bradford's flatboat, laden with another rude printing press and some type cut from dogwood, floated down the Ohio to the road which connected the river with the Kentucky metropolis. On Lexington's *Kentucky Gazette* worked a printer named Elihu Stout, who in 1804 dared to strap a press and type on packhorses and follow the trails that led to the little town of Vincennes deep in the old Northwest.[139]

Many other pioneers of ideas and special competence were quite as daring. They were convinced that behind the thin edge of settlement, slowly cutting into the wilderness, the social soil was already prepared to sustain their particular specialties, that even on the frontier there were communities—literate, prosperous, and expanding—where men and women would cherish the instruments and records of the human mind.

THE CHALLENGE OF LIBERAL THOUGHT

DURING THE EARLY DECADES of its existence the United States of America was a highly dubious experiment. Political independence seemed more shadow than substance, for the encircling territories of Great Britain and Spain emphasized the new nation's economic and cultural dependence upon the European system from which it was striving to escape. With a domain stretching from the Atlantic to the Mississippi, between the Great Lakes and Spanish Florida, Americans faced the task which many foreign commentators insisted was hopeless, of transforming particularistic British provinces into an enduring federal republic. Never had the attempt been made on so grand a scale.

Though the government was republican in form, it was far from democratic in spirit. Its leaders, with few exceptions, were of the older school of English liberalism and they believed that the theories of "the great Mr. Locke" had made clear the intimate connection between liberty and property.[140] If they thought of themselves as interested in the individual man, they were also aware that democratic license could produce such results as Rhode Island's fiat money and the Massachusetts uprising led by Daniel

Shays. Though they were committed by the logic of the Revolution to a government based on the consent of the governed, many remained skeptical concerning democracy. Their republicanism was negative rather than positive. It is true that it embraced not only hostility to monarchy and its attendant institutions, but also distrust of any aristocracy which sought to exploit the many for the benefit of the few. Even John Adams, who was confident of the wisdom of the natural aristocrats, was no believer in unlimited government by wealth.[141] Yet there was little approval of equalitarian doctrines.

In fact, this generation found it difficult to define the proper bounds of its republicanism. In the attempt much ink was spilled, for as men had differed in 1787 over the structure of the new government, so after 1790 they argued angrily over the manner in which it should exercise its powers. Where were the limits beyond which government ought not go lest it invade the rights of the individual? How could property rights best be protected? Could benefit for the many arise from special privilege for the few? Who should determine the extent of the area in which the federal government was competent to act?

Out of such questions arose differences of opinion not unlike those which had marked the struggle over the ratification of the Constitution. The division was accentuated by the financial program of Secretary Hamilton, who found the new climate of opinion in commercial circles responsive to the needs of the rising capitalist order. Though he may have failed to understand the deeply rooted prejudices of rural America, he appreciated the fact that the common man throughout the country still respected the gentleman. The day of the tiewig aristocracy was waning but it had not yet closed. It was possible, therefore, to plan in terms of a philosophy which held that the masses would prosper if the interests of the rich and well-born were properly protected. Hostility to such an assumption rose slowly in a day when men were weary of strife and disorder, of business depression and political uncertainty.

As Hamilton's measures became law, the opposition took form. The well-disciplined Federalists, committed to business enterprise, sound finance, and a vigorous foreign policy, faced a loose union of groups, known variously as anti-Federalists or Republicans, who cherished ideas of an agrarian republic, suspected the methods by which Hamilton had reached his objectives, and resented the broadening of governmental powers so easily covered by the mantle of liberal interpretation of the Constitution. Like their opponents, they rejoiced in the establishment of the national credit and the enhancement of American prestige, but they felt that Federalist policies, however admirable the ultimate goal, were designed to exploit planters, farmers, and laborers so that merchants, manufacturers, and bankers might profit.[142]

Though Republican leaders talked much of the rights of man, the phrase had chameleon qualities. It might mean the rights of "honest" farmers against their city creditors, as William Manning thought; or it might mean the rights of Virginia gentlemen against a domination of Northern businessmen, as John Randolph of Roanoke suggested.[143] If there were many who believed it meant the right of all men equally to share in government, their influence at the close of the eighteenth century fell short of their numbers.

No such leveling principle belonged to the political theory of Thomas Jefferson. "The people," whom he cherished, were not European mobs recruited from down-trodden peasants and exploited city workers. He thought and spoke in terms of the America of his day. A sound majority should be composed of farmers and villagers busy on their small freeholds or laboring earnestly to obtain such a stake in society. Social distinctions between the gentry and the others, or property qualifications for suffrage and officeholding, did not greatly disturb him. He had confidence that the politically active citizens in the United States would move steadily toward a more democratic system, for their domestic economy was relatively simple, being free from the complexities of Europe's stratified social arrangements.[144] More surely than Hamilton, Jefferson caught the spirit of the generation at the turn of the century. The former made use of a temporary reaction against popular excesses and economic maladjustments, while the latter based his philosophy upon that "fierce love of liberty" which Burke had once remarked. This it was which made him the great leader of the Republican forces.[145] In Virginia, Pennsylvania, and New York local organizations had felt the quickening influence of his spirit and realized that his idealistic faith in humanity was tempered by a realistic sense of what was politically possible.[146]

The French Revolution made a momentous impact upon the direction of thought and action in the United States. As slow-sailing vessels brought belated news of the events of 1792—the proclamation of the French Republic, the victory at Valmy, and the November decree of the "war of all peoples against all kings"—American rejoicing became almost hysterical. Dispatches from Paris, published in the gazettes from Maine to Kentucky, stirred men's thoughts and filled their conversation.[147] In Savannah, Newport, and Philadelphia there were dinners and balls, and the bands played *"Ça ira"* and "Yankee Doodle."[148] In Boston the words "Liberty" and "Equality" were stamped on children's cakes, while merchants ostentatiously addressed one another as "citizen." At a great civic celebration the school children appeared in national cockades to watch their elders consume a huge roast ox, two hogsheads of punch, and a cartload of bread in the name of the French Republic. "Citoyen S. Adams" presided over a more select banquet in Faneuil Hall.[149] The intensity and persistence of this feeling revealed a discontent which had been slowly spreading under the surface. Few could doubt that, whatever the outcome in Europe, the French upheaval had laid bare social antagonisms and democratic longings in

America. It had given impetus and direction to the friends of the rights of man.

The equal measure it had aroused the friends of law and order to a sense of their danger. By 1794 there were many, like Noah Webster and the Reverend William Linn, who repented of their early enthusiasm for revolutionaries and turned to the defense of conservative principles. The Federalists classified all who disagreed with their philosophy of government as promoters of Jacobinical excesses.[150] Alexander Graydon complained of the "torrent of fanaticism" raging through Harrisburg and eastern Pennsylvania, with complete disregard for the "dictates of justice, humanity and consistency."[151] "There can be but two parties in a country," observed the editor of the *Massachusetts Mercury,* "the friends of order and its foes. Under the banners of the first are ranged all men of property, all quiet, honest, peaceable, orderly, unambitious citizens. In the ranks of the last are enlisted all desperate, embarrassed, unprincipled, disorderly, ambitious, disaffected, morose men."[152]

Standards of journalistic propriety sank lower as the political disputation grew more intense.[153] Probably at no period in American history unless it be immediately after the Civil War has the language of public controversy so constantly hovered on the verge of scurrility. John Fenno's hope that his *Gazette of the United States* might become the dignified journal of the "court party" soon vanished before the necessity of meeting the brilliant sarcasm of Philip Freneau in the *National Gazette* and the virulent abuse of Benjamin Franklin Bache in the *Aurora.*[154] In a generation which remembered the polemics of the Revolutionary era it was easy for party service to degenerate into vituperative attacks. From Europe came journalists already trained in the excesses of partisan warfare, and political leaders seldom restrained them.[155] Country printers, imitating their city breathren, found their readers more amused than shocked by the batteries of slander. Bache's *Aurora* described even Washington as a cheat and an embezzler and, when the president retired from office, exulted that his name would cease "to give currency to political iniquity, and to legalize corruption."[156]

If one fixes attention on the partisan politics, it is easy to picture American society as servilely copying the quarrels of Europe. But the great majority of the people were attached to no country but their own. Cutting through the verbiage, a French observer reported that Republicans as well as Federalists accepted the Constitution, but that each group was learning how to use the document for its own designs.[157] Ideas concerning constitutional interpretation were still in flux. The line between "strict" and "loose" constructionists was meaningless, for circumstances constantly dictated shifts across it, as New Englanders were to learn in the first decade of the new century. Though all accepted the work of the Convention of 1787, few held that the document was sacred. The cult of the Constitution was yet to be developed.[158]

Despite the dismay of the extreme Federalists as Thomas Jefferson took office in 1801, most Americans felt less apprehensive concerning the nation's future than they had when George Washington became president. Out of the tumultuous decade had come confidence in severely tested processes of government. Free discussion seemed to bring that change which is necessary if government is to remain sensitive to the popular will. Experience with the alien and sedition laws tended to confirm belief in freedom of speech, of the press, and of association, rights which the amendments to the Constitution in 1791 had specifically guaranteed. The Virginia and Kentucky resolutions of 1798–99, whatever their implications for the political theorist, had suggested that minority interests could be safeguarded without resort to violent revolution. The rude electioneering of the Republicans had stirred many voters from their apathy.[159] In New England, where the proportion of actual voters to the entire population was the lowest in the country, activity at the polls increased notably.[160] Rotation in office, based upon a belief in the need of change, had challenged the long tenures characteristic of many communities. Of course, annual elections did not necessarily mean new incumbents, but they clearly denoted that the party system was not an evil and that no governmental arrangement, however wise its sponsors, should be permanent. The Federalists in their alarm and the Republicans in their elation probably exaggerated the immediate significance of what Jefferson was wont to call "the great revolution of 1800." Yet the party with a creed had succeeded the party with a program, and that creed looked toward the establishment of a more democratic way in America.[161]

There were no stauncher defenders of the old order in politics and in religion than the Congregational clergy of New England. Closely allied with merchants, lawyers, and the whole hierarchy of officialdom, they had become accustomed to wielding political influence in the interests of orthodoxy, to which they added Federalism in the decade before 1800.[162] The compact groups in Connecticut and Massachusetts, believing that they governed by divine right, were menaced by the rising democratic spirit.[163] Hence clerical voices quickly denounced the "atheism" of French revolutionaries and their Republican friends in America. From Charlestown, Massachusetts, Jedidiah Morse wrote of the "malignant aspect" which brooded over the country; he trembled in fear of a reign of American Jacobinism.[164] Timothy Dwight at Yale angrily questioned what the end of French influence would be: "Is it that we may change our holy worship into a dance of Jacobin phrenzy, and that we may behold a strumpet personating a Goddess on the altars of Jehovah?"[165] Some carried political controversy into the pulpit, which became a sounding board for party propaganda.[166] That their influence was potent is apparent from the bitter resentment of the Republicans, whose counteroffensive was weakened by their reluctance to be branded as enemies of religion and good morals.

Yet the social position as well as the religious authority of the clergy, even in rural New England, was waning. Among laymen they were no longer accorded the respect which had been theirs before the American Revolution. This they blamed upon foreign importations—English Deism and French rationalism—indiscriminately described as infidelism. It is probable that early American Deism, like the English, owed as much to the indirect influence of Locke's essays, especially his *Letters on Toleration* and *The Reasonableness of Christianity*,[167] as it did to the direct impact of the Enlightenment.

However that may be, Deistical inroads were apparent late in the eighteenth century. President Charles Nisbet of Dickinson College complained that there were few who read the Bible or continued the custom of family prayers.[168] The Reverend William Linn of Rutgers College looked out upon a nation endangered by the decline of the family altar, the profanation of the Sabbath, the ostentation of those enriched in neutral trade, and the growth of infidelity.[169] Ethan Allen's coarsely written attack on the clergy may not have influenced many, but it betokened the direction of Deistic thought.[170] With revolutionary doctrines from the Paris faubourgs came French rationalism to reenforce this trend. Deistical clubs such as the Theophilanthropists in New York and the Druidical Society at Newburgh were formed, with many recruits enrolling from the Democratic Societies.[171] Students at Yale and Princeton took the names of favorite European rationalists, using them in preference to their own.[172] It was thought, though erroneously, that many were imitating that aggressive anticlerical organization, the Bavarian Illuminati.[173] With "youth in revolt" the earnestness of the rebels occasionally bordered on the absurd.[174]

In their attack on revealed religion the Deists pretended to be scientific, but they could launch no scientific attack except along Copernican lines, for their data were inadequate. The Rosetta Stone had not yet crushed the old chronology of Archbishop James Ussher; Sir Charles Lyell had not yet raised the curtain on the immense *Antiquity of Man;* modern biology had not yet brought its challenge against the separate-creation theory as it did, for instance, in Charles Darwin's *Origin of Species;* the critical apparatus of the Germans had not yet been turned against certain Scripture texts; the possibilities of the comparative method in studying the world's great religions were unexplored.[175] Deists, therefore, relied upon a "commonsense" exposure of revelation, supplemented in the manner of Voltaire by denunciation of the church as a social institution.

Their most popular apologist was Thomas Paine, whose *Age of Reason,* completed in 1796, created a greater sensation than his *Rights of Man.* It was largely a popularization of the older Deistical writers from the days of Lord Herbert of Cherbury to his own. Paine affirmed his belief in a God whose only revelation was "in the immensity of the creation" and "the unchangeable order by which the incomprehensible whole is governed."[176]

There were some, though not many in America, who recognized in this God of Nature the deity whom Jefferson had invoked in the Declaration of Independence. New York, Philadelphia, and Baltimore were centers of rationalism, with active societies, frequent public addresses, and periodicals. In the dissemination of tracts and cheap editions the Deists rivaled the Christian tract societies, and their influence extended far beyond a few seaboard cities. Travelers found French infidelity openly professed in western New York and western Pennsylvania, while Virginia earned the reputation, especially in the North, of being in the hands of skeptics and avowed unbelievers.[177]

In the eyes of professing Christians conditions had become alarming. The pulpits of Calvinism from Massachusetts to Kentucky thundered defiance, and the reverberations were heard for years.[178] Yet such sermons as Timothy Dwight's *Discourse on the Genuineness and Authenticity of the Old Testament* (1796) would not have been necessary for the generation which preceded or that which followed.[179] The "deistical fever" ran its course quickly, leaving not weakened but invigorated Christian sects behind it. Much that was regarded as French skepticism was probably little more than enthusiasm for French political liberalism. As the excesses of revolutionaries in France terrified some and the victories of Republicans in America satisfied others, Deism declined. Philosophic rationalism could scarcely compete, except among intellectuals, with the emotionalism of evangelical religion.

More subtly subversive of traditional Christianity than the frontal attacks of European rationalism were the heresies which came to be known as Universalism and Unitarianism. In the transit of ideas the accident of the carrier is often of primary importance. So John Murray from London, thinking to bury his ruined life in the American wilderness, discovered that some persons in New England were ready for the gospel of universal salvation which he was under compulsion to preach. At Gloucester in 1779 and at Boston in 1793 he formed Universalist societies which became centers of his itinerant ministry.[180]

Murray clung to the essential tenets of trinitarianism, but insisted "that *every individual* shall in due time be separated from sin, and rendered fit to associate with the denizens of heaven."[181] In 1791 at the New England General Convention of Universalists he met for the first time Hosea Ballou, who argued that society could well dispense with such doctrines as the deity of Jesus and human depravity. It was this form of Universalism which reached New Hampshire, Vermont, and western New York in the wake of Ballou's successful preaching. The confession of faith adopted at Winchester, New Hampshire, in 1803 was broad enough to include his ideas, which within a decade dominated the first Universalist periodical, the *Gospel Visitant,* and represented the position of the Association.[182]

If Universalists thought that God was too good to damn a man, the

Unitarians felt that man was too good to be damned. Long before an open break occurred in the ranks of Congregationalism, the ancient Socinian heresy had appeared among New England Calvinists.[183] The Boston Association was particularly affected, for James Freeman, having led the Episcopalians of King's Chapel in repudiating the doctrine of the Trinity,[184] busied himself with distributing Unitarian tracts and encouraging liberalism among the Congregationalists. By 1797 he reported that a "number of ministers . . . in the southern part of this state" were preaching Unitarian sentiments, while others were cautiously leading their hearers to embrace them.[185] Orthodox Calvinism was finding liberalism far more dangerous than French rationalism.[186]

In 1803 controversy came into the open, for Dr. David Tappan, Hollis professor of divinity at Harvard, had died and the conservative clergy were determined that no unorthodox person should replace him. The liberals in Boston proposed the name of Henry Ware, pastor at Hingham, whose Unitarian leanings were pronounced, even if he did not accept the humanitarian view of Christ. After a protracted struggle, in which the opposition was belligerently led by the Reverend Jedidiah Morse of Charlestown, Ware was appointed in 1805. Within a few months Professor Samuel Webber succeeded the deceased Joseph Willard as president, and Harvard was lost to the Calvinists. Some thought the loss had occurred when the works of Priestley, Toulmin, Price, and other English Deists had first been received into the college library.[187]

Liberalism, though triumphing at Harvard, won few notable victories beyond the borders of eastern Massachusetts during the first decade of the nineteenth century.[188] However democratic in its implications, it failed to stir the popular imagination. Even the colleges were apathetic or resistant. In New Haven, Timothy Dwight rejoiced at the renewed interest in the Scriptures, while he marshaled the forces of Congregationalism and Presbyterianism in Connecticut to support the standing order. Throughout the Atlantic seaboard, especially among the Presbyterians of the Middle and Southern states, there was a growing determination to combat heretical teachings.[189]

In Kentucky, where Republican political philosophy became manifest in a state constitution providing for universal manhood suffrage, liberal theology had strong supporters. Though various shades of heterodoxy existed, none exerted more influence than that associated with Unitarianism. Its ablest exponents were Harry Toulmin, son of Joshua Toulmin, the English Unitarian leader, and Augustin Eastin, a former member of the Elkhorn Baptist Association. Supported by such politicians as Governor James Garrard, Senator John Breckinridge, and John Bradford, publisher of the *Kentucky Gazette,* who had fought in Virginia for the act establishing religious freedom, they dominated Transylvania Seminary for a decade after 1794, and for a generation carried on a struggle with the champions of orthodoxy for control of education in the state.[190]

Here, as in many other sections, the Presbyterians with their high regard for an educated clergy, their strong dogmatic emphasis, and their middle-class constituency assumed the lead in intellectual conflict. Baptists and Methodists, on the other hand, eager to meet the spiritual needs of unlettered folk, strove to overcome the easy morals of frontier communities rather than to combat heterodox speculations. The contrast was dramatically revealed in the Great Revival. Though it first became manifest in Presbyterian churches, the Methodists and Baptists nurtured it and secured its best fruit.[191]

The Western revivals, unlike the quiet return to the religion in Eastern villages early in the nineteenth century, were marked by phenomena which seemed distinctively American. In fertile river valleys against the background of forest and hills, preachers and people grappled clumsily but earnestly with an ancient problem, man's relation to the unseen world, and its corollary, man's fortunes in eternity. It was drama on a grand scale. The participants, many of them Scotch-Irish acutely conscious that they had fallen far short of the standards set by Calvin and Knox, were of energetic stock, intense and quick to respond. The content of their religious meditations has been captured in the words of an old hymn:

> My thoughts on awful subjects roll,
> Damnation and the dead;
> What horrors seize a guilty soul
> Upon a dying bed![192]

Cowards they were not, yet they lived in perennial fear of dangers—the caprices of Nature, Indian attacks, the scourge of starvation, illness without benefit of medical aid. The terrors of hell they found easy to imagine. Most of them were lonely, especially the women, starving for human contacts and exciting incidents. Some were exiles from civilization: weaklings and criminals, who lacked self-control and fell easy victims to cumulative suggestions. Out of such lives came the emotional extravagances of the frontier revivals, miraculous to some, fantastic to others.

After 1800 the camp meeting became a regular feature among Western Methodist and Baptists. In a region where large towns were few and the roads leading to them poor, it was necessary to hold such a religious fair in order to accommodate the crowds. The gathering usually assembled near some church, which might afford lodging for visiting clergy. After a rude platform had been constructed at one end of a nearby clearing, planks were laid across the tree stumps to furnish seats for some of the multitude. Around the edges of the space the wagons and tents arranged in somewhat irregular rows, gave the appearance of a village sprung up in the forest. At night, blazing bonfires, lamps suspended from the trees, and hundreds of flickering candles in the tents illumined the scene. "The uncertain light upon the tremulous foliage . . . the solemn chanting of hymns swelling and falling on the night wind; the impassioned exhortations; the earnest prayers" kindled the highly emotional. Weeping and sobbing gave way to shouts and shrieks; some were seized by the "jerks," their bodies torn by convulsions; others fell to the ground as in a trance, to lie for hours while friends sang and prayed over them. Occasionally barks were heard from those caught up in the exercise popularly known as "treeing the devil," or the "holy laugh" rang out, high-pitched and mirthless.[193] If falling was the most prevalent of these outbursts, jerking was the most spectacular.[194] To some these manifestations were the miracles of Protestantism.

Evangelism had its critics as well as its heroes. The Presbyterians particularly scorned the hysterical outbursts. Falling, jerking, rolling, and barking, they insisted, indicated that a doctor, not a preacher, was needed. Moreover, the wholesome intercourse of friendly family groups at the camp meeting, which has played so large a part in the American tradition of public gatherings, was sometimes marred by obscene conduct and sexual irregularities which raised ugly doubts concerning the spiritual gains. In crowds so highly charged with emotion it was not difficult for vagrant men and women of easy virtue to cloak their vices in the respectable garb of religious ardor.

Americans who feared that uneducated exhorters ministering to the multitude might breed popular scorn of sound learning mistook the temper of their generation. An education was the goal of an increasing number, though many a boy at the beginning of the nineteenth century found it more difficult to obtain than had his father or grandfather. This did not arise from indifference on the part of political and religious leaders. In some communities it resulted from the limitations of a frontier environment; in others, it reflected the decline of education through the new apprenticeship which accompanied the growth of factories. Except for sections of New England, education in America, as in Europe, had always been a function of the family and the church. The creation of a republican government emphasized public responsibility for the instruction of youth, but the transition from private and parochial control to state support was slow and awkward.

"A people who mean to be their own governors," James Madison argued, "must arm themselves with the power which knowledge gives."[195] Education, therefore, could not remain the privilege of the few; it must become the possession of the many. Little doubt existed concerning objectives. Most educational reformers wished to end cultural dependence upon Europe, create an American social consciousness, and inculcate patriotic devotion to the new nation.[196] It was high time, thought Robert Coram, to check all blind adherence to transatlantic policies and to reject every European idea that would hamper human thought.[197] Benjamin Rush, who held a degree from the University of Edinburgh, agreed with Thomas Jefferson, graduate of the College of William and Mary, that American boys should not be educated in Europe. Rush feared that their minds would be poisoned against political democracy, while Jefferson doubted that America would accept foreign-trained leaders.[198] There were even suggestions that a prohibition be erected against American youth enrolling in European universities. Had it been taken seriously, an insignificant number would have been affected during the quarter-century after 1790.

Probably no educator in this generation was so determined as Noah Webster that the thought and action of his countrymen should have a distinctively American cast.[199] "As soon as he opens his lips," so ran Webster's prescription for the education of an American, "he should rehearse the history of his own country; he should lisp the praise of liberty, and of those illustrious heroes and statesmen who have wrought a revolution in her favor."[200] Education was the mold in which the national character would be formed and Webster labored mightily to help determine the pattern. This inspired much of his arduous work on his spellers and dictionaries, for he believed that uniformity in the pronunciation and use of words would break down provincial distinctions and that a simplified and regularized orthography would promote nationalism. His grammar included many examples of American prose writings, especially those dealing with the Revolution.[201]

There was substantial agreement among the articulate theorists that an educational system adequate for the United States should be national in scope and nationalistic in emphasis.[202] Samuel Knox, principal of Frederick

School Discipline

Academy in Maryland, received an award from the American Philosophical Society for an essay which stressed the necessity of teaching youth to submerge sectional prejudices. Samuel Harrison Smith, editor of the Jeffersonian *New World* and founder of the *National Intelligencer,* proposed an extensive system of public schools. Less insistent than Knox upon uniformity in textbooks and curricula, he urged his country to take the best from all lands and use it for the world's benefit.[203] At the top of the ideal educational system stood the national university, a subject of much wishful thinking. Washington and Madison warmly endorsed the idea, the latter maintaining that a national "seminary of learning" could be established out of funds available from land sales in the District of Columbia.[204] In response, Dr. Samuel Latham Mitchill of New York prepared an elaborate report on the way in which a central school at the seat of government could roll "the flood of useful information throughout the land," but he found no constitutional warrant for such an appropriation of national funds.[205] Similar constitutional scruples may explain why Jefferson worked out the plans for his university in the state of Virginia.

Educational performance during the quarter-century after 1790 lagged far behind theory. John Adams might insist that the instruction of children of every rank and class, down to the lowest, was a public responsibility, but few taxpayers were eager to underwrite either a national or a state system of schools open to all without tuition. That legislators were aware of new forces demanding the democratization and secularization of education is apparent from the statutes which they enacted. But legal phrases did not describe actual conditions. The Massachusetts legislature, for example, in 1789 recognized the discrepancy between expectation and performance by providing that towns, which had long been obliged to establish elementary schools wherever there were 100 families, might in the future defer such provision until the number of families had increased to 200.[206] Of the sixteen commonwealths in 1800, seven had written into their constitutions general statements concerning the state's duty to educate the people, but the laws to particularize such generalities were of various sorts. In New England the district schools were largely supported either by local taxes or, as in the case of Connecticut, by proceeds from the sale of Western lands. In the Middle Atlantic states public funds generally went to private or parochial schools to supplement their slender resources, or to charity societies which sponsored educational work for the poor. In the South some states diverted revenues from lotteries and license fees into "literary funds" to be used for school purposes.

Despite the volume of legislation between 1790 and 1815 no part of the country had a comprehensive school system except on paper. Most of the laws were temporary expedients or were not enforced. Virginia, for instance, in 1796 authorized three "aldermen" in each county to set up districts, employ teachers, and construct schoolhouses where all free children, male and female, might receive instruction without cost for three years; five years later not a single county had acted.[207] Delaware's legislature of 1796 directed that for ten years the money received from tavern and marriage licenses should be used for the erection of local schools, but within a year the legislators repented and devoted most of the revenue to other purposes.[208] The general common school law of 1795, whereby New York appropriated £20,000 annually to be allotted to counties which voluntarily raised amounts equal to one half of the state grant, remained in effect only five years. Not until 1812 did a law inaugurate a permanent state subsidy for elementary instruction.[209]

The district schools which received public support were "free" only in the sense that no white child was excluded because of the family's social position or financial status. The local taxes, even when supplemented by state subsidy, seldom sufficed to pay the teacher's salary, purchase fuel and other supplies, and maintain the schoolhouse in serviceable condition. Whatever additional sum was needed to balance the annual budget was assessed against the families of the district according to the number of youths of school age. Parents unable to meet the rate bill were usually permitted to enroll their children with the understanding that they were "charity pupils." In Pennsylvania this stigma was made official by the preparation of a special list of those who requested exemption from payment. Throughout the rural districts, and to some extent in the cities, this regulation resulted in keeping many poor children away from school.[210]

In the cities the educational facilities for the poor were still largely provided by private and sectarian charitable associations, which occasionally received assistance from state or municipal treasuries. In 1801, for example, the free charity schools of eleven Protestant religious societies in New York City benefited from moneys which had become available under the law of 1795, and an equal amount was granted several years later to the school maintained by the Catholic Church. But it was chiefly children without church connections who were in need of free schooling. Their plight prompted the organization of nonsectarian groups which proceeded to mobilize benevolence for this purpose. Schools for both boys and girls were established in Philadelphia, Baltimore, New York, and other cities.[211]

Education beyond the elementary subjects depended chiefly upon private enterprise—upon clerical tutors, preparatory schools, or tuition academies. In New England the Latin grammar school of colonial days, with its emphasis on college preparation, was being challenged by the academy. At Andover, Massachusetts, and Exeter, New Hampshire, there were models which other institutions with small endowments and no comparable prestige strove to copy. By 1815, Massachusetts had thirty academies and New York thirty-seven. South of Pennsylvania the progress was even more rapid. As early as 1783, Georgia had undertaken to establish one in each county. The academies varied widely in organization and control, and their educational programs expanded rapidly. Many were founded upon endowments raised solely by popular subscription or by generous gift of a few philanthropists; some drew their support from particular religious sects; still others obtained public subsidies in addition to private funds. In New York, for example, the act of 1787 authorized the board of regents to incorporate academies and those which met state requirements received periodic appropriations from the state.[212] In some communities academy students ranged from boys and girls who had just learned to read to young men ready to enter college.

As late as 1830 public support of education was still largely "a gift to the destitute." This was as true of the Western states as of the slaveholding South.[213] In view of the provision in the land ordinance of 1785 setting aside the sixteenth section of each township in the Northwest Territory for public schools, the rapid development of a common-school system might have been expected. But not until 1824 did a reluctant Ohio legislature face the problem of how such a system could be created out of mere land grants. So it was in the sister states. Indiana in 1816 and Illinois in 1825 permitted the electors in each county to tax themselves for the maintenance of schools free to all, but few counties actually took advantage of the opportunity. The sale or leasing of land to pay the tuition of poor children at private schools was not abandoned until after 1830.

The secularization of education likewise proceeded slowly.[214] Eighteenth-century skepticism, as we have seen, had been largely overcome by the emotionalism of the revivals. The upswing of religious sentiment influenced the schools and in turn gained new strength from them. Not only did the churches maintain considerable supervisory power over elementary education—in Connecticut, for example, the schoolmaster had to be certified by the nearest minister of the established Congregational Church—but the curriculum stressed religious and moral precepts. In Noah Webster's spellers, Jedidiah Morse's geographies, and John Pierpont's readers the Christian spirit permeated the pupil's lessons, constantly reminding him of the hand of God in human affairs. Mingled with instruction on American governmental forms were suggestions that existing republican institutions had been divinely inspired. So patriotism had its religious side. There was a moral order in the universe, the student learned, upon which sound government rested, and that moral order was based upon revealed religion. Nowhere was this philosophy more explicitly stated, as we shall see in a later chapter, than in the colleges.

THE DAY OF THE MERCHANT

THE ABOUT-FACE which seemed to follow the "second war for independence" was more a state of mind than a reflection of economic realities. In their business activities, if somewhat less in their political concerns, Americans were constantly affected by forces emanating from the Old World. However much they wanted to concentrate upon the problems of their own expanding economy, they could not escape the fact that success for them often depended upon conditions across the Atlantic. The price of cotton at Liverpool, of tobacco at Le Havre, of flour at Lisbon or Cádiz, vitally concerned American producers. So, too, the movement of goods, whether in foreign or domestic commerce, responded in part to the London money market. After 1815, European balances in American banking houses began to accumulate, and within a decade such New York brokers as Romulus Riggs and Nathaniel Prime faced strong competition from the resident agents of British bankers.[215] Short-term commercial credit, granted by London merchants to stimulate their own exports, was subsidiary to the investment of capital funds in various American enterprises.[216] Between 1815 and 1827 more than $43 million worth of securities—government bonds, bank stocks, canal bonds—were sold in England. Already complaints were heard that foreigners had gained control of American industry.[217]

While the townsfolk of the Atlantic ports were still drinking toasts in celebration of the treaty concluded at Ghent, shipwrights and riggers were busy reconditioning the merchantmen which had been lying idle during the blockade. Some of these ships had not cleared for a foreign port since the days before the embargo. Now their owners proposed to carry on in the tradition of the prewar years. Commercial circles talked of clearances for Canton and Bombay as well as for Havana, Belfast, and Liverpool. The waterfronts of Boston, New York, and Philadelphia resounded with the shouts of longshoremen unloading goods which the British had decided to "dump" upon a relatively empty market at rock-bottom prices.[218] For several years after 1815, the American economy was bolstered by crop failures in Europe. But by the end of 1818, a general depression had settled upon the nation's businesses and industries.

In years of business depression social maladjustments appear in sharp definition. Then men give thought to the individual's responsibilities to society and the obligations of society to the individual. So it was in the crisis of 1819–22. Much writing occurred on the role of government in the promotion of human welfare. Though Americans had never before faced such insistent problems of unemployment and pauperism, many nevertheless agreed with John Quincy Adams that government could do nothing but wait for "the healers and destroyers, Time and Chance," to bring either "catastrophe or the cure."[219]

In the East, private philanthropy provided a safety valve for discontent. Urban poor were fed at soup houses supported by generous citizens and the charity organizations of the churches, while societies for the prevention of pauperism undertook to study the subject systematically.[220] Their proposals generally took the form of platitudes concerning industry, sobriety, and frugality. Humanitarian motives, as well as considerations of thrift, led to the founding of additional savings banks. The Savings Fund Society, created at Philadelphia in December 1816, was followed within the year by the Provident Institution at Boston. In July 1819 the New York Society for the Prevention of Pauperism sponsored a nonprofit savings bank, paying 5 percent on deposits and soliciting the business of laborers, mechanics, and tradesmen. Its first annual report showed more than $300,000 in about 3,000 accounts.[221]

During the twenties, American business seemed in the doldrums. Except for sharp rises in 1821 and again in 1825, wholesale commodity prices drifted steadily, though not alarmingly, lower, a trend more noticeable in the products of the factory than of the farm. The fluctuation of industrial prices corresponded rather closely with trends in Great Britain.[222] Public land sales fell off greatly. Only Indiana in 1824, Michigan in 1825, and Illinois two years later showed remarkable activity in this respect after the 1819 collapse.

Though foreign commerce also reflected the general decline of business, these years were rich in incidents of shifting trade routes, rising commercial centers, and new forces in transportation.[223] Despite the enemy's solicitude for New England during the War of 1812, the British blockade, following hard upon embargo and nonintercourse, had taken a heavy toll. Salem, proud of her 182 merchantmen engaged in foreign trade in 1807, had only 57 eight years later.

Meanwhile, Americans were making greater use of steam navigation. Its possibilities had been demonstrated on August 17, 1807, as Robert Fulton's *Clermont* moved slowly up the Hudson, sparks flying from her smokestack and the clanking of her steam-driven machinery drowning out the splashing of her paddle wheels. The speed was not impressive, for the trip from New York to Albany took slightly more than thirty hours. Yet even those inclined to scoff sensed the great changes in transportation were in the making.[224]

It was the inland waterways, however, rather than the safe reaches of New York Harbor and Long Island Sound, that witnessed the most notable triumphs of this new form of navigation. The first steamboat west of the Alleghenies was built in 1798 at Bardstown, Kentucky, by John Fitch. For another fifteen years most of the hardy woodsmen, who annually floated downstream to New Orleans to dispose of their agricultural surpluses, were compelled to make the long journey back on foot or, at best, on horseback. It was cheaper and easier to haul merchandise from Philadelphia to Pittsburgh in wagons at $125 a ton than to force it against the current of the Mississippi.[225] But in 1811, Nicholas Roosevelt, in association with Fulton and Robert R. Livingston, the first chancellor of the state of New York and an ardent supporter of steam navigation, persuaded the Louisiana legislature to grant an exclusive use of the lower Mississippi for steamboats. Their first vessel, the *New Orleans,* built at Pittsburgh, steamed down the river to

Scene on the Erie Canal

reach New Orleans early in January 1812. Four years later the *Washington,* equipped with stern paddle wheels and cleverly piloted by Captain Henry M. Shreve, made two round trips between New Orleans and Louisville, cutting the time upstream to a quarter that required by the barges and keel boats. It was an event, wrote Salmon P. Chase many years later, "of more momentous consequences to the West than the issues of a thousand battles."[226]

But the steamboat did not solve the country's transportation problems. Its usefulness was greatest upon rivers, lakes, and the protected bays and inlets of the Atlantic seaboard. But water transport lines failed to connect Eastern ports with trans-Appalachia. Those links, begun by the turnpikes and the towpaths of canals, were later completed by the tracks of railroads.

Tangible progress toward this objective commenced in 1824 when the Pennsylvania Society for the Promotion of Internal Improvements sent William Strickland across the Atlantic to investigate particularly the application of steam locomotives to tramways. Stricklens's fifty-page report, published with numerous plates in 1826, was freely copied by Eastern newspapers.[227] A few American engineers were prompted to see the developments for themselves.[228] Strickland's opinions were sensationally confirmed by the success of George Stephenson's *Rocket* when tried on the Liverpool and Manchester Railway in the fall of 1829.

Merchants, watching the expansion of their markets, seemed slow to realize what steam locomotion on land might mean to them, yet they were generally men of large vision. Among them a certain hierarchy had developed during the first quarter of the nineteenth century, though the lines were not rigid and a fusion of functions was much more common than specialization. Foreign textiles, for instance, might flow along such a channel as importer-jobber-retailer-consumer. The sequence was similar for American-made drygoods, if one substituted "domestic wholesaler" for "importer." But only in the larger cities were these gradations clearly defined. In such centers there might be two types of wholesalers—merchant middlemen and agent middlemen. The former took title to the various commodities which they handled, while the agent middlemen—commission merchants or factors, brokers, and auctioneers—avoided the risks normally involved in ownership.[229] Some wholesalers did a job-lot business, buying from importers who specialized in a single line of goods. Thus Joseph Hertzog of Philadelphia bought up varied assortments from importers in order to supply retailers along the Ohio and in St. Louis.[230]

Both foreign and domestic producers relied chiefly upon commission merchants, brokers, and auctioneers to establish contacts with retailers. The decade following the War of 1812 marked the heyday of the auction system. It cut into the business of importers and wholesale jobbers, who were quick to protest. Beginning in 1817 they vainly petitioned Congress for heavy duties on auction sales, but the delegates at a convention of the

The "Paragon," on the Hudson, about 1812

United Dry Goods Mercantile Association in New York in 1821 admitted that there was small chance of success without the cooperation of "those from populous towns, and sister cities, more or less remote," who frequented sales in New York and other seaports.[231] The popularity of auctions waned only when improvements in transportation made it possible for many inland towns to become wholesale centers and when manufacturers began to send aggressive agents into all parts of the nation to solicit business from country merchants who had once flocked to the Eastern sales.[232]

The general commission merchant frequently performed the services also of shipper, warehouse proprietor, insurance company, and banker, utilizing his own facilities rather than bringing his principals into contact with specialists in these several functions. The Neilson brothers of New Brunswick, New Jersey, for example, found that their shipping between the Raritan and New York City was more profitable during the twenties than their wholesale and commission business.[233] Christian Wilt, trading out of St. Louis on his own account and as a commission merchant, owned a fleet of riverboats at the close of the War of 1812.[234]

As an embryonic banker, the commission merchant stood in his most intimate relation to retailers, urban and rural. Usually he sold on credit of from four to six months. When prompter payment was required he often made a financial advance in order to facilitate exchange. By the late 1820s it was becoming customary to grant Western retailers six months' credit without interest and then to extend the period for another six months at a charge of from 6 to 10 percent.[235] Southern planters expected advances as high as three fourths of the market value of their cotton, tobacco, or sugar. In addition to financing the transfer of goods, the agent middlemen performed other banking functions. They might occasionally be called upon to buy or sell securities or specie, and they were frequently authorized to draw, endorse, accept, or sell bills of exchange, for which they received 2.5 percent. While it is impossible to determine the precise influence of these merchants upon commercial activities, by 1830 they were probably handling the major portion of the goods exchanged in this country on the basis of money payments.

Along the lines established by the commission houses capital flowed into all sections of the nation. Retail merchants were the transformers making it available for commercial transactions, individually unimportant but in the aggregate significant.

At the opening of the nineteenth century few retailers could afford to confine their stocks to a particular kind of goods. Typical of the limited market with slow means of transportation and communication was the general store, exchanging goods for goods and providing an outlet, however small, for the community's surplus produce. Its stock was always varied, sometimes inferior and seldom large. Observing the small country stores in western Pennsylvania in 1806, Thomas Ashe was reminded of a well-stocked magazine where one could find "both a needle and an anchor, a tin pot and a large copper boiler, a child's whistle and a pianoforte . . . a glass of whiskey and a barrel of brandy."[236] When Jedediah Barber opened the Great Western Store at Homer, New York, in 1813, he managed to crowd his merchandise into a room twenty-two feet by thirty. Fifteen years later his establishment, consisting of three stories besides an attic and a cellar, contained an assortment of drygoods, staple and fancy, "equal to any in the western country." Though the opening of the Erie Canal had cut down the long haul for Albany goods from 150 miles to thirty, from seven days to one, the Great Western continued to carry the same wide variety of articles.[237] Indeed, the general store in America changed little in a half-century. The descriptions of it at the time Abraham Lincoln was born are not inappropriate for the Offut establishment in Salem, Illinois, where he later worked, or for the country store flourishing in the year that he became president.

Though the rural retailer based his business largely on barter, certain articles could not be purchased without cash. Among them were tea, coffee, and powder and frequently leather, iron, and lead. On the other hand, some products were so much in demand and so easy to transport that they passed currently as specie. Pennsylvania, Ohio, and Missouri merchants were inclined to place deerskins, furs, feathers, linen cloth, and beeswax in this category.[238] The system of barter held some advantages for the storekeeper. Whatever country produce he accepted was valued lower than the price at which he expected to dispose of it, and he often had complete control of the marketable surplus in his immediate neighborhood. At times, however, this scarcely compensated for the risks of transportation he was compelled to assume.

Whether sales were made for money or goods, the country storekeeper rendered important services to the community. His contacts with distant market centers, domestic and foreign, enabled the people to concentrate upon those forms of production for which they were particularly qualified. For many of them these were the first tentative steps away from a self-sufficient economy toward economic specialization. Not least of the merchant's services was the extension of long-term credits. Probably a majority of his customers settled accounts only twice a year, in January and June, while some expected to be carried from one year's crop to the next.[239] That such concessions did not always prove sufficient is apparent from the yellowed pages of account books of the period.

In our admiration for the frontiersman blazing new trails, or the farmer clearing new land, we are apt to forget the pioneer merchant. He, too, was daring and determined. Many a Western community owed its origin to his decision to start a store at a particular crossroads or on the banks of a certain stream. As often as not, he preceded settlement, spying out opportunities for farm families who later contributed to his own prosperity. Shrewd and aggressive, he rendered signal public service, even when his acquisitive spirit was but slightly curbed by a sense of social responsibility. As his general store grew in size and his goods improved in quality, the range of his interests steadily widened. To farming—usually the initial accompaniment of shopkeeping—he proceeded to add milling and other forms of manufacturing. The grain which he accepted in exchange for wares was not all shipped to New Orleans or Eastern seaports; much of it was ground into flour at his own gristmill. An abundance of timber might lead him to erect a simple sawmill, or the opportunity to process other raw materials might result in his becoming a manufacturer of rope, bagging, paper, or tobacco products.[240]

Much that has been said concerning the general storekeeper applies also to the business of the urban retailer. Yet there were differences. By the opening of the nineteenth century a tendency toward specialization was apparent in the larger towns. City directories in Philadelphia, New York, Boston, and Providence classified most of the retail stores as dealers in groceries, drygoods, hardware, and queen's ware, the favorite combination being groceries and drygoods. The gradual separation of these two branches was a development of the first three decades of the century. Such specialization did not prevent the proprietor from adding to his stock any commodities which he could conveniently handle for his customers. In other words, the urban retailer was a general storekeeper who concentrated upon one or two profitable lines. Specialty stores, which steadily increased in number, were usually closely associated with the work of skilled craftsmen. The cabinetmaker, venturing beyond the limits of customers' advance orders, sold furniture at retail, the cobbler's shop was listed as a shoe store, the clock maker became a jeweler. Similarly, the apothecary shop expanded into the drugstore with a lengthening array of patent medicines upon its shelves. As late as 1830, however, all these stores were artisans' shops rather than specialized retail establishments.[241]

Although the volume of domestic manufacturers rose rapidly after 1815, many American consumers continued to show a partiality for imported goods. Shipments of broadcloths, flannels, and kersey were quickly snapped up at the auction rooms; and retailers vied with one another to obtain Sheffield ware and the motley assortment of articles which ingenious Birmingham manufacturers turned out "for the American trade." That the world of fashion should demand laces, ribbons, silks, and bonnets direct from Le Havre was natural, but the preference seemed to extend also to cheap muslins and calicoes. Price was not the determinant, for Fall River or Waltham could often undersell Manchester across New York and Charleston counters. Tench Coxe, pleading that Americans should manufacture and wear their entire cotton crop, discovered that in this respect at least his countrymen in the third decade of the century had not yet escaped from their colonial-mindedness.

THE CONSERVATIVE TRADITION

IN CALVINISTIC NEW ENGLAND at the opening of the nineteenth century, a reformation was taking place and its challenge was met by an effective counter-reformation.[242] Orthodoxy's champions in New England stubbornly resisted frontal assaults from Deists or flank attacks from liberals of Universalist or Unitarian persuasion, and they were resourceful in extending the areas of their own influence. Foremost in their ranks was the Reverend Jedidiah Morse of Charlestown, who gave and asked no quarter in the columns of his religious journal, the *Panoplist,* constantly striving to lay bare the lines of doctrinal cleavage and to convict the liberals of their Unitarian heresy. Finally, in 1815, when a recent publication of the English Unitarians which referred to American clerical brethren by name fell into his hands, he reprinted the entire passage and declared that the fight was now to be in the open. And so it was.[243]

On many New Englanders the grip of John Calvin was still unrelaxed. Though the trinitarians had lost every Boston pulpit but one, and Harvard's defection was not merely temporary, they yet had the satisfaction of establishing in 1808 a training school for ministers of the old faith at Andover, Massachusetts.[244] The Andover seminary was probably the most important institution of Calvinist orthodoxy in America during the first half of the nineteenth century. Among others, Moses Stuart brought national distinction to its faculty. At a time when Hebrew scholarship had virtually disappeared from American colleges, he learned German that he might read Gesenius's *Hebrew Lexicon of the Old Testament.*[245] In 1813 he published his grammar, the first Hebrew work printed in America, whose type he had set up with his own hand. It was but the first of thirty volumes revealing the scope of his knowledge and the depth of his zeal.

Though the majority of Christians in the United States relied upon a learned clergy, theological instruction was rarely formal and sytematic.[246] In a few colleges ministerial candidates attended lectures by professors of theology, but most received their special training as apprentice-students in the homes of divines for six months or a year, perusing such doctrinal works as were suggested and preparing a few essays in sermon form. Standards of training, of course, varied with the tutor and the requirements of the denomination. Congregationalists and Presbyterians insisted that each applicant submit evidence of a college degree or its equivalent and satisfy a board of examiners as to his proficiency in Greek, Latin, English grammar, mathematics, logic, rhetoric, geography, and natural philosophy.[247] In New England the Baptists strove to maintain similar standards, though their associations in the West and South did not. Few candidates who applied to the appropriate examining board for a license were rejected.

Superficial this sort of training might be, but it kept alive the tradition of a learned clergy at a time when some denominations tended to ignore formal tests of scholarship. In many Baptist associations, especially in the backcountry, a candidate's fitness to preach was decided by his neighbors in the congregation and depended upon personal attributes quite unrelated to sound learning. Frequently the Methodists likewise found among farmers and artisans men, like Paul of old, powerful in preaching the Word. Such self-trained exhorters became the circuit riders of trans-Appalachia at the beginning of the nineteenth century.[248] They prided themselves on being alumni of "Brush College"—that is, the school of practical experience. Most of them possessed no more of a library than their saddlebags could hold, yet a few, reading as they rode, gained a knowledge of the great works in English literature.[249]

The coming of the theological seminary foreshadowed the secularization of the college throughout America, for a steadily increasing number of ministerial candidates sought their formal training in this type of professional school. The first important seminary was Andover, founded in 1808. Though that institution resulted from dogmatic tensions in New England Congregationalsim, it was quickly copied in other sections and denominations, notably by the Presbyterians, who founded divinity schools at Princeton (1812) and at Hampden-Sydney College in Virginia.[250] Within twenty years of the inaugural ceremonies at Andover seventeen seminaries were founded—the initial group of those institutions which during the ensuing century would impose a distinctive stamp upon American Protestantism.[251]

Among the ventures of orthodox Protestantism none was more thriving than the plan for wholesale distribution of the Bible.[252] A society for this purpose was organized at Philadelphia in 1808. Within two years fifteen others had been formed in America.[253] Women became the effective workers, and the mite societies diverted a portion of their revenue into this affiliate of home missions. Young Samuel J. Mills, who had been the leading spirit of the little band at Williams College, made two extensive tours through the Western wilderness during the second war with Great Britain. In New Orleans, where he could not buy a Bible, he made arrangements for distributing 3,000 copies of a French translation of the New Testament. More than 76,000 families in the Southwest, he estimated, lacked access to the Scriptures.[254] As his report became available in print, men began to ask how the Bible societies could supply such a demand without cooperative effort. Having created a movement out of sentiment, they proceeded in typical American fashion to institutionalize it. While nationalist feeling ran high at the close of the War of 1812, delegates from thirty-five societies meeting at New York in 1816 established the American Bible Society. Within a decade there were glowing reports that through an intensive campaign virtually every family in the United States which lacked a Bible and desired one had received a copy of the King James version.

Ordination of the First American Foreign Missionaries

The First Planned Campus in America

More effective in reaching uninstructed minds were short, simple stories of Christian triumph over evil. In 1795, Mrs. Hannah More, the English essayist, had started a movement which fruited in the London Religious Tract Society, an organization which prompted emulation in America.[255] The first tract society, formed in Connecticut in 1807, was quickly followed by others in Vermont, New York, Pennsylvania, and Maryland. Nationalization among interdenominational lines, though deterred by local prejudices, finally resulted in 1825 in the American Tract Society with headquarters in New York. Judicious editing, though without sacrifice of fundamental orthodoxy, rendered the texts of pamphlets acceptable to all constituent sects. While many were reprints of little essays which had been popular in England, some were of American authorship, even by such eminent divines as Timothy Dwight and Gardiner Spring. There was a message for everyone: *An Affectionate Address to a Married Couple; Advice from a Master to His Apprentice; To Christian Females on Simplicity of Dress; Advice to the Keeper of a Turnpike Gate; The Well Conducted Farm* —and in large editions with woodcut illustrations. In 1827 the Society was printing more than 53 million pages annually and consigning them to local centers as far west as Illinois.[256]

Highly important in the new Christian propaganda was the Sunday school, which began as an educational philanthropy for poor children. In 1790, Philadelphia had a "First Day or Sunday School" sponsored by admirers of Robert Raikes's achievements with the neglected youths employed in the pin factories of Gloucester, England. It was copied the next year in Boston, and presently New England manufacturers such as Samuel Slater and David Humphreys set up such schools for their mill families, following the custom of using the Bible as a reading text and placing emphasis upon writing and simple arithmetic. By 1815 the Sunday school existed in a score of places from New Hampshire to Maryland.[257] This advance was not made without struggle, for some disliked the institution because of its origin in England, while others doubted the propriety of conducting schools on the Sabbath. To the latter it was pointed out that the exclusive use of the Bible as a textbook should be sufficient justification, and this educational feature began to stir the interest of churchmen.[258] Lyman Beecher, deploring the disappearance of the catechism from the schools, urged his parishioners at Litchfield, Connecticut, to enroll their children in regular attendance on Sabbath lessons.[259]

While the Sunday school was bringing thousands within the orbit of revealed religion, other organizations sought to lay restraints upon the conduct of the unchurched. Moral socieites, sounding a warning against Sabbath breaking, profanity, intemperance, and other human frailties, gave expression to a neo-Puritanism, in some repsects more rigorous than the Puritanism of the preceding generation. The Connecticut Society for the Reformation of Morals, formed in 1813, soon had local auxiliaries throughout the state.[260] The religious journals reported similar groups in other parts of the country.[261] As always, reform had its fanatics. Some communities now intensified their hostility to the theater and frowned upon even dancing and card playing, which had gone largely unrebuked earlier in the century. Horse racing, as it grew more popular in the North, encountered similar opposition. Pennsylvania in 1820 not only prohibited racing, but forbade any person to "print or cause to be printed, set up or cause to be set up, any advertisement mentioning the time and place for the running, trotting or pacing of any horse, mare or gelding."

The protest against intemperate drinking made the greatest headway. In 1810 it was estimated that 14,000 or more distilleries produced over 25 million gallons of ardent spirits annually. Ten years later the census enumerators reported that it was meaningless to classify distilling as a separate industry since it was carried on generally throughout the rural districts.[262] Inspired largely by the writings of Dr. Benjamin Rush, who had begun declaiming against distilled liquors while holding the post of physician general during the Revolutionary War, Dr. Billy J. Clark in Saratoga County, New York, brought together forty of his neighbors in a formal society early in 1808 and set a precedent of organization to diminish the use of strong drinks.[263]

Rush based his arguments mainly on grounds of hygiene. Others warned of the waste of money, time, and labor efficiency. It was Lyman Beecher who infused the aggressive spirit of evangelical Protestantism into the movement. Of his first Consociation meeting in Connecticut in 1810 he reported, "the sideboard, with the spillings of water, and sugar, and liquor, looked and smelled like the bar of a very active grog-shop. None of the Consociation were drunk; but that there was not, at times, a considerable amount of exhilaration, I can not affirm."[264] Aroused to action, he helped organize the Connecticut moral society in order to set a higher standard of conduct among the clergy as well as to wage war generally on "Sabbath-breakers, rum-selling, tippling folk, infidels and ruff-scruff."[265]

From Maine to the Mississippi the movement spread, easily blending its crusading spirit with the rising missionary zeal of the Protestant churches. Wherever a religious revival deeply stirred village and countryside, there the friends of temperance found fertile soil in which to sow their seed; and it multiplied abundantly. In 1826 the Boston leaders nationalized the movement by forming the American Temperance Society, which had jurisdiction over state, county, and village auxiliaries.[266] Its membership significantly overlapped those of the national tract and Bible societies and the missionary boards, and its most effective propagandist was the Protestant clergyman, who indicted intemperance as the great barrier to the church militant as it marched on to become the church triumphant.[267]

The temperance leaders won their most notable victories either in New England or in sections settled by Yankee stock, for community control of individual conduct had been a folkway in New England from the start.[268] Now, social welfare was to be advanced by moderation in the use of ardent spirits. Some even wished to go further. In 1825, pledge signers were asked to place the letter *T* beside their names if they would promise to avoid all ardent spirits. Within a decade the attitude of the "teetotalers" had become the objective of most societies and had been endorsed by the national convention after several stormy sessions.[269] By that time the word "temperance" had acquired a peculiarly American meaning: abstinence from the use of all alcoholic beverages.

The religious revival gave impetus to so many humanitarian reforms that enthusiasts thought they had Satan on the run. The millennium, which American students had repeatedly predicted from their meticulous exegesis of the Scriptures, seemed to be at hand.[270] Religious journals told of renewed interest in Bible study and the spread of the "concert of prayer" throughout the land and declared that the Great Revival of 1801 now was being enacted on a national stage.[271] Most inspiriting of all were the evidences of joint efforts in Christian work. "Various denominations," wrote Sereno Dwight, "already commune together at the sacramental table; and those who do not are relaxing in their rigidness. While the great divisions of the Church are thus growing truly liberal toward each other, they unite more cordially than ever in opposing fundamental error."[272]

In the story of the religious and humanitarian enterprises of this period the figure of the evangelical clergyman looms large. It was not otherwise in education. "The Christian College," said the Methodist Episcopal Conference in 1824, "is the bulwark of the Christian Church." Few discerned any conflict between such a view and secular learning; indeed, the dominant note in most colleges was religious, if not sectarian. Though less attention than formerly was given to training for the ministry, faculty members tended to feel they were churchmen first and scholars afterward.

The American college president was, in the language of biology, a throwoff from the clergyman, and early in the nineteenth century he was very imperfectly detached. More than nine tenths of the college heads during the forty years after 1790 were ordained ministers, who saw life from the sacred desk quite as steadily after their induction as before.[273] Originally the president had been the entire staff or, at best, had had one or two tutors or instructors under him, but by the close of the eighteenth century differentiation of function had separated from him three or four "specialist" professors. Still he remained chief executive with all that that implied in keeping records, maintaining discipline, raising money, and promoting cordial relations between the institution and its constituency. He also served as college pastor and taught theology or ethics or moral philosophy, sometimes all three.[274] Few carried their burdens with the easy dignity of Timothy Dwight of Yale, who became a great exemplar of the tradition which brought immense prestige to the college president in the United States.[275]

It would be difficult to describe the typical professor, whatever caricatures may have caught the fancy of alert undergraduates. The staff of the Western University of Pennsylvania (1822), to take an extreme example, consisted of the local clergy in the town of Pittsburgh.[276] In nearly all instances churchmen were numerous. The professor, then, evolved from the clergyman, either directly, like the college president, or indirectly through the slow division of the president's teaching functions into specialized fields of instruction. Toward hastening this process and ensuring that science would not undermine faith, Timothy Dwight made an influential contribution. He encouraged young men like Jeremiah Day, Benjamin Silliman, and James L. Kingsley, who could accept the Westminster Catechism and the Saybrook Platform, to devote their lives to the advancement of learning in nontheological fields.[277]

The traditional college curriculum consisted of four divisions: the classics; mathematics and natural philosophy; rhetoric and belles-lettres; and metaphysics and moral philosophy.[278] The crowning glory of the last year was the course in which the "moral professor," usually the president, ranged widely over the whole field of knowledge, pausing wherever he was interested. It was from this side of the college president that there developed in the course of time the political science, economics, sociology, and philosophy departments of the modern university. At Pennsylvania the "moral professor" in 1826 taught logic, philosophy, metaphysics, theology, natural and political law, and during his spare moments dabbled in composition and rhetoric.

The preponderant emphasis upon classical studies caused vehement controversy. It was raging as early as 1790. Dr. Hugh Williamson thought that Columbia College should substitute natural history for some of the required Greek and Latin, pointing out that the ancient Greeks had had the good sense to study their own language and literature.[279] Dr. Benjamin Rush voiced the fears of those who saw pagan immorality undermining Christian virtue.[280] Others insisted that the ancient languages symbolized the dead hand of tradition—students needed more time for the component parts of natural history; for modern languages, which were growing ever more important with the expansion of international trade; and for political philosophy and allied subjects, which were peculiarly useful to the citizens of a republic.[281] Of the numerous answers to such attacks none was more convincing than that of the eminent scholar Moses Stuart at Andover Seminary.[282] Though the ancient classics might seem remote from practical problems in the United States, the study of them, he argued, led to clear thinking, an appreciation of beauty, and a sense of literary form. Latin, long the living language of scholarship throughout Christendom, was basic to an understanding of English and many other modern languages, while Greek was the great avenue of approach not only to the life of an ancient people of remarkable intellectual vigor but also to the truths of the New Testament.

Preoccupied with classical studies the colleges may have been, but the instruction was surprisingly superficial. In 1825, George Ticknor, head of the department of foreign languages at Harvard, asked,

Who in this country, by means here offered him, has been enabled to make himself a good Greek scholar? Who has been taught thoroughly to read, write, and speak Latin? Nay, who has been taught anything, at our colleges, with the thoroughness that will enable him to go safely and directly onward to distinction in the department he has thus entered . . . ?[283]

Even if allowance be made for Ticknor's own foreign sojourns and his exceptionally high standards, it seems obvious that college boys were not being trained for scholarly work.

Attempts to modify the traditional college curriculum accomplished little. Jefferson's plans for the University of Virginia, designed to admit scientific interests and provide superior professional schools, proved more alarming than inspiring. Conservatives even frowned upon Eliphalet Nott's modest proposals at Union College, where he established a parallel course in which modern languages might be substituted for Greek.[284] His example may have encouraged Amherst in 1827 to give credit for modern languages, English literature, history, political economy, and experimental work in natural science in lieu of the classical courses.[285] It would be possible to list other innovations, yet as the third decade of the nineteenth century ended the classicists were still in control. A Yale report on the curriculum in 1828 eloquently defended the place of ancient languages and literatures in the whole scheme of a liberal education. Faculty and trustees alike endorsed it.

College authorities apparently spent more time discussing disciplinary than instructional problems. In some institutions the students lived in drab quarters under a "benevolent despotism" more efficacious in promoting rebellion than in maintaining order. Riots in commons over unsatisfactory fare suggest that income from inadequate endowments was sometimes eked out by economies at table. Furthermore, no intercollegiate athletics or compulsory physical training existed to take some of the mischief out of exuberant youth.[286] In most colleges extracurricular activities were neither numerous nor varied, but it was only the unsocial student at Harvard who could not find amusement or instruction in the musical, literary, and religious societies, or in the clubs dedicated exclusively to nonsense.[287] On every campus rough-and-tumble games were played without violating college rules. By 1830 some variation of "four-old-cat," or "bat and ball" as it was called in New England, had become popular. Primitive football, a crude adaptation of the English sport, often provided the means for settling differences between classes. Like their elders, American boys were eager to test individual prowess, but they lacked indoor facilities to measure and compare strength and skill. The gymnasium was still a curiosity on the college campus.[288]

Colleges were rapidly increasing in number. At the opening of the century there had been twenty-two degree-granting institutions; three decades later they totaled fifty-six, not counting those that had failed to survive.[289] This increase came out of a complex in which religious zeal, educational aspiration, local pride, political rivalry, and real estate interests were closely commingled. Sectarianism, reenforced by a desire to keep learning close to the people, was a major factor in scattering colleges widely over the country. In the opinion of the American Education Society, this was indicative of a democratic spirit "which will not rest till it has brought within the reach of every enterprising youth, the means of a liberal education."[290] Some, however, regretted that Americans had not followed the example of the British and the French in creating a few great centers of learning. Others felt that no further additions should be made to the "multitude of colleges."[291]

According to Jedidiah Morse's Geography Made Easy (1802), the colleges were "generally well furnished with libraries, apparatus, instruments and students." The trustees of these institutions, however, would scarcely have recognized the description. The productive funds of the twenty-two colleges in 1800 were estimated at slightly more than $500,000. In 1804, when Nott became president, the expenditure of Union College was only $4,000, but the income was even less—a situation which he promptly corrected by conducting several lotteries under state authorization. As late as 1830, Yale had only about $20,000 income from endowment, while Harvard secured half its total revenue of $45,000 from student fees and rents. These were the more substantial schools. From the West came incessant pleas for books, equipment, and funds.[292]

Following the depression of 1819 there were numerous complaints that student enrollments were declining. A survey made by the American Education Society in 1829 listed Yale first with 359 undergraduates drawn from a geographic range wider than that of any other college. Harvard stood second with 247, followed by Union (227), Amherst (207), and Dartmouth (137).[293] Fifty colleges had fewer than 135 students each. The professors were peculiarly interested in fluctuating enrollments at a time when salaries were partially based upon fees in courses. Though Columbia abandoned the fee system in 1810, offering its professors $2,500 annually and the use of a dwelling house, many colleges, especially in the West and South, continued to eke out fixed salaries with fees, whenever income from endowments and special gifts seemed uncertain.[294]

The library was the weakest point in any comparison of American colleges with European universities. At the beginning of the century Dartmouth reported 4,000 volumes while Princeton had no more. Both institutions, like many others, also relied upon the collections of the literary societies.[295] To its 2,700 volumes in 1790 Yale added more than 4,000 in thirty years, making its entire collection no larger than the magnificent private library built up by Thomas Jefferson. Like many other institutions, Yale specialized in theological works, almost a third of the titles falling into that category. From Göttingen, George Ticknor wrote in 1816, "I cannot better explain to you the difference between our University in Cambridge and the one here than by telling you that here I hardly say too much when I say that it *consists* in the Library, and that in Cambridge the Library is one of the last things thought and talked about."[296] Yet Harvard had been singularly fortunate on this score. In 1812 its library contained some 15,000 volumes—a number not reached by Columbia until after the Civil War— and in 1830 more than 35,000 books, maps, and other items. No other college could match its treasures.[297] In 1790, Thomas Cooper had remarked that American libraries consisted "almost entirely of *modern* books" and did not contain "the means of tracing the *history* of questions," but he lived long enough in academic circles to see the changes as college librarians tardily became aware of the slowly expanding curricula.[298]

"I cast my eye, for a moment," wrote Moses Stuart in 1828, "on the catalogues of the New England Colleges, which contain *exposées* of the course of study. Here I see navigation, surveying, gauging, spherical trigonometry, fluxions, integral and differential calculus, conic sections, calculation of eclipses, chemistry, mineralogy, the law of nations, political economy, and many other studies of the like nature. . . ."[299] He could have added to this lengthy list. Yet the curriculum still revolved about the classics, moral philosophy, and "evidences of Christianity." Alexis de Tocqueville might well have used the colleges to give point to his observation in the early thirties that, despite the lack of a national church, religion was the foremost institution of the country, more influential in America than in any other land.

LAWYERS AND DOCTORS

At the close of the Revolution the legal fraternity was notoriously unpopular—nowhere more so than in New England. "The most innocent and irreproachable life," remarked John Quincy Adams in 1787, "cannot guard a lawyer against the hatred of his fellow citizens."[300] The reasons were various. As the lawyers who remained loyal to the Crown either retired from active practice or fled the country, pettifoggers took the vacant places and soon found more than a living in collecting debts contracted during the wartime inflation. Attorneys and counselors came to be regarded as hirelings of the creditor interests, English as well as American. There was muttering also against prominent lawyer-politicians who aided returning

Loyalists in suits to regain possession of their property.[301] But while these prejudices lingered long among mechanics and small farmers, the early years of the nineteenth century brought a remarkable change of sentiment. European visitors now noted that the lawyer was "the first man in the state," occupying a social position alongside clergymen and physicians and wielding great political power. Some commentators shrewdly attributed this prestige to the rapidly growing demand for legal services in business and land affairs.[302]

But the professional status of the lawyer was still precarious. No group in the United States corresponded to the upper bar in England, possessing special privileges and prerogatives by reason of affiliation with the Inns of Court. The Revolution had swept away the aristocracy of American barristers trained at the English Inns, who had been notably strong in the Southern provinces.[303] For several decades thereafter the term "barrister" was frequently used, but it became an honorary title accorded by common consent to outstanding lawyers.[304] The English distinction between the practitioner in law (attorney) and in equity (solicitor), faintly persisting in New Jersey and Delaware, generally disappeared; and the functions of the counselor or barrister were also assumed by the attorney. In New York, for example, the leaders of the bar apparently intended to follow the English system, but the provision that solicitors might easily become counselors and the subsequent requirement that counselors in chancery must also be attorneys gradually modified distinctions once more sharply defined.[305] Out of the modifications of English and colonial precedents there emerged the general practitioner, whose sign read "attorney and counselor at law."

Control over admissions to the bar varied. In 1800, Kentucky, Virginia, and North Carolina were the only states where neither rule of court nor legislative act fixed definite periods for legal training. While no uniformity existed, the court regulations usually called for a clerkship of from three to seven years with appropriate credit for courses completed in college. The preparatory work in several states was below the standard set during the colonial period, and from time to time the training term was shortened during the early decades of the nineteenth century.[306] Ohio's first constitution (1802) included every clause of the territorial code except that relating to the education of lawyers. Indiana in 1817 substituted a superficial system of examinations for the traditional clerkship. These were but straws in the wind. The general decline in standards came after 1830 as frontiersmen and urban workers demanded that the lawyer's special privileges be made more easily available to ambitious young men.[307]

The clerkship was usually an informal arrangement. In some parts of the East, particularly New England and New York, the bar associations, motivated by self-interest as well as concern for the profession, undertook to regulate the relation between clerk and counselor. Of the attorneys practicing in Massachusetts between 1800 and 1830 more than 90 percent were college graduates and began their legal education in law offices.[308] The value of such training depended upon the time which the attorney, busy with the details of his private practice, was willing to devote to instruction, however unsystematic. Few preceptors were so inspiring as George Wythe, who during his Richmond years taught young Henry Clay, or so methodical as Lemuel Shaw, who became chief justice of Massachusetts. Shaw prescribed a regular program based upon his clerks' previous reading and designed to acquaint them with the routine of local practice as well as with the philosophy of the law.[309] Most young men "reading law," however, spent their time copying papers, looking up cases, preparing abstracts and briefs, and learning legal procedure by haunting the county courts. Even Joseph Story, fortunately apprenticed in Samuel Sewall's office at Marblehead, complained he had little opportunity to ask for explanations "to light up the dark and intricate paths."[310]

If the student turned to his preceptor's library for help, he was apt to be disappointed. Few of the texts possessed sufficient literary merit to make subtle refinements easy for him. After a careful reading of Bacon's *Pleas and Pleading* John Quincy Adams found the subject "so knotty" that he would have to read the work "one or twice more."[311] Story, having finished Blackstone's *Commentaries,* was directed by Sewall to read Coke on Littleton. He "took it up, and after trying it day after day with very little success . . . sat down and wept bitterly." For a time he was completely confused by the "intricacies of the middle ages of the common law, and the repulsive and almost unintelligible forms of process and pleadings."[312] In most offices books were few, especially in the days before court reports were widely published, but the student-apprentices read earnestly, if not extensively. Webster went through Vattel's *Law of Nations* three times, while John Quincy Adams devoted the same attention to Blackstone's *Commentaries.*[313] Less widely read than Blackstone, but well known, were Ward's *Law of Nations,* Lord Bacon's *Institutes,* Hawkins's *Pleas of the Crown,* Pufendorf's *Of the Law of Nature and Nations,* and Rutherforth's *Institutes of Natural Law,* which was really a commentary on Grotius. No comprehensive commentary on American law was available until James Kent's four volumes appeared between 1826 and 1830.

From a well-conducted office with two or three students trying to master a few texts, it was but a short step to a small private law school. That step was taken late in the eighteenth century. Sometime between 1782 and 1784, Tapping Reeve at Litchfield, Connecticut, began a series of formal lectures to students in his office and announced that he would conduct a law school.[314] For a half-century he or his associates, James Gould and J. W. Huntington, trained young men from every part of the country, more than a thousand in all. Students who completed the course spent fourteen months—eight in the first year and six in the second—attending lectures, reading cases, writing weekly examination papers, and participating in moot court or the programs of the forensic societies. Though Reeve was not a vigorous lecturer, judged by the oratorical standards of his generation, he possessed the qualities of an inspiring teacher. A goodly number went out from Litchfield to win recognition in private practice or in public office, and if they were not Federalists it was no fault of their preceptor. Fifteen became U.S. senators and ten governors, two were appointed to the Supreme Court, and forty were named to the state judiciary. High on the list stand the names of John C. Calhoun, Horace Mann, George Y. Mason, and Levi Woodbury.[315] It was said that the student learned more at Litchfield in one year than could be gained in five by the "ordinary method of securing an acquaintance with legal principles."[316]

Whatever his legal education, the neophyte became familiar with judicial procedure by frequenting the county courts rather than by reading treatises and reports. There was much to be learned—the functions of the various court officials, the possibilities in challenging potential jurymen, the rules of evidence, the nuances in handling witnesses, and the legal erudition sometimes paraded in the charge to the jury. Ceremonial precedents were few and simple, causing foreign observers to deplore the failure to maintain the dignity of the courts. Judges were abandoning the English custom of wearing carefully curled wigs and scarlet robes.[317] Black suits and black gowns were the only distinguishing costume of bench and bar in most parts of the country. Sporadic attempts to preserve the judicial garb of colonial days were discountenanced as incongruous in a simple republican government, or as unseemly survivals of English practice.

Court time was frolicking time. Taverns at the county seat were filled with litigants, attorneys, and spectators who had come to enjoy the sparring of rival counsel and to participate in the wrestling, gambling, drinking, and horse racing which filled the intervals between sessions. Even the judges spent the evenings in smoking, drinking, and "cracking jokes indifferently with all."[318] James Kent, riding the western "eyres" of New York, was often distressed by the easy informality of lawyers, litigants, and jurymen, especially in "democratic" counties, but he admitted that court procedure, however lacking in pageantry, was orderly and marked by a simple dignity.[319] On a small platform in the courtroom sat the judge behind a high desk with the clerk below him, quill behind his ear and armed with the papers of the case. On either side of the clerk's desk attorneys for plaintiff and defendant sat at tables, while the jury occupied hard wooden benches close to the witness box and the prisoner was seated on an enclosed bench guarded by the sheriff or his deputies. A conspicuous iron stove made court sessions during the winter months endurable, if not always pleasant.[320]

In most states the attorneys and judges of both appellate and county courts rode circuit. For the beginner this proved excellent schooling since he learned from the conversations of older practitioners, often in reminiscent mood, lessons which would help him handle difficult cases of his own.

But circuit riding put lawyers, young and old, to the test. Its physical discomforts were slight in comparison with its professional disadvantages. There was little opportunity to confer with clients and witnesses, and reference to legal authorities frequently was limited to whatever could be conveniently carried in one's saddlebags. So aggravating was the situation in Berkshire County, Massachusetts, that in 1815 the members of the bar formed a Law Library Association to provide books for use during court sessions.[321]

Lawyers, everywhere, engaged in a fierce hunt for clients. Except in New England, where maritime questions frequently arose, they found their most lucrative practice in serving the interests of the landed gentry and land speculators. At the same time, however, the ramifications of expanding domestic and foreign commerce; the extraordinary problems imposed by nonintercourse, embargo, and war; and the growing investment in machine industry steadily emphasized the importance of the law merchant. Legal business was increasing so rapidly, especially in the port cities, that conditions seemed favorable for specialization within the profession. It was retarded, however, by the fact that in most communities the personnel of the landowning and mercantile groups was closely related and by the inclination of both groups to make investments in industrial enterprises.[322]

Country lawyers, quite as much as their colleagues in the cities, used the law as a gateway to business opportunities. The small town, often the frontier village, beckoned to the beginner. If he was not already a qualified attorney, a season of teaching school might precede the day when he had satisfied all requirements and could hang up his shingle. However that might be, his ultimate success depended upon his ability to withstand months of anxious waiting for clients and other tedious months of filling out writs and serving summonses or of drudgery over deeds, conveyances, and bad debts. Once he had won the confidence of his neighbors, there came a period of widening business activity as he learned of mortgages to be foreclosed or of choice tracts of land where a small speculative investment might return proportionately large profits. Political preferment, at first a welcome supplement to insufficient income, came to be valued as a badge of power and prestige. Many country lawyers built their lives into the communities where they first sought clients; others regarded the small town as merely a way station to the city. Rufus Choate, starting practice in the busy port of Salem, quickly moved to Danvers, where he would not have to face the eminent lawyers of Essex County. When he ran for Congress, it was charged that he did not reside in the district since he was only stopping there "while he oated his horse" for Boston.[323]

The income of the legal profession in America varied greatly. George Ticknor, visiting Philip Barbour, an eminent Virginia lawyer, found that he was making less than $7,000 in 1824.[324] A few years later William Wirt, U.S. Attorney General (1817–29), was told that $6,000 or $8,000 was a good

The Pennsylvania Hospital, in 1802

practice in New York City while $10,000 was the maximum. Even such figures must have seemed astronomical to small-town lawyers, especially when farm prices sagged and speculative land values broke sharply.

Medical societies strove to formulate codes of professional conduct and to ensure compliance. Modeling their bylaws on the Englishman Thomas Percival's *Medical Jurisprudence or Code of Ethics* (1803), they suggested the precepts that should guide the physician in his relations with patients and colleagues. If he hit upon an efficacious formula, he was expected to share it with the profession. Few, however, resisted the temptation to keep their prescriptions secret. In 1797 the Connecticut Medical Society gave nationwide publicity to Elisha Perkins by expelling him because he had patented "painted metallic instruments" which, he alleged, possessed inherent powers of curing many diseases. Expulsion apparently did not prevent the discoverer from reaping a small fortune from the sales of "Perkins Tractors."[325] After considerable deliberation the physicians of Albany dropped Dr. Elias Willard's name from their rolls because he refused to reveal the nature of his reputed cure for scrofula and cancer.[326] Likewise, Massachusetts expelled Dr. Lyman B. Sarbin of Wrentham who had the patents to Dr. Lee's Gravel Specific and Peges Vegetable Cyrup.[327]

Suspicion of motives hindered the work of the societies, for many felt that the primary purpose of such organizations was purely selfish—to increase patronage and maintain high charges for service. In New Haven and elsewhere it was said that the way to bring a full attendance at a meeting was to advertise a discussion of fees. But there is no conclusive evidence to indicate how closely individual physicians followed the rate schedules so determined.[328]

Practitioners who failed to meet the standards of allopathic medicine proved a perennial source of trouble. It was not easy to draw the line between harmless herbalists and dangerous quacks.[329] Probably no irregular commanded more followers than Samuel Thomson, who in 1813 patented a system combining steam baths with the use of varying vegetable compounds in which the emetic properties of lobelia leaves were important. From "Thomsonism" stemmed a host of "botanics" and "steam doctors," whose regimen may have helped, if it could not cure, perennially hopeful patients. Dr. Benjamin Waterhouse of Boston, openly endorsing Thomson's ideas, was criticized by a profession which dared not discipline him for his temerity. Even Benjamin Rush and Benjamin Smith Barton of Philadelphia had a good word for the "botanics."

As the list of irregulars—botanic, regular botanic, Thomsonian, reformed Thomsonian, magnetical, electrical, rootist, herbist, florist—steadily lengthened, state legislatures began to retreat from their attempts to promote higher standards in medicine.[330] There was an impression abroad that some sort of conspiracy existed in medical circles to deprive the poor man of his cheap cures. As a Massachusetts farmer wrote in 1798,

The Doctors have established their Meditial Societyes . . . by which they have
so nearly enielated Quacary of all kinds, that a poor man cant git so grate
cures of them now for a ginna, as he could 50 years ago of an old Squaw for
halfe a pint of Rhum. The bisness of a Midwife could be purformed 50 years
ago for halfe a dollar & now it costs a poor man 5 hole ones.[331]

Here was the crude but forceful expression of the spirit which from that
day to this has resisted advances in medical science.[332]

Self-interest spurred the licensed practitioner in his running fight with
the patent-medicine industry. In America, as in England and the German
provinces, there was fear that the competition would undermine the position of the medical profession.[333] The Medical Society of the City of New
York in 1827 carefully investigated Swain's Panacea, Potter's Catholicon,
Columbian Syrup, and other popular "remedies" for rheumatism, syphilis,
scrofula, and chronic eruptions. They reported most of them to be ineffective, nothing more than compounds of sarsaparilla and varying amounts of
harmless drugs.[334] Manufacturers of such concoctions found golden rewards in indulging man's eternal craving for cheap and painless cures.
Others, equally reprehensible in the eyes of the medical societies, published books of prescriptions guaranteed to cure two types of diseases:
those which baffled the scientist and those which the victim in shame
wished to conceal.[335]

At the close of the eighteenth century the leaders in American medicine
were men with European training, most of them having studied at Edinburgh or Leyden. In 1803, however, the editor of the *Medical Repository,*
glancing over the latest list of Edinburgh graduates, noted that of the
twenty-four candidates "there was not a single one from the United States.
The schools of Philadelphia, New York, Cambridge, Baltimore, Lexington
[Kentucky], and Dartmouth are engaged in the business of medical education to an extent that is pleasing and surprising."[336] It was being loudly
proclaimed, and increasingly believed, that one could become a first-class
doctor without studying abroad. In fact, the American medical schools
were not only well established, but they were sending their graduates
into distant parts of the country, there to found new schools and to raise
professional standards. It was one of the achievements to which Americans
constantly pointed in their boasts of cultural independence.

Though such training determined the nature of leadership in the profession, only indirectly did it affect the rank and file of American physicians.
The vast majority in 1800 had gained their skill and knowledge not in a
medical school but by apprenticeship. In a physician's office the apprentice, besides sweeping floors and keeping fires, read his master's books,
pounded out the powders with his master's pestle, and made up pills. From
it he followed his master to the sick room, handed him the necessary tools,
and watched his practice, much as a plumber's helper does today.[337] As his

knowledge grew, he took a hand himself, but the master was entitled to such fees as came from the apprentice's extracting of teeth, bleeding, or other minor operations. In return the master taught the pupil everything he could. Occasionally a successful doctor might take several young men into his office and lecture them as a class. Such opportunities, however, were exceptional. Instruction of apprentices in medicine, as in law, was usually casual and fragmentary.

The inadequacies of the American doctor's office as a training school strongly impressed all who had studied in Europe. Chemistry required an "elaboratory," Dr. Samuel Bard of New York observed, botany a garden, and, above all, diseases could not be systematically studied save in a hospital.[338] These considerations pointed to the desirability of well-equipped medical schools located in the larger cities. But not all schools sprang from such sound motivation. Some resulted from professorial jealousies and professional quarrels. In New York City, where these disputes were particularly intense, three schools were founded—in 1792, 1811, and 1826—whose graduates received their degrees through Rutgers College in New Brunswick. So inharmonious was the medical faculty at Columbia that the College of Physicians and Surgeons was chartered in 1807. Well might DeWitt Clinton lament, "Look at New York . . . three contended where there should have been one grand temple dedicated to the healing art."[339] That grand temple was long in building, for after Physicians and Surgeons had absorbed the Columbia medical faculty in 1813 and had crushed the Rutgers school a few years later, it still had to face another rival in the twenties and the vigorous competition of New York University in the next decade. A similar schism produced a school to challenge that of the University of Pennsylvania, but Philadelphia's doctors, however vehement their disagreements, never equaled their New York colleagues in acrimonious dispute.

During the two decades after 1810 medical faculties were established with unprecedented rapidity, most of them granting their degrees under the charter of some liberal arts college.[340] Except for those in New England —at Brown (1811), Yale (1813), and Bowdoin (1820)—these newer schools generally ministered to the needs of frontier regions or rural communities. The one at Winchester, Virginia, served the valley of the Shenandoah, while as early as 1813 young men from the Mohawk Valley were attending courses instituted by Lyman Spalding, who had come from Dartmouth to Fairfield, New York. The medical department of Middlebury College opened at Castleton, Vermont, in 1818; about the same time Lexington, Kentucky, welcomed the medical department of Transylvania University; and the restless spirit of Daniel Drake, who held a degree from the University of Pennsylvania, found a temporary abode in the Ohio Medical College at Cincinnati before moving farther west.[341]

Prior to 1830 the South's medical dependence on Northern schools and hospitals was almost compete. During colonial days Southerners interested in medicine, as in law, had formed a disproportionately large contingent among the provincials studying in Europe. At the opening of the nineteenth century, however, Edinburgh was being supplanted by Philadelphia, New York, and other American institutions.[342] But neither foreign study nor Northern schooling was thought to fit young doctors to meet the challenge of diseases which were peculiarly Southern. Furthermore, the Southerner, coming from a "Yankee" school, had to revise many of his notions in the light of native conditions. It was Charleston, where scientific interest had long flourished, which finally established in 1823 the Lower South's first medical school—the Medical College of the State of South Carolina.[343]

The mushroom growth of training institutions pleased Americans like Daniel Drake, who felt that such activity would free the country from European influences, but the *Boston Medical intelligencer* in 1826 viewed "the multiplication of medical schools" with alarm. "In all England," the editor wrote, "there is but one medical school, one in Ireland, in Scotland two (for that at Aberdeen scarcely deserves the name); and in all France but three. In the United States there are already 17, and scarcely a month but we learn of the establishment of a new one."[344] What the *Intelligencer* failed to realize was that the settled parts of the United States in 1826 extended over an area of nearly three times that of France and the British Isles combined, and that distance was an important factor in the availability of medical instruction.

As new schools reached out to serve a rapidly increasing and perennially migrant population, it became difficult to maintain earlier standards. Gradually the degree of bachelor of medicine was abandoned, and the doctorate was cheapened by bestowal on those who met little more than the former bachelor's requirements. At the very moment Edinburgh was lengthening its medical course from three years to four, American schools were accepting two terms, each of which had been shortened from four months to twelve or thirteen weeks to suit the convenience of students who had to travel long distances from their homes. Standards suffered also from the failure to retain natural history and natural philosophy as a background for the young doctor's science and from the withering of the dissertation, that guild masterpiece long essential to the doctorate. One melancholy critic said that a medical diploma was as "little respected as the license of many of our county medical societies."[345]

A perusal of medical school circulars and catalogues reveals virtual uniformity at any given time in the arrangement and sequence of courses. Despite some evidence of progressive differentiation in subject matter, most professors, as well as most physicians, took all medicine for their province. At Dartmouth, Nathan Smith was the entire faculty for almost a dozen years.[346] James S. Stringham taught chemistry in the Columbia medical faculty, but later in the College of Physicians and Surgeons he taught medical jurisprudence. David Hosack was considered equally proficient in botany, midwifery, theory and practice of physic, and clinical medicine.

Basic for the student was the work in anatomy, physiology, and chemistry, followed by more advanced courses in therapeutics, botany and materia medica, midwifery, diseases of women and children, and medical jurisprudence. Slowly the schools followed the lead of the University of Pennsylvania after 1805 in separating the course in surgery from that in anatomy. Not until 1813 was the lecturer on midwifery, whose subject was still regarded as folklore of women, given equal standing with other members of the medical faculties.[347] By 1820 the requirement was well established that each student should attend lectures, sometimes five or six a day, in all subjects during his first term and then go to the same lectures during his second year. This regulation probably had originated at a time when textbooks were so scarce and lecturers so few that a return engagement by each professor was necessary in order to cover the subject matter properly.[348] Later, as repetitive attendance on a professor's lectures became conventional, there were few protests in faculties where aggregate fees determined salaries.

Although the importance of dissection in the study of anatomy had been clearly recognized since the days of Vesalius, this phase of medical training, even in the larger American schools, was seriously handicapped by lack of adequate equipment and by popular prejudice against the use of cadavers in teaching the subject. In April 1788, some boys, noticing a severed human limb hung out of a New York City hospital window to dry, straightaway raised a riot which required the combined efforts of governor, chancellor, mayor, and militia to quell.[349] An especially aggravating case of body-stealing at the Yale school in New Haven necessitated a two days' military guard for the professor of anatomy. At Berkshire, choleric Major Butler Goodrich threatened to burn the college down unless corpse-snatching ceased. While medical faculties sought to quiet the public by promising expulsion for "any attempt, proved on a student, to disinter the dead," such appeals as that of Dartmouth, offering $50 for each corpse, not only spurred irrepressible youngsters to activity but also sent surreptitious merchants of cadavers to medical college doors. The bodies of executed criminals had long been available, but not until 1830 did Massachusetts take the lead in devoting to science those of unclaimed paupers dying in state charge. Though the law was slowly liberalized in other states, the popular aversion to dissections long persisted, handicapping the "clinical professor" in his systematic research and often preventing the autopsy in private practice.[350]

Other barriers discouraged the search for the true nature of disease. Medical men were distracted, and their work was often disrupted, by the recurrent pestilence which ravaged American cities in the three decades after 1790. To the profession these visitations were a terrific challenge, not only exacting a heavy toll in human lives but subtly influencing medical theory and practice. When yellow fever or typhoid or malaria struck in epidemic form, the insistent demand was for immediate treatment to forestall death. The yellow fever visitation of 1793 in Philadelphia was one of the worst the United States has ever experienced. The unadorned narrative of Mathew Carey describes it no less vividly than the fictionized account in Charles Brockden Brown's *Arthur Mervyn*.[351] There had been sporadic outbreaks of this disease, particularly in New York in 1702 and again in the early forties.[352] But in 1803 a Philadelphia journal could say: "Till the year 1793, we, in this part of America, at least, the present generation, had only heard and read of pestilence. Since that period it has visited us five years out of ten . . . by which the city would be, for two or three months, almost entirely depopulated. . . ."[353]

There and elsewhere, especially in the Atlantic ports, its periodic returns continued until the 1820s. The horror of those times when cities lost thousands of their residents, when corpses were hurried through the night-black streets or abandoned where they lay, when rows of houses bore the tragic chalk mark, when impromptu hospitals were rigged up at the town's edge to be tended by heroic men who volunteered as nurses, when every desperate expedient at prevention and cure was tried on hearsay, when crime flourished amid the prevalent distraction — such horror could not be overstated. Nor was the dread destroyer confined to the seacoast. Between 1797 and 1803 the *Medical Repository* reported epidemics, diagnosed as yellow fever, in western New York, central Pennsylvania, southeastern Ohio, and several settlements along the Mississippi. In neighborhoods where poverty prevented flight the list of victims was always long. "A poison," remarked a journalist in 1801, "which, in the city of New-York, has destroyed, within three months, the lives of more than twenty practitioners of medicine, well deserves to be traced and understood by the survivors."[354]

If understanding was not vouchsafed to this generation, speculation concerning probable cases and cures was voluminous.[355] These variant explanations seemed to support two contending schools of thought. The "importationists" insisted that yellow fever was brought by ships from the tropics, while the "domesticians" attributed it to poisonous acid gases arising from rotting refuse or foul ships. Dr. Samuel Latham Mitchill, spreading fear of this lethal agent, which he called septon, recommended that it be counteracted by alkalis, especially lime.[356] But not all domesticians subscribed to the "septon theory." Some associated fevers with the cosmic maladjustments that produced droughts, meteors, earthquakes, and volcanic eruptions. Noah Webster wrote a 700-page history showing the relation between disturbances in the physical world and the incidence of pestilence — a work which Benjamin Rush warmly recommended to Joseph Priestley, for it confirmed the Philadelphian's own observations concerning epidemics and earth tremors.[357]

Less fantastic was the suggestion that fever, or at least malaria, was generated in stagnant water and some even mentioned the mosquitoes which bred there. A writer in Savannah held the surrounding marshes responsible for the "autumnal insalubrity" while a North Carolinian blamed the swampy land near Edenton.[358] But many scoffed at such theories. The editor of the *Medical Repository,* pointing out that "writers have been very fond of considering a plentiful generation of insects to be the forerunner or concomitant of epidemic diseases," concluded: "Common as this opinion is, and strenuously as it has been urged, the careful observer of the seasons in America has now acquired satisfactory proofs that insects, even in great variety and number, are not the necessary harbingers or companions of popular distempers." The agency of the *stegomyia calopus* in spreading yellow fever and that of the *anopheles* in malaria were not to be known for many decades.

Catastrophe is often the prelude to social change. Just as the Chicago and San Francisco fires cleared the way for more carefully planned cities and the tidal wave at Galveston and the Dayton flood brought new forms of municipal government, so the yellow fever induced doctors and laymen to undertake new researches and investigations. Observation of climatic conditions in various sections of the country became more scientific. Vital statistics, not yet carefully recorded under government auspices, assumed a new social significance. The campaign for health through cleanliness received a prodigious impetus;[359] there were demands that streets be widened, paved, and cleaned at municipal expense; that slaughter pens and boardinghouses be placed under rigid inspection; that wells be dug deeper and more adequate water supplies be provided.[360] Philadelphia began to harness the Schuylkill into an effective public water system, the first in the country, while New York incorporated the Manhattan Company to serve its own metropolis.[361] Skeptics pointed out that an increase in public and private cleanliness was followed by even more violent epidemics; nevertheless, sanitation—the word was not yet in use—made steady headway, largely at the insistence of the doctors.

There was also much complaint by 1830 that the profession was overcrowded. A Cincinnati journal thought there were twice as many doctors as were needed and suggested that some return to farming.[362] It is impossible to determine whether the average income of physicians was lower than today, but it was estimated in 1833 that rural practitioners seldom received more than $500 yearly in money and in kind. Account books of city physicians tell a different story. The most successful doctors, who professed competence in minor surgery, probably earned more than $8,000 a year in New York and Boston, where fees were largest.[363]

If professional prestige was not so high in 1830 as it had been in 1790, public esteem for the family physician had not declined. From Maine to Louisiana there were general practitioners who touched so intimately the lives of their fellows that they became the confessors of the families to which they ministered. Confidence in their advice was unlimited and that advice was often more valuable in healing the spirit than the body. Unable to summon skilled specialists to their aid, they took all medicine for their province and met each new problem as best they could. With meager instruments—knife, lancet, forceps, and probe—they faced the multiform hazards of surgery and did not always lose. Their heroism reached out to the fringe of frontier settlements, where they rode through miles of almost pathless forest to stake energy and skill against death in a lonely cabin. Out of their ranks rose a William Beaumont, whose years of patient observation brought an epochal analysis of the digestive process; a Samuel Guthrie of Jefferson County, New York, discoverer of chloroform; and an Ephraim McDowell, practicing in Kentucky and performing the first ovariotomy a decade before Europeans attempted it. It was men like these who finally made medicine a science.

CULTURAL ASPIRATIONS AND ACHIEVEMENTS

THE DESIRE for cultural independence was strong. Though a lively sense of indebtedness to the Old World still persisted, it was overshadowed by the hope that American art and letters would soon break through the bonds of imitation and make original contributions commanding respect in foreign lands. That hope was briefly stimulated by John Trumbull's paintings, Samuel McIntire's houses, and the public buildings inspired by Thomas Jefferson.

Adequate patronage of the arts came tardily in a country where there was neither royal court nor established church to assume responsibility. "A people must secure a provision of absolute necessaries," wrote one magazine editor, "before they think of convenience, and must enjoy conveniences before they indulge in the agreeable arts of life." Only when accumulated wealth provided patronage for painting and sculpture could native talent escape the need of quitting the country in order to be suitably trained and rewarded.[364] Some interpreted Gilbert Stuart's return in 1793 from study with the Pennsylvania-born Benjamin West in London as evidence of an imminent change.[365] American youth might continue to seek instruction in the Old World, but an increasing number would find teachers as well as patrons at home.

The artistic achievement of Americans was not necessarily a measure of their cultural separation from Europe. Whatever the reasons for Gilbert Stuart's return to his native land, he repudiated little that he had learned in England. His portraits, invariably revealing manual brilliance and a distinctive style, nevertheless encouraged European mannerisms among his imitators and exalted Old World standards of taste among his numerous admirers.[366] Neither his great portraits nor his career contributed much to the growth of an indigenous artistic tradition. That growth really depended upon scores of nonprofessionals. Lay painters, concerned with the typical in their environment, carried on in the manner of colonial limners; master craftsmen in carpentry found time to plan and execute ornamental designs in building; hewers of wood, like William Rush, who fashioned figureheads for ships, and workers in stone, like John Frazee, who carved tombstones, became pioneers in arousing interest in the plastic arts.[367] The contribution of these laymen, whose work may be regarded as folk art, was generally ignored, but some of them finally earned the right to professional status and helped direct European influences into American channels.

In architecture two forces were important during the republic's early years. One flowed across the Atlantic, either with those European architects who sought favor in the United States or with Americans returning from foreign study. The other originated with native carpenters and master builders, whose practical experience led them to study the function of design. The subtle fusing of these forces resulted in the modification of older models along utilitarian lines. Though that adaptation was far from unimaginative copying, there was genuine cultural continuity, well exemplified in the creation of the national capital on the Potomac.

American architects and builders were inclined to turn from Tudor and Georgian models and to find their masters in the admirers of ancient Greece and Rome. There was an intensely personal quality about Jefferson's classical enthusiasm, but he was far from unique.[368] Ever since the Revolution popular conversation had been filled with allusions to republican Rome, and correspondents in the public prints had delighted in signing their communications with the names of legendary Roman heroes. The Society of the Cincinnati indicated that this interest was not confined to aggressive democrats. Roman influence in architecture was strengthened by the desire, not peculiar to Jefferson, to be free from the domination of English art forms. The spirit of independence was admirably expressed in the Capitol at Washington, the great country house at Monticello, and the new university at Charlottesville. It was manifest also in state capitols and other public buildings from New York to Savannah.[369] Foreign visitors during the early decades of the nineteenth century were impressed by Philadelphia's banks and mercantile houses and New York's churches, designed chiefly by amateurs whose architectural apprenticeship had been served as carpenters or builders' assistants.[370]

In New England, more than in any other section, the colonial tradition was honored and English precedents remained basic. On many a village green in Massachusetts and Connecticut, Congregational churches rose with delicate towers and slender white spires. Some of the most beautiful symbols which Calvinists and Episcopalians ever erected were made possible by profits from neutral trade during the Napleonic era. There was usually a suggestion of ancient models in the English manner of Robert Adam, but few were so patently in the classical tradition as Ithiel Town's Center Church at New Haven.[371] In New England also there was abundant evidence of a somewhat independent American style. Samuel McIntire, erstwhile wood carver, became architect extraordinary to the Salem merchants in the fabulous years of the Old China trade. His contemporary, Charles Bulfinch, one of the first Americans to deserve the title of professional architect, finally convinced Boston of his outstanding ability after he had remodeled Faneuil Hall, designed the state houses in Boston and Hartford, and assumed charge in 1818 of the work on the national capitol. Though Bulfinch and McIntire were deeply indebted to English masters, each contrived to adapt contemporary European forms to the conditions peculiar to the region in which he was working. Originality in detail enabled each to rival the classical enthusiasts in their contributions toward a distinctively American school.[372] Bulfinch, more than any other, transformed boxlike Puritan meetinghouses into austere but beautiful churches.[373]

Throughout the first quarter of the century there were numerous indications of an interest in Greek design, which was to dominate the architectural taste of the next generation. Before 1800, Benjamin H. Latrobe, lately arrived from England, had written, "Wherever, therefore, the Grecian style can be copied without impropriety, I love to be a mere, I would say, a slavish copyist. . . ."[374] This was the spirit in which the Greek revival in architecture came to America. Just as adaptation of English Georgian to wooden buildings in this country had emphasized the beauty of variations in the elaborate main doorway, so modifications of Greek models fixed attention on the majestic simplicity of the column. One did not need to build a complete temple in order to make use of the classic portico. In New England and New York as well as in Virginia and the Carolinas such a portico adorned many a Georgian dwelling. James Madison's Montpelier was thus remodeled and James Monroe set the same example in building Oak Hill. In 1826 a massive Doric portico was added to the mansion at Arlington across the Potomac from Washington. By the 1830s new state capitols and county courthouses were rising in templelike form, while the portico on the more pretentious country houses had become a symbol of dignity and prestige.[375]

Americans resembled Europeans in their enthusiasm for the exquisite beauty of the Greek orders and moldings. Throughout the Western world romantic interest in ancient culture, breaking through mere academic concern with classical languages and literatures, was stirred anew by Lord Elgin's announcement of the removal to London of the Parthenon frieze and the sculptures from the Acropolis, and by the Greeks' heroic revolt against Turkey.[376] But the Greek revival in American architecture was more than an incidental part of a worldwide romantic movement. Laymen as well as professional architects came to think of Greek forms as the media through which distinctively American styles might be developed.[377] In 1830, Asher Benjamin remarked in *The Practical House Carpenter* that since the appearance of his last book some fifteen years earlier the Grecian School had almost completely superseded the Roman. Already Latrobe's able pupils, Robert Mills and William Strickland, were enthusiasts, while Ithiel Town and Alexander J. Davis in New York were convinced that the inspiration of the Greek orders would provide an escape from servile copying of contemporary English and Continental designs.

Though some foreign-trained professional architects, like Latrobe in Philadelphia and Joseph Mangin in New York, had settled in Eastern cities after the Revolution, their colleagues were usually either skilled master craftsmen or talented amateurs who turned to architectural work as an avocation. As late as 1833, Asher Benjamin complained that many who would not think of "instructing a carpenter in the art of sawing boards" essayed the more difficult task of designing buildings.[378] They had learned whatever they knew about drawing plans and elevations either in the school of apprenticeship and experience or from the pages of pattern books. These convenient manuals, simplifying the styles popular in London as well as in Philadelphia and New York, long inspired the best architectural work in rural America.

The pervasiveness of old-world influences became apparent inside the homes of the wealthy. William Bingham's residence in Philadelphia was described in 1794 as furnished in the best English taste, a characterization that would have fit the town houses of the aristocracy anywhere from Boston to Charleston at the close of the eighteenth century. As in London, whitewashed walls were disappearing in a riot of color: either painted plasters or scenic wallpapers.[379] The latter, more common in Northern than in Southern houses, were available in series of tropical scenes, European landscapes, Chinese motifs, or conventionalized designs from classical subjects.[380] At the windows rich damasks and brocades were giving way to printed linen and chintz hangings, while floors, once highly polished, were now completely covered with carpets. Wedgwood ware with its decorative Grecian designs enjoyed as high favor as Lowestoft china, and tables heavy with European cut glass were sometimes lighted by large candelabra moved about on casters.

While many of the wealthy imported their chairs and tables from Seddon's in London, there was no need for them to do so. Native craftsmen, studying the style-books of the great Georgians, Chippendale, Hepplewhite, and Sheraton, modified these English forms with French ornamentation or with American national symbols, and for a quarter-century fashioned furniture which has not yet been surpassed.[381] Bookcases and secretaries usually had two doors, each with thirteen panes of glass in honor of the original states. The gilded eagle perched on the top of countless mirrors and wall clocks, and a carved bust of Washington often surmounted the backs of formal chairs. In New York the Georgian styles were Americanized largely through the work of Duncan Phyfe, a Scotch lad who had served an apprenticeship in Albany before becoming cabinetmaker to Knickerbocker society. But his influence proved scarcely greater than that of Henry Connolly in Philadelphia or John Seymour and Michael Allison in Boston. In New England the unusual success in reproducing the delicacy of Hepplewhite's designs probably came from the fact that artisans who specialized on trim and cabin equipment in the shipyards, spent their slack time in fashioning fine furniture.[382]

Shortly after the treaty of Ghent, French influence, long held back by the Napoleonic wars, moved into American drawing rooms, introducing Empire styles sharply divergent from those of the English Regency. To meet the change of fashion American craftsmen now turned from London to Paris for their models. Thus Duncan Phyfe's pieces in the decade of the twenties were more massive and ornate than anything he had done earlier. There was a suggestion, but only a slight one, of the decline in taste which was to come at mid-century when the aristocratic tradition, still imperfectly understood by the newly rich, no longer commanded the respect of the multitude.

Other artistic standards early in the century were largely borrowed from Europe. In painting, for example, the controlling influence emanated from the London studio of Benjamin West, where many a young artist received his inspiration.[383] Late in the eighteenth century this American expatriate had welcomed Gilbert Stuart, John Trumbull, and Robert Fulton, which his last groups of students included Washington Allston, Samuel Waldo, and Samuel F. B. Morse.[384] But these represented the fortunate minority. Not more than forty-five in all crossed the Atlantic for brief periods of European training during the forty years after 1790. Yet it was difficult otherwise to secure proper guidance.

Such financial support as the painter received grew out of interest in portraiture. Normal human vanity was reenforced, at least among the aristocrats, by rumors of the vogue of portrait painting across the Atlantic. Religious scruples against personal adornment and decorative embellishment, which had never been confined solely to the Quakers 8and other pietistic sects, yielded gradually to the desire to preserve the likenesses of the Revolutionary hero and the republican statesman. An improved market attracted foreign artists. Thus, John Vallence, a Scotch limner, opened a studio in Philadelphia in 1791; from Denmark came Joshua Carter, who settled in Charleston in 1792; two years later Févre de Saint-Mémin, the French refugee, arrived and perfected his profile portraits in crayon.[385] Even mediocre artists, carrying on in the tradition of colonial limners, began to discover that their talents had commercial value. A veritable army of them moved over the countryside, receiving in some districts a welcome not unlike that accorded to the peddler. Most were compelled to eke out a living by supplementary work. Ezra Ames in Albany maintained himself over slack periods by varnishing chairs, engraving silver spoons, painting sleighs, and hanging wallpaper. Others repaired jewelry, conducted dancing schools, or earned what money they could as hairdressers.[386]

Most portrait painters yielded to the "miniature craze," which was at its peak early in the nineteenth century. If Gilbert Stuart could boast he had painted few miniatures in more than 1,150 portraits, at least a score of his contemporaries devoted themselves almost exclusively to this form of art. Edward Malbone of Boston and Charles Fraser of Charleston ranked with the best Europeans of their day. There was also a host of lesser artists in this medium.[387] These delicate small portraits on ivory, so charmingly intimate, were prized as highly by agrarian democrats as by the tie-wig aristocracy in seaport towns. Benjamin Trott toured the regions beyond the Alleghenies on horseback, carrying his materials in his saddlebags, in order to reach remote hamlets which itinerant painters never visited.[388]

The portraitists of these years made an incalculable contribution to the historical record. As a result of their work posterity feels better acquainted with Washington and his younger colleagues than with any American leaders until the photographer's art recorded accurately the features of Lincoln and Lee. Gilbert Stuart's gallery alone included the first five presidents, as well as Samuel Adams, James Otis, Josiah Quincy, Fisher Ames, and other public figures.

Although the professional artist had no literary medium peculiarly his own, his work was discussed occasionally in the magazines, and of these there were many.[389] The typical periodical was general in content and highly imitative of English precedent. Between 1790 and 1800 more than fifty such literary journals were established, but only three lasted more than two years and none enjoyed a wide circulation. Financial difficulties, however, did not deter optimistic editors, for it is estimated that at least 500 were able to get into print during the first quarter of the new century.[390]

Editorial policies varied widely. Isaiah Thomas's *Massachusetts Magazine* (1789-96) contained the best examples of the developing short story, while the *American Register* (1806-10) purveyed political and scientific information. Some quickly became specialty magazines, emphasizing agriculture, theology, medicine, or the drama. Others, appealing to a particular region, featured events of local interest. A few, like Charles Brockden Brown's *American Review and Literary Journal* (1801) and Robert Walsh's *American Review of History and Politics* (1811-17), attempted the critical appraisal of letters, but none deserved to rank with the great British quarterlies until Boston's *Monthly Anthology* was revived as the *North American Review* (1815). Particularly outstanding as an editor was

Joseph Dennie, who enlisted the support of the literary junto in Philadelphia. His forthright Federalism seemed incongruous in the capital of Jeffer-
sonianism, but the *Port Folio* prospered as its list of contributors
lengthened to include such political figures as Richard Rush, Alexander J.
Dallas, Gouverneur Morris, and John Quincy Adams.[391]

Fiction struggled rather feebly for recognition in the guise of the romantic novel, sugar-coated with sentimentality.[392] Its beginnings were manifest
in such moral tales as *The Power of Sympathy* (1789), probably the first
novel by an American,[393] and Susanna H. Rowson's *Charlotte; a Tale of
Truth* (1791, known later as *Charlotte Temple*), which proved the most
popular American book to the time of *Uncle Tom's Cabin.*[394] Though the
familiar formula of English sentimentality was likewise used in Gilbert Imlay's *The Emigrants* (1793), the locale was western Pennsylvania and Kentucky and there were overtones of social reform in the vigorous defense of
American institutions and the proposal for an ideal community in the Western wilderness.[395] Hugh Henry Brackenridge obviously found in *Don Quixote* and the great English satirists of the eighteenth century the models for
his *Modern Chivalry*. A democrat after the manner of Thomas Jefferson, he
took time from political activities and judicial duties to poke fun at lawyers,
doctors, clergymen, and the political opportunists whom he knew so well;
nor did he spare the pseudoscientists and the pundits of the American
Philosophical Society. *Modern Chivalry* was aimed at Western pioneers,
and in large numbers they read it and liked its humor.[396]

In Europe, literature provided a means of livelihood; in the United States
at the close of the eighteenth century it was a diversion for one's leisure
time. Even Mrs. Rowson's popularity did not permit her to discontinue her
school for girls in Boston. It is true that Sally Barrell Wood regarded her
writing as something more than an avocation when she published the
"wholly American" *Dorval; or, the Speculator* in 1801, but neither in
quantity nor quality did her work equal that of Charles Brockden Brown,
America's first native professional novelist. In his best romances—*Wieland*
(1798), *Edgar Huntley* (1799), *Ormond* (1799), and *Arthur Mervyn* (1800)
—Brown strove to "adapt his fiction to all that is genuine and peculiar in
the scene before him."[397] It was the sensational rather than the sentimental
that interested him.

Young Washington Irving may have erred in comparing the life of his
city to that of Addison's London, but he and his associates were eager to
make it comparable. The first number of *Salmagundi*, appearing in January
1807, was avowedly in the style of the *Spectator*. Its gentle satire was but a
prelude to the boisterous humor of *Diedrich Knickerbocker's History of
New York* (1809), which amused Walter Scott as much as it entertained
American Federalists, who were sure they could see the caricature of
Thomas Jefferson through the clouds of smoke emanating from the
Dutchmen's pipes. Irving spent the seventeen years after 1815 in Europe,

publishing *The Sketch Book* (1819), with its Dutch legends of the Hudson Valley, and then *Bracebridge Hall* (1822) and *Tales of a Traveller* (1824), both eloquent of his affection for England.[398] If some Americans were distressed that he had succumbed to European influences, probably more were inspirited by the reports of his increasing reputation wherever great literature was honored.[399]

Like Irving, James Fenimore Cooper quickly gained a large audience following *The Spy* (1821), his novel of the American Revolution. By 1830 he had completed three of the *Leatherstocking Tales—The Pioneers* (1823), *The Last of the Mohicans* (1826), and *The Prairie* (1827)—and had delineated in the frontiersman one of the most picturesque characters in the long gallery of world literature.[400] His Indians may have belonged, as Mark Twain once remarked, to "an extinct tribe which never existed," but at first they seem to have been convincing to most American and all European readers.

Edward Everett, surveying American literature in 1824, was impressed by "an astonishing development of intellectual energy in this country."[401] Probably much that he saw was behind his eyes, for he was under the spell of new forces astir in Boston and Cambridge. It was gratifying to watch the widening influence of the man of letters; to read the essays and reviews of American, English, French, and German books in the *North American Review;* to know something of what was in the minds of Richard Henry Dana, the elder; Edward T. Channing; George Bancroft; and young John G. Palfrey. Boston, self-centered but world-conscious, seemed to sense already that destiny which Emerson described as a summons "to lead the civilization of North America."[402] But where Everett found cause for rejoicing, William Ellery Channing saw need for renewed effort. With an eloquence surpassing that of others who had sounded a similar warning, he reminded his countrymen that "a people into whose minds the thoughts of foreigners are poured perpetually . . . will become intellectually tame and enslaved." The true sovereigns of any country, he said, are "those who determine its mind."[403]

Americans excused their literary deficiencies by referring to their preoccupation with the practical side of life and by boasting of their literacy.[404] Timothy Dwight, late in the eighteenth century, had reported a large and growing reading public in the Northeastern states, and it was said that the great house on many a plantation had a "book room" and a "respectable library."[405] But those who read regularly—and there is no way of knowing how numerous they were—probably did not read extensively. Either through choice or necessity they learned to know a few books well and to meditate on them. David Ramsay observed that South Carolinians outside Charleston had little available save the Bible and the newspapers, and from these two sources they drew whatever they knew of theology, philosophy, history, and science.[406] Where books were more plentiful, John Bunyan's

Pilgrim's Progress and Richard Baxter's *Saints' Everlasting Rest* were often companion pieces to the Scriptures.[407] Theological works still outnumbered secular in New England, but even that section admired Oliver Goldsmith's poems and Alexander Pope's essays and read the *Spectator* and the *Tatler*. Gentlemen who professed no legal aspirations spoke with knowledge of Blackstone's *Commentaries* and Montesquieu's *Spirit of Laws*. If fiction was still suspect at the close of the eighteenth century, *Robinson Crusoe, Don Quixote, The Vicar of Wakefield,* and *Gil Blas* passed even clerical censorship in many communities.

Changes in popular literary taste, though not yet fully revealed, were in the making. Even before the opening of the new century Royall Tyler, jurist and playwright, noticed that in New England "some dreary somebody's day of doom" was being supplanted by lighter reading.[408] In 1811 a Pittsburgh book dealer advised Mathew Carey, the Philadelphia publisher, that new novels were "all the rage" in the West. It was creditable to Americans that they quickly recognized the merits of Scott, Irving, and Cooper. The earlier *Waverley* novels, in which history seemed both romantic and moralistic, were in great demand long before Sir Walter revealed his authorship, and during the 1820s "bookstands almost creaked" under pirated editions of *Ivanhoe, Quentin Durward, Kenilworth,* and *The Heart of Midlo-*

William Dunlap's painting of a scene from the drama based on James Fenimore Cooper's novel "The Spy"

thian.[409] Nowhere were they more influential, then and later, than in the homes of southern planters.[410]

But if one considers all classes and sections of the country, the vogue of romanticism was more accurately represented in the mediocre works of minor novelists. Maria Edgeworth, in America as in England, was generally regarded as "safe," even for impressionable young women. Of Mrs. Rowson's numerous imitators, probably the ablest was Hannah Webster Foster, whose *Coquette, or the History of Eliza Wharton* (1797) was republished as late as 1874.[411] Caroline Warren's *The Gamesters; or Ruins of Innocence* (1805), in which the seducer's snares never failed, enjoyed an unmerited popularity for several decades. Somewhat better were novels based upon American themes: John Neal's *Logan* (1822), a tale of Indian life in colonial days; James McHenry's romance of Fort Duquesne, *The Wilderness, or Braddock's Times* (1823); and Timothy Flint's *Francis Berrian* (1826), a sentimental story of a New Englander in the Mexican revolt of 1822, faithfully portraying the Southwestern border.

The literary culture of Americans depended in certain respects on the book trade, which in turn was at the mercy of inadequate transportation and defective organization. Distance sometimes established a prohibitive barrier. Philadelphia, New York, Boston, and Baltimore had almost mutually exclusive hinterlands so far as booksellers were concerned. Convenience of shipment justified the development of smaller publishing centers, such as Worcester, Hartford, Albany, Lancaster, Richmond, and a score of others.[412] There was little differentiation of function in the trade, the modern specialties of printing, publishing, distributing, and retailing usually being handled by the same proprietor. The printer-editor-publisher in the larger towns sometimes maintained a reading room in conjunction with a circulating library, where his customers might examine the latest books received. To create a well-balanced wholesale market on a nationwide basis Mathew Carey promoted the organization of the American Company of Booksellers, which managed five literary fairs between 1802 and 1806. But it quickly aroused the suspicions of small dealers in regions far from New York and Philadelphia and failed to establish an efficient method of distribution.[413]

Energetic publishers of broad vision strove to reach remote customers by sending out special canvassers. Carey, for example, gave particular attention to the South and Southwest, often employing the Reverend Mason L. Weems, who used the opportunity to push the sales of his *Life of Washington* until it reached its fortieth edition and fixed for generations the legendary figure of the first president.[414] But most printer-publishers were content to follow the conventional methods of accepting a subsidy from the author or of securing an advance subscription sufficient to meet publication costs. When James and John Harper decided to set up on their own account, James solicited orders from various New York booksellers, agreeing to use their respective imprints if each would take 100 copies. Thus the House of

Harper ran no risk in putting a new edition of John Locke's *Essay on Human Understanding* on the market. By 1825 the firm, only eight years old, had so shrewdly gauged the public demand that it was the largest book manufacturer in the United States.[415]

Most of the books sold in America were not only of British authorship but also were printed and published in Great Britain. Of some 400 titles advertised in 1801 by Joseph Nancrede of Boston about 250 bore a London imprint, while fewer than 100 had emanated from the United States. Samuel G. Goodrich estimated that in 1820 approximately 70 percent of the volumes bought by Americans were of British production. A decade later, however, the proportion had fallen to 30 percent, a change which he attributed to a combination of factors—the vigorous enforcement of tariff regulations, the increased activity of American printers and publishers, and the rising national spirit after the War of 1812.[416] But this does not mean that native authors were coming into their heritage, for they continued to be hampered by the absence of an international copyright. It was cheaper for publishers to pirate English "best-sellers" and ignore aspiring American writers. The situation became acute when Scott and then Dickens swept the country, and it was not soon remedied. Carey, knowing well the uncertainties of a transatlantic voyage, engaged fast sailboats to get him copies of new *Waverley* novels before incoming ships touched quarantine. The brothers Harper established a record by reprinting *Peveril of the Peak* in twenty-one hours.[417]

The mechanics of printing had changed little since Benjamin Franklin's youth. Two "partners," as they were called, were still required to run the wooden hand presses.[418] While one applied the ink with hard-stuffed balls, the other laid on the sheets and did the "pulling." In later years Thurlow Weed recalled how he and James Harper, apprentice lads at a New York shop in 1816, managed each day to do a third of a day's work before breakfast, morning after morning, in order to earn overtime.[419] Harper already had established his own publishing house when iron presses, invented in England, began in the 1820s to drive out the wheezy wooden ones and composition rollers began to replace the familiar and foul-smelling ink balls.

Though public collections of literary material were not new, most of them were insignificant. The forty-nine in 1800 probably contained fewer than 80,000 volumes, though the Library Company of Philadelphia and the New York Society Library had been in existence more than sixty years.[420] Within the next quarter-century small collections were established in rapid succession by colleges and academies as well as by literary clubs and learned societies. A writer in the *North American Review* in 1816 thought the best libraries were at Cambridge, Boston, and Philadelphia. The first two were particularly strong in theological treatises, Greek and Latin classics, and American history, while the Quaker City was esteemed for its works on natural history.[421] New Yorkers learned in 1826 that, though their city was three times as large as Boston, its ten libraries contained only four fifths as many books. Even Baltimore, with but four libraries open to selected readers, possessed three fourths as many volumes as the nation's metropolis.[422] No New Yorker understood the situation better or regretted it more than DeWitt Clinton. Convinced that the government should come to the aid of private benevolence, he proposed to the legislature in 1827 that each school district be permitted to tax itself to establish and maintain libraries for the free use of all its inhabitants. It marked the beginning of the long campaign to create tax-supported libraries.[423]

Singularly insensitive to the trend of the times was the critic who complained in 1818 that "all the libraries in America would not furnish materials for a work like Gibbon's *Decline of the Roman Empire.*"[424] He was right, but his fellow countrymen, so far as they wrote history, were much more concerned with the rise of the American republic than with the decline of the Roman Empire. Fixing their attention on the Revolutionary era and its immediate antecedents, some were already engaged in organized endeavors to gather and collate public and private papers. Thus Jeremy Belknap of Boston, John Pintard of New York, and Ebenezer Hazard of Philadelphia, eager to emulate the Society of Antiquarians in London, developed a movement for collecting and preserving American antiquities which finally took form in the Massachusetts Historical Society (1791) and the New York Historical Society (1804).

The increasing accumulation of public documents, pamphlets, newspapers, and personalia only slowly influenced historical writing. John G. Palfrey and George Bancroft began to use the libraries of the East in their zealous researches during the twenties. For the most part, however, Americans read their own history in the rather superficial compilations of David Ramsay, William Gordon, and John Marshall, the stilted chronicles of Abiel Holmes and Timothy Pitkin, the biographical sketches of Mercy Warren, and the pious platitudes of Benjamin Trumbull and Frederick Butler.[425] More widely known, though not necessarily more influential, were the pamphlets and books of "Parson" Weems, who, writing without fear and without research, appropriated oral tradition wherever he found it and embellished it to suit his fancy. But he was not unlike those who set "truth" as their goal, for they, too, believed that history should instruct as well as entertain, that it should preach to the sinner and inspire the patriot.

Such historical effusions amazed, when they did not amuse, a generation of Europeans who still enjoyed the literary artistry of Gibbon and were beginning to appreciate the critical acumen of Ranke. But not all American writing was so lightly dismissed. Though most English reviewers continued to sneer, there were occasional signs of change. In 1824, *Blackwood*'s ran a series of respectful articles on "American Writers," prepared by John Neal, who had been born in Maine.[426] "How wonderfully America is rising in the scale of intellect!" wrote Mary Russell Mitford after reading *The Last of the Mohicans*. "Depend on it that America will succeed us as Rome did Athens." [427] The tribute was mildly patronizing, to be sure, but it seemed sincere, a prelude to the long-deferred recognition of America's intellectual independence.

URBAN INFLUENCES

IN THE BROADENING and deepening of American culture the larger centers of population, as we have seen, exerted a pervasive influence. Cities were growing steadily if not spectacularly during the first three decades of the nineteenth century. If one accepts the highly dubious enumerations of the early U.S. census reports, there were four times as many urban communities of 8,000 or more in 1830 as there had been in 1790, and they represented a fifteenth as against a thirtieth of the nation's inhabitants. The twenty-six cities of 1830, totaling a population close to 865,000, had experienced their most rapid growth during the preceding decade.[428] While none could boast of a status comparable to that of metropolitan London or Paris or Vienna, each was reaching out along the routes of improved roads and newly dug canals to enlarge its economic and cultural hinterland. New York and Philadelphia had passed the 150,000 mark, and the other seaports—Baltimore, Boston, New Orleans, and Charleston—followed in that order. But it was such river towns as Albany, Pittsburgh, Cincinnati, and Louisville that had shown the greatest rate of increase in the fifteen years following the peace of Ghent.

In this period Americans, despite temporary setbacks, were finding additional uses for power derived from waterfalls. Small-scale manufacturing, thriving artificially behind the protective barriers of embargo, nonintercourse, and war, seemed to shrink with distressing speed when exposed to the combined pressures of European competition and the declining business cycle.[429] The tariff of 1816, even with the principle of minimal valuation, did not suffice to keep Rhode Island's cotton mills open, and Pennsylvania and New York ironmasters reported that bar-iron importations doubled during the first year the act was in force.[430] Manufacturers everywhere sought governmental aid, but relief actually came from other quarters. American concern for the practical, which Europeans had often remarked, was happily attended by an awareness of the opportunities in a steadily expanding domestic market, thanks to the constantly improving lines of transportation and to the fewness of governmental regulations. An additional impetus came from the desire, stimulated by the rising nationalistic temper, to be free from dependence on foreign producers.

The result was an impressive growth in manufacturing enterprises, first apparent in the 1820s.[431] Ingenious mechanics, trained in America and abroad, invented new machines and improved old techniques. Merchants and landlords turned from wharf and farm to calculate the possibilities of factory and forge—and were convinced. Occasionally technical skill and financial resources were combined with remarkable effectiveness. In 1814, Francis Cabot Lowell, Boston merchant, and Paul Moody, a mechanic, perfected the power loom and, installing it in the mills of the Boston Manufacturing Company at Waltham, established the first cotton factory to perform every operation necessary to convert the raw fiber into cloth.[432] Just as Samuel Slater's spindles had made deep inroads into household spinning, so mechanized weaving, with its numerous improvements, cast the long shadow of the factory system over the craftsman at the loom. By 1830 probably half the cottons, woolens, and linens used in Eastern communities came from domestic factories. Imports, except the finer fabrics and pattern weaving, had sharply declined while household production was steadily retreating toward the frontier.[433]

The Americanization of the machine in these years contributed only indirectly to the population of the larger cities. Its influence was most palpable in creating new mill villages and factory towns. Even in the Northeastern states, most workers still lived in the rural environment of the small village. Where children toiled long hours, as in Rhode Island cotton mills, there was a marked preference for the family system of employment rather than the English apprenticeship. Parental control relieved employers of many responsibilities and the family group provided a welcome basis for social stability.[434] In Massachusetts, where young women, drawn into the textile factories from the neighboring countryside, constituted more than 60 percent of the operatives, owners strove deliberately to make tending a machine seem as honorable as any other form of decent labor. Far more concerned with the moral welfare of their employees than with hours, wages, and working conditions, they established strict codes of conduct and supervised carefully the company dormitories or boardinghouses in which the young women were expected to live.[435]

The factory's worst features probably were not unlike the evil conditions described in the famous Shaftesbury report to the House of Commons, but what completely differentiated the American from the British scene was the spirit of the workers. Few thought of themselves as perennially dependent on the machine. For the young women, employment meant a small cash income during the years before marriage. The young men hoped it would be an aid to more remunerative positions or to professional careers in the larger towns, and so it was for many of them.

Such organization as American labor achieved before 1830 was among skilled artisans rather than factory and mill operatives. The unions of printers, cordwainers, carpenters, and others in Philadelphia, New York, and Boston represented the attempt of skilled craftsmen to protect themselves against the growing power of merchant capitalists. Relying upon the strike or "turnout," as they called it, in their disputes with employers, they encountered widespread hostility to any policy which encouraged violence and public disorder. Press and pulpit inveighed against any who would spread a spirit of discontent and insubordination among thrifty and prosperous native-born mechanics. More effective, however, in curbing the incipient labor organizations was the fact that, under the prevailing construction of the common law, any combination of workingmen for the purpose of raising wages was illegal. Six times between 1805 and 1815 local associations of shoemakers were charged with criminal conspiracy in restraint of trade and four times they were brought to trial.[436]

When the first city central union—the Mechanics' Union of Trade Associations—was formed in Philadelphia, some believed that labor was becoming class conscious. If by this they meant that American workers viewed with dismay the widening gulf between the rich and the poor, they were correct. Yet there was little agreement among skilled craftsmen and unskilled laborers concerning the methods by which that gulf could be bridged. In Philadelphia the Mechanics' Union advocated political action and in the columns of its journal, the *Mechanics' Free Press,* stated the program of the Workingmen's party. In 1829 they held the balance of power between the two older parties in the city, a success which inspired imitation in New York, Boston, Albany, and other Eastern cities.

Assuming that social inequality and economic exploitation could be corrected in part by legislation, the labor parties generally agreed on what was needed. Saying little about wages, hours, and working conditions in mill and shop, they stressed the importance of free, democratic education, mechanics' lien laws, abolition of banking monopolies, and reform of the judicial system. In New York and elsewhere this program was quickly championed by doctrinaire reformers who knew little about the attitude of American workers and often misjudged the temper of the men and women whose support they desired. Factionalism in New York prevented the party from capitalizing on its local successes. Lacking political experience and baffled by the vigorous counterattacks of conservatives, the trade unionists discovered that their most articulate leaders did not come from the ranks of the workers. They were embarrassed, if not politically injured, by the ardor of Robert Dale Owen, fresh from the cooperative community which his father had established at New Harmony, Indiana, in 1825, and by the vigorous campaigning of Frances Wright, who mingled arguments favoring women's rights and denouncing revealed religion with her pleas for free, public education.[437]

Although these early ventures in politics were local in scope and of brief duration, they brought labor's demands into public discussion. By 1830 a score of publications presented the workers' point of view with fairness. Trade-union membership steadily increased. If the political strength of the

Workingmen's parties fell off, their proposals gradually won the support of both Jacksonians and Whigs, as the strategists in the more conservative parties maneuvered for the vote of enfranchised mechanics in the larger towns.

Factory labor, just becoming significant in the structure of urban society, attracted few foreign-born immigrants. Though the era of reconstruction and repression following the Napoleonic wars sent thousands from Great Britain, Ireland, and the south German states to American shores, most of them represented the substantial middle classes rather than the desperately underprivileged. Merchants and men of professional competence mingled with skilled mechanics and thrifty yeomen in the holds of westbound ships.[438] Peasants who lacked both craftsmanship and resources had to start their New World experience as unskilled laborers, building turnpikes and digging canals. Probably more than 220,000 immigrants arrived in the period between 1815 and 1830, at least three fourths of them from the United Kingdom.[439] At times the Irish equaled the combined English, Scotch, and Welsh contingents, but less than half the Irish were Gaelic and Catholic, for Ulster and other Protestant districts also lost many of their artisans and farmers in this migration.[440]

Relatively few immigrants entered this country south of Chesapeake Bay or northeast of the Hudson except those who landed at Charleston or Boston.[441] New York, Philadelphia, and Baltimore were the chief distributing centers. Here the newcomer, whatever his nationality, was apt to find a helping hand from those of his own kind. Various "national" societies, primarily concerned with combating nostalgia and promoting conviviality among their members, extended financial relief to indigent compatriots and helped them find employment. In New York, for example, the English had the St. George's Society and the Ancient Britons; the Scots made their contributions through the St. Andrew's Society and the Caledonians; while the German Society enlisted support from John Jacob Astor and Stephen Van Rensselaer. The French Benevolent Society, probably because of widespread sympathy for the early refugees, received funds from the common council until 1817.[442] Most active of all were the organizations that aided Irish arrivals.[443] Baltimore's Hibernian Society, the Irish Emigrant Association of Philadelphia, and similar groups in New York, finding their slender resources for charity unequal to the demand, urged Congress in 1817 to set aside certain sections of public lands for Irish colonization. The lawmakers, however, felt that the problem of the needy immigrant could still be handled by private benevolence, especially when lands in trans-Appalachia were attractive to settlers at prices as high as $40 or $50 an acre.[444]

Prudential cooperation also manifested itself in the mutual-benefit societies for native workers. Printers, cordwainers, carpenters, and many others thus sought a modicum of insurance against illness, misfortune, and untimely death.[445] Such organizations, restricted in their charities by the self-interest of members, were welcomed by the property holders of the community, anxious to promote thrift and reduce the tax burden. Their own sense of social responsibility sometimes went no further than the formation of associations to combat petty crimes and protect property.[446] They were more interested in getting rid of the pauper than in curing poverty. This was not, however, the dominant spirit of the period, and accumulated wealth made it possible for a larger number than ever before in America to translate their benevolent sentiments into action.

The humanitarian movement, thus capturing their financial support, was complex in its motivation and comprehensive in its aims. Such unity as it possessed came from a confident belief in human perfectibility and social progress. Its strength derived from the Enlightenment, from the idealism of English liberals, from the reforming zeal of French humanitarians and their converts in Europe, and from the quiet but effective example of the Society of Friends.[447] Christian charity, as interpreted by Protestant and Catholic, by orthodox and liberal, played its part; yet on most fronts humanistic considerations were becoming ever more powerful.[448] Indeed, these early years of the nineteenth century were notable for the advance in the secularization as well as the organization of philanthropic effort.

Reliance on the almshouse temporarily increased, especially after John Van Ness Yates's report of 1824 persuaded New York State to adopt a program of setting up county poor farms.[449] However enlightened the policy seemed at the moment, especially against the background of contemporary British debate over the poor laws, these institutions soon were filled beyond capacity with a motley crowd of unfortunates, young and old, feebleminded and vicious, crippled and diseased. Since the typical almshouse was an appalling place, humanitarians stressed the need for other and better accommodations. Increasing support was given to hospitals ministering to the poor. The Pennsylvania Hospital in Philadelphia, the New York Hospital, the Charity Hospital in New Orleans, and the Massachusetts General in Boston pioneered in applying new methods of caring for the indigent insane, based upon the ideas of Philippe Pinel in France and the work of his English disciples. But little could be accomplished until state appropriations, supplementing or replacing private charity, made possible separate institutions which received charity patients. As a result, the majority of the mentally ill continued to be incarcerated in jails and almhouses or kept in solitary confinement in private homes, the victims of ignorance and indifference.[450] The first institution to care for the physically handicapped was the American Asylum at Hartford, where the Reverend Thomas Gallaudet, lately returned from studying English and French methods, began in 1817 to conduct a school for deaf mutes.[451] New York copied his system and in 1820 the Pennsylvania Institution at Philadelphia undertook to care for such unfortunates from New Jersey and Maryland as well as those within the state.[452]

Upon no inmates did the almshouse leave a more disastrous impression than upon children, whose only refuge it was until they could be bound out to some form of service. Public authorities did little to improve conditions until feminine interest was roused to the point of action. The Boston Society for the Care of Girls, of which Abigail Adams was a member, established a Female Asylum in 1803, which became the prototype of many others in New England's seaports. Likewise a group of pious women in New York, who had secured a charter as the Society for the Relief of Poor Widows with Small Children, enlarged their benevolence and created on Orphan Asylum Society in 1806 which followed the plans of Francke's famous asylum at Halle. Such institutions were an inspiration to the various religious sects, and soon Catholic, Hebrew, and Protestant churches were making at least partial provision for their own children.

Concern for the underprivileged extended to the criminal. The last two decades of the eighteenth century had witnessed reforms in the penal codes of several states. Not all the barbarous penalties of colonial days were swept away, but the pillory, whipping post, and branding iron were less in demand. Moreover, the list of offenses for which one could be hanged was steadily diminishing, while the jail, which had once been merely a house of detention between arrest and punishment, became a house of correction.[453] In 1794, Pennsylvania built a prison at Philadelphia, which may be regarded as the beginning of the penitentiary system in the United States. Within two decades New York, Virginia, Massachusetts, Vermont, and Maryland followed this example, each reproducing the worst as well as the best features of the original.[454]

Penal reform, which was but one phase of the humanitarianism of this period, received particular impetus from the societies organized to aid imprisoned debtors. These unfortunates, incarcerated in foul jails and workhouses perhaps for trifling debts, often depended on charitable groups for food, fuel, and clothing. Their plight, paraded at times in the press, inspired a long campaign to secure revision of state laws governing debtor-creditor relations and to compel public support of those in prison. It also led to investigations of prison conditions in the larger cities and arguments concerning the methods and purposes of punishment. Boston, Baltimore, and New York followed Philadelphia's example in supporting societies that expanded the relief of distressed debtors into a broad program of penal reform.[455]

In the prisons, classification of inmates got little beyond separation of the sexes, but the demand was rising for a logical segregation according to the ages and types of offenders. Brushing aside considerations of cost, philanthropists offered to assist the state, if necessary, in distinguishing between "novices in guilt" and "convicts whose hearts are seared to remorse and penitence."[456] In New York, for instance, the Society for the Prevention of Pauperism, having denounced existing prisons as nurseries of vice and crime, joined forces with the Society for the Reformation of Juvenile Delinquents in establishing a House of Refuge in 1825. This reformatory, modeled on a similar London institution, did not long remain alone in America, for Boston's house of refuge opened its doors in 1826 and Philadelphia followed two years later.[457]

If the literature of reform reveals an awareness of the increase of poverty and vagrancy, it also shows a growing concern over how the less privileged classes used their idle time. By the 1820s the tavern as a social center was rapidly disappearing. Its function of providing food and lodging for travelers was being usurped by boardinghouses and hotels, while the conviviality of its cheerful taproom was cheaply imitated in grogshops and tippling houses. The more reputable of these latter had become poor men's clubs, where apprentices, mechanics, and low-salaried clerks congregated for recreation and refreshment. The lowest elements consorted in dramshops, which, neglecting the little formality of securing a license, hid behind the pretense of greengroceries. Every corner grocery was permitted to sell liquor by the penny's worth regardless of the customer's age. In Baltimore and Philadelphia the oystermen, having retreated from the wharves and the street carts into convenient cellars, throve on the patronage of youthful idlers, their establishments becoming rendezvous for pickpockets and other petty thieves. New York's Five Points district, not far from the old Collect Pond, had more than its share of unlicensed rumshops and gaudily decorated halls, where dancing was free to all who bought ale or beer.[458]

The general disapproval of such tawdry pleasures sprang partly from the fact that Americans tended to regard any sort of frivolous diversion with suspicion. Thus, except in certain parts of the South, where the tradition of gentlemanly leisure flourished, evangelical Protestants as well as the more pietistic sects frowned on any profanation of the Sabbath, the one day when most people could escape the daily grind. Nor were the actions banned on the Lord's Day necessarily encouraged during the rest of the week, for there was widespread fear that harmless games might be carried to excess and that the participants, weary from strenuous exercise, might temporarily drop their guard in the endless battle against temptation. Amusements, said many, led to the gambling hall, the tippling house, and worse.[459] As late as 1827 the editor of the *American Farmer* had to argue that hunting, fishing, and other outdoor sports were beneficial to health and morals, even if they did afford pleasure in addition.[460]

City dwellers unable to seek recreation far afield had nevertheless some opportunity, if they could find time, to test their strength and skill. The English game of fives (similar to modern handball), quoits, ninepins, pitch and toss, battledore, and shuttlecock—all these were popular.[461] A Philadelphia archery club, organized in 1828, the first to follow the English rules, set a standard for other devotees of the bow and arrow. Interest in swimming, or rather in saltwater bathing at the public bathhouses, had steadily increased since the day when Benjamin Franklin had first published his famous treatise; but the furor occasioned by Francis Lieber's swimming school, established at Boston in 1827, indicates that not many men and fewer women really knew how to swim. The feats of Lieber's pupils in distance tests, reported widely in the press, amazed readers.[462]

Except for cricket, which still survived in communities where recent English immigrants were numerous, competition in the various participants' sports was generally on an individual basis. Americans had not yet

Low Life in New England

introduced the cooperative effort of team play into their ball games. New England's town ball, developing out of boyhood's one-old-cat and two-old-cat, so reminiscent of English stool ball, and involving the competition of two "sides" or clubs, contained only a slight hint of modern baseball. Like shinny and hockey, it was primarily a boys' game, played with emphasis on individual skill and without benefit of spectators.[463]

Juvenile Sports

In a generation which had not yet given substance to the concept of sportsmanship the spectators' interest in sporting events was apt to center in the wagering of money on the outcome. The brutal English amusements of cockfighting and animal baiting, which easily lent themselves to the uses of professional gamblers, persisted in America long after they had lost respectability across the Atlantic. New England sentiment forced the promoters to operate undercover. In the Middle states their activities were condoned but rarely publicized. Only in the South, notably Maryland, Virginia, and North Carolina, were these sports publicly conducted and attended by all classes.[464]

By the 1820s, Eastern cities reported a remarkable increase of spectators at such events as foot races, walking meets, and wrestling bouts. Champion wrestlers usually contented themselves with local conquests, but runners from various sections contested on such well-advertised courses as those at Hoboken, on Long Island, and near Philadelphia, where thousands watched races which tested endurance rather than speed.[465] Fashionable society preferred water sports, and boat races, briefly interrupted by the War of 1812, became gala events along the seaboard. Clubs sprang up in all the larger cities to sponsor intersectional as well as local matches. Some, like the Whitehall Aquatic Club of New York or the Savannah Boat Club, gained a national reputation for the graceful lines of their craft and the superiority of their oarsmen.[466]

It was generally believed that anyone who participated regularly in strenuous contests imperiled his health and courted serious injury. Perhaps that explains the fanatical enthusiasm with which the crowds hailed the victors. Particularly in boxing bouts the element of danger was ever present. Tolerant though Americans were of disputes settled by fisticuffs or by gouging in the Western manner, they scorned such commercializing of the fighting instinct as the prize ring represented. Tom Molyneux, the giant freed black who claimed the heavyweight championship of the country at the opening of the century, was more profitable to his promoters in his English fights than in his brief American tour.[467] English pugilists, after encountering the vigorous hostility of the press from Boston to Savannah, frequently abandoned the prize ring to establish "schools" for teaching the "manly science of self-defense." Out of their attempts to encourage amateur boxing arose an interest in systematic exercise at the very moment that several young Germans—Charles Beck, Charles T. Follen, and Francis Lieber— were introducing in New England the program of gymnastics advocated by Friedrich Jahn. Thus the least esteemed of spectators' sports was in part responsible for bringing the public, as well as the private, gymnasium to America.[468]

The most socially significant sport was horse racing, with its appeal to all classes and all sections of the country. Its most enthusiastic devotees, as in colonial days, were in the South and in those districts of Kentucky and

Tennessee peopled by transplanted Southerners.[469] But there was also a growing interest in Northern communities, especially after New York repealed its prohibition against the sport in 1821. The Union Course, built in that year on Long Island, provided a track which soon became famous for its intersectional races, occasionally attended by as many as 50,000 spectators. Here, in 1823, the Northern champion, American Eclipse, defeated the Southern contender, Sir Henry, in two out of three four-mile heats.[470] None of the metropolitan tracks, however, enjoyed the prestige of the Washington Course at Charleston, where the annual racing week was a gala event in February, or the National Course near Washington, which was a favorite rendezvous for Southern congressmen and at times even lured John Quincy Adams from the presidential desk.[471]

Much as the pleasant excitement of the racetrack was justified in terms of improving the breed of horses, so the art and entertainment of the theater was originally sanctioned by many communities only under the disguise of "histronic lectures" or "moral dialogues." The opposition to stage performances was still numerous and resourceful. It was complained that plays and players alike, almost without exception, were from England—"vile minions from a foreign land." It was further pointed out that the theater was at times a disorderly place. The two or three rows of semicircular boxes might be respectable, but in the gallery above and the pit below and at the house bar there was plenty of rowdiness. If the orchestra failed to play a tune demanded by a gallery shout, it was showered with missiles; if the actors failed to please, stale eggs provided an effective form of dramatic criticism.[472] In some playhouses a section was set aside for bedizened women of the town eager to attract attention. Nor could the lives of the performers always stand scrutiny. The Reverend John Witherspoon, president of Princeton, declared in his *Letter Respecting Play Actors* that few of them knew enough of pure love to depict it on the stage. Perhaps nothing was so resented by the clergy as the blasphemous claim that the theater could join hands with the church as a preacher of good morals and an instructor of youth. In 1790 this seems to have been the dominant religious attitude everywhere except in Charleston, where the church was tolerant of polite amusement and one minister actually wrote a play.[473]

Such antagonism to the stage lingered a long time, but counterinfluences worked against it. For many, the patronage of George Washington settled the propriety of the theater.[474] "It is a concomitant of an independent nation," wrote George Clymer, who had helped to frame the federal constitution. Actors and mangers strove to reassure the public by promises of circumspect behavior and by insisting that "the stage refin'd, cleansed of its dross," could "charm, instruct mankind."[475] Soon among the emerging playwrights were such persons as Charles Jared Ingersoll and Hugh H. Brackenridge, political leaders in Pennsylvania; Judge Royall Tyler of Massachusetts and Vermont; Colonel David Humphreys, the Connecticut manufacturer; and William Dunlap, New York's genial artist. But it was the rich and fashionable, slowly overcoming the prejudice of many intellectuals, who made possible the naturalization of the theater in America. Mrs. William Bingham's set in Philadelphia accomplished the repeal in 1789 of the prohibitory law. The comparable social group in Boston, led by the Russells, achieved a like result a few years later. In Providence it was the same sort of Federalist coterie which prevented a legal ban.[476]

So it happened that the young republic welcomed, or at least tolerated, an institution which was frankly maintained by and for the occupants of the boxes, with a glance of respect toward the bachelor critics in the pit. Though the gallery furnished additional income, it was seldom enough to relieve the manager's worries. Prices were so high as to prevent clerks and mechanics from attending regularly. Recurrent epidemics in the Eastern cities, closing theaters with tragic frequency, likewise help to explain the slow growth of a playgoing public.[477]

The most characteristic phenomenon of the American theater was the traveling company, facing hardships along forest trail and primitive woodland roads unknown to its English prototype. But transportation difficulties, however unpleasant, could not keep needy actors from any community where support seemed probable; and after the War of 1812, frontier circuits were organized and supplied with talent, some of it first-rate. In the winter of 1810–11, residents of Lexington and Frankfort, Kentucky, welcomed their first troupe of professional actors, lately arrived from Montreal and Quebec. Soon actor-managers from Albany, Philadelphia, and Charleston competed for patronage along the Ohio and the Mississippi. In the towns where traveling companies stopped en route there was feverish, if not protracted, activity in amateur dramatics. Thespian and Roscian societies, sponsored at times by prominent citizens like Andrew Jackson and Sam Houston, rose and fell in the larger communities from Detroit to Mobile. They did not always overcome a persistent social prejudice, stirred anew by some itinerant revivalist.[478]

The American circus was just beginning to roll out of the cities into the rural villages. It was still in process of evolution. The very word "circus," retaining something of its classical meaning, referred to the building where well-trained performers, usually from England, France, or Ireland, gave demonstrations of expert horsemanship. Often the proprietors conducted riding schools in addition. Late in the eighteenth century English equestrian shows, which became the central feature of the American circus, had begun to emphasize mounted clowning and to fill the interludes with tumblers, jugglers, and artists on the tight wire. From these exhibitions developed the peripatetic shows, of which in the decade after 1815 probably thirty were moving through the Middle Atlantic states, New England, and the upper South. They were small, rarely consisting of more than two or three wagons, six horses, and six or eight performers, including an acrobat, a clown, and an equestrienne resplendent in unclean satin and spangles and a headdress of slightly bedraggled white plumes. A trumpeter, occasionally assisted by fifers, fiddlers, and drummers, performed the function of a band in a rather sketchy parade. Not many troupes could boast, as did Buckley and Wick in 1828, that they had forty horses, eight wagons, and thirty-five people.[479]

This embryonic circus still lacked a menagerie. Americans, like their European ancestors, were fascinated by exotic animals, but they had not yet brought about the union of the menagerie with the "rolling show."[480] Meanwhile, curiosity was stimulated, but never satisfied, by the exhibition of strange beasts at taverns and country stores, usually with highly embellished explanations from trainers or owners. There were numerous small "zoological gardens" such as Dr. King maintained at 28 Wall Street in New York. He advertised as early as 1789 that he had living specimens of the orangutan, baboon, monkey, ant bear, tiger, porcupine, crocodile, and various kinds of snakes.[481] It seems probable that the first elephant was brought from Bengal in 1796 and thereafter in the traveling exhibits quickly surpassed all rivals for popular favor.[482]

The urban dweller in search of entertainment found constant improvement in establishments catering to the multitude. Thousands who could not afford even gallery seats in the theater paid the small admission fee at the waxworks museum. Proprietors might stress the artistic and instructive character of their enterprise, but most of their patrons frankly wanted to be amused. Though humorous subjects gained in favor, biblical scenes and the figures of military celebrities, church dignitaries, American presidents, and British royalty held their places securely.[483] At times, waxwork exhibits went on tour or were established as features of the public gardens during the summer.[484] New Yorkers were fond of the Vauxhall Gardens, described in 1807 as two miles out on Bowery Road, where they could listen to band concerts and choral singing or watch displays of fireworks or attend performances by actors from well-known theatrical companies. Other cities had similar amusement parks, but none so nearly reproduced the European *Kursaal* as did Niblo's Columbian Gardens in New York, with its large trees transplanted from distant woods, its flower gardens and exotic plants, and its fountains playing in the sunlight.[485]

Though rural America spent little time and substance on social recreation, the farmer differed only slightly in his outlook from the merchant and the artisan. That urban-rural cleavage, which was to develop into bitter antagonism later in the century, counted as yet for little. Foreign travelers, quick to notice superficial differences based on ethnic or regional customs, felt that these were less significant than an underlying agreement on standards of conduct and moral codes. Perhaps that unity seemed the more striking because wherever they went they encountered manifestations of neo-Puritanism, inspired by the reinvigorated evangelical sects and their pietistic allies. No other force was so potent during these early decades in determining both the urban and rural outlook in America. As long as the spirit of the city was essentially that of the country village, it retarded the development of a distinctive urbanism.

NEW SECTIONAL TENSIONS

As LATE AS 1830 Americans still thought of the West as the entire section from the Alleghenies to the Mississippi and from the Great Lakes to the Gulf of Mexico. If signs of cleavage between the northern and southern parts of this great valley had already begun to appear, they were generally overshadowed by certain unifying forces. Perhaps the section's most distinctive characteristic was the fact that its social structure had been created out of the experiences of a relatively brief generation of pioneering. Its geographic variations were minimized by the length of the Mississippi and its tributaries, which carried to New Orleans the surplus products of farm and gristmill, of ropewalk and forge. Though the crews that manned the riverboats were drawn from every part of the older union and from many foreign countries, the population of the interior valley was predominantly composed of yeomen from the uplands of Virginia and North Carolina, with large contingents of German and Scotch-Irish pioneers from Pennsylvania and Maryland.[486] By 1830, New Englanders had made good their conquest of the Western Reserve in Ohio and had risen to leadership in many of the river towns north of Kentucky, but theirs was not always the dominant influence even in districts where they had been the first settlers.[487]

Whatever the immediate background of the men and women who built the "new West," they exemplified that "fierce spirit of liberty" which Edmund Burke had attributed to an earlier generation of Americans. Individualists, often in revolt against the laws and conventions of older communities, they learned quickly in their new environment to develop self-reliance. The very abundance of natural resources, especially land, stimulated competition in exploitation and its attendant wastefulness, which in a later day would make governmental regulation imperative. But the restraints of government were not easily borne by the man who felt that his farm had been created with his own ax and plow and could be protected with his own gun. Law offered a convenient method of settling individual disputes and it often had to be taken into one's own hands. It had not yet become an instrument to safeguard one's equality with one's fellows.[488]

Such cooperative enterprises as this highly individualistic western society achieved were generally in the form of extralegal associations. This was true of its religious as well as its economic and political activities. We have already noticed the pervasive influence of the camp meeting in widely scattered communities, where there were few social outlets for normal human emotions. Similarly their economic needs were satisfied in many a plowing contest, stump pulling, barn raising, and husking bee. Such instances revealed the persistence of that spirit of voluntary association so important in the evolution of American institutions. At many points this trait forestalled governmental intervention for decades, but nowhere did it show signs of developing into genuine collectivism. European observers, accustomed to the power of social convention and legal compulsion, agreed with Tocqueville that "in most of the operations of mind, each American appeals only to the individual effort of his own understanding." [489] Nowhere was this more true than in the West.

For over a decade after 1815 these Western traits were generally characteristic of the people of the trans-Allegheny area, but within the section numerous regional differences slowly became evident. By 1830 the discerning eye could see increasing contrasts between the Northwest—roughly bounded by the Ohio, the Great Lakes, and the Mississippi—and the territory south of the Ohio lying between the Mississippi and the Appalachian barrier. The variant influences of geography and climate had been accentuated by the Ordinance of 1787, which denied the slaveholder possession of his human chattels if he carried them north of the Ohio, and by the infiltration of New Englanders and New Yorkers into the larger stream of upland Southerners. [490] In 1830 more than half the people of the Northwest were concentrated in Ohio; most of the others lived behind a frontier line which extended from the vicinity of Detroit through the southern part of Michigan and then cut back across north-central Indiana and central Illinois to the Mississippi. In many Ohio counties no farmer had yet invaded the primeval forest; rumors of the unhealthful character of Indiana's swamplands held settlers in the Ohio and Wabash valleys; in Illinois the pioneer woodsman, pushing up the tributaries of the Ohio and the Mississippi, was prone to avoid the open prairie, however fertile. He preferred the wooded stream. [491] In some districts clearings already constituted a gigantic swath cut through the better timberlands, but no farmer was very far from extensive tracts of unplowed wilderness.

Only along the Ohio did the villages give much promise of developing into cities. In 1830 the cabins near Fort Dearborn, present site of Chicago, probably sheltered fewer than fifty inhabitants. [492] Detroit, incorporated as a municipality in 1824, was merely a village of 2,200 persons with an unsurpassed harbor. Cleveland, about half as large, was just beginning to feel the effects of the new commerce made possible by the opening of the canal connecting the Cuyahoga and Scioto Rivers. [493] Pittsburgh, Cincinnati, and St. Louis seemed destined for greatest growth. Of the three, Cincinnati, though the youngest, was already the largest, second only to New Orleans in the Western country. Its 25,000 residents were busy handling the products of the rich farmlands of southern Ohio and northern Kentucky. If the farmers of the region found it more profitable to fatten hogs than to ship their bulky grain to market, Cincinnati took full advantage of the situation. Not only did its businessmen steadily expand the packing industry until the city was commonly called "Porkopolis," but they built the steamboats to carry their products into the channels of world trade and bring back the fabrics, furniture, and hardware so much in demand in the great interior valley.[494]

Pittsburgh, especially after the use of steam power, likewise built the riverboats that carried its imports and domestic manufactures down the Ohio. Long favored by its unique location at the junction of turnpike and river, it gradually lost its preeminent commercial position, but found more than adequate compensation in the profits from blast furnace and rolling mill, engine shop and hardware factory.[495] Louisville and St. Louis, both smaller than Pittsburgh, drew their support from commercial activities. The former, at the Falls of the Ohio, was a port of transshipment, serving large vessels which could not ascend the river beyond the falls. St. Louis's strategic situation, between the points where the Missouri and the Ohio empty into the Mississippi, enabled its 6,000 inhabitants to levy toll on the fur trade of the upper Mississippi and lower Missouri and on the commerce of the Illinois country.

The growth of these river towns between 1810 and 1830 was one gauge of the rapidly mounting agricultural surplus which within another two decades would help to transform the Northwest. Already the beginnings were noticeable in an increasing concern over transportation and markets, over credits and currency. The panic of 1819, with the subsequent depression, sharply defined the Westerner's dependent position in a debtor section. It quickened his desire to achieve economic independence, not only from Europe but from older America. To get his surplus goods to market more quickly and more cheaply seemed to him the most important consideration, making him willing to borrow heavily for the construction of roads and canals. The added debt, he felt, was but one step on the path to greater freedom.[496]

Western roads and canals in the 1820s still ran toward the Mississippi and its tributaries. Not until the closing years of the decade did the Erie Canal begin to make inroads on the river traffic. By 1830 the Ohio canals were turning some commerce toward the Erie to the great advantage of the port of New York.[497] At the same time the steamboat was revolutionizing trade on the Mississippi. It made the round trip from Louisville to New Orleans in one sixth the time of the keel boat and at a third of the cost per ton. As a result, the pork, grain, flour, and whiskey of the Ohio Valley were shipped downstream in ever increasing volume. In 1830, New Orleans reported it handled $26 million worth of produce from upriver farms and plantations. Its wharves afforded abundant evidence that the produce of the simple agrarian economy of the West was becoming greater in quantity and more varied in character.

While the settlers north of the Ohio were clearing farms for grain and livestock and building towns for small-scale industries, others from the uplands of the old South or from Kentucky and Tennessee were carrying cotton into the Gulf region. By 1830 certain regional differences could be clearly distinguished. Kentucky's Blue Grass basin was safely in the hands of slaveholding planters, who had far more in common with the tidewater aristocracy of Virginia than with the pioneer farmers in less fertile districts of the state. They had monopolized not only most of the good land but also most of the tobacco and hemp production, but for a time they derived more satisfaction and profit from the sale of their thoroughbred horses and their mules to the planters of the seaboard South.[498] Tennessee, also, had its limestone basin in the Cumberland Valley, where Nashville merchants prospered from the cotton and tobacco which they handled for the planters. In 1825 they loaded more than a million dollars' worth of cotton on steamboats for New Orleans. A few years later Nashville had become the metropolis of western Tennessee, its hinterland controlled by wealthy landlords who tried, with some measure of success, to maintain the social standards of South Carolina and Virginia. Their slave-operated plantations, often secured through adroit speculation from less fortunate frontiersmen, formed an economic basis for social gradations, which were less obvious among the small farmers of the eastern counties.[499]

South of the Tennessee boundary cotton was creating a new kingdom in the years after the War of 1812. Those who rushed in to occupy the fertile river valleys were generally aggressive and adventurous small farmers. But they were followed quickly by great and lesser planters, some of whom counted their slaves by scores. If reluctant to do their own "pioneering," they bought out the improvements of others and thus built up their estates. It was a process of land aggrandizement, already well developed in the piedmont, which pushed many a nonslaveholder onto inferior land.[500] So rapidly did settlement proceed that an English traveler in 1821 could describe a plantation in northern Alabama with 100 acres in cotton and 110 acres in corn, where less than two years earlier there had been nothing but wilderness.[501] A few years later, even when cotton prices were sharply declining as a result of sensational increases in production, Timothy Flint decided that "no planters in the United States have better incomes, in proportion to their capital and hands," than those in Mississippi.[502]

Prior to 1830 the incoming settlers preferred the rich bottomlands of Alabama and Mississippi, the alluvial soils on both banks of the Mississippi, and the fertile valleys of the Red and Arkansas Rivers. In two areas—near Natchez and in the Louisiana parishes—they overran fields which had been under cultivation since the days of the French, but in most districts they were exploiting virgin soil. In general they prospered. The entire region had produced only 5 million pounds of cotton in 1811; a decade later it harvested 60 million; and by 1826 the yield had risen to two and a half times that figure. In 1830 both Alabama and Mississippi were picking almost as large a crop as either South Carolina or Georgia.[503]

With such remarkable increases in production it is not surprising that cotton and blacks became a constant theme, "the ever harped upon, never worn out subject of conversation among all classes."[504] A traveler from Charleston to St. Louis reported in 1827 that the fields adjoined one another in close order for fourteen miles along the road out of Montgomery; cotton land speculators were "thicker than locusts in Egypt"; Mobile's wharves, stores, and press houses foamed with white bales; half the streamers and barges on the Mississippi were carrying the crop of the Tennessee and Red River valleys to New Orleans.[505] It was cotton that kept the ties strong between the old South and the Atlantic seaboard and the newer Southwest. The men who waited expectantly for the bolls to ripen in Alabama, Mississippi, Louisiana, and Arkansas Territory had come from the piedmont and, in smaller numbers, from the tidewater. There was evidence of regional preferences. Georgians, for instance, were most numerous in eastern Alabama; Virginians and Carolinians usually sought out the bottomlands of southwestern Alabama and southeastern Mississippi; Tennesseeans congregated in the northern counties of both states.[506]

The cotton and sugar planters of the Southwest built few such thriving towns as lined the banks of the Ohio. Between St. Louis and New Orleans on the Mississippi a community such as Natchez was exceptional. Established by the French early in the eighteenth century, it had been occupied by both British and Spanish before it came under the control of the United States in 1798. By 1830 it was a cosmopolitan river port, the market center of one of the best cotton districts in the Southwest. On its streets one might see descendants of French officials and Spanish dons, younger sons of the first families of Virginia and the Carolinas, lawyers from New York and New England eagerly seeking their first clients among the commission merchants and wealthier planters.

What Natchez meant to its countryside up and down the river was characteristic of villages throughout the Southwest. None were large, but some gained prestige as county-seat towns. Each was the social capital of a surrounding district occasionally twenty-five or thirty miles in radius. Its economic life was supported by the plantations, great and small, and it rendered corresponding services to the planter. If it was primarily the marketplace for his crops, it also helped him to overcome the isolation of widely separated farms and plantations. Here he found the social influence of lawyer, doctor, editor, and teacher, however inadequately represented; here were books and lectures and discussions. Recreation, especially for the women, often meant riding into town in a "showy carriage" to meet friends or to dine at the best tavern or to attend the gala dancing assembly of the season.[507] Where Georgians and Carolinians were numerous, society endeavored to reproduce on a small scale the pleasant hospitality of Savannah and Charleston. Life in the newer Southwest steadily moved toward the stereotype of life in the older South.

Prior to 1830, as we have seen, the South, either directly or indirectly, contributed as much as any other section to the colonization of the new West. Many of these migrants were discouraged over their economic prospects, or disgusted by the political hegemony of the tidewater counties, but their departure did not improve conditions in their native districts. A committee of the North Carolina legislature reported in November 1815 that within twenty-five years "more than two hundred thousand of our inhabitants have removed to the waters of the Ohio, Tennessee and Mobile; and it is mortifying to witness the fact that thousands of our wealthy citizens ... are annually moving to the West." A year later a legislative committee in Virginia somewhat exaggerated the facts in its rhetorical phrases. "The fathers of the land are gone," ran this gloomy complaint, "where another outlet to the ocean turns their thoughts from the place of their nativity, and their affections from the haunts of their youth."[508] During the twenties westward migration was already slowing down population growth in the South Atlantic section. Georgia, opening up some of its Indian lands, showed rapid increase, but the other seaboard states gained fewer than 500,000, less than the growth of New York State. A prominent Virginian explained "the whole secret." New York, he argued, had retained its Genesee Valley while Virginia had ceded its Kentucky lands to form a new state.[509]

The South felt the adverse effect of the Western settlements in other ways than those revealed in statistics of population. In competition with the fertile low-priced lands of the Gulf states, its acres lost in value and its slaves would have been worth three or four times as much on plantations along the Mississippi. Cotton declined in price in the New York market— in 1816 it was thirty cents, but by 1827 it had dropped to nine—and at the same time the price of slaves in certain areas rose. Many a planter in the old South discovered that he had to secure more working capital, since his operating expenses increased as he grew more dependent on Western and Northern farms for his livestock and foodstuffs. His difficulties were further complicated by the fact that his competitors in Western cotton fields had generally better transportation routes, notably along the rivers that flowed to the Gulf. New Orleans and Mobile were drawing this commerce to their noisy wharves. By 1830 both ports had more than doubled their foreign exports on the basis of 1820 values, while Savannah and Charleston were shipping products of slightly less value than a decade earlier. Many planters in the older South who had placed their faith in cotton were bitterly disappointed. They blamed their plight on the policies of the federal government, especially the protective tariff, and the Charleston district was ready to lead the revolt.[510]

But no sectional unity existed sufficient to justify the term "solid South." In 1830 antagonism between seaboard and interior counties was still lively, though South Carolina had tried to quiet it in 1808 by giving the uplands control of one house, while the tidewater retained the other. This compromise, however, left political power in the hands of slave owners. The minority in some interior counties, where slave labor was not only rare but unpopular, seldom had a chance to speak in the legislature.[511] Virginia's concession to its underrepresented western regions was postponed until the constitutional convention of 1829, when acrimonious debate resulted in a reapportionment shifting political power into the piedmont and the Valley.

The pattern of conformity in the South was being broadly sketched, even if many details would be accentuated later. By 1830 it was unmistakably clear that, wherever cotton moved, slavery would quickly follow. As pioneer farming steadily receded before the small and larger plantation, blacks spread into every area except the mountainous districts. Nothing more clearly indicated the economic revolution under way than the changing attitude of the section toward its black inhabitants. That reluctance to accept slavery as a permanent institution which marked the states of the Upper South at the close of the eighteenth century was gradually disappearing. To be sure, most of the antislavery societies in 1825 were located south of the Mason and Dixon line, but 80 percent of the Southern ones were in western North Carolina and eastern Tennessee. Elsewhere in the slaveholding states hostility to the system was being diverted into the American Colonization Society, with the object of sending free blacks to Africa.[512]

No systematic proslavery argument had yet been formulated, but the critics of the institution, resting their case on the Jeffersonian doctrines of liberty and equality, were slowly yielding to those who found a justification in necessity. As late as 1824, Benjamin Lundy won a hearty response for his *Genius of Universal Emancipation* in Maryland, where antislavery sentiment seemed strong. Within four years, however, his subscriptions had so fallen off that he was combing New York and New England for support. In 1829, the very year the *Genius* was temporarily suspended, antislavery forces met a decisive rebuff in the Virginia constitutional convention. At the College of William and Mary, where Chancellor George Wythe had once indoctrinated "young abolitionists," Thomas R. Dew was penning the opening chapters of his defense of slavery on historic and moral grounds.

As the South moved slowly toward an understanding of its own unity, it prepared to protect its interests in a rivalry, not always friendly, with other sections. The growth of the West and its rising power in national affairs threw into bold relief the hopes and fears of other parts of the Union. Missouri's application for statehood, for example, started a debate which raged beyond the halls of Congress and revealed sharp sectional cleavages that discreet politicians would gladly have concealed. The bitterness of the

Harbor View of

New Orleans

controversy filled Jefferson with terror and the compromise seemed to him but a temporary reprieve. "A geographical line," he wrote, "coinciding with a marked principle . . . held up to the angry passions of men, will never be obliterated, and every new irritation will mark it deeper and deeper."[513] Calhoun and John Quincy Adams, alarmed by the heated arguments, discussed the probable fate of Americans if a dissolution of the Union should occur. Even Henry Clay admitted that the emergence of several confederacies in North America was not impossible.[514]

By 1830 the American people seemed to have traveled a long way from the nationalism of 1815. Then they had talked confidently of national preparedness and economic self-sufficiency. Congress had reorganized the army, chartered the Second Bank, and passed the protective tariff of 1816. Under Calhoun's whip the "Bonus Bill" for setting up a systematic survey of transportation needs would have become law save for Madison's veto on constitutional grounds. From the Supreme Court came a series of decisions which not only gladdened the hearts of merchants and manufacturers but also encouraged those who were working to exalt the power of the federal government. Yet beneath the surface old sectional antagonisms revived and new ones appeared. Particularism seemed more rampant as Jackson took office than it had in the days of Thomas Jefferson. Symbolic was the position of Calhoun. Once the champion of the nation's unity, he now hesitated, torn between his devotion to his state and section and his desire to play a commanding role in national affairs.

Meanwhile, in the valley of the Sangamon in Illinois, a young man came of age. He was more sensitive than Jackson to the moods of the West and more catholic than Benton in his intellectual interests. In his thinking there was something of Calhoun's early concern for the preservation of the nation's unity, of Webster's conception of the nature of the federal government, of Clay's enthusiasm for the balanced economy of the American system. When he first announced his political principles, they seemed to stem from the Hamiltonian rather than the Jeffersonian tradition. "My politics," he said, "are short and sweet, like the old woman's dance. I am in favor of a national bank. I am in favor of the internal improvement system, and a high protective tariff."[515] Within thirty-five years, in one of the greatest crises of the nation's history, Abraham Lincoln watched his principles take the form of law. It was in a sense the triumph of Hamilton, but modified, so Lincoln hoped, by the spirit of Thomas Jefferson.

BOOK VI

The Rise of

the Common Man,

1830–50

NEW WINDS

IN 1815 NEW WINDS had begun to blow over the American people. For more than a decade they buffeted the fortresses of old habits and ideas, and then in 1829, with the elevation of Andrew Jackson to the first office in the land, they gained full sweep. In the twenty years from 1830 to 1850 these new concepts were to dominate American life: they became established, respectable, venerated. The brash young men of 1830 became the pillars of society. By 1850, however, other forces were rushing to control, younger leaders were worshiping changed gods. It is this span of years, marking the dominance of the generation that came to power in 1830, that is the theme of this opening section.

One feature of this era was its outstanding Americanism. Americans have from the beginning differed from the world from which they have been drawn, but they have been at no time detached from that world. Relatively, however, this was the period of least vital contact. The spirit of the Monroe Doctrine was so universally accepted among them that diplomatic relationships were reduced to a minimum. Foreign trade was important, but less than usually contentious. Immigration until the late forties was less a factor than in any period except that immediately preceding. Fewer boys than before or since went abroad for their education. The cultural independence of the United States had to a large extent been attained.

Nor was this a mere statement of facts: Americans were vitally conscious

Aristocracy retreats before THE RISE OF THE COMMON MAN—A riotous election, 1844.

of their difference. The Americans of the thirties and forties gloried in their separation from the "monarchical" governments and tax-supported churches which were "enervating" the civilization of Europe. It would not be true, or fair to Americans of other ages, to say that this was the most patriotic of our generations. It was, however, the period of most assertive patriotism, and of a patriotism typical of a certain stage of social development. It was like that which one still finds among the dwellers in new Western towns. Americans had their plans, they knew their power, to them the future was already realized. Their cities did not equal those of Europe, but they would–as they have. They, therefore, resented the criticisms of others, and they bolstered up their own hopes by suppressing their own criticism.

Nor was this aloofness, at least among the thinking, entirely selfish. It is astonishing to find how widespread was the idea, passed on by those who had conceived of American civilization before it existed, that a purified people, with institutions based on the laws of Nature—identified in the words of Webster with the law of God—would, if true to their covenant, found a refuge for the world's oppressed and a model for other nations to copy. In 1848, this generation, now in its old age, believed it saw the world actually copying this model.

Americans were not alone in regarding the United States as unique. No other people have had their opportunity of realizing Burns's ambition to "see oursels as others see us." From about the time of the Revolution until after the Civil War, scarcely a year passed without the publication of a book by some European traveler. A comparison of these accounts of the thirties and forties with those of the preceding period shows one difference so emphatically pointed out that its real existence can hardly be denied. This is a difference in the speed of life. It is clear that it was at this time that Americans became hustlers. The "quick lunch" was introduced, and everywhere people ate in a hurry. They ate abundantly, from tables groaning with the products of a soil teeming beyond all demands. Breakfast, dinner, and supper, practically identical, each with hot breads and meats, and washed down by ice water, confronted nearly all Americans daily, but detained them briefly. The drinking of intoxicants was generally not so hurried, but it was not at the table. It was not always clear what particular task called them away from the board, but there was unquestionably a general urge to be up and doing.

This restless hurry was an outward sign of an inward quality which became apparent as soon as one engaged an American in conversation. This was optimism. Like hustle, this enormous optimism was but newly becoming an American characteristic. It had certainly required faith to bring the first Americans across the Atlantic, but that faith had little of the intoxicating quality of this new spirit. The Indian and French wars of colonial times had severely tested faith and turned many to the habit of fearing the worst. The Revolutionary generation regained confidence, a reasoned philosophic serenity such as Franklin expressed, a belief that America was safe and would be great. Very different was this new exhilaration, this conviction of salvation attained. In matters of politics and economics Americans were nearly all millenarians, believing that they themselves would see the realization of human happiness; in religion the belief that this generation would with their own eyes, living, even see God, went far beyond the confines of the small sect which made that belief an article of creed.

The causes of such optimism are found in the conditions which the new generation encountered. Its basis was the realization of the unlimited resources of the land. These resources had existed from the beginning, but their relation to the American people had changed. Until 1815 the future of the vast valley of the Mississippi could scarcely be considered as definitely determined. Andrew Jackson's great victory at New Orleans on January 8, 1815, bore the same relation to the whole two-century-long contest for this valley that it did to the War of 1812. For the winning of either it was unnecessary, but it put to the result the seal of finality. The door to the boundless spaces of the continent was now open to them.

It was true that each new portion of the continent presented new problems, and called for new methods and new tools. It was, however, precisely in respect to such requirements that the American's training was most efficient. He was not afraid of the new. By this time the disinclination to change, a characteristic of settled civilizations, had reached the lowest point as a deterrent; the lure of the untried has rarely been so general. The American became an inventor not through scientific research or from peculiar mental gifts, but because of a developed spiritual impulse to try new things, and to rebound and try again if they proved unsuccessful. Travelers all noted the moving of houses. Now the moving of houses is not a difficult mental achievement, but it is the work of a man who is willing to take wide liberties with circumstances, a man undeterred by fear or ridicule.

To the American of the thirties and forties, however, unlimited natural resources and acquired fitness for handling them seemed but incidental blessings. Fundamental was the political system which his fathers had created and which he inherited. For him the political wisdom of the preceding generations had been crystallized and condensed into the Constitution. To him that document had become not a mere instrument of government, but the reality behind all government. In the next generation tens of thousands would die for it. It drew to itself not only the strength of people meticulously legal-minded, ready to fight on points, as Webster said, but the devotion of a people who inherited and transmitted a high degree of religious intensity. As the Ark to the Israelites, so was the Constitution to the Americans; and as David, so, in their own way, the American leaders danced before it.

The Capitol from the White House, 1838. In the second quarter of the nineteenth century the Presidency began to seem attainable by every American boy.

Liberty had been a leading ideal of the Revolutionary generation, but then it was a thing to be won or defended; now it was a thing realized, and this realization was impregnated into the very bone and sinew of the Americans. Liberty, moreover, was now linked with another ideal which paired with it in the devotion of the people, and which served to broaden still further the basis of their optimism. Liberty and opportunity, after all, mean responsibility, a sobering thought; one other gift of the American political system involved no personal effort, was complete at birth—equality.

Of course, the notion of equality went back from the Constitution to the Declaration of Independence, but the two blended in the popular mind. When Jefferson wrote "All men are created equal," did he state a fact existing, or an ideal to be made real, or an aspiration to be approximated? Whatever view people took, the phrase had an effective influence on conduct. It is for the historian to discover what it meant in practice.

As far as dress may be taken as an illustration, Americans between 1830 and 1850 ran neither to an extreme of individualism nor to uniformity. Class distinction became less obvious than in earlier days, but did not quite disappear. Gentlemen had by 1830 given up knee breeches and donned pantaloons, but they still wore coats of blue and buff; they had given up lace, but their shirts continued to be frilled. Many tried to look like gentlemen using a shortcut, such as a detachable collar or shirt front. Foreign travelers laughed, but after all, even to look clean was something. As with clothes so with manners. The formal manners of class became less and less common, at least among those who sought popularity; on the other hand, in part, the thought of equality caused many to imitate the courtesy of those to the manner born.

The lower aspect of this belief in equality was expressed by Andrew Jackson in his message to Congress in 1829: "The duties of all public offices are, or at least admit of being made, so plain and simple that men of intelligence may readily qualify themselves for their performance." [1] Americans were only too prone to believe that they were at any moment ready for anything; it was the reverse side of their splendid self-confidence. Failure did not touch them, for with their ready adaptability they turned from failure in farming to banking, from the broken bank to law, from law to mining. The life history of many an American of the period reveals him adept at many trades, while but few excelled in any. There was distinct danger that the ideal of equality would run to seed in futile belief that all men are created the "same."

It is a relief to find one of the brightest boys growing up during the period, William T. Sherman, shunning versatility as a plague, and counseling his young brother John to mix no two occupations, not even engineering and trade, or law and politics. This was not only a reaction from the evil effects of the Jacksonian doctrine which he saw about him but in part due to the fact that among certain of Jackson's contemporaries equality found an interpretation different and less likely to abuse.[2]

Penetrating the quiet recesses of Concord, Massachusetts, optimism and equality flamed in Emerson into the doctrine that all men were divine, and could become as God, thus placing equality upon a superhuman plane. While, however, he flung his challenge into the teeth of that Calvinism which had so dominated American thought, he retained Calvinism's practical teaching. This elevation of mankind was open to all, but it could be attained only by effort. Self-improvement—that it was the duty of man to control his conduct and that he possessed the power to mold his character—had ever been a central feature of Calvinistic discipline and particularly in New England. Now, under the impulse of national elation, this conviction was not merely a solemn duty, with fear of failure always present and with escape from damnation as its most insistent motive; it was a thrilling, almost gay, opportunity, a sure key to treasures of earth and heaven. Seldom have people thronged so merrily to school.

The ultimate tendency of Jackson's view would have been to dull effort by a satisfied sameness. Equality to Emerson was a reward of striving. Andrew Johnson, a child of their generation, combined the two: "I believe man can be elevated; man can become more and more endowed with divinity; and as he does he becomes more God-like in his character and capable of governing himself. Let us go on elevating our people, perfecting our institutions, until democracy shall reach such a point of perfection that we can acclaim with truth that the voice of the people is the voice of God."[3]

It was more immediately important that both Jackson and Emerson realized that equality was not yet existent. Jackson, therefore, and the confrères and disciples of Emerson set themselves to make it so by throwing down the obstacles they saw in the way, fearlessly breaking old habits and customs with the same confidence that American mechanics were discarding old methods and devising new machines. Restrictions as to the suffrage, long terms of office, the barriers of ignorance, the impediments of blindness, such were the hindrances to the equality of man, and to annihilate them was the dominant idealistic aim of this generation.

In the twenties and thirties these aims were developed, first here, then there, now by one individual, then by another. By the forties there was very general acceptance of the validity of such purposes, and to carry them into effect it was only necessary to overcome inertia, unless they touched some substantial interest, such as the liquor traffic, or some division of interest or of culture, as in the case of slavery. To force such obstacles, organization was resorted to in both politics and philanthropy. The most striking thing about all these campaigns, however, is that their strategy was invariably based on the conception that all might be accomplished at once. To deny that the American system of government would be immediately beneficial if adopted in China, was to commit democratic treason; heredity availed not—opportunity plus effort would produce anything at once.

Finally, it must be remembered that the dominant note in all these campaigns was Emerson's. The limit was only at the top. Nothing was to be dragged down. The struggle for equality aimed not at all at transferring one man's wealth to another: no important man thought of an equal division. Nor was there any purpose of limiting any man's liberty. The ideals—that some men's liberty should be restricted because they are not strong enough to use it for their own advantage; that some men's liberty, or at least the liberty of artificial men, corporations, should be restricted because dangerous to other individuals or to the body politic; that the body politic is more deserving of consideration than any of the individuals who comprise it—were never in America so weakly held or apologetically presented. Resources were limitless. Free men could be trusted to want what was right and to get it.

FARM, PLANTATION, AND HIGHWAY

A LIVING—that is, what was generally conceded in 1830 to be the minimum which an American should secure—was decidedly above what was actually necessary for existence. Food was to be unlimited in quantity, and on festive occasions, choice in quality. Drink was to be ordinarily limited by a liberal conception of hygienic consequences, and on festive occasions, unlimited. Dress was to be adequate for protection and was to include a "best" for Sunday use, but was not expected to respond to the demands of fashion. Every family was to own its home, which was to include, beyond the demands of necessity, a "parlor" and at least half a bedroom for each member of the family. On the frontier many lived much less commodiously, but this was considered to be merely a temporary condition. With each home there was to be a "yard," with some flowers and summer vegetables. A fundamental element of a living was liberty, and all Americans were expected to look forward to becoming their own masters. A chance to educate one's children in the elements was considered a just demand. On the other hand, little heed was paid to hours of labor. People expected to work long hours and to work while the power to do so held out. The poor farm was not such a horror as the workhouse in England, and less often pressed the mind, because it was a contingency so much more remote. One was not expected to provide in health complete support for old age or for one's widow, but was expected to accumulate something which would compensate children, relatives, or others for a few years' care at the end of life.

A very large majority of the people of the United States made their living by agriculture. There were two long-established systems of agricultural organization, one in the North and one in the South, each employing approximately one third of the agricultural population. The agricultural methods of the remaining third had not been systematized in 1830.[4]

A New England farm was more apt to consist of over, rather than under, 100 acres, picturesquely varied with pasture, arable, and woodland. On it were raised practically all food products needed for home use, and small quantities of wheat and corn, together with a few cattle and horses, for sale. It was generally cultivated by the farmer and his sons with frequently a hired man who lived and ate with the family. Seasonal stress of harvest work was generally met by exchange of services with neighbors. During the winter, "chores" could be attended to in a short time, and left long hours during which most farmers employed their time at some mechanical work, as the making of hats or harness or furniture, for use or for sale.

The farmer's wife and daughters were equally producers. Except for the killing of the pig, the milling of flour, and the making of cider, the products of the field were fitted for the table by their hands. They made their own yeast and soap, they dried meat and fruits, they hulled corn, they gathered and prepared medicinal herbs, and they tended the poultry and churned butter. In the hill districts they still, in 1830, spun the wool of the farm sheep, in anticipation of the itinerant weaver on his rounds. Where factory-made cloth was bought, they made their own and their husband's clothes, except perhaps his "Sunday suit." Children from the time they could walk were expected to assist. Such tasks as hunting the eggs, unscientifically laid all about the barn yard, belonged particularly to the girls. Keeping up the wood supply for the kitchen fire, habitually "the" fire, was boys' work.

The connection of the farm with the outside world was slight. What it needed was sugar, except in the maple region, salt, and generally tea; then small quantities of cloth, linen, shoes, and well-made, long-treasured tableware and tools; then certain services, as religion, education, the milling of flour and meal, and occasional medical attendance.

For the first time, the wife was beginning to play a part in these exchanges. She had no money, but exchanged rags and the products of her own handicraft with the tin peddler, who, with his glittering wagon, glib tongue, and gossip of distant towns, was reaping fat profits from these unaccustomed bargainers. Otherwise the exchanges of a hundred farms were gathered together in the village to which the farmer hauled his surplus behind his oxen, his solitary nag, or, if he were prosperous, his pair of "Morgans," over the rutty roads, in the maintenance of which he and his neighbors worked out a good portion of their taxes. Few dollars passed in these transactions. The miller received a proportion of the wheat and corn, the general storekeeper, the cobbler, and the minister were paid in large part by produce; balances on the storekeeper's books were carried from year to year. Agents from the larger towns, however, with leather wallets, paid for cattle and horses in coin, which went home to fill a carefully concealed stocking, or, in the case of the more shrewd, to be loaned on mortgage to less successful neighbors.

The village craftsmen generally included the miller; frequently the tanner; the cobbler, who made as well as repaired; carpenters and masons; the tailor; the seamstress; the cabinet and furniture maker—most of them owning a small stock of materials. Trade was represented by one or two storekeepers who performed some of the functions of bankers; the professions by two or three ministers, several lawyers, a physician, and a schoolteacher. It was the function of the village also to collect the surplus products of the farms and to dispose of such of them as it did not need for the foreign and manufactured products which have been enumerated. Periodically the mail arrived over the highway, generally a fairly well-built toll road running to a seaport or to one of the distributing centers of the interior, such as Worcester or Hartford. At seasons, droves of cattle, increasing in numbers though not in succulence as village after village passed, leisurely progressed over the same roads; at other seasons wagons, heavy with products on their way to town, lighter when they returned with the less bulky goods the village needed.

In New England, between 1830 and 1850, this life was slowly breaking down under the influence of changed conditions elsewhere. In 1830 it just about supplied its cities and its merchant fleet. By 1850 wheat from the West, butter and cheese from New York, and other agricultural products were being sold at lower prices than those produced at home, while farm and village handicrafts were being supplanted by factory-made goods. Some farms in Vermont and the Berkshires were united and turned into grazing pastures for sheep, but, for the most part, there was a gradual decay rather than adaptation. Farm boys and girls in increasing numbers left their home communities and sought their fortunes in the West, or in the nearer factories of their own regions. Agricultural New England simply became less important and less self-sustaining than previously.[5]

In the South there was in 1830 a greater variety of method.[6] The greatest change during these years was in the extension and increasing dominance of the plantation system. As compared with the North, the farming units were larger, they were both more highly organized and less independent, and the profits, probably less in proportion to those engaged, were concentrated in fewer hands, so that the agricultural leaders were more wealthy and powerful and cultured. The unit of the Southern system was the plantation, which consisted of from a dozen to several hundred persons, occupied an ample area, and was generally separated from its neighbors by woods and streams. Economically it existed for the production of some staple crop —in Maryland and Virginia, tobacco; in the Carolinas and westward, cotton; in Kentucky, horses; along the South Carolina seacoast, rice; in Louisiana, sugar.

For production it was organized with the owner as merchant and supervisor, generally with an overseer of labor, and with "hands," who were divided into gangs. In marked contrast to colonial times, practically all laborers were slaves belonging to the owner. The bulk of plantation necessities were home-raised. Garden vegetables and poultry were abundant, hunting and fishing brought variety to the diet. Corn was a standard crop; in the form of meal and hominy it furnished one chief item of food and, intermediately, in the form of bacon the other. The plantation force also did many of the necessary odd jobs of carpentering, blacksmithing, and the cruder crafts. The amount of these varied occupations, however, was growing less. Salt pork, cattle, and flour were increasingly imported from the Northwest, and, more and more, imported implements and manufactured materials, even to doors and window sashes, took the place of those produced at home.

The mansion with its dependent village, where all the community lived, was the center of much activity. Corn was made into hominy, and clothes were prepared for all the laborers, chiefly from cotton and other cloths brought from New England or old. Its occupations were less varied than those of a New England village, but more attention was given to the conduct of the rather elaborate life of the owner's family, with its frequent entertainment of large numbers of guests. Not only did the mere process of living require more time and effort than in the Northern farm home, but there was much more demand for things brought from the outside. Practically no portion of the mansion-house equipment was of local origin, and many choice articles, even of food, came from far away.

This was a much more developed organization than that of the North. The very life of the plantation depended on the sale of its products in far distant markets. Commerce and credit, therefore, were its breath of life. In such staple-producing communities there is generally a tendency to concentrate business and wealth in some one dominant city such as Babylon, Alexandria, Sydney, or Buenos Aires. That this was not the case in the South was due in part to the strong social prestige attaching to plantation ownership and the strong credit position which slavery gave planters, and in part to the political division of the plantation area into states.

Next to agriculture as a means of earning a living in 1830 stood shipping.[7] Four fleets—that engaged in foreign trade, the coasters, the riverboats, and the fishing fleet—employed, directly, well over 100,000 men, and indirectly many more. How much more water transportation counted in 1830 than now may be appreciated by noting the work of these groups of vessels. The river and canal boats, crafts of every size and type, did practically all the inland work now done by railroads, sharing it only with the slow and cumbersome wagons on the few practicable highways.[8]

From the ports of New England in the thirties 100,000 tons of little fishing vessels fared forth for the cod and mackerel, of which they brought back all the fish Americans cared to eat, and $2.5 million worth for export.[9] Chiefly from New Bedford, about 90,000 tons of somewhat larger craft sailed forth on voyages adventurous and three years long, to bring back from the Pacific the whale oil, whose use in the better American homes was the first step in the transition from the candle to the electric light.[10]

The conditions of the ocean marine in 1830 were not substantially changed by 1850. The American fleet increased its proportion of the growing trade. The Baltimore clipper and the ocean steamship improved facilities, and Cornelius Vanderbilt developed organization. These changes, however, were small compared with those in inland transportation, which was attracting the interest and the genius of the country.

In 1830 inland transportation was based on water transit and on toll roads and bridges. In some districts the road system was reasonably satisfactory, but few cared to invest in such undertakings far from home, and these roads were rather an evidence of civilization achieved than an aid to its accomplishment. Federal aid had stretched the National Road into the heart of the Northwest, and built military roads in Florida and to the outskirts of settlement across the upper Mississippi.[11] Jackson's Maysville Road veto of 1830, however, put an end to hopes of a comprehensive national system.

More important than the roads were the waterways, which in 1830 were rapidly becoming equipped with steamboats. Their use ideally fitted the needs of this individualistic generation. In the beginning, each boat was a separate investment, so that no large capital was required, and competition stimulated hundreds of ingenious-minded mechanics to devote themselves to improvement.[12]

Many travelers considered the clean-cut, swift Hudson River liners, turned out at such works as those of the Stevenses at Hoboken, as the finest products of American material civilization. On the Mississippi and Southern rivers, the raftlike hulls with their fairylike superstructures, pushed forward by their high rear wheels or by their separately driven side-wheels, did everything human ingenuity could do to take their cargoes over the sand bars, up and down the rapids, and across the snags. Sturdy, wide side-wheelers carried on the trade of the coast and the lakes; screw propellers shot long slim hulls through canals and the narrower streams.

The range of action of the steamboat was fairly clearly determined by the extent of navigable water. This might, however, be increased by reasonably moderate expenditures for the cleaning of streams and for short canals about obstacles. It was characteristic, however, that little was done in this direction. The most successful of such pieces of work constructed during these years were a system of slack-water navigation on the Kentucky rivers, which was created by that state, and a three-mile canal to escape the rapids of the Ohio at Louisville, which was a private enterprise.[13]

The idea of supplementing the natural watercourse system of the country by canals was one which the United States shared with Western Europe.

The preceding generation was impressed by the Duke of Bridgewater's famous Liverpool canal and was not unaware of the Napoleonic development in France. The difficulties of canal construction were not particularly those of engineering but of finance. Each represented a unified investment, instead of large numbers of small ones as in the case of steamboats, and they were infinitely more expensive than roads. To the solution of this problem the earlier generation left the idea that the work be made governmental. In 1830 it seemed that the development of transportation by canals might well become a national function.

In the meantime, under the lead of her great governor DeWitt Clinton, New York had accomplished the simple but imposing task of making a waterway between the Hudson River and Buffalo.[14] This success caused bitter rivalry on the part of other Eastern cities, which saw New York absorbing the trade of the country. Boston, Philadelphia, Baltimore, Charleston, even Portland, Maine, and Portsmouth, New Hampshire, formed visions of tapping the golden stream and sought aid of their state governments.

Three classes of canal projects were undertaken. First were short canals to connect nearby rivers and feed the trade of a wider neighborhood into such ports as Boston and Charleston. These were built generally by private enterprise. One of the most important was that connecting Philadelphia with the anthracite coal region of the Lehigh and the Lackawanna. A second class were the canals connecting the water system of the Ohio with that of the Great Lakes, and so through the Erie Canal to New York. The third class of canals, upon which depended the efficiency of the whole system, were those designed, like the Erie, to connect East and West. Most favorably situated for such an enterprise, after New York, was Pennsylvania. Here the financial problem was undertaken by the state, but the engineering problem was of peculiar difficulty. It is hard to conceive a geographical formation more aggravating than that afforded by the successive ranges of the Allegheny Mountains, rising in obstinate placidity, one after the other, up and down, for nearly 150 miles. The idea of making water run over them was preposterous. This was precisely the kind of problem with which the thirties and forties were at their best. The canal was brought to the foot of one range, and then, by a stationary engine at the top, boat, cargo, and passengers were hauled up and let down on the other side, to resume the slow monotony of canal life until another range interrupted. With five such interruptions, one arrived at Pittsburgh with its choice of the National Road or the Ohio for the further journey. In 1834 this system was complete, at the cost of $10,038,133, and the route was used for a dozen years to the extent of its physical capacity—that is, at the seasonal peak of trade.[15] Philadelphia thus maintained herself against New York. Baltimore's attempt, by the Chesapeake and Ohio canal, in spite of national help, never reached a satisfactory western terminus.

To have provided itself with steamboat and canal transportation was no mean achievement for any generation. The main obstacles of nature had been overcome and the development of the continent might conceivably have gone forward satisfactorily, if somewhat slowly, with no new innovation, but by gradual improvement and extension. "Somewhat slowly," however, did not appeal to the men of the period, and while this system was still far from complete, the generation was expending more thought and capital upon the development of a system quite different, that of the railroad.

The railroad involved two separate ideas. First was that of the economy of friction in transportation by the use of fixed rails. Later, but very soon, came the idea of using steam power to draw vehicles over the rails, and, after very little experimentation, it was found that this should be done by locomotives and not by stationary engines drawing the cars to them. The moving cable was a later idea. To build such railroads involved problems of finance similar to those of the canals, but it was soon discovered, somewhat bitterly, that it involved also another point of public policy quite contrary to the spirit of the age. In 1828 a committee of Congress recommended that monopoly of use should no more be granted to railroad companies than to companies building roads or canals; they should all be open to the use of all, on paying proper tolls. Even in 1839, Governor William Henry Seward of New York clung to this hope. It was soon realized, however, and by the power of ratiocination of which this generation was not devoid, without experiment, that steam locomotives, running on a single track, must be under a single control. One must, therefore, accept railroads with this monopolistic feature or do without them.

The first center of railroad interest was in Baltimore, whose hopes of surmounting the mountains by water were proving so chimerical. In 1826 the Baltimore & Ohio Railroad was incorporated. The best brains of the city were put upon the subject. In 1831 steam was finally chosen for motive power. A locomotive, the "Tom Thumb," was built by Peter Cooper; it ran thirteen miles in an hour and surmounted grades that had been pronounced impossible. Soon Ross Winans established engineering shops which were laboratories of practical experiment and from which year by year came forth improvements by the dozen.

The first roadbeds were probably the most substantial we have ever had, solidly built of granite and ballasted with rock. They were unsatisfactory, however, because they lacked elasticity. Not only was each new line an experiment, but the directors of the longer roads freely laid a few miles of one kind, and a few of another, kept careful reports of each, and studied with care the reports of other roads. By 1840 they had pretty generally become convinced that the roadbed was not a final investment but a continual expense, and construction became generally less costly; but it had been learned how long rails should be, how they should be joined together, and how fastened to the ties.

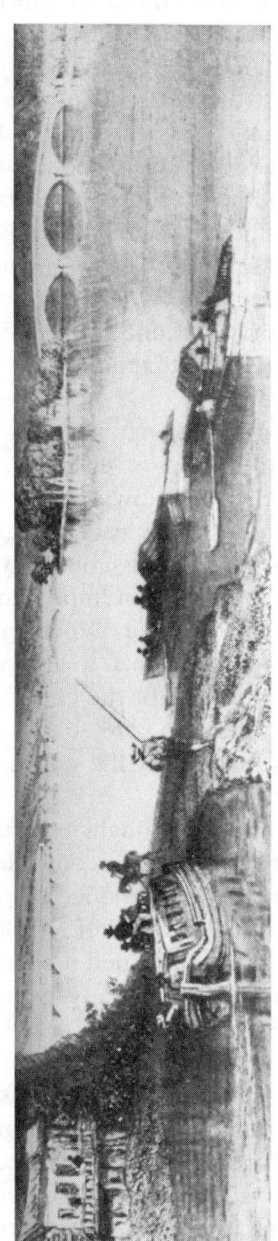 

Three of the types of transportation in use in the thirties: scenes at Northumberland, Pennsylvania, and at Little Falls, New York

There was longer experimentation with the rails because there was a keen desire to use the timber which was so abundant and cheap rather than iron which in the beginning had to be brought for the most part from abroad. The iron-capped wooden rails were in fact so well made that, where used with care, they were really sufficient for the light traffic of early years, and remained on many roads throughout the period. Most people, however, soon realized that they were doomed, and when the tariff of 1842 gave impetus to the domestic manufacture of iron rails, wooden ones ceased to be newly laid. American iron rails did not decrease costs, but it was claimed in the forties that they were of superior durability; and they were modeled on the American designed T pattern, which experiment had convinced American managers was the most desirable. When this generation passed on their tasks to their successors, the chief uncertainty was as to the weight of rail which would prove most efficient, and development was in the direction of greater and greater weight.

After brief experiment with horses, sails, mules, stationary engines, and "atmosphere," steam locomotives were shown to be most desirable, and American manufacturers such as Peter Cooper, the Baldwins, and Ross Winans speedily made them effective. The long life of the earlier engines, some of which served forty years, is a tribute to their makers, but for years scarcely a new one was put out which did not represent an improvement on those that went before.[16] They grew gradually heavier. When in the thirties a locomotive collided with a cow, the locomotive had to be sent to the repair shop; in the forties, the company had to pay for the cow.[17] The losses in both cases caused the development of the elaborate "cow catchers," and finally to the fencing of the railway, so that at the end of the period the number of such accidents was much reduced.

Except in the coal regions, the fuel was wood, although its scarcity was already apprehended. Cinders were not merely an inconvenience but a danger. In 1845 a spark arrester was generally introduced, which netted its inventors what seems now the very modest reward of $45,000.[18] Speed tests were often impressive, but few roads maintained a speed as good as the Hudson River steamer *Oregon*, which made twenty-five miles an hour. Some lines made thirty miles, but from ten to twenty was more characteristic.[19]

The cars began like the English, resembling stagecoaches, at first separate, then joined together, and finally with a running board along which the conductor perilously made his way. This type, however, gave way to the long car, with two double seats divided by an aisle. Just why this change was made it is difficult to say, but it is significant that when it was complete, the American traveled everywhere—whether by canal boat, steamer, or train—in a long narrow saloon, in close association with his fellow travelers, and with the opportunity for general conversation or for the expression of his opinion before an audience, willing or unwilling.

In 1840 such cars were constructed of wood; they were connected by chains, which took up none of the slack on starting and stopping; and their ventilation and heating were of that variety of the primitive which is unsatisfactory. Cars were of first and second class. The first seated about forty people, on double benches covered with horsehair. The Eastern (Massachusetts) road in 1845 put on a chair car, with seventy seats on pivots, and walls of inlaid wood. In 1836 a sleeping car was introduced by the Cumberland Valley Railroad with twenty-four berths that resembled the bunks of canal boats; the type convertible for day use was a later development. Frequent stops made restaurant cars unnecessary, and the usual absence of toilet facilities less inconvenient.

Gentlemen traveling alone were expected to use gentlemen's cars, and in regions where they were numerous, blacks used "Jim Crow" cars. Heavy luggage in most instances was handed over to the company in return for a check, but the generation never arrived at a decision as to whether the company was responsible for damage. Originally passengers were "booked" as on stagecoaches, but by 1840, tickets were coming into use, and passengers were encouraged to purchase them in advance by some slight reduction in fare. Tickets over connecting lines, however, could not be bought until the fifties. They were collected by the conductor, who, in contrast with the European system where the engineer was chief officer, ruled the train. On the main lines he was a lordly personage, dressed in top hat and with a medal proclaiming his number, but scorning both uniform and tips.

By 1840 there was a broken line of railroads from Portsmouth, New Hampshire, to Wilmington, North Carolina. Between 1840 and 1850 the greatest development was in New England. Boston was connected with Albany, New York, and Montreal. Elsewhere railroads were serving useful purposes as connecting links between rivers and canals. Only in one case, however, did they actually cross from the East to West, and that merely duplicated the route of the Erie Canal. They were, however, nosing westward along many other routes, the completion of which was assured. In 1850 the Erie was two thirds of the way to its goal at Dunkirk. The Pennsylvania had reached Johnstown and was confronting its Horseshoe Curve; the Baltimore & Ohio had passed Cumberland; Charleston and Savannah were both reaching westward.[20]

More important was the fact that real difficulties had actually been mastered, and that American engineers were unafraid and investors willing to back them. Asa Whitney was agitating for the building of a railroad to the Pacific within our territory, hoping in part to realize the dreams of Columbus for a western passage to the riches of the Orient. Military and naval officers reviewing the defenses of the United States were suggesting that the national government undertake the construction of railroads for military purposes, as one to the Pacific and one along the coast. William Wheelwright was projecting a transcontinental line from Buenos Aires to Valparaiso, and soon engineers and managers trained by American experience were swarming over South America and surveying the expanses of Russia.

INDUSTRY AND INVENTION

AGRICULTURE AND TRANSPORTATION employed most Americans. Both were self-sustaining occupations, supplying the nation and earning the wherewithal for improvement and purchases abroad. But most Americans of the day were unwilling to be dependent upon foreign nations for their manufactured goods. While, therefore, manufacturing employed a much smaller part of the population, and never during these years reached the adequacy of the two major occupations, it attracted an interest quite as deep.

The most discussed of its problems was that of protecting it from foreign competition.[21] That of the greatest industrial significance was the struggle between individual and factory production.[22] The relation in the factories between labor and capital was far from satisfactory, but during these years the subject was one which attracted interest only to a minor degree.[23] Of labor it may be said that throughout this period no Americans intended to remain laborers in the sense of living all their lives dependent on wages. The only fixed laboring class was in the South in agriculture, and these capital owned it. Moreover, in 1830 the total number of wage-earners in America was relatively very small, and the amount of organized gang labor was slight.

Factories were generally small and the industries were in that condition where even unlettered mechanics often contributed new ideas which gave them standing, and ingenious and industrious youths not infrequently rose to partnership. The New England textile mills were scattered up and down the valleys to make use of the river water power. Their labor they drew from the farms around them. The farmers' daughters did not mind the long hours or hard work, they knew little of the hygiene of congestion, and any money seemed to them a great deal. They did, however, demand conditions clean and moral. If they did not find them, they could return home. Most of them thought their factory experience, as boys did sailoring, an episode introductory to life. For all factory people was the possibility, daily made easier, of migration westward. It was not entirely with an undue devotion to vested interests that orators of the forties dwelt more on protecting the labor supply for manufacturing than on the dangers of capitalism.

In fact, laboring conditions during this period were generally satisfactory except for the long hours. Foreign travelers were usually taken to see the

Printing — a handicraft shop.

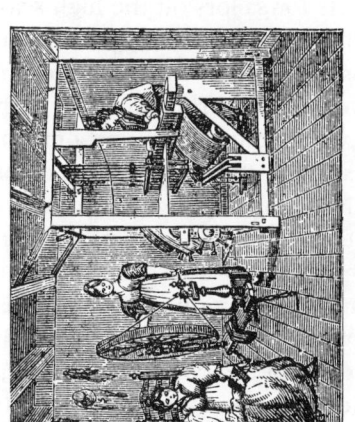

Above: First sewing-machine.

Below: Skyline of Lowell, Massachusetts, 1845.

Cloth making as a household industry.

Lowell mills, and all were enthusiastic over what they found. Dickens waxed lyric in describing the girls he found there and their life. Factories were generally located in villages rather than in cities, at waterfalls and mines, and most laborers lived in separated cottages with gardens or, if unmarried, in boardinghouses. It was with the employment, toward the end of the period, of foreign immigrants, who had no country homes to which to return and who could less easily seek the West, that the pressure of the industrial system began to express itself in unwholesome conditions.[24]

The struggle between factory and individual production was a complicated one. A clear illustration is found in the textile industry. Here factory cottons and woolens had, by 1830, almost driven the spinning wheel from the New England kitchen to the attic. From the mountain area they never quite drove it away. In many cases it is impossible to draw a line between the factory and the nonfactory unit, as in the production of the innumerable novelties that Connecticut inventiveness was turning out. In the boot-and-shoe industry of eastern Massachusetts, work was done in homes, but was so tied by agreements with finishers and agents that the essentials of factory conditions existed. The fundamental conditions of change seem to have been that craft education by apprenticeship was not as good as it had been, that the imagination of the best minds of young Americans devoted to such things was fired rather by the desire to invent and use machines than by the eighteenth-century zeal for expert mastership, that factory-made goods were displacing individual-made goods first in one line, then in another, and that consequently the career of the independent craftsman rising from apprentice to master was becoming less attractive. The shoemaker's apprentice was no match in the city streets for sailors off the high seas, with their trim dress, black silk kerchiefs about the throat, belled trousers, and their pockets full of the wages of a three months' voyage, nor in prospect with the city mechanic from the Stevens engineering works at Hoboken, who might by an inspiration followed with patience become a millionaire.

The chief products of the factories in 1830 were the textiles of New England, the iron goods of Pennsylvania, and the specialties, such as clocks and firearms, of Connecticut. In all these lines the progress during the period seems to the student of today steady; to the manufacturer of the time, it seemed a road of romance and peril, with prospects constantly dependent on the varying prices of raw materials and the variations of the tariff. From 1833 to 1842, under the terms of the compromise tariff, there was a period when government policy was fixed, but this condition of stability was broken by the business panic of 1837. Relatively, textiles throve more than iron, until the last years of the forties, and men like the Lowells and Lawrences were able to make large benefactions.

Of more interest than this steady growth of established industries was the diversification of products by the introduction into America of the manufacture of things previously made abroad, but still more of things newly invented to meet or to tempt American demand.[25] It was to an outstanding degree an age of invention. There was almost no department of life which the inventors left untouched. So universal was their scope that their work defies classification, but it is interesting to distinguish those things which were of the period generally from those which were American by origin, and then those whose purpose was to change the conditions of labor from those that affected chiefly the home.[26]

One of the simplest and most complete was an American contribution, the telegraph. For seventy-five years electricity had been a problem to the scientist and a toy to the public. Its habits had become fairly well understood, and the possibility of its application to communication intrigued many. It was the American, Samuel F. B. Morse, a characteristic son of the time, with many gifts from portrait painting and literature to medicine, who made the successful combination. Morse was an inventor by dint of ingenuity and general information. He was fortunate in attracting the interest of Amos Kendall, who, having contributed more perhaps than anyone else to such administrative success as the Jackson regime attained, was now at loose ends looking for a fortune. Working together they secured the support of Congress, and in 1844 a line was laid between Washington and Baltimore. Comparatively inexpensive to construct and meeting so obvious a demand of the time and particularly of the vast spaces of America, its use was extended with such rapidity that by 1850 the daily receipt of news from one end of the country to the other, excepting the Far West, was an accepted fact of life, and people were confidently expecting the system to be extended across the Atlantic.[27]

Perhaps the most important of all the inventions and the most characteristically American was that of the reaper. The successful experiment was in this case undoubtedly the one best deserving. The father of Cyrus H. McCormick was an active-minded farmer. He was interested in the problem of a harvesting machine, and made some progress toward its solution. In 1834 young McCormick patented an automatic reaper which contained essential new principles. Unlike the majority of inventors, he was remarkable for his business ability as well. Delayed by the Panic of 1837, he continued active in exhibiting his reaper at agricultural fairs and in seeking capital and a strategic location for manufacture. At first he selected a position on the Erie Canal, where 100 machines were turned out, and some profit accumulated. He then moved to Cincinnati, the capital of the West, where German immigration was supplying a population of skilled and unexacting mechanics. In 1847, however, he saw the promise of the future in Chicago, and reestablished himself in that muddy and scattered frontier station, which nevertheless soon proved to be near the center of his developing market.[28]

The reaper was merely the most important of the agricultural inventions of the period. Plows were continually improved, and practically every agricultural process was attacked by some inventor with the hope of performing it by mechanical means. Even a milking machine was patented. Nevertheless, taken together, they did not constitute a system, as those in transportation. Only 3,000 machines were manufactured in 1850, and, indeed, only 20,000 in 1860. Such numbers had no real effect on production, and they affected life on but an infinitesimal proportion of the farms. It is difficult to see why, in spite of the demand for these machines, and the increasing demand for agricultural products—caused by the greater ease of transportation and the growth of the European market as industrial life developed there—agriculture was so much slower to change than transportation. Not much can be attributed to the natural conservatism of the farmer, for the proportion of progressives among the immigrant farmers of the West was large. More was perhaps due to sheer poverty. Probably most important was the enormous swell of immigration which began to roll in by the middle forties and which temporarily met the labor problem. The reaper was bequeathed to the next generation, but mechanical agriculture had yet to be developed, both as to some fundamental principles and as to application.[29]

A characteristic series of inventions were those for the taking of likenesses. Portrait painting was a costly process, and the rise of democracy called for something less expensive. Early in the century the silhouette afforded a new method, cheaper but inadequate. More satisfactory was the process discovered in France by L. J. M. Daguerre. Introduced into America by S. F. B. Morse, it was rapidly developed, and by 1850 as good likenesses were thus taken as have ever been printed, but at a cost in the long holding of a fixed expression. Daguerreotypes became common in a large proportion of American homes, and Americans set themselves to the further cheapening of the process.

A more basic change was with regard to domestic heating. This was a development peculiarly American, perhaps because of the driving power of our cold winters. Franklin had made a practical contribution in his open-grate stove. Still more was accomplished by Benjamin Thompson, Count Rumford, whose study of the physics of heat lie at the foundation of all subsequent development. On the basis of these principles great numbers of American inventors set to work during this period to make more practical stoves for both heating and cooking. All through the Northeast this was the period when kitchen fireplaces were closed up and iron ranges took their places, the first step in a long procession of such changes, each one of which has been regarded by the older housewives as destructive of real delicacy in cooking, but has been welcomed by their daughters, because of increase in the speed of living and cleanliness and the saving of household labor.

Fireplaces elsewhere in the house were at the same time being sporadically supplanted by stoves for heating, of which there were many kinds, some justifying the outcry that they were dangerous to health. Such stoves in railroad cars made traveling possible in winter, which in the stage-coaches had only been endured by heavy wraps, rugs, hand and foot warmers, and by crowding. In churches and public buildings large stoves were employed, and soon these began to be dropped to the cellars and to heat the auditoriums indirectly. By 1850 practicable furnaces were on the market. Some of the enterprising and wealthy began to install them in their houses, to warm the halls and upper rooms which before had generally been left without heat.

In the South the fireplace survived, and in the West iron stoves were too expensive for general use, though their adoption was only a matter of time. The heating system, like the railroads, existed, and remained only to be generally adopted. A new American characteristic, the love of heat, was on the way to development, and a new strain was about to be placed upon the American constitution. Still, in 1850, Fredrika Bremer found the cold bedroom as yet more usual, and complained bitterly of its discomfort.[30] The fuel used depended largely upon locality, though coal, with the aid of vigorous advertising, was driving out wood. Smoke consumption was in its infancy, and the streets still resounded with the calls of the chimney sweep.

A second change of similar character toward which important, though not so great, strides were made was in lighting. The desire for brilliancy was as marked as that for heat, though the need for it was less obvious. In general, it may be said that this generation was born by candlelight, and died by the light of oil lamps. Here again were no fundamental inventions but a continual succession of adjustments. The real interest was less in the container than in the fuel. The best by far was whale oil, but the supply was limited in quantity and the oil expensive. Lard and many other sources were sought, but the petroleum supply, lying just below the surface, was not discovered, and lamps consequently remained a mark of moderate prosperity. When used, they were, in spite of the attention they required of the housewife, another saving of labor in the home; for candles had been generally one of the many products of each household. Whether lamps or candles were used, however, they had come by 1850 to be in most instances lighted by the friction match invented in Europe and first patented in America in 1836. It very soon reached an almost universal use because of its outstanding superiority to the flint or steel and tinder which it supplanted. In the meantime lighting by gas, which had been introduced in the preceding generation, was spreading from city to city and from public uses to private. Gas companies were naturally dependent on a closely populated area, and consequently this illuminant was among the things making for an increasing difference between life in the city and on the farm.

The kitchen, which was not beyond—or below—the ken of practically every American woman, was being transformed not merely by the cook-stove but by new kitchenware. In place of the copper of the Dutch country-side and the ironware of New England were coming the new tin goods. The tin had to be imported, but American cleverness shaped it into so many useful forms that its vendors not only tempted American housewives but exported some of their products. Less substantial than what they replaced, tin goods were so much cheaper that they could be purchased in relative abundance, and so much lighter that they reduced drudgery. They formed the stock-in-trade of the peddler who frequented all the closely settled portions of the country and who not only rapidly distributed the new wares but was an agent for collecting the rags from which to make paper for which there was an increased demand. Such peddlers carried with them, also, all sorts of novelties of a less useful character, as well as forerunners of direct labor-saving devices for the kitchen, such as hand mills to grind coffee, which was rapidly becoming a new national drink.[31]

The dining room was less changed. It, as well as other rooms in the house, was more frequently papered, now that the making of wallpaper had been brought to America and made cheaper, though imported French papers were preferred and constituted a mark of distinction. The service of the table began to be enriched by new implements such as fruit knives,[32] and the whole house from kitchen to attic began to creak with the restless rocking chair, which of all such American-conceived trivialities penetrated perhaps most speedily and widely. More and more in the public rooms carpets were substituted for the earlier rag rugs — carpets, the cheap manu-facture of which was in part an American invention and the manufacture of which throve with the tariff; carpets tacked down snugly against the wall and presenting problems of sanitation which were not to be solved even by the next generation; carpets blossoming with roses of fantastic size and brilliancy and which flashed not only from the floors but on street and railroad from the sides of carpetbags in which the ever-growing number of travelers carried their few necessities. More and more generally, entrance to the house was sought by ringing the modish bell instead of the knocker, which was becoming vulgar but not yet old-fashioned.

Meanwhile the structure of the home was changing. The houses of the rich reflected a greater variety of influences in their architectural styles — all foreign influences though with American adaptations. The building of houses in continuous blocks extended little beyond Boston, New York, Philadelphia, Baltimore, and St. Louis. Here and there over the country the influence of Washington Irving and Scott was seen in the many-gabled cottages which were a distant echo of a growing interest in the Gothic. Toward the end of the period the cult of Italy, which began among the esoteric and throve chiefly among the aristocratic, produced some rather beautiful studies in window spacing and iron grille work. A plan that ap-pealed more to the innovating reformer was that reflecting the teaching of

Fourier and resulted, in many localities, in octagonal houses, which were supposed to afford an economy in heating, and the interior treatment of which was managed with some cleverness. These houses served to give a more varied appearance to the cities of 1850 than those of 1830 had possessed; they were somewhat more complicated by the elementary beginnings of plumbing, and occasionally possessed bathrooms. They seldom equaled in dignity or size those of the preceding generation.[33]

What amazes is their cheapness of construction, even when the subsequent rise of general values is considered. One could build a six-room house, with some evidence of taste, for $800; $1,500 would give a seven-room house with architectural pretensions. Twenty-five hundred dollars secured a town mansion or a country villa of Greek, Gothic, or Italian style. With such prices it is apparent how easily the general housing of the population could improve.

With regard to public buildings, the greatest change was in the churches, where the Gothic was more in evidence, Trinity Church in New York representing a really creditable example of that ecclesiastical type. More common, however, were rather awkward combinations of dome and portico. In church and public buildings the Italian influence also was in evidence. One of the most artistic effects of the period, or rather just following it, was the railroad entrance to Providence, Rhode Island, with a graceful structure in red brick with cloisters and campaniles edged against a round cove, bordered by a double row of elms. In this case the age of individuality had given the control to culture, but lack of taste and indifference had equal rights, and cities lost rather than gained attraction.[34]

Business had not yet generally realized the advantages of display. Banks were impressive, properly advertising their conservative tendencies by using the standard Greek forms. Shops were generally inconvenient and small, but their error in psychology was becoming apparent, and the more successful merchants, as Jordan and Marsh at Boston and A. T. Stewart at New York, were increasing their frontage and window space. The most advanced were the hotel builders. Perhaps the most admired structure of the period was the white granite Astor House on Broadway in New York.[35] It is fairly evident that the majority of Americans were too busy with other things to change their artistic conceptions; to them white was still the essence of good taste and marble the material *de luxe,*[36] though private homes were affecting variations running from cream brick to brown stucco.

On the whole, the contrast in life between 1830 and 1850 exhibits an astonishing fertility of resource and willingness to change. One cannot say that the technique of living was occupying more attention than previously, but whereas Washington devoted his attention to bringing his gardens to an exquisite perfection, the men of the thirties and forties sought novelty rather than perfection. In some respects, as in the use of carpets, ease of heating, cherishing of personality by daguerreotypes, and cheapening of kitchen supplies, these changes decreased, except in the case of the frontier, the differences between the homes of rich and poor. On the other hand, the close of the generation saw greater contrasts between city and country than had previously existed, and a wider variation due to the scattered use of the new inventions. This, of course, was chiefly an accident of time, and the rising generation might expect to see the use of such things practically universal. Taking these changes altogether, they cannot be said, economically or socially, to have produced a satisfactory new scheme of life. They did not accomplish for the home what the railroad did

Architectural Design in the Forties.

for transportation. Many more inventions and developments were needed to complete the revolution in living which this generation began in America and the continuance of which they rendered inevitable.

NEW AMERICANS

BETWEEN 1830 and 1850 nearly 2.5 million foreign immigrants were added to a population that increased altogether from a little less than 13 million to a little over 23 million. Of these newcomers, nearly half arrived in the last five years of the period. It is evident that immigration was an important feature in the life of the time. The attention that it attracted was due not merely to its magnitude, but to its distribution and character, and in part to its relative novelty.

A steady stream, already started and continuing to grow, brought English, Welsh, and Scotch. They were of varied classes and occupations, many had family connections in America, and with their similarity of language, they quickly found a place in American life, which made it unnecessary, if not impossible, to maintain a group life. Thus the Scotchman Alexander Mitchell, establishing himself in Wisconsin in 1839, speedily inspired perhaps the greatest confidence of any banker of the Northwest. As farmers they were to be found throughout the Northwest, but perhaps the largest number were those who continued in the new country to be factory operatives as they had been in the old. These latter naturally belonged at home to the dissatisfied classes, and they contributed something to American sympathy for the Chartist movement at the end of the period.[37]

Much more attention was attracted by the Irish, whose number steadily grew until at the end of the period they taxed the rapidly increasing means of ocean transit. This influx was novel rather because of its rapid increase than its newness, for the Irish had always come; it was chiefly to be attributed to the greater ease in reaching America, for the causes of emigration had long existed. In the late forties, however, it received an enormous impetus from the famine that for several years devastated Ireland. The Irish immigrants consisted of all classes but not all occupations. Few were mechanics, and such as were came from Ulster and properly are to be joined with the Scotch. Some were gentry, with a little money, who sought, often with success, to build up country estates in the West. The great majority, however, had been peasant farmers working under an abominable land system, whose effort reached its limit when they paid their fare to America. They arrived at Boston, New York, Philadelphia, Baltimore, or New Orleans, but chiefly at New York, equipped with the knowledge of a simple tillage, but with no money to secure the land to till or even to journey to the place where land was.[38]

They constituted, therefore, what the new life of America was demanding and what America did not possess—a laboring class with no choice but to accept such jobs as were offered. Fortunately for them such jobs were numerous. Pick-and-shovel work was new in America. Few of the native stock cared to or were forced to engage in it, for nearly all could scratch together a living on some family farm, even if they could not gather the cash to migrate. The Irish, therefore, were welcomed by the new corporations, and stayed in the coast cities to excavate ditches for gas and water mains, or were taken in gangs to dig canals or prepare the track of new railroads, or served as engine crews in the omnipresent steamboats. Throughout the period their brawn was laying the foundation for the new material civilization of America.

While so employed, they stepped on no economic toes and were regarded with general indifference. A second economic stage appeared, however, before the period was over. The railroad gangs, when the work was completed, were apt to settle down in some nearby manufacturing town and to enter the factories on terms which began to drive the natives from their posts. They won the hatred not only of those whom they displaced, but also of the independent skilled mechanics, the demand for whose services was slackening—not really because of the Irish but because of the increased use of factory-made goods. In the cities, too, the Irish girls, who began to come over in almost as great numbers as the men, not only permitted many Americans for the first time to indulge in the luxury of a maid-of-all-work but took the place of native "help."

In addition to this competition, the Irish movement was characterized by several features differentiating it from that of the English and Scotch. The Irish laborers generally settled in groups, whether in the cities or in the factory villages. While they spoke the language of the majority, they were distinguished at this time by their poverty, and secondly by their religion. American tolerance was not a simple trait, and during this period the Roman Catholic Church was becoming more distasteful to the majority as it became more important. The feeling toward it was not merely religious but political, for it was considered as an extension of the great established church of Europe, monarchical in its own organization and the chief prop of civil monarchy as well. When, therefore, the first Catholic church arose in the Irish quarter of city or town, the combination was regarded as a menace.

The cohesion of the Irish extended to politics. The Irish had played a part in American politics since the end of the eighteenth century; Tammany Hall attracted them in the early twenties and in time they came to control that institution. As New York City grew and the public services increased, they showed a capacity for securing appointments and contracts; the typical policeman came to be an Irishman, and policemen were growing more numerous and powerful.

The reaction of the native population to these conditions varied. The combination of religious, political, and economic rivalry became at times intense. In 1834 an Ursuline convent was burned in Charlestown, Massachusetts.[39] The following year S. F. B. Morse returned from Austria deeply suspicious of Catholic enterprise in the United States as propaganda for monarchy and published his small but influential book *Foreign Conspiracy.*[40] Rioting, particularly at election time, was a feature of the life in the more crowded districts of New York and Baltimore. In Philadelphia from time to time during the forties there were attempts to organize an American Protestant party with the idea that the foreigner was the leading problem of the day.[41]

More novel than the Irish immigration was that of the Germans, who were indeed known and numerous in America from the earliest days. There was, however, a virtual cessation of immigration at the Revolution, and a revival about 1830, which separated the population of that stock into two elements. During this period the immigration was of varied classes and types. From a political point of view it represented, as had the Puritan emigration to New England, practically all phases of liberal opinion. From an economic point of view, and this was what influenced the larger number, it brought over the more conservative, who were out of harmony with the rising industrialism of modern Germany.[42]

In many more instances than in the case of the Irish, these immigrants arrived with some money. A large number prepared carefully for the move and had read emigrant guidebooks, such as those of von Gerstner and of Bromme.[43] As time went on, the greater number came over to join friends and relatives from whom they heard intimate accounts, and sought to reestablish in America family and village groups. Consequently, few stayed in the coast cities or in the older portions of the country, where it was difficult to break into American life, socially and economically, except at the bottom. Some, such as musicians, mechanics with some special skill as watchmakers, or merchants interested in developing an import trade in German goods, scattered about the country, and Germans were as familiar as Irish in cities and along routes of trade. The great bulk, however, sought the first and easiest road across the mountains. Like the Irish, they generally eschewed the South, and consequently the majority were to be found in the Ohio Valley and the Great Lakes Region.

In general the Germans, like the Irish, adhered to the Democratic party, but during this period they were by no means so powerful an element. The arrival of so many intellectual and political leaders just at the close of the period began a change. These men were not only concerned with politics but were keenly interested in particular questions of state and national policy. They had ideals in accordance with which they wished to mold the United States. By 1852 they were in the thick of affairs and it was believed that they could swing their fellow countrymen as easily as did the Irish

Bishop Hughes, of New York.

The Charlestown Convent, 1834.

Irish immigration made the "Catholic question"
more prominent.

The Germania Musical Society, about 1850.

Among other things the Germans brought a taste for music.

leaders of the East. At the same time, they were placed even more strategically in the balanced Northwest, which was to be the political battleground of the next ten years; soon Abraham Lincoln was studying German.

While the Irish and the Germans were the most important in number and in the interest they attracted, other elements were of some significance at the time or promised to be in the future. Of the first type were the French, whose number was very small but whose influence on the native population was decided. These newcomers occupied themselves to a large extent with the arts affecting manners and customs. It was a period when French etiquette was supplanting British, and while this was chiefly due to the dazzling influence of Paris, it was assisted by French dancing masters and chefs. During the same years the French Canadians began to drop down from their rural homes to garner in the cash wages of the New England mills. Dutch, emigrating for commercial reasons or distressed at home by fine shades of religious differences, founded towns in Michigan, Iowa, and Wisconsin. Belgians settled in the lake region of Wisconsin, and Swiss about its hills. Curiously, like the Israelites, Norwegian communities sent men and families to spy out the land, and while their numbers were few, the reports returned were being read on many a mountainside farm. On the whole, the impression created by the United States, however contrary to the reports of their consuls who investigated their settlements,[44] was so favorable that in a few years Norwegians, Danes, and Swedes would be coming by the tens of thousands.[45]

The Americans of English descent increased rapidly. The large families of colonial times continued to be the rule and the easier conditions of life allowed more to reach maturity. All settled areas produced a surplus population urgent to move. Cities drew ambitious boys from their neighborhood, but their attraction was small in comparison with that of the new West. From New England there still emerged occasionally complete towns, each with some new idea to germinate. Most emigration, however, was of families and individuals. The greater part came from the outer edges of New England settlements, the Berkshires, the Green Mountains of Vermont, and the hilly country of New Hampshire and Maine.

The impulse for migration was less strong in the middle states, but was reenforced as time went on by the increasing flow of foreign immigration. From New York most followed the natural watercourse of the Hudson and joined the New Englanders at Albany, whose newspapers they continued for many years to read. The highways of Pennsylvania, and the Ohio and Chesapeake Canal, gathered other thousands at Pittsburgh and Wheeling. From these ports some took boats down the Ohio, landing nearly always on the northern bank, while others set out on the National Road, which took them to the interior of Ohio, and later into Indiana and Illinois.

From the older South two streams flowed with increasing strength. The growing monopoly of the best land by the plantations caused a constant exodus of the poorer farmers to the northern bank of the Ohio where slavery did not exist. The second stream was impelled to move by the declining profits of plantation culture. Some planters, such as the Chestnuts of South Carolina, fortified themselves by investing the profits of past years in the bonds of the rising corporations. Others, like the Hamptons of the same state, opened investment plantations to the West. Many sought new fields where they could found anew their plantations on a virgin soil. They moved with their establishments and their slaves, southwesterly, leisurely, over the rough valley roads, into Alabama and Mississippi, Louisiana, Arkansas, Missouri, and even Texas. They soon established a sectional civilization, which became highly self-conscious and distinctive.[46]

Land seemed to nearly all Americans the key to happiness. To start a new Western farm in 1830 required a cash investment of $100 for land alone. Many of those going West lacked this amount and settled on land as yet unsurveyed, from which they might be driven by U.S. authorities, and which they were almost sure to lose when the land was surveyed and put up at general auction. Two ideas were frequent in their thought and conversation. One was that all public land should be turned over to the state in which it lay. The other was that land be given free to actual settlers. This latter idea came to be known as the homestead policy.[47] Both views were opposed by the older states, which feared that their populations would be depleted if emigration were made too easy. The second was particularly objectionable to the South, for public sentiment with regard to slavery had reached the point that, should land be given away, no special consideration would be given, as it had been in colonial Virginia, to settlers carrying slaves with them, but the same unit would be given to all heads of families.

Nevertheless, these frontier wishes were important, for never was so large a proportion of the population migrating as between 1830 and 1850, or dominant in so large an area as measured by congressional votes. This was already true in 1830, and the impulses to migration continued to grow stronger and the obstacles less difficult to overcome as the facilities for transportation improved. While Ohio, Kentucky, Georgia, and some other regions ceased by 1850 to be frontier, the pioneer had advanced by that date into regions unoccupied in 1830, and the frontier was as strong, though probably less proportionately strong, at the end as at the beginning of the period.

The first demand to be met was that for the elimination of the Indians. Two presidents owed their selection to this frontier element, Andrew Jackson and William Henry Harrison. Both had won its support in large measure by destroying the military and diplomatic power, the one of the Indians of the South, the other of those of the Northwest. One of Jackson's firmest determinations on entering office in 1829 was the removal of the Indian population to the Great Plains beyond Missouri, Arkansas, and what was to become Iowa. Legal obligations seemed of small weight to a man whose customary associates had an interest involved and interpreted them from one point of view. That the Supreme Court held another view did not cause Jackson to condemn its chief justice, John Marshall, but to conclude that the president, the executive head of the government, need not be bound in action by the judiciary branch. He protected the states, particularly Georgia, in measures rendering the position of the Indians untenable, and pressed the sale of Indian land to the United States and the acceptance of the government's proposals for migration.[48]

Throughout the period, the process of removal was being carried out. Tribal migrations shepherded by U.S. troops were a feature of the Western picture. Some Indians resisted. In 1831 and 1832 there was the brief episode of the Black Hawk War in Wisconsin. In Florida there was a ten-year struggle with the Seminoles, moated about by their swamps. By the end of the period, except for a number of fixed reservations, the Indians were pretty well cleared out to beyond the first tier of trans-Mississippi states. With true Jacksonian spirit, the Indians of the Plains were left alone except for insufficient lines of forts along the trails of trade or migration to Santa Fe, Salt Lake, and Oregon. This arrangement was by most regarded as final. Jackson himself opposed the rounding out of Missouri by the addition to that state of what is now its northwestern jog extending to the Missouri, for which Congress nevertheless provided in 1837.

The settlers demanded that the land so secured be speedily surveyed. By 1850 the survey had practically been completed in Michigan and in the southern and eastern third of Wisconsin and half of Iowa, was almost complete in Arkansas, and about half finished in Florida. During this period perhaps more than any other the U.S. government owned the land most desired and sold it directly to the settler. The sale price, therefore, became a matter of high concern. Although this question was always at the forefront of politics and forced every party and leader to offer some solution in framing a general political platform, the migrants were not able to have their way. They wished the distribution of land to actual settlers at cost, but the older landless states regarded the public domain as a property to bring in income. The result was, politically, a deadlock in spite of a continual struggle for free homesteads, and the system of offering surveyed land first at auction, and then for sale at $1.25 per acre, was continued.

The land being occupied under such conditions was one of the easiest regions in the world to develop. Many of the new settlers were spared even the long task of clearing by occupying the prairie regions which earlier settlers had avoided because of the absence of wood, or still better, the "oak openings" of southern Michigan and Wisconsin. The development of transportation, however inadequate, produced results superior to that which any inland settlers had previously enjoyed. They were able to bring more with them. Mrs. John H. Kinsie, for example, coming to the wilderness of Wisconsin in 1830, found room for her piano. Those who brought money succeeded in securing carpenters to build homes which were soon adequately furnished. Those without it were able to market their crops with some profit, and few lived long in the one-room log cabins with which they started. Log extensions and porches were gradually added, and by the end of the period, brick making and the development of lumbering enabled a good number to move into real houses and relegate the original cabin to some farm use.[49] By 1850 public buildings, capitols, county courthouses, schools, churches, and colleges were rising not much inferior to those with which the generation had started in the East. Never had a civilization been established so quickly.

The population which came together in the West was a mixed one. At its base was the family ambition for a good farm, which, after hard work, would bring comfort in late middle age and provide for the upbringing of the children. To most communities, however, came families with some wealth and background, who sought to establish themselves in prominence and rise to wealth. Everywhere were young men who sought freer opportunities for distinction in law and politics, for this was a wholesome period when able young men consciously aimed at growing up with a community which would ultimately entrust them with its political destinies. Everywhere were those who had been discredited at home, and sought either opportunity to reform, or to resume under freer conditions careers of varying degrees of dishonesty.

Some sought the West to escape the oppression of uncongenial families or communities, or to secure a greater moral latitude for themselves, or the power of imposing some particular system upon others. As compared with earlier times, however, there was less need to migrate for such purposes, and, with regard to moral and social aims, the frontier was often rather conservative than radical. Always hovering about each new community were numbers of the merely shiftless, endlessly seeking that turn of the wheel which would never come, while some were frankly criminal, who came to prey upon the less protected flocks of a new land.

Before this more solid mass of home seekers and their parasites continued to scurry the fringe of the still more adventurous and fantastic, and of those bent on finding new Utopias. Thus in 1848 the Mormons made their great move out of the U.S. territory into the heart of the Rockies, and every year thereafter saw their thousands crossing the Great Plains to the Salt Lake region, where their new experiment was painfully striking its roots. The American missionaries in Hawaii established themselves firmly and looked back to the United States for protection. The fishermen, and the traders they attracted, were especially interested in the harbors of California, and though few in number, they were, in the early forties, making their presence disturbing to the cabinets of Mexico and Great Britain. Likewise the Texan movement ripened into statehood. Finally, in 1848, the last touch was given to this varied migratory movement by the discovery of gold in California.

In general, as contrasted with earlier migration, there were fewer community movements. As contrasted with later periods, the family, or at least the incipient family, played a larger part. Families with young children were common, newly married couples frequent, groups of brothers with the purpose of sending back for parents and sisters were found in every district. Young men with the plan of sending back for acknowledged sweethearts seem to have been as numerous as those who left home free-hearted. Even the latter, once established, often returned to find a wife, or at least married the daughter of a neighbor from home. During this generation it was much more common for the migrating husband and wife, whether of native or foreign birth, to come from the same home environment and thus to preserve the tradition of their strain than to marry into another provincial culture.

MANNERS AND MORALS

THESE CHANGES in transportation, in conditions of life, and in the composition of the American people naturally produced changes not less important in their habits. Seldom have transformations so great been made anywhere in the lifetime of one generation. To create conditions so new and to make the necessary adjustments of life at the same time is something which is seldom satisfactorily accomplished. The United States of this period was not an exception, and it is doubtful if the surface of life was ever so fantastic and, except to an almost incredibly optimistic eye, so disagreeable. How deep these surface changes penetrated into the character of the people is a question more important but much more difficult, whether for the contemporary or for the historian.

Never before was the surface of life so exposed to the gaze of the public and the future. Never before in America were people so much out of their houses and on the move. Never before were there so many travelers to observe them, with so easy a market for their observations when put into print. Never had the busy reporters of the newspapers been so numerous and so alert to catch the mass or the individual in some unusual pose, some amusing gesture. The generation was exposed to a continual "close-up" without having learned how to appear before the camera. Whether this multitude of snapshots affords a better understanding of its real life than the materials existing for earlier generations is a question. Certainly at the time there seemed to be less sense of direction, a greater variety of tendencies, than usual. Whether this was a fact or was due to variety of report the cautious will be slow to declare.[50]

The travelers represented almost every variety of experience, prepossession, and purpose. De Tocqueville came in the thirties to study the working of our institutions from the point of view of political philosophy. Somewhat the same purpose animated Harriet Martineau, who, in spite of her deafness, had probably the best advantages of all for meeting the ablest minds and entering the finest homes of America. Dickens had a popular reception and best saw America as the dominant democracy wished it to be seen. He came primarily to write a book, and he was probably too insensitive to understand that the Americans who had been laughing at an Englishman making fun of Englishmen would not laugh at an Englishman making fun of his foreign hosts. In America as in England, he saw rather the unusual and the comic than the ordinary.

About some of the more constructive products of this generation, such as the institutions for the blind and the insane, all were enthusiastic. On the great novelty of universal male suffrage perhaps none changed their preconceived ideas. As to the character of our public life, they were divided, but the intimate experiences of Harriet Martineau at Washington are of more value than all the others taken together and are more favorable. Practically all disapproved of slavery; few traveled in the South to observe it.

One thing upon which the travelers were competent to report was the public manners of the Americans. On this point they were almost at one: The manners were bad. Foremost was the almost universal male habit of chewing tobacco and then spitting. Cigarettes had not come in, cigars were limited by social custom to certain times and places, but the "plug" was everywhere, and the bystander was fortunate when it was accompanied by its attendant spittoon. It is not necessary to suppose that there were no homes devoid of these articles, nor American men who were immune from the habit. It was, however, pervasive, and did not cause social ostracism or mark a social class. Equally distasteful was the manner of eating. The prevalent impression derived from hotel and boardinghouse was that the knife was too much in evidence, particularly in the consumption of peas; one noted merchant also used his for ice cream. Here again this habit was not universal, but the circles from which it excluded a person were small, and to most travelers inaccessible.

More general still was the practice of eating rapidly, without conversation. What they ate was again unsatisfactory to the observer and, if one may judge from the medical advertisements of the newspapers, to the digestion also. This impression would perhaps have been varied if more travelers had frequented the South. It was also true that in a country where most cooking was done or closely supervised by the housewife and where time was not considered a factor, there were more dishes of special excellence than there are today. In the church "socials," rivalry was keen in the production of cakes of elaboration and succulence, and if sauces were few, as Talleyrand had earlier remarked, relishes were many and recipes for them highly prized. The defect seems to have been the lack of balance in the ration. Meat was overabundant and fresh vegetables were too few. This generation did indeed learn to eat tomatoes, but not to make salads. The three meals of the day were practically identical.

Still again travelers were unfavorably impressed by the appearance of Americans. The women of the cities they reported as being of pleasing manner and costume but overdressed. New conditions meant that incredible numbers of Americans came to have, at least from time to time, unusual sums of money: the nouveaux riches came to swamp the aristocracy. The spirit of democracy was that all should rise to the top, and the first and easiest method was by overcoming the differences in outward guise. The increasing ease of ocean transportation meant a more and more rapid influx of fashion, in setting which the needle turned steadily away from London and toward Paris. More and more, therefore, the streets were crowded with women dressed in the extreme of fashion, and the shops displayed a greater and greater wealth of foreign goods. Less and less could foreigners distinguish the social position of these women, and on the whole, social position came to be less and less significant.[51]

Such display was distinctly feminine. There was coming into existence that division of functions, which was to characterize the United States for several generations, by which culture was feminine, and masculinity was expected to distinguish itself by a lack of exterior polish. To a considerable degree the men could be more easily classed socially by their attention to their toilet, though such a criterion would have done an injustice to the birth and station of many a Southern planter. While the older men of the generation, such as Webster and Benton, still "dressed," it was becoming less and less desirable to do so. Equality expressed itself in the general vogue of the long-tailed frock coat, accompanied in the South by a broad-brimmed soft hat, in the North by the tall hat, less expensive than formerly now that silk had become its material instead of fur. Individual taste found its expression in the waistcoat, which rivaled the carpetbag in splendor. Still, men whose wives appeared in silks and satins slouched beside them in unfitted suits and dirty linen. For both, the bath was a weekly event, not always observed. Webster, when his second marriage brought him into the aristocracy, began daily to wash his chest, but this had more to do with his nasal troubles than with cleanliness.[52]

One of the first impressions the traveler received on reaching New York in the later days of the period was of the newsboys. During the forties they were almost as characteristic of the city as were the dogs of Constantinople. They were new in America; they were almost unique in the world. It was one of the first occupations in which boys, who had always labored hard enough at home, began to receive money for their work. They were ragamuffins from the growing slums; they were sons of widows helping keep the family together; they were shrewd products of the business instinct who would save their earnings and rise to be financial magnates. They fought, they divided their "beats," they had their regular days at the theater, they were among the most picturesque elements of the city.

The reason for their existence was the new development of the press, which was one of the marked features of the period. The newspaper was, of course, not new. It had always enjoyed unusual advantages in America. Since the Zenger case in 1735 it had enjoyed a freedom of expression which the Federalists in the Adams administration had tried in vain to limit. It was free also from such imposts as the British "paper" duties, which laid so heavy a hand on the press of that country until Gladstone withdrew them. Nevertheless, American papers had but scantily rewarded their owners because of their slight circulation. Many were maintained only by subsidies, direct or indirect, received from political leaders who needed them. Nearly all had been adjuncts, sometimes unimportant, of printing establishments. The most significant had been those of Washington, which relied on the profits of the national printing or on hopes of securing it.

The first new step was the establishment of the *Sun* in New York City by Benjamin H. Day, who, seeing the possibility of maintaining a low-priced paper by advertising based on large circulation, issued it in 1833 at one cent a copy. The *Sun* made a second innovation in seeking to attract readers by the startling character of its news. Its famous moon hoax, detailing astonishing discoveries made by the astronomer Herschel, which were proved by the arrival of the next packet from England to be without foundation, hit the funny bone of the public with a tingling sensation that was remembered and enjoyed. So successful was Day's experiment that in 1835 he began to turn the Napier press, upon which it was printed, by steam, and the need was created which stimulated inventive minds and brought about Hoe's rotary press in 1846.[53] Day's example was quickly emulated by the Scotchman James Gordon Bennett, whose *Herald,* by its collection of news and its brief and snappy editorials, gave an impression of sophistication and cosmopolitanism. In 1841 a Vermont printer's boy, Horace Greeley, founded the *Tribune,* to which he gave distinction by its ardent advocacy of, or opposition to, the movements of the day, outside of politics as well as in that field.[54]

The world as presented by such papers was a peculiar one. It is important to discount both the picture of American life and the effect produced on the American mind. Political editorials were of the most exaggerated bitterness, and did not stop with the condemnation of men's opinions or the actual defects in their character. Their news was selected with reference to the unusual and the sensational rather than with the desire of creating a photograph of life. One may almost conclude that things mentioned in the papers were exceptional, and look elsewhere, or at least read between the lines, for the real life of Americans. Facts were generally presented from the point of view of optimism; the conception of some public improvement was presented as if it were completed. On the other hand, there was little, if any, of the later practice of selecting news with reference to the editorial policy.

Special value must be given to the advertisements which were paid for; one can safely conclude from these that the consumption of patent medicines was immense, and their patentees among the new members of the money aristocracy. The press, too, was so flexible, it cost so little to establish a new paper, and the habit of doing it was so strong, that in time most new ideas and points of view found somewhere an expression, and a survey of the whole press gives at least the elements of which American life was composed, although their proportionate importance must be fixed by other means.

At the time, most Americans read a paper with which they fundamentally agreed, and whose suggestions on small matters they were apt to follow. The respect for the printed word was still strong, and the influence of newspapers was probably somewhat more powerful than it is today. On the other hand, the population was keen, and there was ever present a standard for comparison between the knowledge each one had of local happenings and the newspaper reports. The new press began not only to give the Americans news but to develop their critical faculties. On the whole, the people obtained a better impression of what was taking place outside their personal experience than had their fathers, but it was still strangely and somewhat maliciously distorted.

The theater made no such sensational change as did the newspapers.[55] Actors were still mainly of English birth and training and of theatrical families like the Kembles. As the cities grew, however, they played to a larger proportion of the people and their position became more a matter of debate. On the whole the theater gained in standing, and Americans began to enter the profession without losing caste. In the forties some fifty stock companies were supported in moderation. Stars traveled individually and played in each city with the company established there. The demand for these stars became so great that, at the end of the period, their salaries threatened to reduce managers and regular staff to a very low compensation. Throughout the period Edwin Forrest was the chief hero of the stage. In 1849, Edwin Booth appeared at the Museum in Boston, and already Americans were becoming proud of Charlotte Cushman. Just after this period the dramatization of *Uncle Tom's Cabin* brought to the theater tens of thousands who up to this time had regarded it as the chief weapon of the devil.

Theaters were of all types, and the ancestry of the Great White Way was in full swing in the Bowery. Plays were chiefly, however, of the classic type, all such authors from Shakespeare to Bulwer-Lytton contributing. Melodrama often held the boards. Comedies were often of native authorship and supplemented by impromptu dialogue. The humor tended to be broad and for that reason they were all the more discredited. The outstanding vogue of Shakespeare must be attributed largely to the emphasis given to the action, and to the wondrous mouthing of his verse which hypnotized by its music this oratorical generation. As always, there was the appeal to sensuality made not without response. The chief expression of this was in New York in the forties, in the form of living pictures taken from the Bible and from classical mythology. The exact degree of nudity which they involved was the subject of newspaper discussion and court testimony.[56] Except perhaps on the Bowery, however, it was not absolute disclosure, but the human form revealed by tights.

More far reaching than the theater, which required a permanent roof, was the circus, which indeed needed shelter but now set up its tent in the wilderness and drew in the lonesome farmers from a widespread countryside.[57] It has been said that the modern circus is but a reproduction of the Roman and that the revival took place in Europe and not in America. There are, however, marked distinctions. For one thing the new circus was more humane, not only than that of Rome, but than the traveling shows and street amusements of the preceding generation, with their baiting of bears and bulls, and cockfighting. An indigenous feature, moreover, was the presentation of hoaxes, which delighted this generation, no matter how barefaced they were, perhaps because they gave so many a sense of superiority in fathoming them. The supreme artist in such matters was P. T. Barnum, whose nurse of George Washington, mermaid, mechanical chess player, and similar genial frauds never lost their charm. In fact he brought them to such a point of popularity that he established a permanent museum in New York, as successful and infinitely more amusing than the correct museum of Madame Tussaud in London.[58] More important, however, was the traveling circus, which penetrated almost to the frontier, and brought cheer to laborious millions.

Of sports, the most general was horse racing, which was universally American, though it did not become national in the sense that horses and owners competed from all parts of the country.[59] During this period the trotting race began to press hard on the running race, and in both sulkies were occasionally used. Crowds became larger, and in the North more democratic. Hiram Woodruff acquired fame as a driver, but not so great as that of the horses, the famous blinded Lexington, Flora Temple, and Lady Suffolk, who between 1838 and 1853 ran between 400 and 500 heats and won $35,000.

American men were not devoid of the innate desire to develop and test their strength, but this was rather rural than fashionable and private rather than public. Abraham Lincoln became the chief wrestler of his community, but was not challenged by the champion of the adjoining district, and no one paid admission to see him. Shooting, trapping, and fishing were, except in the Southeast, an occupation rather than a sport. The volunteer fire companies, founded in the preceding period, had an enormous vogue; in the forties, 3,000 members paraded in New York, but their connection with athletics was slight. In fact, few American men had sufficient leisure for much participation in or attendance at games. Rowing was organized on the coast, and there is mention of baseball clubs, although it was not the game as now known. Cricket matches were held between New York, Philadelphia, Montreal, and Toronto. The wealthy did some racing of yachts, "Corinthian" yachting, as they called it, and while some of the generation still lingered, in 1856, the *America* off the Isle of Wight won the cup, the most famous of modern international trophies that still remains with us.

More time was found for the swapping of yarns than for sport. In inns, in country stores, on trains, and in the ubiquitous saloon, there was developing a folklore of humor which had in it something distinctively American and racy of the soil. Practical joking extended to remarkable proportions. It remains a mystery who made and buried the "Cardiff Giant," which on being excavated near Syracuse in 1869 set the scientists agog with stories of a petrified man.[60]

Conditions on the frontier were such as necessity required rather than what people chose to make them. Social life was mainly what could be fitted in with the requirements of labor, and was largely connected with neighborly assistance on such occasions as harvesting, house raising, corn huskings, and the like. Such events were infrequent, and Margaret Fuller, who was sent West by Horace Greeley to report on conditions, gave a sympathetic picture of the drabness of the women's lives and the tragedy of sensitive souls wrenched from the close-knit civilization of the East.[61] Still, in the seasons when farm life was less exacting, parties did occur, and were attended by those within the distance that a farm nag could reach.

In most homes the new lamps aided in creating increased hours for reading. The magazine was in its experimental stage and not a general feature, but nearly everywhere the newspaper arrived daily or weekly and was read from first page to last. Equally important was the religious press. Nearly every denomination published periodicals, which discussed some religious matters, much more the affairs of the churches, with picturesque glimpses of the outside world through the reports of missionaries, and gave a varying degree of attention to secular politics. The effort was to make such periodicals cheap, and some were distributed free; they reached an astonishing proportion of the population.

The increased facility of the printing press was taken advantage of also to turn out literature of the gutter, which was surreptitiously hawked about, and was available for those who wished it in cities and on routes of travel.[62] This seems to have been less sought, however, than the simpering *Souvenirs, Galaxies,* and *Keepsakes,* full of death, attenuated love and moral

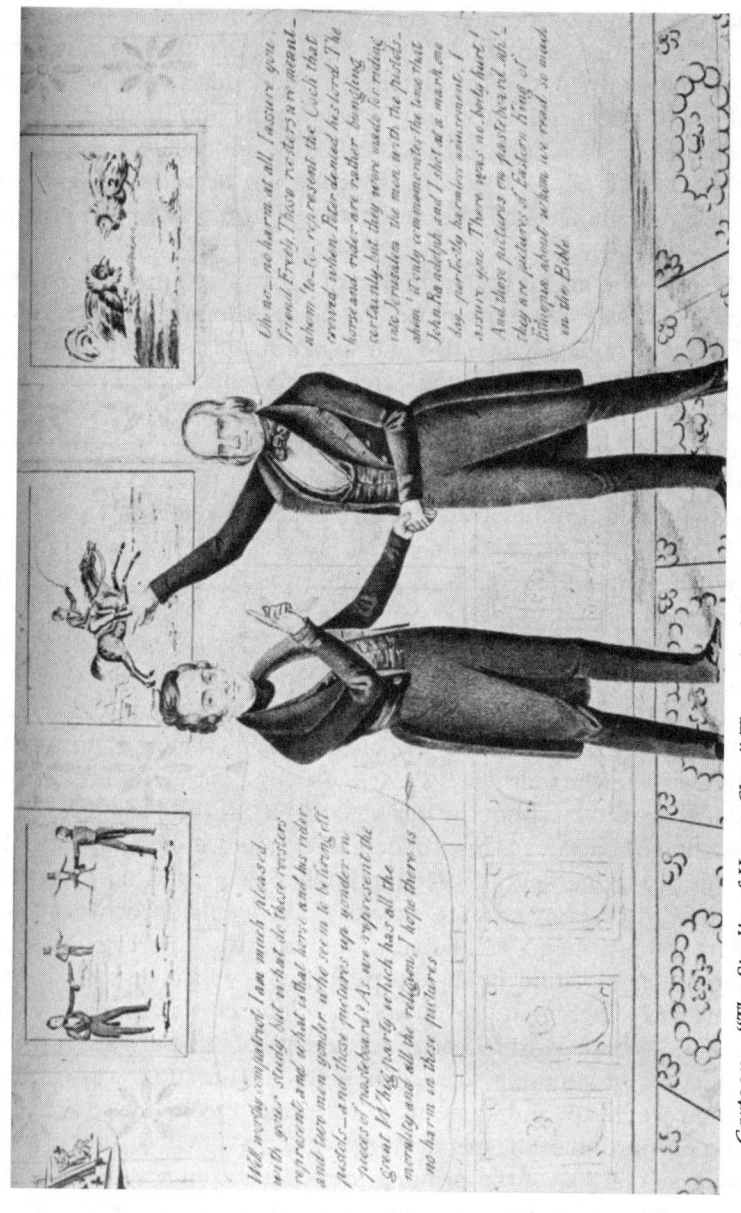

Cartoon — "The Studio of Henry Clay." The typical Kentuckian attempts to explain away bis pet vices in deference to the Eastern standards of Frelinghuysen, bis partner on the Wbig ticket of 1844.

sentiments, which were the appropriate gift of a young gentleman to the lady of his affections. Among the magazines, *Godey's Lady's Book* guided the feminine aspirations of most well-to-do homes, and at the end of the period its popularity began to be shared by Nathaniel P. Willis's *Home Journal.*

The market for good literature was much larger, more varied and active, than previously, although not sufficient to support many authors in more than moderate comfort. Whereas the preceding generation had for the most part ordered such books from England and France, American publishers such as Harper and Brothers, D. Appleton, Lea Brothers, J. B. Lippincott, Little, Brown & Company, and Ticknor & Fields were now publishing not only American but foreign works. Books such as Longfellow's *Evangeline* were known to be forthcoming and sought hot from the press. Among comparatively wide circles the fate of Dickens's characters, as they developed week by week, was a standard topic of conversation. French was less read than previously but translations brought Dumas into many homes. This was a period everywhere in which the chief authorities on such subjects as history, economics, science, and political theory wrote to be read, and to a very large extent they were read. Ideas were more emphasized than facts, and sentiment considered more important than subtlety.

On the matter of sexual relationships the code of the thirties and forties was exceptionally strict. Violation of this code was almost the sole meaning attached to the word "immorality." Marriage was somewhat more optional than in the colonial period when economic necessity rendered a widowerhood of more than one year both inconvenient and unpopular. Once entered into, it was for life. Divorce was legally permitted for causes varying in the different states, but socially was little tolerated. The rural condoning of anticipated marriage, which had been common in some districts during the colonial period,[63] had for the most part passed away, although marriage was still a sovereign balm to wash away past sins. A double code existed in the difference in the punishment meted out to the offending man and woman. In the South there was little reprobation for the incontinent male. Still, everywhere the ideal was complete purity for man as well as for woman.[64]

This code was accompanied by a prudery which was almost universal. The living pictures of the early forties yielded to the public clamor enforced by the police. It was a period in which legs did not exist at all. While Powers's "Greek Slave" was admired by the daring, Edward Everett in Boston draped his copy of the Apollo Belvedere.[65] Probably at no period was an ankle so exciting. With its own peculiar inconsistency, which was actually a little greater than that of most ages, the most conspicuous advertisements of the newspapers related to sex functions with a directness and completeness which would disgust if not shock even the present generation. The presumption must have been that women were protected by their own modesty and ignorance. Yet from the modern point of view the most interesting are of drugs to prevent conception. Despite this glaring exhibition of the facts of life, however, it remains true that most girls and an amazing number of women did pass through life in an ignorance touching if not appalling.

The facilities for the incontinent were almost universal and subject to little disguise. In the leading theater of New York, one of the galleries was a regular place for the making of assignations, and in most towns the house of ill fame was known to boys and men of all characters, sometimes mobbed, but more often jeered at. It was an accepted aspect of life, disapproved but recognized. On the other hand, vice was strictly segregated. Irregular relationships in normal society, of course, existed, but were extremely rare and received neither charity nor tolerance. One can only guess, but by that process one comes to feel that the proportion of male incontinence was large, particularly among the planter class of the South where slavery afforded so many opportunities, and that the proportion of social irregularities among those considered social equals was strikingly small.

On the positive side the picture is more pleasing. The attitude of the American man toward woman was exceptionally good. Women not avowedly for sale were not expected to protect themselves nor to be protected by their male relatives. Any and every man was supposed to protect them at any time and place. Passion was no excuse for a failure of this trust. The charm of social relationships which came from justifiable confidence was something that gave grace even to this awkward age. Even in the case of "fallen women," without place in the social order as they were and with little opportunity even for the gilding which in foreign capitals concealed the fundamental dross of their position, their treatment by the public was not physically brutal. It may be said that an American woman was practically safe in doing whatever she would. According to her character, for which by the men her word was generally accepted, she was placed upon the right hand or the left. Of the attitude of the respectable women toward their fallen sisters little is to be said—they were not supposed to know of their existence, and many, miraculously, did not. Their literature told them little; heroine and hero were spotless, and the unfortunate girl who enters most novels dies, or is made "honest" by marriage. However, Magdalene societies did exist, and the recognized and unrecognized worlds had here and there their contacts.

Of the men it is obvious that large numbers were not pure. On the other hand, there was among them no gospel of "wild oats." While youth was accountable for much of the degradation that existed, it was in general much more true that the men, like the women, were divided into two classes, the pure and the impure. In small communities they were almost as well known. The difference lay in the fact that the sinning man was not excluded from society. With fewer drawbacks to deter, the impure class of men was much larger than that of women. On the other hand, the number of men who responded to the idealism of the time, and kept themselves pure for marriage and devoted to their wives afterward, was very large. It is probable that it was larger proportionately in America than elsewhere, and larger in America than in previous generations.

As difficult to estimate as sexual morality is honesty. Yet some distinctions of the time may be noted. However much they might copy it in the writing books, this generation was little impressed by Benjamin Franklin's dictum that "honesty is the best policy." Honesty was a virtue, a simple virtue existing or absent, not an art requiring knowledge and practice for its successful attainment. It was not a practical device for success. In fact, it was believed, and to a greater degree than in some other times and places, that the wicked flourished mightily.

Honesty was in the Northeast confused to a great extent with legality, and the American distaste for equity in law gave to many individuals a fictitious reputation for the virtue who were zealously weaving webs to catch less legally minded flies. Particularly the novel developments of cooperative business gave a great advantage to the shrewd. The law had not been developed to meet such complexities and yet served to salve the consciences of those who took advantage of its inadequacies.[66]

The general optimism of the times also affected the practice of honesty. Where men believed, in innocence and simplicity, that fortunes were to be picked up from every new invention, or by each new section of land opened up for settlement, there was but a weak inhibition against taking the funds of others to start the flow. The number of thieves was not greater than at other times, but the number who used any money that came into their hands for the purpose of their own speculation, was never so great.

A striking illustration of the working of these tendencies was to be found in the condition of the civil service, already referred to, when the Panic of 1837 dimmed the first glow of these bright hopes. In 1840, Clay stated that of the sixty-seven officials of the land office, sixty-four were defaulters. This statement by the leader of the opposing party was more or less confirmed by the agents of the government who investigated conditions. Hardly an officer had refrained from using the public funds in his possession to buy the land which was rising in value each day; they would sell out, repay the government, and retain fortunes for themselves. Quite as significant was the finding that scarcely an officer could keep books; why worry over dollars when thousands were flowing by?

The ablest of the government investigators was V. M. Garesche. One of his characteristic reports is on an Ohio officer: "The man seems really penitent; and I am inclined to think, in common with his friends, that he is honest and has been led away from his duty by the example of his predecessor, and a certain looseness in the code of morality which here does not move in so limited a circle as it does with us at home. Another receiver would probably follow in the footsteps of the two. You will not, therefore, be surprised if I recommend his being retained in preference to another appointment, for he has his hands full now, and will not be disposed to speculate any more. . . . He has, moreover, pledged his word that, if retained, he will strictly obey the law. . . . Lenity towards him . . . might stimulate him to exertions which severity might perhaps paralyze."[67] The reader will not suppose, as did the historian Van Holst, that the collector had "his hands full" of ill-gotten gains.[68] The point, of course, was that he was so involved by his obligations that he might be supposed to have learned a lesson, and so be apt to observe more caution in the future. In the customs service were defalcations of a different kind. Numbers of mere crooks simply stole the money of the government, and the Panic so overwhelmed them that they were no longer able to cover up their tracks, and fled. The intentionally dishonest always exist. At this period they were a little more apt to secure public office than at present, and inspection was not sufficient to restrain their activity. The involuntary dishonesty, resulting from lack of public standards of conduct, is what was characteristic of the time.

Rather different was the reaction to the somewhat kindred question of gambling. Gambling was in the blood of the time. When such a proportion of the population was taking its future into its hands by venturing forth to seek new homes, when those with little capital were risking it in such precarious new enterprises as railroads and gas companies, it is not surprising that men bet on horse races, and that lotteries were a feature of the day. The very prevalence of this custom, however, began to breed a moral feeling against it, which with some ran to the point of condemning the use of chance, even in cases where all history and convenience authorize it. By the end of the period probably more Americans played cards without stakes than the people of other countries, and the number who condemned cards because some did play them for stakes began to be formidable.

Most significant of all is perhaps the fact that morals were among the most serious interests of the time, and the subject of hot controversy and debate. The preceding pages have treated those questions that are essential to know in dealing with the everyday life of the people. Those problems which by the clamor they aroused called for group or community action will be treated in connection with the reform movements.

POLITICS AND RELIGION

ASIDE FROM THE MAKING of a living or the accumulation of a fortune, the main preoccupation of most American men was politics. Politics was a male function not merely because the vote was confined to them, but because it was supposed to be unsuited to the female mind and inconsistent with that "delicacy" which was the current ideal. It was, however, a time when man proposed and woman disposed. In the South, the social mingling of the sexes made the women of the governing class almost as politically minded as those of the English aristocracy, though without their influence. The glimpses one gets of feminine opinion in the South lead one to suppose that their influence might well have been extended.

The call of politics as a career was not so general as in the preceding generation, and became less compelling as the years went on and opportunity came to be more varied by new inventions and business opportunities. Conditions remained less changed in the South, where the man whose plantation was in running order took to politics as naturally as did the English country gentleman. Some few of the poorer also entered the arena to fight the aristocracy or to make a place in it for themselves.

Though the population somewhat less than doubled between 1830 and 1850, between 1828 and 1848 the vote increased about three times.[69] This increase was partly due to the extension of manhood suffrage and partly to silent organization and noisy advertisement. The increase from 1.1 million to 1.6 million between 1828 and 1836 was, apart from natural circumstances, quite apparently the result of organization, especially the development of the Jacksonian organization in New England and Ohio. Speeches were made and published, newspapers clashed in their scurrilous attacks, broadsides were distributed, "Major Jack Downing" introduced the humorous reaction of the supposedly rustic commentator;[70] but probably more important was the quiet work of the local organizer with his hand on the pulse of every voter in his district.

The increase of 800,000 in the next election was in large part due to the counterattack of the Whigs. Never as successful as their opponents in organization, some genius or geniuses among them evolved the idea of blatant penetrating publicity, pitched in a moral key, but affording a degree of amusement. It was founded on a hoax little more subtle than the articles on the moon in the *Sun* a few years before. Their candidate, quiet old General William Henry Harrison, of one of the first families of Virginia, well-to-do and living as a gentleman, a scholar stored in a rather schoolboyish fashion with historic parallels for modern conditions, was represented as sitting in a log cabin, in a coonskin cap, drinking hard cider. With less untruth, but with exaggeration, the Democratic candidate, Martin Van Buren, was pictured as an aristocrat, eating with gold spoons and maintaining the White House on the scale of a king's palace. A description of its furniture, appalling in very truth to the frontierman, was the leading campaign document.[71]

The Whigs thus appealed to the democratic sentiment of the time, and in a measure even to class hatred. The judicious must have marveled at this spectacle of a party that had boasted its support by gentlemen of both North and South sounding all these phrases of Fraternity. Whatever the

Whigs may have lacked in logic they had psychology on their side; they shouted that a great crusade was on, and called on all to participate in the assault. The parades, which had for many years been held, elongated and decorated themselves with floats and banners to an extent previously unknown. Songs were sung by these great gatherings, some of which caught the popular ear. Gigantic balls, representing the growing Harrison majority, were rolled from city to city. In the West, crowds, sometimes numbering, according to popular report, 100,000, were drawn in from miles around by

GENERAL HARRISON.

The Whigs in 1840 thought it good American politics to represent their candidate as living in a log cabin.

Whereas his home was really that of a typical Ohio country gentleman.

the prospect of what amounted to a circus with a serious aim—something this generation could not resist; in which they did not stand alone but only a little more on tiptoe than their forefathers and descendants.

The Whigs in this election had a perfectly good case. The significance of the campaign is that their leaders recognized that the people ruled but did not trust the people's judgment. Men of aristocratic tendency and of great ability, they hit upon the susceptibilities of the time and played on them with unusual skill. They won the election but not complete control of the government. Their insight, however, into the weaker sides of the American character was correct, and the political methods they introduced lived for over fifty years. This election for the first time brought out the full voting strength of the American people; in the succeeding election, the vote increased only normally.

During the forties practically all Americans were either Whigs or Democrats. Some were sufficiently dissatisfied with both parties to organize on the outside. Some changed their votes from one side to the other. More than nine tenths of the electorate, however, were tagged and proud of their tag. The two-party system never stood higher in the public regard. The Whig party really existed for only about fifteen years, from 1839 to 1854, and yet for twenty years after men were spoken of as Whigs and their political fortunes were affected by their early record.

To have evolved two national parties, even though one was but precariously united, was no small achievement for this generation. While more stable organizations have been attained, never since have both parties been national in the sense of including North and South. While the two parties represented in mass two opposing attitudes toward government, they embodied also many subtler but equally permanent divisions. A study of successive elections in Ohio, for instance, shows that from the period of Federalists and Republicans, through that of Whigs and Democrats, to that of Republicans and Democrats, there has been a continuity of sectional majorities quite amazing. Causes dependent upon original stock, geographical location, religion, migration, immigration, and mere tradition have at all times modified the natural division based on political theory or economic interest.[72]

While politics was the predominant preoccupation of the men, religion was that of the women. This is by no means to say that religion did not interest the men, but merely that, taking them as a whole, it came after politics. This was distinctly and increasingly a religious period. It was not merely that the interest in religion itself was stronger than in the preceding generation, but that the union between religion and morality was so strong that they became practically indistinguishable, and that almost every subject was invested with the religious qualities of certainty and enthusiasm. Every orator had to prove that his position was endorsed by the Constitution and the Bible.

This religion was Christianity. Deism may have been held by as many as in the preceding generation, but at least not so many distinguished men professed it, and the rationalistic attitude of the eighteenth century melted under warmer rays. Atheism was unimportant. The distinction between the two generations was in spirit rather than in form. The outward evidences of religion continued to be for the most part the same. Travelers, except from Great Britain, were impressed by Sunday observance, and this impression was generally favorable even in the case of Catholics. It was a genuine power in the land, and was nowhere more in evidence than in the schedules of the new railroads.[73] For over fifty years after the period only mail trains ran through Connecticut on that day. In the second place, church attendance was general. It was both respectable and fashionable. It included far greater numbers than the rolls of church membership carried. It pressed hard on the facilities provided, and on the frontier was checked only by the lack of churches.[74] Another evidence was the fact that while religious taxes were withdrawn, religion was, on a basis purely voluntary, better supported than ever before.

The call of the ministry was stronger than in the preceding generation. Sainthood for its own sake attracted few, but Christian service was more than usually attractive. More than in the Revolutionary period it afforded a means of distinction as well as of usefulness. Preachers such as William Ellery Channing, Theodore Parker, and Henry Ward Beecher became national figures. At the same time the development of missions added the call of adventure to that of religion itself. Peter Cartwright, the frontier itinerant, and Adoniram Judson, the first great foreign missionary, continued to illustrate how a life of varied experience might be combined with religious service. The number of able boys attracted increased, but the total number of ministers was never sufficient. The opportunity for women who wished to lead a life devoted to religion, which had previously been restricted to sects such as the Quakers and Shakers, was increased by the introduction of Roman Catholic sisterhoods, the semiofficial recognition given by the Protestant bodies to missionaries' wives, and by the open forum which existed for those few women who felt called upon to preach without denominational sanction.

In spite of this revival of interest in religion, the idea remained unchanged that the basis of its relation to the state should be separation. During this period the last taxes for church support were abolished, in Massachusetts in 1833, and nearly the last religious disqualifications for office.[75] In this separation education was the contested field and remained so throughout. This was, however, mainly a contest of competition between public and religious schools, not for elimination. There was some struggle for state support for religious schools but the principle of separation was strong enough to prevent serious controversy. In the free field, opinion, perhaps for practical reasons of expense, swung toward the public rather than the religious schools, although in the realm of higher education denominational colleges continued to be more important than those of the states.

It was undoubtedly true that, in spite of the principle of separation, very large numbers, overlooking minor differences, regarded the United States, some as a Protestant country, more as a Christian country. This latter idea, in fact, infused the speeches and proclamations of nearly every president and governor. It had, however, no tangible result, and Jews were not treated differently from Christians.

Religion was, indeed, too vital a thing to escape connection with politics. The churches paid little heed to the ordinary conflicts of parties, except in New England, although such sermons as that of Robert Little, the Unitarian at Washington, when Jackson was about to be inaugurated—from the text: "When Christ drew near the city he wept over it"—were not uncommon. So many matters, however, began to come before the public which were regarded as fundamentally moral and yet called for legislative action, such as the care of the insane, temperance, and in particular, slavery, that public men found it impossible to ignore them. In fact, during these years the connection of religion with life was more and more emphasized, and preaching took on more and more a humanitarian and social cast.

The mingling of these semipolitical questions with religion was deeply resented by many and caused not a few ministers to lose their places and not a few congregations to divide. This hostility was, however, chiefly due to the political instinct to avoid dangerous discussion rather than to a real desire to restrict religion to its especial field. With opposition the practice grew. More and more ministers took a stand on this question and that, and in the forties the meetings of the governing bodies of the various denominations came to be rent between those wishing their church as a whole to declare itself, one way or the other, and those who wished it to keep silent. This practice was strongest in New England and in New York. It extended gradually West. In the South there was more feeling that ministers should keep out of politics; yet even there on one conspicuous subject, advocacy of slavery, they were encouraged to declare themselves.[76]

This was hardly an atmosphere in which one would expect tolerance, and yet, except in the Eastern cities where religious differences were emphasized by those of race, and riots occurred between a rather rowdy type of Protestants and Catholics, intolerance did not often run to violence. There was, indeed, some development of a broad-minded charity but not enough to account for the lack of strife. Rather, it seems to have risen from the fact that all the sects had come really to stand equal before the law, and that it was so easy for divergent elements to separate and form new sects. This was indeed a period particularly marked by the formation of such new groups.

It is not surprising that in a period so individualistic there developed one important movement that was less a modification of Protestant Christianity than a brand-new religion. This was Mormonism, founded by Joseph Smith, a member of a family of New England migrants that had drifted into central New York.[77] He provided for his followers a new Bible, the Book of Mormon, with a history of the adventures of the Lost Tribes of Israel and with a continual revelation of the divine will through the perpetual presence of a prophet, he being the first of this new line. In 1830 he founded his church. He soon associated himself with Sidney Rigdon, who brought to the church a new element of popularity and strength.

Although the Mormons were not anti-Christians, and although the revelations commending polygamy were not given until 1844, the fact that they represented a new religion in a country which, however tolerant, was Christian, combined with a great variety of other causes to render them unpopular with their neighbors. Their community moved from New York to Ohio, thence to Missouri, next to Illinois, always growing and always hopeful. In 1844, Joseph Smith was killed by a mob. They thereupon determined to move beyond the borders of settlement, and finally, in 1848, under the leadership of Brigham Young, succeeded in occupying the Valley of Great Salt Lake, which they hoped to keep a distinctive land for themselves. To this new home they had brought by 1850 not merely the bulk of their adherents but also the beginnings of a stream of European immigrants which their missionaries persuaded to cross the Atlantic.[78]

Another great change was the enormous increase in the number of Roman Catholics as the result of immigration. Practically all of the Irish immigrants and perhaps a half of the Germans, with the French Canadians, belonged to that faith. Distributed over most parts of the country except the South, they brought a new factor into all populous communities and many of the smaller towns. The Church of Rome was not unaware of this great extension of its influence and responsibilities, and its shifting followers were not left entirely to their own resources for the development of their complex life. Missionary organizations and the orders supplied funds for beginnings, and priests were often designated to the American field. By the end of the period the church was fully established, with archbishops, bishops, monasteries, and convents, and the opportunities for the development of its own priesthood. Although still organized under the missionary department, the Propaganda, its bishops holding commissions as *in partibus infidelium,* the church was fully cognizant of its position of equality before the law, and felt at home in the United States.[79]

The innovations in religious methods during this period consisted chiefly of those brought with them by the Roman Catholics: ritual, contemplation, and the religious life. These were nearly exclusively confined to the members of that church. The Episcopal Church was about to introduce them, but rather as a result of the Puseyite movement in England than of copying their neighbors at home. A change more general was the increase in the use of music in the churches. Many Protestant bodies, and particularly the Quakers, held out against instrumental music and set forms. Nevertheless, hymns, supported by organs or melodeons, rapidly supplanted the versified psalms and the tuning fork.

Much greater use than before was now made of the forms of worship and religious expression developed in the preceding generation. Revivals were constant and took place frequently at the camp meeting which became general and better organized. Few countrysides were without a grove devoted to such uses, and they came to be equipped with open-air auditoriums which were surrounded by the frail cottages of habitues. The Methodists extended their system of itinerant preachers, and colporteurs carried the Bible and local news to thousands of isolated farmsteads on the frontier. Religious manners varied with the locality, and, where necessary, religion sought the soul by acquiescence in exterior crudities. It was probably by the wide extension of these essentially democratic methods that the migrating folks were held, and that the gradual intensification of the religious impulse was carried forward.

One striking manifestation of the religious spirit was the development of missionary work. Christianity has always been a proselytizing faith, but the insistence of the call for extension has varied from time to time. One significant movement began in the last years of the preceding generation, signalized by Bishop Heber's great hymm, in 1819, *From Greenland's Icy Mountains*. Bishop Heber found that though in Ceylon "Every prospect pleases and only man is vile," the fault was rather with the Christians than the heathen:

> Can we whose souls are lighted,
> With wisdom from on High,
> Can we to men benighted
> The Lamp of Life deny?

In 1848, Bishop Doane of Albany expressed the spirit of his time. It was only necessary to let the light be shown.

> Fling out the banner! Heathen lands
> Shall see from far the glorious sight,
> And nations crowding to be born,
> Baptize their spirits in its light.

Most particularly this call was to the distant and the unusual. Perhaps religion shared the spirit of the Jacksonian democracy and felt that those at home, being freed from ignorance, were responsible for themselves and that the first duty was to carry the gospel where it was not known. Something, too, must be attributed to the combination in individuals of the spirit of adventure with the religious impulse. At least during this period there was a wide extension of the range of missionary activity.[80]

Missionaries were active in India, China, and the Mediterranean. In Hawaii (the Sandwich Islands) the missionaries arrived at a strategic moment and, within limits, civilized and christianized the kingdom. In 1842, Webster recognized their accomplishments by declaring that Hawaii lay within the American sphere of influence; just at the close of the period annexation was discussed. Maintaining themselves in the island, their families became the nucleus of the American element which finally gained financial and economic control.[81] Another popular field was among the American Indians, particularly of the South. Here the missionaries per-

Marcus Whitman's mission at Waiilatpu, Oregon, in 1843.

In Salt Lake City, 1847, then the capital of a little Mormon republic.
President Young's house (right), theater (left), mint (in background).

formed what came to be their customary feat—the putting of the spoken language into writing—established schools, and acquired a strong hold which led them to oppose Jackson's policy of Indian removal. After the blow of that defeat they never quite regained their position.

Theologically this period was important, but it is an unsatisfactory one for study. New ideas originated and became potent without affecting the structure of theology. Among the Catholics there was little doctrinal disputation, and little contribution unless one reckons as such the voluminous polemical writings of Orestes A. Brownson, begun in the early forties. Protestant creeds remained practically unaltered. Like the national Constitution they were accepted as fundamental while controversy raged about their interpretation, often breaking up bodies of the same creed, such as the Methodists and Baptists, into many independent organizations, sometimes bitterly opposed. Preaching was often extremely narrow, and it was probably as a reaction from the bitter denunciations and bigoted expositions of the frontier enthusiasts that the young Abraham Lincoln wrote his uncharacteristic attack upon religion.[82]

This instance of Lincoln is an illustration of a situation far more important than most people then realized. Among a people imbued with optimism, self-confidence, and a sense of equality, it could hardly be expected that the dolorous version of Calvinism which had animated so much of the preaching of America could continue to make an appeal. To keep the population religious, it was necessary that some adjustment take place. The direction of this change was indicated by views expressed by a number of the leading minds of the time. From 1833 to 1859, Horace Bushnell preached at Hartford to a congregation of exceptional influence and culture. The characteristic theme of his sermons was the search for truth through multifarious channels. He differentiated intention from attainment, and gave credit to all who earnestly sought. Nor did he claim to see the whole but only one facet of the jewel. He taught that all who asked would be given some glimpse, that the only error was to claim to have the whole. In all religions and sects he could find something, or at least admitted there was something, special and choice. This "comprehensivism," setting sympathetic understanding in the place of either dogmatism or tolerance, developed an intellectual following, but still more was it in harmony with the spirit of equality, and so influenced the tone of preaching of many denominations.[83]

A second development, which was not so much a change of theology as a change of emphasis, is illustrated by the preaching of the Unitarian William Ellery Channing, first at Newport and later at Boston. A man of extreme dignity and reasonableness, with an ability to write as well as preach, he influenced not only his congregation and denomination but a conservative class far beyond these confines. In its earlier stages Unitarianism had insisted most strongly on its denials, not only of the divinity of Christ but of salvation by grace. Channing spiritualized the positive aspects of its teaching, the insistence on the merits of good works. Practically all the reforms of this period found support from his pulpit, and he almost forced those who believed in grace to urge that the works of the righteous must exceed those of unbelievers who relied on works alone.[84] He was probably more influential than any other person in uniting the forces of religion with humanitarian reforms, and in developing the idea of social service by the churches, which has become so characteristic of American Christianity.

More important than either was Ralph Waldo Emerson. Theologically Emerson walked by himself. Absolutely individual, he was yet the most representative of all the aspirations of the people. Whatever their creed, Americans were restive under the constant insistence that they were born in sin. No theology denied the possibilities of men, but American Calvinism had never emphasized it as did the Catholic Church in which men and women might rise to recognized sainthood. This longing for spiritual joy while still on earth had never been absent. Anne Hutchinson had felt it when she proclaimed that the Lord had personally revealed the truth to her. The same possibility of direct sanctification had been one of the compelling graces of Quakerism. Among the Methodists some sects believed such an attainment possible. This feeling Emerson voiced, not in effusive oratory, but in a clear calm voice that penetrated far.

Just what Emerson believed cannot be exactly defined, for its merit was its mysticism.[85] In raising human possibilities to the elevation of divine stature, he certainly did not look to unification with God in a Nirvana; he was too keen an individualist. Perhaps he looked to a divine democracy in which, as all were gods, there would be no strife, and all decisions would be unanimous because all would see alike in seeing all. Historically, at least, this is unimportant, for few were really interested in an Emersonian system. The important point was that he exalted man to the highest point of conceivable attainment, emphasizing that he was born with a spark of the divine instead of in sin, and at the same time he incited to effort, in a way that Jackson's philosophy never did in politics, by raising the goal of human achievement to the skies. While Emerson's influence was much greater in the succeeding generation, even in the forties he influenced the tone of preaching of ministers of all kinds of creeds, and, where they caught his note, they held their self-confident congregations without cheapening religion.

In presenting Emerson as a product of American conditions and as a religious force, it should not be overlooked that his views were influenced by German thought and that he is chiefly regarded as a philosopher. Among the Americans who at this time were influenced by the philosophy of Kant, developed by Fichte and interpreted to the English by Coleridge and Carlyle, Emerson was neither the first nor at this time the most prominent. George Ticknor and a few others brought their interest fresh from their studies in Germany, and they regarded Henry Hedge of Boston as their leader.[86]

Few in numbers, they were very able, and concentrated chiefly in or about Boston. An informal club united such of the interested as George Ripley, Margaret Fuller, James Freeman Clarke, Emerson, George Bancroft, and others. This club was known among its members as the Symposium or Hedge's Club, but soon acquired popularly the name of Transcendentalist. In 1838 it brought out fourteen volumes of *Specimens of Foreign Standard Literature,* and few groups of so small size have attracted so much attention. This association, based on a study of philosophy, was in intent religious only in its purpose to batter down the traditional Calvinism of New England. Quite as interesting is the evident fact that the religious atmosphere of New England enveloped the group, and that Transcendentalism came to be with them for the moment a religion, or at least was held with all the spirit of religion.[87]

The influence which these Transcendentalists exerted must not be even largely attributed to the power of their ideas or their skill in propaganda. As in the case of Emerson's religious views, this philosophy fitted in with the state of the American mind, and Kant was received, as Locke had been earlier, because he gave expression to what Americans thought. The particular phase of his system as developed by his followers and turned into a flame of action by the American Transcendentalists was that problems of reality could best be studied by the subjective consciousness. As a consequence their philosophy appealed strongly to this self-educated generation who loved the abstract and disliked detailed study. It was, too, emphatically the philosophy of the reformers.

EDUCATION FOR THE PEOPLE

THE IDEALS and the resources of one generation determine the education of the next. There are wide differences between the education which the generation reaching its maturity in 1830 had received, that which it devised for its children, and the education which its chaotic maladministration actually gave them. Its own schooling, moreover, was not the embodiment of the ideas of its fathers, for they had been too devotedly concentrated on problems of political construction to revolutionize the schools. Rather it was an inheritance from grandfathers and still earlier ancestors, touched here and there by revolutionary "Liberty" and by more or less unconscious gains or losses from the mere change of conditions. It is not surprising, therefore, to find that educational practices differed widely from section to section, that they were not based upon the sense of equality, and that they were better at the top than at the bottom.

There was, when this generation was growing up, a general expectation that all Americans should receive a primary education in the "three R's," reading, 'riting, and 'rithmetic. In Massachusetts and New York school maintenance was by law compulsory. In all New England opportunity was provided in various ways, by the assistance of taxation, if necessary. In the little white frame schoolhouses scattered over the countryside instruction was carried on with all degrees of efficiency. Teachers' salaries were small, but, eked out by free board and lodging with first one and then another of the patrons of the school, were sufficient to tempt ambitious boys seeking the little actual cash needed to give themselves a higher education. There was no such thing as "grading," but the system had in New England been so long in operation that most of the scholars were of proper school age. Noah Webster's spelling books and "spelling bees" helped fetter one fine freedom which the earlier generations had enjoyed.[88]

In New York the idea of universal education went back to the Dutch. There was in 1830 no general provision for it by taxation, but a School Society spent perhaps $100,000 a year in New York City; the Lancastrian system was an economical method of using some pupils to instruct the others, and on the whole there was little excuse for not learning the fundamentals of social intercourse. In Pennsylvania conditions varied. Nowhere were better schools than those maintained by such religious bodies as the Quakers and the Moravians. On the other hand, absolutely free education was seldom available and some communities were without educational opportunity. In the South was still more diversity in 1830. Here it was a matter of class more than of locality. People of means educated their children regardless of local institutions. On the other hand, there was very little provision for the really poor whites and many grew up in self-respecting and excusable ignorance. According to the will and energy of the mistress, black house servants were taught to read and write, or left in ignorance. Such an ambitious boy as Andrew Johnson left Raleigh at the age of ten unable to write and he seems not to have acquired the art until after his marriage in Greenville, Tennessee. Indeed, desire to learn seems to have been one incentive to his marriage.

The mountain area was practically illiterate. West of the mountains this generation suffered not only from the poverty of their parents but from an economic fallacy of their parents' generation. It was supposed that in all the area where ownership of the land passed through the hands of the U.S. government, that is, north of the Ohio, west of the Mississippi, together with Alabama and Mississippi, education had been provided for by land endowment from the famous "sixteenth section." It escaped notice that unoccupied land does not sprout schools. Probably in no part of America before or since, except in the Allegheny region, was it so difficult to start an education as in this area before 1840. The story of Lincoln shows the difficulties, but it must be remembered that not everyone was a Lincoln to overcome them.

The opportunities for education beyond the primary schools were most numerous in New England in 1830, and its institutions were of more than local importance. Nowhere was the impulse behind education so general and so strong. Unusual numbers consecrated themselves to the carrying of education to others. New England became for a time the seed farm for education throughout the United States, except for New York and Pennsylvania with their self-sufficient cultures.

The oldest establishments for what we call secondary education were the "Grammar" or "Latin Schools," of which the Boston Latin School with its sound drill in the basic branches of languages and mathematics was justly the most famous.[89] In the twenties a few high schools had been established in Massachusetts and at Portland, Maine; and the Massachusetts statute of 1827, requiring a tax-supported high school in every town of 500 families or more, set a pattern that was soon copied by Maine, Vermont, and New Hampshire.[90] Much more numerous throughout this period, however, and certainly in the beginning, were the academies which had been rapidly increasing in numbers since the Revolution.[91] These were generally founded by endowment, were frequently assisted by the towns in which they were located, but also charged tuition. One striking thing about them was that with their independence of each other and the absence of such a governing tradition as bound the colleges, they differed more among themselves, and expressed more readily the new ideas of the time. The most famous, Phillips Exeter and Phillips Andover, by this time considered venerable, resembled the English public schools such as Rugby. Others, with little remark, became coeducational.

For most of their students these academies were finishing schools, and their commencements and exhibitions were the rallying points of educational interest for all the surrounding communities. In New England they were usually held in the Congregational Church, which, of course, had been built originally as a town "meeting house" for all public purposes. Their character reveals in part survival of a Puritanism that has been somewhat misunderstood and in part the new impulses of the rising generation. The pulpit end of the church was boarded over to make a stage, and curtains and sometimes scenery were provided. Here oftentimes exercises were offered all day long to an audience of relatives, friends, and patrons.[92]

More somber were the Quaker or Friends' schools which represented a different type and from which at this time instrumental music was excluded, but where high educational standards attracted many students from outside the membership of the "Meeting." The earlier academies in the South were generally founded by Scotch teachers with little outside assistance and were conducted with less display than those of New England. Nor in general did they become educational centers for the communities, for the youth of the best families continued to be prepared for college by private tutors. In time, however, New England teachers took the place of the Scotch, and the academy life was modified in the direction of New

England habits. Here, however, none were coeducational. Educationally, this was important, for the "female academies" offered a curriculum designed to meet chiefly the ornamental requirements of the Southern lady, whose practical education was given by her mother and her "Mammy." Wax work and hair flowers played a prominent part in her formal schooling. Socially, the difference was not so great as it might seem; for where there was a "female" academy there usually was a male academy also.[93]

The pride and joy of any fortunate community, however, was the college.[94] The college constituency was not purely local. Except for the University of Pennsylvania, the University of Virginia, and state-aided colleges in a few other Southern states, colleges were the creation of religious denominations with the original object of training their clergy. It is from this point of view that their restricted curricula should be viewed. When in the middle of the eighteenth century the interest of the most ambitious youth began to turn from the ministry to the law, the change was reflected not so much by the introduction of new subjects, as by gradual curtailment of the requirements in theology and logic. Some opportunity was here and there afforded for natural science and public law. In 1806, John Quincy Adams became professor of rhetoric and oratory at Harvard, and in 1810 he published his lectures, which had wide effect in introducing this popular subject into college teaching.[95] In the main, however, courses remained grounded on Latin, Greek, and mathematics. Nor can it be denied that the teaching was generally of an uninspiring character, and that the instructional staffs were in many cases inferior in intellectual caliber to the average of their students, and not far above them in training.

Here and there were great teachers, and in the twenties there began to be a few scholars, such as Jared Sparks, among the college faculties. What saved the colleges from dry-rot, however, and what caused them still to appeal to the ambitious and train them for the work they had to do, was the development of extracurricular activities by the students themselves, assisted by the more alert of the professors and tutors. These activities did not take the form of athletics. Students did, indeed, play, but there was nothing resembling the organized sports of later times. As in the preceding period, surplus energy showed itself chiefly in the life of the literary societies. A new development was the growth of the Greek-letter fraternity system in the colleges. Although Phi Beta Kappa had been founded as a secret society at William and Mary in 1776, it had had no imitators until the mid-twenties when three new fraternities, Kappa Alpha, Sigma Phi, and Delta Phi, were founded at Union College in New York.[96] The Greek names reflect the strong classical tone of the higher education of the times. The example once set, chapters of these fraternities spread to other colleges, and what was more important, new fraternities were set up here and there. As early as 1839 students in the Western colleges caught the fever, and Beta Theta Pi was started at Miami University in Ohio.

Despite the Greek-letter designation, the activities of the fraternities did not, in this period, differ essentially from those of the preexisting literary societies. In both cases, their substance was of debates and orations on the current problems of the day, the declaiming of literary selections, and the production of plays, classic or original. It was, however, in the older literary societies that the men of this generation were trained. One of the chief rivalries of these societies was the creation of libraries.[97] In 1817 the college library of Dartmouth consisted of about 4,000 volumes, chiefly antiquarian. A fee was collected for each book borrowed and the library was open one hour a week. In 1825 the libraries of the Dartmouth societies numbered about 6,000 volumes, they were open daily, and books were loaned freely, even for vacation use. One would dislike to say that this was a measure of the relative enlightenment of the faculty and the students, but it is to some extent an indication that the rising generation was taking its education into its own hands.

Training for a livelihood, whether in trade or profession, was still chiefly a matter of apprenticeship at the opening of the period, though the organization of professional education had begun. The senior profession was the ministry. Probably a larger proportion of the ministers were college-trained than of any other professional group. For them, too, the college training was most nearly adequate, while divinity schools like those at Harvard and Andover had now come to a flourishing condition.

Greatest in the eyes of the rising generation, as of their sires, was law. The law school at Harvard had been opened in 1817, and that at the University of Virginia in 1826.[98] More common was office training; almost every prominent lawyer had one or two clerks who were studying and who hoped for partnership. A certain standard of legal learning was maintained by the examinations for entrance to the bar, but these did not keep out young men who relied solely on their assiduous reading of Blackstone, the Constitution, and the statutes of their own state.

Medical schools existed in 1830, as at Pennsylvania and Harvard, and their graduates and those of foreign training were held in much higher esteem than the much larger number who had picked up their knowledge in the office of some old practitioner. On the whole, however, the medical profession had less standing than that of law. The public credited the quack as readily as the honest apprentice-trained doctor; the conservative trusted much to the age-old lore passed down in families from mother to daughter; the speculative indulged first in one "Universal Specific" and then in another. All Americans, stirred thereto eventually by their hastiness of diet, took a deep interest in their own interiors and bought generously and read persistently the many medical books arranged alphabetically by symptoms and drugs, which keen producers furnished to a ready market.

For the learning of trades apprenticeship was the only reliance.[99] An institution affecting the whole structure of society and the lives and happiness of so many of its members could not but undergo constant change and modification. These changes, however, in the period when the generation of the thirties and forties was being educated, had not attracted serious attention and were the result of more or less unconscious yielding to the pressure of circumstances. One was that the authority of the master over the apprentice, except in seamanship, was lessened in law and much more in fact. Another was that the trades had less attraction than in the eighteenth century, when Benjamin Franklin was their typical product. There seemed clearly a greater future in marketing great numbers of articles, such as Connecticut-made clocks, than in laboriously producing a few articles of extraordinary merit, which after all would but come into competition with similar articles more cheaply made in Europe. Moreover, the lure of tending one's own flocks under one's own vine and fig tree, as Webster with an imagination rather poetic than exact described the life of the American farmer, was over all the land. Craftsmanship, therefore, on the whole, decayed and little of the work of this generation is cherished as is some of that of the preceding. In speed and ingenuity, however, the American skilled laborer had few if any equals.

The whole economy of the farm and of the household was taught in the home, and passed on, the first in the male, the second in the female line. In both fields there was some progress. Some planters sent their chefs to be trained in France, and recipes went by favor from family to family. Dress, furniture, fancywork, and table etiquette by slow degrees responded to European influences, chiefly those of London. The farm was subject to the influence of agricultural societies to which belonged many of the leading men of the time, and whose publications were of some influence in sowing new ideas in the minds of farmers' sons.[100]

It is difficult to assess the differences which formal education placed between those who enjoyed it, and those subject only to the casual educational opportunities about them. In the rural districts there was a difference in speech, but there were also marked differences among the educated from different localities. Education meant a livelihood, but all could secure a livelihood. The influence of training upon such minds as those of Webster and Calhoun, as distinguished from the slightly trained native intelligence of such men as Clay and Jackson, is plain to one who studies them. It has seldom been more easy to enforce on the public the spurious brilliancy of an educational veneer, yet the prestige of education has seldom been higher. It brought somewhat grudging respect for those who possessed it; it was considered as the key to success and there was an overwhelming impulse to possess it. The spirit of the times was expressed in a report of workingmen in Philadelphia in 1830. They unanimously resolved "that there can be no real liberty without a wide diffusion of real intelligence; that the members of a republic should all be alike instructed in the nature and character of their equal rights and duties, as human beings, and as citizens; . . . that until means of equal instruction shall be equally secured to all, liberty is but an unmeaning word, and equality an empty shadow. . . ." [101]

The changes which the people so educated desired to make for the benefit of their children were more of extension than of content. It was part of the democratic movement of the time to provide for the education of the children of the common man, but the general satisfaction with things American and the absence of any effective critique of life prevented any systematic and general change in the character and aim of the education afforded. It was part of this condition that people were best satisfied with education at the top, and changes in the colleges were less important than those in the schools—nor did universities really develop in the period under review. [102]

To take up first the colleges with their less vital changes, one notes again the leadership of Harvard and Yale. Both fostered the development of science and literature. By adding irregularly one new subject and then another, they widened the opportunities of their students, but did not weld the whole into any new educational scheme. Some of their professors, as Benjamin Silliman at Yale and Jared Sparks at Harvard, came to be nationally known, and smaller institutions began to take pride in having men of distinction on their faculties. In 1827, Francis Wayland became president of Brown University, remaining until 1855. [103] Stimulating successive generations of students, he thought also profoundly on educational methods and devised an approach to the elective system. In 1826, Mark Hopkins became president of Williams, in which position he remained throughout the period. Hopkins's remarkable influence over the students of Williams for half a century emphasized the value of strong men for such posts. [104]

The multiplication of such colleges was more remarkable than the growth of any one of them. Something like eighty were founded between 1830 and 1850. [105] This was due, in large measure, to denominational rivalry. Each aimed at being represented in each new state. Members everywhere would contribute to such a cause. Within the new states communities were keen to secure the institutions so planned, and people often gave beyond their means. Many colleges that have proved permanent were begun with less than $10,000 in subscriptions; $50,000 was a firm basis. It might have seemed that American youth were to receive their collegiate education in colleges not larger than those of an English university but separated from each other. All these colleges charged fees, which, like the cost of college living, were very low. It was becoming more and more customary for boys to earn their way. A chief purpose of most colleges was still the preservation of a learned clergy. Revivals were habitual, and the pledging for foreign missionary service was frequent. [106] It was, however, already true that most colleges drew more heavily from their community than from their denominations, and each student body was of many beliefs.

The most interesting of the new foundations was the coeducational, coracial Oberlin, which was founded in 1833 by a group of liberal Congregationalists who wished to experiment with new ideas in education and to foster new causes.[107] Another striking institution, not of college rank, was Girard College, founded at Philadelphia under the will of Stephen Girard, from which the clergy were rigorously excluded.[108] But more striking than the gradual improvement of the colleges and their multiplication was the lack of any vital change either to meet their defects existing at the beginning of the period or to tune them to the times. Barring a few scattered brilliant teachers, instruction was poor and laborious. While science was slowly making its way in, there was no general change of importance in the curricula. The thing that boys longed for, and girls envied them the chance for, was the opening of doors of opportunity by language, mathematics, and scientific method and the inspiration of some leader. The persistent few got them, chiefly by their own initiative. What made most persons glad that they had been at college continued to be the training obtained by constant clash and adjustment with their fellows in a society where, on the whole, the majority modeled themselves on the best.

Professional education made more substantial advances. While most doctors and lawyers still continued to receive their instruction by apprenticeship, supervised by the medical societies and the bar associations, an increasing number sought schools of medicine and law. These were generally attached to a college and through them some colleges were on the way to becoming universities. A simple college course was no longer regarded as sufficient training for an educated clergy and theological seminaries increased in number and attendance. The medical school at Harvard was in high estimation, and the University of Pennsylvania drew many from the South, though those who could afford it still resorted to Edinburgh, Paris, and Vienna in some numbers. The great advance, however, was in scientific and in technical training. The Rensselaer and Franklin Institutes, begun in the twenties, grew in influence, but probably the best school of engineering during the period was West Point. Certainly appointments to it were highly prized, and while made by the personal favor of members of Congress and the president, were of high character. As the army was too small to absorb the number who graduated, many went into general business, and its graduates played a large part in the development of the railroad system.

Though in 1830 the principle that education should be provided for those who could not pay for it was accepted in New England and New York, it was not national; it was not yet decided how far such an education should be extended; and in particular, it was not recognized even in the Northeast that education should be free for the children of those who could pay as well as of those who could not.[109] The key state in this controversy was Pennsylvania.[110] Here, labor, which was largely that of craftsmen, strongly urged the adoption of the free system. In Philadelphia such a system was established, and in 1834 a state law was passed. This produced a violent reaction. Petitions with 32,000 signatures were delivered in protest, and a large majority of the legislature was believed to be in favor of repeal. The Senate passed a substitute bill "making provision for the education of the poor gratis." This was opposed by the Democratic governor and by the brilliant young Anti-Masonic, later Whig, and still later Republican leader Thaddeus Stevens. In one of the great orations of American history he stood for a general free public system; he won the legislature, and the act stood.[111] Some states had preceded and most followed, but this contest may be taken as the turning point toward a public school system free to all on equal terms. It must be kept in mind, however, that the Pennsylvania law involved compulsion neither on the community to maintain schools nor the individual to attend. In Massachusetts, which had always stood for compulsion upon the community, a law of 1842 made an additional point by forbidding manufacturers to employ minors of certain ages who had not received a minimum of education.

The adoption of these principles was the most notable educational accomplishment of the generation. The actual practice of tax-supported education made rapid but uneven progress. It was a matter of time and circumstance. It was undoubtedly delayed by the still flourishing hope that education might be supported by land endowments. The newly created Western states received government grants, and when the surplus revenue was distributed in 1837, the older states created permanent funds in hopes of assistance to an indefinite amount, hopes which were speedily dashed by the Panic and consequent change in policy. The actuating motive was the rising desire for better schools, and as plans and systems were made definite and attractive, they steadily won support.

The organization of a system of schools was most largely the work of Horace Mann, although he stood by no means alone. In 1837, Massachusetts created the first real state board of education, which appointed Mann secretary, a position he held from 1837 to 1848.[112] Mann issued a series of annual reports which had an influence far beyond the confines of his state. His first attempt was to improve, or rather create, the teaching profession. American schoolchildren were, here and there, not badly off, for nearly all the distinguished men of the North and West taught school during some portion of their careers. In general, however, teachers were pensioned incompetents. Mann urged the necessity of special instruction in the art of teaching, and secured in 1839 the foundation of the first state-supported American normal school, at Lexington, Massachusetts.[113] In the meantime, a professional spirit was being aroused, and some training was being given by teachers' institutes. In 1845, Mann secured the formation of a state association of teachers in Massachusetts. Other states followed rapidly, and teachers emulated others in taking advantage of the improvements of transportation to meet frequently for the purpose of mutual acquaintance, self-training, and influencing public opinion. How speedily such ideas spread is indicated by the fact that by 1849 fourteen states had appointed superintendents of education. Buffalo was the first, in 1837, to appoint a city superintendent, Providence followed in 1839, New York in 1841, New Orleans in 1843, and by 1850 it showed promise of becoming the custom.

As to the limits of the system one may say that outside of the South, public responsibility was fully acknowledged for elementary education, was strongly felt to extend to secondary schools, and was beginning to extend to collegiate education. The contest was a local one. In the older states it was between the idea of a private academy, supported chiefly by private generosity and fees, and a tax-supported, free high school.[114] The academy still received strong religious support. Protestants were most anxious to control education at this level, whereas Catholics generally devoted their efforts to the separate maintenance of lower schools. Nevertheless the high school gained steadily on the academy.[115] In New England financial

The first state-supported normal school, Lexington, Mass., 1839.

Oberlin College: Ladies' Hall,
First home of college girls.

Oberlin College: Tappan Hall,
Gift of an abolitionist.

stress led in many cases to combinations. Academies were taken over by the public and high schools were assisted by donations. In the West, as cities developed, the general equality of financial conditions caused the high school to outdistance the academy.

While the lines were being laid down on which the school education of the mass of the American people has been developed, the forces that kept them alert and sharpened their faculties after school was over were being strengthened to a notable degree. Before 1830 organized religion, with its regular sermons, its facilities for the publication of books and its innumerable periodicals representing each form of activity of each denomination, was the most potent intellectual influence in the country. The next twenty years merely developed this activity. Political discussion, however, gained enormously in its power of presenting problems to the people. It copied many of the methods of the churches, and it outranked them in its employment of the newspaper press. Between 1830 and 1850 there was also an increase in the influence of the secular and nonpolitical magazine. Besides the "parlor magazines" like *Godey's Lady's Book* and *Peterson's Magazine,* the *New England Magazine* was founded in 1831, the *Knickerbocker Magazine* the next year, and the *Southern Literary Messenger,* of which Poe was for a time editor, in 1834—all of them periodicals of reassuring literary merit. Numerous others were started, especially in the South, but died untimely deaths, though near the close of the period, in 1846, *De Bow's Commercial Review,* a journal of somewhat different type, began a successful career in New Orleans.

Despite these promising developments, however, the most important educational agency touching the lives of adult Americans was the one known as the Lyceum movement.[116] This was originated in Millbury, Massachusetts, in 1826 by Josiah Holbrook. Its main activity was the establishment of lecture courses. Soon it became nationally organized, and sent forth some of the ablest and some of the most specious men of the times, from New England to the far stretches of the frontier. Similar work was undertaken by mechanics' institutes and other bodies. Of single instances, the most important was the Lowell Institute of Boston, endowed in 1836 with a quarter of a million dollars by the will of John Lowell. The fees received for such lectures were an important element in the support of intellectual workers in the United States, who were thus enabled and, indeed, almost forced to carry their intellectual life to the people in a manner never before equaled.

A remarkable feature of the period was the part played by New England in the actual extension of education. Its belief in education, its opportunities, the thrill of its renaissance combined to make it a second Scotland, sending forth countless apostles of intellectual training. Schoolmasters, professors, college presidents, lecturers, and state superintendents swarmed out, generally flying over the mountains and alighting beyond wherever there was a job, often trusting to the future to develop a salary. The influence of this New England element varied in the different sections.[117] In the Lake regions its members at once took the lead in educational affairs, and strongly influenced the region, through education and example, in its attitude toward life. In the Ohio Valley it reinforced the New England elements already there and built up a strong and self-conscious community centering largely at Cincinnati. This was, however, a community among strong rivals, the Southern and the German. Sometimes the three blended, sometimes they stood apart, sometimes they contended. In the South, New England educators were almost as numerous. They took the place of the Scotch tutors of earlier times, and they almost halved the leadership of higher institutions. Their influence, however, was very slight. Most left after a term of years, retaining some mutual relations of sentiment but few of agreement. Those who stayed for the most part, as Sergeant S. Prentiss of Maine and Mississippi, adopted the Southern point of view, although they retained much of their self-discipline and carried the earnestness of their moral conviction to the new views they adopted. Many came to be among the most ardent advocates of the Southern position.

In spite of these diversifications it should remain the last impression that this period saw the acceptance of the fundamental principles of the American public-school system by the nation and that it laid the actual foundations. In 1850 there were in the country at large some 80,000 elementary schools, with more than 90,000 teachers and 3.3 million pupils, and something over 6,000 secondary schools, with more than 12,000 teachers and over a quarter of a million pupils. The income of the former was derived in most part from public sources; and a growing proportion of the secondary schools were on a similar basis.[118] Such an accomplishment is convincing evidence of clear thinking, and forces one to conclude that the unfavorable picture of American life presented by the travelers and the newspapers is a hasty and ill-drawn picture of superficial traits.

LITERATURE

At the beginning of the period New York was distinctly the literary center, already having enjoyed fifteen years of activity. Here the initiative had been taken by a number of the aristocrats who were not dependent upon popular support. First in importance and recognized in the thirties and forties as the leading literary figure in America was Washington Irving. Possessing a strong and individual sense of humor, he had begun by laughing out Dutch customs in his *Knickerbocker History of New York*. His interest, however, was more in developing a style based upon the study of English models. He turned sharply from tales of American life to a sympathetic presentation of foreign lands, first England and then Spain. As he grew older the patriotic impulse of the men of his age turned him again to American themes and he wrote a series of books on pioneer life. Toward the end of the period he started his researches on a life of Washington, which began to appear in 1855, a five-volume biography, excellent but rather admired more than read.

In his desire to write on American subjects but to find such as were heroic and detached from contemporaneous life, Irving may be associated with the prevalent romantic school of the time, and was typical of an impulse very strong among American writers. The American Scott was another aristocratic New Yorker, James Fenimore Cooper. In choosing themes from the conflicts with the Indians, and pioneering, he was dealing with subjects which were actually contemporaneous in American life. They were not, however, contemporaneous in the life of New York, and he wrote from a point of view which never existed on the frontier. His novels, *The Last of the Mohicans* (1826), *The Pathfinder* (1840), and the others, presented material practically before untouched by literature and introduced American scenes to practically the entire youth of Western Europe.[119] His few essays to comment upon the life about him are forgotten except by students.

The literary strength of William Cullen Bryant, a New England boy who came early to New York, was in poetry, which was admired but was not sufficiently profitable to its author. Throughout this period he was editor of the *New York Evening Post.* Highly independent, he gave voice to views held largely by the more intellectual elements of the Democratic party. To his paper he gave a literary tone and to some degree he unified the literary work of New York. More and more New York became a publishing city. The firms of Harper and Appleton were in operation throughout the period, and at the end were in close rivalry with that of Putnam. There existed, therefore, the full equipment of a literary center.

No one city, however, could aspire to be the center. Competition was strong both between cities and between sections. Philadelphia won N. P. Willis, the popular poet of mediocrity, away from New York, and in 1848 he began to edit the *Home Journal,* which represented the tastes and intellectual capacity of the middle class. The firm of Lippincott offered the best of publishing facilities, and that of Lea Brothers, an already established reputation.[120] In Baltimore the very unliterary *Niles' Register* was the best recording agency of political affairs in the country. In Richmond the *Southern Literary Messenger* attempted to develop the talent of the South.[121] In Charleston, William Gilmore Simms wrote historical novels of the Revolution and border wars and encouraged and influenced many younger writers.[122]

Connected with no section or center, the leading poetic figure of these years was Edgar Allan Poe, who was but twenty-one in 1830 and died in

1849. His poetry was the finest expression of the weirdly romantic, and struck one of the most responsive chords of the time. Full of music and mastery of form, his themes were treated with an imagery so far from any reality that ever was in America that they seem artificial. More original was his prose. Here, too, he toyed with the weird and the fantastic, yet in form and subject made the first distinctive American contribution to the scope of literature. Not the first to write short stories or detective stories, he was the first to master the essentials of both arts. Such contributions, being rather personal than the result of national stress, received recognition more promptly abroad than at home. Particularly among the French were his works admired, and from Paris his reputation was reflected back to his home. The inadequate support that brought on his premature death, however, was not entirely the result of nonrecognition. The United States in this generation did not support pure literature. When Poe, as was to have been expected, failed as a magazine editor, the general public felt relieved of further responsibility for his maintenance.

This failure to remunerate American authors properly was perhaps in part due to the fact that much of the reading of the public was supplied to them without any compensation to the authors. The "best sellers" were English—Scott and Dickens. There was no provision for international copyright; in fact, the situation had never before created a serious injustice as no such market as the United States had ever before been open since the days of printing, ready to take the untranslated products of another nation. English works were pirated when the first copy reached America. Numbers of American publishers, such as Harper of New York and Ticknor & Fields of Boston, voluntarily paid large sums to authors like Dickens, but they could not give adequate payment, for the foreign author could give them nothing except priority and a good word to advantage them over other publishers. This situation made it cheaper for publishers to produce foreign than American works, and particularly in magazines and reviews, with the notable exception of the *North American Review,* the American author who must live by his writing was hard driven by foreign competition. The increased guaranty of the U.S. copyright law of 1831, which extended the period of protection from fourteen to twenty-eight years with the former renewal right of fourteen years, was no protection against this competition.[123] Although Pennsylvania iron and New England textiles were able to secure national aid, the public preferred a cheap market to domestic production when it came to literature. Actually the failure of an international agreement, so strongly urged by Dickens on his first visit to the United States, was a greater blow to American then to foreign authors.

The outstanding development of the period was the rise of the New England literary movement, and the organization of Boston, though on the extreme eastern edge of the country, as its most productive literary center. Here Harvard was the nucleus both in training and in maintaining by its professorships the first literary leaders. The earliest to obtain distinction were, as in New York, members of the aristocracy, Alexander and Edward Everett, George Bancroft, and William H. Prescott. Among them they illustrated the tendencies already noted. The Everetts combined politics with scholarship. Alexander was an essayist on many subjects and served as minister to Spain from 1825 to 1829. Edward, after being ordained as a minister, accepted a professorship of Greek at Harvard, and in 1820 became editor of the *North American Review.* In 1836 he became governor of Massachusetts, in 1841 minister to Great Britain, and in 1845 president of Harvard. His chief form of literary expression was the oration, carefully prepared and polished on the most exacting classical models.

Like Everett, Bancroft alternated between politics and literature, but his literary purpose was more persistent.[124] He was the precursor of a new type of American scholar who sought German training. He became active in politics, being that rara avis, an educated Northern Democrat, and served as collector of customs at Boston, as secretary of the navy, and as minister to London and, after the Civil War, to Berlin. In the meantime, he was preparing for his life work, a history of the United States, which should be a justification of the conflict with Great Britain and an exposition of American principles. His first volume appeared in 1834, and through fifty years the appearance of each of its successors was a literary event of the first importance. More detached was the historian Prescott, who sought also an American subject but, like Cooper, wished it to savor of romance. He found his field in the early relations of Spain and America, and while he sank himself in the sources he lost none of the romance his subject afforded.[125] His first work, *Ferdinand and Isabella,* appeared in 1838, and his most famous, *The Conquest of Peru,* in 1847. In the forties his greater successor, the young Francis Parkman, was preparing for his pathfinding work on the other side of our colonial relations, those with the French and the Indians of our own territories.

Perhaps the greatest product of this aristocratic culture was Henry Wadsworth Longfellow, who was born in Portland, Maine, in 1807. In him were combined the scholarly interest, a sense of the romantic, and a choice of American subjects having in them the possibility of embodying American ideals. Becoming a professor of belles lettres at Harvard in 1836, he published his *Psalm of Life* two years later and followed it presently with his *Voices of the Night* and *Evangeline.* By instinct he avoided the realities of life around him, and painted in ready and charming verse a world and human nature in which men delighted to believe. Already by 1850 he had equaled Irving in the popular estimation and exceeded him in the affection of the public.

Of about the same age as Longfellow, but different in spirit, was another group of New England writers. These men were more deeply affected by the impulses of the time. Oliver Wendell Holmes, who was born in 1809, has vividly described their attitudes in his tale of the "wonderful one-hoss shay." This remarkable vehicle, which in the poet's mind symbolized New England Calvinism, was so well built that without repair or defect it ran for exactly 100 years when at once every part went to pieces in complete dissolution. Though the wish may have been father to the thought, there is enough truth in such a conception to justify the poet; still, in the interest of accuracy, the historian must modify the picture. The youth growing up between 1800 and 1830 were indeed exhilarated by the breaking of barriers to thought and the wide new world of speculation; but the discipline of Calvinism was left, with its social order and habits of orthodoxy. However wild the views accepted, the habits of the newly liberated stood in this generation comparatively unchanged, and as this movement centered in the intellectual middle class, these were the habits of "plain living and high thinking." Each new view, moreover, became for its disciples "the" gospel, and the advocacy of "causes" became the chief object of their lives.[126]

What Emerson and the others got from Kant was the supreme importance of the ideal as contrasted with the apparently real, and this led to something of a schism between them and their elder contemporaries in that its temporary effect, at least, was to stay the advance of scholarship laboriously accumulating details and let the mind flow into expression in prose and verse. The American Academy of Lorenzo de' Medici was the democratic and parsimonious Brook Farm. This was a communistic experiment, the outgrowth of the Transcendentalist movement and started by George Ripley in 1841. Beginning as the Brook Farm Institute of Agriculture and Education, it turned into a "phalanx" on the principles of the French philosopher Charles Fourier, and in 1846 it failed. While it existed, however, it was the controversial and joyous meeting place of many members of the rising generation where they associated on terms of equality regardless of social origin and sex.[127]

The greatest of this new group was, as we have seen, Ralph Waldo Emerson. After Emerson, the reputation which has best lasted is that of Nathaniel Hawthorne. While identified with Brook Farm, Hawthorne was more a literary man and less a reformer than most of the rest. He first came conspicuously before the public in his *Twice Told Tales,* published in 1837, but soon turned to subjects purely American. In his *Scarlet Letter,* published in 1850, he produced a work that blended romance with deep psychological study. To him again, the period did not afford support, and petty political offices kept the wolf from the door.

The Quaker John Greenleaf Whittier was the outstanding poet among the reformers. As with Hawthorne, his dominant tendency was undoubtedly literary, but a deep interest in causes and principles affected much of his writing, and he was active in the movements for peace and against slavery. In his *Legends of New England* (1831) is the "King's Missive," a

"Berry Hill," a Parthenon house in Halifax County, Virginia.

Above: Hiram Powers' "Greek Slave."

Below: Brook Farm, West Roxbury, Massachusetts.

Thomas Sully's portrait of Fanny Kemble as "Beatrice."

Classicism and Transcendentalism

stern attack upon the Puritan traditions of Massachusetts; and his *Ichabod* in 1850, an attack on Webster for supporting the Compromise of that year, was among the half-dozen most potent political documents of the period. The younger poet James Russell Lowell first became prominent through his *Bigelow Papers* (1846–48). He followed an old tradition, and one particularly prevalent at the time in America, of putting his wisdom into the vulgate of local dialect and into the mouths of the lowly. With a satire biting yet frolicsome, he attacked the conservatives of his day, and with a strong note of patriotic pride, espoused the new causes, such as peace and the rights of blacks. In his later career, poetry, criticism, a Harvard professorship, and diplomatic ministries to both Spain and England blended to identify him with the best in American effort. The interest excited by these new writers attracted Horace Greeley, who was editing the *Tribune* in New York. He became closely allied with them. Margaret Fuller he employed as a special writer to visit and report on the West—a sensational employment for a woman at the time. In 1848 he made Charles A. Dana managing editor of the *Tribune,* and that paper became to a degree the popular vehicle of the new lights, although it would have been quite different in many respects had it been edited in Boston.

As literature was expected to justify itself by a purpose besides that of art, so purposes were expected to be set forth with some attention to literary effect. Daniel Webster revised his orations with scrupulous care, and they were read by many more than ever heard them. The sermons of William Ellery Channing were finished literary productions. The grand style was affected by most of those who appeared before the public, and the Fourth of July reverberated with periods most unfairly fathered upon Cicero and Demosthenes. With some apology, however, many listened to and read the racy speeches and memoirs of "Davy" Crockett, and the humorous political skits of "Major Jack Downing," the Maine Yankee character presented by Seba Smith and his imitators. In Georgia a group of writers were producing studies of American character: A. B. Longstreet, *Georgia Scenes;* W. T. Thompson, *Major Jones's Courtship;* and J. B. Baldwin, *Flush Times in Alabama and Mississippi.*[128] Beneath the surface was produced and circulated a ribald literature.

On the whole, the aristocratic tradition persisted more strongly in literature than in most other fields of life. It adapted itself to changing ideas and conditions with commendable vigor. Standards were maintained with some effect, and influenced the form even of the more radical school. There was still reverence for that which was not understood, and millions boasted of books they had never read, because the authors were Americans. By the end of the period writers had become almost as numerous as politicians. As in England and France, the public taste had changed from poetry and didactic essays to romances and stories of adventure and travel. It is not too much to say that, as in those countries, fiction had by 1850 triumphed over all other forms of writing in the United States.

REFORM AND SLAVERY

THE WORD "REFORM" was a touchstone which differentiated people more incisively than did party allegiance. It was something rather felt by instinct than defined by reason. There was something fortuitous about it. If one succeeded in getting his particular hobby labeled a "reform," it received the support of certain classes and encountered the opposition of others regardless of its real classification. In general, however, political reforms may be excluded; they were regarded as a mere extension and application of principles already accepted and proved. "Reform" had usually some social implications.

Most reformers were interested in all reforms while specializing on some of their own. The histories of the different movements were differentiated by the reactions which they caused rather than by their internal character, their support or the methods by which they were promoted. Public education was perhaps the most successful of them all during this period, and one reason was that it aroused little opposition, except that of the taxpayers and private-school interests which were so demonstrably based on selfish motives that it was forced gradually to yield before public opinion.

An outstanding reformer was Samuel Gridley Howe.[129] Son of a wealthy Boston merchant, after a frolicsome career at Brown University he studied medicine at Harvard. Caught by enthusiasm for the cause of Greek independence, by dint of persistence he collected funds from Boston friends and devoted seven years of active service to that land. After the Greek cause triumphed, he lingered on the continent to study his particular medical interest, blindness. Back in Boston he installed several blind patients in the home of his father, whose reputation for crabbedness must have been somewhat fictitious. With his ever compelling charm he won support for the establishment, in 1832, of the famous Perkins Institution for the Blind, of which he became superintendent. At one fair in Boston the ladies raised over $14,000 for this philanthropy. Here Howe made his most striking contribution, the opening of the world to Laura Bridgman, who was blind, deaf, and dumb.

In 1843 he won in marriage Julia Ward, a beautiful and vivacious New York heiress, of a family which has contributed many of our leading artists and novelists. Already she was remarked as an illustration of the new type of woman in American life. Together the Howes created a home through which most of the reformer group passed, renewed in their good works and generally unaffected by the counsels of moderation with which their more balanced host endeavored to temper them. Other centers through which most reformers passed were the homes of Arthur Tappan in New York City and Gerrit Smith in central New York, where they received a support more lavish, as accorded with the means of the hosts, and advice perhaps more sympathetic and somewhat less tinctured by wisdom.[130]

Somewhat older than Howe, Dorothea L. Dix was later in appearing on the stage of public life. From her Quaker associations she received a sound education and an unconsciousness of sex inequalities. For many years she supported herself by teaching, her ability enabling her early to secure a school of her own. Meanwhile she was studying the world about her. What most affected her was the inhumane treatment of dependents. Her daily task took her by the prison of Charlestown, Massachusetts. The indifference of the public to the treatment of prisoners and of paupers, and particularly the unthinking inhumanity toward the insane, aroused her pity and indignation. From 1841 she devoted her principal attention to the relief of these classes.[131] Her chief method was public speaking. With stern, commanding determination she set forth the situation and demanded that it be changed. Like Howe, she aroused the generosity of the wealthy. As a result, numbers of insane asylums were reorganized, as the Lunatic Hospital of Boston in 1839, and new ones of high character were established, as Butler Asylum at Providence, Rhode Island.

Before many years she began to appear before legislative bodies, which disapproved of being addressed by a woman but knew not how to get rid of her except by heeding the appeal she made, an appeal which by all the canons of the time touched subjects quite properly within woman's province. She was so successful in securing grants from neighboring states that she was called to Kentucky, where her New England angularity, however it may have failed to charm the gentlemen of the South, did not prevent their yielding to her solicitations. During the last years of the period she was devoting much attention to Congress, from which she ultimately secured a grant of over 10 million acres for the indigent insane, only to have it snatched away by the U.S. Constitution as interpreted by President Pierce.

Miss Dix was not so much the originator of ideas as their advocate. In fact, most of the reforms she urged had long been advocated by the Quakers and by European philanthropists. The actual carrying out of these ideas into practice was the work of many men and many years. The period of the thirties and forties neither sowed the seed nor reaped the full fruit. As in so many lines, however, it was the period of experimentation and of the acceptance of certain reforms as desirable and needing only development. During these years imprisonment for debt practically disappeared,[132] the number of crimes for which the death penalty was exacted diminished, and the idea of abolishing that penalty entirely began to be strongly advocated, although it nowhere gained sufficient legislative support. Everyone accepted the principle that men and women should be separated in prison, but it was not everywhere carried out. In general, the idea of cells, instead of one common room, was accepted, but this plan was too costly for universal use. Practical reformers were much divided between the Pennsylvania or solitary system, in which the outstanding feature was solitary confinement at hard labor, and the New York or silent system, adopted by the Auburn State Prison, in which the cell was used but the prisoners were employed by day in large workshops without being allowed to speak to one another.[133] In Massachusetts and New York, prison associations were formed, and the study of imprisonment as a reforming as well as a punishing measure began to be widely discussed.

The improvement in the condition of the ordinary poor was still less definitive, as it was most largely a matter of local action. In general, the problem of pauperism was much less important than in most countries, for the poor were fewer, though the Irish immigrant wave, for all its value to the country, brought many without means or much ambition who became a burden to the public. Stories were told of poor old Irishwomen in Philadelphia, who in their letters home chiefly recommended the United States because of its palatial almshouses. On the whole, the treatment of paupers, even at the beginning of the period, was rather better than elsewhere, owing to the very fact that the customary "poor farm" was better situated than the English "workhouse." For the most part, however, such farms were let on contract, and much depended on the character of the contractors, who were seldom philanthropists. During the period there was a gradual improvement, and foreigners generally commented very favorably upon conditions. The real change, however, consisted in the withdrawal of the insane poor to asylums for their special care. In fact, the treatment of the insane, in this separation and the beginning of the differentiation of the curable from the incurable, showed more general improvement than that of either prisoners or paupers.

A more spectacular reform was that which went under the general designation of temperance. The success of this movement involved a drastic change in the long established habits of the people, and also a disturbance of the business interests concerned in the liquor traffic, though these latter were not so well organized as in later times. In other words, the reform meant, instead of a mere arousing of the conscience, a conflict of enmity and bitterness. When this generation was in its youth, intoxicating drinks were habitual and excited no moral reaction whatever; even occasional drunkenness, particularly if the occasion was good, scarcely came within the moral catalogue. In a Southern election it was the custom for the candidates to provide the means for celebration. In New York, open house was maintained on New Year's Day by all those with social pretensions, and the debutantes not unsuccessfully urged the young men to take, at each house, quite as much as they could well manage, though well aware of the round of homes that they would make thereafter. Widows and maiden ladies felt embarrassed if they had no sherry to serve the clergyman when he called.

On the other hand, while practically all women drank, none who were respectable were supposed to become drunk; and they rarely did. Moreover, it was coming to be disapproved for the men to become seriously intoxicated in mixed parties, until the dancing was over—a point on which the preceding generation had been less particular. The limits of less polite drinking were determined chiefly by opportunity. The differences between sections of the country were those of the beverage locally produced. In general, Americans drank spirits, except the rich who could afford also imported wines. The tradition of the old English ales had almost passed away, their place being taken, perhaps, in the apple-growing districts by cider. In the Ohio Valley the Germans during this period introduced lager beer and domestic wine.

Whether conditions were worse in America than in northern Europe it is difficult to say. Statistics are absent, and there were not enough American travelers abroad to set against the European comments on American conditions. In fact, the small amount of comment indicates conditions not very dissimilar; Europeans were more shocked at the American consumption of ice water than of spirits. It was a native instinct, and not comparison, that made this generation from its youth dissatisfied with conditions and determined to reform them.

The movement was well under way by 1830, but it had expressed itself largely in mild criticism of excesses.[134] Recently the evangelical churches had taken it up with constantly growing enthusiasm, though they had the opposition of some thorough predestinarians like the Primitive Baptists and the sacerdotalists among the Episcopalians, especially clergymen like Bishop John H. Hopkins of Vermont. It was widely alleged that the reform was a New England enterprise, and it was true that one third of the societies and membership in 1831 were concentrated east of the Hudson, while most of the remainder were to be found in regions settled by that stock. The 700 societies in the banner state of New York constituted half of the total of the country, but the majority of those were located in counties peopled largely from the Eastern states. In order to give the crusade more of a national character a convention was held at Philadelphia in 1833 with more than 400 representatives from twenty-one states in attendance. Here the United States Temperance Union was formed on a federation basis, an organization to be known three years later, after the inclusion of Canadians, as the American Temperance Union, and destined to be far more effective than the American Temperance Society it superseded. The deep interest of politicians in the movement, if not in its principles, was evidenced in the American Congressional Temperance Society under the presidency of Lewis Cass in 1833.

Women were admitted to the societies, later to conventions, and finally many, like Lucretia Mott, Elizabeth Cady Stanton, Abby Kelley, and others, to the lecture platform, on an equality with men; but they had to overcome strong disapproval as to their modesty in thus leaving their own hearths to attend to other people's business, and it may be said that the movement remained chiefly a man's concern throughout the first half of the nineteenth century. There were also hundreds of clubs for children, especially those of the "Cold Water Army" which attracted so much attention in the parades at temperance celebrations. Later there were the Sons of Temperance formed in Teetotalers' Hall, 71 Division Street, New York City, in September 1842, whose local lodges, each performing its ritual under a Worthy Patriarch, spread over much of the United States. The old prudential argument that alcohol destroyed the human system was vigorously exploited and, about 1830, another, that it reduced industrial efficiency, which was ultimately to tell so strongly in a country where everyone worked; in connection with the building of the Baltimore and Ohio Railroad in that year, for instance, the superintendent of construction prohibited all use of spirits. Such considerations, however, were little stressed. People were called upon to reform by releasing themselves from habits that shackled them to a life of sin.

In the last of the thirties there arose a dissension within the ranks. The old advocates had been content to abstain from spirituous liquors, but the extremists now gained more and more support for total abstinence from all that could intoxicate, including, of course, wine and malt beverages. Many thought this impracticable. Then, too, a generation trained to respect so deeply the letter of the Scriptures had difficulty in reconciling such a stigma upon wine with Christ's use of it for the sacred purpose of the Last Supper. But some were ready to match against this the warning that wine was a "mocker"; others with fearless exegesis explained quite seriously that the Master sanctioned only pure wine, which was now so rare an article of commerce that its use could hardly be considered mandatory. A growing number of church congregations were persuaded by Dr. Eliphalet Nott and other scholars to believe that the wine which Christ had used must have been the unfermented juice of the grape. Among the many temperance periodicals, some were established especially to argue out this "communion question." Under the lead of Edward C. Delavan, of Albany, whose zeal, personal fortune, and organizing power made him perhaps the most effective temperance man of his time, the radicals in 1836 were able to carry the general convention at Saratoga Springs for total abstinence. There ensued a bitter pamphlet warfare, and for a time societies which took this stand lost heavily in membership, but the outcome seemed to prove its wisdom. Governor Allen Trimble of Ohio wrote in 1837: "The societies that have adopted the total abstinence pledge are active and increasing their numbers. Those societies that go upon the principle that distilled spirits alone should be excluded, are dragging heavily, and I think retrograding, rather than advancing." [135]

For a period after 1840 the leadership was taken by those who were themselves reformed. The agitation in its new phase was known as the Washingtonian movement, and it had its inception in a small group of hard drinkers in Baltimore in 1840 who had been shown the error of their ways by the exhortation of an evangelist. These men set themselves to reforming other tipplers, and the latter in turn took up the work. Soon the movement infected many parts of the country; everywhere meetings were held, addressed by reformed drunkards, and new recruits from the gutter pushed forward to tell their experiences to an admiring public.

Literature, also, was laid under heavy contribution in the propaganda. Holmes, Willis, and many less distinguished poets brought their muse to embellish the temperance "gift books"; *The Fountain* (1847) had offerings in prose and verse by such writers as John G. Whittier, Lydia H. Sigourney, Horace Greeley, Bayard Taylor, Fanny Forrester, and T. S. Arthur. The six volumes of *Temperance Tales* by Lucius M. Sargent had an immense popularity throughout the country. Mrs. Sigourney wrote innumerable sentimental temperance stories defending the American home in a somewhat stilted style. Timothy Shay Arthur, a native of Newburgh, New York, living in Philadelphia, devoted such talent as he possessed almost exclusively to the subject. In this period he published *Six Nights with the Washingtonians* (1842), and just after it, in 1854, the most famous of the temperance works, *Ten Nights in a Bar-Room,* which was quickly dramatized and had a vogue and influence only a little less than that of *Uncle Tom's Cabin* in later years. To these instruments was added the still more universal appeal of the cartoon, or at least of the picture with a moral, which somehow managed to leave a vivid impression on many a youthful mind.

The change of emphasis from temperance to total abstinence was logical and appropriate to the philosophy of the time. Much more difficult to grasp is the development in the forties of the movement for prohibition.[136] Such a program seems to fly directly in the face of the individualism of the period and that conception of governmental functions which was being reinforced by the laissez-faire doctrine of the only group of British thinkers whose influence reached America. Three considerations helped somewhat to clarify the inconsistency, though it may be a hopeless enterprise to seek logic in a generation so chaotic. The primary aim of reform was to release the individual, to secure a real freedom. It is not surprising that the active minds of enthusiasts came to regard many things as servitudes which the state should end in order to liberate the human soul. To extend this to habits was indeed to lose the general principle in the particular case, but such twists are not unhuman. In the second place, they were under the spell of the millenarian conception, which led them to expect their reforms to be complete in their own lifetime. Their horror was of failing to do their full duty, and they were moved by the spirit of that most self-confident exhortation ever delivered, which was voiced later by one of their distinguished sons, when Edward Everett Hale said: "When in doubt, do it." More important is the third consideration. The prohibition movement was to all intents and purposes a New England movement, and in New England the current philosophies swayed public opinion but within narrow limits.

TEMPERANCE PIC NIC

Father, don't send me after whiskey, to-day!—See p. 26.

Gleanings from the Temperance Literature,
1830–1850

From the beginning to the present, New England, except Rhode Island, has believed in community responsibility.

The lead for prohibition was taken by Neal Dow, a political leader in Maine, a state both radical and radically New England. Here, just at the close of the generation, in 1851, he obtained a prohibition law, which, excepting during the years 1856–58, withstood all buffets of reaction, until swallowed up by the Eighteenth Amendment. In the first years of the new generation, the movement was to spread rapidly, carrying other New England states, and urged upon the new states of the West by their increasing population of New England extraction.

While the millennium did not arrive, the results of this moral reform were not to be despised; in fact, they more nearly justified the hopes of its advocates than the slurs of its foes. In the first place, it almost destroyed drinking among women. It still remained good form in the "society" of the larger cities, and in the South, but here good manners prevented excess. In middle-class America and generally on the frontier, women did not drink. The drunken woman was practically unknown and came to be one of the novel sights recorded by Americans traveling in certain countries abroad. Among men the results were more marked in the number who drank not at all than in the number who moderated their drinking. At no time during this generation did occasional drunkenness offer a bar to political preferment, though later among the children of the generation, in certain localities, it came to do so. Brilliant lawyers could, at least in the West, appear drunk in court and keep their practice. More often such habits might stand between a young man and the girl of his desire, although the majority of girls were willing to take the risk, with the purpose of "reforming" the man after marriage. Still, the number of young men who had never tasted alcohol was probably larger than in any previous place or time, unless in some Mohammedan countries at periods of religious revival.

The most important moral change of the time, however, was not American but general in the European world. This was the continued progress and exceptional accomplishment of the humanitarian movement,[137] which began among the Quakers and became general in the eighteenth century. In colonial Massachusetts, John Winthrop gave up shooting for pleasure, but none of the reasons which he carefully enumerates includes the cruelty of the practice. Representative boys growing up in the thirties and forties, like Abraham Lincoln and U. S. Grant, objected to hunting because they did not like killing animals. While individuals took this extreme view, and fanatics extended their tenderness to fish and even trees, the crowd revolted from many of the brutalities of the preceding generation, such as animal baiting, cockfighting, and the human gouging matches of the frontier described by Thomas Ashe in 1806.[138] Horace Mann even advocated the disuse of corporal punishment in the schools.

While the individual conditions of the time permitted glaring exceptions which shocked visitors and, in the case of the Indians, extended to public practice, it remains true that the Americans on the whole were distinguished by their kindness of heart. This was, however, so dominant a feature of the period, and was so varied in its manifestations, that it can only be referred to as one of the moral accomplishments of the time.

A striking anachronism of American life was the legal and political position of woman. Nowhere was she accorded a higher place in so far as lip service went, and this attitude was not a tribute to particular women but to the sex. Genuine Southern gentlemen extended even to female slaves the ordinary courtesies of social intercourse. European travelers universally commented upon the deferential attitude of American men toward women, even in the more primitive communities. Nevertheless, by law women were given a distinctly inferior place to men in the social organization.[139] Indeed, in the new democracy they seemed actually to play a smaller part than in the old days of aristocratic dominance. Politics was more distinctly a man's business than in Great Britain or France. As in earlier times, married women had no control, that is, legal control, over their property or children. In no state or locality did they possess the right to vote. These contrasts were especially noticeable to women who came from abroad with glowing ideas of the position their sex would occupy. Frances Kemble, an English actress who married Pierce Butler, a Georgia planter, could not long endure the life. Frances Wright, who came over from Scotland in 1818, soon began to devote herself to improving woman's position. Ernestine Rose, a Polish Jew, had the same reaction, and became a speaker in the cause.

Naturally, American women were not behindhand.[140] Their interest was first generally aroused by their desire to cooperate in other movements of general reform. They soon discovered that they were not wanted, but before their persistence the male reformers, representing of course liberal opinion generally, were powerless. In 1840 eight were sent as delegates to a World's Antislavery Convention in London. With debate and commotion they were excluded therefrom, and agreed among themselves that the position of women was pivotal to other measures and that they would devote themselves to it as a cause. The leader was Lucretia Mott, a middle-aged Quaker preacher of Philadelphia. With her was Elizabeth Cady Stanton, a bride of twenty-five. Keenly interested in the movement also was Margaret Fuller, who was already exemplifying the possibilities of women in varied fields of work.[141]

The main object at first was the securing of civil rights for women. Of these the first to win support was the rectification of laws regarding property; and some progress was made. In 1839, Mississippi granted to married women the control over their own property, and similar laws were enacted in the next decade by Texas, Indiana, Pennsylvania, New York, California, and Wisconsin. Encouraged by these successes, a younger group of women began to press the less popular issue of equal suffrage. Thus, in 1847, Lucy Stone graduated from Oberlin at the age of twenty-nine and began at once to fight for the vote. In 1848 a woman's rights convention was held at Seneca Falls, New York, the first in the history of the world. The delegates drew up an impressive declaration of sentiments patterned closely upon the Declaration of Independence. They asserted that "all men and women are created equal," and demanded equality with the men before the law, in educational and economic opportunities and in the suffrage.[142] Though greeted by the ridicule and condemnation of press and pulpit, the gathering was to have almost yearly successors until the outbreak of the Civil War diverted the attention of the feminist leaders for a time to other matters.

The condition of wage-earners during these years differed from that of women in that they had no system of laws to batter down but new economic conditions to contend with. Insofar as they wished legal changes, this desire was for new protective measures, to pass which was contrary to the spirit of the time. The number of wage-earners was continually increasing with the new tasks of engineering and the factories. They included women as well as men, and many children.[143] The employment of children in factories gave no severe shock to the public sentiment of the generation, for children had always been expected to work. Few realized the difference of work at home and on the farm, and work in the rising factories.

The chief objective which the laboring men strove for was the ten-hour day (instead of the prevalent twelve or thirteen),[144] though they never lost sight of their program announced at the end of the twenties, especially the demands for free tax-supported schools and for the abolition of all monopolies such as banks and other chartered corporations. From 1828 to 1832 they sought such reforms through political action, but between 1832 and 1836 they contented themselves with agitating strongly by means of organization and strikes, and many labor papers were published. Among their leaders was George H. Evans who published in New York the *Working Man's Advocate.* In 1836 the union membership of the country numbered nearly 300,000. The movement looked like one of the most promising of the reform agitations of the time, and one might have predicted that within a short period it would achieve reasonable success. The trade societies received a serious blow, however, in 1835 by reason of certain common-law decisions beginning with *People* v. *Fisher,* in New York, which declared strikes illegal, and during the period of depression which began in 1837 they would have been, in any case, useless. The competition for jobs became so keen that wage-earners could not exact conditions. Standards of hours and wages which had been won by organized efforts were sacrificed; leaders were discouraged: Evans, for example, retired to a farm.

Three elements are to be observed in the various reform movements. In the first place, there was the part played by those hereditary reformers, the Quakers. Nearly always there was a Quaker at the start, but the leadership seldom remained with them. The second element was the action and reaction between Europe and America. This was particularly marked in the case of Great Britain. The foreign missionary movement there stimulated that of the United States. American women lectured on women's rights in England, and British temperance workers in America. Prussian education was drawn on for American use, and before the end of the period German and American reformers were fraternizing. The whole movement was presided over by the *Egalité* and the *Fraternité* of the French Revolution. Charles Sumner, the beautiful youth, who was developing into the St. George destined by all reformers to kill all dragons, was equally welcome on both sides of the Atlantic.

The third element was the relentless driving power given by the New England renaissance, curiously like and yet differing from the dominant Jacksonian democracy. As with Jackson, universality was of the essence of their thought. It would be unfair to say that they were in such a hurry to convert the world that they did not worry over converting themselves; certainly, however, they were much less self-searching than their ancestors. Confident of themselves, they devoted their attention to their neighbors with all the intrusive power developed by two centuries of prying village life. As individuals and as a group, they were exceptional for high-mindedness and propriety of habits. One is, however, forever wishing to preach to them from the text: "And why beholdest thou the mote that is in thy brother's eye, but perceivest not the beam that is in thine own eye?"

Embodying these three elements, the movement for the abolition of slavery encountered special conditions which made it the most interesting of all both to contemporaries and to posterity. Long-continued development of European practice hastened by the earlier humanitarian movement of the eighteenth century had created a general sentiment of disapproval in the European world. The idealism of the Revolutionary period had been sufficient to abolish the institution in those parts of the United States where the disturbance of property rights and the social problem of the freed black were not too embarrassing. Before this generation appeared, slavery had ceased, or was in legal process of disappearance, in all states north of the southern boundary of Pennsylvania, which was known as the Mason and Dixon line, and of the Ohio. Moreover, the demarcation line had been extended, omitting the jog made by the slave state of Missouri, to prohibit slavery in the territory north of the parallel of $36° 30'$ to the Rocky Mountains, then the western limits of the United States.

While there was a general belief that this was a temporary division and that slavery would ultimately be eliminated, the only serious movement to bring this about was among the Quakers. Having declared against slavery, they had early adopted a discipline excluding members who held slaves. They continued to work against it, chiefly in the piedmont regions to the east and west of the Alleghenies where they had settlements. Some among them objected so strongly that they migrated to the north of the Ohio, forming a strong center in Indiana. Among the leaders was Benjamin Lundy, who from 1812 to 1836 published a periodical entitled *The Genius of Universal Emancipation.* Beginning his work in Ohio, he moved his head-quarters in 1824 to the slave city of Baltimore.

In the meantime the spirit of the French Revolution was sweeping slav-ery from its last recesses in the Christian portions of Europe and from the Latin American republics, and was buffeting it in the European colonies. Between 1800 and 1815 the slave trade had ceased to be a reputable source of income, and became a discredited and illegal occupation in all the more advanced countries. The Pope added his disapproval, and to these com-bined forces Spain and Portugal were forced to yield. The United States had prohibited the importation of slaves in 1808, and in 1819 declared the trade piracy. Throughout this period the agitation for abolition in the colonies of other countries was in full swing.

As slavery in the United States became more and more an isolated anach-ronism, pride added fuel to the zeal of those who aimed at its extinction here. The slow process of persuasion by example and mild sermonizing no longer sufficed the souls of those interested. To many it became no longer merely an undesirable habit or a political inconsistency but a crime to allow, a sin to practice. To Benjamin Lundy came in 1829 the twenty-four-year-old William Lloyd Garrison, a printer of Newburyport, Massachusetts. Garrison had had few conventional educational advantages, but at that time a printing shop was a university to the printer's devil who knew how to take advantage of his opportunities. Garrison, like Franklin and Greeley, became a cultured man—more so than Greeley, less than Franklin. His particular talent was as editor, and in this respect he has had few equals in America. Later he developed a capacity for public speaking, but his elo-quence was rather an intimate appeal to the few than the swaying of great masses.[145]

Quickly Garrison found the methods of Lundy too slow and compromis-ing. Unable to work under restrictions, he returned to the North, and in 1831 set up a paper of his own, the *Liberator.* In this he adapted the antislavery cause to the new spirit of the time. "I will be harsh as truth, as uncompromising as justice"; slavery was not an evolutionary economic institution but an immorality. He would have naught to do with expedi-ency. With Edwardean logic, every slaveholder became to him a sinner. The U.S. Constitution, by recognizing slavery, became a compact with hell; he would not recognize it until slavery was eliminated. Abolition must be immediate; it must be without compensation. The idea of removing the freed black from the country—a favorite project of Henry Clay and many others—was as sinful as slavery itself. The freed black must be admitted at once to full equality; equal, he would make his own place in society. Garrison's mottoes were: "I will not retreat one inch" and "I will be heard."

Bred in a strong Quaker tradition, Garrison was more keenly interested in the cause of universal peace than in anything except slavery. He would not, therefore, proceed against that institution by force. His interpretation of force, however, was distinctly limited. He encouraged blacks to run away, using the cartoon to reach their illiterate minds. He promoted the formation of what was known as the "Underground Railroad," a series of secret stopping places for the escaped slaves arranged to protect them on their way to freedom across the Canadian border.[146] To stir the latent disapproval of the North to acton, he lashed his audiences with tales of the injustices and atrocities of slavery, and eulogies of the black and of humanity. One of his earliest converts was the son of an aristocratic Boston family, Wendell Phillips, who became perhaps the greatest of our emotional orators after Patrick Henry.[147] The gradually gathering band of his supporters Garrison organized after the custom of the time. The first association was formed in 1831. In 1832 the New England society was organized, and then, in 1833, the American Anti-Slavery Society.

No movement of the time attracted so much attention, engaged so many active workers, or, with the exception of public education, won by the end of the period so wide a range of really interested support in the North. In legislative achievement, however, none seemed in 1850 more futile, nor was this because there were no small preliminary steps to take. In 1850 as in 1830, blacks nowhere lived under the same laws as whites, except in New England. In New York some voted, but beyond that state they were barred from the suffrage. In cities and on all routes of travel, slaves, personal servants of traveling masters, were a familiar sight, and were nearly everywhere held to their service by the law. Aside from a few state laws to protect their free black populations from claims of Southerners under the fugitive slave act of 1792 and a thriving colony of escaped blacks in Ontario, there was no apparent legal gain from the movement.[148] Privately, however, something had been done in the way of greater care and better educational opportunity for blacks in the North.

This relative lack of accomplishment was due to the special conditions of slavery. In the first place, slavery in America was a question of race; this of itself differentiated it from the other reforms. More important was the fact that slavery was sectional, and that the new movement came from the region in which it did not exist. This meant that the attackers had a simplicity of vision which ignored the difficulties of the situation, and that the attacked were not unnaturally stirred to high resentment. In 1835, for example, the people of Charleston invoked federal aid to prevent the post office from circulating abolitionist literature. President Jackson endorsed such local control of its functions, and in spite of action by Congress in 1836, the mails remained practically closed. The South was thus able to a considerable extent to exclude the agitation from its borders.

By 1840 the sectional cohesion of the South was fairly evident. It was to some degree, however, disguised from the eye, and was for twenty years prevented from the full exercise of its power by divergent views on matters of policy. One group of Southern leaders, distinguished by such figures as Calhoun and his youthful disciple, Jefferson Davis, followed the practice of Jefferson in relying upon the noninterference policy of the Democratic party for protection of their institutions. Another group, among whom the brilliant Georgians Alexander H. Stephens and Robert Toombs were, during the forties, becoming conspicuous, relied rather upon the class sympathy

 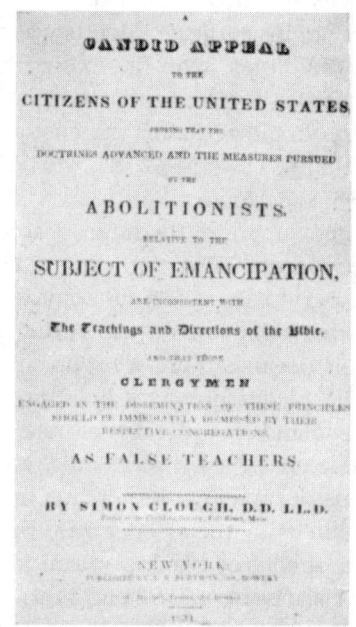

Proslavery men claimed that their institution was authorized by Nature and the Bible;

But even they deplored the necessity of the slave trade, as shown, for example, in this march of a gang to market.

and the general desire for stability which they found among the Northern Whigs. This division of Southern leaders as to the better course with reference to political alliances tended to diminish for a time the full force of the new sectionalism and to keep the political parties national throughout the period.[149]

It was natural that party leaders should exert their full influence to keep questions of slavery out of politics. Thus, in 1847, when John G. Palfrey, a Whig from Massachusetts, refused to vote for John C. Winthrop as speaker because he suspected that certain committee appointments would quash slavery discussion, there was an outburst of partisan wrath that the young James Russell Lowell satirized in a poem beginning

No? Hez he? He haint, though? Wut?
  Voted agin him?
Ef the bird of our country could ketch him,
  she'd skin him.[150]

The more sensitive organizations of the religious bodies were less able to resist.[151] In 1844 and 1845 the more democratic bodies, the Baptists and the Methodists, split on the subject, and there were organized a Southern Baptist Church and a Methodist Episcopal Church, South. The Presbyterians, with their stronger system, prevented separation for the time by agreeing not to meet. In a similar way periodicals became sectional or abstained from reference to sectional differences.

By the late 1840s, political developments had overtaken all hopes of achieving a national consensus of slavery. The Compromise of 1850 may reasonably be taken as the end of an era. History, of course, does not lend itself to division and all attempts are arbitrary; convenience, however, demands it, and from the point of view of presentation there is the justification that it renders possible a certain emphasis on forces which rise to dominance and fade. The year 1850 is least satisfactory from the material point of view, for the new economic forces continued with acceleration until 1857, when they encountered a debacle from which recovery was slow. The reform movements continue beyond 1850 with no conspicuous change until the organization of the Republican party, in 1854, when they merged for a time with general politics. The striking change of 1850 is in the controlling leadership. A few years before and after mark the passing of the group of men who emerged into national politics with the War of 1812, who assumed control in 1829, and who kept their grip on national affairs until they died. Jackson died in 1846, Calhoun in 1850, Clay and Webster in 1852. In the small span of life left the last two after the Compromise, all thought their earlier constructive program had vanished, and all their efforts were directed to maintaining their last work.

Their last work was in no sense the culmination to which they had looked forward. Certainly the brash young men who had taken it on themselves to run the nation in 1830 did not expect that the final work required of them would be the sacrifice of their ideals. It may be held, indeed, that in accepting this necessity they showed spiritual growth, but their sacrifice lacked the inspiring quality of finality. It is arguable that the Compromise saved the Union, but certainly not in the sense in which they conceived it.

There died, then, with its political leaders something of that geniality and universality that had characterized the optimism of this generation in its youth. There remained among the reformer element a sufficiency of élan, confidence in still obtaining their hopes in their own day, but more bitterness and hysteria. The conservatives gave over their struggle for a program and pessimistically tried to decide which was the lesser of two evils. They gave little evidence even of the catastrophic philosophy of Hamilton and George Cabot, that by hastening evils to run their full course they would promote the return of sanity. After 1850 one seems to be in a nation held together in part at least by reticence and restraint instead of by the free and trusting belief of 1830 that all good could be simultaneously pushed to rapid accomplishment.

THE BALANCE SHEET

IN CONTRASTING the picture of the United States at the beginning and at the end of the thirties and forties it is important to differentiate between the changes which had been made and those which were in process. The greatest change of all was the increase of diversity. It had not been an age of striking originality or of complete realization; it was—and this was inherent in its philosophy and its politics—an age of experimentation. Ideas which had long been formulated were taken into the laboratory and workshop and put into usable form. Not many of them were put into general use but they were made ready for use.

In brief comparison with the analysis of conditions in 1830 it may be said that no substantial change had been made in ideals. There had been some hammering into practical shape, some rise of skepticism; but no new elements had seriously entered into American thought. Population had increased from 12,866,020 to 23,191,876.[152] The material inheritance now passed on represented a substantial accumulation. The majority of the people were better housed and had more domestic conveniences; roads of all kinds had remarkably improved;[153] manufacturing equipment incomparably advanced and extended; luxuries had been turned into necessities; public institutions multiplied.[154] With the exception of some use of water and steam power, this had been accomplished by concentration on work and by labor-saving devices rather than by exploitation of natural resources, which remained as vast and now even more obvious than in 1830.

With regard to social inheritance, the case was different. It had been one of the purposes of the generation to break the aristocracy which had been so powerful in its youth and which so contrived to influence its taste. In this it had to a considerable extent succeeded. At least, the aristocracy was driven from power, except in the South, and its alliance with the rising moneyed class had not created a new body able to set standards of conduct. The provincial middle-class cultures had proved more stubborn; many of their props, however, had been torn from them. The Dutch, "Pennsylvania Dutch," and Quakers had distinctly lost ground. New England was expanding its influence, but was suffering dilution. The creation of a general American culture was lagging, though it was in process of formation. Its mandates were felt by those who violated its sensibilities, but it was as yet impossible to define its code or to separate the essential from the trivial in its habits.

In the matter of getting an education the change was one of the greatest in our history, and yet its effect may easily be exaggerated. The new thing was the evolution of a system. As, however, this began to develop only in the late thirties it had not been sufficiently carried into effect to have greatly influenced the education of those who were to receive the torch when this generation passed it on. Indeed, owing to the large influx of foreigners, the percentage of adult white persons who could not read and write increased from 3.77 to 5.03 in the two decades from 1830 to 1850.[155] Spasmodically, in certain districts, the rising generation were more ready with the pen and in handling books than their parents but one could not yet declare that the average American would know certain things, as was later to be the case. In higher education the change was not one of system but of development. Here and there young Americans were receiving in college an inspiration that twenty years earlier they had to bring to college with them. The foundation of small colleges had also run ahead of the increase of population, and a larger proportion of the people were receiving a college education. New ideas and methods of higher education, however, were still a whole generation away. Of an importance perhaps more immediate than any of these things was the spread of the means of adult education through all the new paraphernalia of publicity, which was making it increasingly difficult for the average citizen to escape some knowledge of things that the earnest had previously labored to secure.[156]

In the matter of making a living two striking changes had taken place. In agriculture a new era was beginning with the introduction of machinery. This, however, was of the things which as yet affected but a small proportion of the population. The important fact was that the chaotic agriculture of the West had taken form, or, rather, two forms. The frontier which had united to elect Andrew Jackson was in the process of division into the Northwest and Southwest, which were soon to fight each other, and the Ohio Valley, which this fight was to rend. Of all the forces making for this division none was more powerful than that of agricultural institutions. Into the Southwest had entered the plantation system of industrialized cultivation based on slavery, not indeed everywhere dominant in practice but universally dominant as an aim and hope. In the Northwest the scattered frontier farms had developed according to the model set by the Northeast: small farms cultivated by the owners with a minimum of hired help, each forming part of a community centering in a village. In the whole West there was, however, a common difference from the parent institutions of the East in that the aim was less to be self-sustaining and more to produce a selling crop. This meant that transportation was of fundamental importance. The South was a little better served by its river system, but this was not satisfactory. By 1850 the idea of canals had been dropped and all were looking with confidence to the railroads.

The other change in means of livelihood was that a continuously increasing number of Americans were relying upon wages, and that the community was accepting the idea of a permanent wage-earning class. Pick-and-shovel jobs were everywhere laying the material foundations of a new kind of civilization. Wage-earners increased also in the rapidly expanding business of internal transportation, and particularly in the developing factory system, which was not only steadily diminishing the dependence of Americans upon imports but, within the United States, displacing the handmade goods that had supplied most of the needs of 1830. Craftsmen were disappearing, but from the best among them was arising a class of skilled mechanics, who continued to exhibit standards of fine workmanship as well as an aptitude for invention.

Industry was obviously producing so much more wealth than had heretofore existed that there was comparatively little dissatisfaction. Several tendencies did, however, deserve attention. For one thing American prosperity was becoming more involved with that of Europe. As a crude index of this, it may be noted that American imports were valued at $70,876,920 in 1830, and at $178,138,318 twenty years later. In the same period the export trade of the United States grew in value from $73,849,508 to $151,898,720.[157] The increased consumption of American-grown cotton and the new demand for American-grown food products were the key to the rising high wages and profits. Again, the distribution of wealth was becoming more unequal. There was no decline in the general minimum, although, owing to causes social rather than economic, slums were becoming a problem in the large cities. The fortunes of the rich, however, were beyond anything previously dreamed of in America.

In the third place, this new wealth was beginning to exercise a control in the free states which the old aristocracy had not possessed.[158] The attack on banking had displaced the old aristocracy only to substitute another, a moneyed class. In the Northeast the relative desirability of well-located city land had created for certain families, such as the Astors, fortunes which aroused the emulation of speculators in the West. The development of the transportation system, chiefly by private corporations, gave small groups of directors a hold upon the fortunes of communities which had previously been unknown in this country. Most important of all, the factory system, as yet practically unchecked by legislation or by the organization of labor, made a few the arbiters of destiny for the many.

Among specific achievements, probably the greatest was the realization of Manifest Destiny in the rounding out of the territory of the United States. To the 1,787,159 square miles held in 1830 had been added 1,194,007.[159] With very slight exceptions the area over which the American people have chosen, or been able, to expand their civilization was in 1850 under the American flag. Little as this was accepted in 1850 as final, it corresponds in the main with the original ideas of the generation.

Next in importance, among material things, was the actual occupation of the Mississippi Valley and the establishment of far-flung posts in Oregon, Texas, Utah, and California. By 1850 the people had run their first plow over the colossal region that Jefferson had thought would occupy them for a thousand generations, had advanced beyond it, and were actually being held back from certain portions by the law rather than by lack of vitality for the work.

An accomplishment of a different kind was the completion of the railroad system, which had reached a point where it could, and soon would, be spun like a web over the vast expanse of the nation. In 1830 the steam railroad could hardly be said to exist; by 1850 it had attained a mileage of more than 9,000.[160] If after 1850 no improvements had been made, the railroad would nevertheless be one of the greatest factors in the life of today. The same may be said of its handmaid, the telegraph. Less progress, however, was made in the case of the other great utilities. Agricultural machinery was well started, but did not yet constitute a system. The sewing machine was invented, but still needed to be applied to leather. The ocean-going steamship reached a high point of usefulness, but was rather a gift to America than a native production. In fact, the lavishness of American productivity at this time is evinced by the fact that, at the very period when steam was beginning to rule the ocean, our shipwrights were sending out the most superb wind-driven craft the world has ever seen, the Baltimore clippers.[161]

Already in 1850 the railroad, the telegraph, and the ocean steamship were affecting the life of practically every American home. Just over the line, in 1851, letter postage was made three cents for 3,000 miles instead of five cents for 300 miles. Whatever may be its effect, it is at least a change to have news promptly, and news of Paris could reach New Orleans in less than half the time possible in 1830, and did so more regularly.[162] Owing to the general economic situation of the day, these new instruments reduced the prices of things dealers bought, and increased them for things they sold.

Without notable change in methods of construction the population was nevertheless better housed than twenty years before. In the Northwest but few years elapsed before the original log cabin became a corncrib, pigpen, or kitchen and a first real house arose. Therefore, while there was no marked change in the character of the American house, fewer Americans were living in temporary structures.

Inside the house the amount of furniture had considerably increased, but its character had already begun to deteriorate with the employment of factory-made products. There was some increase in gaiety; more floors were covered with carpets instead of rag rugs; more rooms were decorated with wallpaper, which began to blossom into wilder colors; while lithographs and process-produced chromos spotted the wall spaces. Lighting had generally improved. While gas was rare and poor, lamps were common, and there was more effort to light rooms instead of lighting merely one's work or book. While lamps did little to diminish the labor of the housewife, matches almost universally removed one long-standing source of ill-temper.

The most important change in living conditions, however, was to be found almost solely in cities, and that was the running of water out of faucets from city mains and the draining of sewage into central systems. From these already began, for the more well-to-do, the blessings of indoor toilets and baths. Indeed, the effect of such changes was more widespread than one might suppose. One could hardly imagine in 1830 what happened in 1851, when two students of the pioneer Lawrence College at Appleton, Wisconsin, rigged up a shower bath of perforated tin through which they doused each other with ice-cold water from frozen pails. One certainly reads also of more enjoyment of open-air bathing, not only on the beaches of the East but in the forest streams and lakes of the West, and one gathers that Americans began to be somewhat cleaner than heretofore.

In the whole matter of food and clothes, changes were rather in the nature of fashions than of methods. Food indeed changed little except for the gradual increase of coffee drinking. This new habit may have been the result of South American independence or of the temperance movement, or perhaps merely the discovery of an agreeable aroma. Stoves, however, were better and more common. Dress became less distinguishing as to class, though it still marked city or country origin. The women of the cities followed with increasing nervous pleasure the changes of fashion, the standards shifting during the period from London to Paris.[163] Not yet were the originals chosen in the foreign capital by their wearers. Dressmakers constructed the first examples from models and plates and, with a skill of eye and finger which seems to have been universal among American women, they were cheapened and multiplied until American city crowds were already among the most uniformly and fashionably dressed in the world. For men and women all this was still the result of the hard-driven needle of housewife, dressmaker, or tailor. Such clothes were more substantial than those of today and intended for longer wear. It is only in comparison with 1830 that the changes were quicker, and the most notice-able thing is the democratic spread of fashion over a larger portion of the population.

Americans were somewhat more gregarious in habit than they had been, which was obviously due, in large part, to the improvement in the means of transportation. There is evidence also that a larger number of them had some leisure time and energy. In both cases instinct was still controlled by

Fashions for 1844.

Smart gentlemen of the period not only learned the Polka, but began to grow beards.

past conditions and habits. Except for the small group of city rich, they were apt to spend their leisure on production, such as fancywork, rather than on cards or sport, and to assemble for some useful and convenient purpose. On the frontier a houseraising was still a social event. Increasingly the church social gave the odor of sanctity, and the convenience of a necessary meal, to pleasant gatherings. Idling was still unpopular and was possible only to those who could set others to work for them.

The art and science of the period had as yet little effect on the life of the community. They were generally respected in the abstract, but appreciation and support for them came almost entirely from the discredited aristocracy, which thus found a new field for the activity previously given to politics. In music there was some improvement in the popular taste, but this was confined for the most part to such forms as hymns and songs suited to parlor use, in which many could take part. The literature produced by the generation, if inferior to that of England or France, was certainly far superior to anything produced in America before; and the foundations were laid for something of choice and lasting value.

Foreign travel for pleasure, on a considerable scale, began about the middle of the forties. Perhaps the founding of the Collins Line in 1847 with a subsidy from the U.S. government may be taken as the beginning.[164] Foreigners in America were a much more common sight in 1840 than in 1830, and at the very end of the period they became a factor and a problem. While they were soon to create one of those violent reactions of nativism which have from time to time occurred in the United States, there seems in this generation little foundation on which to build an expectation of such a movement. Violent feeling against them was confined to a few large cities. On the whole the attitude toward them seems to have been condescending and kindly.

In few periods of American history did conscious borrowing of European ideas, as in the case of education and communistic experiments, excite so little hostility. The temporary and fading superiority of the material civilization of Europe and the fact that in political matters that continent would ultimately sit at the feet of the American Gamaliel were accepted by the majority as axioms. Equally axiomatic was the belief that for the United States to assume what garb of Europe it wished and for Europe to digest the American political system would both be easy tasks.

While laying the foundations for the industrial America that was to come, this generation showed that it had not lost that genius for constructive political practice which had characterized their ancestors. Far less versed in political thought than their forebears and less able to concentrate on such problems, they nevertheless effected, in the convention system, a compromise between pure democracy and representative government, which must be considered as among the real contributions to the forms of government, and which, while it became later clogged in some of its main manifestations, still operates with an efficiency so smooth that it is seldom recognized.

Equally important, though not so new, was the evolution of the business corporation in such a form as to secure capital from one district to spend in another under a central control. In fact, no decision of the generation was probably so important as that limitation of the functions of government which forced the development of this machinery. In 1850 the corporation stood almost as complete as the railroad system, ready to assume the gigantic tasks the next two generations would thrust upon it.

With less evidence of result, this generation was attempting to solve the problems, always joined in the American mind, of a circulating medium and of a banking system. On the surface its accomplishments were destructive. Taking advantage of the federal system of an Independent Treasury, however, men of affairs in the states were trying out ideas and conducting experiments. As practical ideas, worked out were the licensing and inspection of banking institutions, the clearinghouse method of quickly detecting a lack of solvency, and the plan of a paper currency resting upon publicly controlled funds. It was on these foundations that a satisfactory national system was ultimately constructed in the sixties.

Perhaps more amazing than these contributions to material life and to organization was what the generation did to its character—the traits which it acquired and passed on to its descendants. It is not necessary to assume that human nature changed; it was rather that blindness in certain directions was rendered no longer possible. At any rate, one becomes conscious of a certain general humaneness to a degree not previously observable. In part this was, like the progress of invention, a world movement. It had, however, certain characteristics distinctively American. The most remarkable demonstration was to be given when the Civil War came on and was fought in an atmosphere of thoughtfulness which had been unknown in all previous wars.

Kindred to this was the ability which large numbers of the generation showed to change their own habits. Particularly, the adoption of total abstinence was a striking illustration of a power of self-control, which would not have been expected by the casual observer, but which the student must have predicted for a generation which reduced government to a skeleton and yet ran to construction rather than to anarchy.

Among the conscious purposes of the generation was the preservation and strengthening of the Union. In the development of its material program and of new organizations, it was spinning a web which seemed to render separation more and more difficult and was actually to prove the foundation of a much closer national life. It must be remembered, however, that closer contacts and intimacies may mean fiercer disagreement instead of harmony. Increasing communication might in time smooth away some of the provincial differences, but was more apt immediately to intensify them. It would certainly be long before it could blend the rival material interests of the physiographic sections into a whole conscious of the mutual dependence of their several prosperities. It was certainly these more disastrous immediate results of the more closely knit life of the nation that became more obvious as the decades waned.

More striking was the change in the larger sectionalism based on a combination of elements material and immaterial. In 1830 the outstanding sectionalism of the country was that between the East and the West, the old and the new, the parent section and the colony, whose divergencies were at the root of so many of the problems of party politics and the main issues of political campaigns. The development of the period decidedly lessened these antagonisms, which indeed the American colonial system and the Jeffersonian code of politics tended to reduce to a minimum. By 1850 the Mississippi Valley was ceasing to be frontier, and was settling into a consciousness of its more permanent interests based on its nature and the characteristics of its population.

Meanwhile a new sectionalism, of which much slighter evidences had previously existed, was coming to the forefront of politics and of American life with such momentous steps that as many of the patriotic were endeavoring to be deaf to its advance as were racking their brains for a way to stop it. This was, of course, that of the North and South, with the issue of slavery as the chief, though not the only, irritant. Still held apart by a middle region of doubt and of mediation, the extremes were approaching each other with hostile mien, and the Mason and Dixon line was becoming a division between two purposes apparently more permanent, and infinitely more bitterly opposed, than had been the East and West in 1830.

When one considers the tendencies working through this period and its genuine accomplishments, one must rise from its study with a feeling very different from that of the travelers who hastily observed a cross section of all these slightly bound and so greatly different movements, or from that of the reader of the newspaper who read each day what was sensational and picturesque. Never was the surface of American life so chaotic; seldom has a nation been more absurd, and the absurdity was part of the reality. One could walk up Broadway and visit Barnum's Museum, and that was America. One could, if one had permission, visit the machine shops of the Stevens family across the river, and that was America. One could spend a day at Concord and talk philosophy with Emerson and visit Agassiz's laboratory on the way, and that was America. One could drink a mint julep with Robert Toombs of Georgia and damn New England, or 'midst the splashing of ink, hear from Garrison a logical demonstration that the difference between the slaveholding Bishop Polk of Louisiana and the inmates of the penitentiary at Auburn was all in favor of the latter; and both were evidences of America. Of course, such contrasts may be found at all times and places, but in this period their existence denoted the lack of a common standard by which to evaluate these differences. They were equal contemporaries in a life that recognized all as equal—whatever they might think of each other.

The generation of the thirties and forties did not evaluate, it destroyed taste; it produced, and let time value its products. It saw the acme of a particular development of individualism which had for some time been gaining ground and from which there was to be a rapid change to a more rigid system of community control. It presents one of the outstanding instances in history of the working of individuals trammeled by a minimum of law and convention. Its accomplishments were almost unprecedentedly the work of individuals, for leaders had little to enforce their leadership; they were the result of the independent work of more individuals than had ever before been free to work by and for themselves, at what they chose, and how they pleased.

BOOK VII

The Irrepressible

Conflict,

1850–65

THE LAND OF CHIVALRY

IN THE 1850s the black belt of the South, the region of heaviest slave population, attained its highest development, spreading over nearly one third the territory of Dixie. Black chattel became part of the agricultural economy not only of the plantations in the fertile river bottoms but also of many small upland farms. Yet never had the lines of social cleavage been so closely drawn. The plantation oligarchy had its nucleus in some 300 planters, each of whom owned 200 slaves or more; a group of 2,300 others were lords over 100 each; while fewer than 200,000 owned as many as ten slaves and 77,000 could each command the labors of but a single black. In all the region there were scarcely 384,000 slaveholders in 1860 out of a population of over 8 million whites. This meant that slightly more than one out of every four whites was directly or indirectly connected with slaveholding as against one out of three in 1850. Of this number only a quarter of a million enjoyed the full fruits of a plantation system that required a working unit of at least twenty field hands.[1] Many Southerners like Joseph E. Johnston, A. P. Hill, and Fitzhugh Lee never owned a slave.

Nevertheless, the plantation ideal more than ever dominated the South. To become a larger planter was the aspiration of every ambitious youth. Some nursed this ambition in the squalor of humble hill-country cabins, others in the luxury of comfortable city homes, while the elect awaited their inevitable inheritance on their paternal estates. The planter-aristocrat on his broad acres represented a leisure class that was genial, picturesque, and patriarchal. Not all took part in public affairs; even some of the largest planters like Samuel Hairston of Pittsylvania, Virginia, or J. C. Johnson of North Carolina dwelt in contented obscurity.[2] The result is that time has left few traces of men like William B. Goulden, who was reputed to be the largest slaveholder in Georgia.[3] The plantation was the center of social life in the South, though the winter months usually brought a shift to the gaiety of a nearby city—Baltimore, Richmond, Charleston, Mobile, or New Orleans—and summer a brief respite at some Northern resort or Southern watering place.

One feature of this aristocracy in former times had been its flexibility, evidenced by the ease with which a small farmer, town merchant, or sometimes even an ambitious mechanic rose into its ranks. The coming of the railroads led the professional men in the cities sometimes to purchase rural estates and, in the occasional visits of an absentee proprietor, to taste the pleasures of plantation ownership. In general, however, the fifties found the landed gentry chary about admitting newcomers to their circles. Not only did the price of slaves and worthwhile land steadily mount, but the parvenu was not always welcomed into an aristocracy in which a generation or two of slaveholding had fostered a tradition of birthright.

The best contemporary picture of social stratification is that drawn in 1860 by D. R. Hundley, an Alabama planter. At the top stood the plantation aristocrats. Then came the middle class made up of smaller slaveholding planters, professional men, tradesmen, and skilled mechanics. Next followed the yeomen, while separated from them by an almost impassable chasm were the "poor whites." Underneath all were the blacks, slave or free. Members of the middle class were usually deficient in culture and refinement and, according to Hundley, they "sometimes, from sheer envy and jealousy, entertain a most cordial hatred of those whose attainments and good-breeding they despair of ever being able to emulate."[4] Of this group the skilled artisans were least likely to be slave owners. Their contact with slaves—and with free blacks—was almost exclusively with those with whom they competed in their work. In the fifties they demanded legislation to prevent such competition, a demand effectively launched at a mechanics' state convention in Georgia on July 4, 1851.[5] But while the proposal was considered in several states, slaveholders were averse to any effort to prescribe the way in which they might employ or hire out their slaves.[6] Signs abounded in the late fifties of an increasing class consciousness among white workingmen, which might have marked the beginning of a revolt against the institution. Thus, in North Carolina, an organized workers' movement challenged a twenty-year-old revenue system because it taxed mechanics' tools twenty times as heavily as slave property.[7]

The yeomanry consisted of small farmers on the hilly fringes of the black belt, where they raised varied crops and lived mainly on "hog and hominy."

They represented the surviving influence of the later stages of the frontier. Usually tall, lean, crude, tobacco-chewing, profane, they were also honest and pious, and in number they constituted the backbone of Southern society. Sometimes owning, sometimes hiring, a slave or two, they worked with their children side by side with the blacks. Their greatest ambition was to become slaveholders; whenever they achieved that status, even on a small scale, they were extremely proud. As they acquired more slaves, they rose in social standing to the middle group. It was from this class, too, that the plantation overseers were usually recruited. In the fifties, however, many of the yeomen, weary of wringing a scant subsistence from a scrap of hillside land, tended to become discouraged and to settle down to habits of sloth and idleness.[8] Traveling through the backcountry of the South from the Mississippi to the James, Frederick Law Olmsted never observed in their homes a "thermometer, nor a book of Shakespeare, nor a pianoforte or sheet of music, nor . . . reading lamp, nor an engraving, or a copy of any kind, of a work of art of the slightest merit."[9] It was to this group and its supposed discontent that Hinton Rowan Helper appealed when in 1857 he published *The Impending Crisis of the South,* in which he challenged "the lords of the lash" as foes "of all non-slaveholding whites, whose freedom is merely nominal, and whose unparalleled illiteracy and degradation is purposely and fiendishly perpetuated."[10]

Helper's failure to arouse the white masses emphasizes the chief paradox of the Southern social system. Though slavery raised ever higher barriers against nonslaveholding whites and in many ways sacrificed the latter to its own prosperity, a greater number of the people than ever before—from the planter capitalists at the top to the willing peasant hangers-on at the bottom—were drawn into some sort of active support of the "peculiar institution." Less than ever before, apparently, did the gentry need to dread leveling agrarian tendencies, or to fear lest they be unhorsed politically by the introduction of the "white basis" of apportioning representation in place of the "mixed" or "federal" system. Indeed, a slaveholding leadership, which included many of the wildest fire eaters in the South, was marshaling in political array the ranks of the unprivileged.

And yet all was not well in the South. The planter leaders realized they could not rely absolutely upon the contentment of the nonslaveholder, especially as, in the fifties, the poor-white class took on more definite outline. An original pioneer stock, drained by the westward movement of its most energetic and ambitious elements, it found itself isolated in the mountainous Appalachian backcountry and in the piny sand barrens of south-central Georgia and eastern Mississippi. Physically undermined by attacks of what was called "malaria," and by a wide range of disorders now known to have been due to the hookworm, some of its members degenerated until they became satisfied with the barest human necessities and with few social enjoyments. At their best, with simple piety and frugality, they eked out a precarious livelihood by tilling a scrubby farm, supplementing its yield with hunting and fishing or by doing occasional chores for a nearby planter. At their worst they ate clay, chewed resin and snuff, drank fiery "rot-gut" whiskey, and dreamed on in blissful ignorance of the contempt with which the outside world regarded them.

The planters showed no desire to employ these "hillbillies" at farm labor, nor would the latter have been willing to toil alongside the slave, whom they thoroughly scorned but over whom they could not always show a marked superiority. Pioneer manufacturers saw in them an available labor supply to bring about in the South the industrial revolution which they foretold. William Gregg employed them in his cotton factory at Graniteville, South Carolina, and gave them a chance to settle the question as to whether ignorance, shiftlessness, and contentment with poverty were inherent qualities or the result of circumstances. Most critics of the poor whites, however, saw little hope for them. Scorned by the groups that surrounded them, the highlanders of western Carolina and of the eastern parts of Kentucky and Tennessee failed to share the general enthusiasm for the "peculiar institution" of the South. Indeed, sometimes they revealed a bitter hatred toward the slaves as well as toward the slave barons. In this attitude the poor white was often encouraged by those who sought his political support. Many a politician wallowed in a demagoguery that attested a degenerate conception of democracy both by the voter and the candidate.[11]

At the very bottom of the social pyramid stood the blacks, numbering in 1860 over 4 million. Of these, 3,838,765 were enslaved.[12] The institution of chattel slavery can best be interpreted historically as an educational as well as labor system in which, without his consent and in return for his forced labor, the black was given his keep and taught some of the elementary lessons of white civilization. By 1850, however, it should have been an open question as to whether or not the institution had outlived its usefulness. There was certainly little in the system to make it keep pace with the march of events; more and more the planter was in a position to realize its economic unsoundness. In a detailed analysis of the Southern system one of the editors of the *Southern Cultivator* frankly admitted that "the amount of labor used on an ordinary Southern plantation is greater per productive acre than the amount of labor used in the most perfectly cultivated portions of Europe" and that "the negro is the investment rather than the land."[13] Under slavery land was soon worn out in an exhausting one-crop agriculture and scrapped. It remained only for the Southerner to realize the significance of the fact that the heavy capital investment in labor had no equivalent under a wage system.

Moreover, while the essential needs of the black were cared for, the system had little to teach those slaves who displayed signs of initiative and ingenuity. Individuals, to be sure, profited from contact with their masters or from the mechanical employments into which they drifted, either on the home plantation or when hired out to others. But if some were given wide latitude of self-expression, most were lost in the system of absentee ownership with overseer control, such as was common throughout the Lower South. The overseer, generally a semiliterate representative of the humbler white element, was all too often a mere slave driver. Naturally enough, he kept his accounts in terms of dollars and cents and not in human values. Yet one half of the slaves were held in parcels of less than twenty and hence labored under the eye of the owner. From a maze of conflicting testimony by contemporary observers, mainly travelers, it is reasonably clear that the average slaveholder was genuinely concerned for the physical well-being of his "chattels." Some would not allow their slaves to go into the field to pick cotton while the dew was on the plant; some employed white laborers, usually Irish floaters, to do strenuous and unhealthful work such as ditch digging and draining.

As the sectional controversy sharpened, life in thralldom lost many of its mitigating aspects; Southern hearts were hardened by the mere thought of outside dictation or interference.[14] Laws against teaching slaves to read no longer remained dead letters. Police regulations and precautions for the control of slaves were revised and extended while the machinery for enforcement was strengthened. The curfew became an insistent reality, in Charleston for free blacks as well as for slaves. Bondsmen attempting to run away were flogged with less mercy than ever. "Judge Lynch" punished the black's more serious crimes, sometimes at the stake, with the active approval of sober citizens. All too often the atmosphere reeked with fear and suspicion. As a result, greater brutality colored the authority of master over slave.

Yet the lot of the enslaved black was probably not much more unfortunate than that of his free brother in the South. Indeed, an occasional black, given his choice, preferred slavery to the uncertainties of freedom.[15] It was hardly for this reason, however, that in 1860 the free colored population of the slave states was only 260,000, a number which represented a smaller rate of increase than that of any other group in the nation. Of these about half were to be found in Virginia and Maryland. Probably the more aggressive and capable ones migrated to the North. At any rate, those who remained had the reputation of being "the most vicious and corrupting element in southern life."[16] They were charged with most of the crimes; nor could the numerous convictions be explained entirely as the result of prejudice or by their lack of civil rights.

Free blacks were generally confined to menial employments scorned by the whites. From certain skilled occupations they were excluded by law. In some states, like Georgia and Mississippi, they virtually lacked school facilities, less than ten black children being enrolled for the two states according to both the census of 1850 and that of 1860.[17] Inevitably they drifted townward to find employment and escape the restraints of the plantation regime; in the crowded black quarters of Washington and New Orleans they developed their own churches, schools, and mutual improvement societies. In New Orleans, where the mulattoes outnumbered the pure strain, they were largely skilled workers and, in a community essentially cosmopolitan, received unusual consideration.[18] Both here and in other large cities individuals among them attained a high degree of prosperity and culture. Economic opportunities enabled 360 free blacks of Charleston to accumulate sufficient property to have it listed on the tax duplicates of 1860, while their real estate holdings were valued at $724,570. One hundred and thirty even owned slaves, to a total of 190.[19]

In all, Southern free blacks in 1860 owned property valued at $25 million. James P. Roper, natural son of an eccentric English planter, added by his own efforts to his inheritance until he became the largest landowner and the wealthiest man in Jefferson County, Virginia.[20] At least one in every 100 free blacks owned a "chattel" or two, a few controlling parcels of fifty and more. In some cases they purchased relatives to free them; often, however, it was a purely business transaction—nor were they invariably generous masters. In Louisiana, certain opulent and refined planters of black-French ancestry claimed and were duly conceded the status of Southern gentlemen.[21] In the crisis of 1861 some of the black masters publicly declared their unqualified loyalty to the Southern institutions which had enabled them to rise on the shoulders of their fellow blacks.

The presence of free blacks, however, came increasingly to be regarded by the dominant race as a menace.[22] Many of the 20,000 slaves manumitted during the decade were set free upon condition of migration to the free states. A demand even arose for legislation to reenslave any blacks who failed to leave. Arkansas enacted such a law to take effect on January 1, 1860. Similar measures were considered in other states, but in Missouri the bill was defeated by the governor's veto, while in Maryland, where the large free black population intensified the fugitive-slave problem, the voters in 1860 rejected an exclusion proposal submitted by the legislature. Louisiana and Kentucky forbade the further immigration of free blacks. As the day approached upon which the Arkansas law was to go into effect, a general exodus of blacks began. While a few preferred the authority of a master to the uncertainties of seeking a new home, the majority poured into Kansas or took passage up the Mississippi.[23] On January 3, forty-three exiles landed at Cincinnati where a committee representing the black population bade them welcome. But Illinois and Indiana, the two nearest free states, had long since closed their doors to such migrants; nor did the whites of any other Northern state invite their coming. The pitiful appeal of a group of these helpless exiles soon appeared in the public prints; it suggested that many probably regretted not having accepted their fate in Arkansas.[24]

The South was also becoming troubled about what had formerly been deemed a highly desirable addition to her population. Thanks to the part played by Northern-born citizens, certain Southern towns had come to be characterized as "Northern towns." Indeed, many of the largest slave owners as well as of the influential business and professional men and prominent political leaders had originally hailed from Pennsylvania, New York, or New England. For a time the push and enterprise of these Yankees had been a spur to many Southerners to go and do likewise. As sectional bitterness increased, however, more and more concern was felt over the presence of "outsiders." It was soon evident that a type of espionage was developing by which recent comers were kept under surveillance. After John Brown's raid upon Harper's Ferry the tension became especially strong. Travelers of all sorts were stopped and compelled to give an account of themselves and their business in the South. Alleged abolitionists were tarred and feathered and expelled, while certain unfortunates were subjected to the extreme penalty of lynch law.[25] Such conditions not only checked the flow of population into the South, but caused many local agents of Northern business firms to leave in order to avoid annoyance, if not positive maltreatment. In this way, too, the years immediately before the war led to a gradual severing of social and economic connections between the sections.

Militant Southerners were not averse to erecting a Chinese wall against the barbarians of the North. They claimed that their section enjoyed the superior opportunities for culture and refinement that only a leisure-class society based upon the exploitation of a servile race could assure. Others, however, pointed to the scanty returns upon the planters' capital, complaining that they could not surround themselves "with comforts and luxuries, and the advantages of education, like other men."[26] In any event, the narrow confines of this culture could not be denied in the face of prevailing illiteracy.

The long-haired Southern youths, served by their black valets, had for years attended colleges and universities in greater numbers proportionately than their Northern contemporaries; yet few were inspired to carry on the torch. Higher education in the South, inadequately supported and, perforce, modest in its standards, was largely in the hands of instructors drawn from the North or abroad. The cultural poverty of Dixie caused extensive patronage of Northern and foreign universities. The sectionalism of the fifties, however, bred a demand for greater educational self-sufficiency. Southerners were exhorted to cease sending their youth to Northern institutions, to hire Southern teachers whenever possible, and to utilize schoolbooks published in their own section. As a result, nearly every college and university doubled in attendance, institutions were accorded a more generous support, and new ventures were launched.[27] Most ambitious was the dream of the bishops of the Southern dioceses of the Protestant Episcopal Church, who, under the leadership of Leonidas Polk and with the support of eminent Southerners, projected the "University of the South." In the fall of 1860 the cornerstone of the main building was laid on the chosen site at Sewanee, Tennessee, and contributions toward an endowment of $5 million were coming in when the war interrupted the promising undertaking.[28]

Yet it was clear that this movement for more colleges and universities would not assure the South a sound educational development. The glorification of the status quo, the defense of social and economic institutions already threatened by crumbling foundations, could not wisely have been substituted for the search for truth and the spirit of open-mindedness. When Professor B. S. Hedrick of the University of North Carolina was dismissed for having favored the election of Frémont, his academic brethren plodded on in humble subserviency lest they, too, share the same fate. In 1857 the University of Virginia, forgetful of its rich Jeffersonian tradition, was advertising for a professor of history and literature at a handsome salary, but there were few applicants. Who wants a professorship without freedom of teaching? it was asked.[29]

In the same way the South cut itself off from other intellectual contacts with the North. Northern publishers noticed a decline in the sale of their works in the Southern states after 1850, although it was observed in 1851 that there was a sudden increase in orders from South Carolina for works on military tactics.[30] Yet there was no corresponding development of Southern publishing. The recurrent Southern conventions repeatedly endorsed proposals for a publishing agency within the section, and in 1857 even went so far as to provide for a committee to select and prepare a series of Southern schoolbooks "in every department of study, from the earliest primer to the highest grade of literature and science, as shall seem to them best qualified to elevate and purify the education of the South."[31] But the very magnitude of the undertaking stood in the way of success. Somewhat later a protagonist of the South, impressed by the influence of works issuing from Harvard scholars in molding opinion, expressed a pious hope that a similar "university press" might be established in Dixie.[32] But it was a byword in Southern literary circles that the planter failed to sustain the various mushroom periodicals that sought his attention. Even the excellent *Southern Literary Messenger* received an uncertain support, while the *Southern Quarterly Review,* started in 1842, reached the end of its resources in 1856.[33]

Cultured Charleston produced little creative literature; its social set looked askance even at William Gilmore Simms who, proud Southerner that he was, persisted in his efforts to give the South an indigenous literature. No wonder then that the youthful and rebellious Sidney Lanier chafed at the limitations of his homeland and found a more appreciative Northern audience. Nor did the antebellum South really glimpse the poetic genius of

Henry Timrod and Paul Hamilton Hayne, whose talents were discovered and duly heralded by the generous Simms. Though all these spoke as loyal Southerners, they wrought their success without encouragement from the planter aristocracy.

Similarly, the aristocratic ideal did little to make even a common-school education generally available. Though there were beginnings of public education in Maryland, Virginia, South Carolina, and Louisiana and in the cities of certain other states, these only faintly reflected the educational awakening which had swept through the North and West in the preceding generation.[34] Secondary schools, supported by taxation, existed in such cities as New Orleans and Charleston, but the white youth of the South largely attended academies and private schools.

With the increasing tension of the sectional controversy the supply of Northern teachers dropped off. There was much talk of filling the need locally, but there were available in the whole section only two normal schools, one in North Carolina, which in 1859 became Trinity College, the other in Charleston, dating from 1857. For one reason or another many Southern schools declined visibly during the decade. A writer in *De Bow's Review,* after perusing the *Annual Report* of the superintendent of public instruction, announced that a "ten years' trial" of public education in Louisiana had revealed that over half the families of that state would not avail themselves of such opportunities and that the New England system was "not adapted to Louisiana and the South."[35] Some, in their subserviency to the dominant institution of the South, probably shared the bitterness of the critic who declared:

> We have got to hating everything with the prefix free, from free negroes down and up through the whole catalogue—free farms, free labor, free society, free will, free thinking, free children, and free schools—all belonging to the same brood of damnable isms. But the worst of all abominations is the modern system of free schools, which has been the cause and prolific source of the infidelity and treasons that have turned her [Northern] cities into Sodoms and Gomorrahs, and her land into the nestling places of howling Bedlamites. We abominate the system because the schools are free.[36]

The average white southerner busied himself with revamping the now threadbare arguments in defense of slavery. For his convenience the efforts of its chief protagonists were assembled and published in 1852 under the title *The Pro-Slavery Argument.* Southern slavery, it was iterated and reiterated, was a humane and beneficent system that well supplied the needs of the black chattels. It extended its patriarchal care to the weak and aged while Northern industrialism callously threw its used-up free labor upon the scrap heap. It guaranteed law and order to the South while Northern almshouses, jails, and prisons were filling. It cleared the way to a genuine liberty for white freemen, for it laid the foundations of a cultivated and refined society, intelligently organized in contrast with the sprawling anarchy of the North. Human bondage, moreover, had the stamp of Holy Writ: Was this not the testimony of the tenth commandment and the numerous other scriptural references to servants and their duty of obedience to their masters? Slavery had erected the magnificent temple of Solomon; instead of rebuking the practice in abolition sermons Christ and later St. Paul and St. Peter had repeated the injunction of obedience. The wise men of the past, in general, Aristotle and the rest, had proclaimed its value. The Roman Empire had wrought much with slave labor. Indeed this institution had been an essential of every successful and well-ordered society in history.

As his contribution to the cause, William R. Smith, then president of Randolph-Macon College, published in 1856 his oft-repeated *Lectures on the Philosophy and Practice of Slavery.* Albert J. Bledsoe followed with his *Essay on Liberty and Slavery* and Thomas R. R. Cobb brought out his *Inquiry into the Laws of Negro Slavery.* There was an increasing use of the ethnological argument—helped by the first intimations of Darwinism—to the effect that blacks were an inferior race. Abolition, it was argued, meant the Africanization of the South and the end of white civilization there. Though it was a fundamental proposition that only Southerners could understand the problems of race relationship that lay at the root of their social system, the most intensive analysis of this issue was that of a Northern writer, Dr. John H. Van Evrie, who with pseudoscientific gusto declared the black to belong to a debased race and slavery to be his normal condition.[37] Other champions, resenting the insinuations of antislavery writers

An ideal plantation home.

like Harriet Beecher Stowe, entered the lists. In the three years that followed the publication of *Uncle Tom's Cabin* fourteen proslavery novels appeared picturing more favorable aspects of domestic slavery.[38] Somewhat later, with more concern for authentic data, Edward A. Pollard submitted the racy realism of his *Black Diamonds Gathered in the Darkey Homes of the South.*[39]

The Jeffersonian creed of human equality was frankly repudiated by all champions of the Southern system. Slavery was declared the only sure foundation of republican government because of its success in uniting capital and labor. Indeed, the argument logically pointed to the spread of slavery throughout the American republic. The South thus supplemented its defensive tactics with a vigorous offensive. Perhaps the most versatile and provocative advocate of this point of view was George Fitzhugh of Port Caroline, Virginia. Residing in the rural isolation of a tiny community in tidewater Virginia, he boldly wielded the cudgel in behalf of the "peculiar institution" in a manner quite without a parallel. In the early forties he "became satisfied that slavery, black or white, was right and necessary." He undertook to arouse the South to taking "higher ground in the defense of Slavery; justifying it as a normal and natural institution, instead of excusing and apologizing for it, as an exceptional one." Proclaiming himself an enemy to free society, he warned Northern capitalists against abolitionism as the handmaid of a radicalism and agrarianism that was threatening their own vested interests. He urged their alliance, offensively as well as defensively, with the South to stem this tide; slavery is the normal status of the laborer and the Northern states may yet have to introduce it, he argued.[40] This view had just enough currency in the Southern press to act as a boomerang, for Northern agitators seized the opportunity to exhort the wage-earners to scotch the viper, slavery, before it struck at their own freedom. Indeed, for proclaiming this doctrine an editor of the *Charleston Mercury* had the distinction in 1854 of being burned in effigy by the indignant mechanics of the capital of his state.[41]

By this generation also the finishing touches were put upon the biblical argument for slavery.[42] In its behalf the Southern divine invoked the strictest literalism; indeed, the section was well on the road to a religious fundamentalism that repudiated the old Jeffersonian free-thinking tradition. With missionary zeal, on Thanksgiving day, 1860, the Reverend Benjamin Morgan Palmer proclaimed from his pulpit in New Orleans that God had imposed upon the South the duty of maintaining and spreading over the continent the Southern social system.[43] The brilliant but erratic William G. Brownlow, the "fighting parson" of Knoxville, Tennessee, was a staunch defender of slavery, as he was later of the Union and the flag. Lecturing at Memphis in January 1858 he announced his intention to go on a proselytizing mission to the "heathen of New England." Later in the year he met the antislavery clergyman Abram Pryne in public debate at Philadelphia and ran the whole gamut of the scriptural argument.[44] Representing the nonslaveholders of eastern Tennessee, this doughty champion demonstrated the role which the yeomanry of the South had come to play in defending the institution.

Brownlow was not the only Southerner to carry the fight into the enemy's territory. Fitzhugh, who enjoyed friendly relations with several abolitionists, keenly relished a battle of words; in 1856 he lectured with some acclaim before the students at Yale, urging for their consideration some of his advanced theories of class relationship. In the same year Senator Robert A. Toombs of Georgia repeated in Tremont Temple, Boston, the thoroughgoing defense which he had made the subject of an earlier address at Emory College, Georgia. Among other points he maintained that slavery would cease only when wages descended to a point barely sufficient to support the laborer and his family, so that capital could not afford to own labor; American slavery therefore would "find its euthanasia in the general prostration of all labor."[45] Other spokesmen twitted Northern industrialists with charges of hypocritically evading the fundamental fact that they, too, were practicing slavery. Capitalism, they held, was slavery under the guise of freedom. In palliation of their own "peculiar institution" professional Southerners shed crocodile tears over the pitiful condition of Northern "slaves without masters."

Thus did the South proclaim for a decaying institution more virtues than it had ever before been supposed to possess. Thus did a society deeply fissured by forces of social stratification acquire coherence, if not unity, on the eve of a struggle that was to determine its very right to exist.

THE STRUGGLE FOR THE NEW WEST

THE TRADITIONAL Western suspicion of the older settled areas had come by mid-century to yield to forces, physical and spiritual, which linked the upper Mississippi Valley to the Atlantic seaboard. The embattled legions that were to overwhelm the forces of Southern chivalry gained their decisive strength from recruits that poured forth from the farms of the Northwest. The fifties beheld the flood tide of the westward movement. In that decade the total population grew from less than 23 million to nearly 31.5 million. About one tenth of this gain occurred in states and territories not even listed in the census of 1840, while a million and a half were added from the only slightly older trans-Mississippi states. It is significant that the South, despite its apparent zeal for territorial expansion, was not producing a serious population pressure along its own frontier. Texas, to be sure, experienced a significant growth, and the rush to its lands attracted attention, but there the slaveholders from the older South were outnumbered by the mixed stream of Northerners and foreigners seeking the plains of west Texas.

Each spring throughout the free states a teeming mass of humanity, cattle, and wagons pushed over the east-and-west highways and the prairie roads of Illinois and Iowa to new homes in the West. "Movers' wagons! More movers' wagons!" chorused the small boys as they spied another approaching train of migrants. Old settlers turned their homes into taverns with simple accommodations for the travelers. River steamboats, now in their heyday, carried their crowded human cargoes down the Ohio and up the Mississippi. For weeks in 1854 the ferry at Burlington, Iowa, daily transferred some 600 or 700 passengers, many from the older states of the Mississippi Valley—Ohio, Indiana, and Illinois. The railroads connecting the Atlantic seaboard with the Mississippi ran trains of fourteen and fifteen cars, carrying those able to afford the more rapid method of transit.[46]

Minnesota was in 1850 a frontier outpost of 6,000 souls; St. Paul, capital of the newly organized territory, a yearling town of a thousand. Soon, however, settlers poured in, ruthlessly expelling the Indians before a fair treaty adjustment could be completed. Villages and towns sprang up and land speculation was rampant. The Panic of 1857, a blessing in disguise, brought the collapse of a fictitious prosperity, followed presently by development on more solid foundations. By 1858 the population of Minnesota was sufficient to win recognition, even from a reluctant South, of its right to statehood. In 1860 its inhabitants numbered 172,000, a cosmopolitan mixture of foreigners and of settlers from the older Northern states.[47]

Farther south the agricultural frontier lingered at the bend of the Missouri. The land beyond the river—the "Great American Desert" of early travelers—was too scantily supplied with water and timber to compete with the fertile unsettled areas of the old Northwest. It was the home and hunting ground of the American Indian, many of whom had earlier been transported across the Mississippi to make way for the oncoming tide of white settlers. Pioneers following the great trails to the Pacific had sometimes paused to sell forbidden firewater to the Indians, but otherwise they had shown little interest in the region. Occasional raids on the creeping white-canvased caravans raised howls of indignation from the settlers and their proponents in Congress. To ease the situation the newly created department of the interior brought together the tribes along the overland trails in a great council in the summer of 1851. In return for presents and the promise of an annual payment of $50,000 for fifty years, they consented to settle upon designated ranges, agreeing not to commit depredations upon emigrants and recognizing the right of the federal government to build roads and posts at will. It must be said that the Indians observed their obligations, moral as well as legal, more scrupulously than did the government agents.[48]

Hardly had the agreement been made before squatters began to penetrate this region, hoping to acquire legal rights to land. Restless spirits in neighboring states, tempted by high prices offered for their farms, also looked expectantly toward it. Meanwhile, the increasing interest in a transcontinental railroad created a demand for organizing this region into the territory of Nebraska. Missouri advocates of a central route and Stephen A. Douglas, the great champion of a northern route connecting with Chicago, were equally anxious to remove the Indian barrier and to throw open to settlement the lands through which the road would pass. Placating Southern hostility to the Missouri Compromise restriction, Douglas now proposed the application to Nebraska of the democratic doctrine of popular sovereignty. On May 30, 1854, his measure, the Kansas-Nebraska Act, as it was finally called, was duly enacted, providing for two territories north of the thirty-seventh parallel.[49] In the territory of Kansas, it was believed, the South could test the strength of the slave institution in the onrush of westward expansion. Nebraska, it was expected, would be commercially tributary to Iowa and, with the aid of a transcontinental railway connecting the North Platte Valley with the rail and water routes out of Chicago, be identified with the North and freedom.[50]

The peopling of Kansas at first differed little from other movements into fertile lands freshly thrown open to settlement. While territorial legislation was pending, immigrants on the left bank of the Missouri impatiently awaited the opportunity to cross over into the new territories. In the middle of March four steamboats descending the Ohio picked up 600 men, women, and children from Pennsylvania, Ohio, and Kentucky; reaching St. Louis they found other arrivals competing for transportation up the Missouri.[51] Not long after, large companies of emigrants, old rangers, and prospective settlers inexperienced in pioneering were moving through the states of the old Northwest with the destinations "Kansas" and "Nebraska" proclaimed from the canvas coverings of their wagons.

A new incentive, however, soon entered into the migration to Kansas. In Worcester, Massachusetts, Eli Thayer aroused the foes of the extension of slavery to the need of filling the new territory with inhabitants who would dedicate the region to free labor. In April 1854 he arranged with Amos Lawrence and other wealthy opponents of slavery to incorporate, as a business venture as well as a philanthropic enterprise, the Massachusetts Emigrant Aid Company; the plan was to colonize free-soil settlers in Kansas and provide them, at a profit to the promoters, with land, equipment, and supplies.[52] When the original project, a $5 million corporation, failed to attract the necessary capital, Thayer and his fellow promoters went ahead with a more modest philanthropic venture designated as the New England Emigrant Aid Company. Endorsed by leaders like Horace Greeley, this colonizing idea spread to other communities. New York City soon had three organizations: the Kansas League, the American Settlement Company, and the Western Emigration League.[53] News of these activities aroused the people of the frontier towns of Missouri. Kansas, they asserted, should be reserved for the institutions which Missourians would naturally carry with them across the western boundary of their state. Organizations were formed to remove any "abolitionists" who arrived under the auspices of Northern aid societies.

Meanwhile Missourians crossed into Kansas. Some of them, settling upon lands not yet ceded by the Delaware Indians, founded the town of Leavenworth, which, in six months, became a thriving community of several hundred inhabitants. For a time free-state emigration could not keep up with the tide of proslavery squatters. Most Northern settlers came, and continued to come, unassisted from Ohio, Indiana, and Illinois. It was midsummer before the first party sent out by the Massachusetts group arrived; when winter set in, only 600 settlers had thus been placed in Kansas. These, pitching their tents on the Kansas River, established the town of Lawrence at some distance from the settlements of the Missourians. There, lodged in hastily constructed log cabins, sod hovels, and board shanties, this handful of Northerners struck terror to the hearts of proslavery zealots. They were regarded as the vanguard of a horde of mercenaries bent on winning Kansas, not as true pioneers but as the military agents of a fanatical corporation of limitless resources.

Threatened with the exclusion of their human chattels from a territory they claimed as their rightful own, western Missourians organized in secret oath-bound societies to cross into Kansas at a moment's notice to save the "peculiar institution" at the polls. In this way some 1,600 men, many of them armed with pistol and bowie knife, entered the territory in November 1854 and contributed—unnecessarily, as the sequel showed—to a proslavery victory in the first territorial election. In certain border towns the entire male population—doctors, lawyers, merchants, and editors as well as the ne'er-do-wells—joined the invasion. When the election of a territorial legislature took place, they again appeared at the polls and swept all before them. The legislature so chosen adopted a drastic slave code based directly upon Missouri statutes.

The struggle, however, had only begun. Northern champions of freedom conjured up in their minds a picture of ruthless "border ruffians" ready for any act of desperation at the behest of the slavocracy. They hastened, therefore, to organize additional colonization companies and aid societies all the way from Maine to the Mississippi. Everywhere volunteers were enrolled, so that by the summer of 1855 Northern settlers formed the majority. Organizing a Free State party, they held a convention at Topeka and drafted a free-state constitution. In the autumn the Kansas Emigration Society of Missouri made a frantic appeal to the South to speed to the rescue. The response came in the formation of Kansas associations in older states like South Carolina, Georgia, and Alabama. Major Jefferson Buford of Eufaula, Alabama, recruited a company of 300 under military organization, selling forty slaves to raise the $20,000 he had personally pledged to the enterprise.[54] This and other companies arrived in Kansas just in time to swell the military forces of the proslavery authorities who were determined to crush the Free State party.

On May 21, 1856, acting as a posse, they entered the town of Lawrence and left behind a path of destruction. Conceiving himself divinely appointed to avenge the lives lost at Lawrence, John Brown, beginning the train of events which would end at Harper's Ferry, led his sons and a few neighbors to the cabins of proslavery settlers along Pottawatomie Creek, and, dragging five men from their beds, butchered them in cold blood. The entire territory and the Missouri border were soon aflame with exaggerated tales of the sacking of Lawrence and of the Pottawatomie massacre. Both sides rushed to arms. The martial bands of the proslavery party were matched by companies of young Northerners prepared, with Sharps rifles in their hands and the plow and sickle among their baggage, for either peace or war. Henry Ward Beecher, regretful that "anything else should be needed but moral instrumentalities," sent to a colony forming at New Haven not only his blessing and twenty-five Bibles but "the arms required for twenty-five men."[55] Soon Sharps rifles, listed as "Beecher's Bibles," were regarded as standard equipment for every emigrant company.

The Southerners countered with a strict embargo upon traffic up the Missouri River. At various points armed bands stopped, searched, and plundered parties of Northern migrants. A Chicago company of seventy-eight men under military organization was twice held up, disarmed, and finally taken to Alton under guard. Such incidents fanned the zeal for aiding the cause of freedom in "Bleeding Kansas." Chicago, where a meeting promptly subscribed a relief fund of $15,000, became the headquarters of a National Kansas Committee organized by delegates from aid societies all over the free states. The Chicago company and other emigrant parties were again fitted out and sent to Kansas by a safer route through Iowa and Nebraska.[56] Meanwhile among the older settlers of Kansas blood was flowing. Fanatics and ruffians on both sides ranged about stealing, pillaging, burning, and killing. Two hundred lives lost, $2 million worth of property destroyed—this was only part of the cost of "Bleeding Kansas." At length, in November 1856, to the relief of all, federal forces under a more capable governor brought the reign of terror to a close.

Members of the Free State party had been the chief sufferers, but they were gaining in number every day. The enthusiasm aroused by the Kansas relief activities caused a considerable revival of unassisted emigration in the spring of 1857.[57] Confident of President Buchanan's support, the proslavery settlers therefore hastened to press for the admission of Kansas as a slave state before the reins of political power slipped from their hands. But the Free State men, at last exercising their rightful influence at the polls, upset this plan by participating in territorial politics and, in August 1858, rejecting the proposed Lecompton proslavery constitution by a vote of 11,300 to 1,788. As a result, admission to statehood was delayed until January 1861, a time, as it happened, when stark famine, following a devastating drought, menaced the 100,000 inhabitants.

While these ill winds were blowing over Kansas, the twin territory to the north had shown steady progress. By 1860 nearly 30,000 people were scattered over the timberlands along the Missouri. The fertile soil produced grain in great abundance, often, however, only to be harvested by the grasshopper. Of a chain of villages, Nebraska City was at first the most important, but Omaha City, designated as territorial capital, claimed 4,500 inhabitants in 1865. By that time its growth was proceeding rapidly, partly in anticipation of the completion of the Pacific railroad. In another year, its sidewalks "thronged with returned gold seekers, discharged soldiers, farmers selling produce, speculators, Indians, and other strange characters of border life," it seemed to some "the liveliest city in the United States." [58] To the west lay the undulating prairies and the sand hills with their grasses, still the ranging grounds of innumerable buffaloes. Asked in 1864 whether they considered the territory ready for statehood, the people of Nebraska modestly voted no.

Meanwhile, in 1858, the Indians of the Dakota country in upper Nebraska were induced to sell their old hunting grounds and remove to a reservation. In the next year a few white families arrived and erected pioneer cabins. On March 2, 1861, the region north of the forty-third parallel was cut from Nebraska and, together with the wedge-shaped tract between the Big Sioux and the Missouri Rivers, formed into the territory of Dakota. [59] The 5,000 people listed in 1860 dwelt mostly in the lower part of the older area east of the Missouri, which had been cut from Minnesota when it became a state. Conditions in Dakota were soon recognized as peculiarly favorable for wheat growing, Red River grain, often averaging sixty bushels an acre, being unexcelled. Though the frontier normally looked eastward for a market, Dakota farmers sold their produce mainly to Indian agencies, military posts, and mining camps upriver, while those of the Red River valley sent their products downstream on the steamer *International* to the forts and trading posts of the Hudson's Bay Company in the interior of British America. Agricultural products, including cattle and horses, brought higher prices in Dakota than on the Mississippi River.

The farther West continued to lure the adventurer in ways only less dramatic than the gold rush of the forty-niners. [60] California, the new El Dorado, did not find its stride in gold production until 1853 when $65 million worth was taken from the mines. By this time life in mining settlements had been rendered more orderly by the activities of vigilance committees. In a commonwealth so favored by nature agricultural development was inevitable as disillusioned fortune seekers reverted to the field labors they had abandoned. Farm acreage more than doubled in a decade, while the value of farms and of farm implements leaped at least fifteenfold; the wheat yield, already over 5 million bushels in 1860, doubled in another five years. In southern California the orange, the fig, and other semitropical fruits were found to flourish as in their native clime. The grapevine, free from its common destructive diseases, came also to be cultivated extensively; by 1863 the vineyards of the state totaled nearly 3.5 million plants.[61] Much of this development centered in the region of Los Angeles, a city of 5,000; in the absence of the real estate promoter unimproved agricultural lands were available at prices of one or two dollars an acre. Many old Spanish rancheros sold sections of the 40,000- or 50,000-acre tracts which they had exploited in rude feudal ease.

Made a state as a part of the Compromise of 1850, California quadrupled its population in a decade, reaching nearly 400,000 in 1860. The mingling of people from all parts of the globe made the commonwealth the most cosmopolitan in the Union. Contacts of California with the East were unusually close. San Francisco prices were quoted in New York papers, some of which published regular California editions. The *New York Herald* claimed San Francisco as the daughter of New York: her merchants were from the Eastern metropolis, her financiers from Wall Street, and her leading journalists from the office of the *Herald.*[62] The city on the Golden Gate had a population in 1860 of about 57,000, which nearly doubled by the end of the Civil War. The journalist Samuel Bowles was impressed with the prosperity, culture, and refinement of the Pacific Coast and hazarded the guess that San Francisco possessed more college graduates proportionately than any other American city.[63]

North of California the vast agricultural empire of Oregon continued to entice the emigrant.[64] Soon the timber and fishing resources attracted attention; their development was delayed only by the problem of communication with the markets of the world. The population of Oregon increased from 13,000 in 1850 to over 52,000 in 1860 despite the fact that Washington territory, organized in 1853 out of the region north of the Columbia River, embraced about 12,000 inhabitants in 1860. Seeking statehood, the people of Oregon on their own motion held a constitutional convention in 1857 at Salem. Remote from the scene of the slavery controversy, these Westerners saw little appeal in the new Republican movement and chose rather to affiliate with the traditional party of the frontier. This fact commended their plans to a national administration generally favorable to Southern interests, and the new state with reduced boundaries secured recognition early in 1859.

Meanwhile, the recently arrived Mormon exiles in Utah reared their desert commonwealth. Under the able leadership of Brigham Young they directed their patient industry toward the agricultural conquest of the arid Great Salt Lake valley.[65] New proselytes to the Mormon faith, with its generally unpopular doctrine of polygamy, were recruited, partly in the British Isles and other foreign fields. Each year large caravans, arriving by the Mormon trail, were systematically placed as well-organized colonies upon carefully chosen sites. The tracts contiguous to streams were promptly made fruitful by a well-planned irrigation system. By 1865 the system included 277 main canals which, built at a cost of less than $2 million, totaled over 1,000 miles and watered 150,000 acres. The farms, small in size, were tilled intensively. Along the canals, connected by good roads, stood tidy towns and villages which boasted of sobriety, industry, and excellent school facilities. The humbler followers of the faith toiled with remarkable industry and perseverance. Those endowed with qualifications for leadership, largely from the more educated and refined minority, held places in the ecclesiastical hierarchy which was dominated by Young, a shrewd and benevolent despot. He was president of the Mormon Church and governor of Utah territory.[66]

Under the unique system of social control the solitude of "Deseret" began to glisten with golden fields. No ready market for the surplus had originally been contemplated, but the gold rush to California provided purchasers at unexpected prices. The Mormons salvaged, or purchased when necessary, discarded baggage, implements, furniture, and livestock. They fattened the emaciated beasts of burden and resold them to immigrants who refitted in the Utah settlements. In due time the crops of the Great Basin were transported by ox and mule team to mining camps in Montana, Colorado, and Nevada 500 miles distant. The future promised a transcontinental railroad connection with both the Pacific Slope and the older states.

Salt Lake City was in the sixties a beautifully laid-out community of over 15,000. Public edifices of stone and wood attracted favorable notice. A theater, in which amateurs performed with a skill equal to that of the professional troupes of the day, ranked architecturally with the playhouses of the metropolitan centers of the East.[67] Utah more than trebled its population in a decade, attaining a total of over 40,000 in 1860, a growth based on solid foundations. Its very prosperity presaged the passing of that isolation which the Mormons had deemed necessary for security and independence. "Gentiles" came in to represent the federal government or to head business enterprises, at first with a doubtful welcome from the "saints." The latter desired to rule the territory to their own ends, and federal officials found themselves not only helpless but virtually defied by territorial authorities.

When President Buchanan in 1857 undertook to clear up the situation by displacing Brigham Young as territorial governor, Young and his Nauvoo Legion, composed of all male Mormons from eighteen to forty-five years, attempted to prevent the "invasion" of Utah by the new governor and his 1,500 federal troops. During the course of the "Mormon War" that followed, Mormon militia joined with a band of Indians in the cold-blooded slaughter at Mountain Meadows of 120 men, women, and children, emigrants to California. The news of this massacre and of other outrages upon non-Mormons aroused belligerent feeling in the states, especially in those which had previously expelled the Mormons from their midst. Buchanan and his representatives, however, found that Mormons were evacuating Salt Lake City, leaving to its defenders instructions to apply the torch to every house if the troops entered. After an exciting year the issue was adjusted amicably. Young and the Mormons promised to respect federal authority and a general amnesty was granted. While the tension between Mormons and Gentiles continued, the latter steadily grew more numerous and, as they approached the 5,000 mark, they organized social contracts of their own.

Meanwhile other groups of settlers were drawn into the mountainous country. When the ebbing of the California fever awakened prospectors from their dreams of glittering wealth, there began an exodus of those unwilling to settle down to agricultural and other normal pursuits there. One group of adventurers, refusing to give up hope, sought the yellow metal in the nooks and crannies of the great American divide. It was they, the backwash of the gold rush, who in time spread the mining frontier over the entire region of the Rockies.[68]

Repeated false rumors of gold discoveries were followed in the fall of 1858 by stories of fabulous finds in the "Pike's Peak Country," identified by the one point of mountain geography generally known on the frontier. While the metal found in the sands of Cherry Creek proved an uncertain reward for the privations and sufferings encountered by the early comers, in the following summer rich quartz veins were discovered in what came to be known as the Gregory district. Even before this, the new rush had reached its height. Seasoned prospectors closed in on this new field; border communities sent their restless spirits; and in the Middle West the old scenes of 1849 were reenacted. Thousands left for the gold fields with the slogan "Pike's Peak or Bust" emblazoned on the canvas of their prairie schooners. Many others had scarcely completed preparations when the news came in May that the fortune hunters were returning in droves with the cry of "humbug."

As a matter of fact, success and disappointment alternated in the new gold country. Rich placer diggings proved limited and yielded few fortunes. When prospecting parties, exploring the nearby mountain range, found gold-bearing quartz veins over a large area, the ore was so firmly embedded in the rock as to require unexpected outlays of labor and capital in setting up stamp mills. The mining company perforce entered the field. Bonanza days seemed over for the average gold seeker, and the exodus threatened to develop into a stampede. Meanwhile, Denver City had been established, a busy, compactly built settlement in a fertile river valley at the very heart of what had been called the "Great American Desert." The census enumerators reported 5,000 there in 1860 and found 34,000 more in its general vicinity. With the first rush of settlers a spontaneous movement for local

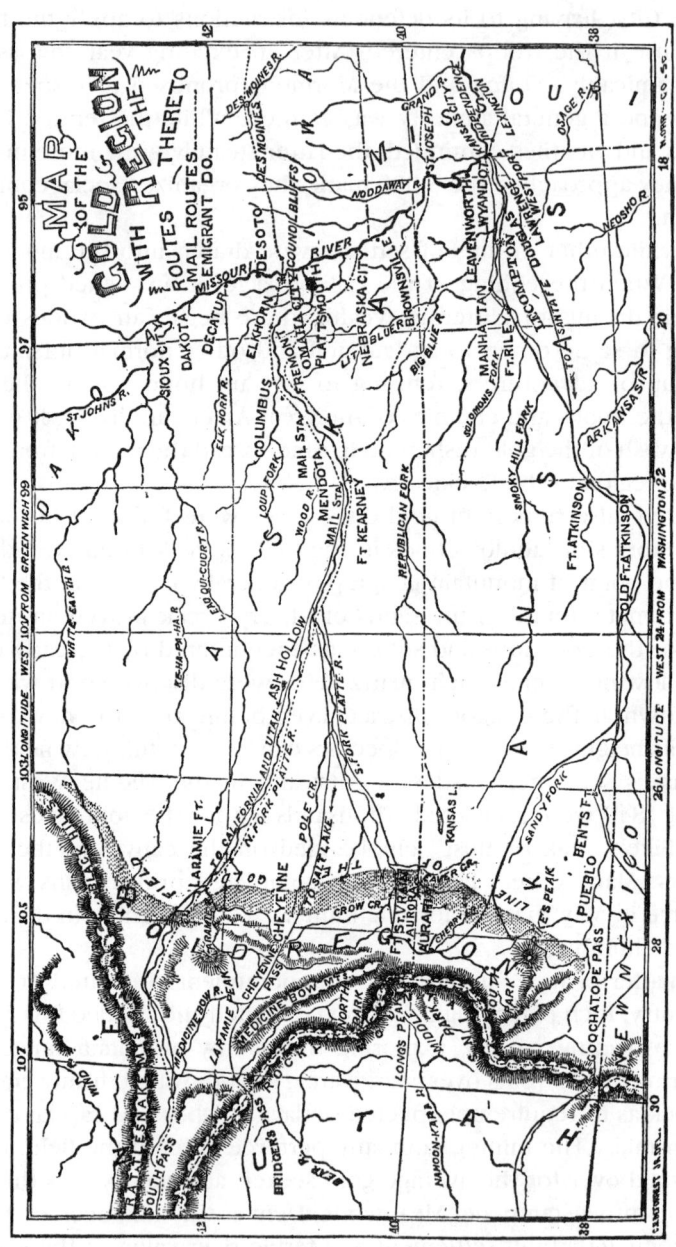

self-government developed, but an early dream of statehood vanished with the dwindling population of the gold fields. Late in 1859, however, the autonomous territory of "Jefferson" was in full operation.

The early years of Colorado, as this territory with reduced boundaries was formally christened by Congress in February 1861, helped confirm the Eastern concept of the "wild and woolly West." Outlaws and desperadoes, flocking to Denver and the mining camps, for a time held sway. But the order-loving citizens of Denver, as in many other smaller towns, soon organized a vigilance committee which drove out or tamed the rougher elements. Presently came a different source of division, over the question of secession. Rebel sympathizers were active and influential; plot and counterplot became the order of the day. When the crisis passed and the danger of Indian uprisings was allayed, the settlers of Colorado turned more and more to agricultural pursuits. The valley of the South Platte River soon instanced yields of sixty bushels of wheat to the acre, sixty-six of barley, sixty-five of oats, and four tons of hay. Mineral wealth and agriculture proved the combination which at length broke up the great mountain empire that had thus far stood in vast isolation.[69]

Meanwhile a new commonwealth was in the making immediately to the west. In 1858 and 1859 gold prospectors combing the eastern slopes of the Sierra Nevada discovered valuable silver deposits on the sides and at the foot of Mount Davidson, the loftiest summit in the Washoe range. The most important find was the Comstock lode. Miners promptly poured in from all quarters of the compass. Carson City, a flourishing town just off the California trail and a product of the first rush, quickly demanded an independent existence for this new mining frontier. Though the natural associations of the settlers were with California, the silver deposits were largely within the territory of Utah, and neither government was near enough to reflect adequately their wishes or needs. In 1861, therefore, Congress created the territory of Nevada with headquarters at Carson City. Thither came Mark Twain as private secretary to one of the territorial officials; in the mining camp he found ample opportunity for "roughing it" and ample local color for his later volume under that title.[70] Virginia City, with the Comstock lode partly within its limits, was the metropolis of the territory. When the ore-bearing veins of eastern Nevada were discovered in 1862, the thrifty city of Austin grew up at the center of the Reese River mining region. Despite a small and uncertain population, a congressional majority anxious to gain votes admitted Nevada to statehood in 1864.

To the south, in the region of the Spanish settlements along the Mexican border, mining was already an old story.[71] Of the 60,000 citizens of New Mexico in 1850 few were Americans, and these were of the type that find a fascination in isolation, lawlessness, and danger. Most of them were engaged in trading, such as the few hundred at Santa Fe, an almost negligible element in a population mainly Mexican and half-breed. Sleepy, sun-baked Mexican towns revealed plaza, old Catholic church, adobe houses, narrow streets, and naked children. Outside, sheep and goats grazed on the hills; the rancheros knew only the most primitive agriculture. Evidences of mineral wealth recalled the Spanish search for El Dorado. But only the more westerly region responded to the mining excitement of the early sixties. There Arizona territory was created in 1863, although yielding in 1870 a population of fewer than 10,000.

Far to the north, those nomads of the mountains, the prospectors, were opening up a new gold country along the Snake River. Early in 1861, after finds had been made just across the Washington-Oregon line, over 1,000 miners hit the trail for the new field. In 1862 the Salmon River region to the south was the scene of wild excitement; 8,000 to 9,000 miners stampeded to Florence—to leave almost as quickly as they had come. The discovery of the Boise basin drew most of the prospectors to a new district with Idaho City as its main settlement. Boise, at the head of the valley and between the Owykee and Boise mining fields, was founded in 1863 as a staging junction through which nearly all the passengers and supplies had to pass. Soon it gave promise of becoming the commercial center of this region.

Just across the Great Divide miners were prospecting on the upper waters of the Missouri. It was not long before ore was discovered over a wide section about the headwaters of the Columbia, Missouri, and Yellowstone rivers. In May 1863, Virginia City grew up overnight on Alder Gulch, and in 1864, Helena was founded at "Last Chance Gulch," each the center of a valuable mining district. In 1863, Congress organized this new inland empire into the territory of Idaho, including the area of the present states of Montana and Wyoming. Mountain ranges, however, divided the territory into two fairly well-defined groups of camps. In response to the pleas of miners east of the Bitter Root range, Congress in 1864 erected the territory of Montana.

Thus in the period from 1849 to 1865 the mining camp made its first real contribution to the Anglo-American frontier. Over 150,000, with pick and pan, burro, pack, and shovel, took part in the quest. Ready to brave almost any hardship to attain sudden wealth and then go back to the East for its enjoyment, few actually returned. The call of the wilderness, the lure of the great out-of-doors, alone detained many. Others found their success bound up in the permanent development of the Far West—in cultivating the fertile valleys or grazing stock upon the nutritious native grasses, in handling supplies, or in selling their labor. Erstwhile miners thus became home builders and the vanguard of a new frontier.

Meanwhile the older regions of the upper Mississippi Valley were becoming the social and economic, as well as the political, heart of the nation. "Westward the star of empire takes its course," truly sang the contemporary Yankee bard.[72] A great influx of new settlers more than replaced those lost to the trans-Mississippi West. Yankee stock from the rock-strewn farms of New England, enterprising sons of other seaboard states, and restless pioneers from the upper Ohio Valley, together with sturdy, ambitious, and freedom-loving refugees from the Old World, combined to make their contributions to the Midwest and to hasten the passing of the frontier.

New Englanders often migrated in parties or in well-organized colonies. They first sought their kind in the old Yankee belt along the Great Lakes, thus avoiding the antipathy of critics who charged them with being "sniveling, hypocritical, rascally, white-livered Yankees" afflicted with "cant, humbug, Pharisaism, bigotry, abolitionism, red republicanism."[73] It was not long, however, before they spread out in all directions, even into lower Illinois, that "land of ignorance, barbarism, and poverty."[74] There the Southern bias of the earlier settlers made them less welcome, but missionary zeal inspired many to carry the torch of freedom to light up the darkness of "Egypt." Migrating New Yorkers, Pennsylvanians, Ohioans, Hoosiers, and the rest also played an important part. As in the case of Yankee settlers, the older Eastern influences which they brought with them, far from succumbing to frontier experiences and prejudices, came to make a deep impress upon the new environment. Thus the mingling of peoples aided further in breaking down Western suspicion of the Atlantic seaboard.

The North-South line of cleavage, on the other hand, grew steadily more rigid. Only a few settlers hailed from the states south of the Ohio River, and these, primarily from Virginia, Tennessee, and Kentucky, cherished growing doubts concerning the virtues of slavery. This stream remained insignificant until the oncoming war enlarged the flow, bringing many who felt bitterly resentful toward the South and its institutions. The heart of the South had shifted with the culture of cotton to the Gulf states. A common frontier experience no longer bound these states to those north of the Ohio. The barrier between freedom and slavery was fast becoming more effective than the old mountain barrier between the seaboard and the West.

THE GROWING PAINS OF SOCIETY

FOREIGNERS SWELLING THE RANKS of the wage-earners helped to advance the labor movement. If immigrant workers by their numbers tended to depress the wage scale, at the same time they provided some of the most effective labor leaders of the 1850s, men trained in the industrial struggle abroad. For a time the American movement seemed bogged in a discussion of the relief to be gained from free homesteads. This panacea constituted a major topic of discussion in the series of industrial congresses held during the early fifties, gatherings which more often represented the white-collar reformer than the wage-earner. As the years went on, however, the worker increasingly turned his attention to coping with the more exigent problems of his employment, such questions as wages, hours of labor, and conditions of work.

While local unions had come and gone in the preceding decades, especially with the awakening of labor in the late twenties and early thirties, the modern type of union originated out of a heightened emphasis upon efficient and nationwide craft organization. In 1852, after two years' planning, the printers organized the International Typographical Union. Two years later the stonecutters launched a similar body, and in 1859 the Iron Moulders' Union of North America grew out of the energetic efforts of William H. Sylvis, the most forceful figure in the mid-century labor world. After a walkout in his own foundry Sylvis joined the iron molders' organization and, as its recording secretary, directed its expansion over the United States and into Canada until on the eve of the Civil War the Iron Moulders' Union was credited with being "the largest mechanical association in the world."[75] The year 1859 also saw the formation of the National Grand Union of Machinists and Blacksmiths, a body incorporated by Congress, its charter being the only one ever so conferred upon a labor organization.

There was little concern in this new movement for the common cause and solidarity of the working class. The increasing particularism of the skilled crafts contrasted sharply with the glowing ideals of the humanitarians who had recently been proclaiming in the abstract the dignity and the rights of labor. The unskilled and the unorganized were left to shift for themselves. Meanwhile the new unions set about to attain their own objectives, including exclusive control over conditions in their own crafts. The workday in the fifties varied from the eight-hour schedule of a very few well-organized local groups to the fourteen or fifteen hours often demanded of mill hands in New England. A new downward pressure, however, was being exerted along political as well as economic lines. In Massachusetts a long struggle took place for a ten-hour day, and in 1852 and 1853 employers in that and other states saved themselves from more drastic reductions by conceding the eleven-hour day.[76] In certain other states the ten-hour system was legally established, if not effectively enforced. The new speeding-up processes, however, notably through the use of labor-saving machinery, guaranteed enterprising manufacturers against any loss of productivity.

The worker's daily wage for eleven or more hours allowed him usually but a frugal existence with no provision whatever for possible misfortune. The great mass of unskilled labor received a dollar or less a day; trained mechanics seldom more than two dollars. Wage returns, of course, tended to reflect the ups and downs of the general economic situation. For a time in 1850 and again in the dull periods following the business recession of 1855 and the Panic of 1857 wage reductions took place. In the decade as a whole the general level of pay showed an inconsiderable increase of 8 percent.[77]

To seasonal fluctuations of work and total shutdowns in hard times were added the complications of technological unemployment. The sewing machine in its various forms was revolutionizing the manufacture of clothing and even of shoes, forcing the little handicraft shops to give way to more productive processes. Labor-saving inventions were likewise playing havoc with the more exclusive status of the machinist and blacksmith. Machines tended by apprentices or unskilled workers turned out more goods than did trained artisans who hence often found themselves without jobs. This was a new and potent argument for unionization.

As the years rolled by, labor acquired a steadily growing sense of its strength. Even liberals like Greeley, hitherto censorious of the strike and hopeful that labor would solve its problems by producers' cooperation and land reform, came to champion its cause. Collective bargaining spread through the leading trades while the strike was resorted to with increasing frequency. The year 1853 was a veritable strike year.[78] When, in February, workers won a significant victory over the Baltimore and Ohio Railroad, the contagion promptly infected other parts of the country. In May over thirty trades walked out in New York City. Even waiters in the metropolitan hotels, and later in Pittsburgh, struck for higher wages. While success in these movements varied, they generally tended to impress upon the thoughtful public the conclusion drawn by the St. Louis *Missouri Republican,* January 10, 1854, after a local epidemic of walkouts, "that labor is too poorly paid in proportion to the high rates demanded for the marketing of produce."

The industrial disturbances in 1855 and those following the Panic of 1857 proved less successful in preventing wage reductions. The walkout on the Erie Railroad was the first in the annals of great railway strikes. A modern note was sounded when certain strikers on the Marietta Railroad were arrested on a charge of obstructing the mails. Successes won in 1859 in strikes in Massachusetts shoe factories led to a general statewide movement early in 1860.[79] Previously unorganized, the workers revealed an unsuspected solidarity, with even some of the women operatives joining. At length 10,000 out of the 40,000 shoemakers of the state quit work. The strikers held meetings and demonstrations; at Lynn on March 7 several thousand men and women marched in procession carrying flags and banners, accompanied by bands and military and fire companies. Sympathy ran high on both sides, and troops were employed to quell riotings. In the course of the excitement the Reverend G. W. Babcock, pastor of the Unitarian Church in South Natick, was dismissed because of his sympathetic aid to the strikers. The disturbance was extending into adjacent states when the men began to return to their jobs. Despite favorable adjustments with certain manufacturers the strike in the main failed. In terms of material gain the American labor movement on the eve of the Civil War had little improved its position since the beginning of the decade. Yet progress had been made in self-confidence and in a knowledge of tactics, and the foundations laid for more promising advances in the days of wartime prosperity.

The uncertain rewards of labor were reflected in a new problem of urban poverty. Unemployment in a period of high prices brought the helpless and unorganized workers and their families to dire straits. The early winter of 1854, marked by financial depression following a bad drought and high food prices, compelled the "friends of the poor" to devise alleviative measures.[80] Besides the appropriations of local governments, private charity lent a helping hand, benefit performances were staged, fairs and relief meetings held. Meantime the jobless in New York met almost daily in the parks and listened to the remedies proposed by socialist leaders.

The Panic year of 1857 yielded an even greater harvest of unemployment. In the midst of plenty, with barns and storehouses full of foodstuffs held back because of low prices, 20,000 workers and their dependents in Chicago faced starvation. In New York and other Eastern cities the distress was, if possible, even more acute. The jobless held hunger meetings and organized demonstrations. "We want work," "Work or Bread," they shouted. Mobs threatened to raid the banks, "plundering shops," as they were branded; one procession marched to Wall Street. Rich men, it was proclaimed, must share with the poor, or muskets would be used. Yet in spite of the alarm of the authorities, who finally stationed police and soldiers to guard public buildings, no violent outbreak took place. Remedies, such as municipal works, municipal bakeries, and soup houses and the sale of foodstuffs at cost by the city administration, were discussed from many angles, but little effective relief was accomplished. In the main the workers struggled through the winter as best they could. Unemployment continued well into the spring.[81]

Simultaneously with the appearance of poverty and unemployment the newspapers chronicled a startling crime wave in the larger cities. Petty theft and robbery, previously uncommon, seemed to spread with amazing swiftness, while juvenile offenders multiplied. Young boys were caught picking pockets, shoplifting, pilfering wharves and warehouses, and even in more serious criminal acts. Crimes against property became especially numerous, though deeds of violence also increased until it seemed that little value was placed upon human life. New York City was alleged to be the most crime-ridden city in the world, with Philadelphia, Baltimore, and Cincinnati not far behind.[82]

Gangs of youthful rowdies in the larger cities, sometimes under the guise of political clubs, threatened to destroy the American reputation for respect for law. Actuated by group loyalty and a spirit of bravado they operated in New York under appropriately picturesque names like the "Bowery Boys,"

"Plug-Uglies," "Highbinders," "Swipers," and "Dead Rabbits." Philadelphia and Baltimore had their own assortments of hoodlums and turbulent bands. The Maryland metropolis with its "Rough Skins," "Rip Raps," "Blood Inks," "Bloody Eights," and "Butt Enders" enjoyed the unenviable reputation of having more gangsters, and more reckless ones, than elsewhere.[83] The "Crawfish Boys" of Cincinnati and their like saw to it that Western cities could not claim exemption from such ills.

These ruffians found the two great holidays, New Year's and the Fourth of July, peculiarly suited to their purposes. Saturating themselves with liquor, they demanded complete right of way, rejoicing in the opportunities for fisticuffs when someone, preferably a rival gang, disputed their claims. A regular amusement consisted in attendance upon fires which they were often accused of having started; there they lent their aid to the volunteer companies and rewarded themselves by appropriating everything that struck their fancies. On election day, often in the name of native Americanism, they drove voters from the polls or fell upon groups of foreign-born citizens who banded together for self-protection.[84] Before their boisterous demonstrations the crude police forces of the day were often helpless.

Prostitution stalked abroad at night, overrunning Broadway and adjoining streets. There flourished saloons and dingy dance halls where amidst a tawdry glitter the ten commandments were forgotten and "pretty waiter girls" drank with the patrons they enticed. In the basement haunts along the Bowery there existed, under police protection, a shameless exhibition of vice. Apparently many property owners rejoiced in the opportunity to secure a double rent for such miserable quarters. In gorgeously furnished mansions on Mercer Street beautiful women followed the same ancient calling with a refinement that attracted little notice, except that of the Broadway dandies whom they undertook to ensnare.[85]

The moralist attributed the situation to the laxity that prevailed as a result of the growing inclination toward extravagance and dissipation. According to certain sober critics the relation between crime and poverty could not be denied, especially since the winter months with their heavy expenses and unemployment found lawlessness more rife in the cities than other seasons of the year. Some amateur criminologists found cold comfort in the fact that much of the criminality could be traced to the foreign-born, especially in the seaport cities.

Police connivance and misplaced executive clemency aggravated the problem. At any rate, conditions had passed beyond the control of the primitive official systems of the time. In cities where policemen were at all in evidence they appeared in ordinary attire except for the official badge, lounging at grocery corners, reading a newspaper, or talking politics with some acquaintance. In times of need they were usually conspicuously wanting, some said because in cowardice they removed their badges and so concealed their official status. In November 1853 an order of the police commissioners required the policemen of New York, despite vigorous complaints upon their part, to wear an official uniform consisting of a blue cap bearing the number of the officer, a blue swallow-tailed coat with brass buttons, and gray pantaloons.[86] Less than three months later the same attire was imposed upon the protesting police force of Philadelphia. In 1855 uniforms were introduced into Boston, this city adopting a system of surveillance upon the European model, which made Westerners and Southerners call Massachusetts a "police-ridden state." In New York, where the metropolitan police were responsible to police commissioners appointed by the governor, the latter failed to cooperate. Early in 1858 the mayor, complaining of the vice prevailing under police protection, organized a special squad under his own direction which conducted a series of raids upon certain notorious gambling houses, lottery offices, and other nuisances.

In Western towns and cities police facilities were limited and uncertain. Although well-established places seemed to have surprisingly little crime, upon the mining frontier the gambler and the desperado enjoyed full license until the community took the law into its own hands and by its vigilance committee meted out crude but effective justice. In the rural districts of the Mississippi Valley horse stealing continued to arouse the wrath of impromptu committees which often dispensed lynch law to the thief as promptly as they applied a coat of tar and feathers to the violator of the community standard of morals. In 1854 when the rustlers concentrated their operations upon Missouri, the National Anti-Horse Thief Association was organized to supplement the efforts of local societies.

Nor were the Southern states immune to criminal proclivities. Desperadoes, gamblers, thieves, and murderers, operating upon the Mississippi River boats and in the towns that lined the banks, became more and more in evidence as one penetrated the South. In New Orleans crime was so prevalent that the local sheriff declared it "a perfect hell upon earth";[87] arrests were at times proportionately more numerous than in New York. In other Southern towns somewhat similar conditions existed. Among the dominant groups of the South no formally dispensed justice was swift enough to deal with crimes against white women: prevailing sentiment ruled that the offender be shot down like a dog.

The extent of crime conditions, particularly in the cities, suggested a connection with the "demon drink." Under the prevailing American custom of "treating," intemperance had long been a feature of community life. There seemed to be a certain freemasonry in tippling—as William H. Herndon put it, "a peculiar tie that binds men together who have drunk bouts together."[88] Liquor establishments of all sorts abounded: saloons with mahogany cases and cut glass, grog shops, "bunghole-doggeries," wine shops, summer gardens, and the rest, while the well-stocked barroom was a prominent adjunct to every hotel. New York City possessed from 7,000 to 15,000 dispensaries;[89] like Chicago and many smaller communities, it had at least one for every 100 inhabitants.

Aroused by the evils of drink and the ostentation of the liquor traffic, a great temperance wave swept across the nation. The apostles of moral suasion still held the field in 1850. They spoke on the open squares of New York on Sunday, often to audiences of sailors and street walkers, and from this center they reached out into the provinces. In 1850, John B. Gough was adding pledge signers in Buffalo and Detroit to the thousands already on his list,[90] while Father Mathew, the Irish apostle of temperance, was enrolling teetotalers with 3 million signatures as his goal. Pledge-takers belonged to the Sons of Temperance, a secret ritualistic organization, which became a vast "Cold Water Army," their processions in elaborate regalia and their public exercises a feature of nearly all holiday celebrations. From the East the movement spread to the Mississippi Valley and even into the South, "the land of Dixie and whiskey."[91] In the North Carolina legislature applications for charters of the Sons of Temperance were granted in spite of opponents who "quoted from the Bible, Shakespeare, and Hudibras."[92]

The more aggressive temperance advocates, desiring a complete purging of society, urged political action to strike at the root of the evil. The general assembly of Maine led off in 1851 with a statewide prohibitory enactment known as the Maine liquor law, the first great landmark in this new phase of the crusade.[93] Encouraged by this victory the temperance forces throughout the country began a vigorous agitation to induce other states to take like action. Its most aggressive expression took the form of Maine-law alliances with township and county divisions and active state organizations. Practical men, who at first frowned on the proposal as the propaganda of traveling tract peddlers and of reformers identified with all the incipient "isms" of the day, came increasingly to look upon it as a force that might work incalculable good.

Vermont, Rhode Island, and Massachusetts promptly followed in the footsteps of Maine. Soon the fight was raging in every state.[94] By 1855 every Northern state legislature except New Jersey had approved some form of prohibition. Where laws were upheld there was still the problem of enforcement. In most communities success in this was only temporary.

Probably one of the greatest obstacles to real success was the increasing popularity of lager beer. Scarcely known in America before 1850, this mildly alcoholic beverage attained in ten years a wide popularity.[95] Many an American of older stock joined the German immigrant in favoring this thirst-quenching drink. In 1858, suits involving the question of its intoxicating character came before the courts of New York and Massachusetts. When witnesses in the New York case testified to their ability to drink gallons without inebriating effects, the jury acquitted the defendants of illegally selling intoxicants on Sunday, "believing that lager beer, which does not contain more than 3¾% alcohol, does not come within the provisions of the statute in relation to intoxicating drinks."[96] The Massachusetts supreme court, however, held beer to be intoxicating in the sense of the law.

Of greater moment was the movement by which American women went forth in quest of fresh laurels. American women probably spent two or three times as much upon dress as their sisters in England and the Old World. In fashionable circles in the cities there was reflected a steady gain in the influence of French styles, as set forth in *Le Follet* and profusely copied in *Godey's Lady's Book* and similar journals. Parisian gowns and bonnets together with copies of American fabrication were conspicuously displayed by strollers on Broadway and Fifth Avenue. In the very early fifties ladies' dresses steadily increased in length until they became long dangling "street-sweepers." The ridiculousness and expense of the inconvenient, untidy garments awakened a minority protest among the women. Mrs. Amelia Bloomer, editor of the *Lily*, a reform paper advocating temperance and woman's rights, donned a new costume, the chief features of which were an overskirt reaching somewhat below the knees and a pair of moderately full "trousers" gathered in at the ankle with an elastic band or fastened into the boot top.[97] This style was more an adaptation of the pantalette costume worn for years by young girls than an imitation of male attire. It promised, however, emancipation from a garb which did not permit vigorous physical activity and which had caused the men, thus denied the society of women in many of their labors and pastimes, to regard the sex as inferior.

Woman's rights advocates led the way in adopting bloomers. Elizabeth Cady Stanton, daughter of an austere and distinguished judge, wife of a New York senator, and mother of four fine boys, shocked all three generations when she performed the surgical operation upon her costume. Her young son wrote from boarding school that he did not want his mother to visit him "in a short dress," while at home the street urchins screamed in chorus:

> Heigh! ho! the carrion crow,
> Mrs. Stanton's all the go;
> Twenty tailors take the stitches.
> Mrs. Stanton wears the breeches.[98]

In the spring of 1851 the new costume took on a sudden popularity. The fashionable set in the cities evinced an interest, qualified only by the fact "that it did not originate in Paris."[99] Newspaper editors commented upon the favorable contrast "with the *pavement-sweeping* robes that were . . . gathering up the dust and mud at every step."[100] Upon the Fourth of July, especially at certain resorts, bloomers, it was said, were out "in full bloom."

One editor noticed a number whose garb "did not extend below their 'courtesy benders.' Well, whose business is it?" he asked.[101] Bloomer parties were held to keep up the courage of the innovators, who braved the gaze of the curious and the sharp tongues of the town gossips rather better than they faced the obvious discomfiture of fastidious husbands and relatives. But even the most courageous grew weary of suffering for their convictions. By the summer of 1853 the new garb was being abandoned by all but an occasional zealot in the woman's rights movement who religiously attended its conventions in full regalia, and by a few who, safe from the public eye, enjoyed the comfort and convenience which the new dress afforded for housework.[102]

It has been customary to speak of the bloomer craze of the early fifties and to ignore the hoopskirt mania that succeeded it. The hoopskirt was introduced with the credentials of the beautiful Empress Eugénie who set the style for the French court in 1853. Originally fashioned in a stiff fabric known as crinoline and set off by billowing petticoats, the garment aimed at a barrellike effect, which it was found could better be achieved by the use of cane or whalebone reinforcements. Soon other refinements were attempted like gutta-percha cord and wire framework; watch-spring steel hoops were on the market at five cents a hoop. The newspapers chronicled embarrassing experiences of hoopskirt wearers upon crowded sidewalks, in trains and street cars, and even in church pews. In spite of caricature, ridicule, and male disgust the hoopskirt style, with variations like the floating-bell and the watch-bell skirts, persisted through the Civil War.[103]

The extravagance of feminine toilette and attire evoked considerable comment. Gowns at $100 and more were frequent purchases; expensive shawls, lace scarfs, and other wraps were a common sight; and modish bonnets for street and house wear, generously trimmed with "love-ribbon" and other frills, graced matrons and misses. Low-necked gowns aroused the indignation of moralists. "Women who wear such dresses are seducers," declared "Justitia" in the *Cincinnati Enquirer,* June 11, 1859; ten or fifteen years ago such dresses would not have been tolerated except in the theater, added this critic. Some journals were ungallant enough to attribute the Panic of 1857 largely to the extravagance in personal adornment of the fair sex.[104]

Male attire, by contrast, revealed itself essentially stable. The well-to-do and middle classes continued to be partial to loose-fitting black frock coats, often seedy in appearance, but the uncomfortable stovepipe hat began to pass out in the sixties. Meanwhile colored satin, velvet, or brocaded vests had a period of popularity. Trousers were usually narrow except when some dapper specimen of Young America returned from Paris to "startle the town" by the looseness of his bags. The chief field of experimentation for males was in beards and mustaches. Among the younger generation goatees and imperials competed for popularity with the full beard, which seems to have received considerable support from the influx of German immigrants and from the tonsorial deficiencies of the mining frontier. Creams and unguents were advertised with assurances of a crop of whiskers and of mustaches in six weeks. In due time the mustache cup was invented "to meet the exigencies of the unshaven lip." [105] When, following his election, Abraham Lincoln decided to introduce a beard into the White House, the issue of beards or no beards seemed to be settled for many who had hesitated. Lincoln's results were so conspicuous that a *Vanity Fair* caricature showed a druggist proudly commending his jars of "Lincoln Whiskeropherous": "Try one of them pots, and in three weeks you'll be as 'arry and 'ansom as 'im." [106] In due time the uncertain toilets of army life were to add an additional argument for beards; never before or since have whiskers had such a vogue in America.

Into the American home many a comfort and luxury was being introduced. Well-to-do abodes ordinarily possessed hot and cold running water, bathrooms, cookstoves, and perhaps even hot-air furnaces. Moreover, the drudgery of housework was often turned over to servant girls who worked at a wage of a dollar or two a week. Previously domestic employment had existed upon an essentially democratic basis, the menial status belied by the use of the term "help" instead of "servant." Now, with a mass of Irish and German immigrants available, the native-born abandoned the field and the term "servant," or "hired girl," began to come into general use.

The family, indeed, seemed to many in process of disintegration. Early marriages were still the rule, brides of fourteen being far from uncommon. The editor of the *New York Herald* deplored runaway matches, especially of young girls who "are as worldly minded as men of thirty." [107] Matrimonial agencies like the Caroline Fry Marriage Association and the Bloomer Marriage Association undertook to arrange suitable matches for those unable to do it themselves. Marriages easily and lightly entered upon frequently ended in failure. Some sought relief in a second marriage, often without a dissolution of previous ties, for with easy escape to the Western frontier bigamists were not easily punished. The laws of California made bigamy a mere misdemeanor, and the offender could not be prosecuted unless indicted within one year of the second marriage. A foreign-born observer held that Mormonism was the natural outgrowth of American conditions. However this may have been, over 3,500 men were openly practicing polygamy in Utah in 1859, although Congress was becoming increasingly disposed to enact legislation against the custom. [108]

Many of those disposed to test the success of a marriage by the kind of offspring it produced were depressed by the behavior of the younger generation. Emerson quoted a contemporary as saying it was a misfortune to have been born in an age when children were nothing and to have spent his mature life in an age when children were everything. [109] Youngsters of all ages seemed irrepressible. Foreigners were unanimous that modesty and shyness were unheard of, that children were selfish and willful, spoiled beyond all discipline. A few admired their sturdy independence, the remarkable development of self-reliance and self-management. American moralists lamented the decay of parental discipline and the alarming development of juvenile depravity. "What have the parents or the community to hope from such children?" they asked in despair.[110] Others undertook to reassure them, to set such gloomy observations in a proper perspective, pointing out that under the milder parental regime most of those no longer subjected to the old grim discipline were working out their own salvation.

In any event, family limitation seemed a desideratum to many parents if one may judge from the advertisements, in daily papers and even in the religious press, "of professed abortionists; of pills which 'are sure to procure abortion,' from which 'miscarriage will certainly ensue,' & etc."[111] But a movement of protest against such practices arose, which was supported by Walt Whitman, who, in his editorial condemnation, included those "infernal inventions," "warranted 'to regulate or limit offspring, without injuring the constitution,'" which were said to be patronized by "ladies of fashion and social position." It may be noted that foreigners felt scandalized at the American laxity in regard to the transmission of birth control information.

The increasing frequency of divorce was widely deplored as a sign of declining morality. Courts and legislatures seemed to be besieged by applicants for matrimonial relief. Divorce laws varied from complete prohibition in certain Southern states to the easy processes of nearly every Western state and territory. Indiana had a statute which a local judge declared was virtually all that the advocates of free love could ask. Introduced by the idealist Robert Dale Owen, this law had made that state free soil for unhappy wives and husbands, while outsiders went there to dissolve undesirable unions.[112] In Nebraska a divorce could be had from the legislature for the asking. The probate courts of Utah had full and unlimited power to issue divorces.[113] In New York, on the other hand, divorces were granted only upon proof of adultery. This seemed to many unduly drastic; in 1858 and successive years bills were introduced into the legislature to make willful desertion, separation for a term of years, or cruel or inhuman treatment by a husband endangering life, cause for divorce. When these efforts failed, divorce lawyers advertised in the daily papers their services in obtaining without publicity or change of residence legal divorces from some other state.

The most active champions of "marriage reform" in New York were to be found in the ranks of the feminists. To Elizabeth Cady Stanton the "whole question of woman's rights" seemed to turn "on the pivot of the marriage relation."[114] Her active ally in this cause was Lucy Stone who, in wedding Dr. Henry B. Blackwell in 1855, required the omission of the word "obey" from the ceremony and set an example of retaining her maiden name.[115] Stanton introduced a series of resolutions for more liberal divorce at the national woman's rights convention of 1860, triumphing over the eloquent Wendell Phillips, who pronounced her resolutions irrelevant to the feminist cause. Stanton, moreover, addressed the New York legislature in favor of a liberal divorce bill, which Lucretia Mott and others supported before the committee. Most of the advocates, however, were silenced by a broadside of editorials in the *New York Tribune* in which Greeley opposed liberalization.

Above everything else, the times demanded fuller educational opportunities for women. Many chafed at a situation that left leisure-class women content to while away their time in the everlasting rocking chair, ready to lay aside fan, light novel, or "fancy work," only to indulge in trifling gossip.[116] In spite of the increasing excellence of the contemporary female seminary or college they insisted that the same opportunities be made available for young women as were found in colleges and universities for men. In response to this demand, but not without extensive criticism and ridicule, Elmira Female College was launched in 1855, the first woman's institution to grant academic degrees. In 1860 at the request of an invalid niece, a schoolteacher, Matthew Vassar, prepared to establish the institution which, delayed by the Civil War, now bears his name.[117]

Meanwhile the demand grew for the admission of women to regular colleges and universities. Oberlin no longer occupied a unique place as a coeducational institution, although it continued to bear the reputation, based upon its lack of race or sex discrimination, of being "a sort of fanatical way-station between the district school and Harvard University, where men, women, and 'colored people' are all taught together."[118] Gradually the doors of Midwestern institutions began to open. Antioch College was founded in 1852 with Horace Mann, an aggressive exponent of coeducation, as its first president. Though other colleges followed Antioch's lead, including the State University of Iowa in 1860, the University of Michigan and the legislature of that state coldly rejected pleas for the admission of women.[119] Many felt that such action was entirely sound. On the other hand, Thomas Wentworth Higginson declared in the *Atlantic Monthly* in 1859 that the real issue was, "Ought women to learn the alphabet?"; that "woman must be a subject or an equal: there is no middle ground."[120] It was to be long, however, before this simple logic would be accepted by the many who felt that education would unfit women for domestic duties and social graces.[121] Meanwhile, in 1852 an American Women's Educational Association was organized.[122]

The champions of the new day became more and more insistent upon the right of women to participate in any honorable and remunerative field of employment. In 1850, women teachers outnumbered their male associates in Massachusetts more than two to one, but the situation there was exceptional. By 1855, however, their pressure upon the teaching profession was being felt generally.[123] In spite of the frequent citation of the traditional doctrine, "It is a shame for woman to speak in the church," she began also to appear in the pulpit. Antoinette L. Brown, an Oberlin graduate of 1847, after having first been refused a license to preach, was ordained pastor of a church in South Butler, New York, where she began a long and active career. Among those who followed her example were Olympia Brown and Lydia A. Jenkins, active Universalist preachers, Phoebe Hanaford, and others. An occasional preacher's wife, like Caroline H. Dall, substituted for her husband during periods of illness or absence.

Dr. Elizabeth Blackwell and other women pioneers in medicine who by sheer persistence had secured their own professional training made numerous converts among the younger generation. The regular medical colleges, however, were not as yet open to women students. In an address at the opening of the new Harvard Medical Building, Oliver Wendell Holmes declared: "If here and there an intrepid woman insists on taking by storm the fortress of medical education, I would have the gate flung open to her, as if it were that of the citadel of Orléans and she Joan of Arc returning from the field of victory.[124] Not all, however, shared his generous impulse. Accordingly, separate medical colleges for women were established at Boston in 1848 and Philadelphia in 1850. Yet as late as 1859 the Pennsylvania Medical Society went on record recommending "the members of the regular profession to withhold from the faculties and graduates of Female Medical Colleges all countenance and support."[125]

Women writers and editors like Jane Grey Swisshelm, Paulina Wright Davis, Anna E. McDowell, Ellen Wentworth, Minnie Myrtle, and Fannie Fern urged with their pens a broader field of woman's rights. Bolder spirits like Elizabeth Cady Stanton, Susan B. Anthony, and Lucy Stone mounted the lecture platform to plead their many causes. Male prejudice was encountered at every turn; grave professors sometimes refused to address lyceums which scheduled an occasional female lecturer. Most "females" themselves were indifferent or antagonistic. Women delegates, refused the right to speak at a New York state temperance convention, arranged for a women's state temperance convention at Rochester on April 20, 1852. On the other hand, notable representatives of the male sex, generally liberals and radicals like Horace Mann, Wendell Phillips, and T. W. Higginson, joined in presenting the plea for woman's rights before the public.

No more outspoken critic of feminism could be found that James Gordon Bennett of the *New York Herald.* He characterized Lucy Stone "and all like her . . . fit inmates for some well conducted private lunatic asylum" and advised her husband to put her there, "where medicine and soothing treatment will extract from her brain that maggot of desire to exhibit herself at the polls."[126] "It is the settled and fixed sentiment of this and all civilized countries," he insisted, "that the rights of women, like her duties, are bounded by her household, that the votes she has to cast must be polled at her own tea table, that her politics must be the principles of domestic economy and that her authority must be over her own children and her servants."[127] This was a widely prevailing masculine point of view.

The woman's rights agitation excited fresh determination to secure for married women the separate control of their property. By 1860 this movement had succeeded in a number of states, sometimes to the point of granting them control over their own earnings. At the same time feminist leaders kept alive the question of widening the suffrage franchise and of rendering women eligible for officeholding. Strenuous but unsuccessful efforts were made in certain Eastern states, notably Massachusetts and Connecticut, and the question was considered somewhat in Ohio, Wisconsin, and Kansas. The one tangible gain of the decade was the granting by Kentucky of the right to vote for school trustees to any widow having a child of from six to sixteen years. The editor of the Montgomery *Alabama Journal,* rejoicing that such heresies were generally confined to the North, published a facetious account of a women's convention at Boston in which he characterized the principal speakers as disappointed old maids who had embraced the excitement of politics because they had no husbands to embrace; two weeks later, however, he found it necessary to print a petition addressed to the Alabama legislature to give women the franchise and the privilege of holding office.[128]

The "isms" that ravaged the country during the fifties evidenced the growing pains of an adolescent nation. Largely confined to the North, their local critics, like Walt Whitman, were usually willing to concede that they were "significant of a grand upheaval of ideas and reconstruction of many things on new bases."[129] Proud Southerners, on the other hand, rejoiced that the land of chivalry had largely escaped the taint of the fads that were sweeping Yankeedom. In less complacent mood they sounded the tocsin of alarm against vagaries of Yankee fanaticism that found their most portentous expression in a militant abolitionism.

HEALTH AND HAPPINESS

The health of the American people in the middle of the nineteenth century reflected the survival of pioneer optimism and neglect. Although the traditional ague and fever prevailed only on the frontier and in rural backwaters, careless and uncleanly conditions in the more thickly settled towns and cities bred diseases which quickly assumed an epidemic character. Hardly any town possessed an adequate drainage system. In bad weather the unpaved streets approached the condition of a quagmire, with dangerous sinkholes which only the boatman's phrase "no bottom" fitly described.

Absence of civic pride made the gutters the dumping ground for the community rubbish, while backyards and alleys reeked with filth and offal, the environs of public buildings and stores being especially offensive. If the few pavements of the larger cities somewhat simplified the problem of drainage, they did not solve the problem of cleanliness since they were often hidden from sight by accumulations of filth. New York City had perennial difficulty in securing street-cleaning contractors with a real sense of obligation to the community.

Then, too, nearly every city—from the national capital to some budding Western porkopolis—had its hog nuisance or some equivalent.[130] The streets, squares, and parks amounted to public pens, hog holes offending the eye and nose at every turn. Local sentiment, as in Springfield, Illinois, often sharply divided over the question of discontinuing this inexpensive system of scavenging. While the hog and antihog forces in city councils debated the issue his swineship contentedly pulled himself out of his gutter wallow, threatening to upset pedestrians as he carefully chose a freshly painted fence to rub off the unctuous matter with which he was plastered. In the fall of 1853 porkers were more numerous on the streets of Springfield than in the pens at the state fairgounds. The nearby town of Urbana had a record of more hogs than people, and they had at least equal rights with citizens upon the streets.

Hydrophobia was the natural consequence of the packs of dogs that roamed the streets. Ordinances against allowing them to run at large were seldom enforced, for the city dweller was not willing to dispense with the former guardian of the isolated farmhouse and assistant of the shepherd. At times of mad-dog panics men were often employed to kill off the surplus animals at twenty-five cents a head. Troops of rats lived under the wooden sidewalks and were accepted as an inevitable part of the population of public buildings until the horror of an episode like the devouring of a newborn babe in Bellevue Hospital, New York City, aroused the public to action.[131]

Community waterworks increased but slowly, there being only eighty private water systems and sixty-eight public ones when the war began. Yet this number represented a marked gain over the total of eighty-three in existence in 1850.[132] In 1862 the new 100-acre Croton reservoir, which had been four years building at a cost of $2 million, assured the nation's metropolis an ampler supply though, unhappily, the tenement districts were often without access to it. Important places like Milwaukee, Providence, and Portland had no public provision whatsoever. On the other hand, a public system did not ensure pure water. Thus Chicago's water, drawn from Lake Michigan, was often contaminated by filth which the rain washed from manure heaps upon the lake shore; indeed, the zealous apostle of cleanliness was often served with "chowder in his bathtub." Besides, much of the milk sold in Chicago came from cows "fed on whiskey slops with their bodies covered with sores and tails all eat off," a circumstance which enabled an editorial critic to explain "Why so many children die in Chicago."[133] New York's milk supply was also largely a by-product of the local distilleries and the milk dealers were charged with the serious offense of murdering annually 8,000 children.[134]

While the larger cities possessed handsome residential districts in which the streets were paved and kept clean and the sewage was properly cared for, there were also crowded foreign quarters, veritable hives of humanity lacking ordinary comforts and often even necessities. New York in 1850 had 8,141 cellars sheltering 18,456 persons. There, as in Boston, about a twentieth of the population lived in damp, dark, ill-ventilated, vermin-infested, underground rooms.[135] By the end of the war 15,000 tenement houses had been built in New York, many of them hardly more than "fever nests." Great blocks of slums were owned by men who resisted all sanitary improvements by securing from the Tammany-ridden city health department appointments as "health officers" in a system of sanitary police provided for in 1860.[136] In protest a "citizens' committee" appealed to the state authorities at Albany and secured an investigation that led to some relief. It is not surprising that New York had the highest death rate of all American cities. It nearly doubled that of London, although the rate for the country at large was probably not much more than half that of England. Other cities like Baltimore, which made rapid strides in reducing the percentage of mortality, seemed to have surpassed the metropolis in provisions for sanitation.[137]

"Narrow and crooked streets," asserted a contemporary critic, "want of proper sewerage and ventilation, absence of forethought in providing open spaces for the recreation of the people, allowance of intramural burials and of fetid nuisances, such as slaughterhouses, and manufactories of offensive stuffs, have converted cities into pestilential enclosures."[138] The actual record went far to sustain this sweeping indictment. Smallpox was a dread visitor liable to appear anywhere during the winter months; vaccination was possible only to a limited degree and was not compulsory. In the winter of 1860–61 the contagion raged in Philadelphia, Jersey City, and later in New York until summer, when the police department checked its spread by providing free vaccination at appointed places.[139] It broke out again in Washington in 1863, especially afflicting blacks. President Lincoln had already experienced a mild form of the disease and carried the disfiguring marks upon his face.[140] Yellow fever, for years a threat to the midsummer peace of Southern communities, raged in all its fury in 1855 at Norfolk and Portsmouth, Virginia, and in Louisiana and Mississippi.[141] In the Virginia plague area one out of five died of the fever, its victims often being buried wholesale in trenches without coffins. Its ravages ceased with the arrival of cold weather, in part because by that time nearly everyone had already contracted the disease. Relief for the fever-stricken district was organized in Northern communities, New York alone subscribing a quarter of a million dollars.

The pestilence that left behind the widest path of destruction, however, was the cholera. A year of special calamity was 1849. Making its appearance in the South in the early spring, the disease spread rapidly through the country, decimating the population of many a town and village. Thousands fled panic-stricken before the scourge, while days of fasting, humiliation, and prayer were appointed in view of its probable advent. Almost everyone felt, in fact or in apprehension, the unusual depression and other premonitory symptoms. The streets were empty except for the doctors rushing from victim to victim, and the coffin makers and undertakers following closely on their heels. Huge piles of wood were burned in the hope of purifying the atmosphere, the smoke hanging low on the heavy midsummer air. Cold weather brought relief, though Chicago and other Western cities suffered heavy mortalities in the summer of 1850. In 1851 and the succeeding years the disease extended to the Pacific Coast and to communities that had previously enjoyed relative immunity. But in 1854 it recurred in even more destructive form in Chicago and New York City, taking a toll of nearly 2,500 lives in the latter place.[142]

To bar the influx of such epidemics from abroad, New York State revived its quarantine station on Staten Island with regulations for the rigid inspection of every incoming vessel. During a yellow fever scare in 1858 mobs twice set fire to the hospital buildings which they considered a menace to health; they were at least successful in forcing their removal to a more remote point. A sense of the magnitude of public health problems led to a series of quarantine and sanitary conventions in the years immediately preceding the Civil War and prepared the way for more adequate measures of protection.[143]

The touching faith of the people in blatantly advertised patent medicine "cure-alls" continued strong, although the German migration, by bringing the trained prescription druggist, exercised a steadying influence upon American pharmacy. The *Deutsche Apotheke* with its German-script signboard appeared in many communities; in New York City there was one such institution for about every fifty families.[144] Dr. Oliver Wendell Holmes, however, declared in 1860 in a startling address before the Massachusetts Medical Society his firm belief that, in view of the prevailing dependence of his profession upon medication, "if the whole materia medica, *as now used,* could be sunk to the bottom of the sea, it would be all the better for mankind—and all the worse for the fishes."[145]

Even in the more provincial interior towns there seemed to be a ready hearing for lectures upon diseases and sanitary subjects, often announced in lurid posters. This lent encouragement to the numerous systems of medicine that promised to correct the "shocking barbarity" of old-school practice. Besides the well-known allopathic and homeopathic sects, usually in hostile array against each other, hydropaths were active and successful in the East and in parts of the Middle West. The virtues of water were proclaimed as a stimulant and a sedative, as an astringent and an aperient, and indeed as a universal agent for producing beneficial changes in the human organism. The "water cure" became the refuge of many who sought relief from strenuous living, while New Yorkers frequented Dr. R. T. Trall's Hydropathic Establishment, making it a sort of reform center.[146] Dr. Trall was also a moving force in a flourishing local Hygeiotherapeutic Medical School. In addition there were those who expounded the virtues of galvanic treatment and of electrochemical baths, while still others espoused a broad eclecticism in medicine. A contemporary critic found the medical profession a bedlam of "allopaths of every class of allopathy; homeopaths of high and low dilutions; hydropaths mile and heroic; chrono-thermalists, Thompsonians, mesmerists, herbalists, Indian doctors, clairvoyants, spiritualists with healing gifts, and I know not what besides."[147]

Without improved facilities for medical training the science of healing could not hope to forge rapidly ahead. In May 1848 the American Medical Association was organized at Philadelphia in the effort to elevate and systematize medical education by setting up standards higher than the prevailing ungraded courses of at most three terms of from twelve to sixteen weeks.[148] A young New York physician Dr. Nathan Smith Davis, who had taken the lead in this movement, accepted an appointment to Rush Medical College in Chicago in 1849 in the expectation that it would inaugurate the reform. Defeated after a prolonged contest, he joined in founding the medical department of Lind University and, when the first term opened in October 1859, he had the satisfaction of initiating a three-year graded course of study.[149] Davis was a pioneer in a field which even the well-established medical colleges of the East were not as yet ready to enter.[150] Hospitals, on the other hand, were beginning to appear in the larger cities. Though their total number remained small, they were credited with being an important factor in keeping down the death rate. Not only the state and municipal governments but also religious denominations in the bigger centers displayed an interest in this field. Yet as late as 1873 there were only 149 hospitals in the country, of which one third cared for insane patients.[151]

Despite the improved outlook for community and individual health, signs of a serious physical decline attracted thoughtful critics. Personal habits failed to reflect an adequate readjustment to the somewhat leisurely life that appeared with the recession of the frontier and of frontier conditions. Shrunken limbs, crooked spines, weak joints, and disproportionate bodies seemed everywhere in evidence. To the editor of *Harper's Monthly* Young America was "a pale pasty-faced, narrow chested, spindled-shanked, dwarfed race—a mere walking manikin to advertise the last cut of the fashionable tailor."[152] Abetted by the national habit of rapid eating, disorders of the stomach multiplied as the people continued to stuff themselves with a rich diet of badly cooked food. Only a negligible minority accepted the teachings of Sylvester Graham, apostle of vegetarianism and especially of the use of whole-wheat bread, who died in 1851. The unique advances in dental surgery reflected the ravages of disease in the wake of a faulty diet.

Thoughtful men pondered what Emerson referred to as "the invalid habits of this country." It came increasingly to be believed that the sorest need of the people was some recreation that would offer relaxation from business cares and sedentary employments. The example of England pointed to the value of out-of-door exercise and sport, for Young America in 1850 had not learned how to play in the modern sense. "To roll balls in a ten pin alley by gaslight or to drive a fast trotting horse in a light wagon along a very bad and very dusty road, seems the Alpha and Omega of sport in the United States," declared a contemporary English observer.[153]

Sports found no less worthy champions in New England than Oliver Wendell Holmes, the statesman Edward Everett, and the authors Bayard Taylor and Thomas Wentworth Higginson. Holmes, a puny, asthmatic type, was fond of horse racing, knew the records of the prize ring, and could often be seen rowing upon the Charles River; but the "Autocrat of the Breakfast Table" admitted that a reputation for athletic prowess might easily lead to ostracism from "good" society.[154] Everett enthusiastically advocated "noble, athletic sports, manly outdoor exercises, which strengthen the mind by strengthening the body, and bring man into a generous and exhilarating communion with nature."[155] Higginson, a strenuous young apostle of the cause, launched a series of articles in the *Atlantic,* beginning with his "Saints and Their Bodies."[156]

So strenuously did he press the merits of skating that rigid-minded people sneered at its increasing vogue as "Higginson's Revival." This sport was one of the few that required little inspiration from old-world customs. Popular with old and young and with both sexes, advocates of woman's rights seized upon it as a means of ushering in the new day; some found it an excellent argument for the bloomer costume. Crowds of 10,000, 20,000, and even 50,000 frequented the ponds in the new Central Park in New York. Rinks were built in towns like Roxbury, Massachusetts, while special excursion trains carried 1,000 or 1,500 Boston skating enthusiasts to Jamaica Pond and other nearby waters.

The fifties also ushered in a new boating era. Races were scheduled, college crews organized. Two of the greatest college presidents of the next generation, Andrew D. White of Cornell and Charles W. Eliot of Harvard, were members of crews in which Harvard and Yale began the tradition of intercollegiate athletics. Optimists even predicted that "if the boating era shall continue for the next five years, the coming generation will relieve America from the odium of physical decline."[157] At a time when graceful

A Summer Resort

clippers carried the flag in record-breaking voyages through the seven seas, it is not surprising that yacht sailing should have become popular along the Atlantic and in the ports of the Great Lakes. Particularly after the *America* returned victorious in 1851, the sport received a great impetus.[158] Yacht clubs were organized in every large city and regattas regularly scheduled.

Hunting and fishing had always been a common American diversion, if only as a means of obtaining a supply of food. To some extent, too, they were a business. Venison, selling for three cents a pound in Midwestern communities, was offered in large quantities in the New York market at around ten cents. From as far west as Wisconsin large shipments of game birds were sent to Eastern cities. The element of sportsmanship was better represented in Dixie where planters were apt to spend much of their time in field sports, especially the fox chase and the deer hunt. The game hunting of the Carolinas was known to sportsmen the world over.[159] On the lagoons of Chesapeake Bay wild-fowl shooting was followed with such ardor and success that canvasback duck was a famous Baltimore delicacy. The big game of the Far West attracted parties of British sportsmen who matched their wits with the American buffalo and elk. But the Prince of Wales during his visit in 1860 was content to fill his bags with the prairie hens and other wild fowl of Illinois.[160]

Boxing or prizefighting gained thousands of followers who felt an instinctive admiration for "the manly art of self-defense." Others, however, joined the press in condemning it as "un-American," a brutal importation from England where it held favor as the amusement of a degenerate nobility. Bouts had to be arranged secretly in out-of-the-way places where the authorities would be least likely to intervene. Oftentimes under cover of excursions into the country a large attendance was secured for a match. A boxing festival managed by John C. Heenan, the prizefighter, at Jones's Woods outside New York drew a crowd of 30,000.[161] Fights, usually continued until a knockout, often went to twenty-five rounds or more. One, in 1860, ended in a fifty-nine-round draw.

On October 20, 1858, John Morrissey, destined to be a future member of Congress, won from Heenan, called "Benicia Boy," an eleven-round contest for a purse of $5,000 at a point in Canada eighty miles from Buffalo.[162] In April 1860, following Morrissey's retirement, Heenan met in England the British favorite, Tom Sayres, in a championship bare-fist match which lasted two hours and twenty minutes, although Sayres's right arm was badly injured early in the fight. In the thirty-seventh round the crowd, sympathizing with the plucky Englishman, invaded the ring and stopped the contest. Both battered fighters claimed the victory in this most celebrated prizefight of modern times, but the match was officially declared a draw. Three years later Heenan returned and lost any claims he might have had to the championship and a $10,000 purse to the Briton, Tom King.[163]

From across the seas also came the game of racquet. Clubs were organized, but it found favor only among the wealthy. Cricket, another importation, had enough followers to make possible contests between local clubs and international games with British and Canadian teams. It, too, failed to interest the average American. Football was played, but as then conducted the game was apt to start or end as a free-for-all fight. Foot-racing appealed to many, while Edward Payson Weston in 1861 began his long-enduring reputation as a pedestrian by walking from Boston to Washington in 208 hours.[164] Bowling, with easy access to liquid refreshments, was a popular pastime both of idlers at watering places and of small-town loafers. Abraham Lincoln sought to while away the time waiting for news of the Republican national convention at Chicago by a game at a Springfield alley, but found the local resources for bowling and billiards entirely exhausted.

At this favorable moment in the annals of American athletics the game of baseball made its appearance. At first a modification of "Old Town Ball," in the early fifties it took on essentially its present form, though with from eleven to thirteen men on a side. It throve as an informal sport among the youth of the land, played largely on cow pastures without gloves or suits. Clubs were organized and spectators turned out to support the home team whether it registered a victory or a defeat. Scores ran large, one of seventy-five to forty-six for a twenty-five-inning game played upon the Boston Common in 1855 being a matter of record.[165] The organization of the National Association of Baseball Players in 1858 marked the beginning of a more regulated development under a definite code of rules; players from cities all over the Union sought admission to its ranks. Every community of any size soon had its own team and the competitive spirit assured a large attendance. High school and college teams were also organized. Baseball was well on its way to becoming the national game.

Except in New England where horse racing was supposed to have been prohibited in the decalogue, the racetrack offered entertainment and vicarious exercise to thousands, as it had for many years. Even Boston in 1862 turned out in force to witness its first horse race in half a century.[166] Classic events of distances of from one half to four miles were held on hundreds of tracks; when twenty-mile races were attempted they were found too exhausting to be profitable or humane. Tar River, a Southern horse, demonstrated unquestioned excellence in the three- and four-mile events; Ethan Allen, reputed to be the fastest trotting stallion in the world, was finally defeated in 1859 by Flora Temple, a gangling, disjointed mare of surprising swiftness. Horse racing and breeding were important industries, and followers of the track doubted whether American horses could be outdistanced. But in November, 1857, the S. S. *Arabia* brought news that the American horses Prioress and Babylon had been badly beaten in Newmarket.[167]

Along with outdoor sports came facilities for indoor athletics, a movement which reflected a strong German influence. As has been said, the revolutionary refugees of 1848 and the years that followed brought with them their *Turnvereine* or gymnastic unions, which met in Turner halls for gymnastic drill. By 1860 over 150 societies with a membership of nearly 10,000 were scattered over the country. Meanwhile, the thickening population of the cities encouraged experiments with gymnasiums on a commercial basis, while the Y.M.C.A. and similar organizations provided further opportunities. Just on the eve of the Civil War, too, while the older generation shook its head and pointed significantly to the backyard woodpiles, facilities for physical training and education were furnished in institutions like Amherst, Oberlin, Yale, and the U.S. Naval Academy.

But the older generation was not to be immune from the contagion. In 1860, Dr. Dio Lewis, a young Buffalo physician trained at the Harvard Medical School, who had developed a system of "light gymnastics," moved to Boston to offer the boon of exercise to those in greatest need, "old men, fat men, feeble men, young boys, and females of all ages." [168] A year later he opened his Normal Institute for Physical Education, the first school in the country to train teachers of physical culture. The zeal of a former advocate of prohibition and woman's rights entered into Lewis's numerous contributions to periodicals and into his work on *The New Gymnastics* (1862).

At the same time it must be remembered that most Americans were content with less strenuous amusements. For the younger generation this was the day of the spelling match and of the autograph collector, when few of the great and near great denied requests for a signature with a rebuke such as Horace Greeley administered to the youthful Frances Willard. [169] For a time a "coin fever" ran unabated among young and old and numismatic collections sold at fancy prices. [170] Social centers with equipment for checkers, dominoes, and other games made their appearance. But the post office and the depot (pronounced dee-poe) served with the church as the chief social centers of smaller communities. When the evening train or the mail arrived, the current of life set in and social amenities were eagerly exchanged.

Meanwhile the mystery of the secret fraternal society strengthened its hold on city folk, and prefigured the place it was later to occupy in the social organism. [171] Usually it was the Masonic order or the Odd Fellows, but newer organizations like the Improved Order of Red Men, the United Order of Friends, the Independent Order of United Brothers, and the Sons of Malta also attracted a following. The secret ritualism was one explanation of the remarkable popularity of the Know Nothing party and of the Sons of Temperance. Apart from certain clergymen few seemed to share the hostility of President Jonathan Blanchard of Knox College who classed not only the fraternal orders but even the Sons of Temperance as "anti-Republican in their tendencies and subversive of the principles both of the Natural and Revealed Religion." [172]

Summer tours through this nation of magnificent distances attracted an ever increasing patronage. Rail lines and their steamship connections carried the traveler in luxury to the scenic beauties of the upper Mississippi. The wonders of Niagara were at length within easy reach; there vagrant Indians in gaudy attire lent color to the scene. The visitor was guided down long flights of stairs until he stood where he could observe the full rush of the torrent above him. The *Maid of the Mist* carried passengers to the very vortex of the falls until in the summer of 1861, when the war curtailed the tourist traffic, it evaded seizure for debt by running the rapids only to be sold at the mouth of the river.[173] Meanwhile swaggering Americans were thronging to Europe in great crowds, giving foreigners "a capital notion of our progress in intellect and refinement," sarcastically commented Walt Whitman.[174]

While the middle class was finding amusement in such ways, no provision met democratically the needs of all classes. For this reason the rougher element and the youth of the large cities avidly responded to the appeal of the public dance halls, which reaped a golden harvest. Some critics of "such sinks of iniquity," "these branches of Satan's den," demanded their immediate extirpation,[175] others their more effective police regulation at the expense of the keepers. It was nevertheless noted that "those cities which extend the largest amount of patronage to amusements, do the greatest amount of business and attract the most visitors."[176] Chicagoans were only human, therefore, in taking pride at the close of the Civil War in the expenditure of a half million dollars a year for the city's organized amusements.

At the same time the upper social crust was reshaping itself again. In the Northern states leadership fell to a new aristocracy of wealth. Fortunes made in trade and industry, in railroad building and in Western land speculation lined Fifth Avenue with brownstone and marble palaces. Even in Boston, worth was coming to be measured in terms of dollars. An "Office of Heraldry," set up in New York, sought to indulge the vanity of those who wished to claim a share in the aristocratic tradition.[177]

Membership in the upper 10,000 required participation in the fashionable summer hegira to approved seaside resorts or to Saratoga Springs. Newport, once a thriving commercial town, was now in its glory as an American Brighton, the most fashionable sea-bathing resort in the country. Originally visited chiefly by Southern planters and their families, it found increasing favor with New York patrons. More and more the wealthy notables built their own summer homes — cottages, villas, and mansions stretching along the beach for two miles. Dressing, flirting, dancing, riding, and bathing furnished the chief amusements. Of these bathing was the newest and the most distinctive pastime, the women clad in clumsy white ankle-length pantalettes and red frocks with long sleeves, the men in costumes rather more abbreviated but less picturesque. So garbed, mixed bathing of men and women seemed harmless enough. Ordinarily the male companions took charge of the ladies in the surf, at times "handing about their pretty partners as if they were dancing water quadrilles." [178] A resort at Old Point Comfort, however, confined the men to one stockade built out into the water, while alongside in another, shrieks, screams, and laughter betrayed the ladies at play.[179] At certain beaches nude bathing, indicated by a red flag fluttering in the breeze, was provided for the men during the early afternoon—or napping—hours.[180]

Wealthy Southerners had long furnished a valuable patronage to the Northern resorts. Summer Newport was often referred to as a Southern community; a conservative proslavery atmosphere prevailed in the hotels they patronized and even in the churches they attended. In 1858, Senator Jefferson Davis of Mississippi joined a congenial group of prominent Southerners who regularly sojourned near Portland, Maine. As sectional feeling grew sharper, however, the Southern fire eaters insistently demanded a boycott of Northern resorts. Dixie had mountain and seaside attractions of her own, they pointed out. At the same time sensitive Southerners reported an increasingly rude reception upon Northern visits. "We are treated worse in the North than if we were foreign enemies," lamented the editor of the *Richmond Whig.* "Let us with one accord stay home and spend among our own people." [181]

Under this impetus wealthy planters began to erect summer places at the already popular mineral springs in the Virginia mountains, Fauquier White Sulphur Springs becoming especially fashionable. In 1855 a number of Southerners formed a stock company to develop Southern resorts, particularly a spring at Montgomery, Virginia, a few miles from the Tennessee line, where they hoped to create a "Southern Saratoga." [182] A few years later a number of small watering places with attractive summer residences grew up along the Gulf coast of Mississippi, a convenient location for inhabitants of New Orleans and for planters of the interior.[183] Thus, as the decade drew to a close, the spirit of sectionalism was invading even the sphere of pleasure and recreation. Formerly, leisure-class Americans from both sections rubbed elbows and learned the lesson of tolerance as they exchanged social courtesies and ideas at Saratoga and Newport. But unobserved by the statesmen, coming events disclosed how badly frayed had become the bonds of fraternal feeling and mutual esteem.

EDUCATIONAL AND CULTURAL ADVANCE

IMPROVING ON THE PIONEER LABORS of the preceding generation, the Americans of mid-century strengthened and extended the democratic system of education which they inherited. The West, which Horace Mann believed destined to be the "seat of empire," was eager to secure the benefits of the victories recently won in the older states.[184] In 1850 only a few schools were available in the West and terms were often three months or less. Over two thirds of the buildings were log houses, many of the rest mere shanties or temporary shacks. In one Illinois county the average worth of twenty-one buildings was $65. Now, however, came rapid development. The organization of a public system under state superintendents of instruction and the principle of free education were promptly adopted. Wisconsin's first constitution (1848) opened the doors of the schools freely to all. Indiana and Ohio followed in 1852 and 1853. The next year Illinois made provision for a state school tax, for unlimited taxation, and for a free school term of six months in every district. The number of schools doubled and trebled, while enrollment increased even more rapidly. Soon Illinois was boasting that only one child of school age in fifteen was not in attendance and that the average term was nearly seven months.

This expansion produced an inevitable dearth of available instruction. The National Educational Society therefore, through its agent, ex-Governor William Slade of Vermont, cooperated in enlisting well-trained Eastern young women as missionaries in the cause of education. In a period of eleven years nearly 500 "Yankee school-marms" were sent into the West, which welcomed them with salaries only half those of their male associates, many of them, too, New Englanders. The complaint of Western advocates of education was not only that the supply of young women was insufficient, but that once arrived they married. "Instead of teaching other folk's children, [they] soon find employment in teaching their own."[185] Others, however, had deeper doubts as to the plan. Some educational leaders suggested that such teachers were bound to bring in a spirit of condescension growing out of their lack of sympathy with Western habits, customs, and feelings. Certain Democratic politicians, including the great Douglas who had himself come to Illinois as a Vermont schoolmaster, expressed fear that these selected emissaries of New England, and therefore probably of abolition, would mold the youth into the likeness of "canting, freedom-shrieking" Yankee demagogues.

Such ungenerous criticism proved unwarranted, but at any rate it furnished an argument for a local supply of teachers. The colleges of the West were not able to meet the demand, nor were their graduates specifically trained for teaching. This situation led to the founding of normal schools, the West following along the paths marked out by aggressive Eastern leaders.[186] Michigan acted in 1849, Illinois in 1857, Minnesota in 1860, with other states presently doing the same. Teachers continued, however, to be sadly underpaid though salaries advanced greatly during the decade. In Wisconsin, for example, the average pay of men rose from $15.22 a month in 1850 to $24.20 in 1860, of women from $8.97 to $15.30.[187]

In most Eastern states the "rate-bill" lingered in whole or in part. This practice involved a charge upon parents to supplement the school revenues and prolong the school term, and was assessed in proportion to the number of pupils in each family. While provision was made for its remittance in the case of parents who could not pay, there were many whose pride kept them from declaring their need and whose children were therefore kept out of school. In New York State the issue of free schools was fought out in a series of popular referenda in which the city voters advocating tax-supported schools met heavy opposition from the rural counties and from the supporters of the parochial system. The result was a compromise which continued the state rate bill in effect—it was not repealed until 1867 —and at the same time authorized such school districts as wished to do so to provide free schools by local taxation. Under this arrangement New York City organized a system of free schools. In June 1853, therefore, the Public School Society of that metropolis, which had maintained an extensive system on its own account, decided that its goal had been achieved and agreed to surrender its schools to the local board of education. Nowhere, aside from a mild requirement in Massachusetts, was there as yet the feature of compulsory attendance.[188]

For the average boy and girl of 1850, public education ended in the common schools. Some fortunate few continued their training in the private or semiprivate academies that were just reaching the zenith of their development. But the city high school was steadily increasing in importance. The number of such public institutions rose during the decade from a few dozen to some 300. The son of the day laborer and of the artisan began to share educational opportunities that had often been regarded as a peculiar monopoly of the privileged minority. Except in a few conservative communities like Boston, girls took their places in the classrooms devoted to this more advanced training. The high school had its early origins in New England, but the democratic West promptly appropriated the idea and established secondary schools in its growing cities.[189]

The high schools, like the academies, were generally college preparatory schools. Simultaneously in this decade before the Civil War nearly 100 institutions of higher learning were founded, a record unrivaled in the annuals of American education. Most of the new colleges were located in the South, with its growing distrust of the North and Northern schools, and in the West, the newer parts of which were now ready for refinements undreamed of during the frontier stage. These were largely denominational colleges which adopted the traditional curriculum and the prevailing methods of study. Yet the spirit of innovation and revolt was also abroad. Many attacked the existing form of higher instruction and called for a more practical education on the European model. Scores of American students, most of them destined to become college professors, had studied in German universities.[190] From them and others came a demand that the colleges, which seemed to many "the headquarters of conservatism," keep pace with the rapid progress of human knowledge; that science be given a place alongside classical studies; that better libraries and laboratories be provided; and that more freedom in the choice of studies be allowed.[191]

Henry P. Tappan, president of the University of Michigan from 1852 to 1863, proclaimed the virtues of the German universities and of European systems of thought until critics branded him the most completely for-eignized specimen of an abnormal Yankee that they had ever seen, and in due time forced his dismissal.[192] But under his aggressive administration progress was the order of the day. A course in civil engineering was estab-lished, the first chemistry laboratory in America was set up in 1857, and in the same year Andrew D. White was appointed to one of the first chairs of history to be created in an American university.[193] These and similar pion-eering ventures caused the enrollment to jump in a decade from a mere handful of students to more than 500 in 1860; in another five years it more than doubled again. Students flocked from all parts of the country to what an Eastern educator, an orator at the Harvard triennial festival in 1866, called

the only seminary in the country whose liberal scope and cosmopolitan outlook satisfy the idea of a great university. Compared with this, our other colleges are all provincial; and unless the State of Massachusetts shall see fit to adopt us, and to foster our interest with something of the zeal and liberality which the State of Michigan bestows on her academic masterpiece, Harvard cannot hope to compete with this precocious child of the West.[194]

But Harvard, with a faculty made up of men of scholarly distinction, some of them of international repute, remained in the foreground of higher learning. It showed its ability to outgrow old traditions by creating a chair of modern languages to which first Henry Wadsworth Longfellow and later James Russell Lowell were appointed. The vitality of collegiate education in this era, indeed, seemed to depend upon courage to break new ground. Graduate work had its faint beginnings. In 1861, Yale awarded the first American degree of doctor of philosophy. In many places mathematics and the ancient languages were compelled to yield to the demands of the age and make room for modern languages and the new physical sciences.

The advance of knowledge became increasingly indebted to members of college faculties. When Darwin's *Origin of Species* was published in 1859 the entire first American edition sold within a fortnight. Professor Louis Agassiz of the Harvard faculty promptly reiterated his loyalty to the theory of immutability and proclaimed Darwinism "a scientific mistake, untrue in its method, and mischievous in its tendency."[195] At the time, Joseph Le Conte, an American scientist trained under Agassiz, was working at the University of South Carolina on a theory of the origin of species by natural selection. Agassiz's own scientific labors attracted such favorable notice that a bequest of $50,000, supplemented by popular subscriptions totaling $75,000 and by a legislative grant of $100,000, made possible at Harvard University a permanent museum of comparative zoology to house the collections of this indefatigable worker.[196] Astronomical science as practiced at Harvard, where extensive experimentation in stellar photography was being undertaken, aroused the interest of a trio of wealthy Chicago merchants to the point of causing them to provide a local observatory with a telescope somewhat larger than the instrument at Cambridge.[197] In the meantime, while Asa Gray, the noted Cambridge botanist, was writing the *Botany of the United States Pacific Exploring Expedition,* and pleading for a fair and favorable consideration of Darwin's theories, Henry Shaw, a retired St. Louis merchant, devoted his time to building up a botanical garden near his home which was to develop into an invaluable laboratory for scientific study. The Smithsonian Institution, too, rapidly expanded its work and its influence as a national clearinghouse for scientific activities. When a disastrous fire in 1865 destroyed building and records, its evident value ensured its prompt replacement.

Inevitably the hydraheaded slavery question made its way into nearly every college community in the land. In the East, where traditions were conservative, college faculties generally frowned upon antislavery agitation, advocating compromise. President Theodore Dwight Woolsey of Yale was one of the few outstanding leaders in that section who braved public sentiment by condemning the fugitive-slave law and other concessions to slavery. In the Midwest, on the other hand, many colleges were hotbeds of antislavery feeling. Oberlin, which long since had opened its doors to the few blacks who applied for admission, saw its enrollment under the impulse of the controversy leap to over 1,200 in 1850, a new record in college attendance. But Horace Mann with a similar but more radical venture at Antioch College in the same state met with serious obstacles which hastened his death in 1859.[198]

Many an American gleaned his education and drew his inspiration chiefly from the printed page. In the cities the tax-supported free library began to take hold. In 1854 the Boston Public Library, authorized in 1848, opened its doors, and within fifteen years was dispensing 100,000 volumes. In 1854, too, the Astor Library in New York City opened. Made possible by a generous bequest from John Jacob Astor and aided by later gifts from the Astor family, it was long the largest library in the country. In 1857 the Peabody Library in Baltimore was established. When a disastrous fire in 1851 destroyed two thirds of the collections of the Library of Congress, a new and safer building was acquired and annual appropriations of $10,000 enabled it to add in eight years 50,000 volumes. By 1863 the country contained 104 libraries of over 10,000 volumes each, a decided gain from the forty in 1849.[199]

The enthusiasm was shared by the West, where libraries were soon set up in communities as remote as Leavenworth, Kansas. Township libraries, often direct adjuncts of the schools, were provided for by law in several states. Their avowed object in Michigan was "to diffuse information, not only or even chiefly among children or minors, but among adults and those who have finished common school education."[200] It became traditional in Indiana that such collections helped to develop the literary talent and the intelligence of the reading public of that state.[201] In a decade the public libraries of the nation increased eightfold, to over 1,000, while their volumes multiplied fivefold, reaching a total of nearly 8 million. In 1856 a group organized the Chicago Historical Society, which, after a year, reported a collection of 11,000 volumes, largely the gift of members and friends. In time its accumulating bundles of maps and papers and its shelves of books were proudly displayed to distinguished foreign travelers like the Prince of Wales.[202]

Books were being purchased by private individuals at a rate that contributed to the increasing prosperity of the American publisher. The bookstore in New York or such an establishment as that of Ticknor and Fields in Boston was the natural resort of cultured patrons and of literary celebrities, but even Albany, the gateway to the West, had several extensive shops that provided for the intellectual wants of travelers on the line of the great trek into the interior. Chicago had three thriving bookstores, including one which claimed to be the largest in the Middle West. The shops of this and other Western cities often carried an extensive line of English classics and current publications, while the Yankee book peddler sold sets of standard works in the more isolated communities.[203] Even the humble frontier cabin generally had "some newspaper, some book, some token of advance in education."[204]

Transappalachia, indeed, was revealing an amazing if uncertain zeal in literary self-expression. Its political, agricultural, and even family journals had from an early day shown marked leanings in that direction. But during the forties special publications with literary interests sprang up in quick succession, Chicago alone witnessed at least one such venture every year. The Western interest was vigorously proclaimed by editors of Yankee origin in successive salutatories and editorial statements. "The GREAT WEST," announced the *Literary Budget* of Chicago on January 7, 1854, "in her undulating prairies, deep-wooded highlands, mighty rivers, and remnants of aboriginal races, presents topics teeming with interest to every reader, and big with beautiful scenes for the artist's eye. The West is full of subject-matter for legend, story, or history."[205] It seemed clear, wrote a poet and compiler of poetry, that the West had "a symphony to utter, whose key-note is already struck, and which is to make the world pause and listen."[206] But that Eastern ties and influence remained was evident in 1860 when Moncure D. Conway, a young native of Virginia, set up in Cincinnati, the oldest literary center in the West, *The Dial: A Monthly Magazine for*

Literature, Philosophy, and Religion. This journal frankly aspired "to be an Avatar" of the earlier Boston organ of the same name, a fact which Emerson recognized when he sent a succession of contributions to it.

The "cracker-box philosophers," with their homely sallies about the foibles of the day, also made their contribution to Americanism in literature. Their efforts were characterized by a crudity and exaggeration that sacrificed accurate portraiture to achieve a humorous effect. The average reader of the fifties still enjoyed *The Sayings and Doings of Samuel Slick*, the Yankee clock maker and peddler, or the pungent humor in the *Letters of Major Jack Downing of the Downingsville Militia.* A new crop of American humorists also made their appearance. In 1856 was published *Plu-Ri Bus-Tah, a Song by No Author, Perpetrated by Q. K. Philander Doesticks* (Mortimer Thompson), and in the next year the excellent social satire of William A. Butler, *Nothing to Wear*, a popular humorous poem which was promptly followed by *Nothing to Do, an Accompaniment of Nothing to Wear.* The pretentious ignorance of the garrulous Mrs. Partington who played with words too large for safety added to the general merriment.[207] "Partington Pearls" became the chief stock in trade of the American wit.

Next to riotous fun the average American craved hair-raising thrills. Nor did writer and publisher fail to cater to this need. Beginning in 1850 the country storekeeper found it easy to sell cheap paperbound tales of city wickedness and of the thwarted attempts of side-whiskered villains of sartorial perfection to seduce innocent maidens.[208] The earlier success of certain Western romances suggested another field. A restless literary swashbuckler named Edward Z. C. Judson set out in the late forties to retail the products of his own experience and imagination in the pages of a weekly story paper called *Ned Buntline's Own,* on the theory that "trash for the masses" instead of art for the critical few was the secret of literary success. The adventures of his gallant hero and of other similar worthies were soon appearing serially in Eastern weeklies, and "Ned Buntline" with an income of $20,000 a year was living in ease in New York.[209] In 1860, too, the enterprising publishing house of Erastus F. and Irwin P. Beadle, following successes with the *Beadle Dime Song Book* and the *Dime Joke Book,* launched the large-scale distribution of cheap paperback novels. Their editor Orville J. Victor overhauled the manuscripts of varying merit that poured in and paid $50 or more for the tales he selected. The flavor of American life, especially of the frontier, was in these thrillers. One of the most popular was Mrs. Metta V. Victor's *Maum Guinea and Her Plantation Children,* a pathetic tale of slave life which Lincoln, Seward, and Henry Ward Beecher read and praised and the English edition of which ran up to 100,000 copies. In four years 5 million were put into circulation, including several volumes of biography, largely of frontier heroes.[210]

Meanwhile the more dignified historic muse took pride in the productive pens of her devotees, largely New Englanders. Richard Hildreth completed in 1856 the *History of the United States* which he had begun in the preceding decade, while George Bancroft after a twelve-year interruption resumed a similar task, the end of which was to prove nearly a quarter-century away. Younger historians impelled by the same patriotic interest also gained recognition. Francis Parkman began his life study of the romance of the colonial frontier, the first fruits of his labors appearing in his *Conspiracy of Pontiac* (1851). In 1858 the initial volume of John G. Palfrey's *History of New England* was published, but failed to prove an immediately profitable venture. When John Lothrop Motley began in 1856 to bring out his *History of the Rise of the Dutch Republic,* he also gained a place among American historians. Meanwhile, the skillful pen of William H. Prescott was depicting the fortunes of *Philip II.* Most of these writers had stylistic distinction that made their work popular. They were part of that galaxy of literary talent that bespoke for the American republic an era of real cultural achievement. Every bookstall in Britain, said an English writer, was beginning to groan under "the products of the American mind."[211]

No such product was more influential than Harriet Beecher Stowe's *Uncle Tom's Cabin* (1852), dramatic versions of which, heralded by sensational headings of theatrical placards, threatened to monopolize the stage in the North. For night after night and week after week it held the boards in the cities, while companies toured the provinces with tents capable of seating as many as 5,000 spectators. In the closing years of the decade the temperance play *Ten Nights in a Bar-Room,* adapted from T. S. Arthur's book of the same title, began a long career. Greeley must have discounted these two pieces when he asserted that the stage, the traditional ally of liberty and humanity, had failed to support the antislavery cause and the temperance movement.[212] Indeed, the injection of moral purpose into histrionic performances helped break down the ancient prejudice against the stage. When a Hartford judge in 1852 refused a permit for theatrical presentations on the ground that they were dangerous to morality, several newspapers spoke out in protest. Even the church took a more tolerant attitude toward the drama. A prominent clergyman actually proposed a Christian theater for the production of the right type of plays, although a critic suggested that this was like a proposal to establish a "holy Hell."[213]

Besides *Uncle Tom's Cabin,* other plays dealing with slavery scored successes, notably J. T. Trowbridge's *Neighbor Jackwood,* a fugitive-slave tale which held the Boston stage for eight years, and, especially, *The Octoroon* (1859), one of a number of popular dramas from the pen of Dion Boucicault, a young playwright of Irish birth who in 1853 with his actress wife, Agnes Robertson, cast his lot with the American stage. Boucicault aided in the movement which secured more adequate protection to dramatists in the copyright law of August 18, 1856.

Popular interest in the stage reflected a craving for entertainment rather than an enjoyment of artistic form. All indications pointed to a slow development of an appreciation of art for its own sake. Art stores in New York existed for the sale of mirrors and gold frames, or of steel engravings, lithographs, and cheap oil paintings, in standard sizes turned out wholesale under factory conditions.[214] The firm of Currier and Ives sold untold thousands of colored lithographs of racehorses, clipper ships, locomotives, and other aspects of the American scene. Little did their owners think that they would be dug from storeroom and attic to serve a twentieth-century vogue![215] More pretentious were the huge rolls of painted canvas that were exhibited throughout the country — the "Panorama of Eden," the "Classical Panorama of Roman History," a "Panorama of China," the "Sacred Panorama of Pilgrim's Progress," the "Panorama of the Mississippi River," the "Moving Mirror of the Overland Route to California." Ball's "Pictorial Tour of the United States," an antislavery work, depicted in 23,000 feet of canvas the scenic beauties of the country and the woes of slavery. At the same time the "instantaneous" photographic art of the fifties found a skilled exponent of the new wet-plate process in Mathew B. Brady, a former master of the daguerreotype. At his New York studios and the Washington branch established in 1858, the most eminent Americans of the day sat for their likenesses.

If the American nation had become by 1860, as some friendly foreign visitors admitted, "the most generally educated and intelligent people on the earth,"[216] this was due not only to the operation of the rapidly expanding public school system but also to the less formal intellectual and cultural influences that ramified in almost every direction. Carl Schurz ascribed the high average of intelligence in large part to the fact that "the individual is constantly brought into interested contact with a greater variety of things, and is admitted to active participation in the exercise of functions which in other countries are left to the care of a superior authority."[217]

Less reassuring was the circumstance that the cultural advance of these years was sectional in character. For the most part the South, hampered by its caste system, its undigested mass of poor whites and enslaved blacks, its growing antagonism to the free states, remained unaffected by the new currents of civilization. It did not share in the movement for popular education; it took a negligible part in the lyceum movement; it supported few magazines or publishing houses; it had little of a creative nature to contribute to science, scholarship, letters, and the arts. More and more it lived to itself, closed in by tradition and by loyalty to a social institution which it alone in all the civilized world maintained and defended. The widening breach between the sections thus reached beyond political acerbities into the very substance of life itself.

THE CHALLENGE TO THE CHURCH

THE AMERICAN CHURCH of the fifties enjoyed its greatest development in the upper Mississippi Valley where it represented one of the refinements that followed in the wake of the frontier. In the flush times of this decade 1,000 church edifices were built annually, most of them simple frame structures. Many congregations were still without provision for regular preaching, but the humble, zealous itinerant preacher, pioneer in the work of evangelizing the raw West, reached a large scattered constituency by "riding circuit." The quaintly heroic Peter Cartwright was at the age of seventy still duplicating upon the Illinois prairie some of the feats of his prime. On one occasion he rode ninety-four miles through almost incessant rain, preached to several congregations, and received as quarterage fifteen cents and, by way of table expenses, a dozen apples.[218]

Nearly all denominations expanded in membership, at the same time meeting rivalry in a proliferation of minor sects. In the country at large the Methodists stood in the lead, although Methodism in the West seemed to suffer from neglect by the central organization. After a decade of controversy which caused their leaders to be expelled from the fold, the Free Methodist Church was organized in 1860 out of a group of western New York dissenters known as Nazarites. Meanwhile, in 1858, two reform elements among the Presbyterians effected a union which produced the United Presbyterian Church. The Baptist churches continued to display a strong frontier influence, while the Disciples of Christ, even more typical of the pioneer spirit in religion, experienced steady growth.[219] Renewed enthusiasm was inspired by the Western tour in 1853 of the Reverend Alexander Campbell, founder of the denomination. By the end of the Civil War the membership of this denomination approached the half-million mark.

German and Scandinavian immigration into Middle America hastened the growth of Lutheranism in northern Illinois and in Wisconsin, Iowa, and Minnesota. The German settlers replaced the losses in the East of their countrymen who had dropped away, while the Scandinavians formed congregations and, in due time, synods of their own. In 1853 the Norwegian Evangelical Church of America was organized by representatives of Wisconsin congregations; seven years later the Scandinavians of northern Illinois withdrew from the northern Illinois synod of the Lutheran Church and formed the Scandinavian Augustana Synod.[220]

The extensive migrations of the New England element brought large numbers of Congregationalists into the West. The first general convention of American Congregationalism, held in Albany in October 1852, formally declared at an end the old "Plan of Union" with the Presbyterians and called for $50,000 for the erection of new churches in the states west of

Ohio.[221] Congregations under their own name began to increase rapidly, especially in the "Yankee" belt along the lower Great Lakes.[222] Already in April 1851 a Congregational church had been organized in Chicago when the repudiated antislavery members of the Third Presbyterian Church, most of whom had New England Congregationalist antecedents, set up for themselves. Two other congregations established places of worship in the city during the decade.[223] The Midwest also helped train one of the most influential Congregational ministers of the East. Young Henry Ward Beecher, fresh from Indiana where his triumphant revivalism had led to a call to Plymouth Church, captivated his sedate Brooklyn congregation by his oratory and received a salary that rapidly mounted to $5,000 and, later, to $12,500. Beecher was soon a collector of paintings, bronzes, books, and precious stones, and lived in an atmosphere of refulgence, if not extravagance. Every seat in his immense church was usually occupied; pew rentals went at a premium at the annual auction. High-salaried preachers, high pew rentals, paid singers, and expensive organs made stern moralists wonder whether the worship of Mammon had not crept into organized Christianity.[224]

The Episcopal Church had its stronghold in the East; the West was less hospitable to its ritualism and elaborate ceremonial. When Bishop Henry J. Whitehouse succeeded the popular pioneer Bishop Philander Chase of Illinois in 1852, a heated controversy soon waged between the new bishop and low-church critics who attacked him as teaching "Tractarian and Semi Romish Errors."[225] In 1858 the low-church party set up an organ in Chicago, the *Western Churchman,* to combat the influence of the official publication, the *Chicago Herald.*

The Roman Catholic Church grew lustily in the larger cities, mainly from recruits of Irish and other immigrants. In cities as diverse as New York and Cincinnati, from a third to a half of the population were Catholics. Particular efforts were made to ensure religious provision for the Midwest. Certain leaders, including Archbishop Hughes of New York, hoped that Catholic colonization beyond the Appalachians might save the poor and degraded Irish from the grog shops and squalor of Eastern cities and, at the same time, strengthen Mother Rome. Meanwhile the Jesuits undertook an active educational campaign through their rapidly increasing colleges, seminaries, and female academies. These were in many ways in the vanguard of female education, a fact which, together with the low cost, led many Protestant families to send their daughters to them.[226]

The mental excitability of Americans seemed to lend itself to many kinds of religious fervor and metaphysical inquiry. Thus the cult of spiritualism experienced a rapid rise. It originated in Rochester with the Fox sisters, the young children of a western New York family, who claimed to act as media for communication with the dead through certain mysterious rapping sounds by which questions put to them were answered.[227] The fame of the

Rochester spirit rappings spread over the nation. In 1850 the Fox sisters gave exhibitions in New York City with some of the most eminent men of the nation among their visitors. Persons like William J. Stillman, the artist, and Thomas Appleton, the publisher, became sincere spiritualists, while Horace Greeley gave generous space to the movement in the columns of the *Tribune* and professed at least to maintain an open mind.

Soon a veritable craze was abroad, spreading from Maine to California.[228] Mediums appeared everywhere ready to exhibit spirit manifestations. In 1852 spiritualists began to hold a series of conventions at Boston, Worcester, and Cleveland. By the end of the year a dozen or more spiritualist periodicals were in circulation, including the *Seraphic Advocate,* the *Spiritual Telegraph,* the *Spirit Messenger,* and *Light from the Spirit World.* The printing press groaned under the pamphlets and books that were being issued, with their exciting tales and their "research" data. In 1853 a great conference was held at Springfield, Massachusetts, with some 300 or 400 "rappers" and other mediums communing with spirits of all ages, all countries, and all languages. To many it seemed religious fanaticism gone mad. Indeed, the newspapers began to chronicle numerous instances of suicide and insanity growing out of the excitement. Insanity seemed to increase where the movement was strongest. Presently, however, spiritualism went the way of other "isms." In 1854 the national Senate refused to give serious consideration to a petition signed by 15,000 asking for the appointment of a commission to investigate the phenomena of "occult forces." Within a few years a mere handful remained of the million or more adherents which the cult had optimistically claimed in 1853.

Although violent religious emotionalism was becoming more and more a rarity, the revival continued to be an accepted pastime of the closing weeks of the long, dreary rural winter, just as the camp meeting was an escape from dull summer monotony. But the sudden and widespread distress occasioned by the financial crisis of 1857 sharpened the consciousness of sin of many who felt that the Heavenly Father was visiting divine vengeance upon a selfish and materialistic nation.[229] As the theaters closed and other normal means of amusement slipped from the impoverished grasp of habitual seekers of diversion, a new religious interest gripped persons usually least susceptible to such an influence. In the early part of 1858 a spiritual awakening was perceptible throughout the country. Revival meetings attracted community-wide interest; tens of thousands of conversions were reported. For a time only one class seemed immune. "While pugilists, rowdies, and burglars are converted, the revivals have not made the slightest impression upon the hardened sinners of Wall Street," lamented a New York editor.[230] Soon, however, it was evident that the spirit of prayer had penetrated even the countinghouse, where the pious hoped that it would continue to dwell.

"Prayer meetings sprang into existence in private houses, stores, shops,

A Camp Meeting

theaters, and even in lofts and cellars," noted one observer.[231] But the particular feature of the "Great Revival of 1858" was the large daily union prayer meeting held in nearly every city. Suddenly despoiled of their prosperity, the people turned to God and began to pray. Spontaneity and sincerity marked these gatherings; the pastors did not need to take the initiative. Neither ecstasies nor convulsive sobs were necessary to show that the human soul had been reached. Except in rural communities there was a singular freedom from the extravagances and the wild excitement that had formerly attended such awakenings. The freedom from sectarianism and the perfect cordiality with which preachers and laymen of different churches labored together seemed to herald a new day of religious cooperation.[232]

The "Great Awakening" of 1858 called attention to the growing secularization of the Sabbath, a relaxing of time-honored practices due to the cosmopolitan spirit that prevailed in the large cities and the frontier carelessness that lingered in the West. If Boston still had compunctions against allowing theatrical performances on Saturday night, New Orleans went so far as to impose no Sunday restrictions upon the drama, horse racing, or other forms of amusement. Even smaller communities sometimes took on a gala atmosphere on the Lord's day, militia companies in uniform parading to music while groups of young folk spent the day in merrymaking, and their elders quenched their thirst through the side-door entrances of the liquor shops. Conditions in other cities were often like those in Chicago:

> Here in Chicago, we have fifty-six churches open on Sunday . . . but at the same time, there are no less than eighty ball rooms, in each of which a band plays from morning till midnight. . . . In addition to these activities we have two theaters, each with its performers in tights and very short garments. . . . Saloons . . . do a thriving business through side entrances.[233]

Other conditions also menaced the church's monopoly of the Sabbath. Railroads and newspapers represented the encroachments of commercial enterprise. A Northwestern Sabbath Convention at Chicago in May 1854 denounced the danger of desecration by Sunday trains as more appalling than that from any other source. Objection was also made to the running of horse railway or omnibus lines. As the Sabbatarian movement gained strength from the "Great Awakening," Horace Greeley joined the reformers in their protest against the sale of newspapers on Sunday. But his rival James Gorden Bennett rejoiced that a concerted campaign of Sabbatarians and the police commissioners had not caused the circulation of the *Sunday Herald* to decrease.[234] The editor of *Harper's Monthly* deplored the narrowness of the Sunday restrictionist, insisting that urban life required a new version of the Christian conception, that the Sabbath was made for man "for his moral, intellectual, and physical good."[235] It became more and more evident that on this score the Sunday-observance movement could not stay the hands of the clock of time.

The Christian church of the North wavered as it faced the even more serious challenge flung by the abolitionist crusaders. Leading divines, even in the North, denounced the abolitionists as apostles of atheism and anarchy and proclaimed that the institution of chattel slavery had the sanction of Holy Writ. President Nathan Lord of Dartmouth College appealed to his fellow preachers of all denominations to stem the tide of abolition, while Bishop John Henry Hopkins built up an elaborate defense of slavery on scriptural and historical grounds.[236]

The antislavery forces found it no easy matter to meet the scriptural argument for slavery. William Jay, the veteran abolitionist, contended that the proslavery texts were incorrect translations;[237] but this did not undermine the confidence of theological doctrinaires who accepted without question the verbal inspiration of the King James text. The leaders of the American Anti-Slavery Society in 1858 agreed without any real enthusiasm to a proposal by Harriet Beecher Stowe that a tract be issued concerning the Bible and slavery; all present seemed relieved to learn that the task could be delegated to the proponent's brother, Charles Beecher. In 1860, too, an able work appeared from the pen of the Reverend George B. Cheever on *The Guilt of Slavery and the Crime of Slaveholding.*

As early as the 1840s two major denominations had split upon the rock of slavery and driven their Southern brethren into independent organization.[238] Only the Roman Catholic Church seemed free from the agitation,[239] although its next of kin, the Protestant Episcopal Church, proud of its conservative spirit, also succeeded in steering a safe noncommittal course.[240] It was an easy matter for churches organized in independent congregations without central legislative bodies to practice the gospel of "no fellowship with slave-holders." Moreover, most Baptist, Congregational, and Unitarian churches were controlled by elements unequivocally committed to the gospel of freedom.

Official spokesmen of the Methodist Episcopal Church North commonly pointed to the record of its earnest but conservative protest against the evil of slavery. On the other hand, probably as many as 200,000 slaves were owned by its members. Many zealous antislavery men from Northern conferences demanded that the general rule in regard to slavery be made more drastic so that the church might be freed entirely from its "criminal" connection with the institution. This issue was pressed against a declining opposition until the general conference at Buffalo in 1860 adopted a new rule in which, without excluding slaveholders from its communion, it admonished members "to keep themselves pure from this great evil, and to seek its extirpation by all lawful and Christian means."[241]

While the Old School Presbyterians, true to their traditional conservatism, ignored the slavery question, the New School group continued in the early fifties the tactics of trying to appease the antislavery forces by mild condemnations of slavery.[242] The radical element, however, proposed to refuse fellowship to the slaveholder, a program much too strenuous for the cautious leaders of the church and influential laymen like Cyrus H. McCormick, patron of the Theological Seminary at Chicago. Finally, in 1857, when the general assembly voted strong condemnation of a proslavery report of a Kentucky presbytery, six Southern synods with about 200 churches and 15,000 communicants withdrew. With the opening of the Civil War the Old School Presbyterians of the South organized a separate church of their own.[243]

Meanwhile the common cause of freedom was tending to break down the denominational barriers that separated the Christian antislavery forces. Deprecating the adoption of expediency as a substitute for the spirit of Christ, the crusaders could not but feel that the slavery issue was of more importance than sectarianism. As a result a Christian Anti-Slavery Convention assembled at Cincinnati in April 1850; in July 1851 an even more enthusiastic session of 250 delegates met at Chicago with Jonathan Blanchard of Knox College in the chair. Though the Christian Anti-Slavery Convention disappeared as the conservative reaction set in, it was revived in October 1859 as the Northwestern Christian Anti-Slavery Convention.[244] Again Blanchard was a leading figure, calling the assemblage to order and justifying his support of the Republican party.

On less drastic tests of their devotion to human liberty the clergy of the nation spoke out with greater courage. Though ministers were oftentimes silent or apologetic, a strong note of protest sounded from many pulpits at the passage of the fugitive-slave law of 1850. Four years later the clergy burst out in wrath against the Kansas-Nebraska act as an assault on freedom. A memorial signed by 500 clergymen of the Northwest denounced Douglas for "want of courtesy and reverence toward man and God."[245] Promptly conservative editors and politicians deplored the tendency of churchmen to leave their sacred calling and incite partisan strife. "When ministers enter the arena of politics, and associate themselves with the corrupt and lying hypocrites who lead the black republican party, and utter seditious harangues from the pulpit, they are no longer entitled to that respect that their sacred calling commands," declared the *Signal* of Joliet, Illinois, when four of the local clergy participated prominently in a Republican meeting of Knox College.[246] Such warnings probably restrained the timid at a time when radical abolitionists were wondering whether the cause of freedom could triumph except upon the ruins of the church.[247] Henry Ward Beecher, a brilliant barometer of popular progressive currents, answered critics by advancing the doctrine that any topic introduced into the pulpit became thereby consecrated. Mock slave auctions at his church vividly dramatized many of the horrors of chattel slavery.[248]

Thus the outbreak of the war found most branches of the Christian faith embroiled by the slavery controversy. As the paramount moral question of the day it was regarded by churchgoers on one side of the Mason and Dixon line predominantly from one angle and by those dwelling on the other side predominantly from another; and both groups of Christians espoused their convictions with a sense of inner righteousness and high scriptural sanction. However reluctant organized religion may earlier have been to enlist in the sectional strife, it failed to stay the tide of revolt and division when the national crisis appeared.

FANATIC AND DOUGHFACE

THE OUTSTANDING FACT in the antislavery cause of the fifties was the awakened conscience of the masses of the free states. Yet at the beginning of the decade public opinion, wearied of agitation, was susceptible to nearly any appeal for political quiet. Not only conservatives and compromisers, not only businessmen with Southern connections, but most Northern critics of slavery were, for the time, ready to sacrifice their ideals in order to maintain their loyalty to the Constitution and the Union. Many could say with Abraham Lincoln: "I confess I hate to see the poor creatures hunted down and caught and carried back to their stripes and unrequited toil, but I bite my lips and keep quiet." [249]

To be sure, minority elements continued to agitate. The enactment in 1850 of a fugitive-slave law which denied the black not only trial by jury but the right to testify or to summon witnesses in his own behalf, and which imposed drastic penalties upon persons who attempted to assist him, caused consternation in the North. Many thoughtful citizens refused to condone such a clear violation of the principles of common justice. "I say solemnly that I will do all in my power to rescue any fugitive slave from the hands of any officer who attempts to return him to bondage," cried the outraged Theodore Parker. [250] Massachusetts abolitionists mentioned by name heroic fugitives living in Boston and defied efforts to return them to slavery. "The edict of Nebuchadnezzar, setting up the golden image to be worshipped, on pain of the rebellious being cast into the den of lions, was just as obligatory as is the fugitive-slave law of Congress. . . . Its enforcement on Massachusetts soil must be rendered impossible." [251] Even conservative journals prophesied that the law would be a dead letter.

In other parts of the North friends of freedom also rallied in indignation meetings and circulated petitions for an immediate repeal. Thus, the Chicago common council with only two dissenting votes pronounced the law cruel, unjust, and unconstitutional, a transgression of the laws of God. Yet two days later a popular audience in the same city which greeted Douglas, a supporter of the statute, with hostile jeers and hisses, was actually won over and induced by his bold defense to vote an express repudiation of the common council.[252]

When the fugitive-slave measure was enacted, probably 20,000 blacks were quietly dwelling in the free states, in comparative safety from the masters whose authority they had fled.[253] They constituted less than a tenth of the Northern free black population. Its growth in a decade to a quarter of a million represented in considerable part the normal expansion, for there was no unqualified welcome in the border free states for the surplus free black population of the states across the Ohio.[254] Indeed, Illinois in 1853 reenforced its black code by imposing a heavy fine upon every black who entered the state and provided that, in default of payment, the black should be auctioned off to the person bidding the shortest period of service in return for payment of the fine. This seemed, even to a Southern journal like the *New Orleans Bee,* "an act of special and savage ruthlessness," and within the state it found few open champions. The *Ottawa Free Trader,* claiming that it would establish a peonage system more heartless and cruel than Southern slavery, declared, "We should like to see the man that would mount the auctioneer's block in this town and sell a free man to the highest bidder."[255]

Such a law could never have been enforced against a hostile public opinion. But the electorate of the state had in 1848 given authority for black exclusion by a vote of 50,261 to 21,297. The law, therefore, was actually applied in certain cases, and blacks seeking homes on the prairies of Illinois were put upon the block. In 1857 a free mulatto named Jackson Redman was arrested in St. Clair County and found guilty of violating the act; notices were accordingly posted about the streets of Belleville offering Redman for sale at public auction. Only the interposition of Gustave Koerner, the German Republican leader, who advanced $62.50 to cover the fine and costs, saved the victim from the penalties of the law. Such cases generally aroused widespread indignation in Illinois, although apologists were not altogether lacking.[256] In other border districts, too, Northerners were alarmed at the heavy burdens caused by a sudden influx of free blacks. In 1860 citizens of western Pennsylvania circulated petitions to the legislature requesting the enactment of legal restrictions.[257]

The decade of the fifties was an era of marked progress for the blacks in the North. Without large accretions from outside, they were more free from disintegrating forces and were better able to justify their presence in communities where they had established themselves. They became, in private homes and in hotels, "the pleasantest servants in the country," said the Englishman Dicey, echoing a general testimony.[258] Both the proud mistress of a Fifth Avenue mansion and the Mercer Street "Madam" insisted upon black maids.[259] At times at an approved hotel a black head waiter with quiet dignity directed a staff of white waitresses;[260] more often, however, he marshaled a squad of assistants of his own race and sex. The mulatto barbers at Willard's Hotel in Washington and elsewhere plied their trade with the assurance that comes only from birthright. New accomplishments in mechanical fields overcame some of the prejudice against black artisans. Occasionally successful black merchants, bankers, and lawyers climbed to prominence and in some instances married white women. John V. De Grasse, a Boston physician educated both in America and in France, was formally admitted to the Massachusetts Medical Society in 1854.

In the main, however, blacks had to be content with the humble role of hewers of wood and drawers of water, despised if not degraded. In spite of Frederick Douglass's ringing admonition, "Learn trades or starve!" many of those who had trades were compelled to abandon them on account of prejudice against their color.[261] Though "the one picturesque element in the dull monotony of outward life in America," they formed "a race apart, a strange people in a strange land."[262] Living in wretched hovels in obscure corners of the towns and cities, they were generally excluded from hotels, from streetcars, and from cabin passage on boats. The color line was also drawn in the theater, at the lyceum, and even in almshouses, schools, and churches. Thrifty and sober or not, they were scorned by white workers, even by the crudest of the newly arrived immigrants.[263] The latter feared as well as resented black competition. Race hatred often broke out in towns along the Ohio; in 1857 the populace of Mound City, Illinois, undertook to drive out black residents once and for all.[264]

As these facts suggest, the growing antislavery sentiment in the North did not necessarily imply a wholehearted acceptance of blacks by whites. The voters of Iowa rejected a black-suffrage clause drafted to form a part of the constitution framed in 1857. Elsewhere efforts to secure for him equal rights before the law proved abortive; even many members of the Republican party were frightened by the specter of "Negro equality" which their opponents charged them with harboring. There were Northern Democrats like D. J. Van Deren, editor of the *Mattoon (Illinois) Gazette,* who frankly declared his preference for the enslavement of the black in Northern states to the extension of civil and political equality. In 1857 came the great blow of the Dred Scott decision in which the Supreme Court ruled that a black could not be a citizen.

Meanwhile, abetted by antislavery extremists, blacks developed a greater race consciousness and assertiveness. Meeting in convention at various points in the North they shouted defiance at the fugitive-slave act. Their celebrations on August 1 of the anniversary of West Indian emancipation became a regular event.[265] A number of ex-slaves, supplementing the work of Frederick Douglass with harrowing tales of their experiences, made their contribution to the abolitionist movement.[266] While certain black leaders rejected the idea of colonization in all its forms, others looked more favorably upon the scheme, some even joining the ventures at Haiti and in Liberia.

Marked progress was made in educational facilities. Humble ventures of the race itself were followed by separate public schools. In 1855, Charles Sumner and other opponents of "caste schools" secured a Massachusetts law which proclaimed that there must be no distinction in the educational system on account of race, color, or religion.[267] Several institutions for higher education were soon available, the fruits of the philanthropy of patrons like Gerrit Smith or of certain religious denominations. Wilberforce University near Xenia, Ohio, was a notable Methodist contribution of this period. In 1858, blacks rejoiced in the ordination of one of their race as a bishop in the Methodist Episcopal Church.[268]

A new menace to the tranquillity of the Northern black man came when the fugitive-slave law excited to activity not only the slave hunter but also the kidnapper. Southern Illinois was for a long time the special hunting ground of man stealers. Scores of free men of black skin were sold into bondage by organized bands which operated the more boldly because blacks could not be admitted to the witness stand. Matters became so serious in the vicinity of Cairo that the mayor called out the citizens to break up the operations of a local gang of armed kidnappers who worked in league with a Missouri band.[269] In 1860 the kidnappers found easy victims among the free blacks of Kansas who had fled the Arkansas exclusion-or-reenslavement law.[270]

Meanwhile there had occurred an active revival of the antislavery movement. The year 1854 marked the turning point. In March, Joshua Glover was rescued from the authorities at Milwaukee by a mob whose leaders, afterward arrested, were acquitted by the state supreme court on the ground that the fugitive-slave law was unconstitutional.[271] Later in the same year, the hot-headed young idealist Thomas Wentworth Higginson led an infuriated band in a vain attack upon the federal courthouse at Boston for the purpose of freeing Anthony Burns, an arrested fugitive; all attempts to visit upon Higginson the penalties of the law failed.

The year 1854 also saw the leadership of the antislavery cause taken out of the hands of the abolitionist extremists and transferred to practical politicians. Before this date the antislavery movement in politics had seemed a failure. Now, in the popular disillusionment and party chaos that came when Stephen A. Douglas sponsored the Kansas-Nebraska measure, a way to real success was opened through the launching of the Republican party. The new party proclaimed its unalterable purpose to check the canker of slavery that seemed likely to eat out the vitals of the nation.

The Republicans were enemies of the further extension of slavery, not abolitionists. They generally admitted that the South could justly claim an adequate fugitive-slave law. Yet with perhaps ironical respect for the law they placed tantalizing obstacles in the way of the slave catchers by withholding the cooperation of state authorities. Statutes known as personal-liberty laws were enacted in virtually every state that fell under Republican control. These laws undertook to nullify the effect of the fugitive-slave act by such devices as guaranteeing jury trial, by authorizing writs of habeas corpus to alleged fugitives under arrest, by forbidding state officials to cooperate in the process of rendition, and by prohibiting the use of local jails for the confinement of fugitives.

Northern Democrats, when charged with being "doughfaces," trucklers to the slave power, generally retorted that the "Black Republicans" or "kinky-heads" were converts to rank abolitionism. In reality, the abolitionists would have none of such timid brethren; they were made of stronger stuff. They not only bore witness to the sinfulness of slavery, not only refused fellowship to slaveholders and defenders of that institution, but they scorned all compromises with "tyranny." Declaring a union which sanctioned slavery accursed of God, William Lloyd Garrison in 1854 publicly burned a copy of the U.S. Constitution and proclaimed the slogan, "The Union must be dissolved." [272] Yet few moderate abolitionists agreed with Garrison when he editorially gibbeted Lincoln as the "slave-hound of Illinois" because he had admitted the South's right to an effective fugitive-slave law![273]

The Republicans were strong enemies of disunion from whatever quarter it was proposed. They found valuable recruits in working-class elements previously devoted to the Democracy. Northern wage-earners had thus far displayed little sympathy for the Southern slave. But now they were made to see the slave power standing across their own path, not only thwarting their demands for free land or equal rights to the soil but threatening the very social and economic foundations of free society.

Republicans seemed to be coming slowly to a conclusion long since reached by Southern champions of slavery on the one hand and by their abolitionist enemies on the other. " 'Tis not possible that our two forms of society can long coexist. . . . Social systems, formed on opposite principles, cannot endure," wrote George Fitzhugh, Virginian.[274] From the North, Ralph Waldo Emerson could paraphrase the Southern philosopher: "I do not see how a barbarous community and a civilized community can constitute a state. I think that we must get rid of slavery or we must get rid of freedom."

Republicans were thus drawn into even more advanced ground upon the slavery issue. On June 17, 1858, Abraham Lincoln, the prophet of the Illinois prairies, declared in his famous "house-divided" speech his belief that "this government cannot endure permanently half-slave and half-free." Somewhat later in the same year William H. Seward, the outstanding Republican leader, declared that the radically different social systems of the North and the South were headed for a collision, "an irrepressible conflict," as a result of which the United States would, "sooner or later, become either entirely a slave-holding nation, or entirely a free-labor nation." For this forecast—and Lincoln strenuously insisted it was a forecast rather than a program of action—the Illinois leader denied for himself and Seward any originality. "That same idea was expressed by the *Richmond Enquirer,* in Virginia in 1856—quite two years before it was expressed by the first of us," he declared.[275] In 1860, Seward, perhaps with working-class votes in mind, again pointed to the fundamental conflict between what he now chose to call the "labor states" and the "capital states." Lincoln, who had frequently expressed fear lest in this conflict "the white man's charter of freedom" be at stake, rejoiced, as he told Connecticut audiences during a shoe strike, "that a system of labor prevails in New England under which laborers can strike when they want to. . . . I like the system which lets a man quit when he wants to, and wish it might prevail everywhere. One of the reasons why I am opposed to slavery is just here."[276]

Under the pressure of such arguments many wage-earners, previously attracted to the Democratic party, entered the ranks of the much-reviled "Black" Republicans. At the same time, as Lincoln and the Western leaders forced a repudiation of nativistic doctrines, the Germans of the Midwest made complete their revolt from the Democracy. The Republicans organized the moderate antislavery forces about the proposal to confine the "peculiar institution" within existing limits. The party found itself the special beneficiary of the Panic of 1857, responsibility for the hard times having been laid at the door of the Democratic administration. The elections that followed revealed Republican gains from the spirit of discontent. In Pennsylvania, where the party had previously made slight headway, the unemployed iron workers joined the leaders of the industry in a demand for tariff protection from foreign competition. Making this the issue in the fall elections of 1858, they accomplished the defeat of all but three of the Democratic candidates for Congress. Though the Philadelphia district did not join in repudiating what had for decades been the dominant party, the conservative leadership, economic and political, there as elsewhere was thoroughly frightened.

Now at length the relationship of Northern capitalism to the slave power of the South was made entirely apparent. On the one hand stood those industrial forces of the North which were demanding a protection that they could not expect the South to concede. On the other hand stood the merchants with large credits upon their books to Southern purchasers, the bankers with extensive loans in the South, and the manufacturers whose products found a ready sale there.

It was quite obvious that the business interests of Philadelphia and New York were bound up with the economic life of the cotton states. New York, the chief broker of Southern cotton, seemed in many ways "a prolongation of the South."[277] There were some who extravagantly pointed out that, with the loss of Southern trade, the great metropolis would be "no more than a fishing village."[278] As the crisis approached Wall Street cried out: "Without the South we are ruined."[279] So also orders from Dixie played an important role in the economic life of Boston. The *Boston Post* reckoned the sales of New England products in the South at $60 million annually besides the impetus given to shipbuilding by the Southern trade. "In every point of view," it declared, "New England seems to have been made for the South, the South for New England. How could either live and flourish without the other?"[280] The countinghouses of State Street, in the mother city of the Puritans, set a conspicuous example of groveling servility to "King Cotton."

The excitement that developed in the South following John Brown's raid upon Harper's Ferry very much disturbed the normal business relations between the two sections. As has been said, Yankee peddlers and traveling representatives of Northern merchants and manufacturers were received with growing suspicion and even hostility. The cry, "Don't trade with the North," went up and orders began to fall off. The *Atlanta Confederacy,* with the aid of "*true* Southern born men in New York," published a black-list of antislavery firms in the Northern metropolis and announced its intention to supervise the boycott locally. A "white list" of "sound, Constitutional houses" was also prepared from which Southern merchants were urged to purchase their goods.[281]

Throughout the presidential campaign of 1860 powerful forces of Northern capital were arrayed against the candidacy of the Illinois rail splitter. Conservative fears seemed borne out early in November when the news came of the suspension of the oldest banking house in Baltimore. "The panic of 1860 has commenced in earnest," commented a New York journal. "This state of things is the harbinger of what may be expected in case Lincoln should be elected. . . . The merchants of New York should give heed to those signs of the times, and strive, with might and main, for the success of the Union ticket."[282] The belated meeting on November 5 of a group of New York merchants favorable to Lincoln's election was a rather equivocal demonstration of Wall Street support.[283] The Illinois standard-bearer was privately under powerful pressure from the commercial and manufacturing interests of New England "to barter away the moral principle involved in this contest, for the commercial gain of a new submission to the South."[284]

The Republican victory on election day seemed a great blow to American prosperity. Trade with the South reached a complete standstill; the wheels of industry ceased for the moment to turn; securities at the stock exchange went topsy-turvy; money became excessively stringent as the banks, fearful of another panic, called in their loans. The future was dark and uncertain. Was the economic development of the nation to be sacrificed to maudlin sentimentality and blind fanaticism? This was the question upon the lips of conservative men of affairs.

The moneyed interests of the North, hysterical at the thought of secession, favored preserving the Union at any price, particularly since disunion was likely to be accompanied by the forfeiture of Southern debts.[285] There was owing upon the books of Northern merchants and bankers a Southern debt of $200 or $300 million; nor was there any evidence of a disposition to pay those obligations as they fell due. Indeed, as Southerners beheld the utter terror of Northern creditors at the specter of repudiation, disunion began to offer even greater attractions than mere relief from long-continued economic exploitation and a time-worn crusade.[286] Journals like the *Clayton (Alabama) Banner* advanced the argument that it was *"treason to the South to pay money,* or in any way *encourage,* aid or abet the transfer to the hostile section of so important a weapon of attack and defense."* Many were induced to favor a general "smash-up" that would wipe out their liabilities to Northern creditors.[287]

Lincoln's election, indeed, inaugurated a revolution which played havoc with many existing institutions—political, social, and economic. But the brunt of the upheaval fell upon the states that had taken their stand for a static, agrarian civilization in which the institution of chattel slavery held the place of paramount importance. Some Southerners consoled themselves with the thought that they were of the blood of a master race, a noble Norman stock not to be crushed by Northern Puritans of vulgar Saxon origin. They repudiated all thought of brotherhood with the Yankees; this was no fratricidal war but a renewal of the hereditary hostility between the "two races engaged." Let not the "Saxonized maw-worm" bring his taint to the soil of the South.[288] Others, like Senator Wigfall of Texas, accepted as compliment and not reproach the description of their section as a primitive but civilized agricultural community. If, they claimed, it lacked not only a commercial marine, manufacturing, and the mechanic arts but also any real cities, literature, or even press, it was by choice.[289] In such an atmosphere, of course, the plantation system and the institution of chattel slavery might flourish, although then only with the reins of power in the hands of its ardent exponents and champions. But amid the whirl and rush of modern industrial civilization its doom was certain.

MARSHALING THE GRAY HOST

DURING THE PRESIDENTIAL CAMPAIGN, in anticipation of Lincoln's election, companies of "minute men" were formed in South Carolina; blue-cockaded recruits drilled and paraded in the principal centers of the state. With the news of the "Black Republican" victory, organizations of "minute men" also appeared in New Orleans and other cities while efforts were made to transform into effective military units the militia that had existed largely on paper. Orders for weapons and munitions were placed with dealers in New York and New England as well as in Baltimore. These developments, together with movements to boycott other Northern goods and to expel suspicious Northerners, stirred the popular pulse and created something of a mob spirit on which the advocates of succession promptly capitalized. The news of the South Carolina ordinance of secession was hailed by noisy salutes and enthusiastic demonstrations which brought new recruits. Confederate flags were flung from private dwellings and public buildings, even in states that had not yet seceded.[290] Home guards were organized in nearly every city or town, ready to act upon rumors of incendiary fires and servile insurrection which the existing nervous tension bred. In some communities the secretly organized "chivalry leaders" varied their excited discussions with target practice, using as a mark a board roughly hewn into the shape of a man and designated as "Old Abe." Meanwhile the state legislature gave legal authorization for properly equipped military forces.

The celebration of the Sumter victory was followed by more serious tasks. War had to be made in earnest if the Southern Confederacy was to take its place in the family of nations. Previously there had been idle talk, even in Richmond, of a grand march on the capital at Washington.[291] Now it was urged that Southern hearth and home be safeguarded against "the invading hosts of the damned Abolitionists."[292] President Jefferson Davis called for 100,000 troops, later for four times that number. Volunteers poured into the recruiting offices from plantation homes and yeoman farms. Clumsy yokels as well as sleek, dandyish youths with long, flowing locks enlisted in the ranks to fight the battles of Southern chivalry. Within a year half the eligible male population had responded to the appeal to arms.

In six months the South had achieved an apparent unity out of the diversity of sentiment that had prevailed at the time of secession. Most of those who had urged that the sectional fight should be continued within the Union had acquiesced in the separatist decision of their respective states. The conservative planter who still shook his head and quietly lamented the passing of better days was left undisturbed in his rural isolation, but the zealous Union man quickly felt the adverse judgment of the community, visited upon him perhaps by vigilance committees and other emissaries of King Mob. In due course conscription and exile reduced the numbers of both types; some Louisiana Unionists even preferred refuge in the swamps to involuntary service in the Confederate army.[293] Of those who remained at home many kept silent, hoping to escape the penalties of disloyalty to the Confederacy.

Throughout the war the mountain fastnesses and valleys of "Alleghania," centering around western North Carolina, northern Alabama, and eastern Tennessee, formed the chief stronghold of the Unionists.[294] This was an isolated region of little cotton culture and slaveholding where a mild anti-slavery sentiment had earlier cropped up. In communities torn by dissension the Union sympathizers awaited the succor of the federal army; meanwhile their ranks were depleted by refugee migration to Northern states, by enlistments in the Union forces, and by the ravages of a guerrilla warfare which they waged mountain-style with their Confederate neighbors.

Lurid tales were recounted in Northern parts of the mistreatment and sufferings of these loyalist dissenters.[295] In eastern Tennessee both sides intermittently harassed and abused their opponents and at times burned, pillaged, and murdered. Two or three thousand local Union noncombatants were said to have suffered martyrdom. In 1863, James Longstreet's hungry army cleared the country of its food supplies; when it retreated before A. E. Burnside's forces, starvation and destitution stared the rejoicing Unionists in the face. Only generous contributions from the North rescued the unfortunate from their plight.

Although certain venerable and distinguished sons of the South like James L. Petigru of South Carolina and Judge Garnett Andrews, a large Georgia slaveholder, refused to have any part in the war that they opposed and were left unmolested out of respect for their gray hairs or because they were regarded as amiable and harmless dotards, younger blood was given no choice. Under the circumstances many preferred to fight for the Union. The advancing federal armies brought Northern state recruiting agents who operated in active rivalry to credit the new recruits to their own commonwealths, sometimes offering bounties greater than those available to their own citizens.[296] In the course of the struggle nearly 300,000 white Union soldiers were enrolled from the slave states.

But a year of war, with little in the way of definite accomplishment, dulled the enthusiasm of many for participating on either side of the struggle. Yet the Southern forces that had suffered and fought in trench and camp sorely needed reinforcement. Accordingly, in April 1862, despite their strong state's-rights predilections, the legislative representatives of the Confederacy adopted a policy of conscription which, amended in September, rendered liable to draft all able-bodied males between the ages of eighteen and forty-five. Numerous exemptions were authorized, including state and Confederate officials and persons engaged in war industries or in what were deemed essential occupations. Under these arrangements many continued to evade military service. By one device or another, including in some cases self-imposed physical disabilities, probably 150,000 persons were exempted from active military service in the area east of the Mississippi River.[297]

Professions like teaching, when twenty or more pupils were under tutelage, acquired new popularity even with those who had previously scorned the art of the pedagogue. The privileged status of apothecaries resulted in shops that boasted of "a few empty jars, a cheap assortment of combs and brushes, a few bottles of 'hair dye' and 'wizard oil' and other Yankee nostrums"; soon they anticipated their modern counterpart in having even greater resemblance to variety stores or produce depots.[298] Some found no way out except through the employ of substitutes. Here was a profitable field for brokers, as the market price of a soldier soon mounted to $1,500 and $3,000; professional misfits and deserters found their places as raw materials of the trade. Under the "twenty-nigger" clause many slaveholders escaped for a time the hardships of camp and battlefield while resenting any suggestion that this was "a rich man's war and a poor man's fight." It was estimated in September 1864 that "over 100,000 landed proprietors and most of the slaveholders are now out of the ranks," a condition which, though doubtless exaggerated, caused ominous mutterings to reverberate through the Confederacy.[299] In due time the government remedied the more flagrant abuses, and in the last year of the war the manpower of the South was more effectively mobilized. The government maintained in active service a fighting machine that averaged about 400,000 men. Probably a grand total of well over a million served under the Stars and Bars in the course of the bloody struggle.[300]

The Confederate soldiery did not, however, constitute an altogether enthusiastic fighting force. Caste barriers were felt to exist not only between officers and privates—with an often "shameful disregard" of the humble musket bearer by those in authority[301]—but also among the rank and file where the sensitive exemplar of chivalry chafed at having to share the lot of rough, uncouth countrymen.[302] The latter, conscious that those who had no direct stake in slavery constituted three fourths of the defenders of the Confederacy, in turn resented the implied superiority. Smoldering class hatred sometimes flared up on the arrival of rumors that wealthy exempts at home were "grinding the faces of the poor with their extortions and their speculations."[303] There were increased mutterings against the conscript officers of the "Jeff Davis Secession Aristocracy."[304]

Hunger constantly menaced the gaunt recruits of Dixie. Regular rations were scant enough from the start and, because of the poor management of the commissariat, often failed of delivery. After the spring of 1863 reduced allotments became a necessity. The generosity of the country people often supplemented the deficiency, and shipments from home sometimes broke prolonged fasts just when starvation seemed at hand. Raids upon Union supply centers and foraging also supplemented local stores. The Confederate cavalry, to which no beef was issued over a period of eighteen months and more, subsisted chiefly on corn, with an especial fondness for roasting ears in season.[305]

In other particulars as well the Confederate forces suffered from inadequate arrangements for their health and physical well-being. Many of the better-trained city physicians promptly enlisted and were given commissions for active service. On the other hand, in the rural areas anyone who possessed a small stock of medicines, a few recipes, and a knowledge of how to bleed a patient was accepted as a military doctor.[306] Then, in the fall of 1862, yellow fever decimated the population of Wilmington and smallpox soon raged violently in the Confederate capital. Supplies of quinine and other necessary medicines threatened to fail despite some success in smuggling from the North and through the blockade.

After a battle all the doctors who could be spared from cities like Richmond hurried off to the field. For miles around every dwelling served as a hospital. In Richmond public buildings and even tobacco factories sheltered the sick and wounded, sometimes to a total of 30,000 or more. Overworked army surgeons became hardened to the neglect which they were often powerless to correct. In general, little attention was directed to the most elementary sanitary precautions. To be sure, many an angel of mercy appeared among the volunteer nurses; Sally Tompkins, the Florence Nightingale of the South, was commissioned captain for her unwearied ministrations.[307] But the South never developed an elaborate civilian volunteer organization to parallel the Sanitary and Christian Commissions of the North.

With all the hardships of field and camp and with the enemy penetrating farther and farther into Dixie, the drain of desertion impaired the strength of the Southern legions. The urge to desert was not a matter of simple disloyalty. Ill-fed, barefoot, homesick, and war-weary soldiers could not have been expected to maintain a satisfactory morale. Discontent made rapid headway. Backcountry farmers and mountain yeomen increasingly resented the mandates that issued from the ruling class of the black belt. Often under the impelling need of their families for food and clothing they fled to the rescue. At times they sought relief from military routine in swamp and forest or mountain fastness. There, in desperate bands, they resisted the efforts of the Confederate authorities to hunt them down. Some sought the enemies' lines to taste the more generous treatment of federal generals. In all, at least 200,000 deserters were lost to the Confederate ranks. It was desertion that virtually undermined the conscription policy of the Southern Confederacy.[308]

Although the people of Dixie, fighting for hearth and home, were prepared to make their many sacrifices to the cause of Southern independence, they did not achieve—or at least maintain—that high degree of unity and morale which was essential to a successful revolution.

In response to Lincoln's call for volunteers, there came an outpouring of native sons from all parts of the North. Yet to many the Union army seemed "an amalgam of nations." Indeed, to William H. Russell the nativeborn seemed slow to enter the ranks while the Irish and German elements were, he thought, "fighting con amore and pro dolore (viz. 11 per mensem)."[309] Military adventurers—Hungarians, Austrians, Poles, Spaniards, Italians, and others—flocked to America to secure commissions.[310] The government scarcely dared refuse their requests for fear they would seek service with the Confederates. Certain military units, dubbed Les Enfants Perdus because of their inclusion of "black sheep" soldiers of fortune from every nation, were officered mainly by foreigners. In the case of General Louis Blencker's division commands were given in four different languages.[311]

It was not for love of, or pity for, the enslaved African that the Irish poured into the army. Indeed, emancipation of the black was the great bogy of Irishmen who feared that the Northern states might be flooded with free blacks with resulting competition for jobs.[312] In the hearts of these sons of Erin there burned a consuming passion for Irish freedom. Many an Irishman felt that service in the Union army was but a preparation for the great day of Ireland's deliverance. When the war began Colonel Michael Corcoran of the Sixty-ninth New York militia promptly took the field with his Irish battalion; over a year later, after his exchange by the Confederates as one of the prisoners of Bull Run, he raised an Irish legion and was made brigadier general.[313] Companies and regiments for an Irish brigade were promptly tendered in the summer of 1861 from cities like Cleveland, Detroit, Boston, and Philadelphia to serve the endangered Union in preparation "for the cause which is still more desperately in peril."[314]

Doubtless thousands of these foreign-born defenders of the Union, like countless of the native-born, were reluctant, if not unwilling, recruits. The bounties so generously offered by federal, state, and local governmental units lured many into service and tempted not a few repeatedly to enlist and desert for the profitable returns of "bounty-jumping." When in 1863 the counterattractions of an industrial boom forced the federal government to resort to conscription, many reluctantly acquiesced in the necessity of a military service that offered meager rewards compared with wage-earning.[315] Still others employed all the arts of evasion to escape the necessity of an enlistment which the well-to-do were able to avoid by paying the $300 exemption fee. In the early months of the draft the enrolling officers encountered all sorts of obstacles to the performance of their duties from every ingenious artifice to open violence. The extensive opposition in New York City led to the draft riots of July 1863, which were finally quelled only by drastic employment of military force. In the course of the war over 2.5 million men served under the colors with mingled emotions as well as doubts as to whether the objective of their efforts was to preserve the Union or to free the black chattels of the South.

The problem of the conscientious objector to military service was a relatively small one but none the less vexatious.[316] Earnest Quaker apostles of peace not only proclaimed "the plain scripture testimony against all wars," but some even refrained from voting because to do so might indirectly implicate them in violations of their principles. In the draft of 1862 some states exempted all Quakers and members of similar sects, while certain other states permitted exemption in return for a payment of $200. Elsewhere no distinction was made. In November 1863, after considerable pressure from the Friends, Secretary of War Stanton proposed a commutation fee for objectors that would provide a special fund for freedman relief;

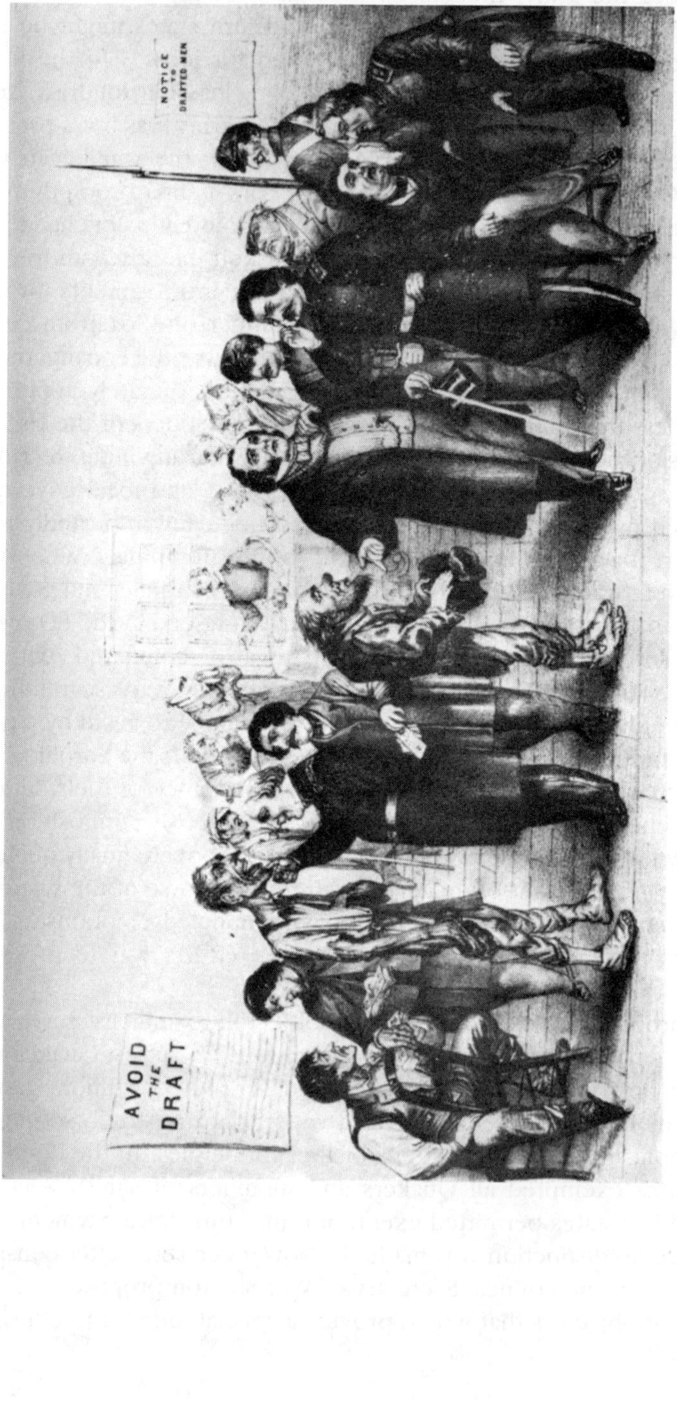

Offering Substitutes

when this was rejected by spokesmen of the dissenters, Stanton professed to be annoyed by their abstractions. In the conscription law of February 24, 1864, however, provision was made for assigning conscientious objectors to hospital work or to caring for the freedmen. Even this concession did not satisfy the more extreme of the dissenters. In general, the war department tried to avoid making an issue of specific cases. Sterling champions of their rights were found in Senators Sumner, Wilson, Ten Eyck, and Lane and in Thaddeus Stevens in the lower house. Lincoln himself showed sympathy with, and understanding of, objectors and promised Eliza P. Gurney to do "the best I . . . can, in my own conscience, under my oath to the law."[317] Few subscribed to the harsh formula that they should be made to "fight, pay, or emigrate."[318] In the South, where the issue was more closely drawn, leaders like Assistant Secretary of War John A. Campbell did what they could to alleviate the sufferings of pacifists who were caught in the toils of conscription.

More troublesome than the problem of the conscientious objector was that of the deserter. Soldiers deserted singly and in groups of varying size. The second winter of the war opened with over 100,000 absent without leave from the Northern armies; the average monthly desertion for the remainder of the war was over 5,000. The grand total was roughly 200,000.

While each side encouraged desertions from the enemy, desperate efforts were made to check it in their own ranks. Thousands of troops were detached to hunt down absentees, an unpleasant task in which the "tears and screams of wives and children" often touched the tender chords of those detailed to that duty.[319] The death penalty was increasingly applied in the later years until executions became an almost daily occurrence. Deserters from both armies were scattered over the Confederacy, especially in the mountain region and in backcountry districts, where bands of them often held sway or added their contribution to the local guerrilla warfare.[320]

Those who fought suffered untold privation. In winter they shivered in the cold and wet, floundered and wallowed in the mud of the roads and trenches, while in summer they sweated under torrid skies amid the stench of camp and battlefield and writhed with vermin that infested their bodies and clothes. Uncertain food supplies left the gnawing pangs of hunger or drove foraging parties to participate in raids that exceeded the bounds of authority, if not of decency. After a bloody contest the scarred and ravaged fields strewn with corpses and abandoned arms and equipment gave further testimony to man's inhumanity to man.[321] Only the photographs of Brady's field representatives can begin to reproduce this sight, and they omit the terrible sounds of suffering that rent the air after gun and cannon had been silenced.[322]

Brave men, suffering the first agonies of their wounds, whined and shrieked like babies as they were carried to the ambulances. Meanwhile, hardened veterans remained deaf to the cry of expiring comrades for a swallow of water; elsewhere callous captors eagerly appropriated articles of clothing from their wounded prisoners. An armistice to allow for the burial of the dead removed from sight bloody corpses "with their eyes and noses carried away; their brains oozing from their crania; their mouths shot into horrible disfiguration," "heads off, arms off, legs off, and great swarms of flies and gnats buzzing around the open mouths, froth-lined and horrible," or perhaps "horses and men chopped into hash by the bullets, and appearing more like piles of jelly than the distinguishable forms of human life." Hogs overnight "mangled many of the bodies" or ghouls stripped them, leaving the naked forms all the more bloody and ghastly. Under the excessive Southern heat corpses swelled to twice their natural size and decomposed amidst the buzz of gyrating insects that attacked them. At the end of the war thousands of dead on both sides lay unburied in swamp and wilderness while whitening bones and skulls were visible from many a roadside.[323]

"The genius of destruction is let loose in war. Soldiers acquire a passion for destruction," lamented a Northern participant as he saw his comrades break up for firewood the mahogany chairs and rosewood piano of an abandoned Southern mansion.[324] Many a time did the federal troops, according to their own testimony, "drive to the rear every pony and mule, every ox and cow and sheep. They did not leave, on an average, two chickens to a plantation. Wherever they encamped, the fences served as beds and firewood." This was war with all its penalties and all its horrors, boasted a preacher aide-de-camp to General N. P. Banks, betraying little sympathy for the helpless victims who cursed, whined, or cried.[325] It was especially difficult to control the numerous stragglers, or "bummers," who concentrated upon spoils as they went about marauding and committing every sort of outrage.[326] A tender-hearted Yankee officer deplored "the desolation and misery, and poverty and woe, that fell upon the inhabitants of every town, village, hamlet, and homestead wherever this army moves." "Our train of confiscated Horses mules and negroes was nearly two miles long. . . . Now nothing remains but the occupied dwellings and negro shanties," wrote one of the participants in a fifty-mile raid "through the Garden of Miss[issippi]."[327] "I send out parties of cavalry here & there, and instruct men cooly to burn, kill and destroy," wrote an officer engaged in suppressing guerrilla warfare in Missouri.[328]

Early in the struggle federal generals were intent upon protecting civilians and private property and upon preventing plundering.[329] It soon seemed sound policy, however, to break the rebellion by a systematic appropriation of enemy property. On July 22, 1862, the war department authorized military commanders to seize and convert to their use any property belonging to inhabitants of the Confederacy.[330] Generals Pope, Grant, and Sherman pressed this policy until they became the most feared and hated of federal commanders.

Political Brigadier-General and the masked battery.

Sherman's "Bummers" in South Carolina

War in the Field

The most elaborate application of this policy of systematic devastation was made by William T. Sherman. To "make old and young, rich and poor, feel the hard hand of war" Sherman's army left a path of destruction "thirty miles on either side of the line from Atlanta to Savannah." Most of his officers tried to keep the work of devastation within the limits set. But there was often no restraining the rank and file, and many an officer looked on sympathetically. As a result there were many scenes of indiscriminate pillage. "Everywhere," wrote a Yankee colonel to his wife, "the houses of the wealthy are pillaged, clothes torn up, beds torn to pieces, barns and gins and their contents given to the flames. . . . I have no doubt that fifty thousand dollars worth of silk dresses were found buried and were exhumed and torn to pieces by the men."[331] When Sherman's forces reached South Carolina the work of ruin attained its height. The whole army was "burning with an insatiable desire to wreak vengeance" upon the state that had led secession; its path was marked by the smoky clouds of burning towns and homes.[332] Meanwhile General "Phil" Sheridan was in his own way accomplishing the devastation of the Shenandoah Valley and rendering it untenable for a hostile army.[333] By such methods was the Confederacy finally brought to its knees.

Southerners have ever since pointed proudly to the contrasting scrupulous regard for private property shown by their invading forces. Lee's men knew that his " 'touch not, taste not, handle not' orders were something more than mere idle words."[334] Even the fact that Ben Butler's troops had looted and burned his ancestral homestead did not alter the fine regard of the gallant General Pickett for the amenities of civilized warfare, while that dashing raider "Jeb" Stuart took justifiable pride in his generous treatment of enemy civilians.[335] Yet it cannot be denied that there was frequent difficulty in restraining Southern cavalry forces from despoiling not only the enemy but also their own people.[336] War, the destroyer, loosed all his macabre forces in these four terrible years of fratricidal strife. Fifteen years later "the million dead . . . strewing the fields and woods and valleys and battlefields of the south" still troubled the conscience of the ex-war nurse Walt Whitman, whose pen recounted the tale of human destruction.[337]

The continued good health of the soldier was from the start menaced by crowded transportation in cattle cars and by filthy and unsanitary conditions in camp. Mud and stench seemed all pervasive; mosquitoes of apparently "secession sympathies" swarmed everywhere. It was not long before disease, from "camp fever" to smallpox, decimated the ranks. The former under the label of the "Chickahominy fever" was a serious factor in the final delay in the Peninsular campaign; its steady toll kept the twenty coffin makers working night and day at the specially improvised army shop.[338] After a year of fighting, 40,000 Union troops were away on sick leave, and enlistment did not proceed fast enough "to compensate for the emasculation of the army by disease."[339] Of the total of over 300,000 deaths in the

Union army, two men succumbed to disease for every one that died of wounds.[340]

Two hundred and thirty-three general army hospitals were established to take care of the sick and wounded, while Washington was described as "one vast hospital." In the battle area each bloody conflict caused the temporary conversion into hospitals of not only schools, churches, and stately mansions but even "cow-houses, wagon-sheds, hay-barracks, hen coops, negro cabins, and barns."[341] In such shelters bare-armed surgeons with bloody instruments added steadily to the growing heaps of human fingers, feet, legs, and arms. For months after a major battle like Gettysburg there were not enough "good Christian praying men" at the general hospital "to point the two thousand mangled and dying men still remaining to the Lamb of God who taketh away the sin of the world."[342]

More comforting, perhaps, were the tender ministrations of the nurses, especially the women recruited under the dauntless leadership of Dorothea L. Dix, who labored untiringly despite her advancing years and shattered health.[343] So courageously did these angels of mercy face conditions that made many a hardened man wince that they promptly established their claims to control over the new profession. The U.S. Sanitary Commission, established in June 1861 to cooperate with the army, used its income from private gifts and from a series of great fairs to relieve sickness and suffering and to improve the sanitation of camp and hospital. It spurred on the official agencies but encountered numerous obstacles from governmental authorities. The Sanitary Commission set up depots for the collection of sanitary stores, supplied diet deficiencies and delicacies, established soldiers' lodges, and directed its criticism to the improvement of the medical department of the army. Not the least important of its contributions was its directory of the 600,000 men invalided in the numerous hospitals.[344]

The problem of keeping a united public opinion behind the administration became more complex as the original purpose of the war broadened to include emancipation. The loyal border states, themselves slaveholding commonwealths, were averse to the new departure. Antislavery extremists, on the other hand, insisted that Lincoln was moving too slowly. They found allies in generals in the field, editors and politicians who had not long since boasted of their antiabolition sentiments. When Lincoln, busy at the helm of the ship of state, tried to restrain them within the limits of what seemed to him sound policy, they came to doubt his wisdom and his statesmanship, if not his patriotism. Even when the emancipation proclamation of September 22, 1862, announced the new objective of the war, some of the Radicals, dissatisfied with the limited application of the proclamation, denounced the president's "quarter loaf" as wholly inadequate to the occasion.

Meanwhile the vast mass of slaves continued loyally to serve their masters and mistresses even after word came to them, by direct or devious channels, that the armies of "Abe Linkum" were penetrating the South, bringing to the black freedom from his bondage.[345] Though wartime uncertainties greatly undermined the value of the black chattel, there was considerable buying and selling of slaves within the Confederacy.[346] Some traders operated in the war zone of Virginia, "running off" blacks to the South in chains to prevent their escape.[347] Many slave owners in exposed areas transferred their holdings to Texas, where they hoped to find greater security. Prices in the slave market dropped rapidly until they were outrun by the rapidly depreciating Confederate paper. It was not long before they had only one fourth their prewar value.

Freedom under these conditions was no less precious to the many chattels who, chafing under their bonds, now found that the prospects of escape had become better than ever before. During the first year of the war, despite numerous preventive enactments, the border slave states lost at least 50,000 slaves, two thirds of them the property of Virginians.[348] In the spring of 1862 many Maryland slaves sought refuge in the District of Columbia, just as District slaveholders were carrying their property into Maryland to escape loss from the local emancipation scheme decreed by federal statute.[349] But safety from rendition as fugitive slaves was greater in more remote parts, a fact which caused Philadelphia, Detroit, Cleveland, and the other cities to witness a new influx of blacks, some of whom did not stop until they achieved genuine security in Canada. Distant Kansas, in which the slaveholder had never found adequate protection for his human property, also witnessed a sudden immigration of self-emancipated chattels.[350]

At the same time thousands of black chattels sought sanctuary within the easy reach of the federal lines. In the early months of the war General Butler at Fortress Monroe found himself deluged by such a flood and gave his self-assigned charges the designation of "contrabands," which recognized some obligations for their care. It was soon necessary to establish a number of camps in the Potomac area for their relief.[351] With the best of intentions on the part of the federal authorities, however, there was much hardship and suffering in the lot of these refugees. After Lincoln's emancipation policy went into effect on January 1, 1863, the victorious Union armies proclaimed freedom to the slaves of invaded districts, and crowds of blacks, welcoming the troops with joyful demonstrations, threw themselves upon their bounty.

In no accessible Northern state was there an unqualified welcome for blacks, bond or free. Everywhere critics objected to their presence, usually on the ground that black labor would "steal the work and bread of the honest Irish and Germans" and that wages generally would drop disastrously as a result.[352] Various states tried to erect new barriers against them, while Illinois as late as 1862 reenacted her constitutional provision against the immigration of free blacks. Almost at once, however, by arrangement

between the secretary of war and the military commander at Cairo, contrabands began to pour into that town until the levees were "so dark with
negroes that pedestrians found it difficult to peregrinate without lanterns."[353] From Cairo, which was under martial law and legally amenable
to such a policy, the Illinois Central carried one or more carloads northward
daily and distributed them over the state. After Lincoln's emancipation
proclamation there were many Illinoisians who hoped that the black man
would henceforth "shape his bearings and route by the Southern Cross
instead of the North Star." Some Northern blacks did go South to rejoin
their kith and kin, but Illinois repeatedly found it necessary to invoke its
law and sell for their fines blacks illegally residing within the state.[354]

Wartime idealism, in fact, broke down few of the barriers against the
race. In the spring of 1862, Congress repealed the black code of the District
of Columbia, but despite the tragic need for educating the freedmen in and
about Washington they were denied access to the city's educational system
and had to be content with the inadequate facilities of the makeshift
schools set up by the various missionary and relief agencies.[355] Senator
Sumner, backed by Secretary of the Treasury Chase, protested with little
result against the color line drawn on the streetcars of the capital. Ardent
New York friends of the black man proclaimed his right to "ride in the
Eighth-avenue cars, to sit in the parlor of the New York Hotel, to hire the
best pew in Grace Church, to run for Congress . . . and to be a candidate
for the next presidency of the United States"; but most people shared with
Lincoln "the ordinary American opinion" adverse to the possibility of black
and white associating on terms of social equality.[356]

Some efforts were also made to secure the suffrage for the black in the
Northern border states, which generally denied him any political rights. A
special legislative committee in Ohio reported favorably in 1864, pointing
out that the ignorance and degradation of the black man was the inevitable
result of past oppression, but the minority protested that the idea of suffrage was "suicidal madness" and the assembly withheld action.[357]

The services of the "degraded race," however, could be very useful in
wartime. Eight or ten thousand black teamsters were soon hauling supplies
for the Army of the Potomac. Five times that number of contrabands were
put to work upon the fortifications guarding Washington. There was much
difference of opinion as to whether the black should be allowed the privilege of sharing the dangers of the battlefield. Abolitionists warmly advocated giving him this starting point from which he might rise to a
recognized place among men.[358] But their opponents wished to reserve for
the "superior" race the right of defending the flag, and talked glibly, now
of the black's inherent lack of courage, now of the danger of bloody servile
insurrection. Lincoln himself actively advocated colonization of blacks, hoping that therein would be found the ultimate solution of the race problem;
but he was forced to recognize that there was a good deal of "itching to

get niggers into our lines."[359] Congress voiced its share in this sentiment when in the second confiscation act on July 17, 1862, it authorized the enlistment of persons of African descent.

General David Hunter had already in the preceding May tried without success to organize a black regiment in South Carolina, an attempt abandoned after months of slow recruiting and drastic camp discipline. General Butler at New Orleans had reorganized as Union troops the regiment of "Native Guards, Colored," that the Confederate governor had previously recruited, but these were wealthy free mulattoes, the darkest of whom was "about the complexion of the late Mr. Webster."[360] The first regular regiment of ex-slaves was the First South Carolina Volunteers recruited in the Sea Islands under federal control, followed soon by a similar Kansas regiment.[361] These were the first of a series of units which, together with colored regiments recruited in the Northern states, made a black contribution to the war of 186,017 soldiers.[362]

These black troops generally served under black noncommissioned officers with white superiors, and they were usually denied the full regular pay of white soldiers.[363] Some of their critics never abandoned the emotions that impelled a Broadway mob to attack Sergeant Prince Rivers, a jet-black six-foot trooper whose chevrons seemed a special invitation to an outburst of race prejudice.[364] But competent military authorities, former slaveholders on the one hand and abolitionists on the other, testified to their general competence, courage, and at time conspicuous gallantry, and the principal problem was to get them in sufficient numbers.[365] Lincoln soon impressed this upon his military representatives in the South, telling Governor Andrew Johnson of Tennessee that there was no greater specific need than that he, as a Southerner and a slaveholder, take up this work.[366] The Corps d'Afrique thus became a recognized and important adjunct of the federal forces, contributing to the success of the conflict for which the black man had unwittingly been so largely responsible.

NORTHERN LIFE BEHIND THE LINES

NORTHERN LIFE behind the military front was profoundly affected by the contest. The disruptive impact of civil war bore down at the start with cataclysmic force upon the industrial machine just recovering from the Panic of 1857. Business, paralyzed during the months of fearful waiting that preceded Sumter, next faced the chaos caused by the violent breaking of economic ties that had previously bound the nation.[367] Trade with the South came to an abrupt end. Property values, even in the case of real estate, dropped rapidly. Besides Southern debts on the books of Northern merchants and bankers, a considerable amount of the bonds of Southern states was held in the North. The paper currency of Western banks, issued upon such securities under the state free-banking laws, depreciated rapidly as those bonds declined in value. Panic swept the West as dozens of banks failed and the bonds held in security sold at auction at from sixty to seventy cents on the dollar.

The closing of the Mississippi by the Confederates threatened to be an even more serious blow, particularly to cities on the upper river and on the Ohio. Ruin threatened St. Louis especially, as its river trade stopped and the values of accumulated commodities collapsed. Even in central Illinois corn sold in the autumn at eight and ten cents a bushel and was often found more valuable for use as fuel. All land and water routes eastward were soon choked with traffic.[368] Prices declined as freight rates soared. It cost nearly as much to carry grain by water from Chicago to Buffalo as it did for the transoceanic freight to Liverpool.[369]

But after the first summer's hostilities the alluring spectacle of a general wartime prosperity appeared upon the horizon. A shrewd Northern financier read in the battle of Bull Run, with its promise of a long war and resulting expenditure and inflation, the signs of a fortune for every man in Wall Street "who is not a natural idiot."[370] Portents of a reanimation of all branches of industry and trade were soon in evidence in the large cities. Even in border towns like Cincinnati stringency was ended by the army contracts awarded to their citizens.[371] Despite the threat of heavy taxation, a general rise in land values was well under way when Lewis A. Cass found an undeveloped holding of 300 acres in Detroit worth over $400,000.[372] In another year or two the cautious business leaders of 1861 would be reminded that the loss of Southern trade had not after all proved a vital blow to the national economy. New York revealed at every turn the full glory of the new prosperity. Travelers swarmed into the metropolis, crowding its hotels until beds were set up in billiard parlors and barrooms. Many of these were merchants from North, East, and West in search of goods to replenish their stocks. New York was "never more crowded, more brilliant, more extravagant."[373] To Alexander T. Stewart, entrepreneur extraordinary, was attributed the largest income in the country, if not in the world; for 1864 he paid an income tax of $250,000 on a net of $5 million.[374]

The full swing of prosperity was not evident until the autumn of 1862. It took time to wipe out the lessons of the Panic of 1857 and the bad times of 1861.[375] But the improvement in stocks noted in the first autumn of the war proved only the harbinger of a general boom market. Stock values rose an average of 40 percent in 1862; many popular shares more than tripled their prewar value. During 1863, transactions in the stock exchange totaled nearly a billion and a half dollars, and in the two boom years stock operators were said to have realized profits of a quarter of a billion.[376] By 1864 the industrial profiteer was transferring his activities to the stock market and to lead in an even greater rage for speculation. "The city exchanges and their approaches are already crowded with a frenzied throng of eager speculators," reported a critic.[377]

> Streets are blocked up by a mass so frenzied by the general passion for gain that almost all regard for personal safety and respect for personal propriety seems lost. . . . The number of brokers has more than quadrupled in a few months, such has been the enormous increase of stock-jobbing. Their aggregate business, in the city of New York alone, has arisen from twenty-five to more than a hundred million a day.

The rapid appreciation in stocks was attended by a disposition to purchase and hold property for the inevitable rise. Metals and many articles of merchandise were the objects of such speculation. A "Washington party," a clique of politicians and bankers, were thought to secure advance inside information in regard to political and military developments and thus to harvest enormous profits.[378] Gold was a favorite investment and rose rapidly, with some interruptions resulting from treasury operations, until in the summer of 1864 it reached the figure of 285 and seemed likely to be forced by energetic operators to 300.[379]

The thrift and frugality of the average American home which responded with its contribution to the sinews of war contrasted strangely with the luxury which, led by the "Sybarites of 'shoddy,'" stalked unashamed through the great cities. Silks and satins, laces and costly jewels, heads powdered with gold and silver dust, were flaunted at opera and theater, in the parks and on the streets, until at length the conscience of some of the fair sex was pricked into organizing a "national covenant" to discourage lavish expenditure, particularly for imported luxuries.[380] Among their male companions, who buttoned their waistcoats with diamonds of the first water, there was no corresponding movement for the abandonment of reckless indulgence at the gaming table or in wines and spirits. For the wealthy and especially the newly rich the war seemed a continual carnival of abundance and dissipation.

Meanwhile most branches of manufacturing responded to the wartime prosperity, being assisted by protective duties that far surpassed the rosiest dreams of a Clay or a Webster.[381] The chief exception was the cotton-spinning industry which, after two years of profitable production based upon the surplus raw stocks of 1860, was prostrated by the effects of the wartime shortage. In its place, however, rose a new prosperity in the manufacture of woolens that quite balanced this loss. Under the encouragement of actual or possible government contracts factories multiplied their output, while new companies were organized and new plants were erected with incredible speed. At the same time, the making of ready-made clothing expanded from a petty business largely in the hands of German Jews in the Eastern cities into a huge industry chiefly for the manufacture of soldiers' uniforms, but the labor-saving operations of Elias Howe's invention, the sewing machine, did not as yet take the manufacture of clothing out of the home or the shop. The government was responsible for employing thousands of women, who received five and three-quarter cents for making a pair of drawers.[382] Thanks to the ingenuity of L. R. Blake and Gordon McKay the machine was also adapted to the sewing of uppers to the soles of shoes. The result was the development of the modern shoe industry, concentrated, like the preceding handicraft, largely in eastern Massachusetts.

Other sources of newfound wealth were realized in sugar refining, which became the ninth most important industry in the nation; in the making of whiskey, which was pushed to capacity on a speculative basis in anticipation of increased taxation; and especially in iron and steel manufacturing, which, increasingly freed from foreign competition, found profitable markets in wartime railroad development and government needs. Nor did the government leave all its manufacturing to private enterprise. The federal armory at Springfield produced a standard rifle at $9, less than half of what contractors asked, and turned them out at a rate that contributed significantly to victory.

Meanwhile, despite transportation handicaps and the drain on farm labor due to army recruitment, agriculture prospered, acreage increased, and good crops were harvested. From the outset farmers were lured by the promise of "war prices."[383] Agricultural values soon reflected not only the new demand for foodstuffs to feed the Union armies but also, thanks to poor European harvests in 1860, 1861, and 1862, enlarged purchases by foreign countries. Indeed, the amount and value of grain exports increased many fold in 1861 and reached their height in 1863. During the war years Europe purchased a third of a billion dollars' worth of breadstuffs.[384] Such periods of extreme uncertainty in diplomatic relations as the Trent affair were used by grain buyers to force lower prices.[385] On the other hand, the dependence of England upon the American crop was soon realized to be an important factor in foreign affairs. It was not long before sturdy champions of the West, declaring King Cotton dethroned, hailed a new sovereign—"Corn is King!"[386]

Northern resources in horses and cattle were considerably reduced by war demands, but the sheep and wool output reflected distinct gains at handsome prices, and the hog crop was the particular pride of seven Western states. Especially in areas not favored by transportation facilities, local prices often made it wise to market the corn crop in the form of fat hogs. The peak of production was reached in 1862–63 when over 4 million porkers were listed.[387] In the packing industry as well as in the grain and lumber market, the war accelerated the growing supremacy of Chicago, the new "porkopolis" of the sixties.[388]

Since the war cut off access to Southern staples, efforts were made to find a Northern source of supply. Soon Indiana, Illinois, and Missouri were the scenes of extensive experimentation with growing cotton. Individual successes led to a "cotton mania" in southern Illinois in which the "procottonists" worked with infectious zeal. As a result, a seed problem arose and the federal government undertook to secure seed and distribute it through the offices of the state agricultural societies.[389] The resulting crops, harvested when prices had climbed from sixty cents to $1.50 a pound, in large part took care of local needs, but failed to solve the fundamental problem raised by the war. Nor did outside sources of supply like South America afford much relief, while the increased production of flax availed little since linen could not be made with the existing machinery for cotton manufacture. The problem remained unsolved even after enterprising Yankees entered the field in the wake of the Union armies as lessees of Southern plantations.[390]

One of the most remarkable features of the agricultural contribution to the war was the fact that so much was achieved despite the reduced manpower on the farm. From certain districts nine tenths of the young and able-bodied men promptly enlisted. The shortage of farm labor was soon reflected in increased wages and in appeals for help. Wages rose to $2 per day, and were then forced still higher by the depreciation of paper money. In some instances farmers turned their cattle into the grain fields rather than pay the rates required to harvest. In many cases women and children, in the pioneer spirit, took their places as farmhands, and a grown man at work in the fields came to be pronounced "a rare sight."[391] Reviving immigration offered some additional relief although the newcomer was often more interested in establishing his own farm upon the public domain.

Invisible labor units were added by the installation of agricultural machinery, especially the reaper, which saved many a Western crop. Even conservative farmers were forced to replace the supplement manpower by machines. Orders for reapers and other farm machines often consumed the entire output of factories. Midsummer made the upper prairie districts almost a continuous wheat field with hundreds of reapers harvesting the golden crop.[392] Oxen were found to be too slow for hauling expensive farm implements and, in spite of the scarcity and high price of horses, were steadily discarded.

The agricultural area of the North increased extensively as the government granted free homesteads under the act of 1862. By 1865 nearly 2.5 million acres were parceled out. In addition, many purchases were made from the state governments and from private holdings. The Illinois Central Railroad made new records in its sales, dispensing virtually a quarter-million acres in both 1863 and 1864.[393] "Every day sees new settlers arriving and fresh lands subjected to the plough," testified an observer.[394] New England rural communities dwindled as their residents joined the foreign immigrant in the new westward movement. At the same time the thrifty pioneer farmer acted to clear his farm of mortgage or to reduce his indebtedness. In six months 600 mortgages totaling some $240,000 were paid off in one Wisconsin county.[395]

One of the inevitable corollaries of the prosperity that spread from the industrial East to the Western prairies was a rise of prices to unprecedented levels. In the national capital, with its wartime congestion, food costs and house rents advanced to such exorbitant figures that several hundred government clerks decided to take up their residence in Baltimore and commute over the B. and O.[396] The cost of living generally increased, at first by 50 and eventually by over 100 percent.[397] But this represented commodity prices in a paper currency, which in the later years of the war was worth only half its face value. There was some tendency on the part of wages to adjust themselves to the new price levels, if only because of the scarcity of workers with so much of the manpower of the country in the army.[398] But wages did not keep pace with the rapidly mounting prices of food and clothing. Even in the later years of the war, when labor's greatest gains were made, there was a continued decline in real wages until they stood at about a third less than in 1860.

Labor, therefore, did not enjoy, along with industry and agriculture, its full share of the prevailing prosperity. Indeed, its standard of living declined materially, sometimes to the point where there was acute difficulty in making ends meet. The shortage of labor that followed the hectic summer of 1861 was partly offset by labor-saving machines and by new recruits to the industrial army from the ranks of women, blacks, and immigrants. Seward utilized all the resources of the state department to induce unemployed workingmen in Europe to come to the "land of opportunity" where a great labor deficiency prevailed. The homestead act of 1862 opened the public domain to foreign settlers as well as to the native-born, and, in addition, Lincoln recommended federal legislation for the direct encouragement of immigration. Congress responded with the act of July 4, 1864, which authorized the importation of wage-earners by contractors under supervision of a commissioner of immigration.

By this time immigration had already more than doubled the 1861 mark. The hungry surplus of Ireland had scored this gain a year earlier, and it was reasonably evident that concentrated efforts had been made to stimulate their coming, whether or not the methods included the direct and questionable efforts at military recruiting that were charged by Southern and British critics, including Foreign Secretary Lord John Russell.[399] It was not long before staid Bostonians were deploring the fact that their beloved city was overlaid by Celts from across the sea and that Catholics were beginning to occupy the historic strongholds of liberal Protestantism in America.[400] Meanwhile New Yorkers rejoiced that their metropolis had become the third largest German city in the world, and the nation generally took pride in the foreign contingent of over 400,000 which helped to fight the battles of the Union.[401]

The war came just as labor had begun to achieve a certain amount of self-consciousness and self-expression. Certain leaders, like William H. Sylvis, foreseeing the menace of war to their class as well as to the general welfare, had called a series of meetings terminating in a national working-man's convention at Philadelphia on February 22, 1861, which deplored the prevailing spirit of sectionalism and urged an adjustment by compromise.[402] They left little doubt, however, as to their devotion to the Union, and when the war broke out they loyally rallied to the support of the government. Some labor unions enlisted to a man and adjourned their activities for the duration of the conflict. But in the face of the danger that the working classes might be ground between the upper and nether millstones of industry and agriculture, there was a growing realization of the power of labor as well as a disposition to make use of it.

The warning went out that capital was trying to assume the right to own and control labor for its own greedy ends. As a result, with "self-preservation the first law of nature," the workers launched numerous local unions in all the Eastern states.[403] A number of new national bodies were also brought into existence, including the American Miners Association (1861), forerunner of the United Mine Workers' organization; the Brother-hood of Locomotive Engineers (1864), originally organized in Detroit as the Brotherhood of the Footboard (1863); the Cigar Makers' National Union (1864), which came into being just when Samuel Gompers, a young English immigrant, was joining a New York local; the Iron Molders' International Union (1864), reflecting the indefatigable efforts of Sylvis; and the Bricklay-ers' and Masons' International Union (1865).

By the end of the war, trades' assemblies existed in every important city. They not only undertook to link together the local bodies and to encourage the formation of unions in unorganized trades but assisted in the establish-ment of cooperative stores, in the creation of workingmen's libraries and reading rooms, and in the development of a labor press.[404] They also made their existence felt in efforts to influence legislation, especially for an eight-hour day. In 1864, under the lead of Sylvis and the Iron Molders, an attempt was made to join these city federations into a national organization. But a convention at Louisville brought out only a small attendance, and the meet-ing set for May 1865 in Detroit never occurred.[405]

The organization of a union usually evidenced a determination to influ-ence some adjustment of wages to prices. Employers therefore ordinarily found it wise to make some concession to stave off labor difficulties. Certain employers, however, were disposed to charge the economic problems of the day to the unreasonable demands of the unions[406] and showed a stubbornness that yielded only after a test of strength. As a result the number of strikes increased rapidly after 1863, totaling well over 100 in the following year. In general, such disturbances were attended with little violence. Most serious passions were aroused when black strike breakers were employed to take the places of Irish workers. The Irish dock laborers especially resented such competition, with bloody affrays often the result.[407] Conditions in the industrial world in 1865 were still such as to make a militant reformer like Wendell Phillips feel that, now chattel slavery had been destroyed, it was the inevitable logic of events to transfer the attack to wage slavery.[408]

The distress of the working class was symptomatic of unsettled conditions that ramified in many different directions. As people looked about them in the large cities, they found much evidence to belie the dictum "Peace enervates and corrupts society; war strengthens and purifies."[409] Aside from the abolition movement it was manifest that the strength of prewar idealism had withered before the hot breath of war. Humanitarian movements in general underwent a rapid decline, and reformers who did not throw their energies into the war found themselves isolated, if not discredited. This was the lot not only of the peace crusade but also of the temperance movement and the feminist cause.

Many, indeed, agreed with the New York board of metropolitan police that "a state of war is a school of violence and crime."[410] Newspapers chronicled with horror the growing prevalence of licentiousness and criminality.[411] Vice of every sort found safe refuge in the great cities and in communities that had large military establishments. Wrangling, profanity, and intoxication were common among soldier and civilian populations alike. Rowdiness and bloody brawls among the soldiers led at times to organized attacks upon persons and property. There was a marked tendency toward crimes of violence. What else could be expected, commented a contemporary, when men go about with arms in their hands?

Intemperance thrived upon war's numerous abnormalities. For the time the crusading John B. Gough turned into a lecturer upon "London Life" and "Eloquence and Orators,"[412] while innocent youths in uniform who had previously known little of alcohol found increasing pleasure in its use. When efforts were made to curb drunkenness by the denial of liquor to common soldiers, they often found reason for resentment in seeing the confiscated gifts of well-wishers at home "staggering about afterwards with shoulder-straps on."[413] Apparently on the theory that important transactions of state were facilitated by the aid of alcoholic lubricants, liquor was served in the congressional refreshment room at the capitol, to the point where reformers began to conclude that there were too many drunkards in office.

Women came to Washington on various errands—to visit soldier relatives, to claim bodies of those who had been killed, to seek work—some with small funds, if any. In not a few cases the more comely of them were set upon by certain graceless petty officeholders offering to buy them for pleasure, the bargain being accepted as an alternative to destitution. Nor did politicians hesitate to put their mistresses into government clerkships. Moreover, the military segregation of healthy males who longed even for the sight of anything suggesting femininity invited the attention of female camp followers who flocked by the hundreds to the national capital and to the environs of military encampments. Fallen women were believed to constitute a quarter of the civilian population of Washington where a good Samaritan established a foundling hospital which saved many a despondent soul from suicide.[414]

Everywhere the "painted lady" seemed to ply her ancient calling with increasing patronage from soldier, profiteer, and roué. Border cities on the Ohio declined to add to their swollen prostitute population in 1863 when the military authorities at Nashville planned to deport the 300 or 400 female hangers-on who thronged that base. A scheme was therefore adopted by which the prostitutes were allowed to pursue their profession under a system of licensing and medical inspection. The arrangement, which was self-supporting, reduced materially the amount of venereal disease, although it regularly increased with every fresh arrival of troops from the front or from the North.[415]

Nymphes du pavé, soliciting soldier patronage on the streets of Cincinnati, "nearly succeeded in elbowing all decent women from the public promenade." The street corners and walks of Chicago became so infested by gay and flashing damsels, brazen-faced courtesans, and their parasites that the newspapers—including the *Chicago Tribune,* with its estimate of 2,000 lewd women—set up a cry of protest. Broadway boasted some 200 supper and concert saloons with their "pretty waiter-girls," who represented the upper stratum of the 20,000 prostitutes of that prosperous metropolis. Even Boston, home of the Puritans, "absolutely swarms with strumpets," a contemporary traveler announced. Matters came to a climax in 1865 when the soldiers were mustered out and paid. In New York and elsewhere "city sharpers" joined the women in the process of exploitation. The small capital city of Illinois was so "overrun with black legs, burglars, garroters, and harlots (male and female), who have congregated to rob the soldiers . . . of their hard earned wages," that General John Cook detailed two additional companies to act as a provost guard.[416]

In a quite different fashion the ever-present fact of war colored the intellectual life of the times. The lyceum, adapting itself to the new conditions but catering to a dwindling public, added patriotic propaganda to its educational function. The schools were left to carry on largely from their own momentum, although frontier states like Minnesota and Nevada found energy to organize their systems from the ground up. The annual sessions of various educational agencies, like the National Educational Association, were suspended during the first two years of the war. The teacher was often prompt to volunteer his services upon the field of battle. Ohio alone sent to the front in 1861 over 2,000 schoolmasters of whom some 100—topped by two brigadier generals and seven colonels—received commissions.[417] Those teachers who remained at their desks found their pupils at first inclined to desert their lessons to enjoy the excitement of military show and parade. Children who attended were taught songs and poems that excited their young heads and fired their young hearts. In the later years of the war the upper classrooms were quite bereft of their male contingent, for, in the absence of compulsory-attendance laws, boys found profitable employment waiting for them in many fields. The teachers sometimes shared in the adjustment of wages to soaring prices, if not in the general prosperity, but they often had to organize their request for increased pay.[418]

More serious was the invasion of the schools by wartime hysteria. Patriotic school boards sometimes forced the resignation of allegedly disloyal teachers and some states—such as Oregon, Kentucky, and West Virginia—required educators to take an oath of fidelity to the government.[419] There was a sudden plea for military instruction, especially since it was assumed that under impulse of the Civil War Americans would henceforth become to a greater extent "a military people."[420] A leading religious journal expressed sympathy with the notion of connecting drill with intellectual development and shared the conviction "that the future of this country is to be stamped with a more decidedly military character."[421] Accordingly, many private schools added martial instruction to their curricula, a number of new military schools were founded, and boards of education made provision for drill.[422] It is significant of the times that Elizabeth Cady Stanton shared in the contemporary conversion of many pacifist reformers. Recognizing that "the age of bullets has come again," she found the war "music in my ears" and was anxious to prepare her son Henry for a soldier's career with the aid of "a scientific military education" at West Point.[423]

The field of higher education even more violently experienced all these new disturbing forces. In the first flush of the war, college presidents hastened to offer their services to the government. With equal fervor undergraduates signed up for companies under the tutelage of favorite professors turned soldier, or of drillmasters who had had previous military training. In the four years of the war, attendance at Yale, then the largest institution, fell from 521 to 438, at Harvard from 443 to 385, at Dartmouth from 275 to 146, at Lafayette from 87 to 51, and at Ohio Wesleyan from 157 to 119.[424] For those who remained behind, military drill was added to the usual round of studies.[425]

It was not strange that a clause requiring offerings in military training insinuated itself into the Morrill act for land grants to agricultural and mechanical colleges. No protest was offered in Congress though there was grave doubt in the minds of many advocates of land-grant colleges as to the place of military training in a college curriculum. R. W. Taylor, auditor of state in Ohio, argued that the inclusion of military tactics would make the colleges "contain elements incongruous and destructive." "The teaching of agriculture and the mechanic arts, in a college where military science is also taught, would be almost as difficult as their peaceful pursuit in a country occupied by an army."[426]

In a different way the antagonism of war to education was brought home to Professor Oliver Wendell Holmes when he was reminded "that a ship of war costs as much to build and to keep as a college, and that every port-hole we could stop would give us a new professor."[427] Such considerations, however, inevitably yielded to sentimental ones, as when a crippled veteran returned to a Harvard commencement to become the hero of the day.[428] Still more serious was the threat to intellectual honesty and freedom when students were forbidden to wear Democratic badges, when Copperhead papers were banned from college libraries, when the faculty of Denison University refused to accept the "disloyal" oration of a senior on the suppression of civil liberties, and when the trustees of Dartmouth College, who had long acquiesced in the proslavery fulminations of their veteran president Dr. Nathan Lord, unwittingly forced his resignation in listening to the insistent ministerial declaration that the "*moral* and *religious* interests and material prosperity of Dartmouth College imperatively demand the removal of the presiding officer."[429] It was perhaps ominous of tendencies that the board of visitors of the University of Michigan found that certain valuable professors had resigned and that uneasiness prevailed among others because the regents had assumed the executive administration of the college which really belonged to the faculty.[430]

With the literary talents of the nation stunned by the awful realities of war or enlisted in support of the national cause, American letters suffered a decline. Of "Eighteen Sixty-One" Walt Whitman wrote,

> Armed year—year of struggle
> No dainty rhymes or sentimental love verses for you, terrible year.

The news of a wounded brother summoned the poet to the front and to service in army hospitals, where war lost much of its heroics for the bearded 200 pounder who, by his own admission, came to resemble "a great wild buffalo."[431] His volume *Drum Taps* (1865) proclaimed, along with "the blast of the trumpet and the drum pound," "the whirl and deafening din . . . the unprecedented anguish of wounded and suffering, the beautiful young men in wholesale death and agony, everything sometimes as if blood-color and dripping blood."[432]

Longfellow was shocked by hearing the pulpit thunder war sermons with glorified unction. Whittier's doubts concerning the righteousness of "this terrible war" were not resolved when he learned that an antislavery poem of his, set to the music of Luther's famous hymn, had been banned from the Army of the Potomac.[433] From the pen of Whittier came some slight contribution to the small quantity of good poetry that the war evoked, but much of his *In War Time and Other Poems* (1864) and of his *National*

Lyrics (1865) reflected his passionate desire to find in the unfortunate cataclysm the way of destruction for chattel slavery.

Heading the popular poets of the day was Henry H. Brownell who shortly admitted that his *War Lyrics,* which first appeared in the daily papers, were "but ephemeral expressions . . . of the great national passion." [434] Esteeming the historical, if not literary, value of such effusions, the journalist Frank Moore culled them for republication in his *Rebellion Record* (twelve volumes, 1861–68), which appeared in weekly installments from the very beginning of the struggle. His catholicity of interest was strikingly revealed in his special collections of *Lyrics of Loyalty* and of *Confederate Rhymes and Rhapsodies,* both published in 1864.

Nickel and dime joke books also found new favor perhaps as an escape from wartime horrors. Petroleum V. Nasby, Private O'Reilly, and Mrs. Partington were loved for their pungent sallies, and Lowell revived his erstwhile pacifist Hosea Biglow, dedicating his homely philosophy to the winning of a "righteous" war. But it was Artemus Ward whose lectures and articles in *Vanity Fair* supplied society with its best sayings; [435] Abraham Lincoln found him a homespun champion of the administration as well as an unofficial dispenser of mirth at the White House. All of this, indeed, was good tonic for wartime hypochondria; democracy had need of laughter.

Music for the masses found expression largely in the patriotic songs and martial tunes that filled the air, belying the rumor that Congress was considering banning military bands and leaving the soldiers to find inspiration in whiskey rather than in song. [436] Over a third of a million copies were sold of *Beadle's Dime Song Book,* the most popular collection. Two thousand songs were published during the first year of fighting and the musical deluge continued. Twelve hundred entries were considered by a national-anthem committee which conducted a $500 prize contest but made no award. [437] "Dixie" retained much of its earlier favor, and the tune was said to be as popular in New York as in Richmond. [438] It was not long, however, before the great Northern marching song, "John Brown's Body," was being "hummed and whistled and ground and played all over the loyal land." [439] The melody was that of a popular hymn by Southern composer William Steffe; to it were set in due time the words of Julia Ward Howe's "Battle Hymn of the Republic," which also achieved an immediate popularity. The later years of the war brought intensely partisan songs like "Marching Through Georgia" and those of a more sad and mournful note like "Just Before the Battle, Mother."

THE BELEAGUERED CONFEDERACY

GRADUALLY HEMMED IN by the serried battalions of the North and by the vessels of the blockading squadrons, the people of Dixie struggled for independence against overwhelming odds. The conflict had begun in an atmosphere of enthusiasm and confidence. But as the fight dragged slowly on and defenses were penetrated or pushed back, hope yielded to a despair which by the fall of 1864 was writing the epitaph of the Confederate States of America. Proclaiming the supremacy of King Cotton, Southerners at the outset had urged a cotton embargo which they believed would compel an acknowledgment of their independence, either because of the resulting economic breakdown of the North or because of intervention by foreign countries to prevent the bankruptcy of their own textile interests. The federal blockade threatened more isolation than was desired, but few planters thought it would long persist; they and the factors at the start agreed to the policy of keeping the cotton crop on the plantations until the blockade was abandoned, a policy which state legislatures and executives warmly supported and which found favor with the Confederate Congress.[440]

Along with the embargo, which was gradually relaxed after a year's trial, went a policy of crop curtailment. Only about a million and a half bales were produced in 1862, one third of the crop of the previous year, while the combined crops of 1863 and 1864 fell to only half that amount. Meanwhile hundreds of thousands of bales had been put to the torch partly to increase the leverage upon England and France and partly to keep cotton from capture by the enemy. The amount, however, was greatly exaggerated in the Confederate propagandist statements, although, as the war progressed, probably 2.5 million bales were destroyed before the advancing federals.

Many cotton lands were in the meantime sown to corn, wheat, and other foodstuffs. Some of the largest planters of the Gulf states met in convention during the first winter of the war and agreed to set the example of greater food production. A year later the governors of Georgia and North Carolina urged this policy even more insistently. The more enthusiastic were not averse to a policy of mild coercion. Committees of safety waited upon their neighbors to urge cooperation. It was rarely, indeed, that a planter defied such pressure with the determination that General Robert Toombs put into a telegram from Richmond: "I refuse a single hand. . . . You may rob me in my absence, but you cannot intimidate me."[441]

Champions of Southern independence found the food problem an argument for curtailed production of alcoholic beverages. Whether or not as a result, within a year whiskey mounted to five times its prewar price. It was a regular component of the navy ration except for a period of some months beginning late in 1863 when the navy department was unable to obtain the needed supply. Soldiers in the field were issued whiskey only under circumstances of great exposure and protracted fatigue. In view of the increasing deficiency of the meat ration, however, General Joseph E. Johnston ordered a regular issue of whiskey to the Army of the Tennessee as it stood off the federal invasion of Georgia. Efforts were made generally, however, to keep strong drink from demoralizing the soldier in camp. The Confederate Congress twice passed acts to discourage drunkenness in the army, while several state prohibitory laws, intended primarily to safeguard the grain supply, were enacted after 1862.[442]

Cut off from new sources of supply, Southern merchants experienced in the early days of the war a flush of prosperity based on the sales of their rapidly ebbing stocks. Some made haste to acquire the goods of the stores of smaller interior towns to resell at enormous profits. Soon many had sold out their wares and closed their doors. Unscrupulous traders made their appearance, however, scouring the country in all directions and setting their purchases at prices that often aroused bitter criticism. High charges, abetted by the redundant currency, only accentuated the misfortunes of the widows and orphans, the unemployed, and the thousands from the devastated regions who fled to Richmond. The Y.M.C.A. and other relief agencies wrestled with these problems; the city government set up depots for the sale of goods at cost and dispensed poor relief with a necessary caution. There was much squalor and suffering in the cities of the beleaguered Confederacy.[443]

The morale of the South was increasingly undermined by the fear of starvation. On the very eve of the war Southern emissaries were actually soliciting Northern corn for the victims of the drought of 1860.[444] The food problem early became pressing in the Virginia area which, in the absence of proper transportation for outside supplies, had to assume the chief burden of feeding Lee's army, meanwhile watching while Northern troops consumed or destroyed much of the crop yield. Elsewhere supplies were generally adequate. The parched summer of 1862 aroused many fears, but the large surplus of corn and bacon from the yeoman farms of North Carolina helped relieve the acute shortage in the following spring when, with the railroads and riverboats choked by the transport of troops, Confederate soldiers were on half rations and famishing women led bread riots in Richmond and other cities.[445] The crops of 1863 and 1864 were good enough to terminate the threat of famine, but there was always the serious problem of adequate transportation and of its efficient use while hungry mouths anxiously waited to be fed.

The food problem was aggravated by the difficulty of obtaining a store of salt adequate for the preservation of the meat that had to be held in readiness for the insistent demands of the army. The average Southerner seemed to care little for fresh meat when salt port or bacon was available.[446] Previously dependent upon a Northern or foreign supply, the South made significant headway under difficulties; by desperate efforts the states contracted for supplies which, however, it was necessary to distribute under careful regulation.[447] Ice, a luxury in the antebellum South despite the huge shipments regularly floated down the Mississippi, was no longer available at any price, even to chill the fiery beverages of the gentry.

Items in the newspapers bore quiet testimony to wartime sacrifices. Editors generally lent ready aid to the cause. Many of them abandoned their desks and went to war in person. Those who remained found it necessary, on account of paper scarcity and high costs, to reduce the size of their sheets and to raise their price, with a resulting decline in circulation. Some papers soon gave up publication while others were eliminated by mergers. But the services rendered, even by the crude half-sized sheets printed on a single side, were deemed sufficient to warrant the exemption of newspapermen from the draft. News, of course, was highly colored to favor the Confederate cause. Items from the North were published under the heading, "Foreign Intelligence." Wide scope was left for journalistic dissent. A frankly Union paper like Brownlow's *Knoxville Whig* was duly suppressed, yet a moderate amount of freedom of the press remained as an official ideal. When Georgia troops sacked the office of W. W. Holden's antisecessionist Raleigh *Standard* and provoked a mob to retaliate against the *State Journal*, an administration paper, Governor Z. B. Vance demanded of President Davis the punishment of the officers of the Georgia brigade.[448]

Since the regular prints offered little literary pabulum apart from the humorous skits of "Bill Arp" (C. H. Smith) on "Abe Linkhorn" and his generals, a *Southern Illustrated News* was launched at Richmond early in the war, and a weekly *Record of News, History, and Literature* made its appearance there just before Gettysburg, only to expire before the end of the year. Another shortlived venture was the *Southern Punch*, replete with humorous woodcuts. Few books were published, if only because of the paper shortage. Some English and French novels were reprinted by firms in Richmond and Mobile, but the local products like the Reverend E. W. Watson's novelette *Nellie Norton or Southern Slavery and the Bible* and "the great Southern novel," *Macaria or, Altars of Sacrifice,* by Augusta J. Evans were frank proslavery appeals. In the same cause, but in a spirit critical of the Davis administration, the opinionated Edward A. Pollard, editor of the *Richmond Examiner,* undertook in a series of volumes to interpret the developments of the war from a Southern standpoint.

As in the North, the schools were expected to reflect a sectionally patriotic outlook. The traditional demand for Yankee textbooks was laughed to scorn. The Methodist Book Concern at Nashville promptly issued an edition of McGuffey's *Readers,* the compiler of which could now be claimed as a Southerner by adoption. New texts purged of Yankee ideas were put out in "Confederate" or "Dixie" series. Illustrative material was taken from Southern life or, in arithmetic books, from comparisons greatly to the disadvantage of the North and its soldiers. Mrs. Marinda Branson Moore's *Primary Geography* admitted that the people of the "hellish Yankee nation" were "refined and intelligent on all subjects but that of negro slavery" upon which they were "mad."[449]

In further protest against the prevailing vice of "Yankeeism" in education, arguments were advanced for encouraging Southern women in the teaching profession.[450] Partly for this reason many girls' seminaries carried on successfully during the war. The Central Female Institute of Clinton, Mississippi, never closed its doors a single day in spite of successive Union and Confederate occupation of the town. When teachers were accorded exemption from conscription, male recruits readily offered themselves even for country schools in the remoter districts. Widespread complaint arose, however, when the pedagogue tried to adjust his tuition charges to the enhanced prices that he had to pay for commodities.[451]

It was inevitable that education should be sacrificed to wartime conditions. "Literary funds" were frequently diverted to military defense. The lower schools suffered least, for it was logical, as the *Charlotte Democrat* pointed out, that children should "be taught to read and write, war or no war."[452] North Carolina authorities therefore struggled desperately to maintain and even to improve the nascent educational system of that commonwealth. But the Southern youth, like his mentors, promptly deserted books and the classroom for the adventures of camp and battlefield. Some academies and colleges were closed for lack of patronage. Enrollment at the University of Virginia dropped from 600 in 1861 to less than 40 two years later. What students remained were usually mere boys not yet arrived at military age, joined later on by wounded soldiers incapacitated for further service, who were sometimes tendered free tuition.[453] Many college buildings were converted into hospitals. If invading armies found them convenient and necessary for military quarters, only occasionally did they visit upon them the wrath of the conqueror.

Religion and its houses of worship also suffered from the ravages of war. Promptly after secession Southern Christians completed the dissolution of ecclesiastical relations with their brethren of the North. As has been said, Protestant denominations generally achieved their own independent organization within the Confederacy. The organ of the Roman Catholics of New Orleans, announcing a boycott of Yankee schools and colleges, departed so far from the spirit of the Church Universal as to declare, "The social bonds between us and the Catholics at the North have been severed by them."[454] With the advance of the Northern armies, however, many of the Protestant clergy were suspended from their functions and the churches turned over to the ecclesiastical control of Northern bodies.[455]

Meanwhile the pulpit did all in its power to glorify the cause of the Confederacy. Prayers were offered for the success of the army and collection plates were passed for its support. Hundreds of preachers served gallantly in the ranks; a few recruited companies of their own. "We fight," proclaimed Bishop Leonidas Polk of Louisiana, now a dashing major general, "for our hearth stones and our altars; above all we fight for a race that has been by Divine Providence entrusted to our most sacred keeping."[456] In this cause another Louisiana clergyman, one of five in a single company, announced his willingness to slay any Northern minister who accompanied an invading army "with as hearty a good-will, and with as clear a conscience, as I would the midnight assassin."[457]

While some thought that churchmen in general could do more good on the battlefield than "in preaching to empty meeting houses and old maids and grannies," others were of the opinion that "the minister and the priest [should] remain at the altars; [and] continue their warfare against the Devil (who is perhaps the strongest ally of the Yankees)."[458] If his satanic majesty was really "stalking at large in every village and city in the Confederacy," it soon became easy to enlist recruits to attempt his rout. After a year of fighting, a wave of religious emotionalism swept through the South. The churches were aglow with revivals. "The force of example, and the contagion of the ungovernable emotions" brought thousands of converts.[459] Hardened veterans in the camps also sought comfort in prayer and worship. Under the inspiration of leaders like Generals Polk and "Stonewall" Jackson rest periods often became huge camp meetings. Evidence came to Lincoln that "the rebel soldiers are praying with a great deal more earnestness . . . than our own troops."[460] Soon, despite rather uncertain evidence of Divine aid on the battlefield, perhaps as many as 50,000 professed to have found salvation in Christ.[461]

If religious faith gave courage to many, all were stirred by the martial airs that voiced the national spirit of the Confederacy. "Yankee Doodle," hissed and forbidden at Southern theaters, was promptly abandoned for the throbbing strains of "Dixie." Soon the inspired words of James R. Randall's impassioned lyric, "Maryland, My Maryland," made it the "Marseillaise of the Confederacy," rivaled only by Henry McCarthy's "The Bonny Blue Flag." In the cities one popular air after another—a "Beauregard's" and a "President's" march, a "Palmetto" and a "Jeff Davis" waltz—followed in quick succession. The new tunes spread to the army, but the military bands—and the marching columns—often preferred the sentimental strains of "Nellie Gray," "Annie Laurie," "Alice, Where Art Thou?," "Swanee River," and "Home Sweet Home."[462] Such songs of home and sweetheart formed a strange contrast to the "rebel yell" of victory or defiance that shrieked the determination of the warriors in gray.[463]

With fiery enthusiasm Southern maid and matron spurred on husband and brother to do or die for fireside and country. Some patriots in crinoline not only donned "secession bonnets" and blue revolutionary badges, but organized target practice with pistols, "vowing to shoot the first 'Yankee' who came within sight of their homes."[464] Some volunteered for cartridge making and for filling shells and fuses. Some like the reckless young spy Belle Boyd undertook at the risk of their lives to supply the Confederacy with important military intelligence.[465] Some languished for a time in federal prisons in penalty for their active "treason." But others, more in keeping with the traditions of Southern womanhood, contented themselves with carding lint and preparing bandages. Many gladly contributed their money, plate, and jewelry to the "Ladies' Gunboat Fund." Most of them accepted new domestic burdens—managing farms and gardens and developing substitutes for imported articles—and answered the call to service in soldiers' aid societies or in other relief work. But while the grand dame and her younger sisters were glorifying the Confederacy and its militant legions, in many a humble Southern home wives and mothers refused to reconcile themselves to the ruthless sacrifices of war and even refused to believe that the cause for which their men were fighting was more glorious than that of the Union which it challenged.[466]

Ere the final collapse before Grant's armies, the Confederacy had decided upon a desperate expedient, the arming of the slaves. By their agricultural labors these patient servitors, knowing little of the issues of the war, had contributed substantially to the fighting resources of the white population, and their work upon fortifications and in other noncombatant fields had added even more directly to Southern military strength. Now Robert E. Lee became one of the strongest advocates of their enlistment for active service, believing that the slaves could "with proper regulations . . . be made efficient soldiers."[467] Besides giving such recruits immediate freedom, he further favored "a well digested plan of gradual and general emancipation."

In the face of the serious disintegration of their armies the Confederate authorities on March 13, 1865, enacted a law authorizing the employment in military services of as many as 300,000 slaves. The revolutionary character of this decision may be judged from the argument of Howell Cobb: "The day you make soldiers of them is the beginning of the end of the revolution. If slaves will make good soldiers our whole theory of slavery is wrong." But he added, "They won't make soldiers."[468] The arming of the slaves was the last expedient of despair. By it possibly, just possibly, might the South evade the conqueror's heel. Defeat, proclaimed Congress in a final appeal, with no thought of anticlimax, meant having to "drink the cup of humiliation even to the bitter dregs of having the history of our struggle written by New England historians!"[469]

The South had given generously of its blood and treasure to the fight for independence. Careful calculation reveals that the equivalent of well over a half-billion gold dollars, nearly a sixth of the true wealth of the South in 1860, not counting slave property, was cast into the fiery furnace of civil strife. A section which had an economic strength less than a third of that of the North made material sacrifices more than half as great as those which carried the Union arms to victory. When peace at length settled upon the weary land with its charred ruins of rural homesteads and of wrecked towns and cities, the remaining personal property in the South—only one fourth that of 1860—revealed losses equal to the entire official expenditures for the struggle. Aside from the confiscation of slave property the total wealth of Dixie had shrunk to less than one third of that upon which

*A Southern cartoon on how to deal with
extortioners.*

Richmond in ruins.

The Collapse of the South

Southerners had hoped to lay the foundations of a separate nation. And yet the full story is not quite told. The defeated had still to assume their proportionate share of the federal war debt which, augmented by pensions to veterans of the successful armies, totaled fully a billion dollars. The per-capita cost of the war eventually fell thrice as heavily upon the vanquished Southerners as upon the prosperous victors.[470]

The news of the collapse of the Confederacy, marked by the surrender of General Lee, was celebrated in the North amid the wildest enthusiasm—with no hint of the national tragedy that lay just ahead. In the language of a contemporary journalist,

> there was a smile on every face—happiness in every heart. Booming guns, clanging bells, streaming banners, and the tumultuous cheers of a happy populace told the public joy and proclaimed it to the world. But in a few short hours all this was changed. The people went about the streets mournfully, the bells tolled, the flag of the Republic was hung at half mast, and the hope of immediate Peace, which made the country glad, vanished like a beautiful vision of the night—for ABRAHAM LINCOLN, who in the days of his triumph had become the champion of the pacification of the South by conciliation, had fallen under the hand of an assassin, just as he was about to accomplish the grandest and most solemn problem of statesmanship in the world.[471]

With Lincoln, indeed, passed the hope that the South could be dealt with generously in defeat. Assassination seemed "the crowning fruit of slavery," according to the mixed metaphor of a young New England intellectual who was basking under the sunny skies of an Italian spring: "In our admiration of the soldierly virtues of Lee and his army, we felt like embracing our enemies and welcoming them back to Peace and Country. But here is the most dastardly of crimes thrown across the path of conciliation. It is the last proof that our struggle is a struggle of humanity against barbarism, but how shall we redeem or get rid of the barbarians."[472]

After four years of armed strife neither victor nor vanquished was in a mood to view in perspective the bloody struggle and assess the forces that had produced it. The South, its fields ravaged, its homes in smoking ruins, nursed a "lost cause," and mourned that righteousness had fallen before brute strength. Nor had war, "the avenger," satisfied the holy indignation of the North, for "treason" not only had struck at the foundations of the Union, but had loosed the assassin's knife in the final hour of its triumph. It was difficult to recall that but a decade and half before Northerners and Southerners had proudly formed parts of the same great people, lying on opposite sides of the boundary between freedom and slavery. Both groups had found it wise to court or pacify the maturing West, but, as the frontier moved ever onward, the free North found it easier to assimilate the Western provinces and, at the same time, to make necessary concessions to their demands. The spirit of democracy and the cause of free land spread their influence over the industrial North. The railroad pushed its iron bands across the country binding together the young commonwealths and the old. The fruits of a new and glowing prosperity were tasted in the great agricultural empire as well as in the Eastern marts of trade and manufacture. The throbbing forces of enlightenment, culture, and humanitarian reform spread over the North, while free labor, girding its loins, began to feel its power.

South of the Ohio's murky waters a plantation oligarchy basked contentedly in the waning sun of property. For the few, life was easy and pleasant; culture, measured in terms of a passive leisure-class enjoyment and not in science and the creative arts, was within ready reach. An army of black vassals and a dependent white class made obeisance to planter rule, though the white yeomanry stirred restlessly as its opportunities of rising to a share in the plantation regime steadily declined and slave labor threatened to become a fatal incubus upon the back of Dixie. The revolutionary victory in 1860 of the forces that challenged the social institutions of the South severed the last bonds that held the cotton kingdom within the Union. Since the North and the administration that represented it refused to "allow the erring sisters to depart in peace," the issue was staked upon the arbitrament of arms. Workshop, farm, drawing room, press, and pulpit—all the gentle arts of peace were dedicated to the shrine of Mars. In the fiery furnace of war and the crushing defeat of the South the permanence of the Union was welded. Yet dislike, suspicion, and fear remained; the gaping wound lingered. Only when it could be bound up and healed could real peace and happiness come to the nation. Then emerged at length the glories of a modern America.

BOOK VIII

The Emergence of

Modern America,

1865–78

THE SOUTH "RECONSTRUCTED" (1865-73)

THE ELEVEN STATES over which defeat spread its black wings in the spring of 1865 contained slightly fewer than 5 million white inhabitants and 3.5 million blacks. Of this number, about a million were men who had served in the field, many of whom were left crippled or debilitated by the war. A full quarter of a million had died in the armies, either in battle or from wounds or disease. The number who were actually left with the colors when the war guttered out was smaller than might have been supposed. At Appomattox, Lee surrendered 26,765 men, the discouraged remnant of about 50,000 with whom he had begun the final hopeless campaign. These troops dispersed immediately to their homes. Within the next few weeks the remaining Confederate armies, Joseph E. Johnston's, Richard Taylor's, and E. Kirby Smith's singularly destitute force west of the Mississippi, surrendered also. The whole number of troops who turned their faces toward their families and the tasks of peace was 174,233, a body which was quickly absorbed by the remaining 8.25 million Southerners.[1]

A determination on the part of Northern generals to cripple the resources of the South in every way had added greatly to the destruction which always attends a clash of armies. Virginia had suffered in almost every section. From Harper's Ferry to Newmarket the Shenandoah Valley had been turned into a desert by Sheridan and Hunter.[2] The barns, mills, and haystacks were all burned with many of the houses; the bridges had been demolished; the livestock had been destroyed; and fences had disappeared. Eastward, the whole region between Alexandria and Richmond had been overrun again and again, and villages, farmhouses, churches, and timber swept away. Much of the country was a mere commons with all landmarks obliterated save here and there a blackened chimney keeping watch like a grim sentinel over the desolation.[3] Through the Carolinas and Georgia, Sherman's army had cut a broad swath of destruction—destruction so complete that one federal officer had boasted that agriculture and trade could not be effectively revived in a generation.[4] Wide areas in northern Alabama had been ravaged by contending armies and guerrilla bands, and the Valley of the Tennessee in particular showed scenes of appalling ruin. Other states had suffered hardly less. In Arkansas, Governor Murphy reported that the desolations of the conflict were beyond description; guerrilla bands and scouting parties had pillaged the country so savagely that two thirds of the counties were full of destitution.

The South from Virginia to Texas was dotted with towns which had been partly or completely ruined. The business section of Richmond had been laid waste by the fire which accompanied the Confederate evacuation, and other parts of the city plundered. In Columbia, South Carolina, eighty blocks, with 1,386 buildings, had been turned into a chaos of crumbling walls. Charleston had suffered from two disastrous conflagrations and from repeated bombardments; and to Northern visitors the summer after the war, seeing it half in ruins, with vacant houses, rotting wharves, grass-grown streets, and pavements torn up to make fortifications, its old-time beauty and pride seemed as dead as those of Athens.[5] Atlanta, a thriving little mushroom city when the war began, was now half in ashes, with thousands of tons of debris strewing the ways and 35,000 people in the immediate vicinity dependent upon charity for sustenance. In Mobile a terrible explosion had converted nine blocks into a smoldering waste; the wharves were partly torn up for firewood; the harbor had been obstructed by the federal forces; and an atmosphere of decay enveloped the narrow, dirty streets, in which men loafed dispiritedly.[6] So the story went. Even in New Orleans, which had suffered little physical damage, the energy and confidence of the people were gone. Many of them were exiled, half the stores were locked and empty, and flashy gamblers furnished the chief sign of animation.[7]

Everyone, with the exception of a small class of speculators and war profiteers, was impoverished.[8] Not only had the whole property in slaves, estimated at almost $2 billion, been swept away, but land values had become incredibly low. The banks of the South had been submerged beneath a sea of worthless Confederate paper, and their capital, another billion dollars, was gone. The Southern insurance companies were bankrupt and dead. Mills, factories, and mines were closed, and had little prospect of reopening in the near future. Many plantations were heavily mortgaged, and their owners knew that unless they got upon their feet at once they would lose their homes. This gave rise to an atmosphere of nervous anxiety, which infected those not engaged in agriculture. Worst of all was the irretrievable human ruin, physical and moral. Mississippi alone had fully 10,000 orphans; a family there which had not lost a member seemed a rarity, and observers said that half of the adult male population appeared to be gone. The destruction of character and courage—the effect of ruin, camp dissipation, and guerrilla warfare—was more saddening than poverty or death.[9]

It was no wonder that, as Carl Schurz reported, many men who were stripped of all their available means, with nothing but perhaps some infertile land left, seemed sunk in despondency. But there were many more whose courage created their own opportunities, men like General W. N. Pendleton of Virginia, who, settling down on a farm near Lexington, began tilling it in such ragged clothes that passersby took him for a farmhand; or men like Washington Duke, a hill farmer of North Carolina, who drove a covered wagon laden with hand-manufactured tobacco to the Capehart herring fishery on Albemarle Sound—a week's trip over rough and muddy roads—bartered his tobacco for salt herring, and traded the herring in turn for fresh pork, which the Raleigh merchants bought at a good price. Out of his profit he bought a dollar's worth of brown sugar and took it home to his hungry boys, one of them James B. Duke who was to become the founder of the American tobacco trust.[10]

In many Southern communities the reign of violence and terrorism continued after the war. Thus in southeastern Alabama guerrillas and deserters from both armies continued for a year to plunder helpless countrysides; the Saunders gang was especially active until 1866, when Saunders was killed after fleeing to Georgia. The rivers were infested with cotton thieves, who landed at flourishing cotton fields, stole the cotton, and carried it down to market. A band of outlaws even took passage upon an Alabama river steamboat and overcame the crew and the passengers. Throughout the South horse and cattle thieves were active. Beyond the Mississippi, in the wilder parts of Arkansas and Texas, desperadoes scoured the country, driving off livestock, robbing men, and cutting throats.[11] Most alarming of all, the relations between whites and blacks were tinged by a steadily increasing turbulence, which showed itself not only in isolated affrays and murders but also in such bloody and frenzied race riots as that which disgraced New Orleans in July 1866.[12]

The first twelve months after the war saw a hectic and deceptive flush of activity spread through most of the towns of the South. The need for the commonest articles of life was exigent and there was a modest amount of cotton for sale at the famine price of $125 a bale. A summer which began in stagnation thus ended with a brisk trade. By September 1865, cotton was pouring into New York and Boston in unexpected quantities, while a stream of necessities—clothing, groceries, farm machinery, household wares, schoolbooks—flowed south. A. T. Stewart, Claflin & Company, and other New York firms reported that the section was taking about one fourth as much as in 1860 in bulk, or, because of the inflated prices, an equal amount measured in dollars.[13]

In Richmond, the late autumn found scores of business houses in process of construction, and the mechanics fully employed. When Grant's troops entered the city there had not been $10,000 in federal currency within it; now there were millions.[14] Visitors to Mobile the same month rubbed their eyes at the sight of bustling streets, overflowing hotels, and warehouses rising on the ruins of former structures. New Orleans was slower in catching the stride, but by the new year trade had approached its old volume, and the ballrooms, theaters, and opera were crowded. But it was Atlanta which offered the most encouraging spectacle. The four railways centering here were burdened to their utmost; the trade of the city, measured in currency, was already one third greater than before the war.[15]

But at bottom, the prosperity of the Southern towns was dependent upon that of the rural regions, and the farmers and planters had to climb a steep and flinty path to recovery. The materials with which to create capital —livestock, machinery, and seeds—were largely gone. For example, Georgia in 1860 had 232,000 horses and mules, and six years later only 132,000, a loss of three draft animals in seven. It had possessed more than a million cattle, and was left with little more than half that number. Louisiana likewise had lost more than half her draft animals.[16] For the first time many Southern farmers used oxen for plowing, and there were instances in which the plowshare was drawn by men and women. What seed existed was poor, the harness was a patchwork of strings and wires, and the craziest homemade implements had to be used.

Above all, the problem of labor tormented the agriculturist with anxieties he had never anticipated. Neither the whites nor the blacks had any practical acquaintance with the wage system, and circumstances impeded their efforts to learn. On each side was an attitude of distrust, the whites frequently believing it impossible to make blacks work without compulsion, and the blacks sullenly suspecting that the whites would browbeat or overreach them. In many areas the result was a temporary demoralization of farming.

The difficulties of Southern agriculture were accentuated by the onerous direct taxes laid by the federal government, and by the plundering and cheating practiced by federal officers.[17] Under the circumstances, the first three years after the war were inevitably, among whites and blacks alike, years of the direst destitution which has ever been witnessed under the American flag. The very hand of nature seemed against the South. The crops of 1865, owing to the shortage of labor and implements and a terrible drought, were calamitously poor. The yield was less than half as much as in the crop year just before the war.[18] The same story was repeated in 1867, when not only did the crops come to grief through bad weather, insects, and the idleness of black hands, but prices fell to less than half the expected level, completing the ruin of many planters.[19]

The result of these bad seasons was profound discouragement and the sharpest want. By the close of the crop year 1867, innumerable blacks and many whites had no money, no decent clothing, and not a week's supply of any food except cornmeal. In the four years after Appomattox, the Freedmen's Bureau alone had to issue nearly 22 million rations, of which more than 15 million went to the freedmen.[20]

Although the destitution was visible throughout the South, it was worst in Georgia, South Carolina, and Alabama. In Alabama the ravages by the armies and by guerrillas contributed to such a paralysis of agriculture that the first crop was hardly one tenth of that raised before the war, and not before 1880 did the improved acreage equal that of 1860. During the first winter of peace many white families near Talladega lived in the woods, with no shelter save pine boughs, and when spring came three fourths of the 80,000 widows of the state were said to be in want of the bare necessities of life. Many instances of outright starvation were reported in the northern part of the state of Alabama. Federal, state, and private agencies had to distribute food unstintingly, the Freedmen's Bureau reporting in the fall of 1867 that 10,000 whites and 50,000 blacks were without means of subsistence.[21] In South Carolina many once wealthy families, especially in Charleston, parted with their plate and other heirlooms to buy bread; here, too, some actually starved to death. In Georgia during 1865 pitiful scenes were described by the press correspondents. "In many whole counties," wrote one observer, "the merest necessaries of life are all any family have or can afford, while among the poorer classes there is great lack of even these." Early in 1866 the legislature appropriated $200,000 to buy food. In Mississippi the year after the war Governor Humphrey recommended that one fifth of the state revenues be applied immediately to the succor of widows, orphans, and other needy persons.[22]

Mentally and spiritually the white South suffered the most in these dark three years; physically the black South endured the most. In the "contraband camps" and the mushroom black colonies in the cities, the sanitary conditions were horrifying. Inevitably epidemics, of which smallpox was the deadliest, swept away great numbers, while the ravages of tuberculosis were heavy. The black children, without proper care or diet, died like flies and for several years almost none were to be seen in some districts. It was remarked that some new Herod would seem to have slaughtered the innocents.[23] The Freedmen's Bureau, which gave at least a million ailing people medical assistance, established hospitals and dispensaries, but they could not check the epidemics. Just how great was the loss of life it is difficult to determine, but some clue is afforded by the statistics of Charleston. Here, where the two races were not far from equal in numbers, there were years between 1866 and 1871 when the black mortality was twice that of the white citizens. The relative mortality of black children under five was even more shocking. Thus, in 1868 there were 136 deaths of white children and nearly three times as many—372—of black; in 1869 the figures were 181 and 461.[24] In some crowded, unhealthy communities of the South one fourth or one third of the blacks died during the first years of readjustment.[25]

But in spite of all the handicaps, Southern blacks began to show evidence of definite progress. As the months passed, more and more of them saw that they must work or starve, and heeded the admonition of General O. O. Howard and other Freedmen's Bureau officials to prove themselves industrious. The Bureau settled itself to the task of finding places for the blacks and encouraging them to sign contracts. Those who had special skills or unusual energy were not long in making themselves better homes than they had occupied in the slave quarters of the plantations.

Every Southern state established normal schools for the race, and some even set up so-called universities for them. In Washington, the school that later became Howard University was incorporated in 1867, with public-spirited residents of the capital as founders, and in the same year, Atlanta University was chartered, with funds from the Freedmen's Bureau and other sources. Berea College in Kentucky, for whites and blacks alike, Straight University in New Orleans, and Shaw University at Raleigh, North Carolina, all came into existence shortly after the war. So did Fisk University at Nashville, which, by 1870, was already doing much to supply Tennessee with a corps of colored teachers.[26]

The attitude of the whites, too, rapidly changed for the better. Many of them, embittered or discouraged, thought at first of expatriating themselves. Scores of families left the South for Europe, some, like Judah P. Benjamin, going to England, and others, including certain South Carolina Huguenots, to France.[27] Some more adventurous spirits, such as Henry W. Allen, the war governor of Louisiana, who had been badly crippled at the battle of Baton Rouge, set off for homes in Mexico, while a steady stream, particularly of ambitious young men, poured into the Northern cities. Both Lee and Jefferson Davis protested against abandonment of the section, but in vain. Equally futile was the tendency of many Southerners to cast about for some method of replacing black labor with white. They talked, with a certain traditional horror of free blacks, of transporting the freedmen to Africa; a clamor went up for foreign labor, and men suggested bounties and direct steamship lines to the emigrant ports of Europe.[28] However, though thousands of immigrants arrived in New York every week, the high wages and the peace and prosperity of the North and West kept substantially all of them from going below Mason and Dixon's line.

This ill-natured and petulant spirit necessarily gave way before the realization by intelligent citizens that the future of the section must be carved out by a partnership of whites and blacks. Some states achieved a partial success with free labor at the very outset. For example, in Virginia and North Carolina and along the border, the great majority of freedmen were placed at fairly regular work during 1865–66, and the planters of Tennessee also employed most of the available hands.[29] In Louisiana, free labor succeeded wherever the whites gave it a fair trial and had money enough to pay cash at frequent intervals. But in South Carolina, Georgia, Alabama, and Mississippi the problem was more difficult, partly because of the higher proportion of blacks and partly because of the general poverty. Everywhere, naturally, the former slaveholders soon showed themselves to be the best friends of the freedman. They needed him more, understood him better, and did not fear his competition. In lowland Tennessee, for example, the planters gave the Freedmen's Bureau cordial cooperation, while the poor hill-dwellers of East Tennessee were malevolent, often killing free blacks with great glee—"the buzzards can't eat 'em up as fast as we kill 'em," as one old Union adherent put it in 1866. In some sections the blacks were shamefully bullied or cheated by rascally farmers, while they were widely preyed upon by sharps, peddlers, and rural storekeepers.

But real progress, little by little, was made toward a sound economic basis for labor.[30] Some Southerners tried renting their land for cash; some paid a money wage to their hands; and others rented out their land on the share system. Though each method had its advantages and disadvantages, powerful forces began to make the third the favorite. Most planters had little money to pay the blacks, and the blacks had even less to spend for rent. The chief defect of the share system was that it accentuated the devotion of the South to the production of cotton alone. Placing cultivation in the hands of untaught and unguided blacks, it retarded the diversification of crops, the growing of a proper amount of livestock, the introduction of deep plowing, and the making of physical improvements. The wretched crop-lien system became more deeply rooted than ever. The black renter almost invariably, and the planter landlord too frequently, had to obtain advances from the merchant, who took a mortgage on the harvest and who, since cotton alone was sure to bring ready money, usually insisted that cotton be planted. Moreover, the planter was frequently in a position to bully his poor tenant; "It is more like a halfway slavery than any relation of capital and labor of an advanced type," wrote one observer. But we must remember that blacks would have fared badly anyway, and that under the conditions of the day the crop-lien system was ineradicable. The great merit of the share plan was that it furnished a transition to independence. It constantly raised blacks from the lowest rung to a position where they could rent land from the whites for cash and crop it themselves, or could even buy land.[31]

A revolutionary break-up of Southern plantations and farms into smaller units was certain under the new labor conditions. The blacks during slavery had lived in compact "quarters" or rows of cabins, usually near the master's house; now each worker needed his individual corncrib, hogpen, and mule stable, while it was convenient for him to be near his own land allotment. Little farmsteads sprang up by the dozens on what had been large single plantations, and a genuinely able body of black farmers began slowly to emerge.[32] Their number, however, was very small compared with that of the new white farm owners. Poor men all over the South, whether they came from the Appalachians and the hill districts, from the ranks of the overseers and small shopkeepers, or from the small holders of the lowlands, found their opportunity in the high price of cotton and the low price of land. Cheap as good soil had always been, it was now far cheaper still, and for a time after the surrender, and again in the darkest Reconstruction days, plantations in some states could be had for a song. Many proprietors had to let part of their land lie fallow or rent it free to anyone who would pay the taxes, and the constant foreclosure of mortgages helped to drug the land market.[33] We read of good land in the lower South selling just after the war at $3 to $5 an acre, one fifth or one sixth of what it had brought before 1860. A plantation three miles from Corinth, Mississippi, sold for thirty-five cents an acre.[34]

These low prices and the ensuing transfers marked the downfall of a ruling class. Nearly all the patrician families of the old South had been country gentlefolk and they suffered so heavily from the war that their names almost disappeared from public affairs for a generation. The Pickenses, the Allstons, the Mannings, the Middletons of South Carolina; the Carters, the Pages, the Tazewells, the Barbours of Virginia; the Forsythes and Cobbs of Georgia, represented a social stratum that was broken up and churned into the heterogeneous society of the new South.[35] The ambitious, hard-working middle class—farmers, lawyers, merchants, manufacturers— pushed forward to take their places. Poverty-stricken though the South was, it had its men of comparative wealth, for some had prospered by the rolling mills, foundries, and factories of wartime, and some had made large profits by food speculation. By the spring of 1866, more than 1,200 Georgians, who had been excluded from the general amnesty as being worth more than $20,000, had received special pardons. Here was the nucleus of a new leadership. In antebellum days the wealth and prestige of the South were in the hands of landed or professional men; now commerce received a large share, and city life gained in importance as compared with the country.[36]

The misfortune of the South seemed the opportunity of the North and the low land prices brought a notable influx of Northerners to engage in farming. A considerable colony of Ohioans was formed in Noxubee and Lowndes counties in Mississippi, and its glowing reports resulted in fresh arrivals.[37] Every other state had its fortune hunters, sure that they could show the indolent Southerner how to raise cotton at $100 a bale. Whitelaw Reid and General Herron of Iowa removed immediately after the war to Louisiana, John Hay invested in orange groves in Florida, and Colonel Henry Lee Higginson with two comrades went to Georgia and bought a plantation of about 5,000 acres, thirty miles from Savannah, for $27,000. But three out of four of these self-confident Northerners failed ignominiously. Reid, dosing his ague with quinine in a damp cottage, met with one disaster after another—floods, the army worm, and trouble with his 150 black hands. Hay never received a cent from his orange trees. Higginson and his comrades, after encountering heavy rains, insect plagues, labor difficulties, and a vexatious lawsuit, sold their plantation for $5,000 and, returning North, found that their experience had cost them about $65,000.[38] So the story went. Much more significant to the South than this Northern invasion was the vast migratory movement of both white and black farmers toward the Southwest. Energetic men of the old slave states, longing for a new chance, were drawn to Texas and Arkansas as by an irresistible magnet, and opened tens of thousands of fertile new farms there. The land was cheap, the soil productive, cattle-raising and mixed farming were easy, and the society was progressive. The rapid development of this region was one of the important factors in the emergence of the new South.[39]

Under these rapidly changing conditions of land tenure and labor, the dark skies above the South showed a roseate gleam of dawn in 1869. The cotton crop marketed in that year was so abundant and the price so good that Northern financial authorities estimated that it furnished the impoverished section with $250 million in currency, a sum swelled by easily $50 million from the sale of sugar, tobacco, naval stores, and other products. For the first time, many planters felt comparatively independent.[40] Southerners made more purchases from the Northern cities than at any time since 1860 and paid for them more promptly.[41] New buildings were erected, houses were painted, worn out furniture was replaced, and exhausted fields were fertilized. The new stir of prosperity brought an enthusiastic industrial congress of 700 delegates together at Mobile. This feeling of buoyancy continued with the bountiful crops of the following years. The yield of 1871 amounted to the amazing total of 4,347,000 bales, one fifth again as great as the crop in the last year before the war. When cotton could be grown for ten cents a pound, as was coming to be the fact, and its average price was not far from twenty, such totals spelled new hope for the dejected Southern people.[42]

This increased production and higher prosperity were permanent, for they rested upon a remarkable and continuing growth in the number of farmers. The far-reaching revolution in the very basis of Southern agriculture was made startlingly evident by the census returns of 1870. Tennessee, with its large Northern immigration and mountaineer class, had 118,141 farms, against only 82,368 a decade earlier. In South Carolina the number increased from roughly 33,000 to 52,000, in Mississippi from 43,000 to 68,000, and in Louisiana from 17,000 to 28,000, these being the states in which the great planters suffered most heavily. But not a single state failed to show a decided gain. All this, of course, meant a marked decline in the average acreage. The typical Louisiana agriculturist, for example, had tilled 536 acres just before the war, and now held only 247, while even in North Carolina, where the small farmer had flourished from colonial days, the average farmstead fell from 316 acres to 212.[43] Frequently these so-called farms were mere patches of a few acres that blacks had acquired, along with a mule and cabin, as the first step toward a larger property.[44]

Picturesque and far-reaching changes also resulted in the mercantile organization of the South. The great slaveholders had once bought goods for their entire retinue of hands. They corresponded, in the commercial world, to so many jobbers or extensive retailers, obtaining their supplies at wholesale from the nearest large city—Mobile, Charleston, or Richmond. When the slaves became independent purchasers, all this ended. A host of small stores sprang up throughout the South, and Northern wholesale firms now made the acquaintance of customers in innumerable villages and cross-roads stations. The Yankee drummer became familiar on Southern trains, and goods suited to small farms, as distinguished from large plantations, came into demand.[45] Freedom meant a very substantial elevation in the living standards of hundreds of thousands of blacks, and this also increased the retail market for widely assorted commodities sold in small lots.

A similar change took place in the method of selling Southern crops. Before the war the factor who took the produce of a wide plantation made but a single advance on the crop of 1,000 acres. Now the same quantity of cotton was grown by the united efforts of perhaps a score of farmers, each of whom had to have his individual credit at the factor's, and a tribe of small money lenders sprang up and flourished. The great planters before 1861 had consigned their crops to commission men in the principal cities. Now most landholders did not know enough about marketing to ship so far, and sold their crops to the local dealers who, as the network of railways increased, constituted a more and more numerous class.[46] Economically, the section was taking on a modern color; its commercial system was approaching that of the North and West.[47]

Politically, the Southern whites were pushed brusquely to one side to make way for a class government. Their property, their institutions, their revered traditions were made the prey or sport of Northern adventurers. The blacks, whom the North should have protected and helped forward one step at a time, were partly debauched by being made the participants in a corrupt and incompetent administration, in which lawless and selfish men stole the public moneys, bribed the legislatures, treated the dignity of office with ribald contempt, and mismanaged every public trust. A surer method of delaying the black's preparation for the really stern tasks of

Columbia, S.C., after the passing of Sherman's army.

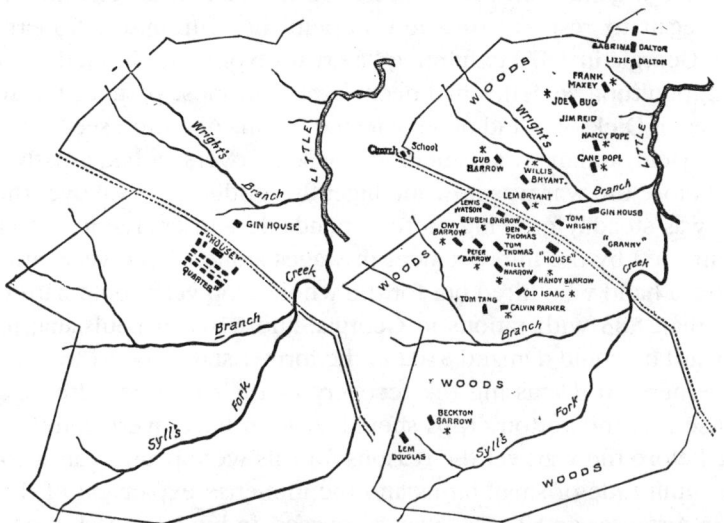

A Georgia Plantation — 1860 and 1880.

The Negroes found new liberty in the camp meeting.

Chivalry among the Southern whites — a tournament.

self-government could hardly have been devised. The result, as might have been predicted, was an uprising by the angered white population of the South, which in its violence and force swept away much of what constructive work had been done.

But the confusion and agony of the late sixties and the first years of the seventies should not be allowed to obscure the fact that beneath the surface a steady process of healing and growth was going on. The social readjustment was surer and more continuous than the political readjustment. The blacks were establishing themselves as tenants or even small landowners, a considerable number of them were gaining a rudimentary education, and they were taking the first halting steps with their own schools, churches, and social organizations. Agriculture, backward and unscientific though it was, began to respond to a few hopeful new impulses. Robert Somers found Georgia in 1870 exhibiting "a great revolution" in methods of farming. Agricultural societies had been formed in most parts of the state, the planting of Dickson's and other selected brands of cotton seed was increasing the yield, and many a plantation that some overseer had grossly mismanaged before the war was now intelligently conducted.[48] All over the South, labor was steadily growing more dependable and energetic, a fact which was attested by the improvement in wages alone. Three years after Appomattox, a hand who hired out for the whole crop year could hardly expect more than $83 with rations in Georgia, and $104 in Louisiana; ten years afterward he could demand $102 in the former state, and $136 in the latter. Southerners, in discussing the recovery of their section, often expressed surprise that the cotton crops should so soon have overtaken the records made before the war; yet the reasons for this were plain to all who looked at the multitude of small farms and the immense expansion of the cotton area in Arkansas and Texas. New resources, in lumber, marl, tobacco, and naval stores, were being exploited.[49]

Little by little, traces of the conflict were being erased, and visitors to the South five years after Appomattox found Richmond, Atlanta, and other cities already so well rebuilt that few marks of the war remained. Even Charleston showed the same bustle as of old. The cobblestones rang to the succession of carts hauling cotton and other produce down the river streets; the clang and wheeze of the cotton presses mingled with the shouts of the stevedores and whistles of boats; and the hotels, with their stately colonnades of white pillars and troops of ebony waiters, were full of visitors. The fine residences around the esplanade, long neglected, were being rapidly renovated. New quays and wharves and new lines of counting rooms had risen to meet fresh departments of trade. In cities like these could be caught the clearest glimpse of the new South that was destined slowly but irresistibly to rise to view.[50]

THE INDUSTRIAL BOOM IN THE NORTH (1865-73)

MEANWHILE, the industrial North was pressing forward with a speed which seemed to leave all old landmarks behind and which year by year wrought new social changes. David A. Wells wrote in 1889 that to a generation whose memory covered only the years following 1860, "the recitation of the economic experiences and industrial conditions of the generation next preceding is very much akin to a recurrence to ancient history."[51] Economically the nation of 1865—a nation which had hardly advanced to the Missouri, which used iron alone, which had a modest railway system and but $1.5 billion invested in manufacturing—was a world away from the nation of 1878—a nation which had pressed to the Pacific, which was producing huge quantities of steel, which had the finest railway system in the world, and which had invested nearly three billions in manufacturing. The impetus behind this stride was at its greatest in the years 1865-73; Northern industry was booming when the war ended and the boom had eight years to run.

The victorious end of the war and the return of labor from the armies gave increased buoyancy to enterprise in every field. A leading Northern manufacturer, testifying under oath, said that his rate of profit in 1865 had been "painfully large"; and the special commissioner of revenue reported at the end of the following year that the returns of business had been almost unprecedentedly high.[52] Scarcely a record in industry escaped being broken during the next five years. More cotton spindles were set revolving, more iron furnaces were lighted, more steel was made, more coal and copper were mined, more lumber was sawed and hewed, more houses and shops were constructed, and more manufactories of different kinds were established than during any equal term in our earlier history.[53] Moreover, the improvements in the quality of manufactures equaled the increase in quantity.

The high prices which wartime demands and the issue of greenbacks had brought about continued in nearly all markets. The elation of Northern victory, the feeling of recuperative power, the sense of enormous Western wealth waiting only to be unlocked, were reflected in industry. "The truth is," John Sherman wrote his brother in the fall of 1865, "the close of the war with our resources unimpaired gives an elevation, a scope to the ideas of leading capitalists, far higher than anything ever undertaken in this country before. They talk of millions as confidently as formerly of thousands."[54] Sherman himself thought of leaving politics to engage in railroading, banking, or manufacturing in Ohio. The home market was steadily expanding, partly through the inflow of immigrants from Europe, partly through the rapid settlement of the Western prairies. The war had tended to break down the previous economic dependence upon Europe, and behind a high tariff wall a host of new manufactories were making articles formerly shipped from abroad. In 1859 there had been 140,000 manufacturing establishments; in 1869 there were 252,000 with a commensurate increase in the number of employees.[55] A succession of foreign wars, beginning with the Austro-Prussian War of 1865–66 and the coalition of Brazil, Argentina, and Uruguay against Paraguay, also benefited American trade.

Although the modern steel age was born in 1856, when Henry Bessemer in England invented his process, it did not gain a real foothold in America for a decade. Till after the Civil War steel was rare and costly, used chiefly in cutlery and fine tools. The demands of the conflict gave manufacturers no taste or time for experimenting, so that not until 1864 was the Bessemer process first used, at a short-lived plant in Wyandotte, Michigan, and even in 1867 only 2,600 tons of steel ingots were produced.[56] Then, steel making expanded with striking speed. Steel quickly became as cheap as cast iron, and its cheapness created such a keen demand that by 1875 a dozen important Bessemer works had been established. The years 1865–73 also witnessed the emergence of the American meat-packing business on an international scale. Even more Aladdin-like was the development of the Pennsylvania oil fields. Petroleum was destined to be the foundation for a host of new industries, and though few of its uses were discovered between 1865 and 1878, these few were important in themselves and still more important for the vistas they opened up.[57]

Almost every field of business witnessed a consolidation of industrial enterprises. Not until the Civil War did any cotton mill have 100,000 spindles, or any iron furnace produce more than 300 tons a week.[58] The success of the Waltham enterprise in making watches by factory methods, instead of slowly and expensively by hand, led to the establishment of the American Watch Factory at Elgin, Illinois, in 1865. The sewing machine factory, the farm implement factory, the piano and organ factory all improved their processes, their subdivision of labor, and their capacity for quantity production in these flush years. Many small businesses sprang into a hothouse life, for money was abundant,[59] but all the while the principal manufactories — those at the top — grew astonishingly. Less and less did the American people consume goods made in small and simple establishments managed by individual proprietors; more and more did they use goods from large factories managed by corporate boards.

A pronounced westward thrust of industry became evident quite apart from the birth of the meat packing and flour milling undertakings of the Northwest. George Pullman founded the Pullman Palace Car Company in Chicago. William H. Seward remarked of McCormick's reaper that through its use "the line of civilization moves westward thirty miles each year," and it was natural that the makers of agricultural machinery should move west, too. McCormick's own factory stood on the north bank of the Chicago

River. Two of the heritages of the war were a beet-sugar industry in Illinois and Wisconsin, and a flourishing tobacco industry in the latter state. Particularly interesting was the progress of the brewing business in St. Louis and Milwaukee, with their large German population, for the nation was beginning to appreciate the fact that beer was less harmful than ale or spirits, while the excise tax placed upon it was comparatively small.

This westward march of manufacturing was plainly indicated by the census of 1870. It showed that in the nation as a whole the number of establishments had increased in the decade almost 80 percent. But in Indiana they had more than doubled, in Illinois they had trebled, and in Missouri they had more than trebled. Before the war the great states along the upper Mississippi had been almost wholly agricultural and their cities had depended upon the trade of the farms; now the smoke of factory chimneys showed that they were definitely passing out of the pioneer stage. In the East, the agglutination of industry in strategically placed centers interested every observer.

Financial institutions responded to the buoyant expansion of the time like vegetation to a tropical sun. The inflation of credit made banking a business which tyros could enter with success. The federal government established a great new national banking system, and between the fall of 1864 and the fall of 1865 the number of such banks rose from 584 to 1,566.[60] But even more remarkable was the multiplication of savings banks. The workmen were enjoying what seemed high pay, and needed repositories for it. In Massachusetts there were 93 savings banks in 1862, and 180 in 1875; in New York State in the same period the number increased from 74 to 158. Costly offices were rented and fitted up, high rates of interest were promised, and extravagant salaries were granted.[61] Insurance companies, many of them speculative ventures with insufficient capital, incompetent management, and a shocking inattention to sound actuarial principles, rose on every hand. Until these years, trust companies had been almost unknown in the United States, but now there sprang up a sudden realization of their usefulness and opportunities, and between 1864 and 1875 no fewer than forty came into existence.[62]

In answer to the heavy demands of industry upon the labor market, and to the alluring spectacle of prosperity, comfort, and opportunity presented by American life, the stream of European immigration rose rapidly to a torrent. The Fenian movement and land troubles in Ireland, the panic of 1866 in England, and the Austro-Prussian conflict gave tens of thousands of Europeans a special incentive to emigrate to the United States. For the first time American manufacturers combined in considerable numbers to send agents to Europe to stimulate emigration, and their efforts advertised the opportunities open to active men. The increasing speed and cheapness of transatlantic travel was also a factor of importance. In 1856 a mere handful of European newcomers, some 5,000 in a total of 131,000, had arrived in steamships, the others using sailing vessels, but in 1865 the great majority were transported by steam. Not quite a quarter of a million immigrants were admitted in 1865, and thereafter the number rose year by year until in 1873 it reached the then amazing total of 460,000.[63]

In this fresh surge of old-world population certain novel, interesting, and valuable elements appeared prominently. When, in 1850, Fredrika Bremer, the Swedish novelist, visited the Northwest, she found a large advance guard of Scandinavians; now the central host was coming, and by 1870 there were almost 45,000 of them in Illinois alone. The first Swedish secular journal, the *Svenska Amerikanaren*, was established in Minnesota in 1866, edited by Colonel Hans Mattson who became known as an active agent in Europe to induce Scandinavians to migrate.[64] About 125,000 Scandinavians entered the republic in the first half of the seventies. Some Slavs, German-Russian Mennonites, and Bohemians also arrived. Decidedly more important was the accession of Italians from Sicily and Naples; for in the same half decade slightly more than 100,000 people of Latin blood, most of them Italians seeking work in the construction gangs on the railroads and other rough employment, were admitted. But it was the British, Irish, and German immigration which continued the heaviest, these nationalities leading in the order named. The result of the inflow was that by 1875 the nation had about 7.5 million of foreign-born among its 40 million people.[65]

It would be expected that the position of labor, in this period of thriving industry, would be one of great prosperity; and viewed superficially, this seemed the fact. Work was abundant and wages were firm or rising. Men talked with wonder of the high pay skilled employees were receiving. Rumor exaggerated the returns obtained by labor, while employers, as ever in flush periods, had much to say of the money the working class spent on liquor, fine clothes, jewelry, and parlor organs.[66] But when investigators looked beneath this bright surface they found a very different state of affairs. It can be summarized in Commissioner Wells's succinct statement at the close of 1866 that while the average wage had risen about 60 percent since 1860, the increase in the cost of commodities was about 90 percent, while in computing the cost of living a still greater rise in house rents had to be considered. Wells found that only a single working group, the copper miners, enjoyed the advantage of doubled wages in facing a doubled cost of living a doubled cost of living. Innumerable workmen—the ready-made clothing workers, the farm laborers of the North and West, and so on— obtained only half again as much as before the war.[67] Nor was this a merely transient pinch. Two years later, when a momentary depression was making businessmen uneasy, it was still more evident that the workingmen had actually suffered a loss from the economic changes produced by the war. For all their apparently enhanced reward, skilled employees could be found living in shabbier and less sanitary homes than formerly—sometimes eating plainer fare. Commissioner Wells again asserted that the great majority of wage-earners were worse off than in 1860.[68]

Ordinary workmen of intelligence in the larger cities were glad to get $2 a day. The whistles everywhere sounded at 7:00 A.M., an hour was allowed at noon, and at six in the evening the ten-hour day was finished. In some trades the hours were a little shorter, but in others a good deal longer. Thus, in New York the drivers of horse cars and stages labored, in blazing heat or biting cold, twelve or even sixteen hours a day for $2, while hotel or livery drivers toiled an equal period for from $10.50 to $12 a week. The lot of women employees was often bitterly hard. When peace came, New York had not less than 15,000 working women whose weekly pittance did not rise above $3.50 or $4. They were employed in shops, factories, and large stores and they had reason to count themselves happier than the thousands of wretched women who carried materials home and made shirts and overalls for seventy-five cents a dozen. Girls in the drygoods stores of the great Eastern cities, where civilization was proudest of its achievements, toiled from seven-thirty in the morning till the closing hour of nine or ten, without seats, without rest rooms or facilities for a quiet lunch, without more consideration than dumb animals received; and for this health-ruining drudgery many were paid $5 a week.[69]

It was therefore no impulse of perversity, as some employers suggested, which led at once to a concerted movement for shorter hours and better pay. Ira Steward, a self-educated Boston machinist, indignant at the overwork he saw all about him and imbued with the ideas of John Stuart Mill, became the foremost apostle of a widespread agitation for an eight-hour day.[70] Eight Hour Leagues were formed in various states, a national congress met at Baltimore in 1866, and labor pressure carried through six legislatures laws which established eight hours as the legal day, unless other hours were agreed upon. These statutes proved futile, but the movement, by calling forcible attention to some of the grave abuses which labor endured, had its decided value. Another expression of the growing labor discontent lay in the vigorous movement for distributive cooperation on the Rochdale plan, an outgrowth of Socialistic and Fourieristic philosophy. Cooperative stores were set up to sell groceries, meat, drygoods, and footwear to workmen, while many workers, in the years 1866–69, tried to open small factories and produce wares cooperatively. Bakers went into the breadmaking business; coach makers combined to make and sell vehicles; coal miners, shipwrights, glass blowers, hat makers, tailors, printers, and many other embarked in business for themselves. Most important of all were the cooperative stove foundries established in Rochester, Troy, Pittsburgh, Louisville, Cleveland, Chicago, and other cities in 1866–67 under the leadership of William H. Sylvis, president of the Molders' International Union.[71] Some of these undertakings were financially successful, but the basic difficulty was that they tended to turn into old-style capitalistic enterprises, the owners hiring new workmen on a wage basis.

The best weapon of underpaid, overworked labor was, after all, not legislative action or cooperation but a trade union powerful enough to call an effective strike. Though by 1870 there were more than thirty national unions with a total membership of perhaps 300,000, and though the year 1866 witnessed the formation of the National Labor Union as a result of Sylvis's efforts, there was still little militant labor action. Strikes were few in number, frowned upon by public opinion, and for the most part abortive. Many organizations fell into quick decay, the National Labor Union going to pieces in the years 1870–72.[72] In many respects the most impressive of the bodies formed in the first decade after the war was the Knights of St. Crispin, the shoemakers' organization. It was a natural response to the introduction of the factory system into the shoe industry and its chief initial object was to protect the skilled journeyman against the competition of green hands and apprentices. Established in Milwaukee early in 1867, it spread like a prairie fire before a gale, until by the spring of 1872 there were no fewer than 327 lodges. The Crispins for a time conducted strikes with impressive success, waging a series of victorious battles in Lynn, Worcester, Philadelphia, and San Francisco; but after an unsuccessful strike at Lynn in 1872, the order was gradually beaten back by the employers.[73] Throughout these years the organization of unions and the conduct of strikes were grievously hampered by the inrush of immigrant workers, many of them skilled and all ready to accept employment under conditions which American labor found unsatisfactory.

This sullen discontent on the part of a great mass of workers, these attempts to seize upon one remedy after another—of one, the organization of the Knights of Labor in 1869—represented part of the dark reverse of the bright shield of industrial prosperity and expansion. Another gloomy aspect of the business rush and whirl lay in the frequent dishonesty, the sharp manipulation, and the ever-growing tendency toward speculative excesses, which accompanied it. Still another lay in the private extravagance, the relaxation of moral standards, and the vulgarization of taste which it encouraged from Boston to Omaha. The war, which had done so much to create the era of inflation and abounding prosperity, had also introduced many elements of confusion and recklessness into American life and thrown off old restraints. But, for the time, the great body of Americans, intent upon dipping their cups into the golden stream, overlooked all this. They thought only of the humming mills, the smoking factories, the magic birth of new cities and towns all over the West, the throng of immigrants from Europe, the atmosphere of optimism and cheer. The nation had never seemed so busy, its future never so bright. There was faith everywhere, but after the stunning disasters of 1873, so suddenly to follow, men wondered how they could have been so credulous.

URBAN LIVING

A NATURAL CONSEQUENCE of the great industrial prosperity of the time, with its multiplication of mills and railways and its growing stream of European immigrants, was the rise of the city to a new importance in American life. East of the Mississippi an ever-larger proportion of the population lived in towns. New York in 1870 had almost a million people, Philadelphia nearly three quarters of a million, Chicago 300,000, and Cincinnati 216,000.[74] All of these centers were expanding at a rate which pressed painfully upon their housing accommodations. Meanwhile, the greater ease and swiftness of communication made urban modes and manners much more widely influential, while the abundance of money bred in every Northern community a desire for urban luxuries and conveniences such as the American people had never before known. The cities were full of wealthy newcomers of rural antecedents, like W. D. Howells's sterling but crude Silas Lapham, who was so proud of his magnificent new residence on the water side of Beacon Street, and who boasted to his friend Corey: "Yes, sir, give an architect money enough, and he'll give you a nice house every time."[75] More and more the texture of American civilization was becoming urban in character, though the great transformation was not to occur until later in the century.

The large-scale industrialization of the North would alone have assured a multitude of the changes characteristic of city, as distinguished from country, modes of life. Clothing was altering to conform with the exigencies of a machine civilization. The ordinary man still had his best suit tailor-made of sooty broadcloth, but for everyday wear his suit was ready-made and his shoes and congress gaiters came from the factory. As the seventies wore on, Americans grew used to meats sent from Chicago, canned salmon from Oregon, and canned tomatoes from Maryland; they learned, especially after the Centennial Exhibition gave popularity to Vienna rolls and other hard-crusted breads, to patronize the commercial bakeries. Invention played its part in the introduction of novelties. Washing machines, still regarded by many people as a failure when the war closed, were rapidly improved—fifty patents were granted in the latter half of 1868—until they sold in enormous numbers. Sewing machines were being distributed by a half-dozen manufactories of national repute, like Singer, Wheeler and Wilson, Wilcox and Gibbs, and Grover and Baker, in addition to many smaller firms; and several sewing-machine millionaires were as well known as the petroleum capitalists. At the end of 1866, sewing machines were being made at the rate of 1,000 a day, and were selling for an average of $60 apiece. Though half were exported, American shops and homes were absorbing 180,000 annually, and their busy whir was heard in every prosperous household throughout the land.

Kerosene brought in its train a wide array of new lamps, and the ground glass globe was as characteristic of the ordinary American home as the base-burner with red coals shining through its mica windows; the more pretentious dwellings had Argand gas lamps. The two objections to kerosene were the frequency of explosions, which led to legislation to regulate the quality of the oil, and the readiness with which the glass chimneys cracked. As the use of anthracite coal increased with the marked development of the Pennsylvania fields, cooking ranges and heating stoves were rapidly improved. The large office buildings and flats of the seventies had to be heated by steam radiation, and the hot-water furnace in the late seventies was making its way into many of the finer city homes. Refrigeration and artificial ice were becoming well known in many quarters; New Orleans in 1871 boasted an ice factory which was making seventy-two tons daily from distilled water and which had reduced the price, to the dismay of Northern ice importers, from $40 or even $60 a ton to $15. Even at that price its large profits were encouraging the formation of similar companies in other Southern cities.

While the urban household was becoming a much more comfortable abode, many innovations were contributing to the convenience of business life. Thus the earliest safety-deposit vaults came into use just after the war. Meanwhile, the use of the passenger elevator, first designed for an exhibition tower adjacent to the Crystal Palace in London in 1853, was becoming common. It was indispensable for such comparatively tall structures as the new Bryant Building and the Lord and Taylor department store in New York, and in all the great cities it permitted contractors to raise their buildings first to eight and then to ten or even more stories.[76]

The best hotels, like the Tremont House in Boston, the Astor House in New York, and Willard's in Washington, had long been the most elaborately fitted in the world, and they maintained their high standards, but though they impressed everyone by their size and magnificence, their service was not always equally good. The novelist Anthony Trollope found that the clerks were frequently inattentive, that the "extras" cost too much, and that the meals, brought on all together in their flock of birdbath dishes, were greasy and badly served. In New York some striking improvements were embodied in the great Park Avenue Hotel, which A. T. Stewart began late in life with the aim of erecting a fireproof house possessing a homely comfort, yet with magnificent public rooms. It was a quadrangular edifice of seven stories, with a spacious courtyard upon which the interior rooms opened, and the stonework and broad arches bore witness to its nonflammable character. The Hoffman House, which was finished just as the war closed, became famous for its grand banquet hall, sixty feet square, and its art gallery.[77] In many cities the hotels tried to fill a larger civic purpose and devised more ambitious entertainments. The Fifth Avenue Hotel in New York was well known for its political meetings and banquets to public figures; the Grand Pacific Hotel in Chicago served annually a game banquet to invited guests, turning its dining hall into a miniature forest, crowding its tables with stuffed animals and beautifully arranged birds' nests, and placing every meat and fowl of the West, from bear to reedbird, on the generous menu.[78]

Without exception, the cities still depended upon horsepower for transportation. In some instances this elementary means of transit was highly developed. The New Yorker, for example, had at his disposal in 1866 some 1,400 hackney coaches; 7 lines of omnibuses, employing perhaps 300 vehicles on regular routes; 16 separate lines of horse railway, with 800 cars and nearly 8,000 horses; and a few hansom cabs.[79] Yet the slow-moving horse vehicles crowded the main thoroughfares of the largest cities to suffocation, they littered the pavements with dirt and cruelly overtaxed many dumb beasts. So limited was their range that the outlying districts remained totally undeveloped while the central streets were congested. Thus in New York the most desirable parts of the island, the sections abreast of and above Central Park, were largely given up to pigs, ducks, shanty squatters, and filth, while lower Broadway was so jammed that a man in a hurry almost lost his reason.[80]

Only in New York were the beginnings of a reform effected. Here, after much talk of sunken railways, subways, and elevated lines running over the housetops, construction of an elevated railway on pillars was actually begun in 1867. The fiercest of fights was waged against it. Horsecar interests and property holders brought suits; its charter was attacked as unconstitutional. Businessmen declared that the noise would kill trade, that the unsightly structure overhead would ruin the city's appearance, and that the moving trains would frighten horses. But the railway was finally completed from the foot of the island up Ninth Avenue to 30th Street in 1870, and within a short time was being operated with such success that its immediate extension and the building of another on Sixth Avenue were called for.[81]

The cities were equally patient with the wretched street paving of the time, though they recognized its inadequacy and the New York press spoke wistfully of the day when all thoroughfares might be as smooth as a specially laid section of concrete on Nassau Street. The close of the seventies found surprisingly little done.[82] Philadelphia, with 900 miles of paved streets at this date, had 500 miles of cobblestones—rough, noisy, and impossible to clean. Most of the remainder was rubble stone and broken stone. New York paved the greater part of its streets with stone blocks, which were uneven, held mud and dust in their cracks, and were ruinous to vehicles, while for the rest, macadam and cobblestones were used. Boston had resort to cobblestones, trap blocks, and broken stones, though in the late seventies by far the greater part of her ways were merely graveled. Many cities used wooden blocks, especially in the West, where stone was scarce, lumber cheap, and the subsoil favorable. Washington spent

Scene from "The White Fawn,"
New York City

"Two Sides of the Way"—Common on Fifth Avenue,
New York City.

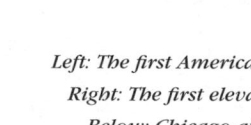

Broadway
Swell.

Left: The first American sleeping car.
Right: The first elevated railroad.
Below: Chicago after the fire.

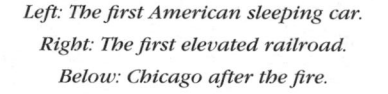

Philadelphia
Quakers.

Section of the carnival pageant,
Louisville, Kentucky.

1865—Glimpses of the Cities—1878

more than $5 million in laying chemically treated blocks in the early seventies, so that by the Centennial year it was called the best-paved city in America. Everywhere the really best materials were neglected. Asphalt was extensively used in Paris after 1854, and in London after 1868, and was there found smooth, durable, and clean; but an opinion prevailed in the United States that it was too costly and that stone remained the best of all pavements. Even by the close of the seventies, Boston, Philadelphia, and New York did not have ten miles of asphalt among them.[83] But happily concrete sidewalks were coming steadily into favor.

A far graver failure of the cities was their neglect to insist upon fire-resisting buildings. *Harper's Weekly* pointed out after the war that the dense masses of wooden houses and offices in New York invited a repetition of the disastrous conflagration of 1835.[84] When Portland, Maine, suffered her terrible fire of July 4, 1866, which began with a match tossed into a boatbuilder's shop, a cry of warning was raised.[85] But these voices went unheeded. Until 1871, Boston made no attempt whatever to regulate the construction of buildings, while Chicago was equally negligent. Both paid a memorable penalty.

Chicago's great fire of 1871 burned over an area in which many buildings were fondly believed to be fireproof, reducing them to ashes and fragments. The conflagration, originating in a small wooden barn in De Koven Street on a Sunday night in early October, was driven by a strong wind through the squalid shanties of that quarter and gained momentum in the large lumberyards on the Chicago River. Leaping eastward across the stream, the flames swept north into the main business district, closely built up with structures of stone, brick, and iron. No Chicagoan would have believed that they would yield to the fire like tinder, but they did.[86] The flames pushed through this section from the southwest, eating a path a mile wide, and then debouched upon the scattered buildings farther north. Banks, theaters, newspaper offices, hotels, grain elevators, the courthouse, and the waterworks all disappeared in the holocaust. The deafening roar of the flames and the overpowering heat made the scene an inferno. When Frederick Law Olmsted visited the ruins three weeks later, he found that a man standing on an omnibus could see people walking three miles distant across what had been the densest, loftiest, and most substantial part of the city. This destruction of 17,450 buildings, leaving almost one third of the population homeless, was an unforgettable object lesson in the necessity for fuller safeguards against fire.[87]

The much smaller fire in Boston a little more than a year later also swept the business section, and destroyed hundreds of brick and granite buildings which the people had supposed entirely safe. Here the fierceness of the flames owed much to the mansard roofs, which along the narrow streets burst into an instant blaze and were inaccessible to the firemen, while, as in Chicago, the fire department lacked discipline and its apparatus proved imperfect.[88] The shock produced throughout the country by these conflagrations caused a powerful movement in favor of fire-resistant materials, and laws were passed which forced the question of safety upon the attention of architects and builders. One innovation after another aided the movement. Concrete buildings were unknown in America just after the war, though Napoleon III had used concrete in the erection of workmen's houses in Paris and it had been employed in business edifices in England. But within a few years concrete was exciting keen interest in all parts of the United States, and in 1870 the first dwellings of that material were erected in Belleville, New Jersey. Plate glass was at this time just coming into general use in stores and offices, and it did away with the necessity of much wooden-sash work. Most of it was imported, though by 1870 there was one American factory which produced unpolished plate glass.[89] Asbestos, too, began to be known in the late seventies after large mines were discovered in Canada. Above all, the manufacture of steel by the Bessemer process made it possible to use it in place of wrought iron for buildings and prepared the way for the coming era of fireproof steel construction.

The multiplication of cities and towns and the increasing congestion of population within industrial areas furnished new problems in communication. The mileage of American telegraph lines was trebled within a few years, and far-reaching improvements were made in the postal service of the nation. City after city was adopting the free-carrier service which Congress had authorized in 1863. The urgency of the need was best illustrated in New York, where some 6,000 boxes had represented 30,000 names, and the sorting clerks had to be able to recall and associate any one of these names with the proper box on the instant. Carrier delivery, which Europe had long employed, led for the first time to the extensive directing of letters to streets and numbers. By 1871 there were fifty-one cities with carrier service, and though the work of the postmen did not yet command universal confidence, it was rapidly improving.[90] Two years later the postal card was introduced from Europe. Thomas A. Edison, the future magician of light and sound, was soon at work improving the telegraph and using it to print stock quotations.

Yet nothing did more to expedite communication than two widely different inventions upon which in the early seventies two modest geniuses were laboring all unnoticed: the typewriter and the telephone. Each answered a strong, though ill-realized, social demand, and each did much to change important phases of business and urban life.[91] The telephone was the work of a mercurial young Scotch-American named Alexander Graham Bell who at the outset of the seventies was conducting a school for deaf mutes in Boston and laboring over the dream of a musical telegraph. The typewriter we owe chiefly to a middle-aged printer of Milwaukee named C. L. Sholes, a dreamy, erratic man who just after the war was giving his spare hours to a device for numbering serially the pages of a book. Each was led step by step to an achievement far beyond his first ambitions.

Sholes had completed his device for printing numbers when his attention was called to an article by Alfred Beach in the *Scientific American,* expatiating on the value which a practical typewriter would possess. The immense growth of business and official affairs, Beach pointed out, had made letter writing and record keeping by pen deplorably inadequate; the time was ripe for a quicker, clearer, more permanent method.[92] Sholes set to work in his dingy two-story machine shop and with the help of several friends, notably Carlos Glidden, made, by the autumn of 1867, a machine which would write with a fair degree of accuracy and rapidity. One of the letters written by his typewriter fell into the hands of a businessman of Meadville, Pennsylvania, named James Densmore, who was so interested that he asked to buy a share in the invention. It was Densmore who, pointing out that the machine was full of the gravest defects, insisted that they must be corrected. Between 1867 and 1873, Sholes, Densmore, and Glidden built model after model, each showing some improvement, until, in the latter year, the device was deemed good enough to be manufactured for general sale. We find Mark Twain in December 1874 composing a letter upon a machine which had cost him $125 and explaining its many virtues. "I believe it will print faster than I can write," he declared. "One may lean back in his chair and work it. It piles an awful stack of words on one page. It don't muss things or scatter ink blots around. Of course it saves paper."[93]

The year 1874 also saw Bell laboring in his basement workshop in a Salem dwelling with the idea of speech transmission by wire ever more prominent in his mind but with the means still quite unforeseen. He took a long step forward when, with the advice of a friendly surgeon, he began experimenting with an apparatus of which a dead man's ear formed a part.[94] He noticed how the delicate eardrum set the heavy bones behind it to vibrating. "Why," he asked, "should not a vibrating iron disk set an iron rod or electrified wire into vibration?" It was on a hot June afternoon in 1875, while patiently toiling over the complicated mechanism which he and his assistant, Thomas A. Watson, had set up, that he heard a feeble sound, a faint twang, come over the wire from a similar machine in the next room. It was the birth cry of the telephone. While Sholes in 1875 was slowly marketing his first crude typewriters, Bell was puzzling out the mechanical details which made his invention workable. It was to be only a few years until in every city office the two most familiar noises would be the ring of the telephone bell and the click of the typist's key.

Equally striking were the improvements in the comfort and safety of long-distance traveling. When an American entered a railway car at the beginning of the period, he could seldom find a window that opened easily, a stove that warmed his body, or a seat secure from the tobacco juice and talk of rowdies.[95] The railway waiting rooms were usually small, dirty, and insufferably close, with no more facilities for comfort than a police station. A pleasant restaurant was nowhere to be found; instead, the passenger who entered the hot, noisy "refreshment saloon" had to lift himself to a high stool and bolt the viands which, badly cooked, were literally thrown at his plate. Once embarked on a train, no matter how long the journey, he could have no food save stale popcorn, apples, and candy.

But within the space of a half-dozen years first-class travel was completely transformed. The agent who produced this change was an enterprising young New Yorker, still in his early thirties, named George M. Pullman. He had carried an unusual eye for opportunities into his business as cabinet maker and contractor, and had given some attention to the refitting of ordinary railway cars with berths. As the war was ending, he invested more than $20,000 in building in Chicago the first Pullman car, a sum four times as great as had ever been spent upon a railway coach.[96] The "Pioneer" possessed improved rubber-bearing trucks, was a foot wider and two and a half feet higher than any other car, and showed resplendently ornate furnishings. The dimensions of railway platforms and bridges would not permit its passage over any existing line, but the needed changes on two routes were hastened by the request that it be attached to Lincoln's funeral train and be used to carry General Grant from Detroit to Galena. Pullman, confident that the public would welcome the innovation, asked only that the railway superintendents give his cars a fair trial. This was first done on the Michigan Central, where several of the new cars were attached to trains together with the old-style sleeping cars, the charge being $2 a berth on the one, and $1.50 on the other. The success of the Pullmans was immediate. Lines competing with the Michigan Central found that many travelers preferred the railway which had the Pullmans, and they hastened to install them.[97]

As the number of Pullman cars multiplied, their designer prepared to bring forward fresh luxuries and innovations. In 1867 he introduced the first "hotel car" or rudimentary diner, a sleeping car with a built-in kitchen from which meals were served at tables placed in the sections. When in that year the gauge between New York and Chicago was standardized by the addition of a third rail to the Great Western, and the first "through" train ran between the two cities, the hotel car was coupled to the train.[98] Others were soon running between Chicago and Boston or New York, and the dining car proper, devoted exclusively to restaurant purposes, followed in 1868.[99] Later still came the drawing room cars and the reclining chair cars.

Not only did the American travel more comfortably, he traveled more safely. In 1866, George Westinghouse, a shrewd young New Yorker, had his attention directed by a railway wreck near Schenectady to the difficulty of stopping trains in motion, and began working at a power brake. A magazine article on the use of compressed air in driving rock drills on the French-Italian Mont Cenis tunnel gave him a brilliant idea, and the result was the air-brake patent issued to him early in 1869 when he was not yet twenty-three.[100] Westinghouse's invention, which included a steam pump on the locomotive to compress air to about seventy pounds a square inch, was first tested near Pittsburgh in the fall of 1868. His train had not emerged from the city when a drayman was espied on the track just ahead and the engineer applied the new brakes with an abruptness that hurled all the guests to the floor. The train made demonstrations throughout the country, and orders at once came in. Almost immediately young Westinghouse became president of an air-brake company capitalized at a half million dollars, with leading railwaymen of the country, such as A. J. Cassatt of the Pennsylvania system, as directors. He continued zealously to perfect his invention, patenting (1872) an automatic air brake, which was so constructed that when the train broke in two the brakes set of themselves upon the detached cars. By 1876 nearly two fifths of all the locomotives and passenger cars of the country were equipped with his appliances.[101]

Nor were Westinghouse's devices by any means the only contribution to railway safety and convenience. Just after the war Miller's car platform, coupler, and buffer, the first noteworthy improvements in this equipment, were adopted on all passenger trains. They brought the platforms into close contact, thus minimizing the jolt in starting and stopping trains and lessening the danger of telescoping.[102] Meanwhile, steel or steel-capped rails were fast being substituted for iron, and iron bridges, Carnegie's first large business venture, for wooden structures. Wood was used as fuel upon important trunk lines of the East, even near the Pennsylvania coal fields, until after 1870, and one of the improvements which Jay Gould wrought upon the Erie lay in the introduction of coal in adequate quantities. A highly important step in railway safety, the invention of the automatic railway signal, came early in the seventies, when David Rousseau's device was brought into use on the New York Central.[103] Every wreck in these years—for example, the great Revere catastrophe upon the Eastern Railroad of Massachusetts in the summer of 1871, which revealed astounding negligence—was seized upon by the press as the text for an argument in behalf of the new safety appliances.[104] By 1878 it could be said that railway travel in the United States had passed out of the stage of fumbling youth into that of sophisticated young manhood. The American rightly boasted that he could travel with less discomfort and greater safety than anyone else in the world.

THE TAMING OF THE WEST (1865–73)

THE BUILDING of the transcontinental railway, the filling in of a great transportation network behind it, and the rapid advance of settlement all pronounced the doom of the wildest West—the West of hostile Indian tribes, enormous bison herds, unexplored mountain ranges, and unnavigated rivers. There were approximately 300,000 Indians in the United States when the war closed, of whom 32,000 lived in the region east of the Mississippi (including Minnesota) and 48,000 upon the Pacific slope.[105] The northern Indians on the Great Plains numbered more than 60,000 and included four nations of the first importance—the Sioux, the Crow, the Northern Cheyenne, and the Arapahoe. Of these, the Crow, like the Pawnee, were usually friendly to the whites, and they were enemies of the fierce and warlike Sioux and furnished many scouts to the government. But the other three nations needed the most tactful and generous treatment. The southern tribes of the plains included not only the peace-loving and industrious Cherokee, Creek, and Choctaw, well-settled on reservations in what is now Oklahoma, but the Kiowa, the Comanche, the Southern Cheyenne, and the Southern Arapahoe. They were tinder for any blaze of hostilities, and they numbered about 85,000 in all.[106]

Certain main characteristics stamped the life of these plains Indians. They were physically of fine stature, strong and active. They lived by the hunt, and their habitat, their government, their social institutions, and their beliefs were affected, above all other factors, by the buffalo. Agriculture played a comparatively small role in their economy.[107] Their chief elements of wealth consisted of their herds of ponies and of their weapons and ammunition, while they were quite unable to understand the desire of the white man to monopolize any part of the earth.[108] Their government was simple and, in a sense, democratic, consisting in a leadership of chiefs who attained their primacy by skill and courage and whose sway was most stringently exercised in time of war or other emergency.

These proud, stern, and really formidable peoples, who had many faults but whose courage and fortitude even their enemies admired, were now caught as in a gigantic vise. The Missouri frontier and the Pacific frontier, shaped like a pair of parentheses, tended constantly to contract. On the east the advance of the settlers had by 1872 crept up to the semiarid region of the Texas, Kansas, and Nebraska cattle range, where tillage was difficult; on the west, it pressed up to the Sierras.[109] A marked restiveness developed among most of the plains tribes during the Civil War—a restiveness not the result of Confederate machinations, as many observers believed, but of the irresistible thrust of settlement. From 1865 to 1870 there was almost constant war, and long after 1870, when the West had been fairly subdued and policed, there were sporadic outbreaks of a bloody nature. The Indians would have been tame indeed had they not rebelled. Their food supply in the herds of elk and buffaloes was being cut off, their reservations were reduced, they were constantly shifted to less desirable territory, and individually they were often cheated and maltreated. The almost universal testimony along the border was that the only wise policy toward them was extermination, and even so liberal an American as Samuel Bowles could say that if this policy alone was feasible, the sooner and quicker it was carried out the better.[110]

Moreover, the government's plans for their disposal were weak and fluctuating. Up to 1851 the whole immense region between the Missouri and the Rockies had been officially recognized as an Indian domain, but the successive gold discoveries in California and Colorado, with the rush of prospectors and other emigrants across the plains, had caused the tribes to be partitioned off into ever smaller and more barren districts. In 1861 the restive Cheyenne and Arapahoe of the south agreed by treaty to restrict themselves to a region along the Arkansas River and the northern boundary of New Mexico.[111] In return, the United States was to protect their lands, pay $30,000 to each tribe annually for fifteen years, and supply them with stock and farm implements. Finding themselves in a poor and inhospitable region, their discontent was immediate. Meanwhile, the Sioux to the northward had driven the Crow into the Montana country and had taken sole possession of the area between Montana and the Missouri, with parts of Minnesota. But this was not so wide a range as they desired. They felt irritated and alarmed. So did the Northern Cheyenne and Araphoe.

The first hostilities on a general scale were inaugurated by the Cheyenne uprising of 1864. They began in August, with an attack upon Ben Holladay's stage and freight line east of Denver, and with raids upon scattered farms, ranches, and stagecoach stations. For 370 miles every ranch but one along Holladay's route was deserted; the frontier was reduced almost overnight to a state of abject terror.[112] At this juncture occurred the barbarous Sand Creek massacre, throwing a lurid illumination upon the attitude of most Westerners and military men toward the Indians. Colonel J. M. Chivington, at the head of nearly 1,000 Colorado volunteers, suddenly fell upon between 500 and 600 harmless, unsuspecting, and friendly Cheyenne and Arapahoe, mostly women and children, and slaughtered them with sickening barbarities.[113] When news of the massacre reached the East, a passionate wave of indignation swept all humane circles. But in the West, where the Indians were hated like serpents, Chivington received general applause.[114] For the moment, as the news spread, the whole frontier was ablaze.[115] The Platte route was raided from a point near Denver almost to the Missouri; telegraph lines went down; trains were captured; and men and women killed. For six weeks no mail passed east or west.

At the close of 1865, after a summer of arduous campaigning, the state of Indian affairs was dismaying to all observers. Not fewer than 25,000 troops were in the field against the tribes. They were employed along the frontiers of Minnesota and Dakota, in the Black Hills and the Powder River country, all over the Nebraska plains and along the Smoky Hill route in western Kansas and in New Mexico and Arizona. This large army was performing important services to the settlers. It was holding open the great central and southwestern mail routes; it was protecting 2,000 miles of the navigable Missouri above Kansas City; it was keeping the overland telegraph from Omaha to the Carson Valley uncut; and under the shield it raised, emigrants were thronging toward the West.[116] Nevertheless, the question arose whether this tremendous outlay of capital and appreciable expenditure of blood was necessary or even justified. Secretary of the Interior Harlan estimated that every regiment thrown upon the plains to fight the Indians cost the treasury $2 million a year, and that all the campaigns of the preceding year had not wiped out more than a few hundred braves.[117]

It was plainly cheaper, not to say more humane, to feed the Indians than to kill them. But was it necessary to do either? Could not the Indian Territory be made a really inclusive reservation; could not treaty stipulations be honestly fulfilled and the trade in Indian supplies fairly conducted; could not justice be enforced against the ruffianly white man and the hostile Indian alike? Under pressure of these considerations, the government made an earnest effort to deal constructively with the problem. There was a congressional inquiry; two peace commissions were dispatched westward in 1865, one to bargain with the Southwestern Indians and the other to make a treaty with the Sioux and their allies.[118] Agreements were actually concluded and the Cheyenne and Arapahoe gave up their reservation along the Arkansas in return for the privilege of ranging the unsettled plains for buffalo. But none of the deeper causes of the Indian hostility were removed or even softened. The Indians felt crowded on the south by the new Kansas and Nebraska settlements and on the east by the steady thrust from Iowa and Minnesota, while they saw a new stream of white migration strike across their best northern hunting range to the mines of Montana and Idaho.

While the Indians were being thrown back from the country which the white newcomers wanted, the destruction of the great buffalo herds was being relentlessly organized. Of all the wild quadrupeds that have ever lived, the bison marshaled the greatest numbers.[119] Our most careful estimates place the number of buffaloes in the trans-Mississippi West just after the war at 15 million.[120] A single herd seen by Colonel R. I. Dodge on the Arkansas River in 1871 has been estimated to have contained at least 4 million. Their range lay between the Canadian plains on the far north, and the Gulf on the south, and they swept back and forth in spring and autumn as the line of pasturage advanced and receded. The building of the Union Pacific separated the bison into northern and southern herds, and other railways stretched rapidly into the most populous buffalo regions. Coincidentally there arose a general demand in the East for buffalo robes and hides, while the armies released a host of men with new and accurate breech-loading rifles and fixed ammunition.[121]

The destruction of the southern herd, ranging south of the Union Pacific and east of Pueblo, came first. By the building of the Santa Fe, the Kansas Pacific, and shorter lines, every part of the buffalo range was made easily accessible. Railroad workers, teamsters, professional hunters, trappers, guides, and unemployed men turned out to share in the harvest of free hides and free meat, and during the years 1870–74 buffalo killing became one of the chief industries of the Southwestern plains.[122] The first large shipments from the Western terminals were bales of buffalo skins, and at Dodge City at one time there were to be seen 120 cords of them in a single corral. Prominent among the hunters were sportsmen from the East and Europe. The youngest son of Czar Alexander III, the Grand Duke Alexis, with a large entourage, traveled across the plains in 1871–72, and for his benefit a grand buffalo chase was arranged on the plains of western Kansas under Buffalo Bill, General Custer, and General Sheridan.[123] The approved commercial party consisted of four men: one shooter, two skinners, and an assistant who stretched hides and cooked. It has been carefully estimated that in four years, 1871–74, 3.7 million buffalo of the southern herd were slain, and that of the total more than 3,150,000 were killed by professional white hunters.[124]

By the end of the hunting season of 1875 the herd passed out of existence, utterly annihilated as a body, though a few vestiges had fled to remote parts of the range. So overstocked was the market for robes that by 1875 the hunters received only sixty-five cents each for an ordinary buffalo-bull's skin and $1.15 for a cow's. The consequence was that whenever it became difficult to skin an animal, it was simply left in its tracks. According to Colonel Dodge, each buffalo skin which reached the East represented five slain buffaloes in 1871, three in 1872, and one and a fourth in 1874. Though the meat might have fed hundreds of thousands of people, little of it was preserved. Probably no great American resource has ever been quite so wantonly and completely destroyed within so brief a time.[125] The main northern herd was smaller, and in its greater isolation it persisted somewhat longer. It was not until the opening of the Northern Pacific in 1880 that its fate was sealed. Within a few years thereafter almost the only surviving bison were those on the cold Canadian plains. The American people had all the buffalo robes they needed for sleighing, and buffalo heads had become a commonplace ornament of homes and public buildings. But one of the most picturesque and impressive forms of wildlife the world has ever seen was left virtually extinct.

Meanwhile, the new policy of keeping the Indian tribes within bounds and laboring to "civilize" them was yielding encouraging results. By 1871 the board of Indian commissioners was able to describe "the remarkable spectacle seen this fall, on the plains of western Nebraska and Kansas and eastern Colorado, of the warlike tribes of the Sioux of Dakota, Montana and Wyoming, hunting peacefully for buffalo without occasioning any serious alarm among the thousands of white settlers whose cabins skirt the borders of both sides of these plains."[126] The tribes had greatly "improved" in temper and docility. Another step of great importance was taken that year, when Congress passed an act ordering that no more treaties with Indian tribes should be made by the president and Senate.[127] The fiction that the Indian chiefs held a sovereign treaty-making power was thus abandoned and Congress as a whole, not the Senate alone, assumed jurisdiction over the entire field of Indian administration. Henceforth the West gradually lost

An attack on the Overland coach.

Shooting buffalo from the train.

The Invasion of the West.

all apprehension of another general Indian war; the tribes were too widely scattered and weak, while the railways made it easy to throw troops into vital positions. The Cheyenne of the South and some of the remoter Sioux still showed a great deal of turbulence and the Apache were almost utterly intractable. But a good many of the Arapahoe were already engaged in farming; in Nebraska, the Pawnee and Omaha had made encouraging progress; and with the extinction of the buffalo from the plains, it was believed that nearly all the tribes would settle down in earnest to agriculture.[128]

As the Indians were pushed aside and pacified in the period from 1865 to 1873, the stream of migrants to the trans-Missouri region steadily increased in size. During the summer, river towns like Kansas City, Leavenworth, and Omaha were scenes of bustling confusion as crowds of settlers prepared to face the perils of the long journey into the farther West. An Eastern newspaperman who traveled on horseback across the plains in 1866 found that though the prairie might be solitary, the trails were as busy as Eastern highways.[129] He was scarcely ever out of sight of long ox teams or shorter mule teams, and in one week after leaving Leavenworth, passed 680 creaking vehicles. Samuel Bowles remarked the same procession of heavy wagons and carts, going east empty or rolling west full of emigrants and the supplies needed by ranchers and miners. Covered with dirty white cloth, the separate trains frequently stretching from one quarter to one third of a mile, they looked at a distance like Oriental caravans. At night the wagons were drawn into a circle as a protection against Indians or storms, and the animals turned loose to graze.

An effort might be made to exhibit the growth of population graphically on the motion-picture screen by showing the West as it became peppered with spots representing 1,000 people. We would see the spots first appearing sparsely at railheads and the intersection of trails and streams, then following the ramifications of the railways, and finally stippling the prairie lands. As they move westward, they push before them the black and sinuous frontier line, from Dakota to Texas. Upon the map of Minnesota for 1870, we may fancy 436 such spots massed largely in the south and east, an agglomeration of 30 representing St. Paul and Minneapolis.[130] Though only a third of Iowa's farmland was under the plow and the northwest corner was yet unsettled, that state would show 1,200 spots. It was already one of the chief agricultural units of the nation—the fourth state in corn production, the fifth in wheat, and the sixth in livestock. Kansas was hard on the heels of Minnesota, with about 380 spots, growing sparser and sparser toward the west.[131] Western Missouri shared in the influx of new settlers brought by the railways; thus Jackson County, in which lay Kansas City, would show 23 spots on the screen for 1860, and 55 for 1870.

Where did this tide of population get its homes?[132] The public lands had been thrown wide open to settlers by three great enactments during the Civil War: the homestead act, the Morrill land-grant act, and the act giving the Union Pacific a princely domain. When Grant was preparing his move on Vicksburg, the earliest homesteaders had made their entries, and after the war the entries increased rapidly. During the fiscal year 1871-72 nearly 6,000 homesteads passed into the possession of settlers; during 1872-73 more than 10,000, and in 1875-76 no fewer than 22,530.[133] The public lands were, for the most part, occupied by families with no spare cash, who built their sod houses or frame shanties and toiled like slaves, saving every penny to obtain stock and machinery. Those settlers who wished to buy land from private owners found it abundant and cheap. Under the Morrill act, each state had received, for the endowment of colleges of agriculture and the mechanic arts, 30,000 acres for every member in Congress, with the result that New York, for example, had 990,000 acres to sell or rent. And enormous though the railway land grants of the fifties had been, they were now far surpassed. All the great transcontinental lines— the Union Pacific, the Santa Fe, and the Southern Pacific—received twenty sections a mile on each side within all territories traversed and ten sections within all states, while other railways were given lesser amounts. The last railway land grants were made in 1871, the year in which the outburst of Western hostility to grasping rail corporations resulted in the "Granger legislation" of Illinois. But by this date the whole area thus given away by the government had reached the colossal total of 129 million acres, an area three times the size of New England.[134]

Nearly all the grantees were eager to dispose of their land holdings. Thus the Illinois Central, given 2.5 million acres by the state, which had received it in turn from the federal government, sold all but a third of a million acres before 1871, at an average price of $10.61 an acre. Up to November 1, 1872, the Union Pacific reported land sales of 650,000 acres, at an average of $4.72 an acre, while it was widely advertising its unsold area of almost 11.5 million acres.[135] A skilled mechanic in the cities, discontented with his lot and eager to own his own farm, could earn the equivalent of an acre of land in a day. All the railways understood the wisdom of developing an immediate freight business by selling land to farmers rather than to speculators and were seldom inclined to cling to their acreage for the unearned increment. The average price of the huge volume of railway lands disposed of before 1881 was only $4.76 an acre.[136] Unfortunately, the land departments of the transportation systems, with glowing promises and advertisements, often induced inexperienced colonists to push into spots remote from neighbors or markets, or to buy poor land. The destitution and semi-starvation suffered by farmers along the Republican and Solomon rivers in Kansas early in the seventies was blamed in large part on the Kansas Pacific Railroad. But on the whole, the lines played an invaluable role in Western farm development.[137]

Nearly all the tillable lands went to small holders—war veterans, Eastern clerks and artisans, German and Scandinavian immigrants, and farmers' sons, all men of limited capital. Some few large farms were acquired by rich men. There was an 80,000-acre estate in Bureau County, Illinois. Much more famous was M. L. Sullivant's 70,000-acre farm a short distance to the east in Champaign County, the owner of which employed from 100 to 200 laborers and lived as on a manorial estate.[138] In the Northwest, large holdings were more common. As southern Minnesota became settled, it contained one farm—the property of the Rock County Company—with 50,000 acres, and others of from 2,000 to 7,000 acres. Near Fargo, in the Dakotas, was the 40,000-acre farm of J. L. Grandin, nearly three times the area of Manhattan Island. But such concentrated holdings, apart from the large ranches of the cattle country, were rare until the failure of Jay Cooke in 1873 threw large tracts of Northern Pacific land into the hands of the security holders, some of whom kept them intact for farming. They required altogether too much capital for operation, and as the lands increased in value the interest charges on the investment became excessive.[139] All the Western states made strenuous efforts to attract immigrants of more limited means. Thus Minnesota, in 1868, appropriated $10,000 for the use of an immigration board, printed pamphlets in a half dozen tongues, inserted advertisements in the Irish press, and maintained agents in Milwaukee, Chicago, New York, and Germany.[140] Everywhere was heard the strident voice of the booster.

Cities sprang up as if by magic on the central plains, the waving prairie giving way in a half dozen years to blocks of stone and brick structures and fine residences. Some of these thriving communities were made by the government, most of them by private energy. Lincoln, Nebraska, and Wichita, Kansas, will serve as examples, both of them towns which were nonexistent when Grant's administration began and well known to every American when it ended. In 1867, legislative commissioners, searching for a capital site for Nebraska, pitched upon the little settlement of Lancaster, consisting of ten crudely built stone and log houses almost 100 miles distant from the nearest railway. For their initial task the commissioners had to sell enough lots to provide at least $50,000 for a capitol building, which the law required to be ready in a little more than a year. The first two days' sales at Lincoln, with a meager crowd and many scoffers, were so dismal a failure that the commissioners saw their plans collapsing. In a spasm of energy they mustered all their friends and ready cash and sold $34,000 worth of lots on the third day. A later auction at Nebraska City netted $10,000. With this money they found a contractor, imported skilled labor from the East, and hauled all the material by teams for from forty to sixty miles. The capitol was finished on time and the next legislature met in it. Thereafter Lincoln grew by a series of rapid leaps.[141]

When the Panic year began, the frontier had crept up to central Minnesota and the semiarid region of central Nebraska and western Kansas.[142] This filling up of the plains meant an increase in wheat production which was very shortly to upset the markets of the world. Even more remarkable than the swift settlement of the prairies was the rapidity with which the people succeeded in reestablishing the essentials of the civilization they had left behind them. They demanded churches, schools, newspapers, smart clothing, and the newest novels. "They want to hear Froude lecture," said the *Nation*, "would like a chance of listening to [Austrian soprano Pauline] Lucca, and wonder what the Emperor of Austria will think of the Illinois schoolhouse at the Vienna exhibition."[143] The little sun-baked, blizzard-chilled hamlet that was talking of Indian raids one day might be talking of the *Atlantic Monthly*, the suffragist lecturer, and Paris fashions the next. University towers began to catch the bright ray of the future. By 1873 the University of Minnesota had 278 students, the agricultural college in Iowa had graduated two classes, and several scores of young men were studying in the halls which Nebraska had hastened to erect at Lincoln.

THE WEST AT WORK (1865-73)

STOCK BREEDING and agriculture were the two chief concerns of the settlers in the region between the Mississippi and the Rockies. The rise of the cattle range, one of the most romantic chapters of American history, occurred simultaneously with the building of the transcontinental lines, the birth of cities like Wichita and Cheyenne, the destruction of the buffalo, and the suppression of the hostile Indians. The whole wide expanse where the bison had ranged became, save where the homesteader invaded it, a great cattle region. It was admirably adapted to the purpose. The dry winter climate of the Northern plains permitted the snow to be blown off the hillsides to expose the dead grass, the coulees and ravines gave shelter during the blizzards, and the bunch grass covering most of the country offered nutritious pasturage. Shrewd Texas cattlemen perceived, as soon as the plains were opened up by the railwaymen and infantry, that the northern ranges were superior to their own;[144] and furthermore the war had left them heavily overstocked with cattle.[145]

Hence there sprang up a great annual northward drive of cattle, following well-beaten trails to the feeding grounds along the railways and to sections farther north.[146] As early as 1856, large Texas herds had been driven through Missouri to St. Louis to find a northern market. When nine years later the railway system reached Kansas City, the drive was made shorter still. But the first decisive step toward developing the upper range country came with the opening of a great cattle market and shipping point at Abilene, Kansas.

The news that an outlet had been established there spread as by electricity through the Southwest. The first year, 1867, some 35,000 cattle were driven into Abilene and thence shipped east over the new Kansas Pacific, which had been persuaded to make favorable rates and furnish yards.[147] Thereafter, as the rival railways pushed west, new markets, or "cow-towns," were established from point to point—Newton, Wichita, and, later, the picturesquely vicious Dodge City, on the Santa Fe; Ellsworth, on the Kansas Pacific; and Baxter Springs, on the Fort Worth and Gulf. Of course, some Texas cattle were sent to market from the coast, while others were driven to points on the Red River, whence they could be dispatched north by steamer and rail. But the great majority were driven, in numerous independent herds ranging in number from a few hundred to 10,000 each, into Kansas, Nebraska, and Colorado.[148]

So profitable was the business that by 1870 the livestock industry showed an activity never before witnessed in Texas. Men scoured the country, contracting for herds of longhorns to be delivered in time for the next spring drive, buying horses and hiring cowboys, while numerous companies were formed to obtain capital for investment.[149] During the early seventies the northern herds grew rapidly. The possibilities of gaining wealth were so tempting that adventurous men came flocking from the East and Southwest. Young cattle could be bought cheap, driven to the plains at very little expense, matured on "free air," as free grass and water were called, and sold in favorable seasons for four or five times the original cost. The stream of Texas cattle driven northward increased as steadily as did the herds bred and fattened on the upper plains. In the year 1871 more than 600,000 cattle crossed the Red River for the northern markets that were opening up all along the transcontinental lines. In the decade 1869–79, the golden age of the cattle drive, not fewer than 4 million beeves were driven up, an annual current that slackened only in the years 1874–75 when the financial panic checked it.[150]

The main paths of this drive naturally shifted to the west. At the outset they led through the eastern part of the Indian Territory (colloquially called the "Nations") to southwestern Missouri, while a little later the Chisholm Trail from Texas to Wichita was the most famous. Some years afterward, under the constant pressure of the railways and farms, a new channel for the drive was established up the Pecos River Valley of New Mexico into Colorado. There arose at one time a demand for congressional protection of a fixed right of way from south to north, but this was impracticable.[151] The drive was always an adventure, sometimes a very dangerous one. From southern Texas the start would be made about the first of March, the riders or "brush-poppers" usually gathering together cattle of many brands, for which they gave a very loose accounting. Later on a system of state inspection of trail herds at different points before the Texas boundary was crossed made the division of proceeds more careful. The men toiled incessantly, sometimes going for several days with scarcely a wink of sleep when wind and rain made the cattle uncontrollable. They had to fight roving Indian bands, ford great rivers like the Red and Arkansas at flood, check night stampedes that meant many a fall and broken limb, and encounter desperadoes and rustlers.[152]

Let us look at a typical ranch of the southern range—a ranch which centered about a roughly built log house of generous size, set in some sheltered nook with shade and abundant water.[153] This house contained a single large room lined with bunks; its furniture was a table or two and a few stools or broken chairs; and the men's clothing hung on wall pegs or was stuffed under the bunks. The rough domicile was unfinished and open to the weather at a hundred cracks, but comfortable in its rude masculine way. An open front passage, infested by the numerous dogs used for wolfing, led to the cookhouse, where the men ate hurriedly at a long pine table, seated on two or three wooden benches. Branding pens stood near, as did stables for the horses and a woodpile. The grub wagon, with the cook busy about it, might be seen making ready for a trip. Sometimes the ranch bore the owner's name—the Keith or Martin Ranch—sometimes the name of his brand—the Diamond Ranch or Bar-4 Ranch. At such a ranch house the stranger, whether hunter, traveler, or fleeing horse thief, received unquestioning hospitality. Sometimes the ranch, especially in long-settled parts of lower Texas, would be more elaborately equipped.[154] In addition to the cowboys' bunkhouse, there would be a frame dwelling for the owner—a long, low, one-story structure with large airy rooms, a wide hall to keep it cool, and comfortable furniture. Farther to the southwest, in the vast region between the Pecos and the Rio Grande, where the Spanish civilization of Mexico had left an enduring imprint, the Mexican or American ranchero would have an adobe dwelling with walls three or four feet thick.

The central buildings of a Northern ranch were even more varied in character.[155] The house might be a mud dugout or a log shack of timbers planted upright in the ground. It might be a sod house on the semiarid plains, where the unresting summer wind seared the skin with its alkaline touch. More frequently it was a commodious, well-built structure of hewn oak or cottonwood, far more nearly windproof than the ranch houses of the South. For the bitter winter weather, there would be both a huge fireplace and a big "cannon" stove, stoked red-hot. Here, too, bunks would line the walls, but buffalo robes as well as blankets would be everywhere in evidence, while the floor would be overlaid with furs and skins.[156] Only Easterners, like Theodore Roosevelt on the Elkhorn Ranch, would insist upon a separate bedroom and an easy chair.

North or South, a ranch might cover a million acres, of which the ranchman perhaps held legal title to a single quarter section. To maintain the ownership of his huge herds he relied primarily upon branding and secondarily upon "out-riding" by his employees. Daily, the cowboys went out to "ride sign" around the territory recognized as their special range and to turn back any cattle that seemed to be wandering from it. Every spring, after the grass had grown lush and the calves were large enough, there was a roundup for branding that might last for weeks.[157] Naturally, upon a range that was common property for many ranchers, this was a cooperative enterprise. By a general agreement—for as the industry developed, the state or territorial cattle associations divided the range into roundup districts—a group of cowboys selected from the various ranches met under a captain who ruled the work like a czar. The cattle, perhaps 2,000 or 3,000 in all, were driven together in a tumultuous mass into some valley or corral, the cows bellowing, the calves bawling, and the horses whinnying amid a thick cloud of dust. When a little order had been restored and the mothers had found their calves, the work of cutting the calves out, dragging them to the fire, and marking them with the brand and perhaps the knife began.[158]

The social life of the Western range was pitched to a key of conflict.[159] There was conflict between the rival cattle barons, particularly in the lawless Southwest; conflict between the cattlemen and sheep herders, whose flocks destroyed the range grass and tainted the water; conflict between honest ranchers and the "rustlers"; conflict with the Indians; and conflict, finally, with the irresistible current of homesteaders or "nesters," whose barbed-wire fences[160] turned back the roving cattle and whose irrigation ditches robbed the ranches of water. The face of the West changed from year to year, and every element in that change produced friction. Desperadoes sometimes gathered in gangs in sparsely settled regions and with a dozen rifles swept before them every herd of cattle not safely corralled. Many a rancher saw his whole property driven away before his eyes and if he resisted was shot dead. Sometimes the range witnessed a dramatic feud waged for years, like the famous Lincoln County War of the seventies in the Pecos Valley of New Mexico—a contest between two violent factions, one led by a powerful rancher named John Chisholm, and the other by a great supply firm called Murphy and Dolan, which embroiled a third of the territory and required the use of federal troops under General Sherman to restore order.[161] It was in the course of this affair that there sprang into prominence the notorious man-killer "Billy the Kid" (William Bonney), a desperate youth who perpetrated sickening outrages—his gang once killed seven inoffensive Mexicans "to see them kick"—before an officer of the law hunted him from lair to lair and finally shot him dead.[162] Raw towns of the "cow country," like Newton, Kansas, and later Dodge City, were haunts of shameless vice; saloons, gambling dens, and dance halls sheltered a dissolute and desperate set of men who preyed on the cowboys as they came in from the ranches.[163] The term "stiff" for a corpse is said to have been invented in Dodge City, and its main cemetery was, significantly, called Boot Hill. But with comparative rapidity, vigilance committees and law officers brought law and order.

The ranchmen and cowboys were essentially transitory occupants of the plains. They utilized its wealth in pasturage while it was waiting for the farmers who should put it to more profitable employment. It was evident to everyone that a more intensive use of the soil was desirable, yet the ranchers yielded only after a bitter struggle. Homesteaders in the semiarid regions naturally sought to preempt sufficient water for irrigation, and frequently they would construct irrigation ditches serving a whole tier of farms. Little by little the tillers of the soil seriously interfered in many sections with old-style ranching.[164] The enraged stockmen used threats, tore down the farmers' fences, and occasionally killed stubborn men; but the homesteader had the government behind him, and his enclosures steadily crept snakelike around the watercourses while his irrigation ditches dried up the running streams. Sections like that north of Great Bend in Kansas were settled by farmers who, when they obtained a land claim, would simply plow a furrow about it; and since the state law declared this a fence, heavy damages were invariably claimed against drovers whose cattle crossed it. Western and central Nebraska became dotted over with farming communities which the ranchers had to avoid. "Free air" steadily contracted, and the open tracts that were left became more and more congested, though in many parts the old-style ranching managed to survive into the eighties.

One of the services which the range performed for American life can never be forgotten: It created a unique, picturesque, and extraordinarily hardy type of manhood in the cowboy and furnished a spectacle of free and fearless activity with horse, rifle, and lariat that had a powerful influence upon the national character. From the boodling, extravagance, and financial recklessness seen in Eastern cities we can turn to no more refreshing contrast than the wild West that Owen Wister and Frederic Remington have celebrated. It had its faults, but even these were often healthily different from the corruptions wrought by ease and wealth. Here American virility appeared as nowhere else since the battlefields of the Civil War. "We felt," the greatest of cowboys has said, "the best of hardy life in our veins, and ours was the glory of work and the joy of living."[165] In time the range country developed a lore and a balladry all its own. The cowboy songs, composed around the campfire or in the ranch house, recalling the daily routine or the thrilling events of the cow country, or trolled in minor key to soothe the steers on the march, were a distinct addition to the folk literature of the American people; and they helped keep alive the flavor and spirit of a heroic interlude that is almost as dead as Atlantis.[166]

If farming and ranching were the chief interests of the region lying east of the Rockies, mining may be regarded as the great magnet that drew settlers farther West. The main foundation of the mountain and Pacific states had been laid by a series of mining rushes, of which the California gold rush in 1849, the Comstock Lode rush during 1858–59 in what became Nevada, and the Montana gold rush just after the war were typical. As the successive mining fevers died away, the immigrants would perceive the rich farming or stockraising opportunities about them. But the distance of the Far West from the main centers of population and the inadequacy of its transportation facilities retarded agricultural development prior to 1873. Outside of California, Oregon, and Utah, the Far West was exploited only for minerals, with the prospector always in the vanguard. This meant that it had a jerky, wasteful, and, in striking degree, an evanescent development, without much direct profit to the territories involved. The hectic gold or silver rush commonly resulted in drawing an excited mass of men to a single barren spot, where a rough and vicious town rose like magic, where money was spent like water in digging shafts and installing machinery, where get-rich-quick companies flourished and whence for a time a stream of bullion flowed to the world outside.

Nevada is the best example of the mining boom in its spasmodic phases. Here, in 1865, the new Golcondas were the wonder of the world. Five years earlier the region had been a desert, but the discoveries at Virginia City, Austin, and in the White Pine district, assisted by Lincoln's need for political support in Congress, had brought it into the Union in 1864 as a full-fledged state. Nowhere in the West were the social conditions and results of the rush for wealth better exhibited than in these three centers, the first of which will forever be remembered as the site of the Comstock Lode, one of the globe's richest mines. They made Nevada, but they did not make it a populous, stable, steadily growing community.[167]

Virginia City affords perhaps the best illustration of the indomitable energy with which the miners flung themselves against the difficulties in the path of their operations. In the winter of 1866 the towns and mills along the Comstock Lode were using 200,000 cords of wood for fuel, while the time soon came when 80 million feet of lumber a year went down into the chambers and drifts. Since the mountains about were naked rock, flumes had to be built from the forested slopes of the Sierras, and by 1880 there were ten of them with an aggregate length of eighty miles. The town's water supply presented an ever-increasing problem, until in 1873 a gigantic siphon was completed from the high Sierras at a cost of $2 million.[168] The Gould & Curry, the largest mine, had by 1865 invested almost a million dollars in its stamp mill alone, and when it exhausted its first vein, it boldly sunk a new tunnel and shaft 1,000 feet into the mountain to find another. Most stupendous of all was the great undertaking known as the Sutro Tunnel, the conception of Adolph Sutro, who owned a quartz mill on the Carlson River. He saw the practicability of constructing a three-mile-long tunnel into the mountain to intersect the Comstock Lode at a depth of 1,600 feet, draining all the mines to that level, and affording an economical means of carrying the ores to the river, where cheap waterpower and abundant fuel were available. In 1866 he obtained contracts from twenty-three of the principal mining companies on the lode, binding them to use the tunnel and pay for its services; after incessant effort, in which any man of less marvelous pluck and energy would have failed, he raised sufficient capital to begin the project. In 1869 he broke ground for the tunnel and set a corps of drillers upon the task that was to occupy them for eight weary years. It was the labor of a giant.[169]

The nation gazed upon Virginia City after the war as one of its chief

A cattle shoot at Abilene, Kansas.

Gold and silver mines in a Colorado mountainside.

Work in the Far West, 1865-1878.

marvels.[170] In the twenty-one years between 1859 and 1880 the various Comstock companies extracted a mass of bullion valued at $306 million. The Belcher mine alone produced a gross yield of $26 million and the Crown Point $22 million. During the eight flush years after the war the average annual production exceeded $12 million. These were days when elated stockholders walked the streets of Virginia City as if pacing the roof of an inexhaustible treasure house. A superintendent of one mine filled his water tank with champagne for his guests at a wedding; another mining magnate fitted his entire house with door handles of solid silver; and mansions luxurious enough for an Oriental monarch studded the raw Nevada hillsides.[171]

California, not Nevada, reaped the richest profit of this vast output of wealth. Most of the original capital invested was Californian, most of the managers came from California, and the seat of control for most of the companies was San Francisco, the natural center for trade in their stocks.[172] Not a single promising city, no counterpart of Denver or Sacramento, was created in Nevada by the whole wealth of the Comstock, whose flush paled in the western sky like a brief sunset. When the seventies ended, the magical history of the lode was almost over. The stock of its mines, which had been valued in 1875 at more than $393 million, had sunk in the spring of 1880 to less than $7 million. No approach was ever again made to the discoveries of early days, and the population slowly ebbed away. Nor did the other mining camps in Nevada, such as the gold fields at Austin and the strange community in the White Pine region, where a city of 20,000 leaped into brief existence on the harshest of mountain sides, accomplish anything more for the state.[173]

When we turn to the other commonwealths of the Far West, we meet with agricultural rather than mining communities. Even California learned during the seventies that the riches locked in her mountains were as nothing beside those obtainable from her fertile plains and valleys. Lincoln had called Utah "the treasure-house of the nation," yet after the war it was known preeminently as a farming population.[174] Indeed, Utah gave the West by far the best example of the farsighted development of a new land. This was due principally to the fact that the people had to be self-sufficing and to the fortunate circumstance that their destinies were guided by a real statesman, Brigham Young. Theirs was essentially a Mormon state, peopled and ruled by members of that faith; of the 120,000 people estimated to be living there in 1866, only a handful were "Gentiles." Salt Lake City was the metropolis, though it contained fewer than 20,000 of the well-diffused population. Here, travelers found, in a matchless physical setting between lake and mountains, the largest city between St. Louis and San Francisco. In addition to the overland telegraph, it had stage lines plying in every direction. Indians and Mexicans jostled with prospectors laying in supplies and with eager converts fresh from Europe. With its wide and symmetrical streets, its flashing streamlets running down the gutters, its fine public buildings, its shade trees and bright gardens, the capital was one of the most attractive cities to be found anywhere in the nation.[175]

This self-contained theocracy had an efficient and highly centralized economic system. All the great business enterprises of Utah were in Brigham Young's hands.[176] He kept a close control of the medium of exchange, confining most transactions among his people to a virtual system of barter. The payments he made for the innumerable services rendered him or the church were calculated in dollars, but actually granted in orders on the tithing office, where all the necessities of life, from firewood to potatoes, were to be had. Mechanics and farmers found it easy to obtain every comfort but very difficult to accumulate funds for a rainy day, or for emigration. As long as the community grew food and made simple wares for its own use alone, this system served well; but with the springing up of mining camps all over the Rockies, where the Mormons sold their products, it began to weaken. When the transcontinental railway arrived its doom was clear. Gentile shopkeepers and middlemen crowded into Salt Lake City, and as a desperate measure to prevent trade with them, Brigham Young incorporated in 1869 the Zion Cooperative Mercantile Institution, to which almost all the retailers in the territory were forced to sell out. But such steps were futile.[177]

The Mormon state presented its most attractive side in the attention it paid to cultural institutions. The 380,000 settlers who dwelt in Kansas in 1870 could boast no prouder list of educational and artistic undertakings than the population, only one third as great, of Utah. Elementary schools flourished under wise territorial laws and town patronage. Congress had appropriated $5,000 for a library which was duly sent out from New York; a university, fifteen years old in 1865, had gained some vigor. No architectural achievement of the time beyond the Mississippi equaled the Tabernacle, erected between 1864 and 1868—a huge structure in the shape of an oval, 250 feet long and 70 feet high, the interior presenting one of the largest unsupported arches in the world.[178] Yet there were two markedly depressing factors at work in this strange Mormon society: the tyrannical centralization of Brigham Young's administrative system, which had a paralyzing influence, and the institution of polygamy. Young's will was law, and it was impossible to obtain needed reforms for which he lacked sympathy. Social conditions favored an absolute rule, a large proportion of the community being poor, poorly educated, and industrious foreigners. But the absolutism was carried too far. A citizen who incurred the enmity of his Mormon rulers had no choice but to flee Utah, for once he was excommunicated, Mormons were forbidden to associate with him or to succor him. As between Mormon and Gentile, the administration of justice was utterly lacking in fairness. Worst of all for the territory, individual initiative was sorely hampered by the rulers.[179]

Picturesque as Utah was, California presented a civilization far more varied, active, and full of historical and racial color. Here the conquest of 1846–47 and the gold rush of 1849 had superimposed an American culture upon the old Spanish culture of Mexican days. With a population approaching a half million, already in 1865 California was one of the great states of the Union. The casual visitor was surprised to find towns and cities fully armed in the paraphernalia of civilization, wanton with the luxuries of the East, rich in social amenities, supplied with colleges and libraries, and even affecting high art. The state was a most striking example of the rapidity and completeness with which Americans could colonize a new land, organize its society, and provide themselves with comforts and superfluities.[180]

The Western slope had yet but one metropolis and did not dream of the day when Los Angeles would rival San Francisco. With 150,000 residents in 1870, "Frisco," as it was already called, sprawled irregularly for several miles over the bare, brown-white sand hills above the bay. The scene was one of strange contrasts and rapid changes. In the background was a line of rocky heights—Telegraph Hill, once the site of a criminal settlement; Nob Hill, where the mining and shipping magnates were building their mansions; and Pacific Heights.[181] In the foreground the tumbled dunes and slopes were being steadily altered as men cut streets through the bluffs and sliced the tops of hillocks away. The business district was shooting far out into the old residential area; dignified mansions overlooked the "tin-can" houses of the Chinese, wooden shanties roofed with beaten-out tin cans; and transportation facilities were being outgrown.[182] Socially the city exhibited a strange combination of hard-headed industry and speculative extravagance. There were no more farsighted and sagacious men of affairs anywhere than those who built up the machine shops of Pacific Street, the great banking firms, the Wells-Fargo Express, the Pacific Mail Line, and the California Steam Navigation Company.

Despite the exhaustion of the rich placer deposits, California's mining just after the war was still the most important industry and chief source of wealth; for the output of the quartz mines was steadily growing, and enabled the state to assert in 1866 and again in 1867 that its gold yield exceeded $25 million.[183] But by the commencement of the Panic year, agriculture, stimulated by the transcontinental railway, had definitely emerged as the leading California interest.[184] The cosmopolitan character of California's population, the varieties of soil and climate, and the tendency of each newcomer to experiment with the crops he knew best, ensured a singularly diversified agriculture in specialized farms.[185] For some years grain and livestock, which required comparatively little labor and capital, were the main products. Meanwhile, fruit-growing developed steadily.[186] Canning and preserving flourished as production outstripped home needs; dried fruits of fine appearance appeared, and by 1868 large shipments East were being made. In the first year after the war the orange orchards near Los Angeles were already supplying San Francisco with 250,000 oranges. California wine, though still in the experimental stage, with the vine planters "prospecting" for a soil that would bring forth a Clos Vougeot or Lafite, was hopefully regarded. By 1867 the state could boast that some of its vineyards rivaled the largest in Europe, with 30 million vines set and more than 6 million gallons of wine produced. Hock, port, sherry, champagne, and other varieties were all sold in the East.

In California everything seemed on a larger scale than elsewhere, and because great areas were purchasable at low rates from the holders of Mexican titles, the number of extensive ranches was a marked feature of the state's agriculture. Some that were partly tilled covered 30,000 acres, and a traveler could hear a farmer mention casually that he was holding 120 tons of wheat for a rise in the Liverpool market.[187] Half a dozen years after the war there were 120 Californians who possessed 5,347,000 acres in tracts of from 20,000 to 335,000 acres apiece, and 231 owners whose holdings ranged between 5,000 and 10,000 acres. At this time it was supposed that such large areas, even for farming, paid better than moderate units intensively cultivated, an opinion that was soon to be decisively refuted. Meanwhile, the existence of these huge ranches retarded the process of bringing the best California lands under the plow.[188] In aridity we meet another factor that delayed the development of farm lands, for the right principles of irrigation were not understood till about 1870, and this hindered the use of the vast interior plains and mesas from which California's distinctive products now chiefly come.[189]

That same rich flow of investment-seeking capital from the mines which fertilized farming gave a steady stimulation to manufacturing. Easterners approaching San Francisco through the Golden Gate were surprised to see the lower town enveloped in dense smoke, pouring out in volumes from tall chimneys burning Mount Diablo coal. The isolation from the East and the variety of natural products fostered a wide array of enterprises. Thus the fine malts and hops, and the difficulty of shipping beer in good condition, encouraged local breweries; the fruit and salmon led to the establishment of canneries; the proximity to Hawaii's raw sugar gave birth to refineries. An Englishman in 1870 found saw factories which rivaled those of Sheffield and locomotive and steam-engine works comparable with Philadelphia's and Newcastle's.[190]

The one alien and unassimilable element in California life was the Chinese population, which by the close of the war presented a harsh but by no means baffling problem, a problem of the sort that American heedlessness is always letting arise. Fifty thousand or more Chinese were scattered through the large towns and mining regions, and more were arriving. Comparatively few were coolies, the great majority being a sturdy peasantry from near Canton and Hong Kong.[191] They were busied in mining, railway building, farming, and fishing and as cooks and house servants; they made nine tenths of the cigars, almost monopolized the laundry business, and furnished many hands for the woolen factories. In short, they were highly useful, if not actually indispensable. The Chinese evinced an orderliness that was never questioned, yet their rapidly growing numbers made their presence a sharper and sharper irritant.[192]

This irritation was chiefly economic, for the workmen of the state resented their willingness to labor long hours for perhaps three fifths of a white man's pay. They had no families to support, no children to educate, and no apparent desire for luxuries and refinements.[193] They obstinately remained Chinese in dress, diet, and ways of thought, and the Christian missionaries were resentful because they could not convert them. They unquestionably had some repugnant vices: They were addicted to gambling, their opium dens were numerous and foul, and they imported many prostitutes. They were also accused of treacherous murders. Yet three fourths of the agitation against them was artificial and false, being very largely the work of demagogic politicians appealing to a set of bar loafers and hoodlums. "The people who actually earn the bread they eat," wrote a New York journalist, "do not persecute the Chinese." Discriminating taxes were laid upon them, and before they were found unconstitutional, they largely benefited the treasury. Indeed, from 1850 to 1870 about half the state's income came from the anti-Chinese levies.[194] They were forced to live in the most squalid quarters of the large towns, and in San Francisco particularly they occupied, for the most part, a set of decayed rookeries that would have disgraced the Five Points in New York.[195] Fortunately, the Chinese problem was far less serious and intricate than it often seemed, and the irrepressible growth of the state alone did much to solve it.

Farther north, in Oregon and Washington, there was growth also but without the varied social background that distinguished California. Most of the population was collected in a few fertile valleys: the beautiful Willamette Valley in southern Oregon, the Columbia Valley, the Walla Walla Valley in eastern Washington, and the Grand Ronde.[196] Of these the Willamette, with its neat towns of Salem and Portland, was easily the most important. The leading element — the clergy, teachers, traders, and professional men — was largely of New England blood; the Sabbath was kept in Portland as in the staid Connecticut Valley, and academies and colleges thrived in this region as in the East.[197] In the far Southwest, on the other hand, growth was comparatively slow, though there was a steady drift of Southerners into New Mexico after the war. The migration of the American settlers into New Mexico and Arizona accentuated a dramatic social conflict with the old Mexican order. Possessing more capital and energy than the Spanish-speaking aristocrats and quite as determined, arrogant, and quick on the trigger, the newcomers rapidly seized the government and the best of the wide areas devoted to semifeudal ranches.[198]

No treatment of the Far West of this period would be complete without some reference to the psychological effect which the mere existence of this vast, romantic, half-known treasure house had upon the remainder of America. It was a porch opening upon wide free vistas. It gave national life a sense of spaciousness and adventure that it would otherwise have lacked. Men listened with wonder to Major Powell's story of the first perilous voyage down the Grand Canyon, to Clarence King's descriptions of the Sierras, to Custer's narrative of his campaigns. They could feel that the age of almost boundless opportunities in America had not yet come to an end. The stagecoach and immigrant train, mining rush and cattle roundup, Mexican mission and salmon fishery, Chinatown and Indian agency made up a varicolored panorama that added breadth and brightness to the American scene. They, and the kaleidoscopic bustle that was month by month altering the face of the huge region, were a constant stimulus to the imagination and energy of Americans whose lives were narrowed into parlors and countingrooms thousands of miles away. And beyond the passing day, the social contrasts of the Western scene, its types and incidents, were destined to become a lasting part of American folklore, influencing the mind and enriching the fancy of the nation for many generations to come.

THE EVERYDAY LIFE OF AMERICANS

AMERICAN LIFE between the war and the Panic of 1873 was characterized throughout the North, except for the depressed rural districts and some underpaid labor groups, by a decidedly greater prosperity and comfort than ever before. The Panic, of course, brought grinding economy and privation into millions of homes, but this burden was gradually lightened and the old level restored. Taking the period as a whole, the real wealth of the population attained a higher average than before the conflict. The heavy production of cheap foodstuffs, the progress of invention, the application of factory methods of manufacture, all brought increased ease and well-being to the public. In what we may call the typical American town or city home —the dwelling of a fairly well-to-do clerk or shopkeeper or businessman— there was better food, better furniture, better clothing, and more books and magazines. The domestic economy of the time offers much that now appears stuffy, tasteless, and repellent, but in part these very qualities grew out of a higher standard of living. Men had money to spend without knowing very well how to spend it.[199] In this period the late Victorian modes and manners came into their full bloom, and they make a curious study.

There have been few decades in which ugliness so prevailed in the building of houses as that just before the Centennial Exhibition; yet it was an ugliness that spoke of wealth and was associated with comfort. Jay

Cooke's huge mansion, Ogontz, was not untypical of many rich men's residences.[200] A vast gloomy pile of granite, 175 feet long, with seventy-two rooms, it cost $2 million; and the *Art Journal* rightly dismissed it as "inharmonious, heavy, and confusing,"[201] Bayard Taylor's Italian villa at Kennett Square, also near Philadelphia, showed how badly a literary man building a costly house quite beyond his means could do. An Italian villa, its main body square and ugly, it possessed a tall tower with spire, dormer windows, and a veranda in it.

Yet the artists themselves proved no better. Albert Bierstadt built a house on Haverstraw Bay, on a fine commanding site overlooking the widest part of the Hudson, that in its weird medley of towers, turrets, and jigsaw work in iron and wood was an atrocity. It did not quite equal, however, the residence of the painter F. E. Church on the same noble river.[202] This was in a bastard "Persian" style, with four towers, several minarets, Moorish arches, much glaring mosaic work in red, yellow, and black bricks, and a glittering crescent above all for a weathercock. It was an outrage upon taste that could hardly be paralleled in the East. When men of distinction indulged themselves in such architectural nightmares, it is hardly surprising that the ordinary American with money to spare lived in an altogether tasteless house. Only at the close of this period did new tendencies show signs of driving the mansard roof, the heavy ornaments, and the rococo lines into the past.

The interior of the typical urban home of the North was somber, crowded, and deficient in simple refinement but quite comfortable to the occupants. Floors were usually covered to the edges with carpets, nailed down tight with straw beneath, and swept with heavy brooms till worn out. The *Nation* tried to convert housewives to the European fashion of throwing a few rugs loosely upon hardwood floors, but with slow results. Visitors at the Centennial contrasted the American carpets, poor in material and design but protected by a high tariff, very unfavorably with the imported Axminster and Indian carpets. Late in the seventies a new floor covering, linoleum,[203] was being extensively advertised. The great majority of homes were of course still heated by stoves or fireplaces, and even Franklin stoves survived here and there. In the cities most of the better houses were warmed by hot-air furnaces, with pipes leading to large iron registers in the floor, but the public had begun to apprehend an unhealthfulness in this system and to demand steam heat. Even in small towns many newly built houses were now supplied with gas and running water. One observer of the wealthier classes tells us that by 1869 it was unusual to find a town home without a comfortable bathroom, but the bathtub was certain to be a zinc-lined structure of black walnut or pine.[204] The fine pictured wallpapers of the past had been universally displaced by cheaper and gaudier print papers of questionable design.

The furniture of these homes tended to be elaborately decorative. The

A Rogers group.

An "Italian" villa.
Bayard Taylor's house.

A typical American
courthouse.

In the best taste of the period—the Roosevelt parlor, New York City.

Atlantic states were filled with the work of a New York cabinetmaker named Marcotte and his imitators, who produced ornamental curving tables covered with chocolate-hued marble, while fashionable people bought the much better square-patterned pieces called the Eastlake, with incised lines of gilt tracing elaborate figures.[205] A happy influence that grew stronger in the seventies was that of the Englishman William Morris, who had established furniture workshops in 1861 on the principle that "decoration involving rather the luxury of taste than the luxury of costliness will be found to be much less expensive than is generally supposed," and whose designs were known in America ten years later.[206] Most people felt that a parlor was incomplete without a Rogers group of statuary, and a popular anecdote of a later day told of a tramp who assured his benefactress, "You can realize how poor we were, ma'am, when I tell you that my parents could never afford to buy Rogers's 'Weighing the Baby.' " Wealthier householders used, instead, an ornamental bowl of alabaster called a "tazza." But everyone delighted in the portiere, the lambrequin, the whatnot, the antimacassar, and Berlin wool work; everybody thought it proper for daughters to learn to decorate china or paint on a brass plaque or on crimson plush; and in the late seventies nearly everyone deemed iron statuary on the lawn a mark of taste and means.[207] Crocheting was a constant feminine employment, and crocheted match holders and dog muzzles were not unknown. Plush albums were universal. Even the White House had its hand-painted china with fruit, fish, or poultry portrayed on each dish. Late in the 1870s came the "aesthetic movement" from England, bringing gilded chair legs, vases filled with cattails, embroidered "throws," and Japanese fans tacked to the walls.

The remoter the communities the more likely they were to be filled with excruciating household materials. Mark Twain in 1874 described with rare gusto the typical well-to-do Southern home as it still survived, scattered in towns and villages along the Mississippi.[208] Here was the parlor with its ingrain carpet, its mahogany center table, its polished airtight stove with a pipe passing through the painted board which closed a discarded fireplace, its piano with a beribboned guitar tilted against it, and its pyramidal whatnot in a corner. Tupper, Ossian, and a copy of *Friendship's Offering* represented literature; the current number of *Godey's Lady's Book,* with painted fashion plates as double-page illustrations, showed an interest in periodicals; and the piano was piled with such selections as "The Battle of Prague," "The Last Link Is Broken," and "Long, Long Ago." On the walls were hung a variegated array of drab steel engravings, Landseer being especially popular, lithographs, amateurish crayon drawings, a family group in oils, and a pious motto done in faded grasses. The bric-a-brac included shells with the Lord's Prayer or a carving of Washington, several alum baskets of various colors, a pair of bead moccasins from some relative who had crossed the plains, several daguerreotypes spread open in folding covers, and under a glass dome a large bouquet of wax flowers. Somewhere in the house, if not in this sacred parlor, would be a number of horsehair chairs and a slippery horsehair sofa.

Such homes continued to exist in diminishing numbers down to the end of the century, and a few may be found today.[209] Naturally they were most numerous in the conservative South, the section which actually found diversion after the war in holding what it called "tournaments," after the model of that described in *Ivanhoe*. Crowds gathered at these entertainments to watch young men who were dressed in fantastic costumes and who called themselves "disinherited knights" or "knights of the sword," tilting at a ring to win a prize offered by some young woman who was styled the "queen of love and beauty."

In New York City an important innovation just after the war was the construction of many "French flats" or modern apartment houses of which the first was erected in 1870 at 142 East 18th Street by the architect Richard M. Hunt.[210] It was said to be better than most of those in Paris and, at rentals of from $1,000 to $1,500 a year, offered sixteen suites of six rooms and a bath. G. P. Putnam, the publisher, and other men of means lived here. The demand for these convenient homes, with their saving in servant hire, rapidly increased. They filled a keenly felt need, for previously all well-to-do New Yorkers had known but two modes of residence: They must either take a full single house or consent to live in a dismal boardinghouse. Builders vied with each other in putting up costlier and better-equipped buildings. A block of flats was shortly overlooking Central Park from the east at 68th Street, and gave each tenant eight rooms and a bath, black-walnut floors, elevator service, and his own kitchen range and hot water heater for from $75 to $150 a month.[211] By 1874 the *Evening Post* thought that the new apartment houses "may now be considered almost perfect," and by the close of the following year the *World* could state that there were 198 of them in New York, accommodating about 3,000 families.[212] The Haight Building, at 15th Street and Fifth Avenue, offered flats renting for from $2,000 to $3,000, with an elevator, an internal telegraph, and a restaurant. Among the notables living there were Henry M. Field, the traveler; Colonel W. C. Church, editor of the *Galaxy;* E. L. Youmans; and the Spanish consul.

Across dress, as across architecture, the meretricious splendor of the Second Empire threw its influence even after the empire had fallen into ruins. Eugénie invented, or at least revived, the crinoline skirt which became universal in the sixties and which Anthony Trollope found far more vulgarly excessive in size in New York than in Europe. She also gave vogue to the horizontally striped stocking which appeared in all its gaiety in 1865 and was soon followed by solid colors.[213] There were Empire bonnets and hair was dressed in the Empire style, while Zouave jackets were much in fashion, and the *robe impératrice* also showed the French influence. In the late seventies came the bustle and the barber-pole skirt, while throughout the decade the sealskin coat was the height of elegance. Women cultivated the absurd posture called the Grecian bend, while the chignon and waterfall—the latter a heavy bag of hair which most girls were sensible enough to lay aside on hot days—were familiar everywhere. A powder called "gold-dust" was frequently sprinkled on the hair for evening parties.[214] Shawls were much used by women, but men had dispensed with them. All well-dressed little boys appeared in kilts and in boots with black tassels, while little girls wore Garibaldi suits. Men's clothing still tended to the somber in color and cut, black broadcloth being the approved material for everyday business wear, and bright waistcoats having faded from the scene. Full dress, which included tight "doeskin" trousers and a stovepipe hat, was regarded as merely a matter of choice at even very formal evening gatherings, while it was not infrequently worn at other times of the day; at the famous breakfast in honor of Holmes's seventieth birthday in Boston in 1879, served at noon, a few guests appeared in evening garb.[215] Men pomaded their hair and regarded trouser creases, a sign of the store shelf, with distaste. It was the era of universal, luxuriant, and variegated beards.

The American diet altered slowly. One of the principal changes was the more and more general introduction of oatmeal, called "grits" or "Irish oatmeal," as a breakfast dish. It tended to lighten that repast, which still usually comprised not only fruit, coffee, and rolls but steak, chops, or ham and eggs, and frequently in addition fried potatoes. Even Emerson, as we wonder now to learn, habitually ate pie for breakfast. Through large parts of the North men found it hard to rise from breakfast without a stack of buckwheat cakes, while New Englanders retained all their old fondness for baked beans and pork on Sunday morning.[216] This heavy meal betrayed the persistence of rural habits. So, too, did the prevalent habit of making dinner the midday repast and the fact that most prosperous American families thought that two dishes of meat, or one of meat and one of fish, were none too many. A half-dozen vegetables were frequently served. Supper, or tea, was a much simpler refection, and was served early, for the English fashion of eating after 7:00 P.M. was followed only in a few highly fashionable circles. Nearly every family still made its own bread, and the hotels usually had a baking establishment of their own. Among the novelties of the seventies were oleomargarine and butterine, which appeared soon after the establishment of meat packing as a highly centralized industry and which within a few years found a large export trade.[217]

As for drinks, wine was seldom served except upon ceremonial occasions and even then was frowned upon by good American families. It was practically unknown on the table of city hotels, where it was customary for men to repair to the bar for a drink or two of spirits before or after eating. In some private houses there was a genial practice called "taking the oath,"[218] which meant finding a little bourbon and ice water in the recesses of a bookcase or behind a statuette of Powers's "Greek Slave"; but outside the large cities spirits were regarded with stern disapproval. Beer was no longer treated as a foreign beverage; the war record of the Germans, as well as the low excise tax already mentioned, commended it to growing numbers. In Milwaukee, the home of the Schlitz, Best, and Pabst breweries, its production thrived so well that the output rose from 36,000 barrels in 1860 to 260,000 barrels in 1873.[219]

The rigidity of private morals and the primness of convention were still striking. Sunday was generally observed with strictness throughout the Northern and Middle states. No theaters could open their doors; all liquor sales were forbidden though evasion was frequent; and businesses were tightly closed, even drugstores sometimes falling under the prohibition. The British journalist G. A. Sala found that the observance of the day was "more than Scotch in its severity" and felt fortunate in Baltimore that he could hire a carriage for a drive.[220] The rural South was even more rigid, but in some Southern cities such light refreshments as tobacco and confectionery were purchasable, and in New Orleans the fish market was open for an hour or two on Sunday morning to dispose of its perishable wares. Even charitable work for the poor was often considered a desecration of the Sabbath, and Maurice Francis Egan found that sewing in their behalf would have created a scandal in the Washington of 1875.[221] At least two states, Vermont and South Carolina, were so straitlaced that throughout these years they had statutes making church attendance compulsory. Still, steady inroads were being made upon the bleak Puritan Sunday, for men were beginning to realize that the toiling masses in the cities needed the day for unfettered relaxation.[222]

The utmost regard was paid in the better social circles to the proprieties. Among many families of the Eastern cities chaperons were considered indispensable, and in Philadelphia young men like James Huneker found that for a girl to go alone with her suitor to a theater or ball would have riddled her reputation.[223] Elsewhere young people were allowed a freedom based on a complete and justified confidence that the rules of good behavior would be instinctively observed. The novels of Charles Reade were regarded as shocking, and *A Terrible Temptation* was denounced by press and pulpit as "carrion literature." Swinburne and Whitman were declaimed against with equal fervor, and Whitman's removal from his clerkship in the interior department in 1865 on the ground that he had published improper poetry was a deplorable example of moral rigidity pushed to Pharisaism and intolerance. Throughout the seventies John Burroughs and other devoted friends had to champion Whitman against the running attacks of journals like the *New York Tribune*.[224] Such family magazines as *Scribner's* and *Harper's* never printed a word which could be considered objectionable by the most prudish taste, and Howells in the seventies commenced a series of novels so dominated by a respect for what "nice" people wanted that their realism totally neglected the uglier aspects of American social life.

Much was said about what Mrs. Lynn Linton in England called "the girl of the period," who was thought then, as always, a little faster than her mother; much was said about the corroding effect of prosperity and luxury upon morals. But sexual morality was still, as Rhodes declares it was in the fifties, kept at a high level.[225] To be sure, the great cities had scandals enough; those feminist crusaders, Victoria and Tennessee Claflin, published a weekly which for a time specialized in exposures of double life in New York. But the nation as a whole met fairly rigid moral standards.

This was partly because of the force of public opinion and rooted Anglo-American standards; partly because men worked hard; and partly because marriage came early and home life was well protected. It is true that observers still commented upon the popularity of the boardinghouse and residential hotel. Even in the Far West many a young couple began their life together in this wise. E. L. Godkin thought it worthwhile in 1868 to fulminate in the *Nation* against the married couple who, though able to own a home, deliberately boarded to save trouble, as citizens who were "enemies of society and deserve clerical reprobation in almost equal degree with the purchasers of Indiana divorces."[226] It was not the mere chilly aridity of the boardinghouse that made it objectionable. It was accused of leading to indolence, promiscuous friendships, a disregard for family ties, and immoral relations between the sexes. J. D. Burn wrote that, from his observation, "I have no hesitation in saying that many of these houses are hotbeds of vice and every species of immorality." However, the extent to which Americans patronized the residential hotel and the restaurant was greatly exaggerated by the foreigners who were entertained in many such institutions and in few private homes. Their patronage represented in the main a transitory mode of life until a family could find permanent occupation and a settled home. American boardinghouses were, as a native commentator said, chiefly asylums for bachelors, spinsters, widows, and young couples who longed ardently for love in a cottage.[227] Moreover, they were typical of the great centers rather than of the smaller cities.

The healthy domesticity of Americans was, in fact, unquestionable. The old usage of early marriage continued, though of course not so early as in colonial times, and we are assured by Von Glosz that the ages of twenty-three for men and seventeen for girls were regarded as perfectly normal for contracting a union. As a Frenchman put it, before the young Americans had passed twenty they were "thinking of establishing themselves, taking a wife, founding on their own account a banking or mercantile house, and of quitting the temporary hospitality of the paternal roof." Sir George Campbell formed a decided impression in the late sixties that Americans married earlier and trusted more to their wits to support a family than did the British.[228] Some Americans took a different view, but the *Nation*'s editorial of 1868 on "Why Is Single Life Becoming More General?" referred primarily to New England and to the upper tenth there.[229] As for divorce, there was as yet very little of it, though it was increasing. In the year 1867 there were 9,937 divorces in the whole nation, and we have evidence that the number rose with great uniformity to 16,089 in 1878. This was an increase of more than 60 percent.[230] But when it is realized that in 1867 there were only twenty-seven divorces in the country for every 100,000 people, it will be seen that the situation was far from disquieting. Divorce has its beneficent side in that it reflects a higher independence and self-respect among women and is preferable to a jangling and loveless marriage. Nations with little divorce are commonly nations with numerous irregular establishments and in which the domination of the husband overrules any incompatibility. With the drift toward the cities, where couples had less neighborhood disapproval to fear if they separated, with the growing economic independence of women, and with the restless movement of the population, it would have been astonishing if divorce had not increased.[231]

In only two states, Connecticut and Indiana, was the legislation governing divorce liberal to the point of laxity, and here it was gravely censured by the rest of the Union. The statutes in Connecticut allowed the dissolution of a marriage for "any such conduct as permanently destroys the happiness of the petitioner, and defeats the purpose of the marriage relation," but public opinion compelled its repeal in 1878. It was to Indiana that divorce hunters usually proceeded, as at a later date to Nevada. A year's residence qualified for a petition, the case could be tried thirty days after a published notice, and the defendant was often ignorant of the proceedings. In *A Modern Instance* W. D. Howells gives a vivid picture of an Indiana divorce trial and of the frustration of a wife-deserter's effort to procure his release by perjury.[232]

Americans after the war were keenly interested in all forms of amusement. The growing urbanization of the country brought summer resorts into increased favor and caused the rapid multiplication of seashore cottages. Newport in 1866, a city whose permanent residents numbered only 15,000, had about 3,000 summer visitors who took cottages, 6,000 or 7,000 who stayed at hotels and boardinghouses, and tens of thousands who came for one-day excursions.[233] Here, as well as north of Boston and at other watering places, the crowds were so great that many, disgusted by the heterogeneous company at hotels, erected their own villas. This new departure was most evident at Long Branch, New Jersey, where the many summer houses were supplemented by hostelries of an exclusive type. When Grant became president, he began spending the hottest weeks in Long Branch, building two modest cottages, one of which he rented; taking his horses with him the second year, he spent hours in driving.[234] The popularity of the White Mountains grew rapidly, and in 1866–69 a railway on the cogwheel principle was built to the summit of Mount Washington, making possible the erection there of a comfortable inn called the Summit House. Saratoga, after suffering a temporary loss of prestige and gaiety through the absence of the Southerners who had given it so much life before the war, made a steady recovery.[235] Meanwhile, increasing crowds were seeking the Rockies and the South. Denver became a place of resort for tourists and pleasure seekers as soon as the Indian hostilities died away, while Colorado Springs at the foot of Pike's Peak, boasting a climate better than that of Davos, was founded in 1871. By 1874 the population of several Florida cities, notably Jacksonville, doubled every winter.[236] The summer vacation, which before the war had been largely an indulgence of the well-to-do, now rapidly became general among nonmanual workers.[237] In the Northeastern states the practice of summer camping in the woods was noted in 1873 to be on the increase, having the advantage of cheapness as well as the opportunity to live close to nature.

Everyone commented on the popularity of the theater in Eastern cities just after the war. In 1866 it was estimated that the total receipts of the New York playhouses were between $2 million and $2.5 million—Niblo's Garden alone took in nearly $350,000.[238] The opera flourished, with its fashionable audience arrayed in decorative opera cloaks and gay rich dresses, with jeweled fans and marvelous chevelures. Even New Orleans, it must not be forgotten, had its opera. It had also its great Mardi Gras festival, which toward the close of this period annually drew strangers by the thousands from the entire lower South, but especially from Alabama. Henry Adams was a little depressed by a new postwar Boston in which fortunes of $4 million did not seem extraordinary, but it was, above all, in New York that, as one observer put it, the social type was "that of a brilliant, ostentatious, sprightly, pleasure-seeking kind." Here the desire was keenest to outdo one's neighbors, to have the most gorgeous drawing rooms, equipages, and dinners, and to follow an unceasing round of glittering gaiety.[239] The newcomer found that the more recherché his manners, the more piquant his conversation, the purer the breed of horses he drove, the more fashionable his criticism of pictures, books, and music, the better he was liked; but above all it was money that was indispensable.

Immediately after the peace, racing attained a new popularity and dignity, chiefly because it was taken up by the leaders of fashion in New York. The American Jockey Club, founded by Leonard W. Jerome, W. R. Travers, August Belmont, and other wealthy sportsmen, purchased a beautiful site of 230 acres in Westchester County, which was named Jerome Park, and in 1866 built there a grandstand accommodating 8,000 people. The sale of liquor was prohibited, and everything that money could effect was done to give the place an air of gentility fit for ladies.[240] At the opening races General Grant was present. The towns north of New York promptly built a fine broad drive to this racecourse so rich citizens could trot their pacers over the Harlem River and through the green country. Belmont and others set themselves to horse breeding with great assiduity, and racing was soon entrenched as a pastime of the best society. Very shortly newspaper prince

James Gordon Bennett, Jr., was introducing polo into the United States at Newport.

It was due to the war that outdoor sports showed in the late sixties a vigor never before approached. Baseball, a popular pastime in the camps, promptly established itself as the national game.[241] Club after club was formed until hundreds were represented at the annual convention of the National Association of Baseball Players. The meeting of 1867 showed fifty-six in Illinois alone, and forty-two in Iowa; while in the Eastern cities great crowds gathered throughout the summer to watch the matches. Young men of future distinction on the diamond were emerging—A. G. Spalding of Rockford, Illinois; Adrian C. Anson of Marshalltown, Iowa; and James White of Sutton, New York. It was not long before intersectional contests were arranged. Arthur Pue Gorman of Maryland, a crack player whose executive talents later placed him in the Senate, helped to arrange a triumphant Western tour of the National Club of Washington in 1867; and three years later Spalding's club of Rockford made a trip through the East, winning fifty-one games out of sixty-five played. At first an effort was made to keep the sport on a thoroughly clean amateur basis, but amateur standards quickly collapsed as betting on games became prevalent and players were bribed to "throw" matches. City clubs arranged to give coveted small-town players high-salaried positions in commercial and industrial enterprises, and we find Spalding early in his career offered $40 a week, ostensibly to clerk in a wholesale grocery in Chicago but really to be a member of the Excelsior Club there.

The public began to lose its former confidence and to grumble. The result was that the Red Stockings of Cincinnati took a revolutionary step in 1869, frankly turning themselves into a professional team under the management of a veteran player named Henry Wright. That summer they made an Eastern tour, the first tour of a professional club, in which they won every game. It demonstrated at once and decisively the superiority of a team chosen, trained, and paid for the work they did over any set of amateurs brought together for mere exercise and amusement. Professional baseball immediately overspread the whole nation, and names now long familiar to every lover of the sport became for the first time well known: the Chicago White Stockings, the Philadelphia Athletics, the Washington Nationals. In 1871 ten such clubs entered a championship contest.[242]

But while the important teams were thus being professionalized, and the way paved for the organization in 1876 of the National League of Professional Baseball Players, an agency which dealt severely with the evils of betting, game-throwing, and contract-breaking, purely amateur teams were multiplying everywhere. Every town and every school had its nine; all young America learned to play. Year by year the game was improved in its rules and its material. At first a very "live" ball was employed, which bounced erratically and led to the running-up of enormous scores; then the

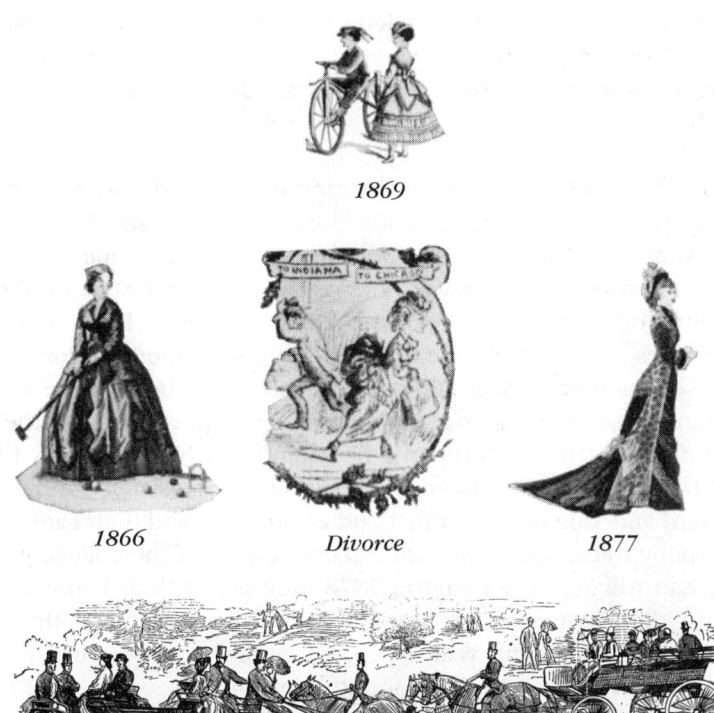

1869

1866   *Divorce*   *1877*

On the road to the Jerome Park races.

The Grant family at Long Branch.

Costumes for lawn tennis—1878.

other extreme, a very "dead" ball, and finally a happy medium. Gloves and masks were introduced and the swollen hands of the early catchers became a thing of the past, while bats were perfected. In 1865 the New York press had thought it a matter for some wonder that 5,000 spectators frequently gathered for a match at Hoboken, but now tens of thousands collected at the games.[243]

Cricket, which in 1865 was played by various New York and Philadelphia clubs and by teams at Newark, Bridgeport, and other small cities, was naturally stunted and thrust to the wall by the overwhelming success of baseball.[244] Meanwhile football was developing, slowly but steadily. One of the first intercollegiate matches was played in the fall of 1869, with very uncertain rules, between Princeton and Rutgers. A modification of the English Association game was fairly well known to all boys of the period, and early in the seventies a code was drawn up to govern it. But the real birth of the sport dates from the middle seventies, when the rugby game, imported from Canada to Harvard and other colleges, assumed the leadership. Harvard and Yale held their first contest in 1875, and their game, with modified rugby rules, was soon a spectacular feature of the college year.[245] Both also had rowing crews, and in 1878 they began their famous series of races on the Thames above New London. There was an enthusiastic demonstration in the same year when a Columbia crew returned from England after defeating Oxford, Cambridge, and Dublin.

The college youth could no longer be a mere grind, whose only outdoor recreations were walking and swimming. Nor, for that matter, was youth anywhere left in the deplorably unathletic position of the fifties. The organization of Young Men's Christian Association branches all over the country gave an impetus to organized sports, outdoor and indoor, for their city buildings contained gymnasiums and their directors taught gymnastics after the German model. Moreover, the growing wealth of the cities, the emergence of a large class of men with leisure, and the needs of sedentary life led to the systematic establishment of athletic clubs. The great leader and prototype in this field was founded in 1868 in New York. This, the New York Athletic Club, rented a field for games at Mott Haven, on the Harlem River, which soon became famous. It grew and flourished for almost twenty years on the stern regimen of athletic games alone; its boathouse, track, and field becoming centers of general sport, while its annual contests for young athletes furnished an array of records that was an incentive to emulation the nation over.[246]

All in all, the nation took a very different attitude toward sports after the war from that before. No longer could a man like Edward Everett deplore, as he did in 1856, the almost complete inattention to "manly outdoor exercises, which strengthen the mind by strengthening the body." No longer could Holmes assert that "society would drop a man who should run round the Common in five minutes." The whole country watched with bated breath the efforts of the English yachtsmen who brought over the *Cambria* in 1870 in the vain hope of capturing the America's Cup, a trophy closely guarded by the New York Yacht Club, and the later equally unsuccessful attempts of the *Livonia* (1871) and the *Countess of Dufferin* (1876).[247] It watched lawn tennis become a sport of such importance that a few years later it had its national association. It saw organized field "meets" begin in the colleges—the earliest one at Yale in 1872—and outside, the first great amateur handicap meet taking place in New York in 1876. What Charles Kingsley called "Muscular Christianity" was coming into its own.

Twice during this period the country was conquered by sudden popular crazes in recreation; the first time by croquet, the second by the velocipede or bicycle. "Of all the epidemics that have swept over our land," the *Nation* exclaimed in the summer of 1866, "the swiftest and most infectious is croquet."[248] Every lawn from the Atlantic to the Mississippi seemed to be impressed into service. Expensive English sets of balls and mallets found a large sale. Four years later the bicycle had become an equally universal passion. It was as yet a crude vehicle of locomotion, one variety having a very high front wheel fitted with pedals, a low rear wheel, solid tires, and a seat so placed over the large wheel that the rider was likely to be pitched over the handlebars if he met even a slight obstacle. Schools opened for instruction in the large cities. At one in New York, according to the *Scientific American,* the visitor could see every evening "upward of a hundred and fifty gentlemen, doctors, bankers, merchants, and representatives from almost every profession, engaged preparatory to making their appearance upon the public streets."[249] The craze subsided, only to be revived a decade later. Improvements were rapidly introduced, tricycles and ladies' bicycles were devised, and late in the seventies wheelmen's clubs began to be formed in large numbers. But for the average American of sedentary habits the chief outdoor amusement, as in earlier years, was driving. The most prominent social line was that which parted the family with a carriage from the family that had none. The sleigh was as prominent in winter as the wheeled vehicle in summer, and in city, town, and village it was seen in every variety—shell-shaped, basket-shaped, and box-shaped.[250]

During these years also the circus attained its mature stature as an American amusement. Shortly after the war the business genius of P. T. Barnum lifted it to a new scope and popularity.[251] In 1871 he formed a traveling tent circus which offered many more attractions than any predecessor, including wax works, dioramas, Swiss bell ringers, a new Cardiff Giant, dwarfs and monstrosities, and among many other beasts, a real giraffe —still a rarity in the United States. In 1872 he showed his acumen by two additional innovations. One was the introduction of a second ring, a development soon imitated by his rivals but making his claim to "the greatest show on earth" doubly secure. The other was the transportation of the circus by rail instead of by wagon, thus by long trips eliminating all towns where the receipts did not promise to reach $5,000. The details were so perfected that the establishment could be carried 100 miles in a single night, could give a street parade in the morning, and present an afternoon and evening performance before packing up again for travel. Since a much larger show could be carried over a much greater extent of country, for the first time the circus became a really national institution. Financial success crowned Barnum's experiment, and in the first season with the railroad the receipts exceeded a million dollars.[252] It is an indication of American tastes and character in this era that Barnum heavily emphasized the wholesome and ethical element of his circus. It was always advertised as "Barnum's Great Moral Show"; clergymen as well as editors were given passes.

Whatever can be said against the manners and morals of the time, it was a larger, fuller life that people of the North and West lived after the war. Education was better diffused, the conflict had given birth to new ideas, and the growth of wealth purchased new refinements.[253] Americans, shrewdly remarked Godkin, "are far less raw and provincial than their fathers; they have seen more, they have read more, they have mixed more with people of other nationalities, they have thought more and had to think more, they have spent more for ideas and given more away."[254] They were also beginning to travel far more. It is interesting to note how many of these years a long list of our literary men—Bryant, Bayard Taylor, Lowell, Charles Eliot Norton, Mark Twain, and others—spent in Europe; and it is significant that the first overseas tour of an ex-president, Grant, occurred in the seventies. Increasing colonies of American expatriates were to be met abroad, including such distinguished figures as W. W. Story and Henry James, and it will be recalled that James's fine novel *The American,* with its picture of a Western businessman who had made a small fortune and gone to Paris to imbibe culture, appeared in the seventies.[255] Directly or indirectly, the daily life of the American people was thus achieving a greater variety and breadth, and yet the very rapidity of its expansion bred some glaring defects. Its greatest fault was its lack of depth, of cultivation, and of established canons of taste, permitting the frequent display of what Godkin aptly called a "chromo civilization." There was something recurrently flashy and cheap in its activities, which only a more thorough culture could eradicate.

This cheapness was due less to the effects of the war than to the crude, aggressive growth of the republic and its defective social organization.[256] The West, with its heterogeneous population busy with the rough work of subduing the country, was peculiarly liable to a relaxation of standards. The great Eastern cities also, melting pots of Irish, Germans, Italians, and other races, with a froth made up of grasping businessmen and newly rich families, suffered from similar tendencies. The belief that a $25 plaster statuary group representing the "Courtship in Sleepy Hollow" was fine art was a mark of a "chromo civilization." So was the insistence upon equipping every hotel and steamboat with a gilt monstrosity called a bridal suite. So was the devotion of boulders, cliffs, and barns to glaring advertisements of Rising Sun Shoe Polish, Schenck's Pulmonic Bitters, and Dr. Brandreth's pills.[257] A distinct mark of a "chromo civilization" was the action of the Plymouth Church in Brooklyn, on the day Henry Ward Beecher came to trial for his alleged intimacy with Mrs. Tilton, in sending flowers to decorate the courtroom; like placing wreaths, said Godkin, about the open manhole of a sewer. Only a "chromo civilization" could have produced the expansive people who, in 1876, could not see that Blaine's railway transactions, even if admitted, were to his discredit. "He showed his smartness in it," they said, "and that is just the smart man we want."[258]

Nevertheless, despite passing maladies, despite grave scandals, the life of Americans at this period was fundamentally wholesome, progressive, and fruitful. Its chief faults were less of quality than of tone, less of structure than of finish. James Bryce's arraignment of our national weaknesses a few years later was substantially valid.[259] We wished, he said, to keep abreast of the best thought of the world and to achieve much in art and letters, but we also showed an excessive fondness for bold and striking effects. Lacking refinement of taste, we were disposed to regard anything brilliant as superior to really admirable work in a quiet style. We demanded quick, showy results and constantly tended to identify bigness with greatness. Fortunately, however, there were countervailing tendencies at work which were steadily growing in vigor and usefulness. These conditions and influences it will now be instructive to examine.

THE BROADENING OF AMERICAN CULTURE

INTELLECTUALLY, a new maturity was stamped upon the country by the grim struggle for the Union and the stern problems which had to be solved after it was over. Millions of people, the fighters and their families, were left with a deeper sense of the values of life, a wider interest in national affairs. This ripening process was assisted by the new cultural breadth which came with the conquest of the Far West and the vigorous emergence of the Midwest. Intellectual interests which had been focused before the war in comparatively small groups in New England and the Middle Atlantic states—in the literary circles of Boston and Concord, New York and Philadelphia, the faculties of Harvard and Yale and a few other centers—now played over a wider field. What was in some respects the most alert and progressive university was found as far west as Ann Arbor.[260] Among authors, Mark Twain, Edward Eggleston, and W. D. Howells suddenly came forward from the Midwest; Bret Harte and Joaquin Miller from the Pacific; and George W. Cable and Mary N. Murfree from the South.

For a brief period after the war, before these new impulses had had time to appear, there seemed a pause in the nation's cultural life. The colleges, chilled by poverty and the blow that recruiting had struck at class enrollments, hesitated to plunge into the bold innovations that were to re-create many of them. Literature seemed to produce nothing original. Hawthorne died at the close of the war; Bryant was seventy-one, Longfellow nearly sixty, and Emerson, sixty-two.[261] It seemed an evidence of the palsying effect of the conflict that the best poets turned to translation, and within a half dozen years after 1866 the country was given Longfellow's, Norton's, and T. W. Parsons's translations from Dante, Bayard Taylor's from Goethe, C. P. Cranch's from Virgil, and Bryant's Homer. Not a novel of importance appeared in the four years following the war. Although Lowell and Holmes produced some enduring literature, and the patriotic odes and "Democracy" of the former seemed to catch the new note of the period, it was not until the year 1869 brought *Innocents Abroad* and 1870 Bret Harte's *Luck of Roaring Camp* that the fresh era could be said to have commenced.[262] In science, also, the changed outlook did not come until, at the opening of the seventies, E. L. Youmans established the *Popular Science Monthly,* and John Fiske devoted himself to propagating the doctrine of evolution.

There was a crying need for fresh impulses, for the intellectual sway of the great New Englanders and Victorians, which belonged to the prewar period, was still dominant. Rebecca Harding Davis speaks of the pride in Emerson especially, as an American prophet, which in the sixties pervaded the nation.[263] "In the West and South there was no definite idea as to what truth this Concord man had brought into the world. But in any event it was American truth and not English." Holmes was equally popular. "Everybody who cared for books, whether in New York clubs, California ranches, or Pennsylvania farms, loved and laughed with 'the little doctor.' " All of the West settled by New England stock sat at the feet of these writers with especial fervor, and Hamlin Garland's thrill when he first found the train carrying him over the Massachusetts boundary was felt by thousands of Western travelers.[264]

Since the moral tone of the American reading public was perfectly assimilated to that of the English, the sway of the eminent Victorians was even more powerful than that of the New Englanders. There was a Dickens worship abroad in the land. Sets of his books and Scott's and Thackeray's were to be found in the remotest hamlets. Dickens's second visit, in 1867, though it did not evoke the callow, unbalanced demonstrations of 1842, was a prolonged ovation.[265] In Boston the demand for tickets to his readings was so great that Harvard undergraduates could not obtain a single seat; in New York, where people stood all night in the December cold, there were two lines nearly a mile in length when the box office opened, and speculators hovering near the head offered $20 for anybody's place. His earnings during a tour that did not take him outside the East amounted, after the deduction of $40,000 for expenses, to $100,000. The year of his visit saw thirty-one different editions of Dickens's collected works published.[266] Wilkie Collins was paid $7,500 each by Harper for his successive books *The Moonstone* and *Man and Wife.* Of Disraeli's *Lothair* (1869) 80,000 copies were sold in America. Charles Reade commanded $5,000 for so poor a novel as *A Woman Hater,* and in 1867 the same sum was paid for Trevelyan's *Macaulay.* Such remuneration, above the reach of any American author, attested to the prestige of English works.[267]

From its four years' preoccupation with the war the younger public turned eagerly to ideas and doctrines that had already become familiar abroad. In 1865, says Henry Holt, "I got hold of a copy of Spencer's *First Principles,* and had my eyes opened to a new heaven and a new earth."[268] Charles Francis Adams, Jr., coming out of the army a colonel, tells us that he chanced one day upon a copy of John Stuart Mill's essay on Comte. "My intellectual faculties had then been lying fallow for nearly four years, and I was in a most recipient condition; and that essay of Mill's revolutionized in a single morning my whole mental attitude."[269] For the first time, he, with millions of others, heard of Darwin. Carlyle was receding into the past, his voice less potent than in the fifties; Mill, succeeding him, was the chief influence for a few years until Darwin, Spencer, Tyndall, and Huxley, as leaders of the new scientific movement, and Arnold, in criticism and theology, took his place. Thinking Americans were about to pass from the theological stage into the scientific.

Popular literary taste, which of course reached no such lofty level, continued to be remarkable for the vogue it gave to authors who combined commonplace entertainment with a rigidly Victorian code of morality. The *Nation* remarked upon the immense number of families which had just five secular books on their shelves: Abbot's *Napoleon,* Headley's *Washington and His Generals,* Ingraham's *The Prince of the House of David,* an illustrated giftbook on the Orient, and Tupper's *Proverbial Philosophy.*[270] The same audience wanted popular didacticism offering no such difficulty as Emerson. Dr. J. G. Holland, under the pseudonym of Timothy Titcomb, obtained a wide reputation by truisms insipid enough for a young ladies' boarding school and religious enough for the most bigoted sectarian. All together, nearly a half million copies of the Titcomb letters were sold. His long narrative poem *Katherina* (1867) enjoyed a similar vogue, selling 35,000 copies in its first three months and soon passing its fiftieth edition. Holland's novels were rivaled in circulation by the moral tales of E. P. Roe, who studied at Williams College, served as a chaplain in the war, and until 1874 was a minister in a Hudson River village. His first novel, *Barriers Burned Away,* with its topical interest growing from the Chicago fire, made him famous among semieducated readers who enjoyed a love story weighted with a religious purpose; and thereafter a new book appeared almost yearly, until his death in 1888. Three popular didactic essayists of the day were Carl Benson, Fanny Fern, and Gail Hamilton.

It was creditable to American society that Motley's *United Netherlands,* the third and fourth volumes of which appeared in 1868, should within a year sell more than 15,000 copies; it was creditable that Parkman's books were eagerly hailed.[271] But looking at the people as a whole, several minor authors were more truly characteristic. The Reverend Dr. Henry M. Field, a circumlocutory writer with some talent for description, catered to the taste for the "instructive." Elizabeth Stuart Phelps, of an equally able New England family, expressed several tendencies in postwar fiction. Her *Gates Ajar,* with its glimpses of Paradise, comforted many who mourned dead soldiers, and her *Silent Partner* dealt in a philanthropic spirit with the wrongs of New England workingpeople. T. S. Arthur continued to deal out tracts in fictional form with astonishing success.[272] There were thousands who supposed E. P. Whipple a great critic, Noah Porter a great moral teacher, and J. W. Draper a great thinker, and even in the pages of the *Atlantic* there was asserted a comparison between Macaulay and James Parton. Such saccharine nonsense as Theodore Tilton's novel *Tempest Tossed* (1874), the tale of a family which lived for twenty-six years on a calm-bound but fortunately food-stocked ship in the South Atlantic, and which came ashore just in time to give the young daughter a romantic marriage, found an eager audience.[273]

Worse still, the managers of the Boston Public Library in 1872—Boston!—named as the most popular authors of the day Mrs. E. D. E. N. Southworth, Carolina Lee Hentz, and Mary J. Holmes, while Mrs. A. D. T. Whitney was a close competitor in the suburbs.[274] Indeed, four years later, when *Publishers' Weekly* asked the bookstores of the country to state which works of fiction were most salable, such titles as *St. Elmo, The Wooing O'T, Infelice, My Wife and I, Barriers Burned Away,* and *The Opening of a Chestnut Burr* crowded out all but a few really good novels, like *Jane Eyre* and *The Scarlet Letter.*[275] And when in 1879 the libraries of three representative New England cities reported on the circulation of various novelists, the showing was equally unpleasant to lovers of the classics. In Bangor, Mary J. Holmes, Mrs. Southworth, and Charles Reade were first in the order named; in Lawrence, Mrs. Southworth stood first and Dickens third; while in Quincy, where Mrs. Southworth's trash was excluded, Mrs. Whitney held second place, against fifth for Dickens.[276] Most of the novel reading, it is clear, was done by the women of the country—and college women were almost unknown. Some of the books imported from abroad were of the same stripe: This was the period of Louisa Mühlbach and Ouida. In 1868 the sale of the romances of the former outstripped all competitors —Henry Ward Beecher's *Norwood,* Rebecca Harding Davis's *Dallas Galbraith,* Reade's *Foul Play,* and Auerbach's *On the Heights.* The novels of Spielhagen were also popular. If he and Miss Mühlbach were approved because they taught history, the stories of the Reverend George MacDonald, such as his portrait of an ideal Calvinist philanthropist in *Robert Falconer,* achieved a wide circulation for their moral and religious tone.[277]

One curious phenomenon of popular taste deserves a word. The Civil War had given a remarkable vogue to the dime novels published in New York by Beadle and Company, which the soldiers passed from hand to hand in literally millions of copies. Erastus Beadle, the astute head of the firm, had at first directed his corps of writers—not all of them hacks, for Mayne Reid and Edward S. Ellis were active—to themes from Eastern pioneer life and the Revolution. Now he turned to the Far West, enlisted the pens of numerous Western explorers, Indian fighters, and plainsmen, and began issuing enormous numbers of "yellowbacks" which bore such titles as *Deadly Eye* by William F. Cody, *Idaho Tom, the Young Outlaw of Silverland* by Oll Coomes, and *Spitfire Saul, the King of the Rustlers* by Joseph E. Badger. Among the contributors were Captain "Bruin" Adams, Major St. Vrain, Captain Jack Crawford, and others whose years of personal knowledge and actual adventure were woven into their volumes. Adult Easterners looked upon these lurid tales as dangerous trash, and youngsters who devoured them in secret were taken to the woodshed if caught. Nevertheless, many of the volumes possessed genuine merit as a presentation of the Wild West of the explorer, cowboy, and prospector, and their picture of pioneer life and character is more accurate and vivid than that of many a formal historian. The books, too, were ethically sound, the authors inculcating lessons of manliness and avoiding scenes of vice. Beadle, in his tens of millions of dime, half-dime, and quarter-dollar publications, covered a large field, from songbooks to popular biographies, and shortly had a flattering number of imitators.[278]

Then, as afterwards, the masses were nourished chiefly upon periodical literature. Robert Bonner's *New York Ledger* was the great bourgeois success of the time, able, with its high prices, to capture poets like Longfellow and divines like Beecher. It paid $3,000 for "The Hanging of the Crane," and maintained an adroit mixture of eminent names with tales of the "Demon Cabman" and the "Maiden's Revenge." *Hearth and Home,* a languishing periodical, was revived early in the seventies by Edward and George Cary Eggleston, who also compounded religion and thrilling stories according to an infallible formula. *Godey's Lady's Book* still pursued its blithely decorous way, the indispensable feminine magazine, but it lost vigor in the late seventies. As earlier, a prominent place in American life was occupied by the atrociously moral and gossipy family weekly of religious tendencies. The best of the religious publications, because the broadest in interest, was the *Independent,* which in political opinions lived up to its name, and which a succession of men—Beecher, Tilton, Edward Eggleston, William Hayes Ward—edited with ability.[279]

One of the factors to be marked in considering the literary culture of the day was the bad organization, evinced chiefly in two defects, of the book trade. There was no systematic method of distributing new volumes from publisher to retailer, and a spring book sale in New York and other centers still partly took the place of modern methods. Retail buyers crowded to the auction rooms on lower Broadway, where each publisher sold his stock on consignment, not at a fixed trade discount. Not till the eighties did the book auction die. Another indication of weakness was the success of the subscription plan of publication, reduced to a secondary role in the eighties by better methods. The leading house in this field for some years was the American Publishing Company of Hartford, which sold 31,000 copies of Mark Twain's *Innocents Abroad* within five months at $3.50 or more, paying him 5 percent royalty. At the end of the year the total sales had reached 77,000. For *Roughing It,* Clemens obtained better terms, 7.5 percent royalty, and again there was a heavy sale, nearly 40,000 copies in three months.[280] But even the old, established publishers, in order to reach the public in great areas bare of bookstores, used the subscription plan. Thus Appleton had Bryant edit a superb two-volume collection of steel engravings of scenes in the republic, called *Picturesque America*—published in portfolio parts—of which nearly a million sets were sold. The subscription system flourished not only because of the lack of retailers and good book advertising, but because it lent itself to a species of "star system" in literature; yet a method which gave Mark Twain financial independence and a large audience was not wholly a bad method.[281]

Prominent among the agencies which contributed to the general broadening of culture was the lyceum, of which the thirteen years after the war witnessed the spectacular reorganization and decline. It was James Redpath, an able journalist of English birth, who took the chaotic lecture system of prewar days, and in 1867 opened a central booking office through which local lecture committees might engage the speakers they wanted.[282] For a 10 percent commission he assured the lecturers ample remuneration while saving them troublesome correspondence, and at the same time he was able to offer lyceum managers programs of a high character. Under Redpath's influence the whole character of the lyceum steadily altered, becoming commercialized and of wider popular appeal. Taking charge of John B. Gough, he enabled that temperance orator to clear $40,000 for the year 1871–72, and $30,000 or more in succeeding years. Redpath paid Beecher $1,000 for a single Boston appearance in 1872. A number of men whose fees had formerly been $50 or $100 now discovered that they could command $250 or even $500 a night. The cartoonist Nast lectured for the season 1873–74, engaging Parton to prepare his discourses and delivering them sometimes five nights in a week.[283]

In this popularized form the lyceum had a few years of radiant prosperity, but by 1874 it evinced decided signs of fading. Many of its best figures disappeared. Sumner died, Emerson's mind failed, Curtis was busied editing *Harper's Weekly,* and Colfax and Beecher were lost in clouds of scandal. It was necessary to turn to music to bulwark the failing institution, and in a single season the Redpath agency paid Max Strakosch $10,000 for ten

concerts. But the irretrievable decline of the lyceum was significantly revealed by the immortal Gilbert and Sullivan operas. These two masters
began their collaboration in 1871 with *Thespis,* and in the years 1878–81
produced *Pinafore, The Pirates of Penzance,* and *Patience,* which were
shamelessly pirated and became enormously popular throughout America.
People whose moral scruples prevented their attending plays went to hear
the operas, and in New England especially they so appreciably took the
place of the lectures that many lecture halls were remodeled to make their
presentation possible.[284] Meanwhile, the Chautauqua movement had been
founded in 1874 as an effort to promote the intensive training of Sunday
school teachers, and rapidly broadened into a partial substitute for the
old-style lyceum of instructive aims.[285]

Nor did the newspaper, as an instrument of popular education, show
just the progress after the war that was hoped of it. Progress there was, but
it was chiefly in news gathering and commercial enterprise, with editorial
tutelage less and less important. Fresh young men of ability, it is true, were
called into the profession. In the decade from 1869 to 1879, Raymond,
Greeley, the elder Bennett, Bowles, and Bryant died; and as successors
there appeared Charles A. Dana of the *Sun,* Manton Marble of the *World,*
Whitelaw Reid of the *Tribune,* Henry Watterson of the *Louisville Courier-
Journal,* Murat Halstead of the *Cincinnati Commercial,* and Joseph Pulitzer
of the *St. Louis Westliche Post.*[286] Though these men had talents sufficient
to support the tradition of "personal" journalism established before the
war, two tendencies of the day were inimical to it. One was the fact that
during the war newspaper readers had been taught to value the news
columns far above the editorials. Now astute editors, profiting from the
new methods taught by wartime necessities, paid their principal attention
to the rapid, accurate, and effective reporting of events. In assuming the
editorship of the *Sun* (1868), Dana promised that "it will study condensa-
tion, clearness, point, and will endeavor to present its daily photograph of
the whole world's doings in the most luminous and lively manner."[287]
Indeed, the pungency, cynicism, and sensationalism of Dana's news columns gave his journal its success. The other tendency was the decentralization of the press. No journal after the war wielded as great an influence as
the *Tribune* had done just before it. Throughout the West and South a
multitude of new papers sprang into existence, and by means of the Associated Press supplied their readers with intelligence almost as full as that of
the New York dailies.[288]

As yet the bookstore was but a feeble institution, and throughout large
areas of the country the public library was not merely unknown but un-
thought of. Parton in 1867 commented with surprise on the fact that Chicago boasted of three bookshops, which offered an assortment almost as
large as any in the Atlantic cities and which had sold more than 1,700 sets
of *Appletons' Cyclopaedia* and the *Britannica.* Visitors to San Francisco

felt the same astonishment in seeing H. H. Bancroft's fine Market Street bookstore. But outside of the very largest cities there were usually no bookstores in the true sense of the word at all. Nor were there many libraries in the modern sense of the term; no American collection of books in 1870 yet reached 200,000 volumes, though Europe counted more than twenty of that size. Indeed, there were only six libraries with as many as 100,000 volumes each—one the Library of Congress, with 183,000; three in or near Boston—the Boston Public Library with 153,000, the Harvard library with 118,000, and the Athenaeum library with a few more than 100,000; and two in New York—the Astor Library with 138,000, and the Mercantile with 104,500.[289] Of city and town libraries there were in 1875 about 2,000 in the whole country with 1,000 or more volumes each, and many of these were rubbish.[290] Even in the largest cities, moreover, the library privileges were restricted by unhappy rules. The Boston Athenaeum collection was accessible for reference purposes, but only those who purchased shares at $300 each could borrow books. New York's largest library, the Astor, was not open for reference at night, and lent no volumes. Chicago had no provision for a free public library until 1868, when the merchant Walter Newberry died leaving a fortune estimated at $4 million for one; Philadelphia was similarly handicapped until the following year when Dr. James Rush left about $1 million as an endowment.

It was largely upon this cultural basis, and against these difficulties, that the new forms of intellectual betterment had to make their advance. The first clear manifestation of these forces came in the establishment of magazines which offered a medium for a broader, more realistic literature, and which created and guided a large new reading public. One weekly, the *Nation,* and four monthlies—*Scribner's, Lippincott's,* the *Galaxy,* and the *Overland*—were founded at almost the same time, while *Putnam's Magazine* was reestablished.[291]

One change of far-reaching significance, resulting largely from the establishment of the new magazines and the founding of energetic publishing houses like those of Henry Holt, Charles Scribner, and E. P. Dutton, was the creation of a really solid economic basis for authorship. Lowell, in an address in New York near the end of his career, remarked that in his boyhood only two Americans, Irving and Cooper, could have lived upon their literary incomes, and they fortunately had other sources of revenue. "There are now scores," he said, "who find in letters a handsome estate."[292] The most important literary periodical in New York just after the war was the *Saturday Press;* to be accepted by it had been, as Howells said, nearly as signal a brevet of merit as to be accepted by the *Atlantic;* yet it paid contributors not a cent. It was quickly shouldered aside by *Scribner's,* which paid well.[293] No longer was it possible for a writer of Poe's originality and genius to starve for lack of a few dollars while he hawked his poems, tales, and criticism from one miserly editor to another. Thoreau was a greater writer, if not a greater naturalist, than John Burroughs, yet Thoreau's income from his books and papers was zero while Burroughs was able to take advantage of a varied and eager market.[294]

The task of providing the United States with adequate literary criticism fell squarely upon the shoulders of E. L. Godkin, the brilliant Anglo-Irishman of thirty-three who on July 6, 1865, began publishing the weekly *Nation*. It enlisted as contributors Longfellow, Lowell, Whittier, Howells, Frederick Law Olmsted, Bayard Taylor, Richard Grant White, Norton, and a long list of academic worthies. From the beginning it was doubly a power —a power in the critical domain, an even greater power, thanks to Godkin's acute, mordant, and fearless pen, in the political world.[295] Godkin's British education gave him a novel point of view and an acquaintance with more mature institutions which were of the utmost value in his criticism of American life.[296] Editors, clergymen, lawyers, and professors read his sound opinions on politics and transmitted them, in form dilute but recognizable, to a popular audience. Literary men read the *Nation*'s comments on books and immediately profited.[297] It was shown incidentally that the weekly, not the monthly or the daily, was the best agency for criticism.

The same forces which gave vigor to a peculiarly American type of fiction were felt more feebly, but still realistically, in the drama. In 1874, Mark Twain made a play from *The Gilded Age* which he called *Colonel Sellers,* and to which the capable actor John T. Raymond, playing the title role, gave a considerable success. It contained a broad satire upon American political and social corruption. The following year was produced B. E. Wolf's *The Almighty Dollar,* which W. J. Florence made famous by his characterization of Judge Bardwell Slote, the congressman from Cohosh district—a typical American politician.[298] The stock companies were steadily waning, and the "star system" was slowly rising, as the years passed, but the best of the companies, like Wallack's in New York, Mrs. John Drew's Chestnut Street Theater in Philadelphia, and the Boston Museum, were admirable even in decay.

A postwar era which, amidst boodling, scandal, and money grubbing, could produce *Scribner's* and the *Nation, Life on the Mississippi* and *Old Creole Days,* Edwin Booth in *Hamlet* and the Boston Museum of Fine Arts, was an epoch full of healthy and irrepressible growth in every cultural field. They represented achievements of enduring value, and indicated powerful and promising currents flowing beneath the surface of the life of the new nation.

THE DEEPENING OF AMERICAN CULTURE

NOTHING WAS MORE TYPICAL of the intellectual immaturity of the United States in 1865 than the state of its higher education. Harvard, as Bryce said later, was a struggling and poverty-stricken college, with vague relations to learning and research, loosely tied to a congeries of professional schools. Many of its courses were on the level of a present-day high school, and, except in science, it was impossible for any of its students to push beyond the weak training for the A.B. degree.[299] Yale's facilities were even more wretchedly insufficient. Its policies were shaped by a little group of Congregational ministers and a narrow church atmosphere stifled the teaching.[300] Its curriculum was antiquated, and the oldest professors were paid less than the youngest ministers in New Haven, while the scanty library fund was always exhausted before it was paid in. Princeton followed a course of study almost identical with that pursued by undergraduates when Madison was in the White House. The students recited in rooms that were "mostly ill-conditioned cellars and attics," and when, in 1868, Dr. James McCosh became the head he pronounced the scientific apparatus and collections fit only to be burned. The University of Wisconsin had two or three very dilapidated buildings, a tiny uncatalogued library, five professors, and a few tutors; its critics declared that it was merely an academy for the village of Madison.[301]

There was everywhere an antediluvian flavor about the courses of study which explains Henry Cabot Lodge's remark that, in all his four years at Harvard, 1867–71, "I never really studied anything, never had my mind roused to any exertion or to anything resembling active thought"—with the exception, he adds, of Henry Adams's course in medieval history.[302] Electives were virtually unknown outside the universities of Michigan and Virginia; and the hard-and-fast curriculum emphasized the ancient classics, ethics, and rhetoric. In many institutions there were no modern languages taught, not even French and German. There was little science and laboratory practice was everywhere confined to a few experiments performed by the professor before his class. T. R. Lounsbury in all his college courses at Yale never heard mention of any English author. Brander Matthews at Columbia had just one term in the history of English literature, but was not even introduced to the writings of any authors or told to read them for himself. G. Stanley Hall at Williams was given no English literature save a driblet taught by the professor of rhetoric.[303] The colleges were used to the spectacle of professors filling several or even a half-dozen chairs at once. Thus Yale had one heroic savant expounding physics, astronomy, meteorology, and mechanics, while at Columbia an intellectual Hercules dealt with moral and mental philosophy, English literature, history, political economy, and logic.[304] The method of teaching, for the most part, could not have been duller. The students recited in much the same parrot fashion as in grade schools, for in general they were expected to acquire information rather than the ability to think. Brander Matthews tells us that he was never encouraged to go outside the textbooks, that no collateral reading was ever suggested, and that the professors lived in a splendid isolation from their students. "All the exercises," testifies Dr. Hall regarding Williams, "consisted in hearing recitations."

Equally striking in a survey of higher education was the fact that the very branches most important to the future growth of the nation were those most neglected. There was no scientific instruction in agriculture anywhere. The first school of mines, that at Columbia, was only two years old when the war ended, and gave a slender three-year course.[305] Instruction in technology was yet in its infancy, and the view still obtained that the proper function of the engineering college was to give students a superficial knowledge of technical methods and formulas, leaving them to be licked into shape by practical experience. Shop practice in technical schools was almost unknown. In medicine there were, by 1870, more than fifty schools, but by present-day standards they were all wretched. As yet there was little real distinction between surgeon and physician, as in England. Many of both the medical and law schools were wholly or in part proprietary—that is, moneymaking trade schools—and only nominally attached to the colleges whose names they borrowed. In women's education, when the ambitious girl of 1865 looked about her, she found only three or four institutions, Oberlin the most notable, of worthy standards.[306]

To produce the upheaval which changed and modernized the domain of higher education within two decades, three primary causes interacted. The emergence of a half-dozen statesmen of education—Andrew D. White of Cornell (inaugurated 1867), James McCosh of Princeton (1868), Charles W. Eliot of Harvard (1869), Noah Porter of Yale (1871), James B. Angell of Michigan (1871), and Daniel Coit Gilman of Johns Hopkins (chosen in 1875)—provided the personal force that was needed. It was noteworthy that one of these men was a Scotchman, while the other five had studied or traveled extensively in Europe. Moreover, an outcry for a fresher, more practical and more advanced kind of instruction arose among the alumni and friends of nearly all the old colleges and grew into a movement that overrode all conservative opposition. The aggressive "Young Yale" movement appeared, demanding partial alumni control, a more liberal spirit, and a broader course of study.[307] The sons of Harvard simultaneously rallied to relieve the university's poverty and demand new enterprise. Likewise, as an impulse toward greater social breadth and increased practical usefulness in university work, came the establishment of the land-grant institutions under the Morrill act. Education was pushing toward higher standards in the East, throwing off hidebound church leadership everywhere, and in the West, finding a wider range of studies and a new sense of public duty.

The old-style classical education received its most crushing blow in the citadel of Harvard, where a young captain of thirty-five, the son of a former mayor of Boston and treasurer of Harvard, led the progressive forces. Five revolutionary advances were made during the first years of Dr. Eliot's administration.[308] They were the elevation and amplification of entrance requirements; the enlargement of the curriculum and the development of the elective system; the recognition of graduate study in the liberal arts; the raising of professional training in law, medicine, and engineering to a post-graduate level; and the fostering of greater maturity in student life. Most of these we may dismiss briefly. Standards of admission were sharply advanced in 1872–73 and 1876–77. By the appointment of a dean to take charge of student affairs, and a wise handling of discipline, the undergraduates were led to regard themselves more as young gentlemen and less as young animals. One new course of study after another was opened up—science, music, the history of the fine arts (with Charles Eliot Norton as lecturer),[309] advanced Spanish, political economy, physics, classical philology, and international law.

In organizing postgraduate instruction upon a well-ordered basis, Harvard was acting in response to a need which was clearly recognized at other institutions as well. True graduate training was unknown in America until after the war. Young men like Andrew D. White, G. Stanley Hall, and Edmund J. James went naturally to Germany for their advanced study.[310] In 1871, however, Yale led the way for American institutions by concentrating all her nonprofessional graduate work into a distinct school. The next year Harvard went a step further by stiffening the requirements for the degree of A.M. and providing that the two new degrees of Ph.D. and Sc.D. might be conferred after three years of residential study. It was not, however, until the Johns Hopkins University was opened in Baltimore in 1876, as the result of the bequest of a wealthy merchant of that city, that an American university devoted itself primarily to research and the training of scholars.[311] Under the presidency of Daniel Coit Gilman a notable faculty was gathered there, and young college graduates soon began to feel that it was not necessary to go abroad for their intensive training, though the old tradition continued strong for another generation.

But if the increased breadth of higher education owed much to a half-dozen Eastern leaders, it owed still more to the Morrill act of 1862, which both re-created Western education and added a new wing to the Eastern edifice. Primarily, of course, its purpose was the provision of education in agriculture and engineering, but actually its effects touched all branches of instruction. It led to the reorganization in 1866 of the University of Wisconsin, by which that university was given a strong president in place of a weak chancellor, while the curriculum was broadened with the practical studies fairly in the foreground. It caused the founding of the University of Illinois (1867), which, in the words of its chief parent, the rugged Jonathan B. Turner, was intended to be "a peculiar university," one which "our posterity can erect into the strongest, broadest, and best university on the face of the earth."[312] From it, also, sprang the universities of California (1868), of Minnesota (1868) and Kansas (1864), the Massachusetts and Texas Agricultural colleges, and other institutions. Most strikingly among its results, it brought to fruition the plans for a new, broader, and better university which Andrew D. White, a wealthy young New Yorker, had been forming during his years of teaching at Michigan and of study and observation at Oxford and in Germany.

The rapid rise of Cornell University, under the double impetus of the Morrill land endowment of 960,000 acres and an initial fund of $500,000 presented by Ezra Cornell, was the most remarkable phenomenon in higher education during the postwar decade.[313] The institution opened in 1868 with about 400 students and an adequate faculty. President White laid down four "foundation ideas": a close union of practical and liberal instruction, nonsectarian control, a fruitful alliance between the university and the state school system, and the concentration of revenues for higher education. He called also for other innovations—for the steady development of scientific studies and for partial alumni control of the government. The university had to contend with much detraction, misrepresentation, and poverty, but it was blessed by the vision of both White and Cornell.[314]

Coeducation was given national breadth and irresistible impetus by the land-grant colleges. Nevertheless, the distrust of higher education for women remained so keen, especially in the East, that T. W. Higginson felt it necessary to publish in the *Atlantic* a sarcastic essay, "Should Women Learn the Alphabet?" An eminent Boston physician, Dr. E. M. Clarke, issued a volume on *Sex in Education,* which presented "proof" that the physical impediments to sex equality in higher education were insuperable.[315] Influential leaders of opinion maintained that women would unsex themselves and lose every feminine grace if they undertook the same routine as men; they would soon be wearing bloomers and going in for rough outdoor sports!

The chief blow against these paleolithic beliefs was struck by the establishment, in the very heart of the conservative East, of three colleges exclusively for women: Vassar in 1865,[316] and Smith[317] and Wellesley[318] just a decade later. Various "female colleges" had been scattered throughout the country, but not even the best offered courses of true college grade. Vassar was established by a rich brewer of Poughkeepsie; Smith by Sophia Smith of Hatfield, Massachusetts, who in 1870 left about $365,000 for an institution to give young women advantages equaling those of men; and Wellesley by Henry Towle Durant, a wealthy Boston lawyer. A brewer, a spinster, and a lawyer—the diversity of these figures illustrates the breadth of the new movement. Of the three colleges, Smith insisted from the outset upon standards precisely as high as those of the best men's universities, and maintained these standards despite the difficulty of obtaining adequately prepared students. The other two rapidly raised their requirements.

It was in these domains just outlined, if anywhere, that the texture of American life was proof against the charge of superficiality. That charge might be brought against the hectic rush of business to skim the cream from the natural resources of the continent; it might be brought against our literature, which was for the most part but skillful reporting. It might also be brought against our social thinking—we had no counterpart for the English group represented by Carlyle, Ruskin, Mill, and Leslie Stephen. But it could hardly be brought against the undaunted and fairly surefooted efforts of the colleges to keep pace with the rapid growth of human knowledge and to anticipate the needs of the nation for better-trained men and women.

TWO MEMORABLE YEARS: 1873 AND 1876

LIKE A BLACK DIVIDING LINE, the Panic of 1873 cuts across the history of the thirteen years following the Civil War. On the one side lies the sunshine of buoyant commercial prosperity; on the other the gloom of depression, economy, and poverty. When the struggle ended at Appomattox, the economic strength of the North had sufficed to throw off immediately a slight reaction which manifested itself in 1865, and a somewhat greater trade depression in 1868. From 1869 to 1873, however, business showed an abounding prosperity;[319] and the crash of Jay Cocke's banking house in the summer of the latter year seemed to many almost unportended.

Factors which were felt throughout the world played a prominent part in causing the depression, and the United States did not stand isolated in facing this storm.[320] In nearly every part of the globe the same sharp dividing line marked off a period of expansion from one of stagnation and poverty. Germany had a panic at precisely the same time as the United States, which spread at once to France and Belgium and thence to England and all parts of the world. This profound check was evident in new communities based on agriculture like Australia and South Africa; it was felt in all the populous industrial regions like New York, Lancashire, and Westphalia. It even manifested itself in Japan and South America. Certain causes of a worldwide nature, as well as merely national impulses, must therefore be sought. Among them stands prominently a costly epidemic of wars. Our Civil War, the disastrous French invasion of Mexico, the Austro-Prussian conflict, England's quixotic assault upon Abyssinia, the South American wars centering about the dictator López, and the Franco-Prussian War piled up a heavy economic debt. There was also an excessive construction of railways in Central Europe and Russia. The heavy indemnity which France paid Germany, $1.1 billion, and the opening of the Suez Canal also resulted in profound economic dislocations. Everywhere currency inflation, with rising prices, wages, and speculation, made itself conspicuous and provoked a sharp reaction.

In America, cautious observers had expressed a fear that the currency was inflated too much, that railways were being overbuilt, that there was overtrading, and that a luxurious mode of life was demanding excessive importations from Europe. Federal extravagance, complained the critics, had become outrageous, while state extravagance was equally bad. David A. Wells, as special commissioner of the revenue, pointed with alarm in 1869 to the rapid drift of energetic men from pursuits directly productive of wealth to occupations connected with commerce, trade, or speculation.[321] The consequences were seen in a marked growth of population in the commercial centers, a striking increase in the number and cost of business buildings, and a spirit of trading and gaming rife everywhere. The number of business firms in the United States in 1870 was 431,000; in 1871 it had leaped to the astonishing total of 609,904.[322] All this, as Wells said, indicated not a healthy growth but an unhealthy fever induced by inflated paper currency.

The financial situation became more and more plainly perilous as the seventies moved on. By February 1873 the best commercial organs were expressing their apprehension of a crisis. The inflation of credits had by this time reached an unprecedented height; in the five years from 1868 to September 12, 1873, the national bank deposits increased only $44 million, but the bank loans for the same period rose by $283 million. That is, the aggregate debt had risen 50 percent, while the aggregate circulating capital had increased only 7.5 percent. Since all the debts of the country had to be paid out of its circulating capital, the danger was clear. Moreover, fires in Portland, Boston, and Chicago had caused a demand for floating capital to take the place of that which had been annihilated. It took credit to finance the rebuilding; and during 1872, Chicago alone was estimated to have borrowed $50 million in the New York market. Finally, the burden of railway paper grew constantly heavier; the wildcat methods and frequent exposures undermined the confidence of foreign investors and the companies had to obtain their credit at home.[323] The *Nation* might point out in 1872 that, of the 364 listed railroads, only 104 paid dividends at all, and 69 of these paid less than 10 percent; but the dazzled citizen fixed his eyes on the 35 which paid 10 percent or more.[324]

Harbingers of the oncoming storm slowly multiplied. During 1871 there were only 2,915 failures in the United States, but in 1872 the number suddenly leaped to 4,069, involving a loss of more than $121 million.[325] There had been danger of a general panic after the Chicago fire in the fall of 1871. Nearly a year later, when the Grant-Greeley campaign was rising to its height in September, grave disturbances were avoided only by the intervention of the government, Jay Cooke, and other strong financial interests. In the spring of 1873 the money market was again so badly shaken that some of Jay Cooke's associates begged him not to carry forward the Northern Pacific syndicate, then being formed.[326] Throughout the first half of the year the Crédit Mobilier scandal was gathering force, throwing Congress into a state of demoralization and accentuating the general distrust of big business. Meanwhile, New York had been deeply agitated by insurance and banking scandals,[327] causing a severe strain upon the money market, already inadequate to sustain the top-heavy structure of debt.

The crash came in September. An atmosphere of dread was created when on September 8 the New York Warehouse and Securities Company and five days later Kenyon Cox and Company, in which Daniel Drew was a special partner, failed. The gloom thickened as rumors spread that George Opdyke and Company were in grave danger.[328] On Wednesday the seventeenth, stocks came down with a run on the New York market; and consternation reigned in all the offices that had burdened themselves with unmarketable collateral. Grave reports spread to Boston, Washington, and Philadelphia, where President Grant had just arrived to spend the night at Jay Cooke's home at Ogontz. Still, Jay Cooke's firm, the pillar of the nation during the Civil War, was generally considered unshakable. Yet just before eleven the next morning, before business had fairly begun, the doors of his New York office were suddenly closed.[329] This step, taken by the partner in charge after consulting with a group of bank presidents, electrified the city. When the news was laid before Jay Cooke at the Philadelphia office, he ordered the doors of the house closed, and then turned his face away from his associates, tears streaming from his eyes. A few minutes after noon his Washington branch and the First National Bank in Washington were shut, making the suspension complete.

The failure was a financial thunderbolt, stupefying the country. The New York Stock Exchange, after a moment of startled silence, was thrown into an uproar such as the oldest member could never remember hearing.[330] In Philadelphia the telegraph bulletin from New York caused the entire stock board to rush pell-mell into the street and down to Jay Cooke's doors to verify the report. A newsboy shouting an extra "all about the failure of Jay Cooke" was arrested by a horrified and incredulous policeman. In Washington, word of the failure reached a criminal court during a murder trial, and it was hastily adjourned, the judges, lawyers, witnesses, and spectators hurrying into the avenue to learn further news.[331]

In itself the failure was a blow certain to cause widespread but not universal demoralization. The real fright and dismay of the failure lay in its disclosure of the half-suspected fact that the aggregate indebtedness of the business world was far too great to be paid out of the circulating capital. The instant this disclosure came that bright September day, every business-man clutched simultaneously at the means of payment. This frenzied rush for ready money, with the weaker trod ruthlessly underfoot, constituted the panic.[332] Nothing could be done, in essentials, but let the storm blow itself out. Several houses failed the same day as Jay Cooke, and thereafter came a steady succession of crashes. Fiske & Hatch went down in New York, carrying with them all hope of an immediate financial reorganization of the prostrate Chesapeake & Ohio; the Lake Shore Railroad failed; the Union and the National Trust companies were forced to suspend. At eleven o'clock on the third day of the Panic, September 20, the governing committee closed the New York Stock Exchange, taking this unprecedented step "to save the entire street from utter ruin."[333] President Grant, Secretary Richardson, and other high government officers hurried on the fourth day to the Fifth Avenue Hotel and summoned Commodore Vanderbilt and other financial leaders to their apartments to offer advice. Grant remarked that the first need of the situation seemed to be for "a week of Sundays," but more heroic measures had to be taken. For ten days the Stock Exchange was kept closed; the banks, pooling their resources, for the first time issued the now familiar clearinghouse certificates; and the government, acting on the counsel of men who believed the chief cause of the Panic was a lack of money, released $13 million of greenbacks from the treasury for the purchase of government bonds.[334] But these steps proved the merest palliatives. The country was like a debilitated patient, who rallied from a sudden stroke of illness to face a slow convalescence. Before it lay a long era of prostration, which was simply "a period of painful and impossible effort to pay a large amount of indebtedness with a relatively small amount of capital"—a period in which business had to readjust itself to a much smaller, narrower, but more solid basis.

As the weeks passed, the evil effects of the Panic made themselves felt in widening circles. Five national banks in Chicago suspended, and other Western business and financial houses failed as disastrously as those in the East. Jay Cooke and Company was found to have assets worth $15,996,212 to balance against its liabilities of $7,939,409, but it was long before it could pay all its creditors—so great was the difficulty of realizing on its assets—and Cooke never resumed business in his old capacity.[335] The year ended with more than 5,000 commercial failures in the United States for the twelve-month period, the liabilities aggregating to $228,500,000, or nearly twice as much as the preceding year. Still, the gloom over the country thickened, and firms continued to fall like lines of dominoes, each toppling over some neighbor.[336]

The actual panic, naturally, was of brief duration, and in a few months anybody with good collateral could borrow money at 4 percent.[337] But the crisis, the Fury outraged by the violation of the laws of sound finance, was pursuing innocent and guilty alike with her vengeance and bringing her heaviest lash upon the backs of the poor—the laboring factory hand, the sweated garment worker, the small savings-bank depositor. The first disastrous effects were evident in a stoppage of work on long lines of railway. The mileage built in 1874 was only 1,940, less than one third the average of the preceding five years.[338] Nearly a half million laborers were thrown out of work, partly or wholly, by this suspension. Rolling mills, machine shops, foundries, and other industries connected with rail transportation followed. When the ironmasters of the country met in Philadelphia late in the spring after the Panic, they found that, of the 666 furnaces in the United States, only 400 were in operation. Subsidiary industries, one by one, shut down as demands and payments for their goods failed. Unemployment steadily mounted.

As the winter of 1874–75 came on, long bread lines and demands for outdoor and indoor relief in New York, Boston, and Chicago testified to a chilling drop in the social temperature. Despite the abundant harvest, wrote B. F. Nourse, "many thousand families will be nearer to hunger than for many years for lack of employment, and the circle of enforced idleness, disability, and poverty widens daily."[339] Radicalism was appearing among the unemployed of the great cities, and there was a grim significance in the demands which some socialistic bodies were making—demands for work on public enterprises, advances of money or food for one week to all who were in actual want, and the stopping of all eviction for nonpayment of rent. Immigration ground sharply toward a stoppage, and workless aliens began departing by tens of thousands. From nearly 450,000 in 1872, the arrivals dropped to 130,000 in 1877, the lowest number since the tide of the Civil War was turned at Gettysburg.

Work was not only hard to obtain, but what work could be got paid lower and lower wages.[340] In Massachusetts a particularly careful survey of wages for this period shows that all the wage-earning groups in the year 1872 were receiving some 36 percent more than in 1860, but that immediately a sharp decline began. By the end of 1875, wages had dropped nearly 10 percent, and by the close of 1878 they had fallen more than 5 percent further, near which level they remained until 1880 brought a turn for the better.[341] Professional men—doctors, dentists, lawyers—reduced their charges by one half, and the churches were compelled to cut the salaries of their already ill-paid ministers. There was an alarming increase not merely in penury but in all that it entailed—illness, ignorance, discontent, crime. It was quickly reported that the city streets showed a distinctly larger number of young women driven to prostitution, and the jail records more men driven to theft.[342]

One consequence of the depression was the sudden emergence of the "tramp evil." The "bummer" of the Civil War had been succeeded by a small vagrant class after peace came, but it was never troublesome. Now the countrysides swarmed with hoboes. In some Eastern sections, like the Berkshires, they formed an organized brigandage, associating with professional criminals and beggars, camping in the woods, stealing, drinking, and fighting. Their ranks were recruited by reckless young men wandering about in search of employment. From all over the East came reports of thefts, incendiary fires, rapes, and even murders committed by vagrants. In some New England towns during 1877 people on the outskirts were forced to abandon their homes, and in Massachusetts alone there were said to be a thousand vagabonds roaming the rural communities. In parts of the Midwest the nuisance was almost as great, and every summer brought stories of outrages by small cohorts.[343] Late in June 1876, some 200 tramps stopped a train on the Rock Island Railroad and ran it into Beardstown, Illinois, where the city marshal and his constables had a bloody encounter with the invaders. Another threatening gang temporarily occupied and terrorized Jacksonville, Illinois. Elsewhere in these states during 1876 revolver fights between trainmen and tramps became so frequent that trains on some railroads had to be especially guarded.

A natural consequence of the reduced consumption of goods and the accompanying "glut" was a marked and sometimes astonishing fall in the prices of commodities. It would not be too much to say that the cost of articles used by the average American family dropped about one fifth or one sixth in the five years after Jay Cooke's failure.[344] House rents fell slightly in most cities, and heavily in some, while in the East the charge for table board dropped by one fifth or even one fourth. Real estate suddenly found a stagnant market, and in innumerable instances became worth less than the mortgages it bore. Luxuries like silks and jewelry had almost no sale at the most astonishing reductions. The market for pianos and organs was kept active only by a combination of price-slashing and the introduction, for the first time in American history on a large scale, of the installment system of buying; furniture and clothing grew steadily cheaper. But perhaps the most striking single item was pig iron, which sold for $53 a ton in Philadelphia in the fall of 1872, and six years later was worth just $16.50.[345]

The skies seemed for a time to grow steadily blacker. During 1874 there were 5,830 business failures in the United States, during 1875 no fewer than 7,740, and in the Centennial year the number climbed to 9,092.[346] The sections which enjoyed the largest measure of prosperity were the farming districts of the Central West and the mining regions of the Far West. Business was weighed down by a millstone of bad debts and debilitated by the rottenness inherited from previous years. There were very nearly 9,000 failures for the year 1877. In the closing months the rapid succession of frauds, forgeries, disgraceful failures of several banks and trust companies, and embezzlements of securities cast an increased shadow over the financial community.[347] Not only were the actual losses from these breaches of trust heavy, making everybody suspicious of business, but they produced an angry and exaggerated outcry against Wall Street as a den of robbers. Indeed, the year 1877 may rank as one of the blackest in the nation's annals. It had opened with the country in the throes of a disputed presidential election, threatening civil war, and it had brought disastrous labor revolts and a hot discussion of the silver question, producing a fear of rash currency legislation. When the year ended economist Horace White wrote that the industries of the nation were never, in the memory of living men, so smitten with paralysis. The farmers almost alone held up their heads. "All else is a weary and aching mass of unemployed or half employed capital, misdirected talent, and underpaid labor, to which commerce gives the generic name of glut."[348]

The year 1878 seemed to many people to leave the United States at the bottom of a deeper gulf than ever before. The number of failures reached an unprecedented total. There were no fewer than 10,478, and the liabilities totaled $234,383,000, or more even than in the black year 1873.[349] More than half the iron and steel furnaces were idle the whole year, while the price of their product was lower than at any time since colonial days. Unemployment seemed to be increasing rather than decreasing, while the relations of capital and labor were more inflamed than ever before.[350] Yet actually the nation was at the turning of the tide and the skies were about to brighten rapidly. One great process essential to recovery, the process of deflation, had now been completed—a deflation both industrial and financial.

In the midst of this period of hard times, and three years after the Panic, there came a year when the people for a time sought deliberately to cast aside their cares, and gave themselves up to an impressive commemoration of their country's birth. All could agree that a century's perspective yielded genuine cause for national pride whatever temporary difficulties America might be facing. The celebration took the form of a great exposition, formally opened for its five-month career on May 10, 1876, in Fairmount Park in Philadelphia with imposing ceremonies.[351] This sixth of the world's great fairs, and the first to be held in the United States, was in most respects an exhibition of which the United States might feel proud. Though its architecture was mediocre, Americans were, as might be expected, pleased by its mere size. They boasted that the Main Exhibition Building was the largest structure in the world, and that with four other great halls and fifty or so smaller buildings scattered through the 236 acres of grounds overlooking the Schuylkill, the exposition surpassed the previous Paris and London fairs.[352]

On a single day, Pennsylvania Day, no fewer than 274,919 visitors entered, the greatest throng that any exhibition had ever attracted. There were very nearly 10 million visitors and more than 8 million paid admissions. At the outset, a fierce debate raged around the question whether the Exhibition should be open on Sunday. Among church members, those who regarded the Exhibition as a place of amusement, took one side, those who thought of it as an educational institution the other.[353] In the end the management bowed to the guardians of the old Puritan Sabbath and followed British precedent in deciding for Sunday closing. Perhaps it was, as the *New York Tribune* said, all the more truly a national exposition in thus conforming to the national habit.[354] But in one respect the directors were thoroughly "liberal": They allowed the sale of liquor and turned a neat penny in auctioning the privilege to the highest bidder.

The best exhibits of the Centennial were unquestionably those of industrial and commercial interests, for European manufacturers were eager to enlarge their footing in the American market. British exhibits of furniture and household decorations aroused admiration by their completeness and beauty. Here was presented evidence of the astonishing renascence in household taste which England was experiencing, and the fine Lambeth faience, Eastlake furniture, and Minton tiles, together with the examples of exquisite cabinetwork in Jacobean and Queen Anne's days, delighted American women. Germany sent an arresting display of fine porcelain and France specimens of her best textiles. Excited attention was also given to the bronzes, porcelains, and lacquerwares of the Japanese, which had been an almost complete novelty but now found a growing favor in American homes.[355]

The essential symbols of American talent and progress were in Machinery Hall. There stood the majestic Corliss engine, a mighty athlete of steel and brass, the enormous flywheel revolving with the power of 1,600 horses and making the whole building quiver. Another symbol lay in the sewing machines with which this hall seemed flooded, cramming every corner and overflowing from every alcove. Still another was the Woman's Pavilion,[356] with its acre of products of feminine industry, from textile designs by women trained at MIT to a complete materia medica from the Women's Medical College of Philadelphia. Never before had a collective display of women's work been attempted, and its scope impressed many a scoffer at the feminist movement. Another symbol of America's essential interests lay in an exhibit of ores and mining processes by the Western states. Still another was the demonstration of the work of the Waltham watchmakers, busy with their fine machinery, and of the Trenton ceramic workers.

It was an exposition, as it was an anniversary, which could not but stimulate a patriotic pride in American achievement, and yet reflecting people were painfully aware that in many respects the year 1876 was an infelicitous time for America to place herself on exhibition. Not only was economic distress still widespread, but the epidemic of political scandal and corruption which began in Grant's first administration had not yet run its course. Lowell expressed this thought by the speech he put into Brother Jonathan's mouth when Miss Columbia asked him what she should display at the Centennial:

> Show 'em your Civil Service, and explain
> How all men's loss is everybody's gain; . . .
> Show your new bleaching-process, cheap and brief,
> To wit: a jury chosen by the thief;
> Show your State Legislatures; show your Rings;
> And challenge Europe to produce such things
> As high officials sitting half in sight
> To share the plunder and to fix things right;
> If that don't fetch her, why, you only need
> To show your latest style in martyrs—Tweed.[357]

Tweed was indeed exhibited to Europe in dramatic fashion. Escaping from jail in the closing days of 1875, he found his way to Cuba and Spain, and the next autumn was recognized in Vigo, through one of Thomas Nast's internationally circulated cartoons, and captured. The frigate *Franklin* brought him home to the Ludlow Street Jail,[358] and in this prison he shortly after died (April 1878).

Into the whole reeking series of exposures which crowded upon one another during the spring and summer of 1876 it is unnecessary to go in detail. The first event, the acquittal of Babcock upon the charge of sharing the Whisky Ring's profits, brought no comfort to the public, since few were assured of his innocence or of the propriety of the president in upholding him.[359] Then came the impeachment of Secretary Belknap of the War Department on the charge of taking money for the grant of a post tradership in Indian Territory; the issuance of an official report upon General Schenck's misconduct while minister to England; the publication of the Mulligan letters, which indicated that Blaine had accepted improper favors from railway interests[360] and the exposure, by committees which the Democratic House had appointed, of the rottenness which had honeycombed half of the executive departments. President Grant's own display of nepotism, his acceptance of lavish gifts, and his carelessness of appearances were all open to censure.[361]

Month by month, too, corruption was still being stripped bare in the states and cities of the land. Governor Tilden in March reported upon his overthrow of the notorious "canal ring" in New York, which in the preceding five years had stolen or wasted close to $15 million. Yet Albany was still far from clean, and that spring the lobbyists of the horse railways of the metropolis had no difficulty in defeating the Husted rapid-transit bill by purchasing votes at from $250 to $1,500 each.[362] In Maryland, a Democratic ring was proved to have stolen right and left; in Connecticut, the Democrats who controlled the legislature sold a U.S. senatorship to William H. Barnum, an illiterate politician, for a gift of $20,000 to the state committee.[363] A legislative report upon crime in New York City showed that many officers of the police department and district attorney's office were working hand in glove with thieves, gamblers, and keepers of brothels and sharing in their plunder. In Washington there was a hot debate upon the frauds of the District ring, which "Boss" Shepherd was accused of heading. Shepherd, as the chief force in a new District government created in 1871, had done a wonderful job renovating the ill-paved, ill-built, unsanitary capital, and had earned the title of the Baron Haussmann of Washington, but his and his associates' financial methods left much to be desired.[364] Worst of all was the corruption exposed in Philadelphia itself, where a "gas ring" had stolen nearly $8 million within a few years.[365] Throughout the year the Beecher-Tilton scandal kept recurring and left the immense public influence of Beecher—who if not guilty of the adultery charged was certainly guilty of weakness in other regards—temporarily shattered.[366]

Closing the Stock Exchange, New York City, 1873.

The narrow victory of the Republicans, 1876–1877.

President Grant visiting the foreign delegations at the Centennial Exposition.

It was a year to make Americans ashamed rather than proud, and the most hopeful fact of the time was that this sense of shame, this appreciation of the contrast between the pretentious national Exhibition and the seamy, shabby aspect of American civic life, was earnestly expressed. A change had come over the national temper, and the easy tolerance of the late sixties was being replaced by a new sternness. The editorial columns of the press harped constantly upon the national humiliation, and great Republican organs like the *New York Tribune* and *Chicago Tribune* bitterly assailed the corruption in the administration. The pulpit, the civic organizations, the professional leaders, the men of letters of the nation, all showed their mortification and resentment. The country was awakening, and this fact was itself a sign of convalescence from the long moral sickness which had followed the war. The evils were superficial rather than deep-seated, and they had at last aroused so deep a revulsion that a cure was seen to be indispensable. An era of reform was about to open.[367]

HUMANITARIAN STRIVING

WHEN THE THIRTEENTH AMENDMENT was assured of victory, and William Lloyd Garrison locked the forms of the *Liberator* for the last time, the veteran abolitionist turned to the advocacy of temperance, "free trade," and woman suffrage.[368] This change of front was a symbolic act. It evinced the compelling reason why humanitarian zeal should manifest itself in a variety of new ways after 1865. The idealistic energy which had formerly been largely absorbed by the antislavery cause was now free to express itself in solicitude for the poor, the defective, and the defenseless. The increasing urbanization of the nation, moreover, in connection with the hard times following the Panic, thrust certain problems more insistently into the foreground, such as poverty, public health, sweatshop abuses, and child labor. The nation awoke after the war to find conditions existing in its largest cities which till then it had fondly thought confined to Manchester, Paris, and Naples. As a result, the late sixties witnessed the first large and concerted movement against the city slums, the first scientific efforts in behalf of public health, the opening of a new chapter in penal reform, and the movement for the prevention of cruelty to animals. The seventies brought the organization of the Women's Christian Temperance Union and the first national ticket of the Prohibition party, the efforts of Clara Barton in behalf of the Red Cross, the rise of the National Association for Woman Suffrage, and the founding of the State Charities Aid Association in New York.

The slum, recently a mere name, had become a firmly rooted American institution. New York City had 100,000 slum dwellers, sheltered in nearly

20,000 tenement houses, many of which were the vilest rookeries.[369] The cellar population alone approached nearly 20,000 people. In some districts there was a congestion which had probably never been equaled in any other great city of Christendom. The tenements, erected by grasping speculative builders, were crowded together in solid blocks, with rear houses jammed in behind those facing the street. They were unheated, and most of the houses had no connection with the sewer. In such an immense and notorious rabbit warren as Gotham Court on Cherry Street each home consisted of two rooms and housed an average of from five to seven people.[370] In Boston, where the slum district was smaller than in New York but hardly less repellent, the construction of tenements after the war amazed all observers. By the time of the Panic more than one fifth of the whole population, or about 60,000 people, dwelt in the 2,800 registered tenement houses. What tenement life sometimes meant in human misery can best be suggested by a brief excerpt from an official report describing a tenement home not a half mile from the Boston City Hall.[371]

> The room was unspeakably filthy; the furniture two or three old chairs and an old dirty table. No fire, and the room damp, dark, and cold. It was the only room the family occupied except a little dark box in the corner with no window in it—a part of the room itself partitioned off for a bedroom. And such a bed! The two oldest children were dirty and ragged and leaning against the window on the side of the room. . . . The youngest was . . . about worn out and apparently half starved. . . . Its only clothing was an undershirt scarcely reaching to the waist, and the child's body, face, hands, and hair were reeking with the vilest filth; and the child was pinched with the cold.

Many mill towns of Massachusetts and other Eastern cities were just as shockingly overcrowded. Fall River, a conspicuous example, reported tenements where a dozen people dwelt in three rooms, or fifteen in four.[372]

Throughout the slums of the cities, so few were the sanitary precautions that death stalked almost unchecked. In the congested parts of New York, typhoid, smallpox, scarlet fever, and, above all, typhus fever were never idle. A wretched building in East 17th Street, a stone's throw from the mayor's house, sent thirty-five typhus patients to the city fever hospital in a single year, while nearly 100 more were treated at home.[373] Garbage was allowed to collect in many streets until they became almost impassable; in 1866 some 1,500 loads were removed from the Fourth Ward in a few days, and yet some streets were still ridged two feet high with the deposits. The city sewers, unconnected as yet with any main trunk lines to carry the contents far out into the tide-scoured bay, simply emptied under the piers of the Hudson and East Rivers. The nation's second city, Philadelphia, presented a spectacle that was not a whit better. A large slum district existed on Bedford and St. Mary Streets, crowded by people exhibiting a revolting squalor and vice. The town was so exceedingly dirty that in 1870 the street authorities removed 1,000 loads of filth a day over a period of two and a half months.[374] Hogs still roamed a large area of the city. A considerable part of the population was supplied with drinking water from the Delaware River, into which the sewers threw 13 million gallons of waste daily, which was carried by the tides to the induction pipes.[375]

The result was writ large in mortality figures that seem barbarous by the standards of a later era. During the winter of 1864–65, New York had more than 2,000 cases of smallpox and more than 600 deaths. Philadelphia in the first year of peace lost 773 victims to typhoid fever and 334 to typhus. A year later, in 1866, cholera appeared and claimed 910 lives. During 1869 and 1870, Philadelphians suffered from a scourge of scarlet fever, which was responsible for 1,755 deaths in the two years and left hundreds deaf, crippled, or mentally enfeebled. Then, in 1871, a terrible smallpox epidemic ensued which threw both New York and Philadelphia into mourning. It killed over 800 people in New York, more than ever before in its history, while in Philadelphia the total deaths nearly reached 2,000.[376] Boston, Baltimore, and Washington were all ravaged by the same powerful epidemics. The most casual investigation showed that a great part of the deaths would have been preventable by better housing and a few elementary measures of sanitation. Thus, in the reeking slums of the Fourth Ward of New York, it was found in 1863 that one resident in twenty-five perished, while in the open, well-built Fifteenth Ward, only one resident in sixty.[377]

The necessity for reform was one to which no intelligent body of citizens could long remain blind, and public-spirited men arose in the largest Eastern cities to demand action. New York City, leading the way, obtained in 1866 a state enactment creating an efficient municipal health board, which was headed by the public-spirited merchant Jackson S. Schultz. Within four years it had closed virtually all the cellars and basements used for foul lodgings.[378] It had completed a survey of the tenements and ordered the owners to effect alterations making them decently habitable. Vaccination had been applied to most of the population without resorting to compulsion, and the causes of cholera had been vigorously dealt with. In 1868 the board forced the removal of all downtown slaughterhouses, of which there had been twenty-three in a single half-ward, to points above 40th Street. At the same time the first collecting sewer to free the pier slips from the accumulation of waste was built, and others rapidly followed.[379] Meanwhile, Massachusetts was being persuaded to create her state board of health (1869)—a far-reaching step which stimulated all the cities of the Bay State to improve their sanitation and to attack disease.[380] Two years later the legislature gave Boston a tenement-house law far in advance of the old code. It was also necessary for Boston to attack the problem of sewage disposal, and in 1875 the city established a commission to prepare a plan for main sewers stretching far out into the harbor.[381] Philadelphia already had a board of health, which labored as vigorously as a corrupt administration would let it.

If these conditions existed in the three largest and wealthiest cities of the East, the state of affairs in backward Southern centers and the raw, fast-growing Western municipalities may be easily imagined. Memphis in 1870, a city of 40,000, had practically no sewage arrangements or health administration at all, though built in part on swampy soil. New Orleans, then easily one of the most insalubrious cities in the world, was, despite the establishment of the Louisiana board of health soon after the war, in even worse shape. "The soil is saturated almost to its surface," ran an official report in 1880, "and saturated very largely with the oozings of foul privy vaults, and the infiltrations of accumulations on the surface of the streets and in the rear of houses." The drainage was totally ineffective.[382] Charleston and Mobile presented the same spectacle. All the Southern cities were habituated to frightful epidemics. Memphis in 1873 was attacked from three quarters at once—by yellow fever, smallpox, and cholera. The people fled in a panic, leaving half the houses vacant. Some 7,000 cases of yellow fever were reported and about 2,000 deaths; cholera attacked 1,000 and slew 276; and smallpox reaped a heavy harvest among blacks.

Among the people who filled the slums of the large cities there was one large group which is deserving of special notice. A product partly of the war, partly of the trend toward city life, the sweated woman worker suddenly appeared in large numbers. In the North the invasion of the industrial field by women did not halt in 1865, for the shortage of labor remained acute; the competition with discharged soldiers simply pushed these women lower in the economic scale.[383] Both East and West their lot was frequently pitiable, for they were protected neither by the laws nor by trade unions. In New York City alone there were 75,000 women workers who lived on the ragged edge of misery. In the first year of peace, with prices rising to an unprecedented height, 15,000 or more, employed in shops and factories, earned only from $2.50 to $4 a week. Yet they were far more fortunate than the wretched stratum of women employed as pieceworkers on cheap garments.[384] In the Midwest women were glad to earn from $3 to $5 weekly, and those in the Chicago and Cleveland sweatshops labored for even less. A union movement was inevitable. Susan B. Anthony became head of the Workingwomen's Protective Association;[385] women's labor organizations were born in the cigar-making, printing, and shoe-making trades. Yet these protective efforts, taken in the aggregate, could accomplish little.[386]

Despite the poverty which stared every city dweller in the face, remedial or relief institutions were few and painfully weak. The settlement house was unknown; the slum mission was just taking root; the institutional church and the Salvation Army were unborn. Efforts at the erection of cheap model houses, though familiar in England, were unheard of in

America. In Boston, Dr. H. P. Bowditch, of the state board of health, was spurred by the misery of the tenements to incorporate a cooperative building company, which opened the first of five groups of "cottage-flats" in 1872. In Brooklyn, Alfred T. White, a philanthropic gentleman who had studied housing in England, built in 1877–78 two admirable sets of model tenements.[387] But this was all. A. T. Stewart's model hotel for working girls, with its excessively rigid rules, proved a failure. As yet, refuges, shelters, and asylums were few, and the free clinic and "milk station" were unknown. Not until about 1870 was there even so obvious a form of philanthropy for children as the fresh-air work in Boston and New York, undertaken in the former city by the North End Mission, and in the latter by the newspapers cooperating with religious workers.[388]

On the other hand, agencies of vice and impoverishment carried on their work with only the slightest impediment. New York officials in the late sixties confessed to 697 disorderly houses in the city and 2,574 prostitutes, but these figures were notoriously too low, and one authority placed the entire number of such resorts at about 775 and that of the fallen women at fully 12,000. Outside of a few states, the saloon flourished in nearly every town of any size. The census of 1880 showed that the 492 cities of the country with a population of more than 5,000 each supported about 80,000 liquor establishments; and the census authorities estimated the whole number of drinking places in the country at perhaps 100,000, or one for about every fifty inhabitants. This was a showing distinctly discreditable to the habits of the nation. No fewer than 185 towns admitted having houses of ill-fame, while 94 boasted that they were quite free from them; 215 furnished no information whatever.[389] It was believed that they should be "regulated" instead of stamped out. A sanitary committee in New York reported in 1867 in favor of controlling the social evil as in continental Europe, with official inspection and regulation; and this recommendation, written by three able physicians, was emphatically endorsed by the *Nation*.[390]

There were two groups, the pauper insane and the pauper children, whose lot was especially painful. The New York poorhouses sheltered 1,842 such unfortunates in 1867, who were confined sometimes in heavily grated cells, sometimes in gloomy cellars, and sometimes in bare dungeons as dark as midnight; while more than 200 of the helpless creatures were in chains or otherwise tightly secured.[391] Ohio officers reported finding some insane patients in nudity and filth and others with feet frozen off. As for the children, two years after the war New York had more than 1,200, many of whom had been born in the poorhouses, and all of whom suffered physically and spiritually from debasing contacts. The official reports speak of small children confined in rooms near the cells assigned to maniacs and crying with horror and fright at their situation. A similar account comes from Ohio.[392] Those children could count themselves fortunate who were bound out, like Riley's "Little Orphant Annie," to families who needed their labor and made at least a perfunctory promise of giving them kind treatment.

Reform was bound to come, even though slowly. The most powerful impulse was furnished by the rapid creation of state boards of charities to supervise all institutions of relief, public and private, and to suggest means of improving them.[393] The Massachusetts board, established in 1863, was followed during the five years after the war by the formation of similar bodies in New York, Rhode Island, Pennsylvania, Ohio, and Illinois. The Bay State body quickly distinguished itself in the establishment of two schools for teaching deaf mutes by articulation—one in Boston, the other the Clarke Institution at Northampton. In 1868 the board in New York brought out a report on poorhouses and almshouses which the press used in a campaign for reform. This report demanded the building of a state institution adequate to care for the insane, a demand met by the completion of the Willard Asylum, which had been authorized in the last year of the war. In 1873 the board also made an effort to arouse public sentiment for the better care of destitute children. Meanwhile, in Illinois, the officers were exposing county abuses of a terrible nature: the inhuman practice of farming out the patients to the lowest bidder, who systematically starved them; the insufficient medical care of the sick; the neglect of children, "almost without exception uninstructed and untrained"; and the failure to separate the two sexes, so that the number of illegitimate children within the poorhouse walls was shocking.[394] The Ohio board called not only for better treatment of juveniles and the insane but for the establishment of district workhouses for vagrants and petty criminals and of reform schools for wayward girls. This last was one of the crying needs of the time everywhere.

States that neglected their poor in this fashion, it is not surprising to find, paid little attention to their prisoners. During the latter years of the war the jails had been but half-filled, the commitments of male convicts falling off enormously.[395] But when the war closed, the amount of crime increased alarmingly, from one half to three fourths of the new convicts in many penitentiaries being former soldiers or sailors.[396] At this moment an inquiry was made into the condition of American prisons and reformatories by E. C. Wines and Theodore W. Dwight and presented to the New York legislature as a 500-page report (1867). They found that the United States was far behind Europe in the convict systems used. The American prison industries, once so boasted, were now poorly managed. In some states, including New York, the politicians had laid hands on all prison appointments. In the Southern states the convicts were leased to contractors in gangs, and nobody could travel through the section without hearing, as Sir George Campbell did, terrible stories of outrage and abuse.[397] Nowhere was there a proper inspection of the lower prisons; the county jails were, as a

Michigan report said, "moral pest-houses, foster-places of idleness, and schools of crime"; and in every state the lack of classification was glaring. Even Massachusetts had no satisfactory system until 1870.[398]

What a thoroughly bad penitentiary might be was revealed in 1878 by a report in Tennessee upon the state prison in the heart of Nashville. Two men and sometimes three were locked in a cell seven feet long and three and a half feet wide, compelled to breathe air tainted by the open buckets used for wastes; and the sick were "thrown into a hospital lacking in the decency and comfort of a pig-sty." The mortality rate was fearful, for scurvy and typhus fever were almost constant, and epidemics spread with fearful rapidity, until the prison became a menace to all Nashville.[399]

The two great principles of prison reform about which the discussion of the postwar years centered were the indeterminate sentence and the adaptation of penal discipline to the regeneration, rather than the punishment, of the offender. Here the influence of the British example, and especially of the so-called Irish prison system instituted by Sir Walter Crofton, was potent.[400] Two important events in the field of penal reform occurred almost simultaneously: the establishment of a prison where the new reformative principles could be applied, and the formation of a national body to enunciate and expound them. The New York legislature authorized the Elmira Reformatory in 1869, and the state commission which drew up plans for it reported that the new name would be given genuine meaning. "We propose to make the sentences substantially reformation sentences," they said. "We propose that, when the sentence of a criminal is regularly less than five years, the sentence to the Reformatory shall be until reformation, not exceeding five years." In 1870, Dr. Wines was instrumental in forming the National Prison Association.[401] Its declaration of principles called for a progressive classification of prisoners, a system of rewards for good conduct, a constant insistence upon reformation, and the indeterminate sentence. Already the walls of Elmira were rising, and with Z. R. Brockway of Detroit as its able manager, the new plan was given partial scope when the institution opened in 1877.

It is a singular fact that the organized protection of children was, in large degree, an outgrowth of the protection of dumb animals. In 1874 a little girl of nine, beaten, gashed, and starved by her foster mother in a New York tenement, was brought into court as an animal—for the law sanctioned no interference between parent and child—on the complaint of the Society for the Prevention of Cruelty to Animals. Jacob Riis has described the scene on that bitter winter day, when the unclothed mite was brought into the courtroom, "carried in a horse blanket, at the sight of which men wept aloud. I saw it laid at the feet of the judge, who turned his face away, and in the stillness of that court room I heard a voice raised claiming for that child the protection men had denied it, in the name of the homeless cur on the streets." In the dingy courtroom was born the New York Society for

Clearing out a rookery in New York City.

Henry Bergh begins the work of the S.P.C.A.

the Prevention of Cruelty to Children.[402] Other cities adopted the idea. Children had been trained to beg and steal; they had been whipped into hazardous occupations; they had been exposed to surroundings of vice and obscenity. All these abuses, together with physical cruelty to minors, were attacked. Like its predecessor, the new society was criticized for officiousness, but it quickly made itself respected.

But such undertakings, commendable as they were, were of less importance than the temperance movement and the woman's rights movement, two mighty causes destined to enlist millions and within half a century to write their results into the Constitution. Both were revivals of prewar movements which, thrust into the background by the slavery struggle, now emerged with greater strength than ever. Both entered upon new phases, including a far more aggressive part in politics than had been previously attempted.

The liquor evil just after the war seemed to be attaining formidable proportions. The reliance of the federal government upon liquor taxes for revenue gave drinking a new respectability.[403] Immigration assisted its growth, for the Germans of the Midwest checked the prohibition legislation which had been attempted there, and the Irish and Italians of the East supported the saloon. The capital investment in liquor grew from $29 million in 1860 to $67 million in 1870 and $193 million in 1880. With this prosperity to embolden them, the liquor manufacturers and retailers entered politics to protect themselves against heavier taxation or anti-saloon enactments. In cities like New York they allied themselves with the dominant gangsters, and the Whisky Ring frauds showed that they were able to corrupt high federal officers and reach their polluting hands into the very precincts of the White House. The old-fashioned warfare against the dramshop was seen to be quite ineffective.

The prewar movement for state prohibitory laws, so successful in the North during the fifties, had suffered serious reverses during the conflict. When the war ended, only Massachusetts and Maine were "dry," and a vehement popular revolt in the former commonwealth led to the restoration of the license system in 1868.[404] In Maine, prohibition continued in force, and the question whether it was a success or not was one upon which national opinion was sharply divided. Several Central states, notably Michigan, Ohio, and Illinois, stood vacillating at the end of this period between license and prohibition. However, the antisaloon forces labored strenuously for local-option legislation, and before 1878 a considerable list of cities, including Cincinnati and Dayton in Ohio, and Gloucester and Portsmouth in New England, allowed no dramshops. In some other places saloons were forced to operate under costly licenses.

Meanwhile, a militant prohibition party had come into existence throughout the East and Midwest. This party, state and national, grew out of the order called the Good Templars, which, founded about ten years before the war, was by now the country's largest and most powerful temperance organization.[405] The first state political organization was formed in Ohio during the summer of 1869, and that fall 500 delegates met in Chicago at the call of the Templars to perfect a national party. The platform demanded statutory abolition of the liquor traffic, and supported woman's suffrage as the most effective means of reaching that goal. It was a bold step, for during a half century temperance leaders had insisted that the movement would be wrecked if it ventured on the tempestuous sea of party politics. Nationally the early results seemed disappointing. John Black, Green C. Smith, and Neal Dow, the three presidential candidates in 1872, 1876, and 1880, failed to receive 26,000 votes among them. But in certain states the party showed an impressive and increasing vigor, and a long list of towns went "dry" under local option.

Much more spontaneous was the emergence of a powerful woman's temperance movement. The seed of the Women's Christian Temperance Union was dropped as if by accident. Late in 1873 a well-known health reformer of Boston, Dr. Dio Lewis, delivering a series of temperance addresses, urged the women of Jamestown and Fredonia, New York, and Hillsboro, Ohio, to begin a praying crusade to close the saloons. This effort, though a failure in New York, succeeded at Hillsboro, and spread through southern Ohio with astonishing effects. The country was startled to hear that in city after city squads of women were singing hymns before the saloon doors and even entering to hold prayer at the bar.[406] In Dayton and Chicago the women were insulted by street loafers; in Cincinnati they were received with respect; in Zanesville they persuaded the city council to stop the sale of drink. A hundred women marched in Chicago to the city hall to ask the council to keep the saloons closed on Sunday. Along the Eastern seaboard and as far west as San Francisco, the strange outburst manifested itself. Its direct effects were evanescent, but indirectly it accomplished a great object. The church women of Chautauqua, New York, called a national convention of temperance women in Cleveland, which in the late summer of 1874 organized the Women's Christian Temperance Union. It grew swiftly, and when five years later Frances E. Willard was elected its head, it could already claim to be one of the real powers of the land.

This formidable participation of women in the temperance struggle was, from one standpoint, merely a part of the growing emancipation of the sex. In view of the services women provided during the war, feminist leaders, when the war ended, believed they had as good a title to the ballot as liberated blacks. Bombarding Congress with petitions, they tried to obtain for their sex the right to vote as a part of the proposed Fourteenth Amendment. They were totally unsuccessful, for though such leaders as Gerrit Smith, G. W. Curtis, Garrison, and Greeley believed theoretically in equal suffrage, even they objected to imperiling the amendment by making it too broad.[407] But despite their failure in getting the word "male" omitted from the second section of the Fourteenth Amendment, the women steadily pushed their campaign for the vote. Susan B. Anthony and Elizabeth Cady Stanton were in the forefront of the effort. The year 1867 found them fighting in New York for the admission of women to the state constitutional convention; it found them conducting a hot struggle in Kansas for an equal-suffrage clause in the new constitution. "We speak in schoolhouses, barns, sawmills, log cabins with boards for seats and lanterns hung around for lights, but people come twenty miles to hear us," wrote Miss Anthony. On election day the suffrage amendment got 9,030 votes out of a total of about 30,000—the first votes ever cast in the United States for the enfranchisement of women.[408] Then the devoted pair established a suffrage weekly called the *Revolution*. Despite some help from the eccentric George Francis Train, it soon died, leaving Miss Anthony $10,000 in debt— a sum which she gallantly paid to the last cent by lecturing and writing.[409]

One difficulty with the movement was that at first many people refused to take it seriously. Most intellectual circles would have regarded it as freakish had it not possessed the advocacy of John Stuart Mill, who lent it the dignity of a great philosophical reform.[410] In May 1869 the National Association for Woman Suffrage was born, with Mrs. Stanton as president, and its annual conventions in Washington aroused great interest. Senator Hoar and Vice President Wheeler were among the early converts. Almost simultaneously the Woman Suffrage Association was established, with Henry Ward Beecher as head, to demand equal suffrage through a federal amendment.[411] The opponents of the movement objected that under equal suffrage women would no longer be regarded with reverence, that family life would be unsettled by sex equality, and that the feminine intellect was incapable of dealing with civic issues. The suffragists, said the *Nation*, shirk one point discreditably: "the existence and enormous influence in life and manners, and above all on the social position of women, of the sexual relation."[412] The only substantial gains came when Wyoming and Utah territories gave women complete political equality, while a few states granted them the vote in school elections.

In reality, there were two sides of this woman's economic movement. One was represented by the irresistible forward thrust of countless daughters of farmers and wage-earners, eager for a life of light, clean, and sedentary labor that would leave their evenings free for recreation or rest. They had no journals or lecturers, made no noise, held old-fashioned ideas about marriage, and cared nothing about "independence" from men. Yet they raised the number of women over sixteen working in factories, offices, and stores to 364,819 in 1870, and 644,208 in 1880. The more vocal side of the movement was represented by the women's rights advocates who insisted that their sisters should become brokers, lawyers, ministers, and editors, thus asserting their equality with men in ambition and capacity.[413]

If the humanitarian activities of these years, seen as a whole, betray many glaring gaps and strange oversights, we must remember that the labors and agencies of our own time will seem, to the view of posterity, very nearly as ragged and inadequate. Social needs always outrun social provision to meet them. The seventies were strangely indifferent to many other evils. They paid no attention to the fraudulent and health-wrecking nature of the patent-medicine business, with its enormous sale of kidney pills, tonics, bitters, and blood purifiers. Though nearly all groceries were commonly adulterated, sometimes in the most unhealthful way, there was no movement on foot for purer foods.[414] Cream was mixed with gums and white glue; oleomargarine was frequently adulterated with horse fat; baking powders were largely made of alum; and it was said that at least half the vinegar sold in the large cities contained poisonous preparations of lead, copper, or sulphuric acid. There was no systematic effort to reduce the high infant mortality of the time, and dark ignorance was manifest everywhere in the care of young children. Yet despite all reservations, the thirteen years after the war may be pronounced years of creditable progress in liberal and humanitarian fields.

RECOVERY IN SOUTH AND WEST (1873-78)

THE SOCIAL and economic evils flowing from the mismanagement of Reconstruction were enormous. The embitterment of racial relations, the destruction of white morale, the interference with labor readjustments, the strengthening of the old Southern curse of violence were in all a calamity that defies measurement. No other part of the Union was half so poor as the South; yet the South groaned under levies that were unapproached elsewhere. The first census after the war showed that, despite a much lower per-capita wealth, the state charges in Louisiana were $21.85 for every thousand dollars' worth of property, against $7.47 in New York; in Mississippi they were $17.86 as against $6.44 in Pennsylvania. With every year until the Reconstruction governments were overthrown, the burden tended to grow heavier.[415] When computed according to wealth, it was a more oppressive taxation, in all probability, than has ever been borne before or since in the United States. The consequence was a general inability of property values in the Lower South to rally as they should have done.

Yet the depression could not continue. In the elections of 1874, Alabama and Arkansas were carried by the Conservatives, who also came close to victory in Louisiana and Florida, while in South Carolina a Radical governor pledged to reform was chosen. Early in 1875 the Conservatives made good their claim to control of the lower house in Louisiana.[416] Not even a state like Mississippi, where the black majority was overwhelming, could long resist the tide. Armed clubs, organized by white leaders, showed themselves ready to plunge the state into racial warfare to redeem its government, and the Radical governor was reluctantly forced to compromise with them. In the fall of 1875 the Conservatives carried the state elections by a majority of 30,000, and their legislature immediately forced the resignation of the governor and superintendent of education.[417] Thus by the summer of 1876 the political revolution which gave the white Southerners full control of their states was seen to be approaching completion. Only Florida, Louisiana, and South Carolina remained in Radical hands. That fall the Conservatives waged a desperate struggle with such success that the election left in each of the three states two sets of claimants for office. In Florida the Democratic candidates were promptly seated, but in Louisiana and South Carolina they were not permitted to take control until the newly elected President Hayes made it clear that he would refuse to allow the use of federal bayonets to compel acceptance of the Republican nominees.[418]

Everywhere the white Southern population felt a new impulse of hope, a sense that now their land, with the last hated Northern garrison withdrawn, belonged to themselves. They had time to breathe freely and to look about them. Within a year or two it was borne in upon them that, after all, progress had not been halted in even the darkest Reconstruction days. A great part of the producing area had been little affected by the Reconstruction maladies, while for the obvious reason that Southern wealth rested upon agriculture, it felt the effects of the industrial depression after 1873 much more slightly than the North. The cotton yields rose almost steadily and prices remained good.[419] Farmers who had not turned a profit since the war did so during these years, and every season the South emerged with less debt than before. In 1875 the *Financial Chronicle* pointed to the wonderful change in a half-dozen commonwealths, and predicted that the North would some day be surprised at the wealth quietly developed in the section.

In the South in general the number of small farmers continued to increase, partly through the break-up of old plantations, partly through the occupation of neglected lands. It was a section in which the poor man, white or black, found it remarkably easy to establish his independence. Not merely Arkansas and Texas but Louisiana, Georgia, and Florida each had millions of acres lying uncultivated at prices so low that the farmer could pay for his holdings from the profits of two first-rate cotton crops.[420] In North Carolina, a half-empty commonwealth, fair cotton land even in 1878 could be had for $5 an acre and up. The small farmers of Georgia were observed by the Centennial year to be a remarkably prosperous class. They had little or no debt, money circulated rapidly, and steady improvements were seen in their buildings, implements, and methods. Across the Mississippi River a pioneer agriculture was fast pushing west and south. The movement of settlers virtually doubled the population of Texas in the seventies and almost trebled the number of farms, while it sent the population of Arkansas past the million mark early in the eighties.[421] The whole social texture of the South was changing. Year by year it was becoming a more democratic region, one decidedly more modern and alert in its outlook and much more like the Midwest in its manners and psychology.

The sturdy growth of manufacturing gave the South an entirely new social and economic class, composed of the mill operative, the miner, and the foundryman. Particularly did the textile industry confer invaluable advantages upon the poor whites who furnished most of its hands. It gave employment to girls and women who would otherwise have remained household drudges; it increased the family income and raised the standard of living; and it was the means of offering a rather abject and miserable rural population a taste of a wider, livelier town life. The child-labor evil which accompanied it was not yet regarded with much reprobation. All over the South the income yielded by the new industries had a stimulating effect, and by 1878 the worst phases of poverty were vanishing. "Within the last year or two," one Southerner wrote, "broadcloth is often seen and ladies wear costly outfits." Carriages were still little used, as being too costly, but well-kept buggies were numerous. A strong taste for travel had revived, and mountain resorts, watering places, and mineral springs were finding a large custom, while the practice of going to Northern centers was being resumed. Indeed, the love of travel was now more widely spread than before the war, having been stimulated by the campaigning of the conflict and the breaking up of old homes and associations. In cities like New Orleans, Richmond, and Charleston the antebellum festivities were fast reviving.[422]

Not merely the worst of the poverty but the worst of the old provincialism, aristocratic arrogance, and quarrelsomeness was disappearing. It was now possible to engage in trade or the baser professions without loss of caste. In the antebellum South a gentleman could be a planter, a lawyer, or an officeholder, but little else; now young men crowded into business with alacrity, and felt pride in attaining distinction as physicians, journalists, teachers, or engineers. The section was no longer dominated by a semifeudal set of rural ideals. The spirit of lawless individualism which had long been one of the curses of the section could not be stamped out in a few years, and manifested itself in countless personal affrays, duels, and murders based upon a mistaken idea of "honor." But little by little, the social, ethical, and, intellectual codes of the South were being modernized.

No element in this revolution was more remarkable than the change in the status of women, a change produced primarily by the rough buffets which sent Southern girls to work outside the home. In the old days they had moved in an atmosphere compounded of Cavalier tradition, the *Waverley* romances, and pure moonshine. But the outcome of the war compelled them to become equals instead of weak dependents.[423] It forced tens of thousands of sheltered women to do all the washing, cooking, and sewing; it sent innumerable widows and orphaned daughters to support themselves by opening boardinghouses, acting as dressmakers, or managing shops. In rural districts the oversight of many a plantation and farm fell upon feminine shoulders. A multitude of Southern girls married the crippled wrecks who came back from the battlefields, and helped establish new homes by labor in the schoolroom, over the counter, and in garden and field. Thanks to the rebirth of Southern education, within a generation it was asserted that the public schools had made it possible for every maiden, however humbly born, to become independent. This new outlook of womanhood seemed to many old-fashioned people profoundly disturbing, and they asserted that the young men no longer paid women a proper deference; but shrewd observers perceived that the change in standards was wholesome.[424]

The rise of a new Southern culture, of a society that knew and cared about books, newspapers, and schools far more than before, was also evident by 1878. After all the educational turmoil and errors of Reconstruction days, an uneven but distinctly valuable school heritage had been left all the same. For the first time, mandatory provisions for free public education were generally found written into Southern constitutions. For the first time, too, provision was made for a uniform system of school taxation and for the education of black children. Such a state as South Carolina, which had kept its public schools on the pauper level before the war, was now forced to give them respectability, place them under adequate state supervision, and raise their enrollment year by year. By the Centennial year more than 50,000 white and 70,000 black children were in the South Carolina schools.[425] All over the section there was a rapid strengthening of public education.

Thus, all together, when the nation took stock of its resources at the end of the seventies, the "New South" was already a reality. Many of its people were better educated, better clothed, better governed, and more thoughtful and alert than when the incubus of slavery, with all the fictitious wealth it represented, rested upon their shoulders. Yet they still faced a multitude of problems dismaying in their complexity and gravity. Great numbers of whites remained, as they had been during Reconstruction, poor, ill educated, overburdened, and filled with resentment against the North. The old kindliness and pleasantness of Southern life seemed to have disappeared. Under pressure of the war and its aftermath, and of the fiercer competition of the new era, the former hospitality, geniality, and individualistic flavor of existence had been lost. But the section as a whole was upon an improved basis, adjusting itself to a sounder economic system, and responding to higher social and intellectual ideals.

However amazing the recovery of the war-stricken South, it was surpassed by the construction of a wholly new America in the West. Month by month, settlement thickened and the comforts of civilization increased. The wild meadows were fenced; lanes of barbed wire replaced the winding wagon trails; groves of Lombard poplar and larch took the place of aspen, hazel, and cottonwood. Baseball nines sprang up, and the Eastern newcomers brought fairs, conventions, and Fourth of July picnics. Here and there a farmer added an ell to his house and painted his barn. The crops were enormous and the prices good; only when the weather turned against the farmer, or the chinch bug, debouching from northern Illinois and southern Wisconsin, threatened the prairie wheat, did the pinch of poverty return.

These were years of increasing crop yields, of fair if not steady prices, and of dropping transportation costs, during which it became evident, both abroad and at home, that America was immeasurably the world's greatest single source of food.[426] The fertile prairies, netted by a railway system which brought them next door to the European capitals, were forcing the yeoman farmer of Yorkshire and the Junker of Prussia to the wall. American bread was baked for the table of the Berlin workman, American cheese was eaten by the French artisan, and American bacon used for the breakfast of the British clerk. The farmer still endured a multitude of hardships and many injustices, but he had an interlude of five years of lighter burdens and increased compensations.

In Oregon and Washington the number of farms more than doubled in the seventies and the value of livestock more than trebled. This region plainly needed only clear railways to California and the Great Lakes to leap forward in startling fashion, and the railways were coming. But it was in Utah that the changes of the decade were most important. These changes preceded the death of Brigham Young, and were traceable to the steady seeping in of an immigration which gave Utah 144,000 people by 1880. Brigham Young's death on August 29, 1878, removing the last of a great group of state builders—for Heber Kimball had died in 1868 and George Smith in 1875—merely attested to the durability of the Mormon institutions. His funeral occasioned such an outburst of popular grief as the West has seldom witnessed.[427] But those who had supposed that his death would result in church schisms and disintegration found themselves mistaken.[428] After a brief interregnum, John Taylor, an Englishman by birth and the president of the Twelve Apostles, became head of the church. The real weakening of the Mormon theocracy was caused by the steady increase of the Gentile community in strength. Utah would have grown still faster than it did but for the difficulty of marketing agricultural products.[429]

On every hand occurred kaleidoscopic changes in population and development throughout the West. Not merely the larger cities—Chicago with 500,000 people, St. Louis with 350,000, San Francisco with 235,000, Kansas City with 56,000, Minneapolis and St. Paul with 88,000—showed unceasing growth, but new cities emerged all over the West. By 1878 settlement in Kansas and Nebraska had overspread all the well-watered area, and along the streams—the Republican, the South Platte, the Kansas, and the Arkansas—had reached the western boundaries. In Minnesota in 1870 the frontier line of population still clung to Lake Michigan on the north, but now it thrust west along the Canadian border until it met the ninety-seventh meridian. The tide of farmers overlapped into eastern Dakota, green each spring with wheat, and was steadily pressing west and north. Colorado, the Centennial state, made an amazing growth, the belt of settlement widening from a narrow strip along the immediate base of the Rockies to cover the greater part of the mountains and plains—nearly 200,000 people.[430]

California, a nation in itself, stood apart from the remainder of the West in the complexity of its social scene. The growth of population, the depression consequent upon the Panic and the decreased flow of gold from the mines, and the liberation of an army of Chinese from the work of railway building all combined to produce a critical social situation which came to a climax in 1877-78 at a period of unprecedented distress among the laboring people. The crash of mine stocks and the Eastern depression had thrown on the streets thousands of ignorant workmen responsive to any incendiary agitator. They had genuine grievances. There was some truth in the charge that the Chinese, nearly 150,000 of whom were now under the control of six great Chinese companies, had forced down wages and narrowed the scope of employment; in the shoe factories, for example, the Chinese outnumbered the whites four to one, and the pay had declined from $20 a week in 1870 to $9 in 1878.[431]

Although hardly one quarter of the 850,000 people of the state lived on farms, California dated the ascendancy of the farming interest over all others from the early seventies. Not only did the small farmers and fruit growers steadily encroach upon "cow county" but also upon the vast farming estates, which the passing years were steadily proving to be unprofitable.[432] These estates were an unquestionable evil, stunting the growth of the commonwealth, and limiting opportunity and equality to an extent which inspired in Henry George—a California editor during these years—the zeal for land and tax reform which found expression in *Progress and Poverty* (1879). Some of the largest farms, like that of Dr. Glenn at Jacinto, were famous. Lying on the west bank of the Sacramento, 23,000 acres of this enormous holding were under cultivation and a much larger area lying fallow. Glenn kept hundreds of men, 1,500 horses and mules, and a line of 50 gang plows busy at one time.

One social trait of the fast-growing West, its deference toward women, was of increasing national importance. The freedom of the West offered women new careers and broadened activities, and because women were so badly needed, they attained a new dignity in the social scale. California just after the war had three men for every woman, Washington had four, Nevada eight, and Colorado twenty. So great was the demand for a feminine element in the Pacific Northwest that a whole shipload of women was sent

California laborers had no welcome for the Chinese.

The Ku Klux Klan operating in North Carolina.

White Supremacy in the Seventies

out from New York, by special arrangement, to be teachers, clerks, and housekeepers. Women were "objects of a sort of crude, fierce worship" and were treated not merely as men's equals but "as a strange and costly creation," whose whim ought to be law. If unmarried, the attractive woman had suitors without end; if married, she could warn her husband to be deferential—"if he don't, there's plenty will." Women workers in a town like Denver commanded pay four times as high as in Chicago, with board and room thrown in. The pioneer woman of the West, moreover, in facing frontier conditions necessarily developed an individualism, resourcefulness, and courage that made men regard her with respect. She fought Indians, she managed ranches, she preached, doctored, and taught. It was with good reason that the West exalted woman to sovereignty, granting her social privileges unknown in the East, and that the Western school of fiction paid her the same honor. When Wyoming gave universal suffrage to women in 1869, they at once set to work and purged Cheyenne of its brothels and gambling saloons and forced the nomination of better territorial officers.[433]

In a hundred diverse ways it was evident by the close of the seventies that the West was gaining maturity. To attest the variety of its resources it had innumerable new industries—salmon packing, wine making, fruit growing, a great Northwestern lumber business, coal mining in Colorado,[434] borax shipments from the Mojave Desert. It had come into the closest contact with the East in the decade since the completion of the transcontinental railway, and tourists were familiar with its scenic wonders from Estes Park to the Yosemite. James Gordon Bennett demonstrated in the Centennial year just how close the two oceans had drawn by paying half the cost of a special train which made the New York–San Francisco trip in eighty-three hours and thirty-four minutes. If the South showed where the reconstructive energies of the nation were working most vigorously, the Far West showed where its capacities for new construction were being most effectively expressed.

EMBATTLED INDUSTRY
(1873-78)

THE PANIC OF 1873, like every other panic since 1837, was accompanied by convulsions in the field of labor. Indeed, the constant growth of unemployment, the cruel drop in wages, and the general hopelessness of the industrial outlook produced in 1877 one of the most violent revolts of labor in American history. Somewhere between 2.25 and 3 million people were idle who would gladly have worked,[435] and as all times of labor surplusage necessarily are, it was a black period for labor unions. Strikes were easily defeated, and the threat of a lockout was usually sufficient to enforce the acceptance of a wage cut. Employers, seeking to free themselves from the restrictions labor had imposed in the boom years after the war, resorted to blacklists and legal prosecutions, so that it became difficult for unions to find men of ability and energy to serve as their leaders.[436] During the depression the number of really effective national trade unions fell from about thirty to eight or nine, most of which were nearly penniless.[437] In New York City, where the roster of union men had once reached 44,000 it dropped to about 5,000, and in Cincinnati to about 1,000.

Most important of all was the Knights of Labor, which had been founded in Philadelphia as early as 1869.[438] But the one which attracted the most attention in the mid-seventies was a sinister body among the Pennsylvania coal workers called the Molly Maguires.[439] It was a product, on the one side, of the harsh conditions under which the miners worked and, on the other, of the naturally lawless temper of the Irish miners. At first the criminal activity had been unorganized, but the Molly Maguires arose as a secret group which controlled the several lodges of the Ancient Order of Hibernians in the anthracite counties and directed and concealed the crimes. Its operations centered in Schuylkill and Carbon Counties, though it was known throughout the anthracite area. It began resorting to secret acts of violence as early as 1862, and until it was crushed in 1876 through the efforts of James McParlan, a Pinkerton detective who was employed by the enterprising head of the Reading Railroad, it made increasing use of assassination, mutilation, and destruction of property.

To add to the discontent, one strike after another since the Panic was ruthlessly crushed. Of a long series of labor defeats, one strike involving the anthracite workers of Pennsylvania[440] and another the toilers in the textile mills of New England,[441] attracted wide attention. Each occurred in 1875 and was the result of successive reductions of wages to starvation levels. Each resulted in the grimmest misery, the anthracite strike, especially involving women and children in a protracted ordeal of hunger and destitution. Workers the country over, watching them, were wrought up to a high pitch of uneasiness and indignation.

Such industrial battles as these were the prelude to the first great nationwide conflict in American history: the railway strike of 1877. The signal for the battle was a cut of 10 percent in railway wages, ordered in June and July 1877, with peremptory suddenness for most lines east of the Mississippi. The first conflict came on the Baltimore & Ohio. On July 18, the day after the reduction became effective, strikers took possession of the B&O lines at many points and refused to let any freight trains leave. The governor of Maryland called out the whole militia force, and President Hayes[442] at once sent 250 regulars to Martinsburg, West Virginia. At once the rail system of the nation north of the Potomac and east of the Mississippi was half-paralyzed. The three other trunk lines to the west, the Erie, the New

York Central, and the Pennsylvania, with their subsidiaries, were tied up; so were the coal roads, such as the Lackawanna and the Reading.

As the strike spread, it was accompanied by such destructive and bloody riots as the country had never before experienced in connection with labor troubles. The desperation of the strikers, the presence of a large body of tramps, and the increase in the "dangerous classes" from the industrial malady, all furnished fuel for the blaze. The first alarming outbreak occurred in Baltimore. Here on July 20 two regiments of the Maryland militia were ordered under arms, one to proceed to Cumberland, Maryland, to restore the passage of trains, the other to remain at the Baltimore armory. The former, reaching Cumberland, was hemmed in there amid scenes of disorder and asked for reinforcements from the Baltimore troops.[443] When the latter marched out from the Baltimore armory, they were greeted with brickbats, stones, and clubs. Revolver shots followed and the soldiers returned the fire. Many of the troops, pursued by the infuriated crowd, had to take refuge in private homes and escape by the back door or in civilian dress. When the remainder entered the railway station in headlong disorder, the structure was promptly set in flames. Only the arrival of the entire police force of the city, which stayed all night and repeatedly charged the mob, rescued the militia. The next day, when federal troops arrived to restore order, nine persons had been killed and more than a score lay wounded in Baltimore homes and hospitals.[444]

While the country was reading with alarm of this riot, a far graver disturbance had commenced in Pittsburgh.[445] With local feeling already highly inflamed, 650 soldiers arrived on the scene from Philadelphia on Saturday afternoon, July 21. At five o'clock they came into collision with a large mob at the 28th Street crossing, where the missiles of the rioters were met by several volleys of musketry; about twenty-five persons were slain and many wounded. As night fell, the troops were ordered into the roundhouse and machine shops to seek shelter. A fierce assault at once began on the roundhouse, and continued for hours by the light of blazing buildings and freight trains. The mob had broken into the gun shops, and volley after volley was poured into the windows. At dawn the roundhouse was set on fire by cars of flaming coke that had been pushed against it, and the military were in imminent danger of their lives. "Tired, hungry, worn out, surrounded by a mob of infuriated men yelling like demons, fire on nearly all sides of them, suffocated and blinded by smoke, with no chance to rest and little knowledge of what efforts were being made for their relief . . . the wonder is that they were not totally demoralized."[446] Yet they marched out and, under a hail of bullets, retreated across the Allegheny River like veterans.

There had already begun a scene of shameful pillage, and with the mob now complete master of the situation, it steadily increased. Long lines of freight and passenger cars were broken open, looted, and set afire. The streets near the yards were filled with rioters carrying off furniture, cloth-

Union men taunting the "Blacklegs," Mahonoy City, Pa., 1871.

The great railroad strike of 1877—The Baltimore riot.

ing, and provisions. Barrels of liquor were tapped and drunk on the spot; women appeared and seized laces, silks, parasols, and small gas stoves. The incendiarism extended until 2,000 freight cars, the machine shops, two roundhouses with 125 locomotives, a grain elevator, and other property had been destroyed. At three o'clock on Sunday afternoon the Union Depot, a large four-story building, was set aflame.

But within a surprisingly brief period the whole movement utterly collapsed. The ill-paid men knew they did not have the means for a sustained effort, and the psychological effect of this knowledge had made many eager to strike a hard, violent blow. On July 26, the day of the rioting in Chicago, St. Louis, and San Francisco, the workers showed signs of weakening in the East. Under the protection of the troops the trains quickly began running. The New York Central resumed full traffic on the twenty-sixth, and the Erie and the Pennsylvania on the twenty-seventh. By August 3 the revolt was ended on the most severely interrupted lines. "The property losses have to be made good by the taxpayers," said a Western newspaper. "The strikers have finally gone to work at the wages they refused. The dead are the only lucky ones in the entire affair." [447]

While labor was suffering a succession of misfortunes and defeats, capital found the hard times a blessing in disguise. From the standpoint of the business world, the dark years following 1873 were, in their enduring results, highly constructive. They took the whole excessive commercial structure built up during and after the war, knocked away the false and superfluous elements, strengthened those which were left, and began a drastic reorganization. Business was put on an athletic regimen; it became spare and fit and learned to use its wits to keep alive. The results were not long in showing themselves.

A natural process of concentration and consolidation in industry had been interrupted by the flush times after the war, and now it was suddenly accelerated and strengthened. Year by year thousands of weak, ill-managed businesses were thrown into bankruptcy—an average of no fewer than 9,500 for the three years 1876–78. Those that survived had the most capital, the greatest efficiency, and the best marketing facilities. At the same time, such leaders as Rockefeller perceived that cutthroat competition menaced the vitality of even the largest, best-managed plants. The result was the first slow and hazy shaping of those tendencies which in the eighties and nineties were to bring the trust problem before the nation as a giant menace. As yet there were no trusts anywhere, but there were pools and marketing or rate agreements, and they pointed out a broad highway toward monopoly.

Not only the trend toward consolidation but also technical advances and inventions were stimulated by the Panic. Industry had to save money and utilize neglected materials as never before. Little by little, business was making use of the newest applications of chemistry, physics, and engineering; little by little the sway of the rule-of-thumb superintendent was passing away and that of the expert technician arising. It now seems incredible that in the late sixties chemistry was virtually unknown as an agent in the manufacture of pig iron and steel; the blast-furnace manager of those days was a rough fellow who relied upon instinct to show him the condition of his furnace, as the dowser relied upon a hazel twig to locate oil. Nor was chemistry better known in the manufacture of soap, oil, or paints. It is an attested fact that a leading oil refiner spent thousands of dollars just after the war in mixing perfumes with petroleum in an effort to deprive it of its offensive odor.[448] Half the value of crude oil was still thrown away, not merely because the gasoline engine was as yet unknown but because industrial chemists had not brought their test tubes to the discovery of its secrets.

But as the year 1878 came to a close there were indications here and there that the tide of depression had definitely turned and that a period of prosperity was near at hand. Railway building had revived. This was the year in which James J. Hill, with Canadian capital behind him, began the actual work of constructing what he called the St. Paul, Minneapolis, and Manitoba Railroad, destined to grow into the Great Northern. Another railway builder of eminence was stepping upon the stage in the person of Henry Villard, who in the years 1876–79 was taking the steps in Oregon and Washington which were to enable him to complete the Northern Pacific. Foreign trade was mounting steadily. Immigration had begun sharply to increase, a sure evidence that employment was easier to find. The nation, in short, was emerging from one of the darkest half decades in its industrial history.[449]

If we were to select the one outstanding characteristic in which the America of 1878 differed from that of 1865, it might be summed up in the word "unity." When the war closed, the North was divided by a seemingly impassable line of hostility from the South; the Eastern states were farther removed from the Pacific slope than from Europe. The social conditions in Massachusetts and Alabama, in Pennsylvania and Colorado, were utterly dissimilar. Within these thirteen years important strides were made toward knitting the nation into closer unity politically, economically, and culturally. The continental railways made it more compact; the newspaper, the magazine, and the public school tended to make it more like-minded; the growth of wealth and the progress of industry gave it a greater identity of outlook. Sectional characteristics persisted, but even in the South, where the humiliations of Reconstruction still rankled, there was an increasing tendency for people to pride themselves on being participants in the common life of a great country. This growth of common traits and interests was to be greatly strengthened in the period of material and intellectual expansion just opening.

The chief element which supported this increased homogeneity was the economic revolution now evident throughout a great part of the nation. The North had emerged from the Civil War a full-panoplied industrial giant. Its people awoke to the realization of innumerable smoking factory towns, great slums, a strangely variegated tide of aliens pouring into the seaboard cities. This industrial conquest strode over the wide West, and even threw outposts into the new textile towns of the South. The Panic of 1873, which seemed to check the exuberant new commercial era, simply confirmed its sway, for the ensuing depression sheared away what was weak and false in the business structure and compelled a reorganization on stronger, more careful lines.

Yet the new industrialism was only the greatest among a hundred facts and tendencies which were remolding American life. Despite its losses, the South could count an inestimable gain in the fact that, for the first time in history, it was adjusted to the healthful competitive forces, economic and social, of American life. The West of the Indian and buffalo had given way to a new West that was steadily losing every trace of wildness. The farmers had not merely shown a strength and cohesion undreamed of before, they had taken the lead in declaring that, if the industrial era had arrived, the excesses of industry must be checked by firm political control. The vicious tendencies of postwar readjustment were yielding to the idealism and progressivism typified by the civil service reform movement of Curtis and Schurz and by those reformers who, like Tilden, purified states and cities. The universities had been transformed; the women's movement and the labor movement were rising to a new aggressiveness. New forces in literature and art caught their color from the quicker, more vital tendencies of the time. The Civil War had marked the end of one great era in American life; the dozen years of reorganization and readjustment which followed it marked the emergence of the new and modern republic.

BOOK IX

The Nationalizing of Business,

1878–98

PEOPLING THE NATION

THE WEALTH over which the people of the United States were struggling in 1878 had been drawn from a magnificent estate of over 3 million square miles, not counting Alaska. Fully a third of this area still belonged to the federal government. The rest was in the hands of the states, corporations, or individuals. Of this residue the farmers owned nearly half, approximately 537 million acres. The most densely inhabited section was that known as the North Atlantic division, embracing New England, New York, New Jersey, and Pennsylvania. Here a land surface of 162,000 square miles accomodated 14.5 million people. The most sparsely settled was the Western division, made up of eleven states and territories. There, on a land surface of 1,176,000 square miles, was scattered a population of a million and three quarters, about one to the square mile.[1] Outside of the Western division there was more unsettled land per man in Dakota Territory than elsewhere in the country. The center of population lay in Kentucky, eight miles southwest of Cincinnati; in twenty years it had moved 102 miles. To attain its ambition of rapid development, the nation must push this center farther westward—in other words, fill in its waste places with people.

The national government led in the drive for settlers. The one million square miles it owned was what was left of an immense public domain originating in the eighteenth century in gifts by the states made on condition that these lands be held and used for "the common benefit of the

United States." How best to secure that benefit? The government had adopted the policy of distributing the land on easy terms and in small parcels to actual settlers, but by 1878 it was apparent, as President Cleveland was to tell the country a few years later, that

> Laws which were intended for the "common benefit" have been perverted so that large quantities of land are resting in single ownerships. . . . It is not for the "common benefit of the United States" that a large area of the public lands should be acquired, directly or through fraud, in the hands of a single individual. . . . A rapidly increasing population creates a growing demand for homes, and the accumulation of wealth inspires an eager competition to obtain the public land for speculative purposes.

And Cleveland added this prophetic word: "In the future this collision of interest will be more marked than in the past. . . ."[2]

The states went along with the federal government in its effort to entice settlers to the unoccupied lands. As each had come into the Union, Congress had bestowed upon it as a dower a part of the public domain within its boundary, to be used "for the common benefit." Where large tracts still remained in the states' possession, strenuous efforts were made to bring in settlers. Official immigration bureaus were set up for this purpose.[3] Missouri, for example, established a bureau charged with the duty of preparing maps, articles, and pamphlets concerning the resources of the state, its undeveloped farm lands, its minerals and timber, its railroads, and its waters.[4] Even some of the Eastern states were concerned with the problem. In their case it was not, as in Missouri, "land which has never been brought under cultivation." It was a growing anxiety about an increasing exodus from disadvantaged farming districts.

The railroads, particularly those west of the Mississippi, were among the most active of the land boosters. Their future prosperity depended on peopling the country and developing its resources. "Each mile of railroad constructed in a new country is a kind of centrifugal pump furnishing for exportation hundreds of tons of the products of such country."[5] The drive for settlers was conducted largely through, or in cooperation with, the steamship companies and land companies. At one time the Inman Steamship Company had 3,500 agents in Europe and as many more in this country, selling tickets to be sent to friends and relatives of immigrants already settled in the United States.[6]

In 1880 there were about 6.7 million foreign-born in the nation. Because of the depression following the Panic of 1873 the annual number of newcomers during the decade 1870–80 had averaged but 280,000. In the single year 1878 only 138,500 had come, the smallest number since 1862. But with the turn to better times the tide began rapidly to mount again. The year 1882 saw 789,000 arrivals, nearly three times the average annual increment of the seventies and the greatest influx yet recorded in a single year. Of this number three out of every five were adults between fifteen and forty years of age, excellent brawn for the task of developing America's natural wealth.[7]

It is little wonder that Andrew Carnegie exclaimed in amazed approval at this addition to the nation's labor force. "These adults," he said,

> were surely worth $1,500 (£300) each—for in former days an efficient slave sold for this sum—making a money value of $710,000,000 (£142,000,000), to which may be safely added $1,000 (£200) each, or $315,000,000 (£63,000,000) for the remaining forty per cent. of the host. Further, it is estimated that every immigrant brings in cash an average of $125 (£25). The cash value of immigrants upon this basis for the year 1882 exceeded $1,125,000,000 (£ 225,000,000).

In a final word he claculated that the average yearly augmentation of the country's wealth from immigrants "is now more than twice as great as the total product of all the silver and gold mines in the world."[8] The decade 1880-90 brought nearly 3 million foreigners to Amercian shores.

Western Europe made the largest contribution to the incoming flood, over two thirds of the total druing the 1880s. The country from which America drew most heavily in the early years of the decade was Germany. Nearly a third of all immigrants from 1880 to 1884 were Germans. Another third was recruited from the British Isles, Sweden, and Norway. The remaining third consisted of "new immigrants," those from southern and eastern Europe, notably from Italy, Austria, Russia, and Hungary. The banner immigration year 1882—when more came than in any year until 1903 —witnessed the climax of the movement from western Europe and the advent of noticeable numbers from the southern and eastern nations. This shift in the sources of immigration became steadily more marked. From 1885 to 1889 western Europe furnished 1.5 million newcomers; from 1895 to 1899 it sent but 495,000. From the southern and eastern countries, on the other hand, came 493,000 in the former period and 747,000 in the latter. The reasons for this change are many: the overcrowded conditions in southern and eastern Europe, anti-Semitic persecutions in Russia, the establishment of new steamship connections between Mediterranean ports and the United States, and the unexampled opportunities for employment in America. At the same time, the industrial advance of western Europe made it less worth while for the people there to try their luck in a new land.[9]

However much a Carnegie might rejoice at the boundless extent of the influx, others were beginning to question the traditional national policy of welcoming all comers without discrimination or restriction. Organized labor was particularly alarmed because of the competition for jobs by immi-

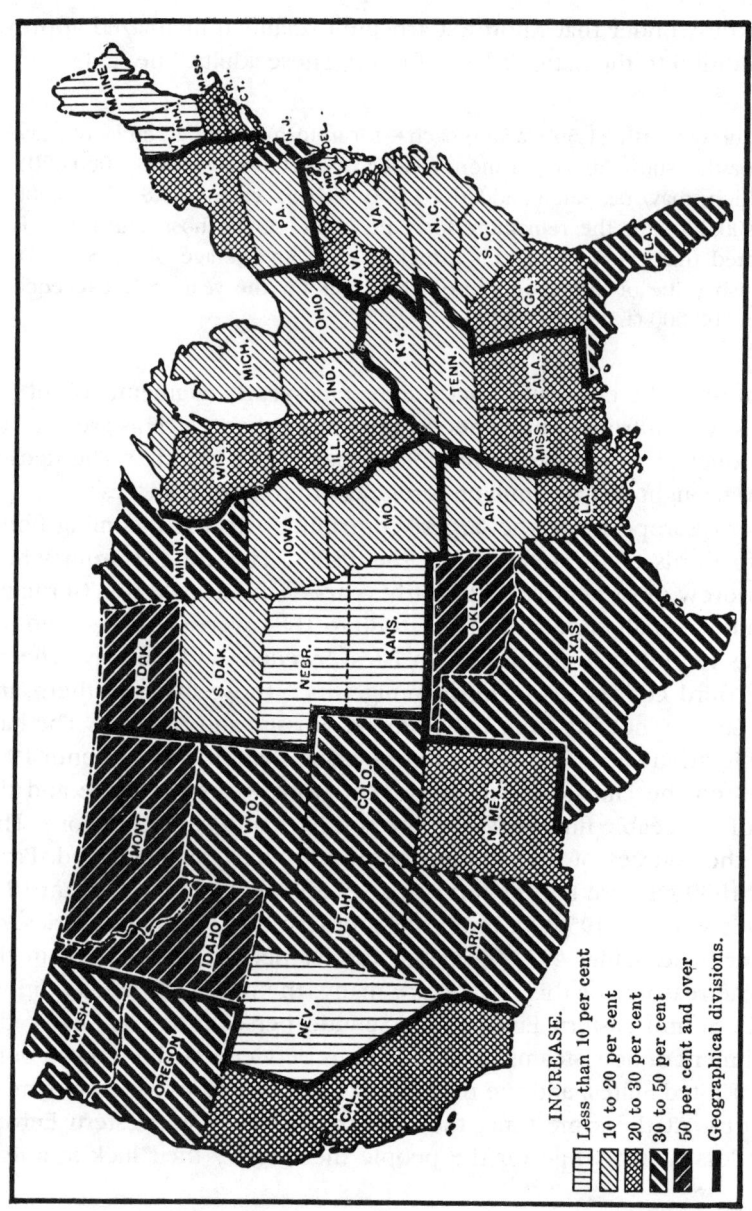

INCREASE.

Less than 10 per cent
10 to 20 per cent
20 to 30 per cent
30 to 50 per cent
50 per cent and over
Geographical divisions.

The Rate of Population Increase at the End of the Nineteenth Century

grant workers used to a lower standard of living. As a result, Congress began, somewhat haltingly, to apply tests of fitness to arriving aliens.[10] The first act of this kind, that of 1882, excluded lunatics, convicted criminals, and persons likely to become public charges. Three years later a law was passed which prohibited employers from importing foreign workers under previous contract. This practice had contributed to the rapid increase of immigration from southern and eastern Europe. Subsequent statutes stiffened the administration of these provisions and added new restraints. As a special act of discrimination against immigrants of the new type, Congress in 1897 passed a bill for excluding aliens between the ages of fourteen and sixty who could not read and write English or some other language. Two days before his official retirement President Cleveland vetoed the measure on the ground that literacy was a test of youthful opportunity, not of mental capacity.[11]

Meanwhile, an immigration problem of a special kind had arisen on the Pacific Coast. The Workingmen's party, headed by Denis Kearney, an Irishman who owned a draying business, stood at the forefront of the agitation. In Sunday afternoon meetings on sand lots near the San Francisco city hall, Kearney delivered fiery harangues against Oriental cheap labor, always closing his address with the exhortation, "The Chinese must go!" So effective was the propaganda that a new state constitution in 1879 forbade corporations to hire Chinese, prohibited their employement on public works, and directed the legislature to impose conditions on their residence.[12]

Though the agitation in its more violent form spent its force with the adoption of the constitution, organized labor kept the issue alive. In the eyes of labor leaders the question had a national bearing because of the employment of the Chinese as strikebreakers in some parts of the East. As the presidential election of 1880 approached, old-party leaders in Congress saw in the issue an opportunity to capture the electoral vote of California. As a result, the Democratic House and the Republican Senate in 1879 joined in passing a bill revoking the Burlingame treaty and restricting Chinese immigration.[13] Though President Hayes approved of the purpose, he could not approve of the method Congress had chosen. He therefore vetoed the measure and sent a mission to China to sound out the Manchu government as to an alteration of the treaty of 1868.

The outcome was the treaty of 1880, which permitted the United States to "regulate, limit, or suspend," but "not absolutely prohibit," future Chinese immigration.[14] Under its terms Congress, two years later, adopted the first Chinese exclusion law, to remain in effect for ten years.[15] Subsequent acts renewed the suspension from time to time, and in 1902, Congress made the prohibition indefinite.[16] Although difficulties of enforcement were experienced, the shrill fears of the "yellow peril" were effectively silenced.

Meanwhile, the dispersion of European immigrants through the country had been proceeding apace. While many of them settled in the industrial centers, others went into the new agricultural regions. There they were joined by countless numbers of disillusioned Eastern farmers, victims of the long depression of the seventies. These native folk came from the Western Reserve of Ohio, from middle and western New York, from New England, Pennsylvania, and elsewhere. Not always did they travel long distances: Missouri men sought the Red River of Minnesota, Kansans went to Colorado at the news of irrigation, people from North Carolina, South Carolina, and Georgia moved over into Florida.

Sometimes it was rocks that had caused their migration: "You pick 'em up one spring and the next there they are agin." Sometimes it was the lure of the lands that did not need clearing: "Nary a tree to grub out and I reckon a body could plow a furrer a mile long and not strike a rock as big as a hen's egg."[17] Sometimes it was incorrigible optimism and love of change and adventure. More frequently, however, it was the saddening conviction that they would never get on where they were. The explanations for their failure they found outside themselves: the "times," the banks, the trusts, the tariff. They would begin over. They did, and often with the same results.

To assist the ready movement of this mass of settlers four transcontinental railways were soon in operation and a fifth was under construction. The first of these, the Union Pacific, had been opened in 1869. In 1881 the Atchison, Topeka & Santa Fe joined the Southern Pacific at Deming, New Mexico, forming a second somewhat irregular route. Two years later it straightened itself out by running its line due west from Santa Fe to California, while the Southern Pacific reached eastward to New Orleans. This gave two roads, roughly 300 miles apart, south of the midcontinental route.[18] Another through line, lying north of the Union Pacific, was the Northern Pacific, opened in 1883. The Great Northern, paralleling the Canadian border, was still in process of building under the direction of James J. Hill.

Equally notable were the attempts to rehabilitate public lands hitherto classified as waste. The area affected comprised the Mountain and Pacific region, aggregating fully two fifths of the entire country, Alaska excluded. The inhabitants of these eleven states and territories numbered 1,751,000 in 1880, nearly half of them in California. The second most populous state was Colorado, and the most thinly settled section was the territory of Wyoming, where there were but 16,500 over ten years of age.

Hitherto the miner and the cattleman had been the principal ones to profit by the resources of this great region. In 1877, Congress had passed a somewhat ambiguously worded act by which tracts of 640 acres of desert land were offered at $1.25 an acre to individuals on condition that irregation be attempted within three years.[19] No one perceived the inadequacies of this legislation and the need for constructive action more clearly than

John Wesley Powell, head of the federal geological survey of the Rocky Mountain region, who, in 1878, submitted an official report on the possibilities of developing the arid public lands.[20] Already famed for his exploration of the Colorado River and his thrilling descent of the Grand Canyon, Major Powell was a man who spoke with authority. He pointed out that the so-called desert country contained a goodly percentage of public lands which could be made arable by appropriate treatment. Too much attention, he said, had heretofore been paid to the chemical constituents of soils, too little to those physical conditions by which moisture and air are supplied to the roots of the growing plants. He insisted that nearly all soils are suitable for agriculture when properly supplied with water.

Unfortunately, Powell's recommendations won no immediate response from Congress, but it did encourage a veritable irrigation boom in the arid region during the eighties. Companies were formed to take up land, irrigate it, and invite settlement. The country was flooded with agents offering securities in this or that scheme. The rosiest possibilities were presented: sure wealth for investors, quick prosperity for settlers. There were no warnings that time, money, and courage were needed; that the best of the projects were freighted with difficulties, many of them incalculable. In response to the offerings, not only were large amounts of stock sold, but throngs of people were soon finding their way across the plains—sometimes hundreds of miles from a railroad—to land which they expected at once to see blossoming like a rose.

These cooperative undertakings, as they were misleadingly called, quickly showed the same weaknesses as stock companies in many other economic fields of the time. Just as in oil, coal, ore, and certain manufacturing industries, the promoters often had little knowledge of how to put their undertakings on a solid basis and frequently little desire to do anything more than to reap profits from stock sales. And just as in other undertakings, many rushed in not as bona-fide farmers but as speculators, eager to make a quick turnover. Every unsound and dishonest exhibit in the use of capital, common in the country, manifested itself in these irrigation schemes.[21] Weld County, Colorado, where the success of the Greeley colony naturally attracted capital, soon became threaded with more canals than the water supply could take care of. Grave disturbances, intense bitterness of feeling, and large losses of crops resulted.

Wyoming dealt more successfully with the problem. Her law of 1890, founded on the experience of other commonwealths, was generally considered the best and most practical of those that had been adopted so far. It recognized what virtually no state up to this time had recognized: that the first step in any sound irrigation scheme is to know how much water is available for a given territory. It further took into account what was called the "duty of water," that is, how much land, say, an inch of water could be expected to irrigate.[22] The statute required that it be decided who had a right to water and provided agents to see that the proper persons were served. Every settler had a paper showing the order of his priority, just how much he was to receive, and the number of acres on which the water was to be used.

Meanwhile, in 1888, the federal government had begun a series of surveys of the arid region. The purpose was to measure the flow of streams, big and small, and to estimate the volume of water that could be depended upon over a given period. The work was in the charge of Frederick Haynes Newell, a graduate of the Massachusetts Institute of Technology, who had had large field experience in the Southwest under Major Powell's direction and who had just been appointed assistant hydraulic engineer of the U.S. Geological Survey. Under Newell's direction the investigation went on for a number of years, winning for him the title of the "Father of Irrigation." His first and most important report, that of 1894, embodied all the experience of the settlers, favorable and unfavorable. It showed that, if there had been exploitation and injustice, there had also been an accumulation of important practical knowledge. It also showed that, whatever the failures and difficulties, there had been a good deal of real achievement. The number of bona-fide irrigators by 1890 had increased to 52,584, and the number of irrigated acres from less than one million in 1880 to over three and a half.

The great achievement of this twenty-year period was that it taught the thoughtful and intelligent among legislators, developers, and settlers what was necessary to establish and conduct irrigation projects. This knowledge had come mainly from two sources. One was the successful demonstration made by men, singly or in groups, who had redeemed a few desert acres by continuous effort. The other was the scientific work done under the direction of such men as Powell and Newell. It was this work which gradually convinced Congress that, if any great stretches of the arid region were to be redeemed by irrigation, larger undertakings than those possible through cooperative labor or private capital were necessary. It was gradually becoming clear to those who were studying the problem that the federal government itself must go into the business of irrigation.

The degree of success resulting from these varied efforts to people the sparsely settled parts of the country was in part reflected in a growth of the total population of the United States from 50 million in 1880 to 76 million at the century's close. The Great West became organized into self-governing commonwealths. Washington, Montana, and the Dakotas entered the Union in 1889; Idaho and Wyoming in 1890; and Utah, her case prejudiced by the Mormon practice of polygamy, finally in 1896.[23] With the system of states extending in an almost solid array from sea to sea, with railroads and other means of communication binding them together, with a vast population undivided by tariff walls or other political barriers to the free exchange of goods, the stage was set for a gigantic industrial development such as the United States had never before known.

THE FARMERS ORGANIZE

THE DRIVE to people unsettled land, particularly in the region west of the Mississippi, resulted during the eighties in enlarging the number of farms in the United States from 4,008,907 to 4,564,641.[24] The average farm increased in size from 133.7 acres in 1880 to 136.5 in 1890. More important was the 4 percent gain in the amount of improved land. The contribution of the farmer to the national wealth grew by some $4 billion. In numbers, the farmers far exceeded any one of the four classes into which the census of 1880 divided the country's wealth producers. Out of 17,392,099 engaged in "gainful and reputable occupations," 7,670,493 were in agriculture. This was almost exactly twice as many as in manufacturing and mining and over four times as many as in trade and transportation.[25] The value of what these farmers sold, consumed, and had on hand was estimated at nearly $2.25 billion.[26]

Not only did agriculture provide the food supply of the nation and, to an increasing extent, of Europe, but it formed the basis of some of the country's biggest industries. Thus, in 1880, the flour and grist-mill industry stood first in the United States with a total value of over $505 million, and meat packing and slaughtering ranked second with an output of more than $303.5 million. The milling industry was the outcome of the efforts of a few manufacturers in and near Minneapolis to make a better grade of flour with less waste of grain than had been possible by the old-fashioned method of grinding between an upper and nether millstone. The first step had been taken in 1870 with the invention of the middlings purifier, a machine for removing the thick coat between the bran covering of the wheat kernel and the stock centers.[27]

But the real revolution came with the introduction of a machine for breaking the grain by rollers. The inventor of the process was John Stevens, son of a Welshman who had brought his family to Neenah, Wisconsin, in 1854. At the age of fifteen the boy had gone to work in a flour mill and from the first he had taken an intelligent and critical interest in what was going on about him. Later he was able to buy a share in the mill and became its manager. Having seen a fellow miller getting more efficient results through using rough instead of smooth stones, he began experimenting, keeping his conclusions to himself until, in 1880, he produced a machine in which a roller of corrugated chilled iron broke the grain. Attached to it was a valuable device for feeding in the wheat. With this machine Stevens could get 500 barrels of flour where his competitors at best got 200. Moreover, he was able to produce a much higher proportion of "good" flour than they did.

A new industry built on a product of the farm was glucose. Started in the 1870s, it had developed so rapidly that by 1881 there were nineteen factories in New York, Ohio, Illinois, Michigan, Iowa, and Missouri with an estimated capital of $2 million. Together they consumed about 35,000 bushels of corn a day and between 11 and 12 million a year, and they employed 2,100 persons.[28] By 1884 it was estimated that the yearly manufacture and sale of glucose amounted to about ten pounds per capita. It was used chiefly in the making of table syrups, strained honey, confectionery and the cheaper grades of sugar, also as food for bees and in the manufacture of condensed milk and mucilage. With continued expansion the glucose trust was formed in 1897 under the name of the Glucose Sugar Refining Company, including all the plants but one in the country, at a capitalization of over $40 million. According to the testimony of H. O. Havemeyer, head of the sugar trust, before the U.S. Industrial Commission, "the sirup made from glucose has virtually knocked out the consumption of refined molasses in this country."[29]

In the extraordinary increase of the national wealth the farmer felt that he was not getting his share, that too large a percentage went to the agencies which had been built up to serve him: the railroads, the banks, the marketing agencies, the industries based on his raw products. All this economic machinery bewildered and antagonized him. By habit and conviction he was deeply individualistic. He believed that the most satisfactory material results, as well as the finest individual development, came from self-reliance. Yet he saw himself growing more and more dependent upon an economic order which was yielding to a form of irresponsible collectivism. Moreover, he resented the increasing predominance of the cities whence the masters of capital and Big Business directed the course of economic conquest, frequently to his disadvantage, and where the people enjoyed social and intellectual advantages denied to himself and his children.

At one time, the cycle of growing, harvesting, and distributing his crop had been largely in the farmer's own hands. He understood its problems — bad years, inefficient labor, wayward sons — and he had learned in a practical way to deal with them. He had hauled his produce to town where in the open market he traded it in and returned home with the fruit of his labor in calico, sugar, seeds, and new implements. It was an intimate, personal process which gave him a sense of adequacy and control. Now all this was over. His market was made elsewhere and with its making he had nothing to do. His prices rose and fell according to the operations of those whom he considered gamblers. By what right did James R. Keene and his associates attempt a corner in wheat in Chicago? Though it failed with great loss to the manipulators, why should they be allowed to juggle what he had produced? How did the farmer benefit when Armour & Company in the same year, 1880, cornered his pork, controlling the supply for months to reap huge profits in the fall?[30]

For a similar reason he distrusted the railroads. During rate wars they carried his produce at a loss to themselves, but when they effected an agreement, it usually entailed a loss to him. Moreover, the instablity of rates was unsettling to the marketing of his crops. He was coming to look on the railroad as his enemy, not as the friend he had expected it to be in the days when the government aided it with huge grants of land, presumably for his benefit. Particularly did he fear the steady consolidation of the roads into systems by which one man or group of men controlled the transportation and trade of a great area.

Only less was the farmer disturbed by the newly formed industrial combinations which handled many of the necessaries of his life. He saw with anxiety that the process of consolidation was beginning to touch the small neighborhood crafts on which he had depended. The grist mill was being put out of business by the great milling centers. The number of carpenter shops, of cooper shops, of blacksmith shops, decreased before his eyes.[31] At the same time, he saw the number of middlemen multiply. On them he blamed, in part, the high prices he was obliged to pay for the manufactured articles which he and his family needed. In all this the farmer sensed a concentration of the growing wealth of the community in fewer and fewer hands, and he feared power in wealth even as he feared it in government.

The growing restlessness of farm dwellers deeply troubled him: the ease with which his neighbors sold out, moved west or south, went into new deals and new places, gave up the land for the factory, the country for the town. Something was wrong when a whole countryside was abandoned, as sometimes happened, and rural communities were left to fall apart. The waste involved in the breaking up of traditional ways, the change, the instability of men, disturbed the thoughtful. They had been reared to what Horace Bushnell called

> a closely girded habit of economy. Harnessed all together into the producing process, young and old, male and female, from the boy that rode the plow-horse to the grandmother knitting under her spectacles, they had no conception of squandering lightly what they all had been at work, thread by thread and grain by grain, to produce.[32]

Yet such conditions were the inevitable outcome of the economic burdens which every year bore more heavily on the farmer's shoulders.[33] Because of the enormous expansion of Western agriculture and of stiffer competition in the world's markets with the grain-growing regions of Russia, Australia, and the Argentine, farm prices fell disastrously during the eighties. Much the same thing held true of Southern cotton, which had now to compete with cotton raised in India and elsewhere. Corn, which commanded sixty-three cents a bushel in 1881, sold for twenty-eight in 1890. Wheat averaged but seventy-three cents a bushel from 1883 to 1889. Cotton fell from fifteen cents in the period 1870–73 to about eight in 1886–89. Overproduction as an explanation of the farmer's ills was cold comfort.

He could not very well adjust his production to market needs as could the Standard Oil Company or the cordage trust. On the contrary, he urged that no real overproduction existed when low prices caused farmers to burn corn for fuel while at the same time thousands of people elsewhere were facing hunger and even starvation.

To carry on his business, the farmer found it increasingly difficult to obtain money at what seemed to him reasonable rates of interest. Obliged to borrow in the spring to put in his crop, he claimed that short-term credits cost him more than they did other wealth producers such as the railroads and industries. If he had not been heavily mortgaged, the cost of money while he was growing his cotton or corn or wheat would have been less of a burden, but in certain states the weight of debt was mounting alarmingly. By 1890 the majority (64.4 percent) of Kansas farms were mortgaged up to 38 percent of their value, and thier owners were sweating under interest rates averaging 8.1 percent. It is not remarkable that a large increase in tenant farmers occurred. Though no other state was quite so deeply in debt as Kansas, there were several where the situation was threatening. In Minnesota, 46.4 percent of the farmers carried mortgages at 8.2 percent; in Iowa, 53.8 percent of the farmers paid an average interest charge of 7.3 percent.

The *New York Evening Post* ascribed the Western predicament to "a credit system which enables farmers to borrow heavily where tradesmen in like circumstances cannot. Such borrowers take the chances. . . . "[34] Yet conditions not unlike these also existed in certain parts of the East. Vermont, Massachusetts, and New Jersey farmers carried almost as many mortgages as those in the Western states named, but at a lower interest charge, under 6 percent. A similar situation prevailed in the cotton-growing South, where the crop-lien system constituted the chief mortgage evil. In the words of a song widely sung by distressed Southern farmers,

> My husband came from town last night
>   As sad a man could be,
> His wagon empty, cotton gone,
>   And not a dime had he.
>
> Huzzah—Huzzah
>   'Tis queer I do declare:
> We make the clothes for all the world,
>   But few we have to wear.

Gradually the farmer was driven to the conclusion that it was necessary for him to take things into his own hands and seek to regain control of the essential factors in his problem. To do this he must employ the principle that the railroads and industries were using to such good effect: national consolidation. By 1878 the Grange was beginning to be replaced in many sections by more radical ogranizations known as alliances. The first of these had been formed in 1875 in Lampasas County, Texas, originally for the purpose of protecting farmers against the depredations of horse and cattle thieves. Similar alliances later started in other parts of the state, and in 1880 these groups coalesced and were chartered under the name of the Texas Farmers' State Alliance. Spreading rapidly over the state, it united in 1887 with the Farmers' Union of Louisiana to form the National Farmers' Alliance and Cooperative Union of America. Into this new body soon came alliances which had been forming in ten or more other states of the South and Southwest.[35]

In 1889 a merger was effected with the Agricultural Wheel and the name changed to Farmers' and Laborers' Union of America, though popularly the organization was known as the Southern Alliance. Begun in 1882 by W. W. Tedford, a farmer and schoolteacher, the Agricultural Wheel had increased rapidly in membership, and in 1886 had launched the National Agricultural Wheel.[36] The constitution of the merger was general and theoretical with no more specific a demand than "equal rights to all and special favors to none," no more direct pledge than to "suppress personal, local, sectional, and national prejudices, all unhealthy rivalry and all selfish ambition" — in which pledge no doubt it was expressing its opinion as to what had made earlier efforts of the alliances no more successful than they had been.[37] The leaders, however, had pretty definite notions of what needed to be done to improve farm conditions.

Meanwhile, in the Northwest, there had developed a similar movement. The National Farmers' Alliance, or Northern Alliance as it was generally called, began with a local organization formed in Chicago in April 1880 by Milton George, editor of the *Western Rural,* an aggressive farm journal.[38] By October the movement had so spread that it was possible to hold a convention in Chicago to which 500 representatives came from various local alliances, farmers' clubs, and granges. The gathering drafted a constitution declaring that its object was to unite the farmers of the United States against "class legislation, and the encroachments of concentrated capital and the tyranny of monopoly; . . . to oppose, in our respective political parties, the election of any candidate to office, State or national, who is not thoroughly in sympathy with the farmers' interests. . . ."[39] Though growing sporadically for a few years, the alliance profited greatly from the agricultural depression of the late eighties and became a power to be reckoned with throughout the whole Northwest.

From the beginning the state alliances accepted cooperation as the one practical method of escaping the middleman whom they charged with taking an unfair percentage of their profits and overcharging for commodities sold over the counter. The Texas Alliance first tried a plan called the contract store. A committee of trusted members in each county made a

contract with a chosen merchant by which he agreed to sell at a discount
to alliance members on condition that they would buy only from him.[40]
The result, in most cases, was price-cutting warfare against the contract
store by those merchants of a community who had build up a farmer trade
largely by means of direct barter coupled with credit and cash advances.
The merchants felt it a violation of an established relation. The consequence
too often was that the farmers, tempted by lower prices, deserted the
contract store.

In 1886, after a year's trial, the plan was abandoned, and the Texas
Alliance advised the farmers within each county to eliminate the middlemen by cooperating in the sale of their products. Growers were to turn
over to alliance cotton yards their entire crop, and sale days were fixed
when it was expected city buyers would compete with one another and
bid up the price. But the buyers did not like the new attempt at cooperation
any better than the merchants had the contract store. So few of them
attended on sale days that at the end of the season large stores of cotton
remained on hand.[41]

This unanticipated outcome proved less discouraging than it might otherwise have been because by this time the Texas Alliance had a new idea,
that of selling cotton direct to the mills. This notion had originated with
C. W. Macune, chairman of the executive committee of the state alliance.
A reflective, self-educated man, he had seen enough of conditions as a farm
laborer in the Far and Middle West to persuade him that the only hope for
profitable farming lay in cooperation. Macune now went to New England
and, after discussing the scheme with mill owners in Fall River and Boston,
he returned convinced that his plan was sound, but that in order to succeed
it must be carried out on a large scale. He proposed an organization called
the Farmers' Alliance Exchange of Texas with a capital of $500,000, to be
paid in installments. With this money the buildings and equipment necessary for the enterprise were to be provided, together with supplies sufficient to carry the farmer until his crop was ready to be sold.

The cotton merchants who had been accustomed to advancing money
to growers, taking more mortgages on the crop, did not abandon business
because of the proposed Alliance Exchange. In fact, they made so many
contracts with their old customers that it was crippled from the start. The
first installment of the $500,000 amounted to but $56,000 in cash and
$40,000 in notes. It was not enough properly to finance the plan, and
although Macune did his best to rally the farmers and to convince the banks
that the future of the Alliance Exchange provided adequate security, he
was unable to obtain the loans he needed. The exchange opened its doors
in September 1887; within twenty months it had gone to pieces. Like
the earlier cooperative undertakings, it failed because it lacked proper
preparation and a sound financial foundation, and did too much business
on a credit basis.[42] In the opinion of W. S. Morgan, of the Agricultural

Wheel, the farmers needed further education in cooperation before the movement could succeed.[43]

The cooperative efforts of other state alliances were very like those of Texas, and when they failed, it was usually for the same reasons. The "Macune business system" spread until in 1890 it had been introduced into eighteen states. Not all these attempts were as short-lived as the parent exchange. That in Georgia operated successfully until 1893.[44]

The disappointing results of cooperation turned the thoughts of the organized farmers more and more to political measures as a means of securing relief. A long period of drought, beginning in 1887, and attended by infestations of chinch bugs, brought fresh despair to the farming population and prepared the way for more decisive action.[45] In 1889, representatives of the Northern and Southern alliances met for the purpose of uniting.[46] For a number of reasons, however, the plan came to naught. The Southern Alliance was secret and wanted to remain so; the Northern was open to all. The Southern Alliance wanted a complete merger, the Northern a federation. There was, besides, a difference of opinion as yet as to the extent of political activity that was wise. A surviving sectional antagonism also contributed to a lack of complete understanding. Nevertheless, the gathering made the leaders better acquainted with one another and emphasized the common goals which the two groups were aiming to achieve.

The pressure for political participation grew constantly stronger. Thus, in April 1890, the U.S. Supreme Court in the Minnesota Rate case decided that state commissions and state legislatures had no unrestricted right to fix rates even for railroads within state borders, for the final determination as to the reasonableness of charges lay with the courts.[47] The decision came while the executive committee of the Minnesota Alliance was in session. It meant "the subjection of the people and the states to the unlimited control of the railroad corporations of this country," declared the committee, and a resolution was adopted to the effect that the alliance would "appeal from this second Dred Scott decision to the people of the nation . . . with a request that they unite with us in an effort to so amend the constitution as to abolish this new slavery."[48]

By the end of the year the Southern Alliance had promulgated a list of measures which it proposed to demand of the existing parties. This program included the free and unlimited coinage of silver, an increase of circulating medium to not less than $50 a person, abolition of the national banks, the establishment of subtreasuries for granting easier credit to farmers and others, legislation against stock-market speculation, a graduated income tax, stricter regulation of railroads or government ownership, and the popular election of U.S. senators.[49] These demands were, in the main, agreed to by all other agrarian groups, including the Grange, the Northern Alliance, and the Colored Alliance.[50]

The farmers' grievances were genuine even if the manner of statement was exaggerated and violent, often to the point of absurdity. It was a fact that the machinery of the economic order favored industry, finance, and the railroads at the expense of agriculture. The government alone had the power to restore a just balance; therefore the farmers felt they must control the government. Resistance to their demands by the old parties showed that this could be done only by forming a new party. When a call was issued to the leading farmers' organizations, the Union and Confederate soldiers, and the Knights of Labor to attend a conference at Cincinnati in 1891, 1,400 delegates appeared.[51]

This body organized the People's party and, in the next year, held a mammoth convention at Omaha to select a presidential ticket. The convention turned to James B. Weaver, an Iowa lawyer who had fought in the Civil War. Originally a Republican, Weaver had been an early leader of the Prohibitionists, and in 1877 had joined the Greenback party, serving as its representative in Congress for several terms.[52] In 1880 he had been its presidential candidate. His change to Populism was natural, for the new movement included most of the old Greenbackers. For second place on the ticket the convention chose James G. Field of Virginia.

The platform, written in part by Ignatius Donnelly, contained a flaming denunciation of the abuses of capitalism:

> The fruits of the toil of millions are boldly stolen to build up colossal fortunes for a few, unprecedented in the history of mankind; and the possessors of these, in turn, despise the republic and endanger liberty. From the same prolific womb of governmental injustice we breed the two great classes of tramps and millionaires.[53]

As cures for this condition the party offered free silver; the subtreasury plan of the Farmers' Alliance; a graduated income tax; government ownership of railways, telegraphs, and telephones; restriction of "undesirable" immigration; a shorter workday for urban wage-earners; and the popular election of senators.

The extent to which the Populists frightened the Republicans and Democrats can be seen from statements included in their platforms.[54] On the money question the Democrats declared: "We hold to the use of both gold and silver as the standard money of the country. . . . We insist upon this policy as especially necessary for the protection of the farmers and laboring classes. . . ." In a similar spirit the Republicans asserted: "The American people, from tradition and interest, favor bimetallism, and the Republican party demands the use of both gold and silver as standard money. . . ." Both parties eagerly claimed for themselves the role of champion of the oppressed, opposed unrestricted immigration, and pledged their earnest efforts against the exactions of trusts and combinations. Their main interest, however, was the tariff question, which they represented as

The Leaky Connection

involving the vital interests of the masses. The nomination of the protectionist Benjamin Harrison by the Republicans and of the "free trader" Grover Cleveland by the Democrats made this the paramount issue in the campaign.

The outcome of the election demonstrated impressively the extent of the agrarian unrest. The Populists polled over a million popular votes. Moreover, for the first time since 1860, a third party secured electoral votes —22 out of a total of 444.[55] In addition it elected five U.S. senators, ten congressmen, fifty state officials, and 1,500 county officials and members of the state legislature. Small wonder that Weaver was happy over the result. "Unaided by money," he wrote, "our grand young party has made an enviable record and achieved surprising success at the polls."[56] But the old-party leaders anxiously asked themselves: What of the future?

THE NATIONAL CONSOLIDATION OF LABOR

PARALLEL WITH THE GROWTH of agrarian organizations went a rapid consolidation of labor. In 1878 the most powerful labor body was that known as the Noble Order of Knights of Labor. The significant feature of the organization, that which distinguished it from the trade unions, was the miscellaneous character of its membership. It admitted anybody who worked without regard to occupation, color, nationality, or religion. By 1878 its "local assemblies" had become so widespread and so vigorous that a convention of delegates met at Reading, Pennsylvania, to effect a central national organization of the Knights.

The dominating figure in the gathering was the then mayor of Scranton, Terence V. Powderly. The labor life of Powderly was typical of the day. Born of Irish parentage in 1849 at Carbondale, one of twelve children, he had gone to work at the age of thirteen as a switch tender. Later he learned the trade of a machinist. While working in the railway shops at Scranton, he became a prominent member of the strong Machinists' and Blacksmiths' Union, a connection which cost him his job in 1873 and put him on the employers' blacklist. Leaving Scranton, he worked in various places in Ohio and western Pennsylvania and finally returned to Scranton. Everywhere he went he identified himself with labor interests, with the result that he was soon marked as a nuisance and dismissed. In turn, he was active in the Machinists' and Blacksmiths' Union, the Indistrial Brotherhood of the United States, and the Greenback-Labor party. It was as a candidate of the last orgainization that he was elected mayor of Scranton in 1878.[57]

The keynote of the constitution which the convention adopted was a quotation from Edmund Burke: "When bad men combine, the good must associate, else they will fall, one by one, an unpitied sacrifice in a contemptible struggle." A highly centralized organization was provided for, and a list of fifteen demands drawn up. These were later added to until in 1895 they numbered twenty-three. They give a broad view of the labor aspirations of the period. The aims of the Knights were asserted to be

I. To make individual and moral worth, not wealth, the true standard of individual and national greatness.

II. To secure to the workers the free enjoyment of the wealth they create; sufficient leisure in which to develop their intellectual, moral and social faculties; all of the benefits, recreations and pleasures of association; in a word, to enable them to share in the gains and honor of advancing civilization.

As specific measures, the Knights pledged themselves to the "establishment of cooperative institutions productive and distributive" and the substitution of arbitration for strikes whenever possible, and demanded the creation of bureaus of labor statistics, the abolition of all laws bearing unequally upon capital and labor, the prohibition of child labor, equal pay for the two sexes, a graduated tax on incomes and inheritances, and other provisions of like import.[58]

As soon as the consolidation of the Knights had been achieved, Powderly, as Grand Master Workman, threw himself energetically into building up the order. On a meager salary, paying his own traveling expenses, he gave all his time to strengthening and enlarging the sprawling and idealistic undertaking. The order grew rapidly in membership. From about 28,000 in 1880 it numbered nearly 52,000 in 1883 and approximately 104,000 in 1885.[59]

To Powderly, cooperation promised the greatest hope for the organized worker. It was, in his opinion, destined to be "the lever of labor's emancipation," a means which would eventually "make every man his own master, every man his own employer."[60] In 1883, at his urging, the national organization bought a coal mine at Cannelburg, Indiana, in order to sell coal at reduced prices to the members. A more common plan was for local assemblies, or groups of members subsidized by their assembly, to establish cooperative workshops and, to a less extent, stores. Most of these undertakings were run by the stockholders, though, in some instances, the assemblies managed them. A notable example of the latter arrangement was the Solidarity Cooperative Association, set up and conducted by District Assembly 49, New York. The committee in charge, investing the money as it saw fit, financed a cigar factory, a leather shop, a printing shop, a watch-case factory, a building association, and a plumbing shop as well as certain other enterprises.[61]

The movement reached its peak in 1886, though it had not wholly spent itself by the close of 1887. At least 135 cooperative ventures were set going, the largest number in mining, cooperage, and shoe manufacturing —industries in which starvation wages prevailed.[62] Most of these enterprises were conducted on a small scale. As a "lever of labor's emancipation" cooperation never materialized, but as a means of enabling some ambitious and energetic wage-earners to become independent, it proved fairly successful. Too often, however, the success assumed a form harmful to the very cause which copperation was intended to serve, for the well-managed undertakings sooner or later became joint-stock companies.

The causes which brought disaster to most of the cooperative undertakings were the same as those which ruined the farmers' similar enterprises: inefficient management, internal squabbling, inadequate capital, and discriminations instigated by competitors.[63] The coal mine at Cannelburg, the order's sole experiment of a centralized kind, met the common fate. After $20,000 had been spent on improving the property and $1,000 worth of coal had been dug, the mine was obliged to lie idle for nine months until the railroad company saw fit to connect it with the main track. Other obstacles quite as unexpected appeared. The available funds being exhausted, the order succumbed to the pressure and sold out. Only three or four years after it had begun, the Knights' adventure in cooperation came to an ignominious end.

In its political program the order was somewhat more successful. Powderly was instrumental in securing the establishment of labor bureaus in a number of states and also in inducing Congress to pass the law forbidding the importation of labor under contract.[64] The Knights had at first been reluctant to oppose unrestricted immigration, but presently they changed their minds. Was it fair, they asked, that articles made abroad should be imported only by paying a duty while a foreign workman came in free? If the employers were to be protected, why not the wage-earners? Drafting their own bill on the subject, the Knights had it introduced into Congress. The House passed it in June 1884, and the Senate in February of the following year.[65]

The hard times, beginning with the Panic of 1884, produced great labor unrest. Fresh recruits swelled the ranks of the Knights of Labor until the membership in 1886 reached 700,000.[66] The rapid expansion brought into the order many men impatient of the conservative methods which Powderly stood for. Their demands for immediate action forced the leadership increasingly to countenance the use of the weapons of industrial warfare: the boycott and the strike. During 1885 the boycott reached equidemic proportions, affecting all parts of the country. No less than 196 were conducted, nearly seven times as many as in 1884.[67] A notable instance was the boycott against the Dueber Watch Case Company. The company had discharged all its employees who were connected with the Knights and refused to discuss the matter with any representatives of the order. Thereupon the order's official organ, the *Journal of United Labor,* instructed the members not to buy watches with Dueber cases or patronize jewelry stores which sold them. The pressure proved effective, and the company soon reversed its former position.

Strikes occurred with increasing violence and frequency. The most extended series in which the Knights were directly involved took place on the Gould railway system. The first began in March 1885, when some 4,000 workmen of the Missouri Pacific in the states of Missouri, Texas, and Kansas struck for a restoration of wages which had been cut without warning. The walkout was short-lived, being ended by the efforts of the governors of Kansas and Missouri. The shopmen received more than they had asked for: not only was the former wage scale restored, but one-and-a-half pay for overtime was granted. The company further agreed not to change rates thereafter without thirty days' notice. This settlement was due largely to the sympathy of the public. Reducing wages at a time when there was believed to be no decline in the company's earnings outraged the Southwest. The rail officials, quickly realizing this, had the good sense to yield.[68] Six months later a second strike, caused by discrimination against workers belonging to the Knights of Labor, ended triumphantly for the men.[69]

The third and greatest of the disorders resulted in their utter rout.[70] It began in March 1886, when a foreman, a prominent Knight, was laid off without notice in the car shops of the Texas & Pacific at Marshall, Texas, for alleged incompetence. This action, the strikers claimed, violated the settlement of the preceding year. The federal commissioner of labor, discussing the strike in his third annual report, held that this claim was not well founded since the agreement referred to dealt only with wage rates. Moreover the Texas & Pacific was now no longer in the Gould system, but in the hands of receivers who were free to run the road according to their best judgment. Martin Irons, who directed the walkout, saw in the receivership merely a legal device revealing Gould's grim determination to destroy the power of the Knights at any cost. In a manifesto he declared this view and added that the strike was designed to defeat "these contemptible and blood-sucking corporations and their governmental allies. . . ."[71]

Irons called on the shopmen of the entire Gould system to quit work, and some 9,000 obeyed. The disturbance affected more than 5,000 miles of railway in Missouri, Kansas, Nebraska, Arkansas, and Indian Territory. The men not only quit work, they undertook to stop all freight traffic on the roads. They invaded yards and shops and, when attempts were made to take out a train, promptly "killed" the engine by removing some indispensable part. Within two weeks practically all the locomotives at every strike center were dead, and no freight moved over the vast territory affected. Passenger trains carrying mail, however, were not molested, the strikers apparently fearing to provoke federal interference. In the opinion of an acute observer, "The strike was a stuggle for power. The Knights . . . thought that they were irresistible. They had 'downed Jay Gould' once, and they were going to do it again. In order to win their victory, they were determiend to choke the railroad company, and, if need were, the community also."[72]

For a time hatred of Jay Gould was sufficient to ensure popular sympathy for the fighters regardless of the merits of the case. But when business came to a standstill for lack of supplies, factories closed for want of coal, houses were cold, and tables short of eggs and butter, the public began to demand that order be restored. Once again the governors of Missouri and Kansas sought to settle the trouble, but the Knights, calling their offers interference, declined to negotiate. Thereupon the governors of four states ordered the companies to run their trains and forbade all persons to interfere. Attempts to intimidate crews and cripple rolling stock ensued, but the people along the lines, now thoroughly aroused, transferred their sympathy from the strikers to the railroad. On March 28 the strike was temporarily halted by Grand Master Powderly, who wished to submit the dispute to arbitration, but no agreement could be reached with Gould. Early in April hostilities resumed with a bitterness and a violence far greater than before. But the men never regained the old backing of the public, and in May surrendered unconditionally.

Side by side with the Knights, a second great national labor body had been forging to the front, an organization which from its birth in 1881 had been the chief competitor of the Knights. Known originally as the Federation of Organized Trades and Labor Unions of the United States of America and Canada, the body changed its name in 1886 to the American Federation of Labor. Conflict between the two groups was inevitable. The American Federation of Labor, believing that only the members of a given craft or trade could properly protect and develop its interests, guaranteed the autonomy of each trade union belonging to the Federation, its activities being directed only toward improving the condition of those unions which joined. The Knights of Labor, on the other hand, were organized on the principle of "one big union," and were usually hostile to trade unions, holding that they sacrificed the general interests of labor to the selfish principles of temporary advantage.[73] Basically the conflict was one between the practical and the idealistic, the hard-headed common sense of Samuel Gompers, the American Federation's foremost leader, and the all-embracing humanitarianism of Terence V. Powderly.

The new organization was at first set on achievement through legislation. Its chief objectives were compulsory education laws, the prohibition of child labor, sanitary and safety regulations for factories, uniform apprentice laws, a national eight-hour law, the prohibition of contract convict labor and of the truck system of wage payment, the repeal of conspiracy laws, a national bureau of labor statistics, and the protection of American industry against cheap foreign labor.[74] After a few years, however, it subordinated its legislative program to economic action, regarding the strike as the wage-earner's chief weapon and the trade agreement, by which collective bargaining was to be accepted, as the ultimate goal of unionism.

In 1884 the Federation called upon its affiliated bodies to direct their energies toward the establishment of an eight-hour day by May 1, 1886.[75] The long day was one of the oldest grievances of American labor. The first call for eight hours seems to have been in Maine where a slogan, "Eight hours for work, eight hours for sleep, and eight hours for God and the brethren," was sounded as early as 1844; but it had come to nothing.[76] Though some states took favorable action, the laws always left loopholes by which employers could escape their obligations. Nevertheless conditions in the course of half a century had in some respects improved. Thus, in 1830, four out of five wage-earners had worked more than ten hours a day; in 1880 only about one in four.[77] The eight-hour day, however, was virtually nonexistent.

The Federation had allowed two years in which to educate the public as to the need of the shorter day. Reluctant employers it expected to whip into line through the strike. Its most important ally should have been the Knights of Labor, but after considerable hesitation Powderly refused to cooperate. He was reluctant to resort to the strike until all other means were exhausted; besides, he did not think that the people most concerned were sufficiently educated. It may be, too, that he saw more clearly than Gompers that most industries of that day were too badly managed to stand a change to shorter hours. Gompers himself wrote thirty-nine years later that in 1886 there were "hardly twelve industries in the United States sufficiently organized to establish an eight-hour day," but that he considered the campaign valuable as an "educational influence."[78]

The approach to employers was carefully planned, conferences were sought, and many employers promised to cooperate. While most of them were doubtless actuated by fear of the consequences of refusal, others, more enlightened, believed that a shorter day would make the workers more productive.[79] Labor was so convinced of this that it had a slogan:

> Whether you work by the hour or work by the day,
> Decreasing the hours increases the pay.

The main argument for the reform, however, was to provide work for the jobless, of whom a million were to be found in the nation. Apart from the direct benefits so accruing, it was urged that the employment of this great number "would necessarily increase the number of consumers, and thereby enlarge the market for commodities to that extent."[80] While the intelligence of the country generally supported the cause, there were also violent critics—newspapers like the *Illinois State Register,* which declared the eight-hour movement a "consummate pice of humbuggery . . . too silly to merit the attention of a body of lunatics. . . ."[81]

Preparation for the general strike was left largely in the hands of the local labor organizations. Workmen throughout the country were urged to lay aside a certain sum of money each week, invest it in the necessities of life before May 1, 1886, and thus be in a position to defy defeat. By this time the goal of the movement had changed to a demand for shorter hours, not necessarily an eight-hour day. When May 1 arrived, 150,000 secured a reduced workday (eight or nine hours) without striking, and 190,000 struck, of whom only 42,000 were successful.[82] The advantage of many of these gains, however, was lessened by the practice of employers of paying smaller wages for fewer hours. Moreover, *Bradstreet's,* June 12, six weeks after the strike, reported a withdrawal of one third of the concessions, with a prospect of more to come. This result was in part due to the public hostility to labor excited by the Haymarket riot in Chicago.[83]

Chicago, with 80,000 wage-earners participating in the strike, had been the storm center of the eight-hour movment. There the tension between capital and labor was rapidly reaching the breaking point. Not only were aggressive employers determined to break the growing power of the unions, but the labor movement in Chicago was shot through with all kinds of European radicalism. In hysterical rhetoric the *Illinois State Register* described one labor demonstration as consisting of "Communistic Germans, Bohemians and Poles, representing the lumber-yards, coopers, bakers, the cigar shops, the breweries, and the International Workingmen's Association . . . the Nihilistic character of the procession was shown by the red badges and red flags which were thickly displayed through it."[84]

Among the leading industrialists of the city was Cyrus H. McCormick, Jr., head of the harvester works. In February he had locked out his 1,400 employees when they tried to enforce the principles of unionism. "I told them," he said, "that the right to hire any man, white or black, union or nonunion, Protestant or Catholic, was something I would not surrender."[85] He declined to consider either compromise or arbitration. When "scabs" replaced the locked-out workers, disorder became rife, guards were taken into the factory, and the police were continually called on to break up threatening meetings. McCormick decided, however, to concede the eight-hour day demanded by organized labor. The decision was announced on May 3 and a half holiday was granted to celebrate it. As the workers came out of the factory they were greeted with hoots of contempt and derision by the union men assembled near by. Not far away, in a vacant lot, striking lumbermen were holding a meeting which August Spies, editor of the radical *Arbeiter Zeitung,* was addressing.[86] The two groups joined forces. The owner summoned the police, and, in the fighting that followed, several workingmen were killed and a score or so wounded.[87]

That night 5,000 copies of a circular, printed in English and German, were scattered over the city. "Revenge! Revenge! Workmen to arms!" it shrieked:

> Men of labor, this afternoon the bloodhounds of your oppressors murdered six of your brothers at McCormick's! Why did they murder them? Because they dared to be dissatisfied with the lot which your oppressors have assigned to them. They demanded bread, and they gave them lead for an answer.[88]

Meetings of protest were at once called by the strikers, the most important one for the evening of May 4 near Haymarket Square. Three leading anarchists addressed the gathering, which numbered perhaps 1,500. Mayor Carter Harrison attended and, finding it orderly, went home. The crowd had begun to break up when a squad of police appeared with Inspector John Bonfield at their head. As they reached the crowd, ordering it to disperse, there occurred a terrific explosion. It was a bomb thrown from no one knew where into the ranks of the police, killing one and wounding many more. Instantly an indiscriminate firing opened on both sides. When it was over, sixty-eight policemen were so injured that seven died and many were crippled for life, while of the crowd four were killed and about fifty wounded.[89]

What followed that awful night's work is an illuminating demonstration of what a city and its forces of law and order are capable when in the grip of fear, suspicion, and a lust for revenge. The almost universal, and probably true, conviction was that the bomb came from the hand of a member of one of the small bands of anarchists which for months had been urging upon strikers the necessity of direct action. But such apostles of violence were few. Charles Edward Russell, who, as a reporter, covered the Haymarket riot and in 1907 made a detailed investigation of the affair, declared that Chicago in 1886 possessed "a very small group, comprising perhaps fourteen in all, of physical force anarchists, depraved and desperate men of the type that assassinated Sadi Carnot and the king of Italy."[90] Even more sinister to conservatives than the anarchist philosophy was the fact that its adherents were tolerated, included even, by many unions which, while decrying the doctrine of direct action, were willing to use the threat of it to wring concessions from the employing class. Businessmen sympathetic with the eight-hour demand saw in this alliance with violence proof that what labor really sought was an overturn of the industrial order.

"Those who threw the explosives that resulted so disastrously," declared the *Chicago Inter Ocean,* May 5, "aimed to destroy the law. They have made the issue and they should be hunted to the ends of the earth." On the Sunday following the outbreak the ministers of the city dealt with the affair under such titles as "Anarchy," "Dead Policemen," "Protection against Anarchy," and "Our Foreign Population."[91] The press did not report a single pulpit as advising the use of Christian moderation in dealing with the offenders. In other parts of the country public opinion was quite as febrile. The *Indianapolis News,* May 5, held that the "Chicago police would have been justified in wholesale slaughter." The *Louisville Courier-Journal* of the same date impatiently demanded that the "blatant cattle" be "immediately strung up." The *Philadelphia Times,* May 6, gave Chicago definite orders "to kick the anarchists out." Even the usually even-tempered *Springfield Republican,* May 8, declared,"It is no time for half measures."

Meanwhile, the police, egged on by popular sentiment and blind with rage at the slaughter in their ranks, set out to find the guilty parties. "For days," remarks Charles Edward Russell, "the police stations were filled with suspected persons, rigorously examined in the method of the third degree; persons for the most part that had no knowledge of the bomb nor of the meeting, nor of anything connected with either, and could not have."[92] In the end, the authorities settled on eight well-known anarchists, men conspicuous for their advocacy of social revolution. These were Albert Parsons, editor of the *Alarm;* August Spies, Michael Schwab, and Adolph Fischer of the *Arbeiter-Zeitung;* and Samuel Fielden, George Engels, Oscar W. Neebe, and Louis Lingg.[93] All but Parsons and Neebe were of foreign birth. On June 21 the eight were brought to trial and, after many weeks of almost frenzied public attention, all were found guilty. Seven were sentenced to death and the other, Neebe, to fifteen years' imprisonment. No one of the eight was proved to have had any hand in making or throwing the bomb: The men were condemned because of their revolutionary opinions. As Joseph E. Gary, the presiding judge, later declared, the defendants "had generally by speech and print advised large classes of the people . . . to commit murder, and . . . in pursuance of that advice, and influenced by that advice, sombody not known did throw the bomb. . . ."[94] Yet Judge Gary's opinion was not more than an assumption, for the fact was not established by court evidence.

The death sentences aroused strong opposition in and out of Chicago. Leonard Swett, one of Chicago's ablest lawyers, held the verdict legally wrong. Lyman Trumbull, friend of Abraham Lincoln, wrote Governor Richard Oglesby that he knew of no other state trial in history where eight men were tried together for their lives on an indictment containing sixty-nine counts. He declared that not an enlightened nation on the globe would permit it. From the East, William Dean Howells wrote of the condemned men, "I have never believed them guilty of murder, or of anything but their opinions, and I do not think they were justly convicted."[95] In many parts of the country meetings were held urging clemency. The Knights of Labor at their general assembly in 1886 took similar action, and so did the Chicago Central Labor Union. These appeals were harshly criticized by the press of the country, which was almost unanimous in approving the verdict.

The case was carried to the state supreme court and the verdict sustained. The hanging was fixed for November 11, 1887. On the day before, the sentences of Fielden and Schwab were commuted to life imprisonment. Lingg escaped the penalty by blowing out his brains with a bomb believed to have been given him by his sweetheart, who had visited him in his cell.[96] The four remaining men were hanged. "The time will come," declared Spies as the noose was placed about his neck, "when our silence in the grave will be more eloquent than our speeches."[97]

Six years later Governor John P. Altgeld, a few weeks after his inauguration, pardoned the men who had been sentenced to life terms. He accompanied the act with a thoroughgoing analysis of the evidence and a scathing arraignment of the unfair and partial methods of the judge.[98] "If I do it," he had told Clarence Darrow, "I will be a dead man politically."[99] He was right. The act, prompted by an uncompromising love of justice, brought down on his head a flood of vituperation such as few men in public life have ever received. Advertised by the nation's press as a friend of "anarchy," he faced political oblivion.

The year 1886, which brought so many setbacks to the labor movement, led Terence V. Powderly to make futile efforts to stay the process of disintegration which had begun in the Knights of Labor. His most difficult task was to combat the widespread belief that the order reeked with radicalism and anarchism. In the period of rapid expansion, anarchists and socialists had been admitted to membership and many of them had cunningly used the order as a recruiting ground for their doctrines. Some of them, Powderly believed, had been "hired by monopolists to become members . . . so that public opinion might be turned against the order." On one occasion the attorney of a manufacturers' association frankly told him, "We have paid Anarchists to become members of your assemblies that they might stir up the devil and bring discredit upon your whole movement."[100]

In place of the discredited methods the general assembly now endeavored to stress education "on the great question of labor." Not only was militancy to be discarded but also politics. It proved as difficult, however, to keep the local assemblies out of political struggles as it had been to keep them out of strikes. Though their national officers warned them "so surely as we run into politics we shall be destroyed," few remembered the warning when a fight occurred for some law which they favored. Both their wide sympathies and their itch for political action made the Knights of Labor a natural ally of the Farmers' Alliances.[101] In the Knights' opinion, the two sets of interests were alike: the interests of those who labored. In 1891 the Knights were strongly represented at the Cincinnati convention which formed the People's party, and in the campaign of 1892 they also took an active part. By this time, however, the organization was only a shadow of its former self. Its membership had fallen from 700,000 in 1886 to less than 260,000 in 1888 and to 100,000 in 1890, with the downward tendency unchecked.[102]

While the Knights were declining, the American Federation of Labor was increasing its hold on the labor movement and strengthening its position in American life. At a meeting in Columbus, Ohio, in December 1886, the organization took stock and decided it needed a thorough overhauling, a headquarters, full-time officers, and salaried organizers.[103] Samuel Gompers was elected president at a salary of $1,000 a year, occupying as his first office a room eight by ten, its desk a kitchen table, its chair a box, and its filing cases tomato cans. Under his vigorous direction the Federation eschewed politics, avoided the pitfalls offered by radical doctrines, and stressed trade-union methods.

In 1888 the Federation decided to launch forth on a new general strike for the eight-hour day, to begin on May 1, 1890. But the plan was later changed for one by which a single well-organized union, that of the carpenters, should make the first effort, supported with financial contributions from members of the Federation.[104] The strike proved moderately successful. An attempt in 1891 to repeat this feat, with the miners, fell through, however, because their union, rent with internal dissension, failed at the last moment to act as agreed. The number of national unions affiliated with the Federation steadily increased, and from 1886 to 1898 the membership rose from about 140,000 to 278,000.[105]

The eighties and nineties proved a crucial period in the history of the American labor movement. Two great experiments in the nationwide organization of wage-earners had been tried and tested: one involving the amalgamation of all workers and the other the federation of those already combined in separate crafts. The events of these years decreed the greater acceptability of the federative type of structure. This decision involved, further, an emphasis on organizing skilled labor rather than all grades of labor. Unskilled workers, representing the bulk of the wage-earners, remained ouside the fold of the unions.

THE COMING OF THE PANIC OF 1893

THE OPENING of the last decade of the century found an increase in the wealth of the United States over that in 1880 of nearly $21 billion.[106] Unfortunately this did not indicate an even pace of economic advance. Agriculture had fallen back relatively. Instead of producing about 26 percent of the national wealth, as in 1880, it was down to nearly 21 percent. On the other hand, manufacturing, transportation, urban real estate, and wealth abroad all registered substantial gains.[107] It was clear that the essential elements of the national economic structure were changing shape and size, and that these changes were going on without regard to the stresses and strains on the structure as a whole. Each considered only its own form, its own gain. Those who watched the process realized that a sudden shock might topple over the edifice and bring on a severe panic and depression.

Iron and steel suffered sorely from the bad economic conditions which, for various reasons, began to plague the country. Early in 1890 the price of rolled-steel products started to fall. Steel billets, which had sold in Pittsburgh around $35 a gross ton at the beginning of the year, declined to $25 at the end and to $22 early in 1892.[108] Iron and steel men began saying that wages would have to be cut. This was the conclusion of H. C. Frick, general manager of the Carnegie Company, as in the spring of 1892 he faced the expiration of the three-year contract with the members of the Amalgamated Association of Steel and Iron Workers employed in the Carnegie plant at Homestead, near Pittsburgh. The contract followed a model which Andrew Carnegie had approved: a sliding wage scale, going up without limit as prices rose, and falling as they fell though never below a minimum of $25 a ton for steel billets.[109]

In place of the old contract Frick offered one which lowered the minimum pay to $22, with a reduction in tonnage rates whenever new machinery and improvements substantially enlarged output. In the matter of wages the men contended for a $24 minimum, and Frick raised his offer to $23 but refused more.[110] He also refused further conference with the Amalgamated.

June was a month of growing bitterness among the laborers and citizens of Homestead. When finally Frick was hung in effigy, he closed the plant and deputy sheriffs were sworn in to guard the property. The men ordered them out of town, saying that they themselves would guard the plant. There is reason to suppose they would have done so. It was their all; the jobs were theirs, they felt, a contention in which they had always been upheld by Andrew Carnegie.

But Frick recognized no vested right of labor in industry. At midnight on July 5 he sent up the Monongahela River to Homestead two barge loads of Pinkerton detectives armed with Winchester rifles. When they attempted to take possession of the mills, the strikers, entrenched behind piles of steel billets, met them with volleys of fire, picking off the members of the invading force as rapidly as they showed their heads. The detectives made repeated efforts to land, but the defenders had the advantage of numbers, position, and weapons. On the second day of the battle the workers endeavored to destroy the barges with brass cannon, planted behind breastworks of railroad ties. This attempt failing, they sprayed the barges with oil and poured barrel after barrel of it into the river above the mooring place in order to set the boats afire. After seven detectives had been killed and twenty more wounded, the Pinkerton force surrendered. They were guaranteed safe conduct out of the community on condition that they give up their arms and ammunition. Notwithstanding this promise, the maddened mob fell upon them with fists, stones, and clubs. From the sixth to the twenty-seventh of July eleven workmen and spectators were also killed and many others wounded.[111] The reestablishment of order proved too much for the sheriff and his deputies. On the twelfth the governor of Pennsylvania sent in a force of militia, the town was placed under martial law, and the plant was reopened with a small force of nonunion workmen. In November the strike was declared off. At that time not more than 800 of the old employees had been reinstated.

For Andrew Carnegie, retired and busy at his castle in Scotland, but in contact with the management as befitted one who owned over half the company's capital stock of $25 million, the upheaval was a devastating experience. To William E. Gladstone, who in September wrote him a sympathetic note, he replied:

> This is the trial of my life (death's hand excepted). Such a foolish step—contrary to my ideas, repugnant to every feeling of my nature. Our firm offered all it could offer, even generous terms. Our other men had gratefully accepted them. They went as far as I could have wished, but the false step was made in trying to run the Homestead Works with new men. It is a test to which workingmen should not be subjected. It is expecting too much of poor men to stand by and see their work taken by others. . . . The pain I suffer increases daily. The Works are not worth one drop of human blood. I wish they had sunk.[112]

Declining prices in the steel industry proved danger signals of a much greater economic catastrophe. The long depression of agriculture in the West and South had steadily curtailed the purchasing power of a large section of the population, thus contracting the domestic market for manufactures. The continued economic instability abroad after 1890 also lessened the demand for American products and, at the same time, caused further withdrawals of foreign gold invested in American enterprises. Another disturbing influence in the business world was the new silver policy adopted by Congress in 1890, which threatened to force the country off the gold standard.[113] Behind all such factors lay the vast amount of speculation in railways and especially in industrial corporations, which had been going on at an accelerating tempo.

By the opening of 1893 there was great uneasiness in the stock market because of signs, particularly in railroads, of overstrained credit. The first startling event was the failure of the Philadelphia & Reading, a railroad which had been in the hands of receivers several times in the previous decade—a victim, as one shrewd financial observer said, of a management alternating between "visionaries and plunderers."[114] But the blasting shock to public confidence came in May 1893 with the failure of the rope trust, the National Cordage Company. The company was unsound in its structure, but few of those who speculated in its stock had taken pains to inform themselves about the character of the securities. They were interested only in their market performance and that had been highly successful. It had long been the practice of the management to borrow money on its stocks of binder twine to tide over the winter and spring. Early in 1893 the trust had over 5 million worth on hand and no worries about the future. Then came the Reading failure and the bankers notified the concern that they could not take care of the usual loans. In order to secure the necessary working capital the company made a new issue of preferred stock. This alarmed the market, producing a panic in National Cordage stock and causing all its creditors to jump on it.

The failure of the rope trust marked the beginning of the general collapse. Banks, corporations, mortgage companies, fell on every hand. New York banks refused to rediscount notes offered by interior institutions, and this tightening of credit led to a suspension of banks and business houses thoughout the West and South. Terrible sacrifices of supposedly valuable properties were made. Thus a Boston mortgage concern was obliged to sell for $9,000 a mortgage which it regarded worth $220,000. In July the Erie Railroad failed, in August the Northern Pacific, in October the Union Pacific, and in December the Atchison and the New York & New England.[115] No part of the country escaped the blows of the economic disaster. Industries refused by their bankers the money to meet payrolls save at excessive premiums resorted to all sorts of expedients, often issuing scrip.

The hard times beginning in 1890 formed a prolific breeding ground for labor troubles. When the continued fall in prices reacted on the wage scales, organized labor was aroused to strong and often violent resistance. The year 1894 saw nearly 750,000 wage-earners involved in industrial warfare, an even larger number than in 1886.[116] Moreover, unlike the earlier year, the workers now fought on the defensive. One of the most destructive and significant disturbances was the Pullman strike. The Pullman Palace Car Company had suffered from the beginning of the depression. A labor force of over 5,800 at the beginning of 1893 fell to 2,000 before the year was out, and wages were cut 25 percent. In order to build up business, George Pullman, head of the concern, began taking orders at a loss.[117] By this means he returned some 2,200 to the payroll.

In May 1894 the men asked for a restoration of their wage scale. The works were busy; the company was paying dividends; but their pay had not been restored, nor had their rents in the town of Pullman been reduced. Their request, made through an employee's committee, was refused, Pullman explaining that the company was losing money in order to keep the plant going. As for the complaint that the rents charged at Pullman were higher than the employees could afford and should be lowered since wages were cut, he contended "that none of the reasons urged as justifying wage reduction by it as an employer can be considered by the company as a landlord."[118] The day after the interview three of the committee were discharged on the plea of no work. They belonged to a local chapter of the

American Railway Union, a body organized by Eugene V. Debs at Chicago in 1893 for the purpose of embracing all railway workers born of white parents in "one great brotherhood."

When the Pullman local learned of the dismissals it called a strike on May 11. The company promptly laid off its entire labor force and closed the works; Pullman announced great relief at the removal from his shoulders of the responsibility for the bread and butter of over 4,000 men and their families.[119] The men, however, were allowed to remain in their homes. This was the situation when in June a convention of the American Railway Union in Chicago proposed arbitration to the Pullman Company. The company refused to consider any communications from the body and thereupon the convention voted that after June 26 the members should handle no Pullman cars on any railroad until the Pullman Company should consent to arbitration. Members might handle trains of which Pullman cars were not a part and it was particularly asked that such cars be separated from mail trains.[120]

The strike was thus transferred to the national field. Its principals became the railways under contract to move Pullman cars and their employees who refused to move them. As Eugene V. Debs, president of the American Railway Union, saw it, "The contest is now on between the railway corporations united solidly on the one hand and the labor forces on the other." Accepting this issue, the *Chicago Herald* declared on July 4, "The necessity is on the railroads to defeat the strike. . . . If the strike should be successful the owners of the railroad property . . . would have to surrender its future control to the . . . labor agitators and strike conspirators who have formed the Debs railroad union." In the East, the *New York World* joined in calling the action of the strikers a "war against the government and against society . . . iniquitously directed by leaders more largely concerned to exploit themselves than to do justice or to enforce the right."[121]

The extension of the strike by the American Railway Union involved some twenty-four railways centering in Chicago, operating about 41,000 miles and capitalized at over $2 billion. These roads as a group were represented by an organization formed in the troubled days of 1886, called the General Managers' Association. Its business was the "consideration of problems of management arising from the operation of railroads terminating or centering at Chicago."[122] In the opinion of the federal commission later appointed to investigate the strike, the association had no standing in law: "It cannot incorporate, because railroad charters do not authorize roads to form corporations or associations to fix rates for services and wages, nor to force their acceptance, nor to battle with strikers." It denominated the association "an illustration of the persistent and shrewdly devised plans of corporations to overreach their limitations and to usurp indirectly powers and rights not contemplated in their charters and not obtainable from the people or their legislators."

It was this organization which faced the American Railway Union and refused to deal with its representatives—an action which the federal commission called "arrogant and absurd when we consider its standing before the law, its assumptions, and its past and obviously contemplated future action." [123] Feeling that no alternative remained, the switchmen on June 26 refused to attach Pullman cars to trains. When they were discharged, the train crews quit in a body. By the first of July nearly every road west and northwest of Ohio was tied up. [124] Thus, in less than a week, a large part of the nation's business had been effectually stopped by the refusal of an unincorporated organization, claiming to represent 40,000 miles of transportation, to arbitrate a labor grievance in a manufacturing company.

The railways called loudly on the federal government to protect them in running trains. The strikers contended that the government should not interfere with strikes, and when a resolution was introduced into Congress forbidding such interference, they asked Senator C. K. Davis of Minnesota to support it. "You might as well ask me to vote to dissolve this government," he replied. [125] Governor Altgeld of Illinois, confident that he had the situation well in hand, declined to call on Washington for assistance. Unfortunately the federal government had no machinery for compelling arbitration. It had only armed force, and it was fairly certain that the use of force to set the trains in motion would provoke resistance. The body of strikers was still in the main orderly, but the makings of a mob were at hand: hoodlums, embittered men vainly seeking work, hoboes, and criminals. There was, besides, a sprinkling of direct-actionists wanting nothing more than to set a match.

The first force employed by the government was unfortunate, consisting of some 3,600 special deputies sworn in by the U.S. marshal in Chicago. According to the federal investigating commission, these men were selected by and appointed at the request of the General Managers' Association; they were armed and paid by the railroads and, while exercising governmental authority, were under the direct control of the railroads, not of any public official. Thus, as a first step, the federal government gave over its local police power directly to the railroads, allowing them to recruit (chiefly through detective agencies) a considerable body of reckless and irresponsible men and to arm and send them out in the guise of U.S. officers to do whatever the railroads required. [126]

With the activities of the special deputies, rioting began. Many believed it was started by the railroads themselves, seeking to break the control of the situation which the strikers had established. The charge, however, can neither be satisfactorily proved nor disproved. In view of all the conditions, rioting was, in any case, inevitable. It took the form of frenzied mobs burning cars, looting railroad property, imperiling all law and order. As a result, federal troops entered the city on July 3. President Cleveland found warrant for this unprecedented action in the constitutional obligation to safeguard the mails and protect interstate commerce.[127] On July 6 state troops made their appearance.

At the time special deputy marshals were authorized by Washington, Attorney General Richard Olney had appointed a special counsel for the government. The man chosen was a Chicago attorney, Edwin Walker, whom Cleveland described in his account of the strike as "able and prominent." Walker, however, was at that time, and had been for over twenty years, the legal representative of important roads leading out of Chicago. On July 2 he secured from the federal circuit court a blanket injunction forbidding Debs, his fellow strike leaders, and "all other persons whomsoever" to interfere in any manner, direct or indirect, with the operation of the rail lines.[128] Eight days later Debs and three others were indicted for obstructing the mails and interstate commerce. Released on bail, they were rearrested a week later and indicted for contempt in disobeying the injunction. This time they did not give bail, with the result, as Debs said, that the men "became demoralized, and that ended the strike."[129] By July 20 all federal troops had been withdrawn. Eleven days later the Pullman Company issued its annual report. It had done a business of about $9.5 million during the year and had accumulated a surplus of some $2.5 million, less by $1.7 million than the year before because of the strike, the report said. It was employing 2,640 men, of whom but 300 had been newly engaged.

Had the Pullman upheaval been the only evidence of social unrest, popular sentiment would not have been so deeply stirred. In every industrial center hordes of men were out of work, and in the West and South the farmers lifted up their voices in the general chorus of despair and exasperation. The economic and social order built by the capitalists in the 1870s and 1880s was being weighed in the balance and found wanting. Among the few million unemployed the spirit of discontent spread like a contagion. Presently they began to form "armies" to make personal presentation of their grievances to the government at Washington.

The most conspicuous of these armies was the one led by Jacob S. Coxey of Masillon, Ohio. A quiet, unassuming man of forty, he had worked for ten years in the iron mills of his native state of Pennsylvania before going to Ohio where he became a farmer, quarryman, and horse breeder. So successful had he been that by 1894 he was reputed to be worth $200,000.[130] Despite his profitable business career Coxey was a congenital reformer. Like scores of others in depressions, he had his own plan for ending unemployment: The government should set the jobless to work constructing highways and others public improvements and pay them with irredeemable legal-tender notes.[131] Failing to arouse an interest in his plan in Congress, he decided to lead a "petition in boots" in its behalf. "The aim and object of this march to Washington," declared Coxey while the army was en route, "has been to awaken . . . the whole people to . . . their duty in impressing upon Congress the necessity for giving immediate relief to the four million of unemployed people and their immediate families, consisting of twelve million to fifteen million more."[132]

Coxey started out with a band of 122 men which, by April 30 when he reached Washington, had grown to over 400. The police allowed them to parade, but kept them off the Capitol grounds, finally arresting Coxey when he broke through their lines and attempted to make a speech on the Capitol steps.[133] "Up these steps," he said in a written protest which he had ready,

| *Browne* | *Jones* | *Coxey* |

Three Leaders of Protest Armies

"the lobbyists of trusts and corporations have passed unchallenged on their way to committee rooms, access to which we, the representatives of the toiling wealth producers, have been denied."[134]

After this experience at the hands of the police, Coxey's army presently disbanded and scattered, but by this time at least seventeen other armies were headed for the capital. The largest of these was Kelly's Industrial Army, numbering some 1,500, which the state and local authorities in California had loaded into trains of box cars and headed eastward.[135] Its leader, a thirty-two-year-old printer named Charles T. Kelly, had been elected by the unemployed as "general." At Council Bluffs, Iowa, the railroad dumped the men and took away the cars. On the outskirts of the town they camped a week in the mud, fed by a great body of sympathizing townspeople and laborers. In vain they waited for the railroad to furnish transportation, and finally the army took to the road afoot. Through all this pathetic journey Kelly kept order in his force, but not all of the divisions were manageable.

The Montana contingent of the Industrial Army, made up of nearly 650 miners, mountaineers, and hoboes, when refused a lift by one of the line managers of the Northern Pacific, proceeded to capture a train and run it themselves. They were followed by a trainload of deputies, and at Billings a fight ensued in which the deputies were worsted with the help of the people of the town. Eventually a band of federal troops surrounded the train at night and the men surrendered without a fight.[136]

Through May and June remnants of the various armies straggled into Washington. They appeared too late, however, and were too few in number to make the impression on Congress that their cause deserved. Of the 100,000 men whom Coxey had predicted, never more than 1,000 were in the capital at a given time. Congress ignored them; the local authorities harried and harassed them. While some tried to jest at the new "American pilgrims bound on a merely fantastic and adventurous journey,"[137] thoughtful persons realized that a germ of deadly earnestness underlay the movement. "The Coxeyites, ridiculed by the classes, have the sympathy of the masses," declared an English observer. "Organized labor, and labor not organized, has cheered the armies on their way."[138] There could be no doubt, to use the language of another contemporary, that the movement, despite its farcical ending, was "a symptom. Symptoms . . . mean always internal disturbance, they mean the possibility of diseases that may threaten the vitals."[139]

AFTER TWENTY YEARS

As a matter of fact, the long depression of the nineties had not paralyzed the productive energies of the nation, however much it had temporarily weakened them. If 4 million men were thrown out of work, 20 million had work. Though a continuous succession of bank and industrial failures had occurred, wealth grew steadily through the decade as a whole. The total wealth of the country rose from $78.5 billion in 1890 to $126.7 billion in 1900, up to that time the greatest gain ever made in a single decade.[140]

The return of normal times in the closing years of the twenty-year period since 1878 afforded a clearer view of the laborious road which this genera- tion had had to traverse. The most notable development had been an extraordinary unification of the nation's economic life. This had proceeded with accelerating tempo until the single year 1898 beheld the formation of twelve huge business combinations.[141] The outstanding example of the so-called franchise trust was, in 1898 as in 1878, the Western Union Tele- graph Company. Its 206,202 miles of wire had grown to 874,420. Instead of carrying 24 million messages, it now transmitted over 62 million.[142] Its only competitor, the Postal Telegraph, acted, in matters of rates and treat- ment of the public, as its ally. The two of them constituted a practical monopoly. As for industrial amalgamations, the Standard Oil Company, which the congressional committee had termed in 1888 "the incentive to the formation of all other trusts and combinations," was still the almost perfect monopoly. Thus the end of the period witnessed the triumph of that process of interlocking and combination which at its opening had been so generally challenged. Neither appeals to the philosophy of democracy, nor political agitation, nor restraining laws, nor even the recurring depres- sions which had disclosed the overexpansion and exploitation of industrial mergers had halted their progress.

The triumph of industrial consolidation knitted the country together in ever-closer bonds, increasing the feeling of nationhood. Since each aggrega- tion strove to enlarge its market, offering more and more people something they wanted and could pay for, each worked systematically to push its organization into fresh territory. The people of the Great West had added a huge new population of potential customers. From 1880 to 1900 the eleven states and territories of what the census called the Western Division had grown by nearly 2.5 million. At the same time Texas had gained a million and a half; the two Dakotas nearly 600,000; Nebraska and Kansas each a half million.[143] Makers of farm machinery, representatives of the telephone, salesmen for the great electric-equipment companies, the sugar trust, and the oil trust penetrated to the remotest communities, weaving a network of mutual interest. Not only did they build up custom locally, but they almost invariably added a local agent to their far-flung organization.

In this immense task of building a nationwide market it was more obvi- ous in 1898 than it had been in 1878 that the strong man, whom Andrew Carnegie had celebrated, played a more essential role in great undertakings than did capital. Still clearer was it that the leadership of strong men was the price the country was paying for its rapid development as well as for more abundant comforts and cheaper luxuries. Nowhere was this truer than in the case of the railroads. In spite of the setbacks which reckless speculation and overbuilding had forced on the railroads in 1883–84, and again from 1893 to 1896, they had grown in mileage and had solidified the territorial divisions already well defined in 1880. There were now six recognized rail groups: the Morgan, Vanderbilt, Harriman, and Pennsylvania interests, controlling approximately 20,000 miles each, the Gould-Rockefeller group 16,000, and the Hill interests 5,000. The control of these giant systems did not rest on so simple a method as direct ownership. Ownership of mileage was combined with leases and "community-of-interest" arrangements. In the conduct of these systems a powerful financier or speculator acting as director—a Gould, a Morgan, a Harriman— exerted more influence than a weak individual or group of individuals even though owning a bigger block of stock.

The interlocking of consolidations in different economic fields had caused grave uneasiness in 1878. By 1898 many accepted it fatalistically as inevitable. The telegraph lived off the railway; the railway could not operate without the telegraph; while the size and wealth of certain monopolistic industries made servants of them both. All these undertakings, moreover, were equally dependent on those who controlled large sums of money, whether they were bankers looking for investments or industrial magnates who, like Jay Gould or the Standard Oil group, had made greater profits than were needed for their own businesses. It was the direction which these interested groups of bankers, railway men, and industrialists—these strong men—had given the country that in twenty years had so swiftly nationalized its resources and, for good or ill, had changed the whole structure of the land.

The chief complaint against this system was that its leaders had taken too big a share of the profits for themselves. The country was prone to forget the benefits it had derived. It complained of the cost of telegraphing, but failed to remember that in twenty years the number of offices had increased from 8,000 to more than 22,000, thus giving hundreds of thousands more men and women the advantage of quick communication. Moreover, the service was cheaper, the average charge per message having fallen from 38.9 cents in 1878 to 30.1 in 1898.[144]

One enormous benefit, little appreciated at the time, was the example of efficient organization and operation which the big combinations were setting the country. Under the old individualistic methods of doing business each proprietor, each employee, worked along in his own way, but as undertakings enlarged and consolidated, systematized practices began to be the rule. Order, economy, and stability became the ideals of operative heads, especially those touched by Taylor's new science of management. An undertaking was analyzed as never before, and each function given proper attention. At the same time improvements in office equipment added to business efficiency. The typewriter, still regarded as a novelty early in the period, became before many years an important adjunct to the conduct of every enterprising business office. In the single year 1890 a little over $3.6 million worth of typewriters and supplies were sold; ten years later nearly twice as much.[145] After the typewriter had come the adding machine, invented in 1886 and made practical in 1891. In 1892 the first addressograph appeared. The filing case, the card catalogue, and the tabulating machine followed rapidly. Business offices were coming to have their special technology as did the farm and the factory.

The temptation to condemn industry as a whole because a few powerful men became inordinately rich not only prevented a proper weighing of the advantages the public was receiving, but it prevented cool and effective dealing with the roots of the evil. Popular attention fastened on the conspicuous or wicked individual rather than on the nature of his practices, which the existing economic and political system made possible. In the twenty-year period two major attempts to correct basic wrongs had been made: the interstate commerce act dealing with railroad abuses, and the Sherman antitrust law. Although both statutes proved unsatisfactory in operation, they at least committed the government to the principle of regulation, and as their weaknesses became clear to the public, it was certain that there would be amendments by Congress and judicial decisions which would strengthen the arm of the government.

The farmer, despite many ups and downs during the two decades, enjoyed a distinctly improved position in the national economy as the century drew to a close. The prices of his products had advanced. Money was easier than ever before. In ten years the per-capita circulation of the country had increased from $22.88 to $25.15; at the same time his credit facilities had improved. He had used these advantages to lift the load of mortgages, which had so shocked the country when revealed by the census report of 1890, and to better his farming methods. Labor-saving devices played an ever-greater role in his operations. In 1900 he had $750 million invested in implements and machinery.[146] From the state agricultural colleges, experiment stations, and farmers' institutes he was learning more scientific methods of tilling the soil and breeding livestock and of combating plant diseases and pests. Food factories were beginning to appear in his district, taking his products in bulk. The handling of milk, the making of butter and cheese, the canning of fruits, the packing of apples were being increasingly industrialized.

It was necessary that the farmer be on the alert, for he had 25 million more mouths to feed than in 1878. To be sure, he had placed more acres under cultivation, nearly a third more, but on this land he was asked to raise not only food for America but an increasing amount for overseas. The nation's prosperity depended, in large measure, upon the sum total he could export. By the end of the period his produce made up nearly

70 percent of the country's total exports. That this represented a relative fall of nearly 13 percent in twenty years was due to the tremendous increase at the same time in the output of America's factories and mines.

Not all was rosy on the farm, however. The question of uncontrolled production, of crop surpluses in the future as in the past, continued unsolved. Moreover, many farmers, preferring traditional to the new scientific methods, were storing up trouble for the years ahead. The spirit of haste, of indifference to waste, affected the agriculturists as it did every other class, causing them often to work the land to the utmost without proper provision for replenishment. At the same time they complained bitterly of the greed and wantonness of lumbermen who cut timber over wide stretches of the country, hastening soil erosion and leaving stumps and brush to feed destructive forest fires. The farseeing realized even then that such methods were preparing for one of the greatest tragedies in land history: the ravages of the wind which nothing but abundant and properly placed timber and grass could prevent.

On the whole, the conditions of the wage-earners had also greatly improved in the twenty years. After trying the "one-big-union" type of organization sponsored by the Knights of Labor, the labor movement had turned to the form of organization represented by the American Federation of Labor, one consisting of a league of nationwide craft unions. By 1893 the Knights had dropped to less than 75,000, and their activities had become political rather than economic.[147] Membership of the American Federation, on the other hand, showed a steady growth, standing at 275,000 in 1898.[148] Under the leadership of Samuel Gompers it had become a compact, militant body, intent on spreading unionism among skilled workers and alert to encroachments on the part of the employing class.

At the beginning of the score of years most labor leaders had favored the legal incorporation of unions. This demand, for example, appeared in the original platform of the Federation of Organized Trades and Labor Unions. There were various reasons for this desire. Incorporation would protect unions against embezzlement of funds by officers, remove them from the possible operation of state conspiracy laws, and, by giving the organizations greater stability, make employers more inclined to deal with them. Peter J. McGuire, secretary of the Brotherhood of Carpenters and Joiners, in urging such action on a congressional committee in 1883, pleaded that, if Congress lacked the power, "it shall assume the power; and, if necessary, amend the constitution to do it."[149] But later experience with the courts in industrial disputes convinced laborites that the disadvantages of incorporation would outweigh the advantages. By the close of the period they had completely reversed their position.

The American Federation of Labor credited labor's gains to militancy. The unions had learned much from their experience in fighting organized capital—not to go into a strike without preparation, to keep within the law, to avoid violence, to educate the public as to an understanding of labor's grievances. Over 6.6 million persons were out on strike for longer or shorter periods in the twenty years from 1881 to 1900, at a cost to industry of about a half-billion dollars, of which two thirds was in wages. On the whole, labor issued from these conflicts more successfully than capital, primarily because what it sought was so often just. Moreover, organized labor succeeded better than unorganized. The proportion of victories, according to the labor bureau, was 51 percent for labor, 36 percent for the employer, and the rest undetermined.[150] Did industrial warfare pay? The answer depends on whether the real grievances could have been settled by conciliation or arbitration to the satisfaction of both sides. In a considerable number of cases undoubtedly this might have been done. The gain in developing a sound technique for threshing out common problems and adjusting them by peaceful means would have been tremendous. But nei-

The Trouble of Labor

An unfriendly view of a walking delegate's visit to a construction job

ther side, unfortunately, was interested primarily in a peaceful industrial life. Both strove to achieve their immediate material ends and used those methods which promised the quickest results.

If labor and capital had changed but little in ambition and methods, the attitude of the public toward these dominant forces in the nation's economic life had changed. A continuous stream of official investigations by the state and federal governments, of private lawsuits, of reports from courts and commissions, supplied a body of data such as the people had never before known. This mass of information lay behind the legislation which increasingly manifested the government's tendency to intervene in economic concerns. An ever-larger element of the public was growing to realize that the doctrine of laissez-faire too often cloaked the greed of the strong. "Our civilization," declared Henry Demarest Lloyd, "has followed the self-interest of the individual to learn that it was but one of the complex forces of self-interest. The true *laissez-faire* is, let the individual do what the individual can do best, and let the community do what the community can do best."[151] It was this latter principle, which Lloyd termed the "*laissez-faire* of social self-interest," that had bred such legislation as the interstate commerce and antitrust acts.

There was, moreover, a deepening conviction that ethical and humanitarian considerations had a vital relationship to economics and that a failure to observe them constituted a continuing menace to social stability. This conviction was, in part, the intellectual contribution made by the socialists, the single taxers, the Populists, and other minority groups which refused to admit that poverty was a legitimate concomitant of progress. On all sides experiments in education, technological training, economic cooperation, the shorter day, better wages, the model factory, better housing, attested the belief that life could be made more tolerable for the masses.[152] But Carnegie's strong man still occupied the saddle. He had fashioned a vast nationwide industrial order and he had no intention of resigning the kingdom which he had so laboriously prepared.

BOOK X

The Rise of the City, 1878–98

THE NEW SOUTH

AMERICAN CIVILIZATION in 1878 was, in one essential respect, like that of earlier times: it rested upon the farms and country towns of the nation. An American Sully of that day might truly have remarked, "Tillage and pasture are the two breasts of the state." His observation would have applied no less to the sources of material prosperity than to those subtler currents of thought and aspiration which from the beginning had given tone and color to American life. The generation destined to dominate the scene during the next twenty years was to be responsible for turning the needle of national interest from the country to the city, but as the period opened there was little to show that so momentous a change impended. Of the 50 million people counted in the census of 1880, three fourths, or nearly 40 million, lived on the open land or in villages of less than 4,000 inhabitants.

As of old, the vast majority of Southerners were farmers and the typical farmer was addicted to the staple-crop system.[1] If he lived in the Lower South he cultivated cotton, or perhaps rice or sugar cane. If he lived in the Upper South he was apt to make tobacco his main reliance. Yet every year showed that the people were learning the unwisdom of pivoting their prosperity on one or two staple crops. Corn, hay, wheat, potatoes, and other products began to count in the Southern agricultural list during the 1880s. The demand of the swiftly growing urban centers of the North for a greater abundance and variety of fruits and vegetables led to the rapid spread of orcharding and trucking in the lands along the Atlantic from Maryland to the Gulf. The Albemarle pippin of the Virginia piedmont and the peanut of the tidewater, the Scuppernong wine grape of North Carolina, the luscious watermelon of Georgia, soon commanded a nationwide patronage. Stimulated by the example of California, Florida awoke to the golden possibilities of developing her subtropical fruits; and her oranges, lemons, and pineapples began to vie on Northern fruit stands with those of the Coast and far-off Sicily.[2] These years demonstrated the ability of the South to raise almost any crop that could be grown in the United States.

Equally striking was the continuance of the postwar trend toward smaller units of cultivation. The attempt to resume agriculture on a large-scale basis had generally broken down after the war because of the heavy taxes, lack of operating capital, and the lack of farm laborers. The impoverished aristocrat eagerly seized the opportunity to sell or lease "parcels" or "cuts" of ground to blacks or landless whites. Already in 1880 there were 1.5 million farms of all kinds in the South, more than double the number when the war broke out. By 1890, 300,000 additional ones had come into existence and the process was far from halted.[3] Some of the new holdings resulted from clearing the forest from land that had never known hoe and plow, or had known them so long since that a new growth of pine or hickory had replenished the worn-out soil. But most of them represented further subdivision of the great plantations. A marked decline in average acreage resulted. The Georgia farmer who in 1880 tilled 188 acres held but 147 ten years later. In Mississippi in the same decade the typical holding shrank from 156 to 122 acres, and in Tennessee and Kentucky from 127 to about 118.

The effects of this democratizing process were far-reaching both economically and socially. In increasing number the patrician families which had traditionally dominated Southern life and politics fled the countryside for the towns. Cut off from the expansive life on their great estates, the members of the younger generation gave their attention to the professions or, in continuance of an old tradition, to politics. The pursuit of agriculture, once a badge of social distinction, suffered a serious loss of prestige.

On the other hand, the partition of land offered a new footing to the unprivileged folk, not only to the former slaves but also to the mass of white people. A minority of the latter consisted of a sturdy yeomanry who for generations had tilled their small farms in the fertile backcountry valleys, usually without the help of slaves and always without the social and political rewards that accrued to the large planters. In sharp contrast to them stood the poor whites of the black belt, a numerous folk who had always occupied the lowest rungs of Southern white society.

The plight of the former planter class gave all who would a chance to share in a new partition of the kingdom. While the yeoman farmers, able to outbid their poorer rivals, succeeded in securing the choicest cuts, in the long run the poor whites were the chief beneficiaries. For the first time since their forebears ventured into the section they were able to escape their piney-wood solitudes and take a self-respecting part in the life of the countryside. Normal social relations became theirs; schools began to touch the lives of their children; glass panes in the windows and carpets on the floors evidenced an increasing sense of pride and taste.

The road to economic independence, however, was a steep and rocky one, conditions in the eighties showing little improvement over those which had prevailed in Reconstruction days.[4] The aspiring but poverty-stricken husbandman must first become a "cropper" or share tenant, obtaining tools, seed, and draft animals from the landlord and usually giving him half of the crop grown. To safeguard his interests the landlord often retained a measure of centralized control. Sometimes, as on the D. C. Barrow plantation near Oglethorpe in central Georgia, the oversight was loose and general;[5] but more typical was the arrangement whereby the landlord or his manager planned and directed the work, kept the implements and mules at a central barn, and controlled the marketing of the crop.[6] This system, while lending itself to many abuses, had the advantage of providing a period of apprenticeship for the unskilled and protecting them from destitution in times of low prices or crop failure. It also preserved the benefits, enjoyed under slavery, of large-scale operation. The plan was more characteristic of the Lower South than of other parts and more workable with the ex-slaves than with the white toilers.

Given favorable conditions and the exercise of thrift, the cropper might advance to the position of renter or cash tenant and, in time perhaps, to full ownership. The chief obstacle in his path was the vicious credit system which constantly tempted him to borrow from the local merchant or banker at excessive rates of interest in anticipation of his harvest. This "lazy 'descent into hell,' " as Ben Tillman called it, plunged him into a bog of debt-peonage from which extrication was heartbreakingly difficult.[7] It was also an important deterrent to the rapid development of mixed farming, for the money lender insisted upon the one-crop routine—cotton or tobacco —with which he had always been familiar. Perhaps 80 or 90 percent of the cotton growers—tenants and proprietors, whites and blacks—were normally enmeshed in the crop-lien system.[8] Despite all discouragements, however, the number of farmers who graduated from share tenancy to cash renting, as well as those who became freeholders, grew steadily through these years.[9]

Many believed, however, that the South might more profitably devote its chief energies to the development of factory industry. The idea appealed to a variety of motives. How better to retaliate on the late enemy than to fight the devil with fire? "If we have lost the victory on the field of fight," declared the *Columbia Register* in 1881, "we can win it back in the work shop, in the factory, in an improved agriculture and horticulture, in our mines and in our schoolhouses.'' [10] More important, however, was the belief that economic salvation rested upon the exploitation of the raw materials, water power, and cheap white labor which lay immediately at hand. The South, relieved of the incubus of slavery, had at last a chance to take its place in modern industrial society. Efforts in that direction were urged forward by the doubling of the Southern railway net in the twelve years after 1878. But many were not ready for the change; much inertia had to be overcome. The enemies of progress, asserted the *Register* in the same editorial, ''are the prejudices of the past, the instincts of isolation, the brutal indifference and harmful social infidelity which stands up in our day with the old slave arguments . . . on its lips, 'I object' and 'You can't do it.' ''

Nascent industrialists were cheered by the success which greeted tobacco manufacturing in the Upper South. From humble beginnings shortly after the war the industry had already, by 1878, reached a position of importance. The new decade brought fresh enterprise, more economical production, improved methods of marketing.[11] Through skillful advertising, brands like Bull Durham and Duke's Mixture, made at Durham, North Carolina, became known throughout the world. Across the Atlantic, Tennyson was a devotee of Bull Durham, to which he had been introduced by James Russell Lowell. Thomas Carlyle likewise found its pungent aroma congenial to his taste. For a time misguided zeal even caused the taurine lineaments of its trademark to decorate the pyramids of Egypt. The Dukes' business was based upon the making of smoking tobacco, snuff, chewing tobacco, and cigars, but they saw interesting possibilities also in the cigarette, which prior to 1867 had been produced exclusively in Europe. Early in the 1880s when they effected a satisfactory means of making the white tubes by machinery and invented a sliding pasteboard box for their sale to smokers, the cigarette trade began to add materially to their revenues. In the three states of North Carolina, Virginia, and Kentucky the value of tobacco manufactures rose from about $21 million in 1880 to nearly $31 million in 1890.[12]

The enthusiasm for manufacturing was even more strikingly shown in the so-called cotton-mill campaign of the eighties. Only a feeble start had been made at cotton manufacturing before 1878. Now something akin to a religious fervor swept over the seaboard states, directed toward the establishment of local factories for utilizing the basic Southern crop. Newspapers, large and small helped propagate the new gospel, none more effectively than the *Charleston News and Courier* under the editorship of the brilliant Anglo-American F. W. Dawson.[13] Soon the rallying cry, ''Bring the mills to the cotton!'' was echoed from village to village and from hamlet to hamlet. Money for launching the enterprises was not to be had from the North where, for example, such a man as Edward Atkinson, biased perhaps by his Massachusetts mill connection, publicly counseled his Southern friends against the new departure.[14] Capital had to be raised from the people of the neighborhood out of their meager savings. While a few upcountry mills such as Piedmont, Pacolet, Clifton, and Pelzer were financed in part by Charleston investors, this was the exception rather than the rule.[15] The zeal often outran prudent business considerations, but everywhere it evidenced a heartening spirit of enterprise and a resolve to rescue the community from the slough of agricultural distress.

Leading cities like New Orleans and Louisville were the natural centers of the new industrial development. Other places such as Atlanta, Memphis, and Chattanooga forged rapidly ahead in population and manufacturing importance, though without attaining a size that would have been considered large according to Northern standards.[16] No champion of Southern industry failed to take pride in the meteoric rise of Birmingham. Without existence until 1871, its location in the heart of the Alabama iron and coal district had by 1890 caused it to become a bustling town of 26,000, the center of rolling mills, foundries, iron furnaces, and machine shops.

Generally speaking, however, Southern manufacturing was conducted on too small a scale to breed important urban communities. Even Durham had less than 6,000 residents as late as 1890. The typical mill village possessed but a few hundred people, mostly laborers and their families gathered for the purpose of working in a particular factory and living in unpainted shanties along a single street ankle-deep with dust. The entire South in 1880 contained only ten cities of 25,000 or more inhabitants and this number had grown to but nineteen in 1890. Historic old cities like Charleston and Mobile showed little sign of new life, resting tranquilly in the autumnal glory of their past renown.

In emulating the industrial course of the North, the South had never been more truly Southern. Unlike New England or Great Britain she depended for her basic supplies entirely upon the tobacco produced in her own fields, the cotton grown on her own lands, the coal and iron mined in her own hills, the timber cut in her own forests. Not a dollar's worth of raw materials did she need to buy from outside her own borders. Moreover, apart from the railways, the new undertakings were nourished largely by her own capital, usually in the form of an aggregation of petty savings. It was only after the path had been blazed and the certainty of profits demonstrated that Northern investors began to show an active interest. The turning point perhaps came in the mid-eighties when the important Thomas Iron Company of Pennsylvania constructed a million-dollar branch plant in Alabama, one of the finest in America.[17] In 1889 a large party of Northern capitalists and bankers, including Andrew Carnegie and the two leading partners of Cooper, Hewitt & Company, toured the South and brought back glowing reports. Soon an increasing stream of Northern capital began to flow southward.

What was true of financial support was even truer of the human energies devoted to the new developments. Northern promotion played a negligible part. The editor of the *Manufacturers' Record* could well say in 1890:

"Southern energy and enterprise mainly are entitled to the credit for what has been accomplished."[18] In the South itself the drive toward industrialization came chiefly from the former nonslaveholding class, for, as we have seen, the members of the old landed gentry turned to the professions rather than to manufacturing. The typical entrepreneur, as he may be generalized from a few hundred random instances, was the son of a country merchant.[19] Beginning as a clerk with perhaps a common-school education, he rose in time to storekeeper and petty money lender, laid by his profits and, with his savings, aided in starting a local factory or mine which he headed as president. When it is recalled how much of the leadership and financial strength of the prewar South was monopolized by the slavocracy, this change may be regarded as little short of revolutionary.

Similarly the manual labor was supplied by the South. This was not wholly a matter of choice, for ever since the close of the war an active campaign had been waged to make the section attractive to foreign immigrants. Most of the states had passed laws to encourage their coming, boom literature was circulated under official auspices, and recruiting agents were dispatched to European countries, Virginia, it is said, sending several hundred to Great Britain and Germany in 1870.[20] Not discouraged by the negligible results, renewed efforts were made in the eighties as the industrial possibilities of the section were disclosed. State immigration bureaus were reestablished or given enlarged powers; and official endeavors were supplemented by the activities of popular conventions, land companies, boards of trade, and, most important of all, the new railways eager to build up their satellite territories. In 1883 a Southern Immigration Association was formed for the purpose of redoubling such exertions and to press for the opening of direct steam communication between Southern ports and Europe.[21]

Immigrant wage-earners, however, continued to prefer the North and the West where their countrymen had long been accustomed to go and where they need fear no competition from cheap native labor. Thus Southern manufacturing development had to rest on the brawn of the poor whites. By the same token it opened a fresh road of escape for this submerged element. The new industrialism did for the unprivileged commoners of the upland South what the breakup of the great plantations was doing for those of the lowland districts. As fast as factories were set up, labor was drawn from the foothill and mountain country to operate them Employers, somewhat to their surprise, discovered that as workers they were industrious, self-improving, and reliable, thus giving color to the belief that the highlanders were not degenerate but simply unstarted.[22] Machine shops, the cotton industry, and furniture factories were wholly dependent upon their labor. Only in the sawmills, tobacco factories, and a few other less skilled employments did they find it necessary to compete with blacks for jobs. With every factory owner a law unto himself, the workday was long, wages were low, conditions wretched. Yet even so, the new job in the busy mill village, with its opportunities for human fellowship, held more attraction than the bleak life in a distant mountain cove.

Since the whole family had worked together on the farm, it seemed natural to comply with the wishes of the mill proprietor to have the family as the working unit in the factory. So arose the evil of child labor—not the healthful outdoor choring of the farm, but the steady, benumbing toil of the ill-ventilated, ill-lighted mill—and its concomitant evil, the idle father living off the working child. By 1890, 23,000 children were employed in industry in the thirteen states.[23] A distinct "factory people" was in process of creation—a folk whose life was shaped by a common origin and a social experience not reaching beyond the sound of the factory whistle. When all was said and done, however, the mill hand was a part of the pulsing world; he had gained a real foothold in the struggle for existence. A few became superintendents of the new instrumentalities that had called them from their long sleep. Even the most wretched of them were unwilling to return to their mountain solitudes.

Though far fewer in number than the tenant farmers of the lowlands, the mill workers were like them in constituting a new economic and social class in Southern life. Together, these two sections of the poor-white population formed a Third Estate of which the earlier South offered no counterpart. The mill people were too new to their situation and too scattered to be alert to their grievances—the "damn factory class," Tillman impatiently called them—but each year marked increasing restiveness among the small-farmer contingent.[24] Politically untrained, they had, since the overthrow of the Carpetbaggers, accepted the leadership of the old gentry. This leadership, however, little heeded the critical conditions which beset the rural majority, such as the nefarious credit system, "landlordism," high transportation costs, and low crop prices.

While the brave attempts at factory industry foreshadowed the future, the section retained its predominantly rural character during the decade of the eighties, a time of economic distress and political upheaval. Agriculture passed through a period of storm and stress which aroused the agrarian masses to organized activity and eventually to political triumph. For better or for worse the Third Estate mounted the saddle. Southern politics was no longer to be merely government of the people and for the people but also by the people.[25] But it was equally clear that the people must be white people, for legal disfranchisement of the black, was one of the first fruits of the new dispensation. Though the farmers' difficulties were largely of local origin, they were similar in kind to those of the other great agricultural region of the nation, the Great West. Thus, as the decade ended, the Southern agrarian leaders were ripe for cooperation with their Western brethren in demands upon the federal government for remedial action.

If the changes which the section underwent during this critical decade made its way of life more nearly like that of the remainder of the United

States, the responsibility rested squarely upon the South itself. The homogeneity which characterized the white population in slavery times continued unaltered. The dominant race in the thirteen states advanced in the ten years from 9.5 million to nearly 12 million.[26] The number of Americans born outside the section who lived in the South in 1880 was 450,000 and the total had increased to probably not more than 600,000 in 1890. As for foreign infusions, at no time during the decade did aliens number more than one in fifty of the entire population. In 1890 fully seven eighths of the white inhabitants were of Southern nativity. On the other hand, the section contributed to the upbuilding of other parts of the nation a wealth of human material that it could ill afford to lose. The blacks, while increasing at a slower rate than the former master class, advanced from 5.5 million to 6.5 million.

In view of the frantic efforts made to attract immigrants, an incident at the close of the decade caused many Southerners to question the wisdom of such endeavors and rejoice at their lack of success. Sometime during the 1880s a compact colony of Sicilians settled in New Orleans where they worked mainly as longshoremen, forming a turbulent and lawless element. The bloody clashes of their secret oath-bound societies led finally to the assassination of the Irish chief of police. When a trial of three of those accused of the crime resulted in their acquittal, a mob of citizens formed on the morning of March 14, 1891, and strung up all eleven.[27] The affair precipitated an international crisis, caused the withdrawal of the Italian minister, and eventually brought the payment of an indemnity by the Washington government.

Within the section itself there was considerable shifting of population during the decade, notably toward the rich farming country of the Gulf region and particularly into the half-developed state of Texas.[28] Railroads were penetrating the Texan interior; the great ranches in the western section were slowly crumbling before the farmer advance; cotton was asserting its primacy among agricultural crops. As heavy beef cattle and dairy cows crowded out the longhorns, so Merinos and Shropshires replaced the old Mexican sheep, and stocky, quickly grown hogs the lean and voracious razorbacks. Despite the great drought of 1886, which lasted twenty-three months and affected thirty-seven western counties, the total number of people in Texas increased by 750,000 reaching 2.25 million in 1890 drawn from many parts of the country as well as other portions of the world. What had been a thinly inhabited region ten years before had become well populated and the edge of settlement had reached the escarpment of the Staked Plains. This phenomenal growth, however, betrayed the essential kinship of Texas with the Great West rather than with the South.

THE GREAT WEST

MOST OF THE GREAT WEST in 1878 lay as yet beyond the pale of statehood.[29] Five states had indeed been formed as a result of mining rushes, partisan exigency at Washington, or other fortuitous circumstance. The bulk of this vast region, however, consisted of eight great territories—Dakota, Montana, Idaho, Wyoming, Washington, Utah, New Mexico, and Arizona—and of a special reserve, Indian Territory, set aside for the red men. These eight territories embraced nearly a third of the total national area and already contained 600,000 white inhabitants. Over twice as many settlers scattered through this region in the years from 1880 to 1890 as in the two picturesque decades preceding. Wealth, adventure, health, wanderlust, the desire for an easier living, all played their part in swelling the tide of migrants.

Except in early colonial times, Western growth had always been a drain on the older American communities from which the migrants came. The familiar story was repeated once more, and for the last time, as the trans-Missouri country passed under the hand of the settler. Broadly speaking, the Middle West was the motherland of the newer states and territories. Her children fared forth to face the hardships and hazards of life in strange parts with the same dauntless spirit that their fathers and mothers had once set forth from the still older lands to the east. To their ranks were added many from those counties of New York and Pennsylvania bordering on the Ohio Valley. It is significant that these colonizing areas were also the parts of the North where the white population was breeding its largest families and which, according to the standards dictated by a simple rural economy, were threatened with overpopulation.[30]

The restless Midwesterners were at home in all parts of the region.[31] They flocked into Kansas in such numbers that by 1890 one fifth of the inhabitants consisted of natives of Illinois and Ohio. Farther to the west, the major strains in the population of Colorado and California derived from Iowa, Missouri, Illinois, Ohio, New York, and Pennsylvania; and a similar situation prevailed elsewhere. From Illinois alone a third of a million persons settled in the newer commonwealths. This was a "wandering of the nations" that was none the less notable because confined within the boundaries of a single country. It involved a transplantation, not only of men and material possessions but also of ideas and institutions, which, in spite of different conditions of geography and climate, were, after the initial shock of adjustment, to shape the lives of Westerners along traditional American lines.

In making the journey westward the "prairie schooner" was rapidly giving way to swifter means of travel. Many, however, clung to the time-tried mode. But the old-fashioned ox team had now been supplanted by horses or mules, the necessity for carrying large stores of food no longer existed, and few or no cattle were driven along. Mr. and Mrs. C. D. Ide and a large party from Mondovi, Wisconsin, made such a journey in the spring of 1878, reaching their destination at Dayton in Washington territory four and a half months later. Despite the better trails and other ameliorations of travel, Mrs. Ide's diary shows that hardship and excitement remained aplenty.[32]

The number who went in this way, however, steadily diminished. Railways advertised their advantages, offered special rates, and sometimes, as in the case of the Northern Pacific Railroad, temporarily gave free transportation to persons intending to settle upon railway land.[33] "Without the railroad," declared a prominent Dakotan in 1884, "it would have required a century to accomplish what has been done in five years under its powerful influence."[34] The Ide party made such a strange appearance while moving through southern Minnesota as to cause people in a passing train to mistake them for a circus. The space-conquering locomotive inevitably rang the death knell of the covered wagon.[35]

The spell of the Great West was felt not only within the national borders but across the seas as well. Though a majority of the alien newcomers to America stopped in the industrial centers to the east, others sought the farming life with which they were familiar in their homelands, and special immigrant trains distributed them by the thousands through the remote trans-Missouri country. In a single week in the spring of 1882, according to the *Chicago Tribune*, 9,000 foreigners arrived in Chicago, most of them destined for Dakota.[36] Robert Louis Stevenson, short of funds and in search of health and a bride, boarded a transcontinental immigrant train in 1879, carrying with him a minimum of luggage and Bancroft's *History of the United States*.[37] The trip was marked by greater discomfort than the passage by immigrant ship from the Clyde to New York.[38] After many stops and transfers he and his bewildered polyglot companions reached the Pacific Transfer Station, near Council Bluffs, where they changed to the Union and Central Pacific railways for their ten-day trip to the Coast.

Every passenger was sold a board and three straw cushions; when darkness fell, the seats were rearranged and the distance between each pair bridged with the boards, thus forming a perilous couch for two sleepers in a cramped position. For food and comforts the travelers relied chiefly upon the newsboys who noisily peddled fruit, canned beans and bacon, coffee, soap, and tin basins. A single flat-topped stove at the end of the car provided cooking facilities. Stevenson good-naturedly took part in the rough camaraderie of the train. He even succeeded in attaining the democratic distinction of a nickname, no less a one than "Shakespeare," bestowed perhaps because of his accent and the erudition implied by the six volumes of Bancroft. None too robust when he began the adventure, Stevenson reached his destintion "feverish and sick," looking "like a man at death's door."

The business of transporting immigrants was eagerly sought by the railroads, not so much because of the immediate returns of the passenger traffic as because of their desire to hasten settlement, develop a shipping business, and enhance the value of their land holdings. After a period of relative quiet during the five hard years following the Panic of 1873 the railway immigration departments in the Atlantic ports and Europe resumed their activities with redoubled energy.[39] In 1883, for instance, the Northern Pacific had 124 agents stationed on the Continent and 831 in the British Isles. Over half a million copies of its publications, printed in five languages, issued from its Liverpool office within the year.

By 1890 one in every five persons in the Great West was foreign-born. The total number of immigrant settlers had increased three quarters of a million in ten years. In particular places, as in Dakota, Montana, or Nevada, every third or fourth person might be of alien birth.[40] No other section of the country contained so high a percentage except the North Atlantic states where the proportion was about the same. To an Eastern student of Western conditions it seemed that "No such experiment in the blending of the different race of men into one homogeneous nation, has ever been attempted, on a scale so grand and extensive."[41] Yet despite the strong foreign admixture, the West impressed James Bryce as "the most distinctively American part of America."[42] He, of course, was thinking not of racial origins but of qualities of character, conduct, and ideals. In all these respects, though it is often forgotten, the immigrant on the frontier had, from earliest times, contributed significantly to a genuine Americanism.

Economically, the Great West at the close of the seventies was passing out of one era into another. The older industries, mining and ranching, were being obliged to assume new forms and agriculture was about to take its dominant place in Western economy. Just as the period opened, a silver rush to Leadville, Colorado, transformed that place in three years from an unnamed settlement of six log cabins in April 1877, to a busy hive of 30,000 inhabitants.[43] Such stampedes, however, occurred with rapidly diminishing violence and frequency. Indeed, mining was losing its earlier spirit of individualistic adventure. That picturesque nomad, the prospector, was giving way to the trained metallurgist employed by a mining company; the rocker, the sluice, and other primitive devices for obtaining ore were yielding to the hydraulic process and great rock-crushing and smelting machines.

The new system required large investments of capital and the formation of mining corporations. Already by 1880 groups of capitalists controlled not only the Leadville district but also the richest mines in Nevada. One gigantic California company owned all the best mines near Deadwood in the Black Hills, while similar conditions prevailed in Utah and Montana.[44] Emigrant guidebooks cautioned the tenderfoot against the hardships, risks, and almost certain losses of seeking previous metals by rule-of-thumb methods, pointing out that most of the mining kings had had comfortable fortunes to begin with.[45] Such advice did not go unheeded. So far as mineral wealth was concerned, the typical American of the 1880s preferred to get his thrills vicariously, risking his money (rather than his life) by buying stock in mining corporations which, alas, too often defaulted their dividends. One hundred and forty such companies, located at San Francisco in 1880, had already assessed their stockholders $47 million in addition to their original investment and had paid a total of but $6 million in dividends.[46]

No less notable was the change that took place in the conduct of the cattle industry. As the decade began, stock raising seemed to be at the noontide of its prosperity. The northerly push of longhorns along the trails from Texas was as great as ever while on the northwestern ranges the herds increased in size and value. Huge cattle companies were formed, often with English and Scotch capital, and in many sections of the Western range the cowboy began to receive his orders from a boss appointed by a board of directors in New York or London—a man who kept ledgers and gave serious study to cattle breeding and market conditions. As ranching sobered down to a businesslike basis, the position of the cowboy became steadily less that of a romantic hero and more that of a plain hired hand.

The abounding prosperity, however, was doomed from the outset, for it rested upon the rancher's possession of unfenced and unsettled public domain—obviously a temporary condition.[47] As the homesteader or "nester" advanced into the open range and the prairie was "cleft by skirmish lines of fence," the zone of free pasturage steadily dwindled. An angry desultory warfare occurred between the upholders of two types of civilization, the herdsman and the husbandman, with all history tilting the balance in favor of the husbandman. Each spring saw new homesteads marking the plains like a checkerboard and erecting prickly barriers against the free movement of the herds. Each year, too, the Long Drive from Texas was being slowly blotted out of existence, an event hastened by the Cattle quarantines laid in 1885 by Kansas and Colorado. The federal government also sided with the farmer. Thus the tortoise once more defeated the hare. The last half of the decade witnessed the collapse of the old range industry. In order to survive, the stock raiser was obliged to reorganize his business on a new basis—own his grazing grounds, fence them, provide winter feed, and breed better and fewer cattle.[48]

As the mining and cattle industries settled down to an orderly routine, the social disorders characteristic of the rawer, early days subsided. To be sure, Leadville in the first flush of the boom reproduced all the elements of a tumultuous mining town—saloons, dance halls, gambling hells; ruffians, prostitutes, criminals. But the advent of the railway in 1880 quickly and quietly gave the forces of civilization the upper hand, and the citizens presently began to boast of their schools, churches, newspapers, and banks.[49] A similar fate befell Dodge City, Kansas, last of the border "cow towns" and magnet of a turbulent, bird-of-passage population.[50] The settlement of a hinterland of farming communities and the effects of the state quarantine in keeping away the cattle drives caused this "Bibulous Babylon of the Frontier" to lose the chief source both of its prosperity and its wickedness.

Sporadic flare-ups of criminality continued to occur, but generally at points remote from the centers of law and order. The chief breeding ground was central and eastern New Mexico. Here in 1879 the Lincoln County cattle war dragged to a weary and gory close after the intervention of federal troops, though the principal killer, Billy the Kid, escaped a violent death for two years more.[51] Other bad men—Joel Fowler, Jesse Evans, Billy Wilson—had their day of truculence and death-dealing before they themselves became victims of their own system of private justice or else, surprisingly enough, changed their names and localities and settled down to become respected and useful citizens.[52] Undoubtedly much of the old border wildness—the "desperado complex"—was a result of social sanction. When times changed, men changed with them.

The plague of banditry also came to an end in that part of the Mississippi Valley most exposed to lawless influences.[53] Though temporarily disorganized by their bloody repulse three years before when trying to rob the Northfield (Minnesota) bank, the most notorious gang, the James Boys, resumed their depredations in 1879 in Missouri, holding up trains and robbing or shooting the passengers. Public opinion was so aroused that in September 1881 the governor of the state joined with various railway and express companies in setting a price on the heads of Jesse and Frank James. Tempted by the heavy reward, a member of the gang treacherously killed Jesse several months later. Frank voluntarily gave himself up and, after several futile attempts to convict him, quietly lived out the rest of his life as a decent member of society.[54]

The evil that the old West had done continued to live after it, highly romanticized in song, dime novel, and cheap melodrama. The substance, however, was gone. This satisfactory condition had been hastened by the spread of agricultural life through most parts of the Great West—by the coming of people who built houses and lived in them and were not content with blanket for a bed and the sky for a roof. The typical miner or cowboy was a bachelor and a rover, but with the farmer came his womenfolk, homemakers, supplying the Great West for the first time with the "right kind of girls" in sufficient quantities. There were twice as many women there in 1890 as in 1880. In certain parts, such as Wyoming, Idaho, and Oregon, their number tripled and in the cases of Washington and Montana, quadrupled.[55] Quickly the family hearth took the place of the ranch house or the camp saloon as the social center of Western life. It was a change which, however much for the better, involved for men a lessening of desirable simplicities and freedoms as well as of moral laxities. We can at least spare a transient tear for the last surviving longhorn who declaimed with his dying breath:

I little dreamed what would happen
　Some twenty summers hence,
When the nester came with his wife, his kids,
　His dogs and his barbed-wire fence.[56]

As the better and more accessible lands were occupied, the tidal wave of migration in the early eighties pushed great numbers of prospective farmers into districts which a few years before would have been avoided. Thus the zone of settlement spread into western Nebraska, Kansas, and Dakota, eastern Colorado, and Wyoming, places where the soil was fertile but the rainfall uncertain and the rivers shallow and inconstant. A wet season meant smiling crops and reduction of the farmer's mortgage, but the dice of nature were loaded against him and what was won one year was wiped out the next. Harried by droughts and other afflictions and ignorant of the possibilities of dry farming, thousands abandoned their hard-earned homes in the late eighties and returned East. It was this uneven duel with nature which injected much bitterness in to the farmer's soul and helped goad him into movements of protest.

Though the small farm was everywhere the typical unit of cultivation, this accustomed American system was for a time threatened by a spectacular new development in agricultural management. This was the bonanza farm, which had first appeared when Jay Cooke's failure in 1873 dumped large quantities of Northern Pacific land on the security holders. By the early eighties scores of great tracts of from 5,000 to 100,000 acres in Kansas, Dakota, Minnesota, Texas, and California had gravitated into the hands of individuals or companies, many of them absentee owners.[57] On one such farm near Colusa in the Sacramento Valley, California, nearly ninety square miles were under cultivation, principally in wheat, most of the laborers being Chinese. One of the famous Red River farms at Casselton in Dakota, managed by Oliver Dalrymple, half-owner in partnership with some directors of the Northern Pacific, spread over 115 square miles. It was conducted with the efficiency of a railway. The principal buildings were connected by telephone, a central clerical staff kept accounts, and free medical service was maintained for the workers. Though only a third of the area was as yet under the plow, an army of 600 were employed during the harvest. A formidable line of 115 self-binding reapers attacked the ripe wheat, cutting a swath of one fifth of a mile; then the grain, after passing through seventy-one steam threshers, was loaded into waiting trains that every night puffed away toward Duluth. With land bought at from forty cents to $5 an acre yielding an average of fifteen or twenty bushels, and with the wheat grown at a minimum cost and commanding special shipping rates, the profits were enormous.

The bonanza farm was a revival, under unexpected conditions, of a type of agriculture reminiscent of the plantation system of the prewar South but really allied to the mass-production methods that were transforming the Eastern factory system. Alarmed by the new development, students of the social trend did not hesitate to predict that rural America was approaching the condition to which Europe had been reduced by "a thousand years of feudal robbery and tyranny of wealth—with the lands concentrated . . . in the hands of the few and cultivated by a people who are dependent upon the rich.[58] Such fears, however, proved premature. The same decade that saw the greatest efflorescence of large-scale farming saw its fading. After the riches were once skimmed from the soil by the staple-crop system and when land values began to rise, the large holders inevitably yielded to the pressure to sell their farms in units small enough for more intensive cultivation. The Census of 1890 showed everywhere, except in the grazing sections, a marked tendency to return to medium-sized holdings.[59]

While the westward extension of the wheat and corn belts was the most striking development in Western agriculture, almost equally significant was the increasing diversification of farming through most parts of the region. California, for example, was in 1878 not only the greatest wheat-growing state in the Union, but also the banner state in wool production.[60] Sheep raising, however, waned in importance as new settlers appeared, eager to invest in more intensive agriculture. Orange groves, peach farms, prune orchards, vineyards, chicken ranches, bee farms, and similar undertakings attested the diverse interests of the later comers. Although fruit culture had been tried earlier, it was the decade after 1878 which, by means of irrigation and better marketing facilities, changed it from a highly speculative venture to a settled business.

Over the broad and sometimes wrinkled face of the Great West there were two spots which, though in many respects peculiar to themselves, were nevertheless profoundly affected by the new economic forces at work. One was the religious commonwealth of Utah, which by 1878 the Mormons had transformed from a sand-girt solitude into a cultivated domain rich in flocks, herds, farms, and orchards and threaded with highways and railroads. The fanatical ardor which had fired the original colonists already showed signs of cooling as Brigham Young passed from the scene in 1877 and a new generation came into control. Thanks to its ready access by rail, Salt Lake City exhibited a lusty growth—from 20,000 in 1880 to nearly 45,000 in 1890. While some of the newcomers were Mormon converts from Great Britain and the Scandinavian countries, many more were "Gentiles" utterly at variance with the Mormon creed and seeking their share of this world's goods. Under the circumstances the contagion of new ideas was not to be avoided. The *Deseret News,* the church organ, dating from

1850, now had rivals in the independent *Salt Lake Herald* and the anti-Mormon *Tribune*. Even in the religious field proper the Latter-day Saints, as they called themselves, were challenged by the efforts of other sects, notably the Presbyterians, Methodists, and Congregationalists.[61]

Looked at apart from their theology, the Mormons were a canny practical folk, hard working, temperate, and clannish.[62] The plague of saloons, brothels, and gambling dens was apparently introduced by the non-Mormons, though the latter insisted that the Saints were the sinners.[63] How many Mormon marriages were polygamous it is difficult to ascertain, but the Mormon figure of about 3 percent is probably nearer the truth than the feverish guesses of their opponents.[64] The church, however, did not recede from its earlier attitude that polygamy was a divine institution, designed by the Hebrew patriarchs to produce a eugenically superior race. It was this stubborn contention which, more than anything else, hindered the growing friendliness between Mormon and Gentile, sharpened the long-standing antagonism of the rest of America, and for many years kept Utah from statehood.

Though Congress in 1862 had prescribed fine and imprisonment as penalties for polygamy and twelve years later had strengthened the enforcement provisions, the legislation had remained virtually a dead letter. Prior to 1882, when a more drastic act was passed, only three final convictions had been secured by the government, largely because of the difficulty of obtaining proper testimony. The Edmunds law of that year aimed to cure the defects of earlier legislation and at the same time destroy the temporal power of the church.[65] While legitimating children born in polygamy before 1883, it threw out safeguards about the jury system and the testimony of witnesses, and added to the previous penalties for polygamy the loss of the right to vote and hold office. An even more direct blow at the Mormon theocracy was the provision for placing the conduct of Utah elections under a federal commission. Though this stringent measure brought gratifying results—there were over a thousand convictions by 1888[66]—public opinion was not yet appeased. As a result, the Edmunds-Tucker law in 1887 empowered the United States to take over all the property of the church except such as was used exclusively for religious purposes.[67]

The resentment of the Mormon leaders knew no bounds. Despite Supreme Court decisions to the contrary, they rang all the changes on the charge that they were being denied their constitutional right of freedom of worship.[68] They faced a crisis of national proportions, however, which could no longer be met either by open defiance or by passive evasion. Some of them went into hiding temporarily rather than submit, but this was a gesture of futility. It was clear that the days of polygamy were numbered and that the church must soon take the necessary steps to bring itself into harmony with the spirit of the age.

The region now known as Oklahoma presented a different kind of problem. All of it but the narrrow strip, "No Man's Land," north of the Texas panhandle had been set aside as a protected area for the Indians in the period before the Civil War. The original colonizing tribes—the Cherokee, Creek, Chickasaw, Choctaw, and Seminole—had developed an orderly and prosperous farming life and established schools, churches, and governmental institutions.[69] As a result of choosing the losing side in the Civil War, however, they had been forced to give up the western half of their lands. The ceded region was in part assigned to newly conquered bands of the plains and mountains, such as the Kiowa, Apache, Cheyenne, and Ponca Sioux, but a great district near the heart of the present state, known to the Indians as Oklahoma ("the beautiful land") and two thirds as large as the state of Connecticut, remained unoccupied.

The existence of this vacant central tract was a constant source of irritation and temptation to land-hungry Westerners, and shrewd railway promoters, eager to hasten white occupation, helped to keep this irritation at the boiling point. Moreover, since federal laws did not apply to the Indian country and the tribal authorities lacked jurisdiction over vagrant whites, the territory had become a threat to the peace of the older Western communities by the use horse thieves and other desperate characters made of it. The Indians, on the other hand, suspicious of any move to tamper with their existing status, preferred to bear the ills they had than to fly to others they knew not of. In this position they found ardent allies in the cattlemen to whom they had leased vast unused acres for grazing purposes.[70]

As in the South, so in the Great West the decade of the eighties was significant as marking the end of one cycle and the beginning of another. The trans-Missouri country was like a well-favored woman who, having given her adolescent years to an exciting and somewhat dubious round of gaiety, decides while the conventions still permit to settle down to a life of sober respectability. The West looked back over its shoulder toward a glamorous and romantic past, cherishing memories which have become a part of the national folklore, but bent its energies to the rewards of a life of steady habits and prosaic toil. It was no mere coincidence that border heroes like Buffalo Bill, Texas Jack Omohundro, and Wild Bill Hickok forsook the rapidly paling drama of Western life to take part in blood-curdling frontier melodramas on the mimic stage.[71]

Yet the eighties also taught the Westerner that hard work was not enough. Like his Southern brother, he was caught in the toils of an economic transition which too frequently denied him the legitimate fruits of his labors. Low crop prices, grinding debts, high freight rates, droughts, and insect visitations made him feel that the hand of both man and nature was raised against him. Thus the settling down of the Great West was, paradoxically enough, attended by multiplying evidences of agrarian unrest. Just as in the South, the farmers, despite their traditional individualism, turned increasingly to organized action. The Farmers' Alliances by 1890 controlled many of the legislatures and even had spokesmen in both houses of Congress.[72]

These loudly declaimed grievances, however, did little to halt the movement of settlers into the region. As the population enlarged, demands for statehood were made with ever greater vehemence. Only the inevitable jockeying for party advantage delayed appropriate action by Congress. In the summer and fall of 1889 conventions in North and South Dakota, Washington, Idaho, Montana, and Wyoming drew up constitutions reflecting the agrarian dislike of railroads and other corporations and embodying sundry demands for reform.[73] In 1889 and 1890 the six new states were admitted to the Union. The economic ills of the people remained, but the Great West was now in a position to join with the South and other discontented groups in pressing for relief through national action.

THE LURE OF THE CITY

IN THE MIDWEST and the North Atlantic states rural America, like a stag at bay, was making its last stand. The clash between the two cultures—one static, individualistic, agricultural; the other dynamic, collectivistic, urban—was most clearly exhibited in the preceeding section, for the march of events had already decided the outcome in the East. Agriculturally the Midwest, unlike the Great West, was beyond its period of growing pains. Farming was no longer pioneering and speculative; save in some of the newer districts the tendency everywhere was toward stabilization and a settled routine. Though the corn belt cut a wide swath through the lower tier of states and wheat predominated in the colder climes, the individual farmer was apt to supplement his main product with hay, orchard fruits, and vegetables and to raise horses, cattle, and hogs as well as crops, meantime guarding his soil resources through systematic rotation and the use of fertilizers.

The maturity of agriculture was mirrored in the physical appearance of the farms, particularly in the older regions. Neat frame dwellings housed the owners. Barns of increasing size and solidity, built of trimmed painted boards and perhaps protected below the ground line by stonework, sheltered the livestock and crops in place of the pioneer's slender framework of poles covered with straw. Instead of the oldtime zigzag fences of split logs, orderly rail fences or the new-fashioned wire variety appeared. One observant visitor from the Old World formed a distinctly favorable impression of Middle America as it flashed by his car window. "The tall corn pleased the eye," he wrote afterwards, "the trees were graceful in themselves, and framed the plain into long, aerial vistas; and the clean, bright, gardened townships spoke of country fare and pleasant summer evenings on the stoop." That this "flat paradise" was "not unfrequented by the devil" was suggested to him only by the billboards along the car tracks advertising cures for the ague.[74]

As urban communities increased in number and importance, the farmer's feeling of isolation was deepened by a knowledge of the pleasant town life not many miles away. The craving for solitudes is not as natural as the craving for multitudes, and the companionable sense of rubbing elbows, even if anonymously, with one's fellows compensates for many of life's repulses and frustrations. If the chief historian of the Scandinavian Americans is correct, the cheerlessness and hardships of farm life accounted for the uncommonly high proportion of insanity among the Norwegians and Swedes in the Midwest.[75] Certainly where families of different nationalities occupied the same neighborhood social intercourse was at a minimum, though a homogeneous immigrant community sometimes succeeded for a time in keeping alive the friendly social customs of the homeland.[76]

Despite such drawbacks many farmers valued the free open country life above all else and would not willingly have exchanged it for any other type of existence. Rural life, too, had its occasional cherished diversions for both young and old: its picnics and its gatherings at the swimming hole in summer, its nutting and hunting expeditions in the fall, its annual county fair and horse races, its family reunions at Thanksgiving, its bobsled parties of merrymakers in winter, its country dances in all seasons of the year.[77] Even its religious revivals might be so regarded. Funerals, too, were as much social events as solemn obsequies, attracting people from miles around and affording a treasured opportunity for brushing shoulders and exchanging gossip on the doorstep of the church or under the horse sheds. For those with eyes to see, nature itself in its vagrant moods and infinite variety was a never-ending source of pleasure. A field of growing wheat—"deep as the breast of a man, wide as a sea, heavy-headed, supple-stalked, many-voiced, full of multitudinous, secretive, whispered colloquies"—was to the aesthetic "a meeting-place of winds and of magic."[78]

But such pastimes and diversions paled before the bright attractions of the city, for, after the manner of human nature, the country dweller was apt to compare the worst features of his own lot with the best aspects of urban life. Nor, in the thinking of many, especially the younger folk, did these occasional pleasures repay for the drudgery and monotony which attended much of the daily toil, only to yield in the end a modest living. Farm work in former days had been spiced with greater variety. Now the advent of railroads and the lowered cost of manufactures led the farmer to buy over the store counter or through the mail-order catalogue multifarious articles which he had once made for himself. With no apparent reduction in the amount of labor, the kinds of tasks were fewer and often less appealing to his special interests and aptitudes. In contrast, the city offered both better business openings and a greater chance for congenial work.

The parents of Hamlin Garland, after a taste of Iowa village life, returned to the farm, to the resentful disappointment of their two sons (one of whom had clerked in an "ice-cream parlor"), who compared unfavorably the "ugly little farmhouse" and the "filthy drudgery of the farm-yard" with the "care-free companionable existence" of the town. Herbert Quick's mother pleaded in vain with her husband to leave their Iowa homestead for a place where their children might attend better schools. About the same time, in Wisconsin, Grant Showerman's farmer father told him, "I hope you won't have to drudge the way I've had to. . . . I want you to be a lawyer. I might have been a lawyer if I'd only had an education." [79] Men and boys, however, were probably less sensitive to the shortcomings of rustic life than the women, who, as Herbert Quick recorded in later years, "in many, many cases . . . were pining for neighbors, for domestic help, for pretty clothes, for schools, music, art, and the things tasted when the magazines came in." [80] It was the city rather than the unpeopled wilderness that was beginning to dazzle the imagination of the nation. The farmer, once the pride of America, was descending from his lofty estate, too readily accepting the city's scornful estimate of him as a "rube" and a "hay-seed." [81]

Different from Australia, where a few great centers gathered in the city-wending throng, the tendency was to move from the countryside to the nearest hamlet, from the hamlet to the town, and from the town to the city. [82] The reasons that impelled a person to leave the farm to go to a crossroads village were likely to cause the ambitious or maladjusted villager to remove to a larger place, or might in time spur the transplanted farmer lad himself to try his fortunes in a broader sphere. The results were seen in the records of city growth. The pyramid of urban population enlarged at every point from base to peak, and the countryside found itself encroached upon by hamlet, town, and city. The typical Midwestern urban community was a small town varying in size from a few thousand to 10,000 to 15,000 people. [83] Amid such surroundings, it may be noted, youths like George Ade, Charles A. Beard, Meredith Nicholson, and Charles H. Mayo grew up and had their first taste of life's sweets and bitters with no foreknowledge of that greater world where their names were to gain repute. [84]

The extraordinary growth of its bigger cities was one of the marvels of Midwestern life in the eighties. Chicago, which best represented the willpower and titanic energy of the section, leaped from a half million in 1880 to more than a million ten years later, establishing its place as the second city of the nation. The Twin Cities trebled in size; places like Detroit, Milwaukee, Columbus, and Cleveland increased by from 60 to 80 percent. [85] Of the fifty principal American cities in 1890, twelve were in the Midwest.

The rapid urbanization was of course, accelerated by the swarming of foreigners into the section. During the eighties the immigrant population of Middle America increased nearly 900,000, reaching a total at the close of the decade of 3.5 million.[86] Every fifth or sixth person in 1890 was of alien birth. Though the Scandinavians generally preferred the farm to the city, 70,000 of them were working in Chicago in 1890, the men as mechanics or factory hands, the daughters usually as domestic servants. Fifty thousand more dwelt in the Twin Cities. The Germans also divided their allegiance. James Bryce heard German commonly spoken on the streets of Milwaukee; the Teutonic element in Chicago, while thrice as numerous, was less conspicuous because of the babel of other tongues. As skilled workers, the newcomers from the *Vaterland* were generally found in such trades as photography, tailoring, baking, locksmithing, and lithography.[87] The nationalities which most thoroughly identified themselves with city life, however, were the Irish and particularly the increasing stream of Russian and Polish Jews and Italians who constituted the "new immigration."

So great was the influx of all races into Chicago that its foreign-born inhabitants in 1890 numbered nearly as many as its entire population in 1880. A writer in the nineties, analyzing its school census, pointed out that "only two cities in the German Empire, Berlin and Hamburg, have a greater German population than Chicago; only two in Sweden, Stockholm and Göteborg, have more Swedes; and only two in Norway, Christiania and Bergen, more Norwegians."[88] If the "seacoast of Bohemia" was a figment of the poet's imagination, the third largest city of Bohemians in the world could at least boast an extended lake front.

These and other immigrant groups huddled together in dense colonies like islands in a sea of humanity. They jealously maintained their own business institutions, churches, beneficial societies, foreign-language newspapers, and often their own parochial schools. In the small district about Hull House on South Halsted Street, eighteen nations were represented. As individuals ventured forth from these racial fastnesses into the bewildering world outside, they generally found it their lot to perform the disagreeable or arduous work which Americans of older stock disdained. The sweatshops in the garment industry were recruited largely from Bohemians and Russian Jews; the rough unskilled jobs in the building trades fell chiefly to Irish and Italians; while the business of peddling became a specialty of Jews.

Assimilation went on at an uneven pace, being notably slow in the case of the new arrivals from southern Europe and Russia. Timidity and ignorance on the part of the immigrant, suspicion and contempt on the part of the native-born, constantly retarded the process. Even the American-born children, if reared in an old-world atmosphere and taught their school lessons in an alien tongue, were more apt to be second-generation immigrants than first-generation Americans. But sooner or later the influences of the new land began to penetrate. Perhaps unusual business success or the liberalizing effect of membership in a labor union helped break down the barriers. More often, however, the change reflected the influence of the public school carried into the immigrant home by the children. Though a regrettable breach sometimes resulted between the older and younger generations, the democratic school system was a major force for rapid Americanization. The number of American-born immigrant children in Chicago in 1890 nearly equaled that of the total alien-born, thus increasing, though not by that proportion, the foreign character of her population.[89]

As was Chicago, so in a measure were Cleveland, Minneapolis, and Detroit. Yet Chicago's 450,000 foreign-born, Cleveland's 100,000, Detroit's 80,000 and Minneapolis's 60,000 formed only two fifths of all the people in those cities in 1890. In places like Columbus and Indianapolis, seven eighths of the population continued to be of American nativity. Many of the native-born, however, were of foreign parentage and still in the process of learning American ways.

Insofar as the swiftly growing urban localities drew population away from the countryside, the effects were severe enough to threaten many rural districts with paralysis. A map of the Midwest, shading the counties which suffered the chief losses between 1880 and 1890, would have been blackest across central Missouri and in the eastern half of Iowa, northern and western Illinois, central and southeastern Indiana, southern Michigan, and central and southern Ohio.[90] Though some of the depletion, particularly in Iowa and western Illinois, was connected with the building up of the agricultural country to the west, much of it was due to the cityward flight. In Ohio, 755 townships out of 1,316 declined in population; in Illinois, 800 out of 1,424. Yet during the same decade, every Midwestern state gained substantially in total number of inhabitants—Ohio about one seventh and Illinois nearly a quarter—an advance only in part to be accounted for by immigrant additions and the natural increase of population.

Such indications of rural decay, however, were mild as compared with conditions in the North Atlantic states. In this great seaboard section stretching from the Potomac to the St. Croix, the city had completed its conquest. Already in 1880 about half the people—7.5 million—lived in towns and cities of 4,000 or more inhabitants; within a decade the proportion grew to nearly three fifth, or 11 million.[91] In 1890 about two out of every three persons in New York and Connecticut were townsfolk, four out of every five in Massachusetts, and nine out of every ten in Rhode Island. Only the states of northern New England preserved their essentially rural character. In the East, too, most of the nation's great cities were to be found. New York City, with already more than a million people in 1880, reached a million and a half in 1890 without the help of Brooklyn, which contained 800,000 more. Philadelphia attained a million in 1890, though since the previous census Chicago had supplanted her as the second city of the United States. Boston, Baltimore, and Washington had about half a million each, Buffalo and Pittsburgh a quarter million each. Countless smaller places spotted the landscape and gave to the entire region a strongly urban cast.

In striking contrast were the rural backwaters. "Sloven farms alternate with vast areas of territory, half forest, half pasturage"; an observant foreign traveler wrote of Pennsylvania and New England, "farm buildings, partly in ruins, testify at once to the former prosperity of the agricultural industry and to its present collapse." Then, "all at once, on rounding a hill, one comes upon a busy valley, its slopes dotted with charming cottages, while at the further end rise the immense blocks of buildings and chimneys that tell of the factory.[92]

The census of 1890 first revealed the extent of the rural exodus.[93] Two fifths of Pennsylvania, a good quarter of New Jersey, nearly five sixths of New York State, and much of New England had fallen off in population during the decade. The eclipse of the Eastern countryside had, of course, been long in process, indeed ever since the old farming districts of the Atlantic states first felt the competition of the virgin lands of the interior.[94] After the Civil War the pressure became even greater, for the opening of new railway lines enabled the prairie farmers, with the aid of favoring freight rates, to undersell Eastern farmers in their own natural markets. The normal drain on the older agricultural districts was intensified by the drift of country boys and girls to the towns and cities as industry boomed and the lure of the nearby metropolis captured their imaginations. Far removed from the free lands of the Great West, the rural youth was now less inclined to ask "Where is the fittest farm?" than "Where is the fitter vocation?"

New England was hardest hit of all, especially those parts in which agricultural retrogression was not offset by corresponding urban development. Three fifths of Connecticut, three fourths of Vermont, and nearly two thirds of New Hampshire and Maine declined in population. Out of 1,502 townships in all New England, 932 had fewer people in 1890 than at the start of the decade.[95] Cellar holes choked with lilac and woodbine, tumbledown buildings, scrubby orchards, pastures bristling with new forest growths, perhaps a lone rosebush—these mute, pathetic memorials of once busy farming communities attested the reversal of a familiar historic process, with civilization retreating before the advancing wilderness.

Official inquiries at the end of the eighties revealed more than 1,000 farms in Vermont abandoned for agricultural purposes, over 1,300 in New Hampshire, nearly 1,500 in Massachusetts and more than 3,300 in Maine.[96] Vermont farms with good buildings went begging at $5 or less an acre. Nor did the upland villages escape the general debacle. "The proportion of abandoned wagonshops, shoeshops, saw-mills and other mechanical businesses has far outstripped the abandonment of farms," wrote one contemporary.[97] Judge Nott of Washington, D.C., happening upon a stricken village in southern Vermont, found that the church was abandoned, the academy dismantled, the village deserted. The farmer who owned the farm on the north of the village lived on one side of the broad street, and he who owned the farm on the south lived on the other, and they were the only inhabitants.

All others had fled—"to the manufacturing villages, to the great cities, to the West." Where once had dwelt "industry, education, religion, comfort, and contentment," there remained "only a dreary solitude of forsaken homes."[98]

Generally the people of push and initiative migrated while the less enterprising stayed at home. Thus Yankee energy, though continuing to contribute vitally to the upbuilding of America, did so at a terrible cost to the stock it left behind. Ministers and humanitarian workers in the country districts were appalled by the extent of inbreeding, the prevalence of drunkenness, bastardy and idiocy, the lack of wholesome amusements and the almost universal poverty. In nearly the same words two Congregational preachers reported, "My people are degenerates; the people all through my district are degenerates."[99] It may well be believed that such characterizations applied to the most neglected communities rather than to typical ones. Yet everywhere, the process of folk depletion was going on at an alarming rate, lending color to the assertion that New England's woods and templed hills were breeding their own race of poor whites.

Despite the decline of rural population in New England and other parts of the East the attractions of city life were so great that from 1880 to 1890 the section in general gained 20 percent in number of inhabitants. By the latter year, 19 million, or somewhat less than a third of all the nation, lived there. Urban growth, even more than in Middle America, was nourished by foreign immigration.[100] A larger proportion of the alien arrivals settled in the East and fewer of them took up farming as a livelihood. The census of 1890 disclosed a million more immigrants than a decade earlier. In the section as a whole, one out of every five persons was foreign-born.

Nor could one assume, as ten years before, that any immigrant he met was likely to belong to the older racial strains that had fused into the historic American stock. The Eastern commonwealths with their great ports and thriving industries were the first to feel the impact of the new human tide that was setting in from southern and eastern Europe. While in 1890 they contained more Irish and Britons than did any other section—a total of 2.3 million—and with 900,000 Germans ranked in that respect next to the Midwest, they also embraced more Italians, Russians, and Hungarians than any other section, to the number of 250,000.

A fourth of the people of Philadelphia and a third of the Bostonians were in 1890 of foreign birth. New York-Brooklyn was the greatest center of immigrants in the world, having half as many Italians as Naples, as many Germans as Hamburg, twice as many Irish as Dublin, and two and a half times as many Jews as Warsaw.[101] Four out of every five residents of Greater New York were foreigners or of foreign parentage. Different from Boston and Philadelphia, the newer type of immigrant had become a considerable element in the city's population though the Germans and Irish still greatly predominated.

These latest arrivals, ignorant, clannish, inured to wretched living conditions, gravitated naturally to the poorest quarters of the city—the tip of Manhattan—and gradually pushed the older occupants into the better sections to the north.[102] Lower New York was like a human palimpsest, the writing of earlier peoples being dimmed, though not entirely effaced, by the heavier print of the newest comers. Through the eighties the Italians crowded into the old Irish neighborhoods west of Broadway, while the Russian and Polish Jews took possession of the German districts to the east with the tenth ward as their center.[103] The Hungarians settled thickly east of Avenue B, about Houston Street, and the Bohemians near the river on the Upper East Side from about Fiftieth to 76th Street. Smaller groups like the Greeks and Syrians also had their special precincts where picturesque old-world customs and trades prevailed, and in the heart of the Lower East Side grew up a small replica of San Francisco's Chinatown.

Quite as strange to Americans as the south Europeans were the French Canadians who began their mass invasion of New England shortly after 1878. For over two centuries these descendants of the pioneers of New France had tilled the soil of the province of Quebec where, intensely race-conscious and devoted to Catholicism, they had stubbornly maintained their identity and language apart from the conquering English. Harried, however, by hard times from the 1860s on and tempted by better opportunities elsewhere, many of them sought escape in migration.[104] Some moved westward to set up farm colonies in Ontario and Manitoba. Others, feeling the pull of the busy mill towns across the international border, succumbed to *le mal des Etats-Unis*. Presently the trickle of population into New England became a flooding stream. About 14,000 had removed to Rhode Island by 1875, 64,000 to Massachusetts ten years later. Northern New England made less appeal though occasional settlements of farmers and lumberjacks were to be found. By 1890 the French Canadians, then numbering 200,000 formed approximately a sixth of the entire immigrant population of New England.[105] Nearly half of them were in Massachusetts.

Hiving in the manufacturing towns, they were eagerly welcomed by employers who found them not only hard workers but also slow to give trouble even when conditions were galling. Added to the already large Irish Catholic contingent, their presence seemed to threaten the traditional Puritan and Protestant character of the section. "Protestant New England will soon have within itself, A Roman Catholic New France, as large as, if not larger than itself," cried one alarmist.[106] As a matter of fact, the language barrier and the desire of the newcomers to import their own priests caused more friction than friendship between them and the resident Irish-American clergy.[107] It was said that French-Canadian support of the Republican party at the polls was due to no reason so good as that the Irish preferred the Democrats.

A race so resistant could hardly be expected to adopt new ways of life overnight. Yet scattered in 100 different communities and obliged constantly to rub elbows with people unlike themselves, the chemistry of Americanization worked as quickly with them as with most other foreign-born groups. Intermarriage, while not common, took place most readily with Anglo Canadians.[108] Less adept politically than the Irish, they nevertheless gradually found their way into local offices and by 1890 thirteen French Canadians were members of New England legislatures.[109] Different from other immigrant peoples, however, they massed themselves in New England, few of them going into the Midwest or even into other parts of the East.

As a lodestone for both immigrant and native-born the city had decisively placed the East under thrall. Its hand already lay heavily upon the Midwest. Even in the farther West and the South its power and distant allure were strongly felt though society as yet lingered in an agricultural state. Through the nation in general every third American in 1890 was an urban dweller, living in a town of 4,000 or more inhabitants.[110] Cities of from 12,000 to 20,000 people had since 1880 increased in number from 76 to 107; cities of from 20,000 to 40,000 from 55 to 91; larger places up to 75,000 inhabitants from 21 to 35; cities of yet greater size from 23 to 39.[111]

Moreover, the concentration of population had been attended by a significant concentration of wealth. This latter circumstance furnished ample basis for the agrarian contention that the rural districts were not sharing proportionately in the advancing national wealth. In 1880, according to the census, the value of farms was equal to that of urban real estate, about $10 billion for each. In 1890 the value of farms was returned as $13 billion while other real estate—mostly urban —was listed at $26 billion. Nor did the people on the farms and in the rural hamlets of the East fare better than those of the West and South. On the contrary, the farms in the Eastern states declined in absolute value during the decade.

If personality were included, the contrast between city and country became even sharper, particularly since the tangible personality on the farms was in considerable degree offset by mortgages held in the towns and cities. The most careful contemporary student of the subject estimated that in 1890 the average wealth of families in the rural districts did not exceed $3,250 while the average wealth of city families was over $9,000.[112] The wider implications of urban growth, however, reached far beyond exigent considerations of wealth and income. These, as they affected the character of American civilization for good or ill, remain yet to be examined.

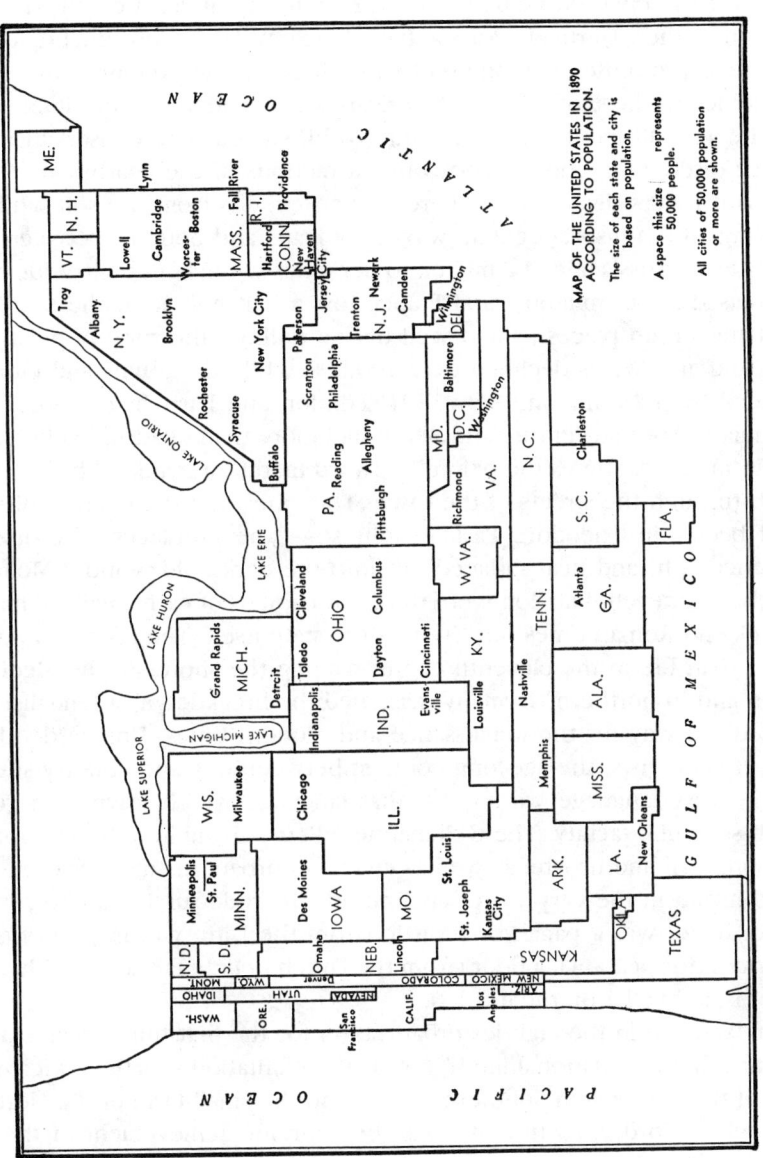

The Populous States in 1890

THE URBAN WORLD

THE CLASH of country and city was not a phenomenon peculiar to America. All over the civilized globe the rural regions lay under a cloud—in Great Britain, France, Germany, Russia, Italy, Belgium.[113] The introduction of farm machinery and the opening up of virgin fields in the Argentine and Australia, added to those of the new American West, rendered unprofitable much of the agricultural labor of the Old World, stirred rural conservatism into fierce discontent, and enhanced the attractions of the nearby city for the peasant toilers. Everywhere there was an exodus from the soil while the trading and industrial centers waxed by leaps and bounds. Between 1881 and 1891, Prussia added 2 million to her cities while her countryside barely increased a half million; rural France lost a half million at the same time that her urban places gained well over a million; the rural population of England and Wales declined over 200,000 while the towns and cities advanced by 3.25 million.[114] By 1891, London and Paris had doubled their population of mid-century and Berlin had more than quadrupled hers.

From earliest times the painful, upward march of mankind had beaten a path through the streets of the town. The cities, not the country districts, had been—in Theodore Parker's phrase—"the fireplaces of civilization whence light and heat radiated out into the dark cold world." Memphis, Thebes, Nineveh, Babylon were the great capitals of early civilized man. In Greek and Roman times the city was the state itself. The revival of a vigorous urban life in the eleventh century, along the shores of the Mediterranean and in northern Germany, hastened the breakdown of feudalism and paved the way for the Renaissance and modern times. Unregarded by all but etymologists, the age-long contrast between city and country survives in the very language we speak—that language which townsmen coined with such glib facility. The well-mannered *civis* living in *urbs* was, for that reason, civil and urbane as well as civic and urban; his manner of life was epitomized in the very word, civilization. His rude rural neighbor, on the other hand, was a pagan or a rustic (from the Latin words, *paganus* and *rusticus*, for peasant), a boor (from the Dutch *boer*, a farmer), or a heathen (that is, a dweller on the heaths).

In America in the eighties urbanization for the first time became a controlling factor in national life.[115] Just as the plantation was the typical product of the antebellum Southern system and the small farm of the Northern agricultural order, so the city was the supreme achievement of the new industrialism. In its confines were focused all the new economic forces: the vast accumulations of capital, the business and financial institutions, the spreading railway yards, the gaunt smoky mills, the white-collar middle classes, the motley wage-earning population. By the same token, the city inevitably became the generating center for social and intellectual progress.

To dwell in the midst of great affairs is stimulating and broadening; it is the source of a discontent which, if not divine, is at least energizing. In a populous urban community like could find like; the person of ability, starved in his rural isolation, might by going there find sympathy, encouragement, and that criticism which often refines talent into genius.

Moreover the new social needs created by crowded living stimulated inventors to devise mechanical remedies—appliances for better lighting, for faster communication and transit, for higher buildings—which reacted in a thousand ways on the life of urban folk. Density of population plus wealth concentration also facilitated organized effort for cultivating the life of mind and spirit.[116] In the city were to be found the best schools, the best churches, the best newspapers, and virtually all the bookstores, libraries, art galleries, museums, theaters, and opera houses. It is not surprising that the great cultural advances of the time came out of the city, or that its influence should ramify to the farthest countryside.

But the heirs of the older American tradition did not yield the field without a struggle. To them, as to Jefferson, cities were "ulcers on the body politic." In their eyes the city spiritual was offset by the city sinister, civic splendor by civic squalor, urban virtues by urban vices, the city of light by the city of darkness. In politics they sought to preserve or restore their birthright of equality by stoutly belaboring their capitalistic foe embattled in his city fortress, but against the pervasive lure of metropolitan life, felt by their sons and daughters, they could do no better than invent sensational variations of the nursery tale of the country mouse and the city mouse. Urban growth evoked a voluminous literature of bucolic fear, typified by such titles as *The Spider and the Fly; or, Tricks, Traps, and Pitfalls of City Life by One Who Knows* (New York, 1873) and J. W. Buel's *Metropolitan Life Unveiled; or the Mysteries and Miseries of America's Great Cities* (St. Louis, 1882). It may be questioned, however, whether such exciting accounts with their smudgy but realistic pictures did more to repel than entice their breathless readers to partake of the life they depicted.

To traveled persons familiar with the distinctive personalities of European centers, American cities presented a monotonous sameness. Apart from New York, Boston, Washington, New Orleans, and a few other places, Bryce believed that "American cities differ from one another only herein, that some of them are built more with brick than with wood, and others more with wood than brick."[117] Most places possessed the same checkerboard arrangement of streets lined with shade trees, the same shops grouped in much the same way, the same middle-class folk hurrying about their business, the same succession of unsightly telegraph poles, the same hotels with seedy men lounging in the dreary lobbies. Few foreign visitors stopped to think, however, that American cities were the handiwork not of many national states but of a fairly uniform continentwide culture. If they lacked the colorful variety of ancient European foundations, they also lacked the physical inconveniences and discomforts which picturesqueness was apt to entail. But it could not be gainsaid that a tendency toward standardization, as well as toward higher standards, was one of the fruits of American urban development.

While in the European sense there was no single dominant city in America—no city both metropolis and capital—yet all agreed in according the foremost position to New York. Nowhere else were there such fine buildings, such imposing financial houses, such unusual opportunities for business and recreation. No other place had such an air of rush and bustle, the streets constantly being torn up, dug up, or blown up. An unending stream of visitors discovered some pretext to go to New York each year; in it many foreign travelers, going no farther, found material for pithy, if ill-informed, comments on the whole American scene. "The streets are narrow," wrote one observer in 1883, "and overshadowed as they are by edifices six or more stories in height, seem to be dwarfed into mere alley-ways."[118] At that time the well-populated district did not extend much beyond 59th Street, and Madison Square at the intersection of Broadway and Fifth Avenue had recently supplanted Union Square as the nerve center of New York life. But the period of growth and expansion was at hand. The corporate limits, which before 1874 had not reached beyond Manhattan Island, spread rapidly until in 1898, as Greater New York, they embraced Bronx County, Kings County (Brooklyn), Richmond County (Staten Island), and a portion of Queens County (on Long Island).

As earlier, Broadway was the main artery of New York life, lending itself successively to wholesale trade, newspaper and magazine publishing, retail shopping, hotels and theaters, as it wended its way northward from the Battery. Manhattan's other famous thoroughfare, Fifth Avenue, offered a continuous pageant of "palatial hotels, gorgeous club-houses, brownstone mansions and magnificent churches."[119] Different from most American cities, the finest residences stood side by side without relief of lawn or shrubbery; only on the striking but as yet unfinished Riverside Drive, with its noble view of the Hudson, was architecture assisted by nature. Merchant princes and Wall Street Millionaires vied with one another to sustain Fifth Avenue's reputation of being the most splendid thoroughfare in America, "a very alderman among streets." During the 1880s a dark brown tide swept up the avenue. The late A. T. Stewart's marble palace at the corner of 34th Street, long a magnet for sightseers, was eclipsed by the newer brownstone mansions of the Vanderbilts and others farther up the avenue, enclosed by forbidding iron fences. In the late afternoon Fifth Avenue churned with "a torrent of equipages, returning from the races or the park: broughams, landaus, clarences, phaetons, . . . equestrians in boots and corduroys, slim-waisted equestriennes with blue veils floating from tall silk hats."[120]

Yet New York was a city of contradictions, reminding one visitor of "a lady in ball costume, with diamonds in her ears, and her toes out at her boots."[121] Against the splendors of Fifth Avenue and the show places of the metropolis had to be set the rocky wastes of Shantytown, extending during the 1880s along the East Side from 42nd to 110th Street and inhabited by Irish squatters, goats, and pigs living promiscuously together. Contrasting with the pillared citadels of wealth in Wall Street was the nearby slum section, a festering spot of poverty and immorality, finding a tawdry outlet for its life in the notorious Bowery.[122]

The New Yorker was already famed for his provincialism: his proud ignorance of the rest of the nation and lofty condescension toward cities of lesser note.[123] Yet foreign tourists found much to interest and detain them in these other centers, and at least one felt a native New Yorker to be "less American than many Westerners born on the bank of the Oder or on the Shores of some Scandinavian *fjord.*"[124] Boston charmed with the quiet tenor of her life, her atmosphere of intellectuality, her generally English appearance.[125] With the reclamation of the Back Bay, a great engineering project completed in 1881, the city acquired over 100 acres of filled land which made possible its expansion southward and the development of straight, wide thoroughfares to Copley Square and beyond.

Even more than Boston, Philadelphia impressed her visitors as a city of homes, with row upon row of prim brick houses with white wooden shutters, owned by their occupants. "If there are few notable buildings, there are few slums."[126] In Washington the traveler found America's most beautiful city, "one of the most singularly handsome cities on the globe."[127] Its parks and wide shaded avenues, its spacious vistas, the dazzling white of its public edifices, were reminiscent of great European capitals. In the absence of an army of factory workers the general tone was one of dignified ease in pleasing contrast to the feverish anxiety typical of other cities. "The inhabitants do not rush onward as though they were late for the train . . . or as though the dinner-hour being past they were anxious to appease an irritable wife. . . ."[128]

Farther to the west lay Chicago, "the most American of American cities, and yet the most mongrel," a miracle city risen Phoenix-like from its great fire of 1871.[129] Its business and shopping district, rivaling New York's in high buildings, noise, and impressiveness, was fringed by three residential areas: the north side, its broad streets lined with handsome abodes, churches, and club houses overlooking the lake; the south side, a newer and hardly less aristocratic section, studded with stately mansions and spacious parks; and the vast west side, more populous than the other two combined, where dwelt the immigrants and laboring folk. Like every other great city, Chicago offered a study in contrasts: squalor matching splendor, municipal boodle contending with civic spirit; the very air now reeking with the foul stench of the stockyards, now fresh-blown from prairie or lake. A "splendid chaos" indeed, causing the roving Kipling to exclaim, "Having seen it, I urgently desire never to see it again."[130]

No better example could be found of what one contemporary called "urban imperialism." The surrounding prairie was for miles laced with railroads, and a large portion of the city and its suburbs was made up of a series of huge stations, car yards, grain elevators, cattle pens, and storehouses. As the world's greatest corn, cattle, and timber market, Chicago completely dominated the Mississippi Valley and, to some degree, the farther West as well. Other places like Milwaukee, Kansas City, Detroit, and the Twin Cities rose and flourished largely by its sufferance or favor. Even the older entrepôts—Cincinnati, St. Louis, New Orleans—lay under tribute to the Lake city, and Denver and San Francisco were not too remote to escape its influence.[131] Yet these and other cities had their own economic and cultural spheres of influence, and astonished Europeans found in them a level of material comfort typical only of the principal foreign centers.

Certain problems growing out of crowded living conditions vexed all municipalities, differing among them in degree rather than in kind. None was more important in 1878 than that of adequate traffic facilities. Even in the major cities streets were ill paved, if paved at all, and in the business sections were apt to be choked with rushing, jostling humanity. "The visitor is kept dodging, halting and shuffling to avoid the passing throng . . . ," asserted one timid contemporary. "The confusing rattle of 'busses and wagons over the granite pavement in Broadway almost drowns his own thoughts, and if he should desire to cross the street a thousand misgivings will assail him . . . although he sees scores of men and women constantly passing through the moving line of vehicles. . . ."[132] Cobblestones and granite blocks were the favorite paving materials in the East because of their local availability, just as wood blocks were in the Midwest.

But streets so constructed soon wore rough and uneven, and the eighties marked an era of experimentation with more satisfactory types of surfacing.[133] The discovery of natural beds of pitch on the Island of Trinidad directed attention to asphalt, already widely used in Paris and London. When Washington laid 400,000 square yards of it between 1878 and 1882, that city set a pace soon followed by Buffalo, Philadelphia, and other places. By 1898 the United States possessed nearly 30 million square yards of asphalt paving. The imported material, however, was rivaled by a native product, brick. Charleston, West Virginia, and Bloomington, Illinois, had tried it in the previous decade, but it was not until the mid-eighties that it came into general use, notably in the Midwest. By 1898, Des Moines, Columbus, and Cleveland stood first in the proportion of brick paving to population, though Philadelphia with its 2 million square yards had more than any other one city. In most cities, macadam, a much cheaper material, was deemed sufficiently durable for residential and suburban roadways. Smaller towns contented themselves with dirt or gravel.

Horsecars, omnibuses, cabs, and other similar vehicles had suited the needs of simpler days, but the age of the great city called for swifter conveyance. The old "bobtail" cars, modeled on the stagecoach and pulled by horses or mules, did not suffice for moving an enormous mass of people to and from their places of work at about the same hours of the day. Already New York had shown the utility of an overhead railway, four-car trains being drawn by diminutive steam locomotives which scattered oil and live ashes on the heads of unwary pedestrians. In 1878 a second unit, the Sixth Avenue Elevated, extending nearly the length of the island, was added to the original line. The "El" three years later was transporting 175,000 passengers daily or, if you prefer, "12,000 tons of human flesh, averging each person at 140 lbs."[134] Under the spur of faster transit, the population spread rapidly northward. New lines were projected and built, reaching beyond the Harlem River into the northern suburban districts.[135] Kansas City also elevated some of her tracks in the mid-eighties and Brooklyn built an extensive system the same decade. But Chicago did not open her first line until 1892, and Boston, which in the meantime had begun to burrow underground, not until 1901.

The slow adoption of the overhead system was due partly to its ugliness and noise, but even more to the initial cost of construction. Of greater popularity in the eighties was the cable car, first contrived by a Scotch immigrant, Andrew S. Hallidie, in 1873 to solve the problem of transit over the hilly streets of San Francisco. The car moved by means of a grappling device which descended from the floor to an endless steel cable moving in a slotted trench between the tracks.[136] After a few years the system was taken over by cities which lacked San Francisco's peculiar need. In 1882, Charles T. Yerkes laid a cable road in Chicago, achieving not only a success for the city but a fortune for himself. Philadelphia followed the next year and New York in 1886. By the mid-nineties Eastern cities had 157 miles in operation, the Midwest 252, the Far West 217, and the South 6.[137]

While the cable system was yet in its heyday, this generation made its most substantial contribution toward solving the problem of urban transit. For many years — at least since 1835 — inventors in America and abroad had been working on the idea of an electrical railway. Until the development of a practicable dynamo in the 1870s, however, they had been baffled by the lack of an adequate supply of cheap current. The 1880s saw the launching of trial lines at points as far removed as Boston and Denver,[138] but the credit for the first American electric railway successfully operated for profit over city streets belongs to Lieutenant Frank J. Sprague. In 1887–88 he installed two and a half miles of track in Richmond, Virginia, the cars securing their current from an overhead trolley wire fed from a central powerhouse.

Its instant success started a veritable revolution in urban transit. Not only were electric-propelled cars fast and comfortable but they were relatively cheap to construct and maintain. Fifty-one cities installed the new system by 1890, and five years later 850 lines were in operation, mostly in the East and Midwest, with a total mileage of 10,000.[139] Though horse and cable cars lingered on many streets, their doom was sealed. European cities lagged far behind those of America in adopting electric transit. At the close of the century, Germany, with a trackage as great as all other European countries combined, possessed only one ninth the mileage of the United States.[140]

Hardly less urgent than the need for better transit was the need for readier communication. In 1878 the recently invented telephone was hardly more than a scientific toy.[141] To use it a person, after briskly turning a crank, screamed into a crude mouthpiece and then, if the satanic screechings and groanings of static permitted, faintly heard the return message. There was no central exchange station, telephone users being directly connected with one another by separate wires.

As population centers grew, social and business needs caused the telephone to be perfected rapidly and made the public forget its earlier prejudices. An important obstacle to success was removed in 1879 when the Western Union Telegraph Company, which had bitterly fought the Bell group by fair means and foul, came to terms and sold out its own telephone interests to the Bell Company.[142] Had Western Union been able to invalidate Bell's claims as prior inventor before the courts, it is almost certain that the development of the telephone would have been sacrificed to that of the telegraph and hence its extension greatly retarded. Under the circumstances, however, mechanical improvements quickly ensued.[143] Francis Blake's invention of a carbon transmitter in 1881, an advance over Emile Berliner's and Edison's devices of four years before, greatly improved the carrying qualities of the voice. Two years later another young man, J. J. Carty, exorcised the mysterious noises of the wires by a simple mechanical arrangement known as the metallic-circuit system.

Hardly less important was the contriving of a central switchboard, the work largely of Charles E. Scribner, who installed the first commercial board at New Haven, Connecticut, in January 1878 for the use of twenty-one subscribers.[144] When Scribner followed this in 1885 with the invention of a multiple switchboard, the nerve center of the telephone was complete. At first, boys were employed at "central," but being addicted to fighting one another and swearing at their unseen customers, they were soon superseded by girls, who thus found a new vocation.[145]

In 1880, eighty-five towns had telephone exchanges with nearly 15,000 subscribers and about 35,000 miles of wire. Ten years later the number of subscribers had grown fivefold and the wire mileage sevenfold.[146] From the first intercity line joining Boston and Lowell in 1879, the reach of the telephone grew constantly greater until, by 1892, Boston and New York were talking with Washington, Pittsburgh, Chicago, and Milwaukee and a few years later with Omaha.[147] As presidential candidate, McKinley sat in his home at Canton, Ohio, and talked with his campaign managers in thirty-eight states. When, in 1893, the monopoly held by the Bell Company expired, many independent companies sprang up, especially in the smaller towns of the Midwest where the Bell system had not found it worthwhile to extend its service.[148]

Nearly 800,000 phones were in use by 1900, one for every ninety-five persons as compared with one for every 923, twenty years before; the United States had twice as many telephones as all Europe. In two decades Bell's invention had, from a mechanical curiosity, become a necessity of American life. That it added to the speed of living and the breaking down of personal privacy cannot be doubted. That it helped make the American people the most talkative nation in the world is likewise clear. On the credit side of the ledger, however, must be put the enormous gains resulting from the facilitation of social and business intercourse and from the extension of urban influences into areas of rural isolation.

If the nation made great strides in communication, the cities repeatedly stumbled over the problem of waste accumulation. Since the middle of the century and earlier, places like New York, Boston, and Chicago had had public underground conduits for discharging sewage into nearby bodies of water. But their facilities lagged behind the growth of population and most other cities employed village methods of surface-draining their streets and of using private vaults and cesspools for family wastes. In 1877, Philadelphia had 82,000 such vaults and cesspools, Washington 56,000 and Chicago, despite its sewerage system, 30,000.[149] Two years later a noted sanitary engineer called proper sewage disposal "the great unanswered question of the day."[150] Its solution involved grave problems of community health, for dense populations made private uncleanliness increasingly a public concern.

In the two decades following, however, sewerage facilities were greatly extended, while important improvements were effected in sewer construction and in methods of ultimate disposal.[151] This last problem was an especially difficult one. Cities with waterfronts usually discharged their sewage into sea or river with always a danger of water pollution, especially where there was a tidal backwash; elsewhere, filter beds and farm irrigation systems were commonly used. Progress was very uneven. While Boston and Washington spent millions in improving their sewerage works during these years, Philadelphia and St. Louis had at the close of the period little more than half as great a mileage of sewers as of streets, and Baltimore, New Orleans, and Mobile continued to rely for drainage mainly on open gutters.[152] The allied problem of garbage disposal was taken care of hardly better.[153] In New York, Boston, and other ports such matter was carried in scows and barges several miles out to sea and discharged upon an outgoing tide. A common practice in inland towns was to contract for its collection by farmers who fed it to swine. Since animals so fed were subject to trichinae, with a consequent danger to meat eaters, furnaces began to be introduced, after 1885, especially in Midwestern cities, for the reduction of garbage by fire.[154]

The growing volume of urban wastes complicated the problem of a potable water system. This generation, however, gave less heed to the quality of the water than to its quantity. Only about 600 cities had public waterworks in 1878, but in the next two decades their number grew nearly sixfold. At the same time some of the greater cities enlarged their existing facilities.[155] Thus between 1885 and 1892, New York, at a cost of $24 million, constructed the New Croton Aqueduct with a carrying capacity of nearly 300 million gallons a day.

Gradually, however, as a result of European example and the advance of the germ theory of disease, attention was also given to the purity of the water. The Massachusetts board of health in 1886 was granted by law general oversight of all inland waters of the state with power to advise municipal authorities in regard to water supply, sewage disposal, and methods of preventing pollution.[156] Within the next few years careful investigations were also made by the state health boards of Connecticut, Minnesota, New Jersey, New York, Ohio, and Rhode Island.[157] Cities differed greatly as to the purity of their water supplies, and public-health guardians were not slow in pointing out corresponding differences as to mortality from typhoid fever. Between 1880 and 1890 about half as many people proportionately died of typhoid fever in New York and Boston, where the water was comparatively pure, as in Philadelphia and Chicago, where the supply was contaminated.[158] Pollution by sewage and manufacturers' wastes was especially serious in the case of cities drawing their water from rivers or other natural sources.

The quality of urban life was profoundly influenced by one's lodgings, and these varied according to income. For well-to-do transients, the great cities offered hotels constantly increasing in number, size, and sumptuousness.[159] Already famous in the eighties were such hostelries as the Grand Union, Park Avenue, and Murray Hill in New York; the Stratford and the Lafayette in Philadelphia; Young's and the Vendôme in Boston; the Grand Pacific, Palmer House, and Auditorium in Chicago; the Brown Palace Hotel in Denver; and Baldwin's in San Francisco. Among the new ones in the last decade of the century were the Plaza, Savoy, and Waldorf-Astoria in New York; the Jefferson in Richmond, Virginia; and the Raleigh in Washington.

Such hotels, gorgeously decorated and furnished, with a steadily diminishing emphasis on the "steamboat style," made a special appeal with their private baths, electric elevators, electric-call service, and other up-to-the-minute conveniences. Though the incessant "tinkle, tinkle, tinkle of the ice-pitcher" proved "positively nauseous" to the British compiler of *Baedeker*, he otherwise thought well of the American institution and had even a word of praise and commiseration for that "mannerless despot," the hotel clerk.[160] Every large city also had hotels of second and third class or of no class at all, falling as low in New York as lodging places in Chatham Street (now Park Row) and the Bowery where one could secure sleeping space for a few pennies a night.[161] In general, hotels in the South were apt to be poorer than in any other section, while in the West, even in the newer towns, they were unexpectedly good.

If the traveler did not wish to patronize his own hotel dining room, he could usually find in the larger cities excellent restaurants at hand. In Delmonico's, at Fifth Avenue and 26th Street, he could eat the best meals in America, at the highest prices. There, important political conferences were held, college societies celebrated their reunions, and distinguished foreigners were feted. The Brunswick and the Brevoort were hardly less fashionable, the former receiving its summer patrons in an attractive garden in the rear. While other centers were not as well served as New York, Chicago boasted of the Richelieu and Kingsley's and the French restaurants in New Orleans—Moreau's, Mme. Venn's, Flêche's, Victor's—were justly famed the country over.

City dwellers who wished to escape the drudgery and responsibility of housekeeping usually lived in boardinghouses. With the opening of the Buckingham Hotel in New York in 1877, however, an increasing number of attractive apartment hotels for private families made their appearance. At the same time the swifter means of transit and communication caused a flow of population into suburban districts, where shaded streets, ample lawns, and neighborly friendliness gave everyday living something of a bucolic flavor. This dispersion was particularly noticeable in the last ten years of the period, far out-distancing the rapid extension of official municipal limits.[162] By the end of the nineties New York's suburbs held over a million people, one third as many as the city proper, while more people actually lived on Boston's outskirts than within her corporate confines. Pittsburgh, Providence, and Cincinnati had similarly acquired strong satellite colonies.

In contrast to this agreeable picture must be placed another, that of the living conditions of the less prosperous classes and particularly of the immigrants. Of the great cities of the land, Philadelphia and Chicago were least scarred by slums. Boston, Cincinnati, Jersey City, and Hartford had badly diseased spots, but the evil was most deeply rooted in New York City, where land rentals were highest and the pressure of immigrants strongest.[163] In all Europe only one city district, in Prague, was half as congested as certain parts of Manhattan. Bad as conditions had been earlier in New York, they became worse in 1879 with the advent of a new type of slum, the "dumb-bell" tenement, so called because of the outline of the floor plan. This became virtually the only kind erected there in the next two decades.

Five or six stories high, the bleak narrow structure ran ninety feet back from the street, being pierced through the center by a stygian hallway less than three feet wide.[164] Each floor was honeycombed with rooms, many without direct light or air and most sheltering one or more families. Almost at once such barracks became foul and grimy, infested with vermin and lacking privacy and proper sanitary conveniences. The sunless, ill-smelling air shafts at the sides of the building proved a positive menace during fires by ensuring the rapid spread of flames. In rooms and hallways, on stairs and fire escapes, in the narrow streets, dirty half-clad children roamed at will, imbibing soiled thoughts from their soiled surroundings. The dense slum district bounded by Cherry, Catherine, Hamilton, and Market Streets was known as "lung block" because of the many deaths from tuberculosis. No wonder such rookeries were nurseries of immorality, drunkenness, disease, and crime. The real surprise is, as the state tenement-house commission pointed out in 1900, that so many of the children grew up to be decent, self-respecting citizens.

In 1879 the total number of tenements in New York was estimated at 21,000, their inhabitants at more than half a million. A census taken in 1888 showed over 32,000 tenements with a population exceeding a million. By 1900 the number of buildings had grown to nearly 43,000 and their occupants to over 1.5 million.[165] From time to time philanthropic citizens like Ellen Collins and Alfred T. White built model tenements in New York and Brooklyn to demonstrate that decent lodgings for the poor comported with fair profits for the landlord. Organizations like the State Charities Association and the Association for Improving the Condition of the Poor insistently agitated for stricter housing laws. To their aid came a young Danish American, Jacob A. Riis. As police reporter on the *Sun* he had gained a firsthand knowledge of slum conditions, which he used with great literary effect in a series of newspaper and magazine articles beginning in the eighties. His first book, *How the Other Half Lives*, published in 1890, came to Theodore Roosevelt as "an enlightenment and an inspiration for which . . . I could never be too grateful."[166]

Remedial legislation, following the first tenement-house statute of 1867, was passed in 1879, 1887, and 1895.[167] But in spite of the reformers the laws contained loopholes and enforcement was sporadic. The tenement-house commission of 1900 felt that, on the whole, conditions were worse than they had been fifty years before. Yet one year later a comprehensive statute was adopted which showed that the humanitarian energies of this generation had not been spent in vain. The act of 1901 not only ensured real housing reform in New York, but prompted other states and municipalities to a fundamental attack on the evil.

The problem of urban lawlessness and crime was deeply rooted in that of the slums. Vile places like "Misery Row," "Poverty Lane," and "Murderers' Alley" were both continuous recruiting grounds for juvenile delinquents and hiding places for criminal bands. Lacking normal outlets for play, the tenement waifs naturally drifted into gangs in which what might have been a laudable spirit of group loyalty was twisted into an ambition to emulate the lawless exploits of their elders. Beginning as beggars, sneak thieves, and pickpockets, they graduated all too quickly into the ranks of shoplifters, robbers, and thugs.[168] The foreign origin of many of the slum dwellers made this transition all the easier because of prior unfamiliarity with American traditions and laws. In particular, the Irish and Italians contributed more than their proportionate share of the country's prison population, though it was the American-born immigrant children, lacking proper parental guidance and wholesome surroundings, who turned most readily to underworld life.[169] One student of the problem, observing that most of the men, women, and children in the jails and penitentiaries he had visited were native-born, concluded: "We have ourselves evolved as cruel and cunning criminals as any that Europe may have foisted upon us."[170]

Criminologists and publicists pointed with alarm to the portentous increase of lawlessness in the United States. A census inquiry disclosed a 50 percent rise in the number of prison inmates from 1880 to 1890.[171] Statistics collected by the *Chicago Tribune* revealed a growth of murders and homicides from 1,266 during the year 1881 (24.7 to a million people) to 4,290 in 1890 (or 68.5 to the million) and to 7,840 in 1898 (or 107.2 to the million).[172] Such figures were all the more startling since most other civilized countries showed a declining homicide rate, the ratio in England and Germany being less than half that of the United States. Students of the subject were agreed in placing the fundamental blame on unhealthy urban growth, unrestricted immigration, the saloon, and the maladjusted black.[173] In addition, Lombroso pointed to the lingering habits of frontier lawlessness even in the more settled states, the new opportunities for crime afforded by discoveries in chemistry and toxicology, and the evil effects of sensation-mongering newspapers. Another writer stressed the undoubted fact that violence and criminality had come to be regarded "as a sort of natural and inevitable concomitant" of every great labor disturbance.[174]

Unfortunately, urban delinquency had its repercussions on the countryside, most notoriously in the case of the "tramp evil," which had first appeared in America in the hard years following 1873.[175] While the return of prosperity after 1878 somewhat diminished the number of such vagrants, habit, uncertainties of work, difficulties of personal adjustment, wanderlust, and the ease of stealing rides on the railroads caused many to continue in their old ways. Pitiful caricatures of the restless hardy pioneers of earlier times, these aimless wanderers were freely spawned by the great urban centers, particularly in years of unemployment and industrial conflict like 1885–86 and 1892–94.[176] An unofficial tramp census taken in 1893 indicated that three out of five were between twenty and fifty years of age, about the same proportion were native-born and trained to skilled trades, five out of six enjoyed good health, and nearly all were literate and unmarried.[177] If, as the investigator estimated, the total number of tramps then in the nation was 45,845, they represented an army larger than Wellington's at Waterloo and their vagabondage involved the withdrawal of a quarter of one percent of the male population from productive work, not to mention the burdens thrown on the public in the form of alms, police supervision, and hospital care.

These nomads developed a manner of living, a culture, peculiar to themselves. A well-marked caste system distinguished between the hobo, forced temporarily "on the road" by lack of work, and the habitual tramp in his ascending social scale from "gay-cat" (tenderfoot) and harmless wanderer to expert criminal.[178] By cabalistic chalk marks on gateposts the elect were informed as to chances for a "handout": a rigid code of ethics governed their conduct toward one another; and an argot, characterized by such expressions as doss (sleep), elbow (detective), mooch (beg), and shack (brakeman), marked their common speech.[179]

If we consider only the sordid aspects of urban life, the American city of the period seems a cancerous growth. But the record as a whole was distinctly creditable to a generation which found itself confronted with the phenomenon of a great population everywhere clotting into towns. No other people had ever met such an emergency so promptly or, on the whole, so successfully. The basic facilities of urban living—transit, lighting, and communication—were well taken care of by an outburst of native mechanical genius which helped make these years the Golden Age of Invention. Some places moved forward faster than others, of course, and all lagged in some respects while advancing in others. If the rural spirit of neighborliness was submerged in the anonymity of city life, there developed in its place a spirit of impersonal social responsibility which devoted itself, with varying earnestness and success, to questions of pure water, sewage disposal, and decent housing for the poor, sometimes taking the extreme form of municipal ownership. Moreover, what the great cities felt obliged to do under the whip of necessity, smaller towns undertook in a spirit of imitation, so that the new standards affected urban life everywhere. What most impresses the history student is the lack of unity, balance, and planfulness in the advances that were made. Urban progress was experimental, uneven, often accidental—the people were, as yet, groping in the dark.

WOMEN AND THE HOME

THE AMERICAN WOMAN reigned if she did not govern. She was in transition—as she always has been—and while the American man was too gallant to regard her as a "problem," her unusual restlessness in the eighties and nineties proved a constant source of worry to the old-fashioned of both sexes. It was as mistress of the home and dispenser of its hospitality that she was most favorably known, and in this role she inspired masculine visitors from Europe to a catalogue of such adjectives as vivacious, fascinating, candid, unaffected, intelligent, self-reliant. With an effort at statistical restraint the musician Offenbach at the opening of the era declared, "Out of a hundred women, ninety are perfectly ravishing"; while another artist, Soissons, observing America twenty years later, could agree that the "modern American woman is charming and almost superior to the majority of European women." [180] Even Matthew Arnold, who saw little to relieve the drab monotony of the transatlantic scene, accounted the unusual measure of feminine charm as an authentic touch of civilization.[181]

Nothing more sharply set off the American woman from her sisters abroad than the deference paid her by men and the unaffected social relations between the sexes. "It is the pride of Americans," noted one foreign observer, "that a woman, unaccompanied, can travel from one end of their country to the other without being subjected to any unpleasantness or to a vestige of impertinence." [182] This attitude, of course, had long been a national characteristic, but as a product of frontier and rural influences it was subjected during these years to a new and unexpected strain as greater numbers of people came to live under urban conditions and women entered the world of men as breadwinners.

In correct social circles of the Eastern cities the practice of chaperonage took root during the 1880s, stimulated by the example of the Old World with which an increasing number of traveled Americans had become acquainted. "The duties of a chaperon are very hard and unremitting, and sometimes very disagreeable," wrote an editor of *Harper's Bazar* in 1884.

> She must accompany her young lady everywhere; she must sit in the parlor when she receives gentlemen; she must go with her to the skating rink, the ball, the party, the races, the dinners, and especially to theater parties; she must preside at the table, and act the part of a mother, so far as she can; she must watch the characters of the men who approach her charge, and endeavor to save the inexperienced girl from the dangers of a bad marriage, if possible.[183]

Three years later another authority noted that the chaperon was "slowly but surely extending her sway," and in 1898 it was announced that the practice was so generally observed in the East that "a girl of the present generation would not venture to combat it without the risk of sharp criticism from alien tongues.[184]

Despite the undoubted spread of the new custom its well-wishers overstated the facts. As Mrs. Sherwood ruefully acknowledged, the "vivacious American girl, with all her inherited hatred of authority, is a troublesome charge. All young folks are rebels." Not appreciating "what Hesperidean fruit they are," they "dislike being watched and guarded." [185] And the young lady found an ally in her young man, who, besides sharing her libertarianism, objected to the extra drain on his purse which the presence of a third party at dinner or the theater entailed. In the smaller towns and rustic parts of the nation the two sexes continued to mingle socially, go buggy riding in the moonlight and pay court unvexed by the attentions of a duenna. Even in the cities, spinsters or "elderly girls" of twenty-five years or more were generally regarded as exempt from the requirement, for "with the assumption of years" had they not safely left behind them "the wild grace of a giddy girlhood"? Yet an "elderly girl," though, of thirty-five, was deemed to act unwisely if she visited an artist's studio alone, even though "there is in art an ennobling and purifying influence which should be a protection."[186]

Despite new social and economic conditions marriage continued to be the cherished goal of the majority of women, all the more so as the numerical excess of females over males steadily climbed in the urban parts of America.[187] Nevertheless the growing practice of seeking matrimonial mates through the advertising columns of the newspapers was generally frowned upon as betraying an unmaidenly zeal. Though in a few Eastern cities the "woman bachelor," as she called herself, gained steadily in standing and public respect, in most parts of the country the "elderly girl" was looked upon as a creature of frustrated purpose.[188] A fragile clinging vine was the ideal of an age which little dreamed a later generation would prefer the rambler.

The Americans were, in fact, one of the most married peoples in the world, being surpassed in Western Europe only by the French. There was a difference, however, between city and country. Matrimony generally took place earlier in the rural districts, was likely to endure longer, and, whether ended by death or divorce, was more often followed by fresh nuptials.[189] In the cities the higher cost of living, together with the greater economic independence of women and the many substitutes for the sociability of the fireside, served to delay marriage or to prevent it entirely. Higher education also proved a deterrent, at least so far as women were concerned. It was widely noted that fewer college-bred girls married proportionately than did their less-educated sisters, though the graduates of coeducational institutions showed less reluctance in this respect than those of women's colleges.[190]

From the later marriages of middle-class urban folk came smaller families, due partly to an increasing resort to the practice of birth control. One medical authority dared assert openly that such conduct was "not only not in itself sinful" but even "under certain circumstances commendable."[191] The result, as Bryce and others pointed out, seemed a reversal of the principle of natural selection, for the progeny of poor and undernourished parents multiplied while the better-nurtured classes barely held their own. In general, the membership of the average household steadily shrank. In 1890 the most usual size was four members; in 1900 three.[192]

All the moral preachments of the time pointed to the wife and mother as the one upon whom rested the chief responsibility for connubial bliss. It was her duty "to embellish the home, and to make happy the lives of the near and dear ones who dwell within it."[193] Addressing her in the *Christian Herald*, the Reverend T. DeWitt Talmage declared:

> Whether in professional, or commercial, or artistic, or mechanical life, your husband from morning to night is in a Solferino, if not a Sedan. It is a wonder that your husband has any nerves or patience or suavity left. . . . If he come home and sit down preoccupied, you ought to excuse him. If he do not feel like going out that night . . . , remember he has been out all day. . . . Remember, he is not overworking so much for himself as . . . for you and the children.[194]

Nevertheless the law, more charitable, it would seem, than the pulpit, accorded married women larger rights than they had ever before enjoyed in America. The old common-law discriminations, already beginning to crumble prior to the Civil War,[195] continued to fall before the assaults of new legislation. By 1898 the special disabilities of wives had been wholly removed in Mississippi, Oregon, and Washington, and in most other states they could own and control their property, retain their earnings, make contracts, sue, and be sued.[196] Here and there, however, inequalities of civil status remained. Thus in Georgia, Louisiana, New Mexico, the Dakotas, and California the law still expressly designated the husband as head of the family and wife subject to him. Furthermore, in all but seven states, the father continued to enjoy prior authority in the guardianship of minor children, and a few commonwealths—North Carolina, Kentucky, and Texas—ordinarily permitted divorce for adultery only when the wife was the offender. So widely was the principle of civil equality recognized, however, that only time was required to remove the remaining discriminations from the statute books.

If woman's chief sphere was the home, complaint was general that she had failed badly in one department of her duties, that of training her children. European visitors invariably described them as "pert and disrespectful," one Frenchman maintaining that a composite photograph of American youth would reveal *"le plus terrible de tous les enfants terribles."*[197] Even American writers admitted that filial irreverence was "the greatest blemish that exists on the childhood of this country today," and one suggested that "the present problem of the children is the painless extinction of their elders."[198] Nevertheless, the gradual disappearance of corporal punishment from the home was regarded even by such critics as a sign of increasing civilization.[199] Whether the slump in manners was due to parental indulgence or to a desire to give children a freer and more self-reliant start in life, the experts were not agreed, though doubtless both elements entered into the situation. One thoughtful European was obliged to confess that "the fruit does not by any means correspond to the seed. . . . The unendurable child does not necessarily become an intolerable man."[200]

Perhaps no factor affected a child's life more than the growth of cities. In the rural districts boys and girls continued to live in the customary manner, close to nature's bosom, but not so in the urban centers. An investigation conducted in 1880 by G. Stanley Hall, then a lecturer in psychology at Harvard, showed that over half the children entering Boston's primary schools had never seen a plow or spade, a robin, squirrel, snail, or sheep; they had never observed peaches on a tree or growing grain and could not distinguish an oak tree from a willow or poplar.[201] In place of these traditional experiences of American childhood the city youth must arrange his play with reference to paved streets, telegraph poles, and iron lampposts. Instead of collecting birds' eggs he collected the small picture cards of burlesque queens and prizefighters, which came in cigarette packages. His greatest thrills centered in the clang and clatter of the passing patrol wagon, fire engine, or ambulance.

While the swift panorama of the streets more or less colored the manners and outlook of all city children, it was, of course, the center of existence for the waifs of the tenement districts. With such homes particularly in mind, many cities in the 1880s followed New York's earlier example by forming societies for the prevention of cruelty to children. It was due to the activity of such bodies, for instance, that the vicious practice of selling Italian children into the slavery of *padroni,* who compelled them to become beggars or strolling musicians, was stamped out or driven under cover.[202]

Less successful were humanitarians in coping with the growing evil of child labor in factories and sweatshops. Though the census undoubtedly understated the facts, the number of boys and girls from ten to fifteen years old engaged in gainful work was recorded as having increased from a million in 1880 to a million and three quarters in 1900. They were employed mostly in the textile industry, and in the new Southern mill towns often began work as young as seven or eight. In Northern cities children also thronged the streets as newsboys and, with their mothers, formed the mainstay of the sweating trades. In Chicago, large numbers of them toiled as meat packers in the stockyards. State legislation, somewhat more restrictive than in the previous generation, ordinarily forbade child labor under the ages of twelve or fourteen, but even such laws were lacking in most Southern states and in few parts of the Union were they effectively enforced.[203]

In an effort to recover for childhood a part of its natural heritage of outdoor recreation, a Boston society in 1885 tried the experiment of providing sand gardens for youngsters. The success of the undertaking led to an ampler provision of public playgrounds there and to imitation on the part of other municipalities. By the end of 1898, however, the movement had spread to only thirteen cities, mostly in the East.[204] As a special provision for poor and invalid children, the Reverend Willard Parsons of Sherman,

Pennsylvania, devised the scheme of "country week" in 1877 to secure a blessed respite of blue sky and pure air during the stifling hot season—a plan quickly taken up by charitable organizations in leading cities and assisted by the "fresh-air funds" of enterprising newspapers.[205] For sons of the well-to-do, summer camps began to be established where city-bred boys were taught the ways of the woods under skilled instruction. The success of the first camp, at Squam Lake, New Hampshire, in 1881, caused others to be set up in New England, New York, Pennsylvania, and elsewhere until by the close of the period nearly a score were in operation.[206] If this generation did little more than glimpse the problem of conserving childhood under the new conditions of American life, at least it laid foundations upon which its successors were to build more soundly.

One pleasure the city could give young America which the country could not rival. This consisted in the variety and savoriness of the comestibles at hand.[207] Nor was the child specialist yet come to judgment, intent on turning into Dead Sea fruit the dainties most appetizing to juvenile palates. On the Northern farm the long winter usually meant an uninterrupted routine of heavy foods without fresh fruit or green vegetables, followed by a general "spring sickness" which sent the people helter-skelter to the village druggist for tonics and "molasses 'n' sulphur." The city, on the other hand, with its concentration of wealth and population, supplied a market for the ready sale of myriad food products brought from all parts of the world by means of ever-swifter transportation and improved methods of refrigeration.[208]

Moreover, the sedentary habits of many urban dwellers, calling for a diet less burdened with meat, made them eager to diversify their fare, and caused them to rely more on vegetables, salads, fish, and fruit. In the mid-century fresh fish had been available only to persons living near bodies of water, but in the eighties and nineties fish, caught in the Northern Pacific and transported several thousand miles, was daily supplied fresh to the markets of the Midwest and the Atlantic Coast.[209] Most tropical fruits— oranges, lemons, red-skinned bananas—were as abundant and cheap in the city as domestic fruits, sometimes cheaper, and their consumption increased greatly throughout the period.[210] After the attractive exhibit of grapefruit at the Chicago World's Fair epicures began tentatively to add that dish to their breakfast menu.

Steadily the factory invaded the precincts of the city kitchen, lightening the drudgery of the home and enriching the family diet. Quaker Oats, Wheatena, and other package cereals began to take the place of cornmeal mush and similar concoctions at the breakfast table. The prejudice against baker's bread as the mark of a lazy housewife waned in the face of the greater convenience of commercially prepared loaves, though even town women usually continued to make their own cakes and cookies. Factory-canned foods also came, for the first time, to occupy an important place in the housewife's activities. After 1878, canning factories multiplied in the East and the Midwest while improved machinery cheapened the cost and increased the variety of the foods packed.[211] By the mid-nineties the principal canned goods, in the order of their importance, were tomatoes, corn, milk, oysters, corned beef, salmon, sardines, peaches, peas, and beans. "Housekeeping is getting to be ready made, as well as clothing," rejoiced one woman, who predicted that "Even the cook book may yet be obsolete, for every can of prepared food has a label with directions how to cook."[212] At the same time, synthetic food products made their appearance. The rapid spread of the use of oleomargarine in place of butter threatened a serious rift in the ranks of the Farmers' Alliance movement in the 1880s, with the dairy farmers opposing the cattle raisers and the Southern cottonseed crushers.[213] Not content with the restrictive measures adopted by nearly twenty states, the dairy interests induced Congress in 1886 to pass a law taxing oleo and regulating its sales.[214]

American cooking was not favorably regarded by foreign travelers, though their opinion may have been influenced by national prejudices. The worst conditions prevailed in the country where the frying pan remained the mainstay of all cooking. But even in the cities the ordinary American family cared more about the quantity than the quality of the food set before them. In such centers, however, inherited frontier culinary habits were becoming modified by contact with foreign peoples. Italian spaghetti and olives, Hungarian goulash, and Chinese chop suey (unknown in China) were gastronomic contributions of the newer immigrant stocks as surely as the white potato and sauerkraut had been of earlier ones. More important was the attention which Americans began to give to the subtleties of seasoning. In the five years following the removal of the tariff on unground spices in 1883, the amount of pepper, pimento, cloves, and nutmegs imported into America doubled.[215]

That cooking was a subject worthy of scientific study was recognized when the New York Cooking School was opened in 1874 and the Boston Cooking School three years later. The former had 1,200 students enrolled in the winter of 1877–78.[216] Other schools were established in Philadelphia, Washington, and elsewhere and courses were even introduced into the high schools. At the same time, dietary studies were undertaken by official and private agencies and the printing press groaned with the production of new and improved manuals and cookbooks.[217]

Nor did the pleasures of between-meal eating escape attention, especially on the part of commercial caterers to the popular palate. The simple candies of yore—peppermint sticks, gum drops, candy hearts inscribed with sentimental mottoes—were supplemented by boxed confections such as Gunther's (Chicago) and Lowney's (Boston). Chewing gum won an army of addicts, notably among children and the "vulgar classes."[218] Ginger beer, pop, and other "soft" drinks acquired a new popularity, partly as a result of discoveries which made the artificial production of ice a commercial success.[219] Soda fountains, introduced by the previous generation, grew rapidly in number until, at the close of the period, perhaps 60,000 were in use.[220] Constructed imposingly of marble, onyx, and various decorative metals, some of them cost as much as $10,000. Few courtships lacked the odorous adjunct of the soda fountain. The young lady and her escort, having made their choice of syrups, waited in palpitant ecstasy while the attendant pulled the faucet first this way for the broad, silvery, foaming stream of soda, and then that for the sharp hissing spurt which crowned the glass with iridescent bubbles.

As the cost of manufactured tobacco steadily declined and its quality improved, the tobacco habit affected an ever-greater proportion of people. Red-blooded men smoked cigars and pipes and chewed tobacco, the latter habit being shared by men otherwise so dissimilar as James Whitcomb Riley, President Cleveland, and the eminent zoologist Professor W. K. Brooks of Johns Hopkins. The newfangled cigarette, on the other hand, bore the taint of the dude, the sissy, and the underworld. Notwithstanding this stigma and the belief that the "insane asylums . . . are being constantly recruited from excessive smokers of the cigarette," its use grew nearly nine times as fast as that of the cigar during the period.[221] Perhaps as a quick nervous smoke it accorded better with the increasing tension of urban life. In the world of fashion smoking in any form was frowned upon as a reprehensible masculine habit not to be practiced in the presence of the other sex. It was even "bad form for a gentleman to smoke on streets . . . at the hours at which he will be likely to meet many ladies."[222] At the dinner parties of the 1890s, however, an increasing number of hostesses permitted their male guests to smoke, though any woman who ventured to join them would at once have placed herself beyond the pale.

The interior of the home showed signs of emerging from the reign of terror which had afflicted it in the preceding generation.[223] In the early 1880s the typical middle-class abode was still likely to be a museum of aesthetic horrors, the choicest rooms cluttered up with easels, bamboo stands, gilded rams' horns, hand-painted rolling pins, and inverted glass domes sheltering wax flowers and china statuettes. To complete the chaos, Japanese lanterns often hung from the ceiling and a painted iron heron stood one-legged amid cattails beside the marble mantel. Such a home, for example, the Marches in Howells's *A Hazard of New Fortunes* found themselves obliged to take after six weary chapters of house hunting in New York.[224] But better things portended. While Mrs. John A. Logan, writing from Washington in the decorous traditions of senatorial conservatism, continued to hymn the advantages of turning cupid-decorated tambourines into photograph frames, another widely read authority, the sister of President Cleveland, was announcing that "every room in the house should be arranged for occupancy, having nothing too good for use," and no room should be overcrowded.[225]

American taste was steadily improving as Americans traveled more widely, as art museums and art schools multiplied, and as women's magazines such as *Ladies' Home Journal,* founded in 1883, and *Good Housekeeping,* dating from 1885, devoted increasing space to sanity in household decoration. The Philadelphia Centennial in 1876 gave an important stimulus to better standards of home furnishing, particularly in the East, equaled only by the influence of the far superior exhibits of the World's Fair of 1893 on the minds of countless thousands of Midwesterners.[226] At the same time, the aesthetic doctrines of the Englishmen Charles L. Eastlake and William Morris swept like a fresh breeze through American drawing rooms, helping to clean out much of the debris, and the efforts—not always successful—of manufacturers in Grand Rapids, Chicago, and New York to duplicate the superior furniture at lower cost brought better-designed pieces into the homes of the masses.

Undoubtedly, too, the servant problem—"the great unsolved American Question," according to one domestic authority—had a wholesome effect on the situation.[227] Whether, as some maintained, the arrogant mistress was the problem rather than the impertinent maid, servants were hard to get and harder to keep despite the enormous immigration of these years.[228] Accordingly, common sense dictated greater simplicity in furnishings and the adoption of labor-saving devices to lighten housework. The introduction of courses in domestic science in high schools and universities helped also to raise housekeeping from a traditional folk exercise to somewhat the dignity of a profession. Whatever the causes, the results were so marked that Judge Robert Grant described the typical American home of the mid-nineties as "intended for every-day use by rational beings."[229] He was referring, of course, primarily to city abodes because in smaller towns and in the country the older customs still held sway.

The changes can be followed in greater detail. Nothing was more revolutionary, perhaps, than the widespread abolition of the parlor, a ceremonial room which, darkened with drawn shades and closed doors, had hitherto served as a sort of mortuary chapel for the reception of guests. As the normal life of the family reached into all parts of the house other improvements were inaugurated. More and larger windows made the home cheerier, as did also the replacement of dark gloomy wallpaper with pale tints and simple chintz designs, and the substitution of lighter furniture for ponderous mahogany and black walnut. Upholstery of glossy black horsehair, once the pride of every middle-class household though always a mortification to the flesh, gave way rapidly to rep coverings or even to cretonne and plush.[230] In many homes metal bedsteads, for better or worse, replaced the old top-heavy wooden ones with their elaborately carved headboards reaching almost to the ceiling. Carpets continued to stretch from wall to wall in the average house, but as the rough board floors were succeeded by evenly joined, polished ones, rugs became increasingly popular, commending themselves by reason of greater cleanliness and the possibility of more artistic effects.[231]

At the same time, better arrangements for plumbing and heating enhanced both comfort and safety. The primitive plumbing of the 1870s, by conveying noxious odors into the rooms, was often a threat to the family health,[232] but with the introduction of improved methods and appliances, adopted under the prod of state and municipal inspection laws, a great change resulted in domestic sanitary equipment in the 1880s.[233] Plumbing could no longer be installed in a first-class dwelling for about $250, as in Civil War times, but was more apt to cost from $2,000 to $4,000. Nowhere was the change more welcome than in the bathroom, which at the beginning of the period was usually small and gloomy, its atmosphere tainted with sewer gas. As plumbing fixtures became more tasteful and the bathtub shed its zinc lining for white enamel or porcelain, the mistress of the house began to take a special delight in keeping this room spotless and airy.

Less alteration occurred in methods of heating. The base burner, with funereal urns on top and mica windows showing the blaze within, continued to be the chief resort of most homes, and any woman considered herself fortunate who owned a Crown Jewel, a Hub, or an Art Garland. Yet well-to-do families usually aspired to a hot-air furnace and, as the price of steam-heating and hot-water systems fell with the expiration of the basic patents, there was a notable expansion in the use of such furnaces as well.

In the kitchen, the housewife learned to rely increasingly upon a wide assortment of new conveniences, such as the steam cooker, double boiler, Dover egg beater, gas toaster, asbestos stove mat, triple saucepans, and cake tins with removable bottoms. More important perhaps was the introduction of aluminum-ware shortly after 1890 in place of the iron or tin or granite variety. New metallurgical processes had made the metal almost as cheap as tin, and it won quick favor by reason of its lightness, durability, and freedom from poisonous alloys.[234] Improved makes of washing machines also appeared and, thanks to the genius of Mrs. Potts, a practicable flatiron with a detachable handle was added to the equipment of the laundry. Even greater relief was promised by the enlarging patronage of commercial laundries by private families.[235] One form of drudgery, however, resisted all efforts at abatement: the washing of dishes.

The progressive liberation from household routine left the middle-class woman with more leisure on her hands than ever before and opened the way for a wider participation in the world that lay beyond domestic walls. The wives and daughters of the poor had long been swelling the ranks of industry, and the five-year depression following 1873 had shown that women even of the comfortable classes might unexpectedly be obliged to supplement the family income. At the same time the colleges and universities were training increasing numbers for pursuits hitherto followed chiefly by men, while the new conditions of American life were opening employments to them wholly unknown to previous generations.

Though the old prejudice against self-support for women lingered, its doom was rendered more certain with the passage of each year, "We have reached a new era," declared a women's magazine in 1883. "Slowly as woman has come to her inheritance, it stretches before her now into illimitable distance, and the question of the hour is rather whether she is ready for her trust than whether that trust is hampered by conditions."[236] Never before had such attractive and multifarious occupations been within reach. Women who would have shrunk from factory work and domestic service or even from teaching trooped forth with a sense of adventure to become typists, telephone girls, typesetters, bookkeepers, nurses, librarians, journalists, lecturers, social workers, doctors, lawyers, artists. Even in the realm of mechanical invention, a time-honored monopoly of men, they were displaying noteworthy capacity in a variety of fields.[237] Miss Faithfull reported that in Massachusetts alone there were in 1882 nearly 300 branches of business and industry in which women could earn from $100 to $3,000 a year.[238] It is not surprising that the number of feminine bread-winners in the United States rose from 2.5 million in 1880 to 4 million in 1890 and to 5.3 million in 1900, or that legislatures in the chief industrial states began in the 1880s to give serious attention to acts for regulating factory conditions of female toil.[239]

Nowhere was the change in the position of the sex more striking than in the old Confederacy. There the "nobility of helplessness in woman" was still cherished as an ideal by many survivors of the old regime, but postwar realities—the goad of poverty, the opportunities of city life, the shiftlessness of hired help—caused the younger generation to discover the ideal of self-reliance and self-support. "The crowning glory of the present age is that every woman is free to develop her own personality," proclaimed one daughter of Dixie in the early 1890s. In contrast to former times, "a woman is respected and honored in the South for earning her own living, and would lose respect if . . . she settled herself as a burden on a brother" or hard-working father.[240] It was noted that a larger proportion of girls, even of the poorer classes, were going to college than formerly and that more of them stayed on to take their degrees.

Not all American women used their new found time in bread-winning pursuits, many of them, especially of the upper middle class, found an outlet in club activities. "We have art clubs, book clubs, dramatic clubs, pottery clubs. We have sewing circles, philanthropic associations, scientific, literary, religious, athletic, musical, and decorative art societies," testified one writer.[241] "The absence of men," observed a visiting French woman, "would make French women feel . . . as if they were eating bread without butter."[242] But such extramural contacts were the best means the average housewife had of learning about the complex world in which circumstances were forcing her to play a part. By 1889 the clubs were so numerous and influential that they became linked together in a great national system under the name of the General Federation of Women's Clubs.[243]

Conservative folk were not at all certain that the widening range of feminine activity denoted progress. "What is this curious product of to-day, the American girl or woman?" asked one woman writer. ". . . is it possible for any novel, within the next fifty years, truly to depict her as a finality, when she is still emerging from new conditions . . . , when she does not yet understand herself . . . " She added, "The face of to-day is stamped with restlessness, wandering purpose, and self-consciousness." [244] As the years passed the note of disapprobation was sounded more and more frequently. "The great fault of the girl of to-day," declared another member of the sex in 1890, "is discontent. She calls it by the more magnificent sounding name of ambition, but in reality she is absolutely restless and dissatisfied with whatever may be her position in life." [245]

Nothing more excited both male and female disapproval than the energetic attempts of certain women to claim for their sex equal political rights with men. In the opening years of the period even the historian Parkman was tempted away from his cloisters long enough to deliver some smashing blows against this effort to overleap "Nature's limitations," disrupt the home and give women excitements and cares "too much for their strength." Especially in the "crowded cities," he pointed out, woman suffrage would be "madness," a certain means of making bad government worse. [246] Five leading feminists joined in a powerful counterblast: Julia Ward Howe, Thomas Wentworth Higginson, Lucy Stone (Blackwell), Elizabeth Cady Stanton, and Wendell Phillips. [247] Reaffirming the principles of the Declaration of Independence, they declared that women as well as men had contributions to make to public life and denounced the failure to accept the consequences of woman's altered position as an effort to "put the bird back into the egg." "One of two things is true," asserted the forthright Phillips, "either woman is like man—and if she is, then a ballot based on brains belongs to her as well as to him; or she is different, and then man does not know how to vote for her as well as she herself does."

This widely read debate marked the lines on which the great battle over the ballot was fought in periodicals, public gatherings, legislative halls, and constitutional conventions. While the majority of women remained somewhat indifferent spectators, the militant "antis" did not feel that their disapproval of feminine political activity precluded them from organizing committees and societies in opposition. In effectiveness of organization, however, they were completely outdone by their antagonists, many of whom had been trained in the old days of the antislavery struggle and the Sanitary Commission. Already two strong woman-suffrage associations were in the field, the American and the National, one seeking the ballot through state action, the other through a federal amendment. New branches of these bodies were organized in the various states, and in 1890, when it became clear that the parent societies were but two blades of the same scissors, they united under the name of the National American Woman Suffrage Association.

Meanwhile, campaigns were being hotly waged on every front and with many weapons. As Colonel Higginson pointed out, "Mrs. Stowe helps to free Uncle Tom in his cabin, and then strikes for the freedom of women in her own 'Hearth and Home.' Mrs. Howe writes the 'Battle Hymn of the Republic,' and keeps on writing more battle hymns in behalf of her own sex. Miss Alcott not only delineates 'Little Women,' but wishes to emancipate them." [248] Prominent men lent their pens and voices to the cause: George W. Curtis, Senator G. F. Hoar, the venerated Whittier, and others. Both the Knights of Labor and the American Federation of Labor rallied to the banner. In 1878, Senator A. A. Sargent of California introduced into Congress an equal-suffrage amendment, drafted by Susan B. Anthony in the very language which forty-two years later was to find lodgment in the Constitution. [249] In the next two decades Senate committees reported five times and House committees twice in favor of the proposal, but action went no further. The platforms of the major parties ignored the issue, and the Prohibitionists perhaps hurt it by associating it in the public mind with their battle against rum. In 1884 a group of suffragists launched a political party of their own, the Equal Rights party, defiantly nominating for president a woman lawyer, Mrs. Belva A. Lockwood of Washington, D. C.

The policy of divide-and-conquer brought more encouraging results. Campaign after campaign was conducted in state after state under the inspiration of veteran leaders like the angular Anthony and the motherly Stanton, aided by such new recruits as Dr. Anna Howard Shaw and Carrie Chapman Catt. [250] The initial gains, as in Britain and the Scandinavian countries during these same years, took the form of obtaining the vote in school elections and sometimes also in regard to municipal or taxation questions. Thus, in 1878, New Hampshire and Oregon, following the earlier example of a few other states, authorized school suffrage. Massachusetts, New York, and Vermont acted in the next two years, and by the close of 1898 thirteen additional states and territories, representing all parts of the Union but the old Confederacy, had fallen into line. [251]

The cause of full equality in voting, on the other hand, showed signs of losing ground when Congress, by the Edmunds law of 1887, deprived the women of Utah territory of the ballot as a means of destroying polygamy and when, two years later, the voters of Washington refused to authorize the reestablishment of equal suffrage at the election for adopting a state constitution. [252] The next year, however, Wyoming was admitted into the Union with the universal suffrage she had practiced since 1869, and three of her neighbors after achieving statehood—Colorado in 1893 and Utah and Idaho in 1896—ranged themselves by her side. Nevertheless the closing years of the decade showed an apparent decline of interest in the movement. For some years to come most Americans were to regard "ballots for both" as an aberration of the wild and woolly West.

Feminism, with considerably less success, sought to play a role in the reform of women's clothing. In this domain Paris ruled supreme, and the law and the prophets required that the human figure be used to display clothes, not clothes the figure. Most American women in the late 1870s, tightly imprisoned in wasplike waists, reveled in flounces and frills, their long, trailing skirts, drawn in at the bottom, making a quick gait impossible. The "street-cleaning-department style" it was called by a writer in *Harper's Bazar*[253] Underneath they were stuffed out with layers of garments known collectively as "unmentionables." Young women dressed like their elders and, by a natural law of descent, even the children were clad to look like premature grown-ups.[254] About 1880 began the vogue of the pannier, an overskirt draped up at the hips or back by means of a bustle. With each season pannier draperies grew more "bouffant," dress extenders or cushion bustles with steel springs being used to produce the desired effect. A walking costume, described in *Cosmopolitan* for October 1887 called for fifteen and a half yards of material twenty-two inches wide; a stylish frock for eighteen and a half yards. But at the close of the decade the pannier was on the decline, while the skirt was worn wider at the bottom and the sleeves, hitherto tight, had become high and full.[255] The new mode reached its climax in 1896 in the leg-o'-mutton sleeve, puffed out balloonlike from a tight band below the elbow and projecting beyond the shoulder.

Recurrent protests against the tyranny of fashion were based partly upon considerations of cost,[256] but much more on the presumed unhealthful effects of long, heavy skirts, tight, high-heeled shoes, and, worst of all, the breath-taking, steel-reenforced corsets. "Woman by her injurious style of dress," asserted one physician, "is doing as much to destroy the race as is man by alcoholism." "Niggardly waists and niggardly brains go together," agreed Frances Willard.[257] In the 1870s the New England Women's Club, led by Elizabeth Stuart Phelps, had raised the banner of revolt, declaring war in particular against the corset, and had even opened a shop for the sale of "dress-reform garments."[258] Though a limited number of women, presumably in the vicinity of Boston, adopted the new "health waists," evidence is overwhelming that, in general, the corset continued to hold its own.

Yet each year, by emphasizing anew the cramping effects of the prevailing styles upon the enlarging activities of women, prepared the way for a new rebellion. In 1891 the National Council of Women of the United States, meeting in Washington, gave the matter of rational attire particular consideration. Its committee reported the following year in favor of a model based upon the "Syrian costume adopted by the English Society for Rational Dress, the short-skirted gown with leggins, and the new gymnastic suit."[259] While no change so radical could hope for adoption, a wider vogue of "mannish styles" such as tailored suits and shirt waists, an increasing use of discreetly shorter skirts for business and even, in some cases, the wearing of divided skirts for bicycling gave promise of a better day.[260]

The growing absorption of women in interests outside the home, whether as social butterflies or as breadwinners or reformers, seemed to some a sufficient explanation of the waning sanctity of the marriage relation. Whatever the reason there could be no doubt as to the fact. With 16,000 divorces granted in 1878, the number rose to nearly 29,000 in 1888 and to almost 48,000 in 1898. The rate of increase was far greater than the rate of population growth—indeed, in the last decade of the century, three times as great—and the proportion of divorces granted in the United States far exceeded that of any foreign country except Japan.[261] In 1890 one divorce was granted for every sixteen marriages solemnized, in 1900 one for every twelve. Since the practice was forbidden Roman Catholics, the frequency of divorce among those not of that faith was even greater than these figures indicate.

The situation excited the widespread alarm of press and pulpit. As a result of the activity of the National Divorce Reform League, formed in 1881, the federal government undertook, in 1887–88, a comprehensive collection of data concerning marriage and divorce. The findings confirmed a cherished notion of the reformers that one fruitful source of the evil was the diversity of state legislation. In some states marriage was permitted as early as twelve or fourteen years; in most a civil ceremony would suffice; and, in perhaps half, a ceremony could be dispensed with altogether under the general principles of the "Scotch law of marriage," which required merely mutual consent.[262]

The lax standards of the law were largely an inheritance from a rural age when early and easy marriage was desired for population growth and community disapproval prevented reckless recourse to the divorce courts. The phenomenal increase of divorce was largely an outgrowth of urban conditions: the anonymity of city life, its distractions and temptations, the growing practice of living in boardinghouses and flats, the harsh struggle for existence, the opportunities for self-support afforded women.[263] Not only was the divorce rate higher in large cities than in small ones and country districts, but the rate of increase was also greater there than elsewhere.[264] Since twice as many divorces in the period 1878–98 were granted upon the wife's complaint as on the husband's, it is likely that the increase reflected, in part, a greater self-respect among women and an unwillingness to put up with conditions which their mothers would have accepted in silence.[265] Legislative changes during the period were in the direction of greater strictness, Connecticut leading the way in 1878 by repealing her "omnibus clause." But the gains were not impressive, and no headway was made toward the reformers' goal: a uniform divorce law for all the states.[266] The more thoughtful perceived that what was needed was not so much a change of legislation as of ethical attitudes.

Even more shocking to most people was the growth of commercialized immorality. Primarily an urban phenomenon, it throve most extensively in the great population centers where unmarried men congregated in largest numbers and out-of-town visitors were numerous. In New York, for example, vice catered to all tastes and purses—in "palatial bagnios" as well as in widely scattered medium-class houses and places of assignation, not to mention basement dives on the Bowery where, we may well believe, the business was "divested of the gaslight glare and tinsel of the high-toned seraglios."[267] As in the seaboard metropolis, "sporting houses" existed in all parts of Chicago, though the traffic was most boldly carried on in the district between Harrison and Polk and between Clark and Dearborn Streets.[268] There, as in the red-light districts of other cities, the male passerby after dark was almost certain to be hailed from curtained windows or accosted on the street by pert sauntering women.

The number of such wretched females cannot be known, but the circumstances which brought them to their life of shame and eventual disease are not difficult to understand.[269] As one brothel keeper in Chicago told W. T. Stead, the English journalist, "Prostitution is an effect, not a careless, voluntary choice on the part of the fallen." Some of them were country newcomers to the city, starved for companionship and lacking the wholesome restraining influence of neighborhood opinion. Others were shopgirls or housemaids eager for the pretty clothes and good times which their meager wages denied them. Many more perhaps were the hapless victims of evil youthful surroundings in the slums, while still others were girls of feeble mentality who in a better-ordered society would have been under institutional care. In the opinion of Stead's informant, "the real cause lies not in the girls who fall, but in the social conditions that make the fall easy and the men who tempt to the step. . . . "[270] The situation was made worse by the growth of an organized traffic in "white slaves," intercity in character, which often involved forcible induction into a life of vice.

Everywhere in the nation the law placed a ban on prostitution, but while municipalities outlawed the evil to prove themselves respectable, they condoned lax enforcement to prove themselves liberal.[271] In some places the authorities raided the vice resorts every month or so, imposing fines that amounted to an irregular license fee. Elsewhere the police were apt to be in collusion with the keepers of disorderly houses, levying blackmail on them for their private gain. Though without warrant in law, segregation was permitted or required in many cities, and in a few isolated cases, like that of Cleveland, the experiment was briefly tried of introducing the Continental European system of police registration and medical inspection. The recurrent upheavals of civic reform generally disclosed the alliance of commercialized vice with corrupt politics and the liquor interests, and brought about a temporary improvement of conditions. In general, community sentiment upheld the time-honored double standard of morality, which conceived of sexual promiscuity as permissible only for the male. Few reform officials were willing to emulate Police Commissioner Roosevelt in treating the men taken in vice raids precisely as their female companions, so far as the law allowed him to do so.[272]

Serious as was the social evil, there was little spread of licentiousness upward through society, and foreign observers were justified in rating American standards of sexual morality as superior to those of most European countries. Indeed, in spite of the whips and buffetings of circumstance, the American woman had substantial cause for pride in the advances made by her sex. Though, as the writer in the *Atlantic Monthly* had said, she might not yet understand herself, she was responding to her highest instincts in struggling toward an easier, more self-respecting and self-reliant footing in American society.

THE EDUCATIONAL REVIVAL

THE CLOSING DECADES of the century saw an educational renaissance comparable in many respects to the great days of Horace Mann and Henry Barnard.[273] While the cities were the chief beneficiaries, the country also shared in the movement and the South for the first time became a part of the national educational order. Nor was the awakening one of the schools alone, for countless other agencies of a less formal sort began to play a significant role in shaping popular culture. Lewis Miller, Frederick W. Poole, S. S. McClure, Joseph Pulitzer, and Edward W. Bok, no less than the professional educators, helped instruct the people and mold their outlook on life.

The ideal of free tax-supported elementary schools had been accepted in the North already by mid-century, but even there practice had lagged behind theory while in the South such facilities hardly existed at all. In the dozen years after the Civil War, though enrollments grew, operating expenses were generally held down in the North, school buildings kept simple, and few new features added to the curriculum. The South, obliged by the Reconstruction constitutions to set up public school systems, was handicapped by poverty, Carpetbag exploitation, and the very magnitude of the task.[274] But with the widespread economic recovery following 1878 and the end of Reconstruction in the South, a new era opened for both sections. Though the North and West now faced the duty of caring for hordes of immigrant children, the vast accumulation of taxable wealth and the growth of cities facilitated accomplishment. If the visible progress was less spectacular in the old slave states, the difficulties overcome were even greater.

Taking the nation as a whole, improvement of the educational system occurred at every point from top to bottom. Congress had evidenced its interest in 1867 by creating a special department (later bureau) of education which, under able leadership, served as a national clearinghouse, gathering statistics, disseminating information, and holding up the torch for the more backward commonwealths. After 1870 compulsory-attendance laws began to spread over the North and West, nineteen states and territories taking this step by 1881, and twelve more by 1898.[275] Rhode Island, for example, had been notorious as a haven for immigrant parents who preferred their children's wages to their education, but this condition was corrected in 1883.[276] The typical statute required children from eight to fourteen years of age to attend school from twelve to sixteen weeks a year; as late as 1890, Connecticut was the only state to exact attendance for the full session. Enforcement, however, was another thing. With notable exceptions it was only the older, well-established communities which compelled parents and children to observe the law.[277] Elsewhere social custom and parental pride were more influential than legal coercion in keeping youngsters at their tasks.

The number of pupils in the common schools of the nation rose from 9.5 million in 1878 to 12 million a decade later and to 15 million in 1898, somewhat outstripping the growth of population. Kindergartens, public and private, increased from less than 200 in 1878 to nearly 3,000 at the close of the period when perhaps 200,000 children were tasting the delights of learning through play activities.[278] Even more remarkable was the growth of high schools from less than 800 in 1878 to 5,500 in 1898. For the first time, the American public, at least in the North and West, squarely accepted the responsibility of extending the benefits of free education upward from the elementary grades. With less than 100,000 pupils in the secondary schools in 1878, over half a million were so accommodated in 1898.[279]

Educational development, of course, varied from section to section and even more between country and city. The concentration of wealth and population in urban centers and the greater spirit of progress ensured higher salaries for teachers, longer school terms, better buildings, and, in general, superior organization and methods of instruction. It was the cities which promoted the kindergarten movement and were most active in providing high schools. Some places like St. Louis under the superintendency of William T. Harris (1867–80) became the generating centers of ideas that helped revolutionize the theory and practice of teaching throughout the land.

In the rural districts, on the other hand, ungraded schools were the rule. The single schoolmaster shepherded students of all ages and degrees of advancement and, in intervals between chastising unruly charges, listened to the halting recitations of individual pupils whenever they were ready. The rural schoolmaster in his value to the community might be compared to the country doctor, but he seldom enjoyed the same neighborhood respect, and if opportunity offered, he fled his employment for something more rewarding. The school year also ended sooner than in the cities and large towns, where in 1891 the typical session lasted from 180 to 200 days as compared with from 70 to 150 in the country.[280]

In the North and West the rural school situation was the subject of constant recommendation by state commissioners of instruction. A basic difficulty was the dissipation of meager resources among many small, independent school districts. Under a Massachusetts law of 1882 abolishing the district system, such schools began to be consolidated, the scattered pupils being daily carried by wagon to a centrally located, graded school. Before 1898 the idea made some headway elsewhere—in Ohio, New York, New Jersey, and a few other places—but, in general, rural conservatism was slow to yield and the country schools remained in an unsatisfactory condition.[281]

The rural school problem in the South was, in a sense, the problem of the entire section. With relatively few cities and a country population more thinly distributed than in most parts of the North, the South had also a greater number of children in proportion to adults than did the North and a net taxable wealth considerably less.[282] The burden of educational support on adults in such a state as Mississippi was about twice as heavy as in Vermont. The situation was further complicated by the lingering financial effects of Reconstruction and the cost of maintaining separate racial schools. For these and other reasons, little or no trace of a state school system existed in Virginia, South Carolina, Georgia, Mississippi, and Texas until 1870 or 1871. In several other commonwealths public schools were confined chiefly to the larger towns.

Nevertheless, the expansion of the common-school system in the South was characterized by the federal commissioner of education in 1890 as probably "without a parallel." The enrollment grew from 2.7 million in 1878—less than one quarter blacks—to nearly 4.5 million in 1888, including a somewhat larger proportion of blacks. "At present," the commissioner asserted, "the schools of the South, taken as a whole, enroll a larger percentage of the population than those of the older States of the North, and furnish to every child an opportunity to acquire at least the essential rudiments of a school education."[283] The rise of the agrarian elements to political power in the late eighties and the nineties gave added momentum to the cause of free education, especially in the rural districts. By 1898 the total enrollment had risen to more than 5 million.[284]

However bright the picture may appear against the former darkness, the South throughout the period lagged behind the rest of the nation. Its chief energies were necessarily absorbed in the basic task of abolishing illiteracy, the curse of the white masses as well as of the colored race. In many rural districts schoolhouses were often mere log shacks without windows, desks, maps, or blackboards. The school term averaged about 100 days in 1890 as compared with 150 in the Midwest and 174 in the North Atlantic states.

When the assertion might still be heard that "it is robbery to tax one man to educate another man's children,"[285] the time was not yet ripe for a forward thrust along all lines as in the North. At most, education was regarded in the South as an opportunity for the individual child and not as a civic obligation, for not one of the states of the former Confederacy applied the principle of compulsion to attendance.

Even in the North teachers were often badly underpaid, the worst conditions prevailing in the rural regions and among women. The state superintendent of Iowa reported in 1883 that teachers of ungraded schools did not average $150 a year, though an ordinary farmhand with no obligation to dress well or pay institute fees received $200 with board.[286] For the country as a whole the average monthly salary for a male teacher in 1888–89 was $42.43, for a woman $34.27; by 1898–99 these amounts had advanced to $45.25 and $38.14.[287] The displacement of men by women teachers, already marked in Civil War days, continued at an accelerating rate, partly because of the lower price at which women would work and partly because of the higher rewards for men in the business world. In 1878 about three out of every five teachers were women, in 1898 two out of three.[288] Women won recognition also as educational administrators. By 1897 over 200 were county superintendents, while twelve were city superintendents and two were state commissioners of instruction.[289] For better or for worse—and educational writers were not certain which—the youth of the nation were receiving their instruction increasingly from that sex which hitherto had had least contact with the world of affairs.

For both men and women, teaching was too apt to be a mere stepping-stone to something more congenial or profitable. The federal commissioner of education, noting in 1887 that twenty-six changes occurred yearly in every 100 positions, estimated the average term of service at less than four years.[290] Such conditions militated against the conception of teaching as a life career, a profession to be cultivated as was law or medicine. Another deterrent to the attainment of professional standards was the active meddling, not only of politicians but also of schoolbook publishers, in teaching appointments and the selection of textbooks.[291]

Nevertheless, the increase of normal schools, the progressiveness of city systems and the waxing strength of teachers' associations helped offset some of these baneful influences. As public schools grew nationwide in their reach, the American people were exalted by a lyric faith in education that rivaled an earlier generation's zeal for democracy. In a time of low political morality it was expected to be the solvent of all governmental ills. Indeed, reformers urged that its precepts be directly applied to officeholders through the examination system of appointment.

The period was marked not only by a physical expansion of the school system, but also by a spread of new ideas, the addition of fresh subjects to the curriculum, and a marked improvement in textbooks. In the late 1880s a number of young Americans who had studied under Professor William Rein at the University of Jena brought back with them the Herbartian conception of instruction.[292] Charles De Garmo's *Essentials of Method* (1889) and C. A. McMurry's *General Method* (1892), by popularizing the new ideas for American educators, did much to change the teacher from a mere drillmaster and disciplinarian to a person charged with the responsibility of interesting his pupils through an effective presentation of subject matter.

It is easier to record the outer aspects of educational development than to appraise its results. Like religion, the influence of education cannot be gauged by a count of buildings, the amount of capital invested, or the sheer number of persons reached. European visitors were deeply interested in the unfolding American experiment, and no less a person than James Bryce believed that, due to its effects, "the average of knowledge is higher, the habit of reading and thinking more generally diffused, than in any other country."[293] Of course, many members of this generation owed their formal training to the schools of an earlier time, and by the same token, the schoolrooms of the 1880s and 1890s were cradling the intellectual life of the early twentieth century.

Certainly, in accomplishing their primary task, the schools made an impressive record, for the proportion of illiteracy in the nation declined from 17 percent in 1880 to 13 percent in 1890 and to less than 11 percent in 1900.[294] The large cities made a better showing than the small towns and country districts, the North and West better than the South, and the children of immigrants better than their parents. Indeed, the American-born children of the European newcomers were more literate than the white children of native parentage, chiefly perhaps because of their concentration in cities. If the ability to read and write may be supposed to have any relationship to political intelligence, conservative folk must have been dismayed to observe that, of the nine states that stood highest in literacy, all but one voted for Bryan and free silver in the notable "campaign of education" of 1896.

Despite the remarkable growth of educational facilities since the 1830s, the comparative newness of the system in many parts of the country left vast numbers of adults with a pitifully inadequate share of systematic instruction. In 1880 the total amount of schooling received by the average person in his entire lifetime was less than four years; in 1898 it amounted to exactly five.[295] In other words, the average American had not advanced, in his formal training, beyond the attainments of the fourth or fifth grade of the elementary school. The varied literary aspirations and attainments of the time were conditioned by this fundamental fact. Fortunately the constant tendency to pull literature down to the level of the half-educated masses was somewhat offset by the fact that more people than ever before were pouring from the halls of the high schools and colleges.

If the schools were primarily concerned with the instruction of children, their elders had a special opportunity of their own in the contagious spread of the Chautauqua movement. This novel institution gave countless middle-class folk a chance to make up for the deficiencies of their youthful education. Founded in 1874 by an Ohio manufacturer, Lewis Miller, and a Methodist minister, John H. Vincent, as a sort of camp meeting for the training of Sunday school teachers, the annual summer gatherings on the forested shores of Lake Chautauqua, New York, quickly developed broader educational functions whose influence ramified to many parts of the country.[296] "Any man who loves knowledge and his native land," observed Professor G. H. Palmer of Harvard,

> must be glad at heart when he visits a summer assembly of Chautauqua: there . . . attends the swiftly successive Round Tables upon Milton, Temperance, Geology, the American Constitution, the Relations of Science and Religion, and the Doctrine of Rent; perhaps assists at the Cooking School, the Prayer Meeting, the Concert, and the Gymnastic Drill; or wanders under the trees among the piazzaed cottages, and sees the Hall of Philosophy and the wooden Doric Temple shining on their little eminences.[297]

Of more lasting value for the diffusion of culture was the multiplication of public libraries. Though dating back to mid-century, tax-supported free libraries had remained few in number outside of certain Eastern cities. Neither in these nor in college and society libraries did proper catalogues exist to indicate the contents of the collections, and the tired ex-teacher or ex-preacher who served as librarian was usually more interested in hoarding books than in having them used. But all this was forced to change as an eager public stormed the reading rooms and demanded untrammeled access to the republic of the printed word. In 1876 a group of progressive librarians, meeting in Philadelphia, formed the American Library Association, which thereafter proceeded aggressively to foster the ideal of providing "the best reading for the largest number at the least expense."[298] Leaders in this body—such as Justin Winsor of the Harvard Library, F. W. Poole of the Chicago Public, Charles Cutter of the Boston Athenaeum, and Melvil Dewey, librarian at Columbia—were responsible for developing those ingenious methods of cataloguing, shelf classification, and book circulation, which have helped make the American library the most efficient in the world.

At the same time the establishment of new libraries was promoted by both public and private agencies. Between 1878 and 1898 eighteen commonwealths authorized the use of taxation for such purposes, and in 1895, New Hampshire went so far as to make its permissive law obligatory.[299] Private munificence for library construction is inseparably connected with the name of the steel magnate, Andrew Carnegie, whose first benefactions went in 1881 to the city of Pittsburgh and nearby towns. Widening his field of activity, he presently paid for the erection of buildings in many parts of the country, stipulating only that a site be furnished and maintenance provided by taxation. By the end of 1898 he had given nearly $6 million to the cause, a mere hint, however, of what was to follow.[300] Carnegie, though the greatest giver, was not the only one. During the two decades a total of not less than $36 million was contributed for library purposes.

Though book knowledge had never before constituted so large a part of the common intellectual stock, the mental world of the average man continued in large measure to consist of a mélange of information, lore and gossip culled from the periodical press. Even the magazines catered to the most diverse tastes. If the score of years from 1878 to 1898 did little to increase their variety, it added to their number and adapted their manner and matter better to the stratified reading public. Monthly periodicals increased from about 1,200 to 1,800, while their more sedate quarterly contemporaries grew from about 100 to well over 200.[301] The chief gains occurred in periodicals devoted to transportation, business (including trade journals), and fraternal organizations. Magazines for general readers were less remarkable for their growth in number than, as we shall see, for their greatly expanded circulations.

Of the better-class periodicals this generation could hardly improve upon those it had inherited from earlier years: *Harper's Monthly*, the *Atlantic*, and *Scribner's Monthly* (changed to the *Century* in 1881 when the Scribner interests withdrew). An enlarging clientele, however, made it possible for Charles Scribner's Sons to launch in 1887 a new monthly of similar appeal, *Scribner's Magazine*. Distinguished in typography, dignified in tone, careful in diction, these journals, the *Atlantic* excepted, also took special pride in their illustrations. Indeed, the triangular rivalry was responsible for important improvements in the art of engraving and the technique of printing pictures. On the literary side they were aided by continuity of editorial policy, Richard Watson Gilder serving throughout these years as editor of the *Century*, as did H. M. Alden and E. L. Burlingame respectively of *Harper's* and *Scribner's Magazine*.[302] A citizen attained a certain prestige merely by having one of these periodicals on his library table.

A flock of new publications bespoke the widening interests of women who no longer needed to content themselves with old-fashioned journals of the *Godey* type. Of such magazines none was so influential as the *Ladies' Home Journal*. Established in 1883 by Cyrus H. K. Curtis, it began its astonishing success six years later when Edward W. Bok, an aggressive journalist of Dutch birth, took the editorial helm.[303] Bok, without neglecting familiar household concerns, introduced many fresh features: fiction by the best writers, articles on interesting personalities of the world, attractive illustrations, inexpensive house plans, and special departments like "Ruth Ashmore's Side Talks with Girls" which brought an average of 10,000 letters a year from maidens troubled with affairs of the heart. And for such riches the reader paid but ten cents a copy. A feminine rather than a feminist magazine, the *Ladies' Home Journal* not only kept in stride with the intelligent middle-class woman, but walked several paces ahead.

Bok's success called attention to the existence of a mass of readers, suckled largely on newspapers, whom fiction magazines selling at twenty-five and thirty-five cents had never been able to reach. What Bok had done to interest women, might not others do for this greater public of both sexes? New manufacturing processes, large-scale production, and the possibility of unusual advertising revenues suggested the means of accomplishment. Armed with this bold idea and savings of $7,300, Samuel S. McClure in 1893 launched a new periodical, *McClure's*, which sold for only fifteen cents a copy. Within a few months *Munsey's* and *Cosmopolitan* went him one better, lowering their rates to ten cents.[304] The great popularity which all of them achieved rested almost as much on their ability to attract able authors and illustrators and on the crisp manner of writing as on the low cost to readers. Ida M. Tarbell's careful articles on Napoleon and Abraham Lincoln in 1894 and 1895 helped increase the circulation of *McClure's* by the tens of thousands. By 1898 the popular-priced magazine had enlarged the number of magazine buyers from about 500,000 to nearly 3 million.[305]

Just as more people read magazines than books, so a greater number read newspapers than magazines. The nineteenth-century American had long since come to regard the newspaper as second only to the church and the school in importance; indeed, in many a pioneer settlement it leaped into lusty manhood while the other two were still gasping for birth. The sweep of population into the Great West, the gargantuan growth of cities, and the increasing literacy of the masses now afforded newspapers new areas for conquest. The result was seen in a multiplication of papers, tremendous competition in news gathering, and a growing vulgarization of the press. Between 1880 and 1900 the number of dailies advanced from 971 to 2226, and the weeklies and semiweeklies—published chiefly in rural towns—from less than 9,000 to nearly 14,000. At the latter date the United States was fathering more than half the newspapers in the world. Yet the growth of subscribers outstripped even the increase of journals.[306]

While the newspapers clustered most thickly in the states possessing large cities, the two new commonwealths carved out of Dakota contained 25 dailies and 315 weeklies at the close of the century, and even Oklahoma territory could boast of 9 daily papers and nearly 100 weeklies. Indeed, it is worth recalling that, though the dynamic forces in journalism emanated from the cities, the average American remained addicted to a weekly or semiweekly journal. As late as 1900 42.5 million took such papers as compared with 15 million who bought dailies.[307] The country weekly of 1900 was, however, a far different sheet from its counterpart of twenty years before.

Newspaper readers were kept abreast of the passing show as never before in American history. If a fifty-mile radius represented the approximate distance to which a city daily had a general sale, there were twenty-one principal newspaper-distribution areas in the United States, embracing a population of nearly 19.5 million or about a third of all the people in the nation. Here were found three fourths of the dailies with the greatest circulation.[308] At the same time, the country press moved closer into the orbit of metropolitan journalism, and, seconded by the magazines, city standards and interests were ceaselessly dinned into the ears of the rural audience—a telling example of urban imperialism in the cultural sphere and indirectly the source of much rustic unhappiness.

New forces were also at work in the colleges and universities. Not only did institutions of higher learning grow in number, endowment, and quality of instruction, but for the first time they began to take seriously their obligation to enrich the world's store of knowledge. "Nothing more strikes a stranger who visits the American universities," declared an English scholar familiar with Oxford and Cambridge, "than the ardour with which the younger generation has thrown itself into study, even kinds of study which will never win the applause of the multitude."[309]

Colleges and universities increased from 350-odd in 1878 to nearly 500 in 1898, the combined student body from about 58,000 to approximately 100,000.[310] Mere growth in number of institutions, however, did not necessarily denote progress, except on the theory of the misguided patriot who exulted, "There are two universities in England, four in France, ten in Prussia and thirty-seven in Ohio." Particularly in the rural South and the Midwest, the country was wretchedly overstocked with institutions making pretensions to the name of college or university, at a time when higher standards of instruction and research called for a concentration of funds. In 1881 the total income of all the colleges and universities in Ohio fell considerably short of that of Harvard alone.[311] Most institutions of this kind had been planted by denominational zeal, and catered to local rural constituencies. Once pioneers in the westward march of higher culture, they were now fallen on bitter times, for the state universities, with constantly increasing legislative support, superior equipment, and richer curricula, were drawing away their students and undermining their position of influence. In many a Western and Southern state legislature the tax-maintained university won its appropriations only in the teeth of hardy opposition from those who decried its "godless" character.

But in an age of the glorification of public education such diehards contended against the spirit of the times. Between 1885 and 1895 the number of students in eight representative state universities—Michigan, Illinois, Wisconsin, Minnesota, Iowa, Kansas, Nebraska, and California—

trebled, while the gain in eight equally reputable church schools of the Midwest was scarcely 15 percent. In the latter year there were more Presbyterian students in seventeen state universities than in the thirty-seven best Presbyterian colleges.[312] Moreover, ten commonwealths of the West and South which, for one reason or another, had not earlier seen fit to set up their own universities now proceeded to do so.[313] To the University of Michigan more than any other was due the constant improvement in state-university standards during these years. One of the first to free itself from the hampering influence of politics, it vied with Eastern institutions in introducing new educational methods and was the first to link the public schools with the university by admitting graduates of accredited high schools without examination.[314]

When Emily Faithfull, the English social worker, visited the University of Michigan in 1883, she was told by President J. B. Angell that, though coeducation was still on trial in the East, the question was definitely settled in the West. Moreover, he assured her, "none of the ladies had found the curriculum too heavy for their physical endurance. . . ."[315] All the new state universities in the West and South, as a matter of course, were coeducational and the strength of the tide was such that most of the Southern state institutions which had hitherto held aloof now succumbed.[316] While the practice continued to be less common in the older parts of the nation than in the West, the proportion of mixed colleges in the United States grew from 51 percent in 1880 to 70 percent in 1898 and the number of women students from 2,750 to more than 25,000.[317]

To meet the challenge of coeducation the East established new women's colleges of high rank and improved existing ones. Thus Bryn Mawr, near Philadelphia, was opened in 1885 with ample resources and excellent scientific equipment, while three years later Mount Holyoke Seminary was converted into a college with degree-granting powers. Most interesting of all was the grudging compromise by certain men's institutions, of setting up affiliated colleges for the other sex—cooperation without entanglement —after the manner of Oxford and Cambridge. Starting in 1879 with twenty-seven students, an organization, informally known as the Harvard Annex, enrolled studious young women who, under the guidance of such professors as William James, John Knowles Paine, and Ephraim Emerton, were enabled to take the same courses as the men at Harvard, though not in their company. By the time this undertaking ripened into Radcliffe College (1894), Tulane University, Western Reserve, and Columbia had created coordinate women's colleges and Brown University was in the process of so doing. By 1898, four out of every five colleges, universities, and professional schools in the United States admitted women. Their right to as complete and diversified an education as men was no longer seriously questioned.

Meanwhile, the old-fashioned, hard-and-fast college course was everywhere rapidly crumbling under the hammering blows inflicted by President

Charles W. Eliot of Harvard and his ilk. However valid were the pedagogical reasons for the elective system, the reform was in any case inevitable because of the great advances in science and scholarship and the sheer impossibility of a student's taking in four years all the courses offered. The world had changed, and as life itself became more diverse, more complex, it was fitting that education, as a preparation for life, should take on greater richness and variety. The elective system, moreover, was the practice of German universities, where many American professors had studied. At Harvard, freedom of election went farthest; in most other places the principle of liberty in the choice of subjects was introduced gradually, the first two years being largely prescribed with options thereafter.[318]

Under the new plan the college curriculum offered a variety of appeal which accounts in part for the swelling stream of students.[319] The time-honored courses in Latin, Greek, and mathematics lost favor in competition with such newer subjects as English literature, certain laboratory sciences, modern languages, history, economics, and political science.[320] While critics deplored an irrational scattering of choices by students and a tendency to concentrate on "snap" courses, Dean LeB. R. Briggs maintained, after many years' experience, that, "as a body, the students of Harvard College use the elective system with some sense of responsibility and with reasonable intelligence."[321] The system had one unanticipated result: By making possible greater specialization of teaching by the faculty, the diversity of offerings contributed indirectly to the increase of productive scholarship.

Curricular changes were attended by changes in student life and conduct. While hazing continued to make the first months of the freshman year a rough apprenticeship, in other respects there was greater soberness, a less excitable class spirit, fewer outbreaks of rowdyism and violence, than in former times.[322] The effect of the elective system in destroying class unity, together with the greater age at which students were entering college, was partly responsible.[323] Equally important was the increasing absorption in intercollegiate athletics. The ancient loyalty to one's class was supplanted by loyalty to the college as a whole. Typical displays of undergraduate spirit thus took the form of mass meetings, athletic celebrations, rooting on the side lines, and perhaps pitched battles after the game with supporters of the other team.

Next to athletics, the chief focus of undergraduate interest was to be found in the clubs and fraternities. The older institutions in the East had their exclusive local societies of long standing, while throughout the West and generally in the South the Greek-letter fraternity system dominated student social life and, to a considerable extent, campus politics as well. To meet the needs of ever-expanding enrollments the national fraternities increased the number of their chapters from 462 in 1879 to 781 in 1898 and their total membership from about 63,000 to over 130,000.[324] Ex-

President White of Cornell defended the Greek-letter system as a means of developing group responsibility and higher personal standards, but others deplored its snobbish tendency and objected to the brutality of the initiation ceremonies.[325] The entrenched position of the fraternities is indicated by the fact that the efforts of the University of California in 1879 and of Purdue in 1881 to ban them were thwarted by an appeal to the courts. On the whole, it seems fair to say that, while fraternities generally exalted social above intellectual attainments, leadership in undergraduate activities usually came from their ranks, and their worst features were accentuated where college authorities were hostile.[326]

Only a relatively few college graduates went on to more advanced study. Postgraduate instruction represented the culmination of the Teutonic influence in higher education. The graduate school was the American counterpart of the *philosophische Facultät*. Its quick and firm rooting in the national soil attested the missionary zeal of hundreds of young scholars who, returning home with German doctorates, resolved to replace American superficiality with the Teutonic ideal of patient thoroughness. During the 1880s over 2,000 Americans were studying in German universities, twice as many as in the preceding ten years and considerably more than in the next decade.[327]

It was not hope of material reward that fired these youthful pilgrims, for the highest salary they could hope to attain was $2,000 in a small college, in a large one perhaps $3,000 or $4,000.[328] It was something different, something which never before had had so ample an expression in American life: a passion for truth born of knowledge; an eagerness to do a few things supremely well instead of many things well enough; perhaps also an unconscious withdrawal of sensitive spirits from the soiling materialism which characterized the ethics of the great captains of industry and colored the whole business world. Moreover, the broad diffusion of worldly goods made it possible for middle-class sons to take advantage of opportunities which an earlier day had restricted to the wealthy few.

These returning Americans made their influence felt in faculties far and wide.[329] The Johns Hopkins University, which had opened in Baltimore in 1876 primarily for the promotion of graduate study in the Teutonic sense, had scarcely anyone on its staff of fifty-three in 1887 who had not studied in Germany. To this bracing center went troops of youths who in turn were to help spread the new ideals to all corners of the land: Josiah Royce, John Dewey, Joseph Jastrow, in philosophy and psychology; Henry C. Adams, Davis R. Dewey, John R. Commons, in political economy; Charles H. Haskins, J. Franklin Jameson, Woodrow Wilson, Frederick J. Turner, Charles M. Andrews, in history and political science; Albion W. Small and E. A. Ross in sociology; Edmund B. Wilson, T. H. Morgan, E. G. Conklin, in biology; and Edwin H. Hall, Joseph S. Ames, and A. L. Kimball in chemistry.[330]

Spurred by the example of Johns Hopkins, the older foundations of the

East placed their graduate work on a stronger basis.[331] Not a few state universities made starts in the same direction, the interest in research there usually spreading outward from the department of agriculture. Assisted by an increasing provision of fellowships, the number of students pursuing nonprofessional graduate work in American universities rose from a little over 400 in 1878 to nearly 5,000 in 1898. So rapid and sound was the development that before the end of the eighties the primacy of Hopkins was already seriously challenged, and by the mid-nineties, she was outstripped in number of registrants by Chicago, Harvard, and Yale. It was no longer necessary for talented young men to seek their higher specialized training across the sea, for a dozen American institutions now offered opportunities as rich as could be found anywhere in the world.

For most Americans, the most important advances in knowledge concerned the medical sciences. The phrase "science and health" was a potent formula even for the new religious sect which rejected medicine as the science of health. For the man on the street the words implied fresh safeguards against the ravages of sickness and greater certainty of recovery. This new posture of affairs was, in large measure, the result of an epochal discovery as to the cause of communicable diseases. First worked out by the Frenchman Louis Pasteur in the 1860s and 1870s, the germ theory in the early 1880s was rapidly widened in its application to human ills by the German Robert Koch's invention of improved methods and his isolation of the microbes of tuberculosis and Asiatic cholera. Then, in 1884, G. T. A. Gaffsky introduced a better knowledge of the typhoid bacillus and Friedrich Loeffler discovered the diphtheria bacillus.[332] Americans also made primary contributions to medical bacteriology, notably in the work of Theobald Smith and F. L. Kilborne on Texas fever, a plague which was decimating Western cattle herds.[333] With the development of the serum treatment of infectious diseases, so strikingly exemplified by the use of antitoxin in diphtheria, the healing art attained possibilities undreamed of a few years before. Medical practice in the United States was profoundly affected as respects both the diagnosis and treatment of sickness and also, as we shall see, as regards the science of epidemiology.[334]

America's original contributions to medical science were perhaps better represented by the attention given to the nervous ailments which tightened their hold on the people as the social order became more urban and complex. In this field George M. Beard of New York, who coined the term "neurasthenia" was a pioneer.[335] His researches, however, were less influential than those of S. Weir Mitchell of Philadelphia, who originated the familiar "rest cure," and of William A. Hammond in New York City. At the same time, the practice of psychiatry was enriched by the work of Shobal V. Clevenger in Illinois, his treatise *Spinal Concussion* (1889) gaining international repute. The new science of laryngology was similarly advanced by the efforts of F. H. Bosworth of New York and J. Solis Cohen of Philadelphia, whose publications on throat and nose diseases also had a deep influence abroad. In a related field, A. H. Buck's *Diagnosis and Treatment of Ear Diseases* (1880) was for many years the vade mecum of otologists.

Among general practitioners and the public at large, medical sects continued to thrive. Besides "regulars," homeopaths, and eclectics, there was a profusion of magnetic healers, physiomedicalists (who prescribed only botanical remedies), vitapaths, hydropaths, electropaths, sun curists, and the like. Some states explicitly banned nonmedical healing, but others, like Illinois and most of the New England states, were on much the same footing as the Cherokee Nation in Indian Territory, which permitted "enchantments in any form." Of the new sects, osteopathy, whose principles were first formulated in 1874 by Dr. Andrew T. Still of Baldwin, Kansas, possessed the greatest vitality. By the close of the century its practice had express legal sanction in the Dakotas, Iowa, Missouri, Michigan, Tennessee, and Vermont.[336]

Many people preferred self-dosing in the form of pills, tablets, and liquids, obtained as proprietary medicines from drugstores.[337] While some of these nostrums were harmless, others were habit-forming opiates or thinly disguised alcoholic stimulants. The enormous demand for "cures" for "lost manhood" and alleged remedies for venereal diseases sheds an interesting, if somewhat puzzling, light on the moral conditions of the time. The use of patent medicines, stimulated by high-pressure advertising, was also assisted, especially in rural towns, by traveling medicine shows. These reached their greatest vogue in the 1880s and 1890s. Gathered about the medicine wagon in a circle dimly lighted by a flickering kerosene torch, the gaping crowd listened approvingly to the banjoist's vocal rendition of such ditties as "The Animal Fair," and then, as the long-haired, self-styled doctor harrowed their feelings with tales of the fatal results of certain symptoms common to all, showered the boards with coins for his famous "Indian" remedy.[338] The addiction of untold numbers to fantastic "cures" forms a splendid testimonial to the basic robustness of the American stock.

As in medical science, so in surgery the germ theory wrought a transformation, largely through the efforts of the Englishman Joseph Lister, a follower of Pasteur, who about 1865 established the principle of cleanliness in wound treatment. By opening up new opportunities for operative skill, antiseptic surgery, as it was called, gave American practitioners for the first time ample scope for their manual dexterity.[339] Intestinal operations had seldom been attempted earlier because even accidental wounds of internal tissues might cause destructive inflammations, but now the whole domain of abdominal surgery was explored and conquered, in large part by Americans. Appendicitis was robbed of most of its terrors, and the removal of the appendix reduced to almost a minor operation, as a result of the researches of Reginald H. Fitz at Harvard.[340] Great advances were also made in the surgery of eye, ear, and brain.

The germ theory registered its greatest triumph in the new direction given to community efforts for health conservation. Recurrent epidemics had caused most of the large cities and fifteen of the states to set up boards of health prior to 1878.[341] In 1878–79 yellow fever swept through the Gulf states, Tennessee and, in some measure, Kentucky and Missouri, exacting a toll of 16,000 lives out of about 74,000 afflicted.[342] At Memphis, where the scourge raged most fiercely, over 5,000 died while 20,000 others, fleeing in terror before an effective quarantine could be established, helped spread the plague to other communities. Although the transmitting cause of the disease continued to elude scientists, Memphis hastened to repair its criminal neglect of the past by laying out many miles of sewers and drainage tiles, and the nationwide horror was reflected in the prompt creation of additional state boards of health. Twelve commonwealths acted before 1882 and fifteen others followed by the close of 1898.[343]

To the service of public-health agencies medical bacteriology brought a rational or scientific knowledge of disease prevention in place of the older empirical methods.[344] Early and definite diagnosis of infectious ailments became possible; new and effective systems of control were devised. Quarantine was extended to other ills than the traditional ones of smallpox and yellow fever, and port cities were barred against the admission of dangerous imported plagues like cholera and typhus. Progress was made also in providing special hospitals for the isolation and treatment of infectious cases. Equally important was the fact that, through a well-sustained publicity, the average citizen came to accept personal cleanliness as an ally of health as well as of godliness. Smooth-shaven jowls began to emerge from behind the unhygienic whiskers of Civil War times, and the constant drive against tuberculosis led to a steady banishment of the national vice of spitting, noted by foreign travelers since colonial times.

Such efforts, it will be recalled, were supplemented by the enterprise of municipalities in constructing water and drainage systems, inspecting milk supplies, undertaking pure-food measures, and the like. Sanitary engineering, though it had its own reasons for being, was an indispensable arm of the public-health movement. The war against disease, of course was hampered by the limited knowledge of the age, especially in regard to methods of immunization, and sometimes also by the interference of time-serving politicians. Yet despite these handicaps and the further difficulty presented by the herding of immigrants in the worst quarters of the cities, the mortality rate in the United States fell nearly 10 percent from 1890 to 1900, and the average age at death rose from thirty-one years to thirty-five.[345] This gain was due largely to the lessening mortality from tuberculosis, diphtheria, and children's diseases. The benefits of public-health efforts fell chiefly to the cities where, of course, the need was greatest. It was a fortunate conjunction of circumstances for America that, when the age of large cities arrived, medical science made it possible to protect the dense population centers from the terrible scourges which for so many centuries had ravaged Europe.

THE PURSUIT OF HAPPINESS

JAMES A. GARFIELD, pausing at Lake Chautauqua for a nonpartisan address during his presidential campaign in 1880, declared: "We may divide the whole struggle of the human race into two chapters; first, the fight to get leisure; and then the second fight of civilization—what shall we do with our leisure when we get it."[346] There can be no doubt that the closing decades of the century marked a great advance on the part of the American people in gaining freedom from bread winning toil. Nearly all classes were affected: the extremely rich whose idle wives and children knew so well how to "make amusement into a business";[347] the wage-earners who benefited from the gradual shortening of the workday; the salaried workers who were coming to consider a two weeks' summer vacation part of the normal conditions of employment. Only the tillers of the soil continued to live very much as of yore. To the farmers, more toil, rather than less, seemed necessary to pull them out of their slough; and constant contrast with the frivolous aspects of urban life deepened the conviction of the older generation that leisure was a polite name for laziness.

It was, indeed, in the city that the people were squarely engaged in "the second fight of civilization." With more leisure at their command than so large a body of mankind had ever before enjoyed, their use or abuse of its opportunities would give at least a provisional answer to the question as to the capacity of the masses to achieve the arts and graces of living. Certainly the new freedom caught many methodically ordered lives in a state of dishabille. Life under American conditions had taught them how to work but not how to relax.[348] They were inclined to pursue their avocations with the same feverish intensity that had won success in their other undertakings. As Matthew Arnold remarked in 1883 while in New York, "Old Froissart, who said of the English of his day, that 'they take their pleasures sadly, after their fashion,' would, doubtless, if he lived now, say of the Americans, that they take their pleasures hurriedly, after their fashion."[349]

For the average person no use of leisure so well suited his taste as that afforded by the ubiquitous fraternal orders which sprang up during the last quarter of the century. Earlier organizations of this character had been few in number and usually imported from abroad.[350] Now Americans turned with furious zeal to the creation of secret societies cut to their own pattern. In the large cities some form of organized social commingling seemed called for to replace the spontaneous friendliness of small rural towns. Liberty and equality this generation was willing to take for granted, but fraternity filled a compelling human need. Moreover, the romantic opportunity to posture before a mystic brotherhood in all the glory of robe, plume, and sword restored a sense of self-importance bruised by the anonymity of life amid great crowds.[351] If further inducement were needed, it was supplied by the provision made by most lodges for sickness and death benefits for their members.[352]

Although some important indigenous orders, like the Knights of Pythias and the Elks, had appeared in the sixties, in the two decades after 1880 their number became legion. At least 124 new secret societies were founded between 1880 and 1890, 136 between 1890 and 1895, and 230 more by 1901.[353] The nomenclature of fraternalism will doubtless some day offer interesting material for the student of suppressed desires and wishful thinking, but to one of less imaginative endowment there seems little enough in common among such names as the Knights and Ladies of the Golden Rule, the Royal Society of Good Fellows, the Modern Woodmen of America, the American Order of Druids, the Owls, the Prudent Patricians of Pompeii and the Concatenated Order of Hoo-Hoo.

As was to be expected, membership was greatest in the urbanized sections of the country. By the end of the period there were over 6 million names on the rosters of fraternal bodies.[354] America possessed more secret societies and a larger number of "joiners" than all other nations. The "big four" were the Odd Fellows, the Freemasons, the Knights of Pythias, and the Ancient Order of United Workmen, which collectively embraced more than one third of the entire lodge membership. Nor did students of religion fail to note that in all the large cities the lodges outnumbered the churches, Brooklyn and Boston each having twice and St. Louis and Chicago three times as many.[355]

The great increase of city dwellers also provided wider patronage for the theater. As the nation's metropolis, New York was the chief producing center; its supremacy in matters histrionic was unquestioned.[356] There money could be found for new theatrical ventures, there actors' reputations were won or lost, there aspiring playwrights flocked to offer their wares. There, too, in the field of the polite drama, were to be found the three greatest producing managers of the 1880s: J. Lester Wallack, Augustin Daly, and A. M. Palmer. At their theaters they maintained stock companies which gave the best performances of the era and included such finished players as Fanny Davenport, Ada Rehan, Stuart Robson, Charles Coghlan, James O'Neil, and Annie Russell.

Throughout the decade, however, the resident stock-company type of production was losing ground to the traveling company and the "star" system.[357] Easier and cheaper means of transportation led newer producers to reach out for the patronage that awaited in the cities of the hinterland. With this in view it was more profitable to employ a featured actor, supported by nonentities, than to maintain the standards of performance which a sophisticated New York audience expected at a place like Daly's or Palmer's Madison Square Theatre. The new system also benefited local managers by relieving them of the greater financial risks of a stock company.

As road companies multiplied, the supply of actor talent could not keep up with the demand.[358] Some of the pathetic or ludicrous mishaps which befell the roving thespians were less attributable to the arrested mental development of their audiences than to their own histrionic deficiencies. A performance of a perennially popular play was dismissed by a Minnesota paper in the 1890s with the laconic comment: "Thompson's Uncle Tom's Cabin company appeared at the opera house last night. The dogs were poorly supported."[359] A favorite subject with cartoonists in *Puck* and *Judge* was the hollow-cheeked actor attired in a mangy fur-collared overcoat and straw hat, indulging in delusions of grandeur before a group of his fellow artists similarly arrayed. "We notice of late, said the *New York Dramatic News* of March 19, 1884, "that professionals returning by rail to New York after the company has 'busted up' have got past complaining of this mode of travel. . . . They admit, however, that it is exceedingly annoying to have to get off the track so often to allow the trains to pass up and down." Yet so great was the lure of the footlights that between 1880 and 1900 the number of actors increased from less than 5,000 to nearly 15,000.[360]

Just as the reading public demanded fictional treatments of American life, so theatergoers were increasingly eager to see plays about themselves —plays depicting American types, American backgrounds, and humorous or exciting situations compatible with American conditions.[361] Departing from the custom of older producers like Daly and Wallack, venturesome young managers—David Belasco, Charles and Daniel Frohman, and others —perceived the box-office possibilities of the native drama and used it as a means of climbing to a position of financial stability and eventual theatrical dominance. Though some of the plays like *Pudd'nhead Wilson* and *Editha's Burglar* were dramatizations of popular novels, every year saw a greater number prepared in first instance for the stage. *Hazel Kirke,* written by Steele MacKaye, had a New York run of 486 nights, beginning on February 4, 1880. This record was exceeded only by another play of native authorship, Charles Hoyt's *A Trip to Chinatown,* which started its career of 650 nights on November 9, 1891. The successive offerings of Bronson Howard, the foremost American dramatist of the time, were also usually certain of a cordial reception. *The Young Mrs. Winthrop,* produced in 1882, continued uninterruptedly in New York for more than 150 nights, while three years later, *One of Our Girls* held the boards for 200 nights. *The Henrietta,* produced in 1887, ran for sixty-eight weeks, earning admission receipts of nearly half a million dollars.

Though MacKaye's greatest success and some of Howard's pieces had a European setting, native playwrights turned more and more to purely American themes and materials. Like the local-color novel, the drama of rural life made a special appeal to nostalgic city dwellers desirous of renewing their childhood memories. A prime favorite was *Joshua Whitcomb* (later renamed *The Old Homestead*), which toured the country almost continuously with Denman Thompson, who had helped write it, in the title role of the simple, lovable old farmer. Two other popular hits were *The County Fair,* by Charles Barnard and Neil Burgess, first staged in 1889, and Lottie Blair Parker's *Way Down East,* produced early in 1898, each of which enjoyed an initial New York run of more than a year. Thickly buttered with sentimentality and rural heroics, such offerings suffered artistically beside James A. Herne's *Shore Acres,* first performed in Chicago in 1892. Herne was an apostle of realism in the drama in much the same sense that his friends, Howells and Garland, were of realism in literature.[362] *Shore Acres,* though largely devoid of theatricalism and dealing primarily with the fundamentals of human character, was nevertheless long in demand.

In general, however, the public did not care to see real life on the stage. One could hardly have guessed from the serious drama, as he might from the serious fiction, that industrialism and the growth of cities were thrusting forward acute problems to plague society. For purposes of stage presentation all such matters had to be given a comic turn. By exploiting humorous possibilities of immigrant life, Edward Harrigan succeeded in writing a series of hilarious comedies about the relations of the embattled Mulligans with their friendly enemies, the Lochmüllers—pieces which incidentally shed much light on the feudal character of New York machine politics.[363] Other aspects of the passing scene were caricatured by Charles Hoyt, who turned out a succession of rapid-fire farces that reached its climax in *A Texas Steer* (1890) and *A Trip to Chinatown* (1891), already mentioned. Profiting by his experience as paragrapher on the *Boston Post,* he paraded before his delighted audiences all the stock characters of comic journalism: the temperance crank, the mannish feminist, the social climber, the chronic joiner, the spiritualist, the baseball hero, and their like.

The comedy of contemporary manners was also cultivated with notable facility by Howard, Belasco, and, starting in the 1890s, by the youthful Clyde Fitch. But as the generation which had fought the Civil War died off, such dramatists turned to romantic plays based on the sectional struggle and its outcome. William Gillette's *Held by the Enemy* (1886), Howard's *Shenandoah* (1888), Augustus Thomas's *Alabama* (1891), and Belasco's *The Heart of Maryland* (1895) proved to be among the most popular offerings of the closing years.

A great many playgoers, however, demanded stronger meat than the polite drama offered. Nourished on the dime novel and the yellow press, they saw life in terms of startling contrasts and swift sensational action. *Uncle Tom's Cabin,* greatest of all native melodramas, retained its accustomed following only by introducing novel features.[364] A half-dozen or more troupes, in the eighties and later, gave performances featured by two Toms, two Evas, two Topsys, and two Simon Legrees. In the nineties the black pugilist Peter Jackson played Uncle Tom in one company, sparring three friendly rounds with Joe Choynski who played George Shelby. A rival company presented John L. Sullivan in the part of Simon Legree. Meantime *East Lynne* retained its earlier vogue, and *The Two Orphans,* a French adaptation first produced in 1874 with Kate Claxton as the blind orphan, reached its twenty-five-hundredth performance at Dayton, Ohio, on May 6, 1884.[365]

More distinctive of the changing national scene were the gun-and-gore dramas of Western life in which, it will be remembered, Buffalo Bill and other actual frontier Bills strode the boards.[366] These presently gave way to a plethora of melodramas depicting the dangers and wickedness of metropolitan life, endless variants of the theme of honest Nell and the city slicker. Although the better dramatists occasionally indulged, such pieces were ordinarily concocted by specialists in the genre like Charles Gayler, C. H. Foster, and Bartley Campbell. Foster was responsible for more than seventy-five thrillers, including *Bertha, the Sewing-Machine Girl, The Gun-maker's Bride,* and *The Turf Digger's Doom.* Campbell, before he went insane in 1886, produced *The Galley Slave, The White Slave,* and other smashing hits, besides composing the deathless line, "Rags are royal raiment when worn for virtue's sake."[367] On Campbell's letterhead were displayed portraits of himself and Shakespeare with the legend, "A friendly rivalry." Any lack of plausibility in such effusions was compensated for by the scenic effects: snowstorms, raging fires, shipwrecks, the thundering approach of the fast mail. The standard admission price was ten, twenty, and thirty cents, and the plays proved quite as popular in the great cities as in the country villages where they were often presented, with nightly changes, under canvas.

The principal attraction in the rural towns, however, was the circus, which reached the zenith of its popularity in the last quarter of the century with nearly forty organizations annually on tour.[368] Traveling by train or wagon during the warm seasons, the human freaks and exotic animals were exhibited in the ubiquitous dime museums during the winter while the acrobats dispersed into the vaudeville circuits. When the two principal circus magnates, P. T. Barnum and J. A. Bailey, combined their shows in 1881, they set a new pace for their competitors, signaled further by acquisition of the elephant Jumbo from the Royal Zoological Gardens, a piece of Yankee enterprise loudly resented by the London populace. Intense rivalry with the Adam Forepaugh circus led in 1882 to a short-lived agreement for a division of routes between them and later to the purchase of the Forepaugh outfit. American circuses, notably Barnum & Bailey's, also met with great favor abroad, and one, W. W. Cole's Colossal Circus, in 1880–81 made a 30,000-mile tour to Australia and New Zealand.

While circuses grew bigger, it is doubtful whether the Toby Tylers of the time thought they grew better, for the increasing size of the "big top" diminished the importance of the clowns whose fun-making under the new conditions was reduced mainly to broad pantomime and slapstick acrobatics. The chief new development in tent entertainment was the advent of Buffalo Bill's Wild West Show in 1883, a truly native circus exhibiting to the descendants of pioneers stirring glimpses of vanishing frontier life, including real cowboys, Indian attacks, bronco busting, and stagecoach holdups.[369] When Buffalo Bill took his show to England in 1887, the tour netted $700,000 and it is said that Gladstone witnessed the performance no less than six times.

It was the production of the Gilbert and Sullivan operas in America, beginning with *Pinafore* in 1878, that brought music into general favor as a form of light entertainment. The delightful nonsense of these two British masters of the art not only set a high standard but also helped break down a popular disapproval based on the supposed naughtiness of musical shows of the "Black Crook" type,[370] inspired by Charles M. Barras's *The Black Crook* (1866), musical spectacles, featuring "indecent" displays of the female leg. A veritable *Pinafore* craze ensued, with amateur productions galore, an endless number of hastily assembled road companies, and, at one time, in 1881, five simultaneous New York presentations. The chief home of comic opera was the New York Casino, opened in 1882 under the direction of Rudolph Aronson.[371] His presentation in 1886 of *Erminie,* an English operetta with Pauline Hall and Francis Wilson in the leading roles, enjoyed a phenomenal run of 1,256 performances. It was the Casino stage which established the reputation of such favorites as Lillian Russell, Fay Templeton, DeWolf Hopper, and David Warfield, making it possible for them in time to go forth as stars heading their own companies.

People living or visiting in the cities could hardly escape the contagion of the latest popular tune. If they avoided the theater and the amusement park, the strains assailed their ears from the Italian organ grinder or the roving German street band. Each year, too, saw improvements in the phonograph, first put on the market by Edison in 1877–78. The original instrument, consisting of a tinfoil cylinder record turned by a hand crank, emitted loud, scarcely recognizable sounds, but further experimentation by Edison, C. A. Bell, C. S. Tainter, Emile Berliner, and others led to the use of flat waxlike disks operated by spring or battery motors and resulting in much clearer tone reproduction.[372] How many of these contrivances invaded American homes in the 1880s and 1890s it is impossible to say, but in the single year 1900 over 150,000 machines and nearly 3 million records were sold.

The rage for popular music was without precedent in the earlier history of America. Chosen by a spontaneous universal suffrage, these melodies were subject to the proverbial fickleness of democracy. Most of them were composed by self-made bards who did not venture beyond the average person's singing range of eight notes or less. However trivial or trite the words, they are of continuing interest to the student of American life as current memoranda of manners, emotions, morals, and absurdities. The same thick vein of sentimentality mined by the yellow press and the writers of sentimental romances and melodrama found musical outlet in an endless succession of moralistic ballads, characterized by such "hits" as Jennie Lindsay's "Always Take Mother's Advice" (1884):

> To you in this world she is dearest,
> At your downfall her grief is severest;

Charles Graham's "The Picture That Is Turned to the Wall" (1891)—the story of why one girl left home; Charles K. Harris's "After the Ball" (1892):

> Many a heart is aching,
> If you could read them all;
> Many the hopes that have vanish'd
> After the ball;

Gussie L. Davis's "The Fatal Wedding" (1893)—"Just another fatal wedding, Just another broken heart"; James Thornton's "She May Have Seen Better Days" (1894); Joe Stern's "My Mother Was a Lady" (1896):

> I've come to this great city
> To find a brother dear,
> And you wouldn't dare insult me, Sir,
> If Jack were only here;

and Paul Dresser's "On the Banks of the Wabash" (1896).[373] Few of such songs, however, attained the musical distinction of De Koven's "O Promise Me," which, popularized by Jessie Bartlett Davis in *Robin Hood*, soon became a melodic accompaniment of every well-conducted American wedding.

Hardly less popular than the theme of misplaced affections was the spirited balladry that centered around life in the city tenements—such songs as "The Mulligan Braves" (1879) and "The Widow Nolan's Goat" (1881), from the Harrigan and Hart comedies; J. J. Sullivan's "Where Did You Get That Hat?" (1888); Joseph Flynn's "Down Went McGinty" (1889); Frank Harding's "Throw Him Down, McCloskey" (1890):

> And future generations, with wonder and delight,
> Will read on hist'ry's pages of this great McCloskey fight;

and C. B. Lawler's "The Sidewalks of New York" (1894). While blacks continued to be a subject of the white man's compositions, the slow-paced, wistful melodies of the plantation type gave way to the "coon song," written in syncopated time to suit the quicker tempo of urban life and designed to stir people's feet instead of their hearts. The first genuine "ragtime" pieces were Barney Fagan's "My Gal Is a High-Born Lady" and C. E. Trevathan's "The Bully," both written in 1896. Their appeal was so great that they set a fashion which lasted into the second decade of the next century.

It remains an open question whether music of the lighter and more ephemeral sort debases the public taste or whether it breeds an appreciation of the nobler forms. The relationship between the two in the eighties and nineties may have been wholly fortuitous, but there can be no doubt that the craze for popular songs was attended by a remarkable growth of interest in serious music. The public schools helped by imparting a knowledge of the rudiments of music; by 1885 seven out of every eight pupils were being taught singing and the ability to read notation.[374] Private teachers also abounded in almost every locality, and piano playing was an ordeal which fond parents customarily imposed upon their offspring, musical and unmusical alike. "There is no country where there are so many pianos and players on them," commented Soissons with not entire approval.[375] A traveler observed a Chickering piano in a miner's tent at Leadville, Colorado, in 1878,[376] and no self-respecting home in the more settled sections was without an instrument of some make or other.

If the record of these years is mainly one of the growth of musical appreciation, yet America began in a modest way to repay a part of its debt for the rich stores of melody it had derived from Europe.[377] Paine, Chadwick, and Horatio Parker all achieved a transatlantic reputation for their orchestral and choral scores, setting a high standard for the next generation to emulate. Similarly, the compositions of Dudley Buck exerted a profound influence for good on American choir music. Ethelbert Nevin and Edward A. MacDowell, on the other hand, devoted their talents to art songs and piano selections. The latter was the most original composer America had yet produced. He had a genius for catching the moods of forest, field, and ocean and expressing them in a musical idiom exquisitely his own. "To a Wild Rose" and "To a Water Lily," published in 1896 as a part of his *Woodland Sketches*, quickly became a precious folk possession of America.

While music and the drama were extending their dominion over men's leisure time, open-air recreations attained a new and stronger hold upon the public. "The disappearance of the backwoods and the growth of large centres of population have created the demand for an artificial outlet," wrote a contemporary, "and the games are the natural successors of the youthful activities of a pioneer period."[378] Indeed, with an increasing proportion of mankind cooped up for long hours in factory and office, working a single set of muscles or benumbing their minds with columns of figures, some form of outdoor diversion was indispensable. But the pioneer inheritance unfortunately did not ordinarily include pioneer biceps. Most people were therefore content to take their more strenuous forms of exercise by proxy, a tendency zealously stimulated by sports promoters who coveted the gate receipts which gladiatorial contests made possible. The audience habit, cultivated by the theater, thus came to infect sports lovers as well.

Much of this new play life reflected the athletic revival which had been taking place in England since the middle of the century. In the United States, however, the new games were not deemed a special perquisite of the upper classes but rather a boon to be enjoyed by all. Nor did the Americans hesitate to modify the rules when it suited their pleasure so to do. In only one instance did they invent a sport of their own; yet that effort was conspicuously successful. Basketball, an indoor game devised by James Naismith in 1891 at the Y.M.C.A. Training College in Springfield, Massachusetts, quickly spread to other countries.[379]

Of the older sports, thoroughbred racing enjoyed an era of unparalleled prosperity.[380] Capital was lavishly invested in new clubhouses and courses, faster tracks were built at the county and state fairs, stakes were increased in size and the great stables sent horses to meets in all parts of the country. In 1876 the record for the mile was set by Ten Broeck at one minute thirty-nine and three-quarters seconds, where it remained until Salvator in 1890 brought the crowd to its feet at Long Branch by clipping the time by four and a quarter seconds. One of the noted racing horses, Hanover, sired by Hindoo, also a great racer of the 1880s, won thirty-two events and finished second thirteen times, earning for his owners, Philip and Michael Dwyer, over $120,000 in a four-year turf career. Despite its wide popularity, however, racing failed universal favor because of the evils of betting and fraud which ordinarily attended it, and which neither the true friends of the sport nor the enactments of legislatures could suppress.

Even more was professional pugilism viewed askance by the respectable elements. Generally banned by law, the fighting was usually with bare fists, the bouts often lasting forty or fifty rounds. In 1882, John L. Sullivan, a slugging fighter of great power, won the heavyweight championship from Paddy Ryan in a battle marked by hitting, wrestling, scratching, and biting. Five years later, while fighting Patsy Cardiff at Minneapolis, he broke his right arm in the third round, but continued to a six-round draw. In 1889,

> Nigh New Orleans
> Upon an emerald plain
> John L. Sullivan
> The strong boy
> Of Boston
> Fought seventy-five red rounds with Jake Kirlain,

winning $20,000 and a diamond belt offered by the *Police Gazette*.[381] His admirers now talked of running him for Congress, but he undertook a boxing tour to Australia instead, coming back only to lose his title in a twenty-one-round bout to the young Californian James J. Corbett. "Gentleman Jim's" victory in 1892 marked a turning point in the sport, for it demonstrated the superiority of scientific boxing over sheer brute strength. His reign, however, was ended in 1897 when, in the fourteenth round of a match with "Bob" Fitzsimmons at Carson City, his Cornish opponent in less than three seconds "accomplished three epochal feats: he had knocked out an Irishman on Saint Patrick's Day, he had won the heavyweight championship of the world, and he had invented the terrible 'solar plexus punch' " that is always associated with his name.[382]

Baseball reached a far larger number of people than either racing or pugilism. Though a vacant-lots sport, it was in its professionalized aspects that it took on the dimensions of "the national game."[383] Alert to stamp out gambling and dishonesty, the National League, formed in 1876 by teams representing four Eastern and four Western cities, made professional baseball respectable at the same time that it offered the most expert playing that could be witnessed anywhere in the country. Minor or "bush" leagues also existed in profusion, and in 1882 a rival to the National League appeared in the American Association.

As competition between nines and leagues grew keener, constant modifications of the rules gave greater scope for both individual skill and team play. Following 1875 the umpire was given power to call strikes and balls, three of the former and four of the latter being made the limit for the batsman. The removal in 1884 of all restrictions on pitching led to the rapid development of the outcurve, incurve, drop, and fadeaway, aspects of the game of which J. B. Clarkson of Chicago and Boston and Timothy Keefe of New York were the particular masters. Protective equipment was also adopted such as the catcher's mask, breastpad, and mitt. In the demonstration of the possibilities of team strategy and coordinated play no nine equaled the Baltimore Orioles, which, under Ned Hanlon's leadership, won the National League pennant for three successive years after 1893.

Rivalry between the major leagues led in 1884 to the inauguration of postseason battles between the pennant-winning teams, an annual event which continued until the collapse of the American Association in 1891.[384] Beginning with Providence's triumph over the New York Metropolitans, victory in the World Series, as it was called, usually rested with the National League. That the world whose championship was yearly at stake might actually learn of America's premier sport, A. G. Spalding in 1888 arranged a series of exhibition matches around the globe between "Pop" (A. C.) Anson's Chicago White Sox and an all-American team. At Kensington Oval grounds the Prince of Wales (later Edward VII) was an excited, if somewhat uncomprehending, spectator, while in Egypt a game was played on the desert close enough to one of the pyramids for it to serve as a backstop. At home, ever greater throngs found the baseball season the most zestful period of the year. The unprecedented number of 40,000 paid admission to the four games between New York and Chicago in 1885 at the Chicago Club grounds. The World Series in 1887 between Detroit and St. Louis had a total attendance of over 51,000.

In the closing years of the period another sport threatened the supremacy of the national game. As long as bicycling was confined to gymnasts whose courage was not daunted by an occasional header from the lofty perch over the high front wheel, it tended to remain in the hands of professionals. Nevertheless, as early as 1880, the League of American Wheelmen was formed with a steadily enlarging membership, and in 1883 a California amateur, Thomas Stevens, undertook a four-year cycling tour of the globe.[385] The real vogue of the sport, however, began a few years later with the introduction of the "safety" bicycle—possessing low wheels of equal size—and the substitution of pneumatic tires for solid rubber ones. At the same time, a drop frame was designed for the sake of the gentler sex who could, if they wished, reassure themselves further by attaching a folded screen to the front of the bicycle "to protect the feet and ankles from view when mounting or riding.[386]

By 1893 a million bicycles were in use.[387] It seemed as though all America had taken to wheels. Frances E. Willard, the temperance leader, fell prey to the craze, announcing her conversion in the book *A Wheel within a Wheel: How I Learned to Ride the Bicycle* (1895). By physicians the therapeutic benefits were declared to be beyond compare, while dress reformers welcomed cycling as an aid to more rational fashions.[388] The new means of locomotion carried people to and from their work; it sped mail carriers and physicians on their rounds; for countless thousands it renewed the forgotten pleasures of open road and countryside. The historian Claude H. Van Tyne, while an undergraduate at the University of Michigan, made a 3,500-mile trip from Ann Arbor over the Rockies in 1894. Meanwhile, bicycle clubs were formed which pedaled together in a body for pleasure, or conducted meets in which professional riders strove to set new records for speed or endurance.

Other forms of physical recreation, while attracting fewer devotees, resembled cycling in their essentially amateur character. Roller skating was an epidemic which raged intermittently and affected all ages; in 1885, skating rinks represented an investment of over $20 million. Croquet made a wide appeal by reason of its simplicity and leisurely pace, though it was objected to by some because of the opportunity it afforded for flirtation.[389] With the hope of converting the game into an exhibition of skill, the National Croquet Association was formed in 1882 and held annual tournaments. Lawn tennis, introduced from England in 1875, was at first also regarded merely as a pleasant pastime, but with the formation of a national association six years later, uniform rules were adopted and the annual tournaments at Newport and elsewhere quickly brought to the fore such masters of the racquet as R. D. Sears, James Dwight, and H. W. Slocum. Meanwhile, the formation of the American Canoe Association in 1880 popularized this water sport. Within a dozen years there were some sixty canoe clubs in the East with over 5,000 members.[390] Skiing was a contribution of Norwegian Americans, who organized the first ski club at Red Wing, Minnesota, in 1883 and held the first tournament the following year.[391]

Rifle shooting also had its addicts, and since 1874 international matches had been held with picked teams from Ireland, England, Australia, and other lands. Fishing and hunting, which belonged to the older American tradition, had now to be carried on with due regard to the laws for preserving wildlife. In the last quarter of the century anglers' associations and sportsmen's clubs appeared everywhere; in the East the members were usually city dwellers who journeyed long distances to find their pleasure. To discourage the indiscriminate slaughter of game birds, George B. Grinnell brought about the formation in 1886 of the Audubon Society, which soon had 50,000 members, and the following year Theodore Roosevelt, an expert hunter, helped organize the Boone and Crockett Club for the protection of big game. Though less adventurous, trap shooting also enjoyed considerable vogue, the first national tournament being held in 1886 at New Orleans.

The athletic awakening of the 1880s and 1890s added a new dimension to American life. Though primarily of concern to men, outdoor play increasingly enlisted the interest of the gentler sex, and in sports like tennis and archery they established excellent records for skill. Sometimes it seemed as if the mass of people could take a serious interest in nothing else. F. B. Opper, the *Puck* cartoonist, drew a phrenological chart, dividing Uncle Sam's cranium among such interests as football, bicycling, tennis, and golf, with the biggest bump of all assigned to baseball.[392] That Uncle Sam did have sport on the brain seemed conclusive to the English visitor who found that, of two events occurring on September 7, 1892, his American newspaper gave one column to the death of John Greenleaf Whittier and nearly a dozen to the Corbett-Sullivan prizefight.[393]

If the generation did not solve the problem of leisure, it at least succeeded in dodging it. The "second battle of civilization," as Garfield called it, found the average citizen in an attitude of nonresistance toward the forces that rushed in on him from every side. He did as others did and hence discovered himself without leisure. The pursuit of happiness tended to become a breathless chase, the provision of recreation an organized traffic. Yet such is not the whole story. Human beings, even when regimented for purposes of historians' generalizations, have a way of remaining annoyingly individualistic and self-willed. It is important to recall that the deeper values of leisure were also explored and by an ever larger number of people. Only in this way can one understand some of the most striking developments of the time: the longer years spent in school and university, the phenomenal growth of the reading habit, the increased enjoyment of good music, the deepened interest in works of mercy, the growth of transatlantic travel, the wider appreciation of the role of art and beauty in life. And these were enduring gains of which any age might be proud.

THE CHANGING CHURCH

DESPITE THE MULTIPLYING demands on their leisure hours a majority of the people, at least in the rural sections, continued to find time to go to church each Sunday and many of them also to midweek prayer meeting. Judging not only from this habit but also from other indications—the sale of theological works, the general respect paid to Christian precepts and ministers, the lively interest in doctrinal questions, the religious coloration of so much philanthropic effort—Bryce considered the influence of the church deeper and stronger than in any European nation.[394] Most professed Christians accepted unhesitatingly what the Reformation had handed down, provided it bore a Protestant label, whether the Nicene doctrine of the Trinity, the Augustinian theory of man's fall, Calvin's insistence upon God's arbitrary will, or less exacting modern variants of these traditional dogmas. With over 150 denominations from which to choose, no country in the world so well exemplified Frederick the Great's principle that everyone should be allowed to go to heaven in his own way. Save in rural neighborhoods and particularly in the South, differences within Protestantdom, however, had lost their ancient fierceness. Religious attendance and church work were often hardly more than "a kind of sacred amusement," a social rather than a spiritual fellowship.[395] In the new communities of the Great West the dearth of churches eased the passage from one denomination into another, a trait characteristic also of the great cities.

A disposition to distinguish sharply between the sacred and the secular tended to divorce religion from everyday thought and conduct. So far as the mass of churchgoers were concerned, this made possible the survival, into a critical and scientific age, of theological ideas which the more progressive clerics were questioning or had already rejected. After the feverish labors of the week, Americans generally displayed a "docile acquiescence" in any teachings which freed them from mental disturbance and satisfied their emotional need of belief.[396]

Yet above these quiet depths the winds of controversy were chopping the theological seas and affrighting conservatives as to the eventual survival of revealed religion. The new findings of science and scholarship impelled intellectual people to reconsider their transitional attitude toward the Bible, while the devout were driven to blind resistance or a new apologetics. Religion, in other words, was engaged in one of those recurrent conflicts between orthodoxy and heterodoxy, between fundamentalism and modernism, which have formed a law of its growth. In the eyes of stalwart believers the foundations of faith were imperiled by three grave heresies: the doctrine of Darwinism, the science of biblical criticism, and the new interest in comparative religion.

The religious controversy over biological evolution reached its most critical stage in the 1880s, for by that time American scientists stood a solid phalanx in its support and many of the thoughtful public had been won over by the persuasive writings of Spencer, Huxley, and Fiske.[397] It no longer sufficed for theological disputants to castigate Darwinism with such epithets as materialistic and atheistic. If evolution was the "bestial hypothesis" of man's origin, it was only too easy to retort in kind that the biblical account was the "mud-man theory" of creation. Reason must be appealed to as well as inherited belief.[398] An analysis of the turbid flood of argument which poured from the press during the decade reveals a steady advance —or retreat—from a position of pure emotional obscurantism to one of concession and accommodation. Some found the way out by asserting that religion and science belonged to mutually exclusive spheres, that the Bible was a rule of conduct and a guide to faith, not a scientific cyclopedia.[399] Others held that the account in Genesis, when allegorically construed, really anticipated and supported Darwin's thesis.[400] Still others contended that genuine religion remained unaffected by what was, at most, a conflict between science and theology.[401]

While ministers and churchgoers accustomed themselves to changed readings and often changed meanings of treasured passages, liberal theologians wrote books and articles to disseminate the teachings of the higher critics. President Orello Cone of Buchtel College, for example, published in 1891 his *Gospel Criticism and Historical Christianity*, the ablest work in its field from an American pen. All was not smoother sailing, of course. Dwight L. Moody, the famous evangelist, venting contempt on those who found inconsistencies and contradictions in the Scriptures, shouted to vast audiences with all the force of his 280 pounds: "The Bible was not made to understand."[402] Professor W. H. Green of Princeton Seminary stoutly defended the orthodox position in a notable debate with President Harper of Chicago, and many a household and congregation continued to find solace in an unquestioning acceptance of the King James version. Yet the reception accorded Washington Gladden's *Who Wrote the Bible?*, published in 1891, indicates the broad appeal of the more advanced attitude. A summary and popularization of the newer studies, it not only enjoyed the largest sale of any of his widely read books, but became a manual for Bible classes and Young Men's Christian Associations.[403] Sober reflection was convincing even many of the earlier objectors that, if critical analysis stripped the Bible of its vesture of infallibility, it revealed it as a work of literary, spiritual, and ethical power, a veritable book among books.[404]

Traditionalism, however, maintained a stubborn front where it could. In 1878, the geologist Alexander Winchell was dismissed from Methodist-controlled Vanderbilt University, with the exultant pronouncement of the Tennessee Methodist conference—anticipating the state of mind behind the Dayton "monkey trial" of 1925—that "our university alone has had the courage to lay its young but vigorous hand upon the mane of untamed Speculation and say, 'We will have no more of this.' "[405] Not to be outdone in good works, the Southern Baptist Seminary at Louisville followed Vanderbilt's example within a year by forcing Professor C. H. Toy's resignation because of his attempts to interpret the Old Testament from the viewpoint of modern science. Five years later, Dr. James Woodrow was driven from his post in the Presbyterian Theological Seminary at Columbia, South Carolina, for avowing the truth of evolution, and in 1891, W. J. Alexander was dropped from the chair of philosophy at the state university because of unorthodox views regarding the divinity of Christ.[406] In 1886, a fire that for several years had been smoldering at Andover Theological Seminary (Congregational) in Massachusetts burst into flame when the board of visitors tried five professors for theological liberalism and declared one of them guilty.[407]

The harm to the cause of religion inflicted by such incidents was greater than that to the cause of science and learning. Yet the wayward religious tendencies of the times help explain the fears of the pious that, once old moorings were cut, the people would drift into uncharted seas. Untold thousands listened receptively to the eloquent and pungent discourses of Robert G. Ingersoll, the "notorious infidel." A relentless foe of dogmatism and illiberalism, he inveighed against Old Testament terrors and New Testament miracles, finding good in all the great religious systems and extolling science as "the only true religion, . . . the only Savior of the world." Starting from much the same position, Dr. Felix Adler, like Ingersoll a clergyman's son though of the Jewish faith, rejected Ingersoll's negative attitude and sought to erect ethical purpose as the vital principle of living without reference to any kind of theological doctrine.[408] With this as his aim he founded in 1876 the Society for Ethical Culture, which presently attracted small bands of intellectuals, usually of Hebrew extraction, in the great cities of the East and Midwest.

Whatever Ethical Culture lacked in mysticism was supplied in full measure by another sect which sought disciples during these years. Originated by Helena P. Blavatsky, an obese Russian woman of somewhat unsavory antecedents, Theosophy was a curious blend of spiritualism and certain occult doctrines derived from the Brahmanic and Vedic literatures of India.[409] The Theosophical Society, formed in New York in 1875, was to be the spearhead of the new movement, but, converts remaining few, Madame Blavatsky three years later transferred her colorful activities to India and Europe. Meanwhile the cult managed to maintain a tenuous existence in

America and was temporarily stirred to a flurry of activity in the 1890s by the arrival of numerous swamis at the time of the World's Fair.

If these new systems lacked warmth of appeal, their plight was shared to some extent by the older, Protestant sects whose ministers, immersed in intellectual controversy, often failed to satisfy deeper spiritual needs.[410] Even more harmful was the failure of the church to adjust itself to the unprecedented conditions created by rapid urban and industrial growth.[411] American Protestantism, the product of a rural, middle-class society, faced a range of problems for which it had neither experience nor aptitude. In the cities, the building of church edifices lagged behind the advance of population, while the shifting of residential districts left once prosperous houses of worship stranded and abandoned on the bleak shores of factory and slum neighborhoods. In the twenty years preceding 1888, seventeen Protestant churches moved out of the district below 14th Street in New York, though 200,000 people crowded into it.[412] In the decade after 1878 22,000 residents in the thirteenth ward of Boston were without a single Protestant church, and it was said that in the heart of Chicago 60,000 people had no church either Protestant or Catholic. It was generally true of large cities that those parts which needed the most religious attention got the least.

When better accommodations existed, the working class commonly regarded the church—with its fine upholstery, stained-glass windows, and expensive choirs—as an institution where ill-clad worshipers were unwelcome and the Nazarene himself would have been rebuffed. As someone has observed, in religion nothing fails like success. The pulpit, increasingly beholden to contributions from the rich, ordinarily ignored or condoned the terrible injustices from which the wage-earning multitude were suffering. In one instance, reported by Professor Ely, when the bakers' union petitioned 500 clergymen of New York, and Brooklyn to preach sermons against compulsory Sunday labor, all but half a dozen ignored the appeal.[413] Even popular sects like the Baptists abandoned their contempt for wealth. In 1890, the Indiana state Baptist convention "thankfully recognized the rich blessing of the Great Head of the Church in the recent gift of Brother John D. Rockefeller to the Baptist Seminary in Chicago."[414] To laborites, religion seemed a sort of capitalistic soothing-syrup. Samuel Gompers bluntly charged that the intellect and talent of the ministry had been suborned by the plutocratic oppressors of the poor.[415]

Another token of alienation from the church appeared in the growing secularization of the Sabbath. This, too, was largely a city phenomenon, for in rural communities, and notably in the South, the people continued to regard the day as one set aside for religious observance and rest.[416] In urban centers, on the other hand, the pressure of life turned the toiling masses to thoughts of pleasure on their one free day while, to satisfy their desire, thousands of their fellows needs must operate trains and streetcars and provide the means of recreation.[417] The altered attitude owed much to the practices of immigrant groups unfamiliar with the straitlaced American Lord's Day—the Germans with their Continental Sabbath, the Irish and other aliens with their Catholic Sunday, and the Jews who observed Saturday as their holy day. "Where is the city in which the Sabbath day is not losing ground?" asked one sad voice. "To the mass of the workingmen Sunday . . . is a day for labor meetings, for excursions, for saloons, beer-gardens, base-ball games and carousals."[418]

The portentous spread of Sabbath desecration brought a revival of militant efforts to restore its sanctity. In 1884, the Women's Christian Temperance Union established a department of Sabbath observance, and four years later, the American Sabbath Union, formed by several evangelical churches, began organizing local branches to arouse opinion. In addition, the International Sabbath Association and the Sunday League of America were in the field. But even such bodies reflected a changed attitude on the subject. Their main plea was less a religious than a humanitarian one: Sabbath breaking was condemned not so much as an offense against God as against man.[419] In other words, a rational regard for a secular day of rest was supplanting the old idea of a day exclusively for religious consecration. For this reason their efforts often won support from powerful labor groups like the Knights of Labor, the Brotherhood of Locomotive Engineers and the American Federation of Labor.

Whether or not a more vibrant religious message would have kept more people within bounds on the Lord's Day, the older Protestant churches were not prepared to give it. To help the common man rekindle the altar fires of his faith, however, two new religions made their appearance. One was a British importation, the other an authentic American creation. The Salvation Army had been organized in London by William Booth in an effort to adapt the Methodist revivalistic technique to the needs of the city wilderness. Extended to America in 1879, it grew by leaps and bounds in the next two decades.[420] Its uniformed bands, parading the downtown districts with bass drum and trombone, gathered knots of the curious at the street corners and preached to "rumdom, slumdom and bumdom" the exciting gospel of repentance and reform. After 1889, the Army added social service to its evangelism. By means of its employment bureaus, "slum brigades" to work with tenement families, cheap lodgings for vagrants, and rescue homes for fallen women, it carried on an essential work of Christian service.[421]

The rise of Christian Science is inseparably bound up with the life and personality of its founder, Mrs. Mary Baker Glover Patterson Eddy.[422] Of New England Puritan descent and a prey from childhood to ill health and recurrent hystcria, she had dabbled in mesmerism, spiritualism, and hydropathy until she found relief from a distressing spinal malady at the hands of P. P. Quimby, a mental healer of Portland, Maine. Upon his death in 1866 she set up as a practitioner in her own right. At first an avowed Quimbyite, using one of his manuscripts as the fount of her teachings, she gradually evolved a system which she came to regard as wholly her own and which she put into print in 1875 under the title of *Science and Health.*[423] "Disease is caused by mind alone" and matter is an illusion—this was the essence of the newly proclaimed Christian Science. "You can prevent or cure scrofula, hereditary disease, etc., in just the ratio you expel from mind a belief in the transmission of disease" by working in harmony with the Eternal Mind as revealed through Jesus Christ.[424]

The founder gathered about her a small band of adherents in Lynn, Massachusetts, consisting mostly of factory workers and other artisans, "their hands stained with the leather and tools of the day's occupation."[425] She also provided for the training of healers by setting up the Massachusetts Metaphysical College in 1881, with herself as the faculty. Converts coming too slowly to suit her, she next changed her base of operations to Boston, eight miles away. Though the period of struggle was not yet over, the removal to a large population center proved the turning point. Attacked by foes both within and without the church and harried by delusions of persecution, this frail, spectacled, ill-educated woman, already past sixty, proceeded to build up a solid support in Boston and to spread her doctrines afar. As a philosophy, Christian Science would probably have had little appeal, but as a system of therapeutics it assured nerve-racked urban dwellers of the immediate cure of their bodies as well as the ultimate cure of their souls.

By 1890 there were over 200 Christian Science groups with nearly 9,000 members, a majority of them in the larger cities of the Midwest. The number of local bodies doubled in the next decade while the membership perhaps quadrupled.[426] Meanwhile, as Mrs. Eddy became increasingly well-to-do and many of her practitioners acquired economic security, the cult sloughed off its working-class origins and directed its chief appeal to members of other denominations at higher income levels. This transition to a religion of the comfortable may be said to have been completed in 1895 when the First Church of Christ, Scientist, built at a cost of $200,000, opened in Boston as the "Mother Church" of the faith.[427]

Unlike the Salvation Army, the Christian Scientists did not develop social work as one of their interests, since poverty, like disease, was regarded as an illusion of mortal mind. In the meantime, leaders in some of the older Protestant sects were awakening to a sense of responsibility for the world about them. Those most active in the effort to liberalize religious thought were usually also at the forefront of the effort to socialize religious practice. Notable among them were Lyman Abbott, Beecher's successor at the Plymouth Church in 1888; his neighbor in Manhattan, R. Heber Newton; and Francis G. Peabody, who from 1886 occupied the chair of Christian morals at the Harvard Divinity School. Particularly influential were Josiah Strong, general secretary of the Evangelical Alliance from 1886, and author of an eloquent book on social religion, *Our Country* (1885), which sold a half-million copies in twenty years; and Washington Gladden, Congregational minister in Columbus, Ohio, whose voice and example made him perhaps the great outstanding leader.[428]

Gladden showed how actively a minister might concern himself with industrial relations without forfeiting the confidence of even a well-to-do congregation. During the Hocking Valley coal strike of 1884, he preached the "right and necessity of labor organizations" to a congregation which included high officers of the corporation involved. Two years later, while a fierce streetcar strike raged in Cleveland, he journeyed there from Columbus and spoke to a great meeting of employers and employees on "Is It Peace or War?" again declaring the right of wage-earners to organize. A little later he headed a committee of Ohio Congregationalists to investigate employment conditions in the state in an effort to promote better understanding between capital and labor. He visioned the solution of the difficulties in an "industrial partnership" in which the toilers would receive "a fixed share of the profits of production."[429]

Despite the many difficulties, theological and practical, which beset the path of religion, the last two decades of the century witnessed a substantial gain in church membership. Protestant communicants increased from 10 million to nearly 18 million; the Roman Catholic population from well over 6 million to more than 10 million; the number of Jews from less than a quarter million to approximately a million. It was a striking testimonial to the vitality of organized religion that the growth was proportionately greater than the general advance of population, though, as was to be expected, less than the rate of increase of the urban wage-earning class.[430] Of the Protestant communicants, the Methodist bodies represented a third of the total throughout the period, followed in order by the Baptists, Presbyterians, Lutherans, and Congregationalists. At all times, however, the Catholics greatly outnumbered any Protestant group.

Roman Catholicism garnered the richest harvest from among the immigrant newcomers, notably those from Ireland, Germany, Austria-Hungary, Italy, Poland, and French Canada.[431] The heightened importance of the American church was signally recognized not only by the creation of a pontifical university but also by the appointment of an American cardinal and, in 1893, the sending of an apostolic delegate to Washington.[432] On the other hand, many Americans, particularly in the Midwest, viewed with mounting alarm the rapid accretion of Catholic power. They took amiss the agitation to secure public funds for parochial schools and regarded even the labor encyclical of 1891 as a sinister move by the Vatican to gain American working-class support.

As in the 1830s and 1840s, the fear and misunderstanding took the form of organized bigotry, embodied this time principally in the American

Protective Association, a secret oath-bound order founded in 1887 by H. F. Bowers, a sixty-year-old lawyer of Clinton, Iowa.[433] Cradled in the heart of agricultural America, the anti-Catholic animus was vaguely mingled with the long-standing rural antagonism toward the great cities where, of course, the citadels of Romanism were to be found. The A.P.A., gained adherents slowly at first, having only 70,000 members in 1893. Then, spurred by fear of immigrant competition for jobs during the hard times and a sudden flaming resentment on the part of urban dwellers against Irish machine politicians, the movement had a mushroom growth in the cities, probably commanding a million members in 1896.[434]

All the familiar phenomena of the earlier Know-Nothing movement were reproduced. The members of the order swore not to vote for or employ Catholics. "Escaped nuns" and "converted priests" told their harrowing tales to any who would listen. Forged documents were circulated to expose the designs of Rome against free America, one of them, an alleged papal encyclical, ordering the faithful to "exterminate all heretics" at the time of the feast of Ignatius Loyola (July 31) in 1893.[435] In a similar spirit, stories were whispered of the gathering of arms in the basements of Catholic churches; and in at least one instance, that of the Toledo council of the A.P.A., a quantity of Winchester rifles was purchased as a measure of self-defense—a fact revealed by the dealer's suit for nonpayment.[436] At Dallas, Keokuk, and elsewhere, mob outrages occurred, the riot in East Boston on July 4, 1895, causing the death of one man and the injury of forty others.

As the movement turned to political action, its stronghold was shown to be a zone extending through northern Ohio, eastern Michigan, and northern and central Illinois into the southern half of Iowa, northern Missouri, and eastern Kansas and Nebraska, an area originally peopled largely by religionists of New England Puritan background.[437] The anti-Catholic groups held the balance of power in many local elections, controlled the Ohio legislature, and helped pile up a triumphant majority for William McKinley in 1893 when he ran for governor.[438] By 1896, however, free silver and Bryanism made the Catholic menace seem the veriest specter. Both major parties snubbed the A.P.A., and the movement withered as suddenly as it had grown. By bringing to the defense of Catholicism and fair play such respected figures as Gladden, Roosevelt, and Senator Hoar, the church issued from the conflict in a stronger position before the public than when the attack began.[439] Within a few years it could be written, "Old feuds between Protestant and Catholic have ceased to be as important as their united battles against moral decay."[440] Organized religion had made great strides in the two decades, not the least of which was an enhanced appreciation of the common spiritual ideals for which all faiths stood.

SOCIETY'S WARDS

IF THE CHURCH as such was slow to engage in works of social amelioration, the humanitarian leaders of the day were deeply imbued with the Christian spirit, and most of them were loyal church members. The zeal to serve afflicted humanity, receiving impetus from the prolonged depression following 1873, was intensified by the hardship and misery which, even in normal times, befell the lot of many city dwellers. To Professor Sumner, the uncompromising individualist, there seemed "an unlimited supply of reformers, philanthropists, humanitarians, and would-be managers-in-general of society." Bryce with kindlier intent opined that no other country equaled the United States either in the sums spent or the personal effort devoted to beneficience.[441] Megalopolis, having crushed the human spirit with its million iron hoofs, became suddenly sorry, wept from its innumerable eyes, and strove ardently to make up for its carelessness and greed. The driving force behind much of this effort came from women, and the personnel who carried on the work was drawn increasingly from them.[442]

The most striking example of this commitment was the migration of resident colonies of social workers to the worst quarters of the larger cities. Anticipated in part by the institutional church, the social settlement was more immediately indebted to the example of Toynbee Hall in East London, which many American pioneer workers knew at first hand.[443] The initial settlement to open its doors was the Neighborhood Guild, started in New York in 1886 by Dr. Stanton Coit, an Amherst graduate, but the most famous one was Hull House, founded three years later in Chicago by Jane Addams and her coworker Ellen G. Starr.[444] Reared under Quaker influences, Addams while yet a student at Rockford College had evinced an ardent interest in social questions. A trip to Europe during which she was irresistibly drawn to Toynbee Hall deepened her concern for the plight of the poor and made her resolve to set up a similar institution in the metropolis of her native state.

Hull House was planted on South Halsted Street amid a factory and tenement district swarming with Russian and Polish Jews, Italians, Bohemians, Germans, and Irish and containing nine churches and missions along with 255 saloons. At first the founders contented themselves with inviting the street waifs and strays to take part in clubs and kindergartens. But as relations of mutual confidence were established, they branched out into myriad activities such as men's clubs, a day nursery for working mothers, courses in arts and crafts, a gymnasium, a penny savings bank, an employment bureau, and an orchestra.

Though only four settlements were established before 1890, they increased rapidly in the years thereafter, particularly in the train of the Panic of 1893. By 1895, over fifty were to be found in the principal Northern and

Western cities, and by the close of the century their number had perhaps doubled.[445] Not every one of these, of course, was equipped to perform the varied services of a Hull House or a South End House (Boston), but all of them, within the limits of their resources and opportunities, gave convincing demonstration of the truth of the adage that a fence at the top of a precipice is better than an ambulance at the bottom. The settlement movement appealed strongly to the idealism of young college men and women. Everywhere they were active in the work. The New York College Settlement on Rivington Street, begun the same year as Hull House, was initiated by Smith College students, while enterprises under similar auspices were launched in Boston, Philadelphia, and Chicago.

Whether engaged in putting up fences or providing ambulances, humanitarian workers could not avoid seeing that the social maladjustments with which they dealt were often conditioned by forces and influences of which the individual was a hapless victim. Their aggressive altruism thus caused them to support all movements for uplift—better working conditions, abolition of child labor, sanitary housing, public-health reform, penal reform, campaigns against municipal corruption.[446] In particular, they perceived in the ubiquitous saloon a relentless foe; and without caring whether poverty caused intemperance or intemperance poverty, they cooperated with those groups in American society which had long been battling against the evil.

The mainspring of the temperance movement had always been rural sentiment.[447] When the period opened it was four rural states—Maine, New Hampshire, Vermont, and Kansas—which had statewide prohibition. Likewise, it was the churches most deeply rooted in the farming regions— the Methodist, Baptist, and Presbyterian—that furnished the shock troops for the "dry" assault. Most important of all was the Women's Christian Temperance Union, founded in 1874 by women dwelling mainly in country towns. When Frances E. Willard became president in 1879, she changed its emphasis from moral suasion to an insistence upon outright legal proscription. The W.C.T.U. under her energetic direction became the leading force in the antiliquor movement.[448] Soon no community in the land was without its corps of "white ribboners," ready at a moment's notice to join battle for the cause.

The principal battlements of the "wet" interests were in the cities. There the strains and stresses of existence made the ordinary man seek solace in the flowing cup after a hard workday. There the immigrant found no reason to surrender cherished folk customs in a land of freedom. There the saloon with its free lunch and rough sociability took the place that the lodge and the club filled in the lives of those higher up the social scale.[449] New York in 1890 possessed 7,500 saloons, or one to every 200 people. Chicago was proportionately well supplied, while smaller places like Albany, San Francisco, and Cincinnati had an even greater relative number.[450] In the cities, too, the liquor industry was firmly entrenched, representing millions of capital and employing countless persons not only in the retail traffic, but at every stage of manufacture and distribution. Besides, the liquor interests had their state and national organizations, formidable by reason of their funds. With the formation of the National Protective Association in 1886, these forces were enabled to present a united front to the common enemy.

Yet some counteracting influences were at work in the cities. As the trade unions waxed in strength, their policy opposed the abuse, if not the use, of alcoholic beverages.[451] A few, like the Order of Railroad Conductors and the Brotherhood of Locomotive Firemen, refused membership to persons connected with the sale of intoxicants. The International Typographical Union in 1894 even demanded "the state and national destruction of the liquor traffic." Had the Knights of Labor, instead of their rival, the American Federation of Labor, inherited the kingdom, the labor movement might have become a militant force for temperance. The Knights in 1878 denied admission to liquor employees, and in 1886, the year that marked the crest of their strength, Terence V. Powderly, head of the order, secured 100,000 signatures to a five-year teetotal pledge.

Business leaders here and there also began to sense the advantages of a sober working force. George Pullman, in establishing his model industrial town in 1880, banned the drink traffic through his control of the title deeds to the land. Before the decade ended, the Philadelphia and Reading, the Lake Erie and Western, the Northern Pacific and the Missouri Pacific railways had forbidden the use of intoxicants by men on duty. An inquiry by the federal commissioner of labor in 1897 disclosed that 5,300 employers out of 7,000 customarily inquired into the bibulous habits of job seekers, while 1,800 "prohibited, more or less strictly, drinking."[452]

Yet the embattled drys were able to wrest few lasting gains from the forces arrayed against them. The question of statewide prohibition was submitted to popular vote in eighteen states between 1878 and 1898, but only one commonwealth, North Dakota, from 1889, continued long with the four which had already taken that stand.[453] The drys turned with redoubled zeal to that method of divide and conquer known as local option— local prohibitory enactments by popular vote. Centering their efforts first upon rural counties and villages, they pressed forward a policy of encirclement of the larger towns and cities. But beyond this point they were seldom able to get. From year to year the saloonless area expanded or shrank as the fortunes of battle veered. The most notable progress under local option was made in the South and the Midwest. Sometimes it seemed as though communities changed merely for change's sake, but even in such cases the recurrent public discussions kept voters primed as to the merits of the issue.[454]

The chief difficulties of enforcing liquor restrictions occurred in places where public sentiment was hostile or sharply divided. Local prohibition was often tolerated merely because of the accessibility of nearby city dram-shops. In states dry by statewide enactment, it was constantly necessary to make the enforcement provisions more drastic. Maine, the vaunted Eden of prohibitionists, found it impossible to keep applejack produced in local cider mills away from rural tipplers. In Portland, her chief city, "blind tigers" and "pocket peddlers" (bootleggers) plied a brisk trade alongside saloons, hotel bars, apothecary shops, and bottling establishments where, as a result of collusion with the police, "customers lounged about, smoking and drinking, with an apparent sense of freedom and security." In 1893, no less than 161 dealers paid federal liquor taxes in that city.[455]

To the observer in 1898 the temperance forces appeared to have been fighting a losing battle. The growth of cities and the increasing tension of living constantly raised up new adherents of the doctrine of "personal liberty." Moreover, though both the W.C.T.U. and the Prohibition party favored woman suffrage, none of the equal-suffrage states took the dry side. The two decades saw an enormous increase in alcohol consumption, from 386 million gallons in 1878 to 1.25 billion in 1898. The annual consumption per capita rose from a little over eight gallons to more than seventeen.[456] Since there was also probably a larger proportion of teetotalers at the end than at the beginning of the period, it is clear that the habit of drinking to excess had greatly increased. Yet in spite of the dark outlook, Willard spoke truly when she said, "While the enemy has brewed beer, they [the drys] have brewed public opinion."[457]

If the efforts of temperance reformers and humanitarian workers were designed in part to check the impulse to crime, others made it their main concern to look after the welfare of those who had run afoul of the law. The condition of jails and prisons in the late seventies remained as bad as in the years immediately following the Civil War.[458] The structures were generally antiquated and unsanitary, the officials in charge politicians igno-rant of penal science, and the discipline stupid or brutal. Of the Kentucky state prison Governor L. P. Blackburn asserted, "The Black Hole of Calcutta, so abhorred in history, was not much worse than this."[459] Throughout the South generally the practice prevailed of leasing convicts, usually blacks, to railways, lumber camps, and mines, where they were subjected to condi-tions often worse than those of prewar slavery.[460] Counties and even states operated their own chain gangs for road construction and repair.

The progress of prison reform owed much to the activities of the state boards of charities and correction, much also to the work of educating public opinion carried on by leaders of the National Prison Association, notably the Reverend E. C. Wines, Dr. Theodore Dwight, Franklin B. San-born, and Zebulon R. Brockway. In line with the best European penological thought, these men stressed reformation, rather than retribution, as the prime object of imprisonment as well as the best guarantee of future law observance. Make the convict good, they said, and make him good for something. Such ideas, while too far in advance of the times in respect to habitual criminals, appealed strongly as a means of reclaiming juvenile offenders of twenty years or younger, a class which, in 1880, formed over a fifth of the prison population.

The new program was first put into effect with the opening of the New York State Reformatory at Elmira in 1877 under Brockway's superintendency.[461] Young men of from fifteen to thirty years of age who had been convicted of a first offense were admitted under indeterminate sentence. There, free from association with hardened criminals, the length of their stay (up to the maximum period set by the statute) depended largely upon their good conduct and their earnest application to means of self-improvement. When released they were sent to places of employment previously arranged, and continued under parole until their discharge was made absolute. It was claimed after ten years' trial that four out of every five Elmira graduates showed complete reformation.[462] The merits of the system commended themselves so strongly that before 1898 it was adopted, in more or less modified form, by Massachusetts, Pennsylvania, Ohio, Michigan, Illinois, Minnesota, Kansas, South Dakota, and Indiana. Reformatories for girls apart from older women developed less rapidly, New York again leading the way with the Western House of Refuge at Albion in 1893.

Not all the social questions confronting this generation stemmed from the maladjustments of city living or the perversity of nature or nations. Two far-reaching problems, heritages from America's rural past, were localized in the two great agricultural sections of the country. One concerned the "civilizing" of the American Indian, the other the assimilation of the ex-slave to conditions of freedom. By 1878, Indian outbreaks had become the exception rather than the rule. The fierce Apache in the Southwest fought desperately from 1882 to 1886 to resist being penned up in reservations; in 1889–90, the unregenerate Sitting Bull, conqueror of General Custer, helped propagate the Messiah craze among the Dakota Sioux, culminating in the battle of Wounded Knee and a loss of over 500 lives; and as late as 1898 a Chippewa band in Minnesota were stung to warlike reprisals.[463] But every mile of Western railroad enhanced the military effectiveness of the United States, while the spreading zone of settlement reduced the Indian's chances of living solely by the chase. The typical Indian of the 1880s was a pensioner of the government, living a tribal life within the narrow limits of a reservation, his health impaired by the white man's contagious diseases and his self-reliance sapped by annuities and rations provided by the Great White Father.

At the beginning of the eighties there were a quarter of a million Indians in the United States, the vast majority west of the Mississippi, dwelling on 120 different reservations aggregating an area as large as Texas. Many of the government agents to whose care they were confided were deplorably inefficient when not outright corrupt, and the Indians were further victimized by unscrupulous licensed traders who grossly overcharged or otherwise duped them. The remnants of about thirty tribes had been herded into Indian Territory, often by methods violating every dictate of humanity. The removal thence of the peaceable Cheyenne of the Upper Missouri is a story of the ill-deserved sufferings of a band taken from an invigorating northern climate to a fever-infested district where the rascality of the agent exposed them to slow starvation. When in the fall of 1878 300 of the Indians—men, women, and children—escaped in an attempted flight to their old home, the fugitives after a desperate resistance surrendered upon condition of being restored to their former reservation. Confined in mid-winter in a Nebraska fort without food or fuel, they broke prison only to be shot down by the troops until but sixty remained.[464]

Equally shocking was the treatment accorded the Ponca, whose story, told to audiences throughout the East in 1879 by Standing Bear and an educated girl Bright Eyes, appalled the humane.[465] Their pathetic recountal prompted Helen Hunt Jackson to write her widely influential *A Century of Dishonor* (1881), a passionate indictment of long-continued Indian mistreatment based upon a study of official records. Shortly afterward Eastern humanitarians formed two organizations—the Indian Rights Association in 1882 and the annual Lake Mohonk Conference of Friends of the Indians in 1883—to influence public opinion and official action for reform. In the next few years the legislatures of Maine, Connecticut, New York, Pennsylvania, Delaware, and Michigan memorialized Congress on behalf of a peaceable and constructive solution.[466]

President Cleveland, whose sympathies had been deeply stirred by Jackson's volume, actively interested himself in the problem.[467] Moreover, the philanthropic incentive to reform was now reinforced by a growing Western demand for the breakup of reservations in order to open virgin tracts for white occupancy.[468] The humanitarians sought rights for the Indians, the Westerners lands for themselves. This combination of forces resulted on February 8, 1887, in the adoption of a general allotment law, sponsored by Henry L. Dawes of Massachusetts, Charles Sumner's successor in the Senate and a leading spirit in the Mohonk Conference. By its provisions the president was authorized, whenever time and circumstances seemed ripe, to end the tribal government and parcel out the lands of any reservation among individual owners according to certain fixed amounts.[469] The private owners were thereupon to become American citizens, though, in order to protect them from white avarice, they were denied the right to sell or mortgage their holdings for twenty-five years. The land remaining undivided might be bought by the government for sale to actual settlers, the money to be held as a trust fund for educating and civilizing the Indians concerned. Although the Five Civilized Tribes in Indian Territory preferred to remain outside the scope of the statute, systematic pressure was exerted to get them to accept its underlying principles, an end finally attained in 1898.[470]

As the benefits of the Dawes law were extended to an increasing number of tribes, the results attested the wisdom of the policy. An official inquiry five years after its passage showed that a large proportion of the favored Indians were tilling the soil or raising stock.[471] While the older generation often clung tenaciously to tribal traditions and customs, the younger men tended to break away from the chief's influence and adopt the ways of whites. This tendency grew markedly with the extension of educational facilities.[472] Some of the children attended neighborhood day schools, but the majority were taken from home influences and placed in reservation boarding schools, or in training schools outside the reservation as at Carlisle, Pennsylvania, or at Haskell Institute in Lawrence, Kansas. Everywhere stress was placed upon vocational training and an appreciation of the values of white man's civilization.

Though school accommodations lagged behind the need, nearly 20,000 youths were enrolled as pupils in 1898. Between 1878 and that year the annual government appropriations rose from $30,000 to well over $2.5 million. Meanwhile the breakup of the reservations had been proceeding apace. Between 1887 and 1906, when important changes were made in the Dawes act, 75 million acres, or nearly three fifths of the total, were disposed of. About 7 million acres were allotted to 58,000 Indians, and over 50 million were acquired by the government for sale to white settlers.[473] In addition, before 1906, 92,000 members of the Five Civilized Tribes received allotments aggregating 14.5 million acres.

Despite this gratifying progress, certain evils attended the application of the law. Allotments were sometimes made before the Indians were ready for the responsibility. In other instances, capable and self-reliant individuals chafed at the inflexible twenty-five-year restriction. Cases were also numerous in which well-meaning Indians were induced to enter illegal leasing arrangements with powerful cattle interests.[474] As voters, moreover, the adult males were preyed upon by unscrupulous politicians who taught too many of them to regard the franchise as a "merchantable article to be disposed of in the best market."[475] Nevertheless, the "Emancipation Act of the Indians," as the Dawes law was called, may be rated as perhaps the generation's most notable humanitarian venture.

Without any regard to consistency, the Americans of the eighties and nineties were resolved that the black question was one for the South to solve, not for the politicians in Washington.[476] President Hayes's recall of the last garrisons in 1877, after a decade of ceaseless governmental activity on behalf of black equality, was a tacit admission of the white South's right to manage its own race relations, as well as a symbol of the North's increasing absorption in the exigent problems arising from its new industrial order. When a belated flare-up of radical fervor in 1890 secured from the House of Representatives the passage of a "force bill" for facilitating federal inter-vention in congressional elections, party leaders in the Senate quietly quashed the measure mainly because of their greater concern for the enact-ment of a new tariff law.[477]

Partly in response to the Republican party's desertion of their cause, a mass movement of blacks set in toward the North and West in the spring and summer of 1879, directed chiefly toward Kansas.[478] For several years Benjamin ("Pap") Singleton, a Tennessee ex-slave, and Henry Adams of Louisiana, a colored veteran of the late war, had been sowing seeds of unrest, and the agents of Western railway and land companies, for their own reasons, vigorously seconded their efforts. Crop failures and low cot-ton prices in 1879, added to the usurious credit system and increasing election brutalities, brought matters to a head. By the thousands blacks, ill clad and often penniless, threw down their hoes in Louisiana, Mississippi, Tennessee, Texas, and elsewhere, crowded toward the river wharves, and, by hook or crook, made their way to the new Canaan. Some of them were turned back at St. Louis or Kansas City; others, upon arrival at their destination, were saved only by the exertions of emergency relief societies.

But the great majority, perhaps 20,000 or 25,000 in all, remained in Kansas, winning the respect of their white neighbors by their diligence and self-denial.[479] Meanwhile the Southern planting interests, fearful of losing their principal labor supply, sought by argument and force to stay the exodus. A biracial convention at Vicksburg on May 6 discussed ways and means of improving the lot of blacks in the South.[480] In many localities would-be migrants were dealt with by violence, defrauded of their money, or jailed on false charges. But the movement ended mainly for other rea-sons, chiefly, perhaps, a better understanding by the credulous blacks of the difficulties and hardships which the northward trek involved.

For the remainder of the century the bulk of African Americans stayed in Dixie, content to work out their destiny in the land where slavery had originally planted them. Migration, however, occurred within the area, notably a steady southwesterly trend from the old border states into the Gulf region. While the vast majority clung to the rural districts, local cen-tripetal movements resulted in straggling colonies in the alleyways and poorer quarters of the cities. The total black population of the ex-slave states advanced from 6 million in 1880 to 8 million in 1900, a rate of growth which should not have caused (though it did) fears of impending Africanization, for the whites meanwhile increased from 11 million to nearly 20 million.[481] Though the black birth rate was higher than the Cauca-sian, it was greatly offset by excessive infant mortality and the inroads of diseases. In 1880, they made up a third of all the people of the section and at no time were they less than a quarter of the total. In certain states of the Lower South—Georgia, Alabama, and Florida—the two races were about evenly divided, while in South Carolina, Mississippi, and Louisiana, blacks actually outnumbered whites.

While Pap Singleton was still exhorting tumultuous crowds to flee the land of their oppressor, Frederick Douglass sounded a solemn note of warning. "The exodus the colored people want," he affirmed, "is the exodus from ignorance, vice and lack of thrift."[482] The history of the years that followed is an impressive commentary on his words. For the black, it was a time of painful awakening from Reconstruction. The statesman of this new emancipation was Booker T. Washington, an ex-slave who, as a result of youthful schooling at Hampton Institute, Virginia, was inspired, as he later said, to go into the Lower South and "give my life to providing the same kind of opportunity for self-reliance and self-awakening that I had found provided for me at Hampton."[483] Starting in 1881 at Tuskegee, Alabama, with one teacher, thirty students, and a borrowed log shanty, he succeeded, with state aid and Northern benefactions, in building up his Normal and Industrial Institute until, by 1898, it had about 90 instructors, nearly 1,000 students, 2,300 acres of land, and 40 buildings erected largely by student labor.

Believing that his people must begin at the bottom and that it was to their best interest to perfect the mechanical skills which they had been taught in slavery, he provided training in all the trades and occupations necessary for securing a footing in Southern economic life. Along this path, too, he maintained, lay the best hope for the recovery of legal equality, for "No race that has anything to contribute to the markets of the world is long in any degree ostracized." His reply to those who beat their breasts for immediate recognition of black rights was: "The opportunity to earn a dollar in a factory just now is worth infinitely more than the opportunity to spend a dollar in an opera-house."[484] The scarcely perceptible emphasis on the words "just now" was missed by Southern whites who, thinking it his purpose to breed a race of robots, acclaimed his wisdom and leadership.

Washington's teachings, backed by the visible success of the work carried on at Hampton and Tuskegee and the ever-widening influence of their graduates, made a deep impress on black education everywhere.[485] As we have already seen, the South was too poor to provide enough schools for the scattered inhabitants of the great rural areas and especially so under the policy of separate instruction for the two races.[486] This, perhaps more than white indifference or antagonism, impeded the development of adequate instructional facilities.[487]

Fortunately, Northern philanthropy did something to relieve the situation. A small part of the Peabody Fund was used for training black teachers, while two new benefactions exclusively for blacks—the John F. Slater Fund of a million dollars in 1882 and Daniel Hand's gift of $1.5 million to the American Missionary Association in 1888—stimulated educational effort in every department. Although about half the African-American children had no schools of any kind to attend, the total number of those who did attend rose from 685,000 in 1878 to 1.5 million in 1898.[488] A serious lack was the dearth of secondary schools in which more intensive instruction in manual training and industrial education could be given. The score or more of black colleges and universities, however, were of hardly better than high school rank, and they usually stressed courses of the vocational type. Howard University at Washington was about the only one whose standards of admission approximated those of the better Northern colleges.

As farmers the race continued to be handicapped, on the one hand, by habits learned in slavery and, on the other, by the vicious crop-lien system.[489] All through the black belt they lived in wretched single room cabins, tilling "one-mule" cotton farms of from twenty-five to thirty acres, and managing to pay their rent and buy supplies only by mortgaging their unharvested crops at exorbitant interest rates. For many it was an economic serfdom from which there was no release. Their diet rarely included much more than hominy, corn bread, rank fat "sidemeat," and coffee, while half their clothing was begged from the whites. In Tennessee, Kentucky, and Virginia, the situation was somewhat more hopeful, and a higher proportion of tenants were emerging into the class of farm owners and householders.

In 1890, six out of every ten blacks gainfully employed were husbandmen, while three out of the remaining four were in domestic and personal service, mostly in the towns.[490] Cartmen and porters were ordinarily blacks, and many were doing well as carpenters, barbers, bricklayers, blacksmiths, and mechanics. There were individual cases of conspicuous affluence. Several blacks in Baltimore were reputed to be worth $15,000, and three or four from $40,000 to $60,000. A few doctors and lawyers were also to be found in the larger Southern cities. Of the older professions, the ministry was the only one in which an African American could count on an enthusiastic following of his own color, but success here depended less upon training than upon a sonorous eloquence.

Race antipathy hampered economic progress only when blacks competed with poor whites for the same jobs, particularly in the skilled trades. Although both the Knights of Labor and the American Federation of Labor were willing to have them as members, and white employers valued them as a docile labor force, local working-class sentiment often managed to block their employment.[491] The antagonism sometimes took the form of strikes; yet in thirty-nine recorded instances from 1882 to 1898, only seven strikes had the desired outcome of excluding black workers.

The color line was most rigidly drawn at points where the association of the two peoples might suggest social equality. While white persons might cheerfully work side by side with black employees or be attended in public places by their black nursemaids, they did not voluntarily tolerate such proximity when the blacks were not in a menial relationship.[492] Blacks and whites even worshiped their common God in different churches. Though the law throughout the South prohibited intermarriage, few states expressly forbade irregular sex relations. Yet Philip A. Bruce, a Virginian of the former master class, writing in 1888, deemed it a "remarkable evidence of the social antipathy of the white people" that since abolition "illicit sexual commerce between the two races has diminished so far as to have almost ceased, outside the cities and towns." The reason, he believed, was that since the woman was no longer a slave the relationship implied a kind of temporary social recognition.[493]

Apart from the denial of intermarriage and the provision for separate schools, Southern legislatures moved cautiously in applying the color test to race relations. As early as 1881, Tennessee passed a "Jim Crow" law requiring different coaches or compartments on trains, but it was not until the Supreme Court two years later emasculated the federal civil rights act of 1875 that her sister commonwealths generally followed her example.[494] On the other hand, blacks could at no time and in no place secure accommodations in hotels, restaurants, and amusement places conducted by whites, though such discrimination seldom had statutory sanction. Opinions differed as to whether black citizens received equal treatment before the courts, but their treatment at the hands of self-appointed enforcers of the law was a reproach to Anglo-Saxon ideas of justice. In the period 1882–98, over 600 recorded lynchings, mainly of blacks, took place in the former slave states, the most tragic years falling in the early nineties.[495] Though these outrages were supposed to represent a species of degenerate chivalry, the victims suspected of rape or attempted rape formed but a minority of the whole number murdered.

In the matter of voting, the South allowed the guarantees in the Reconstruction state constitutions to stand for a time. Meanwhile, however, the dominant race actually disfranchised most African Americans by "bulldozing" and other terroristic methods, by fantastic gerry mandering arrangements, and by unfair manipulation of electoral regulations.[496] When, however, the rising agrarianism of the late eighties split the white electorate into two fairly balanced parties, deep-grained prejudices against the blacks in politics temporarily disappeared, particularly when victory depended upon which side could poll the black vote. Thoughtful Southerners, fearing the remoter consequences of such tactics, believed the time had come to disfranchise the race by constitutional mandate provided, of course, that the step could be taken without infringing the letter of the Fifteenth Amendment.

The three states in which blacks outnumbered the whites were the first to act. Mississippi, in 1890, pointed the way by limiting the ballot to paid-up male taxpayers who were able to read a passage from the state constitution or understand it when read to them or give "a reasonable interpretation thereof." The flexible clause was confessedly designed to enable election officials to reject illiterate blacks without rejecting illiterate whites. Five years later, South Carolina followed with a somewhat similar provision and then, in 1898, Louisiana found a means of exempting whites from the property and educational tests by placing on the voting list all male applicants whose fathers or grandfathers had been eligible to vote prior to 1867. Other states were presently to devise ingenious variants of these restrictions. Thus the postwar political importance of the black vanished almost as quickly as it had come. He became once more a negligible factor in Southern public life.

Notwithstanding these many onerous restrictions, even George W. Cable conceded that the African American enjoyed "a larger share of private, public, religious and political liberty than falls to the lot of any but a few peoples. . . ."[497] The most salient rights of all—to accumulate property, establish a home, and acquire some measure of schooling—remained unobstructed by legal barriers. Nor could any disinterested observer deny that the race had taken excellent advantage of its opportunities. By 1900, one black in five owned his home, and the total value of the farms they operated reached nearly half a billion dollars. About 200,000 owned their farms while over half a million more worked as tenants.[498] Fifty-six percent were literate as compared with 30 percent twenty years before, and with the advance of education had gone a slow but steady improvement in morals and family relations. One-room cabins were everywhere beginning to give way to two or even three-room houses, with an occasional parlor organ and some attention to the decencies and comforts of living. We may agree with the contemporary judgment of a young black intellectual that thirty years of struggle and privation had "changed the child of emancipation to the youth with dawning self-consciousness, self-realization, self-respect."[499]

FIN DE SIÈCLE

THROUGHOUT THE 1890s the people of the United States were deeply imbued with the feeling that the greatest of centuries was drawing to a close. Nor was this feeling confined to the American side of the Atlantic. In France, the sense of destiny fulfilling itself was compacted into the phrase "fin de siècle." Early in the nineties the expression found its way into English newspapers and, by this channel, quickly reached the United States where, as Henry Adams tells us, "during this last decade every one talked, and seemed to feel *fin-de-siècle*."[500] To the fashionable and the light-minded, the phrase denoted ultramodernism—an anticipation of the latest mode in artistic decoration and personal adornment, a new orgy of extravagance in manners and social entertainment.[501] To the humanitarians and reformers in general it meant a final opportunity to cure the abuses and injustices which a heedless society had permitted to appear. To the toilers, these closing years afforded fresh hope and a desperate purpose to solve the staggering problems which beset them both in factory and on farm.

Life in America had never before been so complex. An introverted personality like Henry Adams's, out of key with the times, continually sought escape by flight—to the South Seas, Cuba, the Yellowstone, Mexico, Russia, Egypt, Normandy—only to be drawn back each time, fascinated and repelled by a sense of new energies astir in human fate, comparable in his own day to the will exerted on an earlier mankind by the Virgin. "We call ourselves the masters of machinery: are we quite sure that machinery is not mastering us?" wondered Josiah Strong.[502] "Our industry is a fight of every man for himself," warned Henry Demarest Lloyd, who saw the vaunted American gospel of equality yielding "incalculable power and pleasure for a few, and partial existence for the many who are the fountains of these powers and pleasures."[503] "The huge, rushing, aggregate life of a great city," complained another, " . . . curtails man of his wholeness, specializes him, quickens some powers, stunts others. . . . "[504] A cloistered scholar deplored the increasing demands placed upon the educated man: "He must be familiar with magnetism as well as mythology, with evolution as well as elegiacs, with geology as well as genesis."[505] Once it had been easy to be human, Professor Wilson observed, but now "haste, anxiety, preoccupation, the need to specialize and make machines of ourselves have transformed the once simple world. . . . "[506] "Do you really think the 'game pays for the candle'?" queried a publicist. "I get yearly more tired of what we call civilization. It seems to me a preposterous fraud."[507]

The attrition of town on country continued with unabated force. The unbroken frontier was gone and, as Professor Turner pointed out in his memorable address of 1893, "with its going has closed the first period of American history."[508] Yet the impetus to Western settlement was not yet spent, and a seventh state now joined the six admitted to the Union in 1889 and 1890. Utah had been denied the privilege for more than a decade because of the continuance of polygamy. By 1890, however, Mormons and non-Mormons had become about equal in numbers, mutual business advantage was dissolving religious prejudices, and the nation through recent acts of Congress had announced its implacable purpose to stamp out the hated practice.[509] Making a virtue of necessity, Wilford Woodruff, head of the church, on September 30 openly pledged his personal influence in behalf of enforcing the antipolygamy statues, while the general conference of the church a few weeks later unanimously endorsed his stand.[510]

The West in the fin de siècle was less concerned with attracting new settlers than with the problem of adjusting its life to a national political and social order regulated by the people of the Eastern cities. Agrarian leaders, zealous in treating symptoms, talked cheap money, lower transportation rates, the curbing of Wall Street and big business; but behind their bill of particulars lay something less tangible and often unacknowledged: a deepening sense of frustration and defeat. The men, women, and children who gathered in 10,000 schoolhouses to debate the farmers' grievances in the early 1890s had only vague notions about the intricacies of the free-silver question and its relation to prices and prosperity, but they were grimly aware that mysterious new forces in American life were robbing them of their traditional rural heritage of freedom and spiritual and material well-being.

During the decade the western and central parts of Kansas, Nebraska, and South Dakota declined in population, as did also eastern Colorado, a third of the state of Nevada, and eleven counties of California. Similar losses occurred in northern New England and in the backward agricultural parts of New York, Pennsylvania, Ohio, and Michigan.[511] The land of promise was no longer the land of performance unless one joined the backward trail toward the East, as more and more of the ambitious youth of the countryside were doing each year. As the decade proceeded, the nation grew steadily more urbanized, the number of cities with 4,000 or more inhabitants advancing from less than 9,000 to nearly 12,000 and the proportion of urban dwellers from one third of the total to approximately two fifths.[512] In a Farmers' Alliance campaign song a rural youth pleads with his father, before it is too late, to cast his ballot for farmers' rights:

Free land will be gone and naught else can I do
But be to the rich man a slave.

When the father accedes the lad rejoices:

I'll have clothes like the rich boys in town.[513]

Yet the bulk of city wage-earners were equally irked by their lot. While millionaires raised up their gaudy palaces and Ward McAllister led society into ever more extravagant revels, the masses toiled long hours in factory and office, returning at length to their frugal abodes embittered or benumbed. Industrial outbreaks occurred with increasing frequency and destructiveness. The Panic of 1893 cast a deep black shadow across their lives. Presently began the tramp of the unemployed from all parts of the country upon Washington, a veritable petition in boots whose inglorious ending did not hide the gravity of the conditions which had given it rise.[514] James Whitcomb Riley's friend Eugene V. Debs, jailed in Chicago in 1894 for his activities during the Pullman strike, read socialist tracts in his enforced leisure and dedicated himself to the gospel of the abolition of capitalism. Meanwhile, Hamlin Garland and other intellectuals pinned their faith to Henry George's panacea of the single tax. Still others, lingering fondly over Bellamy's utopian dream, banded together in so-called Nationalist Clubs.[515]

The air was full of revolt against things as they were. Howells, deploring the increasing resort to violence and murder by the unprosperous, feared lest a "blood-mist" screen the real issues from the thoughtful.[516] Even the usually mild-spoken Thomas Bailey Aldrich predicted: "We shall have bloody work in this country some of these days, when the lazy *canaille* get organized.[517] What a vision of fin de siècle, cried a magazine poet:

> Strange vision! The land is filled full with the harvest—
>> Hungry men look for the morrow with dread;
> Our hearts swell with pride of our civilization—
>> God! hear that piteous crying for bread![518]

The campaign of 1896 provided vent for an expression of class antagonisms such as the country had never before known. Perhaps, like the new device employed in surgical operations, the occasion gave drainage to pent-up poisons which might have prostrated the body politic. Though embattled conservatism won the election, it could never again ignore questions that vitally concerned the average man and woman or, in Populist parlance, "drown the outcries of a plundered people with the uproar of a sham battle over the tariff."[519]

In reality, the mists and shadows that gathered over America in the beginning years of fin de siècle had always been streaked with light for those with eyes to see. One needed only to look about him to appreciate the justice of Muirhead's characterization of the United States as the "Land of Contrasts." Howells makes a character in one of his books assert that the passion of Americans for doing things on a large scale extended even to their inconsistencies.[520] Thus, while capitalistic greed ground the faces of the poor under its iron heel, individual potentates of wealth lavished millions upon hospitals, libraries, colleges, churches, museums, and art galleries for the good of all. While the Panic palsied the country's industrial energies and turned hordes of the jobless into the streets, an extraordinary outburst of philanthropic relief effort attested the essential humaneness of the American character,[521] and the Columbian Exposition on the south shore of Lake Michigan revealed to a wondering world the summit of American accomplishment in the fine arts and the graces of life.

It was in a mellow mood that Americans in 1898 could look backward and appraise the developments of the two decades just past. Impatient young men might mutter that the deeper economic conflict had only been postponed, that a truce, not a term, had stilled the popular outcry for social justice. But their elders could reply that while wealth and economic power had tended to concentrate at a faster rate than they would have wished, the general condition of the masses had not been materially affected for the worse. If one eighth of the families of the United States possessed seven eighths of the country's property,[522] the enormous growth in aggregate national wealth still afforded ample elbow room for the less favored classes. In support of this contention a leading statistician pointed out that the number of persons in the higher and more skilled walks of life had increased faster relatively than the population, that the laborers' workday was lessening, and that the general tendency of wages was upward and of prices downward. Admitting that the toilers had not got their due share of the enlarged aggregate wealth, he nevertheless concluded that, though the rich were growing richer, "many more people than formerly are growing rich, and the poor are better off." [523]

The improved position of the common man, however, owed far more to the multifold mechanical inventions which these years brought forth and to the enlarged role of public and private agencies in fostering better living standards. Labor-saving devices in the home, improved methods of plumbing, better lighting indoors and out, the commercial development of the telephone, the advent of the safety bicycle, the new conveniences of rapid transit in city and suburbs, showered blessings upon the many as well as the few, though urban dwellers were, of course, the chief gainers. In like manner ordinary folk benefited from the energetic attention given by municipalities to water purification, sewerage, street paving, parks, fire protection, and public hygiene. In both country and city, schools showed steady progress during the twenty years and, in the fin de siècle, a high school education was becoming the normal expectation of most city youths. Poverty continued to exist, but it was treated by the new profession of social workers as a malady that was functional rather than organic. Even the churches began to take a hand in the exigent work of human rehabilitation.

Laymen and physicians alike testified to the altered physical appearance of the people. While the change was most marked in those rural parts once noted for leanness, angularity, and sallowness of complexion, fifty years' familiarity with the streets of New York and Boston caused a careful observer to declare that there, also, "The men are more robust and more erect, the women have greatly improved both in feature and carriage; and in the care and condition of the teeth in both sexes a surprising change has taken place." [524] During the 1880s, dealers in ready-made clothing were obliged to adopt a larger scale of sizes and many more extra sizes, in width as well as in length, than had been needed ten years before. [525] Nor did the reasons for the improvement in physique baffle the inquirer. Apart from the advances in medical science and an ampler provision of physicians, it was generally ascribed to greater leisure, a lessening anxiety by a larger number of people concerning food and shelter, the growing cult of physical exercise and, not least of all, the varied and better-prepared diet which the generation enjoyed.

On the other hand, the restless energy bottled up in the urban centers, and constantly excited by noises, jars, and the rush of crowds, tended more and more to make nervousness the national disease that medical writers were prone to call it. [526] Neurasthenia (to use Dr. Beard's term) and insanity were as characteristically city phenomena as feeble-mindedness and impaired physical vigor were rural complaints.[527] In its milder effects the high strain of urban living robbed American life of much of the repose which increasing leisure should have afforded it and often betrayed artists and writers into giving the world something less than their best.

If, as was widely asserted, women were the particular victims of the national disease,[528] it was doubtless the price they paid for their steadily enlarging share in activities outside the home—in the world of fashion, clubs, industry, the professions, literature, and the arts. In education and in enterprises of social uplift they were often the mainstay. Old notions of family integrity were rudely jarred by the centrifugal forces at work in the home. Outside agencies assumed an ever-greater responsibility for the welfare of city children, and the nation was startled by the leap in the divorce rate. Yet no finite intelligence could know whether even such changes implied a rise or decline in general ethical standards. Though in the large cities commercialized vice flaunted itself as never before and many would have agreed that "human life is rather more secure in Arizona than in the streets of New York," it was Bryce's considered judgment that, taking the country as a whole, "the average of temperance, chastity, truthfulness, and general probity is somewhat higher than in any of the great nations of Europe."[529] Nor is it to be overlooked that organized religion, after a period of doubt and confusion, attained a numerical and relative strength in the fin de siècle greater than at any preceding time in the twenty-year period.

Posterity will remember this generation less for the way it managed the retail traffic of life than for its more permanent contributions to American civilization. While every generation is born with its hands tied by the generation which went before, the constructive work of the 1880s and 1890s was less a fulfillment of the past than a starting point for the future. Apart from the impressive feat of forging a national economic order,[530] the men and women of the time laid the firm foundations for continuing achievement in all the elements of intellectual and aesthetic culture. The spread of graduate schools, with their goal far beyond the reach of the college, evidenced the new emphasis upon the value of pure knowledge. In an age of supposed dominant materialism a larger proportion of Americans consecrated themselves to the cause of science and learning than ever before in history, and a greater number of them attained an eminence that compelled the attention of the world. Literature and the arts had an equal drawing power, with results hardly less fruitful. A Gibbs, a Newcomb, a Ward, a James, a Mark Twain, a Whistler, a MacDowell, a Saint-Gaudens stand out not as unexpected flowers along a scrubby roadside but as among the most perfect blossoms in a well-tended field.

Cultural achievement, moreover, was based on a broadening popular appreciation of creative effort. So diversified a population reflected a multiplicity of standards and tastes, and popular culture contained much that was transitory and cheap. But the steady leavening of the mass was revealed in the unexampled patronage accorded public libraries, art galleries, and the more serious dramatic and musical performances, as well as by the multiplication of literary periodicals and the greatly increased production of books. For the first time in the national annals, creative workers might count upon a receptive public and ample financial reward at home. The few who preferred a foreign abode usually did so because their work was more European than American in spirit.

Underlying all the varied developments that made up American life was the momentous shift of the center of national equilibrium from the countryside to the city. Long foreshadowed, it had at last become an actuality. A civilization traditionally rural was obliged to learn how to come to terms with a civilization predominantly urban. The process was painful and confusing to those who clung to the older mores and even to many who joined the cityward flight. But to untold numbers of others it meant the attainment of a new Promised Land, the release of energies and ambitions which the constricted opportunities of the farm had always denied. The city had come and, it was clear to all, it had come to stay. Was its mission to be that of a new Jerusalem or of ancient Babylon? The answer to this question was the chief unfinished business of the departing generation.

BOOK XI

The Quest for Social Justice,

1898–1914

THE TURN OF THE CENTURY

TO THE AMERICAN PEOPLE wearied by a quarter-century of economic strife, the Spanish-American War came as a welcome relief. If in retrospect the bizarre aspects of the 1890s lend an appearance of "mauve,"[1] to the people then living the decade seemed deeply tinged with red, with the dread menace of social upheaval and revolution. The Panic of 1893, the lengthening bread lines, the pitched battles between capital and labor, the threatening growth of Populism, the class war preached by the Bryanites in 1896— all these made the dying years of the century a time of sober thought and grim endeavor. Little wonder that, with the mysterious destruction of the battleship *Maine* in Havana Harbor, the nation plunged into a great emotional debauch which enabled it, for the moment, to forget its more serious tasks. The conflict at best offered only temporary relief, and as the decade drew to a close the more thoughtful realized that not only were the old problems still before the nation but new ones had been added, notably the exigent one of imperialism.

As a further complicating factor, America awakened to find herself somewhat in the position of a man who had unexpectedly lost most of his fortune. For three centuries the national social, economic, and political life had been dominated by one outstanding influence: an abundance of unoccupied and fertile land. The free land to the west had afforded opportunities for the energetic and an outlet for the discontented. It had absorbed millions of immigrants from Europe and had, by its plentiful eastward shipment of agricultural products, kept the cost of living low. To be sure, the boundless natural resources which were opened up as each succeeding wave of frontiersmen pushed farther westward were exploited in a most wasteful manner, but the incurable optimism and strong individualism which this wealth engendered became a part of the national habit of mind. The mark of the rapidly moving frontier had been strong upon the content and direction of foreign trade, upon the manufacturing, banking, and transportation systems; in fact, upon all phases of our economic life.[2] Already in 1890 the unsettled area was so broken into that the frontier line had ceased to exist, and by the close of the decade the nation faced a situation unlike any that had gone before.[3]

The rapidly diminishing supply of good free land, while only one of the forces destined to mold social growth in the new century, was probably the most important. It gave an impetus to intensive and scientific farming and to a more serious consideration of conservation. It portended a type of manufacturing less likely to be a simple supplement to extractive industry, but rather, by the greater use of skilled labor and improved machinery, to carry its processes much further. With the end of the era of free land, also, the opportunities for the less fortunate to escape from intolerable conditions became more limited; there were evidences of the development of class consciousness and a tightening of the lines of battle in the conflict between capital and labor. With reason, many people feared that American conditions were tending to approximate more closely the class divisions of the economically advanced nations of Europe. According to a study made in 1890, seven eighths of the families held but one eighth of the wealth, while one percent of the people owned more than the remaining ninety-nine;[4] and a decade later there appeared to be little change. A study made of estates probated in five Wisconsin counties during the year 1900 revealed the fact that the poorest two thirds of the population owned only 5 or 6 percent of the wealth and the poorest four fifths scarcely 10 percent, while the richest one percent owned about half of the property probated.[5] As these Wisconsin counties comprised both rural communities and cities, including Milwaukee, and as the findings agree with similar studies made at different periods in Massachusetts, they may be taken as typical. They point inevitably to the fact that fully 80 percent of the people lived on the margin of existence while the wealth of the nation was owned by the remaining 20 percent.

Measured by the standards of today, the wages of the average worker at the conclusion of the last century seem small indeed. According to the carefully tabulated returns of the census of 1900, only occasional groups of workers were paid as much as $18 a week, two thirds of the male workers over sixteen years of age receiving less than $12.50.[6] The interstate commerce commission reported that 82 percent of the million persons, exclusive of officers, employed on railroads received less than $2.05 per day.[7] Throughout the nation the average wage was less than $2 a day, and only the most highly paid skilled worker was able to obtain $3. Specialists studying wage scales in 1904 and 1905 agreed that at least two thirds of the adult male workers failed to obtain $600 a year,[8] and their findings were in part verified by the census of manufacturers of 1905.[9]

In checking the wage statistics against prices to determine the standard of living, the student finds himself in a different world. Those were the days when beef sold for 17½ cents a pound, fresh pork for 14, eggs for 21½ cents a dozen, potatoes at $1.14 a bushel, flour at $4.69 a barrel, and hard coal at $6.65 a ton. A good pair of shoes could be bought for $2 and an excellent suit of clothes for $20.[10] Low as these prices seem, the income of the average wage-earner failed to meet them. Dr. Ryan in 1906 named $600 as the absolute yearly minimum; Chapin in 1909 placed it at $900 for New York City; and Streightoff in 1911 put $600 as the lowest in the South and $650 as the "extreme low limit" in the cities of the rest of the country.[11] Yet these minima were achieved by comparatively few wage-earners. In 1904, after an exhaustive analysis of the available data, Robert Hunter went so far as to conclude that not less than 10 million persons in the United States lived in poverty.[12] Hunter's estimates may have been a little high,[13] but they reveal a situation far different from the roseate picture of the land of promise which immigrant agents had conjured in the minds of the workers of Europe. The oft-repeated statement that the American laborer was better off than his fellow workman in Europe was undoubtedly true for the country as a whole, but the descriptions by Jacob Riis of poverty in New York equaled, if they did not surpass, the statistics collected by Booth and Rowntree for London.[14]

As low as real wages were in 1900, they were destined to decline during the next decade. The years from the Panic of 1873 to the close of the century had seen a fall in the cost of living and a rise in the purchasing power of wages. Postwar deflation, combined with currency contraction and rapid exploitation of natural resources as the frontier moved onward, had been primarily responsible, but as these conditions were modified, the cost of living began to mount. Population and demand were catching up with production, and at the same time, the discovery of gold in 1897 in the Klondike region of Alaska and the introduction of improved methods of extracting gold from inferior ores tended to inflate the currency.[15] To these primary causes economists suggested contributory influences, such as the rising standard of living; the exhaustion of natural resources; the relative decline of agriculture and the urban trend; uneconomical and wasteful production and distribution; the increasing burden upon society of accident, disease, pauperism, crime, and militarism; the high tariffs and the arbitrary rising of prices by trusts and of wages by labor unions.[16] If the last three items are discarded as controversial, there still remain sufficient forces to explain an era of rising prices. The federal commission on industrial relations reported that, while the nation's wealth between 1890 and 1912 had increased from 65 to 187 billion, or 188 percent, the aggregate income of wage-earners in manufacturing, mining, and transportation had risen only 95 percent.[17] Rubinow believed in 1914 that real wages "were rapidly falling."[18] but a more conservative conclusion is that of Professor Woods when he said that, despite higher pay, "the American worker found himself at the outbreak of the World War handicapped by a slight but unmistakable decline in the purchasing power of his wages. They sufficed to buy somewhat less than had the wages of the year 1900."[19] The phrase "high cost of living" was used so universally that it even found its way into popular songs.

The decline in real wages, however, did not necessarily mean a lowering of the standard of living. Improved machinery and large-scale manufacturing decreased the cost of production and helped to overcome the rising prices of raw materials. The nation's wealth was advancing by leaps and bounds, and some portion of it in addition to mere wages benefited the average man. Those common enterprises in which the whole people participated, such as the public schools, roads, water supply, and sewage disposal, showed improvement during the period and helped to diffuse the benefits of the rapid production of wealth. The same was true of the large contributions which the new millionaires were making to higher education, medical research, and other endowments. The ethics of a civilization which allowed comparatively few men to accumulate most of the wealth and then dole part of it back in charity might well be questioned, and indeed it was, but the fact remained that some portion of it did find its way back to the mass of the people.

As important in raising the standard of living as the mere multiplication of wealth were the new inventions which were making life more comfortable. These had to do particularly with time- and labor-saving devices and providentially were of benefit to the housewife and farmer as well as to the factory mechanic. In the home, the gas stove was rapidly driving out the coal range, and electricity was eliminating both the oil lamp and gas illumination, while electric power and the gasoline engine were destined to modify farm life. That great giant, electric power, whose diverse applications were to feature the early decades of the new century, had already speeded city and interurban transportation, pointing unmistakably to a civilization of ever greater mobility. As American life became more complex and economic competition keener, a certain compensation was afforded by myriad inventions which were making the art of living easier and more pleasant.

To a thoughtful visitor, America at the turn of the century must have appeared a land of curious contradictions. Blessed as it was with unparalleled economic resources and opportunities, its wealth, nevertheless, was almost as unevenly distributed as that of Europe and its slums nearly as desperate. In spite of the belief cherished by those who sought our shores that America was inhabited by a prosperous and happy people, the nation was just recovering from a long period of economic unrest which had but recently culminated in the campaign of 1896. In a nation boasting the most widespread system of free education in the world, the census of 1900 found over 6 million illiterates.[20] On the one hand was an idealism and humanitarianism which led millionaires to lavish endowments upon educational and charitable institutions, on the other a carelessness of life which put America behind all civilized nations in the number of unnecessary industrial accidents. In no nation was the status of women higher or the lot of the child better, yet social legislation respecting women was far behind that of other progressive nations, and child labor existed under conditions too horrible to believe.[21] Yet at a time when the successful businessman represented the American ideal and the people seemed lost in a scramble for wealth, the nation was girding itself for a mighty drive against special privilege and for an attempt to achieve some degree of social justice. Crude and chaotic as was this civilization in many respects, its essential soundness became manifest in the next decade and a half as the rising social consciousness of the people directed the national energy into fresh and nobler channels.

BIG BUSINESS GROWS BIGGER

As the nation recovered from the Panic of 1893 and swung buoyantly on the upgrade of a new business cycle, an unprecedented era of prosperity and industrial expansion burst on the country. McKinley, trumpeted before the election as the "advance agent of prosperity," was scarcely inaugurated before he issued a call for a special session of Congress to revise the tariff. The Wilson-Gorman act of 1894 was speedily wiped from the statute books and for it was substituted the high Dingley tariff, destined to a longer life than any tariff law to date.[22] The bitterness of the free-silver campaign of 1896 delayed for a short time the formal establishment of the gold standard, but this came in the currency act of 1900.[23] An administration so receptive to the wishes of "big business" was not likely to enforce either the Sherman antitrust law or the equally feeble interstate commerce act. With the nation ready for another period of economic advance and the political machinery in the hands of a party committed to laissez faire and the Dingley tariff, the way was cleared for an epoch of gigantic industrial development.

Though the prosperity of the new era was shared by the farmer, its richest rewards fell to the industrialist. By 1898 the United States had become preeminently a manufacturing nation, the greatest in the world.

Tendencies long evident were now culminating. From 1850 to 1900, while the population trebled and the value of agricultural products kept close pace, manufactures had increased elevenfold in value. A variety of factors had made this possible—cheap foodstuffs, cheap raw materials, cheap immigrant labor, an expanding market, and a high protective tariff. Financial power shifted steadily from agriculture to industry and from the country to the city, and with the shift in wealth went that of political power.

Industrialization was accompanied by a pronounced movement toward concentration of ownership. After the "trust"—in the technical sense of the term—had been outlawed by the courts in the 1880s, the form usually taken was that of the holding company, a corporate organization set up for the purpose of holding stock in various branches of the same business and, by this means, controlling them. But under whatever form consolidation took place, the process went on with little interruption, and was the outstanding feature of American economic life at the opening of the new century. In 1904, John Moody listed 318 "greater" or "lesser" industrial trusts representing mergers of nearly 5,300 distinct plants and a capitalization of over $7 billion.[24] Seven of the greater trusts—the Amalgamated Copper Company (formed in 1899), the American Smelting and Refining Company (1899), the American Sugar Refining Company (1891), the Consolidated Tobacco Company (1901), the International Mercantile Company (1902), the Standard Oil Company (1899), and the United States Steel Corporation (1901)—boasted a total capitalization of over $2.5 billion and, with a single exception, all were formed after 1898 and all incorporated under New Jersey laws.[25] Though by 1914, establishments doing an annual business of over $100,000 numbered less than one eighth of the total, they employed over three fourths of the wage-earners and turned out more than four fifths of the products in value. Indeed, nearly half the products came from the 1.4 percent of concerns which had an annual output of over a million dollars each.[26]

The overexpansion and speculation which accompanied the great period of trust making brought the inevitable reaction in the depression of 1903.[27] With most of the major industries at least partly integrated, investors had come to learn that neither great size nor virtual monopoly necessarily meant big profits.

The Setback of 1903 was only temporary. Record-breaking crops of wheat, corn, and cotton in 1905 and 1906, combined with rising prices, brought a real prosperity to the farmer, which was in part responsible for the revived industrial boom. Although the consolidation movement slowed, there quickly developed a renewed frenzy for speculation. And this overexpansion and reckless speculation brought the day of reckoning when, in March 1907, the stock market suddenly crashed, bringing ruin to the small-margin speculator and heavy losses to the wealthy. Help from the federal treasury, European gold drawn hither by high money rates, and the natural gravitation of money to New York as the crop-moving period ended, stayed for a time the panic, but relief was merely temporary. Money became so tight during the summer that even the city of New York failed twice to sell a bond issue.[28]

Although in New York City the Panic of 1907 was more severe than that of 1893, its results were not widespread, owing to the fundamental prosperity of the nation. By February of the next year confidence was restored in the metropolis. But if the Panic of 1907 exerted slight influence upon the general economic trend, it did, as is usual with panics, increase the speed with which wealth and power were concentrated. Many of the smaller speculators and capitalists, unable to weather the storm, saw their holdings quickly taken over by the larger interests. And with the end of the "bankers' panic," concentration of the nation's industrial and financial life continued, but more slowly and more quietly than in the hectic days between 1899 and 1904. The panic itself removed many of the lesser speculators from the scene, and the watchful attitude of the Roosevelt administration put a damper on some of the greater plungers. Moreover younger captains were forging to the front who were primarily occupied with the staggering task of keeping in operation the immense machinery which their predecessors had thrown together.

Consolidation nevertheless proceeded, and although the operations of high finance were but vaguely understood by the public at large, suspicion was widespread that the economic power of the nation was rapidly centering in the hands of a small group of New York financiers. The situation was thoroughly ventilated by a congressional committee in 1913,[29] which had no hesitancy in asserting that an increased concentration of money and credit had been effected, largely through the activities of J. P. Morgan and Company, the First National Bank, the National City Bank of New York, and the three bond houses of Lee, Higginson & Co.; Kidder, Peabody & Co.; and Kuhn, Loeb & Company.[30] How far this had gone was suggested by the fact that four allied financial institutions in New York City held 341 directorships in banking, transportation, public utilities, and insurance companies, whose aggregate resources were $22,245 million. "If by a 'money trust,' " said the committee,

> is meant an established and well-defined identity and community of interest between a few leaders of finance, which has been created and is held together through stock holdings, interlocking directorates and other forms of domination over banks, trust companies, railroads, public-service and industrial corporations, and which has resulted in a vast and growing concentration of control of money and credit in the hands of a comparatively few men — your committee, as before stated, has no hesitation in asserting as a result of its investigation up to this time that the condition thus described exists in this country to-day.[31]

During the course of the investigation George F. Baker, second only to Morgan as a factor in the concentration of banking control, admitted on the stand that the financial welfare of the nation was now dependent largely on the type of men who held the reins of power. When asked, "Do you think that it is a comfortable situation for a great country to be in?" he answered, "Not entirely."[32]

Whatever the methods by which the colossal economic power of America became concentrated in the hands of a few capitalists, the result was fraught with important economic and social consequences. Much time was spent by economists in studying its effects upon the quality and prices of products, but little or none in appraising its far-reaching social implications. The small industry, conducted by the man who had built it up and hence entailing an intimate relationship between employer and employee, was rapidly passing. In its place had come the mighty corporation with its thousands of stockholders, dominated by financiers who knew little or nothing of the business, and conducted by delegated managers for the primary purpose of producing dividends. The centripetal movement which culminated in the first decade of the century produced two results of outstanding importance to American civilization. In the first place, it shifted a large portion of the operation and ownership of the common industries from the actual producer to the banker and nonresident stockholder. In the second place, it speeded the concentration of wealth in the hands of the few, thus creating a class more powerful than the people and, indeed, more powerful than the government—a compact group which, often with utter unscrupulousness and disregard of the public welfare, played fast and loose with the nation's wealth. Whether this power could be adequately curbed was one of America's gravest problems.

THE LABOR WORLD

LABOR FACED a new era as the nineteenth century hurried to a close. In earlier years business consolidation had been achieved at the cost of labor disorganization, but now the right of the wage-earner to organize was no longer seriously challenged either by the courts or the employing class. The bitter industrial struggles of the 1880s and 1890s had been a rough school of experience, but from it the American workers learned lessons in organization and tactics that were to give them a new confidence and steadiness of purpose in the years of prosperity and confusion which now lay ahead. Diversity, however, rather than uniformity marked the labor movement.

Of the various national labor bodies which had sprung up in the earlier period, the American Federation of Labor (A.F.L.) under the leadership of Samuel Gompers had far outstripped all competitors. Its ranks included nearly three fifths of the total trade-union membership, which in 1898 numbered approximately a half million.[33] The strongholds of the Federation were to be found in the urban districts and among skilled workers in the mining industry, the building trades, the machine shops, and the trades engaged in the preparation of food, liquor, and tobacco. Of the unions unaffiliated with the A.F.L. the most important were the Railway Brotherhoods, whose well-stocked treasuries and long-established benevolences and traditions made them unwilling to endanger their freedom by any alliances. Notwithstanding the progress which had been made, only a small fraction—less than 4 percent—of the wage-earners were organized, but it was the unskilled, ill-paid, migratory or casual worker, the woman, and the newly arrived immigrant, for the most part, who remained outside the ranks.[34]

Whatever had been the internal divergences of opinion in earlier years, by 1898 the policies of the dominant leadership in the A.F.L. were firmly established. Its leaders were agreed that, for the moment at least, more would be gained by following the lines of the old-fashioned trade unionism, eschewing party politics, and avoiding radical prophets and programs. This policy of old-line unionism was amply vindicated by a rapid growth in numerical strength and public favor. In many respects the years from 1898 to 1905 were the most successful the Federation had experienced.[35] The membership increased from 278,000 to 1,676,000.[36] At the same time the cause of the workingman received unexpected recognition from responsible leaders outside labor's ranks. The most notable example of this was the formation in 1901 of the National Civic Federation with Marcus A. Hanna as president and Gompers vice president. Frankly recognizing unionization and the trade agreement as fundamental in the relations of capital and labor, this body sought to bring employer, employee, and the general public together in the solution of national industrial problems. "It was the harvest," as Gompers put it, "of the years of organizing work which were beginning to bear fruit."[37]

So far did the rapprochement progress, that one labor historian has called the years from 1898 to 1904 "a honeymoon period of capital and labour."[38] Never before had organized labor attained so favorable a position in American society, and never before was the employing class so well disposed toward what John Mitchell called "the hope of future peace in the industrial world"—the trade agreement.[39] The period opened auspiciously in the machinery and metal trades by an arbitration agreement between the National Founders' Association (organized in 1898) and the International Molders' Union of North America. This was followed the next year by a similar pact between the National Metal Trades' Association and the International Association of Machinists. Unfortunately, neither agreement lasted long, and in the succeeding years the metal trades returned to a condition of warfare and chaos.

According to an exhaustive study of strikes called during the period 1881–1905, three fifths of those in 1881 were for increased wages and only one sixteenth for recognition of the union, while in 1905 less than one third were for higher pay and about an equal number for recognition of the union. Furthermore, while the unions were responsible for less than half the strikes in the earlier year, they instigated directly or indirectly three fourths of those in 1905.[40] Between 1898 and 1905 the number of strikes doubled, and the conflicts were often accompanied by violence and bloodshed.[41] This increasing industrial strife and the waxing strength of labor inevitably brought counterattacks from the employing class. To the man who, after great effort over a long period of years, had established a business and developed friendly relations with his employees, it was highly irritating to have a labor organizer or "walking delegate" suddenly appear to tell him how to run his affairs. The more conciliatory employers might join the National Civic Federation and accede to trade agreements with their workmen, but the more conservative stiffened their backs. The leadership in the fight was taken by the National Association of Manufacturers, founded in 1895 chiefly to promote export trade but now boldly declaring war against organized labor.[42] Whatever the cause, the American Federation of Labor entered again on a period of lean years. Not only was its membership less in 1910 than in 1905,[43] but it had seen its status before the law continually whittled away by the judiciary and its right to protest constrained by the state police.

While the labor movement had to be constantly on guard against enemies outside its ranks, its development was also handicapped by internal dissensions. Though Gompers and his lieutenants were able to hold the Federation to a steady course, their policies upon even such fundamentals as political action and form of organization were under constant attack. The Federation persistently refused to countenance a distinct labor party, preferring to work for its demands within the channels of the old parties. Its policy, definitely laid down by the executive council in 1906, called for the defeat of political aspirants who were antilabor, the nomination of a straight labor candidate if neither party was favorable, and the unqualified support of the men "who have shown themselves friendly to labor."[44]

A radical minority in the American Federation still cherished hopes of committing the body to socialism. But, as Daniel DeLeon's attempts in the 1890s had shown, all such expectations were doomed to certain failure. Far from wishing to abolish the capitalistic system, the typical wage-earner desired merely to open the doors wider so that he might share more generously in its benefits. Socialism, however, as a political movement showed signs of steadily increasing strength during these years, partly as a result of a swelling tide of protest votes against the policies of the old parties,[45] and partly because of the ability of new leaders who entered the movement. Earlier, socialist agitation had been largely in the hands of recent immigrants unacquainted with American conditions, but with the formation in 1897 of a new party, presently known as the Socialist party, men like Eugene V. Debs and Victor Berger undertook to broaden the appeal of the cause and to work in such a way as to conciliate organized labor.[46] Its popular vote increased from about 95,000 in the presidential election of 1900 to more than 900,000 in 1912, at which time Socialist officeholders were to be found in more than 300 cities and towns.[47] Officially, the American Federation of Labor continued to maintain its distance and the party made no progress in the rural South. Its support came mainly from among skilled manual workers, clerical workers, merchants, and professional people in the urban districts of Ohio, Pennsylvania, New York, Illinois, California, and Wisconsin. Though the Socialists failed to win a single electoral vote, a political party of some significance, based primarily upon the labor vote, now actually existed, and the pressure to swing the A.F.L. officially into line was persistent. As late as 1914 the United Mine Workers insisted that the time had arrived "for the laboring people to come together in a political labor party."[48]

Another bone of contention within the Federation had to do with the old question of whether the wage-earners should organize as "one big union" rather than be split off in separate crafts. Such bodies as the United Brewery Workers and the United Mine Workers of America, in which industrial unionism had persisted, formed a radical bloc in the Federation inclined to regard dubiously the traditional craft emphasis. One of them, the Western Federation of Miners, was so insubordinate that in 1902 it led in the formation of the American Labor Union. This proved to be the first step toward the founding of a more powerful labor body on the same principle, the Industrial Workers of the World (I.W.W.), which sprang full blown from a meeting of radical socialists and industrial unionists in Chicago in June 1905. Among those in attendance were Debs, the popular standard bearer of the Socialist party; William D. ("Big Bill") Haywood, soon to emerge as the real leader of the new organization; and others of the ablest and most respected labor leaders, many of them American-born and with a long experience in the labor movement.

The delegates, who represented perhaps 50,000 workmen in forty distinct occupations, committed themselves unreservedly to industrial unionism and revolutionary socialism. "The working class and the employing class have nothing in common . . . ," asserted the preamble to their constitution. "Between these two classes a struggle must go on until all the toilers come together . . . and take hold of that which they produce by their labor through an economic organization of the working class, without affiliation with any political party."[49] In a later revision they went even farther, proclaiming that, "Instead of the conservative motto, 'a fair day's wage for a fair day's work,' we must inscribe on our banner the revolutionary watchword, 'Abolition of the wage system.' It is the historic mission of the working class to do away with capitalism."[50] Moreover, unlike the A.F.L., they set about to organize skilled and unskilled alike. "We don't propose," said Delegate Charles O. Sherman, "to organize only the common man with the callous hands but we want the clerical force." While Haywood declared: "We are going down in the gutter to get at the mass of workers and bring them up to a decent plane of living."[51]

Overloaded with strong leaders, the I.W.W. was handicapped from the start by factional quarrels, which eventually left the radical direct-actionist group in control. Its paid-up membership was never large, amounting to but 4,000 or 5,000 at the commencement of its great activity in 1912 and probably never exceeding 60,000;[52] but the activities of its leaders and the revolutionary ardor of its members gave it an influence far beyond its numerical strength until it threatened to become a serious rival of the American Federation of Labor. Its radical appeal won a following among the unskilled factory hands of the East and, in particular, among the migratory "wobblies" who cut the timber and followed the harvests—the wandering casual laborers, exploited, persecuted, homeless, but with grit enough to fight back at a system they had learned to hate.[53] Because of its bitter antagonism to the existing economic order, its willingness to employ sabotage, and its success in handling the unskilled and unorganized toilers, the I.W.W. was vigorously denounced and relentlessly opposed by capital and conservative labor alike. Nevertheless it brought improved conditions in certain industries, and it eventually forced the A.F.L. to give greater recognition to the unskilled worker.

Nothing harmed the cause of labor more than the lessening of public confidence, which resulted from the persistent antilabor propaganda and in part from the extralegal, if not criminal, activities of the more radical labor leaders. Most damaging to labor was the case of the McNamara brothers, an incident in the warfare between capital and labor on the Pacific Coast. On October 1, 1910, the building of the *Los Angeles Times,* whose proprietor was one of the bitterest foes of organized labor, was destroyed by a dynamite charge causing the death of twenty-one people. Through the efforts of the detective William J. Burns, three members of the International Association of Bridge and Iron Workers, John I. and James B. McNamara and Ortie McManigal, were arrested for the crime. McManigal made a confession involving the others, but the McNamaras so vehemently protested their innocence that the American Federation of Labor took vigorous steps for their defense. All over the country liberal opinion was aroused, but in the end the brothers pleaded guilty. Though the Federation promptly repudiated them, Burns talked much about the men "higher up" who were implicated and asserted that Gompers had known for some time of the guilt of the McNamaras.[54] No evidence, however, was ever produced to prove it. The incident did much to discredit the labor cause and the ordeal was one of the most trying that American labor had ever had to face.[55]

The prestige of the labor movement was further affected by humiliating and costly defeats, such as that sustained in the Colorado coal strike, which lasted from September 1913 to December 1914. In the southern counties of Colorado, industrial conditions were found at their worst. Here were mining towns, isolated from civilization, owned or controlled politically, socially, and economically by mine officials representing absentee stockholders—towns devoid of decent living accommodations, elementary sanitation, chances for recreation or medical attention, where drinking water unfit for use was pumped out of the mines and peddled by the companies at twenty-five cents a barrel, and the saloon was the only place of public resort.[56] So absolute was the domination of the companies that even a U.S. congressman asserted, "I myself had to get a pass to enter one of the incorporated towns of the State of Colorado, situated upon the property of the Colorado Fuel and Iron Co., and I had to get a pass to get out."[57] Eighty percent of the 30,000 inhabitants of these mining settlements were unable to speak English. They were described by one of the militia as "essentially as good as the average man," but "being rapidly debauched and degraded by conditions over which they have no control," and "living under a despotism so absolute that the radical labor press is not far wrong in calling them slaves."[58]

These workers were partially organized in 1913 by the United Mine Workers of America and went on strike for recognition of the union, higher wages, and the enforcement of the state labor laws regarding mining. Moving out of the company houses, the miners and their families established themselves in tent colonies. Some armed clashes occurred between the workers and the imported detectives and deputy sheriffs, and the state militia was called out. The friction reached a climax on April 20 when a pitched battle at Ludlow caused the burning of the tent colony there and the death of six men, two women, and eleven children.[59] In response, President Wilson urged John D. Rockefeller, Jr., who controlled one of the largest of the companies involved, to submit the dispute to arbitration, and when the situation got beyond the control of Colorado, he sent 2,000 federal troops to restore order. Again in September the president proposed a plan for a "three-year truce," but, while acceptable to the miners, it was refused by the operators. Undiscouraged, he appointed a commission to settle future labor disputes in Colorado. With the mines thoroughly protected and operated by strike breakers the strike collapsed, though not before it had given the nation a picture of almost unbelievable industrial feudalism—of an employing and exploiting class whose social and economic ideas had hardly advanced beyond the ethics of private warfare conducted with machine guns and dynamite.[60]

In spite of growing opposition without and within, the Federation and its allies, the great Railway Brotherhoods, hung on doggedly to their well-established policies. Profiting by the rising tide of prosperity and the growing humanitarianism of the bourgeoisie, labor could contemplate at the opening of World War I a decided advance in status. The percentage of labor organized had doubled in the decade 1900–1910, and the membership of the American Federation of Labor had grown to over 2 million by 1914.[61] Economists differed over the question as to whether labor was gaining its fair share of the enormous wealth produced, but there was general agreement that the standard of living had risen since 1898. This rising standard in no small measure was due to the immense amount of labor legislation which had been placed upon the statute books. As far as the federal government was concerned, such legislation had been slow in coming; for it was 1912 before Congress passed an effective and far-reaching eight-hour law for government contract work,[62] 1913 before a separate cabinet department was created for labor, 1914 before an effort was made to exempt labor from prosecution under the Sherman act, and 1915 before the La Follette law for ensuring decent conditions for American sailors was passed.

But the chief obstacle in the way of social legislation was the opposition of the courts rather than the indifference of the public. Grounded in eighteenth-century legal philosophy, unacquainted with modern industrial conditions, and conservative by nature, the judiciary at some time or other has held practically every type of labor legislation unconstitutional on the ground that it was "class legislation," or that it took away property without due process of law.[63] Thus, in the first Ritchie case in 1895, the Illinois supreme court held invalid an eight-hour day for women;[64] the Colorado supreme court in 1899 threw out an eight-hour law in the smelting industry as "as unwarrantable interference with the right of both the employer and employee in making contracts";[65] the U.S. Supreme Court in 1905 declared that the Lochner ten-hour law for bakers in New York State had "reached and passed the limit of the police power";[66] and as late as 1907 the New York court nullified a law prohibiting night work for women.[67]

But these decisions were overruled or reversed as time went on. Some years before the Lochner decision, the federal judiciary sustained the right of Utah to limit the hours of work in mines and smelters, and subsequently upheld the Oregon ten-hour law in 1908 and a California eight-hour law in 1915.[68] The state courts likewise showed a change of heart, for the Illinois tribunal in part reversed itself in the second Ritchie case, and the New York State supreme court totally did so in 1915 on the question of night work for women.[69] While the activities of labor continued to be limited by legal interpretations and the wholesale use of injunctions, in other respects the judiciary gave clear evidence of yielding to the humanitarian emphasis of the times as the minds of the judges were touched by the new spirit of the age.

THE NEW DEMOCRACY

To MANY THOUGHTFUL MEN in the opening years of the twentieth century it seemed that America in making her fortune was in peril of losing her soul. What had become of that precious concern of the Fathers, the "general welfare," when affairs of far-reaching social significance were settled outside legislative halls by contests between big business and little business, between capital and labor, between urban business interests and the embattled farmer? The infection indeed had spread to the legislatures themselves where the enactment of important laws was too often dictated by powerful lobbies which did not hesitate to employ outright corruption and bribery to accomplish their purposes. Despite the occasional victories of labor, big business was in the saddle, and it was the unorganized and inarticulate public that was being whipped and spurred. The tocsin of revolt that had sounded in 1896 against "Wall Street" had been hushed by the bewildering new interests and the outburst of prosperity that came with the Spanish-American War. The death of Henry George in the midst of the New York mayoralty campaign of 1897 stilled the voice of the most acute critic of American economic life. Yet the fires of revolt, though burning low, were not quenched. Soon they were to blaze forth into hot and consuming flame.

Nowhere were conditions so bad as in state and municipal politics. Here the party machinery was at the beck and call of railroad and corporation interests which understood all too well the means whereby legislators were made their pliant tools. Indeed, bribery was so common in political life that Judge H. S. Priest of Missouri affirmed extenuatingly that it was, "at the most, a conventional crime,"[70] and the grand jury for one of Folk's trials declared,

> We have listened to the confessions of State senators, and were we at liberty to make known all they have told us, the recital would appall and astound the citizens of this state. . . . Our investigations have gone back for twelve years, and during that time the evidence before us shows that corruption has been the usual and accepted thing in State legislation, and that, too, without interference or hindrance.[71]

"That bribery exists to a great extent in the elections of this state," said Governor L. F. C. Garvin of Rhode Island in a special message to the legislature in 1903, "is a matter of common knowledge."[72] Indeed, General Charles R. Brayton, boss of the Rhode Island "system," freely admitted that he was "an attorney for certain clients and looked out for their interests in the legislature," adding that he was retained annually by the New York, New Haven and Hartford Railroad Company and by other prominent corporations doing business in the state.[73] Such corporations as the railroad just mentioned held the legislature of not one but a half-dozen states in the palm of their hands.

With the multiplying evidences of public betrayal before their eyes, the voters, jarred out of their apathy or complacency, resolved upon drastic measures to reform the law-making departments of their governments. The years from 1898 to 1914 were a time of almost ceaseless constitutional tinkering, and the one constant thought in the minds of the members of the conventions was to curb the powers of the legislatures. In addition to the laws of the new states of Oklahoma (1907), New Mexico (1912), and Arizona (1912), and the comprehensive revisions made in Ohio (1912), Vermont (1913), and other states, five states framed new organic laws.[74] More than 1,500 amendments to state constitutions were, in fact, proposed between 1900 and 1920, of which three out of five were adopted.[75] New York, which had accepted a new constitution in 1894, wrote a modern and scientific revision in 1915 which was voted down. Of the other states where the movement failed, an interesting example is Connecticut. Its legislature, under the control of rural delegates chosen through a "rotten-borough" system, acceded to the popular clamor for a constitutional convention, but made certain that the rural delegations would control it. The resulting constitution consequently offered little relief from existing abuses and was voted down in 1902.[76]

In general, these constitutional changes reveal an effort to strengthen the power of the executives, centralize administration, and increase popular control over the government. So far did the tendency go that one expert queried whether it would "ultimately prove worth while to retain an expensive legislature to exercise its small residue of petty powers"; and when the movement had about run its course, another was led to assert that the "most serious impediment to a right kind of legislature and a proper kind of legislators seems to me to lie in the fact that they are individually and collectively powerless."[77] But if the new constitutions erred in reducing too radically the function of the legislative branch, they made long strides in the direction of greater executive efficiency and in the perfection of democratic machinery.

The traditional leadership for broader popular rights, so long borne by the rural frontier, had begun to pass with the failure of Populism. Though it was the newer states that led in democratic legislation in the new century, Western radicalism reached out to Eastern radicalism—a radicalism emanating from the population centers. Long regarded by political philosophers as sores on the body politic, the great city now began to stand forth as "the hope of democracy."[78] Thus, at a time when municipal corruption was at its height, reformers began to spring up here and there—in Toledo, Cleveland, Detroit, and elsewhere—to battle for the restoration of government to the people.

Though the movement for political reform was in general from the bottom up, the national parties also made their contributions. Indeed, it might be said that in the nineties the discredited Populists had anticipated most of the demands which were carried to victory and popular acclaim by the anointed leaders of the early years of the new century. Roosevelt, to mention no lesser person, was the direct heir and beneficiary of the Populism he had once so bitterly assailed. Suddenly finding himself the leader of a party which had completely succumbed to special privilege during the leadership of Hanna and McKinley, he strove mightily to give it a distinct progressive tone. In this his personal inclinations fitted nicely with political expediency. The nation was ready for a swing to the left, and Roosevelt gave voice to the unspoken aspirations of the common man with an accuracy achieved by few politicians. Instinctively he responded to the widespread desire for a better civilization and, rushing to the head of the movement, he rose to unprecedented heights of popularity as the reform wave surged onward. Assemblyman, police commissioner, civil-service reformer, historian, assistant secretary of the navy, roughrider, governor, vice president—the exemplar of the strenuous life with a long career of public service behind him—Roosevelt typified as have few others the ideal of his generation. What the many would like to be, he was, and his unerring journalistic sense enabled him to dramatize his actions and discomfit his enemies. Children in the nursery played with Teddy Bears,[79] and leading intellectuals considered him one of the greatest men of his day. The very initials T. R. came to have an almost magic symbolism.

From the point of view of uncompromising progressives, like La Follette, his devotion to the progressive cause had in it an element of charlatanry.[80] While many of his political associates accused him of ingratitude, insincerity, and personal ambition. To his friends, however, his railroad legislation, his prosecutions of the trusts, his efforts in behalf of pure-food laws and conservation, placed him in the forefront of the newer statesmen.[81] Whatever may be the final opinion as to Roosevelt's contribution to the newer America, his domestic policies while president were aggressive and forward looking. Not only was he personally influential in the enactment of progressive legislation, but he helped give momentum to forces in our national political life which his more conservative successor in the White House could not stop.

With the great mass of voters the Rooseveltian policies were undeniably popular, representing as they did the hopes of a new political and social era, and the voters had no hesitancy in supporting William Howard Taft, whom Roosevelt had handpicked as his successor in 1908. Although the Taft administration saw the fruition of much advanced legislation[82] and the president himself was far from the whole-souled reactionary that his political enemies pictured him, it was not long before Taft found himself out of touch with the more progressive of the Roosevelt followers. The tariff issue, which his predecessor had so skillfully and persistently avoided, proved, in particular, to be his undoing, and the Democratic success in the 1910 elections was a strong indication of the growing unpopularity of his regime.

As the Taft administration drew stormily to a close, the progressive movement, which had been steadily growing in strength, reached its climax. Roosevelt, returning from a hunting trip in Africa, threw in his lot with the insurgent Republicans and, in a famous speech on "The New Nationalism" delivered at Osawatomie, Kansas, assumed an advanced progressive position.[83] The insurgents, planning to contest the renomination of President Taft, first rallied around La Follette, and then, scenting victory in the air, they stampeded to their old idol, Roosevelt. Though Roosevelt had asserted he would not run again, he yielded to the importunities of his friends and the promptings of his own ardent nature, and on February 26, 1912, announced that he would accept the nomination if it were offered to him by the Republican national convention.[84] To many, the future of political and social reform seemed to rest on the outcome of the ensuing campaign. Charging from state to state in his whirlwind campaign, Roosevelt undoubtly won the endorsements of the rank and file of the Republican voters,[85] but in the nominationg convention he was flattened by the same "steam-roller" which four years earlier had so efficiently cleared the way for Taft. Hot with wrath and loud in their cries of fraud, the Roosevelt delegates launched the Progressive party, nominated their chief for president, and wrote a platform which epitomized the hopes of reformers.[86] "We stand at Armageddon, and we battle for the Lord," shouted Roosevelt in concluding his keynote speech to a convention which in its fervor resembled an old-time religious revival.

Flushed with the hope that the Republican schism might open the way for victory, the Democratic party met to choose its candidate. The political bosses in the convention labored under no illusion that they were battling for the Lord, but the more liberal element under the leadership of Bryan succeeded in mastering the situation and in nominating Woodrow Wilson on a liberal platform.[87] The Socialist party which had grown steadily in power during the previous decade again nominated its hero, Eugene V. Debs, on a platform more radical than that of the Progressives. Even the Republicans were forced to promise reforms which in an ordinary campaign might have given their platform a complexion of liberalism.

For the progressive voter the millennium in national politics seemed to have been reached. Each of the platforms was progressive and three out of the four candidates were reformers—even crusaders. However the election turned out, it appeared, for once, that the cause of reform would win. Reckoned by the popular vote Wilson was elected as a minority president, but gauged by public sentiment as well as by the decsion of the electoral college he represented a majority. For the only time perhaps in its history the nation contained a progressive majority and the new chief executive stood for that group.

The Underwood tariff with its income tax, the Clayton antitrust act, the federal reserve act, and other important legislation which marked the early years of Wilson's presidency may have stopped short of the full progressive program, but they represented an extraordinary advance. The nation had made vast strides since the complacent plutocracy of the McKinley era and since the days when the Populists had been repudiated as dangerous radicals. A "social consciousness" had developed which demanded not only clean politics but a better world in which to live.[88] If the battle waged across a long front can be epitomized in the lives of a few men such as Tom Johnson, Robert La Follette, or Theodore Roosevelt, the fact remains that their efforts would have been largely futile had they not represented the aspirations of the common man.

THE REVOLUTION IN TRANSPORTATION

WHILE THE POLITICAL attention of the nation was fixed on problems arising from the growth of giant industry, active-minded inventors, going about their proper business, were quietly effecting changes in essentials of American living, which had far-reaching social consequences. In the field of transportation the new inventions, in the immediate and remoter effects, amounted to nothing less than a revolution. Just as in the first half of the nineteenth century the speed and ease of travel had been transformed by the application of steam power to locomotion on land and water,[89] so distances were once more dramatically shortened by new applications of electrical energy and the introduction of gasoline as a source of motive power.

To people living at the time, the most significant of the discoveries was the self-propelled motor vehicle. The automobile had no single inventor; its lineage goes back to the first man who conceived the idea of putting an engine on wheels—perhaps Nicholas Cugnot, a French artillery captain, who constructed in 1769 a three-wheeled wagon equipped with a boiler and engine.[90] It came down through such men as the American George B. Selden, who in 1879 applied for a patent on a vehicle driven by an internal-combustion engine; the German Gottlieb Daimler, who in 1883 perfected the "hot-tube" system of ignition; the German Carl Benz, who built the first successful gasoline-driven motor car; and such Frenchmen as Panhard, Levassor, Serpollet, and the Renault brothers, who added many refinements.

The sixteen years after 1898 mark the advance of the automobile from an obsession of tinkering mechanics or a "plaything of the rich" to a widely used pleasure and business vehicle. The mechanical improvement from the "one-lung" motors of Ford, Olds, and Winton to the smooth-running "sixes" and "eights" of a few years later was nothing short of marvelous. Regarded dubiously by the more conservative in its earlier years, the automobile appealed to too many human traits, both good and bad, to languish. The convenience, the feeling of power, the chance for show, made some willing to mortgage even their homes to obtain the coveted car. The 4 automobiles registered in 1895 and the 8,000 in 1900 grew to 2.5 million in 1915, the capital invested in manufacturing from $5,760,000 in 1899 to $407,730,000 in 1914.[91]

It is doubtful if any mechanical invention in the history of the world has influenced in the same length of time the lives of so many people in an important way as has the motor car. As it passed into general use, it took the city to the country and country to the city, mitigating rural isolation and provincialism and widening the business as well as the intellectual life of the farmer. Hardly a phase of American rural life remained untouched, its influence upon education in promoting the consolidation of schools into larger and more effective units being particularly notable. It helped promote the suburban developments which the railroad and "trolley" had already started, while in the nation as a whole it provided work for hundreds of thousands. By 1914 it was obvious that the motor car had not only contributed a new form of recreation but by means of more rapid facilities for social and economic intercourse had accelerated the whole tempo of our civilization.[92]

More spectacular, though less significant in the life of these times, was the progress made in flying. The century opened with much interest in aeronautics, particularly in France, but the experiments were largely limited to various types of balloons. The Aero Club of America, founded in 1905, had as its chief objective "the popularization of ballooning as a sport, especially among the more wealthy class,"[93] and few people, even in aeronautical circles, believed that a practicable heavier-than-air machine could ever be built. Though Sir Hiram Maxim in England and C. E. Ader in France had constructed airplanes in the nineties, the outcome of their efforts was not encouraging. In America, Samuel P. Langley, secretary of the Smithsonian Institution, devoted study to the building of airplanes and devised large steam-driven models which made successful flights of from one-half to one mile in 1896. After a favorable report from a board of army and navy officers, the war department in 1898 granted $50,000 for further experiments. With his assistant Charles M. Manly, Langley built a man-size airplane which in October and December 1903 made two unsuccessful attempts to fly over the Potomac.[94]

The sight of Langley's machine nose-diving into the Potomac aroused more merriment among the public than serious interest. It was now quite evident, said the *Chicago Tribune,* that there was "little possibility" that man would fly "until we became angels," while the *Boston Herald* urged Langley "to drop work on his flying machine and turn his attention to the construction of a diving or submarine craft, his efforts seeming to result in success in this direction rather than upward." [95]

Just nine days after the Langley fiasco, and while the press was still jeering at the Smithsonian scientists for attempting the impossible, Orville Wright at Kitty Hawk on the North Carolina coast made a flight which "lasted only 12 seconds, but it was nevertheless the first in the history of the world in which a machine carrying a man had raised itself by its own power into the air in full flight, had sailed forward without reduction of speed, and finally landed at a point as high as that from which it started." [96] The next day Wilbur Wright stayed in the air fifty-nine seconds.

These revolutionary applications of gasoline power to locomotion were attended by a tremendous development of the sources of electrical energy. Though most of the basic uses of electricity had been discovered by the preceding generation, it was for this one to realize more fully its possibilities. The few tiny power stations of the early 1880s had grown to over 2,000 in 1898 and more than 5,000 in 1914, delivering their current not only to homes but also to factories, and with each new demand for electricity the primary problem of distributing the power took on new significance. [97] The fundamental researches of the brilliant Austrian immigrant Nicola Tesla [98] in the rotating magnetic field and the work of his successors lengthened the delivery point by 1914 to over 150 miles, a factor which gave power producers a wide radius within which to find the cheapest place for manufacture.

The great project to "harness Niagara" had already been accomplished by the opening of the century, and producers turned with increasing interest to water as the cheapest form of power. The decade from 1904 to 1914 was characterized by a widespread development of hydroelectric projects, culminating in 1913 in the successful inauguration of service on the finished half of the great Keokuk Dam on the Mississippi, destined at its completion to be the largest power plant in the world. [99] As in other industries, the dictates of efficiency and the hope of greater profits soon led the power producers to consolidation and to the extension of a network of giant power cables over large areas. [100]

Electricity played its part in solving the transportation problems of this generation, especially in the case of short distances. In the earlier years at least, it seemed little affected by the growing competition of the automobile. As once the nation had turned enthusiastically to the construction of canals and railroads, so now with equal ardor it embarked upon the building of street railways. The annual increase of track averaged well over 2,000 miles in the years from 1902 to 1907, though falling to about half that amount in the next five-year period. [101]

To meet the intolerable conditions of congestion New York and Chicago had earlier built elevated systems,[102] and Boston followed in 1901; but the overhead railroad left much to be desired until electric power replaced steam. The first trains operated by electricity ran on the New York elevated system in 1901 and this power was soon afterward installed in Chicago and Boston. The needs of traffic in the larger cities, however, seemed always in advance of facilities. At the close of the nineties two of them, following the example of London, attempted to solve the problem by building subways. Boston, the pioneer in this respect, completed the first unit of her system in 1898. New York began hers in 1900 and the portion to be put into operation first, that part from City Hall on the south to 145th Street and Broadway on the north, opened by Mayor McClellan in October 1904.[103] A year later trains were running under the East River to Brooklyn and by 1908 connection had been achieved with New Jersey by the tube under the North River.[104]

At first chiefly useful as a substitute for the old-fashioned city horse car, the electric trolley after 1898 spread increasingly into the suburbs and soon came to link one community with another. So far had this development proceeded by 1910 that, in the more thickly settled regions, most towns were connected by electric railways. By the close of the period it was possible to travel from New York City to Portland, Maine, and from New York to Sheboygan, Wisconsin, entirely by electric road.[105] The extension of interurban service reacted upon the steam railways, forcing fare reductions in some instances, the purchase of the lines by the steam roads in others, and eventually in certain cases the actual electrification of the railways.[106] The New York Central began operation by electricity from Grand Central Station in New York City in 1906 and two years later the New York, New Haven and Hartford inaugurated complete electric passenger service between the same terminal and Stamford, Connecticut. Competition from interurban trolleys was, however, but one of the causes of electrification. The electric engine was cheaper, faster, cleaner, and much better adapted to the crowded conditions of the enclosed city terminals than the puffing, smoky steam locomotive, besides being more dependable on mountain grades and in zero weather. Notwithstanding the heavy initial cost, railroads in many sections of the country were laying plans for electrification as the period closed.[107]

Compared with the achievements in the field of transportation, the advances made in the facilities for communication seem less impressive. Yet here, too, this generation improved greatly upon the work of its predecessors. For the first time, for example, the telephone entered significantly into the life of the common man. The 677,000 telephones belonging to the Bell system in 1900 grew to 3.5 million in 1910 and to nearly 6 million in 1915.[108] From being an exception, a telephone installation by the last date had become the rule in the middle-class home, making life easier for the city dweller and helping further to break down the isolation of rural life.

This growth was in part the cause, and in part the result, of the important discoveries of the large research staff maintained by the Bell holding corporation, the American Telephone and Telegraph Company, which was especially active in solving the problems of underground and long-distance communication.

The range of overhead conversation was gradually lengthened until by January 1915, Alexander Graham Bell, inventor of the telephone, speaking in New York into an exact reproduction of his original instrument, was clearly heard in San Francisco by Thomas A. Watson, who thirty-nine years before, as Bell's assistant, had caught the first telephone message ever spoken.[109] Long-distance conversation by underground cable began in 1902 over a ten-mile stretch from Newark to New York. Owing to a disastrous sleet storm Washington was without wire communication on the day of President Taft's inauguration, but the year that his successor took office saw underground installations from Boston to Washington. Nor were these advances all. Wireless telegraphy, still in its infancy in 1898, was so rapidly developed that on December 12 and 13, 1901, its inventor, the Italian Guglielmo Marconi, caught with the aid of a kite at St. John's, Newfoundland, the signal sent from Poldhu Station, Cornwall. This dramatic demonstration seized the imagination of the public, and a Marconi Wireless Telegraph Company of America was established the next year. Wireless installations within a half-dozen years became standard equipment on all large ships; and many scientists, of whom the American Lee De Forest, was perhaps the best known, contributed numerous improvements.[110] Americans living in 1914 might well have marveled at the changes in transportation and communciation that had occurred within their short span of years. How little they dreamed of the miracles that still lay ahead!

WOMEN, HOME, AND FAMILY LIFE

THE NEW CONDITIONS of American life affected the position of women in many vital respects. In the first decade of the century the number of female wage-earners increased both numerically and relatively, though, in contrast with earlier times, the greatest relative advance took place in office and store employments.[111] While fewer women lawyers and ministers were listed in 1910 than in 1900 and but few more physicians and surgeons, women continued to move into the educational field in ever-greater proportions. The enlarging role of the sex in economic life was, however, purchased at a cost. Of the women sixteen years of age and over at work outside the homes and professions, almost half earned less than $6 a week in 1914 and approximately three fourths less than $8.[112] Probabhly the most comprehensive wage statistics on women's labor were those gathered in the years 1907–1909 by the U.S. bureau of labor for the cotton, men's clothing, glass, and silk-manufacturing industries. "One of the most significant facts brought out by the investigation," asserted the bureau, "was the large proportion of women wage earners who were paid very low wages —wages in many cases inadequate to supply a reasonable standard of living for women dependent upon their own earnings for support."[113]

Various explanations were advanced for the low wages; the immobility of the famale labor force; the youth and inexperience of the individual laborer; the large number of immigrant women among the mill workers; and the fact that seven out of ten lived in families where there were other breadwinners. Women's position in industry was still somewhat subordinated to the home.[114] The real labor unit was the family rather than the woman worker, and as a member of the family group she suffered either because it might not be necesasry for her to earn her full way or because she was forced to find work where her family was located. Moreover, many women considered work a temporary expedient until an eventual escape was found in matrimony; at least half the women in manufacture and trade, it was discovered, were under twenty-five years of age. Such conditions retarded the progress of trade unionism among women. To improve the situation, the National Women's Trade Union League was formed in 1903. Composed chiefly of women labor leaders and social workers, the league strove with increasing success to affiliate women wage-earners with the labor movement.[115]

As in the 1880s, and 1890s, the movement of women was not only from the home to the factory and office, but also from the country to the city. Just as the first women operatives moved from rural New England to the mill villages of Waltham and Lowell, so now their granddaughters, aspiring to be stenographers, saleswomen, or librarians, sought the towns and cities, while the newly arrived immigrant girl found her best opportunity in domestic service in city homes. The factory system had already modified the economic importance of the home and it was now changing its physical aspect. The pressure of population on land had so raised its value that the single-family house was rapidly being supplanted in the great cities by apartment houses and even by apartment hotels. The number of private houses annually built in Manhattan dropped from over 1,300 in 1886 to about 40 in 1904 while apartment houses were springing up everywhere, a tendency greatly hastened after 1897 when the cost of elevator service was reduced by the opportunity to buy electric power from the street conduits.[116] The alteration, commented Charlotte Perkins Gilman in 1904, "is so great and so swift as to force itself upon us with something of a shock," and with many others she protested against seeing the American home "lifted clean off the ground—yardless, cellarless, stairless, even kitchenless."[117] Such conditions, however, were little known in the smaller towns.

Whatever the objections to the new type of home, it was of great service in reducing household drudgery. The difficulty of obtaining domestic servants, the rising cost of building materials, and the decline in the size of the American family, all contributed to a distinct reaction from the large houses of the last half of the nineteenth century to the small compact homes of the new era. At the same time mechanical inventions lightened the labors of the housewife. The telephone in 1898 was more commonly found in offices than in homes, but in the succeeding years it became a household necessity.[118] The incandescent light, widely used in the cities by 1898, now spread rapidly into the surburban districts. Installation of wiring for lighting purposes opened the way for such devices as electric irons, washers, toasters, stoves, and vacuum cleaners which ingenious inventors speedily placed on the market. Better plumbing and improved bathroom and kitchen fixtures further simplified housework as did changing styles in house furnishings. Hardwood floors were banishing carpets for the more sanitary rugs, and the smaller rooms of the new type of dwelling had no space for the wondrous arrays of bric-a-brac which so often cluttered up the living rooms of the previous generation.[119]

Of great benefit to women also was the simpler diet that was being widely adopted. The heavy food and groaning boards that had been characteristic of a rural population were less needed as American life became increasingly urbanized. The discussion that accompanied the pure-food laws made the American pay more attention to food values, while the mania for efficiency led him to lend ready ear to the propaganda for the new "health foods" that flooded the market. The change began with the introduction of new and in some cases "predigested" breakfast foods, that were so widely and persistently advertised in the opening years of the century as to be a chief financial support for many periodicals.[120] The legends that accompanied the smiling features of the ubiquitous black chef[121] or the chubby "Sunny Jim"[122] may have exaggerated the merits of their respective wares, but they helped revolutionize the national breakfast table. Not only was the American eating different food but he was eating less. Lunch in the urban business districts declined in importance until a sandwich and a drink at a saloon or soda fountain served to satisfy the noonday hunger. The only meal of importance to many was now the evening dinner and even here there was less consumption of meat.

The smaller and simpler dwelling of the new century amply served its purpose. The father spent his working day elsewhere, the children spent most of theirs in school, and the mother, relieved of much household drudgery, devoted more time to outside interests. Recreation, intellectual stimulation, and the means of subsistence were now so largely obtained away from home that in many instances the city dwelling had become primarily a place to sleep. But important as were the effects of household improvements on the women of the middle class, large numbers of the sex were entirely unaffected. The rapid growth of cities, the flood of immigrants, the unequal distribution of wealth, and inadequate housing laws all contributed to the development of congested areas where thousands of human beings were huddled into unbelievably close quarters and where, deprived of proper light, air, sanitary appliances, and privacy, it was but a question of time before many fell victims to vice and disease.

Although the problem of the slums was an old one and existed to some degree in every large American city, it was most acute in New York. Of the 3.5 million inhabitants of Greater New York in 1900, more than two thirds lived in about 90,000 tenement houses, the majority of them of the so-called dumb-bell type in which but four rooms out of fourteen on each floor had direct air and light.[123] The New York Commission of 1900, in fact, found that New York presented "the most serious tenement house problem in the world," with conditions that could hardly be duplicated in western Europe and that harked back to Manchester and Liverpool of a century before. New York had not been oblivious of the growing evil; official commissions had reported at various times and legislation had been enacted, but it had proved quite inadequate to cope with the situation.[124] In 1898, partly through the influence of Lawrence Veiller, the Charity Organization Society took up the problem, drafted a model law, and in 1900 conducted a model-tenement competition. So much interest was aroused that the legislature appointed a tenement-house commission and in 1901 passed a special tenement-house law for the greater cities (250,000 or over). The new code required that all rooms and hallways be lighted and ventilated, and imposed strict regulations regarding size of rooms, running water, fire escapes, and sanitation.[125] The recommendations of the commission also included a separate tenement-house department for New York City, which was created under the new charter of that metropolis when it went into operation under Mayor Seth Low in 1902.

Although the law was bitterly attacked by the speculators and small owners, its constitutionality was upheld[126] and it inaugurated a new era in tenement legislation. New Jersey passed a law in 1905 modeled on that of New York, but applying to cities of all classes in the state; Pennsylvania legislated in 1903 for cities of the second class and in 1907 amended its legislation for first-class cities by requiring licensing of tenement houses and quarterly inspection; Connecticut in 1905 enacted a general law for cities of over 20,000. While these few commonwealths set up statewide standards, many cities—Chicago in 1905; Boston, Cleveland, and San Francisco in 1907; and Baltimore in 1908—enacted new regulations or revised the existing building codes. By the end of the period the problem of slum housing had been squarely met and notable progress had been made.

From the slum districts came many of the victims of commercialized vice. Though the new building laws constituted an oblique attack on that ancient uncleanness, the leaders of this generation were not content with indirect or halfway measures. Prior to 1898 little of a systematic character had been done in American cities to regulate the "social evil" or to lessen

Old-law shaft before 1901

New-law court after 1901.

Legislation brought light and air to the poor in New York.

A neat simplicity supplanted stuffiness in the homes of the "middle class."

Homes

it, and practically nothing in the way of scientific study. New York was so startled by the spread of prostitution that in 1900 a meeting of citizens appointed a committee of fifteen to investigate the situation.[127] This committee not only presented an excellent report based upon a study of conditions here and abroad, but prosecuted some offenders of the law, presented a series of recommendations for better control and, in fact, inaugurated in America the first serious attack upon the evil. The report had noted especially the connection between the so-called Raines-law hotels and prostitution,[128] and in 1905 a new and permanent organization, known as the Committee of Fourteen, was formed to fight the Raines law, though its work soon widened to include an attack upon all forms of prostitution.[129] A ten-year crusade distinctly improved conditions in New York City. The Raines-law hotels, numbered literally by the thousands in 1905, had practically disappeared; all of the famous resorts had been closed; and disorderly houses which had operated openly by the hundreds were greatly reduced in number and forced to conduct their business with secrecy. A direct result of the work of this committee was an investigation of the courts of minor criminal jurisdiction in New York and the passage of the Page law which revolutionized the procedure in the city magistrates' courts.[130]

Though the experience of New York was watched in other cities, it was not until George Kibbe Turner in a sensational article in *McClure's* laid bare the connection between liquor, gambling, crime, political corruption, and prostitution that other centers were stirred to action. Turner asserted that there were 10,000 prostitutes in Chicago who were exploited by criminal hotels, houses of ill-fame, cheap dance halls, and saloons, and that the whole business was organized from the snaring of young girls to the drugging of older and less salable women out of existence.[131] At the urging of the Federation of Churches of Chicago, the mayor appointed a vice commission in 1910, and similar studies were made by official bodies appointed in Minneapolis; Portland, Oregon; Hartford, Connecticut; and other cities in the next few years.[132]

The wide extent and highly organized character of the traffic in women came as a shock to the public. The Chicago commission believed that there were at least 5,000 in that city who devoted their entire time to prostitution;[133] a Pittsburgh survey found 200 disorderly houses in one section alone in the summer of 1907;[134] and the Portland vice commission in their comparatively small city reported 113 places wholly given up to prostitution or assignation. There was scarcely a city of any size which did not have its "red-light district." These reports, however, by pointing to poverty, liquor, defective mentality, and lack of wholesome places of amusement as contributing causes suggested thereby means of remedy. At the same time they endeavored to break down the complacent attitude of many that organized prostitution and segregated districts were necessary, if not desirable.

The conditions described by the investigations were greatly modified by

1914, and improved even more during the war years as the federal government cooperated with the local police in eliminating open prostitution. More careful efforts were made to regulate places of amusement and to separate the saloon from the prostitute. The new juvenile courts played their part in rescue work and in many cities the red-light districts were eliminated. In the meantime the medical aspect was beginning to receive the attention it deserved through the organization of the American Society of Sanitary and Moral Prophylaxis in 1905.[135] Efforts were also made to check one source of prostitution by laws against the white-slave traffic. After a period of investigation and agitation in America, Roosevelt issued a proclamation declaring the adhesion of the United States to the International white-slave treaty; the immigration law of 1908 was strengthened to provide adequate punishment for those engaged in this traffic, and in 1910 the Mann act sought to deal with it through the federal power over interstate commerce.[136] Beginning with Illinois in 1908 most of the states also enacted stringent legislation against it.[137]

Less successful were the efforts directed from high quarters against family limitation. Not a new phenomenon, the tendency was greatly intensified by the new conditions of life. The woman who had tasted economic independence was slower to marry and insisted on a higher level of comfort when she did so. Nor was she willing to submerge all her interests in motherhood, however precious that estate, when once she took the fateful step. The cramped living quarters of the modern city and the stern "No children or dogs" of the apartment-house owner provided further deterrents to maternity. These and numerous other social and economic causes were producing the inevitable. The rate of population increase had fallen in each decade but one since 1880 and had done so in spite of tremendous immigration.[138] Although the census of 1910 failed adequately to cover the subject of birth rate, it showed a slight loss in each decade since 1890 of the number of "persons to a family." [139]

The decline in birth rate was greatest among the more educated and prosperous classes and among the native stock, although a similar tendency was at work among the second generation of immigrants. In New England the birth rate of the native stock appeared to be less than the death rate,[140] while a study made of Americans of native parentage in the central United States showed a shrinkage of the family between the present generation and their parents of 38.5 percent. Over a tenth of the unions recorded in this study were found to be infertile and about one fifth produced but one child.[141] College women, recruited from the most intellectual group of each generation, married two years later than other girls of the same social class and averaged less than two children; only one out of two married, whereas in the whole population the ratio was nine out of ten.[142]

Generally speaking, the higher the social, intellectual, and economic status, the smaller the family; but the declining birth rate was also evident among the "white-collar proletariat" of the cities. One student of the subject in New York City visited twenty-two apartment houses containing 485 families which possessed but fifty-four children, or about one child to every nine families. Twelve New York physicians practicing among people in comfortable circumstances agreed, in substance, "that the large family does not exist and is not desired," while a woman physician with long practice on the West Side in the upper Sixties went so far as to say that "having a family is not an American ideal. Among my patients I find that the majority do not want any children; certainly not more than one. I should say that as a rule the second is an accident, the third is a misfortune, and the fourth a tragedy." [143]

To many this situation appeared deplorable. Ignoring the influences which made the tendency almost universal and inevitable, they attributed it merely to the selfishness of the "new woman." The leadership in this cause was taken by President Roosevelt when he scathingly denounced "race suicide" and used his great powers to popularize the idea of larger families. Roosevelt's propaganda called attention to the situation, but it obviously did not change it. [144] The primary motive in the restriction of birth appeared to be economic and social, and the views of a wealthy statesman might have little bearing on the problems of a $20-a-week clerk or a $12-a-week laborer. Roosevelt's blast helped, however, to stir up interest in the question of both eugenics and birth control. Already the Carnegie Institution (1904) had established a eugenics laboratory at Cold Spring Harbor, New York, and enough popular interest in eugenics was aroused by 1907 to induce Indiana to pass a law providing for the sterilization of certain types of defectives and criminals, an example followed by eleven other states by 1914. [145]

Meanwhile an earnest movement for scientific regulation of the size of families took form under a small group of reformers, who coined the term "birth control" as best expressing their aims. The idea was not new in America. An important early agitation had occurred in the 1830s, but the modern movement developed during the first two decades of the twentieth century. American and European advocates of family limitation joined in the First International Neo-Malthusian Conference in Paris in 1900; Moses Harmon, editor of *Lucifer,* was sentenced to Leavenworth in 1906 for publishing a serious discussion of matrimonial relations. A forward step was taken in 1912 when Dr. Abraham Jacobi, in his presidential address to the American Medical Association, endorsed the hygienic prevention of pregnancy. But the obstacles confronting the spread of such ideas were formidable. Not only was the circulation of contraceptive information or devices prohibited by an 1873 federal statute and by laws in many of the states, [146] but contraception was opposed by numerous groups, especially the Roman Catholic Church, on theological, moral, and social grounds. [147] The movement awaited vigorous and devoted leadership.

Such championship appeared when Margaret Sanger, a visiting nurse in the East Side of New York, became convinced through her social work of the importance of family limitation, and began in 1912 to study practical methods. In 1914 she published the first issue of the *Woman Rebel,* immediately barred from the mails, and began the formation of the American Birth Control League. Her arrest and indictment under the federal statutes for mailing her pamphlet *Family Limitation,* and her consequent enforced absence from the country for over a year, delayed progress in the movement, but allowed her valuable time for further study. The movement was reorganized as the National Birth Control League in 1915, and other groups under the leadership of Mary Ware Dennett formed the Voluntary Parenthood League in 1918. The two groups coalesced in 1921 to form the American Birth Control League, and worked to legalize the dissemination of contraceptive methods by properly qualified physicians, at the same time preaching the doctrine of better rather than more children, of the child's right to be wanted, of the proper spacing of children, and of the right of the poor to scientific knowledge of contraception, a knowledge obviously possessed by the wealthy. Efforts to change existing laws failed, but in the postwar years the movement was to take on increasing strength and a number of birth-control clinics were established, though always in the face of continued vocal opposition.[148]

The chief advantages of the new age fell to women of the comfortable classes in the cities. Relieved of much of their former work, they found themselves with more leisure on their hands than they had ever before enjoyed and more, indeed, than some of them knew wisely how to use. The new woman, said Charlotte Perkins Gilman, "too ignorant, too timid, too self-indulgent to do other work, simply plays most of the time, or labors at amusement, salving her conscience with charity."[149] "My mountain of mail," wrote a woman journalist, "is often a volcano of seething unrest," an unrest resulting from the questioning of older values as well as from a failure to meet new opportunities.[150] At such a time the age-old complaint that the younger generation were faster and less bound by convention was frequently heard, and it seems probable that in this case the complaints had some foundation in fact, In 1898, if etiquette books are to be believed, no self-respecting girl would be seen at a public restaurant or tearoom with a gentleman, unless a chaperon was present, and in the "same category of offenses" was ranked that of maidens visiting places of public amusement under the escort of young men alone.[151] This sort of convention was pretty largely an importation from Europe, and the earnest efforts of dictators of manners to impose them upon America were doomed to failure except in select circles in the large Eastern cities. "In many parts of the West and South," mourned an etiquette counselor in 1906, "society may grant a girl the privilege of visiting places of public refreshment or amusement alone with a young man, or of accepting his escort to or from an evening party. . . ."[152] Indeed, the standard of conduct in rural and urban parts varied throughout the nation.

More significant of the new position of women was the alarming increase of divorce. Much interest in this question was excited by Roosevelt's special message to Congress in 1905 and by the publication three years later of the results of a federal investigation.[153] This report demonstrated conclusively that the tendencies toward a high divorce rate, already apparent in the 1870s and 1880s, had continued.[154] Thus the rate, which had been 53 per 100,000 population in 1890, was 73 in 1900, 84 in 1906, and 112 in 1916. Although seven of the states and the District of Columbia showed a lower rate in 1916 than in 1906,[155] in others the increase was astounding. Divorces in Oregon had grown over 100 percent, in New Jersey 120 percent, in Idaho 150, in Arizona nearly 190, and in California over 200. With the exception of Japan, the United States had a higher divorce rate than any other civilized country and granted a greater number of divorces than all the rest of the world, Japan again excepted.

The underlying causes were as complex as civilization itself, and as the speed and intensity of life became greater, the marriage tie became increasingly regarded as a convenience rather than a sacred obligation.[156] By some the rising divorce rate was hailed as a favorable sign, but the great majority deplored it as a dangerous tendency. Remedial suggestions, however, were largely futile; neither the fulminations of the clergy nor the warning cry of statesmen appeared to have any effect.

The discussion did, nevertheless, help call attention again to the curious legal situation which existed with reference to divorce. The grounds for divorce varied from none at all in South Carolina to fourteen in New Hampshire, and while a majority of the states recognized the divorce laws of the other states, at least eight did not recognize them unconditionally. The period of residence required for bringing suit ranged from six months to three years, thus encouraging an exodus to Nevada, where the city of Reno became famous for its six-month settlers. At the same time the laws on marriage also differed widely.[157] The chaotic legal aspect of the divorce problem led to an increasing demand that something be done through state agreement or federal amendment to standardize the laws. Leadership in the movement was assumed by Pennsylvania where Governor Samuel W. Pennypacker in 1906 called a National Congress of Uniform Divorce Laws which drafted a model act.[158] Discussed again by the conference of governors in 1913, the problem was presented to Congress in 1915 and again in 1923. Although supported by the American Bar Association, prominent churches, and leading women's clubs, federal action was not achieved.

Probably never before did so large a proportion of American women strive to keep abreast of the latest fashions in dress. As of yore, the styles were set by Paris, but the models once imported were quickly copied by the wholesale garment makers who brought neat imitations of the new modes within reach of the slenderest pocketbook. Even before the period opened, strong influences were at work to modify the cumbersome costumes of earlier years. The coming of the bicycle and the participation of women in sports put an end to the bustle, and the growing activity of women in business and the professions tended to make the skirt discreetly shorter. In the early years of the century well-dressed women still wore large picture hats set on pompadours artificially enlarged, with tight-sleeved, high-necked blouses and bell-shaped ruffled skirts trailing in the dust. With modifications this style prevailed until 1904, when the waist and skirt were separated and the shirtwaist appeared. This innovation was joyfully received, especially by the outdoor girl, and America's only contribution to fashion, the Gibson girl, with her stiffly starched shirtwaist and dark skirt, flourished for a brief span. By 1908 the unsanitary trains had been eliminated and it was now proper to wear dresses at least an inch from the ground, though the vogue a few years later of the "hobble skirt" seemed to be a backward step. At the same time the massive corsets which had been in vogue in the early years of the century grew simpler and the half-dozen starched petticoats which had hung on them in 1900 decreased to one or two. After many decades women again appeared in a costume which revealed their forms, and with the further shortening of the skirt, about 1915, a serviceable costume for a practical age was at last on its way.[159]

While increased leisure merely gave some women additional time to fritter away, for other women it opened new vistas for self-improvement and community service. Many of them made excellent use of their new leisure in athletic sports, in study, in club activities, and in the social welfare, prohibition, suffrage, and peace movements. The rosy-cheeked "athletic girl" with golf club or tennis racquet, whose picture adorned the magazine covers, had an existence in reality, while women's clubs in the churches and elsewhere throve as never before.

As good a barometer as any of the new women is the growth of the General Federation of Women's Clubs, which through its affiliated clubs embraced a membership of 50,000 in 1898 and had increased to considerably over a million by 1914. Working through its standing committees on art, civics, civil-service reform, conservation, education, home economics, industrial and social conditions, legislation, literature, music, public health, and library extension, the organization did much to assist many excellent movements in an era of rapid change. The more advanced leaders tried to laugh out of existence the old literary study clubs, the president-elect in 1904 urging her followers to drop the study of Dante's *Inferno* "and proceed in earnest to contemplate our own social order."[160] "We have no platform," said the president at the tenth biennial convention in 1910, "unless it is the care of women and children, and the home, the latter meaning the four walls of the city as well as the four walls of brick and mortar," and continued in her address to point out the kind of work which women's clubs had undertaken in behalf of child life and health conservation.[161] In some communities the woman's club was the only organization devoted to civic improvement.[162]

As the participation of women in affairs outside of the home broadened,

The ideal American girl in the first years of the twentieth century was both active and statuesque.

The Queen

their political enfranchisement could not be long delayed. Already by the close of the nineteenth century the chief inequalities in civil status had been removed in most of the states. Differences still remained. In general, the status of women was higher in those states where they took an active part in public affairs. Thus Colorado, the second state to obtain equal suffrage, more clearly recognized sex equality whereas the Southern states were by far the most backward in this respect, with Louisiana, still dominated by the old French civil code, bringing up the rear. In that commonwealth the husband received the dowry, controlled his wife's earnings, and was legal guardian of the children; his wife being unable to appear in court, to be an executor, or to execute business pertaining to her own estate without his authorization.[163] The age of consent was still as low as ten years in Georgia and Mississippi although in most of the states it had been raised to sixteen or eighteen.[164] In certain states women were not admitted to the bar or to the practice of medicine, and in some, even at the close of the period, married women had little or no control over property or earnings, and their legal position as respects control of children was inferior to that of the father.[165] Yet even in the backward states, steady improvement was registered during these years, and the feminist leaders were able to center their efforts on securing equality at the polls.

Although this question had been discussed for almost three quarters of a century, the fruits of the agitation by 1898 seemed very small. Partial suffrage existed, to be sure, for specific purposes in many states, but only four, Wyoming, Colorado, Utah, and Idaho, had granted full political power to women.[166] The leaders of the suffrage movement attributed the slowness of the advance to many causes, such as the opposition of the liquor interests and the low standard of political morality in the eighties and nineties;[167] but more potent than any of these influences was the active hostility of a minority of women and the passive indifference of the great majority of both men and women.

A Frenchman's observation that woman's status had "reached its maximum of progress in the Far West of America, on the shore of the Pacific," was tenable as far as it applied to the suffrage movement in this country.[168] It was in the state of Washington in 1910 that the cause was given a new impetus by the adoption of a suffrage amendment to the constitution, a precedent followed the next years by a hard-won victory in California.[169] In the fall elections of 1912 similar amendments were submitted to the voters of six states. Oregon, with suffrage states on three sides of her, carried the amendment by a small majority; in Kansas, where women had been voting in municipal elections since the Populist uprising of the eighties, victory was easy, while in the new state of Arizona the amendment was carried in every county by a vote of almost two to one.[170]

This success in the Far West was not duplicated in the Midwest. Suffrage advocates twice let victory slip through their fingers in Michigan, the proposal was badly beaten in Wisconsin, while in Ohio other problems of more pressing interest prevented a clear decision on this issue and the amendment was defeated.[171] A bill granting presidential suffrage passed the Illinois legislature in 1913 and was upheld by the state supreme court in 1914. In the latter year suffrage referenda took place in seven states, but in only two, Montana and Nevada, were they successful.[172] Notwithstanding these defeats the number of equal-suffrage states had reached eleven by 1914.

But this progress was too slow for the ardent feminists, whose leaders ascribed their failure in many states to "the mobilization of the foreign vote ... under the direction and probable pay of the liquor interests, and with the collusion of local bipartisan election officials, if not that of state central committees."[173] As a result, they decided to concentrate on the federal government. A federal amendment had, indeed, been pending since 1878, but Congress had shown little interest in it. As late as 1908, Roosevelt had refused to recommend women suffrage to Congress and advised a deputation of workers to "go, get another state."[174] During the next administration, however, a petition of 404,000 signatures was presented to Congress (1910), and headquarters for the Congressional Committee of the National Woman Suffrage Association opened in Washington. In the presidential election of 1912, Taft and Wilson side-stepped the issue, but the Progressive party came out unequivocally for it. Roosevelt, who had admitted in 1911 that he was only "tepidly in favor," now supported it enthusiastically.[175]

During the following months the American suffrage movement began to feel the influence of the more militant English tactics. Alice Paul was given the chairmanship of the Congressional Committee and the full backing of the Association in the organization of a suffrage parade to be held in Washington the day before the inauguration of Wilson.[176] Although the parade was broken up and the participants disgracefully abused by the Washington populace, it was successful in advertising the cause.[177] The hostility of the Washington mob was not a true indication of the status of the movement. The pioneer work had been done and success was in sight. Elizabeth Cady Stanton, who for decades had encountered abuse and ridicule, died full of honor in 1902, and her coworker, Susan B. Anthony, when she laid down the reins of office in 1900, had won worldwide esteem.[178] It was left to their coworkers and successors, Carrie Chapman Catt and Dr. Anna Howard Shaw, to complete the task.

On the very brink of success the suffrage movement had to meet squarely in 1912 the question of tactics. Certain of the leaders, notably Alice Paul, advocated the more militant tactics adopted by their English sisters and the English theory that the party in power should be held accountable, but the majority leaders of the National Woman Suffrage Association under the presidency of Dr. Shaw held that these theories were not applicable to American conditions and ousted Paul from the chairmanship of the

Congressional Committee. Paul, however, had already organized a Congressional Union, which, over the next five years, carried on an aggressive campaign by means of picketing and other methods of publicity, and in the end helped force the Wilson administration to take a definite stand for woman suffrage.[179]

Suffrage agitation occupied so much of the attention of the women leaders chiefly because in most other ways the equality of the sexes was established in law and custom. Colleges of the type of Wellesley, Mt. Holyoke, and Bryn Mawr, brilliantly administered by women executives, were giving collegiate training on a par with the leading colleges for men.[180] The best of the state universities had long since opened their professional schools to women and the great Eastern universities, somewhat grudgingly to be sure, were following their example. Columbia admitted them to the Graduate School of Political Science in 1900, though it was not until 1914 that Pennsylvania allowed women in its medical school, followed in 1916 by Columbia and in 1918 by Harvard. As writers they were turning out their share of the "best sellers" of the period. In some spheres of activity, indeed, women had a clear advantage over men. As school teachers and as social workers they were definitely in possession of the field. If in sculpture, painting and music their participation was less, their influence as arbiters of culture and patrons of the arts seemed often predominant.

CHILDREN'S RIGHTS

IT WAS CHARACTERISTIC of the age that the quest for social justice should embrace children's rights as well as women's rights. Perhaps the shrinking size of the family caused parents to value more highly the individual child, and certainly the teaching of the new psychology tended to place increasing importance upon the years of infancy. Most significant of all, however, was the fact that, while the nation had reached a stage where sufficient wealth was available to give greater opportunities to youth, it was still young enough for the industrious and talented child to achieve a brilliant career. The immigrant himself might not go far, but in a land of hope and opportunity there was nothing to which his children, if properly trained, might not aspire, and this same attitude was prevalent in groups higher up the social and economic scale. A society with its eyes on the future very naturally glorified the child.

A community placing new values on child life could not long overlook the appalling rate of infant mortality with its attendant human suffering. In certain states of civilized America, at the turn of the century, it was found that 160 infants died out of every thousand, and that the death rate for children under five years was one in every twenty.[181] Experts affirmed that probably half of this mortality was preventable, and that the causes, which sprang from unsanitary surroundings, improper food, parental ignorance, and other factors, in part or entirely attributable to poverty, might be greatly lessened. The problem had many ramifications; it extended into the field of labor legislation in laws governing the work of prospective mothers; into the whole question of tenements, tenement-house legislation, and city sanitation; into the problem of the milk supply, the proper feeding of infants, and the instruction of the mother in the care of the child; and into the medical care of mother and child. Indeed, it encompassed the whole range of preventive medicine.

The cities, which surpassed the rural districts in the rate of infant mortality, took the lead in the warfare on death.[182] The pioneer was Rochester, New York, where in 1897, under the direction of Dr. George W. Goler, two milk stations were established in which experiments were carried on, pasteurized milk distributed at cost, and mothers instructed in diet and the proper care of infants. The next step was to obtain a milk supply produced under clean and sanitary conditions. Through a wise intermingling of education and compulsion this was eventually secured in spite of political interference and the opposition of private interests.[183] Following the footsteps of Rochester, most of the large cities worked out milk codes covering various aspects of sanitation, pasteurization, and the number of bacteria per cubic centimeter and made investigations into the source of disease bacteria. Most of them also eventually had milk depots where clean milk, upon a physician's certificate, was sold at or below cost or given away to needy mothers. New York City, especially, after the division of child hygiene was established in 1908, did excellent work. Certain of the states, notably Massachusetts, came to the aid of the cities in requiring commercial milk to have a certain amount of butter fat, in requiring cows to be tuberculin-tested, and in providing for dairy inspection.

As an adjunct of the milk depots many cities established baby clinics where the growth and condition of infants could be regularly checked. Supplementing the clinics was the work of the visiting nurse, by whose means state and private philanthropy was carried into the home and the progress of the baby supervised in its normal environment. The extraordinary success attending the work of the visiting nurses in New York City is indicated by the fact that during four and a half months in 1911 only 1.4 percent of the 16,987 babies under their care died, which was less than half the prevailing rate for the entire city. Other efforts were directed along the lines of prenatal care, first attempted by New York City and by the Woman's Municipal League of Boston in 1908; toward more effective control of midwifery; and toward legislation covering the working conditions of the wage-earning mother. That real progress had been made was shown in Rochester, New York, where the death of children under five years was one third less for the decade following 1897 than for the ten preceding years.[184] The census for the registration area of 1911 showed a decline of 22 percent in the death rate of children under one year for the decade, and a decline of 27 percent for those under five years. Whereas approximately one sixth of the children in the registration area under one year died in 1900, only one eighth died in 1911.

Day nurseries where working mothers might leave their infants had been introduced into the United States as early as 1854, but their rapid extension came after 1897. In that year the Association of Day Nurseries of New York City was founded and in the following year the National Federation of Day Nurseries held its first meeting. Following quite naturally after the day nursery came greater attention to community playgrounds, especially where children's play was responsibly supervised. In 1898, Mayor Quincy of Boston opened twenty schoolyard playgrounds and in the following year New York City through its Board of Education opened thirty-one. By 1910 more than 150 cities reported playgrounds and five years later 432 cities were maintaining a total of 3,294 managed by 2,883 men and 4,624 women.[185] The Playground and Recreation Association of America, organized in 1906, did much to integrate the work of local societies and to extend the movement.

Massachusetts set an example to other states in 1908 by making it compulsory for all cities of over 10,000 to hold a referendum as to whether the municipality should provide at least one public playground for the physical education of the minors of the city, and at least one playground for every additional 20,000 of population.[186] Within a year forty-one out of forty-two cities had voted affirmatively.[187] The impetus for such a law came not solely from the desire to promote amusement and health but also from the hope that juvenile crime might be lessened. Whatever the motives, the supervised city playground was a great success. It might lack the spontaneity and charm of "the old swimmin' hole," but it marked a new era in the recreational life of the city youngster.

As important as the city playgrounds were, they fell far short of solving the entire recreational problem of childhood. The instinct of youth to play together in some sort of club and the necessity of turning the gang energy into useful and constructive activities had not been met. The expanding recreational activities of the Y.M.C.A. were of great value, but it was left to the Scout movement to make the chief contribution in this respect. The Boy Scouts originated in England in 1908 through the work of General Sir Robert S. S. Baden-Powell for the purpose of training boys between twelve and eighteen years in self-reliance, manliness, and good citizenship. Immediately successful in England, the organization was quickly introduced into America where two similar clubs—the Woodcraft Indians, founded by Ernest Thompson-Seton, and the Sons of Daniel Boone, founded by Dan C. Beard—coalesced in 1910 to form the Boy Scouts of America and received in that year a charter under the laws of the District of Columbia. These

American forerunners and the phenomenal growth which the organization quickly experienced indicate that one underlying explanation for its success was the desire to restore to American youth the normal experiences of earlier generations of boys.

With almost unanimous backing, including interdenominational church support, and with an undeniable appeal to youth, the Boy Scouts speedily became the preeminent boys' organization of the country, numbering at the end of 1913 about 8,000 scout masters, representing as many organizations, and approximately 300,000 members. The oath of the organization was a promise made by each scout "to do my duty to God and my country" and "to help other people at all times," and the three classes of the order were based upon accomplishments in woodcraft and in various useful activities pertaining to outdoor life.[188] Although the Scout movement was quite democratic, its greatest work was done among the children of the middle and upper classes rather than among the poor and potentially delinquent children of the cities. It, however, brought into its membership the children of many immigrants whose instruction in Indian lore and woodcraft science constitutes perhaps the most curious episode in the current Americanization movement.

The undoubted success of the Boy Scouts resulted in an organization designed to do much the same thing for girls. The Campfire Girls, founded in 1912 by Dr. and Mrs. Luther Gulick, not only served to promote the health of girls by outdoor life but to instill thrift and other excellent qualities among them as well as to develop an interest in the technique of the homely tasks of everyday life. Quite similar were the Girl Scouts founded in the same year by Juliette Low. Their growth was slower than the boys' organization, but they steadily gained in favor.

In its various phases child labor had existed in America from the earliest times, but it did not become a serious menace until the later decades of the nineteenth century when increasing numbers of children were caught in the toils of the spreading factory system. By 1900 the number under sixteen engaged in gainful occupations was at least 1.7 million, and some students of the child-labor problem placed the figure even higher.[189] The majority (60 percent) were agricultural workers who labored under conditions that might not be deleterious, but the reports that came in of the twelve-hour day in the berry fields of New Jersey, of the congestion, overwork, and immorality among the young workers in the vegetable gardens of Delaware and Maryland, the beet-sugar fields of Michigan, Nebraska, and Colorado, and the tobacco fields and stripping farms of Connecticut, Kentucky, Virginia, and Pennsylvania were anything but encouraging.[190]

The worst conditions, however, prevailed in manufacturing in which about 16 percent of the child workers were engaged. The picture of children kept awake during the long night in a Southern mill by having cold water dashed on their faces, of little girls in canning factories "snipping" sixteen or more hours a day or capping forty cans a minute in an effort to keep pace with a never exhausted machine, of little ten-year-old breaker boys crouched for ten hours a day over a dusty coal chute to pick sharp slate out of the fast-moving coal, of boys imported from orphan asylums and reformatories to wreck their bodies in the slavery of a glass factory, or of a four-year-old baby toiling until midnight over artificial flowers in a New York tenement—these were conditions which might well shame a civilized people into action.[191] "Capital has neither morals nor ideals," cried a Socialist critic in 1906; in the United States of the twentieth century it "calls for children as loudly as it called in England a century ago."[192]

The state laws relating to child labor adopted during these years generally fixed a minimum age limit, prohibited certain employments as dangerous to health and morals, limited the hours a child under a certain age might work, and, in many cases, fixed an educational requirement which must be met before children could be released for labor. By 1914 every state but one had some minimum age limit, varying from twelve years in several Southern states to fifteen years in South Dakota and sixteen in Montana. At least twenty-one states had restricted the working day for children in factories to eight hours, and some had extended the limit to other occupations, though ten hours was the usual maximum. A majority of the states prohibited children and young persons from certain occupations and over half of the states forbade night work under a specified age. A majority also made some effort to ensure literacy before the child could be put to work. Certainly the decade which closed with the year 1914 marked a tremendous progress in child-labor legislation. Unfortunately, however, many states still lacked adequate regulations, and even such advanced states as Massachusetts, Illinois, and New York failed effectively to enforce the excellent laws which had been passed. Child labor in 1914 was still a problem and plenty of opportunity remained for the efforts of the Child Labor Committee.[193]

Dilatory as had been the nation in attacking the curse of child labor, it had not failed to appreciate the importance of education. Like other phases of American civilization, education, as it developed during the lifetime of this generation, was the result of numerous and intricate forces long in the making. The industrialization and urbanization of the nation, accompanied as it was by the inundation of millions of immigrants, opened new opportunities to the city schools, but at the same time staggered them by the complexity of the task. The declining influence of the church upon the home and the relaxation of parental discipline raised the question of the role of the school as a moral mentor, while the living conditions of the crowded slums obliged the school to contribute to the solution of such problems as recreation, hygiene, and health. While the needs of a changing civilization forced educational leaders to wrestle with the question of methods and curricula, a rapidly expanding school system confronted civic authorities with problems of architecture and finance. At the opening of our period the American people were more than ever convinced that the hope of democracy rested largely upon a free, tax-supported public-school system, but as to the lines along which it should develop there was wide divergence of opinion.

Educational philosophy in 1898 was decidedly in flux. Most influential in pointing out the direction which the new education would take was John Dewey, for some years head of the School of Education at the University of Chicago and after 1904 professor of philosophy at Columbia University. Following the new psychology in stressing the importance of early environment and training, and holding to the belief that the public school was the chief remedy for the ills of society, Dewey argued that social efficiency and not mere knowledge was the aim of education. To obtain this social efficiency the activities of the school must be closely connected with real life, and the education of the child must go beyond book learning and include play, the use of tools, contact with nature, and the development of personal expression. The school was a place where the child should learn life by living life.[194]

That one of America's leading philosophers devoted his chief efforts and interest to the field of education was of incalculable benefit during this important period of development, but his influence would have been limited without the aid which came from the psychological and other scientific research which played continuously upon the problem of education. Fortunate likewise was the fact that America's foremost psychologists were primarily interested in education. The books of William James in the early nineties embodied "an earnest and direct and scientific attack on the scholastic psychology" then existing;[195] G. Stanley Hall's monumental studies of adolescence marked a milestone in educational psychological research; while Edward L. Thorndike in his *Educational Psychology* (1903) went far to subject old conceptions of education to the acid test of scientific psychology and to open new fields for research. At all events Dewey's philosophy of modern education together with the work of the new psychology was warmly accepted by trained educators, and deeply influenced the trend of twentieth-century educational reform. Henry Adams's cynical observation that "the chief wonder of education is that it does not ruin everybody concerned in it, teachers and taught," was certainly less applicable in the year 1914 than it had been at the beginning of the period.[196]

While philosophers and pedagogues struggled to evolve a more intelligent system of instruction, the nation carried on with unprecedented enthusiasm a program of educational expansion. The children in elementary schools increased between 1898 and 1914 from less than 16 million to more than 20 million while the registration in high schools and colleges more than doubled.[197] For every day of the calendar years between 1890 and 1918 one public high school was established, and the total high school pupils per thousand of population rose from less than five to more than seventeen, and the increase was to gather momentum in the years which followed.[198]

Especially striking was the advance in the South where the states, says Cubberley, "experienced the greatest educational awakening in their history—an awakening to be compared with that of Mann in Massachusetts and Barnard in Connecticut and Rhode Island."[199] Active campaigns for better schools were generally promoted, beginning in North Carolina in 1902, in Virginia in 1903, in Tennessee and Georgia in 1904, and soon spread to the states of the Lower South. Improvement appeared in many ways: the educational provisions of the constitutions and laws were revised and strengthened; school revenues doubled or trebled in a single decade; the enrollment of white children increased almost a third between 1898 and 1914. Impetus was also given to the development of high schools— hitherto neglected by the South—which now, for the first time, came to be accepted by the rural communities as an integral part of the state school system. Though most of the Southern commonwealths continued to lag behind their sister states, the remarkable educational progress after 1898 both in quality and quantity may be regarded as nationwide. In spite of this advance it was disturbing to note that in 1914 the average number of years (of 200 days) of schooling received by the American youth was but 6.16.[200]

The most important feature of the educational system, if judged by the number of pupils directly touched, remained the elementary school. Twenty times as many students attended the early grades as found their way into the high school and the instruction at these lower levels continued to be the only formal education received by well over 90 percent of American youth. Though buttressed by compulsory-attendance laws in two thirds of the states and hailed as the bulwark of democracy, the elementary school at the opening of the century still had wide room for improvement.[201] The average child attended for perhaps 68 days out of a 143-day year a one-room school where he was taught formal subjects in a mechanical manner by a young woman who had had little if any training beyond the elementary grades and whose services were valued at the munificent sum of around $38 a month.[202] The situation by 1914 was far better: the school year had been lengthened to 158.7 days, the average attendance to 86.7 days, and the salaries of women teachers to approximately $66.

More encouraging than the lengthening of the school term was the general improvement apparent. As never before, elementary education was being subjected to scientific study by the teachers and students of the great graduate schools of education, which became veritable laboratories of educational research and experiment. At the same time large amounts of concrete data were accumulated by surveys of educational systems. Chicago led the way in 1897, Cleveland followed in 1906, and their example was soon emulated by several states and numerous cities.[203] An effort was made to raise the educational qualifications of elementary teachers, which were surprisingly low.[204] That real progress was made was indicated by the slightly higher standards set by some states, the establishment of teachers' training classes in high schools, and by the growth and improvement of normal schools.[205] The cities, as usual, showed the chief gains, but the rural districts too shared in the advance, particularly in the tendency to combine scattered district schools into one union school with a better-equipped building, more highly trained teachers, and division into grades. Great impetus was given this movement by the rapid improvement of roads and the increasing use of motor buses.

Even more important in the field of elementary education was the modification of the curriculum. Music, drawing, domestic science, manual and physical training, which since the 1880s had been gradually pushing their way into the schools, were now adopted with real enthusiasm. These practical subjects fitted in with the pragmatic philosophy of the time, and it was Dewey's great contribution to rationalize and popularize these changes. Perhaps the most interesting experiment along the line of the newer education was that made at Gary, Indiana, by William A. Wirt. Forced in a rapidly growing industrial center to economize in space and money, Wirt worked out a scheme for a school plant which contained not only classrooms but playgrounds, gardens, workshops, a library, and a social center. Specialization of instruction and departmental instruction running through the grades; outdoor activities and shop work carried on at the same time as the indoor classes, thus doubling the capacity; the holding of school in all seasons of the year; the use of the plant in the evening for continuation schools and as a social and recreational center—these were some of the features which attracted the attention of administrators seeking to curtail expenses and students of education looking for improved methods.[206]

The doubling between 1898 and 1914 of the number of high schools and of the enrollment of students shows clearly that the American taxpayer accepted the high school as an essential community obligation and as necessary to the success of the democracy. The private secondary schools might continue to attract the children of the wealthy, but they were declining in relative importance,[207] and there were now few cities or towns which did not support a high school. The high school of the nineteenth century had been largely dominated by the idea of training for college, but this old conception, already yielding in the 1890s, declined rapidly with the new century as it came more directly under popular influence and as the followers of Wirt and Dewey gained greater recognition. Old courses were made more flexible and new ones added. Before 1898 commercial and home-economics courses were almost the only nonacademic training provided in high schools, but after that date vocational training of many kinds was introduced, including instruction in agriculture, industry, trade, and commerce. In the larger cities, high schools devoted to commerce and mechanics were established. At the same time some of the older courses, such as those in Greek, geology, and astronomy, began to be dropped. While the extraordinary growth of high schools showed an insistence upon an opportunity for all to get a higher education, the simultaneous development of vocational training indicated a conviction that not all were capable of achieving it.

Though the number of colleges and universities, exclusive of junior colleges, slightly declined between 1893 and 1916, the students in attendance increased threefold, and the financial support fivefold. This remarkable showing was due in part to the normal growth in population and wealth, and in part to the exuberant belief, stimulated by the marvelous development of the high school, that "not only should college education be open to everybody, but that nearly everybody should have it."[208] In 1914 one in every twenty-five of the population between nineteen and twenty-three years was attending college, a considerable increase over the figures of 1898.[209] Although the inundation of students was not nearly so rapid in the years previous to World War I as in the years following,[210] it was sufficient not only to influence the curricula but also to convince even enthusiastic devotees of democracy that many who entered college were debarred by lack of interest or innate mental limitations from achieving much of value.

To meet the demand of the throngs pressing at their gates, colleges and universities widened and subdivided their graduate and professional courses. Although every aspiring university at the opening of the century already embraced a wide variety of specialized colleges and "schools," their number tended to grow rather than lessen during these years. Especially notable was the multiplication of colleges of education, organized under the stimulus of state laws requiring additional professional training of prospective teachers. Equally noteworthy was the establishment of schools of journalism for which the proprietor of the *New York World,* Joseph Pulitzer, set the pattern when he announced in 1903 that he would bequeath to Columbia University $1 million to build and endow such a college. The Pulitzer school at Columbia was opened in 1912 and was quickly followed elsewhere by similar experiments.

Even more significant perhaps was the rapid rise of the business college connected with the college or university. For years, instruction in typewriting, stenography, and rudimentary business knowledge had been given by private agencies and to some extent by the public high schools, but with the exception of the Wharton School of the University of Pennsylvania scarcely any university had entered the field. Now, responding to the commercial trend of the times, colleges generally began what they called the process of "professionalizing business." This was done by combining some of the more "practical" studies of the old liberal-arts curriculum with courses on economics and business and calling the result a professional school. When the oldest of American colleges gave birth in 1908 to the Harvard Graduate School of Business Administration, the odor of exalted respectability invested the new movement. It had yet to receive the stamp of approval of big business, but this came fifteen years later in a gift to Harvard of $5 million from the aged George F. Baker. The business college by 1914 had not yet subordinated the higher learning to a secondary position, but its growing importance was causing alarm among upholders of the older academic traditions.

For the great universities the period was one of change and expansion. Woodrow Wilson (1902-10) strongly but unsuccessfully opposed the establishment of a graduate school at Princeton isolated from the undergraduate institution, and at the same time sought to improve the grade of the undergraduate work by the introduction of the preceptorial system.[211] Nicholas Murray Butler of Columbia (1902-45), who ran "the University with the nonchalance and efficiency of the head of a railroad system or a department store, combined with the ideals of a philosopher," saw grow up around him some of the strongest graduate schools in the country, including perhaps the foremost social science faculty of the period and the greatest college of education.[212] Charles R. Van Hise of Wisconsin, although president (1903-18) of the university which above all others had allied itself with the life of its state, at the same time upheld the highest ideals of scholarship and defended his liberal professors from the onslaughts of reactionary politicians. At Michigan, James Burrill Angell (1871-1907) developed a great institution which set a standard for the state university, while at Chicago, Harry Pratt Judson (1907-23), building on the money of Rockefeller and the genius of Harper, was carrying on educational experiments which rivaled Columbia and was expanding the facilities with a like rapidity. For decades the intellectual freshness of Eliot had prevented stagnation at Harvard, and his successor, A. Lawrence Lowell (1909-33), signalized his administration by the introduction of the tutorial system and the general-examination plan. Ably led, generously supported by gifts and state appropriations, with the democracy pressing at their gates, the universities found the years following 1898 a period of rapid growth and educational achievement.

That there were unfortunate and even dangerous tendencies at work, however, few leading educators would deny. One resulted from the fact that the ultimate control of American colleges had come to rest in a board of trustees, regents, or fellows, composed usually of clergymen, lawyers, and businessmen who conducted the institution through their agent or employee, the college president. In the last analysis this meant that the policies were often determined by outsiders, noneducators, and representatives of the capitalistic interests, a situation which sometimes existed even in the state universities where the legislatures were likely to be dominated by big business or bad politics. In too many instances the result was interference with the academic freedom of those teachers whose economic or social philosophy was liberal. According to one trenchant critic, there was substituted for the old rule of the clergy that "of business men and politicians; which amounts to saying that it is a substitution of business men." [213] It seemed as if almost any economic heterodoxy might result in dismissal though it is only fair to record that the dismissed professor was usually able to secure appointment elsewhere.

The most famous breach of academic freedom occurred at the University of Pennsylvania where the appointment of Professor Scott Nearing, a brilliant and extraordinarily successful teacher, was terminated because, according to the trustees, "his efforts . . . although doubtless perfectly sincere . . . were so consistently misunderstood by the public and by many parents," the "misunderstood" efforts being his advanced social and economic ideas. [214] Even more astonishing was the demand for the resignation of Willard Clark Fisher, for twenty years professor of economics at Wesleyan University, Connecticut, because of an incidental utterance on churchgoing and Sunday observance made in an address, not intended for publication, before a literary club at Hartford. The official reason for his resignation was so absurdly flimsy that those acquainted with the situation were quick to ascribe the real cause to the professor's advocacy of social legislation and his strong position in state progressive politics. [215] The desire to counteract such invasions of academic freedom was one of the causes which led in November 1914 to a call for the organization of the American Association of University Professors to represent the "common interests of the teaching staffs" and consider "the general problems of University policy." [216]

Why was it that the conspicuous cases of dismissal were of professors who were critics of the economic order? Some explanation for the horror with which college trustees looked upon unconventional economic views may perhaps be found in the vast sums which millionaires were contributing to higher education. The enlargement of endowments and college plants was well-nigh universal during the early years of the century, but the philanthropy which had perhaps the most important nationwide influence resulted from the foundation in 1902 of the General Education Board by John D. Rockefeller. Incorporated by Congress in 1903, its object was set forth as "the promotion of education within the United States of America, without distinction of race, sex, or creed." [217] To this foundation Rockefeller gave before 1909 approximately $53 million, of which $13.5 went to the University of Chicago, over $10 million to the Rockefeller Institute for Medical Research, and approximately $16 million to various other activities initiated by the board. These last included endowments to colleges usually on condition that a similar amount be raised, contributions to medical schools, gifts to black education, and cooperation with federal and state agencies in the betterment of secondary education and the carrying out of farm demonstrations. The board was particularly interested in improving the backward educational conditions in the South, and its policy of "cooperation, not interference" had a helpful and stimulating effect wherever it was tried.[218] Gifts of this type not only encouraged other millionaires to contribute in a similar way but induced state and municipal authorities to be more liberal in their educational appropriations.

When the balance sheet is drawn, however, it is clear that the chief educational gains of the period fell to the younger generation. To them also, as we have seen, came other substantial benefits, cultural and physical. Never before had collective childhood been so much the center of the American scene, never before so important a concern of public policy. To a bewildered European visitor it seemed that "children reign supreme in the United States."[219] Yet the record shows that this generation did not succeed in doing all it set out to accomplish, and its unfinished task it had to pass on to its successors.

RELIGION AND REFORM

FOR AMERICAN CHRISTIANITY the years following 1898 fairly bristled with problems. The immense tide of foreign immigration flooding the cities, the extraordinary mobility of population, the draining of rural districts and the abandonment of country churches, and the difficulties of financing new churches, hospitals, schools, and other similar projects in a period of rapid growth created situations which taxed the enthusiasm and skill of religious leadership to the utmost.[220] The Sunday newspaper, Sunday excursions, Sunday ball games, and Sunday moving pictures crowded in to break the erstwhile Sabbath monopoly of the church. Pastors who a few years earlier denounced Sabbath breaking in sermons on such themes as "You cannot serve God and skylark on a bicycle" now had greater competition in the automobile and the golf course.[221]

In meeting these new problems American Christianity displayed striking resourcefulness and virility. Though science continued to give opportunity for theological exegesis and doctrinal controversy, religious leaders wisely turned their attention from these interesting topics to the role the church must play in the new society. Religious activities were directed in many new channels, both social and political. While still maintaining and enlarging the schools, colleges, hospitals, orphanages, and relief organizations typical of the nineteenth century, the church entered actively into the campaign for reform measures, carrying out its own projects for social redemption and participating frequently in politics. The hand of the church seemed everywhere. Its membership increased by approximately 16 million between 1900 and 1914, an advance which can be explained in large measure by its willingness to face squarely the problems of the new day.[222]

Of the growth in membership the Roman Catholic Church was the chief beneficiary. One half of its 5 million new adherents were immigrants from Italy, Austria-Hungary, and other Catholic countries, who tended to concentrate in the great industrial centers of New England, the Middle Atlantic states, Illinois, Wisconsin, and Michigan.[223]

The prestige of the American church was undoubtedly strengthened in 1908 when the pope removed it from the supervision of the missionary department (Congregation of Propaganda), thereby giving it complete ecclesiastical status, and by the creation of three new American cardinals in 1911.[224] The church was particularly fortunate in its leader, the scholarly Cardinal Gibbons, whose enthusiasm for the American Constitution and endorsement of the separation of church and state gave a distinctly national trend to the American branch of his church.[225]

Among the Protestant churches the Methodist group with its seventeen bodies or offshoots continued to rank as the most powerful denomination, but neither its growth of nearly 2 million communicants nor the increase of the Baptists or Lutherans was as rapid as that of the Catholics.[226] The most notable Protestant gains were made in the South, where every state but four showed a greater increase in communicants than in population. The Southern Protestant advance was to no small extent due to black accessions, for their number of communicants grew 40 percent in the two decades 1890–1910, while the race as a whole increased but 31 percent. As a social and intellectual factor the church was undoubtedly declining in certain Protestant communities in the Northeast, but in 1914 in the rural districts of the South and West it was still playing a role hardly less important than in seventeenth-century colonial New England.

Three tendencies in American Christianity during the early years of the period are clearly discernible: a trend toward church unity, a further liberalizing of theology, and an increasing emphasis upon social work and political reform. Interrelated as these influences were, each strengthened the other, with the result that Protestant Christianity was distinctly modified. Practical considerations as well as a softening of theological differences aided the movement toward unity, particularly in the rural districts where denominational splits and the keen religious rivalry of earlier decades had left an oversupply of churches. Many communities which a half-century earlier could support several churches were now barely able to keep one alive. Decline in economic prosperity, the drain of population to the cities or to the West, immigration which replaced Protestants by Catholics, the decline of sectarianism and the development of the community spirit—these and many other influences led to the pooling of the remaining resources in fewer units. A careful survey during the years 1922–25 disclosed 977 united churches in town and country in the Northern and Western states, the majority organized after 1900. These churches included a number of types: federated churches, interdenominational churches, and denominational united churches; but whatever the name, they represented an impressive decline in sectarian spirit.[227]

This tendency toward cooperation would have been impossible without some softening of the harsh lines which had separated the Protestant denominations. The old-fashioned theology had never recovered from the staggering blow dealt to it by the evolutionary hypothesis and the higher criticism,[228] and each new discovery in the realm of science served to put it increasingly on the defensive in spite of the continued efforts of learned men to reconcile science and the old religion.[229] In America the higher criticism was centered primarily in the theological seminaries. Union Theological Seminary, associated with Columbia, and the Chicago University Divinity School went over wholeheartedly to the new theology; Andover, which had been founded in 1808 to counteract the Unitarianism of Harvard, gave up the struggle to be orthodox and returned to Cambridge just 100 years later, where it was soon absorbed by the Harvard Divinity School.[230] Conservatism at the seminaries of the Episcopalians at Cambridge, of the Congregationalists at Hartford, and of the Presbyterians at Princeton was pretty well forced to the wall, while even those time-honored bulwarks of the old theology, the Methodist seminaries, Drew and Garrett, were rapidly crumbling before the onslaught of the new views. From the centers of advanced theological thinking a constant stream of students went forth to man the pulpits of the nation, young men sympathetic with a more liberal theology and willing to lead in the transition. They found in their pews some communicants who through college courses had come to eye critically certain of the old beliefs,[231] but the great majority continued to be more orthodox than their pastors, and, as a natural consequence, tended in most cases to exert a dampening influence on their liberal aspirations.

This modernist trend, although strong in certain circles, was not universally approved. The great mass of churchgoers, whether in city or country, knew little and cared less about it. The average pew holder, living in a hurried and nervous age, wanted a shorter sermon and one unencumbered with theology. Conservative by nature, he was willing to accept the old dogma if it was presented in an attractive form and, as a consequence, services tended to become shorter and more ornate. Furthermore, the new theology, strong as it might be in the scholastic corridors of a metropolitan seminary, hardly penetrated the great hinterland. Here the old doctrine was fervently preached and here evangelism was revamped to suit a rapidly moving age. There had been just enough of sensationalism in the meetings of Moody and Sankey to give them spice,[232] but the methods of those evangelists were mild in comparison with the "high-pressure" tactics used by their successors. The best known of them was William A. ("Billy") Sunday, an ex-baseball player and ordained Presbyterian clergyman, whose circus antics, free use of slang, and general disregard of dignified pulpit procedure attracted large numbers of curious people to his exciting services. Sunday was only one of scores of traveling evangelists who succeeded in maintaining a "spiritual ferment" in the small towns and rural regions of America and who aimed to confound the cunning emissaries of Satan turned out by the theological schools.[233]

Roaring evangelists, soft-voiced teachers of peace, prosperity, and plenty, and Oriental swamis sitting in silent mystery attracted the attention of the casual observer of religious institutions; but the rank and file of the people were little affected, and invoked still the faith of their fathers. Even here, however, new forces were at work. Nineteenth-century theology had been essentially orthodox and religion essentially personal, but a rapidly changing economic and social order called for both a theology less unbending and a church with a more versatile technique. That organized religion was able to maintain itself during this period of readjustment was due in part to a willingness to desert the older methods and face squarely the new social problems, and in part to a willingness to place the emphasis upon the social teachings of Christ. First in the cities, and later in all types of communities, the churches interested themselves in social work, educational activities, and benefit societies. They extended their activities to include the physical and intellectual as well as the purely spiritual welfare of mankind.

The first decided change in the official attitude of the church toward social reform is apparent in its attitude toward the labor movement. The struggle of organized labor for more humane conditions had met with little sympathy from the church and many labor leaders had come to denounce the church as "organized hypocrisy" and an "ally of capital," and considered it hostile to their aspirations.[234] In an effort to break down this antipathy, the Protestant Episcopal Church as early as 1887 had established a Church Association for the Advancement of the Interests of Labor,[235] but its example was not followed until 1901 when the National Council of the Congregational Churches appointed a labor committee, known after 1904 as the Industrial Committee, to study such questions as organized labor, child labor, immigration and socialism, and at its national meeting in 1904 urged its churches "to take a deeper interest in the labor question, and to get a more intelligent understanding of the aims of organized labor."[236] To the same end the Presbyterian Church established in 1903 a department of church and labor under the board of home missions, placing at its head Charles Stelzle, a clergyman who had served an apprenticeship at the machinist's trade.[237] At its general conference in 1908 the Methodist Episcopal Church likewise took an affirmative stand, recognizing

> that the organization of labor is not only the right of laborers and conducive to their welfare, but is incidentally of great benefit to society at large in the securing of better conditions of work and life, in its educational influence

upon the great multitude concerned and particularly in the Americanization of our immigrant population,

and in the episcopal address definitely advocated child-labor legislation, workingmen's compensation, and other reforms.[238]

Taking its cue from this Methodist conference of 1908, the Federal Council from the outset advocated such far-reaching measures as the protection of the worker from dangerous machinery and occupational diseases, the abolition of child labor, the suppression of the sweating system, the reduction of the work day, the six-day week, a living wage, workers' compensation, old-age insurance, and "the most equitable division of the products of industry that can ultimately be devised."[239] If these declarations meant anything, it appeared that the strength of organized Protestantism had definitely allied itself with the labor movement.[240]

Other evidences also appeared. In many cities the ministerial associations appointed "fraternal delegates" to the city central labor union, and in 1905 the American Federation of Labor at its Pittsburgh meeting reciprocated by recommending that its state and city bodies follow this example wherever practical.[241] In the theological seminaries "practical theology" and home missions were stressed as never before; courses in "Christian Sociology" were widely introduced and some effort was made to prepare prospective ministers to become "social engineers."[242] What organized religion could do for the laboring classes in a definite way and in a restricted area was demonstrated by Stelzle in 1910 when he took over an old church about to close at the corner of Fourteenth Street and Second Avenue in New York and speedily made it a humming center of community interest and social service.[243]

The increasing interest of the church in social problems was not accomplished without a certain amount of the same type of muckraking which had brought improved conditions elsewhere. Ray Stannard Baker in a series of articles on "The Spiritual Unrest" pointed out the estrangement between the church and large classes of the population and accused it of failure to grasp its great opportunities.[244] Charles Edward Russell scathingly attacked Trinity Church of New York for the miserable tenements which it owned. "I have tramped the Eighth Ward day after day with a list of Trinity properties in my hand," he declared, "and of all the tenement houses that stand there on Trinity land, I have not found one that is not a disgrace to civilization and to the city of New York."[245] A widely read series in *McClure's* on Christian Science marked the climax of popular attack upon that religion,[246] and a new outburst of denunciation against Mormonism and its economic and political power occurred in 1910.[247] A powerful plea for a new evaluation of Christ's teachings was made in fiction by Winston Churchill in *The Inside of the Cup* (1913), and on the stage by such plays as Charles Rann Kennedy's *The Servant in the House* (1908) and the English drama, Jerome K. Jerome's *The Passing of the Third Floor Back* (1909).

The new attitude of the church represented but a small part of the contribution of Christianity to the movement for social welfare. From the churches, as earlier, came the chief support for temperance and prohibition, for the movement for social purity, for the Salvation Army, the Young Men's and Young Women's Christian associations, and numerous other social and philanthropic organizations; and it was from the churches that the social workers themselves emanated. No public question so greatly affected the problem of moral standards and conduct with which the religious minded were concerned as that involving the liquor traffic. After more than a half century of agitation only five states were legally dry in 1898—Kansas, Maine, North Dakota, New Hampshire, and Vermont—and of these the last two were to revert to local option in 1903. This situation, however, by no means reflected the true strength of the movement. Quite apart from the effects of drinking on the drinker, the liquor business was in bad repute as a prolific source of political corruption. Roosevelt, for example, asserted that "more than half of the political leaders in Tammany Hall have at one time or another been in the liquor business."[248] Although the saloon was called the "poor man's club" and admittedly supplied "a legitimate want in the life of the workingman,"[249] it was so widely denounced as the ally of every evil interest that even the liquor manufacturers agreed it needed reformation.[250] Temperance agitation had advanced beyond the stage of freak reform and now received support from the most conservative sources. An increasing number of thoughtful people were convinced that the consumption of alcoholic beverages was physically and economically wasteful, and therefore the best interest of the nation would be served by its elimination.

Although the prohibition movement commanded a growing support from employers demanding sober workmen and the backing of social reformers who believed it essential in their warfare on prostitution, disease, poverty, and other ills, its chief impetus came from organized religion. Each of the leading denominations, including the Catholic Church, had its temperance committee or abstinence society,[251] but the brunt of the battle was borne by three organizations: the Temperance Society of the Methodist Episcopal Church, the Women's Christian Temperance Union, and the Anti-Saloon League. Though the Methodist Church had been somewhat late in its hearty espousal of prohibition,[252] by 1912 its official representatives were asserting that "all the woes of perdition lurk in the bar-room" and that "the liquor traffic cannot be legalized without sin."[253] Eventually the Temperance Society of that church moved its headquarters to Washington where its lobby became almost as powerful as that of the Anti-Saloon League. "We must realize," said a leading liquor organ in 1914, "that the entire Methodist Church is a solidified, active, aggressive and obedient unit in this war on our trade."[254] The same year the secretary of the Liquor Dealers' Association asserted, "It is only necessary to read the list of those preachers who are active in the present propaganda for legislative prohibition to realize that it is the Methodist Church which is obsessed with the ambition to gain control of the government."[255] Such statements, however, did less than justice to the other two groups.

Quite as ardent in the cause was the Woman's Christian Temperance Union (W.C.T.U.) which, in 1898, after a quarter-century of activity, claimed 10,000 local branches and a membership, including affiliated societies of children, of well-nigh half a million. One of its unique achievements had been the introduction into the nation's schools of antialcoholic propaganda, in the form of "scientific temperance" instruction, at public expense.[256] Even more effective in its practical measures was the American Anti-Saloon League, a union of several state leagues and local organizations formed in 1893. Essentially a religious organization, it insisted that it was not a rival of any sectarian league but was simply engaged in coordinating the work of militant Christianity and directing the legislative battle. Eyed coldly by the Catholic Church, whose leaders eventually repudiated it, but tepidly supported by the Episcopalians[257] and Lutherans, its chief backing came from the remaining Protestant denominations whose churches were opened to League exhorters and whose membership was urged to contribute to the movement. The Anti-Saloon League became "the Church in Action." It was the spearhead of the militant movement.

Ably led by men of the type of Wayne B. Wheeler and William H. Anderson, who had mastered every detail of political action, its methods were quite as sophisticated and much more successful than those of its opponents.[258] It set out to do two things and in the end accomplished both: first, like the W.C.T.U., to convince a majority of the American people that the drinking of alcoholic liquors was morally wrong, and, second, to organize the sentiment of rural Protestantism to ban the liquor trade by political means, a method made possible by the "rotten-borough" system existing in the state and federal governments.[259] Within a decade after its organization the League had a budget of $400,000 a year with 100 well-equipped business offices, a staff of 500 employees, and a reputation so deadly that politicians feared it as the plague.[260]

The fruits of a century of prohibition agitation were at last to be garnered, and the first harvest was to be in the South, where the desire to remove strong drink from the blacks, the willingness to curtail the political power of the liquor trade, and the belief that economic efficiency would be promoted may have played as prominent a part as moral motives in bringing success. Georgia took statewide action in 1907, Alabama in 1907 (wet again 1911–15), Mississippi and North Carolina in 1908, West Virginia in 1912, Virginia two years later, and Arkansas and South Carolina in 1915. The movement now swung to the Middle and Far West. Statewide prohibition was voted in 1914 in Arizona, Colorado, Oregon, and Washington, to go into effect during 1915 or 1916, and the legislatures of Idaho and Utah by statute sought to make their respective states dry by January 1, 1916. It was certain that by that day at least nineteen states would be officially dry, with an excellent prospect that others would fall into line in the succeeding years.[261]

The extension of statewide prohibition, however, did not measure the full success of the movement. Local option, when state prohibition was impossible, had by 1914 largely dried up rural America.[262] The last stronghold of the liquor interests was in the cities. There they were so heavily entrenched that the League, convinced that nationwide prohibition could be obtained only through federal action, exerted increasing pressure upon Washington. The government's liquor policy in Alaska and on the Indian reservations was carefully watched, bills to control liquor more effectively in the District of Columbia were introduced, and on March 1, 1913, the Webb-Kenyon bill was passed over the veto of President Taft.[263] Its purpose was to prohibit the shipment of intoxicating liquors into any state, territory, or district where they were intended to be used in violation of the local law. It marked the first important federal victory of the League. In spite of the delicate constitutional questions involved in the bill itself and in the supporting state legislation, the rapidity with which it was passed over President Taft's veto and the numerous judicial decisions supporting both it and the state legislation demonstrate with great certainty the growth of the movement. The prohibition forces through Senator Morris Sheppard and Representative Hobson presented their first resolution in December 1913 to provide for national prohibition by constitutional amendment, only to have it die in committee. The following year it actually reached the floor but failed of the two-thirds vote. The prohibitionists were forced to wait until America's entrance into the war offered a new opportunity.

SOURCES OF CULTURE

MORE IMPORTANT than the discoveries of scientists and scholars in shaping the cultural background of America, more important even than the public-school system, was the influence of the newspapers and low-priced magazines. The "little red schoolhouse" might teach the youngster how to read and write, but it was the periodical press that provided reading matter for the great majority. "Yes, sir," commented Mr. Dooley, "th' hand that rocks th' fountain pen is th' hand that rules th' wurruld,"[264] and this seemed increasingly evident as the newspapers enlarged their size, the magazines lowered their price, and the popular fiction came more and more to deal with the problems of everyday life. The basic mechanical inventions which went to make the modern newspaper—the high-speed power press, the linotype, the typewriter, and the telephone—had all appeared before 1898, but their technique was improved and their scope widened to meet the needs of a more complex civilization. With the new century also came the wireless, the printing telegraph machine, the motor truck, and other inventions which facilitated the collection of news and speeded its distribution.

While the mechanical processes for printing huge editions were being perfected, editors and publishers were ever on the alert to catch new readers. The great cooperative news-gathering agencies—the Associated Press Association and the Scripps-McRae Press Association, both dating from the 1890s—steadily increased the efficiency of their service, and were joined in 1906 by the International News Service, organized by the Hearst papers. Well-written news items proved less effective in swelling subscription lists than attractive "feature" articles and special departments designed to cater to a wide variety of interests. Under the new impulse the Sunday edition became little less than a bulky, flapping magazine, divisible into many sections for the convenience of all members of the family. The special syndicated articles, the color and magazine supplements, the comic section, and finally the rotogravure pages, introduced by the *New York Times* in 1914, all helped to promote its popularity. When Arthur Brisbane left the *World* in 1897 to join the staff of Hearst, he raised the circulation of the Sunday edition to the unheard-of figure of 600,000. In 1914 the Sunday edition of the *New York American* had 738,943 buyers and the *New York Times* 217,265.[265]

The daily paper was but the Sunday paper writ smaller. Every enterprising journal came to embrace a financial page, a sporting page, a theatrical page, a women's page, puzzles and bedtime stories for the children, and a series of "comic strips," theoretically for children but enjoyed by the simpleminded of all ages. Even the lovesick youth and maiden found guidance in such departments as "Marion Harland's Helping Hand," Beatrice Fairfax's "Advice to the Lovelorn," and Laura Jean Libbey's "First Aid to Wounded Hearts," columns which one sober authority believes "have played no mean part in the social service of the press."[266] Of the various newspaper features none attracted a wider following than the comic strips. Emulating Richard F. Outcault's success in the 1890s in originating the "Yellow Kid" pictures,[267] popular comic artists in large numbers created characters which became household words.[268] To his original creation Outcault now added "Buster Brown" and other favorites, Frederick B. Opper originated "Alphonse and Gaston" and "Happy Hooligan," Carl Shultz delighted the youngsters with "Foxy Grandpa," and Rudolph Dirks with the adventures of the Katzenjammers, while H. C. ("Bud") Fisher provided unfailing amusement with his "Mutt and Jeff." Though usually purveying humor of a slapstick variety, occasionally there were incorporated in these pictures sly digs at current conventions.

It was in the field of humor, if not in comic art, that the feature pages reached their highest development. Through this channel a new brand of

American humor became popular. It was in the *Chicago Record* that George Ade's *Fables in Slang*—Aesop attuned to the times—first began to appear, and in the *Chicago Journal* that F. P. Dunne published his early comments on men and affairs through the medium of "Mr. Dooley," the Irish saloon keeper of Archey Road, Chicago, and his naive but constant customer, Mr. Hennessy. Nor was it without significance that the Irish immigrant, Mr. Dooley, had taken the place of the early Yankee humorist.

The influence of women upon the content of the daily paper, which had been evident since the eighties, reached full flower after 1898. The widening horizon of women as they moved from the home to the factory or office, the development of higher education for women and the suffrage movement which diverted their attention more definitely to current affairs, and the growth of the newspapers as an advertising medium were among the causes which contributed to the feminization of the press. From the time when McClure began in the eighties to syndicate cooking recipes to the day "when every page, possibly with the exception of that devoted to sports, had to be written so that the intelligent woman could understand it," [269] the tendency was evident, and as this policy developed it became possible for a growing number of women to find newspaper "careers" on the larger dailies.

While the typical American continued to read the newspapers with avidity, his confidence in them was shaken. Repeatedly the venality of the press and its subservience to advertisers were described in the magazines. Samuel Hopkins Adams in a famous series in *Collier's* during 1905 and 1906 told how patent-medicine advertisers influenced the press by inserting clauses to the effect that the advertising contracts were void if any material appeared detrimental to the proprietary interests, and Will Irwin five years later showed again the willingness of all types of papers to prostitute their news columns and editorial policy to the wish of their advertisers. [270] How low the standard for advertising had fallen was revealed in 1907 when the *New York Herald* paid a fine of $30,000 for printing personal notices designed to call attention to houses of prostitution. [271]

The stronger newspapers, not so dependent for their prosperity upon fraudulent advertising, made some effort to protect their readers. As early as 1903 the Scripps-McRae league appointed a censor who, in one year, debarred $500,000 worth of advertising, [272] but it was not until 1913 that the Associated Advertising Clubs of America set up a "vigilance committee" to expose such humbuggery. The newspaper division of that organization endorsed some "Standards of Newspaper Practice" which marked out an excellent objective, and shortly after the *New York Tribune* took the bold stand of guaranteeing its readers "absolutely against loss or dissatisfaction through the purchase of any wares advertised in its columns." [273] Falling first upon habit-forming drugs and patent medicines, the crusade widened to include all fraudulent advertising. This heightened sense of social responsibility was not achieved without some prodding on the part of the state and federal legislators. Advertising was more carefully regulated and the libel laws made more drastic, while some of the courts tried to put a suppressing hand upon the sensational handling of divorce and criminal cases. In a similar spirit the postal department under the revised statutes attempted to prevent the delivery of mail and payment of money orders to fraudulent advertisers.[274]

The same influences which were changing the American newspaper were producing a somewhat similar effect upon the magazines. Large advertising sections and improvements in the process of half-tone engraving had made possible the ten-cent popular magazine, of which *Munsey's* was the pioneer in 1893. With the lowering of the price, a sprightlier tone, and engaging illustrations the purchasing public more than doubled in size when the "era of the muckrake" arrived to shoot circulations up again. The timely studies and attacks upon existing abuses which *McClure's* inaugurated provided a ready cue to others until the popular magazines were in keen competition for the most sensational exposés and a new crop of writers appeared to answer the demands. The work of arousing public opinion, formerly performed by the newspapers, was now for a brief period taken over by the magazine press. The old-fashioned polite literary magazine seemed doomed. Conservative publications of the type of *Harper's, Scribner's,* the *Century,* and the *Atlantic* sought to take on a more popular tone, while such magazines as *Cosmopolitan, Munsey's, McClure's, Everybody's, Collier's,* the *American,* and *Hampton's* flourished mightily.[275]

Muckraking, of course, was not the only influence which made the low-priced magazine popular. The *Ladies' Home Journal,* which under Edward W. Bok's editorship attained a circulation of 2 million a month, and the *Saturday Evening Post,* which under the editorship of George Horace Lorimer reached a million a week, managed to achieve this success with a minimum of sensationalism. The former engaged only mildly in moral crusades, but it indisputably unlocked the mystery of what women wanted in a magazine, and undoubtedly had an influence in raising standards of table decoration, gardening, home entertainments, dress fashions, and domestic architecture. The *Saturday Evening Post,* which Cyrus H. K. Curtis bought in 1897 for $1,000 and nurtured for several years with the profits of the *Ladies' Home Journal,* soon became the great American weekly and a true mirror of the views of the multitude. Curtis and Lorimer divined intuitively the middle-class American—his ardent nationalism, his admiration of financial success, his belief in the economic status quo, his gospel of work, and his mid-Victorian attitude toward sex. Although it generally ridiculed all deviations from accepted practices, the *Post* was primarily a business and not a propagandist enterprise, and it published some of the best fiction of the period. It employed the ablest denizens of Grub Street and incidentally gave to the reader a big return for his nickel.[276]

The magazines of the period were legion, for besides those which tried to please everyone there were others which catered to the special interests of groups. A luxuriant growth occurred of periodicals devoted to sports and moving pictures. A more interesting phenomenon was the growth of the adventure magazine, which supplied the demand for vicarious experience as the possibility of genuine adventure grew less. Thus the old Wild-West weeklies and "dime novels" written for the consumption of youth now gave way to magazines which specialized in stories of adventure or the detection of crime—stories which were read by those who, at least in years, were adults.

Many of the influences which affected the magazines also made themselves felt upon other types of literary production. Prior to 1898 few American novels had achieved a circulation of 100,000, while at the turn of the century such a record began to be common. In 1901 at least six novels ran to 150,000 copies and half as many more to 100,000. Indeed, at the end of that year, *David Harum* had sold 520,000 copies, *Richard Carvel* 420,000, *The Crisis* 320,000, and *Janice Meredith* 275,000—sales which led the *Bookman* fourteen years later to refer to this period as the fat years of fiction.[277] Undoubtedly one cause for this expansion of novel readers was the service of the low-priced magazine in familiarizing readers with better fiction or at least with the kind of fiction now published in book form. Other influences were also important. Improved processes of typesetting and binding helped make it possible to sell the average novel for $1 and $1.50. The lower-priced novel, it should be noted, was in part also made possible by a reduction in its size to 150,000 or 200,000 words, an indication that writers were adapting themselves to a more rapidly moving age. At the same time, publishers discovered that display advertising would sell fiction as well as toothpaste and breakfast foods, and appropriated large sums for this purpose rather than for subsidizing the now disappearing book agent. Doubtless, too, a growing proportion of public-school graduates were turning to a better class of fiction to satisfy a taste hitherto appeased by dime novels and the effusions of E. P. Roe.

At least three tendencies are particularly noticeable in the fiction of this period, that toward historical fiction, that toward the rural novel, and that toward the sociological novel. Although Henry James, from the rarefied atmosphere of his London home, continued to contemplate American civilization and William Dean Howells was still recognized as our chief novelist, their philosophizing and leisurely progress no longer satisfied. The public demand was for the quick action and romantic setting of the historical novel, or else for a courageous attack upon existing abuses. The romantic revival may have had its origin in the burst of patriotism and martial feeling which accompanied the Spanish-American War or from the pleasant feeling that the United States had had a long history. It may have come chiefly, as a novelist-historian himself explained it, from a revived interest in American history.[278] The origin of much of it, however, must have been the longing for a romantic escape from the grinding economic problems and conflicts which so completely filled the decade of the nineties, the same urge which made the war with Spain so popular. At any rate, there was never a time in American history when the proportion of fiction to other books published was so large.[279]

Historical fiction, of course, was anything but new, and the revival was under way before the Spanish-American War. The most widely read book in 1898 was Henryk Sienkiewicz's *Quo Vadis,* a translation of which had appeared the previous year, but it had to share popularity with S. Weir Mitchell's *Hugh Wynne,* perhaps the greatest of the American historical novels of the period, and with other books of a different sort. With 1899, however, the historical novel was in full swing. Charles Major's *When Knighthood Was in Flower,* Winston Churchill's *Richard Carvel,* and Paul Leicester Ford's *Janice Meredith* swept the country, their only rival in popularity being Edward Westcott's *David Harum.* Westcott's book was perhaps the most famous of a group of novels dealing with rural life whose raison d'être, like that of historical fiction, may well have been escape from urban reality. The trio of historical novels so popular in 1899 was soon augmented by Mary Johnston's *To Have and to Hold,* which easily led the sales for 1900. The most widely read novels in 1901—Maurice Thompson's *Alice of Old Vincennes,* Winston Churchill's *The Crisis,* and Irving Bacheller's *Eben Holden*—were all historical, although the last also cleverly combined the element of rural life with pictures of Greeley and Lincoln. But these books did not complete the list, for the year also marked the appearance of Bertha Runkle's *The Helmet of Navarre* and of George B. McCutcheon's *Graustark.* McCutcheon's book, a variation of the historical novel, dealt with an imaginary kingdom, a theme made popular by the Englishman Anthony Hope and one which attracted many readers.[280]

With the year 1902 the tide of historical fiction began to ebb. The most popular book was *Mrs. Wiggs of the Cabbage Patch* by Alice Hegan Rice, although it was closely followed by the Englishman Gilbert Parker's *The Right of Way.* Major wrote another book, *Dorothy Vernon of Haddon Hall,* and Owen Wister's *The Virginian* and Emerson Hough's *The Mississippi Bubble* had their meed of popularity. The most widely read book in 1903 was Mrs. Ward's *Lady Rose's Daughter,* an English novel, and most of the popular fiction was not historical. Toward the end of the year, however, appeared John Fox's Civil War story *The Little Shepherd of Kingdom Come,* which shared popularity with Churchill's *The Crossing.* Following 1904 the vogue of historical fiction passed. Fox, Churchill, and others continued their efforts for a while, but the popular fancy was caught by many types of novels: the sentimentalism of Kate Douglas Wiggin or Alice Hegan Rice, the vivid north-woods stories of Rex Beach or Jack London, the legendary-kingdom stories of McCutcheon and Harold McGrath, the college tales of

Owen Johnson and the studies of American character by Booth Tarkington. Mrs. Wharton, Mrs. Deland, and Miss Wilkins, whose work was well known before 1898, continued to be regarded as among the most highly esteemed of novelists. An examination of the best sellers during the next ten years reveals the fact that the great majority were written by Americans and dealt with the American scene, and it is interesting to note the frequent appearance of women's names among the authors.[281]

Fortunately for American letters, not all the literary talent was spent in providing amusement and romantic escape. Throughout there was a small group, influenced by the realism of Tolstoy and Zola, who believed it was the duty of the literary artist to paint his scene with a stark and utter truthfulness. Feeling that the realism of Howells and James was too attenuated, a group of younger writers—Hamlin Garland, Frank Norris, Henry Harland, Harold Frederic, and others—attempted in the late nineties and at the turn of the century to give the American scene a more uncompromising treatment. Of this school no one made so deep an impression as Frank Norris, who planned a trilogy of stories comprising the "Epic of Wheat." Only the *Octopus* (1901), which dealt with the struggle between the farmers and the railroads, and *The Pit* (1903), an epic of grain speculation in the Chicago market, were finished before his death at the age of thirty-two, but his contribution both to the literature of realism and to the social revolt was far-reaching. What Norris did for railroads and wheat, Upton Sinclair did for the packing industry in *The Jungle* (1906) and Jack London for capitalistic society in general in *The Iron Heel* (1907).

None of these novelists more clearly reflected the cross currents of American social life during these years than did Jack London. The son of a Western frontiersman and scout, Jack London had been successively a rancher, an oyster-pirate, and a sealer. For a year he had followed the life of a tramp and had been one of the few who in the winter of 1897 had reached the Klondike over Chilcoot Pass. There were few of the cruder aspects of the modern capitalistic society which London did not know from personal experience, and socialism with him was a living gospel.[282] In his books are to be found the restless virility of the conquering pioneer and the frontier reaction against urbanization; in his fiery pen was fused the long agrarian unrest and the rising proletarian protest against American capitalism.

The American realists of the first decade of the century dealt primarily with political and social corruption rather than with problems of individual morality. Frank acceptance and discussion of sex met almost universal public disapproval. In 1900, the year that historical novels were selling literally by the hundred thousands, Theodore Dreiser's first novel *Sister Carrie* was peremptorily rejected by Harper & Brothers. When finally accepted by Doubleday, Page & Company, that concern attempted upon second thought to break its contract, but finding that impossible issued a small edition with unstamped covers. Condemned to a decade of hack work for Butterick and Street and Smith, Dreiser's next book, *Jennie Gerhardt,* did not appear until 1911, but the intervening years had seen such a change in the public attitude toward sex that Harper & Brothers gladly published it, as they did *The Financier* in 1912. When that house, however, published *The Titan* in 1914 it again became frightened and suppressed the book,[283] but Dreiser's vindication was not long in coming. Under the wet blanket of disillusionment following World War I, a host of followers were to produce work which was to be predominant in the third decade.[284]

Like other cultural influences, that of the public library is difficult to estimate, but it is safe to say that it greatly increased in the new century. By 1898 the more advanced communities had reached the point where free, public, and tax-supported libraries were held, like schools, to be an essential element in the equipment of a democracy. It was for the new generation to improve library facilities and master the technique of service to the community. There were in the United States in 1900 over 1,700 libraries of more than 5,000 volumes, a number which grew to nearly 3,000 by the close of the period. Undoubtedly the greatest single incentive to this growth came from the Carnegie fortune, which had been pouring into the building of libraries since 1881. Carnegie alone was responsible during the decade 1906–16 for the construction of over 1,000 library buildings, most of them in the United States. The largest of his gifts was in 1901 when he wrote that he would "esteem it a rare privilege" to donate $5 million to build sixty-five branches for the New York Public Library. To carry on the work of providing libraries and otherwise promote the advancement and diffusion of knowledge, he founded in 1911 the Carnegie Corporation of New York and shortly endowed it with $125 million.[285] As the facilities increased, library administrators rose to meet the new opportunities. The libraries took up seriously the task of meeting the public needs and, where possible, of improving the public tastes. No longer was the public library a mere repository of culture; it had become by 1914 an aggressive and important factor in the shaping of American civilization.

THE PEOPLE AT PLAY

THE TREMENDOUS INTEREST in sports and outdoor life which characterized this generation can be explained in part by the growth of wealth and leisure and in part by the desire to recapture something of the benefits of rural life which were disappearing for large numbers of Americans. A nation scarcely two decades removed from a fighting frontier was hardly ready to forgo the strenuous life, and Roosevelt's excoriation of the "overcivilized man" and the "life of slothful ease" fell on receptive ears.[286] Exponents of health fads and physical culture fostered the idea of individual exercise for personal efficiency, and the publicity given to amateur sports by the metropolitan press was both a stimulus to further endeavor and an indication of the public's spontaneous interest.[287] Unfortunately, interest in athletics did not necessarily mean personal participation. College sports came to be less a matter of undergraduate exercise and more a means of visual recreation for alumni and others. The common man, especially the city dweller, who had neither opportunity nor energy to take part personally, looked to professional athletics for vicarious exertion.

In an age of rapidly growing cities it was but natural that the most significant recreational developments should concern the urban population. The first need was to provide the crowded tenement dweller with an opportunity to get into the open, but the problem was complicated by the fact that the typical American city had grown with but slight attention to recreational needs. Not until the 1890s had much interest been evinced in public parks, even in the large centers,[288] but the first decade of the new century witnessed the rapid extension of older systems and the creation of new parks and parkways.[289] Among the most notable examples were the Boston Metropolitan Park System extending from the Middlesex Fells on the north to the Blue Hills Reservation on the south, enlarged and improved during these years; the Essex County Park System along the Orange Mountains in New Jersey, including parks in Newark, Montclair, the Oranges, and other towns;[290] and the Palisades Interstate Park, running from a point opposite 179th Street, New York City, nearly to Newburgh, and from the Hudson River to Tuxedo Park. Opened in 1909, it was enlarged the next year by a gift of 10,000 acres from Mrs. E. H. Harriman and further extended in subsequent years.

Such amusement resorts as Coney Island, New York, and Revere Beach near Boston, with their merry-go-rounds, shooting galleries, dancing floors, freak shows, restaurants, and beer gardens, had long since become an important recreational outlet to the factory hand and the office-bound clerk, but they had been limited to the largest cities. The trolley-car companies, however, as they extended into the country, laid out amusement parks to which the public might go in the evenings or on Sunday when the business of the company was normally light. Soon "trolley-parks" were to be found in the outskirts of even the smaller cities, where throngs enjoyed dancing, band concerts, baseball games, bathing and boating, and the usual shows of a typical trolley-park midway.[291] Some of these parks amounted to little more than a trolley station with a nearby pavilion, as at Neff Park near Xenia, Ohio; others boasted large auditoriums. That at Willow Grove, Philadelphia, seated 10,000 and supported the best musical talent of the nation.

An important impetus to this development had been the widespread popularity of the bicycle, but the zenith of the bicycle was rapidly passing. Pointing to a remarkable decline in general riding and club membership, the *International Year Book* in 1899 added that "wheeling as a fad having now died out, a healthy growth is assured for the sport, while the bicycle itself is becoming more and more devoted to business uses, one example of which is the equipment of telegraph boys in New York with wheels."[292] But the vogue of the bicycle was threatened with something more serious than the changing winds of popular fancy; it was soon forced to meet the competition of a new means of locomotion, the automobile.[293] The recreational and amusement possibilities of the automobile were obvious, though with all its advantages it did not furnish the excellent exercise provided by the bicycle. It did, however, along with the bicycle and trolley car, contribute to keep alive among city dwellers an active interest in fishing, hunting, and other outdoor recreations.

Unquestionably the premier position among American sports was held by baseball and it continued as popular on the village green as the city diamond. The expansion of the professional game, however, was distinctly urban.[294] Up to 1898 the parent professional organization, the National League of Professional Baseball Clubs, had succeeded in crushing any league which threatened to become national in scope, but shortly thereafter its hegemony was broken by the advent of the American League. Organized as the Western League in 1893, it became the American League in 1900 and began a bitter war with the older body. Securing a Chicago franchise in 1900, the new league, strongly financed, reorganized its circuit in the following year by abandoning Indianapolis, Kansas City, Minneapolis, and Buffalo for Baltimore, Washington, Philadelphia, and Boston. In 1902 it transferred its Milwaukee franchise to St. Louis and in 1903 the Baltimore franchise to New York.[295] This invasion of enemy territory, accompanied as it was by extensive raids upon the older organization for star players, considerably weakened the latter. The National League replied in kind, its chief coup being the purchase in midseason of the Baltimore club and the transfer of John J. McGraw and most of his players to New York.[296] The election of Harry O. Pulliam as president of the National League in 1902 brought overtures of peace, and in the midseason of 1903 a new agreement was adopted, that included detailed rules for conducting professional baseball and a national commission to enforce them.[297]

Stabilized by this agreement, professional baseball entered upon a new era of popularity and of financial prosperity not to be interrupted again until the attempt in 1914 to organize a new Federal League. Whatever may have been the interest in local teams and minor leagues, the attention of the baseball world was chiefly drawn to the contests in the two major organizations and to the classic "world-championship" series held each year after 1903 between the victors of the two leagues. In the National League the two most important contenders between 1903 and 1914 were the Chicago team, led by Frank L. Chance, which won the pennant in 1906, 1907, 1908, and 1910, and the New York club, managed by John J.

McGraw, which was victorious in five of the remaining years.[298] The noted Chicago infield trio J. J. Evers, Joseph Tinker, and F. L. Chance has rarely been equaled, while the New York team included the famous pitchers "Christy" Mathewson and Joseph McGinnity and catchers Roger Bresnahan and Frank Bowerman. These were also the years when John P. ("Honus") Wagner, believed by McGraw to be the "greatest of all players," played shortstop for Pittsburgh.[299] In the American League the chief honors were divided between Philadelphia, which won the pennant six times, and Detroit, which enjoyed three years of victories after 1906.[300] The former club, under the crafty generalship of Cornelius McGillicuddy ("Connie Mack") and containing such players as Charles Bender, Edward Plank, J. W. Coombs, E. T. Collins, Jack Barry, J. Frank Baker, and John McInnis, also won the world championship in 1910, 1911, and 1913,[301] while the latter, under the leadership of Hugh Jennings and aided by the batting of Tyrus Cobb, was a constant contender for honors. Financial prosperity attended the increasing popularity of the sport with the result that greater stadiums were built and unheard-of prices paid for players. The world series of 1913 had an attendance at the five games of 151,000 and gate receipts approximating $326,000.

Viewed askance by the more respectable elements and circumscribed in many states by legal restrictions, boxing enjoyed immense popularity among the "sporting fraternity" and remained the sport par excellence of the underworld. Although amateur boxing made progress, pugilism was largely professionalized, and the chief interest centered in the championship contests of the different classes, especially the heavyweight championship. The Australian, Robert Fitzsimmons, who had captured the crown from James J. Corbett in 1897 in a fourteen-round battle at Carson City, Nevada, was forced to relinquish it two years later to James J. Jeffries at the old Coney Island Athletic Club. The mighty Jeffries defended his title in subsequent matches with both Fitzsimmons and Corbett until he voluntarily retired in 1905, handing on to lesser men the task of combating for the world's title. The best of these proved to be the colored boxer Jack Johnson, who established his preeminence at Reno, Nevada, in 1910 when he worsted Jeffries, who had been induced to emerge from a five-year retirement as the only remaining "white hope."[302] These matches helped to stimulate an interest in boxing which was quickly reflected in the press. The *New York Tribune,* which had given the Corbett-Fitzsimmons battle two columns on an inside page, gave the Johnson-Jeffries fight six columns and the place of honor on the front page.[303] In spite of the growing popularity of the sport, boxing was denounced as a brutal pastime and vigorous efforts were made either to abolish or carefully regulate it. Thus New York state, the great mecca of boxers, repealed in 1900 the Horton law which permitted twenty-five-round contests, and for ten years professional boxing was outlawed within its limits.

In like manner the reformers of the period turned against horse racing, a sport carried on by the wealthy but supported chiefly by the gambling fraternity. Antibetting laws, of course, existed in many states, but they were either not enforced on racetracks or exceptions were made to horse racing. In the opening years of the century this was notably true in New York State, but following the lead of Missouri and Illinois, which legislated against racetrack betting in 1905, Governor Charles Evans Hughes, after a strenuous fight, succeeded in getting the Agnew-Hart bill enacted in 1908 and in strengthening the law in 1910.[304] Black pessimism seized racing enthusiasts; some sold their horses and others transferred their activities to Europe.[305] The seasons of 1908–11 were disastrous, but gradually ways were found to evade the laws. It was reported in 1912 that nearly 1,600 meetings were held in the United States in which about 15,000 horses participated and $6 million in purses and stakes were distributed. By 1914 the racetracks in New York State had reopened. In the meantime, increasing interest, as well as the recent legislative opposition, had led to the building of courses at Havana, Cuba, Tijuana, Mexico, and Montreal, Canada, the popularity of which was to be greatly increased within a few years by the adoption of the Eighteenth Amendment.

Professional baseball and boxing provided amusement for the masses, but they did not meet the needs of the wealthy and middle classes who in increasing numbers were finding leisure for sport. The gap was filled by the game of golf. Although country clubs with golf links had steadily increased since the introduction of the game in the late 1870s, it was well past the turn of the century before golf took its place as a sport for the people. The early years were the "dude era" when the wealthy, responding to a new fad or sensing the physical benefits for the middle-aged man, expended large sums in constructing excellent courses.[306] At first laid out in wealthy commuting towns near the great cities, like Brookline, Massachusetts, and Morristown, New Jersey, and in fashionable summer resorts, golf links began presently to appear near every good-sized town and city. Large centers like New York and Boston built public courses, and lesser communities in time imitated them. Hundreds were in existence in 1914, when it was believed that more adults participated in golf than in any other outdoor sport, and yet it was only on the threshold of its great popularity. The newspapers, which in the early years had hardly deigned to notice the game, now gave large space to its interests, and followed in detail the matches for the open-golf championship won by J. J. McDermott (1911, 1912), Francis Ouimet (1913), and W. C. Hagen (1914), and the amateur championship won by Jerome D. Travis (1907, 1908, 1912, 1913) and Francis Ouimet (1914). The development of golf between 1898 and 1914 was perhaps the unique feature in the history of American sport during these years.

Tennis, eclipsed during the preceding decade by the popularity of bicycling, experienced a temporary revival as a spectators' game for a few years after 1900 as a result of the American victories of 1900 and 1902 in the international Davis Cup contests.[307] Though appealing to the same general classes as golf, another decade passed before tennis regained anything like its earlier favor with amateur players. By 1911 record-breaking crowds witnessed William A. Larned win the singles championship for the fifth consecutive year and the seventh time. In 1912 and 1913, Maurice E. McLoughlin won first honors and in the latter year, with his teammates Harold H. Hackett and R. N. Williams, regained the Davis Cup which, since 1903, had been in England and Australia.

Of collegiate sports, in 1898 football occupied the leading position, but critical years lay ahead. Loosely supervised by a rules committee representing a few Eastern universities, college football was endangered in the early years of the century by professionalism and by the development of close-formation mass plays which rendered it unnecessarily dangerous. Educators and reformers of various types took pains to point out the exaggerated influence of the game in college life and the increasing toll of fatalities which each season recorded.[308] The death roll in 1903 reached a total of forty-four, and though it dropped to fourteen and twenty-four in the two succeeding years, the improvement was partly offset by the serious injuries incurred by those who lived. While ardent followers of the sport had little sympathy with the fond parents who "objected to having their sons maimed or killed for the greater glory of the college" or with the old-fashioned college president who complained that it took ten weeks out of the student's school year, the public at large took a different attitude.[309] The climax came in 1905 when the condemnation of the press was well-nigh universal and Columbia University abolished the game (restored in 1915). President Roosevelt invited football leaders to a White House luncheon to discuss the situation and Chancellor Henry M. McCracken of New York University issued a call to all colleges to join in a conference on the sport.

The result was the formation in 1906 of a new National Collegiate Athletic Association (N.C.A.A.) with a revision of the rules. The most important features introduced were the forward pass, the on-side kick, the separation of the rush lines, and the necessity of making ten yards rather than five in three downs. The "new football" was denounced by critics on the ground that the game would be spoiled for the spectators, but this effort to open up the game actually made it more interesting. It is doubtful, however, if the new rules greatly decreased fatalities.[310] Some of the most dangerous mass plays known to the game followed the new rules, notably the "Minnesota shift" devised by Dr. Henry Williams of Minnesota, and it was necessary to change them yearly until a second radical revision was effected in 1910.

Some of the big games were being attended in 1914 by crowds of 50,000, and the leading universities were making plans to build monster stadiums to accommodate larger numbers. Football had not only become the king of college games but the support of the lesser ones.

To bridge the long winter gap between football and the summer sports, basketball assumed the leadership among America's indoor athletics during the first decade of the century. Widely popular in Y.M.C.A. and athletic-club circles, it achieved its greatest development among the colleges.[311] Before the coming of basketball there were few large gymnasiums, and the influence of this sport seems to have been paramount in the growth of the huge building with its high ceiling and large arena now found on every college campus. Although the older position of track athletics was challenged by football and basketball, it continued to attract a large following. This was due in part to the constant bettering of existing records and in part to the development of international contests.

Yet there was much in American sport to disturb the thoughtful student. Wherever there appeared the possibility of making a dollar's profit, professionalism seemed to creep in. The most skillful exhibitions of baseball and boxing were almost wholly professional, and professional leagues of basketball, hockey, and other sports were organized. A prejudice against playing for money still persisted in tennis, golf, and other games participated in by the more affluent classes, where strong efforts were made to differentiate the amateur from the professional, but the line between the two in many cases was so attenuated as to be almost indiscernible. College athletics, especially football, was so buttressed by professional coaches and dominated by huge gate receipts that it was coming to be more of a business than a recreation even to the players. "Spring practice and autumn practice, the enlistment of an army of expert coaches, the long blackboard drill in strategy, the despatch of trained watchers to study the peculiarities of rival teams," and the elaborate system of recruiting material from the preparatory schools, said the *Nation,* "have gone far towards removing the silly notion that intercollegiate games are played just for the fun of the thing."[312] Whether professional or amateur, the average American was inclined to take his sport too seriously.

If golf and motoring represented the most notable additions to outdoor recreational life, the moving picture occupied an even more distinctive place within doors. Although animated picture films were projected on screens as early as 1894 and 1895 in the United States, these first attempts were crude, hard on the eyes of spectators, and interesting mainly as a curiosity.[313] Usually the early exhibition rooms were simply stores fitted with seats and a ticket booth, and the transition from these unpretentious places to the more elaborate theaters specially designed for showing pictures was slow until about 1910.[314] The usual admission price was five cents, a charge which was quite compatible with profits in a period when the hall could be run at a total cost of from $150 to $250 a week, a conventional comedy could be produced for $250, actors received from

$15 to $40 a week, and authors of good scenarios from $5 to $30. Before moving-picture houses were regularly established, traveling exhibitions introduced the new amusement, and the annual appearance of such exhibitions as "Howe's Moving Pictures" was one of the thrilling events of the small-town season.

It was not until 1905 that Edison set up "Black Maria," the first studio for indoor production, a flimsy structure made of black tar paper and mounted on a circular track so that it might swing with the sun; but so rapid was the advance that within five years not only had the Edison Company built elaborate studios but the Vitagraph Company of Brooklyn, the Lubin Company of Philadelphia, and the Essanay and Selig firms of Chicago were producing films with an unheard-of dispatch. According to the *Independent* early in 1908, within the previous two years "moving picture theatres or exhibition halls have opened in nearly every town and village in the country and every city from the Klondike to Florida and from Maine to California supports from two or three to several hundred," patronized each day by an average of from 2 to 3 million people.[315] Before the end of the decade there were few Americans out of reach of a movie.

The first pictures widely shown were outdoor scenes, especially travel pictures, but slapstick farce, with the comic chase and the inevitable custard pie used as a missile, was quick in making its appearance.[316] There was little to commend these early pictures, produced as they were by second-rate artists and often "made up on the lot" in the most casual fashion, but crude as the technique was, it gave an opportunity for John Bunny and other unforgettable figures to impress themselves upon picture history. Producers, eager to please the multitude, took a page from the book of the dime-novel writers until the "western" became a part of the stock-in-trade of the business. Here the swift-riding cowboy hero, the gambling-house villain with his Mexican henchmen, the pretty schoolteacher or rancher's daughter, playing their roles with infinite variations in a setting of frontier towns and gorgeous mountain scenery, established themselves as part and parcel of American folklore.

While the moving picture was capturing its tens of thousands, musical comedy was enjoying unprecedented popularity in the cities, but it was a far different type from the exquisite comic operas composed in the eighties by Gilbert and Sullivan. Much of it was little more than refined burlesque with specially written music and a trained dancing chorus intermixed with vaudeville turns. Perhaps the German-dialect comedians, Joseph Weber and Lewis M. Fields, did this sort of thing as well as any, and their imitators were legion.[317] Higher in the scale was the exceedingly popular musical show which aspired to a more sustained musical score and to a touch of romance, achieved perhaps by placing the scenes in some far-off land. The finest of these, *The Merry Widow* by Franz Lehar, first played in New York in 1907, and *The Chocolate Soldier* by Oscar Strauss, produced there in

1909, were Austrian importations,[318] but the prolific Irish-American Victor Herbert in such productions as *Babes in Toyland* (1903) and *The Red Mill* (1906) also set a high standard.

In spite of a tendency toward standardization, American vaudeville, like almost every other form of light amusement, enjoyed unprecedented popularity. Israel Zangwill in 1905 urged that the variety stage provide a medium for that neglected form of art, the one-act play, but he was far from hopeful as to the future of vaudeville, believing that in all probability "the artlessness of the public and the artfulness of the manager will long keep the present pabulum unaltered, save in increasing staleness."[319] His pessimism was more than justified. The one-act play, it is true, became a part of regular programs, but it lacked both seriousness and art. The only important innovation was the introduction of a "moving-picture news reel" to start the program and perhaps a photoplay to end it.[320] The lowly picture, however, which had crept in as a supplement to the vaudeville show only to take complete possession of many houses, was exercising by 1914 a distinct impetus to vaudeville as the movie theaters found it advisable to vary their programs by introducing vaudeville turns.

The pleasures of the theater were obviously limited to dwellers in urban communities. The majority of the people, who still lived in small towns and rural districts, continued to find recreation in church festivals, Sunday-school picnics, clambakes, and neighborhood parties, enlivened by singing and the usual guessing and kissing games. The Saturday night band concert was a regular feature of many small towns and was as great an attraction to the nearby farmers on their weekly trip to town as the barroom of the hotel.

A species of club life for artisans and the smaller professional men was provided in the numerous secret fraternities which flourished during these years. Whether it was the desire for a romantic escape from the drabness of life, an opportunity for relaxation, the ambition of little men to play big roles in a small organization, the childish desire to parade in fancy uniforms, or the hope of business or professional advancement—whatever the causes, fraternal organizations continued to occupy a large place in the everyday life of many Americans, claiming, at the close of 1914, over 15.6 million members in fifty-seven "principal" organizations.[321] The insatiable desire to join something was responsible for the establishment of a new type of social organization during these years: the civic and luncheon clubs. The first Rotary Club, consisting of one representative of each business, profession, and institution in the city, was founded in Chicago in 1905, but further development was not rapid until 1912. When the idea caught hold, it found imitators in the Kiwanis (founded 1915), the Lions, and other clubs.

No diversion was more popular in America during the first decade of the century than attending expositions. So successful had been the World's

Columbian Exposition held in Chicago in 1893, and so great the impression made upon the nation, that a succession of similar enterprises resulted. The Trans-Mississippi Exposition, exhibiting the products, industries, and life of the states west of the Mississippi, was held in Omaha, Nebraska, in the summer of 1898. Encouraged by its success and aided by federal and state governments, the citizens of Buffalo organized a Pan-American Exposition to demonstrate the progress of civilization on both continents and launched it in May 1901. Hardly had it closed its gates in November before the South Carolina Interstate and West Indian Exposition was opened to the public, projected primarily to demonstrate the new industries and commerce of the advancing South. Already ground had been broken for the Louisiana Purchase Exposition to be held at St. Louis to celebrate the hundredth anniversary of the acquisition of Louisiana (opened in 1904); and plans were under way for the Lewis and Clark Exposition at Portland in 1905, the Jamestown Tercentenary Exposition at Hampton Roads in 1907, the Alaska-Yukon-Pacific Exposition at Seattle in 1909, and finally, as a climax, the two expositions at San Francisco and at San Diego in 1915. Nothing comparable was to come for many years.

The motives behind the organization of these expositions were varied. Sectional rivalry played its part, while local pride and desire for profits seized upon the anniversary of some historical event as an excuse. Manufacturers eager to show their wares, localities to exhibit their products, governments or private organizations to carry on education or propaganda, all cooperated to make possible these monster fairs. Each had its special feature—the Indian exhibits of the Trans-Mississippi Exposition, the great electric tower of the Pan-American symbolic of the remarkable electrical advance of America, the Congress of Arts and Sciences at the Louisiana Purchase Exposition, and the marine display at Jamestown. In their essentials, however, they were the same; the Chicago fair of 1893 had set the style and the succeeding expositions followed it. "He sees the same general scheme of department buildings," said Robert Grant in comparing the Pan-American with the great earlier exposition, "a brilliant imposing city towering . . . as by the touch of a necromancer's wand; a kindred profusion of boldly imagined and freely executed groups of statuary; an analogous system of waterways; the same old Midway with a few novel features."[322]

Henry Adams, impressed at St. Louis by the fact that a "third-rate town of half a million people without history, education, unity or art and with little capital" could do "what London or New York would have shrunk from attempting" and amazed at the gorgeous electrical spectacle, saw the new American as "the servant of the power house as the European of the twelfth century was the servant of the Church."[323] To the average citizen these expositions were not so much a subject for philosophizing as an excuse to take a trip or go on a vacation. Although the migration may have been chiefly for pleasure, the journeyings of millions of people to new

sections of the country and their exposure to unusual sights undoubtedly
had an important educational influence upon the generation. It symbolized
on a grand scale the new America, a nation with leisure to play and with a
material culture as yet unmatched in human history.

THE NEW FRONTIER

AMERICA'S ENTRANCE upon the path of imperialism marked her arrival at
economic maturity. But there were other indications pointing to the fact
that America had come of age. The older theories of laissez faire, so beloved
by the classical economists, no longer fit the more intricate civilization of
the new age, and unrestricted individualism was breaking down in every
phase of human activity. It had failed in the economic world, and the great
wave of industrial consolidation which ushered in the new century was in
part a recognition by private business of the disasters of untrammeled
competition. While big business thus sought to save itself, the nation as a
whole demanded protection from these great aggregations of wealth and,
through state and federal legislation, endeavored to extend some measure
of effective public control over economic life. At the same time, the government itself, through the parcel post and the postal-savings bank, extended
its own business operations, and through its various bureaus offered agriculture and industry a service of ever-increasing value.

Its willingness to employ experts and to partake in the conservation
movement was not only a reflection of the spirit of the time but an object
lesson to the nation. Investigations and surveys—official and private—of
labor, immigration, trusts, banking, internal waterways, and other problems
were an indication that leaders of public opinion valued the scientific approach and were finally in a mood to take sober stock of the nation's
resources. And in this greater appreciation of the value of science, private
business was at the forefront.

Not since the decade of the thirties and forties had America experienced
such a wave of reform as flowed over the country in the early years of the
century. Even among leaders of large enterprises a new spirit appeared.
The bitter attacks of the Muckrakers and the drive for social control made
many business leaders see a new light. A sense of responsibility to the
community was developing far different from the economic brigandage
which had ushered in the century. America had become too big and life had
become too complicated for the old freedom and the old independence.

In politics reform no longer concerned itself merely with the uprooting
of personal dishonesty, the elimination of a Ruef; it presented model charters and advocated commission government. It was no longer satisfied with
turning out the villains, but sought to exercise future control through the

initiative, the referendum, and the recall. The new social consciousness did not merely react to the exposures of the Muckrakers, it revealed a humanitarianism committed to intelligent institutional reconstruction. The drive against the slums, against the ruthless exploitation of the labor of women and children, against the waste of life in industry, against the liquor evil and adulterated foods, resulted in legislative codes which did much to improve conditions. Specific measures were often far from perfect, and reform at times overreached itself, but the progress was one of which any generation might be proud.

The willingness soberly to take stock of American civilization and the desire of large elements to improve it also implied an intellectual maturity which introduced a refreshing realism into many institutions. While new sects and strange dogmas continued to find adherents, the older churches turned from theological controversy to contemplate the existing social order, and prospered only as they caught the new spirit. As a whole, the church was less inclined to dwell upon the glories of a future life and more upon the possibility of making this one endurable. Forward-looking educators, eyeing critically the whole educational system, no longer went into ecstasies over the little red schoolhouse, but with the aid of experimental schools and the new psychology tried to improve conditions. Meanwhile teachers and students in the higher institutions were approaching the whole range of social studies with a new realism. Surcharging the whole intellectual atmosphere were the discoveries of science and their practical application, and unconscious as many scientists may have been of the social implications of their work, the generation in which they lived was alert to turn the new knowledge to human betterment.

The quest for social justice was not wholly indigenous either in its conception or in its execution. The transit of civilization so evident in our earlier history continued unabated into the twentieth century. While foreign leadership in the fine arts had always been acknowledged, we now turned to western Europe as a schoolmaster in the field of human relations and as a leader in the development of new governmental institutions. Scientific city government, the initiative, the referendum, women's suffrage, and other forms of the new democracy had already been tried abroad. Western Europe had preceded us with the income tax, the parcel post, scientific banking methods, workmen's compensation, social legislation, and with government control of business. It preceded us with university settlements and Red Cross stamps just as it did with gasoline engines and modernistic art. It speaks volumes for the intelligence and broad patriotism of this generation that it recognized the worth of foreign innovations and so readily adapted them. Probably not since the time of the early colonial period had the importation of European methods been more conscious or so widely approved.

While the spirit of the time was critical, it was not one of morbid probing into the sores of the body politic; nor was it one of discouragement. Like France during her revolution, America set herself to the task of reform with buoyancy and enthusiasm, and the men of this generation applied themselves to the work of reconstruction with the same confidence that their forefathers had shown in the building of railroads and the conquest of the frontier. But sympathetic as were the masses to a better America, their chief energies were concentrated upon the task of carrying on the economic life, and with an ever-increasing tempo raw materials were being exploited and wealth created. The distribution of this wealth may have been as unequal in 1914 as in 1898, but there was relatively more of it per capita, and the constant effort at reform had made the nation a better place for the common man to live.

BOOK XII

The Great Crusade and After,

1914–28

BETWEEN PEACE AND WAR

In counting the annual rings that tell the life story of a fallen tree the forester can sometimes distinguish narrow, crowded lines that testify to years of stress and drought. If trees had memory we can be sure that they would reckon events as they befell before or after the "hard times." The World War of 1914–18 marked five such bands of waste and suffering across the life of nearly every nation in the world. No other recorded human disaster, not even the Black Death of the fourteenth century, so intimately touched each race of mankind or created so general a brotherhood of suffering. Even the few neutral nations which did not contribute to the casualty lists were shaken profoundly by the economic repercussions of the European conflict. For America, as for Europe, it closed one age and began another.

Yet there was a difference. The war came to Europe as illness comes to a man of advancing years and weakened constitution, a disaster native to the system. The war came to the United States from without, from causes for which the United States had little responsibility. The American people have never really accepted it as a part of their national tradition. Ten years after its close they remained still irritated and bewildered by it, rarely viewing it with that sentimental reminiscent fondness that enfolded 1776 and 1861, although there were relatively far more American "Tories" in the former year and Northern "copperheads" in the latter than "pro-

Germans" in 1917. In the many European countries which suffered more deeply than the United States the revulsion from the war took a positive form, such as radical socialism or a militant and uncompromising pacifism. The average American, however, felt that while his government could perhaps not have avoided the war, the war ought somehow to have avoided America; that it was most unpleasant for a quiet gentleman who happened to be the spectator of a street fight suddenly to be forced to use his fists to protect his own head.

The United States of 1914 certainly presented as unwarlike a spectacle as the sun ever shone upon. The problems of politics were economic problems, concentrating in the "quest for social justice," not questions of foreign policy.[1] The president, Woodrow Wilson, was a student and teacher of history, a "scholar in politics," and therefore an anomaly in American political life. He was believed to be strongly a pacifist and had resisted considerable newspaper clamor for a military occupation of Mexico, then in the throes of a revolution which jeopardized local American interests. His secretary of state, William Jennings Bryan, was avowedly a crusader for world peace and a foe of "imperialism." The Democratic party, in power by virtue of a split in the Republican camp, had been, at least since 1860, the party of "no foreign entanglements." Alone among the Great Powers the United States had neither alliances nor morally binding ententes with other nations. The permanent diplomatic policy of the nation, based on the principles of Washington, Jefferson, and Monroe, was that of nonintervention in European affairs combined with a watchful guardianship of American countries from European intrusion. If some exceptions to this policy had been made, particularly in the administration of Theodore Roosevelt, no one supposed that they would be repeated while Wilson occupied the White House.

The first reaction of the American public to the European tragedy was one of sheer humanitarian horror. It seemed incredible that the peace of western Europe, unbroken since 1871, should be so abruptly terminated. Of the diplomatic controversies which led to the crisis only the professionally informed—diplomats, journalists, historians—were aware. American newspapers before August 1914 gave relatively less space to foreign affairs than the newspapers of any European country. They duly recorded, without special emphasis, the assassination of an Austrian archduke, but the baseball season was in full swing and the relative importance of events seems to diminish with distance. For those who took any interest in the doings of diplomacy, President Wilson's difficulties with Mexico seemed far more disturbing than the rise of another war cloud in the Balkans. But the swift interchange of threats among the Great Powers in the last week of July and the outbreak of hostilities in August brought the European crisis to the front page. The *New York Times* in particular distinguished itself by printing in full the official British correspondence, running to more than 100 documents, as soon as the British government made it public. From the outbreak of the war, till the entrance of the United States made necessary a sort of military censorship, the American press continuously laid before its readers the fullest account of current events which could then be obtained anywhere in the world. Eagerly the reading public pored over the newspaper maps, measuring off the gains reported by each side, attempting in vain to reconcile the optimistic German accounts of rapid advance in Belgium and France with French and British statements minimizing every gain. French military terms and the names of Polish towns became more or less pronounceable. The study of geography was resumed by many who had hoped to lay it by forever upon graduation from grammar school.

Though in these early years the average American may have viewed the war too much as a mere interested spectator, unaware of the danger that his own nation might also become involved in a conflict that already extended from Japan to Portugal, at least he was a sympathetic spectator.

But other Americans went beyond watchful waiting and demanded that the nation prepare for war. If the average champion of preparedness was asked why the country must arm, he usually replied with such generalities as "We must be strong enough to maintain American rights," or "Universal military training is an excellent school for democratic citizenship." If you pressed him further, he would say something about Mexican raids along the southwestern border—no votes could be lost by denouncing Mexicans. The Republican and Democratic parties during the campaign of 1916 strangely resembled two little children quarreling in a cage containing a sleeping tiger, but scolding in an undertone so as not to wake the sleeper.

The most popular and interesting aspect of the preparedness movement was the opening of summer training camps for civilians. General Leonard Wood did much to initiate the plan by organizing such a camp at Plattsburg, in northern New York, in 1915.[2] Colleges and universities also laid greater stress than formerly on their courses in military science. Drill was less perfunctory to the student who now foresaw a chance of becoming an officer in an actual war. From the colleges and from the summer camps came many of the officers of the volunteer and drafted troops raised during the war. Under modern conditions it takes several months' intensive training to turn a civilian into a soldier and an even longer time to fit him to be an officer. Obviously the training camps were but a beginning, but at least they selected from the mass of men of military age those who were interested in the army and had the physique and the qualities of leadership which fitted them for the profession. The partial mobilization of the army and the national guard for service on the Mexican border greatly increased interest in military affairs.[3] If there were no big war with Germany there might at least be a little one with Mexico.

The United States had known several somnolent elections, but that of 1916 is rather to be described as somnambulistic. Under other circumstances the closeness of the contest would have made it an interesting campaign, but the real mind of the nation was elsewhere. Who cared to read conventional speeches when he might read daily of the greatest battles ever fought and knew there was constant danger that they might involve America? The one touch of excitement in the campaign came in the week following the election when the result hung in doubt until the final returns were heard from California.

Fresh from his victory, President Wilson made a dramatic play for world peace. He offered the belligerents an opportunity to state the terms on which war might be concluded. The Entente outlined their terms; the Central Powers refused to state theirs but offered to enter a conference.[4] Before the Senate on January 22, 1917, the president reviewed the negotiations and urged a "peace without victory" based on the equal rights of all nations, great and small, and secured by a league of nations.[5]

But his efforts failed either to end the war or to avert American participation in it. At the end of January the Central Powers declared a war zone around enemy coasts in which all ships, neutral or belligerent, might be sunk. The one exception permitted, which Americans took as an additional insult, was the right to send along a narrow sea lane one passenger ship a week, decorated with "zebra stripes," as the press termed them, of alternate red and white. The United States promptly severed diplomatic relations with Germany, but awaited a hostile act before declaring war. As a temporary measure the president advocated the defensive arming of American merchant ships. A pacifist minority in the Senate talked the resolution to death, but the president accomplished the same end by executive action.

Public opinion began to crystallize into war sentiment. Germany's repudiation of her former pledge to spare unarmed merchant ships, the timely exposure of various plots within the country and of Zimmermann's bid to Mexico to help herself to three American states, the German deportation of Belgian civilians, the revolution in Russia (the American press, with virtual unanimity, had been hostile to the old regime in that country), and the continued sinking of American ships in the war zone enabled the president, when the new Congress assembled, to ask for a declaration of war. Many papers which had formerly opposed intervention now thought that armed neutrality was "nothing . . . but a buckling on of a sword for a siesta in a rocking chair,"[6] and applauded the formal declaration of war.

Fifty members of the House and six of the Senate held out against the action, and a coalition of pacifist and socialist societies bombarded Congress with anti-intervention appeals. But with the actual beginning of hostilities most of the opposition ceased. The question of American participation had not been at all a party issue—it was no more a Democratic than a Republican war. Nor was there any division of classes on the question. Pacifism was a matter of individual conviction, pro-Germanism, usually, of family inheritance, and neither proved to be of much significance. There were no draft riots such as had figured in Civil War times. Particularly commendable was the conduct of the German Americans. Though their sympathies had been vociferously for the German cause from 1914 to 1917, few hesitated when the choice became inevitable between the land of their fathers and the land of their children. The melting pot had proved to be no idle metaphor. The many nationalities in the United States recognized themselves as a single nation.

AMERICA IN WARTIME

WAR WAS A SIMPLE MATTER in the days when good Sir Brian could unhook his armor from the wall, mount his charger, and be off in fifty minutes to answer the summons of his liege lord. Even in the eighteenth century, when war had already become a science for specialists, the army represented the nation only as a football team represents its college. The civilian could supply funds, pray for victory, cheer from the sidelines, but did not take an active part in the game. The coming of the "nation in arms" in the days of Carnot, Napoleon, and Scharnhorst meant hardly more—merely that the civilian might be, as an individual, brought into the ranks in case of need. Only with the twentieth century did mine and factory, farm and home, school and laboratory become so many cogs in a single war machine. In the World War an army was not an army without transports, airplanes, motors, tanks, field telephones, entrenching tools, barbed-wire fencing, gas masks, field glasses, and a thousand other accessories whose lack might give the enemy a slight but fatal margin of superiority.

To produce all that was necessary—from such major necessities as coal, oil, wheat, beef, rubber, and steel down to such small details as cherry pits for gas masks and paint for camouflaged merchant ships—thousands of workingmen had to be taken from their usual peacetime tasks to the munition plants; hundreds of thousands of farmers had to alter their crop routine; and millions of men, women, and children in every walk of life had to modify their habits of purchase and consumption. Even the rarest, most unmilitary talents might find use in modern war. Many expert dentists were called into service to perform operations on jawbones broken by shrapnel. Several artists devoted themselves to designing liberty-loan posters. The linguist could work for the censor and examine letters from Persia or Finland. Some college professors developed a latent talent for deciphering the codes of enemy agents. Literary folk who sympathized in any degree with the national effort could find endless opportunities for propaganda, one of the major weapons of modern warfare. Actresses and other entertainers were in demand to keep up the morale of soldiers in cantonments or at the front. Perhaps one reason why the World War brought a relapse toward barbarism in the treatment of noncombatants was that, under the conditions of the time, very few residents in a belligerent country were really noncombatant.

The United States decided for compulsory service almost as quickly as for war, in marked contrast to England, which relied on volunteering until half her war had been fought. The probable reason for this difference, since prejudice against conscription was much the same in both countries, was that at the time the United States entered the struggle it was possible to observe and benefit by the English experience with the voluntary system. England had enlisted recruits in adequate numbers, but it took the wrong men—those who perhaps were more needed as expert mechanicians in the munition factories—or it took the right men at the wrong time. The real advantage of compulsory service was orderliness, the possibility of raising just the numbers who could be trained and equipped at the time and with the least disturbance to the production of war necessities.[7]

On June 5, 1917, 9,586,508 young men between twenty-one and thirty-one registered, thus placing themselves at the disposal of the army. Many were granted complete or partial exemption on the ground of physical unfitness, the support of dependent families, or their special qualifications for necessary industries. The rest were placed in a first class of enrolled men and the order of their muster into service determined by lot. No one was permitted to purchase exemption or hire a substitute; in that respect, at least, democracy had made a great advance since the Civil War. The banker's son and the laborer's son stood an equal chance of being drafted into the service; indeed, if the laborer's son were needed in the shipyards and the banker's son had spent his time in play, it was the latter who went to the trenches. Each district had its quota to fill, and a single drawing of lots in Washington determined the order in which men would be summoned to the colors in each case. Regular army, national guard, and the new army of drafted men were placed under uniform discipline as a consolidated national force. The offer of former President Roosevelt to lead a special expeditionary force of volunteers was rejected by the president, on advice from military experts, because it was feared that such an expedition would withdraw thousands of men of exceptional ability, zeal, and experience from the training camps where they were needed to officer the inexperienced civilians "blown in by the draft."[8]

Life in the training camps came as a revolutionary experience to many. Sons of aliens in the big cities who had barely learned the English language, "poor whites" from isolated mountain hamlets in the South, black laborers from Louisiana swamplands, boys from lonely Dakota wheat farms, all the untraveled classes of the country, were uprooted from their homes. To go to war was an adventure for everyone, but even to go the nearest training camp was an adventure for these. Their trip to camp was often their first railroad journey, their port of embarkation their first experience in a strange city, their voyage to France their first sight of salt water. Drill and discipline seemed harshly restrictive to young Americans accustomed to being their own masters, and homesickness was prevalent.

Yet very soon the recruits adapted themselves to their new social environment. Military discipline and cantonment life, working in cooperation, tended to standardize the raw material even more effectively than a boarding school. Myriad types of drafted men tended to merge, as in a composite photograph, into a single generalized type of soldier. "You're in the army now," the older recruits told the younger at every opportunity. A certain esprit de corps grew up among the drafted men almost as soon as among the volunteers. At first the latter tended to look down on the former with a certain condescension as near-slackers who had to be dragged into the great game, but before long the drafted men were answering the taunt of "slacker" by the counterstroke of "draft dodger!" The same soldier slang was repeated in the accent of forty-eight states. They all ate the same "goldfish" (tinned salmon), wore the same "tin helmets," and perhaps wagered their pay on crap games, more picturesquely styled "African golf" or "the galloping dominoes." Whether we approve and call it socialization, or disapprove and term it standardization, unquestionably this dip into cantonment life did much to make the oncoming generation more like-minded. Back in civil life once more, no longer the American Expeditionary Force but the American Legion, they had a common background of experience that tended to modify sectional or provincial differences.

The training camps were mushroom cities. Instead of merely erecting tent colonies it was decided to build large, well-ventilated wooden barracks equipped so far as possible with water supply, electric light, sewerage systems, and other "public utilities." Sixteen soldier-cities were built for the national army (the drafted men), and sixteen others for the national guard (volunteer militia). The cost of the cantonment cities averaged $8 million each for the national army, and almost a fourth as much for the national guard.[9] Construction was rushed forward with remarkable speed, for until adequate quarters were ready training could not begin. Even as things were, soldiers sometimes came to camp while their quarters were still unfinished and had themselves to take a share in the task of making them habitable. Many criticized the new barracks as needlessly elaborate and presenting too great a contrast to the hardships of the trenches, but housing experts answered that the government was well advised in sparing no pains to keep the camps clean, dry, and sanitary, because they were made to house civilians from superheated city flats, untempered to campaigning in wintry weather.[10] Within a few months cantonments had been built to house 1.8 million men, equivalent to the population of Philadelphia.[11]

Physical and mental tests of the soldiers told much of the national standards in time of peace, for the drafted men represented a very fair cross section of the whole population. A new registration in the fall of 1918 comprised the age limits from eighteen to forty-five; all together, about 26 million men were registered or entered the service before registration. In all, about 3.5 million men were brought into the army, 2 million crossed the Atlantic, and over 1.3 million took part in battle.[12] It was disconcerting to learn that about one young American in every four was practically illiterate, and about one in three physically unfit. The proportion of unfitness was still higher for the manufacturing districts and for the middle years of life.[13] New England, New York, and the industrial Northeast generally had many of the unfit, and the far West also made a poor record, presumably because the health resorts of the Rockies had attracted many men threatened with tuberculosis. But in a belt of prairies and great plains, extending continuously from North Dakota to Texas, over 70 percent of those examined were found fit, and the South and agricultural Midwest generally made a good showing. Once more it had been demonstrated, as among British volunteers in the Boer War, that urban conditions unfit many for a soldier's life. It should be remembered, however, that a man may enjoy excellent health and be capable of steady hard work for ten hours a day in factory or office and yet not pass an army test because of some minor defect such as fallen arches, bad teeth, or nearsightedness.

Mental inspection was more of a novelty in army routine than physical inspection. For several years careful experimentation had been carried on by psychologists to devise tests of alertness, memory, logical decision, and other measurable mental traits, and to some extent these methods had found application in the personnel work of large factories. But never before had they been employed to sift the wheat from the chaff in a great army. Their first use was to make a rough division between those fit for soldiers' work and the minority too dull to be of use in modern war, even in the ranks. But it was equally important to sort out superior degrees of ability among the drafted men so that they might be tried out for special service or fill vacancies among the noncommissioned officers. An "alpha" test was devised for those who could easily read and were accustomed to verbal symbols; a "beta" test for those with little education. Of course, a recruit sometimes had high intelligence and yet was ill adapted to responsible work in the army because he lacked authority, decisiveness, or tact in handling other men. But this happened far less frequently than one might suppose. At Camp Meade a group of soldiers were graded into five classes according to the intelligence tests, and then separately graded by their officers on grounds of soldierly qualities such as reliability, discipline, and initiative. In nearly half the cases (49.5 percent), the men examined fell into the same class on both tests and in most of the other cases the difference was of only one grade.[14] The practical success of the army tests advertised them widely and led to the increased use of such psychological siftings in both academic and commercial life.

The training of the men was as carefully divided into stages as in any school or college. On the average, the soldier had six months of drill in the fundamentals of military life while in cantonments. Here he learned obedience—the first and hardest lesson—drill, and care of equipment, and received the physical training necessary to fit him for active campaigning. He was also given special instruction in the peculiarities of trench warfare, often under the direction of experienced French or British officers who could speak directly from experience. Then he went overseas for two months more of intensive specialized instruction; then for a month into a "quiet" section of the battlefront, which merely meant that he would probably not take part in a general offensive; after that, into an "active" sector and continuous battle.

The story of the campaigns of 1917 and 1918 does not belong to this volume. But before returning to the civilian organization behind the lines it would be appropriate to speak briefly of the experience which 2 million men took back with them from Europe. The soldier of the American Expeditionary Force faced perils much greater than fall to the lot of the civilian, and yet, just because of the inevitable hardships and dangers of his task, he had to be cared for in a most paternal fashion. Early hours are recommended to the civilian by his doctor; the soldier was summoned to rise by bugle. He shaved, cleaned his teeth, brushed his uniform under inspection, and if his clothes became filthy in the trenches he must at his first opportunity visit a "delousing" station to kill the "cooties" with live steam. If he wore out one suit of clothes he must requisition another. He had no choice as to his diet, though until supplies ran low he had the privilege of deciding how many times he would fill his plate. When travel was necessary he went in a freight car guaranteed to hold "forty men or eight horses" and paid no fare. If he had dependents, the government provided him with insurance. If he wanted to spend his leisure time in study, books and classes were provided.[15] His correspondence was carefully censored to prevent any leakage of military information. He carried an identification disk at all times so that he might not be buried as an unknown soldier. The army provided his quarters, his food, his tools, his clothes, his haircuts, his dental and medical work, his burial costs, and practically all other necessary expenses. This was less true of the officers, whose expensive outfits often outran the funds provided to buy them.[16]

This care of the soldier appeared at its best in the work of the Red Cross and the medical officers of the army. In some respects, such as the treatment of burns and the reconstruction of broken jawbones, American physicians and surgeons achieved triumphs which before the war would have been considered impossible. But in all the belligerent countries the care of the sick and wounded showed high efficiency as compared with any previous war. If soldiers wounded in battle lived to reach the base hospitals they generally recovered, and five times out of six could again enter active service. Soldiers were usually inoculated against typhoid and further guarded by rigorous sanitary regulations. During the war with Mexico, in the medical dark ages of 1846–48, disease killed off in one year more than a tenth of the whole American army, and as recently as the Spanish-American War took five lives for each one lost on the battlefield. In France, in 1917 and 1918, less than half as many Americans died from disease as died in battle.[17] Typhoid, dysentery, bubonic plague, typhus, cholera, and other familiar wartime scourges were almost unknown in the American army. Romance has always pictured the soldier as shot through the heart or bleeding from a sword cut; the World War was the first great conflict in which the conventional picture of a soldier's deathbed approximated the truth. For previous wars a far more accurate type of the average soldier's lot would be a sick man stretched on a tumbled hospital cot from the effects of bad diet, foul water, or an infected insect bite.

Yet one terrible plague broke through all the barriers which science could erect. The influenza, inducing the even more fatal pneumonia, appeared in a particularly active and malignant phase in the autumn of 1918. Worldwide in range, it took its victims indifferently from the army at the front, the recruits in barracks, and the civilians at home. In mid-September 1918, all diseases combined were taking soldier lives in the American cantonments at an average rate of 5 out of 1,000 per year, a ratio not high even for healthy young men outside the army. One month later the death rate had risen from five a year to four a week. Fortunately, the epidemic was as brief as it had been severe. With the frosts of late autumn it diminished and with the winter almost disappeared.

Schools and churches were closed for several weeks in many cities. Men and women walking abroad covered their faces with masks to prevent infection; a stranger visiting an American city during that fatal October might have imagined that the Germans had attacked with poison gas, which compelled the wearing of gas masks. The disease had an ugly habit of selecting strong young men and women in their twenties and thirties in preference to the infants or elderly folk who are the first victims of most epidemics. The result was that the influenza inflicted just the same sort of injury on the nation as the war itself, killing off many of those most fit to do the work of the world. The *Survey* editorially estimated the economic loss to the nation from sickness and death during the epidemic at "not less than three billion dollars."[18]

Americans nevertheless contributed mightily to the war effort. The United States was threatened with no famine and did not require to be provisioned. The problem was rather to create a food surplus in America to relieve a food shortage in Europe. No food cards or rationing were introduced and the main reliance was on persuasion rather than compulsion. A special commission, entirely independent of the food administration's grain corporation, established a fixed price of $2.20 per bushel for spring wheat, twenty cents above the minimum guaranteed by congressional act.[19] Millers were not permitted to sell flour for more than a stipulated margin above their costs, and hoarding and profiteering were severely treated. The high and stable price offered for wheat encouraged so much planting that the 1918 crop of 921 million bushels was adequate for the needs of the war.[20] This rapid expansion of the planted area of staple grains had an unfortunate recoil after the war, when the curtailment of European demand brought prices down to half the wartime figure.

The domestic aspect of the food situation was almost as important as the agricultural. Women and boys on vacation formed a "land army" to help in farm work, and the Boy Scouts planted home vegetable gardens in accordance with the slogan, "Every Scout to feed a soldier." Just those foods in which the average American's diet was richest he was now called on to deny himself—the meats, fine flour, fats, and sweets. He was willing, but needed much instruction as to how to set about it. Millers, bakers, and housewives joined forces to devise more or less tempting substitutes for fine wheat bread from coarse-milled "whole wheat," corn, rye, and other grains. In addition, wheatless days were advertised when patriotic Americans forwent altogether the usual slice or two of bread at dinner. Cheaper cuts of meat supplemented the traditional expensive steaks, and some restaurants catered to the national love of novelty by adding horse, rabbit, and even whale meat to the menu. Meatless days were observed as rigorously as Catholic Fridays. Housewives were urged to purchase only as much food as they were certain to use so there might be less danger of its spoiling, and garbage cans which before the war were full of discarded fragments of food now went to the dump half empty.[21] To prevent the more conscientious from overdoing it and trying to live on nothing but hardtack and spinach, the food administration advised all to "eat plenty, wisely, without waste."

But women helped the war effort in many other places besides the kitchen; indeed, one of the main effects of the war on American life was to bring them out of the kitchen. They were particularly in demand for the types of factory work which required delicate discrimination of touch. "I know a woman who has for years been the Northern agent for the woven rugs and homespun made in a certain mountain community in the South," wrote one observer.

> Now she has closed up her business and is going to one of the base hospitals to do work in occupational therapy. . . . The government gas mask factory has proved a most interesting field for many artists, musicians, and stage women. One well-known portrait painter is now spending her days in turning over little brass disks and carefully inspecting both sides. . . . The aircraft factories, too, seem to have an especial appeal to women. It may be because the sewing on the delicate wings of the aircraft is something that is

distinctly women's work. . . . Wireless telegraphy is attracting many women who have the necessary background of physics and mathematics.[22]

This movement of women into "men's jobs" at something like men's wages revolutionized the economics of many a household. Jane Fuller was a widow who worked as a housemaid at $30 a month, and her sixteen-year-old son did odd jobs for the butcher. As the draft took more and more men away from industry, the boy became a machine operator at $3.50 a day and the widow earned as much in a munition factory. "Today this mother and son—and the case is both actual and typical—average forty dollars a week where a year ago their total income was thirty dollars a month."[23]

To carry the cost of war the burden was divided between taxes and loans. Both withdrew capital from expenditure on the comforts and luxuries of peace and were thus really paid in present costs, but because a loan promises a "reward of abstinence" by repaying the bondholder at the expense of the taxpayer, it will call out money that would hide from the taxgatherer. Five great loans were floated, each was oversubscribed, and a total of more than $21 billion raised from more than 65 million subscriptions. The first four were called "liberty loans,"[24] the last, coming after the armistice, a "victory loan."

Labor troubles were among the major causes of delay in making preparation for war. The attitude of union president Samuel Gompers and nearly all other high officials of the American Federation of Labor (A.F.L.) was almost aggressively loyal and few strikes of any importance were directed against the war or intentionally designed to hamper it in any way. The trouble lay in the economic sphere, not the political. With rapidly rising prices, the displacement of trained union men by nonunionists and women, and the wartime disregard of customary limitation on the hours of labor, the trade unions feared that their hard-won gains of the past were being imperiled.[25] Hence they demanded recognition of the union and a higher standard of wages.

Where the Industrial Workers of the World were active in the far West the conflict was most acute. The I.W.W. promoted huge strikes in the copper mines and in the lumber camps, apparently less to oppose the war or better their wages than to strike a blow at the capitalistic system in general. Their lawless violence was met with equal lawlessness on the other side. In August 1917 the agitator Frank Little was lynched in Montana. In the copper region of Arizona nearly 1,200 strikers, about a third of them members of the I.W.W., were deported beyond the state line by force. Attempts to prosecute the kidnappers failed because local sentiment was with them. During and immediately after the war, to be a member of the I.W.W. was to encounter legal penalties for "criminal syndicalism" or sedition.[26] An example of the way in which official "correctness" merged into personal enthusiasm for direct action was the report of a Nevada sheriff to the governor:

> I regret to report to Your Excellency that on such and such a date, such and such a person was forcibly taken from my possession by parties unknown. He was placed on trial by an improvised tribunal and found guilty of lukewarmness toward the cause of the United States . . . whereupon (after tarring and feathering him) they instructed him to leave the country, telling him that if he ever comes back they will lynch him—and if he does, by   , Governor, *we will!* [27]

Another type of opponent to the war was the man whose conscientious scruples forbade him to serve. Members of religious sects teaching absolute nonresistance, such as the Quakers, were exempted from military service by law, but this exemption did not cover all the cases that arose. [28] Some conscientious objectors adhered to no sect and believed in Christianity only as a general teaching of peace and goodwill, or regarded the particular war as unjust or "capitalistic," or merely revolted emotionally against the idea of killing anyone. Again, there was the case of Roger Baldwin, director of the American Civil Liberties Bureau, who refused to obey the draft on the individualistic plea of his "uncompromising opposition to the principle of conscription of life by the state for any purpose whatever, in time of war or peace." [29] Nor were the bewildered draft boards prepared to deal with strange religious sects which not only objected to fighting but had conscientious scruples against saluting, wearing buttons (the Amish Mennonites), donning uniforms, or shaving. [30] Whether these passive resisters were cruelly or humanely treated in the prison camps depended partly on the good nature of the officers in charge, but even more perhaps on their imagination and sense of humor.

One of the most ill-advised expressions of overzealous patriotism was the war on the German language. Even as early as 1915 the unpopularity of the German cause had brought about a decline in the study of German in the high school. Even ten years after the war, German had not quite recovered its relative position in the curriculum of 1914. Some officers of the American Defense Society wanted to go further and suppress all public use of the German language during the war, and even proposed a boycott of it afterwards. The number of newspapers and periodicals published in German in the United States decreased from about 500 to 344 in the two war years. [31] But the feeling against the German language, and the yet more absurd objection to German music, did not long outlast the war, and practically nothing more was heard of hasty proposals to boycott goods "made in Germany" when peace came again.

A more important influence of the war on American life was the lesson it taught in organization. The war came to a lax, individualistic people; a year was wasted in blundering experiment and another year spent in building up a sound war machine. The full strength of the army and its equipment could not have been placed in the field until 1919, and perhaps not until 1920. The sudden, rather unexpected surrender of Germany and her allies left the government with uncompleted contracts on its hands for the expenditure of hundreds of millions of dollars, an army equally divided between training camps and trenches, factories and power plants half completed, and a nation which, having just passed through all the stages from apathy to profoundest enthusiasm, had no appropriate outlet for its emotions.

The abrupt termination of the war, while welcome in every way, was almost as hard to realize as its abrupt beginning. On armistice day or, rather, on the eve of the armistice—for the news had been prematurely announced—all business was suspended and thousands poured into the city streets, at once elated and bewildered. On their heads fell a shower of paper tape and torn scraps of telephone directories flung as confetti from office windows in the great carnival of peace. So deep was this paper snow that a few matches would have set the business districts aflame, and the fire companies remained in anxious readiness for a call. But the mass of the crowd did not want to smoke, and rarely raised a cheer or gave any other outward sign of rejoicing. It was enough to walk for miles along the city streets with 10,000 strangers, and to realize that in that moment of good news not one of them was really a stranger.

SHADOWS OF RECONSTRUCTION

"THE WAR," said a soldier proverb, "will last a hundred years—five years of fighting and ninety-five of winding up the barbed wire." The first days of reconstruction after any great war are at once tragic and tedious; they lack the dramatic quality that partly redeems the cruelties of battle. The patriotic unity which is called into life by war disappears with the emergency that gave rise to it and dissolves in a welter of confusion, bickerings, and recriminations. The decade after Yorktown and the decade after Appomattox include many of the pages of American history which patriots would most willingly forget. The effect of the World War on the people of the United States was apparently less profound than that of either the War for Independence or the Civil War because it was briefer and because it was fought wholly on foreign soil, but the road back to normal life was rocky enough. There was a war-prosperity boom with great inflation of prices, followed by a serious depression. There was some radical discontent, reflected in a number of violent strikes during 1919, and a corresponding conservative panic leading to hasty legislation against aliens and radicals. There was a series of scandals in connection with oil leases and other public business that recalled the days of the Tweed Ring and the Carpetbaggers.[32] Certain forms of crime became, if not more common, at any rate bolder and more defiant. "Robbery under arms" and the almost open warfare of rival gangs of "bootleggers," "hijackers," and "racketeers" attracted alarmed attention. Some have even traced, though perhaps speculating too boldly, the effects of war on national morale in the impassioned frivolities of the younger generation and the pessimistic tone of the new realistic fiction.

The effects of the war on American life were unquestionably important, but most of them were disguised, indirect, rather than openly present to consciousness. For example, the indignation against Germany which mounted from the first news of the invasion of Belgium in 1914 to its climax in the final death grapple of the nations in 1918, had already begun to seek other channels in 1919.[33] The alien forces which menaced America were now pictured as wearing the red cap of revolution rather than the spiked helmet of militarism. Soviet Russia quickly replaced Germany as the villain of international politics.

The "red" panic of 1919 was indeed one of the most curious aftereffects of the war. "No one who was in the United States, as I chanced to be, in the autumn of 1919," declared an English Liberal journalist, "will forget the feverish condition of the public mind at that time. It was hagridden by the spectre of Bolshevism. . . . Property was in an agony of fear, and the horrid name 'Radical' covered the most innocent departure from conventional thought with a suspicion of desperate purpose. 'America,' as a wit of the time said, 'is the land of liberty—liberty to keep in step.' "[34] In a few cases there was, to be sure, a little real fire under the great smoke cloud of "radical" panic. In the Pacific Northwest the so-called One-Big-Union movement looked toward the establishment of a universal workers' soviet to seize industry with the weapon of a general strike and then hold it in the name of the proletariat. An older organization, the Industrial Workers of the World, did not accept so completely the Russian program, but in spirit and tactics resembled it. Both organizations believed that workingmen should unite by whole industries and not, as was the program of the American Federation of Labor, by separate crafts. Both viewed the strike not as a weapon to gain specific concessions of wages, hours, and the right of collective bargaining, but rather as a means to disorganize the whole fabric of capitalist production. The I.W.W., however, probably never much exceeded 50,000 active members and the One-Big-Union movement does not seem to have enlisted more than 30,000.[35]

In the well-organized trades these radical unions played little or no part, but they found a field for action among ill-paid, unorganized casual laborers in the lumber camps, the grain fields, and the textile mills. In some cases the strikes were supplemented by sabotage or destructive action "on the job," such as driving spikes into lumber to wreck saws, burning haystacks, spoiling machinery, and the like. In the far Northwest a number of violent conflicts attracted national attention, such as the attempted general strike of February 1919 in Seattle, which brought Mayor Ole Hanson, who crushed it, into momentary prominence as the "strong man of the hour."

On armistice day of the same year a riot between American Legionnaires and members of the I.W.W. in Centralia, Washington, caused several deaths.

In the prosperous days of 1919 strikes were numerous, widespread, and not infrequently violent. This was due partly to the effort to bring wages up to the new price levels and partly to the general restlessness of the period. Some 4 million workers were on strike at some time during the year.[36] All the fundamental industries—coal, steel, railways, and textiles—suffered in turn. The strike which attracted widest attention was the result of an attempt to unionize the steel industry. It lasted from September 1919 till the following January. The attempt of some of the union leaders, such as William Z. Foster, to give a revolutionary turn to the struggle resulted in creating prejudice against the strikers. The press hardly gave their side a hearing at the moment, but an investigation by a special commission of inquiry of the Interchurch World Movement showed that many of the grievances of the steel workers were very real and demanded remedy.[37] The Church had stepped in where the press failed.

One of their greatest grievances was the long working day and week. Approximately one half of all the employees of the striking mills were subject to the twelve-hour day, and one half of these in turn were subject to the seven-day week, the average week for all the employees being 68.7 hours.[38] Sometimes at the turn of a shift the steel worker would be compelled to stay on duty without relief for twenty-four hours. The methods used by the employers and managers to break up trade-union solidarity were often questionable. Spying on meetings of the union was frequent. The following letter of instructions is significant:

> We want you to stir up as much bad feeling as you possibly can between the Serbians and Italians. Spread data among the Serbians that the Italians are going back to work. Call up every question you can in reference to racial hatred between these two nationalities; make them realize to the fullest extent that far better results would be accomplished if they will go back to work. Urge them to go back to work or the Italians will get their jobs.[39]

Though the strike was a failure in its immediate objectives, the twelve-hour day disappeared within a few years from the steel mills, largely as a result of the intervention of President Harding.

One of the most interesting specimens of the strike fever was the Boston police strike of 1919. The police, whose fixed salaries bore no relation to the rising cost of living, insisted on organizing in affiliation with the A.F.L., and struck to secure the recognition of their union. For a few days the city was stripped of its legal protection, though university lads and others acted as temporary substitutes. No very great outbreak of crime took place—though some shops were plundered—but everyone felt the presence of a dangerous crisis. The grievances of the police were real, but a police strike, raising the classical question "who shall guard our guardians?" seemed, in Governor Calvin Coolidge's phrase, a "strike against public safety." There was a difference of opinion as to the active part played by the governor in crushing the strike, but at least he spoke out clearly against it and won national fame overnight. When he was reelected governor on the Republican ticket, he received the congratulations of the Democratic president.

After 1919 strikes became less frequent and less associated with revolutionary dreams.[40] In contrast to the more than 4 million men on strike or locked out in 1919 there were about 1.5 million in 1920 and about a million in 1921.[41] But they continued vexatiously common in certain industries, such as coal mining. Everywhere in the world, coal mining, for many reasons, was in an unsatisfactory condition. The work itself was dangerous and laborious, and long periods of idleness alternated with busy seasons when the miners toiled for eight or nine hours underground. Conditions of employment and rates of pay varied enormously between good fields and bad. As particular coal beds approached exhaustion and shafts had to be sunk more deeply, the costs of production increased and the profits shrank toward nothing. American miners and mine owners alike were in a better position than their European fellows, for the mines themselves were newer and richer. American miners were less insistent on government ownership as a solution than the British; their objectives were to unionize the entire coal field, to secure a higher rate of pay, and, by means of a shorter working week, to spread production evenly through the year. In the nonunion fields, such as parts of West Virginia, the men complained also that their houses were on mining-company land and their shops company stores, so they were altogether at their employers' mercy. Strikes were frequent in the anthracite fields of Pennsylvania, and in 1922 soft- and hard-coal workers alike dropped tools to fight a proposed wage cut.

In the days of American adolescence, when industries were still on a merely local scale, the public had regarded strikes as private battles between employers and employed. But the huge twentieth-century concentrations of both capital and labor made it possible for a strike in a key industry to throw out of employment thousands of men in other industries dependent upon it. A traction strike that sent John Citizen walking to work, a builders' strike that made impossible his dream of a cheap suburban home, a walkout at the gas works that left the streets to darkness and the footpad, or a police strike that advertised to the criminal element that their time had come, all emphasized the fact that in industrial warfare there were no neutral rights. Perhaps the most daring solution brought forward during these years was the proposal of Governor Henry Allen of Kansas for an industrial-relations court with plenary powers to decide all industrial disputes that threatened the public welfare.[42] Organized labor, however, bitterly opposed compulsory arbitration on the ground that labor contracts imposed by authority and enforced by penalties amounted to slavery. The courts declared the Kansas antistrike law unconstitutional in some of its important features.[43]

On the whole, the influence on the American Federation of Labor, the Railroad Brotherhoods, and other large unions were distinctly conservative.[44] Labor unions might endorse particular candidates, but they refused to enter the political arena as an independent party. The United States was not called upon to face a general strike of all the principal unions at once, such as occurred in Great Britain in 1926. Many of the most vexatious strikes of the reconstruction period were "outlaw" strikes by small local unions, acting in disobedience to orders of the national officers, or spontaneous walkouts that had no official sanction even from a local union. In all public statements on the question the labor leaders denounced the Bolshevist movement in Russia and all attempts to emulate it in other countries, and the public noticed the curious paradox that many conservative businessmen advocated the recognition of Soviet Russia for commercial reasons while the chiefs of organized labor opposed it. The influence of organized labor was thrown successfully in favor of stricter limitations on foreign immigration and unsuccessfully in favor of railroad nationalization and federal regulation of child labor.

American Socialism failed to recover even the very moderate position it had held earlier. The entrance of the United States into the World War divided the party into "patriot" and "pacifist" factions on the issue of open opposition to the national military effort. Those who, from sympathy with the Entente Allies or from a feeling of national solidarity, gave support to the war, for the most part withdrew from the active Socialist movement leaving it in the control of bitter-ender opponents of intervention. The hand of the law fell very heavily upon the latter; Eugene Debs, the veteran party leader, made his presidential campaign in 1920 from prison.

Another party schism took place when the Russian Bolshevist revolution divided American Socialists between a left wing which wished to affiliate with Moscow and establish a "dictatorship of the proletariat" and a more conservative group which remained loyal to the old program of democracy and social evolution. As a consequence, most of the energy which should have gone into a united assault on the high battlements of capitalism was wasted on factional feuds.[45] The left-wing faction usually took the name Communist, but sometimes they were themselves divided on petty points of theory or practice. James O'Neal listed in 1924 no less than sixteen Communist organizations of national scope which tried to wear the mantle of Lenin.[46] Most of these were very short-lived, and many of them were finally swept together into the Workers' party under the leadership of William Z. Foster, hero of the steel strike of 1919. There were only 15,000 or 20,000 members of the communistic groups and the great majority of them could not speak English, the Finns being the largest alien unit. The

Workers' party dropped the former communist policy of holding secret and illegal meetings and came into the open with a regular national ticket in 1924 and 1928.

The most orthodox wing of the Socialist movement, still keeping the copyright of the Socialist party name, joined with many liberal and reformist bourgeois elements in supporting the presidential candidacy of Robert M. La Follette in 1924, but acted independently again in 1928 under the eminently respectable leadership of the Reverend Norman Thomas, pacifist writer and Princeton graduate. All socialistic national tickets combined cast a smaller relative vote after the war than the Socialist party alone in 1912.[47]

The labor unrest of 1919, the communistic movement within the Socialist ranks, lurid newspaper accounts of Russian intrigues in the farthest ends of the earth, and the still undischarged nerve tension of wartime must all be taken into account in explaining the hysteria of the period. The papers, very literally, "saw red" everywhere. The word "radicalism,"which had been rather a compliment in the Bull Moose days of 1912–16 when it implied merely a reasonable progressivism in politics, now had an implication of dynamite. Many states passed laws against "criminal syndicalism" sufficiently drastic to jail any man on the rolls of one of the many more or less secret Communist parties or associations. Prosecutions were especially common in California. The American Civil Liberties Union was kept busy in defending one case after another of bewildered immigrants whose crude political doctrines had involved them somehow in the meshes of the law.[48] In December 1919 the *Buford* sent back a boatload of Russian or near-Russian Communists to Soviet Russia.[49] Postmaster General Albert S. Burleson suppressed one number of the periodical *Masses* and then, with a cruel sense of humor, refused to admit subsequent issues to the mails on the ground that, not being regularly published, it was no longer a "periodical."[50]

Attempts were even made to hold the antiwar Socialists responsible after the war for their former pacifist views. Victor Berger, chosen to represent a Wisconsin constituency in the House of Representatives, was twice debarred from taking his seat in Congress. The New York legislature, while the Lusk committee was solemnly investigating radical propaganda of all shades and considering ways and means of keeping it from the schools, decided to strike yet another blow for national security and barred five Socialists from membership on the direct charge that no Socialist could be considered loyal to the Constitution.[51] Eventually, however, most "political prisoners" held as pacifists, conscientious objectors to war, or sympathizers with revolution were pardoned, and after 1920 there were no further attempts to keep duly-elected Socialists out of office.[52]

One incident of these times, not very important in itself, threatened to become an American equivalent to the French Dreyfus case for the excitement it occasioned, the length of time it remained before the courts and the public, and the alignment of social forces it created. Nicola Sacco and Bartolomeo Vanzetti, Italians with anarchistic views, were accused of murdering a shoe-factory paymaster in April 1920 and were convicted on rather flimsy evidence the following year.[53] After a wait of seven years, during which the men sought in vain to get their case reheard in a higher court, they were executed in August 1927. What gave the Sacco-Vanzetti case its special notoriety was the use of the radicalism of the accused as an argument by both friends and foes. Judge, jury, and community were prejudiced against them from the start; radicals, equally prejudiced, decided that the whole charge of murder was merely a pretext to "railroad" inconvenient agitators. The evidence in the case was confused and contradictory, and even conservative-minded folk questioned whether the accused had received a fair trial. Under pressure of liberal opinion the governor of Massachusetts appointed a committee of three, among them President A. L. Lowell of Harvard University, who reported they saw no reason for advising the intervention of the pardoning power. As the day of the execution approached, bomb outrages took place in protest, not only in the United States but in distant foreign lands.[54] When the last appeal for stay of sentence was pending, huge crowds gathered in front of the American embassy in London and in front of American consulates in Plymouth and elsewhere to agitate in behalf of the accused.[55] In Latin Europe and in Latin America small riots occurred; Soviet Russia honored them as martyrs. Even conservative newspapers in Europe used the case as a convenient text for preachments about the quality of American justice.

The dominant notes in the political life of the time were conservatism and indifference. Evidences of the former may be found in the already mentioned weakness of third-party movements, in the huge majorities obtained by the Republican party in three successive elections, in the fact that both major parties consistently nominated men who had the confidence of the world of business, in the acceptance of the protective-tariff principle by the Democrats in 1928, and in the popular favor accorded to very wealthy men in high political office.[56] The genial standpatter Warren G. Harding, who died in the midst of his term; Vice President Calvin Coolidge, close-mouthed, intent on economy, a typical self-contained Vermonter, who succeeded him; and the energetic apostle of science in business Herbert Hoover represented an ascending scale of ability, but all alike stood for what President Harding had termed "normalcy."

The general indifference to politics was not altogether a new phenomenon. No election after 1896 had brought to the polls a very large proportion of the electorate.[57] But 1920, when only about half of those eligible to vote exercised their franchise, marked the nadir of interest in American politics, and 1924, in spite of a vigorous third-party fight by Robert M. La Follette, made but little better showing. Several causes suggest themselves.[58] There were no clearly defined issues in most of the contests, all party platforms being deliberately vague on the most disputed points. The old party feeling of the Civil War days had faded to a mere tradition, and in the Lower South, with the virtual disfranchisement of the black, a single-party system had made the section so solid that, with the exception of 1928, the only real contests took place at the Democratic primaries. The grant of woman suffrage increased the absolute but decreased the relative vote since more women than men abstained from going to the polls. But probably the most important factor was simply the pressure of competing interests. So engrossing was the complex life of business, and so exacting the obligations of the life of pleasure, that politics was no longer needed as a popular amusement or topic of conversation.[59] The decline of politics is curiously parallel to the contemporaneous decline of the pulpit, and in both cases the fundamental cause seems to have been simply that people in general preferred the automobile and the movies to the affairs of church or state.

Private crimes attracted more attention from press and public than national scandals. No topic was more common in news and editorial columns than the "crime wave." And yet it remains an open question whether there was a crime wave, in the sense of an absolute increase in the total volume of law violation. Statistics were in such confused and unreliable condition that criminologists waged inconclusive war as to whether felonies were really becoming more common or merely remaining at their normal high American level.[60] A comparison of the homicide (murder and manslaughter) rate for the period 1914–18 and the five following years (1919–23) shows but little change.[61] What even the incomplete and partial statistics available demonstrate beyond dispute is the permanently low standard of public security there is in the United States as compared with any other country of comparable general civilization.

According to Dr. Frederick L. Hoffman, statistician of the Prudential Insurance Company, the homicide rate of the United States was sixteen times that of England and Wales.[62] The single city of Chicago had for several years a longer list of killings than all England; other great cities averaged about as badly. The highest death toll in proportion to population was in such states as Florida, Louisiana, Tennessee, Mississippi, and Georgia. But even orderly Massachusetts had a dozen times the homicide rate of Scotland in 1923. Italy had only half the American murder rate; sedate Switzerland one thirty-sixth. Nor is it possible to lay the blame wholly on the pioneer and protest that in a "new country" like the United States frontier tradition prompts a ready resort to self-help and pistol law. Canada and Australia, too, were pioneer countries, but in proportion to population they had about one murder to the American five.

The typical American slayer was also a robber. In spite of the publicity given by the yellow press to crimes of passion, there is no reason to suppose that jealousy and malice were any commoner in the United States than in other countries. The real problem was the professional bandit who killed with the sole motive of overcoming resistance or of removing a

*Many Americans worried about domestic concerns
hesitated to add responsibilities abroad;*

*As Sacco and Vanzetti were carried to their graves many felt that
intolerance had triumphed.*

The Aftermath of War

witness to his theft. Indeed, the American robbery record was relatively much worse than the American homicide record. Burglary-insurance rates in American cities were from fifteen to twenty times as high as in England,[63] and foreign writers often commented on the shock it gave them to see money moved through the city streets in armored cars as though passing through a hostile army. "Every day," said an American criminologist,

> the observer can see an armored car draw up in front of a bank in the financial district. An armed guard jumps off, places his hand on a large pistol in a holster strapped to his side, and stations himself at the bank entrance; another man steps out of the car and, with his hand on a pistol, takes his post at the rear of the car; while a third man with his hand on his pistol steps out with the bag of money or other valuables and hurries into the bank. It is not merely in New York that this is to be seen, but in all our large cities.[64]

Whether the postwar "crime wave" meant a real increase in lawlessness or merely a shift to newer forms of it, the public was much disturbed. Crime commissions were founded in many states. "At the present time," declared an authority on the subject, "they may be said to be epidemic in the United States. . . . They differ from such bodies as the American Prison Association, the National Probation Association, the American Institute of Criminal Law and Criminology in being expressions of what may be called the 'amateur spirit' in the field of criminology."[65] Lawyers and businessmen were their chief backers. Perhaps the most scientific of all the new bodies was the National Crime Commission, organized in 1925 as a fact-finding body. The surveys and studies of the crime situation, though they led to different recommendations, disclosed an appalling degree of incompetence in both the police and courts. The careful survey made by the Missouri Association for Criminal Justice, to take an instance typical rather than exceptional, showed that for each 100 felonies there were only seven arrests and less than five indictments.[66] And the New York State Crime Commission disclosed that of more than 25,000 prosecutions for felonies in 1925, less than 20 percent resulted in any punishment.[67]

In one respect American criminal jurisprudence showed a real improvement. The prison system, still bad enough in many states, was greatly reformed. The efforts of such penologists as Thomas Mott Osborne, George W. Kirchwey, Frank Tannenbaum, and others to substitute productive labor and healthful recreation for idleness met wide response, and the indeterminate sentence and the parole system—though both were greatly abused—at least placed a premium on good conduct during imprisonment.[68] Children's courts created a new technique in handling the offenses of the very young. Several Southern states abolished the evil custom of leasing out convict labor to private employers. In the larger cities psychological clinics were established to discover the quirks of personality that made a man a wolf to his fellows.[69] Dr. L. Vernon Briggs of Boston fathered a law providing for psychiatric examination of persons indicted for capital offenses or repeated felonies. He declared to the National Conference on the Reduction of Crime, held in Washington in 1927, that "Before this law was passed the procedure employed in ascertaining the mental responsibility of persons accused of crime was almost inconceivably futile, cruel and wasteful. Hardly a day passed . . . without the spectacle in some one of our courts, of two or more physicians, possibly graduates of the same medical school and belonging to the same scientific and medical societies, pitted against each other, testifying to diametrically opposite opinions as to the mental conditions and responsibility of the person in question."[70]

A discussion of crimes of violence in the America of the period permits at least two cheerful postscripts. In spite of race riots and Ku Klux Klan activities, there was a great decrease in the number of lynchings.[71] And the same statistical surveys that revealed a constant high level of homicides disclosed also a marked decline in suicides. The death rate from suicide, according to the life-insurance estimates, showed a decrease for all age groups for the whole period 1909-24, especially at the younger ages.[72] Americans were learning to place a proper value on life—when it was their own!

THE EXPERIMENT OF PROHIBITION

OF ALL THE SOCIAL EXPERIMENTS made by the American people in the wake of the World War, the most radical was the attempt to prohibit the production and sale of alcoholic drinks. But drastic as was the national law, it had behind it more than a century of agitation, controversy, and local legislation.[73] So far from being merely a product of sudden impulse and war-fed emotion it was the final stage of a long process of restriction. By 1914, Maine, Kansas, North Dakota, Oklahoma, Georgia, Mississippi, North Carolina, Tennessee, and West Virginia had adopted prohibition, and the autumn elections of that year added Virginia, Arizona, Colorado, Oregon, and Washington. Together with territory in other states "dry" by local option, nearly half (47 percent) of the population and three fourths (74 percent) of the area of the United States had outlawed the saloon. In most parts of the country only the great cities and mill towns remained "wet"; the single city of Chicago had more saloons than all the states of the South.[74]

During the next four years the number of total prohibition states more than doubled.[75] Other restrictions, due to the entrance of the United States into the war, limited liquor traffic still further. One powerful argument was that it was unpatriotic to convert foodstuffs into distilled or fermented beverages at a time when the nation was voluntarily rationing itself to send grain to Europe. In 1917, Congress restricted the use of foodstuffs in liquor manufacture and in 1918 prohibited altogether the wartime sale or manufacture of intoxicants.[76] The fact that some large brewers had been incautiously friendly to the German cause contributed to the prejudice against the trade.[77] Another influence of the war was the attempt to keep liquor away from the training camps and the shipping yards.

When national prohibition was at last established, over two thirds of the American people already lived under local prohibitory laws, and the other third had submitted to drastic wartime regulation.[78] The return of peace brought no alleviation. Before the temporary war legislation could be repealed, the adoption of the Eighteenth Amendment to the Constitution put the whole traffic outside the pale of the law.

Constitutional prohibition was approved by the Senate and by the House of Representatives in 1917. The proposed Eighteenth Amendment forbade "the manufacture, sale or transportation of intoxicating liquors" for beverage purposes, gave to Congress and the states the concurrent power to enact enforcement laws, and contained the unusual provision that the amendment would be inoperative unless ratified by the necessary number of states within seven years.[79] The legislatures of forty-six states acted favorably, only Connecticut and Rhode Island holding out to the end. In the legislatures of South Dakota, Idaho, Washington, Kansas, and Wyoming the vote was unanimous. By January 1919, when thirty-six states had approved the amendment, it became a part of the Constitution.

In accordance with its terms, national prohibition went into effect a year later, in January 1920. Congress passed over President Wilson's veto the Volstead act (named after the Minnesota congressman to whom fell the duty of framing the enforcement statute), which defined as "intoxicating" any liquor containing as much as one two-hundredth part of alcohol[80] and provided machinery for stringent enforcement. The sale of alcoholic liquor was still permitted for industrial, medicinal, and sacramental purposes, and elaborate licensing restrictions proved necessary to ensure that none of it was diverted to beverage purposes. A prohibition-enforcement unit, at first organized as part of the Bureau of Internal Revenue under the Treasury Department, was established with the double duty of regulating the legitimate use of alcohol and of preventing violations of the law.[81]

Four factors, aside from the temporary influence of the war, seem to have been particularly effective in bringing about national prohibition. First, and most important, the spread of state prohibition had already made prohibition almost national, so that it was but a short step (though a daring one) from prohibition by state law to prohibition by federal authority. Next, there was the crystallizing conviction of the South that the race problem was made more grave by the liquor problem. Then the automobile, now becoming almost universal, was a factor. Finally, Congress and the legislatures were increasingly dominated by an energetic and resourceful "pressure group," the Anti-Saloon league.

The variety of ways in which the Volstead act might be evaded or broken was enormous. To mention only the more important channels, beverage alcohol reached the consumer in the following ways: the redistillation of industrial alcohol and its sale by professional "bootleggers"; the misuse of permits for making or using industrial alcohol; private manufacture— "homebrewing" and the old-fashioned "moonshining"; the misuse of druggists' prescriptions; smuggling from Canada, Mexico, the West Indies, and Europe; smuggling from ships stationed just outside the territorial waters of the United States—the famous "rum row"; the use and sale of old private stocks safely cellared before the dry law was enacted; and the manufacture and sale of "near beer" and other "temperance drinks" which secretly overstepped the legal half of one percent of alcohol. By far the most important of these methods, quantitatively, was the redistillation of industrial alcohol to purify it of denaturants. Expert authorities usually estimated that more than half of the consumer's alcohol drunk in the United States under prohibition was obtained through this channel.[82]

Amateur homebrewing attracted many at first because of its spice of adventure. In many of the larger cities shops openly sold copper stills together with yeast, hops, and other accessories.[83] They dared not quite advertise the purposes for which these commodities—legal enough in themselves—were sold, but they could drop carefully veiled hints, even going so far as to depict in a streetcar advertisement a procession of thirsty camels crossing a desert.[84] Where women used to exchange old family recipes for cakes and puddings, men now met in locker rooms at the country club or in "conference" in business offices to exchange recipes for homemade beer and whiskey. There was also an expansion of the moonshine industry in the rural districts, originally an attempt to evade revenue laws.[85] Yet the homebrewer in the city and the moonshiner in his lonely cabin were but minor factors in the situation. Consumers preferred to trust the professional bootlegger who, with unblushing effrontery, represented his redistilled product as "genuine prewar stuff"—a famous Scotch whiskey or a fine French or Rhenish wine.

Though the proportion of genuine European stock available was very small, the liquor smuggled from abroad was in itself a considerable amount. An exact estimate is impossible, as lawbreakers do not keep statistics of their operations, but one can conclude much from the figures of shipment of spirituous liquors to countries neighboring the United States. From 1918 to 1922, Canada increased her British liquor imports almost sixfold; Mexico, eightfold; and the British West Indies not quite fivefold. Most remarkable of all was the increased importation of the Bahamas from less than 1,000 proof gallons to almost 368,000, and of Bermuda from less than 1,000 to over 41,000.[86]

The Canadian border was a weak spot in the enforcement program. Close to such great urban centers as Detroit, with but a short stretch of water to mark the political frontier, smuggling presented a simpler problem than maintaining a rum fleet on the Atlantic fed by supplies from Europe. Slocum Sleeper, head of the river patrol at Detroit, stated in 1928 that his men had captured $2 million worth of liquor in twelve months besides a fleet of fifty or sixty speedboats and numerous automobiles.[87]

The automobile provided the smuggler with a new facility. Huge trucks, moving by night at high speed along the highways, conveyed millions of gallons of liquor into the United States. The hazards were always great, but the greater the risk the higher were the prices and profits on each delivery. Besides the risk of encountering the lawful authorities, the rum runner had to beware a new and lawless enemy, the "hijacker."[88] The hijacker was the pirate of the landward trails. He found his richest source of revenue in holding up rum runners because his victims, themselves outlaws, dared not call in the aid of the law. But bootleggers, not willing to submit to this imposition, often hired professional gunmen to fight or punish the hijackers — a fruitful source of the gang wars in Chicago and elsewhere.

The bootlegging industry became a thoroughly organized one. Professional experts in distilling were highly paid for instructing others in the art. Professional carriers (women retail smugglers) added twenty-five cents a quart for their middleman services.[89] Bribery in many stages was a necessary part of the business and sometimes annulled the expected profit. Class distinctions crept in; there were "respectable" bootleggers who catered to the wealthy and occasionally sold real smuggled liquor, and disreputable thugs and moonshiners who dealt in redistilled denatured alcohol or cheap corn whiskey from the mountains.[90]

With all the widespread defiance of the Volstead act, the strongest opponents of prohibition admitted a diminished consumption of liquor.[91] Just how much less is quite impossible to estimate. There were no direct figures of illicit sales, and such indirect information as is afforded by statistical estimates of drunkenness, hospital cases of alcoholism, and violation of the prohibition laws is incomplete and often contradictory. Nor is it easy to interpret the facts when we have them. A sudden upward leap in arrests may mean either greater law violation or an increased rigor of law enforcement. An increase in hospital cases of acute alcoholic poisoning may mean either a growth in the quantity of liquor consumed or merely a decrease in its quality. In entering the blind jungle of propaganda and partisan statistics one must tread warily. The best antiprohibitionist estimates, such as that by Hugh F. Fox of the United States Brewers Association, placed the per-capita annual liquor consumption at about half as much in 1926 as in 1918, but added the comment that, as most of the illicit liquor was stronger than the average lawful drink of preprohibition days, there might be an actual increase in the consumption of alcohol.[92] The drys, on the other hand, thought 5 or 10 percent of the former alcohol consumption a generous estimate.[93]

Such statistics on drunkenness as are on a sufficient scale to be useful seem to show two facts: a decrease in drunkenness for the whole period as compared with the years before prohibition, in spite of the worse liquor consumed and the stricter standards of the law; and an increase in drunkenness within the period from 1920 to 1923 and a fairly consistent level afterwards. The year 1920 was the soberest the United States ever had. Arrests from drunkenness in 514 cities and towns for the decade 1914-24 show only 60 to a population of 10,000 in 1920 as compared with 169 in 1914, 126 in 1923, and 127 in 1924.[94] Deaths from alcoholism numbered almost 5 to the 100,000 in 1914, only one in 1920, 3.2 in 1923, and 3.6 in 1925.[95] "It cannot be doubted," declared Dr. Matthias Nicoll, state health commissioner for New York,

> that this striking rise in the death rate since 1920 is due, in great part, to the establishment of a vast national and international machinery for the illicit manufacture, importation, and distribution of alcoholic beverages, a large percentage of which is unfit for beverage purposes, and more apt to bring about pathological conditions.[96]

Yet for the entire period 1920-28, no year appears to have equaled the alcoholic death rate of the years before 1917.

Most sensational, though always exceptional, were the sudden deaths from wood-alcohol poisoning. To denature grain alcohol it was customary to add wood alcohol, a deadly poison which produces death or at least blindness in those who use it. Unscrupulous bootleggers sometimes failed to remove all this denaturant from their product. The sudden death in 1928 of thirty-four persons in New York City in four days revived bitter talk that the federal government was a "murderer" and "poisoner" in denaturing industrial alcohol with poisonous agents, although the use of such denaturants antedated prohibition. Even more harmful, because it was more common, was the use of raw, crude alcohol distilled from corn mash or potatoes and mixed with coloring and flavoring agents, themselves often injurious enough.[97]

Prohibition was unequally received in different parts of the United States. Rural America was mainly dry. Though hard cider and moonshine whiskey sometimes qualified rural temperance, in the main enforcement was an urban problem. But there were wet spots even in the dry areas: New Orleans and tourist Florida in the South; Reno and San Francisco in the far West; the river towns of the Mississippi and Missouri valleys; the Ohio mill towns. But along the Atlantic Seaboard, from Boston to Baltimore, the wet spots merged into a continuous belt, and here was the real focus of hostility to the Eighteenth Amendment. A map prepared in 1924 by Mrs. Mabel Willebrandt, assistant attorney general, showed the degree of nonenforcement in different sections of the country to vary from 5 percent in Kansas, Utah and Idaho to 95 percent in New York City.[98]

Since one effect of prohibition was to increase the price of liquor from four to twenty times to the ultimate consumer, prohibition made much more change in the habits of the poor than of the rich. Many of the wealthy had well-stocked cellars before prohibition came,[99] and when the supply at last ran low the bootleggers found new customers. The sale of silver hip flasks for use at country club dances and other convenient occasions became a widespread custom. There was a curious and almost comical inversion of class relations. Instead of Lady Bountiful visiting the slums to redeem the drunkard, the slums were now shocked at the conduct of the gilded youth. A janitor's wife in New York asserted. "It's not our people that are drinking so much. It's the rich bums that come from outside. . . . It used to be some lively down here before prohibition, but that was our own people and you could say to them, 'Jim, you go along home to Maggie 'til you get sobered up.' But these rich bums, you don't know where to tell 'em to go."[100] After studying conditions in Massachusetts, Dr. Richard C. Cabot of Harvard declared: "The rich may, for all we know, be as foolish as ever, but beyond any question the poor are better off. Drunkenness in women of the poorer classes has signally decreased; children under seventeen are much better off."[101]

Prohibition had a great effect on the dietetic habits of the nation. Strangely enough, at first glance, "near beer" (beer containing no more than the lawful maximum of alcohol) proved a financial failure, only 7 percent as much being sold in 1926 as of "real" beer in 1914.[102] The chief causes for this failure seem to have been the competition with stronger illicit beverages,[103] and the failure of the brewers to realize that the Volstead law had come to stay and their consequent neglect of what was to them merely a temporary sideline to their industry. Grape juice, tea, and coffee, also, seem to have been less affected than one might expect.[104] But the sale of milk for the home increased by one half from 1917 to 1924 and an official of a milk-dealers' association estimated that a good third of this gain was due to prohibition.[105] Citrus drinks, ice-cream, and candy sales made enormous advances; ice-cream consumption alone increased by 55 percent from 1916 to 1925. The National Confectioners' Association ranked the industries benefiting from prohibition in the following order: (1) savings banks, (2) soft drinks, (3) moving pictures, (4) theaters, and (5) candy.[106] In total sum, more than 11 billion bottles of nonalcoholic beverages were consumed in the United States each year.[107] Of course prohibition was only one factor in this development; for intensive advertising helped the soda-fountain trade, and the popular health magazines encouraged a more generous use of milk and fruit-juice beverages.

Food habits, too, were changing. The old-time saloon met three human wants: the specific craving for alcohol, the more general craving for something to satisfy the between-meal appetite, and the desire for a convenient hang-out where a man might gossip with his neighbor. Only by violating the law could the drugstores meet the first need, but the other two lay directly in its province. Sugar is an alcohol substitute as a quick fuel, and while ices might lack "kick," they were tasty and cooling. And a so-called drugstore, which sold everything from stamps and ice cream to books and hot-water bottles, and which remained open on Sunday when other stores were closed, made a convenient social center. Moreover, the soda-bar was soon supplemented by the cheap lunch, specializing in salads and sweets. Numerous confectionery shops that did not even pretend to be drugstores also broadened into quick-lunch restaurants. Said one experienced hotel man, "Nibbles are taking the place of bites. Salads and sandwiches are displacing steaks. While good old-fashioned restaurants close their doors, coffee shops, lunch rooms, and sandwich bars open at the rate of several thousand a year." And he added, "Whether or not one believes in the Eighteenth Amendment, we who deal in foods know that there is not only less heavy drinking, but that it has resulted in lighter eating." [108]

The more general social and economic effects of prohibition are hard to estimate. Certainly there was an enormous reduction in pauperism and a great increase in savings-bank deposits and other workingmen's investments.[109] But many factors had cooperated to elevate the standard of living in the United States in the decade following the war. Professor Irving Fisher's estimate that prohibition had added $6 billion a year to the national income[110] may be sound or not; neither he nor his critics were able to isolate the effect of the prohibition law from other causes of prosperity so as to make out a conclusive case. It would be safer to leave the question on a qualitative basis and say merely that there was, in most parts of the country, some reduction of drunkenness and therefore a decrease in the poverty and inefficiency it caused. Questionnaires sent to the members of the National Council of Social Work[111] and to the National Federation of Settlements[112] supported the conclusion of the latter that "There is less drinking; family life has improved—in some places in a quite remarkable degree; children are better fed and clothed and family ties have been strengthened; neighborhood disorder has been much reduced." In a word, the abolition of the corner saloon contributed its share to the elimination of the slum from American life. Whether or not this gain offset the new tasks and perplexities of enforcement was a question which a decade of prohibition still left to the future.

WOMEN AND THE ADVANCE OF FEMINISM

Count Hermann Keyserling, one of the many distinguished European philosophers, authors, and men of affairs who visited the United States after the World War, found as the most noteworthy of transatlantic marvels the complete and assured ascendancy of the American woman. In America, he wrote,

> all *men* are supposed to be equal. But women as a class are candidly accepted as superior beings. Thus America is today an aristocratic country of a peculiar type. It is a two-caste country, the higher caste being formed by the women as such. And this caste rules exactly in the way higher castes have always ruled. . . . Her inspiration and influence stand behind all American educators, as it stands behind all American prohibitionists. Her influence accounts for the infinity of laws and rules. She directs the whole cultural tradition. She also dictates in the field of moral conduct. Who wants to study the real meaning and purport of a caste system, should today not visit India, but America.[113]

Of course there was exaggeration here. The good count came from the country of Schopenhauer and brought with him not only the traditions of central Europe but, as a lifelong student of Oriental cultures, many of the views of eastern Asia as well. At almost any period of American history the position of women would have seemed strange to him.[114] But his words are not too wide of the mark to call attention to the rapid advance of the feminist movement in the United States during and after the war. The most obvious change was the adoption of woman suffrage as the universal law of the nation. But the complete acceptance of the American woman in political life was only one phase of a general movement toward sex equality, older than the war and broader than America. The same generation that saw woman suffrage granted in the United States saw it granted also in most of the nations of northern Europe along with many other legal rights and privileges. Not in the field of politics but in economic status and social prestige did the American woman occupy her unique position. American feminism meant freedom from custom and tradition more than from positive legal restriction. Many European nations, for example, had enacted divorce laws as liberal as those of most American states, but in none of them (with the possible exception of Soviet Russia) were divorces so frequently obtained by discontented wives. European schools and colleges had been generally opened to women, but only in the United States did women look upon a college education as a natural right. Nowhere else in the world could a respectable unmarried girl spend her time and money with so little adult supervision. Nowhere else did the middle-class housewife have so wide a margin of leisure for amusement, self-development, or public work as her fancy might dictate.

Though the entrance of women into industry began long before the war, it was undoubtedly accelerated by it. The census of 1920, coming conveniently just when temporary labor displacements of wartime had been mainly eliminated, showed 8.5 million women and girls over ten years of age engaged in gainful occupations, an advance of more than half a million since 1910.[115] This was not in itself a notable increase, indeed it did not quite keep pace with the growth in the general population; but the decreases were in occupations long open to women, such as farm work and domestic service, while in practically all "masculine" occupations the number of female workers greatly increased both in number and in proportion. There was a marked decline in the number of women employed as farmhands, laundresses, tailors, music teachers, midwives, charwomen, general servants, and cooks, and a corresponding gain in the number of women chauffeurs, cigar makers, bankers, police and probation officers, social workers, lawyers, college professors, elevator "boys," clerks, typists, bookkeepers, and barbers.[116] Almost one woman in four "gainfully employed" was married and presumably running a home as well as an outside job.[117]

For various sorts of routine clerical work employers definitely preferred women; men tended therefore to drift into other occupations rather than face the competition of the cheap and competent woman worker. There were, for example, eleven women stenographers and typists to every man so engaged. The capture of the elementary schools by the schoolma'am had made the old-fashioned schoolmaster an almost extinct type. No doubt the men had a real grievance in the fact that wages were kept down by the hiring of women to do the same work at cheaper rates,[118] but their grievance was rather against the employers who would not pay "men's wages" than against the women who frequently needed their jobs as badly as the men they displaced. Fortunately, the rapid expansion of American industry made it usually possible for any adaptable man to find some occupation not yet unduly "cheapened" by feminine competition. Probably the worst effect of woman's invasion of industry was not economic but psychological; more men, perhaps, left such occupations as teaching and stenography from the feeling that their task was "no work for a man" than because of lowered incomes.

There was a sharp schism in the feminist movement over the question as to whether women should or should not seek special protection for their health and welfare while engaged in industrial pursuits. Most reformers argued that the entire nation had a vested interest in the health of the mothers of the race and should therefore maintain by law wholesome standards for women workers. By 1922 forty-three states had limited by law the hours of labor for women, thirteen states had enacted minimum-wage laws, and sixteen states had forbidden night work in certain occupations.[119] But what appealed to most feminists as legal protection seemed to the more doctrinaire type, represented by the National Woman's party, as legal restriction. These advocated an "equal-rights amendment" to the federal Constitution which would sweep away all the legal disabilities of women, even those designed to safeguard them from competitive pressure in the ranks of industry.[120] Both political parties were urged in 1928 to endorse the equal-rights amendment, but both cautiously refused to commit themselves.

The institution of the home was affected in a myriad of ways by the growing custom of American women to pursue a trade before matrimony and sometimes along with it. In some respects the influence was wholly constructive. No longer was marriage the inevitable way of getting a living. This set a higher standard for husbands than in the days when "old maid" (a term fast disappearing from use) might mean penury as well as loneliness. On the other hand, a conflict frequently arose between the man's desire to support his wife according to the old American tradition and the woman's desire to have "a career." An interesting evidence of the interpenetration of man's world and woman's was the theme of Dorothy Canfield's novel *The Home Maker,* which depicted a woman who had failed as a mother but was a success in commerce, while her husband, kept at home by an accident, found in educating his children the success which he had missed as a man of business.[121]

Other conditions of the time besides the commercial employment of women bore hard against the home as an economic unit. Domestic help had become almost unobtainable. Household servants, both men and women, numbered about one to the hundred of the whole population. Women cooks decreased in ten years from 333,436 to 268,618.[122] The reduced immigration from Europe, the traditional recruiting ground of American domestic service, was certainly a major cause of this condition, but another reason was the opening of new and more attractive occupations for women. The cook might be wiled away from the stove not only by a wealthier neighbor but equally by the chance of a more independent industrial job. Every mistress in employing servants felt the competition of the entire world of business.[123]

To a considerable extent the cook and the housemaid could be and were replaced by mechanical aids. In the decade following the war there was an increase "of over 100,000 in the employés for attending to (not manufacturing) electric refrigerators, oil heaters, and similar household appliances which so vividly typify the liberation of 'Mrs. Workman.' "[124] To get an accurate idea of the transformation of the household economics we must reenforce personal impressions by statistics. Thus, "from the beginning of 1913 to the end of 1927 the number of customers for electric light and power increased 465 percent. In 1912 only 16 percent of the population lived in electric-lighted dwellings, but 63 percent had electric lights in 1927."[125] It is easy to visualize the meaning of such a change: the extension of daily time for work and play, the encroachment on the hours formerly devoted to slumber, the brightening of homes, the individualization of reading and study and the partial dispersion of the former "family group" about the parlor lamp or hearth fire, the adjustment of household temperature by electric heaters, fans, and refrigerators. By 1926 about 16 million homes had been wired for lighting and of these 80 percent had electric irons, 37 percent vacuum cleaners, and more than 25 percent had clothes washers, fans, or toasters.[126]

The costly but clean and convenient oil heater began to displace the coal furnace. In 1926 the twenty-four leading makers of oil-heating apparatus installed in American homes 73,000 heaters; in 1927, about 100,000. The grand total in use in American homes by 1928 was not less than 550,000, to make no mention of some 220,000 installed in hotels, stores, theaters, and other public buildings.[127] Where local costs permitted, gas heating was often substituted for coal and oil alike, though usually it was too expensive to be used for the family heating plant, however freely it might be employed in the kitchen or laundry. Many improvements were introduced into the domestic furnace for those who still relied on coal, such as the "iron fireman" which automatically pushed into the flames as much coal as might be needed to maintain the desired temperature.[128] The traditional icebox, itself a rare luxury in all other countries, was being rapidly supplanted by the domestic refrigeration plant. The census would have done well to cease listing the American housewife as of "no occupation" and to have called her "household engineer."

Yet the servant problem, in spite of the partial solution offered by modern science, compelled certain simplifications in domestic economy. The traditional nineteenth-century home, which survived in many parts of the United States down to the World War, required an amount of labor that would seem appalling to the latter-day urban American housewife. There were kerosene lamps to be filled and trimmed; coal scuttles to be emptied; huge expanses of rugs and carpets to clean; mountains of curtains, tablecloths, doilies, napkins, and other fabrics to require attention; cupboards of preserves to be put up for winter use; an annual earthquake of spring cleaning; and a huge Sunday dinner, requiring hours of preparation and a whole cookbook full of recipes. The visitor to an American home, especially a city home, in the postwar period would have found a very different picture. Instead of the roomy kitchen there would have been a kitchenette with dumbwaiter, sink, and gas or electric range. Small, brightly burnished aluminum pots and pans had replaced the morose array of ironware. The icebox or refrigerator served the purpose of the cool cellar, eliminating one story of the house. Little attempt was made to keep large supplies of food in the home. The delicatessen store around the corner was the accepted substitute for the pickle shelves in the cupboard; the commercial bakery had eliminated breadmaking day, and ice cream was bought from the confectioner instead of being made in the freezer by boy power.

In the living rooms the same tendency toward compactness, convenience, and simplicity prevailed, influenced no doubt by new artistic ideals as well as by labor shortage. The comfortable old American homes had come to seem "stuffy" and "cluttered." In place of the Victorian ideal of a homely coziness the new time emphasized an austere simplicity. The carpet gave way to the small rug on a polished hardwood floor, or to some new floor covering of the linoleum type which could be cleaned with water and soapsuds. Sofas, draperies, family portraits, and miscellaneous paintings were used more sparingly, and wallpaper was often abandoned. The parlor tended to disappear as an institution, if not as a room, for no longer was a special room reserved for curio cabinets, albums, the family piano, and the Sunday afternoon. The whole house was put to use all the time; all rooms were "living rooms."

Upstairs, unless it was a single-floor apartment, were the bedrooms and the principal bathroom (the houses of the well-to-do had usually several bathrooms and toilets). With its white porcelain tub, its shining tiles, and its spotless cleanliness, the bathroom might have been mistaken by a traveler from the past for a hospital room, just as he might have mistaken the kitchen for a chemical laboratory. Ponderous wooden bedsteads with nine-foot headboards gave place to neat pairs of small single beds. Space as well as time had to be spared, for the cost of building operated as powerfully as the lack of domestic service to reduce the dimensions of the average home. Our imaginary Victorian visitor would have found fault with the low ceilings, the small dining room with its round table, and the paucity of bedrooms. Very often the unexpected friend or relative would be "put up" at the hotel instead of being taken into the home. There was hardly room for hospitality in the older meaning of the word.

Period furniture, especially of the eighteenth-century English styles, had come in during the preceding period, but some interior decorators now carried the trend toward simplicity to an extreme. The so-called modernist furniture, largely influenced by postwar experiments in France and Germany, was a severe scheme of straight lines, almost a "cubist" note in decoration. A bedroom mirror became a mere sheet of reflecting glass gripped by naked metal supports. Wall lines ran from floor to ceiling, unbroken by baseboards or molding. But this extremity of the fashion was, for the most part, followed only by the very wealthy who could afford to redecorate each time the mode changed. The middle-class home accepted the style of fewer and simpler lines but refused to eliminate the curve.

The war struck a serious blow at domesticity by restricting the labor available for house building. A crisis in housing naturally resulted and, before new construction after the war could overtake the demand, rentals soared to unheard-of figures. New York City apartments that for many years had cost $40 or $50 a month increased suddenly to $100 or even $200, and the state legislature was forced to adopt emergency laws to prevent the eviction of thousands of tenants who could not meet the new rentals.[129] The decrease in building from 1913 to 1920 (a temporary factor), the great increase in wages in the building trades (a probably permanent factor); the congestion of population in rapidly growing cities—all combined to enhance housing costs. In some places people with moderate incomes had to give up their dream of owning an independent home, or even a good-sized apartment, and content themselves with a three-rooms-and-a-bath suite, in the meantime storing half their goods in some warehouse. Landlords often subdivided apartments, making two families live where one lived before.

In most parts of the country the separate home still remained the standard type, and in rural districts there were almost as many dwellings as families, though there was a slight increase in the number of rented and mortgaged homes. But in a few places, notably New York City, the usual proportion of separate houses to apartments was reversed. On Manhattan Island there were about seven families to each roof, and the few private homes which relieved the monotony of ten-flat apartment houses were counterbalanced by the huge apartment hotels in which hundreds of families lived in great blocks of steel and stone. Manhattan was, however, in this, as in most matters, an extreme case. But the same trend could be noted almost everywhere, different only in degree. From 1920 onwards the Bureau of Labor Statistics collected figures on building permits and in each year except one (1924) the proportion of urban families housed in single-family dwellings decreased and the proportion of those lodged in multifamily apartments increased.[130] In 1928, for the first time, the permits issued for apartment houses showed a larger estimated expenditure than those issued for single-family houses. Average building costs for all types of dwellings ranged from $2,000 or $3,000 dollars per family in St. Louis, New Orleans, and Dallas, to more than $7,000 in the borough of Manhattan. Single-family dwellings varied from $2,671 in Dallas to more than $9,000 in Providence, Rhode Island, and Newark, New Jersey.[131] These averages included, of course, workingmen's homes. Middle-class suburban houses cost usually from $10,000 to $20,000 to build, an amount equal to four or five years' income of the typical owner, an unwontedly heavy item in the home budget.

Various solutions of the housing problem were ventured. Some feminist leaders, such as Charlotte Perkins Gilman, advocated cooperative housing, and the transfer of cooking, cleaning, and other industrial processes of the "home plant" to central units for a whole block of dwellings. New methods of construction made their contribution. Sometimes houses were made in standardized parts, advertised through mail-order catalogues, and assembled according to pattern. The increased use of concrete saved wood and lessened fire risk. For many Americans the automobile became a second home, and the sole family residence for weeks or months of a family camping trip.

In every direction the economic functions of the home had been reduced. Restaurant, delicatessen, and hotel invaded the sphere of the kitchen; the cannery cut down the pantry shelves; the steam laundry proved a formidable competitor to the hired washerwoman; the public school, kindergarten, nursery school, and public playground assumed part of the care of supervising children. Such things, however, mattered little. When social theorists spoke with dread of the coming "breakdown of the American home," they were thinking of the family group rather than of the household "plant"; for so long as parents and children formed a congenial circle, the family would remain the fundamental human institution though its last economic function disappear. But if the family itself were breaking up, as some pessimists proclaimed, it mattered little where or how the homeless drifters found a place to sleep or eat.

The most common argument of those who believed that the traditional monogamous family was disappearing in America was, of course, the very high divorce rate, by far the highest rate for any part of Christendom where statistics were carefully kept. Moreover, this high ratio was not stationary but increasing, and very rapidly. From 1914 to 1928 the annual ratio of divorces to marriages rose from about one to ten to one to six. The increase was too steady over a long period of time to be attributed to the war, for though the war marriages of 1917 and 1918 may have been rash, apparently many civilian marriages were equally so.

The great majority of divorces were for the standard causes of desertion, cruelty, and adultery, but in the interpretation of these terms much laxity was employed. Desertion often meant a collusive arrangement whereby both parties had agreed to separate long enough to make divorce possible; cruelty was interpreted to cover "mental anguish" caused by any misconduct whatever of the party against whom complaint was laid; adultery was often a staged affair to satisfy the technicalities of law. The blunt truth is that almost any American man or woman who was tired of the marriage relation could have it dissolved at the cost of a little time and trouble. About two thirds of all divorces were obtained at the instance of the wife, and this ratio was constant over many years. The freedom to depart at will from the legal ties of matrimony was therefore chiefly a woman's privilege.

Little wonder, then, that a sober sociologist declared: "Our United States family . . . is monogamic in form with an apparent tendency toward term marriage and what is coming to be called the 'companionate.' "[132] "Term marriage" existed wherever a divorce was taken for granted if the venture did not turn out happily. If it were entered upon with no expectation of children the term marriage became the "companionate," a phrase first generally popularized by Judge Benjamin B. Lindsey, whose service in the Denver juvenile court had convinced him that conventional marriage laws were being increasingly disregarded by the oncoming generation.[133] Professor William F. Ogburn of the University of Chicago declared that the American family at least in "its extreme urban form has lost nearly all of its functions."[134] He noted seven ties that had held together the family of the past: economic, religious, protective, educational, recreational, social status, and affectional. The first six of these has been greatly attenuated or snapped altogether by changes in industrial methods and social customs; only affection remained to hold the home together, and where it was absent divorce was apt to be the solution.

There was, however, no general trend in the United States toward increased celibacy; the marriage rate, in contrast to the rising divorce rate, was fairly constant. The very fact that the knot could be so easily undone perhaps encouraged marriage. Nor was there any general increase in the age at which marriage was contracted except, to some extent, among professional men, college graduates, and business employees working for salaries too small to support a family. In these classes matrimony was frequently postponed till the thirties, though sometimes a solution to the economic problem was found by an early marriage and the postponement of motherhood until the joint savings of husband and wife would permit the proper care of children. For the nation as a whole the most common age of marriage for a man was about twenty-five; for a woman, about twenty-two.

The decrease of immigration brought about by the European war and by restrictive legislation was a factor in retarding the rate of growth of the American population, but "even had immigration continued at a record rate," said the expert analysts of the census, "the percentage of the national population increase still would have been lower than that shown by any previous census of the United States." [135] The United States shared with almost all countries of Western civilization in an accelerating fall of the birth rate. The native white stock of the nation was still enlarging at the rate of 11 or 12 percent to a decade, [136] but this increase was made possible only by a decline in the death rate. If the birth rate of the 1920s had been combined with the mortality rate of 1910, the natural increase would have diminished to 3.6 per 1,000 per annum, and had it been combined with the mortality rate of the beginning of the century there would have been virtually no increase at all. [137]

But actual failure to keep up the existing population was confined to a small class. This class included many of the otherwise most successful elements in the nation—well-to-do and educated business and professional men and women. Celibacy, late marriage, and birth control were all alike widespread in this group, as the late President Roosevelt had noted. [138] It was not "race suicide" that he really had had in mind, but the "class suicide" of the upper and middle classes. Although national mailing laws prohibited such public discussion of methods of birth restriction as was common in many European countries, there is no other way to explain the coincidence of a fairly high marriage rate with a decreasing proportion of births than to assume that, nevertheless, these methods were widely known and practiced in the United States.

The small family had, apparently, come to stay. The passing of the open frontier, the growth of the great cities with their cramped housing conditions, the closing of the door to fecund immigrant races, the higher standards of comfort, and the growing cost of education all tended to make a family of two or three children the national standard. At first glance the smaller family seems even more important than mechanical invention and simplified housekeeping in setting feminine energies free for work outside the home. But one qualification must be made. If care for children in the home was less extensive than formerly, it was also more intensive.[139] At no previous period were children tended with such watchful care of their health, diet, habits, and abilities. Never before were magazines of professional parenthood so widely sold or parent-teacher associations so generally attended. Even where the family had but one child, he often received as many hours of attention as had been distributed among the dozen brothers and sisters of his grandfather.

The effects of the changing standards in home and family life may be illustrated by what happened in a typical Midwestern city of 40,000 population.[140] In "Middletown" almost nine tenths of the high school girls declared their intention of "going to work" after graduation, and more than a fourth of all commercially employed women were married.[141] Children were more independent of the family circle; 55 percent of the boys and 44 percent of the girls spent less than four evenings a week at home.[142] Parents on the other hand greatly increased their range of solicitude for their children's welfare, typical statements being: "I accommodate my entire life to my little girl. She takes three music lessons a week and I practice with her forty minutes a day. I help her with her school work and go to dancing school with her," and "Everyone asks us how we've been able to bring our children up so well. I certainly have a harder job than my mother did; everything today tends to weaken the parents' influence. But we do it by spending time with our children."[143] The home was rapidly ceasing to be a unit of economic production, from five to seven loaves of bread out of every ten—according to the season of the year—were bought from the bakery and, in the well-to-do homes, most laundry was done outside the house, although the "advent of individually owned electric washing machines and electric irons has . . . slowed up the trend of laundry work—following baking, canning, sewing, and other items of household activity—out of the home to large-scale commercial agencies. . . ."[144]

Whether moral standards in the United States were improving or degenerating (and this, of course, was the crucial question for the survival of the home) was widely but most inconclusively debated. The issuance in a given year of one divorce decree to each six or seven marriage licenses was alarming if one considered it a symptom of growing marital unrest. But it might merely mean that unions were now formally dissolved by law that in times past had been covertly dissolved by extralegal relationships. The number of illegitimate births remained fairly low,[145] but this encouraging fact may be partly discounted by the wider use of contraceptive methods.

The National Federation of Settlements, after a very wide and impartial investigation, came to the conclusion that commercial prostitution was much diminished. "Report after report says that disorderly houses are gone and there is practically no solicitation on the streets." [146] In nearly all cities the regulated or tolerated "red-light district" had disappeared, dispersed, or hidden itself from casual view. This great improvement might be explained by many causes. The committee of the National Federation of Settlements laid stress on the effect of prohibition. The increase of industrial wages certainly must have made "Mrs. Warren's profession" less attractive to working girls. Reform campaigns and welfare work among the poor cleansed many a sinister street.

But there was another side to the story. While commercial prostitution was disappearing, there was much talk of clandestine love matches, unsanctioned by law, among young people of the most "respectable" circles. Here, unfortunately, one must leave solid statistical ground for general impressions, and these seemed to differ according to the personal bias of each witness. There seemed to be no direct proof that sexual immorality was more common, but the opportunities for it were certainly greater. The game of personal caresses, or "petting," was not essentially different from the old-fashioned "spooning," but an automobile fifty miles from town or an unchaperoned roadhouse dance may have been a more dangerous place to play the game than a domestic parlor or veranda. Some conservative colleges forbade their students the use of automobiles as much to safeguard their morals as to protect their limbs. The necessary spice of intoxication which could no longer be obtained at a saloon might be carried on the hip in a silver flask. Girls were certainly less restrained by conventions and inhibitions from doing whatever boys of the same social set might do. Often their time and latchkeys were their own. Engagements were lightly entered into and usually considered in no way binding.[147] There was an evil cult of "the thrill," whose motto was "I'll try anything once" and which reduced the problem of happiness to the accumulation of the greatest possible number of "new sensations."

Most of what alarmists said of changes in morals, however, should be translated into changes of manners. Even if one grants that shifts in social fashion do not go very deep into the bedrock of moral character, one must admit that these changes were swift enough after 1914 to alarm the elderly and sedate. Consider the question of clothing. Women's fashions have always fluctuated—the waistline moving up and down anywhere between neck and knee; skirts ballooning out till they covered much of the ballroom floor, or again tucked in till they shackled movement, as in the "hobble skirt" so briefly popular about 1911 or 1912; hats towering like mountains or spreading out like pancakes. But usually the new styles came by degrees, so that people could get used to them; they "evolved" like the British constitution. But during and after the war a real sartorial revolution took place. The skirt, in the old sense of the word, disappeared altogether to be replaced by a sort of tunic or kilt barely reaching the knee. Conservative eyes were shocked by this, although the change was in the direction of common sense and, had it taken a century instead of five or six years to complete, would have provoked little comment. Skirts were already "short," ankle-length, in 1914, but the "very short" skirt, knee-length, hardly became general before 1920 and required about three years more to become the accepted mode for all sections, ages, and classes. In 1929 clothing interests, impelled by Paris, made a desperate effort to restore the long skirt at least for evening wear and formal occasions. But many American women refused, for the first time in history, to obey the Parisian dictators of fashion.

With the shortening of the skirt went many other changes. Hampering petticoats were discarded, the corset was abandoned as a needless impediment to free movement, silk or "rayon" stockings became practically universal even among the poor and for a time were often rolled at the knee, sleeves shortened or vanished, and the whole costume became a sheer and simple structure, too light to be the slightest burden. H. G. Wells, writing in wartime, declared that his heroine "at fourteen already saw long skirts ahead of her, and hated them as a man might hate a swamp that he must presently cross knee-deep."[148] But by the time Joan would have been old enough for the long skirts there were none for her to wear. These simplifications of costume started with the wealthier classes but were almost immediately copied everywhere. A survey in Milwaukee of more than 1,300 working girls showed that fewer than seventy wore corsets.[149] The commercial effect of these changes of style was profound. Factories which specialized in petticoats, corsets, or cotton stockings had to change their trade or go bankrupt, but the sale of silk and rayon hose more than doubled in four years, and the sale of bathing suits tripled in two.[150]

During the sartorial revolution men proved to be, as usual, the conservative sex, making only minor changes in costume. A man who was well dressed for Roosevelt's inauguration would have provoked little comment at Hoover's. What few alterations were made were usually in the direction of greater comfort. The soft hat replaced the derby for almost every occasion, warm weather permitted light tropical suitings, and softer shirts and collars passed muster for business wear in the daytime. But men still wore coat and collar in summer, when women were comfortable in scanty one-piece frocks (unless they followed the fashion of summer furs). "Today our American women are in better physical condition than our men," declared Dr. Ephraim Mulford, president of the Medical Society of New Jersey. "And while there are many reasons, we might credit one to the fact that women do not wear too many clothes, especially in the summer. Their garments, light in weight and light in color, permit the ultraviolet ray of the sun to give its full benefit. Men, in their dark clothes which completely cover them from neck to ankle are denied this energy."[151] The tailors and textile factories even had a certain revenge on the male sex for their losses on the skimpier female raiment. Small boys often wore long trousers, and at adolescence they adopted trousers not only long but wide—huge, baggy affairs that moved hardly a step to each two steps of their owner but were raised above criticism by the name of "Oxford." In swimming, both men and women wore the simplest possible one-piece suits, the woman's suit often having less coverage than the man's. On hot summer days many girls went stockingless everywhere.

When the public had scarcely recovered from the shock of the disappearing skirt, it received another. The girls began to cut their hair. The barbershop was the last refuge of masculinity in America, the only spot which had not become "coeducational." The saloon was gone; the polls were now open to women; swimming tanks were crowded with fair mermaids; the very prize ring had its lady guests; and nearly all men's clubs had their ladies' night. But in the barbershop the unshorn male could lean back at his ease in the great chair, unashamed in his suspenders, while the barber lathered his face and gave him the latest gossip of politics and baseball. This last trench was now taken. A fashion started for hair fitting compactly around the head and fluffed or banged over the ears; long tresses were out of style; hence occasional visits to the barbershop. Persons over thirty viewed the fad with some misgivings, but presently began to try cautious experiments in the same direction. The flapper grew bolder. The "boyish bob" appeared, and ears emerged once again from their retirement. Soon there was no difference between a man's haircut and a woman's, unless the man was an artist or a musician and wore his hair long as a professional asset.

The universalizing of the bob simplified the hat problem. Large, broad, and unstably balanced hats were out of the question, as the hatpin found no anchorage. All the new hats took the form of a close-fitting, simple bonnet which a wind would not carry away. Birds and flowers on headgear largely disappeared, and the vanishing of the hatpin ended a major menace in crowded cars.

A third phase of the revolution in fashions, even more disturbing to the traditional than short skirts or short hair, was the freer use of cosmetics. In a way, this was a move in the opposite direction, as it represented a tendency not toward "naturalness" and freedom but toward artificiality and sophistication. If it be considered progress since the times of Victoria, when ladies got along with a little face cream and white powder, it might equally be considered a reversion to the days of Pompadour. Bright orange rouge and lipsticks advertised as "kissproof" were used by young ladies of the most unquestionable respectability. The fashionable "sun tan" was sometimes acquired at the drugstore as well as on the beach. Like the other changes in fashion, the cosmetic urge was democratic in the sense that it stopped at no class barrier. "Progress toward democracy," wrote a journalist,

> has made amazing strides in this matter of personal decoration. Formerly it was the ladies of the court who used it most; today it is the serious concern and dearest pastime of all three estates. It was the spread of the use of furs, to take but one example, to all classes (and also to all seasons) which inspired the just description of woman as America's greatest fur-bearing animal. And nowadays no one can tell, either by the quantitative or the qualitative test, whether a given person lives on Riverside Drive or on East Fourth Street.[152]

The business of the manufacturers of cosmetics and perfumes increased from less than $17 million in 1914 to $141,488,000 by 1925, over eightfold in one decade.[153] The Foucaults (French perfumers) estimated that 71 percent of the women of the United States over eighteen years of age used perfume; 90 percent, face powder; 73 percent, toilet water; 55 percent, rouge.[154] "Beauty shoppes" blossomed on nearly every street of the shopping districts, their proprietors sometimes seeking to professionalize their status with the word "beauticians." Seven thousand kinds of cosmetics were on the market in 1927, a large majority of them being face creams.[155] Fortunes were made in mud baths, labeled "beauty clay," in patent hair removers, in magic lotions to make the eyelashes long and sweeping, in soaps that claimed to nourish the skin, in hair dyes that "restored the natural color," in patent nostrums for "reducing," and in all the other half-fraudulent traps of the advertisers for the beauty seeker.

One manufacturer of dentifrice based a clever advertising campaign on the vogue of the feminine cigarette, with such headlines as "Why Are Men So Unreasonable about Women Smoking?" and "Can a Girl Smoke and Still Be Lovely?" arguing that since women were determined to smoke they should keep their teeth stainless by the daily use of toothpaste. Cigarette advertisers took a similarly ingenious advantage of the craze for the "boyish form"—for example, "And now, women may enjoy a companionable smoke with their husbands and brothers—at the same time slenderizing in a sensible manner. . . . Reach for a *Lucky* instead of a sweet." Thus one fad supported another. Earlier advertisers, not so bold, had usually depicted pretty girls not themselves indulging in a cigarette but in the company of young men so engaged, perhaps pleading, "Blow some my way!" The number of cigarettes sold in the period 1911–15 averaged less than 15 billion annually; for the period 1921–25 sales averaged well over 65 billion,[156] and in 1928 reached 100 billion.[157] As during the same period there was no greater sale of cigars and a much smaller sale of chewing tobacco, the increased vogue of the cigarette did not mean an increased tobacco hunger. Rather, it meant the entrance of the American girl into the ranks of the smokers.

Thus the flapper of the 1920s stepped onto the stage of history, breezy, slangy, and informal in manner; slim and boyish in form; covered with silk and fur that clung to her as close as onion skin; with carmined cheeks and lips, plucked eyebrows, and close-fitting helmet of hair; gay, plucky, and confident. No wonder the house rang with applause; no wonder also that faint hisses sounded from the remoter boxes and galleries. But she cared little for approval or disapproval and went about her "act," whether it were a marathon dancing contest, driving an automobile at seventy miles an hour, a Channel swim, a political campaign or a social service settlement. Eventually she married her dancing partner, that absurdly serious young man with plastered hair, baby-smooth chin, and enormous Oxford bags, and then they settled down in a four-room-kitchenette apartment to raise two children, another "younger generation" to thrust them backstage among the "old fogies."

The Nineteenth Amendment which extended the political franchise to American women, already emancipated in everything save politics, followed about half a year after the Eighteenth, prohibiting the sale of alcoholic liquors. The twin amendments—twin victories for feminism some would say—had much in common. Both prohibition and woman suffrage had roots deep in American history and represented a final triumph obtained after almost a century of continuous agitation. Both were attempted in many places on a statewide scale before they forced their way to the front as national issues. Both were first mooted by Puritan reformers in the Northeastern states, then actually carried into effect by their radical sons who had moved to the Western plains and mountains, and opposed almost to the last ditch by their conservative grandsons who had stayed in the East. But in at least one respect there was contrast. However prolonged and bitter the opposition to woman suffrage, once the amendment was carried the issue disappeared from politics, whereas prohibition remained a bone of contention as much after its victory as before.

By 1914 equal suffrage existed in Wyoming, Colorado, Utah, Idaho, Washington, California, Oregon, Arizona, and Kansas, and during the year Nevada and Montana were added to the number. Many other states had a limited woman suffrage, often for school elections only. Neither of the great parties had either endorsed or opposed the movement, except locally, but the Progressives in 1912 and many other third parties at various times had made equal suffrage a plank in their platforms. Though all the major victories had been confined to a single section of the country, politicians everywhere felt the pressure of the growing movement. It was ably captained, and one of the chief arguments for admitting women into politics was that they were showing themselves adept at the game even before enfranchisement. Carrie Chapman Catt, Anna Howard Shaw, Alice Stone Blackwell, and their lieutenants aroused much admiration, almost envy, among professional politicians, even those who were their opponents.

After 1916 the states rapidly fell into line. Already (1913) Illinois had adopted a curious compromise by which women could vote for all offices except those governed by the franchise stipulation in the state constitution; thus they could vote for presidential electors but not for Congress or most state officers.[158] Many other states followed with similar "presidential-suffrage" laws, and Arkansas permitted women to vote in party primaries which were there, as in most parts of the South, the really important elections. New York capitulated in 1917, the first Eastern seaboard state to grant complete equality.[159] Nowhere else had the fight been so completely organized and well munitioned. Most of the suffrage, and equally the anti-suffrage, associations had New York offices, and for several years the city had been accustomed to the sight of marching armies of suffrage paraders, each larger than the last and viewed by a more sympathetic crowd. The cries of "go home and wash the dishes!," which greeted the first paraders, were replaced by a continuous ripple of applause up and down Fifth Avenue. In 1918, Michigan, South Dakota, and Oklahoma joined the caravan of equal-suffrage states, and interest shifted from the state campaigns to the prospect of a national amendment.

The so-called Susan B. Anthony amendment forbade the restriction of the franchise on the ground of sex. In June 1919 it started from Congress on a tour of the state legislatures, and by the following spring had been accepted in thirty-five states and rejected by ten, all in the Southeast. Tennessee, Connecticut, and Vermont were still doubtful, the national election was rapidly approaching, and neither party wished to appear as an obstacle in the way of the necessary thirty-sixth ratification. The governors of Connecticut and Vermont refusing to call the legislatures into special session to consider the amendment, the honor fell to Tennessee. A frantic effort by Tennessee antisuffragists to reverse the action of the legislature came just too late; in August 1920 the amendment had been declared part of the Constitution.

Two features of the equal-suffrage campaign in the United States are of special interest. One, already alluded to, was the small part played by the parties in securing the amendment. The other was the almost complete absence of "militancy." In England a fairly large radical wing of the suffrage movement had tried to badger the government of the day into action by such means as breaking windows, interrupting public meetings, destroying mailboxes, and other "nuisance tactics." Nothing so extreme occurred in the United States, the nearest approach to it perhaps being the picketing of the White House with banners denouncing President Wilson (himself already a convert to the cause) for not putting more pressure on Congress to hasten the enactment of the proposed amendment.[160] Even this very mild form of militancy was frowned upon by the majority of American suffragists, who used no method except political organization and open discussion. Their speedy success seems to have been due in part to the skill of their political managers, in part to the chivalric tradition in American life which made it difficult to refuse any really sustained demand by women, in part to the rivalry of political parties to seize a popular issue before it was too late, and in part as a tribute to the indispensable services of American women during the World War.

With the ballot in hand most American women found their political ambition contented. Down to 1928 fewer women sought office than in some countries of northern Europe. After Jeannette Rankin of Montana started the fashion (1917–19) there was usually at least one congress-woman. Two women served as governors, but in both cases the office was in some sense a legacy, Miriam A. Ferguson being the wife of a former governor of Texas, and Nellie Tayloe Ross the widow of a former governor of Wyoming. After the elections of 1928 the National League of Women Voters announced that there would be 145 women serving in thirty-eight of the forty-eight state legislatures, twelve of them serving for a fourth term.[161] All political parties gave to women positions of honor—though not always of much influence—on national and state committees. From the best obtainable estimates it appears that about thirty-five women out of every possible 100 voted at important elections.[162]

As the ballot was everywhere secret, one can only guess at the manner in which the woman's vote influenced American politics, but it is at least significant that those states which had lived longest under equal suffrage were usually very advanced in welfare legislation, and especially laws to protect the rights of women and children. On other issues there seems no evidence that women in the mass differed from men. Of all important groupings among voters, by place of residence, wealth, occupation, race, nationality, religion, and sex, the last named made the least difference in the way the votes were cast.[163]

THE WAYS OF PROSPERITY

DURING THE DECADE of reconstruction that followed the World War, the world watched with peculiar interest two experiments on the grand scale in economic revolution. One was a conscious, deliberate, and political movement to shift industry from a capitalistic to a communistic basis, a movement accompanied by much violence and many spectacular incidents, the Bolshevist revolution in Russia. The other revolution had little to do with politics, embodied no particular theory, brought forth no striking events or incidents, and yet it altered the daily life of the average American citizen almost as profoundly as the revolution of 1917 altered the daily life of the Russian peasant. "The economic changes now occurring in the United States," said a keen contemporary observer, "are significant in their relation to the whole history of Western Civilization—as significant perhaps as the Industrial Revolution in England at the close of the eighteenth century."[164] They are, however, less easy to define because they did not arise out of a doctrine, such as Marxian communism in Russia, or out of any one outstanding invention, such as the steam engine in the English Industrial Revolution. The effect, the new American standard of living, was apparent to the whole world, but the causes were endlessly debated.

Western Europe, which had witnessed the Russian experiment with a mixture of interest and misgiving, turned a similarly speculative gaze across the Atlantic. Numerous books appeared in England, France, and, especially, in Germany on the new industrial structure of the United States, praising its achievements, condemning its materialism, but always seeking its secret.[165]

Certainly the change in American economic life in the postwar decade was something more than a mere increase of the national wealth. That increase was evident enough, but its scale was exaggerated by the inflation of prices which multiplied dollars faster than real values and by the relative impoverishment of Europe resulting from the World War. Even the United States of 1914 would have been envied by the Europe of 1918–28. But quite aside from absolute or relative gains in wealth there were interesting developments in the way in which wealth was produced and distributed. Some of these were concerned with such matters as the transformation of the home into a unit of household engineering, with mechanical aids in place of servant labor; the treatment of farming as a speculative commercial enterprise to be handled by industrial methods rather than by peasant traditions; the ubiquitous automobile; the high-pressure salesmanship of modern advertising; and the multiform applications of science to profit and pleasure. Here we will deal more particularly with the tendencies in the world of "business."

In 1922 the census bureau estimated the wealth of the United States at a little over $320 billion, an increase of about 72 percent over the figures for 1912. An estimate for 1925 indicated a further increase to $355 billion.[166] Allowance must be made for a depreciating dollar and a growing population, but even so it is evident that the nation had absorbed the costs of the war and its worst economic aftereffects by 1922 and from that point onward made positive progress in per-capita wealth. Of course, the census figures were only an approximation because, even supposing that the census made no error of fact, economists are not agreed as to what assets can be reckoned as national wealth. The Federal Trade Commission, using the figures of the 1922 census but including also roads, streets, highways, and the site values of railways and public-service corporations, placed the total for 1922 as high as $353 billion.[167] On either basis the per-capita wealth averaged in the neighborhood of $3,000.

Income rather than capital measures prosperity. In 1914 the per-capita national income was $339; in 1920, $703; in 1926, $671. If correction be made for the changing value of money, the "real" income of 1914 was $336; of 1920, $344; of 1926, $396.[168] The increase in real income per person *gainfully occupied* between 1914 and 1926 was 28.7 percent.[169] Had it been possible without injury to the productive process to divide equally the nation's assets in the 1920s, each American family of five might reckon on an estate of about $15,000 and an annual income of about $3,000. Few nations make as careful a survey of their national wealth as the United States, but from such data as can be gathered it appears that the cash value of the nation as it stood—lands, mines, railroads, factories, livestock, manufactured articles, and all the rest—was just a trifle less than that of the whole of Europe and perhaps as much as two fifths of the entire wealth of the world.[170]

A comparison of the wealth census of 1922 with that of 1912 shows also which items of the national Domesday Book were responsible for the progress of the whole and which forms of wealth were stationary or retrogressive. Real estate, the largest single item, accounted for about $176 billion, an increase of more than three fifths. No wonder Sinclair Lewis selected *Babbitt*, the "Realtor," as the typical American to pillory in his novel. The real estate booms in the vacation states of Florida and California, as well as in the fertile farm lands of Iowa, and the rising site values in the growing cities readily explain this increase. The money value of manufactured products, over $28 billion, had approximately doubled. The value of manufacturing machinery, tools, and implements advanced from $6 to nearly $16 billion. The value of furniture, clothing, and other articles of personal use and consumption made a threefold gain. Motor vehicles appeared as a separate item, with a value of over $4.5 billion.

On the other hand, the money value of farm products increased only slightly in the decade—really a loss in actual buying power for the farmer—and the value of livestock decreased. The railroads and most other public utilities showed very slight advance. A small but significant item in the total was a three-fifths increase in the amount of gold and silver coin and bullion, an interesting evidence of the change of the United States from debtor to creditor among the nations.[171] In these figures we see reflected a stationary phase in railroad building, a relative decline in agriculture, a vast expansion of industry, a rapid growth of motor traction, and a greatly increased social surplus for the comforts and luxuries of life.

The fact that the United States was wealthy did not in itself demonstrate prosperity, for averages can be unduly raised by a few large fortunes. Was it true that while the rich grew richer the poor grew poorer? Or had Uncle Sam—in the phrase used by the Progressives of 1912—begun to "pass prosperity around"? Certainly the rich were growing richer. A bankers' estimate of 1926 placed the number of millionaires in the country at 11,000 as compared with 4,500 in 1914.[172] But were the poor getting poorer, either absolutely or relatively? That is a harder question to answer, but every indication points to the negative. A study made of more than 43,000 estates probated in thirteen states over a decade led to the conclusion that "although the tabulations suggest wide variations in the wealth of individuals and a rather high degree of concentration, a comparison of the estates probated in 1912 with those probated in 1923 indicates that this concentration was greater at the beginning of the period covered by the commission's study than at the end." [173]

For the workers in the organized trades we have statistical evidence of prosperity in the comparison of wage scales and price changes. Combining the two index numbers of union rates of wages and the cost of living, the increase in the purchasing power of wages in 1927 was about one and a half times that of 1913.[174] In other words, the buying power of an hour of skilled labor was one half greater in 1927. For labor in general, including the unskilled and unorganized, the improvement was probably nearly 30 percent. Though nominal wages rose more rapidly from 1914 to 1921 than later, the cost of living in some cases rose even more rapidly, so the "real" improvement in the lot of the workingman, like the "real" increase in the general wealth of the nation, belonged to the years 1921–28 and especially the latter half of that period. Farm wages, save for a brief war-prosperity increase in 1918–20, did not share in the gains of labor as a whole, and the lumbermen and tobacco workers were almost equally unfortunate.[175] The average British wage in the 1920s was about half the American, and rates in continental Europe in very few cases rose as high as the British. But this difference in standard was old. More significant was the fact that, while American wages rose well above the increased cost of living, the European workingman little more than held his own within the prewar period.[176]

More interesting to most of us than the average wages of large classes is the picture of what they meant to the single home. Consider the case of a typical workingman in an American industrial town in 1924.[177] He was at the head of a family of five. In the course of a year he spent $548 for food, $237 for clothes, $186 for rent, $74 for fuel and light, $73 for furnishings and supplies about the house, and $306 for all other expenses, besides saving about $79 for a possible rainy day in the future. Of course wages and prices varied from town to town. New York may be selected to represent the large cities with their high rentals. A typical Brooklyn office worker ("white-collar man") would pay out each average week $10 to the landlord; $15 to the grocer, butcher, and milkman; $5 to the clothing stores; and $9 to all his other creditors.[178] His neighbor, a factory worker in the Borough of Queens, paid about $7.30 to the landlord; over $14 to the grocer; $5 for the clothing of himself, his wife, and the three children; and split $8 into sundries. Apart from a higher rent due to the supposed social necessity of living in a "respectable section of the town," and the need for a neat business suit in place of overalls, the office clerk and the factory hand had an almost identical standard of living.

The hours of labor were reduced at the same time that wages were being raised. The six-day week and eight-hour day became thoroughly established as institutions, as part of the "American standard of living." Prior to 1914 an average factory week for mills on full time was about fifty-five hours, after the war it varied from forty-eight to fifty. The working week in mines and railways was about the same as in the factories, for the building trades a little less. From 1916 onward the eight-hour day constituted legal "full time" on the railroads. In 1923 the U.S. Steel Corporation, an old stronghold of the twelve-hour day, shifted to the eight-hour basis, enlarged its working force by over 17,000 men to meet the labor shortage thus created, raised wages, and still showed an increased profit, thus refuting the fears once expressed by corporate chairman E. H. Gary that the iron-and-steel industry could not afford to make the change.

With the marked improvement in labor conditions went a diminished antagonism between capital and labor. To be sure, in the months of reconstruction immediately after the war, what with rapidly changing prices and some radical agitators who mistook the Russian conflagration for a worldwide dawn, strikes were numerous, extensive, and sometimes violent. But in the years of "normalcy" that followed they greatly decreased. The American trade unions followed in the main a most enlightened policy of encouraging rather than restricting production. As President Samuel Gompers of the A.F.L. said in 1917, "The labor movement of the past thirty years . . . has changed that mode of thinking and that mode of procedure among the working people, so that instead of reducing output or opposing the introduction of machinery and new tools of labor we encourage them." And his successor in office, William Green, declared, "We are cooperating with the managements in the elimination of waste because the working man suffers most of all as a result of waste. We are also cooperating with the managements in the elimination of duplication of effort, and we are not opposing the introduction of improved machinery." [179] This was the subject of much favorable comment by foreign observers. A report by Colonel F. Vernon Willey and Mr. Guy Locock, as visiting representatives of the Federation of British Industries,[180] testified:

In view of the shrinkage in the stream of immigration, and therefore more particularly of the pool of skilled labor, it is becoming more and more important for labor-saving devices to be used to the greatest possible extent. To this labor offers no opposition, and the result is a constantly increasing efficiency of production . . . and a comparative freedom from the restrictions on output which hamper us in England.

Such testimony was almost universal.

The trade unions did not cover so great a proportion of the world of labor in the United States as in Great Britain or some European nations.[181]

The A.F.L. appears to have been at its strongest in 1920, with about 4 million members. Shortly afterwards, due probably to the depression of 1921, about a fourth of these ceased to pay their dues. Even with the restoration of prosperity the Federation did not rise again to more than 3.3 million. The next largest labor group, the railway brotherhoods of engineers, firemen, trainmen, and conductors, mustered about 450,000. The I.W.W. in quiet times had hardly 35,000 active members, though a particular strike might swell their numbers for a few weeks or months. The Amalgamated Clothing Workers with about 160,000 members represented a degree of radicalism somewhat between the revolutionary I.W.W. and the evolutionary A.F.L. Some of the largest coal fields were nonunion and several great cities like Detroit boasted of being "open-shop towns."

Though the American labor unions were not coextensive with American industrialism, they represented the most skilled and best-paid trades and held key positions in nearly every industry. The A.F.L. alone had 107 craft unions within its ranks in 1928. Some of these were strongly represented by branches across the Canadian border. Their prosperity was clearly evidenced by the establishment of a series of labor banks.

Child labor continued to be a feature of American industry. The census of 1920 showed a decline in ten years from nearly 2 million to a little over a million for children from ten to fifteen years of age "gainfully employed." [182] After 1920 there seems to have been an increased employment of children, and in June 1924 the National Child Labor Committee estimated that 2 million boys and girls under fifteen were at work.[183] The majority were farm laborers, usually under the care of their own parents. The beet fields, cranberry bogs, and other seasonal branches of agriculture had their gangs of child workers, however, and the canneries found them useful. Thousands were also employed in textile mills, especially in the Southern states. Two attempts, in 1916 and 1919, to regulate child labor by barring from interstate commerce goods produced contrary to federal law were declared unconstitutional by the Supreme Court,[184] and a proposed Twentieth Amendment in 1924, which would specifically grant to Congress power to legislate concerning the employment of persons under eighteen, met with astonishing lack of public interest.

Unemployment was, like child labor, an industrial problem which the "era of prosperity" left partly unsolved. Aside from agriculture, the number of unemployed at different times varied, according to the best estimates, from 5 to 15 percent of the whole body of workers, amounting to over 4 million during the temporary depression of 1921.[185]

Perhaps the fact which most tended to reconcile the conflicting interests of capital and labor was their increasing identification. Many of the larger corporations adopted the policy of placing shares of stock on easy terms in the hands of their employees.[186] This did not mean that the United States had become a land of economic equality, for the single share owned by

John Doe Hunyak cannot be compared with the vast investments of the millionaire. But it did mean that the distinction between "owner" and "laborer" was of degree rather than of kind. The public at large also bought freely of small shares in big business, so that ownership became increasingly distributed. A study of corporations selling shares to their employees revealed that 5 to 85 percent of the whole stock was in the hands of employees, with an average for the larger companies of about 22 percent.[187] In 1922 there were 14.4 million stockholders in American corporations.[188] About 3.4 million of these had been added in the three years following the entrance of the United States into the World War.[189] No doubt the intensive propaganda for the sale of liberty-loan bonds had increased the habit of investment among the general public.

More than a quarter of the employees of the U.S. Steel Corporation held stock, to a total value of over $100 million.[190] Standard Oil and its subsidiary companies had in 1925 over 300,000 shareholders, many of them employees.[191] The railroad and public-service companies showed the same tendency. There were about a million owners of railway bonds, and about 28 percent of all income-producing endowments of colleges and universities were in the form of railway bonds or stocks. As President C. H. Markham of the Illinois Central put it, "It is 'Main Street' and not 'Wall Street' that owns the railroads today." Public utilities, such as electric light and power plants, gas works, and electric trolleys, counted over 2 million owners.[192]

Other evidences of prosperity besides the widespread purchase of industrial securities may be found in the growth of savings in bank accounts, insurance policies, and building-and-loan associations. These were evidences all the more striking because in an age of high-pressure salesmanship thrift was not one of the popular virtues. In place of the three traditional virtues of the Industrious Apprentice—honesty, industry, and thrift—current magazine fiction applauded the ability to carry through a bluff, to put up a huge "front" on small capital, to break out a new path, and to snatch victory from defeat by daring assumptions of risk and defiance of orders—an economic romanticism superseding the economic classicism of Benjamin Franklin's day.[193] Yet in the spendthrift and speculative period from 1914 to 1925 the number of savings accounts increased nearly fourfold, from 11 to 43 million, and their sum from $8 to $23 billion. About half of this was held in savings banks, which specialized in small accounts and were usually limited to them. By the end of 1926 more than 25.5 million ordinary life-insurance policies and more than 76 million industrial policies were in force in the United States, their total assets being $12.5 billion.[194] In ten years, building-and-loan policies increased in number from 3,103,935 to 8,554,352 in 1924. Over 11 million families owned their own homes.

The combination of speculative spirit and prosperous industry, however, led to the investment of an undue proportion of the nation's savings in stocks of fluctuating value. Rash bidding raised stock values in 1928 and

1929 to artificial heights, and the inevitable collapse, in October of the latter year, wiped out "paper" values to a total estimated equal to the entire German war indemnity![195]

Thrift in the sense of just not spending, as distinguished from investment, was indeed at a discount in all classes. The best proof of this was the great increase in consumer credits, the purchase of goods on so much down and so much a month. Before the war such installment purchases were usually for things permanent or very expensive: the house in which a man would spend his life or a diamond ring for the girl with whom he would spend it. But in the postwar period the habit of installment buying had spread to cover nearly every article subject to purchase. "You furnish the girl; we furnish the home," read the skyline sign of the furniture factory. Automobile dealers attempted to keep their industry on a pay-at-once basis, but the installment system captured the automobile. Many Americans felt lost without some running account. Often the radio set, the phonograph, the player piano, the dinner jacket, the new curtains, and the new car were worn out before the final payments were made.

By 1927 some 15 percent of all goods were sold on the installment plan, at retail prices about $6 billion worth, while at any given moment between $2 and $3 billion of outstanding debt could be accounted for by installment purchase.[196] Over 85 percent of furniture, 80 percent of phonographs, 75 percent of washing machines, and the greater part of all vacuum cleaners, pianos, sewing machines, radios, and electric refrigerators were bought in this way.[197] Most of the industries in which installment buying was the rule were new industries based on recent mechanical inventions. As home radios, refrigerators, electric washers, and the like represented a considerable investment, many a housewife would have hesitated at so much expense for a novel luxury but for the seductive argument of easy payments.

Next to installment buying the most noteworthy tendency in American retail trade was the development of the chain store.[198] This was but one phase of the general drift toward standardization that marked the period. From the viewpoint of the consumer, the important fact was not that the stores were under a central management—competitors in the trade had the worry of that—but that they gave a uniform service. After the war there was a greater increase of business in chain groceries, drugstores, candy shops, and five-and-ten-cent stores than in any other class of retail trade. They held a doubly strategic position, combining the advantages of centralization (uniform management, wholesale purchase, and the economies of combination) enjoyed by the city department stores with the advantages of decentralization hitherto enjoyed only by independent shops, a location in every neighborhood, and consequent direct friendly contact with the consumer.

The chain-store movement first triumphed in the grocery field. The Great Atlantic and Pacific Tea Company, both pioneer and champion among its kind, opened 2,200 new stores from 1914 to 1917 and had 5,000 in all by 1922.[199] By 1928 it had 17,500 branches and did an annual business of $750 million.[200] The Kroger Grocery and Baking Company, the American Stores, and the Safeway Stores were at that time the leading rivals. But the most interesting departure was the Piggly-Wiggly system devised and patented by Clarence Saunders of Memphis, Tennessee. The Piggly-Wiggly was a grocery-cafeteria in which the customer entered by a turnstile, walked past the shelves, selected what he wanted from label and price tag, and paid the cashier on leaving. The clerks, like the waiters in self-help restaurants, had little to do except see that the shelves and counters were supplied. The appeal of the Piggly-Wiggly was partly psychological; many housewives, it developed, were flurried at too much attention by solicitous clerks and liked to make their selections at leisure. So keen was the competition of the chain groceries that more than 500 independent grocers in the far West organized the United Grocers, Incorporated, to protect their interests by collective buying and the pooling of good advice and suggestions on retail management.[201]

The five-and-ten-cent stores were usually part of chain systems. Although most of them ran over the ten-cent limit to small multiples up to twenty-five or fifty cents, they always were sufficiently true to their name to appeal to the bargain-hunting instinct. What was for a long time the tallest inhabited structure in the world, the Woolworth Building in New York, stood as a monument to quick turnover sales in nickels and dimes. The F. W. Woolworth Company, selling $272 million worth of "notions" a year through nearly 1,600 branch stores, stood second in importance only to the Atlantic and Pacific Tea Company among all the chains.[202] The S. S. Kresge stores, the result of a Detroit merchant's efforts, established a $100-million-plus business and a $23 million charitable foundation. Other outstanding examples of combination, such as the United Drug Company, the United Cigar Stores, the J. C. Penney department stores, the Childs restaurants, and the Statler hotels, showed the wide applicability of the chain principle. Because of legal restrictions, chain banking, so familiar to the traveler in Europe, did not develop in America, though there were strings of local banks more or less under the influence of certain large metropolitan institutions.

The same desire for cheap goods, wholesale production and uniform quality which caused the rise of the chain store brought increased prosperity to a somewhat older American institution, the mail-order house. Such firms as Sears, Roebuck and Company and Montgomery, Ward in Chicago had long since extended their influence to every hamlet. The isolated station agent brought within the sweep of American life by a fat mail-order catalogue was one of the truest of national types.[203] Its thousand pages of illustrated and animated detail were to his loneliness all that a library of the "world's best literature" would be to the hypothetical literary gentleman on a desert island. Even small business concerns found that the new facilities of the parcel post opened to them a most profitable channel of merchandising. One general store in Temple, Oklahoma, a town of 900 inhabitants—the case is mentioned because it is typical—made over a fourth of its mail-order sales beyond the 100-mile limit.[204] But the independent local dealer generally felt the mail-order house an even deadlier enemy than the chain store, for it even more directly "took money out of the town."

One feature of American business life which greatly impressed foreign observers was the extent to which everything was organized, not only within the factory but even among competitors. To cite once more from the report of visiting delegates of the Federation of British Industries:

> When one examines the number of trade associations in the United States the total is amazing. It is estimated that there are seven thousand associations, Federal, State or municipal, dealing with trade matters. Undoubtedly there is a considerable amount of overlapping, a certain wastage of effort, but at the same time the leading trade associations, such as the Chamber of Commerce, the National Manufacturers' Association, the National Industrial Conference Board, the Merchants' Association, etc., are extremely efficiently organized and are performing valuable national work.[205]

Some of these organizations, indeed, were civic or social rather than purely "business." For example, by 1928 the Rotary Club and its younger brother Kiwanis each counted more than 100,000 members, and the Lions' Club, founded in 1917, grew in a decade to over 50,000. Besides these national and international societies there were many local business clubs of similar type and purport. With all the chambers of commerce, trade associations, civic-betterment clubs, local "booster" societies, church or charity "drives," fraternal orders, and the like, the American businessman often seemed to have time for anything and everything but his own special business. Charles Dickens must have had him in prophetic mind when he said, through the medium of Marley's ghost, "The dealings of my trade were but a drop of water in the comprehensive ocean of my business!"

THE SAGA OF THE MOTOR CAR

IF ANY ONE FEATURE of American life was uniquely characteristic of the nation and the age it was the ubiquity of the automobile. In 1896 there were but four gasoline cars in the United States: the Duryea, the Ford, the Haynes, and the imported Benz.[206] By 1914 more than half a million passenger cars were sold each year; twelve years later about 4 million, besides nearly half a million trucks.[207] In 1928 over 24 million cars, old and new, were in use,[208] and more Americans had automobiles than telephones. The industry employed directly 375,000 workmen in the construction factories and used either directly or indirectly the services of 3.7 million persons, counting factory workers, makers of accessories or supplies, salesmen, chauffeurs, garage attendants, and the like. It was America's largest industry as measured by the money value of its product, outranking even the packing industry and the steel manufacture.[209]

In the postwar years the day of "one family—one auto" had almost arrived, and the general European impression that "in the United States everyone drives an automobile" was at least more nearly correct than most foreign impressions of American wealth. For the continental United States there was almost one automobile to each five persons, and in some Western states the proportion was one to each three or four. Ownership was no longer a class distinction in 1928 as it had been in 1914 and still was in all European countries.[210]

The effect of the rise of the automobile industry on American business as a whole would be hard to overestimate. By 1928 the automobile accounted for more than four fifths of the rubber used in the United States. It had made this nation the world's chief rubber market, and created the great industry of plantation rubber in the East Indies, Dutch and British. The automotive industry consumed also half the plate glass, 8 percent of the copper, 11 percent of the iron and steel, 65 percent of all leather upholstery, and more than 7 billion gallons of gasoline annually.[211]

Not the automobile itself but its universality was the real American contribution. Europe had had imagination enough to envisage the automobile but not enough to picture it becoming almost as cheap as a bicycle, as commonplace as a donkey, and as necessary as the four walls of a house. Many factors favored its growth in the United States, apart from the characteristic American bent for quantity production and a wide market. Most raw materials of manufacture were to be found within the country and usually in abundance. Methods of organization and salesmanship for making and pushing new commodities were more highly developed than anywhere else. The consumer was eager, having an Athenian fondness for whatever was novel in doctrine or in invention. The general prosperity enabled many to buy even in the early days of the industry, and increasingly so as prices went down with more wholesale production. The Yankee tradition for tinkering with machinery, already well practiced on bicycles, farm machinery, and domestic appliances, encouraged even novices to dispense with a chauffeur. The huge size of the Western farms, the distance between farm and market town, the remoteness of the cities from each other, and the national habit of travel, all placed a premium on rapid locomotion. Europe, excepting always impoverished and backward Russia, was at once more crowded and less migratory.

While the automobile as a machine is the culmination of decades of invention, the automobile as a social force is as definitely associated with one man as the steam engine with Watt or the electric light with Edison. Other young inventors in the experimental 1890s had tinkered with motors, but only Henry Ford had had the vision of the automobile as an engine of democracy rather than as a hallmark of aristocracy. His career was the story of the popular automobile at popular prices. The Ford factories were far more novel, interesting, and important than the Ford itself. His famous Model T, a convenient little car painted in sober black like a Venetian gondola, was for a long time his sole product and it sold more widely in its day than all other automobiles combined. The butt of a thousand jokes, in which affection was blended with amusement, the "flivver," the "tin lizzie," became the family pet of the nation.

On May 26, 1927, Henry Ford and his son Edsel Ford drove the fifteen-millionth automobile which had come from his factories. As soon as they reached Dearborn old Number One was brought from the museum, a two-cylinder veteran of 1903. It proved to be still in good driving condition, so short was the space of time that separated the beginning of the automobile from its universal prevalence. But even the Model T eventually joined the pageant of history. In 1927, Ford shut down for several months, thus reducing the aggregate automobile output in America by almost a quarter as compared with 1926. There had been no sign of a satiated market, but competition was keener and Ford had a new idea and it must be tried! Of course the experiment was costly, a conservative estimate was $15 million spent to January 1, 1928, in the preparations for launching the new car.[212] As usual, the car itself was far less novel than the improvements in the methods of production. In some respects the new Ford more greatly resembled rival automobiles than did the old Model T; the great individualist had partly capitulated to current standards of car form and equipment. But the machinery for production was improved beyond recognition. The company boasted that raw iron ore at the docks at eight Monday morning could be marketed as a complete Ford car on Wednesday noon, allowing fifteen hours for shipment.[213]

Certainly up to the end of the twenties the American idea of mass production had never been carried further than in the Ford factories. Many European industrialists from Britain to Russia, but especially perhaps in Germany, made a painstaking study of the Ford methods as literally a "god from the machine" to cure underproduction and all the poverty which it causes. Mr. Ford himself had no doubts on the matter, for in numberless newspaper interviews he expatiated with a certain modest vanity on the reign of universal prosperity that would be sure to follow the adoption of his policies by industry at large, including agriculture.[214]

Centralization of control in the Ford factories was almost absolute. The Ford Company enjoyed the same advantage as France under Napoleon or Prussia under Frederick. There could be no question of conflicting jurisdictions; one man's will wove every strand of policy into a common fabric. His

Wide World Photo

Fords

chief fellow stockholder was his own like-minded son. Rivals within his company withdrew, in some cases to found automobile companies of their own (as, for example, the Dodges). Managers who opposed his policies had to conform or resign. His enemies termed him an autocrat and even his admirers had to admit that he was a "benevolent despot."[215]

The Ford ideas of factory management were the subject of endless comment and not a little criticism. The plant had room for many experts and specialists in machine and tool designing, but the majority of the employed were unskilled and set to the most routine tasks imaginable, tasks that required neither strength (since the machines themselves did all the "blacksmithing") nor skill. Ford dealt frankly with this question of soul-deadening monotony, saying that while he himself could never endure a life of routine, he had many workmen, good, industrous men, who were unhappy at anything else.[216] Other critics complained that the speed of operation was too great, that even with short hours there was a nervous strain that meant short lives. Again Ford replied that he timed his machines by experiment to find the best speed at which work could be done without loss of efficiency.

Certainly there was something almost uncanny in the endless process of a Ford plant. Efficiency experts so arranged the order of operations that no workman need stir from his place or stoop to pick up anything. On principle, no human labor was used for any operation that a machine could perform, and no skill was employed where deft, routine motion would do as well. The workman did become a part of the machine, an adjustable bit of mechanism to connect one operation with the next while the river of motor or chassis parts flowed by at unvarying speed. It became the Paradise of the motion-study expert, and perhaps the Purgatory of the artist soul, but beyond question it was the cheapest way of making automobiles!

Ford's labor policy was equally criticized and commended. It reflected alike the highly individualistic philosophy and the humane temper of the man himself. He disclaimed, with perhaps unnecessary indignation, any reproach of being a philanthropist and mixing business with charity. "Efficiency" was his sole motto. But his conception of efficiency included the prevention of human waste as well as of other kinds. Everyone who wanted work must be given a fair chance in the factory. If he made good he could stay, and Ford would stand by him in fair weather or in foul, as he stood by his German workmen during the World War when many criticized the retention of men of "enemy alien" birth at a moment when the Ford plants were working for the war needs of the government. During a period of slackness in industry good workmen should be retained even at the employer's cost. There must be safe machinery, high wages, short hours, good housing. But factory discipline might not be questioned. Trade unions should be ignored—they did not harmonize with enlightened despotism. In the Ford coal fields, near the border of West Virginia and Kentucky, the average daily wage in 1928 was $7 a day as compared with an average of

$4.40 for rival companies, but the "open shop" prevailed.[217] Detroit was an open-shop town.

In January 1914, the Ford factories adopted the eight-hour maximum working day and the $5 minimum wage. Such an announcement would have created little stir after the war, with the shorter working day the rule and wage scales trebled to meet the enhanced cost of living, but in 1914 it placed Ford operatives in a class by themselves. Liberal bonuses were added for workmen of good conduct, especially those with families to support. Unfortunately the definition of "good conduct" involved an investigation of the home life of employees, which was sometimes resented as paternalistic interference. This bonus-on-conduct system was later modified, but the general principle still prevailed of dividing the profits of the Ford industries with the employees. One interesting phase of the labor policy was the abolition of any sharp distinction between "bench" jobs and "desk" jobs. Very few executives had titles and very often superfluous clerical employees were forced to transfer to the shops. Administration never long remained in a rut—the restless owner of the business was too apt to come around and shake up the whole organization. Ford mentioned as one reason for his success the fact that he wasted no time in "conferences."

Not the Ford car alone but the automotive industry as a whole tended toward standardization during the boom period of the war and the decade following. Cars differed in little save magnificence of accessories and number of cylinders—plebeian fours, middle-class sixes, and aristocratic eights and twelves.[218] In mechanism they were rather more alike than typewriters. The gasoline type prevailed almost to the exclusion of the steam and the electric. It was cheap, convenient, and adaptable to rough roads and hilly country. The very increase in the sale of gasoline cars promoted still more rapid purchase, not only because the imitative American likes to follow his neighbor's example, but because the multiplication of service stations along the main roads made travel safe and easy.

Both the Ford methods of mass production and the standardization of type favored a steady decrease of cost to the consumer. The average sales price for all passenger cars dropped from its peak of $2,123 in 1907 to $820 in 1916.[219] The rapid fall in the value of money during and immediately after the World War obscured the real decline in cost. At almost any time after the war $500 or $600 would buy a new car of the cheaper type, and $1,000 would purchase one of the better grade. Moreover, the purchaser received more for his money than earlier. Most automobile firms strove to introduce each year some improvement over the car of the year before. Some of these changes were merely for the sake of a new fashion, but almost always there was some added advantage or value as well. When the Ford became "dressy" in 1927 to meet the competition of the more colorful cheap cars, it was evident that mere cheapness, convenience, and a good engine were no longer all that the clerk or farmer expected. The spread of luxury was shown in the increased proportion of closed cars: 28 percent of the production in 1922; 74 percent in 1926, and the tendency continued.[220]

Ford's nearest rival for the general market was a company with many strings to its bow, the General Motors Corporation, first established in 1908. William C. Durant, who fathered this combine, abandoned the once profitable manufacture of buggies for the newer field. But instead of becoming more and more concentrated under a single management and confined to a single type, General Motors came to take in more than 70,000 stockholders with very decentralized management under Alfred Sloan as "easy boss," and to develop different types of car for every need. At one time, General Motors produced the Chevrolet, the Pontiac, the Oldsmobile, the Oakland, the Buick, the LaSalle, and the Cadillac passenger cars, besides making trucks, taxicabs, and, last but not least, the Frigidaire domestic refrigerators.[221] The Chevrolet at popular prices rose to about a million customers and had much to do in compelling the manufacture of a newer type of Ford. Third in the industry was the combine of the Chrysler with the Dodge, consummated in 1928. The Ford, General Motors, and Chrysler-Dodge companies controlled in that year about four fifths of the whole industry, a very high degree of trustification for an industry that rests on no natural monopoly. Yet the motor trust, if one may use the word in a popular and inexact sense, did not share the unpopularity of the oil, steel, and meat-packing combines or of the railways and mines. The public felt that in automobiles, at any rate, consolidation meant better values and lower prices for the consumer.

The farmer probably profited more than anyone else from motor traction. The passenger automobile, though rarely more expensive than the Ford, ended his rural isolation and enabled his wife to visit town at will. The truck carried his perishable fruit and vegetables to market, and in 1926, 7 percent of the farmers operated their own trucks, while many others used the common carriers or contract truckers.[222] The tractor made an even greater difference in the farmer's life than car or truck. Henry Ford was prouder of his Fordson tractor than of his Ford car, described it as a "versatile power plant," and boasted that it had not only plowed, harrowed, cultivated, and reaped, but also threshed, run gristmills, sawmills, and the like, pulled stumps, cleared away snow, hauled with tires on the roads and with sledge runners on the ice, and been used in ninety-five lines of service, including the supply of power to get out an edition of the *Dearborn Independent* during a coal famine![223]

The democracy of the road created by the cheap automobile made the American people more than ever a migratory folk. An ever restless people, whose grandsires were immigrants and whose fathers were pioneers, who had almost abandoned the very idea of an ancestral homestead and were accustomed to changing their jobs and their homes a dozen times in the course of a single career, would naturally welcome the new opportunity for independent travel provided by Henry Ford and his fellow manufacturers. In the day of the buggy and the bicycle five or six miles from town was a good distance for a picnic, and a two weeks' vacation camping trip was usually spent at the nearest sea beach or mountain resort. But the automobile opened up 100 miles for the most impromptu picnic, and the whole United States for a serious vacation.

The automobile conditioned every aspect of American life. It greatly complicated the crime problem by giving every criminal who had three hours' warning a circle with a 100-mile radius in which to conceal himself from the police. It gave fresh urgency to the liquor problem by turning the simple drunkard into the more sinister figure of the drunken driver. It multiplied national parks and playgrounds and made tourism a leading industry. It placed mortgages on homes when the automobile was a luxury, and took them off farms when the motor truck became a necessity. It enabled the farmer to use the services of the town physician and send his children to a consolidated town school. It took this farmer, too, straight by the neighboring hamlet to trade in the city twenty or thirty miles away, causing the country store to languish and the mail-order houses to worry. The latter, to meet these new conditions, straightaway set up chain department stores in the smaller cities to recover their losses.

The motor car replaced the parlor and porch as the courting ground of the new generation. It made the American people more than ever a nation of mechanicians and, according to some hostile witnesses (such as Sinclair Lewis), swallowed up all other topics of male conversation from religion to politics. It gave a new aspect to feminism by making the flapper a gay and gallant *chauffeuse*. It freed the nation from provincialism, though at the heavy cost of increasing standardization of manners. It necessitated wider units of rural and suburban administration and, according to one high authority, did "more in two decades to revolutionize the areas of local government than all the events of history since the battle of Hastings."[224] It opened a new age of the nomads. In a word, it is the main subject not of this chapter only but of the volume as a whole.

RACE RELATIONS IN THE SOUTH

THE FACT that during these years sectional differences were less clearly defined than in any earlier period was due only in part to the integrating effect of the war. Even more potent, because more constant, was the influence of industrialism. Land is local; capital is cosmopolitan. The Yankee farmer and the Georgia planter in an agricultural age differed as the factory operative of Boston cannot differ from his fellow workman of Atlanta. Men still spoke of "the West," but they could no longer draw its boundary on the map, for Michigan and Illinois were now as industrialized as Connecticut. The automobile transplanted large numbers of the agricultural Midwest to urban and suburban Los Angeles, and brought a colony of wealthy businessmen from the Northeast to southernmost Florida. The growing habit of travel mitigated provincial differences, and the standardization of goods made all parts of the country more and more alike in dress and manner of life. In the main this leveling process, at least on its economic side, was a leveling upwards, tending to bring to all sections the standards of the most prosperous communities; but it robbed the United States of much picturesque local variety and subjected it to the reproach of being a land of interchangeable citizens whose minds were as alike as the money they used.

Of all the sections of the nation the South was the most persistent in maintaining its collective individuality. The process of standardization was at work here as elsewhere, perhaps more than elsewhere, but the original differences were greater. For over a century, ever since the cotton plantation became the norm of economic life, the South had felt a consciousness of kind wider than the state and narrower than the nation, a regionalism comparable perhaps to that of Catalonia in Spain or Scotland in Great Britain. In each decade since 1865, journalists had repeated the discovery of a "New South," and doubtless each time they were right, for the growth of industrial wealth and educational opportunity had been fairly continuous. The period after 1914 did not change the direction, but it certainly accelerated its momentum. The war played a part by merging sectional with national effort; the boll weevil diminished the relative importance of cotton. At the same time, the textile factories of the piedmont multiplied, the oil wells of Oklahoma and Texas brought a new influx of capital, tourist travel and winter golf became important, and the black population tended townward and northward as the munition factories enticed them from the plantations.

From 1915 to 1928 about 1.2 million blacks moved from South to North, although many made but a temporary stay.[225] The census of 1920, though covering but the first phase of this northward migration, showed a proportionate decrease of black population to the whole in almost all sections of the South, and in a few cases this decline was absolute as well as relative. From 1910 to 1920, Michigan's black population increased from 17,000 to 60,000, while during the same period Mississippi showed a loss of more than 74,000.

The townward movement of the race was even more striking than the northward trek, as it affected all sections of the country. The Northern cities made by far the most rapid and striking gains, but it is worth noting that Southern cities also attracted blacks from the farms. Nearly 235,000 moved from country to city in the census decade in the South Atlantic states, and in the South Central states, east of the Mississippi, "although each state lost Negro population, this loss was wholly rural, for the urban Negro population in the entire division increased over 62,000, or 12 percent." [226]

The northward movement of the black was not to be explained wholly by any single cause. [227] One of the most important factors was the location of the great munition centers in the Northeastern states. The shutting off of European immigration by the war at the very time when cheap labor was most in demand caused manufacturers to look toward Dixie. After the war, stricter immigration laws and the revival of general industry following a period of depression brought a new demand for labor in 1923, and in the first three months of that year a single Pittsburgh concern imported black workmen at the rate of 1,000 a month. [228] Alarmed at the activity of these recruiters, the white South discouraged labor agents by fines, levied on various pretexts, and by counterpropaganda. In December 1923, a Mississippi planter went to Chicago scattering handbills urging blacks to return to the South and sent out a wagon plastered with signs describing the charms of the cotton fields. [229] The expansion of industry coincided with a decline of cotton planting in districts ravaged by the boll weevil. Said one Southern planter, "It was a billion-dollar bug that got behind the Southern Negro and chased him across Mason and Dixon's line." [230]

Certain long-standing grievances of the Southern black made him more willing to listen to the labor agents. These were of three kinds: unequal treatment before the law, mob terrorism, and social discrimination. In Georgia and certain other states the county and police officials were compensated by a fee for their services, which meant they were paid so much a head for every man they arrested. The effect was to render these officials overzealous in rounding up blacks for gambling, drinking, and other petty infractions of the law. As punishment for such offenses, blacks were usually sentenced to work on the county roads. [231] When more serious offenses were brought to book, especially offenses against the whites, the sentences imposed were often disproportionately heavy. [232]

Purely political discriminations seem to have weighed less than these judicial partialities. The issue of the franchise was not very widely agitated during this period; the Fifteenth Amendment remained in the Constitution, which seemed to satisfy Northern sentiment, and it was quietly disregarded throughout the black belt, which seemed to meet the desires of the white South. The federal courts disallowed the "grandfather" test when the issue was raised, and declared unconstitutional the Texas "white-primary" law of 1924 which drew a racial line in party primary elections. [233] But literacy tests, ability to "interpret" the state constitution, the payment of a poll tax, and other similar devices, long in use and in form not discriminatory, were tolerated however unequally they might be administered. On the other hand, in the North where black suffrage was a reality, the black vote, thanks to the great migration, became far more influential than ever before, especially in such urban centers as Chicago, which elected a black congressman in 1928.

Other grievances were local acts of mob violence—it is significant that many emigrants came from the particular localities where such outrages had taken place—inferior school accommodations, injustice in sharing farm profits between tenant and landlord or between borrower and creditor, discrimination on common carriers, the denial of courtesy titles (such as mister, doctor, etc.) to educated blacks, and the lack of opportunity for employment in certain "white" trades. Such incidents as the murder of eleven blacks on a Georgia plantation to keep indebted peons in subjection had wide repercussions.[234] Several Southern white editors, while asserting that blacks ought to remain south of Mason and Dixon's line both for their own good and for that of their section, pointed out that they could not be expected to do so unless they met better treatment. Thus, in South Carolina, the *Columbia State* declared on December 2, 1916, "If the Southern people would have the Negroes remain they must treat the Negroes justly." And the *Memphis Commercial Appeal* in Tennessee urged on October 15 of the same year, "The South needs every able-bodied Negro that is now south of the line, and every Negro who remains south of the line will in the end do better than he will do in the North."[235]

On the other hand, while the South valued the black's services more as he threatened to leave the section, many Northern newspapers expressed apprehension over the arrival of large numbers of blacks. White laborers resented the competition of the cheap black workingmen and out of this resentment grew serious riots. In East St. Louis, Illinois, where black strikebreakers had been imported by the meat packers in 1916, the trade unions in vain protested to the city authorities against their coming. In July 1917, a disastrous riot took place on a scale quite as large as any that had ever occurred farther south. Over 100 blacks were killed or wounded, 5,000 were made homeless, and hundreds of thousands of dollars' worth of property destroyed.[236] Similar but lesser riots took place in factory towns in Pennsylvania and New Jersey in the same year, and in Chicago, Omaha, and Washington, D.C., in 1919. Thus unhappy proof was given of the truth of the old contention of the white South that race violence was national and not sectional and that if blacks moved northward race riots would follow in their wake.

By a curious anomaly, in spite of the prevalence of race riots in the hectic postwar days and the revival of the Ku Klux Klan, the old American custom of lynch law fell into almost complete disuse. In the first four months of 1928 there was not a single recorded lynching, a record without parallel since exact statistics on the subject began to be kept. For the decade 1914–23 inclusive, the average number was fifty-seven annually, a much better record than that of previous years but still unconscionably high. Though the proposed Dyer antilynching bill, which would have given the federal courts jurisdiction in cases of mob violence, failed of action in the Senate after passing the House of Representatives in 1922, it stirred the local authorities to vindicate state rights by greater zeal in law enforcement. There were only sixteen lynchings in 1924 as compared with thirty-three in the previous year, seventeen in 1925, thirty in 1926, sixteen in 1927, eleven in 1928, and ten in 1929.[237] It became the exception instead of the rule for a mob to meet with no effective opposition from the constituted authorities. A notable instance of civic courage was the personal rescue of a black from a mob at Murray, Kentucky, in 1917, by the governor of the state, A. O. Stanley.[238] Noteworthy also was the denunciation of lynching by a committee of white women associated with the Commission on Interracial Cooperation in Louisiana: "We hold that no circumstances can ever justify such violent disregard for law and that in no instance is it an exhibition of chivalric consideration and honor of womanhood."[239] Similar resolutions were passed in many other states.[240]

Blacks reacted in various ways to their unfavorable position in the United States. Some became ashamed of their race and tried to tone down its characteristics as much as possible, and fortunes were made in hair-straightening devices, the reverse process to the white girl's "wave." Others, in increasing numbers, became race conscious and took pride in their African blood. These race-conscious Afro-Americans were, however, divided in policy. Those who followed the tradition of Booker T. Washington, whose work at Tuskegee was ably continued by Robert R. Moton, sought first of all a solid economic position for the race, as educated, trained, property-owning farmers and artisans, for whom the whites would feel a respect which would eventually bring with it political reenfranchisement. To more fiery and impatient spirits this program seemed too slow, and as a result there had arisen in the early years of the century a second type of racial leader, typified by W. E. B. Du Bois, editor of the *Crisis,* and associated with the National Association for the Advancement of Colored People, who demanded the immediate grant of equal civil and political rights.[241] After the war and the return of black regiments from France (where racial discriminations do not follow the American tradition) much was heard of the "New Negro" who would no longer, cap in hand, submit to injustice, but "when the mob moves, meet it with bricks and clubs and guns."[242] One tiny, picturesque group did indeed carry black nationalism far beyond the simple demand of Du Bois for equal rights in America. These were the followers of Marcus Garvey, president of the newly formed Universal Negro Improvement Association, who dreamed of nothing less than the reconquest of Africa as a black man's republic—a sort of African Zionism. "The hour has come," he declared, "when the whole continent of Africa shall be reclaimed and redeemed as the home of the black peoples." He projected a "Black Star Line" of steamers for transporting the American black back to his ancestral homeland, there to erect a racial empire under the banner of black, red, and green to the strains of

Ethiopia, thou land of our fathers,
  Thou land where the gods loved to be,
As storm cloud at night sudden gathers
  Our armies come rushing to thee!

Garvey was later prosecuted and imprisoned for swindling, and nothing came of his enterprise, too vast and vague for a world of solid realities, but at least his movement was a sign that to many blacks their race had become a pride rather than a humiliation.[243]

On the whole, the economic situation of the American black improved during and after the World War. Though due in part to the competitive bidding of field and factory for his services, the improvement came even more from the spread of education, which qualified him for better positions. From 1917 to 1927 the number of institutions for the higher education of blacks more than doubled, and enrollment in them increased more than sixfold.[244] A larger proportion of the race also attended Northern and Western institutions open to all races. The number employed by the federal government rose from 22,540 in 1910 to 52,882 in 1928.[245] More black high schools were built in the South from 1918 to 1928 than in the entire past.[246] In spite of the boll weevil and a bad credit situation, the majority of those who stuck to the farm found themselves better off. William S. Scarborough, former president of Wilberforce University, testified in 1925: "The Virginia Negro farmers may be said to belong to a thrifty group. Virtually all are members of a church and of one or another of the many fraternal societies. . . . Most of the Negroes have automobiles and many own victrolas."[247]

Probably the most successful, certainly the most famous, of the black urban communities was the Harlem district in New York City. By 1928 the black population of New York City was estimated at 250,000, of whom 170,000 lived in Harlem.[248] Not all came from the Southern states, for the West Indies contributed perhaps 40,000. Steadily the black merchants and shopkeepers drove the whites out of business. "A Negro millinery shop offers 'a variety of styles in the latest Parisian shapes created by expert Negro designers.' A Negro apothecary advertises, 'Why not go to our own drugstores? They employ all colored men.' "[249] There was a thriving trade in black doll babies, advertised "Why should a Negro child play with a white doll?"[250] Here one saw the beginnings of race pride and race culture; the Garveyite movement was largely fostered in Harlem. The black artist was also taking himself more seriously; he had long been a favorite in the lighter arts, vaudeville and minstrel-show song and dance, but the dramatic power of such actors as Charles Gilpin and Paul Robeson, the musical art of Roland Hayes, the famous tenor, and the poetry of Countee Cullen were central parts of a celebrated Harlem renaissance.[251]

The general economic progress of the South was even more rapid than that of most parts of the North and West, and this quite apart from such local booms as the oil fields of Oklahoma or the winter-vacation colony of tropical Florida. If we take the section as a whole in its broadest sense,[252] the population of the South increased by about a quarter from 1910 to 1927; and the aggregate value of its property doubled from 1912 to 1925.[253] Cotton spinning shifted increasingly near to the region of cotton planting. In 1910 about a third of the active looms and spindles of the nation were in the South; in 1927 approximately one half.[254] Seven barrels of petroleum were produced in the South in 1927 to each barrel in 1910. Coal production in the same period more than doubled. The rate of increase in the use of electricity for the decade 1913-23 was over 212 percent, while the increase for the remainder of the country was less than 148 percent.[255]

The cotton mills of the piedmont reached out their tentacles and increasingly swept into urban life the most isolated rural communities in America, the Southern highlanders, where the purest English stock in the nation had stagnated for generations on rocky hillside farms in poverty and ignorance. Lowlanders also of the poor-white class came to the factories. The black did not come, or came only as an outdoor laborer for odd jobs of carpentry and the like. The actual textile operatives were almost exclusively of the white race; as in earlier years, many of them were women and children.[256] The issue of child labor thus raised was much debated. Advocates of national action contended that Southern laws as to age of employment, hours of labor, and working conditions were below the standard of other sections. Opponents pointed out that Southern mill owners did so much welfare work among their employees that their health, education, and social opportunities were better secured than if they had remained on the farm, and the many had passed through the mill door to a future of wealth and community leadership.

Curious indeed were the contrasts presented by the advance of the textile industry in the South. A people possessing a strong individualistic tradition were brought under a paternalism almost feudal in character, for in some mill villages the manufacturer owned or controlled all the land, the homes, the shops, and the places of recreation. City ways were quickly copied by the younger generation, while their elders held to mountain customs. As a recent student has pointed out, the mill village "is the link between poverty and prosperity; it is the meeting place of old and new. Granny wears a sunbonnet and came to the mill in a farm wagon, the young 'uns wear georgette and silk hose and own a Ford car. . . ."[257] Similar transitions to the industrial epoch might be observed in northern Alabama, where the Birmingham iron district was rapidly becoming another Pittsburgh.

The political change in the South was even more dramatic, though probably of less real importance, than its economic and intellectual evolution. The fact that a president of Southern birth, with a cabinet half Southern in personnel, and a Congress led in both branches by Southern Democrats as chairmen of important committees, held power during the World War did much to restore the self-confidence of a section which had counted for little in national or international affairs since 1860. As one loyal North Carolinian wrote, "it seemed almost a miracle to see that aged taunt of the Republicans—'The Democrats will put the South in the saddle'—turned into a proud fact at the most crucial moment of modern history." [258] The disastrous rout of the Democratic party at the polls in 1920, 1924, and 1928 did not undo the growing political influence of the section. On the contrary, the Republicans saw an opportunity for winning the South from its Democratic allegiance and more than ever courted its support.

The growing industrialization of the South tended to modify its attitude toward the one fairly consistent test of American party allegiance, the tariff. "Today one sees the Solid South crumbling a bit in its attitude toward the tariff . . . ," wrote one observer, "Cotton mills that rival or exceed those of New England; iron factories, comparable in many ways to those of Pennsylvania; phosphate mines, and petroleum wells, not to mention Louisiana's acre after acre of sugar cane, not only are not averse to protection, but are actually seen clamoring for it!" [259] Other factors, such as the immigration of many Northern voters, especially to southern Florida, the lessening stress of the race question, the equal disregard of both parties when in office for the principle of state rights, divisions of opinion on the Wilsonian foreign policy, the gradual fading of historic antagonisms and the prevalent prosperity, gave the Republicans many victories in the border states and even won ex-Confederate Tennessee in 1920. But in general, the Solid South remained unmelted until 1928.

In that year the Democratic party strained the loyalty of the South to the breaking point by the nomination of Alfred E. Smith, governor of New York, a man of unquestionable ability but bearing the fourfold handicap of being a Northerner, an official of Tammany Hall, an enemy of prohibition, and a Roman Catholic. Not even the nomination for vice president of Senator J. T. Robinson of Arkansas—the first nomination of an actual Southern resident on a major national ticket since the Civil War—quieted the resentment of the section. The result was that all of the border states, together with Tennessee, Virginia, North Carolina, Florida, and Texas among the old Confederate states, went for Herbert Hoover and against Governor Smith, that Alabama was saved by a narrow margin, and a heavy Republican vote was cast in Arkansas and Georgia. [260] Only Mississippi, Louisiana, and South Carolina had anything like normal Democratic majorities. The same election placed in the Democratic column Massachusetts and Rhode Island. Though perhaps with other candidates some of these overturns would not have taken place, the fact that they could happen under any circumstances proved that American politics, North and South alike, was no longer the mere by-product of sectional tradition that it had been since 1856.

THE BUSINESS OF SPORT

NEXT TO THE SPORT of business the American enjoyed most the business of sport. Politics, religion, education, the fine arts, and other human activities had to compete for third prize at best. "Not far from one quarter of the entire national income of America is expended for play and recreation broadly interpreted," wrote Stuart Chase in 1928. "Perhaps half that sum is expended in forms of play new since the coming of the industrial revolution, and requiring more or less complicated machinery for their enjoyment."[261] All forms of amusement required increased outlay, from the $200 million a year spent on sporting goods[262] to the manufacture of 20 million dolls a year for American children.[263]

The high tide of prosperity after 1914 popularized recreation far beyond anything known in any earlier period and made the provision of pleasure the most comprehensive of national industries. Other influences helped in the same direction. There was, for example, the invention of new toys with which the nation could play. Obviously the rapid and almost simultaneous development of the automobile, the moving picture, the phonograph, and the radio opened pleasant ways of killing time quite impossible to any previous generation. Demand may create supply, but supply may also nourish demand. Without these new pleasures many might have been content to put in more time at work, not being sufficiently attracted by the older forms of recreation. Perhaps, too, the continued growth of the great cities with their confining indoor life caused increasing numbers to seek outdoor play to meet the physical needs once satisfied by outdoor labor.

Nor should we forget the skill of the merchandisers of sports in hawking their wares. The same arts of publicity which made bathtubs, face creams, and vacuum cleaners universal were employed to sell sporting goods, and the same press-agenting which helped make the reputation of a grand-opera star or a politician was also at the service of a pugilist. Millions went to see "Babe" Ruth play baseball, "Red" Grange play football, or Jack Dempsey fight in the ring, because they had learned to know these stars in the columns of the press. The sense of proportion thus created was amusingly illustrated in July 1928, when the debarment of the tennis champion W. T. Tilden from the amateur ranks drove from the front pages a presidential campaign, the assassination of the Mexican president-elect, the mysterious death of a Belgian millionaire, and the search for lost aviators in the Arctic. Charges of bribe-taking by the White Sox professional baseball team a few years earlier created wider popular excitement than charges of bribe-taking by members of the cabinet.

The pleasure-loving American, however, did not form a leisure class in the European sense. He carried into sport the same grim seriousness that had served him so well in trade, and the desire to excel was as cruelly competitive in sport as in commerce. This brought to the United States many trophies and world championships, but the spirit of play was lost. There was a technical distinction between amateur and professional athletics in the United States, insisted on with such pedantic precision that a player could be disqualified as an amateur for writing articles on his own sport or coaching a schoolboy for money in another game; but there was little psychological distinction. Both amateur and professional had the essentially professional attitude which takes training seriously, admires technical form, and would make almost any sacrifice for victory.

Football and baseball were close rivals for leadership in the business of sport. Football remained essentially a college game in spite of the attempt to make it a popular professional sport by inducing athletes on graduation from college to enter the commercial teams. Baseball, on the contrary, was the unquestioned leader among professional games. Though amateurs joyfully played it everywhere, from six-year-olds on the vacant lots up to the university teams, not all these amateur contests together awoke a tithe of the interest aroused by the games of the National and American leagues, the leading professional organizations. In 1913 the baseball world series had an attendance of 150,000 and receipts of $325,980; in 1923, the attendance was 300,000 and the receipts more than a million dollars.[264] A single game in the 1928 series attracted over 60,000 spectators and reaped a harvest of more than $224,000.[265]

The world series—justly named, for in baseball the United States was then virtually the world—was the last week's culmination of a whole summer of intense rivalry. Although the baseball teams in no sense really represented the cities after which they were named, so hearty was the American capacity for make-believe that a contest between two financial organizations whose players were assembled from all over the nation became a strife in which the pride of the cities was directly involved, and feeling was as intense as at any college football game, though it no longer found frequent expression in assaults on the umpire who gave a decision against the "home team." From mid-spring to mid-autumn, even encroaching on the season sacred to football, the baseball teams battled around the country, the newspapers carefully recording their percentages, until one team emerged clearly at the head of its league, and then came for one brief week the struggle of the giants. When Washington, D.C., first won world honors in baseball in 1924, the city held such a jubilee as would have done credit to the close of a great war or the inauguration of a president. George ("Babe") Ruth of the New York Yankees, by hitting the ball for fifty-nine home runs in 1921 and for sixty in 1927, made himself one of the best-known individuals in the United States.

Football, with altered rules to encourage open play—running, throwing, and kicking—won a greater following than ever before. Though the most important of the new rules had become established before 1910, the possibilities of the more open game were not fully developed until the years following the World War, which had temporarily deflected interest even from football. But from 1919 to 1928 football reigned supreme in college life. Thirty years earlier only a few schools and colleges played the game, and most of these without expert coaching, so that Walter Camp could make up his list of "All-American" football stars by selecting the best men from Harvard, Princeton, and Yale. For 1,000 players in the whole nation then, there were 200,000 playing in 1926, and from 6,000 to 10,000 professional coaches and trainers to keep them fit.[266] Any school which chose to spend the money could have expert coaching, and Harvard and Yale were sometimes outranked in gridiron efficiency by a score of other schools. No longer could a college claim national ascendancy; the old dynasties of the East had given way to a turbulent democracy of sport. A very small college, like Centre in Kentucky, would blaze as a star of the first magnitude for a single year or two and then sink back to obscurity. The only permanent advantage of the larger colleges was their superior reservoir of manpower for reserves. Games were no longer of team against team but of squad against squad, and the larger institutions had at least two competent substitutes for every man on the field.

One of the differences between the old game and the new was that the older football interested chiefly the students and the alumni; the new game, more spectacular, attracted also the general public. Although the football season, except in California, lasted only from late September to Thanksgiving, 30 million spectators in 1927 paid some $50 million in gate receipts.[267] To accommodate these enormous crowds huge stadiums of steel and concrete were built, seating about 80,000 at Yale and California, and 70,000 or more at Illinois, Ohio State, Michigan, and several others. For the greater part of the year these enormous "lunar craters," as Coach A. A. Stagg of Chicago aptly called them, stood empty, but on the day of a great game they were filled to overflowing with the largest crowds that ever witnessed athletic sports since the fall of Rome. Many went to enjoy the pageantry of the affair as much as the game itself—the gay colors in the stands, the organized cheering under specially drilled cheerleaders, the military parade of the college band, the tense atmosphere of suspense when 70,000 clamorous voices were hushed as a pigskin hesitated in midair above the wooden crossbar. The games played by the West Point and Annapolis teams were always popular, whether they were weak or strong, because the drills, the songs, the uniforms, and the "stunts" of the army and navy boys were particularly picturesque.

The complaints against the new football as voiced, for example, by a committee of the American Association of University Professors, were not so much, as formerly, against brutality or dishonesty, though neither had become wholly extinct, but rather against the danger of transforming an amateur sport into a commercial amusement business run by coaches and alumni for the benefit of the general sporting public.[268] Not even the huge gate receipts reconciled everyone to spending hundreds of thousands of dollars on football equipment, stadiums, uniforms, coaching, and travel, at a time when many departments of the university were starved of funds for teaching and research. It should in fairness be said, however, that a large part of the profits of football were used to make up deficits in general athletic equipment or to support less profitable "minor sports." Gambling was common, and the attitude of alumni and townsfolk often thoroughly unsportsmanlike.

But the public was impatient with these faint misgivings. A typical editorial in the newsstand periodical *Liberty* retorted to the hostile report of the professors that the whole trouble was faculty jealousy of the superior abilities and earning power of coaches and ex-players: "The problem is not the elimination or restriction of football, but how long it will be before red-blooded colleges demand the elimination or the restriction of those afflicted with this inferiority complex." [269] Sometimes alumni were impatient of the increased standards of scholarship when they threatened to interfere with the superior claims of football. "When high-class athletes with a passable and qualifying school record are turned aside as unfit," complained one alumnus, "it is just as foolish as it would be to turn aside high-class scholars who had only a passable record in physical training.[270]

Next to world series baseball or a football game between two great universities, a prizefight drew the largest crowds. After a period of eclipse, the well-staged and decorous contests in a twentieth-century arena more than recaptured the fashionable note of 100 years earlier when English gentry, nobility, and even royalty (as represented by the crown prince who was later George IV) attended bare-knuckle fights and themselves studied the art of self-defense under expert boxers.

In 1926 a world's championship boxing contest took place in Philadelphia as part of the entertainment of the sesquicentennial exposition. The attendance was estimated at 125,000, not including the millions who listened to the thud of the boxing gloves over the radio. The public paid $1,895,000 for admission, of which Jack Dempsey, who was that day uncrowned as king of the pugilistic world, drew $700,000. Thus was celebrated the 150th year of American independence! Other heavyweight contests were almost as plutocratic. Spectators paid $1,626,000 to see Jack Dempsey defeat the gallant French challenger Georges Carpentier in 1921. Two years later he defeated the Argentine giant Firpo before a crowd which had paid more than a million to see him do it. But the record athletic event was Dempsey's return match against Gene Tunney, the new world champion, in 1927, a contest with gate receipts of more than $2,650,000. So rapid was the development of pugilism from a sport into an industry that nineteen fights between 1918 and the end of 1924 yielded more than $100,000 each, as compared with only four such costly contests for all previous history.[271]

The worst feature of the new pugilism was that dishonesty was so rife that, even when an honest fighter was defeated, his disappointed backers were likely to claim that he had been paid to surrender the victory by gamblers on the other side. Wrestling, professional track meets, horse racing in its many forms, shared with boxing the reproach of being "fixed" by gamblers too frequently for the spectator to feel that he was watching a real contest. Hence the popularity of amateur tennis, golf, football, and track, which were usually conducted with a sincere desire to win. Honesty was, perhaps, the only real moral superiority which amateur athletics could claim over professional, and this superiority lasted only so long as gambling could be kept to a relatively unimportant place. There was real commercial advantage in not making sport too commercial.

Golf, tennis, and polo had been the traditional sports of the wealthy amateur. Polo, because of the cost of good ponies, continued to remain a rich man's game, but golf and tennis greatly widened their appeal. By 1928 golf represented an investment of more than $2 billion, and employed over 3,000 professional instructors, 100,000 workers to keep the courses in condition, and half a million caddies.[272] Private courses were often very expensive, but as early as 1924 eighty-nine cities had established municipal golf courses.[273] No other sport suited so well the average American businessman. The increasing popularity of tennis was shown by the attempts to professionalize this most amateur of sports. Suzanne Lenglen, a highly temperamental Frenchwoman who had at various times held the championship of her sex, entered the professional game and her example was followed by other stars to the exaggerated horror of many amateurs.

Of other sports, basketball, ice hockey, and swimming developed most rapidly. As earlier, basketball was the favorite indoor sport of schools and colleges; hockey, once so largely Canadian, became thoroughly naturalized in the United States, and winter sports generally, such as ski jumping, skating, and ice boating, increased in popularity. Swimming enjoyed a double stimulus, from the indoor tanks now provided in most schools and from the growing popularity of the seashore. When Gertrude Ederle and Clemington Corson swam the English Channel in 1926, a feat few men had ever accomplished, they were hailed as treble victors, vindicating alike the country they represented, the physical prowess of their sex, and the interests of their chosen sport. The one-piece bathing suit transformed American women from "bathers" into "swimmers." Wide popular interest was aroused, and deftly commercialized, by the "bathing-beauty" contests, the winner enjoying the title of Miss America and a week or so of concentrated publicity.

Interest in track and field sports was increased by the Olympic Games, international contests in conscious imitation of the intercity contests of ancient Hellas. The World War interrupted the games from 1912 to 1920, but thenceforward they took place at each four-year interval. The well-trained Americans held championships in most forms of running, leaping, and weight throwing, but were compelled to yield honors in the very long runs, requiring patient endurance rather than dash, to the more stolid English, Canadians, Finns, and Scandinavians. Indeed, in the Marathon long-distance race of 1928 at Amsterdam, the winner was a native of French North Africa, who was followed in order of time by a Chilean, a Finn, a Japanese, and an American.

Of less strenuous amusements dancing was the chief. There was nothing new about dancing, of course, but never before had this ancient and natural amusement been forced through such rapid changes. Even before the war the tango and the turkey trot had enlivened the scene and brought with them an imitative swarm of hops, wriggles, squirms, glides, and gallops named after all the animals in the menagerie. After the war, dancing tended to become a mere shuffle in a confined space, "dancing on a dime" with a partner all evening long. This culminated in a climax of folly—the "dance marathon" in which heroic imbeciles entered an endurance contest, keeping their feet in slow motion for several days and nights. Then the pace quickened; instead of the close hug and slow glide the dancers indulged in the violent acrobatics of the Charleston and the black bottom to the imminent peril of neighboring shins. To learn all the intricacies of the hundred new fashions in dancing steps the youth of the nation attended dancing academies by the thousand.

More and more, young people's parties abandoned other amusements and made dancing the entire evening program. Few hostesses dared give parties without providing for dances; churches used the dance to attract and hold the new generation; schools taught folk dances to little children. The finer art of the dance, as exemplified on the stage by Russian artists, won attentive crowds. Henry Ford interested himself in reviving the almost lost art of the old "square dances" of the pioneer days of the republic. "There are thirty million people who dance in the United States, daily, weekly, or frequently," said a statistician in 1924. "A billion dollars for dancing by rich and poor would be a modest bill."[274] To the music of the phonograph, the radio, and the jazz band all the nation paid homage to Saint Vitus.

Jazz music spread with the new dances and each urged the other to fresh triumphs. There have been many attempts to define jazz, but one of the men who did most to give it such artistic expression as it could attain, Paul Whiteman, was obliged to confess, "What a jazz? Is it art, a disease, a manner, or a dance? Has it any musical value? After twelve years of jazz I don't know."[275] His account of its origin, in the same article, was more revealing.

> Jazz is the folk music of the machine age. There was every reason why this music sprang into being about 1915. . . . In this country especially the rhythm of machinery, the over rapid expansion of a great country endowed with

tremendous natural energies and wealth have brought about a pace and scale of living unparalleled in history. Is it any wonder that the popular music of this land should reflect these modes of living? Every other art reflects them.

Technically, jazz was an exaggeration of the tendencies implicit in the ragtime and pseudo-African melodies long popular on the American stage. Jazz combined the older syncopation with a superimposed accompanying rhythm, "and it is this subsidiary, *one*, two, three on top of the underlying tempo that makes shoulder muscles twitch, that bedevils hips, that provokes wiggles and twists on the dance floor, and causes blue noses to cry out that jazz is a great immoral influence."[276] To those accustomed to suave and melodious Viennese waltzes the new music seemed a mere chaos of ugliness, but Europe welcomed American ragtime and jazz as something exotic, original, and interesting, if not wholly beautiful, and in the United States its rule was as wide as the art of the dance. Twenty typical radio stations, ten large and ten small, were "on the air" for an aggregate of 651 hours one week, and it was noticed that 448 hours of this total, over two thirds, were spent playing jazz.[277]

The fundamental melodies and rhythms of the popular music were borrowed largely from the classics without credit or apology. Jazz orchestrations were often original and ingenious, "as well balanced and as effective in rendition as those produced for our symphony orchestras."[278] The words, blasphemously termed the "lyrics," were usually more devoid of beauty, sincerity, and meaning than the respectable songs of any other age or nation. Now and then an Irving Berlin would introduce a welcome touch of humor or pathos, but in the main they were mere sensuous sentimentality expressed in baby-talk jingles.

The rapid succession of new styles in dress, dancing, and music was not more kaleidoscopic than the shift in minor parlor amusements. For a period of about two years mah-jongg, an imported Chinese game played with decorated tiles like dominoes and involving calculations as intricate as an income-tax blank, threatened to wean the bridge enthusiasts from their loyalty and even to menace the smaller but equally fanatical sect of chess players. A few months passed, and mah-jongg was but a fading memory. The crossword puzzle had succeeded to its honors, a more complexly patterned development from the old acrostics.

Crossword puzzles provided an interesting chapter in the history of the American publisher. Richard Simon and Lincoln Schuster, boys in their twenties, ambitiously tried to launch a publishing house of their own. Needing capital, they began as a humble sideline, under another firm name, the first series of crossword puzzle books. "We hired halls. We drafted by-laws and rules for amateur cross-word orgies. . . . We visited editors, urging them to put cross-word puzzles in the papers. . . . Soon we were selling thousands of copies a day and breaking into the best seller lists."[279]

Of course, once the ball was so started it needed no more pushing, but gathered momentum on its own account. For three or four years after 1924 the Egyptian sun god, Ra; eel, "a snakelike fish"; the Oo bird of Hawaii; and the printers' measures "em" and "en," were among the most familiar words in the language, because so convenient to the architects of puzzles. Many of the by-products of the fad were valuable. It boomed the market for dictionaries and thesauri, widened the vocabulary, stimulated study of the recondite terms of science and the arts, and, incidentally, earned enough money for the firm of Simon and Schuster to enable them to become the publishers of serious books.

The crossword puzzle was but one of several such parlor hobbies. "One wonders if anything that has happened to us in America in the past generation is half as important as this latest tendency, this sudden need for intelligent play," declared an acute observer.

> The newspapers are full of games—words to guess, rimes to fill in, ingenious picture autographs to make, novels to identify. Clerks and plumbers and school teachers and school children go home elbow to elbow in the subway, muttering five-letter words that mean "commonplace," or trying to supply the laddergram links between Bride and Groom.[280]

But these excellent brain-teasing diversions were usually all too briefly popular. One of the chief amusements of the American was to change amusements. Yet some of them seemed likely to become a permanent legacy. The arts of the motion picture, the radio, and the phonograph bade fair to be as enduring as the camera, the theater, and the piano.

On the whole, the increased emphasis on recreation was a positive contribution to American life, though the American still needed instruction in the difficult art of enjoying leisure. As Dorothy Canfield told the students of the University of Kansas, American psychology had been framed in a pioneer age and adapted to the problem of meeting work, want, and hardship. "Nobody forearmed us with forewarnings about the dangers from the *lack* of material hardships. . . . We had neither the tools nor the knowledge to deal with the wholly unexpected phenomenon . . . of evenings with nothing to do. . . ."[281] American play was still too strenuous for those who took part and too idle for those who looked on; too expensive for those who bought and too commercially profitable for those who sold; too dominated by fashion, imitation, and advertisement.[282] The highest function of play, the personally creative, was mainly absent.

THE CULT OF NATIONALISM

THE OUTSTANDING SPIRITUAL phenomenon of the times was the remarkable intensification of nationalism. By one decision this generation closed the door to most European and all Asiatic labor. By another the American people placed themselves outside all international unions for world peace. But the same spirit showed itself in humbler forms as well—in a dramatic revival of nativism, in an aggressive watchfulness against unconventional political doctrines, in an exaltation of the virtues of the "Nordic" race, in an extraordinary revival of popular interest in American history and, in general, in a glorification of "one-hundred-percent Americanism." In large measure this efflorescence of nationalism was a product of the war. The epoch which witnessed the climax and collapse of Pan-Germanism and the rebirth of a dozen nationalities in central and eastern Europe was one of intense national feeling everywhere. In many countries, such as Fascist Italy and the states of the Balkans, the Danube, and the Baltic, as well as among the insurgent students of China and Hindustan, the fever rose many degrees higher than in the United States. Its evil side, so tragically illustrated in the Old World, was only feebly reflected in the New. And yet, relatively to the immediate past, the United States was keenly and intolerantly patriotic after 1914.

The direct influence of the war showed itself at first in self-pleasing contrasts between war-torn Europe and peaceful, prosperous America, and later, as active propaganda was carried on by foreign governments among immigrant Americans, in a fear that the integrity of American citizenship was endangered by alien sympathies. Though in the actual test of battle most of the recent comers proved as loyal as the sons of the *Mayflower,* the years of hesitation which preceded the abandonment of neutrality were so marked by "hyphenism" and the echoes of old-world feuds as to awaken pardonable misgivings that a divided allegiance might appear in times of crisis. Theodore Roosevelt spent his last energies in appealing for a united nation. He popularized the phrase, "one-hundred-percent Americanism," though in his mouth it meant a common allegiance by men of all races and not, as so often misused, the supremacy of a single racial type. But as the passions of war mounted the man of foreign accent became as much suspected as the man of foreign sympathies. To be sure, the popular feeling against the "Hun" quickly evaporated after the war, but it left behind it a residual dislike of aliens and "radicals" and a general suspicion of greedy and unscrupulous European diplomacy.

The panic over Russian Bolshevism, needless though it was, served almost as much as the war itself to bring about an antialien sentiment. The activity of so many East Europeans in radical labor agitation and the boast of the Russian revolutionists that their agents were active in all parts of the world undermining the foundations of capitalist society, caused many to see in every humble immigrant a potential spy or rebel. The civil war in Ireland, also, caused some Americans to hate England as an oppressor, and others to hate Ireland as a disturber, and both alike to deplore the injection of the feud between the Orange and the Green into American life. It is not surprising that European dictatorships, civil wars, and class struggles made many Americans feel that their peaceful, wealthy, and stable country stood on another and higher level than the rest of the world. The *Chicago Tribune* flaunted in each day's issue the arrogant motto, "Our country, right or wrong," and the Hearst papers, perhaps to recover a reputation for patriotism somewhat damaged during the war, lost no opportunity to contrast the virtuous American with the sinister European and the quite demoniac Asiatic.

A similar defensive reaction was called forth by the hostile and unsympathetic depiction of American life by such writers as H. L. Mencken, Sinclair Lewis, and the thirty authors of *Civilization in the United States*.[283] These authors performed a useful service in puncturing national complacency, but their manner of doing it merely transformed complacency into irritation. Just as the average American refused to recognize himself in the European mirror as a calculating dollar-worshiper, so he refused to recognize himself in the Greenwich Village mirror as a gloomy, hypocritical Puritan incapable of humane culture.[284] Any competent psychologist could have told the critics that an indiscriminate assault upon a national sentiment makes the nationalist more set in his ways than ever. If his very virtues are derided as faults, he will erect his very faults into virtues.[285]

The fact that the outbreak of the war had temporarily turned aside the flood of immigration led to a reexamination of the traditional national policy of encouraging all who were discontented with their lot to seek a better home in America.[286] Despite an increasing amount of restrictive legislation in recent years, the gates at Ellis Island still stood wide in 1914. The criminal, the contract laborer, the anarchist, the polygamist, the physically or mentally diseased, the pauper with no visible means of support, the Oriental coolie, were all debarred. But there was no fixed numerical barrier. Immigrants might come in whatever numbers economic conditions should determine. But as the sparsely populated parts of the country became more thickly settled and the alien competed with the native-born laborer in the great urban centers, the question became increasingly acute as to whether the future of America could be wisely entrusted to the children of the more recent comers in preference to the children of the men and women whose forefathers had long been here. The problem was rendered more urgent by the change in the national composition of the later arrivals, for in recent years hundreds of thousands of bread seekers from Sicily, Naples, the Slavic and Magyar parts of Austria-Hungary, and the Jewish Pale in Poland and western Russia had formed the bulk of the newcomers.[287] The annihilation of distance by means of transportation had brought the whole world to the doorstep of Uncle Sam.

The new immigration contained much that was valuable to American life, much that it had traditionally lacked.[288] Without these new additions to the workforce of the nation the economic progress of the new century must have been slower and costlier. Many regarded the prospect with as little dismay as Dr. Abraham Flexner, scientist and educator, who declared, "Far from regarding the mixed composition of races in this country as unfortunate, I regard it as a distinct advantage of which not enough use has been made. Every one of the stocks represented in the American people has made to this country its own unique contribution in the establishment of the native culture."[289]

But there was another side to the question. Even granting the good qualities of the new immigrants, could they be assimilated to American life in such quantities and in such variety? The immigrants from southern and eastern Europe rarely understood English on their arrival and often could not read or write in any tongue. They were accustomed to a meager livelihood and could underbid alike native American labor and the immigrant from the more prosperous countries of northwestern Europe. The trade unions advocated laws restricting European and excluding Asiatic immigration. In this they were supported not only by the nativist prejudice which intolerant men always feel against a foreigner, but also by the more considered judgment of statesmen who believed that a temporary stimulus to industry would be too dearly bought if it impaired either the racial quality or the standards of living of the nation. As Dr. H. H. Laughlin expressed it, "immigration is a long-time investment in family stocks rather than a short-time investment in productive labor."[290]

The emergency law of 1921 limited the annual immigration from any transatlantic country to 3 percent of the number of its nationals resident in the United States as determined by the census of 1910.[291] The new plan met with so much popular favor that in 1924 a more drastic measure reduced the quota from 3 to 2 percent and based it on the census of 1890, choosing that date as the turning point when the old immigration from the British Isles, Germany, and Scandinavia was beginning to be largely supplemented by the new immigration from southern and eastern Europe. It was further provided that after July 1, 1927, the annual quota of any nationality should be such proportionate share of 150,000 as inhabitants of that national origin bore in 1920 to the entire population of the United States. But the national-origins basis was not brought into effect until 1930 because of difficulties in making a satisfactory analysis of the very mixed blood of the American nation. Not everyone was subject to the quota restriction, as foreign-born wives and children of American citizens, travelers and students, Canadians, Mexicans, and other natives of American countries were exempted. To prevent the tragedy of broken homes and disappointed hopes, American consular officers abroad were directed to see that intending immigrants obtained certificates before starting for the United States.

One difficult question involved in the law of 1924 was the exclusion of Japanese labor. As a Great Power with a respectable army and navy, Japan did not like to be classed with powerless China. But the far Western states feared Japanese immigration quite as much as Chinese, regarding both as too alien in race ever to become merged into the general body of American citizenship. Since President Roosevelt's time a "gentleman's agreement" between the American and Japanese governments had prevented Japanese of the laborer class from coming to the United States. But in spite of the protests of Japan and the misgivings of President Coolidge, Congress insisted on definitely barring Japanese immigration by law.[292] The dread of a new racial problem on the Pacific Coast prevailed over all diplomatic and political considerations, though the general immigration law would have admitted only 146 Japanese per year.

The new quota system of 1924 favored most the British Isles and Germany. Great Britain and Ireland together could send about 62,000 immigrants a year and Germany over 50,000; no other nation exceeded 10,000. This meant, among other results, that the late enemy was favored over all but one of America's recent associates in the war. Italy's great flood of immigration sank to a mere trickle of less than 4,000 a year. All southern and eastern Europe together could scarcely muster 20,000. In but one respect did the non-Nordics win an advantage. Owing to the fact that American republics did not come within the restrictions of the quota, thousands of Mexicans crossed the border to meet a demand for cheap labor no longer supplied from Europe. Blacks also moved north to take industrial positions that formerly would have gone to Italians or Slavs, but in the latter instance this was a matter of migration within the nation, not of immigration into it.

The rise of the Ku Klux Klan was perhaps the clearest manifestation of the popular belief that Americanism was no longer—as it had been for Jefferson and Lincoln—a gospel to all the nations, but a national secret which could not be shared with those "not of the blood."[293] When the shadow of impending war hung over a yet neutral America, Colonel William J. Simmons, preacher, salesman, and amateur organizer of fraternal societies, determined to revive the Reconstruction organization. On an autumn night in 1915 he led a band of associates, including three members of the original Ku Klux Klan, to the top of Stone Mountain, Georgia, for this purpose. At first the order was hardly more than a sentimental and patriotic reminiscence, an attempt to throw Southern tradition into the scale against alien influence at a moment of national crisis.[294] For four or five years it remained small and mainly sectional; probably it had no more than 5,000 members. But in 1920, when Edward Clarke and Elizabeth Tyler took over the financial management, it was put on a business basis and began a nationwide membership campaign. The $10 membership fee was divided: $4 to the local Kleagle, one to the King Kleagle of the state, fifty cents to the Goblin of the district, and $4.50 to the headquarters of the Invisible Empire at Atlanta.[295] The boom was now of giant dimensions. By 1925 perhaps 4 or 5 million Americans had placed their names on the rolls of the organization.[296] In December 1922, Hiram Wesley Evans, a Texas dentist, became the new Imperial Wizard and Emperor in succession to Simmons.

The Ku Klux Klan was essentially a protest of American nativism against the pressure from alien races, creeds, and social ideals. Though there was no organic connection with the original Ku Klux Klan of the days of recon-struction following the Civil War—its spiritual father was rather the Know Nothing party of the mid-century—the new organization copied, or rather adapted with slight variations, the robes, the mask, the ritual, and the secret-society language of its titular predecessor. Its slogan was "native, white, Protestant" supremacy and it was directed quite as much against the Catholic, the Jew, and the alien white immigrant as against blacks.

The Klan, however, turned to other purposes as well. Indeed, the chief source of its strength seems to have been that it was all things to all men. In one state it would be chiefly a champion of the prohibition law against the bootlegger; in another a stern censor of morals, sending warning notes and even flogging expeditions to punish men and women who had violated the seventh commandment. Often it denounced internationalism and paci-fism, demanding a strong navy and abstention from the wiles of the League of Nations and the World Court, or insisting on a more militantly patriotic tone in school histories.[297] Here and there it allied with the Fundamentalists and denounced evolution as "European infidelity." For brief periods in certain states the Klan was a political machine, concerned chiefly in be-stowing local offices on its members and their friends. And, finally, to many Americans it was merely another secret society whose imposing ritual, with its Imperial Wizards, Kleagles, Klaverns, robes, signs, and burning crosses in the night afforded the same harmless pleasure that a Greek-letter frater-nity brings to the college boy. In the processions of Klansmen who marched in solemn file through the streets of the national capital and many other great cities, there was a sprinkling of alarmed patriots, fanatics, and political schemers, but the rank and file were just average Americans who would join any organization whatever that professed vaguely patriotic aims and promised a social good time.[298]

The anti-Romanist propaganda on which the Klan more and more concentrated[299] was the revamping of an old phobia which dates back to Bloody Queen Mary and the Book of Martyrs. It had been continued in America by the strongly Protestant character of early American Christianity and had found new fuel to feed on in the vast expansion of Catholicism of more recent years. New York and other Eastern centers had long since fallen into the hands of clannish groups of immigrant politicians, usually Roman Catholic Irish or Italians. Many old-stock Americans were also alarmed by the rapid growth of Roman Catholic organizations, such as the Knights of Columbus, with over 700,000 members in 1928, or puzzled by the legal complexities of dual allegiance to the pope in spiritual matters and to the nation in civil matters.[300] Finally, the refusal of many Catholics to enter the public schools and their support of a complete system of Catholic schools and colleges offended people who believed that the "little red schoolhouse," supported by public taxation, was the most potent agency in Americanizing the immigrant. Out of such miscellaneous material a nightmare was fashioned. One paper found in the honors paid to Columbus a "brazen defiance of the fact that America was not discovered by a Roman Catholic but by a Norseman who landed in Vinland nearly five hundred years before the Pope's agent raised the cross of Inquisition at San Salvador." The motion pictures, too, were revealed as a huge conspiracy. "Jews and Roman Catholics own 95 per cent of the big producing and distributing companies. . . . This accounts for so much papal propaganda being displayed before American audiences."[301] Rome also controlled, so Senator Heflin of Alabama asserted, most of the press![302]

The years 1920 to 1922—when the Klan had become a huge profit-making machine, slipping from the bewildered founder into the hands of practical men who "sold hate at ten dollars a packet"—produced the greatest violence.[303] Under the protection of the mask and the added protection of a secret membership list, sinister elements entered the Klan and used it for their own purposes. Between October 1920 and October 1921, revelations by the *New York World* showed four killings, one mutilation, one branding with acid, forty-one floggings, twenty-seven tar-and-feather parties, five kidnappings, and forty-three persons driven into exile.[304] Klansmen said, and no doubt with much truth, that the majority of these outrages were not by Klansmen at all but by private individuals assuming the robe and mask to disguise their identity; yet it was the existence of the robe and mask that made these crimes possible. In 1922 two mutilated corpses charged to the Klan were discovered in the swamps near Mer Rouge, Louisiana. Hardly less merciless were the factional fights within the Klan. In 1923, William S. Coburn, an opponent of Wizard Evans, was murdered by Philip Fox, an Evans adherent. By the new "Western Method" of recruiting, the recommendation of a single Klansman would now admit a new member.[305] Little or no discrimination was used in filling the ranks, and membership became a convenient refuge for criminals who wanted protection and politicians who wanted a ready-made "machine."

The campaign against the Jew in America was far less active than that against the Roman Catholic, although the two were yoked together in the formal denunciations of the Klan—truly a strange association in view of their centuries of opposition to each other. One of the dupes of the anti-Semitic propaganda was Henry Ford, the automobile manufacturer, by nature a kindly man and seemingly one of the last to cherish a racial or religious feud. Yet his newspaper, the *Dearborn Independent,* became simultaneously spokesman for Mr. Ford and for reactionary Europeans who traced all the social ills of modern times to "international Jewish finance."

On the basis of an alleged "protocol of the elders of Zion," repeatedly exposed by historians on both sides of the Atlantic, a Jewish conspiracy for the subjugation of the Gentile world was charged.[306]

Chauvinism found another target in "unpatriotic" schoolbooks. The same type of unhistorical mind that could believe in the enthronement of the pope or the elders of Zion on the ruins of American liberty found it equally easy to believe in an Anglo-Saxon conspiracy for bringing the United States back into the British Empire. The elements in this conspiracy were the late Cecil Rhodes and his Oxford scholarships, the Sons of St. George, the English-Speaking Union, the Sulgrave Institute, the "multiform Carnegie institutions," the universities and the writers of textbooks dealing with the American Revolution.[307] Charles Grant Miller, vocal in the Hearst papers which were always ready for a chance to "twist the lion's tail," was the chief spokesman of the protest against the Anglo-Saxon conspiracy, and he easily obtained the endorsement of veterans' organizations, patriotic-hereditary societies, and some of the more irreconcilable racial groups.[308] The politicians began to be interested. Oregon and even liberal Wisconsin enacted a law forbidding the use in public schools of textbooks defaming or misrepresenting the heroes of the War of Independence or the War of 1812. Mayor John F. Hylan in New York and Mayor William H. Thompson of Chicago gravely conducted investigations of textbooks alleged to be overfriendly to the British cause in 1776. The spirit of these inquiries is indicated in the report of the committee to investigate school histories in New York in 1922, from which we learn that "strictly speaking the textbook writer is not a historian. . . . It is for the teacher to determine what material is needed. It is for the textbook writer to supply it. . . . Truth is no defense to the charge of impropriety."[309]

It would, however, be a gross injustice to the American public of the period to say that they were interested only in the censorship of history. There was a more positive and pleasing side to the general interest in the national past. Single-volume texts on American history appeared annually, and were supplemented by studies in series such as *The Chronicles of America, The Pageant of America,* and the *Dictionary of American Biography.* Biography was especially popular. Certain authors made an effort, sometimes with more zeal than discretion, to "humanize" George Washington, so that he would be liked as a man instead of being revered as a marble statue. Abraham Lincoln, who never needed humanizing, was an even more popular subject—the records of the Library of Congress show about eight new books or booklets on Lincoln for each year of the period 1914–28.[310] A corresponding cult for General Robert E. Lee as the central figure of the Epic of the South reached comparable proportions. Hamilton, Jefferson, Marshall, and many lesser heroes, especially Western pioneers and unconventional figures in the social history of the country, were reportrayed for the new generation.

*Mayor William H. Thompson of Chicago and the
Ku Klux Klan thought that America could keep its
character only by rigorously excluding all foreign
influences.*

An initiation in the presence of the fiery cross and the flag.

Some of the most successful motion-picture films likewise dealt with American history: the Oregon pioneer in *The Covered Wagon,* the building of the Union Pacific in *The Iron Horse,* an earlier generation of Gothamites in *When Old New York Was Young.* There was a notable revival of interest in the "Paul Bunyan" legends of the north-woods lumber camps and similar American folklore. Colonial furniture became more than ever the fashion among the wealthy, and prices were paid for counterpanes and obsolete lamps that would have gone far to purchase a spinning machine or furnish a house with a complete installation of electric lights. State historical societies rescued from oblivion traditions of the pioneers. Historic homes, such as Thomas Jefferson's Monticello estate, were refurnished for public exhibition. Many excellent monuments—from the Lincoln Memorial in Washington, D.C., to the sculptures in honor of the Confederate army on Stone Mountain—commemorated heroic deeds of the past. A typical venture by America's most typical citizen was Henry Ford's restoration of the Wayside Inn of Longfellow's poem, and his "village of yesterday," which aimed to "assemble a complete series of every article used or made in America from the days of the first settlers."[311] Through the munificence of John D. Rockefeller, Jr., work was begun to restore the old town of Williamsburg in Virginia to its colonial appearance.

If this section has been mainly a chronicle of the absurdities and extravagances of American nationalism, the fact should not be taken to imply that there were no compensating gains. One should reckon on the credit side the devotion of all classes and all sections of the country to a common cause in the World War, the extension of federal aid to education and welfare work, the increased civic pride which made many an ugly mill town a garden city. H. G. Wells in the years before the war criticized the American chiefly for his lack of any "sense of the state"—he was too individualistic, selfish, preoccupied with his private business to think of the nation. No such charge was brought against the postwar American citizen, indifferent, perhaps, to party politics but immersed in a tangle of civic duties and welfare movements. Public spirit there was in abundance; only instruction was needed to harness it to useful tasks.

AMERICA AT SCHOOL

THE OUTSTANDING ACHIEVEMENT of the American school during the period from 1914 to 1928 was to make secondary education almost as universal as the previous hundred years had made primary education. In 1914 there were less than 1.5 million high school students in the United States; by 1926 nearly 4 million.[312] By 1927 approximately half of all children of high school age were enrolled in either public or private schools.[313] Most of this expansion was at the taxpayer's expense, for private secondary schools and academies reported an enrollment of a bare quarter of a million, about one sixteenth of the whole.[314] "In every country," wrote Professor Edward A. Ross, "the national education has the outline of a lofty mountain, broad at the base and tapering upward into a peak. Now the peculiarity of American education is not breadth of base, for there are countries which are more successful than the United States in getting children into the public elementary schools. It is not height of peak, for American universities stand no higher than those of certain other countries. But it is *breadth of education in the middle range*—say from the seventh year of instruction to the twelfth—for nowhere else do so large a proportion of the children receive secondary education."[315]

Higher education—the college, the university, and the professional school—showed a proportionate increase comparable to that of the high school, but much less in absolute amount, for while secondary school instruction reached half the population of its age group, higher education reached only about one in eight. The federal bureau of education, comparing American statistics with European, estimated in 1928 that both secondary and higher education were offered to almost as many students in the United States as in all the world besides, although the elementary schools of the nation included less than three tenths of the world's pupils.[316] The expenditure on education in the United States aggregated about half the world's total, and was estimated in 1925-26 at $2,744,000,000.[317] The total cost of the public primary and secondary schools doubled from 1913 to 1920 and doubled again from 1920 to 1926.[318] Only this latter increase was, however, a real gain, for the rapid rise in prices during the war kept more than even pace with the enlarged school appropriations, and, in terms of price levels, the schools were actually poorer in 1920 than they had been five years before.[319]

One of the gravest consequences of this price inflation was the heavy blow struck at the salaries of the teaching profession. These salaries, usually fixed by law, responded slowly to the upward rush of commercial prices and wages. In purchasing power the average teacher's earnings in 1920 were less than those of 1915 or even 1905.[320] As the teacher's pay slumped from the level of skilled to that of unskilled labor, teaching itself ran some danger of becoming an unskilled occupation, and might have done so, particularly in the case of new recruits to the profession, but for the gradual closing of the gap between teachers' income and costs of living. As late as 1924 it was asserted that only half the rural and village schoolteachers had even a high school education.[321] Rural teachers usually earned from $700 to $800;[322] in towns and cities pay tended to vary with the size of the municipality. The median salary in 1926-27 for elementary school teachers in small towns (under 5,000) was $1,169; for high school teachers, $1,542. In the largest cities, elementary teachers averaged $2,000 a year and high school teachers $2,500.[323] Rural education remained, on the whole, distinctly inferior to urban, and only about a third as many country children went to high school as did city children.[324] In hardly any city was a grade school teacher's pay equal to the minimum standard of living as proclaimed by trade unions and social reformers.[325]

One natural effect of the inadequate salaries was to drive family men almost entirely from the ranks of the grade schools. As late as 1915 one public school teacher in five was a man, taking elementary and secondary grades together; in 1920, when the economic condition of the profession was particularly bad, less than one in seven; in 1925, about one in six.[326] Most of these men were city high school teachers, administrative officers, or teachers of some specialty, such as manual training, in the grades. Nearly everyone seemed to deplore in theory the "feminization" of the schools, but the only practical remedy, raising salaries to what a family man in the professional classes expects, would at least have doubled the salary budget, and even the most generous taxpayers did not desire to pay such a price to restore the balance of the sexes.

Apart from the difficulty of securing well-trained teachers at a longshoreman's wages, there was a most encouraging advance in educational standards. From 1915 to 1925—really from 1920 to 1925—the average number of days in the school session increased from 159 to 169 and the average attendance from 121 days to 136.[327] The number of one-room schools decreased by more than 37,000 from 1918 to 1926.[328] This decline meant school consolidation, and was made possible by lavish public expenditure, amounting sometimes to over $20 million a year, for the transportation of children from their scattered homes to large graded schools.[329] Illiteracy decreased from 7.7 percent in 1910 to 6.1 percent in 1920 according to the decennial census, and the Southern states, where illiteracy was most common, made the most rapid progress in reducing it.[330] Though the foreign-born had the high illiteracy rate of 13 percent, so efficient were the school systems of the great cities where they congregated that the children of foreign parents had actually a lower illiteracy rate than white folk of native-born ancestry. As the oncoming generation was almost everywhere in school, such illiteracy as remained was largely among the older folk, a relic of past negligence.

There were many reasons for the enhanced cost of public education quite aside from the readjustment of salary schedules and the prolongation of the average period of schooling. Buildings and equipment were much more costly. The old-fashioned one-room "little red schoolhouse," now so rapidly disappearing, was a cheap affair that any competent carpenter could put up. The modern school, a splendid structure of brick or concrete in several stories, was often better designed than the average college building. School libraries and laboratories, auditoriums, gymnasiums, school theaters, swimming pools, playgrounds, and athletic fields made the classroom the

This building was one of four abandoned

When this consolidated school was instituted.

The Passing of the Little Red School

least costly part of the structure. The classroom itself, with its movable desks, wall blackboards, window boxes of flowers, and reproductions of famous paintings on the walls, was not in the least like the plain little rooms of a previous generation. The almost tripled high school membership, in particular, necessitated the erection of new buildings and, because they were new, they had all the advantage of the latest theory in school construction.

In order to keep the overcrowded school plant in efficient full-time use, many large cities adopted the "platoon system," sometimes called the "Gary system" after the Indiana city where it was first employed on a large scale. By this plan the pupils were divided into three groups, and while one group was using the classrooms another would be at work in the manual-training shops or on the playground or assembled in the auditorium.[331] William Wirt, who had fathered the scheme at Gary, was called by Mayor John Purroy Mitchel of New York City in 1914 to organize a similar system in the metropolis. The emphasis on manual training was disliked by some parents who wanted their children to rise in the world on the ladder of "book learning" and who listened sympathetically to the demagogic cry, "Rockefeller is stealing the schools," voiced by the Hearst press and other opponents of Mayor Mitchel.[332] Partly on the issue of opposition to the Gary system, John F. Hylan, the Tammany Hall candidate, defeated Mayor Mitchel in the election of 1917 and held office for eight years to the dismay of municipal reformers.[333] In 1927, 115 cities had 740 schools on the platoon system and in thirty-four of these cities all the schools were so organized.[334]

With the children themselves the new emphasis on vocational training was very popular. "Boys bring repair work from their own homes; they study auto mechanics by working on an old Ford car; they design, draft, and make patterns for lathes and drill presses, the actual casting being done by a Middletown foundry; they have designed and constructed a house, doing all the architectural, carpentry, wiring, metal work and painting."[335] Teachers of such special courses were usually better paid than those who taught the traditional academic branches. The necessary equipment of a kitchen in a "domestic-science" course for girls, or of a machine shop for boys, was much more expensive than the equipment necessary to teach Latin, mathematics, or even elementary natural science. Hence the diversification of the school curriculum added greatly to the school budget. The addition of doctors, nurses, and physical-education directors or paid athletic coaches to the teaching staff also added to the obligations of the school. There was constant pressure on school authorities, especially in the primary grades, to set aside certain hours for talks on fire prevention, the safe way to cross streets, the use of the toothbrush, the duty of keeping the street clean, kindness to animals, the virtues of milk and spinach as contrasted with the vices of pastry and sweetmeats, and many other worthy but too numerous causes. Traditional courses in European history and American civics tended to yield place to vaguer courses on "world history," "good citizenship," "social problems," and various adumbrations of sociology for the youthful mind.

Changes so many and so rapid naturally provoked a conservative reaction, especially when hard times and high taxes hit the agricultural Midwest, where school expenditure had been very lavish. "In Minnesota, Iowa, the Dakotas, Nebraska, Missouri, Illinois, and other neighboring states thousands of local school boards wiped out of existence their domestic science, manual training, and physical education departments. 'Back to the three R's' became the battle cry." [336] The conservatives contended that the enrichment of the curriculum merely distracted attention from the essentials, and that graduates of the elementary and even of the high school grades were less well equipped for business life than their parents had been. A partial answer to these contentions was supplied when one state superintendent gave examinations in spelling identical with those that had been in use several decades earlier and compared the new records with the old; he also arranged spelling bees between "stars" of the adult community and the children in his schools. Both tests were victories for the modern methods. [337] Some parts of the traditional curriculum stood out against the utilitarian spirit of the age with strange tenacity. Though Greek was rarely taught, Latin remained more prominent than any of the modern foreign languages in most high schools and its survival secured also as a consequence the survival of many courses of ancient history. In a typical Midwestern city 10 percent of all student hours in the high schools were devoted to Latin, as against only 2 percent to French and Spanish. [338] German had hardly recovered from the effects of the temporary boycott of wartime.

The rapid development of the junior high school and the spread of the junior college idea broke up the traditional uniformity of the American public school. In 1914 most public-school systems included an eight-year elementary school and a four-year high school resting on top of it and not forming a separate educational approach like most European secondary schools. Children kept together till about the sixth year of schooling and then began dropping out as family need or inability to meet school requirements or the temptation of an offered job might determine. By 1928 many cities had shifted to the "six-three-three" plan, six years in the elementary school, three in the junior high school, and three in the senior high school. But there were many other combinations. "Six-year elementary schools stand alongside seven-year elementary schools. We have three-year and two-year junior high schools . . . 'regular' four-year high schools and senior high schools. . . . The traditional four-year college is matched by new collegiate units of two years, three years, and six years." [339]

Federal aid to education was greatly extended, though each state maintained a completely autonomous school system, and the prolonged agita-

tion for a separate secretaryship of education in the national cabinet did
not achieve its aim. But much was done by subsidies shared between
national and local funds.[340] The Smith-Lever act of 1914 provided for extension work in agriculture by cooperation between the department of agriculture and the land-grant colleges, and the more comprehensive Smith-
Hughes act of 1917 established a federal board for vocational education and
granted appropriations to aid work already locally undertaken in commercial, industrial, and domestic-science vocational work as well as in agriculture. Equal sums were contributed by the nation and by the states for the
purpose. By 1926 federal aid in agriculture reached nearly one third of the
rural high schools in the nation and in home economics over 8 percent of
all high schools.[341] The bureau of education, the children's bureau, and the
departments of agriculture, labor, and commerce proved useful sources of
information to educators, businessmen, and farmers.

The enormous expansion of secondary schools made possible a similar,
though less striking, expansion of colleges and universities. This increase
was not at all regular. The war brought a temporary halt in 1917–18, when
many students of military age entered the army, but immediately afterward,
in 1919 and 1920, the registration of most colleges and universities suddenly increased by half. Between 1922 and 1924 there was another upward
leap, followed by a period of more normal growth. From 1910 to 1920
the enrollment in institutions of higher education (excluding preparatory
departments) rose from 266,654 to 462,445; in 1926 it reached 767,263.[342]
What would be the "saturation point"? Already collegiate attendance was
about one eighth of the entire population between the ages of eighteen
and twenty-one[343] At least four or five times as large a proportion of American youth as of British, French, or German were attending college. Of
course this was a measure of quantity, not of quality, as no one would
pretend that all of the 975 colleges, universities, and professional schools
listed by the bureau of education ranked in academic merit with Germany's
modest score of historic universities.[344]

The temporary transformation of the American college into a sort of
officers' training camp necessitated much difficult readjustment after the
armistice. The purely military courses were abandoned, or lingered only as
drill offered, usually on a voluntary basis, for the Reserve Officers' Training
Corps. The faculty had to be reassembled from industrial plants, censorship
offices, experimental munition laboratories, the Red Cross, the Y.M.C.A.,
and the advisory staff of the peace commission. The students, in the majority of cases, resumed their interrupted classes, bringing with them a horde
of newcomers: wounded veterans seizing the chance at a college education
which the nation allowed them, farmers' sons riding on the crest of the
brief wave of agricultural prosperity, young businessmen converted by the
war into a belief in the commercial value of college training, high school
boys whose college entrance had been temporarily delayed by war condi-

tions. Lecture rooms that had been more than ample in 1916 offered scant standing room in 1919. Laboratory courses had to turn away students who could not be provided with desks. Quiz sections were offered to young graduate students with any sort of passable academic record.

The greatest, or at least most pressing, problems were all financial. Building costs had doubled and new construction had been patriotically postponed during the war. Nearly every institution in the country found itself in cramped, inadequate quarters and with insufficient funds on hand for the necessary new building. At the same time, the increase in student enrollment necessitated new courses and a larger staff of instruction. The salary of the faculty had been virtually cut in half by the rise in the cost of living, and the universities shared the fear of the elementary and secondary schools of a "flight from the profession." Every endowed institution girded its loins for a campaign among its alumni for new gifts, using much the same methods of persuasive appeal found fruitful in the liberty-loan drives of the war. Every tax-supported institution besieged the legislatures for a more generous share in the public budget.[345]

The need for rapid expansion of educational facilities affected the American teacher unfavorably in several ways. It dispersed over new courses and a larger staff the funds that might have been used to raise the salary of the existing faculty, it made some presidents and trustees timid of offending wealthy givers and thus endangered academic freedom, and it imposed on the university or college an autocratic political structure. Faculty control does very well under European conditions, where an anciently endowed institution has only routine administrative tasks and can devote its main energies to teaching and research. But where an institution is rapidly developing from a college of a few hundred to a university of 10,000, where millions of dollars must be raised within three or four years, where a rigid classical curriculum is being rapidly broadened into an elective system which offers every imaginable course from aeronautics to cemetery planning, where the university is expected to serve a whole state with extension courses, correspondence work, loan libraries, and agricultural demonstration stations, there is imperative need for an executive of the "captain of industry" type. Under such conditions the president becomes a general manager responsible to a board of regents or trustees as "directors," the deans are managers and division superintendents, the department heads are foremen, the rank and file of the teaching staff employees, the students are the raw material, and the alumni the manufactured product, bearing the "college stamp" and, too frequently, standardized on a single pattern.

Against this system many voices of protest were raised. J. McKeen Cattell, Thorstein Veblen, J. E. Kirkpatrick and many others of the "professoriat" advocated the establishment of a system of faculty control.[346] The American Association of University of Professors kept vigilant watch for

An American High School

local violations of academic liberty, and its reports are the most accurate sourcebook for that subject. In the South, the chief danger was the Fundamentalist attack on evolution, which caused three states—Tennessee, Mississippi, and Arkansas—to forbid the teaching of man's animal ancestry in any tax-supported institution. In the North, the attack shifted from the religious to the political and economic front, and internationalism, pacifism, and all the shades of socialism were the chief quarries of the heresy hunters.

The indefatigable crusader Upton Sinclair attempted to show in *The Goose Step* (1923) that all the colleges and universities in the United States were bound hand and foot to capitalism. This thesis was at once exaggerated and inadequate—exaggerated because interference by wealthy donors or trustees was the exception, not the rule, and inadequate because such pressure was but one of many enemies to academic freedom. Yet in the bag of chaff were several grains of truth. The shadow of wealth hoped for was a much greater than the substance of wealth given, for the latter was usually given with few conditions and spent without much deference to the opinions of the donors. John E. Kirkpatrick was dismissed in 1926 from Olivet College in Michigan on the avowed ground that his views on faculty control were displeasing to wealthy friends of the institution, though this degree of frankness was highly exceptional.[347] One of the most thoroughly investigated cases of the dismissal of an admittedly competent professor for his economic views was that of Louis Levine (Lewis Lorwin) at the University of Montana in 1919. At the request of the chancellor, he had prepared some studies of taxation. The conclusions reached favored heavier taxation of the copper-mining interests, and the chancellor, fearing a political fight that would injure the university, forbade the publication of Dr. Levine's findings and suspended him for insubordination when he refused to acquiesce.

There was a strong tendency toward educational innovation and experiment, resulting partly from the dislocation of accustomed methods by the war and the increased student load, partly from the desire to break away somehow from the "education-factory" standardization with which the universities were threatened. Harvard University, as in all periods of American history, was one of the pioneers. Among the devices there tried were comprehensive final examinations for all seniors to test their mastery of an entire field of study, such as economics or literature; a large force of tutors to encourage independent reading outside the formal courses; and a period of term time without lectures to be entirely devoted to study and self-education. Perhaps the most discussed innovation, and one which met with considerable criticism from students, was the construction of dormitory units within the university, not unlike the individual "colleges" inside Oxford or Cambridge. Special independent work for honors, in which reading and consultation with the professor displaced in large part attendance at lectures or examinations in course, was found in many institutions, notably

Columbia and Swarthmore. Independent work for honors was in part an approach to the English distinction between "pass" students who desired only a general cultural education and "honors" students with genuine scholarly interests and in part an attempt to break down the arbitrary slicing of the living unity of education into courses, "points," and "hours," which had given American higher education so mechanical an aspect.[348]

On a small, what might almost be termed a laboratory, scale, some institutions dropped the lockstep of courses altogether. President Hamilton Holt abolished the compulsory lecture system in Rollins College, Florida, and substituted conference work for the whole school. Alexander Meiklejohn, president of Amherst College from 1912 to 1924, worked out a plan which merged the work of several departments into one comprehensive study of classical civilization; after the trustees of Amherst terminated his presidency, disliking his radical innovations as well as his financial management, President Glenn Frank of Wisconsin called him in 1926 to carry through the experiment there.[349] Since Wisconsin was too large a university to remodel its entire curriculum on the new plan, a special experimental college was created within the university and housed in a special dormitory. Bennington College for Women, Ashland College (Michigan), and several other small experimental groups for education by association and discussion rather than by formal instruction were significant new ventures at the end of the period. The summer lectures by distinguished European statesmen at Williamstown, Massachusetts, afforded a type of advanced study in the realities of international politics to professors as well as to students.

The most common complaint against the American college was neither the capitalistic conservatism of the trustees nor the pedagogical pedantry of the faculty, but the lighthearted carelessness of the students, who seemed apt, in the punning popular phrase, to interpret "college bred" as equivalent to a "four years' loaf." As a matter of fact, the attitude of the student body was, on the whole, better than that of the preceding generation. Not only did there seem to be less drunkenness, but there was certainly less hazing and general riotousness. Standards of admission and graduation were almost everywhere more exacting than ever before—the heroes of George Fitch's delightful "Siwash" stories might well have been dismissed from a postwar college in their first semester. Athletic contests were, on the whole, cleaner and less brutal and, though much more costly, were probably not more absorbing.

Yet there were undoubtedly some symptoms which might cause not unreasonable disquiet. Social life in coeducational institutions became yearly more feverishly intense. Dancing was a universal convention, and the formal balls, "proms," and "hops" became extremely expensive affairs. Campus organizations multiplied beyond all reason, some large universities containing several hundred clubs, associations, and fraternities. What with campus politics, social activities, and athletics, the average student was content to keep up with the required reading in his courses and not venture any independent reading above the level of the magazine stand. Debating fell on evil days and, except in a few colleges like Bates, was scorned and neglected. The literary societies and magazines, which two or three generations before had been the chief relaxation from the steady grind of study, now usually languished in poverty or ceased altogether. The only types of publication to prosper were the daily or weekly news sheet, valued for information as to campus doings, and the monthly comic paper. Now and then would appear an "outlaw" paper, such as *Challenge* at Columbia in 1916 or G. D. Eaton's *Tempest,* which ran a brief career at Michigan, as the expression of a small knot of discontented students, but such ventures rarely survived more than a year or two.

The unspoken questions of many parents found voice in an article by I. M. Rubinow, "The Revolt of a Middle-Aged Father," who estimated the average annual cost of sending a student to college at $1,500 a year to the parents, not to mention the social cost of supporting the institutions from philanthropy or taxation and the postponement of active business life for four critical years.[350] Even granting that students were not more idle or mischievous than formerly, their parents were paying more for their good times, and many more were paying. Could society endure the cost of burdening middle age so heavily for the pleasure of the younger generation? Various critics of the article concurred in thinking that $1,500 a year was an overestimate or, at all events, applicable only to the more expensive institutions. For the nation as a whole, $800 a year seems close to the average.[351] Moreover, much of the expense was shouldered by the students themselves. The bureau of education ascertained that nearly half of the men and almost a quarter of the women students earned all or part of their own expense while in residence.[352] Complete self-support was perhaps more rare than formerly, because only the exceptional student could carry a full schedule of classes and earn $600 to $1,200 in leisure hours or during summer vacations.

One asset of the larger American universities was the considerable attendance of foreign students, who flocked to the United States in even greater numbers than the Americans who had gone to German institutions a generation earlier. The Institute of International Education found, in 1923–24, nearly 7,000 foreign students in 400 American institutions.[353] A very large proportion were Orientals. In a single institution within a brief period there was an Egyptian, a Chinese, and a Japanese on the football squad, a Filipino captain of the swimming team, and an East Indian captain of the polo team.[354] European students often came to the United States on traveling fellowships. American postgraduate work was considered by many critics as superior to that in Europe, while the undergraduate work was often inferior.

THE MIND OF A NATION

The aesthetic side of American civilization has usually been its weakest. In the new arts created by science, such as the motion picture, the radio, and the phonograph, the United States did indeed play the leading part, but perhaps this may be attributed rather to inventive skill than to artistic sense. After 1914 there also occurred a marked improvement in artistic appreciation and a demand for greater beauty in household equipment and advertised commodities. It was no less true that American architecture was almost revolutionized in every category from the bungalow to the skyscraper, and that civic-welfare movements made the average small town a far more attractive home for its citizens. Even coins and medals were more pleasingly designed, billboards less offensive, boxes and bottles and binding twine in better taste. Women's clothing—though this reflected a worldwide tendency—was perhaps more beautiful, from an artistic point of view, than at any previous time in American history, graceful in line and rich in color.

But the great improvement in popular taste during the period by no means implied any corresponding development of popular craftsmanship. It remained true that the modern American creative instinct "finds expression in changing the washers on the faucets or tinkering with the Ford." More than ever goods were made in the factory and distributed to the consumer through the channels of trade. The suburbanite meekly accepted a good house design from his architect and less than ever ventured to interject his amateur fancies into the architect's plans. The feminine arts of needlework and cooking were less emphasized; the tendency to leave the plan of a room to a professional decorator and the garden to a landscape designer increased. There was, indeed, less artistic *self*-expression than even in the tasteless Victorian days, when the lady of the house was painting china badly, making pyrographic mottoes for the bedroom wall, and fixing up absurd museums of shells and starfish for the parlor curio cabinet —creating something with however little skill. In artistic creation, as in amusements, the American had never before been so well served and never before done so little to serve himself. Pampered by machinery and surrounded by its often excellent products, the Yankee had almost forgotten how to whittle.

When massed together in a civic regiment under expert direction, however, the American found it possible to participate in an aesthetic crusade. One example was the movement for city planning. From 1914 to 1928, 570 cities created planning commissions.[355] In 1916 only eight cities were subject to zoning regulations, but by the end of 1928 over 700 cities, towns, villages, with a total population of more than 37 million, had adopted the system.[356] The primary purpose of the zoning ordinances was to secure the pleasant residential sections of the towns from the possibility of being swamped by the spreading business sections, but there were many subsidiary regulations designed to secure the maximum light and air to all parts of the community. One aspect of these regulations had a remarkable effect on the development of commercial architecture.

The skyscraper had been familiar for a generation to the sightseer in New York, Chicago, and a few other great cities when in 1913 the Woolworth Building in Manhattan rose to a height of sixty stories, the tallest inhabited structure in the world, 792 feet above street level. For a long time that marked the limit of height, though at the end of the period (1928) there were several buildings in process of erection which would outsoar it. The significant tendency during the intervening years was not toward new records of height but toward multiplication of the skyscraper type and the development, under the pressure of building regulations, of a new style of structure. By 1925 there were over 1,600 buildings in New York City alone of more than ten stories apiece, and Henry H. Curran, a member of the municipal city-planning committee, was denouncing the congestion of mammoth buildings in lower Manhattan as a menace to public health and safety.[357] Yet the Manhattanites had the excuse of peculiar situation, an island of sturdy rock compressed between wide waterways almost to a pencil shape. Other cities on a loose earth soil with wide plains over which to expand took New York as the metropolitan model and out of imitative zeal copied the skyscraper in their own business districts. Very few followed Boston's example of placing an arbitrary limit to the height of buildings. More commonly the zoning laws followed the New York code of 1916 in limiting the height of vertical wall proportionately to the width of the streets but allowing additional towers where walls were set back from the limits of the lot.[358]

The new style, fostered and half compelled by the new building code, implied a massive tower burgeoning into a slenderer shaft, and this in turn into one still slighter, until the final pinnacle was reached. Instead of being a mere rectangular box set on end, the typical skyscraper assumed a terraced or stepping-stone effect often compared to the Babylonian ziggrat. All problems of design were more carefully studied. Much impetus to the treatment of the skyscraper as an art form was given by the *Chicago Tribune* competition of 1922, which brought out 260 designs from twenty-three countries.[359] The winning design, by John Mead Howells and Raymond Hood, was a graceful shaft flaming into pinnacles of Gothic treatment at its crest. Even more interest was aroused by the winner of the second prize, a design submitted by Eliel Saarinen of Finland, which gave an entirely new concept to the skyscraper. "It is the best design since Amiens!" exclaimed one enthusiast.[360] In it the classic traditions of horizontal lines and cornices were wholly abandoned and the vertical masses were given full scope without apology. Saarinen was called to give instruction at the

University of Michigan, and his *Chicago Tribune* design was widely imitated and adapted in the newer structures, which relied entirely on mass
and form for their effect, disdaining superficial ornamentation. The skyscraper idea was applied to other than office buildings. The Shelton Hotel
in New York (1925), the projected "cathedral of learning" of the University
of Pittsburgh, and the huge tower of the new state capitol of Lincoln,
Nebraska, illustrated some of the diverse possibilities of the form. Churches,
apartment houses, university campaniles, and war memorials also adapted
suggestions from the new skyscraper.

The celebration of the city influenced the fiction of the period, which
was critical of the small town. We are, as George Bernard Shaw once called
us, a "nation of villagers," not of peasants, like Russia, and only by exception metropolitans. The widest and most populous section of the nation
was now the Mississippi Valley—appropriately celebrated in Meredith
Nicholson's *Valley of Democracy* (1918)—and as the center of population
moved westward this section increasingly became the norm of American
life, with New England, New York, the old South, and California as its
marginal variations. The rather standardized small-town life on the flat
plains, with its universal public-school system, its ubiquitous commercial
clubs and secret societies, its competitive Protestant sects, its combination
of Yankee business ruthlessness on week days with sentimental aspiration
on Sundays and civic holidays, became the target for a score of literary
archers. Not all Americans, to be sure, were so unfortunate as to live by the
Spoon River of Edgar Lee Masters, or with Sherwood Anderson in *Wines-
burg, Ohio* (1919), or *West of the Water Tower* (1923) with Homer Croy,
or on *Main Street* (1920) with Sinclair Lewis. The novels of Booth Tarkington and the stories of William Allen White painted a better-balanced picture
of contrasted light and shade than these rather one-sided indictments. But
it is significant that most of these grim realists were themselves of the
Western small town by birth and residence, not merely literary slummers
from the metropolis. The Midwest, or one layer of it, was indulging in
the wholesome diversion of self-disparagement. Boosterism led to equal
exaggeration on the opposite side.

Sinclair Lewis's *Main Street* might be called from the historian's point
of view—though emphatically not from that of the literary critic—the most
important book written in the United States in the postwar decade. Stuart
P. Sherman, whose own viewpoint was widely different, declared that
"more thoroughly than any novel since *Uncle Tom's Cabin,* it has shaken
our complacency with regard to the average quality of our civilization."[361]
In a little over two months it sold 50,000 copies and in eight years
800,000.[362] It created, or ushered in, a whole school of fiction. "The appetite of Americans for hearing themselves abused may well rank in history as
the eighth wonder of the world," declared Henry Sydnor Harrison.[363] Some
critics, such as Simeon Strunsky, interpreted the movement as but another

form of the old Midwestern sport of muckraking, with "the Shame of Kiwanis" taking the place of the "Shame of the Cities" and the "Treason of the Senate" in prewar days. An anonymous correspondent in *Harper's* wittily represented the avidity with which the American public devoured the most hostile criticisms of itself as a case of inferiority complex.[364] There was, however, ample evidence of resentment at the acidity of the Lewisite school of social criticism.[365]

The attack on the small town was but one aspect of a general school of mordant naturalism. Sinclair Lewis showed that he was not a champion of the "city slickers" against the "hicks" by treating prosperous Zenith City in *Babbitt* (1922) even more severely than he had the village backwater of Gopher Prairie. His real enemy was commercialism and its ideals, whether in town or country, and his journalistic photography was often excellent though it never rose to portraiture. *Arrowsmith* (1925), his critique of the medical profession, contained his most nearly heroic hero and his only attractive heroine. *Elmer Gantry* (1927), which aimed to perform a similar service for the clergy, fell rather flat because Lewis hated the church and divided his pastors into fools and rogues only, whereas his physicians had included fools, rogues, and sages. *Dodsworth* (1929) put the more selfish sort of American merchant princess in her place, a very low one; Dodsworth himself is a Babbitt to whom is added a code of honor and a gleam of culture. Booth Tarkington's *The Plutocrat* (1927) is another Babbitt, one wholly without culture but with real qualities of power, decision, and energy, an interesting suggestion that even if the American businessman fails as a Greek he may succeed as a conquering Roman.

The greatest of the novels of realistic naturalism in American life was probably Theodore Dreiser's *An American Tragedy* (1925), which succeeded in making an impression by sheer brute force in spite of an almost willful clumsiness of style. It attracted the unfavorable attention of the Boston police authorities and, along with a number of other current novels, was banned from the bookstalls under the amazing legal principle that if a jury finds a single passage in a book objectionable, without reference to the tenor of the book as a whole, it is subject to prosecution.[366] Floyd Dell's *Moon-Calf* (1920), Zona Gale's *Miss Lulu Bett* (1920), John Dos Passos's pacifist novel *Three Soldiers* (1921), Sherwood Anderson's *Poor White* (1920), Edith Summers Kelly's *Weeds* (1924), and G. D. Eaton's *Backfurrow* (1925) are other typical reflections of discontent with the America that emerged from the war.

Another phase of cynicism and disillusionment was the jest at ancient ideals. John Erskine began it with his *Private Life of Helen of Troy* (1925) and *Galahad* (1926), followed later by restatements in the modernist vein of *Adam and Eve* (1927) and *Penelope's Man* (1928). His books had both popular and literary success and of course had imitators, such as Elmer Davis's *Giant Killer* (1928) "debunking" the reputation of King David, with the usual implication that, as a Frenchman put it, "Plutarch lied"—in other words, all the world's heroes were merely adventurers and the world's statesmen merely dead politicians. Biography, though very popular, was most relished when slightly acidulous, stressing the human character of the great man and especially his human weaknesses.

The fact that Thornton Wilder's *The Bridge of San Luis Rey,* a story of the mellow richness of an old Latin-American scene, became a best seller in 1928 was hailed as a revulsion of taste alike from formlessness, from undistinguished journalistic style, and from cynical naturalism, but in truth at no period had the "debunkers" occupied the whole literary stage. Joseph Hergesheimer and Willa Cather ranked equal with them in popular approval and perhaps rather more highly in artistic merit. Willa Cather's *One of Ours* (1922) and *Death Comes for the Archbishop* (1927) entitled her to be considered queen of the novel, but her court had many accomplished maids or matrons of honor, such as Edith Wharton, Corra Harris, Edna Ferber, Dorothy Canfield, and Mary Roberts Rinehart. James Branch Cabell stood a little apart in this period—romantic and even fantastic in theme, but allied to the cynics by a certain disdainful attitude toward moral idealism. His preoccupation with sex in *Jurgen* (1919) won for him the hostility of self-appointed book censors and along with it the exaggerated praise of insurgents against all censorship.

The dominant figure in American criticism was unquestionably Henry Louis Mencken, critic for the *Baltimore Sun* and, after 1924, editor of the *American Mercury.* Although sometimes grouped with the "radical" critics of American institutions, his point of view was essentially that of the disdainful aristocrat, as his ultrareactionary *Notes on Democracy* (1926) should have made plain to his admirers as well as his enemies. The confusion probably arose from the fact that he joined the radical onslaught on prohibition, Puritanism, and the Anglo-Saxon tradition in literature. Because he disliked nearly everything in the United States, he became more valuable as a balance wheel to keep national pride in bounds, to remind America that its greatness is but mortal and sometimes absurd into the bargain. In the *Mercury,* which advertised itself as a "magazine with no dreams of reform; it is concerned only with setting up America as a puppet-show for the entertainment of its civilized inhabitants," he collected all he could find of the crack-brained deeds and words that crept into the press and called it "Americana." Unsophisticated college boys delighted to sip his sophistication, and a whole generation of them tried to imitate his style. For the rest, he was a good philologist,[367] a clever critic, and a "bonny fechter."

But however great might be Mencken's services to American criticism, two major defects threatened to outweigh all his virtues. One was that he scorned so much and admired so little that he lacked the sympathy necessary to an understanding of other men and their institutions and opinions. Timon of Athens is not the best man to give a comprehending account of the great Athenian civilization! His other fault was that, being confined by temperament to the single field of satire, he used his weapons clumsily. Jonathan Swift was equally scornful of the world, but his subtle Irish rapier could get under the shield and between the ribs of the man he wished to wound, whereas the best Mencken could do was to rap him over the skull with bludgeoning epithets of "boob" and "moron" and "yokel."

To the historian of civilization what the American reads is more important than what he writes, for in the nature of things there must be several thousand who listen to each prophet who speaks. A study of the "mind of a nation" is very different from the study of a few exceptional minds in a nation, in much the same way that a study of the national standard of living differs from an account of a millionaire's colony in Newport or Palm Beach. The United States as a whole may safely be set down as a reading nation but not a bookish one. It led the world in the circulation of periodicals and newspapers but lagged behind all the countries of northern Europe in the number of books published in ratio to population and apparently (though here statistics are often incomplete) in the proportionate number of copies sold. Bookstores were less in evidence in American cities than in almost any European capital, though this deficiency was partly made good by the number of public libraries and by the sale of books through mail-order houses, department stores, newsstands, and other channels. The chief novelty in book distribution was the club which offered its subscribers at stated intervals, usually of one month, a new book selected by a committee of expert critics. By the end of this period the Book-of-the-Month Club had about 100,000 subscribers.[368] The activity of the Literary Guild and the Book-of-the-Month Club held first place in the news of publishing during 1927 and 1928, "for the choice of a book by either board puts it in the best seller class immediately."[369]

The number and type of books published remained remarkably constant during the changeful years of 1914–28. During the war the high cost of printing and paper, and perhaps the popular preoccupation with newspapers, cut the number of new titles in nearly every class of work except those, such as history and books on military affairs, which dealt directly with the events of the day. But after the war, normal production and normal distribution were restored. In proportion to the growing population, slightly fewer books of nearly all kinds were being printed in the 1920s than during the three or four years just before the war.[370] This did not imply that the public was doing less reading. On the contrary, the total output of books and pamphlets increased from 175 million copies in 1914 to almost 424 million in 1925,[371] an increase from about two to nearly four per capita.[372] As nearly half these works were pamphlets, however, it would be safe to say that, even by the latter date, book circulation was barely two books a year to each American, or ten a year for a typical family of five. The tendency was evidently toward fewer books but a greater circulation for the average book.

An indication of national taste is the "best-seller" list of individual titles.

In 1913, which is a better index year than 1914 as it eliminates the ephemeral "war books," every one of the best fiction sellers was a romantic and more or less sentimental story. Winston Churchill's *The Inside of the Cup,* a plea for religious and moral reform sugarcoated with narrative, headed the list, followed by Henry Sydnor Harrison's *V. V.'s Eyes,* Gene Stratton-Porter's *Laddie,* Gilbert Parker's *The Judgment House,* John Fox's *Heart of the Hills,* Jeffery Farnol's *The Amateur Gentleman,* Hall Caine's *The Woman Thou Gavest Me,* and Eleanor H. Porter's *Pollyanna,* "the glad book," whose name became a byword for an omnivorous optimism.[373] In the list of nonfiction best-sellers, Gerald Stanley Lee's idealistic essays on *Crowds* stood first, followed by Price Collier's *Germany and the Germans.* President Wilson's *New Freedom,* Lord Bryce's *South America,* Arnold Bennett's courteous *Your United States,* and Mary Antin's *The Promised Land,* an immigrant's view of America, stood high on the list, along with cookbooks and works on auction bridge. Both lists, fiction and nonfiction, reflect a cheerful, aspiring, unquestioningly patriotic, and orthodox age.

The list of 1928 is harder to interpret. The current here flows in no one direction but seems troubled and turbid. The taste in fiction varies between realistic studies, grave and often sad, and the detective novel. Thornton Wilder's *The Bridge of San Luis Rey* leads with the two English novels, Hugh Walpole's *Wintersmoon* and John Galsworthy's *Swan Song,* following. Just when we are about to conclude that the American people were a nation of highbrows, we meet next in line S. S. Van Dine's *The Greene Murder Case,* and are reminded of John C. Powys's statement that "during no age known to the history of our race has there been so immense a flood of crime literature as at the present day."[374] The list resumes with Vina Delmar's *Bad Girl,* Booth Tarkington's *Claire Ambler,* Warwick Deeping's *Old Pybus,* and Anne Parrish's *All Kneeling.* The best-seller nonfiction list is strong on biography, mostly by Europeans, beginning with André Maurois's *Disraeli* and containing two biographies by the German Emil Ludwig, *Napoleon* and *Goethe,* besides the half-biographic *Trader Horn;* Lindbergh's account of his transatlantic flight, *"We,"* and a narrative of *Count Luckner, the Sea-Devil.* Katherine Mayo's *Mother India,* a mordant attack on Hindu civilization, stands second, and Eugene O'Neill's *Strange Interlude* holds sixth place, a rare tribute to the drama.[375] Two generalizations, at least, seem safe: a decline of popular affection for polite romance and comfortable sentiment in fiction, and a growing predilection for biography.

The presence among the best-sellers of such books as Will Durant's *Story of Philosophy,* Lewis Browne's *This Believing World,* and Bruce Barton's *The Man Nobody Knows* and *The Book Nobody Knows,* interpretations of religious history in the terms of modern American commercial life, shows that popular interest in the problems of religion and the church was still active. The word "still" is used advisedly since the impression widely prevailed that the increasing pressure of secular interests was crowding religion out of American life. How far this impression was justified is impossible to say: The straws point simultaneously in too many directions. There was a large increase in church membership, considerably higher for most denominations than what might have been expected from the increase in population. On the other hand, there was some decrease in church building, especially in the rural districts, and a widely prevalent complaint that the use of the automobile on sunny Sunday mornings was reducing average attendance. Pulpit oratory, even now that the radio had extended its range, seems to have had less influence than in the days of Phillips Brooks and Henry Ward Beecher, and it is very doubtful if the partnership of "Billy" Sunday and H. A. Rodeheaver stirred the nation like the evangelistic campaigns of Moody and Sankey. Yet church organizations and associations were never so active in projects of social welfare and civic reform and many complaints were heard, especially in connection with the prohibition question, that the United States was politically ruled by the churches.[376]

An increased tendency toward liberalism in the theological seminaries was balanced by the establishment of various "Bible Institutes" of impeccable orthodoxy. The number of books on philosophy, religion, the church, and the Bible remained fairly constant and reached a wider circle of readers, but often took an unconventional turn. "Perhaps the most striking feature of the stream of new religious books," said Dr. Winfred E. Garrison in 1927, "is the number of them that deal directly with the personality and teaching of Jesus. It is literally true that there is never a week without a new one, and a dozen a month would be a fair average." Though many of these books were written by persons who had more zeal than historical or theological competence, and appealed chiefly to readers who were not ecclesiastically minded, "even so," he added, "it will be a sorry day when the experts get a corner on religion."[377]

According to the estimates of the department of commerce, based on denominational statements, the number of church members increased in the decade 1916 to 1926 from 41,926,854 to 54,624,976.[378] "Every prominent Protestant denomination stands today at the highest point of its history in respect to adherents," declared an observer in 1928. At the same time, in the decade following the armistice, "the Congregationalists 'dropped' 1,046 organizations, the Presbyterians 'dismissed' 61 and 'dissolved' 1,143, a total death list for the two denominations . . . of 2,250 churches; while they had a net gain of 470,348 members. In the country districts the abandoned church edifice is becoming a common sight."[379] This does not mean that church rolls were increasingly padded; the real explanation seems to lie partly in the community-church movement, combining several weak congregations into one strong one, especially in the villages and small towns, partly in the influence of the motor car in extending the size of the parish, and partly in the movement of population toward the great cities where the average congregation was larger than would be possible in a rural hamlet.

New schisms in existing denominations were threatened as a result of the Fundamentalist movement. The Fundamentalists were the ecclesiastical party who proclaimed certain traditional doctrines as fundamentals of the Christian faith—particularly the virgin birth, bodily resurrection and substitutionary atonement of Jesus Christ, the inerrancy of the Bible, and the literal truth of its miracles. They complained, not without reason, that the so-called modernists and liberals had sapped the literal meaning from the creeds by interpreting them in a purely symbolic sense never intended by the founders of the churches. The conflict was not primarily a theological one, like the old controversies between Calvinist and Arminian, Trinitarian and Unitarian. The issue lay rather in the field of history than that of philosophy: whether the scriptural records of the Old and New Testaments were to be taken as an unquestionable record of fact or as a body of ancient literature which had in it an element of legend.

The doctrine of biological evolution entered the conflict because the account of man's creation according to Darwin appeared to differ in several particulars from the account according to Genesis. Though this question had been fought out at a lofty intellectual level in the late nineteenth century, the battle was reopened and waged with astounding bitterness now that the findings of science had come within the purview of the masses of the people. In the Presbyterian, Baptist, and Methodist churches nearly every annual conference brought forth some trial of strength between modernist and Fundamentalist. Of course, there was also a large center party, which Professor Kirsopp Lake of Harvard christened "institutionalist," who cared more for the work of the church than for the prevalence of any doctrine, and this party remained strong enough to prevent the splitting of the old denominations into new sects.

What was the actual status of religious faith among the American people? Here no census can serve us, as in the case of denominational affiliation, and one must trust to random samplings. A poll of 250,000 newspaper readers and 36,000 college undergraduates in 1927 showed, first, a huge orthodox majority and, second, more orthodoxy among the college students than among the older generation.[380] Thus, virtually all the students and 91 percent of the newspaper readers admitted a belief in God; the divinity of Christ was affirmed by 89 percent of the students and 85 percent of the others. Similar plebiscites taken at about the same period in England by newspapers and magazines revealed a much larger proportion of skeptics. In spite of the fantastic propaganda of the American Association for the Advancement of Atheism, chartered in New York in 1925, and the little groups of self-styled "Damned Souls" in a few colleges,[381] most observers agree that rarely in American history was there so little open hostility to the Christian faith. No one, not even Clarence Darrow, was quite big enough to inherit the mantle of Tom Paine or Bob Ingersoll as a popular American champion of anticlericalism. "No man today," say the historians of Middletown, "has his relatives announce over his open grave, as did more than one member of the Ethical Society [in the 1890s], that the deceased believed death to be the end."[382] Yet it is arguable that, in spite of Fundamentalism, Christian doctrines were more taken for granted and less a subject of earnest thought than in the earlier days of the republic, and if there was less theological controversy, it was because there was less theological interest, many of the most active of the clergy and laity being "institutionalists" who viewed the church primarily as an engine of moral and social reform.

A survey of American folkways shows glaring contrasts in religious influence on daily life. The old sabbatarian "blue laws," if somewhat diluted, still remained on the statute books of many states, but were violated almost as a matter of course by every motorist who bought gasoline and every corner drugstore that sold candy and magazines. Standards of personal conduct revealed interesting variations. In one Midwestern city, probably fairly typical of others, about 10 percent of the families investigated had regular family prayers and Bible readings, and the majority of the children were permitted to attend the moving pictures on Sunday. "One family lets the children swim on Sunday . . . but not play golf; . . . others make popcorn on Sunday but not candy; others object to Sunday evening bridge but allow Mah Jong."[383] Some of the churches lost dignity in frantic efforts to show that they were abreast of the times and thoroughly understood the younger generation. One high school girl boasted, "Our Sunday School class is *some class.* Our teacher . . . gives us some slick parties out at her place. Two of the girls in our class got kicked out of their clubs a year ago for smoking—*that's* the kind of class we have!"[384] There is something a little displeasing in the well-meant eagerness of the city clergy and the Y.M.C.A. workers to prove that they were no better than other men and much more interested in baseball, Rotary, and city "booster" campaigns than in religious philosophy.

One cannot assert that America achieved any national philosophy. Contemporary with the full blaze of modern science, "witches" were found in "Pennsylvania Dutch" communities, while Wilbur Glenn Voliva used the radio to broadcast from Zion City, Illinois, all around the terrestrial globe the news that it was flat. More students crowded the universities than ever before in human history, but, as we have seen, some of them were forbidden by law to learn modern biology. Harry Emerson Fosdick, most liberal of the modernists, and John Roach Straton, most unbending of the Fundamentalists, equally found a home within the hospitable confines of the Baptist church. In alternate Sunday newspapers, and apparently with equal belief, the American read eugenic articles on the omnipotence of heredity and "behaviorist" articles on the omnipotence of early environment.

Previous sections have dealt with the more secular beliefs of the American of this period. Usually he was a patriot, with a faith in the destiny of America almost religious in strength and character. The war had taught him that the nation held a claim on his life and property and labor superior to that of any private interest. What else to learn from the war he had not yet made up his mind. World peace was a good thing to affirm, but continuous association with European diplomacy seemed too high a price to pay and perhaps not the best means of getting it. Rather more than formerly, he was on guard against the undue immigration of foreigners and of foreign ideas. This irritated defensiveness, embodied equally in the Senate and the Ku Klux Klan, made him seem narrowly chauvinistic. Yet he read copiously criticisms of his national folkways, and had acquired a wholly new taste for the more depressing sort of realistic fiction. With all his excess of public spirit he remained skeptical of politics and too cynical about politicians to be greatly moved even by proved dishonesty. Not since the Bull Moose days of 1912 had he taken part in a real political crusade, and the "predatory interests" of his neighbors seemed more harmless now that his own economic position was improved.

The average American was more prosperous than ever before and his conservatism and general optimism reflected this prosperity. The actual buying power of his income was, allowing for the unequal progress of different classes, about a third greater than it had been in 1914. It is worth repeating, however, that nearly the whole of this gain belonged to the last six or seven years of the period. The years of uneasy neutrality, 1914 to 1916 inclusive, piled up great fortunes for holders of "war-baby" stocks, and somewhat helped the farmer move his crops, but the rising prices depressed the real income of the bondholder, the clerk, the teacher, and the policeman. The same was true in even higher degree of the battle years, 1917 and 1918, and the big postwar boom of 1919 and 1920. The swift depression that followed stabilized prices, but it inflicted on the farmers an injury from which, in this period, they never wholly recovered. After about 1922 came real improvement in the general welfare, the product not of the war but of such factors as commercial combination, industrial standardization, improved methods of production, and a more careful study of the consumer market. The stock panic of 1929 brought a pause but, seemingly, not a permanent check to this development. Hours of labor decreased in spite of the weakness of trade unionism; prices slowly fell while wages remained stable and salaries rose, thus consolidating the earlier gains of the manual laborers and pulling out of the slough of despond the previously depressed middle classes. The farmer remained the most aggrieved citizen; so, increasingly, he moved to town and let the tractor make up for his going.

Increased prosperity brought increased luxury. The American became more self-indulgent, less inclined than in the past to think pleasure a sin.

He motored on Sunday without shame or stint, played golf in Florida in winter, took holidays from his office to see the ball game, stayed up half the night to dance, bought goods on credit, gave generously to any cause that asked his help, sent his children to college as a mere matter of course, and perhaps spent his salary as soon as he got it. He was not a materialist or moneygrubber. "America is not dollar-mad," said one observer. "It is activity mad. . . . If the possession of money were the real end, America would be parsimonious."[385] The worship of activity and efficiency may be, of course, as damaging to the soul as the worship of money. If the better sort of American be depicted as Nietzsche's vehement *Ja-sager,* the affirmer of Life, the very phrase has an ironical echo in the "Yes-man," the obsequious lieutenant of the captain of industry.

The American's home had greatly changed. He had admitted his wife to full legal equality at the polls and accorded her better than equality in the

"So This Is Progress"

courts of justice and in social affairs. He had almost abandoned parental control over his sons and daughters. His automobile enticed him more to travel, and the business of cooking and cleaning was passing from household to restaurant and laundry. Yet his house, though small in scale, was more costly and usually far more beautiful than the house where his father had dwelt. The city, too, was more attractive and improved in practically every respect except, sometimes, its government. He had, of course, a phonograph, a radio, an automobile, and went about once a week to the moving-picture palace, and therefore had a high opinion of applied science, which afforded so many mechanical pleasures.

Morally it would be hard to say whether the American was better or worse for the war and the national expansion of the postwar decade. He had abolished the saloon, a feat which few nations dared dream of attempting, but he had not altogether permitted public law to change his private habits. Professional vice had certainly decreased; amateur vice had possibly become more tolerated; divorce was clearly more favored. Business methods were, on the whole, more honest and decent. Theft remained common, and took the dangerous form of open brigandage in the largest cities, before which police and courts seemed almost powerless. Yet the American had been able almost wholly to abandon his national bad habit of lynching, and the general lawlessness stirred him to much protest and great, if often futile, legislative activity.

Often in history the acid test of wealth has been applied to a favored class; alone in all nations and all ages the United States of the 1920s was beginning to apply that test to a whole people. Applied science and business organization had made the test possible. Only a strong national morale could make it successful. Other nations, already greatly influenced by American methods, stood ready to shape their future according to the result.

The Historiographical

Legacy of the

History of American Life

DESPITE THE INEVITABLE DIFFERENCES in outlook and temperament of the twelve authors themselves, and the quarter century that separated the publication of the first and last volumes, the *History of American Life* series provided a consistent depiction of America's past. The volumes in the series can be said to constitute the major coherent exposition of what historian John Higham has termed the "progressive synthesis" that has dominated American historiography since the 1920s (*History: Professional Scholarship in America* [1965]).

The progressive historians are to be distinguished from the Progressive party, which was formed in 1912 when Teddy Roosevelt failed to win the Republican nomination. Many of the historians of the *History of American Life* volumes were themselves active in progressive politics, but what made them progressive historians was their belief that the past should be enlisted in contemporary political causes, that human institutions generally move from ignorance to enlightenment, and that human betterment requires the concerted action of the people—of democracy—against specialized and private interests.

The following essay outlines how subsequent historians have developed the period covered by each volume. The general tendency among historians has been toward ever-smaller fields of specialization; many topics that warranted a paragraph or two in the *History of American Life* have themselves become the subjects of long monographs. Merely to list all of these works would require hundreds of pages; I have instead discussed the more general trends in the relevant historiography, making note of influential or illustrative texts.

VOLUME I:
Herbert Priestley, *The Coming of the White Man, 1492-1848* (1929)

THE COMING OF THE WHITE MAN is of enduring interest because of its distinctive position within the debate among scholars over the meaning and legacy of Spanish colonization of North America. This nation's earliest historians, having witnessed and even contributed to the effort that ended the rule of George III in America, had little affection for the Spanish monarchy. Spain was a Catholic country, its rule was more despotic than England's, and, worse still, it remained in possession of lands Americans coveted. These early historians chronicled, in suitably appalling detail, the "Black Legend" of Spanish tyranny and genocide. After the Mexican Revolution had removed Spain as a threat to U.S. territorial ambitions, however, this dark portrait of Spanish conquest began to fade.

During the last third of the nineteenth century, moreover, the stately haciendas and refined customs of the Spanish Far West provided an appealing contrast to the gritty cities and sordid vices of the rapidly industrializing North and Midwest. Hubert H. Bancroft, in his monumental *History of the Pacific States* (1874-90), underscored the contrast by depicting Spanish California as a rosy Eden: "Never before or since was there a spot in America where life was a long happy holiday, where there was less labor, less care or less trouble." Succeeding Bancroft as the scholarly supporter of Spanish colonization was Herbert E. Bolton of the University of California, who wrote at length on "Spain's frontiering genius." Bolton trained over 100 scholars for the Ph.D., and his disciples challenged the historical profession's preoccupation with Puritanism—and New England. Of Bolton's students, the most influential in perpetuating his positive view of Spanish settlement was John Francis Bannon, who went so far as to describe the Jesuits' first century in the New World as "a glorious one." Of the destruction of the native cultures, Bannon was unconcerned. In a characteristic passage, he dismissed the Sonora Indians as having "practically no religion" (*The Mission Frontier in Sonora* [1955]).

Priestley, librarian of the Bancroft and professor of Mexican history at the University of California, worked in an environment where the words of Bancroft and Bolton still echoed, and *The Coming of the White Man* shows clear marks of their influence, particularly when he described the tremendous obstacles confronting Spanish colonization: the vast, inhospitable spaces of the Southwest; the shortage of Spanish settlers and native labor; and the conflicting aims of Church and Crown. Spain sought to make "the wilderness blossom with a European culture"—yet by means of a "simple practicality," the Spaniards had managed to transplant important aspects of their culture to the New World—proof, Bannon's students insisted, of the soundness of Spanish colonization. Many general readers regarded Priestley's words as a novel defense of Spanish colonization. The *New York Times Book Review* of January 5, 1930, for example, concluded that Priestley had proved that the Spanish "colonized so successfully that their civilization still persists."

But careful readers, particularly those familiar with the historiography of the Spanish borderlands, discerned that Priestley's interpretation veered sharply from Boltonian orthodoxy. The reviewer for *The Hispanic American Historical Review* correctly observed that Priestley's book "differed widely" from Bolton's *The Spanish Borderlands* (1921), for Priestley had contended that the Spanish "solution" to the labor shortage—forcing the Indians to work on pain of death—ultimately undermined the authority of the greatly outnumbered Spanish colonists. Spanish colonization was doomed to fail, and thus its chapter in American history was a "long drawn-out tragedy." Priestley concluded that Spanish colonization was only "moderately successful."

Priestley was attempting to reshape the Boltonian argument so that it might somehow fit within the emerging synthesis of progressive historians, among them the *History of American Life*'s principal editor, Arthur Schlesinger, Sr., an urbane—and pro-urban—historian who had little use for Spanish culture as an antidote to modernity. Thus Priestley steered a middle course between the progressives, who regarded Spanish colonial institutions as hopelessly encrusted with superstitution and error, and the Boltonians, who lauded Spanish influence as a means of blunting the hard-edged modernity of American urban-industrial life.

On the issue of the Indians especially, Priestley broke away from Bolton, who minimized Spain's genocidal policies, or justified them as necessary for bringing the fruits of civilization to the "realm of heathendom." Priestley thought it "conclusive" that the Spaniards "ruthlessly and promiscuously" deprived the Indians of their lives and their lands, and that the moral benefits of Spanish civilization were not as great as the Boltonians imagined, for Indian religions and ethical precepts were "comparable" to Christianity. Spanish colonization was thus no better than that of the English, French, or Dutch; none could claim the moral high ground with respect to the other. "The imputation of vice or virtue to the attitude of any white nation surely overlooks the self-interest under which each worked," Priestley wrote. All of the colonial empires exploited those they ruled and claimed to serve, and all, lacking the support of the common people, were thus doomed. Here was history as the progressives understood it.

Priestley's argument did not win over the army of Boltonians in the colleges and universities, but his criticisms of Spanish colonization did begin to take hold. In 1948, Sherburne F. Cook's *The Population of Central Mexico in the Sixteenth Century,* based on tribute and tithe records, contended that the native population of Mexico declined from 11 million to 1.5 million during the sixteenth century, sobering proof that Spanish colonization had been purchased at a terrible human price. But Boltonian scholars challenged these figures, and increasingly shored up the defense of Spanish colonization by underscoring the attractions of its culture. Some approvingly cited Frank Tannenbaum's *Slave and Citizen: The Negro in the Americas* (1947), which argued that Spanish slavery was far milder than the English variant, one reason Latin America was relatively free of the racial strife that increasingly plagued race relations in the United States. All in all, the Boltonian synthesis remained in place well into the 1960s.

Historical orthodoxies of all types were rocked by the social upheavals of that turbulent decade, and the Boltonian synthesis all but collapsed. A new generation of scholars, activated by the civil rights movement and opposition to the Vietnam War, assaulted the Boltonian position from opposite directions. Some rediscovered the "black legend" of unredeemed Spanish villainy but retold the story in contemporary terms: the military-religious complex of imperial Spain had crushed the black slaves and native Indians and destroyed their cultures. Others, such as Charles Gibson (*The Aztecs under Spanish Rule* [1964]) took the opposite view: Historians had *overstated* Spain's influence, and in so doing had missed the more consequential story of the world and culture fashioned by the native peoples themselves. These scholars gravitated to anthropology and ethnography, where they acquired analytical tools for reconstructing native life. See, for example, Raymon A. Gutierrez, *When Jesus Came, the Corn Mothers Went Away: Marriage, Sexuality, and Power in New Mexico, 1500-1846* (1991).

Priestley was one of the first to recognize that Spain's most important contribution to the New World was its flora and fauna—"the plants and seeds and livestock" of Western Europe. This view has been superseded by Alfred W. Crosby, Jr., *Ecological Imperialism: The Biological Expansion of Europe, 900-1900* (1986), which showed the catastrophic impact of European microbes upon life forms that lacked resistance to them. On the environmental effects of colonization, see Henry F. Dobyns, *From Fire to Flood: Historic Human Destruction of Sonoran Desert Riverine Oases* (1981).

Priestley took the middle ground between the attackers of Spanish colonization and its defenders; scholars in recent years have similarly positioned themselves between extremes. But the terrain they now occupy is oddly indistinct. David J. Weber, the foremost of the new scholars and author of *The Spanish Frontier in North America* (1992), concluded: "There are many viewpoints, some of them contradictory and all of them valid. . . .

The past itself . . . has ceased to exist. What remains of importance is only our understanding of it.''

Priestley's account of Dutch and French settlement is of little historiographical importance. Among the important new works on the subject are Karen L. Anderson, *Chain Her by One Foot: The Subjugation of Women in Seventeenth-Century New France* (1991), which shows how French colonization transformed egalitarian gender relations into a system of gender dominance and subjugation. See also Cornelius J. Jaenen, *Friend and Foe: Aspects of French-Amerindian Cultural Contact in the Sixteenth and Seventeenth Centuries* (1976), which examines the social and cultural interpenetrations among settlers and Indians.

VOLUME II:
Thomas Wertenbaker, *The First Americans,* 1607–90 (1927)

NOWADAYS, a book entitled *The First Americans* would be about Indians, and probably they would be identified as Native Americans. Yet Indians appear in Thomas Wertenbaker's volume in only a few instances, and then not as subjects in their own right but as influences on English settlers: ''savage foes'' to be feared or converted, or savvy woodsmen from whom one could learn useful skills. Wertenbaker's neglect of Indian life may strike contemporary readers as particularly unjust because the Indians, though decimated by old-world microbes such as smallpox and measles, nevertheless outnumbered the English along the Atlantic seaboard throughout the seventeenth century.

Wertenbaker was not unmindful of these facts, nor unsympathetic to the plight of the Indians. He seethed at the ''convivial physician'' of Jamestown who systematically poisoned the Indians, and at the hypocrisy of Puritan leaders such as Cotton Mather, who justified the theft of Indian land on the grounds that ''probably the Devil decoyed these miserable savages hither, in hope that the gospel of the Lord Jesus Christ would never come to destroy or disturb his absolute empire over them.'' Nor was Wertenbaker under a dreamy spell about the nobility of the Indians, whom he identified as ''savages.'' But he described the savagery of the colonists as even worse for being cloaked in piety. Wertenbaker passed quickly over the Indians not because he doubted their humanity or regarded their lives as inconsequential but because the march of progress had left them behind, or, rather, run them over.

In this respect, Wertenbaker, like many thoughtful historians of his day, viewed history as a path that rose above superstition, plague, and tyranny, climbing steadily toward enlightened rationalism, sustained economic growth, and democratic political institutions. The Indians, plainly, had been consigned to some nether region; even as he wrote, ethnographic linguists were frantically recording Indian languages before the Indians disappeared entirely. Wertenbaker for the most part neglected the sad story of the Indians because it was extraneous to his main purpose: to trace the origins of a dynamic modern society.

In his belief that history naturally inclined toward human betterment, Wertenbaker was emphatically a progressive historian. Indeed, some modern scholars regard *The First Americans* as "one of the greatest works on American colonial history" precisely because it so neatly articulated the progressive ethos (See for example, Clifford Trafzer, *Journal of the West*, Vol. II, No. 1 [January 1972]). Wertenbaker's progressivism rang out with special clarity in the final chapter, "The Progress of a Century," in which he asserted that the colonists' most important achievement was their advancement of "the cause of liberty." For whether they settled in Massachusetts or Virginia, most colonists soon became a "new order of men": entrepreneurial, self-reliant, "haters of tyrannical restraint." They were, in short, apostles of liberalism who pushed America along the path of progress, climbing over Puritan despots, devil-fearing peasants, and lackeys of old-world traditions. "The first Americans" laid the broad foundations upon which future generations would erect "the mighty structure" of the United States. To progressives like Wertenbaker, America had surpassed other nations because it had set off along the road of liberalism almost from the start.

But what made these first Americans so special? Following the tradition of Frederick Jackson Turner, whose 1893 oration on "The Frontier in American History" attributed the nation's vibrant democracy to the availability of cheap land, Wertenbaker emphasized the distinctive geography of the Atlantic seaboard and the particular economic system that evolved from frontier conditions. Free labor prevailed nearly everywhere: farmers readily acquired their own land; artisans, the implements of their livelihood; and young merchants, the necessities to set themselves up in business. In the North, large stretches of cheap land and limitless business opportunities made it impossible to keep a man long in servitude. In the South, almost anyone could grow tobacco for profit. Wertenbaker argued that the typical Southerner was not a large plantation owner who longed for the comforts and recreations of the English gentry; rather, he was a small landholder, possessing neither slaves nor servants, who cultivated tobacco with an entrepreneurial spirit not unlike his Yankee cousins to the North.

Wertenbaker was a materialist. He insisted that settlers were motivated, above all, by a craving to satisfy their bodies instead of their souls. In this sense, Wertenbaker shared the pragmatism that flowered among intellectuals of his day, an attraction to the hard realities of the world rather than its abstract metaphysics. His was the philosophy of John Dewey, who believed that the measure of an idea was found in its uses, and of George Santayana, who insisted that Americans were a practical people who had escaped from the ideological and religious preoccupations that had long ravaged Europe. Among historians, this view was expressed by James Harvey Robinson, who asserted on the primacy of economic factors in human affairs. The "economic interpretation of history," Robinson wrote in *The New History* (1912), "serves to explain far more of the phenomena of the past than any other single explanation ever offered."

Wertenbaker's materialism was particularly evident in his treatment of New England. He insisted that most of its settlers did not share the Puritan leaders' religious ardor; the Puritan oligarchs became increasingly repressive precisely because "the battle was going against them." They crippled medicine by attributing disease to Satan, and they inhibited intellectual life by burning books with which they disagreed. The mental life of New England "improved," Wertenbaker wrote, in proportion to its abandonment of Puritan beliefs and practices.

Wertenbaker's indictment of Puritanism soon came under attack. In 1928, Samuel Eliot Morison, in a sharply critical review of *The First Americans,* outlined the virtues of Puritan theology, calling it a "burgeoning of genuine intellectual life." This idea became the central thesis of Perry Miller's *Orthodoxy in Massachusetts* (1933) and subsequent volumes, which together constituted a landmark achievement in the history of ideas. Miller's elegant exegesis of Puritan sermons and writings amply demonstrated the "majesty and coherence of Puritan thinking."

By arguing that the Puritans had attained an intellectual depth and complexity rare in the modern world, Miller helped prepare the way among historians for a more general repudiation of modernity following the rise of Nazism and Soviet communism. During the 1950s, historians such as Daniel Boorstin, Edmund Morgan, and Robert E. Brown questioned whether the modern world was a better one, and they found fresh appeal in the stability and community of premodern societies. Wertenbaker's rendering of early America as white-hot crucible out of which emerged Modern Man, or at least his near relations, bore little relation to the tranquillity of the new "consensus" history.

Waves of social unrest during the 1960s carried to the fore a new generation of historians who adopted an activist ethos not unlike their progressive grandfathers. Many desired change—radical change—and they chafed at older colleagues who claimed that human institutions remained static over long stretches of time, or who spoke glowingly of life in premodern villages. Many scholars discovered that behind the tidy facade of the church and the village green there seethed tensions of all sorts: among neighbors, religious sects, economic rivals, and political factions. Other scholars pursued an activist agenda by reclaiming the history of those neglected by the historical profession: women, minority groups, Native Americans, and others. Still other scholars, such as Darrett B. Rutman (*Winthrop's Boston,* [1965]), found that villagers and townsmen, almost from the outset, were seized with a thoroughly modern lust for money. This social history called itself "new," and no one remarked on its similarities to Wertenbaker's writings four decades earlier.

During the past twenty years, the "consensus" depiction of a seventeenth-century world dotted with "peaceable kingdoms" and sleepy peasant societies has been all but abandoned. More research on the Chesapeake societies and the Middle Colonies has somewhat diminished the importance of New England, and suggested that its social patterns differed substantially not only from other American colonies but also from Britain itself. Wertenbaker had overstated the extent to which the settlers were becoming "Americans," and he had not realized that the social transformations he recognized in America were also occurring in Britain, but the direction and pace of change cited in current scholarship substantially accords with Wertenbaker's interpretation. In a summary of recent research, historian Jack P. Greene has concluded that British America was "a place in which free people could pursue their own individual happinesses in safety and with a fair prospect that they might be successful in their several quests" (*Pursuits of Happiness* [1988], 5). Wertenbaker would have offered no dissent.

VOLUME III:
James Truslow Adams, *Provincial Society, 1690-1763* (1927)

MODERN SCHOLARS have been fascinated by the progressives' penchant for identifying with the common man while trying to eradicate his mores and culture. Thus, progressive politicians sought to strengthen democracy even as they sent popular urban bosses to jail, or they empathized with the immigrants while advocating compulsory "Americanization." James Truslow Adams's *Provincial Society, 1690-1763* (1927) provides a neat illustration of this progressive ambivalence toward "the people." At once a progressive and an elitist, Adams sympathized with the "poor, hardworking pioneers" and acknowledged their "very real grievances" against capitalistic landowners and merchants, yet he deplored the common people's "ample" ignorance, bigotry, and generally "low intellectual level." Adams's portrait of the past blended the warm humanism of Jane Addams with the cool cynicism of H. L. Mencken. Long, affecting descriptions were followed by incisive analysis, and extended analysis was punctuated with charming anecdotes from travel accounts or probate records. Detachment and engagement, snobbery and sincerity were the hallmarks of Adams's volume, which Allan Nevins proclaimed the best of the *History of American Life* series.

Provincial Society continued the argument of its predecessor volume by Wertenbaker. Adams believed that Englishmen came to America to acquire better and more abundant food, clothing, furnishings, and housing, along with the status such material goods signified. He doubted that religion or high culture of any sort mattered much to most settlers, even in New England.

Adams's materialistic view of the past was reflected in his own life. He started out in business, went to Wall Street, amassed a tidy fortune as a broker, and retired at thirty-four in order to write history. In 1922, he won the Pulitzer Prize for *The Founding of New England* (1921), an achievement that helped persuade Arthur M. Schlesinger, Sr., and Dixon Ryan Fox to recruit him for the *History of American Life* series. Schlesinger was delighted with Adams's fluent submission, but they had a falling out over royalties. Adams moved to London and for a time rejected Allan Nevins's pleas that he return to the United States, citing the high cost of housing in New York: "Both my grandfathers were millionaires, and for generations we have been used to comely living," Adams wrote Nevins. "I do not mean that at all snobbishly. I merely mean that space, privacy and such horribly expensive matters are in my blood." In *The March of Democracy* (1932– 33), Adams complained of the superficiality and materialism of American intellectual life, prompting Schlesinger's blast in the *Atlantic* that "the commercialization of artistic and scientific effort which Mr. Adams has condemned in his criticism of American civilization is only too patent in the product of his own pen." Adams became more conservative during the Great Depression and attacked the New Deal. "I see no end to the extravagance of Congress and the 'soak-the-rich' policy of the 95 percent of the population which pays no taxes."

Adams's *Provincial Society* was released with Wertenbaker's *The First Americans* in 1927, and these volumes together constituted a formidable challenge to those who believed that New England dominated early America and that Puritanism dominated New England. Adams's chapter on the "Life of the Spirit" opened with a discussion of art and music; it touched on organized religion only long enough to note that it had little effect on the morals of the people, which were lax. In *Builders of the Bay Colony* (1930), Samuel Eliot Morison refuted both Wertenbaker and Adams; Puritanism, he insisted, pervaded the lives of most Massachusetts colonists. Then came Perry Miller's volumes celebrating the rigor and elegance of Puritan thought in the seventeenth century and lamenting its decline in the next.

Adams believed that the colonists had so firmly fastened their attention to the economic prospects of this vast new world that they seldom lifted their gaze to consider their prospects in the one far beyond. In 1967, Richard L. Bushman's *From Puritan to Yankee: Character and the Social Order in Connecticut, 1690–1765* accepted Adams's notion that the material abundance of the New World had undermined the Puritan ideal of a cooperative commonwealth, but Bushman argued that newfound affluence induced feelings of guilt, and many settlers sough solace in an even more demanding faith. Their psychological needs gave rise to and found expression in the Great Awakening of the 1730s and 1740s. Materialism and religion were not incompatible, and thus the eighteenth century did not mark a declension in faith. This argument stimulated a reexamination of religion in the eighteenth century, culminating in Jon Butler's *Awash in a Sea of Faith: Christianizing the American People* (1990), which described a "spectacular transformation of institutional Christianity" during the period.

For Adams, economic growth had a corrosive effect upon community cohesion as well as religious expression. Social and economic differences became more pronounced, and by the mid-eighteenth century, social distinctions based on food, clothing, furnishings, and housing had crystallized into two recognizable classes: "aristocrats" and the "common man." In his emphasis on class differences, Adams, like Wertenbaker, neatly accorded with progressive assumptions about the deep institutional foundations of inequality in American society.

But during the 1950s, consensus scholars such as Robert E. and B. Katharine Brown, Daniel Boorstin, and Forrest McDonald argued that the progressive historians had overstated the extent of class divisions in early America and had refused to acknowledge that communities were bound by widely shared religious and political values. Brown's *Middle-Class Democracy and the Revolution in Massachusetts, 1691-1780* (1955), which described how an egalitarian and democratic people rose up in opposition to England, contained twenty-three references to Adams, nearly all of them critical.

Soon after the consensus historians' had staked out their positions on the cooperative and democratic foundations of colonial America, their claims were overwashed by a new current of historical research, this one surging in from Europe. In 1956, Fernand Braudel became editor of the influential journal *Annales: Economies, Sociétés, Civilisations* and persuaded a group of French historians—they became known as the Annalistes —to set upon the task of creating a *histoire totale,* a portrait of the past highlighting enduring ideas and mores rather than ephemeral events. Braudel's goal was virtually identical to that propounded by Schlesinger and Fox three decades earlier, as Braudel readily acknowledged. But where the *History of American Life* authors lacked theoretical models to draw connections among economics, social organization, and cultural practices, the Annalistes proposed to borrow heavily from other disciplines, especially anthropology, to explore the relation of culture and social organization.

While the Annalistes were recruiting an army of zealous researchers in France, a host of historians across the Channel were gathering under another (albeit similar) banner. Eventually known as the Cambridge Group, they resolved to tackle the problem of how England, which had always lagged behind China and much of the Islamic world, emerged during the seventeenth and eighteenth centuries as a dynamic and innovative society that inaugurated the Industrial Revolution. The Cambridge Group believed that this social dynamism was woven into the entire fabric of social experience. This was of special significance for the study of colonial America, for viewed in this light the American colonies ceased to be *departures* from the European experience, as Frederick Jackson Turner had pointed out in the 1890s, but its most visible creations.

Younger scholars during the 1960s flocked to the study of eighteenth-century America. In 1970, a remarkable year for the study of colonial America, four important books emphasized the cohesion of New England communities in the seventeenth and eighteenth centuries: Philip J. Greven, *Four Generations: Population, Land, and Family in Colonial Andover, Massachusetts;* Kenneth Lockridge, *A New England Town, the First Hundred Years: Dedham, Massachusetts, 1636-1736;* John Demos, *A Little Commonwealth: Family Life in Plymouth Colony;* and Michael Zuckerman, *Peaceable Kingdoms: New England Towns in the Eighteenth Century.*

Although modern social historians have broadened their field of vision, the earlier debate over the extent and direction of social stratification has persisted. In *Salem Possessed: The Social Origins of Witchcraft* (1974), Paul Boyer and Stephen Nissenbaum put forth the idea that the witch-hunts were a product of communitywide social tensions, Adams neglected the middle colonies, but James T. Lemon, in *The Best Poor Man's Country: A Geographical Study of Early Southeastern Pennsylvania* (1972), found the entrepreneurial spirit to be deeply rooted in Pennsylvania.

Adams's discussion of women was perfunctory; his analysis of slavery, on the other hand, written decades before the proliferation of monographs on the subject in the 1960s and 1970s, anticipated Winthrop D. Jordan's seminal *White Over Black: American Attitudes Toward the Negro: 1550-1812* (1968). Jordan maintained that the enslavement of blacks during the eighteenth century led to their being regarded as essentially inferior; racism was a consequence of slavery, not its cause. Adams had similarly argued that prior to 1700, blacks suffered because they were slaves, but after 1700 their "disabilities" were due to their "status as a slave." Here, as elsewhere, Adams found economic foundations for social relations and cultural practices.

Adams's materialism—his belief that market forces prevailed over religious precepts and community bonds—enabled him to break through the regional and provincial barriers that had long circumscribed study of the early colonial era. Some historians have in recent years applied the universalizing forces of the market to all of the British colonies in the Western Hemisphere—see, especially, Jack P. Greene, *Pursuits of Happiness: The*

Social Development of Early Modern British Colonies and the Formation of American Culture (1988). Yet it remains to be seen whether scholars will succeed in synthesizing divergent views on colonial religion, society, and the economy.

VOLUME IV:
Evarts Greene, *The Revolutionary Generation,* 1763–90 (1943)

THE PROGRESSIVE HISTORIANS' earliest achievement was also their most spectacular. The Founding Fathers' lofty rhetoric in defense of democracy had in fact concealed selfish class interests. Wealthy colonial merchants and planters effectively conspired to use popular discontent to eliminate British influence in the colonies, and then seized control of the revolution to consolidate their power in the new nation. In 1909, Carl Becker issued his famous dictum that the Revolution was fought not to determine home rule but who was to rule at home *(History of Political Parties in the Province of New York, 1760-1776)*. It set the tone and argument for classic progressive texts such as Arthur Schlesinger, Sr.'s, *The Colonial Merchants and the American Revolution, 1763-1776* (1918), which held that commercial elites, fearful of the effects of British economic policies, "instigated" the "first discontents" against the Crown, grew alarmed at the "engulfing tide of radicalism" that led to war, and then, in the troubled years afterward, "drew together in an effort to found a government which would safeguard the interests of their class." This last point was driven home by the forceful prose of Charles Beard in *Economic Interpretation of the Constitution* (1913), the most famous of the progressive texts. And J. Franklin Jameson's *The American Revolution Considered as a Social Movement* (1926) was an influential summary of the progressive historians' belief that the Revolution was essentially conservative.

The volumes of the *History of American Life* series that were published in the 1920s and 1930s similarly challenged the hagiographic approach to the origins of American institutions. But in 1943, when Everts B. Greene's *The Revolutionary Generation* was finally published, the progressive indictment of American society had lost its cogency. The desperate exigencies of the war against German fascism and Japanese militarism had transformed the industrial fiefdoms of the American robber barons into the "arsenal of democracy," and the nation's multiplicity of class and ethnic groups had joined as one in defense of freedom. Historians, always mindful of the importunate demands of the present, discovered a suitably patriotic past. The United States, they now proposed, had from the outset embodied the democratic stirrings of the American people as a whole. An exception was John C. Miller's *Origins of the American Revolution,* also published in 1943, which attempted to reinvigorate the progressive indictment of the Founding Fathers by showing that the Revolution had unleashed but failed to satisfy the strivings of the people. Miller's strident peroration that the revolution of 1776 "has not yet ended" was perhaps proof that it had.

Greene was keenly aware of the sharp reaction against progressive history, and on one point after another he retreated from the progressive position without abandoning it entirely. He agreed with the progressives' critics—soon they would be called "consensus theorists"—that on the eve of the Revolution colonial society had "advanced far toward an equalitarian order," yet he adhered to the progressive belief that legal and social inequalities helped fuel discontents among the lower classes, especially urban workers, who provided the "combustible material" that eventually ignited the Revolution. And on the crucial issue of whether economic or ideological factors had animated the rebellion, Greene argued for the centrality of both.

Some critics welcomed Greene's attempt to fuse progressive history to the emerging consensus school. Carl Bridenbaugh called Greene's equivocal account of class tensions "shrewd and judicious" (*New York Times Book Review,* January 2, 1944), and Max Farrand applauded Greene's subtle renderings as those of a "master" *(American Historical Review).* John C. Miller, writing in the *New York Herald Tribune Weekly Book Review* (December 12, 1943), squeezed out of Greene's equivocations a distillate of progressive pronouncements: Greene had described America's first "populist revolt," Miller wrote. But other reviewers were more plausibly struck by Greene's ambivalence on the central historiographical issues of the day. As Thomas P. Abernethy gingerly observed, Greene's book had proven "most conservative in the matter of generalizations" (*Journal of Social History,* 10:1, [February 1944]), while Curtis Nettels remarked on Greene's "aversion to unfounded generalizations." The respectful words betrayed a potent if implicit criticism: Greene's willingness to embrace divergent opinions meant that he had none of his own.

Dispassionate quibblers such as Greene were soon elbowed aside by more energetic proponents of consensus history during the late 1940s and 1950s. Their numbers included Daniel Boorstin, Clinton Rossiter, Robert Brown, Benjamin Wright, and Edmund Morgan. In *The Birth of the Republic, 1763-1789* (1956), for example, Edmund S. Morgan insisted that the Revolution transcended class and regional divisions: "The most radical change produced in Americans by the Revolution was in fact not a division at all but the union of three million cantankerous colonists into a new nation." Even the poorest became democratic citizens, not an impoverished rabble bent on social revolution.

Patriotic exhortations such as Morgan's appealed to the postwar generation, who had tired of the debunking ideas of their progressive parents.

What remained of the progressive interpretation of early America was nearly dashed to bits by the works of two liberal scholars during the 1960s: Bernard Bailyn's *The Ideological Origins of the American Revolution* (1967) and Gordon S. Wood's *The Creation of the American Republic, 1776-1787* (1969). Bailyn described how the Founding Fathers had rediscovered classical notions of citizenship and republicanism, ideas that profoundly influenced their opposition to the corrupt and tyrannical policies of the British crown. Revolutionary ardor was stimulated by ideas, not by the resentments of class, a thesis whose enthusiastic reception was all the more remarkable in that it surfaced amid the roiling racial and political currents of the late 1960s.

The "Republican synthesis" (as it came to be called) not only challenged the progressive historians' belief in the primacy of economic factors and social class in human affairs, but it further contended that Thomas Jefferson, George Washington, and all the rest looked not to the future but back to ancient Rome and Greece, where selfish interests had been chastened by ideals of civic virtue.

Even before the "Republican synthesis" had received an identifying label, it came in for sharp criticism. Joyce Appleby and others insisted on the essentially modern character of the Revolution. In *Capitalism and a New Social Order: The Republican Vision of the 1790s* (1984), Appleby argued that insofar as the motives of the patriots were refracted through an ideological lens, it was to be found not in the classic texts of the ancient world but in the liberal economic doctrines of Locke; and even more compelling than the Revolutionary generation's words were their actions, for they built a society whose foundations were thoroughly capitalistic and liberal. This was not quite the terminology of the progressive historians, many of whom regarded capitalism as akin to feudalism, but opponents of the "Republican synthesis" had nevertheless managed to establish a strong connection between the Revolutionary generation and the modern world.

In recent years, both sides of the debate have conceded that their positions have been overdrawn. Most generally agree that the patriots carried no single ideological weapon, but eclectically fired at the British whatever would serve their purposes at the moment. During the past quarter-century, moreover, scholars have rediscovered another essential element of the progressive interpretation: class conflict. In *The Urban Crucible: Social Change, Political Consciousness, and the Origins of the American Revolution* (1979), Gary B. Nash described how declining opportunity radicalized workers, and in *Distribution of Wealth and Income in the United States in 1798* (1989), Lee Soltow found strong statistical evidence of the unequal distribution of property. That the poor were almost inescapably bound up in poverty was the view of Gregory Stiverson, *Poverty in a Land of Plenty: Tenancy in Eighteenth-century Maryland* (1977), and Edward Countryman, *A People in Revolution: The American Revolution and Political Society in New York, 1760-1790* (1981). From these and other studies, Linda Kerber has concluded that recent scholars have "reinvigorated the Progressive focus on social conflict between classes" — see "The Revolutionary Generation: Ideology, Politics, and Culture in the Early Republic," in Eric Foner, ed., *The New American History* (1990), 28-29.

After hundreds of monographs and dissertations, the debate has now settled upon a middle-of-the-road position not far from the one Greene occupied a half-century ago. Modern scholars have not so much altered Greene's portrait as they have filled it in with rich detail on people who lacked power or inhabited the margins of society. Greene referred often to slaves, servants, soldiers, and women, and he attempted to delineate salient aspects of their lives. But his words seemed muffled, as if he were writing *about* such people rather than on their behalf.

Thus, while Greene accurately noted that many women had "ample opportunity to display managerial capacity" as businesswomen and midwives, he provided little sense of the achievements of hardships of such women as are described in Laurel Thatcher Ulrich's *A Midwife's Tale: The Life of Martha Ballard, 1785-1812* (1990). Greene further failed to perceive how the Revolution undermined deep-seated patriarchal values, the theme of Jay Fliegelman's *Prodigals and Pilgrims: The American Revolution against Patriarchal Authority, 1750-1800* (1982). In *Liberty's Daughters: The Revolutionary Experience of American Women, 1750-1800* (1980), Mary Beth Norton maintained that women contributed to the Revolution and thereby gained economic opportunities. Men's hasty retreat from the privileges and responsibilities of patriarchy left women free to fill the void. That they did, embracing the role and ideologies of the "republican mother," was the seminal thesis of Linda K. Kerber in *Women of the Republic: Intellect and Ideology in Revolutionary America* (1980). On women's work, see Jeanne Boydston, *Home and Work: Housework, Wages and the Ideology of Labor in the Early Republic* (1990), and Daniel Blake Smith, *Inside the Great House: Planter Family Life in Eighteenth-Century Chesapeake Society (1980).*

Among the works on free blacks and slaves, see Gary B. Nash, *Forging Freedom: The Formation of Philadelphia's Black Community, 1720-1840* (1988), and W. D. Piersen, *Black Yankees: The Development of an Afro-American Subculture in Eighteenth-Century New England* (1988). On the profound interactions between Native American and settler cultures, see James H. Merrell, *The Indians' New World* (1989), and Richard White, *The Middle Ground: Indians, Empires, and Republics in the Great Lakes Region, 1650-1815* (1991). The experiences of soldiers are described in Steven Rosswurm's *Arms, Country and Class: The Philadelphia Militia and 'Lower Sort' During the American Revolution, 1775-1783* (1987), and Robert A. Gross, *The Minutemen and Their World* (1976).

VOLUME V:
John Allen Krout and Dixon Ryan Fox, *The Completion of Independence, 1790–1830* (1944)

THAT DIXON RYAN FOX would write the volume on the early national period had been a foregone conclusion from the outset of the *History of American Life* project. Fox's progressive credentials nearly equaled those of the series coeditor, Arthur Schlesinger, Sr. Fox had studied at Columbia with Charles Beard, the dean of progressive historians, and Fox's dissertation, *The Decline of Aristocracy in the Politics of New York* (1919), forthrightly advanced the progressive interpretation by showing the steady democratization of early New York politics. For over two decades Fox taught at Columbia University, the citadel of progressive historiography, where he imbibed a strong dose of economic determinism, class conflict, and a faith in society's advance through determined reform.

Fox's volume was to appear before the close of the 1920s, but he fell far behind, attributing the delays to obligations as a dissertation adviser, as president of the New York State Historical Association, and, after 1934, as president of Union College. In 1940, he enlisted John Allen Krout of Columbia to help with the volume. *The Completion of Independence, 1790–1830* was finally published in 1944, the last of the originally commissioned volumes in the *History of American Life* series. (Dixon Wecter's *The Age of the Great Depression, 1929–1941* [1948] was conceived as a supplement.)

Fox's administrative duties were onerous, but his inability to complete the volume may have reflected doubts over the progressive interpretation. Much as Evarts Greene had, in 1943, backed away from Beard's and Schlesinger's views on the American Revolution, Krout and Fox retreated from progressive orthodoxy one year later: The chief characteristic of the early national period ceased to be the beleaguered advance of the people against well-entrenched plutocrats; Krout and Fox instead proposed that the salient characteristic of the period was the acquisition of a national identity.

This seemed, at first glance, a craven reversion to what historian John Higham has called the "conservative evolutionist" interpretation of America's past — the belief, advanced during the last third of the nineteenth century by Henry Adams, John Bach McMaster, James Ford Rhodes, and others, that the dominant theme in the nation's past was the forging of national unity. The title of the volume certainly resonated with patriotic overtones. Yet Krout and Fox did not so much abandon the progressive thesis as attempt to set it upon more defensible terrain.

Krout and Fox's argument had two distinct components, the first of which had long been a commonplace of American historiography: The nation's dynamic, expanding economy caused it to outgrow English customs and traditions and rip free of them entirely, as evidenced by the demise of apprenticeship and the differentiation of social class by distinctive clothes. In chapters such as "The Atlantic Ports," "The Day of the Merchant," "Agrarian Expansion," and "The Business Scene," Krout and Fox's volume emphasized how mighty economic forces were transforming society. Their second point, and chief claim to originality, was that while the new economy *should* have given rise to political and social democracy, it failed to do so. This was because conservative "strategists" mounted a concerted ideological and cultural counterattack: They conspired to crush workingmen's organizations, and they promoted religious revivals that inhibited advances in education, science, and the arts. (The rise of Sunday schools, for example, was called by Krout and Fox "new Christian propaganda.")

By 1830, the nation was characterized by a vigorous market economy in which nearly everyone (except slaves) directly participated; yet powerful local and regional elites dictated social norms and controlled government. Conservative values reigned supreme, and religion remained "the foremost institution of the country, more influential in America than in any other land." By the end of the period, the nation's conservative social structure and cultural values were at odds with its liberal economic system. During the preceding forty years, society and culture had failed to advance apace with economic progress. Unstated, but certainly implied in the volume, was the eventual rectification of this anomaly.

This reformulation helped salvage the forward-looking thrust of progressive historiography, but it abandoned one of its central precepts: Frederick Jackson Turner's thesis that free access to good land along the vast frontier had allowed Americans to "escape from the bondage of the past." The crucial role of the frontier in promoting self-reliance and democracy figured in most works of progressive history, including Fox's earlier *The Decline of Aristocracy* and the volumes of the *History of American Life* series that had been published in the 1920s. But during the 1930s and 1940s, younger historians chipped away at this cornerstone of the progressive edifice. In one study after another, they discovered that the democratic ethos of the original frontiersmen did not long prevail. Thomas P. Abernethy, for example, a former student of Turner, showed that the Tennessee frontier had been no training field for egalitarian democrats, but a poaching ground for greedy land speculators (*From Frontier to Plantation in Tennessee: A Study in Frontier Democracy* [1932]).

Krout and Fox agreed with this repudiation of Turner. Citing Abernethy, among others, they found "much evidence" that "acquisitive pioneers helped to create an economic aristocracy" and sought to emulate the social hierarchies of the East and Old South. The image of the self-reliant and democratic frontiersman was in fact myth, and its persistence, like the promise of heaven for workers and slaves, hindered efforts to promote change.

If, however, the frontier had not sustained America's distinctive democracy and egalitarianism, what did? Krout and Fox found the answer in the vital economic system that was emerging, most visibly in the growing towns and cities of the early 1800s. There, especially, the people would ultimately and inevitably prevail over special interests, and secularism and knowledge over religion and ignorance.

Subsequent historians have shared Krout and Fox's belief that commercial expansion was central to the early national period. Few, however, have accepted their hypothesis that the early nation's economic underpinnings were incompatible with its social order and cultural values. George Rodgers Taylor's *The Transportation Revolution, 1815-1860* (1951) demonstrated the powerful convergence of economic and political forces in the building of the early nation's infrastructure, and Carter Goodrich's *Government Promotion of American Canals and Railroads, 1800-1890* (1960) expanded on Taylor's thesis to show the feverish participation of municipal and community leaders in economic development at all levels.

Within the past fifteen years, these views have broadened into a school of thought known as the "market revolution," summarized in Charles G. Sellers, *The Market Revolution: Jacksonian America, 1815-1846* (1991). The "market revolution" synthesis holds that capitalist economic developments generated complementary religious and cultural institutions. Self-sufficient farms, formerly enclosed within the traditional bonds of community and family, were transformed by the capitalist market economy, a thesis described in Christopher Clark's *The Roots of Rural Capitalism: Western Massachusetts, 1780-1860* (1991). Two early and influential works on the cultural transformation of artisans into industrial workers were Anthony F. C. Wallace's *Rockdale: The Growth of an American Village in the Early Industrial Revolution* (1978) and Paul Johnson's *A Shopkeeper's Millennium: Society and Revivals in Rochester, New York, 1815-1837* (1978), which depicted the religious revivals of the era as attempts to discipline workers and ensure their effective participation in capitalistic markets. "Market revolution" scholars essentially agree with Krout and Fox that economic elites had employed religious and cultural ideologies to forestall the ascent of the common man, but where Krout and Fox believed that these institutions and ideologies had evolved in *opposition* to the market economy, Sellers and his followers saw them as its inevitable concomitant.

Many labor historians challenged Sellers's notion that capitalism ensured the "irreversible proletarianization" of the workers. Some have documented workers' successful defense of preindustrial work rules and cultural patterns, see Herbert Gutman, *Work, Culture and Society in Industrializing America* (1976); Sean Wilentz, *Chants Democratic: New York City and the Rise of the American Working Class, 1788-1850* (1984); and Susan E. Hirsch, *Roots of the American Working Class: The Industrialization of*

Crafts in Newark, 1800-1860 (1978). Others have shown how workers incorporated religion, self-discipline, and temperance as part of their culture of *resistance* to capitalist domination, see Alan Dawley, *Class and Community: The Industrial Revolution in Lynn* (1976); Paul G. Faler, *Mechanics and Manufacturers in the Early Industrial Revolution: Lynn, Massachusetts, 1760-1860* (1981); and Bruce Laurie, *Working People of Philadelphia, 1800-1850* (1980).

Krout and Fox provided a sympathetic if superficial description of the plight of workers in this era of momentous economic change, but they had none of the recent historians' sense of effective worker agency, nor any understanding of how workers and farmers could themselves wrest control of institutions and value systems that had been devised by powerful economic elites. Krout and Fox, for example, accepted the temperance reformers' claims that they had made "the greatest headway" against intemperate drinking, a thesis that has been shattered by W. J. Rorabaugh's description of a people awash in booze in *The Alcoholic Republic: An American Tradition* (1979).

Scholars of the early national period generally agree that the 1700s were essentially premodern and that the early nineteenth century witnessed sweeping economic, cultural, and social changes, a thesis with which Krout and Fox would have wholeheartedly concurred. But Krout and Fox's top-downward methodology—their reliance on the writings, publications, and institutional accounts of, for, and by elites—blinded them to myriad ways in which people squeeze their own meanings out of obdurate social contexts.

VOLUME VI:
Carl Russell Fish, *The Rise of the Common Man, 1830-50* (1929)

WHERE KROUT AND FOX'S VOLUME depicted a conservative political and cultural ethos at odds with a liberal and modernizing economy, Fish had the simpler task of showing the subsequent flowering of a thoroughly liberal society and culture from 1830 to 1850. Fish explained that forces of liberal change appeared earlier in the century, buffeting old habits and ideas, but gained "full sweep" with the elevation of Andrew Jackson to the presidency in 1829. Yet Jackson quickly recedes into the background, and the "common man" steps to the fore in Fish's vista: entrepreneurial farmers and energetic producers, self-made men with grand ambitions and grandiose schemes, ideologues and reformers intent on fashioning a new society. A "restless hurry" was everywhere apparent, an "outward sign" of the peoples' confidence in their capacity to better their lives. Emerson's mystical faith in the self constituted the era's prevailing ideology, for the generation of the 1830s and 1840s represented the "acme of a particular development of individualism," and its accomplishments "almost unprecedentedly" derived from independent effort. Fish concluded that more individuals than ever before worked "by and for themselves, at what they chose, and how they pleased."

If President Jackson was the symbol of an age rather than its catalyst, however, what forces lifted the "common man" over the conservative obstacles that had impeded his father and grandfather? Like most progressive historians, Fish accepted Frederick Jackson Turner's thesis that the availability of cheap land on the frontier stimulated the nation's acquisitive and democratic zeal. (Fish could hardly have ignored Turner: He first went to the University of Wisconsin as a leave replacement for Turner in 1900 and over the next few decades became a fixture at that Midwestern bastion of progressivism, "the most democratic institution in America," he called it.) But the core of Fish's argument, delineated through an accretion of details rather than explicit argument, was that a distinctly liberal social system resulted from a convergence of economic development, institutional reform, and supporting ideologies. This rendering, though now familiar, was at the time striking. In 1928, Merle Curti wrote: "Perhaps no one before has appreciated so well" Fish's description of the "systematizing" of American life, largely through the transformation of economic institutions and businesses.

Perhaps Fish's thesis was too subtly—or too impenetrably—adumbrated in the details, or perhaps the early critics of progressive history had bigger and bolder targets on which to train their sights—Beard and Becker on the Founding Fathers, most obviously. For whatever reason, Fish's interpretation of the "rise of the common man" during the 1830s and 1840s went largely unchallenged. That changed in 1945 with the publication of *The Age of Jackson,* by Arthur Schlesinger, Jr., the twenty-eight-year-old son of the coeditor of the *History of American Life* series. Schlesinger's white-hot prose, for which he won the Pulitzer, reignited the embers of the progressive interpretation, suggested the relevance of Jackson to the liberal social policies of Franklin D. Roosevelt, and thus drew a host of critics—pundits and politicians as well as historians—to the subject.

Schlesinger's rhetorical power and narrative drama derived in part from his vivid descriptions of the contending historical actors—radical democrats as heroes, and grasping businessmen as villains—but Schlesinger believed, far more explicitly than Fish, that people and events were driven by powerful economic and social forces. Jacksonian democracy grew out of the "new industrialism" of the Northern and Middle states, which imperiled artisans and journeymen, and of the vulnerability of farmers in a market economy controlled by bankers, merchants, and their supporters in government. "The business community has invariably brought national affairs to a state of crisis and exasperated the rest of society into dissatisfaction bordering on revolt," Schlesinger observed, his shift from past to imperfect tense underscoring the relevance of the Age of Jackson to the Age of Franklin D. Roosevelt. He added, for those who missed the pointed analogy to the present: "Every great crisis thus far in American history has produced a leader adequate to the occasion from the ranks of those who believe vigorously and seriously in liberty, democracy and the common man."

But why, if Jackson had indeed wrested government from the hold of the business community, had it proven necessary for Roosevelt to fight the same battle a century later? Schlesinger, anticipating this rebuttal, had proposed a cyclical explanation: social problems accumulated during conservative eras and were then swept away by radicalized masses whose energies eventually became spent, allowing the forces of conservatism to reassert themselves. (Schlesinger's thesis was fleshed out nearly four decades later in his *Cycles of American History* [1986]).

In 1948, Columbia historian Richard Hofstadter, though himself an ardent defender of Roosevelt, challenged Schlesinger's argument and with it the progressive interpretation of the Jacksonian era. Hofstadter noted that for those who had lived through the era of FDR, it was "natural" to see in Jacksonian democracy an earlier version of the New Deal, for the periods had "many superficial points in common." But where FDR had effectively enlisted the power of the federal government to restrain business, the Jacksonian movement attempted to divorce the two. The vaunted democracy of the Jacksonian era's "common man" was in fact the triumph of the petty capitalist. FDR's revolution, Hofstadter insisted, marked the first real ascent of the "common man" over the business interests of the nation *(The American Political Tradition)*.

During the next two decades, scholars generally confirmed the "petty capitalist" character of different Jacksonian movements, see, for example, Walter Hugins, *Jacksonian Democracy and the Working Class: A Study of the New York Workingman's Movement, 1829–1837* (1960). Bray Hammond determined that many of Jackson's supporters in the Bank War were "men on the make," see *Banks and Politics in America from the Revolution to the Civil War* (1957).

During the 1960s, the question of the composition and objectives of the Jacksonians elicited contradictory answers: In *The Concept of Jacksonian Democracy: New York as a Test Case* (1961), Lee Benson found that the Jacksonians were no more likely than their opponents to represent any particular class; their power base depended on parochial issues of ethnicity and culture. On the other hand, Edward Pessen argued that Jacksonian America was increasingly being rent by class conflict, much as the progressives claimed, but he found that the party of Jackson was a sham that failed to bring about meaningful democratic reforms, see *Riches, Class, and Power Before the Civil War* (1973); on this interpretation, see also Jeffrey G. Williamson and Peter H. Lindert, *American Inequality: A Macroeco-*

A HISTORY OF AMERICAN LIFE

nomic History (1980). Stephan Thernstrom, the first historian to undertake a statistical study of occupational mobility over several decades, uncovered data for Newburyport, Massachusetts, that left matters all the more confusing: Laborers rarely climbed far up the occupational ladder, yet they did manage to accumulate some property. Depending on which fact one cited, one could characterize them either as discontented and radicalized workers or as self-satisfied and conservative petty bourgeois, see *Poverty and Progress: Social Mobility in a Nineteenth-Century City* (1964). Complicating the debate still further has been the general acceptance of the inadequacy of the two-class model of "the people" vs. "the business interests." Historians have discovered the rise of a middle class of non-manual workers during the Jacksonian era, see especially Stuart M. Blumin, *The Emergence of the Middle Class: Social Experience in the American City, 1760-1900* (1989).

Fish's own position betrayed a similar confusion, for while he claimed that the distinguishing characteristic of the Jacksonian era was its individualism, he also described the formation of a "permanent class of wage earners," workers who had become dependent on the initiative of others. Yet in recent years the progressive interpretation of the "rise of the common man" has been repackaged and substantially revivified, see Harry L. Watson, *Liberty and Power: The Politics of Jacksonian America* (1990), and Charles Sellers, *The Market Revolution: Jacksonian America, 1815-1846* (1991). Sellers concluded that Arthur M. Schlesinger, Jr., "may yet be judged more nearly right then his critics," an endorsement not just of Schlesinger but of his father's generation of progressive historians who first advanced the class conflict model.

Fish maintained that the ascent of the common man had been abetted by reformers who extended the franchise, built more and better prisons and insane asylums, and, most important, made basic education freely available to nearly everyone. After surveying these reforms, and the careers of the passionate reformers who promoted them with unceasing diligence, Fish concluded that "Americans on the whole were distinguished by their kindness of heart." In this volume, as in the others of the *History of American Life* series, humanitarian reform was nearly synonymous with progress.

This sturdy commonplace was rattled during the 1960s by two mighty storms. The first swept across the Atlantic from France, the work of a French philosopher and historian, Michel Foucault (1926–84), who argued in *Madness and Civilization* (1961) and subsequent works that nineteenth-century reforms, for all their humanitarian rhetoric, were actually attempts to discipline and control workers and outcasts who might otherwise challenge middle-class cultural hegemony. Foucault's cynicism was intensified by student protests over the seeming complicity of American universities in the Vietnam War. Many American historians, inspired by Foucault and mindful of the students who had closed down their universities, concluded that Fish rightly identified the 1830s and 1840s as a seedtime for institutional reform, but they now identified these reforms as a means of class domination. That the public school system imposed middle-class values on workers and immigrants was the thesis of Michael B. Katz in *The Irony of Early School Reform: Educational Innovation in Mid-19th-Century Massachusetts* (1968); Stanley K. Schultz argued in *The Culture Factory: Boston Public Schools, 1789-1860* (1973) that the schools provided an institutional template for industrial work. David J. Rothman similarly found that American reformers "discovered" asylums, prisons, and workhouses as model societies that exemplify "the advantages of an orderly, regular, and disciplined routine" in his *The Discovery of the Asylum: Social Order and Disorder in the New Republic* (1971), p. 129. The historians' criticisms of asylums and schools resounded during the 1960s and 1970s in the demands for "alternative" (i.e., less structured) schools, more humane prisons, and the deinstitutionalization of the mentally ill, issues that today remain at the center of acrimonious public debate. Other scholars continued to applaud the nineteenth-century reformers and chronicle their achievements, see Alice Felt Tyler, *Freedom's Ferment: Phases of American Social History to 1860* (1944), and Carl F. Kaestle, *Pillars of the Republic: Common Schools and American Society, 1780-1860* (1983).

Women, especially evangelical Protestants, contributed to these nineteenth-century cultural reforms. Fish, however, generally assumed that women reformers followed the lead of men. The temperance movement was, he believed, a "Man's concern throughout the first half of the nineteenth century." During the past two decades, women's historians have refuted this supposition. That middle-class women provided the shock troops of reform, if not always the field marshals, was the thesis of Barbara Leslie Epstein in *The Politics of Domesticity: Women, Evangelism, and Temperance in Nineteenth-Century America* (1981). And in *Cradle of the Middle Class: The Family in Oneida County, New York, 1790-1865* (1981), Mary P. Ryan explained how women sought to protect their families by joining public moral crusades.

A staple contention of women's history, recently contested, is whether Victorian culture in fact separated into two distinct gender spheres, with men supervising the economy and politics, and women the home. Fish prefigured this debate when he matter-of-factly stated that during the 1830s "there was coming into existence that division of functions, which was to characterize the United States for several generations, by which culture was feminine, and masculinity was expected to distinguish itself by a lack of exterior polish." Fish further suggested that this new deference caused American women to be "practically safe" among most men. In *Disorderly Conduct: Visions of Gender in Victorian America* (1985), Carroll Smith-Rosenberg offered a withering rebuke: The harshly competitive market economy of the 1830s and 1840s ground down the psyche of many working-class men who then vented their rage by abusing women and racial minorities. On working-class women's resistance to "separate spheres," see Thomas Dublin, *Women at Work: The Transformation of Work and Community in Lowell, Massachusetts, 1826-1860* (1979).

VOLUME VII:
Arthur Charles Cole, *The Irrepressible Conflict, 1850-65* (1934)

OF ALL THE VOLUMES in the *History of American Life* series, Cole's *The Irrepressible Conflict* (1934) was the most sharply focused, and perhaps the one that longest contributed to historical debates. Cole's writing drew strength from his passionate belief that scholars become engaged in the social issues of the day. In this respect, and many others, Cole shared the views of Charles Beard; indeed, if any historian of that era could be called a Beardian, it was Cole. An outspoken opponent of American participation in the First World War, Cole, a professor at the University of Illinois, was investigated by university trustees for antiwar statements. Beard, though a supporter of the war, vigorously defended academics who opposed it, and in 1917, he protested Columbia's actions against antiwar faculty by resigning. For his part, Cole launched a teachers' union at the University of Illinois, became active in the American Civil Liberties Union, and joined Beard in advocating American neutrality in the 1930s.

The *Irrepressible Conflict* was similarly inspired by Beard. Although the title came from William H. Seward's fateful speech predicting the civil war —an "irrepressible conflict between opposing and enduring forces"—the phrase had also been used as a chapter title in Charles and Mary Beard's popular text *The Rise of American Civilization* (1927). Cole's book in fact constituted an extended exposition of the Beards' chapter, which contended that the Civil War, though seemingly caused by disputes over slavery, was really a struggle between socioeconomic systems: the noncapitalistic planting aristocracy of the South, and the capitalistic and wage-earning classes of the North and West.

War was inevitable, as was the defeat of the South, Cole explained. The plantation system, in particular, was doomed. Profits had been declining; labor and capital that might have been invested in more productive enterprises, especially industry, were wastefully poured upon exhausted cotton fields. Slavery had "outlived its usefulness." Moreover, slavery had transformed the South into a retrogressive "land of chivalry" untouched by "the new currents of civilization" that had revitalized the North: the movement for popular education; the flowering of publishing and journalism; the rise of science, theater, and the arts. The South didn't have a chance against the industrializing and modernizing North.

Critical response to Cole's volume seemed to recapitulate the divisions of the war era itself: Northerners liked the book, white Southerners did not. In 1935, the *New England Quarterly* doubted that a "more complete and satisfactory picture" of American civilization could anywhere be found, and the *Pennsylvania Magazine of History and Biography* praised Cole's study as "comprehensive and magnificent." But the *Virginia Quarterly Review* dismissed the volume as "a belated abolition tract." And Avery Craven, who sympathized with the South, wrote a dismissive review in the *American Historical Review.* Cole had failed to understand the reasons for secession and he did not explain, Craven wrote, why the usual sectional disputes had erupted in so terrible a war. Cole, in short, had failed to "justify the title of his book."

In *The Repressible Conflict* (1939) and *The Coming of the Civil War* (1942), Craven expanded his rebuttal. The cultures of the North and South were indeed different, but not inevitably fated to come to blows. Northern "fanatics," however, whipped up emotions, and their Southern counterparts responded with similarly inflammatory invective. The "molders of public opinion steadily created the fiction of two distinct peoples" and thus "led a people into a bloody war." The Beard-Cole thesis, by positing an irresistible conflict, had merely recapitulated the overheated rhetoric of the abolitionists.

Craven was soon joined by James G. Randall, whose three-volume biography of Lincoln appeared in successive years beginning in 1945. Randall concurred that the Civil War was an unthinkable mistake, the product of a "blundering generation" that had transformed a "repressible conflict" into a "needless war." Craven's and Randall's revisionist books appeared in the wake of *Gone With the Wind* (1939), and their books affected scholars much like the movie affected audiences. Beard and Cole's enthusiasm for contemporary reform had blinded them to its failures nearly a century earlier, or so many historians came to believe.

In 1949, Arthur Schlesinger, Jr., counterattacked Craven and Randall at their most vulnerable point: slavery. That the abolitionists had furiously inveighed against the evils of slavery was inevitable. To imagine that Northerners could close their eyes to its evils and somehow compose their differences with an unrepentant South was absurd. Writing several years after the defeat of Hitler, Schlesinger concluded: "The unhappy fact is that man occasionally works himself into a log-jam; and that the log-jam must be burst by violence. We know that well enough from the experience of the last decade" ("The Causes of the Civil War: A Note on Historical Sentimentalism," *Partisan Review,* vol. 16 [October 1949]). In his 1951 presidential address to the American Historical Association, Samuel Eliot Morison similarly declared: "War is better than servitude."

But was American slavery comparable to the genocide of the Nazis? A more troubling question would have been hard to conceive, and it shocked professional historians who had been reared on Ulrich Bonnell Phillips's *American Negro Slavery* (1918), which described the institution as fundamentally benign. "Severity was clearly the exception, and kindliness the rule," Phillips said of plantation slavery. Even a passionate defender of civil rights such as Arthur Cole thought it "reasonably clear that the average slaveholder was genuinely concerned for the physical well-being of his 'chattels.' " But the analogy between the slave South and the Nazis persisted, especially among civil rights leaders during the 1950s.

Among historians, the most provocative exposition of the analogy was Stanley M. Elkins's *Slavery: A Problem in American Institutional and Intellectual Life* (1959). Unlike slavery in Latin America, where representatives of the Crown and the Catholic church placed restraints on slave owners, Elkins believed that slavery in the American South was untempered by mediating institutions, and thus functioned as a "total institution" that, like Nazi concentration camps, shattered its inmates. Slavery ripped black families apart, infantilized adults, and crushed the black psyche for generations. Three centuries of injustice had caused "deep-seated distortions in the life of the Negro American."

Elkins's thesis provided the historical underpinnings for Department of Labor official Daniel Patrick Moynihan's controversial report, *The Negro Family: The Case for National Action* (1965). Moynihan claimed that the federal government's antipoverty programs, especially aid to unwed mothers, unwittingly replicated the cycle of dependency that had originated in slavery. A period of "salutary neglect" on the part of the federal government might spur black initiative and help reconstitute the black nuclear family.

Moynihan's report thrust Elkins into the center of the national debate over the proper role of the federal government and welfare legislation. Historians flocked to the subject, which during the 1970s elicited some of the finest works of modern American social history, including Eugene D. Genovese's, *Roll Jordan Roll: The World the Slaves Made* (1974) and Herbert G. Gutman's *The Black Family in Slavery and Freedom, 1750–1925* (1976). Genovese had been introduced to the subject while an undergraduate at Brooklyn College. His teacher and early inspiration was Arthur Cole, and *Roll Jordan Roll* was consistent with the Beard-Cole view of the South as a distinct civilization whose institutions and values were irremediably at odds with the North. Genovese in particular challenged Elkins's claim as to the psychological debility of slavery. Slavery in the plantation South, Genovese countered, was in fact paternalistic and loose. It provided slaves with enough room to shape their own religious and cultural values, though in accommodation with the institution of slavery. Herbert G. Gutman made the same observation with particular reference to the slave family, which endured despite adversity. These brilliant works were succeeded by many other excellent studies challenging Elkins's thesis, including John W. Blassingame, *The Slave Community: Plantation Life in the Antebellum South* (1972), and Ann Patton Malone, *Sweet Chariot: Slave Family and Household Structure in Nineteenth-Century Louisiana* (1992). For a contrary account, focusing on the slaves' conscious resistance to the planters, see Margaret Washington Creel, *A Peculiar People: Slave Religion and Community-Culture among the Gullahs* (1988), and Norrece T. Jones, *Born a Child of Freedom, Yet a Slave: Mechanisms of Control and Strategies of Resistance in Antebellum South Carolina* (1990).

Cole's sharp criticism of the South was matched by his enthusiasm for the abolitionists. Craven and Randall's characterization of antislavery reformers as overwrought and possibly deranged moralists was supplemented by studies such as Hazel Catherine Wolf, *On Freedom's Altar: The Martyr Complex in the Abolition Movement* (1952), and Clifford S. Griffin, *The Ferment of Reform, 1830-1860* (1967). In *Means and Ends in American Abolitionism: Garrison and His Critics on Strategy and Tactics, 1834-1850* (1969), Aileen S. Kraditor defended the abolitionists for empathizing with the plight of the slaves. During the 1970s and 1980s, historians tended to regard abolitionism as an expression of the free-labor attitudes and reforming impulses of the emerging northern middle class, much as Cole had proposed, see Eric Foner, *Free Soil, Free Labor, and Free Men* (1970); Gerald Sorin, *Abolitionism: A New Perspective* (1972); and Lewis Perry, *Radical Abolitionism: Anarchy and the Government of God in Antislavery Thought* (1973).

Cole believed that antebellum reform "withered before the hot breath of war," a thesis that was confirmed in George M. Fredrickson's fine study, *The Inner Civil War: Northern Intellectuals and the Crisis of the Union* (1965). That the Civil War imparted depth and secular meaning to middle-class Americans was the subtle thesis of Anne C. Rose's *Victorian America and the Civil War* (1992).

Craven and Randall had complained of Cole's "pro-abolitionist" account of cultural backwardness in the South. That Southern white culture was distinct from Northern is best developed in Bertram Wyatt-Brown, *Southern Honor: Ethics and Behavior in the Old South* (1982). On yeoman alienation and class tensions in the South, an essential theme in Cole, see Phillip S. Paludan, *Victims: A True Story of the Civil War* (1981).

Cole's largely anecdotal account of women is supplemented by several excellent recent studies: Catherine Clinton, *The Plantation Mistress: Woman's World in the Old South* (1982); Suzanne Lebsock, *The Free Women of Petersburg: Status and Culture in a Southern Town, 1784-1860* (1984); and George C. Rable, *Civil Wars: Women and the Crisis of Southern Nationalism* (1989).

VOLUME VIII:
Allan Nevins, *The Emergence of Modern America, 1865–78*
(1927)

ALLAN NEVINS was one of the great narrative historians of the mid-twentieth century, author of *The Ordeal of the Union, The Emergence of Lincoln,* and *The War for the Union* (six volumes, 1947–59). He won Pulitzer Prizes for *Grover Cleveland* (1932) and *Hamilton Fish* (1936). A tireless researcher, Nevins founded Columbia University's Oral History Collection, and he complained about muckraking journalists whose attacks on corporate executives had been based on easily accessible court documents; his own studies on American business were derived from company archives: *John D. Rockefeller: The Heroic Age of American Enterprise* (1940) and *Ford: The Times, The Man, The Company* (1954). His volume for the *History of American Life* series, *The Emergence of Modern America* (1927), illustrated Nevins's ability to pluck delicious tidbits from disparate primary sources and arrange them in an appealing narrative.

The colorful details caught the reader's attention, so much so that their overall patterns have sometimes eluded readers and critics. In 1928, Harry Elmer Barnes wondered whether the volumes of the *History of American Life* series, lacking the coherence imposed by political chronology, served as mere social and cultural scrapbooks whose unifying elements were wholly dependent on the artistry of the author. A reviewer in the *Journal of American History* expressed similar doubts about the enterprise: "One is not even sure that there is such a thing as *American life*, or that the lives of the countless Americans are not so determined by individual adjustments as to defy any attempt to fuse them into any single pattern (*Journal of American History*, 14:4 [March 1928]). But most reviewers, these two included, concurred that Nevins had succeeded brilliantly in providing "incomparable description and analysis," better in fact than Charles and Mary Beard's more superficial *Rise of American Civilization.*

But in the following decades, the *History of American Life* series underwent considerable devaluation within the historical profession, and the glittering details and wide-ranging eclecticism of Nevins's volume often attracted the most criticism. Peter Stearns, editor of the influential *Journal of Social History,* singled out Nevins's chapter on urban life and described it as a collage whose images failed to relate to each other or to larger themes. Nevins was "bent on conveying impressions, more than on establishing a sense of structured argument" ("Old Social History and New," in *Encyclopedia of American Social History* [1993], Mary Kupiec Cayton, et al., eds.). This charge would have puzzled Nevins, who himself complained of social historians who contented themselves with the "surface currents" of human life and thereby neglected the "permanent and compelling" forces surging below ("Recent Progress of American Social History," *Journal of Economic and Business History,* vol. 1 [May 1929]).

Stearns's carefully worded indictment is nevertheless fair: Nevins did not in fact structure an argument in the manner of modern academic historians. His broad, thin coatings of detail, especially when examined close up—within paragraphs and chapters—often appear streaky; but when the reader takes in the whole of the book, it is possible to discern a fine, interpretive sheen.

And the main idea is contained in the book's title: *The Emergence of Modern America.* Nevins believed that the Civil War was formative in the creation of a modern nation for two reasons: it greatly accelerated the industrialization and urbanization of the North and Midwest; and, more important, it shattered the "patrician" aristocracy of the South and the "semifeudal set of rural ideals" that had sustained it. During the Reconstruction years of 1865-77, "the social, ethical, and intellectual codes of the South were being modernized," Nevins claimed.

When Nevins wrote about modernization, he made no explicit reference to the great nineteenth-century European theorists on the subject—Henry Maine (1822-88), Emile Durkheim (1858-1917), and Ferdinand Tonnies (1855-1936). These writers conceived of human societies as fitting into either of two types: traditional, characterized by economic stability, fixed social hierarchies, and close personal relationships; and modern, characterized by economic dynamism, status mobility, and bureaucratized personal relationships. Nevins's description of the proliferation of industrial and transportation bureaucracies, of the rise of distinctly "urban" modes of life, and of the replacement of personal contacts by vast new publishing and communications enterprises was in many ways consistent with the European theorists of modernization. But these points of convergence were fortuitous, and in many other instances, Nevins described social processes —the power of urban bosses, the intensification of ethnic divisions, the persistence of early marriage—without explaining how they promoted the emergence of a modern society. For Nevins, modernization was an organizing device—a theme—rather than a theory. Nevins's failure to tap into the insights of the nineteenth-century European sociologists was common among American scholars. Not until two decades after the publication of Nevins's volume did American sociologists wholeheartedly embrace and greatly extend modernization theory, and another decade passed before American historians followed their lead, a subject considered in further detail in the section of this essay on Arthur M. Schlesinger's *The Rise of the City.*

Nevins's discussion of the South adhered more consistently to the modernization paradigm, and this put him far ahead of nearly all of his colleagues in the historical profession. During the early twentieth century, most historians had condemned the Reconstruction of the South from 1865 through 1877 under force of Union arms. The central figures in the attack on federal Reconstruction were two prominent professors at Columbia University, John W. Burgess and William A. Dunning. In *Reconstruction and the Constitution, 1866-1876* (1902), Burgess wrote that the freed slaves were mere children utterly incapable of voting and holding office, for "a black skin means membership in a race of men which has never of itself succeeded in subjecting passion to reason, has never, therefore, created any civilization of any kind." Under Reconstruction, the South was plunged into chaos and corruption, gleefully superintended by ignorant ex-slaves and abetted by uncouth carpetbaggers and rapacious scalawags. The South was "saved" only through the efforts of the Redeemers, mounted white knights who liberated the South from the depredations of the ex-slaves and their radical friends in the federal government. Burgess and Dunning (see the latter's *Essays on the Civil War and Reconstruction* [1897]) taught and inspired scores of graduate students, who provided additional details on black misrule at the state and local level during Reconstruction.

The Burgess-Dunning indictment of Reconstruction prevailed in the public mind largely as a consequence of D. W. Griffith's *The Birth of a Nation* (1915), a triumph of cinematic art and racist caricature. Nearly as popular was Claude G. Bowers's *The Tragic Era: The Revolution After Lincoln* (1929), a fictional work that many took to be factual. "Never have American public men in responsible positions been so brutal, hypocritical, and corrupt," Bowers asserted. "The Southern people literally were put to the torture."

Nevins accepted none of this. While conceding that its "evils" were "enormous," he credited Reconstruction for initiating the modernization of the South. He praised the federal government, especially the much-maligned Freedmen's Bureau, for strengthening public education and retarding the spread of disease. The Southern economy, once cut free from the deadweight of slavery and the plantation aristocracy, began to take on a "modern color." A "new stir of prosperity" could everywhere be felt, and even Southerners, looking back on Reconstruction, had to admit that even during its "darkest days" there had been substantial progress. "Not merely the worst of the poverty but the worst of the old provincialism, aristocratic arrogance, and quarrelsomeness" were disappearing. The replacement of slave agriculture with sharecropping was not without difficulties, Nevins acknowledged, but the practice of working the land for a proportion of the yield provided ex-slaves with "a transition to independence." The rule of the freedmen was often lawless and corrupt, Nevins admitted, but their failures should not obscure the fact that "a steady process of healing and growth was going on." Indeed, a "roseate gleam" prefigured the dawn of a new era in the South, which had at last been set upon a road to the modern world; the tragedy, implicit in that it occurred in the years immediately following Nevins's chronology, was that federal troops were withdrawn in 1877, leading to widespread violence and the reimposition of white rule in the South, a "calamity which defies measurement."

Nevins's mostly positive rendering of Reconstruction was developed during the 1930s by scholars such as Francis B. Simkins and Robert H. Woody in *South Carolina During Reconstruction* (1932) and W. E. B. DuBois in *Black Reconstruction in America* (1935), but their views were largely neglected by historians. This changed during the civil rights movement of the 1950s and 1960s, which spotlighted the persistence of abject poverty and human rights abuses in the South. Many historians now challenged the Dunning-Burgess indictment of Reconstruction. In 1965, Kenneth M. Stampp emphasized the political and social benefits obtained by reformers in *The Era of Reconstruction, 1865–1877.* That same year, in *After Slavery: The Negro in South Carolina During Reconstruction, 1861–1877,* Joel Williamson found something good to say about nearly every aspect of Reconstruction. Of the corruption of the state legislatures, for example, Williamson found heartening evidence that blacks had proven as capable of "executing frauds quite as grandiose as any produced by the white community."

During the 1970s, enthusiasm for Reconstruction abated. Some scholars argued that it failed to precipitate modernization in the South, and others doubted that Reconstruction had substantially improved the position of freemen, see Joe Gray Taylor, *Louisiana Reconstructed, 1863–1877* (1974), and William C. Harris, *The Day of the Carpetbagger* (1979). Still others, most notably Leon Litwack in *Been in the Storm So Long: The Aftermath of Slavery* (1979), juxtaposed the vitality and cohesion of the black freedmen to the indifference and racism of white reformers in the federal government. Even the educational system of which Nevins approved was criticized by scholars who now saw it as an attempt to discipline and control the black labor force, see Robert C. Morris, *Reading, 'Riting, and Reconstruction* (1981), and Jacqueline Jones, *Soldiers of Light and Love: Northern Teachers and Georgia Blacks, 1865–1873* (1980).

Perhaps the most judicious assessment was Eric Foner's monumental *Reconstruction: America's Unfinished Revolution, 1863–1877* (1988). Foner conceded that Reconstruction was ultimately a failure, but given the implacable hostility of the white South, no reforms would have succeeded and far worse outcomes were possible. "Perhaps the remarkable thing about Reconstruction was not that it failed," Foner wrote, "but that it was attempted at all and survived as long as it did."

Nevins despised the Old South for being out of step with human progress; he thus supported democracy and social reform without embracing the mores and culture of freedmen, or of the white working classes. He even deplored the "lack of depth, of cultivation, and of canons of taste" among the American people more generally. For thoughtful assessments of similar issues, see Neil Harris, *Humbug: The Art of P. T. Barnum* (1973), and Karen Halttunen, *Confidence Men and Painted Women: A Study of Middle-Class Culture in America, 1830-1870* (1982). Nevins similarly complained of the "trashy" sentimental novels of E. D. E. N. Southworth and others who catered to women readers. This theme was brilliantly developed by Ann Douglas in *The Feminization of American Culture* (1977). Nevins firmly believed that modernity and cultivated taste would advance apace, an assumption that betrayed his middle-class sympathies. And if Nevins equated modernity with the rise of a middle class, this assumption was also shared by most of his readers.

VOLUME IX:
Ida M. Tarbell, *The Nationalizing of Business, 1878-98* (1936)

IDA TARBELL was in some respects an obvious choice for the *History of American Life* volume on the nation's economic development in the late nineteenth century. A self-trained historian and author of popular biographies of Napoleon, Madame Roland, and Lincoln, Tarbell had herself become a national figure with her indictment of John D. Rockefeller and Standard Oil, which appeared in *McClure's* from 1902 to 1904 and was published as *The History of the Standard Oil Company* (1904). When Tarbell described Rockefeller as a "great villain" whose "big hand reached out from nobody knew where" to steal from his competitors and "throttle their future," she was speaking from painful personal experience, for Tarbell's father, a small independent oilman, had been crushed by Rockefeller's syndicate. Rightly regarded as a highpoint of muckraking journalism, Tarbell's exposé on Standard Oil invigorated the Progressive movement by giving it a perfect target. By adding Tarbell to the roster of contributors to the *History of American Life*, Schlesinger and Fox had seemingly brought a certifiable Progressive into their progressive history of the nation.

Tarbell's volume was to appear in 1925, but she pleaded for more time, and neither of the editors could have been happy with the subsequent trajectory of Tarbell's career. In 1924, Judge Elbert H. Gary, chairman of U.S. Steel, offered Tarbell $20,000 to be his biographer. After pondering the strapped condition of her extended and dependent family, Tarbell accepted Gary's offer. *The Life of Elbert H. Gary* (1925) praised that steelman for rationalizing the industry by eliminating inefficient competitors. The *Nation* rebuked Tarbell, calling it "pathetic" and "sad" that she had "sunk to the reduction of complicated facts into simple falsehoods." Big business, Tarbell lamely suggested, had changed for the better, partly as a consequence of Progressive reforms. Tarbell followed this work with a laudatory biography of Owen Young, the chairman of General Electric.

The timing could not have been worse. By then the nation had fallen into the Great Depression, and neither big business nor the progressive reformers seemed to merit much retrospective praise. The tenor of intellectual opinion was voiced by radical critics such as Matthew Josephson, a Marxist. His *The Robber Barons; the Great American Capitalists, 1861–1901* (1934), a stinging indictment of the men who built the nation's all-too-evidently defective economy, even cited Tarbell's denunciations of Rockefeller, noting that these had come before Tarbell had "turned official apologist for famous capitalists."

Her volume in the *History of American Life,* which finally appeared when she was seventy-nine, contained some of the sharp descriptions that had established her reputation as one of the nation's foremost journalists. But she was not adept at analytical synthesis, and her clarion theme — "the triumph of industrial consolidation" — failed to reverberate amid the economic wastelands of America in the 1930s. She in fact excoriated the greed of the early industrialists but chided the nation for forgetting "the benefits it had derived" from them.

In their forward to the volume, Schlesinger and Fox gamely proposed that Tarbell's account held a "mirror up to the troubled present," but what the beholder chose to see depended on his or her politics. A conservative reviewer in the *American Historical Review* welcomed Tarbell's book for its "absence of condemnation of American institutions." *The Nation,* on the other hand, complained of Tarbell's "saintly portraits" of the Robber Barons, symptomatic of the book's "distressing shallowness."

In *The Age of Enterprise* (1942), Thomas C. Cochran and William Miller confirmed Tarbell's opinion that unscrupulous businessmen posed less of a threat to the late-nineteenth-century economy than excessive competition. The former was in fact a consequence of the latter. More forthright defenses of the captains of industry appeared during the astounding economic boom following World War II. Allan Nevins's *Study in Power: John D. Rockefeller, Industrialist and Philanthropist* (1953) rehabilitated Tarbell's early nemesis in the manner of her later writings, and a spate of similarly laudatory volumes on business leaders came from other scholars and journalists. In 1958, Hal Bridges praised the expansive vision and purposeful creativity of the early financiers and industrialists: Even the term "robber baron" was a misnomer, see "The Robber Barons Concept in American History," *Business History Review,* 32:1 (1958).

During the 1960s, the study of business history followed the lead of Alfred D. Chandler, Jr., in an entirely new direction. Where Tarbell had perfected the sharply etched description of personality and character, Chandler, in *Strategy and Structure: Chapters in the History of the American Industrial Enterprise* (1962), painstakingly delineated the economic strategies and resultant administrative structures that evolved during the early years of the great corporations. Chandler's essential theme—the expansion of the size and scope of industrial enterprises—was similar to Tarbell's in *The Nationalizing of Business,* but Chandler's knowledge of the institutional workings of the great corporations far exceeded Tarbell's. Among the important Chandlerian studies, see Glenn Porter, *The Rise of Big Business, 1860-1910* (1973), and George David Smith, *The Anatomy of a Business Strategy: Bell, Western Electric, and the Origins of the American Telephone Industry* (1985). John N. Ingham argued against the Chandlerian approach by showing the survival of small, specialized firms in his *Making Iron and Steel: Independent Mills in Pittsburgh, 1820-1920* (1991).

Chandler's focus on the top levels of management neglected the broader interpenetrations of society and the business world. On the evolution of corporate middle managers, see Oliver Zunz's provocative *Making America Corporate: 1870-1920* (1990). On the ways in which technology transformed the structures and interpretation of daily life, see David E. Nye, *Electrifying America: Social Meanings of a New Technology, 1880-1940* (1990).

VOLUME X:
Arthur M. Schlesinger, Sr., *The Rise of the City: 1878-98* (1933)

ARTHUR M. SCHLESINGER had studied under Charles A. Beard at Columbia, and was no doubt wounded by his mentor's review of *The Rise of the City* in the *American Historical Review.* After praising Schlesinger's ability to evoke the period for those who had lived through it, Beard ripped *The Rise of the City* for lacking an interpretive edge.

> Apparently [Schlesinger] thinks interpretations are wrong, that none is possible, and that impressionistic eclecticism is the only resort of contemporary scholarship. He may be right. But that, too, is an interpretation, with profound philosophic implications. . . . We may shut our eyes to the abyss of thought that yawns devouringly at our feet, so perilous; the abyss remains. (*American Historical Review,* vol. 38, 4 [July 1933])

Beard's searing rebuke made sense in the summer of 1933, when the nation was mired in the deepest sloughs of the Great Depression. The economy had collapsed, and the political system had proven powerless to prevent its demise or to rebuild it. Radical nostrums filled the air. In this supercharged political climate, the *History of American Life*'s focus on *life*—"with the politics left out," as some put it—seemed hopelessly wrongheaded. Moreover, Schlesinger's faith in modern institutions appeared completely at odds with the great social and economic calamity that had befallen the nation. Beard's voice, which resonated with the anxieties of the nation, rang out loud and true.

But in recent years, as the culture wars have nearly displaced politics in our national debates, Schlesinger's preoccupation with cultural change no longer seems irrelevant. And Schlesinger's thesis goes to the heart of contemporary concerns: the role of the city in modern life; the challenge of retaining order amid cultural diversity; the meaning of modernity to groups fearful of change. (See, for example, Terrence J. McDonald, "Theory and Practice in the 'New' History: Rereading Arthur Meier Schlesinger's *The Rise of the City, 1878-1898*," in *Reviews in American History*, 20:3 (September 1992).

Schlesinger concurred with Beard on the primacy of economic forces in historical causation, but Schlesinger chose to focus on their cultural rather than political ramifications. His strategy had long been in conceptualization. As early as 1923, Schlesinger freed up space in his volume by persuading Ida Tarbell to take on the period's economic developments, a break with the sequential format of the *History of American Life*. He was surely mindful of criticisms that Allan Nevins's 1927 volume, *The Emergence of Modern America*, lacked a sharp argument. Where Nevins had expansively described modernity as a product of myriad forces that touched all walks of life, Schlesinger devised a simpler and more powerful analytical device: the city as both the carrier and embodiment of modernity.

In so doing, Schlesinger hoped to influence, simultaneously, two major intellectual debates. The first had been joined by nineteenth-century European intellectuals who believed that urban life bred alienation. In *Gemeinschaft und Gesellschaft* ("Community and Society," 1887) the German sociologist Ferdinand Tonnies contrasted the emotionally rich ties of tribal and peasant communities to the stiff formal bonds of industrial societies. A decade later, the French sociologist Emile Durkheim concluded in *Suicide* (1898) that urban-industrial economies failed to integrate the self and society; left increasingly to their own—and woefully inadequate—psychic resources, urban dwellers more frequently fell victim to suicide, insanity, or other forms of social dislocation. In 1928, these ideas culminated in Oswald Spengler's *The Decline of the West*, which bemoaned the artificiality and "soullessness" of the great modern city.

The second (though related) debate that occupied Schlesinger was Frederick Jackson Turner's famous thesis that America's distinctively egalitarian and democratic culture had been a product of the (now vanishing) frontier. Schlesinger sought to pull progressive history away from Turner's rueful nostalgia. By focusing on urbanization, Schlesinger sought to reclaim the relevance of progressive history to the modern world. These ideas—the benefits of urban culture and their salience to the modern world—pervaded *The Rise of the City,* but they can be examined with particular reference to three themes: the essential *modernity* of urban culture; the city's role in promoting *assimilation and advancement;* and the evolution in urban life of agencies of meaningful social *reform.*

Schlesinger had grown up in Xenia, Ohio, the son of immigrant parents, and he harbored no romantic illusions about small-town life, whose bigotry and provinciality had become evident during the 1920s, a decade that all too often witnessed Ku Klux Klan cross-burnings, harsh laws restricting immigration, and the absurd prosecution of Darwinian teachings in the Scopes "monkey trial" in Dayton, Tennessee. When H. L. Mencken denounced "this glorious commonwealth of morons," he was referring, usually, to the denizens of its small towns and rural villages. Schlesinger was sympathetic to Mencken, and *The Rise of the City* constituted an astonishingly vehement indictment of rural life and culture. People abandoned the country for the city for good reason, Schlesinger wrote, and his evocation of "rural decay" was vivid: "cellar holes choked with lilac and woodbine, tumbledown buildings, scrubby orchards, pastures bristling with new forest growths, perhaps a lone rosebush" and other "mute, pathetic memorials" of once busy farming communities. When describing urban life, on the other hand, Schlesinger's lyricism soared, as when he described the "untold numbers" of people for whom the city "meant the attainment of a new Promised Land, the release of energies and ambitions which the constricted opportunities of the farm had always denied." Schlesinger hypothesized that the "less enterprising" people remained on the farm, where men of ability were often "starved in rural isolation." But those with "push and initiative" customarily ventured to the city where, in close contact with different people and values, they might find "sympathy, encouragement, and that criticism which often refines talent into genius." The city dweller perhaps longed for the neighborliness of rural life, but he found in the city "a spirit of social responsibility" that caused him to seek the betterment of all mankind. During the late nineteenth century, cities became "the generating center for social and intellectual progress."

The Rise of the City constituted the foundation text for urban history, and a generation of scholars applied Schlesinger's positivist conception of urban culture to a variety of historical contexts. (See, for example, Richard C. Wade's *The Urban Frontier: Pioneer Life in Early Pittsburgh, Cincinnati, Lexington, Louisville, and St. Louis* [1959], which argued that the proto-cities of the frontier "gave a stimulus and sophistication to a young, raw society"; note, too, Wade's acknowledgment of Schlesinger's influence.) During the 1940s and 1950s, Schlesinger's thesis received indirect support from American sociologists, many of whom followed Talcott Parsons in his flight from European sociology's forebodings about modernity. Parsons concurred with Tonnies and Durkheim that modern societies tended toward stratification and differentiation, but he regarded this process as a salutary accommodation of the self to a dynamic form of social organization. Rural, folk communities inhabited a lower, inferior plane in human affairs, much as Schlesinger's prose seemed to suggest.

Postwar suburbanization challenged Schlesinger's abiding faith in urban life, and the accelerated migration of rural blacks to the cities of the North and Midwest magnified racial tensions. The city's capacity for integrating diversity and exploiting human potential seemed to have been overestimated. In *The Uprooted* (1951), Oscar Handlin proposed, in words echoing Tonnies and Durkheim, that nineteenth-century city life shattered the foreign immigrant's values and sense of self; the city did not assimilate the newcomer, but subjected him to a remorseless process of deracination. In *Poverty and Progress: Social Mobility in a Nineteenth-Century City* (1964), another Harvard historian, Stephan A. Thernstrom, provided statistical proof that the overwhelming majority of the inhabitants of nineteenth-century Newburyport failed to climb more than a rung or two up the ladder of success, and many had slipped and fallen. If such people had come to the cities hoping to find, as Schlesinger put it, "a new Promised Land," most were badly disappointed.

In subsequent decades, many scholars followed Handlin and Thernstrom in suggesting that modern urban-industrial life had been purchased at a terrible price. On the emotional costs to workers and immigrants, see Francis G. Couvares, *The Remaking of Pittsburgh: Class and Culture in an Industrializing City, 1877–1919* (1984); Oliver Zunz, *The Changing Face of Inequality: Urbanization, Industrial Development, and Immigrants in Detroit, 1880–1920* (1982); and Alan Dawley, *Class and Community: The Industrial Revolution in Lynn* (1976). In *Families Against the City: Middle-Class Homes of Industrial Chicago, 1872–1890* (1970), Richard Sennett found that even middle-class families were overstrained by the emotional burdens of life in modern cities. Talcott Parsons had failed to see that the tightly nuclear and differentiated "modern" family was incompatible with modern urbanization. And Schlesinger, by extension, had embraced the exuberant freedom and manifest challenge of urban life without adequately reflecting on its shortcomings.

Scholars who were sympathetic to the ethnic revival of the 1970s attacked Schlesinger from the opposite vantage point. They maintained that city culture, and even modernization, possessed neither the assimilative powers Schlesinger had presupposed, nor the corrosive ones described by Handlin. Immigrants in large measure re-created peasant values and mores within nineteenth-century American cities. That "premodern" ethnic cultures and social bonds were astonishingly resilient was the thesis of works such as Humbert S. Nelli, *Italians in Chicago, 1880–1930: A Study in Ethnic Mobility* (1970), and John Bodnar, *The Transplanted: A History of Immigrants in Urban America (1985).*

"Modernization" historians staked out yet another position, and it differed markedly from the other two. The late-nineteenth-century city was not dysfunctional, they insisted, for it operated smoothly within the parameters set by the elites who built it. Some ethnic and working-class enclaves might for a time escape its pervading influence, but this would require heroic effort. An early and influential work in this vein was Robert Wiebe's *The Search for Order, 1877-1920* (1967), which described how the tendrils of corporate and administrative bureaucracies overspread the nation. This was in some ways analogous to Schlesinger's description of the advance of urbanization, but where Schlesinger believed that the power of the city derived from the stimulating cooperation of the people within, Wiebe regarded bureaucracies as the salient feature of modernity. In *The Incorporation of America: Culture and Society in the Gilded Age* (1982), Alan Trachtenberg examined the cultural implications of Wiebe's insight. Within the past decade, historians of sports have seized upon a modernization paradigm to explain the early evolution of professional teams, leagues, rules, and marketing systems; see, for example, Melvin L. Adelman, *A Sporting Time: New York City and the Rise of Modern Athletics, 1820-70* (1986), and Allen Guttmann, *From Ritual to Record: The Nature of Modern Sports* (1978).

Schlesinger approved of most of the substantial cultural innovations of the late nineteenth century: museums, public libraries, compulsory schools for the young, newspapers and magazines, opera and the theater—all of which thrived chiefly in cities and functioned to promote human betterment, or so Schlesinger fixedly believed. But in the past two decades some historians have insisted that such institutions helped ruling classes impose their values upon workers and immigrants, and thereby made them easier to control. In *Cultural Excursions: Marketing Appetites and Cultural Tastes in Modern America* (1990), Neil Harris described how impressive marble museums and opera houses, and well-ordered libraries and retail stores, inevitably devalued the simpler institutions—taverns, amusement parks, or even the streets themselves—that figured so prominently in the lives of workers and immigrants. See also Helen L. Horowitz, *Culture and City: Cultural Philanthropy in Chicago from the 1880s to 1917* (1976), and Roy Rosenzweig and Elizabeth Blackmar, *The Park and the People: A History of Central Park* (1992).

But scholars in recent years often lament the demise of museums, opera houses, and symphony orchestras, and demand the restoration of public funds for parks and libraries. At a time when public agencies are incapable of merely perpetuating institutions that had been created a century ago, the tangible achievements of the institution-builders of the late nineteenth century cannot be denied. Historians of immigration and ethnicity, after initially accepting the "assimilationist" paradigm of Schlesinger and others, and then an opposed "ethnicity forover" paradigm in the 1970s and 1980s, have now moved back to a somewhat more complex version of assimilationism, see Eva Morawski, "The Sociology and Historiography of Immigration," in Virginia Yans-McLaughlin, ed., *Immigration Reconsidered: History, Sociology, and Politics* (1990). And as the generation that grew up in the postwar suburbs approaches maturity, it has often rediscovered the truth of Schlesinger's main insight—the vitality of the city.

VOLUME XI:
Harold U. Faulkner, *The Quest for Social Justice, 1899-1914*

HAVING BEEN BORN IN 1890, the year that witnessed passage of the Sherman Antitrust Act, and having been a graduate student at Columbia University during the heyday of progressivism, Faulkner looked at the progressive era close up and with a sympathetic eye. Its towering achievements filled his vision—its campaigns against the slums, the exploitation of workers and women and children, the crippling accidents in mines and industry, the "liquor evil and adulterated foods," the corrupt bosses and inefficient government. Although his emphasis on social and political reform—on thinking of the period as a "Progressive era"—was somewhat at odds with the "everyday life" thrust of the *History of American Life* series as a whole, his focus on reform was consistent with the views of most historians before and since. Avery Craven, a harsh critic of other volumes in the series (see, for example, his response to Cole) thought Faulkner's "superior" because it took a "broader view" of the relation of everyday life to politics and government *(New York Herald Tribune Books,* September 20, 1931).

The Quest for Social Justice was progressive history as most of the Progressives would have wished it; Faulkner refined and consolidated Benjamin Parke DeWitt's *The Progressive Movement* (1915), an account that linked contemporary reformers with the Jeffersonians, Jacksonians, abolitionists, and populists—representatives of the people against special, private interests. In *Main Currents of American Thought* (1927-30), Vernon Louis Parrington similarly posited a continuity in the ideas of prominent reformers throughout the nineteenth and early twentieth century. Charles and Mary Beard's chapter on the period in *The Rise of American Civilization* (1927), entitled "Towards Social Democracy," anticipated the thrust of Faulkner's *Quest for Social Justice.* But while the Beards referred to the battles fought in "a thousand obscure corners"—city councils, women's clubs, grange conferences—they fastened their narrative onto the careers of Presidents Theodore Roosevelt and Woodrow Wilson, "the most dynamic [personalities] raised to high authority since the age of Andrew Jackson."

Faulkner acknowledged that the political initiatives wrought by Roosevelt, Wilson, Tom Johnson, and Robert La Follette constituted an "extraordinary advance" in American public life, and he dutifully detailed their agendas and accomplishments, but he insisted that these leaders succeeded not because of their greatness but because they represented "the aspirations of the common man." The quest for social justice had been undertaken by politicians and social reformers, of course, but also by inventors and mechanics, teachers and social theorists, clergymen and journalists, trade union officials and corporate executives. A spirit of reform was in the air, and nearly everyone breathed of it deeply. Faulkner's encomnia to the progressives were summarized in the book's final words: This generation's "constant effort at reform had made the nation a better place to live in for the common man."

The chief difficulty with Faulkner's book, as with several others in the *History of American Life,* was its timing, for when it appeared in October 1931, some 12 million of these common men lacked jobs, and as winter set in many had also abandoned hope. Several months later, John Chamberlain's *Farewell to Reform: The Rise, Life and Decay of the Progressive Mind in America* (1932) offered a bitter rebuttal to Faulkner, and to the progressive mind-set in general. Chamberlain maintained that while the reformers imagined they were striding into the future, marching to the brisk cadence of the "New Freedoms," the "New Nationalisms," or some other up-tempo progressive beat, they had actually stumbled backward into the "primitive capitalism of our fathers." The progressives' inability to respond to the modern world—characterized by the consolidation of gigantic economic processes under corporate auspices—ensured that their reforms would fail. Thus, by the onset of the Depression, the power of the trusts remained unchecked, and the fledgling apparatus of the federal government was vulnerable to takeover by syndicalism or fascism.

Chamberlain's insistence on the *backward* character of the progressives was amplified by a spate of books that described the movement's origins within traditional agrarian protest. John D. Hicks, *The Populist Revolt* (1931); C. Vann Woodward, *The Origins of the New South, 1877-1913* (1951); and Russel B. Nye, *Midwestern Progressive Politics* (1951) linked twentieth-century progressives to the populists of the late nineteenth century, and described both movements as popular protests, especially among farmers, against the political and economic power of transportation companies, banks, and other great corporations, a theme as old as the republic itself.

But while agrarian protests had nearly always followed on the heels of agricultural depression, the progressive movement gained momentum during the mostly prosperous years of the early twentieth century. Seizing on this inconsistency, George E. Mowry found that much of the support for the progressive movement came in fact from small businessmen and independent professionals who lived in towns and cities. Well educated and often comfortable financially, this middle class resented the encroachments of the great corporations and the large unions, see *The California Progressives* (1951) and *The Era of Theodore Roosevelt* (1958).

Economic resentments failed to account for the breadth and depth of progressive sentiment in these prosperous times. A more powerful psychological explanation was required, and Columbia historian Richard Hofstadter provided it in his remarkable *The Age of Reform: From Bryan to F.D.R.* (1955). The unthinking fears McCarthyism had evoked during the seemingly untroubled early 1950s provided Hofstadter with an analogue for psychological perturbations of the progressives. Hofstadter contended that middle-class businessmen and professionals were plagued by "status anxiety" over the demise of individual achievement and personal responsibility. They attempted to restore "familiar and traditional ideals" to a vastly changed world, and their nostrums were as old-fashioned as their goals. The progressive movement lacked coherent strategy and clear focus, and dissipated its efforts on moralistic, retrograde crusades such as prohibition, eugenics, and immigration control.

Hofstadter concurred with Faulkner and the progressive historians that the real villain of the early twentieth century was the giant corporation, but in Hofstadter's view the reformers merely swirled about him with Lilliputian frenzy, hurling menacing taunts, binding him up with string, and then fleeing in terror when he broke loose during the 1920s and hurled the nation into the Great Depression. Hofstadter contrasted the cranky, ineffectual moralism of the Progressives with the purposeful pragmatism of FDR's New Deal, crediting the latter with laying the solid foundation for the nation's postwar, bipartisan political consensus.

That consensus evaporated during the 1960s. Among historians, widespread disillusionment with persistent racial inequality and the war in Vietnam coalesced into a radical critique of early-twentieth-century America. The Progressive reformers had failed to control the big corporation because they had desired to use it for their own ends. The radicals contended that Faulkner and the progressive historians were dead wrong, but so, too, was nearly everyone else who had to that point written on the subject. For example, in *Conservation and the Gospel of Efficiency* (1959), Samuel P. Hays described how Theodore Roosevelt's administration supported the large extractive corporations in an attempt to rationalize the utilization of natural resources. In *The Triumph of Conservatism* (1963), Gabriel Kolko further contended that corporate planners in many industries helped create, and eventually seized control of, the regulatory mechanisms of the state so as to limit competition and ensure high profits.

By the 1970s, all that remained of the early, enthusiastic interpretation of progressivism was the movement's opposition to corrupt urban bosses, but even this shred of Faulkner's banner was ripped down by John D. Buenker, who, in *Urban Liberalism and Progressive Reform* (1973), found that the bosses, backed by immigrant constituencies, provided vital support for many progressive initiatives.

Rich or poor, city dweller or farmer, trustbuster or corporate executive, Anglo Saxon Protestant or immigrant Catholic—everybody, it seemed, was a progressive; and the progressive movement, being everything, ceased to mean much of anything, as Peter G. Filene pointed out in "An Obituary for 'The Progressive Movement," *American Quarterly,* vol. 22 (1970). By the 1980s, Daniel T. Rodgers observed, most historians ceased debating the essence of the progressive world—"an era of shifting, ideologically fluid, issue-focused coalitions"—and concentrated on understanding its context. What impressed Rodgers was that throughout the welter of causes and objectives, the era's language and rhetorical strategies persisted with few modifications, see his "In Search of Progressivism," in Stanley I. Kutler and Stanley N. Katz, eds., *Reviews in American History: The Promise of American History* (1982). Rodgers's sophisticated analysis of language was far beyond anything Faulkner or any other progressive historian could have undertaken, but Faulkner's elegiac evocation of the era's "spirit of reform" —a phrase he employed frequently, much to the irritation of such hard-headed realists as John Chamberlain and such demanding social scientists as Richard Hofstadter—in some ways resonates with Rodgers's notion of the progressive era "as users rather than shapers of ideas":

> To think of progressive social thought in this way is to emphasize the active, dynamic aspect of ideas. It is also to admit, finally, that progressivism as an ideology is nowhere to be found.

VOLUME XII:
Preston Slosson, *The Great Crusade and After, 1914–28* (1930)

THE "NEW SOCIAL HISTORIANS" of the 1960s often derided the *History of American Life* volumes, failing to appreciate the historical profession's early skepticism toward social history of any sort. For instance, the 1930 review of *The Great Crusade and After, 1914–1928,* in the *New York Times Book Review,* scored Slosson for omitting "a surprisingly large number of subjects which . . . have been front-page news in every important metropolitan journal and have been seriously debated in business or political circles": the war debts settlements; the debate over the League of Nations; the problems of railways and inland waterways; Coolidge's intervention in the Boston police strike. Of these "larger and deeper things," the reviewer observed, Slosson had written little or nothing, but had instead exhibited a "curious" fascination for the motor car and crime, women and fashion, architecture and housing, music and religion, and similar topics that "do not need much elucidation or discussion to make their immediate significance clear" (topics, the modern social historian must interject, that have each been the subject of scores of scholarly monographs).

A month after this review, Allan Nevins came to Slosson's defense in *The Saturday Review of Literature* (December 20, 1930), albeit in a qualified way. Slosson's book was of "great immediate value," characterized by "scope, color and scholarliness." But in words that anticipated modern criticism of his own volume (see essay in this section), Nevins complained that Slosson saw fit to record facts rather than interpret them, and particularly, that he failed to draw "important sociological conclusions" from his abundant materials. Nevins also criticized Slosson for neglecting the extraordinary advances of the chemical industry (a subject that, nearly two thirds of a century later, has remained obscure).

Slosson's main theme was perhaps dictated by Schlesinger and Fox's decision to include the years from 1914 through 1918—the Great War—as the beginning of his volume, which continued through the 1920s, rather than as the culmination of a volume beginning in 1898 on the progressive era. Slosson accordingly proposed that the crusade of the Great War eclipsed the domestic reforms of the progressive era, and that the decade of the 1920s was characterized by resolute (and remarkably self-conscious) attempts to enjoy oneself rather than improve the lives of others. But Slosson insisted that the twenties also witnessed the marked advance of some progressive causes and objectives: the elevation of the status of women; the improvement of prisons and insane asylums; the widespread extension of secondary education; the "enormous reduction in pauperism"; and the increase in savings as a consequence of Prohibition. It seems that Slosson—a professor at the University of Michigan; a member of the American Civil Liberties Union, American Association of University Professors, and United World Federalists; and the author of over a dozen books chronicling the far grimmer fate of liberalism in Europe—was evidently unwilling to take a dark view of recent American institutions. Schlesinger and Fox, in their introduction to the volume, remarked on Slosson's generally sympathetic judgment of the period, "a wholesome antidote to much that has been written of these years."

The editors' sanguine sentiments, appearing about six months after the stock market crash and just as the cracks in the financial system were widening into the chasm of the Great Depression, did not long prevail. In the next year came Frederick Lewis Allen's, *Only Yesterday: An Informal History of the 1920's* (1931), which rebuked those who, like Slosson, looked approvingly upon the decade. He insisted that the Great War had cast a dark shadow of disillusionment upon the subsequent decade; people seemed to acknowledge that "life was futile and nothing much mattered," and they became absorbed in "tremendous trifles" such as mah-jongg, jazz, crossword puzzles, and other fads. Their blindness to the looming tragedy of the Great Depression rendered their desperately frenetic amusements all the more pathetic. For many readers, *Only Yesterday's* interpretation of their own times rang true; it became a Book-of-the-Month Club selection and quickly sold more than 67,000 copies. By the 1970s, nearly a million copies were in print.

In *The Growth of the American Republic* (1937), Samuel Eliot Morison and Henry Steele Commager added a political gloss to Allen's pessimistic cultural assessment: The 1920s, like the years following the Civil War, were a period of conservatism, an era in which people were "weary of reform and disillusioned by the crusade of democracy." These beliefs—of cultural excess and political reaction—took firm root among historians and political scientists during the 1940s and 1950s, see, for example, F. L. Paxson, *Post War Years: Normalcy, 1918-1933* (1948). The most important restatement of the thesis was Arthur M. Schlesinger, Jr.'s, *The Crisis of the Old Order, 1919-1933* (1957), which described the 1920s as a time when rural America dug in "for its rearguard stand" and the "cult of business' became almost a secular religion. In *Strangers in the Land: Patterns of American Nativism, 1860-1925* (1955), John Higham similarly described the "tribal twenties" and its attempts to "close the gates" of immigration. That same year, Richard Hofstadter's *The Age of Reform* concluded that the decade was significant only as an "entr-acte," a defensive reassertion of traditional values bracketed by more consequential eras of Progressive and New Deal reform.

In *The Perils of Prosperity* (1958), William Leuchtenburg challenged these harsh assessments of the twenties. In repudiation of Allen he wrote that there was "a great deal more to the era than raccoon coats and bathtub gin," and in response to those who had dismissed the twenties as retrogressively conservative, he acknowledged that while the nation "fell far short" of solving problems of state authority, industrial concentration, mass culture, and secularization, it had not done much worse than subsequent eras. Leuchtenburg's views in this respect were not far removed from Slosson's (one of Slosson's chapters was even entitled "The Perils of Prosperity"), but Slosson did not have Leuchtenburg's long perspective. American society, Leuchtenburg explained, had undergone a half century of industrialization and urbanization, and during the 1920s "all of the institutions of American society buckled under the strain," chiefly manifested by a persistent progressivism in the cities, and rearguard traditionalism in the countryside. (This thesis can be regarded as a logical continuation of Schlesinger's *The Rise of the City* [see essay in this section]).

Leuchtenburg's balanced assessment has in large measure endured, although some scholars have challenged his identifying the city with positive change and the countryside with conservative reaction. Scholars have pointed out that during these years farm communities often articulated farsighted reforms while cities gave rise to backward politics, as Kenneth T. Jackson showed in *The Ku Klux Klan in the City, 1915-1930* (1967).

Both Slosson and Frederick Lewis Allen disapproved of the era's gaudy materialism, and in the past two decades leftist scholars have indicted advertising and consumerism as part of a "cultural hegemony" that ensured high demand and sustained corporate profits but failed to satisfy real wants and needs, see, for example, Roland Marchand, *Advertising the American Dream: Making Way for Modernity, 1920-1940* (1985), and T. J. Jackson Lears, *Fables of Abundance: A Cultural History of Advertising* (1995). That consumption could add depth and richness to human experience was a theme of Warren I. Susman's *Culture as History: The Transformation of American Society in the Twentieth Century* (1984).

Slosson's depiction of the advance of middle-class women, especially their gains in economic dependence, sexual freedom, and politics, is thoughtfully summarized in Rosalind Rosenberg, *Divided Lives: American Women in the Twentieth Century* (1992); see also Christine A. Lunardini, *From Equal Suffrage to Equal Rights: Alice Paul and the National Woman's Party, 1910-1928* (1986), and Susan D. Becker, *The Origins of the Equal Rights Amendment: American Feminism Between the Wars* (1981). For the development of youth culture, see Paula Fass, *The Damned and the Beautiful: American Youth in the 1920s* (1977); Helen Lefkowitz Horowitz, *Campus Life: Undergraduate Cultures from the End of the Eighteenth Century to the Present* (1987); and Beth Bailey, *From Front Porch to Back Seat: Courtship in Twentieth-Century America* (1988). No volume in the *History of American Life* series mentioned gays or lesbians. In *Gay New York: Gender, Urban Culture, and the Making of the Gay Male World, 1890-1940* (1994), George Chauncey powerfully delineated a complex and surprisingly public gay culture that peaked during the 1920s.

Notes

Introduction

1. Finley Peter Dunne, *Observations by Mr. Dooley* (New York, 1902), 271.
2. George M. Frederickson, "What Is the New History?" *Dissent,* Summer 1991; David Thelen, "A Round Table: What Has Changed and Not Changed in American Historical Practice," *Jour. of Am. Hist.,* September 1989; Joyce Appleby, Lynn Hunt, and Margaret Jacob, *Telling the Truth about History* (New York, 1994), 154; K. J. Winkler, "Encyclopedia of U.S. Social History Marks the Field's Coming of Age," *Chronicle of Higher Education,* January 20, 1993; Lawrence W. Levine, "Clio, Canons, and Culture," *Jour. of Am. Hist.,* December 1933.
3. Edward Eggleston, "The New History," *Annual Report of the American Historical Association for the Year 1900* (Washington, 1901), I, 39, 44, 47. Emphasis added.
4. James Harvey Robinson, *The New History* (New York, 1912), Chaps. i and iii; the Mathiez quote is from Harvey Wish's introduction to the 1965 paperback edition.
5. Arthur M. Schlesinger, "Oral History" (Columbia Oral History Office, 1960), 1199–1200.
6. Ibid., 1201.
7. Arthur M Schlesinger, *New Viewpoints in American History* (New York, 1922), ix.
8. See Sidney Ahlstrom's comment: "Schlesinger, whose pivotal essays 'The Significance of the City in American History' and 'The Critical Period in American Religion,' along with countless other works which he wrote, edited, or inspired, made him a major figure in America's rediscovery of the city as a vital factor in its religious history. Nor is this tribute sufficient, for Schlesinger also played a major role in the revival of concern for the history of immigration and ethnic minorities. (Ahlstrom, *A Religious History of the American People* [New Haven, 1972], 11.) Or A. Hunter Dupree: "To make a roll of Schlesinger's students, and of the students of Schlesinger's students, who have made contributions to the history of American science is to draw up an incomplete but quite representative bibliography of the subject over the last two decades." Dupree's list, in his paper on "The History of American Science—A Field Finds Itself" at the American Historical Association meeting in 1964, produced the equivalent of twenty-three books by ten students and nine students of students.
9. Schlesinger, "Oral History," 1220–22, 1265.

10. See, for example, Appleby, Hunt, and Jacob, *Telling the Truth about History,* 146.
11. Vernon L. Parrington, "The Culture Americans Have Created," *N.Y. Herald Tribune Books,* January 29, 1928.
12. Allen Sinclair Will, "Our Historians Cut Some Capers," *N.Y. Times Book Review,* February 19, 1928.
13. The quotations regarding the editing of the series are from Schlesinger, "Oral History," 1230-1164.
14. Carl Becker to Dixon Ryan Fox, July 20, 1943, Macmillan *History of American Life* files.
15. *N.Y. Times Book Review,* January 5, 1930.
16. *American Historical Review,* April 1928.
17. *New Republic,* March 31, 1928.
18. Carl Becker to Dixon Ryan Fox, July 20, 1943, Macmillan *History of American Life* files.
19. *N.Y. World,* December 26, 1927.
20. *N.Y. Times,* January 2, 1944.
21. *N.Y. Times Book Review,* January 7, 1945.
22. *American Historical Review,* July 1928.
23. *Political Science Quart.,* June 1928.
24. *American Historical Review,* January 1935.
25. *American Jour. of Soc.,* November 1934.
26. *N.Y. Times Book Review,* April 1, 1934.
27. *N.Y. Herald Tribune Books,* January 29, 1928.
28. *New Republic,* March 21, 1928.
29. *American Historical Review,* April 1928.
30. *Social Education,* January 1937.
31. See this volume, Book X, 873.
32. *Nation,* March 1, 1933.
33. *New Republic,* July 5, 1933.
34. *American Historical Review,* July 1933.
35. Terrence J. McDonald, "Theory and Practice in the 'New' History: Rereading Arthur Meier Schlesinger's *The Rise of the City, 1878-1898*," *Reviews in American History,* September 1992.
36. Ibid., 442.
37. Charles A Beard, "Written History as an Act of Faith," *American Historical Review,* January 1934; reprinted in Hans Meyerhoff, ed., *The Philosophy of History in Our Time* (New York, 1959), esp. 141.
38. Beard to Schlesinger, July 12, [1933]; Schlesinger to Beard, July 20, 1933; Beard to Schlesinger, August 3, [1933]—Schlesinger Papers, Harvard Archives.
39. *American Historical Review,* October 1931.
40. *N.Y. Herald Tribune Books,* September 20, 1931.
41. *N.Y. Herald Tribune Books,* October 19, 1930.
42. *Saturday Review of Literature,* December 20, 1930.
43. *N.Y. Times Book Review,* December 16, 1930.
44. Schlesinger, "Oral History," 1265-66.
45. Carl Bridenbaugh, "The Genesis of Our Pattern," *N.Y. Times Book Review,* January 7, 1945.
46. Schlesinger, "Oral History," 1214-18.
47. W. E. Lingelbach, ed., *Approaches to American Social History* (New York, 1937), 31, 79, 34-35, 41, 84, 100-101.
48. George Steiner, "Cornucopia," *New Yorker,* September 14, 1987.
49. Robert Darnton, "Intellectual and Cultural History" in Michael Kammen, ed., *The Past Before Us: Contemporary Historical Writing in the United States* (Ithaca, N.Y., 1980), 334.
50. Peter N. Stearns, "Teaching Social History: An Update," American Historical Association, *Perspectives,* October 1989.

51. See Arthur M. Schlesinger, Jr., "Intellectual History: A Time for Despair?," *Jour. of Am. Hist.,* March 1980.
52. Richard Hofstadter, "History and Sociology in the United States," in S. M. Lipset and Richard Hofstadter, eds., *Sociology and History: Methods* (New York, 1968), 8.
53. McDonald, "Theory and Practice," 435.
54. Stearns, "Teaching Social History."
55. Thomas Bender, "The New History—Then and Now," *Reviews in American History,* December 1984, 619.
56. Samuel P. Hays, "A Systematic Social History," in G. A. Billias and G. N. Grob, eds., *American History: Retrospect and Prospect* (New York, 1971), 315-16.
57. David Cannadine, "The Way We Lived Then," *Times Literary Supplement,* September 7-13, 1990, and "What Is Social History?" in Juliet Gardiner, ed., *What Is History Today?* (London, 1988), 56.
58. Lawrence Veysey, "The 'New' Social History," *Reviews in American History,* March 1979, 5.
59. Alice Kessler-Harris, "Social History," in Eric Foner, ed., *The New American History* (Philadelphia, 1990), 164.
60. Olivier Zunz, ed., *Reliving the Past: The Worlds of Social History* (Chapel Hill, 1985), 3-4.

BOOK I   The Coming of the White Man, 1492–1848

1. "Cartas de Eugenio Salazar," Fernández Duro, *Disquisiciones Náuticas,* II, 178-200.
2. Ibid., VI, 611.
3. A. de Herrera, *Historia General de los Hechos de los Castellanos* (Madrid, 1601), I, 83-84.
4. J. López de Velasco, *Geografía y Descripción Universal de las Indias* (Madrid, 1894), 37, 91, 337. A hundred years later the total population of English America scarcely exceeded 160,000. Cf. also French and Dutch America treated later.
5. For an excellent article on this subject, see J. A. Robertson, "Some Notes on the Transfer by Spain of Plants and Animals to Its Colonies Overseas," *James Sprunt Hist. Studies,* XIX, 7-21.
6. Puente y Olea, *Los Trabajos Geográficos de la Casa de Contratación,* 375. Much in the following pages is based on Puente, 374-446.
7. Bernabé Cobo, *Historia del Nuevo Mundo* (Seville, 1890-93), II, 406-407. The first geranium in Peru grew six feet tall. Rosemary was cherished in that region as a reminder of home.
8. Francisco López de Gómara, *Historia de México* (Antwerp, 1554), 342; Puente y Olea, *Los Trabajos Geográficos de la Casa de Contratación,* 422.
9. The advent of the horse upon the continent would have had a greater effect upon the social development of the sedentary Indians had it not been for the legal prohibition against their use by the natives. On the nomadic frontiers the ready adaptation of the native tribes to the new mode of travel meant more effective resistance to the whites as well as a more ample food supply. The white man also brought the wheel, greatest of artifacts in the evolution of social economy, but it cannot be said that the aborigines have yet risen to the capacity of using it as effectively as those who introduced it.
10. Pedro de Mendoza, abandoning Buenos Aires, where he settled in 1535, turned loose five mares and seven horses; by the end of the century their progeny overran the country down to the Straits of Magellan. By 1600 uncounted droves of them had overrun the plains and made their way into the mountains. See W. S. Barclay, *The Land of Magellan* (London, 1926), 106.
11. José de Acosta, *The Naturall and Morall Historie of the East and West Indies* (London, 1604), 299.

12. Cobo, *Historia del Nuevo Mundo,* II, 344. A. L. P. P. de Candolle says (in our opinion rather loosely) that of 247 plants cultivated in America, 199 originated in the Old World, forty-five in America, and one in Australia, while the native habitat of two cannot be determined. *Origine des Plantes cultivées* (Paris, 1883), cited by Robertson, "Some Notes," 20.

13. When in 1665 the eight English proprietors received their grant to territory between the parallels thirty-one and thirty-six and "from sea to sea," the Spaniards already had within the area some twenty-five missions serving ninety villages, Santa Fé had a population of 1,000 persons, and the province of New Mexico an effective military and civil government. See the map in H. E. Bolton and Mary A. Ross, *The Debatable Land* (Berkeley, 1925), opp. 32.

14. Authoritative and convenient outlines of the northward movements are in C. E. Chapman, *The Founding of Spanish California* (New York, 1916), chaps. ii–iii; C. W. Hackett, *Historical Documents Relating to New Mexico* (Washington, 1923–26), I, 10–19, II, 3–82; J. L. Mecham, *Francisco de Ibarra and Nueva Vizcaya* (Durham, N.C., 1927), passim; and L. F. Hill, *José de Escandón and the Founding of Nuevo Santander* (Ohio State Univ., *Studies,* no. 9), passim.

15. The most notable contemporary authorities on the contribution of the Franciscans to the northward movement were I. F. Espinosa, *Crónica Apostólica . . . de Todos los Colegios de Propaganda Fide* (Mexico, 1746), and J. D. Arricivita, *Crónica Seráfica . . . del Colegio de la Santa Cruz de Querétaro* (Mexico, 1792).

16. The situation in New Mexico was paralleled in the colonization of Nuevo León, south of Texas, and roughly in the modern state called Nuevo León.

17. The Inquisition in Mexico may be studied in H. C. Lea, *The Inquisition in the Spanish Dependencies* (New York, 1908), chap. vi: *Documentos Inéditos o muy Raros para la Historia de México* (Mexico, 1905–11), V and XXVIII; and J. T. Medina, *La Inquisición en México* (Santiago, 1905).

18. Much in the following pages is drawn from manuscripts translated by the writer of this volume for a forthcoming part of C. W. Hackett's publication of the "Bandelier Papers" in *Historical Documents Relating to New Mexico,* III.

19. Alonso de Benavides, in his *Memorial,* spoke in 1630 of the villa of Santa Fé as the head of the kingdom of New Mexico where the governor resided. The Spaniards numbered, according to his estimate, 250, only about fifty of whom had weapons with which to protect the settlement. Their arquebuses were, however, sufficient to keep the Indians in awe. All the Indians had to pay tribute of a *manta* (thirty-three inches) of cotton cloth and a *fanega* or bushel of corn each year. This meager support was required for the maintenance of the Spanish settlement. There were about 700 Indians in service to the Spaniards and the total population numbered about 1,000. Up until the time of the good friar's writing no church existed in this early settlement within the present boundaries of the United States. There was a miserable shack in which religious services were celebrated, and Benavides began to build a church and monastery in 1662. The instruction conducted by the fathers was for the purpose of teaching the Spaniards and Indians to read and write, play musical instruments, sing, and learn the various usages of civilization. Alonso de Benavides, *The Memorial of Fray Alonso de Benavides* (Mrs. Edward E. Ayer, tr., Chicago, 1916), 22–23.

20. J. W. Fewkes, "The Group of Tusayan Ceremonials Called Katcinas," Bureau of Am. Ethnology, *Fifteenth Ann. Rep.* [1893–94], 251–313.

21. His personal appearance when placed in the dungeons is revealed by the court inventory of his effects. He wore a *faruadina* or short cloak of buff and black wool decorated with fine points of black, a white jacket dotted with blue wool, a scarf of cotton drawn work, and a raincloak of deerskin. In his box were several woolen jackets bedecked with colored spots, some fine shirts, some common ones of Rouen linen, a mixed assortment of socks, a pair of cordovan shoes, a cake of soap, and a little lavender wrapped in an old black rag, a leather cover for

mustaches, herbs to cure mountain spotted fever and to heal wounds, an old black hat, and a quantity of bedding.

22. R. E. Twitchell, *Leading Facts of New Mexican History* (Cedar Rapids, 1911), I, 354-66. The fighting began August 10, 1680.

23. Outside the walls in some places were cultivated fields, but such agriculture was insufficient for the support of the garrison and many supplies had to be brought from Cuba.

24. G. R. Fairbanks, *The History and Antiquities of the City of St. Augustine, Florida* (New York, 1858), 160.

25. For a description of conditions along the northeastern border of Florida under the second Spanish occupation, see Caroline Mays Brevard, *A History of Florida* (Deland, 1924-25), I, chap. i.

26. Francisco Palóu, *Historia de la Vida del... Fray Junipero Serra* (Mexico, 1787), passim; same author, *Historical Memoirs of New California* (H. E. Bolton, ed., Berkeley, 1926), passim.

27. Z. S. Eldredge, *The March of Portolá and the Log of the San Carlos* (San Francisco, 1909), 27-32.

28. Alexander Forbes, *California, a History of Upper and Lower California* (London, 1839), chap. v.

29. T. H. Hittell, *History of California* (San Francisco, 1885), I, chaps., xii, xiii, xiv.

30. Alfred Robinson, *Life in California before the Conquest* (New York, 1846), 103-107, 143.

31. Hittell, *History of California*, II, 236-37; H. H. Bancroft, *California Pastoral* (San Francisco, 1888), chap. xvi.

32. R. H. Dana, Jr., *Two Years Before the Mast* (Boston, 1868), 84-85.

33. Cf. T. F. Cronise *The Natural Wealth of California* (San Francisco, 1868), 59-63.

34. See Alonso de Çorita, "Breve y Sumaria Relación," esp. chap. iii, in J. García Icazbalceta, ed., *Nueva Colección de Documentos para la Historia de México* (Mexico, 1886-92). III, for a charming account of Aztec social philosophy and religion. Cf. Lucien Biart, *The Aztecs* (Chicago, 1887), 110, 213-25.

35. For an excellent summary of Spanish Indian policy, see Lillian E. Fisher, *Viceregal Administration in the Spanish American Colonies* (Univ. of Calif., *Publs.*, XV), 312, 314-15, and citations.

36. Cf. F. M. Stawell and F. S. Marvin, *The Making of the Western Mind* (London, 1923), 163-66; F. S. Marvin, *The Living Past* (Oxford, 1913), chap vii.

37. See this volume, Book II.

38. In 1514, *Colección de Documentos... de Ultramar* (Madrid, 1885-1926), IX, 22. Cf. E. G. Bourne, *Spain in America* (A. B. Hart, ed., *The American Nation: a History*, New York, 1904-18, III), 265. The "Catholic Monarchs" were Ferdinand and Isabella and no others. They alone had this title, obtained from the pope. Later Spanish rulers have been called "Catholic Majesties."

39. If the treasures of Montezuma and Atahualpa had not made the American adventure remunerative beyond expectation, joint-stock-company exploitation might have been undertaken. The possibility had been discussed even in the time of Columbus. Charles V did himself try one such venture, that of the Augsburg Welzers in Venezuela, but neither before nor after their bootless undertaking was the colonizing type of company employed, though in the eighteenth century at least three semiprivate commercial organizations were utilized for both trade and colonial defense.

40. The literature on the *encomienda* is extensive. For a comprehensive treatment see J. de Solórzano, *Politica Indiana* (Madrid, 1776), I, 244-433. Bourne, *Spain in America*, 254, cites a brief note in E. Armstrong, *Charles V* (New York, 1902), II, 100, to the effect that the *cortes* and the communes, taking part in the controversy raised by Las Casas over the *encomiendas*, petitioned for the freedom of the Indians. For lapse of the institution, see the *Recopilación de Indias* (3d ed.,

Madrid, 1774), II, 231, laws xiv and xv, and Alexander von Humboldt, *Political Essay on the Kingdom of New Spain* (London, 1814), I, 183. J. Garcia Icazbalceta, *Obras* (Mexico, 1896-1905), chaps. xv and xvi, has a disquisition on the early phases of the institution. See also F. de Azara, *Viajes por la América del Sur* (Montevideo, 1850), chap. xii. The Jesuit method is described in chap. xiii. Bourne calls the attention of Americans to the parallel between the nonenforcement of the *encomienda* legislation and the history of the Fifteenth Amendment to the Constitution. For a modern evaluation of the Spanish policy in the Indies, see Jerónimo Becker, *La Política Española en las Indias* (Madrid, 1920), esp. pt. i, chap. v, and for the abolition of the *encomiendas* in Chile, pt. iii, chap. xv.

41. Fr. Z. Engelhardt, *The Missions and Missionaries of California* (San Francisco, 1908), II, chaps. xv and xvi.

42. Cf. H. E. Bolton, *The Spanish Borderlands* (Allen Johnson, ed., *The Chronicles of America Series,* New Haven, 1918-21, XXIII), for characteristics of the frontier missions; their place in the scheme of conquest, 188-91; secularization, 282-85.

43. For a judicious estimate of the mission system, see F. W. Blackmar, *Spanish Institutions of the Southwest* (Johns Hopkins Univ., *Studies,* extra vol. x), chaps. vi-vii.

44. M. Galván, *Ordenanzas de Tierras y Aguas* (Paris, 1855), 188-206; the laws included here form the legal basis of the agrarian reforms of 1915-27.

45. Corita, "Breve y Sumaria Relación," Icazbalceta, *Nueva Colección de Documentos para la Historia de México,* III, 95-96.

46. Thomas Gage, *A New Survey* (London, 1677), chap. xix, cited by Bourne, *Spain in America,* 262; Hipólito Villaroel, Enfermedades Politicas (MS. in Bancroft Library, 1785-87), I, 12, 43.

47. Villaroel, Enfermedades Politicas, I, 55-70; see Loretta Wilson (M.A. thesis, Univ. of Calif., 1918).

48. Justin Winsor, *Narrative and Critical History of America* (Boston, 1884-89), II, 34, n. 6. While most writers discredit the claim, Paul Gaffarel, *Découverte du Brésil par Jean Cousin* (Paris, 1847), advocated it.

49. "Lettres Patentes . . . à François de la Roque," *Collection de Manucrits Relatifs à la Nouvelle-France,* I, 30-36, and "Mons' Proposals," same vol., 40-43.

50. Francis Parkman, *The Jesuits in North America in the Seventeenth Century* (Centenary Ed., Boston, 1922), 131 Cf. this volume, Book II.

51. An interesting account of proposed subsidies to Englishmen for marrying Indian women in Nova Scotia between 1719 and 1773 is in a contribution by J. B. Brebner to "Notes and Documents," *Canadian Hist. Rev.,* VI, 33-38.

52. W. B. Munro, *Crusaders of New France* (Allen Johnson, ed., *The Chronicles of America Series,* New Haven, 1918-21, IV), 64-66. Indian policy demanded the same prohibitions against sale of liquor and firearms as prevailed in other colonial areas. Cf. Montmagny. "Ordonnance, July 9, 1644," P. G. Roy, ed., *Ordonnances, Commissions,* etc. (Beauceville, 1924, in Archives de la Province de Quebec), I, 5.

53. W. B. Munro, *The Seigniorial System in Canada* (*Harvard Hist. Studies,* XIII), 21, 159-60; W. B. Munro, ed., *Documents Relating to the Seigniorial Tenure in Canada* [1598-1854] (Champlain Soc., *Publs.,* III), pp. xxii, 1-3.

54. Munro, *Seigniorial System,* 82-84.

55. See J. B. Brebner, *New England's Outpost; Acadia before the Conquest of Canada* (Columbia Univ., *Studies,* no. 293), 140.

56. Émile Salone, *La Colonisation de la Nouvelle-France* (Paris, 1907), 371-73. In 1719 wheat production was 234,566 bushels, in 1734, 737,892 bushels; in the latter year there were 3,462 bushels of barley, 5,223 bushels of corn, and 163,988 bushels of oats. Same vol., 374.

57. Francis Parkman, *The Old Régime* (Boston, 1910), 393-95, summarizes the evidence of Jesuit fur trading, and praises their example in industry.

58. Munro, *Documents Relating to Seigniorial Tenure,* 167-68.

59. Samuel de Champlain, "Brief Discourse," H. P. Biggar, ed., *The Works of Samuel de Champlain* (Champlain Soc., *Publs.,* new ser.), I, 40. The inroads upon Cana-

dian commerce by Frenchmen who had not borne the brunt of colonization injured the settlers, leading the council to limit the season for "marchands forains." Roy, *Ordonnances, Commissions,* II, 12–16 [1683]; *Collection de Manuscrits . . . Relatifs à la Nouvelle-France,* I, 309; Solone, *La Colonisation de la Nouvelle-France,* 381.

60. André Pénicaut. "Relation," Pierre Margry, ed., *Découvertes et Établissements des Français* (Paris, 1879–88), V. 581, describes the coming of eighty-eight women; in 1719, 1720, and 1721 shiploads of profligate women arrived; the last load of marriageable females was sent in 1751.

61. For the strategic value of Chartres and Detroit, see Margry, *Découvertes,* VI. p. xvii, and T. H. Holdich, *Political Frontiers* (London, 1916), 38. Cf. E. G. Mason, *Chapters from Illinois History* (Chicago, 1901), 212–49, "Old Fort Chartres"; and Philip Pittman, *The Present State of the European Settlements on the Mississippi* (Cleveland, 1906), 88–90.

62. Pierre le Moyne d'Iberville, "Journal," Margry, *Découvertes,* IV, 395.

63. Jean de Champigny, *État Présent de la Louisiane,* quoted in J. H. Deiler, *The Settlement of the German Coast of Louisiana* (M. D. Learned, ed., *Americana Germanica,* new ser., VIII), 17–18.

64. Cf. H. E. Chambers, *Mississippi Valley Beginnings* (New York, 1922), 60–68.

65. Pénicaut, "Relation," 576–78; Deiler, *Settlement of the German Coast,* 58–59.

66. Margry, *Découvertes,* VI, p. xv; Alexander Franz, *Kolonisation des Mississippitales* (Leipzig, 1906), 127–28. The most ample summaries of economic and social conditions are in the notes to Paul Alliot, "Historical and Political Reflections on Louisiana," J. A. Robertson, ed., *Louisiana under the Rule of Spain, France and the United States* (Cleveland, 1911), I, 145–232.

67. Deiler, *Settlement of the German Coast,* 68–69 (citing *Concessions,* 18, 448). 106–107.

68. Bernardo Gálvez reported on July 19, 1781, that five new towns had been formed from 300 Acadian families at a cost of 40,000 pesos. (Bernardo to José de Gálvez.) Antonio Ulloa expected to bring into Louisiana 1,000 Catholic families from Maryland on the strength of the Acadian movement. (Ulloa to Grimaldi, New Orleans, February 11, 1768.) See Archivo General de Indias, Papeles de Cuba, no. 608; nos. 109, 119, 137, 181, 187, 573, 576, 608, and 626, *estante* 86, *cajón* 6, *legajo* 6. In 1785 and 1786, 300 families of Acadians were brought out from France and Spain, where they had taken refuge and had been supported after their dispersal along the Atlantic colonies of England; their way was paid; tools, seeds, and lands were given them; and they were maintained until their crops ripened. MSS. cited, Bancroft Library.

69. The edition printed in Paris in 1767 contains in addition to the Code, French colonial administrative legislation between 1671 and 1762. Alcée Fortier, *Louisiana Folk Tales* (Am. Folk-Lore Soc., *Memoirs,* II), pp. ix–x; same author, *Louisiana Studies* (New Orleans, 1894), 149–97.

70. Pittman, *Present State of the European Settlements,* 41–44, describes the city. See also Grace King, *Creole Families of Louisiana* (New York, 1921), 4.

71. King, *Creole Families,* 7, 81, 85, Perrin du Lac in 1803 found the streets unpaved and filthy, with conditions at the quay responsible for the almost annual recurrence of yellow fever. The city stood about eight feet below the level of the river, and fear of inundation was seasonal. See Perrin du Lac, *Voyage dans les Deux Louisianes* (Lyons, 1805), 393.

72. King, *Creole Families,* pp. vii, ix, 3. Thirty families are noted, much intermarried, with notable public records. See also Deiler, *Settlement of the German Coast,* passim, for the contributions of the German creoles. Pénicaut, "Relation," Margry, *Découvertes,* V, 470; cf. Alcée Fortier, *History of Louisiana* (New York, 1904), I, 56; [F. P. Watrin, S. J.], "Banishment of the Jesuits from Louisiana," Edna Kenton, ed., *The Jesuit Relations* (Toronto, 1925), 475–84.

73. Fortier, *History of Louisiana,* II, 155. Slavery in Louisiana in colonial days is

discussed in Amos Stoddard, *Sketches of Louisiana* (Philadelphia, 1812), 331-43. The first press entered New Mexico in 1834, that at Monterey, California, dating from 1835.

74. Cf. J. J. D. de Pontalba, *Mémoire,* quoted in Charles Gayarré, *History of Louisiana* (New York, 1903), III, 333; pages 354-56 present this rising in a more serious aspect.

75. Pontalba to his wife, excerpts in King, *Creole Families,* 89-91.

76. One could buy land more cheaply just outside the city, he further said, and live economically on a capital of $40,000. A lot with 120 feet frontage by 220 deep could be had for $800 on long time; the property was supplied with blacks, animals, and implements, with all the resources needed for the table, a garden, a dairy, and so forth. It was within easy reach of the city, and the purchaser could have his daughters where they could cultivate good society.

77. For the whole account, see King, *Creole Families,* 85-114. Slaves were valuable chattels. Annette, the cook of Madame Pontalba, sold for $900, and she knew how to "make good gombos and calas." Baptiste, a domestic, sold for $400. Other prices mentioned were lower.

78. Pittman, *Present State of the European Settlements,* 82-86. The following pages on the Illinois country are drawn from C. W. Alvord, *The Illinois Country* (C. W. Alvord, ed., *The Centennial History of Illinois,* Springfield, 1918-20, I), chiefly chap. x. Cf. Mason, *Chapters from Illinois History,* 217-18, and notes.

79. Collot, *Voyage,* I, 316-69. Cf. this volume, Books II and III.

80. Alvord, *Illinois Country,* 205-209.

81. Perrin du Lac. *Voyage,* 167-73, found Ste. Geneviève in 1802 a town of 1,300 inhabitants, one third slaves; most of them had come from the left bank at the time of the English and American cessions. Fur export from Canada under the French averaged £135,000 annually as estimated by H. T. Cramahe, 1761, in *Mich. Pioneer and Hist. Colls.,* XIX, 14. For an excellent and easily available discussion of the *coureurs de bois,* see W. B. Munro, *Crusaders of New France* (Allen Johnson, ed., *The Chronicles of America Series,* New Haven, 1918-21, IV), chap. ix. For hostile legislation by Talon and Frontenac, see P. G. Roy, ed., *Ordonnances, Commissions, etc.* (Beauceville, 1924, in *Archives de la Province de Quebec),* I, 107-108, 111-12; cf. same works, II, 7-9, 26-27, and III, 284-86.

82. An interesting picture, by an American, of the condition of the French settlements in and around Detroit is B. W. Bond, Jr., ed., "The Captivity of Charles Stuart, 1755-1757," *Miss. Valley Hist. Rev.,* XIII, 58-81. See also Mrs. N. M. Surrey, *The Commerce of Louisiana during the French Régime* (Columbia Univ., *Studies,* LXXI), 62-63, 82-92.

83. On the work of the Jesuits among the Illinois, see Kenton, *Jesuit Relations,* 333-87, 392-95; H. S. Spaulding, S. J., "The Life of James Marquette, *Ill. Catholic Hist. Rev.,* IX, nos. 1-2.

84. See R. L. Rusk, *The Literature of the Middle Western Frontier* (New York, 1925), I, 6-13, for an interesting treatment.

85. Fourteen of seventy-one Wisconsin counties, four lakes, numerous rivers and six cities as well as seven towns bear French names. Louise P. Kellogg, *The French Régime in Wisconsin and the Northwest* (State Hist. Soc. of Wis., *Publs.,* I), 441. A multitude of similar survivals in many regions is recalled in J. H. Finley, *The French in the Heart of America* (New York, 1915), 394. Americans of French extraction, Huguenot or French-Canadian, will regret no more than the author of this book the lack of opportunity to allude to the wide influence of the French dispersal throughout the United States, which, however, may be traced in other volumes of this series.

86. J. F. Jameson, ed., *Narratives of New Netherland* (same ed., *Original Narratives of Early American History,* New York, 1906-), 3; A. H. van Buren, "Wiltwyck under the Dutch," N.Y. State Hist. Assoc., *Proceeds.,* XI, 133; Ruth Putnam, "An-

netje Jans' Farm," M. W. Goodwin and others, eds., *Half Moon Series* (New York, 1897-98), I, 64; A. J. F. van Laer, *Van Rensselaer Bouwier MSS.* (Albany, 1908), 687-88; F. J. Zwierlein, *Religion in New Netherland* (Rochester, 1910), 78.

87. T. A. Janvier, *The Dutch Founding of New York* (New York, 1903), 2-4. Janvier's point of view is aptly illustrated by A. J. F. van Laer, ed., *Minutes of the Court of Fort Orange and Beverwyck, 1652-1660* (Albany, 1920-23). Some of the controversies seem naive to us, as that over misnaming houses which set Fort Orange by the ears for a considerable time. A citizen amused himself by naming his neighbors' homes "The House of Discord," "The Cuckoo's Nest," "The House of Ill Manners," etc. A large amount of testimony was taken. See Van Laer, *Minutes,* I, 199, 201, 210, 213.

88. I. N. P. Stokes, *Iconography of Manhattan Island* (New York, 1915-28), I, 28.

89. Mrs. Anne Grant, *Memoirs of an American Lady* (New York, 1901), I, 80-87; G. E. Hill and G. E. Waring, Jr., "Old Wells and Water Courses," *Half Moon Series,* I, 315-16.

90. E. B. O'Callaghan and Berthold Fernow, eds., *Documents Relative to the Colonial History of the State of New York* (Albany, 1853-87), II. 222, 430, and *General Index* (XI) at the word "Slavery"; E. V. Morgan, "Slavery in New York," *Half Moon Series,* II, 3-6. The company itself held slaves, keeping them in a little colony by the East River at what is now 75th Street. See Stokes. *Iconography,* I, 21, 104. On Indian Slavery see A. M. Lauber, *Indian Slavery in Colonial Times* (Columbia Univ., *Studies,* LIV, no. 3), 253-571.

91. Morgan, "Slavery in New York," 16-18.

92. Cf. this volume, Book II.

93. Jameson, *Narratives of New Netherland,* 260.

94. Stokes, *Iconography,* I, 11, 27; III, 65. Bakers were closely supervised by law as to the price, quality, and quantity of their bread. Berthold Fernow, ed., *The Records of New Amsterdam from 1653 to 1674* (New York, 1897), III, 285; IV, 218; VI, 30-31; VII, 219, etc.

95. Stokes, *Iconography,* I, 45, 83, 88. To ensure good quality all tobacco had to be shipped through New Amsterdam.

96. A. J. F. van Laer, "Letters of Van Twiller," N. Y. State Hist. Assoc., *Quar, Journ.,* I, 44-50. Wassenaer (Jameson's *Narratives*) observes that some salt was manufactured by evaporation.

97. Stokes, *Iconography,* III, 94. Isolated farmsteads were surrounded by palisades of logs.

98. Adriaen van der Donck, "Description of the New Netherlands," *Old South Leaflets,* no. lxix (Boston, 1896), 16, 18; Cornelius van Tienhoven. "Information Relative to taking up Land in New Netherland," E. B. O'Callaghan, *The Documentary History of the State of New York* (Albany, 1850-51), IV, 21-26.

99. E. R. Hewitt and Mary A. Hewitt, "The Bowery," *Half Moon Series,* I, 371 ff.; Jasper Dankers [or Danckaerts] and Peter Sluyter, *Journal of a Voyage to New York, and a Tour in Several of the American Colonies, 1679-1680* (H. C. Murphy, ed., L. I. Hist. Soc., *Memoirs,* I), 44, 47.

100. The council of New Amsterdam decried the use of seawant and petitioned the directors in Holland, without much effect, to send them silver. For trading purposes they equated a beaver skin with six guilders and a pound of tobacco with four and a half stivers. See Fernow, *Records of New Amsterdam,* III, 383.

101. Reverend Johannes Megapolensis, Jr., "A Short Account of the Mohawk Indians," Jameson, *Narratives of New Netherland,* 174.

102. E. T. Corwin, ed., *Ecclesiastical Records of the State of New York* (Albany, 1901-16), I, 398-99.

103. Stokes, *Iconography,* I, 29. There were also evening schools. See Van Laer, *Minutes of the Court of Fort Orange,* I, 238.

104. Stokes, *Iconography,* III, 78.

105. Van Laer, *Minutes of the Court of Fort Orange,* II, 21.
106. Mrs. Schuyler van Rensselaer, *History of the City of New York in the Seventeenth Century* (New York, 1909), I, 422–23, 425; J. K. Paulding, *The Dutchman's Fireside* (New York, 1868), 11, 243–46.
107. J. H. Innes, *New Amsterdam and its People* (New York, 1902), 16, 61–67.
108. Stokes, *Iconography,* I, 29, 67. At the same time the city purchased 150 leather buckets for fire fighting. See A. E. Peterson and G. W. Edwards, *New York as an Eighteenth-Century Municipality* (Columbia Univ., *Studies,* LXXV), 169–81.
109. Emma van Vechten, "Early Schools and Schoolmasters of New Amsterdam," *Half Moon Series,* II, 324; Peter Kalm, "Travels into North America," John Pinkerton, ed., *Voyages and Travels* (London, 1808–14), XIII, 452, 456–57. See also Earle, *Colonial Days in Old New York,* 98–127; Helen E. Smith, *Colonial Days and Ways* (New York, 1900), 93–101.
110. Quoted in Eunice F. Barnard, "New York Still Has Dutch Habits," *New York Times,* July 4, 1926.
111. *Documents Relating to the History of the Early Colonial Settlements* (*Documents Relative to the History of New York,* XIV), 249. The "popish" variant of this sport in colonial California was to bury a live chicken in the sand leaving only the head protruding, the riders trying to seize the fowl by the neck while galloping past.
112. Van Laer, *Minutes of the Court of Fort Orange,* I, 220, Hamlin Garland gives the primitive Wisconsin variation of this sport in his chapter, "The Turkey Shoot," in *Trail-makers of the Middle Border* (New York, 1926).
113. Van Laer, *Minutes of the Court of Fort Orange,* II, 234.
114. Fernow, *Records of New Amsterdam,* VII, 262. On feasts and fasts in New Netherland, see W. D. Love, *The Fast and Thanksgiving Days of New England* (Boston, 1895), chap. xii.
115. Earle, *Colonial Days in Old New York,* 184–209.
116. The famous Rembrandt, "The Lesson in Anatomy," now in the Mauritshuis at The Hague, has an interesting though indirect relation with New Netherland history in that the central figure of the painting is that of Dr. Claes Petersz before whom the colonists who came in 1624 took their oaths, A. J. F. van Laer, ed., *Documents Relating to New Netherland, 1624–1626, in the Henry E. Huntington Library* (Henry E. Huntington Library, *Publs. Americana,* no. 1), 256.
117. It will be remembered that in 1673 New York was recaptured by the Dutch; the following year, by the Treaty of Westminster, it was restored to the English.
118. Intro. to "Description of the Towne of Mannadens," Jameson, *Narratives of New Netherland,* 419–20; cf. J. W. Redway. "Some Side-Lights on the Passing of New Netherland viewed from Westchester County," N.Y. State Hist. Assoc., *Proceeds.,* IX, 152–59; Adriaen van der Donck and ten others, "The Representation of New Netherland," Jameson, *Narratives of New Netherland,* 305ff.; W. R. Shepherd, *The Story of New Amsterdam* (New York, 1917), 93–100.
119. The influence of New Netherland upon the life of American institutions is discussed by Doublas Campbell, *The Puritan in England, Holland and America* (New York, 1892), but most of his claims are refuted by H. T. Colenbrander, "The Dutch Element in American History," Am. Hist. Assoc., *Ann. Rep. for 1909,* 198ff. "It is impossible to deny that the characteristics which have become typical of the political and social life of America have for the most part produced themselves at an earlier date and in a higher degree in the English colonies than in New Netherland." The people of New Amsterdam complained in 1649 to the States General, asking for civil rights that were enjoyed by their neighbors in New England, where, as they expressed it, the word "patroon," "lord," or "Prince" is not heard, and the people "is all in all. "
120. Cf. J. R. Brodhead, *History of the State of New York* (New York, 1871–72), I, 36.

BOOK II   The First Americans, 1067–90

1. Edmund Burke, "Speech on Conciliation with America," *Works* (rev. ed., Boston, 1866), II, 125–26.
2. R. Rich, *Newes from Virginia* [1610] (J. O. Halliwell, ed., London, 1865). The first iron was mined at Falling Creek, Va., about 1622; see J. A. Mathews, *Economic and Metallurgical Aspects of Iron in Colonial Days* (Pittsburgh, 1923), 6.
3. Anon., "A True Declaration of the Estate of the Colonie in Virginia [1610]." Peter Force, ed., *Tracts and Other Papers Relating Principally to the Origin, Settlement, and Progress of the Colonies in North America* (Washington, 1836–46), III, no. 1, 25.
4. Alexander Brown, ed., *The Genesis of the United States* (Boston, 1891), I, 239.
5. Thomas Morton, "New English Canaan [1632]," *Force, Tracts and Other Papers,* II, no. 5, 44.
6. William Strachey, *The Historie of Travaile into Virginia Britannia* (R. H. Major, ed., London, 1849), 126.
7. A. O. Craven, *Soil Exhaustion as a Factor in the Argicultural History of Virginia and Maryland, 1606–1860* (Univ. of Illinois, *Studies,* XIII, no. 1), 30.
8. "When food was not provided by the employer, the amount of these wages was in each instance doubled. . . . It was estimated that the smallest sum upon which a family could be maintained during a period of twelve months was twenty pounds and eleven shillings, including the cost of renting a cottage and the price of the necessary amount of bread, meat, fuel and clothing." P. A. Bruce, *Economic History of Virginia in the Seventeenth Century* (New York, 1895), I, 578–79.
9. Virginia Land Patents (Register of Land Office, Va. State Capitol).
10. T. J. Wertenbaker, *The Planters of Colonial Virginia* (Princeton, 1922), 41–42.
11. Berkeley to the Board of Trade, C. O. 1: 26–77 (Brit. Pub. Rec. Office).
12. C. O. 5: 1314, Doc. 63 (Brit. Pub. Rec. Office).
13. "The First Land Grants in Maryland." *Md. Hist. Mag.,* III, 158–69.
14. See John Johnson, *Old Maryland Manors with the Records of a Court Leet and a Court Baron* (Johns Hopkins Univ., *Studies,* I, no. 7), for records of St. Clement's and St. Gabriel's manors.
15. "The servants . . . could, on the expiration of their term, reaily obtain land, and need only procure laborers to become planters themselves. . . . These servants either became land-owners, or squatted on unpatented or unused land. . . ." Basil Sollers, "Transported Convict Laborers in Maryland during the Colonial Period," *Md. Hist. Mag.,* II, 17.
16. George Alsop. *A Character of the Province of Mary-land* (London, 1666), 59.
17. "Public Offices in Virginia, 1702, 1714," *Va. Mag. of Hist. and Biog.,* I, 364–73.
18. Surry County Wills, Deeds, etc., 1671–84, 1684–86 (Va. State Library).
19. *Va. Mag. of Hist. and Biog.,* III, 441.
20. J. T. Scharf, *History of Maryland* (Baltimore, 1879), II, 12.
21. Craven, *Soil Exhaustion,* chap. ii.
22. Hugh Jones, *Present State of Virginia* (London, 1724), 124.
23. Anon., "A Perfect Description of Virginia [1649]," Force, *Tracts and Other Papers,* II, no. 8, 14.
24. Anon., "A Perfect Description of Virginia," 3.
25. Little care was taken of the livestock; thus, 25,429 cattle and 62,377 hogs perished in Maryland during the winter of 1694–95. Craven, *Soil Exhaustion,* 33.
26. York County Records, 1694–1702 (Va. State Library).
27. Wertenbaker, *Planters of Colonial Virginia,* 87–88, 115–18.
28. Thomas Ludwell to Lord John Berkeley, C. O. 1:21 (Brit. Pub. Rec. Office).
29. Anon., "A Perfect Description of Virginia [1649]," Force, *Tracts and Other Papers,* II, no. 8, 15.
30. Professor Krapp, working through seventeenth-century town records in prepara-

tion for his two volumes on *The English Language in America,* found certain words then apparently in common use but now obsolete: *spong, spang,* or *spung* meant a meadow strip; *rubbish* meant land overgrown with brush; *doak* meant valley; *folly* probably meant a clump of trees; *homestall* was sometimes used for homestead; *haysill* for the haying season; and *jade* for a horse, whether good or bad. G. P. Krapp, *The English Language in America* (New York, 1925), I, 79–93, passim.

31. William Wood in "New-England's Prospect [1634]," Prince Soc., *Publs.,* I, 52, says that the 4,000 people in 1634 had 1,500 cattle!

32. On the New England farming and town system, see Thomas Lechford, "Note-Book," Am. Antiq. Soc., *Trans.,* VII, 101; H. L. Osgood, *The American Colonies in the Seventeenth Century* (New York, 1904), I, chap. xi; Anne B. Maclear, *Early New England Towns* (Columbia Univ., *Studies,* XXIX, no. 1), chap. i; C. M. Andrews, *River Towns of Connecticut* (Johns Hopkins Univ., *Studies,* VII, nos. 7-9), 5; P. W. Bidwell and J. I Falconer, *History of Agriculture in the Northern United States, 1620-1860* (Carnegie Inst., *Contribs. to Am. Econ. Hist.,* Washington, 1925), 24, 35, 49-58, 107.

33. The Jersey proprietors and William Penn, however, showed that it was possible to develop a colony with small holders by direct sale. See A. C. Myers, ed., *Narratives of Early Pennsylvania, West Jersey and Delaware, 1630-1707* (J. F. Jameson, ed., *Original Narratives of Early American History,* New York, 1906-17), 219; and Samuel Smith, *History of the Colony of New Jersey* (Burlington, N.J., 1765), 512. The New England system itself was extended by settlers from that region to Long Island and part of Westchester County, New York, and to certain counties in New Jersey.

34. J. H. Beale, Jr., *The Origin of the System of Recording Deeds in America* (Boston, 1907), 7.

35. Weeden, *Economic and Social History,* I, 81.

36. George Lincoln et al., *History of the Town of Hingham* (Hingham, 1893).

37. R. F. Seybolt, *Apprenticeship and Apprenticeship Education in Colonial New England and New York* (Teachers Col., Columbia Univ., *Contribs, to Educ.,* LXXXV), 34-41.

38. Cotton Mather, *Diary* (Mass. Hist. Soc., *Colls.,* ser. 7, VII-VIII), II, 112.

39. W. DeL. Love, *The Colonial History of Hartford* (Hartford, 1914).

40. Lechford, "Note-Book," 64, 322.

41. Weeden, *Economic and Social History,* I, 83.

42. Lechford, "Note-Book," 147.

43. Lincoln et al., *History of Hingham,* II, 411.

44. Ibid., III, 254.

45. In 1639, Tyng purchased property from William Coddington worth £1,300. Lechford, "Note-Book," 164.

46. The graduates of Harvard and Yale, far into the eighteenth century, were listed not in alphabetical order but according to their "dignities." F. B. Dexter, "On Some Social Distinctions at Harvard and Yale," Am. Antiq. Soc., *Proceeds,* IX, 50; and W. G. Brooks, "The Rank of Students in Harvard College," Mass. Hist. Soc., *Proceeds.,* IX, 252-54.

47. Weeden, *Economic and Social History,* I, 226-27, 288-89; *Mass. Col. Laws,* for 1651; Alice M. Earle, *Customs and Fashions in Old New England* (New York, 1893), 316-17.

48. Weeden, *Economic and Social History,* I, 75.

49. In addition to Weeden, who has many citations in I, 280, the reader should consult the interesting chapter on "Seating the Meeting," in Alice M. Earle, *The Sabbath in Puritan New England* (7th ed., New York, 1893).

50. The customary charge for milling was one fourteenth part. See D. R. Fox, *Caleb Heathcote* (New York, 1926), 56.

51. The colonists used not only butcher's fat in making soft soap, but also oil from the dead whales washed up so frequently on the shores of Long Island and Cape Cod. See Maverick, *A Briefe Description of New England*, 21; Judd, *Hadley, Mass.*, 378; and R. H. Gabriel, *The Evolution of Long Island (Yale Hist. Publs., Miscellany*, IX), chap. v.

52. Cotton Mather, *Magnalia Christi Americana* [London, 1702] (Hartford, 1853), I, 65, 70.

53. A good discussion of the character and motives of the colonists is found in Carl Becker, *Beginnings of the American People* (W. E. Dodd, ed., *The Riverside History of the United States*, Boston, 1915, I), chap. iii.

54. Cotton Mather, *Magnalia*, 1, 74.

55. Ibid., 76.

56. Ibid., 219.

57. Lindsay Swift, "The Massachusetts Election Sermons," Col. Soc. of Mass., *Publs.*, I, 400.

58. Ibid., 401.

59. Nathaniel Ward, *Simple Cobbler of Aggawamm* (London, 1647), 3–12, passim.

60. Cotton Mather, *Magnalia*, 1, 240.

61. Edward Johnson, *Wonder-Working Providence of Sions Saviour in New England* [London, 1654] (Jameson, *Original Narratives of Early American History*), 41.

62. Thomas Hutchinson, *The History of the Colony of Massachusetts-Bay* (Boston, 1764–1828), I, 437.

63. Cotton Mather, *Magnalia*, I, 252. The biographical chapter on Cotton (252–86) is very interesting. See also E. D. Mead, "John Cotton's Farewell Sermon," Mass. Hist. Soc., *Proceeds.*, ser. 3, I, 105.

64. John Winthrop, *History of New England* (Jameson, *Original Narratives of Early American History*), I, 74.

65. Letter of April 17, 1637, Mass. Hist. Soc., *Colls.*, VII, ser. 4, 10–11.

66. Winthrop, *History of New England*, I, 162.

67. Ibid., 209.

68. J. T. Adams, *The Founding of New England* (Boston, 1922), 171.

69. George Bishop, *New England Judged by the Spirit of God* (London, 1703), 2.

70. It must be remembered, however, that the Quakers were rather trying, judged by any standard. One woman, to evidence humility, was wont to exhibit herself in an old sackcloth gown with her face smeared with grease and lamp black; two others, though generally of modest deportment, went naked to church and marketplace "as a sign." See Bishop, *New England Judged*, 377, 383, and the summary of the *Persecution in New England* in J. G. Palfrey, *History of New England* (Boston, 1892), II, 449, 483; also Charles Deane, "Report on the Belknap Donation," Mass. Hist. Soc., *Proceeds.*, III (1855–58), 320.

71. United Colonies of New England, *Acts*, II, 180.

72. J. R. Bartlett, comp., *Records of the Colony of Rhode Island and Providence Plantations in New England, 1636–1792* (Providence, 1856–65), I, 376.

73. William Sewel, *The History of the Rise, Increase, and Progress of the Christian People Called Quakers* (New York, 1844), I, 338.

74. For a brief general account, see H. L. Osgood, *The American Colonies in the Seventeenth Century* (New York, 1904–1907), III, chaps. xiii–xiv.

75. Cotton Mather, *Magnalia*, I, 66.

76. Johnson, *Wonder-Working Providence*, 254.

77. John Higginson, *The Cause of God and His People in New England* (1663), 11, quoted in Col. Soc. Of Mass., *Publs.*, I, 398.

78. W. S. Perry, ed., *Historical Collections Relating to the American Colonial Church* (Hartford, 1870–78), I, 201, 263–64, 266, 270, 273, 277.

79. Ibid., 326.

80. *Cal. of State Papers, Colon., Am. and W. I., 1677–1680*, 117.

81. [Henry Hartwell et al.], "An Account of the Present State and Government of Virginia," sec. xii., Mass. Hist. Soc., *Colls.* (1798), 164ff.

82. Winthrop, *History of New England* (Jameson, *Original Narratives of Early American History),* 264.

83. Lines from funeral elegy by Reverend John Norton, in Nathaniel Morton, *New-England's Memorial* (Plymouth, 1826), 149.

84. W. Del. Love. *The Fast and Thanksgiving Days of New England* (Boston, 1895), 190.

85. See Increase Mather, *Remarkable Providences* (London, 1852), 2ff., 51ff., for discussions of "Sea Deliverances" and "Lightning."

86. Cotton Mather, *Diary* (Mass. Hist. Soc., *Colls,* ser. 7, VII), 171, 204.

87. The Reverend John Pierpont to Cotton Mather, quoted in Cotton Mather, *Magnalia,* I, 84. This experience together with the imperfections of the harbor discouraged New Haven commerce. See Maverick. *A Briefe Description of New England,* 23.

88. Exodus, xxii, 18.

89. W. H. Browne, *Maryland, the History of a Palatinate* (H. E. Scudder, ed., *Am. Commonwealths,* Boston, 1884), 83, citing William Kilty, *English Statutes* (Annapolis, 1811), speaks of an execution in Maryland in 1685, but the records for 1685 are lost.

90. The Council and General Court, "Minutes for 1622-1629," *Va. Mag. of Hist. and Biog.,* XXVI, 12ff.

91. "Ordeal of Touch in Colonial Virginia," *Va. Mag. of Hist. and Biog.,* IV, 187.

92. "Witchcraft in Virginia," *The Lower Norfolk Antiquary,* I (1897), 56.

93. The records of this case have been carefully printed by E. W. James, ed., "Grace Sherwood, the Virginia Witch," in *William and Mary Col. Quart.,* III, 190-92, 242-45; IV, 18-20; and in *Lower Norfolk County Antiquary,* II, 92-93.

94. P. A. Bruce, *Institutional History of Virginia* (New York, 1910), I, 278-89.

95. Browne, *Maryland,* 83.

96. Maryland General Assembly, *Proceeds, and Acts for 1666-1676* (W. H. Browne, ed., Baltimore, 1884), 425-26, 444-46.

97. G. L. Burr, ed., *Narratives of the Witchcraft Cases, 1648-1706* (Jameson, *Original Narratives of Early American History*), 85-88.

98. Governor and Company of the Massachusetts Bay, *Records for 1628-1686* (N. B. Shurtleff, ed., Boston, 1853-1854), III, 126.

99. H. R. Stiles, *The History and Genealogies of Ancient Windsor* (Hartford, 1891), I, 147.

100. Burr, *Narratives of the Witchcraft Cases,* 408.

101. Ibid., 135-36.

102. H. C. Lea, *Superstition and Force* (4th ed., Philadelphia, 1892), 325ff., gives a description and history of the water ordeal.

103. Wallace Notestein, *A History of Witchcraft in England from 1558 to 1718* (Washington, 1911), 202-203.

104. See K. B. Murdock, *Increase Mather, The Foremost American Puritan* (Cambridge, 1925), 167-70.

105. "Address to the Reader," *Memorable Providences* (Boston, 1689).

106. Cotton Mather, *Wonders of the Invisible World* (reptd., London, 1862), 122.

107. See the readable account in W. S. Nevins, *Witchcraft in Salem Village in 1692* (Salem, 1892), chap. vii.

108. Robert Calef, "More Wonders of the Invisible World," Burr, *Narratives of the Witchcraft Cases,* 350-52.

109. John Hale, *A Modest Inquiry into the Nature of Witchcraft* (Boston, 1702), chap. iv.

110. In taking leave of the subject, however, it may be remarked in some astonishment that the latest author to treat of witchcraft states his belief that contracts with

Satan must be taken as actualities "then and now"! See Montague Summers, *The History of Witchcraft and Demonology* (C. K. Ogden, ed., *The History of Civilization,* New York, 1924-39), as reviewed by Lynn Thorndike, "A Welter of Witches," *The Nation,* CXXIV (1927), 43.

111. F. H. Garrison, *An Introduction to the Study of Medicine* (Philadelphia, 1922), 37.

112. S. A. Green, "Remarks," Mass. Hist. Soc., *Proceeds.,* ser. 2, I, 44-45; and John Eliot, "The Letter . . . to T. S. [Thomas Shepard] Covering the Late Work of God Among the Indians," Mass. Hist. Soc., *Colls.,* ser. 3, IV, 57.

113. W. S. Steiner, "History of Medicine," N. G. Osborn, *History of Connecticut* (New Haven, 1925), III, 664-66.

114. Paracelsus, *De Cutis Apertionibus,* folio 62.

115. "Advice of the Council," Alexander Brown, *The Genesis of the United States* (Boston, 1891), I, 84.

116. William Strachey, "For the Colony in Virginea Britannia. Lavves Diuine, Morall and Martiall, &c. [London, 1612]," Force, *Tracts and Other Papers,* III, no. ii.

117. Anon., "Tobacco in England in the Reign of James I," *Va. Mag. of Hist. and Biog.,* XXIX, 108.

118. G. L. Kittredge ed., "Letters of Samuel Lee and Samuel Sewall Relating to New England and the Indians," Col. Soc. of Mass., *Publs.,* XIV, 142-66.

119. Alexander Young, *Chronicles of the First Planters of the Colony of Massachusetts Bay* (Boston, 1846), 131.

120. James Thacher, *American Medical Biography* (Boston, 1828), I, 222.

121. Danvers Hist. Soc., Colls., IV, 85.

122. A. Brown, *Genesis of the United States,* II, 601, 830, 907, 988; John Smith, *Works* (E. Arber, ed., Birmingham, 1884), 94, 390; Edward Eggleston, *Transit of Civilization* (New York, 1901), 74.

123. Samuel Lee to Nehemiah Grew, June 25, 1690, in Colon. Soc. of Mass., *Publs.,* XIV, 147.

124. John Smith, *Works,* lxxii.

125. D. P. De Vries, *Voyages from Holland to America, A. D. 1632-1644* (New York, 1853), 109.

126. Cf. this volume, Book III, p. 202.

127. Letter of Cotton Mather to John Cotton, November 1678. Mass. Hist. Soc., *Colls.,* ser. 4, VIII, 383-84.

128. Cotton Mather, *Magnalia,* I, 517.

129. Some other examples are equally striking. Thus, Sarah Hawke had seven children, dying at thirty-six; Rebecca Hersey had twelve, dying at forty-five; Joanna Hobart had seven, dying at forty-one; Mary Russell had eleven, dying at fifty; Sarah Lane had five, dying at thirty-four; Sarah Lewis had seven, dying at thirty-seven; Sarah Lincoln had seven, dying at forty-one; Deborah Hersey Lincoln had nine, dying at forty; Deborah Hobart Lincoln had ten, dying at thirty-seven; Mary Loring had eleven, dying at forty; Sarah Pratt had eleven, dying at forty-two; Elizabeth Stodder had twelve, dying at forty-six; Abigail Thaxter had seven, dying at thirty. See Lincoln et al., *History of Hingham,* passim.

130. Cotton Mather, *Magnalia,* I, 517.

131. In J. A. Doyle, *The English in America, The Puritan Colonies* (London, 1887), II, app. C, may be found some interesting records of early marriages and infant mortality. As Doyle remarks (II, 8), the land was "abundantly replenished and ruthlessly weeded.

132. H. E. Barnes, *The Repression of Crime* (New York, 1926), 43, 90-97, 157.

133. L. G. Tyler, ed., *Narratives of Early Virginia* (Jameson, *Original Narratives of Early American History*), 422-23.

134. Cotton Mather, *Magnalia,* I, 70.

135. The vast bulk of the newcomers to Virginia during the seventeenth century were English. An examination of the lists in the Land Office at Richmond shows here

and there an Irish or a Scotch name, but in normal periods fully 95 percent were unmistakably Anglo-Saxon. Even in the years 1655 and 1656, after the Drogheda tragedy, when one sees such names as O'Lanny, O'Leahy, O'Mally, and Machoone, the list is predominantly English. See Wertenbaker, *Planters of Colonial Virginia*, 36.

136. Alsop, *Maryland*, 48.
137. J. T. Scharf, *History of Maryland* (Baltimore, 1879), II, 40.
138. John Noble, "Notes on the Trial and Punishment of Crimes," Colon. Soc. of Mass., *Publs.*, III, 51–66; esp. 59–60, for the examples in the text.
139. C. O. 1: 3 (Brit. Pub. Rec. Office).
140. Barnes, *The Repression of Crime*, 27.
141. Conway Robinson, ed., "Virginia Council and General Court Records. 1640–1641," *Va. Mag. of Hist. and Biog.*, XI, 277.
142. Robinson, "Virginia Council and General Court Records, 1626–1628," *Va. Mag. of Hist. and Biog.*, IV, 246.
143. W. W. Hening, comp., *Statutes at Large of Virginia* (Philadelphia, 1823), I, 75.
144. Ibid., II, 6–77.
145. Thomas Culpeper, "Report on Virginia in 1683," *Va. Mag. of Hist. and Biog.*, III, 231.
146. Alsop, *Maryland*, 49.
147. Thomas Ellwood (1639–1714) in his autobiography gives us a vivid picture of this famous place in the seventeenth century. "In the night we were all lodged in one room, which was large and round, having in the middle of it a great pillar of oaken timber, which bore up the chapel that is over it. To this pillar we fastened our hammocks . . . three stories high, one over the other. . . . The breath and steam that came from so many bodies . . . was enough to cause sickness among us. . . ." The foreman of a jury, which held an inquest over the body of a prisoner who died during the night, lifted up his hands, exclaiming, "I did not think there had been so much cruelty in the hearts of Englishmen, to use Englishmen in this manner." *The History of Thomas Ellwood, Written by Himself* [1714] (London, 1885), 160, 163.
148. *New York Colonial Laws* (Albany, 1894–96), I, 14, 160.
149. J. T. Adams, *Founding of New England* (Boston, 1921), 362.
150. A. W. Lauber, *Indian Slavery in Colonial Times within the Present Limits of the United States* (Columbia Univ., *Studies*, LIV), 124.
151. William Appleton, ed., *The Winthrop Papers* (Mass. Hist. Soc., *Colls.*, ser. 4, VI), 91.
152. Frederick Freeman, *The History of Cape Cod* (Boston, 1869), II, 293.
153. George Bishop, *New England Judged* (London, 1661), 108–12.
154. Hening, *Statutes at Large of Virginia*, II, 299.
155. Ibid., 270.
156. *Middlesex County Records for 1694–1705*, 238, cited in P. A. Bruce, *Economic History of Virginia*, II, 108.
157. J. R. Brackett, *The Negro in Maryland* (Johns Hopkins Univ., *Studies*, extra vol. vi), 142 n.
158. The care of the poor naturally engaged less attention in America than in England. In the South it was the concern of the parish vestry, a self-perpetuating body. In New England it fell under the jurisdiction of the town, whose officials exercised a close surveillance over strangers, bachelors, and others. See E. W. Capen, *The Historical Development of the Poor Law of Connecticut* (Columbia Univ., *Studies*, XXII), chap. i.
159. Sermons and religious proceedings were often taken down in shorthand. See H. R. Stiles, *The History and Genealogies of Ancient Windsor* (Hartford, 1891), I, 11; S. E. Baldwin, "Rev. John Higginson, of Salem," Mass. Hist. Soc., *Proceeds.*, ser. 2, XVI, 487–89; W. P. Upham, "Remarks [on shorthand]," same vol., 475–76. All we know of Thomas Hooker's famous sermons of 1638 and 1639 comes to us

through Henry Wolcott's notes, taken according to his modification of the Willis system. See J. H. T. *(pseud.)*, "Abstracts of Two Sermons by Rev. Thomas Hooker. From the Short-hand Notes of Mr. Henry Wolcott," Conn. Hist. Soc., *Colls.*, I, 19-21. See also John Hull, "Diary," Am. Antiq. Soc., *Trans.*, III, 151-54; and MSS. by C. C. Beale and J. E. Rockwell in N.Y. Public Library.

160. Cotton Mather, *Magnalia*, I, 250.

161. Charles Deane, "Report on the Belknap Donation," Mass. Hist. Soc., *Proceeds.*, III, 311-12. Lechford's own account is found in his "Note-Book," 48-49.

162. For example, the Duke's Laws for New York in 1663 had to be printed in Boston. Isaiah Thomas, *History of Printing in America* (Am. Antiq. Soc., *Trans.*, V-VI), I, 38-75, 290. William Bradford, the first Pennsylvania printer, came in the *Welcome* with Penn himself in 1682, his earliest imprint bearing the date of 1685; in 1693 he established the first press in New York. See G. H. Payne. *History of Journalism in the United States* (New York, 1920), 37, 46. No press was set up in Connecticut till 1709. See Doyle, *The English in America*, II, 195.

163. C. A. Duniway, *Development of Freedom of the Press in Massachusetts* (*Harvard Hist. Studies*, XII), 32.

164. T. G. Wright, *Literary Culture in Early New England* (New Haven, 1920), 37.

165. Duniway, *Freedom of the Press*, 32-33, 35-37, 54.

166. L. C. Wroth, *A History of Printing in Colonial Maryland* (Baltimore, 1922), chap i.

167. W. C. Ford, *The Boston Book Market, 1679-1710* (Boston, 1917).

168. J. H. Tuttle, "The Libraries of the Mathers," Am. Antiq. Soc., *Proceeds.*, XX, 269ff.

169. Harlan Updegraff, *The Origin of the Moving School in Massachusetts* (Teachers Col., Columbia Univ., *Contribs. to Educ.*, no. 17). chap. i.

170. The hornbook was a leaf of paper, usually containing the alphabet, the nine digits, and the Lord's Prayer, fixed to a wooden frame with a handle, and covered over with transparent horn to protect it from destructive fumbling by the child.

171. Eaton went to Virginia and thence to England. J. H. Littlefield, *Early Massachusetts Press, 1638-1711* (Boston, 1907), 70.

172. Cotton Mather, *Magnalia*, II, 12.

173. Edward Eggleston, *Transit of Civilization*, 35-36; see also T. F. Waters, *A Sketch of the Life of John Winthrop, the Younger* (n.p., 1899), 57.

174. Jasper Dankers [or Danckaerts] and Peter Sluyter, "Journal of a Voyage to New York and a Tour in Severall of the American Colonies in 1679-80." L. I. Hist. Soc., *Memoirs*, I. 384-85.

175. Hening, *Statutes at Large of Virginia*, I, 517.

176. Bruce, *Institutional History of Virginia*, I, 299, 304-305.

177. Ibid., I, 331-42.

178. Hening, *Statutes at Large of Virginia*, I, 518.

179. All are reprinted in Force, *Tracts*, I.

180. Bruce, *Institutional History of Virginia*, I, 411.

181. William Fitzhugh, "Will of William Fitzhugh," *Va. Mag. of Hist. and Biog.*, II, 227.

182. Ebenezer Cook, "The Sot-weed Factor [1708]," Md. Hist. Soc., *Fund Publs.*, no. 36, 11-32.

183. T. H. Wynne and W. S. Gilman, eds., *Colonial Records of Virginia* (Richmond, 1874), 9-32, passim. Sumptuary laws regulating private conduct were not an American or a Protestant invention. See J. M. Vincent, "European Blue Laws," Am. Hist. Assoc., *Report for 1897*, 357-72. These laws in Virginia soon became dead letters.

184. Anon., "A Perfect Description of Virginia [1649]." Force, *Tracts*, II, no. viii, 3.

185. Bruce, *Economic History of Virginia*, II, 473.

186. Hugh Jones, *The Present State of Virginia* (London, 1724), 48.

187. Robert Beverley, *The History and Present State of Virginia* (London, 1705), 258.

188. Bruce, *Economic History of Virginia*, I, 223-38.

189. *The Private Journal of a Journey from Boston to New York in the Year 1704. Kept by Madam Knight* (Albany, 1865), 70-71.

190. Alice M. Earle, *Colonial Days in Old New York* (New York, 1896), 203-207.

191. Daniel Denton, *Brief Description of New York* [1670] (Gabriel Furman, ed., New York, 1845), 2-6.

192. Charles Lodowick, "New York in 1692," N.Y. Hist. Soc., *Colls.,* ser. 2, II, 245.

193. See, however, John Cotton's defense of some kinds of dancing, Mass. Hist. Soc., *Colls.,* ser. 2, X. 183-84.

194. Alice M. Earle, *Customs and Fashions in Old New England* (New York, 1893), 18.

195. T. W. Higginson, *Travellers and Outlaws* (New York, 1889), chap. i.

196. Cotton Mather, *Magnalia,* I, 69.

197. John Cotton wrote, "We sometimes upon extraordinary occasions either of notable judgements do set apart a day of humiliation, or upon special mercies we set apart a day of thanksgiving." John Cotton, *The Way of the Churches in New-England* (London, 1645), 70.

198. Love, *Fast and Thanksgiving Days of New England,* 239-55.

199. For the regulation of defense, see H. L. Osgood. *The American Colonies in the Seventeenth Century* (New York, 1904-1907), I, chap. xiii.

200. William Bradford, "History of Plymouth Plantation," Charles Deane, ed., Mass. Hist. Soc., *Colls.,* ser. 4, III, 134-35.

201. Cotton Mather, *Diary,* II, 146.

202. Crachets, or crochets, were posts with forked tops.

203. John Smith, *Works* (Edward Arber, ed., Birmingham, 1884), II, 957. The two volumes are printed in one.

204. Johnson, *Wonder-Working Providence* (Jameson, *Original Narratives of Early American History*), 83. Cf. illustration showing a Kansas dugout about 1867, in this volume, Book VIII.

205. E. D. Neill, *Virginia Company of London* (Washington, 1868), 398, 409.

206. Fiske Kimball, *Domestic Architecture in the American Colonies* (New York, 1922), 6-7.

207. Men of considerable estates in the colonies maintained their own thatch beds. See, for example, N.Y. Hist. Soc., *Colls.* (1892), 411.

208. Alexander Brown, *The First Republic in America* (Boston, 1898), 208-10.

209. Anon., "A Perfect Description of Virginia [1649]," Force, *Tracts,* II, no, viii, 7.

210. *The Winthrop Papers* (Mass. Hist. Soc., *Colls.,* ser. 4, VII), 118-20.

211. Lechford, "Note-Book," VII, 302.

212. Governor Thomas Dudley, "Letter to the Countess of Lincoln [1631]," Mass. Hist. Soc., *Colls.,* ser. 1, VIII, 46.

213. Quoted in J. T. Faris, *The Romance of Old Philadelphia* (Philadelphia, 1918), 53.

214. The *Mayflower* was less than 100 feet long and about 25 feet wide. The *Speedwell,* its companion, which had soon to return to the English port because of a leak, was one third as large. See William Bradford, "History of Plymouth Plantation," Charles Deane, ed., Mass. Hist. Soc., *Colls.,* ser. 4, III, 85. See also Azel Ames, *The May-Flower and Her Log* (Boston, 1901), chap, iv, for the fullest description of the ship.

215. T. F. Waters, *History of Ipswich in the Massachusetts Bay Colony* (Ipswich, 1905), 24, 30, 32, 121, 362, 367, 489, 500-501.

216. L. V. Lockwood, *Colonial Furniture in America* (New York, 1913) II, 4-5. Dr. Lyon, searching the inventories of seventy-five householders between 1641 and 1659, found an average of two chairs each. I. W. Lyon, *Colonial Furniture of New England* (Boston, 1891).

217. Esther Singleton, *The Furniture of Our Forefathers* (New York, 1900). I, 58-60, gives this among many examples. The Rev. John Cotton had twenty-six chairs, thirty stools, six forms and a couch. *Ibid.,* 185, 191.

218. Wallace Nutting, *Furniture of the Pilgrim Century, 1620-1720* (Framingham, Mass., 1924), 190-91.

219. Bradford, "History of Plymouth Plantation." 194-95.
220. J. A. Krout, *The Origins of Prohibition* (New York, 1925), 44-45.
221. John Dunton, *The Life and Errors of John Dunton* (London, 1705), 126.
222. Edward Field, *The Colonial Tavern* (Providence, 1897), 27-28.
223. Bacon's *Proceedings,* reprinted in Force, *Tracts,* I.
224. Earle, *Home Life in Colonial Days,* 202-203.
225. The suspension of the pestle from the elastic bough or sapling as an aid in grinding corn was also in imitation of the Indian. See H. R. Schoolcraft, *Information Respecting the History, Condition and Prospects of the Indian Tribes* (Philadelphia, 1854), IV, plate 21.
226. Among other Indian words which have found a place in English are opossum, raccoon, skunk, and woodchuck. Krapp, *English Language in America,* I, 104.
227. There was a crude beginning of the graphic arts, as is evidenced by Foster's woodcut of Richard Mather. Frank Weitenkampf, *American Graphic Arts* (New York, 1924), 112-13. See also C. K. Bolton, *The Founders; Portraits of Persons Born Abroad Who Came to North America before the Year 1701* (Boston, 1919-26).
228. Geoffroy Atkinson, *Les Relations de Voyages du XVII Siècle et l'Évolution des Idées* (Paris, 1925).
229. F. W. Coburn, "Newly Discovered Painter of the Puritans," *New York Times Book Review and Magazine,* July 24, 1921. Dummer (1645-1718) was son of Richard Dummer, a prominent immigrant, and father of Jeremy Dummer, agent in England of Massachusetts and Connecticut, and also of Lt. Gov. William Dummer of Connecticut. Unlike most colonial painters he was a man of family and influence.
230. E. B. O'Callaghan and Berthold Fernow, eds., *Documents Relating to the Colonial History of the State of New York* (Albany, 1853-87), V, 339, 459.
231. The source of this immigration is interesting. Anders Orbeck took the pioneers of Plymouth, Watertown, and Dedham as a sample and found that approximately two thirds came from the region along the English coast between London and the Wash, mostly from the southern part. Anders Orbeck, *Early New England Pronunciations* (unpublished thesis, Columbia Univ.), chap. v.
232. Only about twice as many as had gone to the island of St. Christopher alone. See map-chart in J. T. Adams, *The Founding of New England* (Boston, 1922), 120.
233. These estimates and reports are taken from W. R. Rossiter, ed., *A Century of Population Growth* (Washington, 1909), 3-10.
234. William Fitzhugh estimated that he had made three times as much in Virginia as he could have made in England. William Fitzhugh, "Letters," *Va. Mag. of Hist. and Biog.,* I, 395-96.

BOOK III Provincial Society, 1690–1763

1. A. M. Schlesinger, "Colonial Appeals to the Privy Council," *Political Science Quarterly,* XXVIII, 440-45.
2. See J. T. Adams, "On the Term 'British Empire,' " *Am. Hist. Rev.,* XXVII, 485.
3. D. R. Fox, *Caleb Heathcote, Gentleman Colonist* (New York, 1926), chap. i.
4. E. B. Greene, *The Provincial Governor in the English Colonies of North America* (*Harvard Historical Studies,* VII), 49. Jefferson in his "Notes on Virginia" testifies to the cultural influence of Governor Fauquier.
5. Pa. German Soc., *Proceeds.,* XVIII, 1; "Journey of F. L. Michel," *Va. Mag. of Hist. and Biog.,* XXIV, 287.
6. *Va. Mag. of Hist. and Biog.,* IV, 71.
7. Mass. Hist. Soc., *Proceeds.,* ser. 2, I, 44.
8. Topsfield Hist. Soc., *Colls.,* XVI, 7.
9. *The Good Old Way* (Boston, 1706), 70.
10. Edward Ward, *A Trip to New England* (G. P. Winship, ed., Providence, 1905), 38.

11. "Letters of Wm. Fitzhugh," *Va. Mag. of Hist. and Biog.,* I, 395.
12. Col. William Byrd, *Writings* (J. S. Bassett, ed., New York, 1901), xxxi.
13. *Va. Mag. of Hist. and Biog.,* II, 271.
14. E. S. Rohde, *The Old English Herbals* (London, 1922), 179.
15. "Journal of William Black, 1744," *Pa. Mag. of Hist. and Biog.,* I, 126.
16. See J. A. Krout, *The Origins of Prohibition* (New York, 1925), 26-50.
17. Ward, *Trip to New England,* 51.
18. Ibid., 39.
19. Manasseh Minor, "Diary," passim.
20. Anon., "Diary of a Voyage from Rotterdam to Philadelphia, 1728," Pa. German Soc., *Proceeds.,* XVIII, 23.
21. Byrd, *Writings,* 78.
22. Ibid., 320, 323.
23. "Boundary Line Proceedings, 1710," *Va. Mag. of Hist. and Biog.,* V, 10.
24. Knight, *Journal,* 24.
25. "Diary of a Voyage from Rotterdam to Philadelphia," 19. Such a case parallels quite closely an earlier one in New England noted by John Winthrop.
26. In such a brief discussion I have not attempted to differentiate between the different types of servants. There were three classes of those who became servants by indenture: convicts sentenced to transportation by British courts; servants who signed a contract in Europe, including several types; and the free-willers or redemptioners who sold their own services voluntarily for a term of years. There were also certain important legal distinctions between servants by indenture and those by "custom of the country."
27. "Diary of a Voyage from Rotterdam to Philadelphia," 23.
28. Gabriel Thomas, *An Account of Pennsylvania and West New Jersey, 1698* (reprinted, Cleveland, 1903), 28.
29. "Early Letter from Pennsylvania," *Pa. Mag. of Hist. and Biog.,* XXXVII, 334.
30. Quoted in Pa.-German Soc., *Proceeds.,* IX, 153.
31. "Early Letter from Pennsylvania," 338.
32. *Cal. of State Paps., Colon., 1701,* 631; Byrd, *Writings,* xii.
33. *Va. Mag. of Hist. and Biog.,* III, 255.
34. Cadwallader Colden, *Letters and Papers* (N.Y. Hist. Soc., *Colls., 1917*), I, 14.
35. Issue of April 9, 1705.
36. Thomas Prince, *Chronological History of New England, in the Form of Annals* (Boston, 1736).
37. G. L. Kittredge, "Cotton Mather's Scientific Communications," Am. Antiq. Soc., *Proceeds.,* new ser., XXVI, 18-57.
38. "Early Letters from South Carolina upon Natural History," *S.C. Hist. and Geneal. Mag.,* XXI, 5.
39. At the close of this period some were going to Edinburgh; see list in *New England Genealogical and Historical Register,* XLI, 391-92.
40. Two years before the English government placed the bodies of criminals at the disposal of doctors (1752). Dr. Peter Middleton and Dr. Samuel Bard gave a lecture on a cadaver cut from the gallows in New York; *Annals of Medical History,* March 1926.
41. "Extracts from the Book of Phisick of William Penn," *Pa. Mag. of Hist. and Biog.,* XL, 475, 478.
42. Quoted by H. F. Long, "The Physicians of Topsfield," Topsfield Hist. Soc., *Colls.,* XVI, 13.
43. C. A. Duniway, *The Struggle for the Freedom of the Press in Mass.* (*Harvard Hist. Studies,* XII), 68-69, 70-73.
44. Quoted by W. W. Kemp, *The Support of Schools in Colonial New York* (New York 1913), 68.
45. Ibid., 67.

46. *An Addition to the Present Melancholy Circumstances of the Province Considered* (Boston, 1719), 7.
47. H. D. Eberlein and Abbot McClure, *The Practical Book of Early American Arts and Crafts* (Philadelphia, 1916), chap. ix.
48. R. R. Drummond, *Early German Music* (*Americana Germanica,* Univ. of Pennsylvania), pt. I.
49. J. H. Morgan, *Early American Painters* (New York, 1921), 8–21.
50. H. B. Adams, *The College of William and Mary* (*Circular of Information of the Bureau of Education,* no. 1), 17.
51. George Keith, *A Journal of Travels from New-Hampshire to Caratuck* (London, 1706), 36.
52. See remarks by William C. Lane on a manuscript volume recently acquired by Harvard College, in Colon. Soc. Mass., *Publs.,* XII, 229.
53. Broadside, August 22, 1728 (Library of Congress).
54. C. F. Adams, "Some Phases of Sexual Morality and Church Discipline," Mass. Hist. Soc., *Proceeds.,* ser. 2, VI, 477–516.
55. H. R. Stiles, *Bundling, Its Origin, Progress and Decline* (Albany, 1869), chap. i.
56. *The Constitution and By-Laws of the Scots' Charitable Society of Boston* (Boston, 1896).
57. M. S. Locke, *Anti-Slavery in America . . . 1619–1808* (Radcliffe College, *Monographs,* Boston, 1901), chap. i.
58. "Letters of William Fitzhugh," *Va. Mag. of Hist. and Biog.,* II.
59. T. J. Wertenbaker, *The Planters of Colonial Virginia* (Princeton, 1922), 153.
60. Quoted by T. J. Wertenbaker from Gooch to the Lords of Trade, Brit. Pub. Rec. Off., CO 5/1321, 1322.
61. See J. S. Bassett's introduction to his edition of William Byrd II, *History of the Dividing Line* (New York, 1901).
62. See pictures in T. F. Hamlin, *The American Spirit in Architecture* (R. H. Gabriel, ed., *The Pageant of America,* New York, 1926, XIII).
63. Issue December 3, 1736.
64. Witherspoon's account, quoted by C.A. Hanna, *The Scotch-Irish* (New York, 1902), II, 27.
65. Quoted by J. A. Waddell, *Anns. of Augusta County* (Staunton, 1902), 77.
66. J. S. Bassett, "The Virginia Planter and the London Merchant," Am. Hist. Assoc., *Rep. for 1901,* 553–75.
67. Conn. Archives, Trade and Maritime Affairs, I, 72.
68. Samuel Mulford, *Speech to the Assembly at New York* (New York, April 2, 1714), 1.
69. Issue of September 2/9, 1731.
70. *N.Y. Gazette,* August 13/20, 1733.
71. *N.Y. Gazette,* February 11/18, 1733.
72. James Birket, *Some Cursory Remarks Made by James Birket on his Voyage to North America, 1750–51* (New Haven, 1916), 12.
73. Dr. Alexander Hamilton, *Itinerarium* (A. B. Hart, ed., St. Louis, 1907), 125.
74. J. T. Adams, *Revolutionary New England, 1691–1776* (Boston, 1923), chap. vii.
75. W. S. Heywood, *History of Westminster* (Lowell, 1893), 76.
76. Quoted from R. H. Morris Papers, by E. J. Fisher, *New Jersey as a Royal Province* (Columbia Univ., *Studies,* XLI), 193.
77. William Shirley, *Correspondence* (C. H. Lincoln, ed., New York, 1912), I, 418.
78. C. H. Lincoln, *The Revolutionary Movement in Pennsylvania* (Philadelphia, 1901), 45–46.
79. *The Vade Mecum for America or a Companion for Traders and Travellers* (Boston, 1732).
80. Hamilton, *Itinerarium,* 185.
81. *Md. Gazette,* March 24, 1747.
82. R. F. Gould, *The History of Free Masonry* (London, 1887), VI, chap. xxxi; Ossian

Lang, *History of Freemasonry in the State of New York* (New York, 1922), chaps. i–iii.

83. *An Historical Account of the Origin and Formation of the American Philosophical Society* (Philadelphia, 1914), 178.

84. The first *Maryland Gazette* ran from 1727 to 1736, to be revived in 1745. The *South-Carolina Gazette* was begun in 1732, lasted only a few months, and began a new and long career again in 1734.

85. C. S. Brigham, "Bibliography of American Newspapers, 1691–1820," Am. Antiq. Soc., *Proceeds.*, new ser., XXV, 193ff.

86. Livingston Rutherfurd, *John Peter Zenger* (New York, 1904), chap. iii.

87. William Seward, *Journal of a Voyage from Savannah to Philadelphia, 1740* (London, 1740), 10, 17, 18.

88. In the same year there was also started in Philadelphia the *American Magazine, or a Monthly View of the Political State of the British Colonies*. It has been stated that there is only one copy of this known and that it ran for only three numbers. It ran for at least twelve copies, all of which are in the Library of Congress. The *Boston Weekly Magazine* and the *Christian History* also belong to this period.

89. Sermon by Mr. Massey [England] quoted in the *Am. Weekly Mercury*, January 1, 1722.

90. Issue of January 24, 1734.

91. Issues of October 15 and 29, 1736.

92. J. T. Adams, *Revolutionary New England*, 177–78.

93. [L. Campbell], *Itinerant Observations in America*, reprinted from the *London Mag.* (Savannah, 1878), 43.

94. H. L. Mencken, *The American Language* (New York, 1923), 49ff., 55ff., 59, 63, 73.

95. Hamilton, *Itinerarium*, 6, 8, 20, 36, 40, 200.

96. *Md. Gazette*, May 10, 24, 31, 1745; *Am. Mag.*, October 1745.

97. *Md. Gazette*, May 17, 1745.

98. These figures were kindly given to me by Mr. H. M. Chapin of the Rhode Island Historical Society, who has been making a study of the subject, and to whom I am also indebted for some suggestions as to the unprofitableness of the ventures as a whole.

99. Tabulated from issues of the *N.Y. Gazette* and *Pa. Gazette*. The file of the *Boston News-Letter*, which I examined for that year, lacked about twelve issues. The incomplete entries totaled only 348 vessels to compare with 578 in 1733. Eight of the missing weeks were from November 5 to the end of the year, so that even making all allowance the total would not seem to have exceeded that of two decades earlier.

100. *Boston Weekly News-Letter*, July 25, 1754.

101. *N.Y. Gazette*, June 4, 1753; June 3 and July 8, 1754; April 14 and October 24, 1757.

102. *Pa. Gazette*, March 20, 1760.

103. *N.Y. Gazette*, January 3, 1757; *Pa. Gazette*, January 3, 1760.

104. "Narrative of Geo. Fisher," *William and Mary Quar.*, XVII, 170.

105. Cf., for example, *Boston News-Letter*, May 6 and July 15, 1731; April 26, 1733.

106. *Ga. Gazette*, February 9, 16, 1764.

107. *Pa. Gazette*, December 25, 1760.

108. *Md. Gazette*, August 6, 1761.

109. As the following list, compiled from scattered sources, including manuscripts, contains more names than any other I have seen, it may be given in full. The dates are either those of the known founding or the earliest recorded notice of the institutions. Library Company of Philadelphia, 1732; Useful Knowledge Library, Pomfret, Conn., 1732; Philogrammatican Library, Lebanon, Conn., 1739; Library of Friends, Philadelphia, 1742; Darby, Pa., a library, 1743; German Library at Germantown, Pa., 1745; Union Library of Philadelphia, 1746; Redwood Library,

Newport, 1747; Library Society of Charleston, S.C., 1748; Library at Providence, R.I., 1753; New York Society Library, 1754; Winyaw Society, Georgetown, S.C., 1755; Hatborough, Pa., 1755; Amicable Library, Philadelphia, 1757; Association Library, Philadelphia, 1757; Albany Society Library, 1758; Lancaster Library (name later changed to Juliana Library Company), Lancaster, Pa., 1759; Social Library of Salem, Mass., 1760; proposals for a circulating library, Annapolis, 1762; Blockley and Merion United Library Company, Pa., 1763; Portland, Me., 1763; Leominster Social Library, 1763; Georgia Society Library, mentioned 1764, probably in existence earlier. In the above list of public libraries founded during this period I have not included those of various institutions of learning.

110. Issue of April 12, 1755.
111. *Pa. Gazette,* April 2, 1758.
112. Cf. *Md. Gazette,* November 16, 1752.
113. *Boston Weekly News-Letter,* June 6, 1754; *Va. Gazette,* July 11, 1751; *Warner's Almanack* (Williamsburg, Va.), 1762; *Ga. Gazette,* October 18, 1764.
114. *Ga. Gazette,* November 8, 1764.
115. *N.Y. Gazette,* January 7, 1754.
116. Reprinted in *Md. Gazette,* February 17, 1747.
117. The first notice I have found of it in either a private library list or a bookseller's advertisement is in the *Mass. Gazette,* December 13, 1764.
118. *Md. Gazette,* April 23, 1761.
119. "State of the Debts," Brit. Mus. Add. MSS. 35909.
120. *Conn. Gazette,* March 20, 1756.
121. Jacques Fontaine, *Memoirs of a Huguenot Family* (Ann Maury, tr., New York, 1872), 374.
122. A. M. Schlesinger, *Colonial Merchants and the American Revolution* (Columbia Univ., *Studies,* LXXVIII), 56–57.
123. Cf. *Obstructions of Trade* (Connecticut broadside of 1764).

BOOK IV The Revolutionary Generation, 1763–90

1. Population estimtes are based chiefly on E. B. Greene and Virginia D. Harrington, comps., *American Population before the Federal Census of 1790* (New York, 1932).
2. Benjamin Franklin, *Writings* (Albert Smyth, ed., New York, 1907), III, 63ff.; [Lord Adam Gordon], "Journal of an Officer's Travels in America and the West Indies, 1764–1765," N. D. Mereness, ed., *Travels in the American Colonies* (New York 1916), 406; D. D. Wallace, *Henry Laurens* (New York, 1915), chap. v; U. B. Phillips, *Life and Labor in the Old South* (Boston, 1929), 224, 228; Kate M. Rowland, *Life and Correspondence of Charles Carroll of Carrollton* (New York, 1898), II, 54; Theodore Sedgwick, *A Memoir of the Life of William Livingston* (New York, 1833), 446; Edward Wigglesworth, "Observations on the Longevity of the Inhabitants of Ipswich and Hingham," Am. Acad. of Arts and Sci., *Memoirs,* I (1785), 565.
3. Emigration lists, Public Record Office, T. 47/9, 10, 11 (transcripts in American Antiquarian Society); M. L. Hansen, *The Atlantic Migration, 1607–1860* (A. M. Schlesinger, ed., Cambridge, 1940), 52.
4. [Janet Schaw], *Journal of a Lady of Quality, 1774 to 1776* (Evangeline W. and C. M. Andrews, eds., New Haven, 1921), app. i; S. C. Johnson. *A History of Emigration from the United Kingdom to North America, 1763–1912* (London School of Econs. and Polit. Sci., *Monograph Ser.,* no. 34), 2ff.; emigration lists, Public Record Office, T. 47/12.
5. Committee on Linguistic and National Stocks in the Population of the United States, "Report," Am. Hist. Assoc., *Ann. Rep. for 1931,* I, 107–25, and "Annexes."

6. M. L. Hansen, "The Minor Stocks in the American Population of 1790," Am. Hist. Assoc., *Ann. Rep. for 1931,* I, 360ff.

7. G. E. Howard, *A History of Matrimonial Institutions* (Chicago, 1904), II, chap. xiii.

8. Ibid., 121-39; Thomas Hutchinson, *The History of the Colony and Province of Massachusetts-Bay* (L. S. Mayo, ed., Cambridge, 1936), I, 375.

9. Howard, *Matrimonial Institutions,* II, chap. xiv; L. W. Labaree, ed., *Royal Instructions to British Colonial Governors, 1670-1776* (New York, 1935), I, 154.

10. Phillips, *Life and Labor in the Old South,* 203-205; Howard, *Matrimonial Institutions,* II, 215-16; this volume, Book III, 202.

11. J. D. Schoepf, *Travels in the Confederation, 1783-1784* (A. J. Morrison, ed., Philadelphia, 1911), I, 100.

12. R. B. Morris, *Studies in the History of American Law* (Columbia Univ. *Studies,* no. 316), chap. iii; W. G. Brown, *Oliver Ellsworth* (New York, 1905), 113-15.

13. Marquis de Chastellux, *Travels in North-America* (London, 1787), II, 131-36.

14. Helen T. Catterall, ed., *Judicial Cases Concerning Slavery and the Negro* (Carnegie Inst., *Publs.,* no. 374), I, 83-84, 93; U. B. Phillips, *American Negro Slavery* (New York, 1918), esp. chaps, vi, xxi-xxiii; Josiah Quincy, "Journal," Mass Hist. Soc., *Proceeds.,* XLIX, 446; *Va. Gazette,* April 21, 1775; *S.-C. Gazette,* September 24, 1772.

15. E. I. McCormac, *White Servitude in Maryland, 1634-1820* (Johns Hopkins Univ., *Studies,* XXII, nos. 3-4), esp. chaps. iv, vi, viii; C. A. Herrick, *White Servitude in Pennsylvania* (Philadelphia, 1926), chaps. vi-xiv.

16. Ibid., 267-73.

17. George Washington, *Diaries, 1748-1799* (J. C. Fitzpatrick, ed., Boston, 1925), I, 214, 276, 282, 366.

18. T. J. Wertenbaker. *The Founding of American Civilization, the Middle Colonies* (New York, 1938), 244-50; A. E. Peterson and G. W. Edwards, *New York as an Eighteenth Century Municipality* (New York, 1917), 289-91; Samuel McKee, *Labor in Colonial New York, 1664-1776* (Columbia Univ., *Studies,* no. 410), chap. i. For a tailors' strike, see I. N. P. Stokes, *Iconography of Manhattan Island* (New York, 1915-28), IV, 784.

19. Cadwallader Colden, *Letter-Books* (N.Y. Hist. Soc., *Colls.,* IX-X). II, 68ff.

20. Devereux Jarratt, *Life* (Baltimore, 1806), 13-15; A. E. McKinley. *The Suffrage Franchise in the Thirteen English Colonies in America* (Univ. of Pa., *Ser. in History,* no. 2), 47, 357.

21. John Adams, *Works,* II, 49, 133, 197; Hamlin, *Legal Education,* 39; McCrady, *South Carolina under Royal Government,* chap. xxiv.

22. F. R. Packard, *History of Medicine in the United States* (rev. ed., New York, 1931), I, 284ff.; Sam Briggs, *The Essays, Humor and Poems of Nathaniel Ames, Father and Son, . . . from Their Almanacks* (Cleveland, 1891), 361, 413.

23. Stanard, *Colonial Virginia,* 160-63; James Rivington to Henry Knox, Mass. Hist. Soc., *Proceeds.,* LXI, 269 and n.; *Pa Gazette,* February 8, 1775.

24. Michael Kraus, *Intercolonial Aspects of American Culture on the Eve of the Revolution* (Columbia Univ., *Studies,* no. 302), 143; Packard, *History of Medicine,* I, chaps. v-vi; T. F. Harrington, *The Harvard Medical School* (New York, 1905), I, 46-50; G. W. Norris, *Early History of Medicine in Philadelphia* (Philadelphia, 1886), 30-35; T. G. Morton, *History of the Pennsylvania Hospital* (Philadelphia, 1895), passim.

25. Packard, *History of Medicine,* I, 322; *Pa. Gazette,* January 11, 1770; Carson, *Medical Department of the University of Pennsylvania,* 217; Norris, *Early History of Medicine in Philadelphia,* 44-45; this volume, Book III, 202.

26. *Pa. Gazette,* January 11, 1775; Garrison, *History of Medicine,* 380; Packard, *History of Medicine,* I, chap. vii.

27. Franklin, *Writings,* IV, 386; Quincy, "Journal," 448 ff.; John Rowe, *Letters and Diary.* (Annie R. Cunningham, ed., Boston, 1903) 174; Sedgwick, *Livingston,* 153.

28. J. H. Tatsch, *Freemasonry in the Thirteen Colonies* (New York, 1929); Rowe, *Letters and Diary*, 141, 176, 180; H. W. Smith, *Life and Correspondence of the Rev. William Smith* (Philadelphia, 1880), I, 107; II, 11, 347, 409.

29. Rowe, *Letters and Diary*, 104, 119; William Eddis, *Letters from America* (London, 1792), 7-9, 112-15; John Adams, *Works*, II, 288-89.

30. William Gregory, "Journal," *William and Mary College Quar.*, XIII, 227; John Adams, *Works*, II, 400, 402.

31. Peterson and Edwards, *New York as an Eighteenth Century Municipality*, 330-36; [Gordon], "Journal," 398; John Adams, *Works*, II, 138.

32. Peterson and Edwards, *New York as an Eighteenth Century Municipality*, 324-26, 339-41; Adams and Adams, *Familiar Letters*, 240; Schoepf, *Travels*, I, 169; Alexander Graydon, *Memoirs of His Own Time* (J. S. Littell, ed., Philadelphia, 1846), 43; [Gordon], "Journal," 411, 415; Justin Winsor, ed., *Memorial History of Boston, 1630-1880* (Boston, 1880-81), III, 152; *S.-C Gazette*, October 24, 1772.

33. *Pa. Gazette*, January 10, 1765; C. H. Lincoln, *The Revolutionary Movement in Pennsylvania, 1760-1776* (Univ. of Pa., *Ser. in History*, no. 1), chap. v.

34. Jared Sparks, *Life of Gouverneur Morris* (Boston, 1832), I, 23-25; John Adams, *Works*, 273, 295.

35. Abigail Adams, *Letters* (C. F. Adams, ed., 4th ed., Boston, 1848), xxi; Eddis, *Letters*, 128; Marquis de Chastellux to Mr. Madison, Chastellux, *Travels*, II, 344-46; Franklin, *Writings*, V, 362.

36. James Madison, *Writings* (Gaillard Hunt, ed., New York, 1900-1901). I, 19-23.

37. M. C. Tyler, *Patrick Henry* (J. T. Morse, Jr., ed., *American Statesmen*, III, rev. ed., Boston, 1898), chap. iv.

38. Herbert and Carol Schneider, eds., *Samuel Johnson, President of King's College. His Career and Writings* (New York, 1929), I, 379.

39. Mary L. Gambrell, *Ministerial Training in Eighteenth-Century New England* (Columbia Univ., *Studies*, no. 428); Alice M. Baldwin, *The New England Clergy and the American Revolution* (Duke Univ., *Publs.*, 1928), chap. i.

40. J. C. Meyer, *Church and State in Massachusetts from 1740 to 1833* (Cleveland, 1930), chaps. ii-iii; Maria L. Greene, *The Development of Religious Liberty in Connecticut* (Boston, 1905), chaps. ix-xi.

41. For Edwards's teachings, see this volume, Book III, 202.

42. W. T. Root, *The Relations of Pennsylvania with the British Government, 1696-1765* (Univ. of Pa., *Publs.*, 1912), chap. viii; Isaac Sharpless, *A Quaker Experiment in Government* (Philadelphia, 1902), pt. i, chaps. v-viii; E. R. Turner, *The Negro in Pennsylvania* (Am. Hist. Assoc., *Prize Essays*, 1911), chaps. iv-v; Carl and Jessica Bridenbaugh, *Rebels and Gentlemen* (New York, 1942), 253-60.

43. P. G. Mode, ed., *Source Book and Bibliographical Guide for American Church History* (Menasha, Wis., 1921), 172-73; Thomas Balch, *Letters and Papers Relating Chiefly to the Provincial History of Pennsylvania* (Philadelphia, 1855), 208-12.

44. C. A. Briggs, *American Presbyterianism* (New York, 1885). 328.

45. A. H. Newman, *A History of the Baptist Churches in the United States* (Philip Schaff et al., eds., *American Church History Series*, New York, 1893-97, II), 284-310.

46. W. M. Gewehr, *The Great Awakening in Virginia, 1740-1790* (Duke Univ., *Publs.*, 1930), chap. v.

47. J. M. Buckley, *A History of Methodists in the United States* (Schaff et al., *American Church History Series*, V), chaps. iv-vi; John Adams, *Works*, II, 401.

48. Buckley, *History of Methodists*, 149, 155; Gewehr, *Great Awakening*, chap. vi.

49. Peter Guilday, *The Life and Times of John Carroll* (New York, 1922), 225-26.

50. Ibid, 59-72; Quincy, "Journal," 472-74; Adams and Adams, *Familiar Letters*, 46.

51. John Adams, *Works*, 1-36, passim; W. C. Ford, "Henry Knox and the London Book-Store in Boston, 1771-1774," Mass. Hist. Soc., *Proceeds.*, LXI, 250-60; Schneiders, *Samuel Johnson*, III, 279; Quincy, "Journal," 476; H. M. Morais,

Deism in Eighteenth Century America (Columbia Univ., *Studies,* no. 397), 70 and passim.

52. Peterson and Edwards, *New York as an Eighteenth Century Municipality,* 308; McCrady, *South Carolina under the Royal Government,* 101; Franklin, *Writings,* IV, 185-86, John Adams, *Works,* II, 35; P. V. Fithian, *Journal and Letters, 1767-1774* (J. R. Williams, ed., Princeton, 1900), 255; Quincy, "Journal," 455; Gewehr, *Great Awakening,* 260.

53. J. A. Krout, *Origins of Prohibition* (New York, 1925), chap. iii; John Adams, *Works,* II, 84-85, 96; Briggs, *Ames, ... Almanacks,* 352-54.

54. Ezra Stiles, *Literary Diary* (F. B. Dexter, ed., New York, 1901), I, 507; Abiel Holmes, *The Life of Ezra Stiles* (Boston, 1798), 79.

55. John Adams, *Works,* III, 456; Thomas Anburey, *Travels through the Interior Parts of America* (Boston, 1923), II, 48; Stanard, *Colonial Virginia,* 262-70.

56. John Adams, *Works,* III, 456-57; Rowe, *Letters and Diary,* 100, 168.

57. Hugh Hastings, comp., *Ecclesiastical Records of New York* (Albany, 1901-16), V, 3614; VI, 3983. Cf. W. W. Kemp, *The Support of Schools in Colonial New York by the Society for the Propagation of the Gospel in Foreign Parts* (Teachers College, Columbia Univ., *Contribs.,* no. 56), with R. F. Seybolt, *Source Studies in American Colonial Education: the Private School* (Univ. of Ill., Bur. of Educational Research, *Bull.,* no 28).

58. M. W. Jernegan, *Laboring and Dependent Classes in Colonial America, 1607-1783* (Univ. of Chicago, *Social Service Monographs,* no. 17), chaps. x-xii; Fithian, *Journal and Letters,* 50; John Harrower, "Diary," *Am. Hist. Rev.,* VI, 65-107; McCrady, *South Carolina under the Royal Government,* chap. xxv.

59. Henry, *Patrick Henry,* I, 8-10; J. C. Fitzpatrick, *George Washington Himself* (Indianapolis, 1933), 19-31; Rowland, *Carroll,* I, 18.

60. Jarratt, *Life,* 15ff.

61. Thomas Jefferson, *Works* (P. L. Ford, ed., New York, 1904-1905), IV, 67.

62. Estimates in this paragraph are based on material in alumni lists and biographical dictionaries collected by Mary S. Benson.

63. Josiah Quincy, *History of Harvard University* (Cambridge, 1840), II, apps. xi, xxvi; Stiles, *Literary Diary,* I, 77, 84; John Maclean, *History of the College of New Jersey* (Philadelphia, 1877), I, 357-67; Brander Matthews et al., eds., *A History of Columbia University, 1754-1904* (N. Y., 1904), 22; John Adams, *Works,* II, 356.

64. John Trumbull, *Poetical Works* (Hartford, 1820), II, 17.

65. Rind's *Va. Gazette,* quoted in *William and Mary College Quar.,* II, 107.

66. Harvard College, *Catalogus Librorum* (Boston, 1773); H. D. Foster, "Webster and Choate in College," in his collected *Papers* (n. p., 1929). 236.

67. S. E. Morison, *Three Centuries of Harvard* (Cambridge, 1936), chap. vi; F. B. Dexter, *A Selection from the Miscellaneous Historical Papers of Fifty Years* (New Haven, 1918), 269; M. H. Thomas, ed., *Black Book; or Book of Misdemeanors in King's College, New York, 1771-1775* (New York, 1931), 4; Dennys de Berdt, "Letters" (Albert Matthews, ed.), Colon. Soc. of Mass., *Publs.,* XIII, 320.

68. For the earlier story of the colonial newspaper press, see this volume, Book III, 202.

69. *N. Y. Gazetteer,* no. 78, October 1774; Isaiah Thomas, *The History of Printing in America* (Am. Antiquarian Soc., *Archaeologia Americana, Trans. and Colls.,* V-VI, Albany, 1874), II, 8; J. F. Watson, *Annals of Philadelphia and Pennsylvania, in the Olden Time* (Philadelphia, 1845), II, 461; Hugh Gaine, *Journals* (P. L. Ford, ed., New York, 1902), I, 41.

70. Thomas, *History of Printing,* II, 170.

71. *Bickerstaff's Boston Almanack for 1774,* preface; Oscar Kuhns, *German and Swiss Settlements of Colonial Pennsylvania* (New York, 1901), 133-34.

72. Charles Evans, *American Bibliography* (new ed., New York, 1941-42), III-V.

73. *Pa. Gazette,* January 6, 1763; March 15, 1770.
74. Maryland Invoices and Letters, 1772–1787 (MSS, Library of Congress); Rowland, *Carroll,* I, app. a; Chinard, *Jefferson,* 26; John Adams, *Works,* II, 3, 37, 86; III, 197; William Tudor. *The Life of James Otis* (Boston, 1823), 16; D. D. Wallace, *Henry Laurens* (New York, 1915), 182; *Royal American Magazine,* April 1774.
75. C. H. Van Tyne, *The Causes of the War of Independence* (Boston, 1922), 343–44; C. F. Mullett, *Fundamental Law and the American Revolution* (New York, 1933), chaps. i–ii.
76. *Pa. Gazette,* March 15, 1770; J. H. Tuttle, "The Bowdoin Library," Mass. Hist. Soc., *Proceeds.,* LI, 362ff.; Stanard, *Colonial Virginia,* 299ff.; W. J. Mills, *Glimpses of Colonial Society* (Philadelphia, 1903), 69, 135; *Bickerstaff's Boston Almanack for 1769;* Mrs. John Adams, *Letters* (C. F. Adams, ed., Boston, 1848), II.
77. Morais, *Deism in Eighteenth Century America,* 48–53; Quincy, "Journal," 455–68; Mayhew to Hollis, January 7, 1766 (Bancroft Transcripts, N.Y. Public Library); John Adams, *Works,* II, 148; III, 454–55; Adams and Adams, *Familiar Letters,* 349; Charles Carroll, *Unpublished Letters* (T. M. Field, ed., U.S. Catholic Hist. Soc., *Monograph Ser.,* I), 131.
78. Fiske Kimball and Gertrude S. Carraway, "Tryon's Palace," N.Y. Hist. Soc., *Quar. Bull.* XXIV, no. 1, 13–24; Helen Hill, *George Mason, Constitutionalist* (Cambridge, 1938) 18–26; T. J. Wertenbaker, *The Founding of American Civilization, the Middle Colonies* (New York, 1938), 244ff.; Morgan Dix, ed., *A History of the Parish of Trinity Church in the City of New York* (New York, 1898–1906), I, 315–18; Winsor, *Memorial History of Boston,* IV, 470; Quinn, *History of the American Drama,* I, chap. i.
79. Fiske Kimball, *Domestic Architecture of the American Colonies and the Early Republic* (New York, 1922), chap. ii; Architects Emergency Commission, *Great Georgian Houses of America* (New York, 1937); Chastellux, *Travels in North-America,* II, 232, 234; Quincy, "Journal," 443–45.
80. R. T. H. Halsey and C. O. Cornelius, *Handbook of the American Wing* (5th ed., New York, 1932), 99ff.; W. C. Lane, "Early Silver Belonging to Harvard College," Colon. Soc. of Mass., *Publs.,* XXIV, 174; John Adams, *Works,* II, 179; Esther Forbes, *Paul Revere and the World He Lived In* (Boston, 1942), chaps. i–v.
81. John Adams, *Works,* II, 179, 349–51, 360–400; Quincy, "Journal," 446.
82. John Singleton Copley and Henry Pelham, *Letters and Papers, 1739–1776* (Mass. Hist. Soc., *Colls.,* LXXI), 174.
83. C. C. Sellers, *The Artist of the Revolution, the Early Life of Charles Willson Peale* (Hebron, Conn., 1939), chaps. v–vii.
84. F. W. Bayley, *The Life and Works of John Singleton Copley* (Boston, 1915), esp. 5–18.
85. O. G. Sonneck, *Early Concert Life in America, 1731–1800* (Leipzig, 1907), 18 and passim; McCrady, *South Carolina under Royal Government,* 525–29; Quincy, "Journal," 441–42; Rowe, *Letters and Diary,* 180–88, 213.
86. Franklin, *Writings,* IV, 210; Stanard, *Colonial Virginia,* chap. xii; Fithian, *Journal and Letters,* 82, 132, 225; Jefferson, *Works,* II, 5, 12.
87. *Pa. Gazette,* January 5, 1764; titles of songbooks in Evans, *American Bibliography,* III–IV.
88. G. O. Seilhamer, *History of the American Theatre* (Philadelphia, 1888), I, passim; Colden, *Letters and Papers,* VI, 281–83; Sedgwick, *Livingston,* 102; Stokes, *Iconography of Manhattan,* IV, 781; George Washington, *Diaries, 1748–1799* (J. C. Fitzpatrick ed., Boston, 1925), I, 384.
89. Seilhamer, *American Theatre,* I, 153–56, 282.
90. Ibid., 155–57, 198, 204–208, 214–15, 278–81, 346–47; Graydon, *Memoirs of His Own Time,* 86–87.
91. Seilhamer, *American Theatre,* I, 32–33; Rowe, *Letters and Diary,* 77, 197, 200; Quincy, "Journal," 478–79.

92. F. J. Turner, *The Frontier in American History* (New York, 1920), chap. iii; Eddis, *Letters from America*, 98–102; C. A. Barker, *The Background of the Revolution in Maryland (Yale Hist. Publs. Miscellany)*, E. W. Spaulding, *New York in the Critical Period* (D. R. Fox, ed., *N.Y. State Hist. Assoc. Ser.*, I), 54–55; Washington, *Diaries, 1748–1799*, II, 66, 144–145.

93. Dumas Malone, "Thomas Jefferson," Allen Johnson and Dumas Malone, eds., *Dictionary of American Biography* (New York, 1928–37), X, 17–35; Archibald Henderson, "The Creative Forces in Westward Expansion," *Am. Hist. Rev.*, XX, 95; Adelaide L. Fries, ed., *Records of the Moravians in North Carolina* (N.C. Hist. Comn., *Publs.*, 1922–30), II, 791–94.

94. John Adams, *Works*, II, 278; sketches of William Findley, John Harris, John Smilie, and Robert Whitehill in J. B. McMaster and F. D. Stone, eds., *Pennsylvania and the Federal Constitution, 1787–1788* (Philadelphia, 1888), 727–29, 733, 752–53, 756–57; R. G. Thwaites, *Daniel Boone* (New York, 1902), passim.

95. Leila Sellers, *Charleston Business on the Eve of the American Revolution* (Chapel Hill, 1934), chap. iii.

96. Eddis, *Letters*, 129–34; Anburey, *Travels*, II, 187: Fries, *Records of the Moravians*, II, 796.

97. H. L. Osgood, *The American Colonies in the Eighteenth Century* (New York, 1924), III, 470; Fries, *Records of the Moravians*, II, 746; Gewehr, *Great Awakening*, chap. v.

98. Lois K. Mathews, *The Expansion of New England* (Boston, 1909), chap. v; J. E. A. Smith, *History of Pittsfield* (Boston, 1869), chap. vii; Albert Smith, *History of the Town of Peterborough* (Boston, 1876), chap. x.

99. W. W. Campbell, *Annals of Tryon County* (New York, 1924), 8; Fries, *Records of the Moravians*, II, 710, 744, 827; McCrady, *South Carolina under Royal Government*, 315–17.

100. Jefferson, *Works*, IV, 18.

101. C. H. Lincoln, *The Revolutionary Movement in Pennsylvania, 1760–1776* (Univ. of Pa., *Ser. in Hist.*, no. 1), esp. chap. iv; W. R. Smith, "Sectionalism in Pennsylvania," *Polit. Sci. Quar.*, XXIV, 208–35; B. J. Wallace, "Insurrection of the Paxton Boys," *Presbyterian Quar. Rev.*, VIII, 627–77.

102. J. S. Bassett, "Regulators of North Carolina," Am. Hist. Assoc., *Ann Rep. for 1894*, 141–212; W. L. Saunders, Ed., *Colonial Records of North Carolina, 1662–1776* (Raleigh, 1886–90), VIII, 75–80; W. A. Schaper, "Sectionalism & Representatives in South Carolina," Am. Hist. Assoc., *Ann. Rep for 1900*, I, 334–38.

103. For varying estimates of the number of Indians, see Greene and Harrington, comps., *American Population*, 194ff.

104. A. T. Volwiler, *George Croghan and the Westward Movement* (Cleveland, 1926), 209–59.

105. C. W. Alvord, *The Mississippi Valley in British Politics* (Cleveland, 1917), II, 112–14; R. G. Thwaites and Louise P. Kellogg, eds., *Documentary History of Dunmore's War, 1774* (Madison, 1905), 371.

106. Jefferson, *Works*, II, 239–40; III, 4–8; Henry Tatter, "State and Federal Land Policy during the Confederation Period," *Agricultural History*, IX. 176–86.

107. Thwaites, *Daniel Boone*, chap. iii.

108. John Adams, *Works*, II, 401.

109. A. S. Withers, *Chronicles of Border Warfare* (R. G. Thwaites, ed., Cincinnati, 1895), 128–49 and passim.

110. J. Hector St. John [de Crèvecoeur], *Letters from an American Farmer* (new ed., London, 1783), esp. 51–53.

111. R. B. Morris, *Studies in the History of American Law with Special Reference to the Seventeenth and Eighteenth Centuries* (Columbia Univ., *Studies*, no. 316), chap. i. For the earlier conditions, see this volume, Book III, 202.

112. Other testimony to the good quality and comparative uniformity of American

English came from the Tory parson Jonathan Boucher and the German physician Johann D. Schoepf. [Lord Adam Gordon], "Journal of an Officer's Travels in America and the West Indies, 1764-1765," N. D. Mereness, ed., *Travels in the American Colonies* (New York, 1916), 411, 449; Eddis, *Letters from America,* 59-61; Nicholas Cresswell, *Journal* (New York, 1924), 271; Jonathan Boucher, *Reminiscences of an American Loyalist, 1738-1789* (Jonathan Boucher, ed., Boston, 1925), 61; J. D. Schoepf, *Travels in the Confederation, 1783-1784* (A. J. Morrison, ed., Philadelphia, 1911), II, 62.

113. G. P. Krapp, *The English Language in America* (New York, 1925), II, 49ff.; Fithian, *Journal and Letters,* 147; Franklin, *Writings,* V, 208-10; Witherspoon, *Works,* IV, 460; *Royal American Magazine,* January 1774, 6-7.

114. Franklin, *Writings,* V. 363; VI, 312; *American Magazine or General Repository,* July 1769, 207-208; Charles Carroll, *Unpublished Letters* (T. M. Field, ed., U. S. Catholic Hist. Soc., *Monograph Ser.,* I), 77-79, 96-97; Wallace, *Laurens,* 185; Samuel Curwen, *Journal and Letters* (G. A. Ward, ed., Boston, 1842), 33; Edward Gray. "Ward Chipman, Loyalist," Mass. Hist. Soc., *Proceeds.,* LIV, 340.

115. [Crèvecoeur], *Letters,* letter iii.

116. Irving Mark, *Agrarian Conflicts in Colonial New York, 1711-1775* (Columbia Univ., *Studies,* no. 469), chaps. iv-v; A. O. Craven, *Soil Exhaustion as a Factor in the Agricultural History of Virginia and Maryland, 1606-1860* (Univ. of Ill., *Studies,* XIII, no. 1), 52-56.

117. A. M. Schlesinger, *The Colonial Merchants and the American Revolution, 1763-1776* (Columbia Univ., *Studies,* LXXVIII), chaps. i-ii; Virginia D. Harrington, *The New York Merchant on the Eve of the Revolution* (same ser., no. 404), 328.

118. Ibid., 319; Thomas Gage, *Correspondence with the Secretaries of State, 1763-1775* (C. E. Carter, ed., New Haven, 1931-33), I, 81.

119. Schlesinger, *Colonial Merchants,* chaps. iv-vi.

120. Stokes, *Iconography of Manhattan Island,* IV, 784; Lincoln, *Revolutionary Movement,* chap. iii, 91-93; A. E. McKinley, *The Suffrage Franchise in the Thirteen English Colonies in America* (*Univ. of Pa., Ser. in History,* no. 2), 290-92.

121. L. H. Gipson, *Jared Ingersoll* (*Yale Hist. Publs. Miscellany,* VIII), 270.

122. Baldwin, *New England Clergy,* chaps. vii-ix; Samuel Adams, *Writings* (H. A. Cushing, ed., New York, 1904-1908), II, 367-68; John Adams, *Works,* X, 185.

123. Suffolk Resolves in Peter Force, comp., *American Archives* (Washington 1837-53), ser. 4, I, 778; Margaret W. Willard, ed., *Letters on the American Revolution, 1774-1776* (Boston, 1925), 67; A. J. Riley, *Catholicism in New England to 1788* (Catholic Univ., *Studies,* XXIV), 88-90; Charles Inglis, "State of the Anglo-American Church," E. B. O'Callaghan, ed., *The Documentary History of the State of New York* (Albany, 1849-51), III, 1049-1066; E. F. Humphrey, *Nationalism and Religion in America, 1774-1789* (Boston, 1924), 78-81.

124. Schlesinger, *Colonial Merchants,* chap. vii.

125. Ibid., chaps. viii-ix.

126. W. C. Ford et al., eds., *Journals of the Continental Congress* (Washington, 1904-37), I, 43-73 and notes; E. C. Burnett, ed., *Letters of Members of the Continental Congress* (Washington 1921-36), I, 1-89; E. C. Burnett, *The Continental Congress* (New York, 1941), 22-54.

127. Ford et al., *Journals,* I, 75-80; Schlesinger, *Colonial Merchants,* chap. x.

128. Force, *American Archives,* ser. 4, I, 983-85, 1138; Schlesinger, *Colonial Merchants,* chaps. xii-xiii.

129. H. J. Eckenrode, *The Revolution in Virginia* (Boston, 1916), chap. ii; C. L. Raper, *North Carolina* (New York, 1904), chap. x.

130. Force, *American Archives,* ser. 4, II, 364-70.

131. John Adams, *Works,* X, 194; Emory Washborn, *Sketches of the Judicial History of Massachusetts from 1630 to the Revolution in 1775* (Boston, 1840), 214-18, 237-38.

132. Justin Winsor, ed., *Memorial History of Boston, 1630-1880* (Boston, 1880-81), III, 128; Dix, *History of the Parish of Trinity Church,* I, chap. xxii; list of clergy in E. L. Goodwin, *The Colonial Church in Virginia* (Milwaukee, 1927), 245-319; McCrady, *South Carolina under the Royal Government,* chap. xxiii.

133. Baldwin, *New England Clergy,* chaps. ix, xi; C. A. Briggs, *American Presbyterianism* (New York, 1885), chap. ix.

134. On the conservatism of the elder Muhlenberg, see T. G. Tappert, "Henry Melchior Muhlenberg and the American Revolution," *Church History,* IX, 284-301.

135. Schlesinger, *Colonial Merchants,* 316-17, 432-40, 591-606; Rowe, *Letters and Diary,* 256-58, 273-304, 315.

136. Harrington, *New York Merchant,* 349-51; A. C. Flick, *Loyalism in New York during the American Revolution* (Columbia Univ., *Studies,* xiv, no. 1), 34 and passim; Isaac Sharpless, *The Quakers in the Revolution* (*A History of Quaker Government in Pennsylvania,* Philadelphia, 1898-99, II), chaps. vi-vii.

137. Edward McCrady, *History of South Carolina in the Revolution, 1775-1780* (New York, 1901), 172; Sellers, *Charleston Business on the Eve of the American Revolution,* 235; Wallace, *Laurens;* Eckenrode, *Revolution in Virginia,* 114ff.; [Janet Schaw], *Journal of a Lady of Quality . . . 1774 to 1776* (Evangeline W. and C. M. Andrews, eds., New Haven, 1921), 323; R. D. W. Connor, *Cornelius Harnett* (Raleigh, 1909), 166ff.

138. Flick, *Loyalism in New York,* 35, 203; W. H. Siebert, *The Loyalists of Pennsylvania* (Ohio State Univ., *Contribs.,* no. 5), chap. v; E. A. Jones, *The Loyalists of Massachusetts,* (London, 1930), passim.

139. Ibid., passim, esp. 58-61, 215-17, 249-60, 297.

140. Flick, *Loyalism in New York,* 33, 34; Sedgwick, *William Livingston,* 231-33; Seibert, *Loyalists of Pennsylvania,* 34-37, 58; Lincoln. *Revolutionary Movement in Pennsylvania,* passim.

141. Eckenrode, *Revolution in Virginia,* 26-27, 38-39, 119-29; I. S. Harrell, *Loyalism in Virginia* (Durham, 1926), 62.

142. Ibid., 26-29; C. A. Barker, *The Background of the Revolution in Maryland* (*Yale Hist. Publs. Miscellany,* XXXVIII), 375; Burnett, *Letters,* II, 233; III, 179; G. H. Ryden, ed., *Letters to and from Caesar Rodney* (Philadelphia, 1933), 178, 183.

143. [Schaw], *Journal of a Lady of Quality,* appendices and passim; McCrady, *South Carolina in the Revolution,* chaps. i, iii, vi; W. A. Schaper, "Sectionalism and Representation in South Carolina," Am. Hist. Assoc., *Ann. Rep. for 1900,* I, 380

144. Lincoln, *Revolutionary Movement in Pennsylvania,* esp. chaps. iv-v.

145. J. S. Bassett, "The Regulators of North Carolina," Am. Hist. Assoc., *Ann, Rep. for 1894,* 209-11; W. H. Siebert, *Loyalists in East Florida, 1774 to 1785* (Fla. State Hist. Soc., *Publs.,* no. 9), I, passim; W. L. Saunders, ed., *Colonial Records of North Carolina* (Raleigh, 1886-90), X, 46, 90, 406.

146. Cf. C. H. Van Tyne, *The Loyalists in the American Revolution* (New York, 1902), 183, with Edward Channing, *A History of the United States* (New York, 1905-25), III, 216.

147. Force, *American Archives* (Washington, 1837-53), ser. 4, I, 1350-55; Gage, *Correspondence with the Secretaries of State,* I, 371-77, 385-86, 389, 394; Channing, *History,* III, 156n.

148. John Adams and Daniel Leonard, *Novanglus, and Massachusettensis* (Boston, 1819), 31-33 226-27. In this edition the name of Jonathan Sewall mistakenly appears on the title page in place of that of Leonard.

149. Force, *American Archives,* ser. 4, VI, 1119; ser. 5, I, 331, 764; II, 449, 907.

150. Fitzpatrick, *George Washington Himself,* 278; various estimates of numbers at Saratoga in Channing, *History,* III. 267; C. H. Van Tyne, *The War of Independence* (Boston, 1929), 434; Hoffman Nickerson, *The Turning Point of the Revolution* (Boston, 1928), app. ii; H. P. Johnston, *Yorktown Campaign* (New York, 1881), 108-16.

151. Adams and Adams, *Familiar Letters,* 230; Force, *American Archives,* ser. 5, I, 938.

152. Margaret W. Willard, ed., *Letters on the American Revolution, 1774-1776* (Boston, 1925), 120, 133; Cresswell, *Journal,* 159, 163; Allen French, *The First Year of the American Revolution* (Boston, 1934), chap. xxix; Van Tyne, *War of Independence,* 394; R. W. Pettengill, ed., *Letters from America, 1776-1779* (Boston, 1924), 110-13.

153. French, *American Revolution,* chap. xxv; G. W. Allen, *A Naval History of the American Revolution* (Boston, 1913), I, esp. 29, 38-52, chaps. ii, vi.

154. Van Tyne, *War of Independence,* chap. vi; L. C. Hatch, *The Administration of the American Revolutionary Army* (*Harvard Hist. Studies,* X), chap. vi; J. C. Fitzpatrick, *The Spirit of the Revolution* (Boston, 1924), chap. viii; Force, *American Archives,* ser. 5, I, 203; C. K. Bolton, *The Private Soldier under Washington* (New York, 1902), 74-76, 98-99; Thacher, *Military Journal,* 158.

155. George Washington, *Writings from the Original Manuscript Sources* (J. C. Fitzpatrick, ed., Washington, 1931-40), V, 192; Hatch, *Administration of the Army,* chap. vi.

156. Bolton, *Private Soldier,* chap. iii; Force, *American Archives,* ser. 5, I, 195; E. C. Burnett, *Letters of Members of the Continental Congress* (Washington, 1921-36), II, 191; Curtis, *Organization of the British Army,* 91.

157. Curtis, *Organization of the British Army,* 10-12; T. G. Morton, *The History of the Pennsylvania Hospital, 1751-1895* (Philadelphia, 1895), 57, 223; F. R. Packard, *History of American Medicine in the United States* (rev. ed., New York, 1931), I, chap. viii; Thacher, *Military Journal,* 112-15.

158. William Winthrop, *Military Law and Precedents* (2nd ed., Boston, 1896), II, app., viii-x; Thacher, *Military Journal,* 186-188, 190, 195; Fitzpatrick, *Washington,* 330.

159. W. A. Ganoe, *The History of the United States Army* (rev. ed., New York, 1942), 38-39; Anburey, *Travels,* II, 252-54; Stedman, *American War,* I, 169; Graydon, *Memoirs of His Own Time,* 304-306; Sedgwick, *Livingston,* 337; Moore, *Diary,* II, 434-36.

160. John Adams, *Works,* II, 461; W. B. Weeden, *Early Rhode Island* (F. H. Hitchcock, ed., *The Grafton Historical Series;* New York, 1910), 338; Schlesinger, *Colonial Merchants* 566-72; Burnett, *Letters,* I, 372ff.; Ford et al., *Journals* IV, 257-63.

161. Isaac Sharpless, *A Quaker Experiment in Government* (Philadelphia, 1902), pt. ii. chap. vii; W. O. Mishoff, Business in Philadelphia during the British Occupation (seminar paper, Columbia University, 1928).

162. Burnett, *Letters,* I, 276, 288.

163. Willard, *Letters on the American Revolution,* 156, 260, 271; W. B. Norton, "Paper Currency in Massachusetts during the Revolution," *New England Quar.,* VII, 43, 69; John Adams, *Works,* IX, 470.

164. R. V. Harlow, "Economic Conditions in Massachusetts during the American Revolution," Colon. Soc. of Mass., *Publs.,* XX, 168ff.; Sedgwick, *Livingston,* 355.

165. Burnett, *Letters,* V, 205, 220 n., 234, 239.

166. Ibid., VII, 502 n.; W. G. Sumner, *Financier and Finances of the Revolution* (New York, 1891), II, 42-47.

167. *Pa. Packet,* July 4, 6, 27, September 12, 1782; Davis, *History of American Corporations,* I, 178-80.

168. W. E. Rich, *The History of the United States Post Office to the Year 1829* (*Harvard Economic Studies,* XXVII), chap. iv; Burnett, *Letters,* V. 494; VI, 113; Channing, *History,* III, 395.

169. Ford et al., *Journals,* IV, 222-25; Clark, *History of Manufactures in the United States,* I, chap. ix; Force, *American Archives,* ser. 4, II, 140ff., 170-71, 563; Moore, *Diary,* I, 267.

170. Burnett, *Letters,* IV, 53, 60-62, 75-128; V, 185-88, 371ff.; Harlow, "Economic Conditions," 177ff.

171. J. A. Krout, "Finance and Army Supplies," A. C. Flick, ed., *History of the State of New York* (New York, 1933–37), IV, 125–27, 142–46; Division of Archives and History, *The American Revolution in New York* (Albany, 1926), 240; Burnett, *Letters*, III, 541.

172. Adams and Adams, *Familiar Letters*, 238, 278; Ryden, *Letters to and from Caesar Rodney*, 327; John Adams, *Works*, II, 433; Burnett, *Letters*, III, 492, 541; IV, 39, 61.

173. L. C. Gray, *History of Agriculture in the Southern United States to 1860* (Carnegie Inst., *Publs.*, no. 430), II, 577, 579, 586–596; Jefferson, *Works*, V, 245, 247; Landon Carter, "Diary," *William and Mary College Quar.*, XX, 175–85; Cresswell, *Journal*, 173–74.

174. William Meade, *Old Churches, Ministers, and Families of Virginia* (Philadelphia 1857), I, 17.

175. Burnett, *Letters*, II, 113, 485; J. M. Buckley, *A History of Methodists in the United States* (Schaff et al., *American Church History Series*, V), chap. vii; Ryden, *Letters to and from Caesar Rodney*, 219.

176. Baldwin, *New England Clergy and the American Revolution*, chap. xi; Rodgers, quoted in E. F. Humphrey, *Nationalism and Religion in America, 1774–1789* (Boston, 1924), 99.

177. Humphrey, *Nationalism and Religion*, 119; Sister Mary Augustina [Ray], *American Opinion of Roman Catholicism in the Eighteenth Century* (Columbia Univ., *Studies*, no. 416), chap. viii.

178. Hugh Hastings, comp., *Ecclesiastical Records of New York* (Albany, 1901–1905), VI, 4302–4304; Chastellux, *Travels* II, 205–207; Henry, *Patrick Henry* II, chap. xxxi; Gewehr, *Great Awakening*, 136; Force, *American Archives*, ser. 4, II, 1415; Dwight, quoted in R. J. Purcell, *Connecticut in Transition, 1775–1818* (Washington, 1918), 9.

179. Christopher Marshall, *Extracts from the Diary Kept in Philadelphia and Lancaster during the American Revolution, 1774–1781* (William Duane, ed., Albany, 1877), 168; Ford et al., *Journals*, XII, 1001–1004; Burnett, *Letters*, III, 451–52; John Adams, Samuel Adams, and James Warren, *Warren-Adams Letters* (Mass. Hist. Soc., *Colls.*, LXXII–LXXIII), II, 59, 82, 157, 184.

180. Force, *American Archives*, ser. 4, II, 1367; *Pa. Packet*, August 1, 1778; Adams, Adams, and Warren, *Warren-Adams Letters*, I, 297.

181. S. B. Webb, *Correspondence and Journals* (New York, 1893), II, 226; Adams, Adams, and Warren, *Warren-Adams Letters*, II, 54; Burnett, *Letters*, I, 417; III, 483.

182. Adams, Adams, and Warren, *Warren-Adams Letters*, I, 195–96, 234; Anburey, *Travels*, II, 214; G. J. McRee, *Life and Correspondence of James Iredell* (New York, 1857–1858), I, chap. ix, 338.

183. W. E. B. Du Bois, *The Suppression of the African Slave-Trade to the United States of America* (Harvard Hist. Studies I), app. A.

184. Force, *American Archives*, ser. 4, I, 334, 1135; Adams, Adams, and Warren, *Warren-Adams Letters*, I, 335–39; Sedgwick, *Livingston*, 298–99.

185. Thomas Woody, *Early Quaker Education in Pennsylvania* (Teachers College, Columbia Univ., *Contribs.*, no. 105), 58, 71, 94, 149; O. T. Barck, *New York City during the War for Independence* (Columbia Univ., *Studies*, no. 357), 164; R. F. Seybolt, "New York Colonial Schoolmasters," N. Y. Educ. Dept., *Fifteenth Ann. Rep.*, I, 666ff.

186. Jefferson, *Works*, II, 414.

187. C. M. Fuess, *Men of Andover* (New Haven, 1928), 1–3, 15ff., 52, 54; L. M. Crosbie, *Phillips Exeter Academy* (Exeter, N.H., 1923), chaps. i–v; G. F. Miller, *Academy System of the State of New York* (Albany, 1922), 18.

188. Morison, *Three Centuries of Harvard*, 147.

189. Josiah Quincy, *History of Harvard University* (Cambridge, 1840), II, chap. xxviii; John Maclean, *History of the College of New Jersey* (Philadelphia, 1877), I, 321.

190. Quincy, *Harvard University,* II, chaps. xxix, xxxi; Stiles, *Literary Diary,* II, 447; Maclean, *College of New Jersey,* I, chaps. xv-xvi; S. F. Batchelder, *Bits of Harvard History* (Cambridge, 1924), chap ii.

191. Jefferson, *Works,* IV, 266ff.; Stiles, *Literary Diary,* II, 447; Edward Warren, *The Life of John Warren* (Boston, 1874), 253; T. F. Harrington, *The Harvard Medical School* (New York, 1905), I, 68-88.

192. E. B. Greene, "Some Educational Values of the American Revolution," Am. Philosophical Soc., *Proceeds.,* LXVIII, 188-92.

193. Ibid.; Thacher, *Military Journal,* 28; F. R. Packard, *History of Medicine in the United States* (Philadelphia, 1901), app. B.

194. Adams and Adams, *Familiar Letters,* 207; John Adams, *Works,* III, 147; IV, 259-61; American Academy of Arts and Sciences, *Memoirs,* I, preface, 542ff., 556ff.; II, pt. i, 43, 170; American Philosophical Society, *Transactions,* II, 239-46.

195. Barck, *New York City,* chap. vii; Thomas, *History of Printing,* passim.

196. Thomas, *History of Printing,* passim.

197. For wartime propaganda, see Philip Davidson, *Propaganda and the American Revolution* (Chapel Hill, 1941), chaps. xvii-xx; Moore, *Diary of the American Revolution,* II, 78-82, 97-100, 457.

198. J. C. Fitzpatrick, *The Spirit of the Revolution* (Boston, 1924), chap. x; Anburey, *Travels,* II, 31; Fannie L. G. Cole, "William Billings," Johnson and Malone, *Dictionary of American Biography,* II, 269-71.

199. M. C. Tyler, *The Literary History of the American Revolution, 1763-1783* (2nd ed., New York, 1898-1900), II, 198-225; Barck, *New York City,* chap. ix. Details for this period are in G. C. D. Odell, *Annals of the New York Stage* (New York, 1927-42), I.

200. *Pa. Packet,* August 1, 1778.

201. Burnett, *Letters,* I, 174; III, 347, 391, 498; Wallace, *Laurens,* chap. xx.

202. *Pa. Packet,* July 6, 14, 1778; John Rodgers, quoted in Humphrey, *Nationalism and Religion,* 99.

203. Phineas Bond. "Letters," Am. Hist. Assoc., *Ann. Rep. for 1896,* I, 648; Anburey, *Travels,* II, 179; Burnett, *Letters,* II, 194; A. B. Faust, *The German Element in the United States* (Boston, 1909), I, 355-56.

204. Flick, *Loyalism in New York,* chap. viii.

205. H. C. Van Schaack, *Peter Van Schaack* (New York, 1842), 313, chaps. xix-xxi; E. W. Spaulding, *New York in the Critical Period* (D. R. Fox, ed., *N.Y. State Hist. Assoc. Ser.,* I), 129, 246-53.

206. Oscar Zeichner, "The Rehabilitation of Loyalists in Connecticut," *New England Quar.,* XI, 308-30; Stiles, *Literary Diary,* III. 70, 109-12; Jefferson, *Works,* IV, 431-32; Rowland, *Carroll,* II, 67-70; Schoepf, *Travels in the Confederation,* II, 204; Spaulding, *New York in the Critical Period,* chap. vi; Aedanus Burke to the Governor of South Carolina, *Am. Museum,* I (1787), 120-22.

207. Spaulding, *New York in the Critical Period,* 132.

208. Bond, "Letters," 581ff., 643; Lord Sheffield, *Observations on the Commerce of the American States* (6th ed., London, 1784), 190ff.; Clark, *History of Manufactures in the United States,* I, 260; Du Bois, *Suppression of the African Slave-Trade,* 50; Burnett, *Letters,* VIII, 141; Tench Coxe, *View of the United States of America* (Philadelphia, 1794), 65-68, 101.

209. Burnett, *Letters,* VIII, 797; Franklin, *Writings,* VIII, 603ff.

210. Max Farrand, "A Nation of Immigrants," *New Republic,* IX, 148 (December 9, 1916); M. L. Hansen, *The Atlantic Migration, 1607-1860* (A. M. Schlesinger, ed., Cambridge, 1940), 53-58.

211. Allan Nevins, *The American States during and after the Revolution, 1775-1789* (N.Y., 1924), passim.

212. Henry, *Patrick Henry,* I, 411, 425.

213. Ibid., I, 425.

214. McRee, *James Iredell,* I, chap. ix.
215. Lincoln, *Revolutionary Movement in Pennsylvania,* 278-87; Nevins, *American States,* 197-200.
216. William Jay, *Life of John Jay* (New York, 1833), I, 70; Spaulding, *New York in the Critical Period,* chap. v.
217. S. E. Morison, *Maritime History of Massachusetts, 1783-1860* (Boston, 1921), 28-29; text of "Essex Result" in Theophilus Parsons, *Memoir of Theophilus Parsons, Chief Justice of the Supreme Judicial Court of Massachusetts* (Boston, 1859), app. i.
218. Schoepf, *Travels,* II, 205; Jarratt, *Life,* 14-15; Kate M. Rowland, *Life of George Mason, 1725-1792* (New York, 1892), II, 77; Stiles, *Literary Diary,* III, 125.
219. Franklin, *Writings,* IX, 489; Jefferson, *Works,* V, 238ff.; David Ramsay, *The History of the American Revolution* (Philadelphia, 1789), II, 323.
220. Jefferson, *Works,* I, 77.
221. C. R. Lingley, *The Transition in Virginia from Colony to Commonwealth* (Columbia Univ., *Studies,* XXXVI, no. 2), 181-89; Chinard, *Jefferson,* 93-95; Jefferson, *Works,* II, 393ff.; Franklin, *Writings,* IX, 1; Benjamin Rush, "An Enquiry into the Effects of Public Punishments upon Criminals, and upon Society," *Am. Museum,* II (1787), 142-154; Michael Kraus, "Eighteenth Century Humanitarianism," *Pa. Mag. of Hist. and Biog.,* LX, 273ff.; Nevins, *American States,* 454.
222. Nevins, *American States,* 453; *The Constitution of the State of New York* (New York, 1777), Article XXXIV; G. B. Adams, *Constitutional History of England* (New York, 1934), 454; Stiles, *Literary Diary,* III, 118, 328; Joseph Hadfield, *An Englishman in America, 1785* (D. S. Robertson, ed., Toronto, 1933), 185.
223. Kraus, "Eighteenth Century Humanitarianism," 272ff.; Blake McKelvey, *American Prisons* (Univ. of Chicago, *Social Service Ser.,* 1936), 5-7; Nevins, *American States,* 458ff.; Richardson, *History of Early American Magazines,* 266.
224. Nevins, *American States,* 456ff.; Stiles, *Literary Diary,* III, 209; Division of Archives and History, *The American Revolution in New York* (Albany, 1926), 236; S. I. Pomerantz, *New York, an American City, 1783-1803* (Columbia Univ., *Studies,* no. 442), 322ff.
225. John Adams, *Works,* VIII, 387; Anthony Benezet, "Letter on the Slave Trade," *Am. Museum,* I, 122-23; Michael Kraus, "Slavery Reform in the Eighteenth Century," *Pa. Mag. of Hist. and Biog.,* LX, 53-66.
226. E. R. Turner, *The Negro in Pennsylvania* (Washington, 1911), chaps. vi, viii, xii; Sedgwick, *Livingston,* 398ff.; Division of Archives and History, *American Revolution in New York,* 237.
227. Du Bois, *Suppression of the Slave-Trade,* 73, 82, 229-32; J. Q. Adams, *Life in a New England Town* (Boston, 1903), 174; William Bentley, *Diary* (Salem, 1905-14), I, 104ff., 384-86.
228. Mary S. Benson, *Literary Women in Eighteenth-Century America* (Columbia Univ., *Studies,* no. 405), chap. v.
229. Ibid.; Stiles, *Literary Diary,* III, 167.
230. Abigail Adams, *Letters,* 175; J. T. Adams, *New England in the Republic* (Boston, 1926), 77-79; Bentley, *Diary,* I, 118; Hadfield, *Englishman in America,* 191; Jedidiah Morse, *The American Geography* (Elizabethtown, N.J., 1789), 148.
231. Morse, *American Geography,* 148; Abigail Adams, *Letters,* 234; Winsor, *Memorial History of Boston,* IV, 359ff.; Pomerantz, *New York,* A. H. Quinn, *A History of the American Drama from the Beginning to the Civil War* (New York, 1923), 61-62.
232. J. P. Brissot de Warville, *New Travels in the United States* (London, 1792), 103; Stiles, *Literary Diary,* III, 284; Pomerantz, *New York,* 468ff.; *N.Y. Directory for 1786.*
233. Tatsch, *Freemasonry,* chap. iv; Stiles, *Literary Diary,* III, 105-106; anon., "The Influence of Free Masonry upon Society," *Am. Museum,* I, 469.
234. J. Q. Adams, *Life in a New England Town,* 46.

235. Texts of constitutions in F. N. Thorpe, comp., *The Federal and State Constitutions* (59th Cong., 2 sess., *House Doc.,* no. 357). C. H. Moehlman, *American Constitutions and Religion* (Berne, Ind., 1938), includes most of the pertinent clauses.

236. For selected references for this and the following paragraphs, see E. B. Greene, *Religion and the State, the Making and Testing of an American Tradition* (New York, 1941), 86-88, 157. The fullest treatment (with documents) is in H. J. Eckenrode, *Separation of Church and State in Virginia* (Richmond, 1910).

237. W. W. Hening, comp., *The Statutes-at-Large, Being a Collection of All the Laws of Virginia, 1619-1792* (Philadelphia, 1823), XII, 84-86.

238. E. F. Humphrey, *Nationalsim and Religion in America, 1774-1789* (Boston, 1924), chap. xiv; James Madison, *Writings* (Gaillard Hunt, ed., New York, 1900-1910), II, 145; Max Farrand, ed., *The Records of the Federal Convention* (New Haven, 1911-37), III, 227; Jonathan Elliot, ed., *The Debates in the Several State Conventions, of the Adoption of the Federal Constitution* (Washington, 1836), II, 148; IV, 199.

239. E. H. Scott, ed., *The Federalist and Other Constitutional Papers* (Chicago, 1894), 871.

240. Humphrey, *Nationalism and Religion,* chaps. vii-xi.

241. Dana Doten, "Ethan Allen's 'Original Something' " *New England Quar.,* XI, 362; anon., "On the Doctrine of Chance," *Am. Museum,* II (1787), 408-10; Stiles, *Literary Diary,* III, 345; Bentley, *Diary,* I, 82.

242. J. W. Thornton, *The Pulpit of the American Revolution* (New York, 1860), 488-89; Stiles, *Literary Diary,* III, 326; Filippo Mazzei, *Recherches historiques et politiques sur les États-Unis de l'Amèrique Septentrionale* (Paris, 1788), IV, 92; J. Q. Adams, *Life in a New England Town,* 112.

243. *American Magazine,* I (1787-88), 420-21, 491-92; Morais, *Deism in Eighteenth Century America* chap. iv; Jefferson, *Works,* V, 324-26; VI, 23; Henry, *Patrick Henry,* II, 198ff.; William Meade, *Old Churches, Ministers and Families of Virginia* (Philadelphia, 1857), I, 175.

244. Stiles, *Literary Diary,* II, 528; W. S. Perry, *History of the American Episcopal Church* (Boston, 1885), II, 101-18.

245. Bentley, *Diary,* I, 98 and passim; Hadfield, *An Englishman in America,* 184.

246. Schoepf, *Travels,* II, 62-63; Morse, *American Geography,* 146-47; Edward Warren, *The Life of John Collins Warren* (Boston, 1860), I, 157.

247. Brissot de Warville, *New Travels,* 202; Schoepf, *Travels,* I, 100-101; II, 92-93; Stiles, *Literary Diary,* III, 201, 213; G. E. Howard, *A History of Matrimonial Institutions* (Chicago, 1904), II, chap. xii.

248. J. S. Bassett, "Development of the Popular Churches after the Revolution," Mass. Hist. Soc., *Proceeds.,* XLVIII, 254-68.

249. Gewehr, *Great Awakening,* chaps. vii-xi; Isaac Backus, *History of New England with Particular Reference to the Denomination of Christians Called Baptists* (2nd ed., Newton, Mass., 1871), II, chap. xxiv.

250. Gewehr, *Great Awakening,* chaps. vi-vii, esp. 168-73; Buckley, *Methodists,* 254, 258.

251. Guilday, *John Carroll,* 235.

252. John Adams, *Works,* IV, 199; VI, 168, 425.

253. Jefferson, *Works,* IV, 60-65; V, 154.

254. G. H. Martin, *Evolution of the Massachusetts School System* (New York, 1894), 74-86; Morse, *American Geography,* 165; *Acts and Resolves of Massachusetts for 1786-87* (Boston, 1893), 509.

255. Mathew Carey and John Bioren, *Laws of the Commonwealth of Pennsylvania, 1700-1802* (Philadelphia, 1803), chap. mccxiii; Division of Archives and History, *American Revolution in New York,* 245; *Laws of the State of New York* (New York, 1792), I; F. P. Graves, "History of the State Education Department," A. C. Flick, ed., *History of the State of New York* (New York, 1933-37), IX, 3-8.

256. Walter Clark, ed., *State Records of North Carolina* (Winston, 1895-1906), XXV,

21–24; A. D. Chandler, comp., *The Colonial Records of the State of Georgia* (Atlanta, 1904–10), XIX, pt. ii, 300, 363; Stiles, *Literary Diary,* II, 165–66.

257. Stiles, *Literary Diary,* III, 247–48.

258. G. F. Miller, *The Academy System of the State of New York* (Albany, 1922), 18; E. T. Corwin et al., *A History of the Reformed Church, Dutch, the Reformed Church, German, and the Moravian Church in the United States* (Schaff et al., *American Church History Series,* VIII), 191.

259. Madison, *Writings,* II, 139, 221, 239; Rowland, *Carroll,* II, 101, 106; Timothy Ford, "Diary, 1785–1786," *S.C. Hist. and Geneal. Mag.,* XIII, 192.

260. Stiles, *Literary Diary,* III, 114.

261. Morison, *Three Centuries of Harvard,* 151–52.

262. Ibid., 82, 164–71; Stiles, *Literary Diary,* III, 127, 130, 135, 142, 155, 167, 258, 346; P. A. Bruce, *History of the University of Virginia, 1819–1919* (New York, 1920–22), I, 51–55; Matthews et al., *Columbia University,* 64, 76.

263. B. C. Steiner, *History of Education in Maryland* (Washington, 1894), chap. iii, 229–45, 273.

264. G. E. Hastings, *Life and Works of Francis Hopkinson* (Chicago, 1926), 418; Morison, *Three Centuries of Harvard,* 175 179; Stiles, *Literary Diary,* III, 59, 121; J. Q. Adams, *Life in a New England Town,* 7; Bruce, *University of Virginia,* I, 54.

265. Morison, *Three Centuries of Harvard,* 171; Matthews et al., *Columbia University,* 332; D. M. Schneider and H. E. Barnes, "Care of the Needy, the Sick and Homeless Children," Flick, *History of the State of New York,* VIII, 312; Pomerantz, *New York, an American City,* 350, 401; W. P. and Julia P. Cutler, *Life, Journals, and Correspondence of Rev. Manasseh Cutler* (Cincinnati, 1888), I, 279–80.

266. American Academy of Arts and Sciences, *Memoirs,* I (1785), preface, pt. iii; Benjamin Waterhouse, *A Synopsis of a Course of Lectures, on the Theory and Practice of Medicine* (Boston, 1786); Emily E. F. Ford and Emily E. F. Skeel, eds., *Notes on the Life of Noah Webster* (New York, 1912), II, 456.

267. Stiles, *Literary Diary,* III, 262 and passim; Bruce, *University of Virginia,* I, 55ff.; H. R. Warfel, *Noah Webster, Schoolmaster to America* (New York, 1936), 185–87.

268. Jefferson, *Works,* III, 431; IV, 209; Madison, *Writings,* II, 28–30; Schoepf, *Travels,* I, 266–70.

269. Franklin, *Writings,* IX, 263–64; X, 75–77; "Druid" papers in M. M. Mathews, ed., *The Beginnings of American English* (Chicago, 1931), chap. ii.

270. Webster, *Grammatical Institute* (1783 ed.), introduction, and his *Dissertations on the English Language* (Boston, 1789), 20–23.

271. Webster, *Grammatical Institute,* introduction, and his *Dissertations,* 288–90.

272. Ibid., 289; "The Taliaferro Family," *William and Mary College Quar.,* XX, 213; Schoepf, *Travels,* I, 86; Franklin, *Writings,* IX, 488.

273. J. B. McMaster, *History of the People of the United States* (New York, 1883–1913), I, 74–79; Charles Evans, comp., *American Bibliography* (Chicago, 1903–34), VII, nos. 20303, 20991; Annie R. Marble, *From 'Prentice to Patron* (New York, 1935), chap. ix.

274. Charles Warren, *The Making of the Constitution* (Boston, 1928), 155–57.

275. Anon., "Thoughts on American Genius," *Am. Museum,* I, 206–209; Abigail Adams, *Letters,* 277.

276. Fiske Kimball, *Domestic Architecture of the American Colonies and the Early Republic* (New York, 1922), 145ff., and his *Thomas Jefferson, Architect* (Boston, 1916), passim.

277. A. P. Whitaker, *The Spanish-American Frontier: 1783–1795* (Boston, 1927), chaps. i–vi; S. C. Williams, *History of the Lost State of Franklin* (rev. ed., New York, 1933), 259–61.

278. Washington, *Writings,* XXVII, 16–18; Justin Winsor, *The Westward Movement* (Boston, 1897), 270.

279. Israel Shreve, "Journal from Jersey to the Monongahela, August 11, 1788," *Pa.*

Mag. of Hist. and Biog., LII, 203; Schoepf, *Travels,* I, 236, 261; T. D. Clark, *A History of Kentucky* (Carl Wittke, ed., *Prentice-Hall History Series,* 1937), 107; Fairfax Harrison, *Landmarks of Old Prince William* (Richmond, 1924), I, 334; I. B. Wilbur, *Ira Allen* (Boston, 1928), chap. xi.

280. Mathews, *Expansion of New England,* chap. vi; B. W. Bond, *Civilization of the Old Northwest* (New York, 1934), 32; Ann B. Wilkinson, "Letters from Kentucky, 1788-1789" (T. R. Hay, ed.), *Pa. Mag. of Hist. and Biog.,* LVI, 33ff.; "Chronicle," *Am. Museum,* II (1787), 1ff. (The "Chronicle" appears with separate pagination at end of volume.)

281. T. P. Abernethy, *From Frontier to Plantation in Tennessee* (Chapel Hill, 1932), 13, 158; Clark, *History of Kentucky,* 92, 115; Williams, *Lost State of Franklin,* 63.

282. *American State Papers* (Washington, 1832-61), *Post Office Department,* 9-12; W. E. Rich, *The History of the United States Post Office to the Year 1829 (Harvard Econ Studies,* XXVII), chaps. iv-v; Wilbur, *Ira Allen,* I, 523ff.; Halsey, *Old New York Frontier,* pt. viii, chap. iv; Williams, *Lost State of Franklin,* chap. xxxii; Abernethy, *Frontier to Plantation,* 149ff.

283. Abernethy, *Frontier to Plantation,* 149.

284. Schoepf, *Travels,* I, 241-46; Bond, *Civilization of the Old Northwest,* chap. ii; W. R. Jillson, *Pioneer Kentucky* (Frankfort, 1934), 90; Gilbert Imlay, *A Topographical Description of the Western Territory of North America* (3rd ed., London, 1797), 152-53; Abernethy, *Frontier to Plantation,* 195; Clark, *History of Kentucky,* 239; U. B. Phillips, *Life and Labor in the Old South* (Boston, 1929), 84.

285. Williston Walker, *A History of the Congregational Churches in the United States* (Schaff, *American Church History Series,* III), 309-11; Mathews, *Expansion of New England,* chaps. vi-vii; Bond, *Civilization of the Old Northwest,* chap. xv; Backus, *Reference to the Denomination of Christians Called Baptists,* II, chap. xxiv.

286. Williams, *Lost State of Franklin,* 94, 270.

287. Ibid., 268ff.; W. W. Sweet, ed., *Religion on the American Frontier, 1783-1850* (New York, and Chicago, 1931-39), I, 21ff.; II, 8ff.; Francis Asbury, *Journal, 1771-1815* (New York, 1821), I, 399ff.; II, passim.

288. Williams, *Lost State of Franklin,* 299, 317, 320; Abernethy, *Frontier to Plantation,* 10.

289. Wilbur, *Ira Allen,* I, 533-34; Mathew Carey and John Bioren, comps., *Laws of the Commonwealth of Pennsylvania, 1700-1802* (Philadelphia 1803), III, 184, 209.

290. J. C. Andrews, *Pittsburgh's Post-Gazette* (Boston, 1936), chaps. i-ii; C. M. Newlin, *The Life and Writings of Hugh Henry Brackenridge* (Princeton, 1932), 71ff.; W. R. Jillson, *The First Printing in Kentucky* (Louisville, 1936), 19-20.

291. Franklin, *Writings,* IX, 523; Burnett, *Letters,* VIII, 401, 799, n. 4.

292. Alexander Hamilton et al., *The Federalist* (H. C. Lodge, ed., New York, 1907), 239.

BOOK V   The Completion of Independence, 1790–1830

1. The extension of political privileges is graphically presented in C. L. and Elizabeth H. Lord, *Historical Atlas of the United States* (New York, 1944), 54-55.

2. William Winterbotham, *An Historical, Geographical, Commercial, and Philosophical View of the American United States* (London, 1795), III, 298; F. M. Bayard, *Voyage dans l'Intérieur des États-Unis* (C. H. Sherrill, tr., Paris, 1797), 47. For the passing of the aristocrats, see Dixon Wecter, *The Saga of American Society* (New York, 1937), chap. iii.

3. T. E. V. Smith, *The City of New York in the Year of Washington's Inauguration* (New York, 1889), 32; H. M. Lippincott, *Early Philadelphia* (Philadelphia, 1919), 76; Mrs. St. Julien Ravenel, *Charleston, the Place and the People* (New York,

1906), 405-6; anon., *The Congregation "Beth Elohim"* (Charleston, 1883), 9. The New York post office was in the home of the postmaster until 1827.

4. H. C. Lodge, *Boston* (London 1891), 167; R. A. East, *Business Enterprise in the American Revolutionary Era* (Columbia Univ., *Studies,* no. 439), chaps. iii, ix.

5. W. L. Stone, *Reminiscences of Saratoga* (New York, 1880), 22-31; Valentine Seaman, *Dissertation on the Mineral Waters of Saratoga* (New York, 1793); J. H. French, *Gazetteer of New York State* (Syracuse, 1860), 591-92.

6. Valentine Seaman, "An Examination of the Account of Ballston Waters," *Medical Repository,* XI (1807-8), 254; review of Seaman's *Dissertation on the Mineral Waters of Saratoga,* ibid., XIII (1809-10), 58.

7. Sixteenth paper (October 15, 1807).

8. See Robert Munro, *A Description of the Genesee Country* (New York, 1804), for a description of the Clifton Springs and "those near the head of the river, on top of which floats Seneca oil [petroleum]."

9. J. K. Paulding, *Letters from the South by a Northern Man* (New York, 1817), II, 237. The hot springs near Harrisonburgh were discovered in 1804. See *Winchester Independent Register,* November 20, 1804, and John Baltzell, *Essay on the Mineral Prospects of the Sweet Springs of Virginia* (Baltimore, 1802).

10. R. H. Gabriel, *The Evolution of Long Island* (New Haven, 1921), 172-73.

11. S. E. Morison, *Harrison Gray Otis* (Boston, 1915), I, 135, 137; J. P. Brissot de Warville, *New Travels in the United States of America* (London, 1794), 95. For pictures of "The Social Background," see the chapter so entitled in C. G. Bowers, *Jefferson and Hamilton* (Boston, 1925), and Edith T. Sale, *Old Time Belles and Cavaliers* (Philadelphia, 1912), 99-171.

12. For example, Lord Chesterfield, *Letters to His Son* (New York, 1775); anon., *Principles of Politeness* (New Haven, 1789); anon., *The American Chesterfield* (Philadelphia, 1827); Alfred Howard ed., *The Beauties of Chesterfield* (Boston, 1828); the character of "Dimple" in Royall Tyler, *The Contrast* (New York, 1787).

13. Anon., *American Chesterfield,* 202; William Pinkney, *The Life of William Pinkney* (New York, 1853), 35.

14. *Medical Repository,* XI, 329. J. T. Scharf, *Chronicles of Baltimore* (Baltimore, 1878), 267-68, and J. F. Watson, *Annals of Philadelphia* (Philadelphia, 1857), are wrong in believing that cigars were first smoked in American streets to ward off yellow fever. Brissot de Warville mentions them in New York in 1787 (*New Travels,* 87). See Benjamin Waterhouse, *Cautions to Young Persons... Shewing the Evil Tendency of the Use of Tobacco upon Young Persons* (Cambridge, 1805).

15. Samuel Miller, *Letters on Clerical Manners and Habits* (New York, 1827), 83.

16. Between 1790 and 1794 the importation of wine increased from about 3.5 million gallons to 5.5 million, whether from the larger prosperity of the country or from the coming of French merchant-importers. Duke de La Rochefoucauld-Liancourt, *Travels through the United States... in the Years 1795, 1796, and 1797* (London, 1799), II, 570.

17. C. F. Volney, *A View of the Soil and Climate of the United States of America* (C. B. Brown, tr., Philadelphia, 1804), 223-24; David Ramsay, *The History of South-Carolina* (Charleston, 1809), II, 409.

18. J. D. Schoepf, *Travels in the Confederation, 1783-1784* (A. J. Morrison, ed., Philadelphia, 1911), I, 110.

19. Adam Seybert, *An Oration... at the Meeting of the Manufacturers and Mechanics of the City of Philadelphia* (Philadelphia, 1809), 14.

20. Noah Webster, *A Collection of Essays and Fugitive Writings* (Boston, 1790), 91.

21. Alice M. Earle, *Two Centuries of Costume in America* (New York, 1903), II, 408-9.

22. V. L. Collins, *President Witherspoon* (Princeton, 1925), II, 154.

23. See illustrations inserted between pages 1023 and 1024 in E. B. O'Callaghan, ed., *The Documentary History of the State of New-York* (Albany, 1849-51), IV.

24. Brissot de Warville, *New Travels,* 133.
25. M. D. Leggett, comp., *Subject Matter Index of Patents for Inventions* (Washington, 1874), 1503. The old form of the word was "gallows."
26. D. C. Gilman, *James Monroe in His Relations to the Public Service* (J. T. Morse, ed., *American Statesmen;* Boston, 1883), 182. Noah Webster was one such incorrigible conservative.
27. Eliza S. Bowne, *A Girl's Life Eighty Years Ago* (New York, 1887), 23. On the older headdress, see Abbé Robin, *New Travels through North America* (Philadelphia, 1783), 14. The transition back to long hair was eased by wigs and turbans.
28. T. G. Fessenden, *The Ladies Monitor* (Bellows Falls, Vt., 1818), 65.
29. Anon., "Hints Respecting Women and Children's Clothes Catching Fire," *Literary Mag. and Am. Register,* IV (1805), 95.
30. Anon., "Picture of London," ibid, II (1804), 283.
31. *Boston Medical Intelligencer,* July 5, 1825; April 18, 1826.
32. H. M. Jones, *America and French Culture* (Chapel Hill, 1927), 134.
33. John Davis, *Travels of Four Years and a Half in the United States of America* (London, 1803), 322-23.
34. The *Courrier des États-Unis,* still flourishing, was founded in 1828.
35. Moreau de Saint-Méry, *Voyage aux États-Unis de l'Amérique* (New Haven, 1913), introduction.
36. O. G. Sonneck, *Early Concert in America* (Leipzig, 1907), 188, 227.
37. On French importers who became rich, see J. A. Scoville (Walter Barrett, pseud.), *Old Merchants of New York* (New York, 1885), V, 351-53, and Abraham Ritter, *Philadelphia Merchants* (Philadelphia, 1860), 23, 71, 108, 198. The greatest of them, Stephen Girard, came before the émigrés.
38. Francis Lieber, *The Stranger in America* (New York, 1835), I, 226, cited in Jone's account in *America and French Culture,* 300-309. See also Fernand Baldensperger, "Le séjour de Brillat-Savarin aux états unis," *Revue de Littérature Comparée,* II, 94-95.
39. For example, Thomas Addis Emmett and William Sampson, the lawyers; William J. MacNevin, the physician; Robert Adrain, professor of mathematics at Columbia; and Bernard MacMahon, the Philadelphia horticulturist. Harmon Blennerhassett's island mansion on the Ohio was the scene of Burr's scheme for empire. Like the Frenchmen, they sometimes taught dancing. See M. M. Bagg, *Pioneers of Utica* (Utica, 1877), 137-42, 376-79. Some went first to Newfoundland, where they unsuccessfully tried raising a rebellion. For a general account, see E. O. Condon, "Irish Immigration to the United States after 1790," Am. Irish Hist. Soc., *Journ.,* IV, 84-89.
40. Tench Coxe, *A View of the United States of America* (Philadelphia, 1794), 441; Timothy Dwight, *Travels in New-England and New-York* (New Haven, 1821-22), IV, 349.
41. Pennsylvania in 1780, Rhode Island and Connecticut in 1784, New York in 1799, and New Jersey in 1804. See L. D. Turner, "Anti-Slavery Sentiment in American Literature," *Journ. of Negro Hist.,* XIV, 371ff., and this volume, Book IV.
42. Samuel McKee, Jr., *Labor in Colonial New York* (Columbia Univ., *Studies,* no. 410), 173-76; D. R. Fox, "The Negro Vote in Old New York," *Polit. Sci. Quar.,* XXXII, 252-75; C. F. Hoffman, *The Pioneers of New York* (New York, 1848), 30-33. There were 21,000 slaves in New York and 12,000 in New Jersey in 1790. H. S. Cooley, *A Study of Slavery in New Jersey* (Johns Hopkins Univ., *Studies,* XIV, nos. ix-x), 19, 26, 30-31; A. Q. Keasby, "Slavery in New Jersey," N. J. Hist. Soc., *Proceeds.,* ser. 3, IV. 90-96; V. 12-19, 79-85.
43. Samuel Breck, *Recollections* (H. E. Scudder, ed., Philadelphia, 1877), 107.
44. When they left service it was thought their character deteriorated. E. R. Turner, *The Negro in Pennsylvania* (Washington, 1910), 129, 135, 145, 152.
45. English ships had been forbidden to carry indentured servants in 1785, but the act

was ill enforced. C. A. Herrick, *White Servitude in Pennsylvania* (Philadelphia, 1926), 254, 266; Phineas Bond, "Letters," Am. Hist. Assoc., *Ann. Rep. for 1897,* 455. The traffic in indentured servants never recovered from the effects of the depression of 1818-19; see M. L. Hansen, *The Atlantic Migration, 1607-1860* (A. M. Schlesinger, ed., Cambridge, 1940), 105.

46. Elizabeth L. Otey, *The Beginnings of Child Labor Legislation in Certain States* (U.S. Bur. of Labor, *Report on Condition of Woman and Child Wage-Earners in the United States,* Washington, 1910-13, VI), 19-20, 50; this volume, Book VIII, 721.

47. Joseph Eckley, *Discourse Delivered before the Members of the Boston Female Asylum* (Boston, 1802), 2, 13-14; Providence Female Asylum, *Charter and Constitution* (Providence, 1802); Abiel Abbot, *Sermon before the Portsmouth Female Asylum* (Portsmouth, 1807); Dwight, *Travels,* III, 464; Moses Stuart, *Sermon before the Female Charitable Society* (Andover, 1815), 18-19, 23, 25.

48. W. E. Woodward, *George Washington, the Image and the Man* (New York, 1926), 433; Anne H. Wharton, *Salons, Colonial and Republican* (Philadelphia, 1900), 109.

49. A. W. Calhoun, *A Social History of the American Family* (Cleveland, 1917-19), II, 147.

50. Hiram Hitchcock, "The Hotels of America," Depew, *American Commerce,* I, 150.

51. See this volume, Book VIII, 721.

52. This quotation was widely used by editors of farm journals. A. L. Demaree, *The American Agricultural Press, 1819-1860* (Columbia Univ., *Studies in the History of American Agriculture,* no. 8), 185, 332.

53. P. H. Johnstone, "Turnips and Romanticism," *Agricultural History,* XII, 224.

54. Bordley, *Essays and Notes,* 3, 451.

55. James Warren, "Observations on Agriculture," *Am. Museum,* II (1787), 347; P. W. Bidwell, "Rural Economy in New England," Conn. Acad. of Arts and Sci., *Trans.,* XX, 392ff.

56. Only a few gentlemen-farmers were experimenting with crop rotation. See *Medical Repository,* V (1802), 311, for a review of Thomas Moore, *The Great Error of American Agriculture Exposed* (Baltimore, 1801). See also George Logan, *Fourteen Agricultural Experiments to Ascertain the Best Rotation of Crops* (Philadelphia, 1797).

57. Dwight, *Travels,* II, 73.

58. Quoted in *Literary Magazine and American Register,* V (1806), 222.

59. C. L. Flint, "One Hundred Years of Progress," in *Report* of the Commissioner of Agriculture for the year 1872 (Washington, 1874), 278-79. Washington sometimes used what was called a duck-billed plow. P. L. Haworth, *George Washington, Farmer* (Indianapolis, 1915), 94.

60. T. N. Carver, "Historical Sketch of American Agriculture," L. H. Bailey, ed., *Cyclopedia of American Agriculture* (New York, 1911), IV, 65, 100.

61. Few farm implements were made in quantity before 1810. Shovel factories were established at Pittsburgh shortly after 1800, and by 1822 one at Easton, Mass., was turning out 30,000 annually. Flint, "One Hundred Years of Progress," 279-86.

62. A. D. Mellick, *The Story of an Old Farm* (Somerville, N.J., 1889), passim, S. G. Goodrich, *Recollections of a Lifetime* (New York, 1856), I, 61-62.

63. Bordley, *Essays and Notes,* 204. See also Lyman Carrier, *Beginnings of Agriculture in America* (New York, 1923), 256.

64. Bidwell and Falconer, *Agriculture,* 105, 110-11.

65. Anon., "Memorandums Made on a Journey through Part of Pennsylvania," *Literary Mag. and Am. Register,* I (1803-1804), 251.

66. H. S. Nourse, *History of the Town of Harvard, Massachusetts* (Harvard, 1894), 77.

67. R. H. Gabriel, *The Evolution of Long Island* (New Haven, 1921), 39. It took 8,000 to fertilize one acre.

68. Benjamin Rush, "Information to Europeans," same author, *Essays, Literary,*

Moral & Philosophical (Philadelphia, 1798), 199; Thomas Cooper, *Some Information Respecting America* (London, 1795), 95, 125-26.

69. Dwight, *Travels,* III, 205.

70. Warren, "Observations on Agriculture," 347.

71. Cooper, *Some Information,* 114. Washington had written in the same strain to Arthur Young. George Washington, *Letters on Agriculture to Arthur Young and Sir John Sinclair* (Franklin Knight, ed., Washington, 1847), 84.

72. Tench Coxe, *A View of the United States of America* (Philadelphia, 1794), 144-45, 266-68; R. M. Tryon, *Household Manufactures in the United States* (Chicago, 1917), 237-39.

73. Anon., *The New American Cookery, or Female Companion* (New York, 1805), 61, 64; Fortescue Cuming, *Sketches of a Tour to the Western Country* (R. G. Thwaites, ed., *Early Western Travels, 1748-1846,* Cleveland, 1904-7, IV), 236.

74. Jane L. Mesick, *The English Traveller in America* (Columbia Univ., *Studies in English and Comparative Literature,* 1922), 103-4; C. F. Volney, *A View of the Soil and Climate of the United States of America* (C. B. Brown, tr., Philadelphia, 1804), 257ff.; Samuel Brown, M.D., "An Account of the Pestilential Disease . . . in the Summer and Autumn of 1798." *Medical Repository,* II (1800), 364; Charles Caldwell, M.D., *Medical and Physical Memoirs* (Philadelphia, 1801), first memoir, pt. iv.

75. Mesick, *English Traveller,* 103-5; C. F. Adams, *Three Episodes of Massachusetts History* (Boston, 1872), II, 808.

76. The latter, picturesquely named the love apple, had been introduced not as a food but as a curious decoration for the garden. The name was a translation of the French *pomme d'amour,* which was a corruption of the Italian *pomo dei Moro,* reflecting the introduction of the vegetable from South America through "Moorish" Spain and Morocco into Italy.

77. Bernard M'Mahon, *The American Gardener's Calendar* (Philadelphia, 1806), passim; J. T. Scharf, *Chronicles of Baltimore* (Baltimore, 1874), 229; J. B. McMaster, *A History of the People of the United States* (New York, 1883-1913), I, 18.

78. See references in anon., *New American Cookery,* 155, 181, 186, and anon., *The Experienced American Housekeeper* (New York, 1823), 48, 113, 159, and passim.

79. J. W. Harshberger, *The Botanists of Philadelphia and Their Work* (Philadelphia, 1899), 118; J. W. Nix, "The Fruit Trade," Depew, *American Commerce,* II, 602-3; S. H. Wandell and Meade Minnigerode, *Aaron Burr* (New York, 1925), II, 199.

80. *American State Papers* (Washington, 1832-61), *Finance,* I, 132; II, 435. In households within the town of Providence alone 24,000 yards of linen were manufactured during the first nine months of 1791.

81. Levi Beardsley, *Reminiscences* (New York, 1852), 31.

82. Goodrich, *Recollections,* I, 74; Bidwell, "Rural Economy," 262-268; Blanche E. Hazard. *The Organization of the Boot and Shoe Industry in Massachusetts before 1875 (Harvard Econ. Studies,* XXIII), 24ff.

83. Tryon, *Household Manufactures,* 203.

84. Green vitriol, copperas, cochineal, and madder were also used.

85. Tryon, *Household Manufactures,* 135; Samuel Williams, *Natural and Civil History of Vermont* (Walpole, N.H. , 1794), 318ff.; Coxe, *View,* 81.

86. Few of these artisans earned a living from their craft. Like the mill owner and the country storekeeper, they depended upon farming for part of their income.

87. Jedidiah Morse, *The American Geography* (Boston, 1789), 148; Goodrich, *Recollections,* I, 86.

88. Washington Irving, *Knickerbocker's History of New York* (New York, 1916), bk. vii, chap, ii, p. 214.

89. Joel Barlow, *The Hasty Pudding* (Brooklyn, 1833), 18.

90. Morse, *American Geography,* 148; Goodrich, *Recollections,* I, 75-76; M. N. Rawson, *When Antiques Were Young* (New York, 1931), 69-70.

91. On the conservatism of farmers, see C. L. Flint, "Agriculture in the United States,"

Flint et al., *Eighty Years' Progress of the United States* (New York, 1861), I, 23;
A. L. Demaree, *The American Agricultural Press,* 48-51.

92. Davis, *Travels* 102-103. See also anon., "The American Character," *Literary Mag.
and Am. Register,* II (1804), 254, and George Sibbald, *Notes and Observations on
the Pine Lands of Georgia* (Augusta, 1801), passim.

93. L. C. Gray, *History of Agriculture in the Southern United States to 1860* (Carnegie
Inst., *Publs.,* no. 430), II, 610-11.

94. John Drayton, *A View of South Carolina* (Charleston, 1802), 125ff.

95. R. H. Brown, *Mirrors for Americans: Likeness of the Eastern Seaboard, 1810*
(Am. Geog. Soc., Special Publ., no. 27), 221-22, citing William Tatham, *An Historical and Practical Essay on the Culture and Commerce of Tobacco* (London,
1800).

96. *American State Papers* (Washington, 1832-61), *Commerce and Navigation,* I,
241-42; *American Farmer,* IV (1822), 347; A. O. Craven, *Soil Exhaustion as a
Factor in the Agricultural History of Virginia and Maryland, 1606-1860* (Univ.
of Ill., *Studies,* XIII, no. 1), 77-78.

97. La Rochefoucauld-Liancourt, *Travels,* III, 52, 113-14. Bordley, *Essays and Notes,*
17-74, emphasizes Maryland's interest in small grain.

98. Gray, *Agriculture,* II, 607; David Ramsay, *The History of South-Carolina* (Charleston, 1809), II, 216-17.

99. Drayton, *South Carolina,* 168.

100. Eli Whitney, "Correspondence," *Am. Hist. Rev.,* III, 99-101.

101. J. D. B. De Bow. *The Industrial Resources of the Southern and Western States*
(New Orleans, 1852), I, 122.

102. See this volume, Book VI, 517.

103. James Hall, *A Brief History of the Mississippi Territory* (Salisbury, N.C., 1801),
passim; Gray, *Agriculture,* II, 683ff.; U. B. Phillips, *American Negro Slavery* (New
York, 1918), 159-60.

104. Bordley, *Essays and Notes,* I, 17-33.

105. Ramsay, *South-Carolina,* II, 448-49; Isaac Weld, Jr., *Travels in North America in
1795, 1796 and 1797* (London, 1807), I, 146-47; Morse, *American Universal
Geography,* 655-56; Phillips, *Negro Slavery,* 161-62.

106. F. A. Michaux, *Travels to the Westward of the Allegany Mountains . . . in the Year
1802* (London, 1805), 322-25, 339-40.

107. Edward Hooker, "Diary," Am. Hist. Assoc., *Ann. Rep for 1896,* I, 893-95, 903;
U. B. Phillips, *Life and Labor in the Old South* (Boston, 1929), 342-43.

108. J. E. White, "Cursory Observation on the Soil, Climate and Diseases of Georgia,"
Medical Repository, X (1806-1807), 121.

109. See this volume, Book XI, 981.

110. White, "Observations," 122; Joseph Pitt, "Observations on the Country and Diseases near Roanoke River, in the State of North-Carolina," *Medical Repository,* XI
(1807-1808), 337-42.

111. John Bernard, *Retrospections of America, 1797-1811* (Mrs. Bayle Bernard, ed.,
New York, 1887), 146-50; Davis, *Travels,* 355-56; Hooker, "Diary," 850, 919-
20. See also Dixon Wecter, *The Saga of American Society* (New York, 1937), 25-
26.

112. Felix de Beaujour, *Sketch of the United States . . . from 1800 to 1810* (William
Walton, tr., London, 1814), 77.

113. Bureau of the Census, *A Century of Population Growth* (Washington, 1909), 13,
78.

114. La Rochefoucauld-Liancourt, *Travels,* II, 376-77; Davis, *Travels,* 107; John Lambert, *Travels through Canada and the United States* (London, 1814), II, 125-26;
Ravenel, *Charleston,* 350.

115. E. S. Thomas, *Reminiscences of the Last Sixty-Five Years* (Hartford, 1840), I, 33;
Ravenel, *Charleston,* 378.

116. Quinine was not yet in general use. Ravenel, *Charleston*, 385-86.
117. Thomas Hunt, *Life of William H. Hunt* (Brattleboro, Vt., 1922), 3-4; Ravenel, *Charleston*, 384-85.
118. La Rochefoucauld-Liancourt, *Travels*, II, 380.
119. Ramsay, *South-Carolina*, II, 389-95.
120. La Rochefoucauld-Liancourt, *Travels*, II, 379, 381; Morse, *American Universal Geography*, 683.
121. Lambert, *Travels*, II, 163-64.
122. Approximately 1,300 out of 1,600 heads of families in the rural counties of the Charleston district owned 42,949 slaves in 1790. Phillips, *Negro Slavery*, 95-96.
123. Hooker, "Diary," 878, contains comments on the process by which large planters acquired and amalgamated small farms.
124. Phillips, *Negro Slavery*, 136-38.
125. Clement Eaton, *Freedom of Thought in the Old South* (Durham, 1940), 19-20.
126. St. George Tucker, *A Dissertation on Slavery with a Proposal for the Gradual Emancipation of It in the State of Virginia* (Philadelphia, 1796), passim; George Buchanan, *An Oration upon the Moral and Political Evil of Slavery* (Baltimore, 1793), 17-18; W. F. Poole, *Anti-slavery Opinions before the Year 1800* (Cincinnati, 1873), 32-42.
127. One of Wythe's most distinguished pupils was Henry Clay. Bernard Mayo, *Henry Clay: Spokesman of the New West* (Boston, 1937), 78ff.
128. Michaux, *Travels*, 75, 93-94; T. P. Abernethy, *From Frontier to Plantation in Tennessee* (Chapel Hill, 1932), 144-63; Phillips, *Negro Slavery*, 169ff.
129. Timothy Flint apparently encountered all these types in his travels. See his *Recollections of the Last Ten Years* (Boston, 1826). For excellent descriptions of these various types, see C. A. and Mary R. Beard, *The Rise of American Civilization* (rev. ed., New York, 1935), chap. viii. Many travelers commented on the homogeneity of the frontier population. Actually there was a considerable class of purposeless folk, carried along by the movement of the real pioneers.
130. Thomas Cooper, *Some Information Respecting America* (London, 1794), 51-52, 105-106; Isaac Finch, *Travels in the United States and Canada* (London, 1833), 318-19.
131. Quoted in S. J. and Elizabeth H. Buck, *The Planting of Civilization in Western Pennsylvania* (Western Pennsylvania Series; Pittsburgh, 1939), 287.
132. Cuming, *Sketches*, chap. xxxvii; L. D. Baldwin, *The Keelboat Age on Western Waters* (Pittsburgh, 1941), 176-78.
133. C. H. Ambler, *A History of Transportation in the Ohio Valley* (Glendale, Calif., 1932), 73ff.
134. The largest settlement in this region, Lexington, Kentucky, was not a river town. In 1805, Espy thought that the "Main Street of Lexington has all the appearance of Market Street in Philadelphia on a busy day." Josiah Espy, *A Tour in Ohio, Kentucky and Indiana Territory* (Cincinnati, 1871), 8.
135. That this equalitarian influence did not break through all legal restraints on the propertyless appears in the constitutions of Kentucky (1792), Tennessee (1796), and Ohio (1802). See I. F. Patterson, *The Constitutions of Ohio* (Cleveland, 1912), 73-97, and B. H. Young, *History and Texts of the Three Constitutions of Kentucky* (Louisville, 1890), 9-48.
136. There is much evidence in the histories of frontier towns, too numerous to list here, that the natural resources of the wilderness in the hands of acquisitive pioneers helped to create an economic aristocracy and that that aristocracy was essentially conservative in trying to reproduce the characteristics of the older communities whence its members had migrated. For a discussion of the acquisitive spirit of the West, see Abernethy, *From Frontier to Plantation*, 358-59.
137. Alexander Wilson, "Letter from Lexington," *Port Folio*, n. s., III (1810), 506.
138. Cuming, *Sketches*, chap, xxvi. See also Bernard Mayo, "Lexington: Frontier Me-

tropolis," E. F. Goldman, ed., *Historiography and Urbanization* (Baltimore, 1941), 25-29.

139. J. C. Andrews, *Pittsburgh's Post-Gazette* (Boston, 1936), chap. i; R. G. Thwaites, "The Ohio Valley Press before the War of 1812-15," Am. Antiquarian Soc., *Proceeds,* XIX, 310-11, 320, 345; Buck and Buck, *Civilization in Western Pennsylvania,* 375, 378.

140. C. E. Vaughan, *Studies in the History of Political Philosophy before and after Rousseau* (Manchester, 1925), I, 168-70; Merle Curti, "The Great Mr. Locke: America's Philosopher, 1783-1861," Huntington Library, *Bull.,* no. 11, 149-51.

141. John Adams, *Works* (C. F. Adams, ed., Boston, 1850-56), VI, 65; M. J. Dauer, "The Political Economy of John Adams," *Polit. Sci. Quar.,* LVI, 546.

142. Analyses of the economic and social alignment appear in S. E. Morison, *Harrison Gray Otis* (New York, 1913), I, 46ff., and C. A. Beard, *Economic Origins of Jeffersonian Democracy* (New York, 1915), 46ff.

143. William Manning, *The Key of Libberty* (S. E. Morison, ed., Billerica, Mass., 1922), 17-18; G. W. Johnson, *Randolph of Roanoke* (New York, 1929), 98.

144. Thomas Jefferson, *Writings* (P. L. Ford, ed., New York, 1892-99), VII, 356, 451. See also his First Inaugural.

145. For the sources of Jefferson's political theory, see Richard Hofstadter, "Parrington and the Jeffersonian Tradition," *Journ. of the History of Ideas,* II, 391-400; Joseph Dorfman, "The Economic Philsophy of Thomas Jefferson," *Polit. Sci. Quar.,* LV, 98-121.

146. George Cabot to Theophilus Parsons, October 3, 1792, in Theophilus Parsons, *Memoir of Theophilus Parsons* (Boston, 1861), 468-70; Alexander Graydon, *Memoirs of a Life* (Harrisburgh, 1811), 331-34; R. J. Ferguson, *Early Western Pennsylvania Politics* (*Western Pennsylvania Series;* Pittsburgh, 1938), 122-31.

147. *National Gazette* (Philadelphia), December 26, 1792; *Columbian Centinel* (Boston), December 29, 1792; *Kentucky Gazette* (Lexington), August 31, November 16, 1793; C. D. Hazen, *Contemporary American Opinion of the French Revolution* (Johns Hopkins Univ., *Studies,* extra vol., XVI), 164-69.

148. *Gazette of the United States* (Phildelphia), February 9, 1793.

149. William Bentley, *Diary* (Salem, Mass., 1905-14), II, 3; Justin Winsor, ed., *Memorial History of Boston* (Boston, 1880-81), IV, 10-11.

150. The conservatives were further alarmed by the influx of Irish rebels who joined French radicals in the Republican ranks. Rufus King, *Life and Correspondence* (C. R. King, ed., New York, 1894-1900), II, 481, 641-42. For the bitterness of the partisan controversy, see C. W. Upham, *The Life of Timothy Pickering* (Boston, 1873), III, 177-79; R. G. Harper, *Select Works* (Baltimore, 1814), 263ff.; G. M. Dallas, *Life and Writings of Alexander James Dallas* (Philadelphia, 1871), 195-97.

151. Graydon, *Memoirs,* 339-40.

152. Quoted in W. A. Robinson, *Jeffersonian Democracy in New England* (*Yale Hist. Publs. Miscellany,* III), 53.

153. In Philadelphia politics destroyed longstanding friendships, induced the boycotting of radical tradesmen, and caused some gentlemen to arm themselves against personal aggression. Marriage across party lines was not always easy. George Logan, *Memoir of Dr. George Logan of Stenton* (Frances A. Logan, ed., Philadelphia, 1899), 54-58.

154. The *Gazette of the United States* was established in April 1789 with financial support from Hamilton and other Federalists. Freneau's *National Gazette* was first published in October 1791 after Jefferson had appointed him to a minor post in the State Department. Bache founded the *General Advertiser,* late the *Aurora,* in the autumn of 1790.

155. James Callender's reputation as a scandalmonger had been established in Scotland before he convinced Meriwether Jones of the *Richmond Examiner* that his work merited recognition; William Duane had been expelled from India by the British

for seditious writings several years before he began to improve upon Bache's invectives in the *Aurora;* the *Gazette of the United States* had been a model of propriety in comparison with the billingsgate which William Cobbett, late from England, brought to the defense of Federalism in *Porcupine's Gazette.* Mary E. Clark, *Peter Porcupine in America* (Philadelphia, 1939), passim.

156. M. W. Hamilton, *The Country Printer: New York State, 1785-1830* (N.Y. State Hist. Assoc. Ser., no. iv), chap. vi; C. A. Duniway, *The Development of Freedom of the Press in Massachusetts* (*Harvard Hist. Studies,* XII), 143-44; W. G. Bleyer, *Main Currents in the History of American Journalism* (Boston, 1927), chap. iv.

157. La Rochefoucauld-Liancourt, *Travels,* II, 526-27.

158. R. H. Gabriel, "Constitutional Democracy: a Nineteenth Century Faith," Conyers Read, ed., *The Constitution Reconsidered* (New York, 1938), 247-48.

159. For details of the Republican rise to political power in various states, see D. R. Fox, *The Decline of Aristocracy in the Politics of New York* (Columbia Univ., *Studies,* LXXXVI), chap. iii; W. R. Fee, *The Transition from Aristocracy to Democracy* (Somerville, N.J., 1933), chaps. iii-iv; D. H. Gilpatrick, *Jeffersonian Democracy in North Carolina, 1789-1816* (Columbia Univ., *Studies,* no. 344), chaps. ii-iv.

160. Between the periods 1792-97 and 1799-1802 the percentage for Massachusetts rose from 3.9 to 7.4, for Connecticut from 2.8 to 5.6, for New Hampshire from 3.4 to 6.7. See J. F. Jameson, "Did the Fathers Vote?" *New England Mag.,* n.s., I (1889-90), 484-90, and J. D. Leutscher, *Early Political Machinery in the United States* (Philadelphia, 1903), 25.

161. Radical though this change was, it had been accomplished without the violence that elsewhere marked the worldwide struggle of which the Federalist-Republican battle was but one phase. See E. P. Link, *Democratic-Republican Societies, 1790-1800* (*Columbia Studies in American Culture,* IX), 41-43.

162. R. J. Purcell, *Connecticut in Transition* (Washington, 1918), 319-23.

163. Of Connecticut, John Adams wrote in 1808, "Half a dozen, or, at most a dozen families, have controlled that country when a colony, as well as since it has been a state." *Works,* VI, 530. The "Family Compact of Connecticut" is ridiculed in *Aurora,* September 12, 1800.

164. Jedidiah Morse, *Sermon on the National Fast, May 9, 1798* (Boston, 1798).

165. Quoted in A. E. Morse, *The Federalist Party in Massachusetts to the Year 1800* (Princeton, 1909), 171.

166. For examples, see David Osgood, *A Discourse Delivered on the Day of Annual Thanksgiving, Nov. 19, 1795* (Boston, 1795); Hezekiah Packard, *Federal Republicanism, Displayed in Two Discourses* (Boston, 1799); and David Tappan, *Christian Thankfulness Explained and Enforced* (Boston, 1795).

167. H. M. Morais, *Deism in Eighteenth Century America* (Columbia Univ., *Studies,* no. 397), 16-17, 29, 35.

168. Nisbet Papers, N.Y. Public Library, *Bull,* I, 118-19.

169. William Linn, *Discourse on National Sins* (New York, 1798). "Defections from the Platonic Christianity," Jefferson remarked, "are to Deism in Protestant countries and to atheism in Catholic countries." Adrienne Koch, *The Philosphy of Thomas Jefferson* (*Columbia Studies in American Culture,* no. 14), 28.

170. *Reason the Only Oracle of Man, or a Compendious System of Natural Religion* (Bennington, 1784).

171. J. W. Francis, *Old New York* (New York, 1865), 130-33; Morais, *Deism,* 133.

172. Lyman Beecher, *Autobiography* (Charles Beecher, ed., New York, 1864), I, 43.

173. See Vernon Stauffer, *New England and the Bavarian Illuminati* (Columbia Univ., *Studies,* LXXXIII, no. 1), passim, and J. K. Morse, *Jedidiah Morse, a Champion of New England Orthodoxy* (*Columbia Studies in American Culture,* no. 2), 51-58.

174. "Striplings, scarcely fledged, suddenly found that the . . . light of wisdom had but just begun to dawn upon the human race." Dwight, *Travels,* IV, 376.

175. D. R. Fox, *Ideas in Motion* (New York, 1935), 122.

176. W. M. Van der Weyde, *The Life and Works of Thomas Paine* (New Rochelle, 1925), VIII, 43. *The Age of Reason* went through many editions in which Moncure D. Conway counted more than 500 variations in the text.

177. Anon., "The American Character," *Literary Mag. and Am. Register*, II (1804), 255; J. H. Hotchkin, *History of Western New York* (New York 1848), 26; William Meade, *Old Churches, Ministers and Families of Virginia* (Philadelphia, 1861), I, 29; Charles Nisbet to Charles Wallace, September 2, 1790, N.Y. Public Library, *Bull.*, I, 118.

178. Isaac Lewis, *The Political Advantages of Godliness* (Hartford, 1797); Jonathan Edwards, Jr., *The Necessity of the Belief of Christianity* (Hartford, 1794), 12-14; N. H. Sonne, *Liberal Kentucky, 1780-1828* (*Columbia Studies in American Culture*, III), 31-32.

179. For attacks on Paine, see also S. S. Smith, *The Divine Goodness of the United States of America* (Philadelphia, 1797), and Michael Hoge, *Christian Panoply; an Answer to Payne's "Age of Reason"* (Philadelphia, 1799).

180. John and Judith S. Murray, *The Life of Rev. John Murray* (new ed., Boston, 1870), passim; Richard Eddy, *Universalism in Gloucester* (Gloucester, Mass., 1892), passim.

181. John Murray, *Letters and Sketches of Sermons* (Boston, 1812), I, 144.

182. J. C. Adams, *Hosea Ballou and the Gospel Renaissance of the Nineteenth Century* (Boston, 1903), 8-11; Richard Eddy, *Universalism in America* (Boston, 1884-86), I, 354; II, 42-62; D. M. Ludlum, *Social Ferment in Vermont, 1791-1850* (*Columbia Studies in American Culture*, V), 26-30.

183. G. W. Cooke, *Unitarianism in America* (Boston, 1902), 75, 80.

184. See this volume, Book IV, 298.

185. Morse, *Jedidiah Morse*, 82-83. The orthodox in New York City were disturbed by a series of Unitarian lectures in 1794. S. I. Pomerantz, *New York, an American City, 1783-1803* (Columbia Univ., *Studies*, no. 442), 391.

186. The trend of liberal thought appears in William Bentley, *Sermon Preached at Stone Chapel* (Boston, 1790), 21. Boston merchants, concentrating on profitable commerce, were not inclined to quarrel with Bentley's contention that "virtue alone secures heaven." His *Diary* traces the development of an emphasis upon a benevolent system of morals as the road to salvation.

187. Sidney Willard, *Memoir of Youth and Manhood* (Cambridge, 1855), II, 117. For the Harvard controversy, see Morse, *Jedidiah Morse*, 82-100.

188. For religious liberalism in Vermont, see Ludlum, *Social Ferment*, 31-33.

189. *Evangelical Intelligencer* (Philadelphia), II (1808), 417; G. P. Fisher, *Life of Benjamin Silliman* (New York, 1866), I, 83; Elizur Goodrich, "Revivals of Religion in Yale College," Am. Educ. Soc., *Journ.*, X (1838), 289ff.; C. E. Cuningham, *Timothy Dwight* (New York, 1942), 328-34.

190. Sonne, *Liberal Kentucky*, 33-44.

191. R. H. Bishop, *An Outline of the History of the Church in the State of Kentucky* (Lexington, 1824), 76ff.; W. B. Posey, *The Development of Methodism in the Old Southwest* (Tuscaloosa, Ala., 1933), 13ff.; W. W. Sweet, ed., *The Baptists, 1783-1830* (same ed., *Relgion on the American Frontier*, New York and Chicago, 1931-39, I), 20-21, 44.

192. F. M. Davenport, *Primitive Traits in Religious Revivals* (New York, 1905), 99.

193. Catherine C. Cleveland, *The Great Revival in the West, 1797-1805* (Chicago, 1916), 60n., 88; P. G. Mode, *Frontier Spirit in American Christianity* (New York, 1923), 54; review of Z. M. Pike's *Account of a Voyage up the Mississippi River*, *Medical Repository*, X (1806-7), 379.

194. Peter Cartwright, *Autobiography* (W. P. Strickland, ed., New York, 1857), 48-51.

195. E. P. Cubberley, *Public Education in the United States* (rev. ed., New York, 1934), 90.

196. James Sullivan (pseud.), *Thoughts upon the Political Situation of the United States* (Worcester, 1788), 18-21; Benjamin Rush, *Essays, Literary, Moral & Philo-*

sophical (Philadelphia, 1798), 7, 10-12; Lafitte du Courteil, *A Proposal to Demonstrate the Necessity of a National Institution in the United States of America for the Education of Children of Both Sexes* (Philadelphia, 1797), 6, 23.

197. Robert Coram, *Political Inquiries* (Wilmington, 1791), 98-99. See also A. O. Hansen, *Liberalism and American Education in the Eighteenth Century* (New York, 1926), 48-63.

198. Jefferson, *Writings*, I, 467-68. But many Republican leaders had been born and educated in Europe.

199. For the schoolbooks he prepared with this purpose in mind, see this volume, Book IV, 298.

200. Noah Webster, *A Collection of Essays and Fugitive Writings* (Boston, 1790), 23.

201. E. C. Shoemaker, *Noah Webster, Pioneer of Learning* (New York, 1936), 187-88; H. R. Warfel, *Noah Webster, Schoolmaster to America* (New York, 1936), 59-60.

202. Merle Curti, *The Social Ideas of American Educators* (Comn. on Social Studies, *Report*, X), 47-48. Sectional prejudices were far too strong for any broadly national system of schools.

203. Samuel Knox, *An Essay on the Best System of Education* (Baltimore, 1799); S. H. Smith, *Remarks on Education* (Philadelphia, 1798).

204. G. B. Goode, *The Origin of the National Scientific and Educational Institutions of the United States* (New York, 1890), 15-19.

205. S. L. Mitchill, "Proceedings Relative to a National University," *Medical Repository*, XV (1811-12), 122-26, esp. 124.

206. *Laws of Massachusetts* (1807), I, 469-73.

207. General Assembly of Virginia, *Collection of Acts* (1803), 354-55; James Monroe, *Writings* (S. M. Hamilton, ed., New York, 1898-1903), III, 309.

208. *Laws of Delaware* (1797), II, 1296-98, 1352-54.

209. *N. Y. State Laws*, 18 sess., April 9, 1795, ch. 75; also 35 sess., June 19, 1812, ch. 222. In 1812, Gideon Hawley became first state superintendent of common schools in the country. Cubberley, *Public Education*, 215.

210. As late as 1835 there were more than 200,000 children, from five to fifteen years of age, who attended no school. F. T. Carlton, *Economic Influences upon Educational Progress in the United States, 1820-1850* (Univ. of Wis., *Econs. and Polit. Sci. Ser.*, IV, no. 1), 103.

211. Pomerantz, *New York*, 422-23, 426.

212. G. F. Miller, *The Academy System of the State of New York* (Albany, 1922), 21-22.

213. In 1818 a Virginia law gave elementary education to those willing to accept the brand of pauperism. W. A. Maddox, *The Free School Idea in Virginia before the Civil War* (Teachers College, Columbia Univ., *Contribs. to Educ.*, no. 93), 90.

214. Curti, *Social Ideas of American Educators*, 13ff.; Purcell, *Connecticut in Transition*, 95.

215. Edward Clibborn, *American Prosperity* (London, 1837), 3.

216. R. W. Hidy, "The Organization and Functions of Anglo-American Merchant Bankers, 1815-1860," *Journ. of Econ. Hist.*, supplemental issue (December, 1941), 53-66.

217. C. K. Hobson, *The Export of Capital* (London, 1914), 105, 110.

218. R. G. Albion, *The Rise of New York Port* (New York, 1939), 11-13.

219. John Quincy Adams, *Memoirs*, IV, 498; V, 129.

220. See first five Reports of Society for Prevention of Pauperism (New York, 1818-22), passim.

221. Superintendent of the Banking Department of New York, "Annual Report," *Bankers' Mag.*, XII (1858), 857-58; O. C. Lightner, *The History of Business Depressions* (New York, 1922), 112.

222. N. B. Smith and A. H. Cole, *Fluctuations in American Business, 1790-1860* (Harvard Econ. *Studies*, L), 60ff.

223. Southern ports interested in the West Indies commerce waged an unsuccessful

struggle with Great Britain to regain their former share in trading with the Caribbean islands. F. L. Benns, *The American Struggle for the British West India Carrying-Trade, 1815-1830* (Indiana Univ., *Studies*, X, no. 56); T. J. Wertenbaker, *Norfolk: Historic Southern Port* (Durham, 1931), 158ff.

224. H. W. Dickinson, *Robert Fulton* (New York, 1913), 217-18; D. L. Buckman, *Old Steamboat Days on the Hudson River* (New York, 1907), 11.

225. Josiah Lawton, *Oration on the Importance of Scientific Knowledge* (Providence, 1826), 7-8; F. E. Dayton, *Steamboat Days* (New York, 1925), 332-33.

226. *Ohio Statutes*, I, 11, cited in E. L. Bogart, *Economic History of the American People* (New York, 1936), 329, 353; Dayton, *Steamboat Days,* 334-36.

227. William Strickland, *Reports on Canals, Railways, Roads, and Other Subjects, Made to "The Pennsylvania Society for the Promotion of Internal Improvements"* (Philadelphia, 1826).

228. Horatio Allen, then engineer for the Delaware and Hudson Canal Company, had an English locomotive, the *Stourbridge Lion,* tested on the tramway of the Carbondale and Honesdale Coal Company in 1829. Philip Hone, *Diary* (Allan Nevins, ed., New York, 1927), I, xiv.

229. F. J. Jones, *Middlemen in the Domestic Trade of the United States, 1800-1860* (*Ill. Studies in the Social Sciences,* XXI, no. 3), 9-10.

230. Sister Marietta Jennings, *A Pioneer Merchant of St. Louis, 1810-1820* (Columbia Univ., *Studies,* no. 462), 11-19.

231. *Niles' Wkly. Register,* XXI, 103 (October 13, 1821). In 1828-29 the New York Workingmen's party condemned the auction system as a form of monopoly "hostile to the equal rights of the American merchant, manufacturer, mechanic and laboring man." Horace Secrist, *The Anti-Auction Movement and the New York Workingmen's Party of 1829* (Wis. Acad. of Sciences, Arts and Letters, *Trans.,* XVII), pt. i., 154.

232. For a summary of state laws controlling auctioneers, see Jones, *Middlemen,* 40-43.

233. Thompson, *Colonel James Neilson,* 36.

234. Jennings, *Pioneer Merchant,* 127-41.

235. Luke Shortfield, *The Western Merchant* (Philadelphia, 1849), 119-20.

236. Thomas Ashe, *Travels in America, Performed in 1806* (London, 1808), I, 108-9.

237. H. B. Howe, "Jedediah Barber, 1787-1876, Merchant of Homer," *N.Y. History,* XVII, 296-97.

238. Michaux, *Travels,* 157; W. C. Howells, *Recollections of Life in Ohio, from 1813 to 1840* (Cincinnati, 1895), 137-38; Jennings, *Pioneer Merchant,* 29-31.

239. Samuel Stoddard, for example, settled his account of $33.78 covering eight months, January to August 1831, by paying the storekeeper at Pinckney Corners, Lewis County, New York, 49 pounds of butter at 14 cents; 3,000 shingles at $1.50; two skins, $1.25; two cords of wood, $1.25; and the balance of one dollar in cash. *Potsdam* (New York) *Herald-Recorder,* May 6, 1932.

240. L. E. Atherton, "The Services of the Frontier Merchant," *Miss. Valley Hist. Rev.,* XXIV, 153-71.

241. C. H. Haswell, *Reminiscences of New York by an Octogenarian* (New York, 1897), 77, 262-63.

242. See D. R. Fox, "The Protestant Counter-Reformation," *N.Y. History,* XVI, 19ff; E. B. Greene, "A Puritan Counter-Reformation." Am. Antiquarian Soc., *Proceeds.,* n.s., XLII, 17-46; C. R. Keller, *The Second Great Awakening in Connecticut* (New Haven, 1942), chap. iii.

243. The *Panoplist* was established in June 1805. Thomas Belsham's *Memoirs of the Life of Theophilus Lindsey* was reviewed by Morse and Jeremiah Evarts in the issue of June 1815, pp. 241-72.

244. William Bentley, *Diary* (Salem, 1905-14), III, 317, 403, 412. See also Leonard

Woods, *History of the Andover Theological Seminary* (Boston, 1885), passim, and W. B. Sprague, *Life of Jedidiah Morse* (New York, 1874), 107ff.

245. Harvard did offer a little instruction in Hebrew.

246. Prior to 1791, American Catholic clergy received their seminary training in Europe.

247. J. H. Hotchkin, *History of the Purchase and Settlement of Western New York* (New York, 1848), 110.

248. See E. S. Tipple, *Francis Asbury, the Prophet of the Long Road* (New York, 1916), 158–82.

249. W. H. Milburn, *The Pioneers, Preachers and People of the Mississippi Valley* (New York, 1860), 355; W. W. Sweet, *Circuit Rider Days in Indiana* (Indianapolis, 1916), 34, 41. For an eloquent tribute to "Brush College," see John Strange, quoted in J. C. Smith, *Early Methodism in Indiana* (Indianapolis, 1879), 38–39.

250. Samuel Miller, Jr., *Life of Samuel Miller* (Philadelphia, 1869), I, 239, 313–15; J. W. Alexander, *Life of Archibald Alexander* (New York, 1854), 399.

251. G. L. Prentiss, *The Union Theological Seminary* (New York, 1889), 3ff. The *Quarterly Register and Journal* of the American Education Society, II (1829–30), 35ff., contains news of the workers seeking endowments for seminaries and scholarships for divinity students.

252. Directing Committee of the Connecticut Bible Society, *Report* (Hartford, 1810); Emerson Davis, *The Half Century* (Boston, 1851), 321ff.

253. Jedidiah Morse, *Signs of the Times* (Charlestown, 1810), 45.

254. S. J. Mills and Daniel Smith, *Report of a Missionary Tour* (Andover, 1816), 35–36, 47.

255. "Distribution of Religious Tracts," Am. Educ. Soc., *Quar. Register and Journ.*, II, 38–41.

256. American Tract Society, *Tenth Annual Report* (New York, 1835); W. A. Hallock, *A Sketch of the Life and Labors of Justin Edwards* (New York, 1855), 182–84.

257. O. S. Michael, *The Sunday School in the Development of the American Church* (Milwaukee, 1918), 51–58; Francis Eddy, *The Sabbath School Century* (Hamilton, Ohio, 1882), 83–91.

258. Ward Stafford, *New Missionary Field* (New York, 1817), 18–19.

259. Lyman Beecher, *The Building of Waste Places* (Litchfield, 1814).

260. *Panoplist*, X (1814), 198–203, 236.

261. Besides the *Panoplist*, the following religious periodicals carried news of the moral societies: the *Religious Remembrancer* (Philadelphia, 1813), the *Recorder* (Boston, 1816), the *Christian Herald* (New York, 1816), and the *Christian Disciple*, a Methodist weekly founded at Boston in 1819.

262. Adam Seybert, *Statistical Annals* (Philadelphia, 1818), 463–64; *U.S. Fourth Census* (1820), *Digest of Manufactures*, 3–4.

263. J. A. Krout, *The Origins of Prohibition* (New York, 1925), 77–80.

264. Lyman Beecher, *Autobiography, Correspondence* (Charles Beecher, ed., New York, 1864–65), I, 245.

265. Cited in R. J. Purcell, *Connecticut in Transition, 1775–1818* (Washington, 1918), 329.

266. American Society for the Promotion of Temperance, *First Annual Report* (Andover, 1828).

267. *Permanent Temperance Documents*, I, 242; Krout, *Origins of Prohibition*, 113–14. This close association of pulpit and reform propaganda quickly led to the charge that the temperance movement was designed to effect the union of church and state. See J. H. Hopkins, *The Primitive Church* (Burlington, 1836), 129–53, and Calvin Colton, *Protestant Jesuitism* (New York, 1836), preface and chap. v. The link between church and state had been broken in New Hampshire in 1817, in Connecticut in 1818, and in Massachusetts in 1833. These were the last states to maintain religious establishments.

268. See map in Krout, *Origins of Prohibition*, 130.

269. *Permanent Temperance Documents,* I, 455, 474.

270. For a discussion of the millennial prophecies, see D. R. Fox, *Ideas in Motion* (New York, 1935), 110-19.

271. For reports of revivals, consult files of *Connecticut Journal,* February-May 1819; *Boston Recorder,* March 1820-22; *Religious Intelligencer,* January 1817-July 1818.

272. S. E. Dwight, *Thy Kingdom Come* (Boston, 1820), 22.

273. Approximately 40 percent of them were natives of New England. G. P. Schmidt, *The Old Time College President* (Columbia Univ., *Studies,* no. 317), 146-47.

274. Ibid., 77-145.

275. C. E. Cuningham, *Timothy Dwight, 1752-1817* (New York, 1942), chap. vii.

276. Buck and Buck, *Planting of Civilization,* 375, 398.

277. C. F. Thwing, *A History of Higher Education in America* (New York, 1906), 258-63; Cuningham, *Timothy Dwight,* 198ff.

278. A view of the course of study at various colleges in Am. Educ. Soc., *Quar. Register and Journ.,* I (1827-29), 228-32. See also L. F. Snow, *The College Curriculum in the United States* (New York, 1907), chap. iv.

279. T. E. V. Smith, *The City of New York in the Year of Washington's Inauguration* (New York, 1889), 193-95.

280. *Literary Mag. and Am. Register,* III (1805), 426-28; IV (1805), 137, 185-91. President Joshua Bates of Middlebury College thought that this problem could safely be left in the hands of pious professors. *An Inaugural Oration* (Middlebury, Vt., 1818), 19ff.

281. Samuel Miller, *A Brief Retrospect of the Eighteenth Century* (New York, 1803), II, 37-40.

282. Moses Stuart, "Letter on the Study of the Classics," Am. Educ. Soc., *Quar. Register and Journ.,* I, 85-98.

283. [G. S. Hillard et al.], *Life, Letters, and Journals of George Ticknor* (Boston, 1876), I, 363.

284. Cornelius Van Santvoord, *Memoirs of Eliphalet Nott* (New York, 1876), 155-56.

285. Snow, *College Curriculum,* 155.

286. E. M. Coulter, *College Life in the Old South* (New York, 1928), chap. iv; K. P. Battle, *History of the University of North Carolina* (Raleigh, 1907), I, 199, 452; Schmidt, *Old Time College President,* 78ff.

287. S. E. Morrison, *Three Centuries of Harvard* (Boston, 1936), 201-5.

288. The first gymnasium in the United States, established by Germans who had fled from Metternich's agents, was at the Round Hill School in Northampton, Massachusetts, in which George Bancroft was interested. See Charles Beck's translation of Friedrick L. Jahn's *Treatise on Gymnastics* (Northampton, 1828).

289. E. G. Dexter, *History of Education in the United States* (New York, 1904), 270; D. G. Tewksbury, *The Founding of American Colleges and Universities before the Civil War* (New York, 1932), chap. i.

290. In 1830, New England had one college for every 1,231 inhabitants; the Middle states one for every 3,465; the Southern states one for every 7,232; and the Western states one for every 6,060. "General Summary of Colleges," Am. Educ. Soc., *Quar. Register and Journ.,* II, 242.

291. *Analectic Magazine,* II (1813), 310-11; R. S. Baldwin, *Considerations Suggested by the Establishment of a Second College in Connecticut* (Hartford, 1824).

292. Thwing, *Higher Education,* 271-80.

293. Am. Educ. Soc., *Quar. Register and Journ.,* II, 238. Ten years later the figures were Yale, 411; Union, 286; Virginia, 247; Princeton 237; Harvard, 216.

294. Brander Matthers et al., *A History of Columbia University 1754-1904* (New York, 1904), 92.

295. Thwing, *Higher Education,* 410.

296. When he returned to Cambridge, Ticknor was shocked by the inadequate collection of books and manuscripts. [Hillard et al.]., *George Ticknor,* I, 72.

297. President of Harvard University, *Fifth Annual Report to the Overseers* (Cambridge, 1831).

298. Thomas Cooper, *Some Information Respecting America* (London, 1794), 65.

299. Am. Educ. Soc. *Quar. Register and Journ.*, I, 199.

300. John Quincy Adams, *Writings*, I, 37.

301. Charles Warren, *A History of the American Bar* (Boston, 1911), 213-14.

302. John Bristed, *America and Her Resources* (London, 1818), 293-95; Achille Murat, *A Moral and Political Sketch of the United States of North America* (London, 1833), 146. Fortescue Cuming remarked in 1807 that the lawyers constituted "a very numerous class which assumes an air of superiority throughout the whole country." *Sketches,* 71.

303. E. A. Jones, *American Members of the Inns of Court* (London, 1924), xxviii-xxix.

304. Anon., "The American Character," *Literary Mag. and Am. Register,* II (1804), 255.

305. P. M. Hamlin, *Legal Education in Colonial New York* (New York, 1939), 131, n. 16.

306. Ibid, 125-26.

307. A. Z. Reed, *Training for the Public Profession of Law* (New York, 1921), 83-87.

308. This is based on data compiled by Austin L. Moore.

309. F. H. Chase, *Life of Lemuel Shaw* (Boston, 1918), 120.

310. W. W. Story, *Life and Letters of Joseph Story* (Boston, 1851), I, 73.

311. J. Q. Adams, *Life in a New England Town* (Boston, 1903), 158.

312. Story, *Life and Letters of Joseph Story,* I, 74.

313. F. A. Ogg, *Life of Daniel Webster* (Philadelphia, 1914), 56.

314. S. H. Fisher, ed., *Litchfield Law School, 1784-1833* (Litchfield, 1900), passim. More than 100 students were trained in the law school established by Peter Van Schaack in 1786 in his home at Kinderhook, New York. H. C. Van Schaack, *Life of Peter Van Schaack* (New York, 1842), 443ff.

315. D. C. Kilbourn, *The Bench and Bar of Litchfield, Connecticut, 1709-1909* (Litchfield, 1909), 178-215.

316. *United States Law Journal* (1822), 400-401.

317. G. M. Towle, *American Society* (London, 1870), I, 89; Theophilus Parsons, *Memoir of Theophilus Parsons* (Boston, 1859), 154.

318. John Palmer, *Journal of Travels in the United States of North America . . . 1817* (London, 1818), 203-6; Chase, *Lemuel Shaw,* 44-45; Warren, *American Bar,* 206-7.

319. J. T. Horton, *James Kent* (New York, 1939), 126- 30.

320. Towle, *American Society,* I, 103-105; James Stuart, *Three Years in North America* (London, 1833), I, 330; Rufus Choate, *Works* (S. G. Brown, ed., Boston, 1862), I, 280.

321. Anon., *History of the County of Berkshire, Massachusetts* (Pittsfield, 1829), 109.

322. Business interests and their legal advisers constantly sought judicial recognition for the unincorporated association. Their efforts gave a certain semblance of specialization to the work in some urban law offices prior to 1830. For a discussion of legal aspects of the problem of business organization in this period, see Shaw Livermore, *Early American Land Companies* (Columbia Univ. School of Law, *Publs.,* 1939), chaps, vii-viii, and Julius Goebel's "Introduction."

323. Choate, *Works,* I, 18.

324. [G. S. Hillard et al.], *George Ticknor,* I, 347-48.

325. *Medical Repository,* I (1798), 115; Connecticut Medical Society, *Transactions* (1796), 40; (1797), 50; B. D. Perkins, *The Efficacy of Perkins Patent Medicine Tractors* (n.p., n.d.), passim.

326. S. D. Willard, *Annals of the Medical Society of the County of Albany, 1806-1851* (Albany, 1851), 24.

327. Massachusetts Medical Society, *Medical Papers,* VII, 88-90.

328. *Boston Medical Intelligencer,* II, 151-52.

329. Regular practitioners were often more distressed by evidence of empirical folk science than by the vagaries of supersitition. *Medical Repository,* IV (1801), 285ff.; Joseph Johnson, *Oration before the Medical Society of South Carolina* (Charleston, 1808), 24–25.

330. The herbalists, attacking regulatory legislation, helped to perpetuate belief in the efficacy of the rabbit's foot, the beaver's tail, the snake's skin, and scores of weird concoctions in the cure of disease. Some paraded as "botanists," who should have been called sorcerers. See the prescriptions in *The New and Complete Medical Family Herbal* by Samuel Henry, botanist (New York, 1814), and Daniel Ballmer, *A Collection of New Receipts and Approved Cures for Man and Beast* (Shellsburg, Pa., 1827).

331. William Manning, *The Key of Libberty* (S. E. Morison, ed., Billerica, Mass., 1922), 26.

332. For the decline of state regulation after 1830, see C. B. Cartwright, "History of Medical Legislation in the State of New York." *N.Y. Journ. of Medicine,* IV, 160. R. H. Shryock discusses its relation to the general philosophy of laissez-faire in his "Public Relations of the Medical Profession in Great Britain and the United States, 1600–1870," *Annals of Medical History,* n.s., II, 322–23.

333. *Medical Repository,* XV (1811–12), 113; *Literary Mag. and Am. Register,* II (1804), 233ff.; *Boston Medical Intelligencer,* February 28, 1826.

334. Medical Society of the City of New York, *Report on Nostrums or Secret Medicines* (New York, 1827), 29–35.

335. Shafer, *Medical Profession,* 202–203.

336. *Medical Repository,* VI (1803), 434.

337. Asa Greene's *Life and Adventures of Dr. Dodimus Duckworth, A.N.Q.* (New York, 1833), I, 239–40, contains a satirical description of the medical apprentice who learns by just watching the doctor.

338. *Am. Medical and Philos. Register,* II (1811–12), 369–70.

339. DeWitt Clinton, "Introductory Discourse," Literary and Philosophical Society, *Transactions* (1815), I, 19ff.

340. For a summary of medical schools founded between 1800 and 1830, see Shafer, *Medical Profession,* 38–39.

341. Drake's ability as a physician was marred by his contentiousness. He held eleven chairs in six different schools between 1817 and 1852. E. D. Mansfield, *Memoir of . . . Daniel Drake* (Cincinati, 1855), passim.

342. Edward Hooker, "Diary," Am. Hist. Assoc., *Ann. Rep. for 1896,* I, 916.

343. R. H. Shryock, "Medical Practice in the Old South," *S. Atl. Quar.,* XXIX, 166–67.

344. *Boston Medical Intelligencer,* III (1826), 40.

345. *Medical Repository,* XIII (1809–10), 176.

346. Davis, *Contributions to Medical Education,* 26.

347. Where the instructional staff was small, physiology, anatomy, and surgery remained one branch; botany, materia medica, and pharmacy another; and theory and practice of medicine a third. Shafer, *Medical Profession,* 55–56.

348. Committee of the American Medical Association, *Circular Addressed to Medical Colleges of the United States* (Philadelphia, 1856).

349. *American Museum,* III (1788), 389–90.

350. E. E. Atwater, ed., *History of the City of New Haven* (New York, 1887), 271; C. R. Bardeen, "Anatomy in America," Univ. of Wis., *Sci. Ser. Bull.,* III, 139.

351. Mathew Carey, *Short Account of the Malignant Fever* (Philadelphia, 1793).

352. *Medical Repository,* XIV (1810–11), 182.

353. *Literary Mag. and Am. Register,* I (1803–4), 7. See also James Hardie, *An Account of the Malignant Fever, Lately Prevalent in the City of New-York* (New York, 1799).

354. *Medical Repository,* V (1802), 182.

355. In the first six volumes of *Medical Repository* (1797–1803) more than ninety

essays or papers discussed the history and phenomena of pestilence. American treatises, with learned commentaries appended, were translated in German, Spanish, and Italian medical journals.

356. *Medical Repository,* IV, 91-93; C. R. Hall, *A Scientist in the Early Republic; Samuel Latham Mitchill* (New York, 1934), 53.

357. Noah Webster, *Brief History of Epidemics and Pestilential Diseases, with the Principal Phenomena of the Physical World, which Precede and Accompany Them, and Observations Adduced from the Facts Stated* (Hartford, 1799); *Medical Repository,* V, 32ff.; J. L. E. W. Shecut, *Medical and Philosophical Essays* (Charleston, 1819), chap. iii.

358. *Medical Repository,* XIII, 154-57; *Am. Medical and Philos. Register,* I (1810-11), 323.

359. The Anonymous author of *The Town and Country Friend and Physician* (Philadelphia, 1803) believed that more people ought to bathe: "I mean here to inculcate the indispensable necessity of *domestic baths,* so well known among the ancients."

360. *Am. Medical and Philos. Register,* II, 14ff.; *Medical Repository,* VI (1803), 37ff.

361. *Medical Repository,* III (1800), 65.

362. *Western Journ. of the Medical and Physical Sciences,* II (1829), 495.

363. Shafer, *Medical Profession,* 167-69.

364. *Literary Mag. and Am. Register,* VI (1806), 76-77.

365. William Dunlap, *The History of the Rise and Progress of the Arts of Design in the United States* (Boston, 1918), I, 229; Oskar Hagen, *The Birth of the American Tradition in Art* (New York, 1940), 146-47.

366. G. C. Mason, *The Life and Works of Gilbert Stuart* (New York, 1879), 89-91.

367. Wilfred Jordan, "William Rush, the Earliest American-Born Sculptor," *Art and Archaeology,* XI, 145-46; Dunlap, *History of the Arts of Design,* III, 34-38.

368. Fiske Kimball, *Thomas Jefferson, Architect* (Boston, 1916), 81-83.

369. I. T. Frary, *Thomas Jefferson, Architect and Builder* (Richmond, 1931), 43-54 and plates.

370. John Duncan, *Travels through Parts of the United States* (Glasgow, 1823), 189; Peter Neilson, *Recollections of a Six Years' Residence in the United States* (Glasgow, 1830), 14; R. T. Coke, *A Subaltern's Furlough* (New York, 1833), I, 30.

371. Timothy Alden, Jr., *An Account of the Several Religious Societies in Portsmouth* (Boston, 1808); C. A. Wight, *Some Old Time Meeting Houses of the Connecticut Valley* (Chicopee Falls, Mass., 1911), plates opp. 94, 116; Aymar Embury II, *Early American Churches* (New York, 1914), 5-6.

372. See William Bentley, *Diary* (Salem, 1905-14), III, 256-57; Fiske Kimball, "The Elias Hasket Derby Mansion in Salem," *Essex Inst., Colls.,* LX, 273-92; C. A. Place, *Charles Bulfinch, Architect and Citizen* (Boston, 1925), chap. iii.

373. Bulfinch's influence was particularly noticeable in the work of Asher Benjamin, carpenter-builder, whose publications between 1797 and 1833 bulked large in the literature of the developing profession. A. J. Wall, *Books on Architecture Printed in America, 1775-1830* (Cambridge, 1925), passim; Aymar Embury II, *Asher Benjamin: a Reprint of the Country Builder's Assistant, 1805* (New York, 1917), 1-3.

374. B. H. Latrobe, *Journal* (New York, 1905), 139.

375. Howard Major, *The Domestic Architecture of the Early American Republic: the Greek Revival* (Philadelphia, 1926), 17-50.

376. Myrtle A. Cline, *American Attitude toward the Greek War of Independence* (Atlanta, 1930), 19-51; E. M. Earle, "American Interest in the Greek Cause," *Am. Hist. Rev.,* XXXIII, 44-63.

377. Talbot Hamlin, "The Greek Revival in American Architecture," *Columbia Univ. Quar.,* XXXI, 171-75; Rexford Newcomb, "Ithiel Town of New Haven and New York," *Architect,* XI, 519-22.

378. Asher Benjamin, *The Practice of Architecture* (Embury Reprint), 139-40. The first pattern book published by a native American was Benjamin's *Country Builder's Assistant* (Greenfield, Mass., 1797).

379. By 1800 the product of domestic paper manufacturers was almost as highly esteemed as the imports from Paris. Nancy McClelland, *Historic Wall Papers* (Philadelphia, 1924), 255, 266-67.

380. *Salem Gazette*, August 6, 1822. See also Essex Institute, *Historical Collections*, LXII, 4-7.

381. Thomas Hope, *House Furniture and Decoration* (London, 1807); C. M. Stow, "The Influence of the Great Georgian Designers," J. M. Bell, ed., *The Furniture Designs of Chippendale, Hepplewhite and Sheraton* (New York, 1938).

382. C. O. Cornelius, *Early American Furniture* (New York, 1926), 100-179; Nancy McClelland, *Duncan Phyfe and English Regency, 1795-1830* (New York, 1939), 91ff.; T. H. Ormsbee, *Early American Furniture Makers* (New York, 1930), 63-73.

383. See this volume, Book IV, 298.

384. Dunlap, *History of the Arts of Design,* I, 143-44; J. H. Morgan, *Early American Painters* (New York, 1921), 63ff. Morse forsook England for France, where John Vanderlyn, protégé of Aaron Burr, also studied. Carleton Mabee, *The American Leonardo* (New York, 1943), chap. iii.

385. Dunlap, *History of the Arts of Design,* II, 112, 283; III, 332. Of 200 portrait painters, selected at random, who worked between 1790 and 1830, forty-four were foreign-born. G. C. Groce, Jr., ed., *American Poetry Inventory, 1440 Early American Portrait Artists, 1663-1860* (Newark, N.J., 1940), passim.

386. Ezra Ames, Yearly Expense Books, covering years 1799-1826, in New-York Historical Society; William Kelby, "Notes on American Artists," N.Y. Hist. Soc., *Quar. Bull.,* III, 67, 112; IV, 114.

387. Theodore Bolton, *Early American Portrait Painters in Miniature* (New York, 1921), 54ff., 99ff.; H. B. Wehle, *American Miniatures, 1730-1850* (Garden City, 1927), 64-65.

388. Dunlap, *History of the Arts of Design,* II, 204; Richardson Wright, *Hawkers and Walkers in Early America* (Philadelphia, 1927), 134ff.

389. The journals devoting most space to art were the *Port Folio, Analectic Magazine,* and the *American Museum* in Philadelphia; the *American Monthly Magazine and Critical Review* and the *Monthly Magazine and American Review* in New York; the *Athenaeum* and the *North American Review* in Boston.

390. Probably 12 magazines were being issued regularly in 1800, 40 in 1810, and 100 in 1825. F. L. Mott, *A History of American Magazines, 1741-1850* (New York, 1930), 120-21.

391. A. H. Smyth, *The Philadelphia Magazines and Their Contributors* (Philadelphia, 1892), 93.

392. H. R. Brown, *The Sentimental Novel in America, 1789-1860* (Durham, 1940), chaps. i-vi.

393. It was published anonymously and its author has never been positively identified as Sarah Wentworth Morton. Milton Ellis, "The Author of the First American Novel," *Am. Lit.,* IV, 356-68.

394. By 1812, 50,000 copies had been sold. E. L. Bradsher, *Mathew Carey, Editor, Author and Publisher* (New York, 1912), 51. By 1933 the various editions of the novel numbered 161. R. W. G. Vail, *Susanna Haswell Rowson, a Bibliographical Study* (Worcester, 1933), 18, 21.

395. *The Emigrants* was probably written after Imlay left America. R. L. Rusk, "Adventures of Gilbert Imlay," Indiana Univ., *Studies,* X, no. 57, 13-15.

396. *Modern Chivalry* was published serially between 1792 and 1815. See C. M. Newlin, *The Life and Writings of Hugh Henry Brackenridge* (Princeton, 1932), 112-23.

397. *Weekly Magazine,* I (1798), 202–3.
398. S. T. Williams, *The Life of Washington Irving* (New York, 1935), I, 208–10, 220–22.
399. J. D. Ferguson, *American Literature in Spain* (New York, 1916), 8–31. *The Sketch Book* was translated into fifteen languages.
400. H. W. Boynton, *James Fenimore Cooper* (New York, 1931), 106–25.
401. *An Oration Pronounced at Cambridge before the Society of Phi Beta Kappa* (New York, 1824).
402. *Natural History of Intellect and Other Papers* (Boston, 1894), 79.
403. "On a National Literature," *Christian Examiner,* VII (1830), 269ff.
404. *Literary Mag. and Am. Register,* I, 419–24; Samuel Miller, *Brief Retropsect of the Eighteenth Century* (New York, 1803), II, 404–10.
405. Dwight, *Travels,* IV, 355; Ravenel, *Charleston,* 389.
406. David Ramsay, *History of South Carolina* (Charleston, 1806), II, 211–12. If the farmers' almanacs are added, this brief list would be characteristic of many rural districts from Georgia to Maine.
407. U. P. Hedrick, "What Farmers Read in Western New York, 1800–1850," *N.Y. History,* XVII, 283.
408. Cited in Lillie D. Loshe, *The Early American Novel* (Columbia Univ., *Studies in English,* ser. 2, II, no. 2), 1–2. See this volume, Book II, 95, for an explanation of the reference.
409. Bradsher, *Mathew Carey,* 80–81.
410. Edward Everett noticed in his tour of the Southern states that many names of stagecoaches, steamboats, etc., were taken from Scott's novels. P. L. Frothingham, *Edward Everett* (Boston, 1925), 119.
411. R. L. Shurter, "Mrs. Hannah Webster Foster and the Early American Novel," *Am. Lit.,* IV, 306–7.
412. *N. Y. Daily Advertiser,* May 26, 1802.
413. Carey had hoped that "many a musty volume . . . would find a ready market, when transported to the banks of the Susquehanna, the Potomack, or the Santee." Ibid. See also *Gazette of the United States,* July 16, 1802; *Aurora,* June 29, 1803; Bradsher, *Mathew Carey,* 15–22.
414. E. P. Oberholtzer, *Literary History of Philadelphia* (Philadelphia, 1906), 343–44.
415. J. H. Harper, *The House of Harper* (New York, 1912), 15–18.
416. S. G. Goodrich, *Recollections of a Lifetime* (New York, 1856), II, 388–89.
417. Bradsher, *Mathew Carey,* 80; Harper, *House of Harper,* 23–24.
418. Ibid., 8–9.
419. Thurlow Weed, *Autobiography* (Harriet A. Weed, ed., Boston, 1883), 57.
420. "Public Libraries in the United States," Bureau of Education, *Special Report* (1876), xvi.
421. *North American Review,* V (1817), 430–31.
422. DeKay, *Anniversary Address,* 74.
423. G. W. Cole, "Early Library Development in New York State, 1800–1900," N. Y. Public Library, *Bull.,* XXX, 854–55.
424. *North American Review,* VIII (1818), 199–200.
425. For example, David Ramsay, *History of the United States* (Philadelphia, 1816); Abiel Holmes, *The Annals of America* (rev. ed., Cambridge, 1829); Timothy Pitkin, *A Political and Civil History of the United States* (New Haven, 1828); Benjamin Trumbull, *General History of the United States of America* (Boston, 1810); Frederick Butler, *History of the United States to 1820* (Hartford, 1821).
426. Neal was not modest about the merits of his own works, and English editors may have regarded his boasting as characteristically American. Bradsher, *Mathew Carey,* 66–67.
427. Mary Russell Mitford, *Life . . . Told by Herself in Letters to Her Friends* (A. G. K. L'Estrange, ed., New York 1870), II, 60.

428. *U. S. Tenth Census* (1880), *Manufactures,* xxii; A. F. Weber, *The Growth of Cities in the Nineteenth Century* (Columbia Univ., *Studies,* XI), 22–23.

429. *American State Papers* (Washington, 1832–61). *Finance,* II, 666ff.; Adam Seybert, *Statistical Annals of the United States* (Philadelphia, 1818), 8–9; K. W. Rowe, *Mathew Carey, a Study in American Economic Development* (John Hopkins Univ., *Studies,* ser. LI, no. 4), 44–46.

430. F. W. Taussig, *The Tariff History of the United States* (New York, 1923), 17–18, 31, 35.

431. *U.S. Tenth Census, Manufactures,* 542–44.

432. Nathan Appleton, *Introduction of the Power Loom, and Origin of Lowell* (Lowell, 1858), 8–10; Caroline F. Ware, *The Early New England Cotton Manufacture* (New York, 1931), 60–63.

433. The data for such estimates were later compiled in Louis McLane's report for 1832, 22 Cong., 1 sess., *House Exec. Docs.,* no. 308.

434. Ware, *New England Cotton Manufacture,* 63–65.

435. H. A. Miles, *Lowell as It Was and as It Is* (Boston, 1845), 67–166; J. R. Commons et al., eds., *A Documentary History of American Industrial Society* (Cleveland, 1910–11), VII, 137.

436. J. R. Commons et al., *History of Labour in the United States* (New York, 1918), I, chap. iii; Mary R. Beard, *Short History of the American Labor Movement* (New York, 1920), 84–89.

437. W. R. Waterman, *Frances Wright* (Columbia Univ., *Studies,* CXV, no. 1), chap. iv.

438. William Faux, *Memorable Days in America* (London, 1823), 29–30; M. L. Hansen, *The Atlantic Migration, 1607–1860* (A. M. Schlesinger, ed., Cambridge, 1940), 97–98, 121. It should be noted, however, that there were complaints concerning the poverty of newly arrived immigrants throughout the decade of the twenties. See McMaster, *History,* VI, 82–84.

439. The peak years were 1817 and 1818, during the decade that followed the Congress of Vienna. Europeans looked with some disfavor on the United States for several years after the depression of 1819. Hansen, *Atlantic Migration,* 107–19. See also S. C. Johnson, *History of Emigration from the United Kingdom to North America* (London School of Economics and Politics, *Studies,* no. 34), 16.

440. W. F. Adams, *Ireland and Irish Emigration to the New World from 1815 to the Famine* (*Yale Hist. Publs. Miscellany,* XXIII), 158.

441. Oscar Handlin, *Boston's Immigrants, 1790–1865* (*Harvard Hist. Studies,* L), 41–42; Ravenel, *Charleston,* chap. iv. By 1825, New Orleans was becoming important as a port of entry.

442. Common Council of the City of New York, *Minutes, 1784–1831* (New York, 1917), VII, 256; VIII, 121, 454.

443. James Hardie, *Description of the City of New York* (New York, 1827), 291–92.

444. McMaster, *History,* IV, 390–92; Hansen, *Atlantic Migration,* 93–94.

445. One of the most successful was the General Society of Mechanics and Tradesmen, incorporated in New York in 1792. Hardie, *Description of New York,* 294.

446. R. T. Thompson, *Colonel James Neilson* (New Brunswick, 1940), 291–95.

447. Philanthropic effort also owed much to the humane societies established in imitation of Dutch and English societies for the purpose of administering aid to "persons who meet with such accidents as to produce in them the appearance of death." In New England this life-saving activity long persisted; elsewhere the humane societies frequently became nuclei for a wide variety of charitable enterprises. William Tudor, *A Discourse Delivered before the Humane Society* (Boston, 1817), 19–64; *Medical Repository,* IX (1805–6), 328; *Sketch of the Origin and Progress of the Humane Society of the City of New York* (New York, 1814); H. M. Lippincott, *Early Philadelphia* (Philadelphia, 1859), 219.

448. The "charity" sermon, which most congregations expected at some time during the church year, received more attention from the press than any other pulpit pronouncements. For examples, see Abiel Abbott, *A Discourse Delivered . . . on*

the Lord's Day, August 9, 1807 (Portsmouth, 1807); J. B. Romeyn, *The Good Samaritan* (New York, 1810); P. M. Whelpley, *A Sermon Delivered on the Fourth of February, 1816* (New York, 1816); John Pierce, *A Discourse Delivered on the Ninth of November, 1817* (Boston, 1818).

449. The Yates report is reprinted in New York State Board of Charities, *Annual Report for 1900*, I, 937-1145.

450. *Medical Repository*, XV (1811-12), 87-88; New York Academy of Medicine, *Transactions*, I (1847), 2-31; H. B. Shafer, *The American Medical Profession, 1783-1850* (New York, 1936), 116-19.

451. T. H. Gallaudet, *A Discourse Delivered at the Dedication of the American Asylum* (Hartford, 1821), 9-15; H. W. Syle, *A Biographical Sketch of Thomas H. Gallaudet* (Philadelphia, 1887), 16-25.

452. Emerson Davis, *The Half Century* (New York, 1851), 107-11.

453. H. E. Barnes, *The Repression of Crime* (New York, 1926), 86ff.; J. S. Taylor, *A Comparative View of Punishments Annexed to Crime in the United States of America and in England* (London, 1831).

454. O. F. Lewis, *The Development of American Prisons and Prison Conditions, 1776-1845* (Albany, 1922), 30; Blake McKelvey, *American Prisons* (Univ. of Chicago, *Social Service Series*, 1936), 5-7.

455. *Am. Medical and Philos. Register*, IV (1813-14), 632-37; S. L. Mitchill, *The Picture of New-York* (New York, 1807), 112ff.; McMaster, *History*, IV, 532-34.

456. Lewis, *Development of American Prisons*, 16-17.

457. McKelvey, *American Prisons*, 13-14.

458. Society for the Prevention of Pauperism in the City of New York, *Annual Report for 1822: American Daily Advertiser*, June 5, 12, July 9, 1821, cited in McMaster, *History*, IV, 537-39; W. F. Barnard, *Forty Years at the Five Points* (New York, 1893), 1-4.

459. Examples of this attitude may be found in the *New Magazine*, V (1794), 656-57; *American Museum*, XII (1792), 159; *Massachusetts Missionary Magazine*, I (1803), 465-66; *Christian Examiner*, VIII (1830), 204-5.

460. *American Farmer*, IX (1827), 55-56.

461. Jennie Holliman, *American Sports, 1785-1835* (Durham, 1931), 72, 78-84.

462. T. S. Perry, ed., *Life and Letters of Francis Lieber* (Boston, 1882), 77, 95.

463. W. R. Wister, *Some Reminiscences of Cricket in Philadelphia* (Philadelphia, 1904), 4-5; A. G. Spalding, *America's National Game* (New York, 1911), 29-39.

464. *Virginia Argus*, March 20, 1800; *Literary Mag. and Am. Register*, VI (1806), 266; *American Farmer*, IX (1829), 79; *Evening Post*, February 8, 1830.

465. Ibid., July 6, 1824.

466. Ibid., November 13, 1820; December 9, 1824.

467. Alexander Johnston, *Ten and Out!* (New York, 1927), 18-23.

468. *Evening Post*, November 27, 1826; June 24, 1830; Friedrich Jahn, *Treatise on Gymnastics* (Charles Beck, tr., Northampton, 1828); J. A. Krout, *Annals of American Sport* (R. H. Gabriel, ed., *The Pageant of America*, New Haven, 1926-29, XIV), 207.

469. G. W. Ranck, *History of Lexington, Kentucky* (Cincinnati, 1872), 130.

470. Josiah Quincy, *Figures of the Past* (Boston, 1910), 96-99.

471. Ravenel, *Charleston*, 129-30; John Quincy Adams, *Memoirs*, VII, 162.

472. W. W. Clapp, *A Record of the Boston Stage* (Boston, 1853), 11, 23; G. C. D. Odell, *Annals of the New York Stage* (New York, 1927-42), I, 380.

473. Oscar Wegelin, *Early American Plays, 1714-1830* (New York, 1900), 67.

474. P. L. Ford, *Washington and the Theater* (New York, 1899), 35-44.

475. William Dunlap, *History of the American Theater* (London, 1833), II, 360-64; D. R. Fox, "The Development of the American Theater," *N. Y. History*, XVII, 29.

476. Charles Blake, *An Historical Account of the Providence Stage* (Providence, 1868), 79; Clapp, *Boston Stage*, 5; Dunlap, *American Theater*, I, 105-109.

477. At New York's Park Theater in 1798 the scale of prices was: boxes $2.00; pit,

$1.50; gallery, $1.00. Arthur Hornblow, *History of the Theatre in America* (Philadelphia, 1919), I, 246. See also G. O. Willard, *History of the Providence Stage* (Providence, 1891), 38, and Odell, *Annals,* I, 348.

478. N. M. Ludlow, *Dramatic Life as I Found It* (St. Louis, 1880), 96-113, 150-59. Contemporary press notices of the frontier theater are numerous in O. S. Coad and Edwin Mims, Jr., *The American Stage (Pageant of America,* XIV), 125ff.

479. I. J. Greenwood, *The Circus, Its Origins and Growth* (New York, 1898), 17, 78, 87, 113-16.

480. Odell, *Annals,* I, 338.

481. T. E. V. Smith, *The City of New York in the Year of Washington's Inauguration* (New York, 1889), 183; *Columbian Centinel,* April 28, 1810.

482. Sydney and Marjorie Greenbie, *Gold of Ophir* (New York, 1925), 53.

483. Smith, *New York,* 185-86; J. T. Scharf and Thompson Westcott, *History of Philadelphia* (Philadelphia, 1834), II, 950-51.

484. *Cleaveland Herald,* October 25, 1823.

485. Mitchill, *New York,* 156-57; Hornblow, *History of the Theatre,* II, 96-97.

486. James Hall, *Letters from the West* (London, 1828), 48, 91; Timothy Flint, *Recollections of the Last Ten Years* (Boston, 1826), 93-94; F. J. Turner, *The United States, 1830-1850* (New York, 1935), 18-19, 31; J. M. Miller, *The Genesis of Western Culture (Ohio Hist. Colls.,* IX), 38-45.

487. Lois K. Mathews, *Expansion of New England* (Boston, 1909), 181. F. J. Turner, *Rise of the New West* (A. B. Hart, ed., *The American Nation: a History,* New York, 1904-1918, XIV), 76, points out that in the Ohio legislature of 1822 there were thirty-eight members of Middle-states birth, thirty-three of Southern (including Kentucky), and only twenty-five of New England.

488. An excellent description of the characteristics of Western communities appears in F. J. Turner, *The Frontier in American History* (New York, 1921), chap. xiii.

489. Alexis de Tocqueville, *Democracy in America* (Henry Reeves, tr., New York, 1838), II, 2. See also I, 170-72, 175-77.

490. In Indiana and Illinois the position of the black was anomalous during the early years of statehood. What amounted to slavery existed under the guise of indentured servitude. Victory for the antislavery forces was not certain in Illinois until the latter part of the decade of the twenties. B. W. Bond, Jr., *The Civilization of the Old Northwest* (New York, 1934), 96, 163-71; T. C. Pease, *The Centennial History of Illinois, The Frontier State, 1818-1848* (Springfield, Ill., 1918-20), 77-91.

491. Thomas Ford, *History of Illinois* (Chicago, 1854), 102-103.

492. Bessie L. Pierce, *A History of Chicago* (New York, 1937-42), I, 44n.

493. *Fifth Census,* 122-23, 152-53.

494. Benjamin Drake and E. D. Mansfield, *Cincinnati in 1826* (Cincinnati, 1827), 70ff.

495. C. H. Ambler, *A History of Transportation in the Ohio Valley* (Glendale, Calif., 1932), 149-60.

496. Turner, *Rise of the New West,* 98-99.

497. C. P. McClelland and C. C. Huntington, *History of the Ohio Canals* (Columbus, 1905), 30-32.

498. E. G. Swem, ed., *Letters on the Condition of Kentucky in 1825* (New York, 1916), 68-74.

499. T. P. Abernethy, *From Frontier to Plantation in Tennessee* (Chapel Hill, 1932), 277-84.

500. Phillips, *American Negro Slavery,* 173-74.

501. Adam Hodgson, *Letters from North America* (London, 1824), I, 269.

502. Timothy Flint, *History and Geography of the Mississippi Valley* (Cincinnati, 1832), I, 229.

503. Turner, *Rise of the New West,* statistical table on p. 47.

504. [J. H. Ingraham], *The Southwest* (New York, 1835), II, 86.

505. *Georgia Courier* (Augusta), October 11, 1827, reprinted in U. B. Phillips, *Plantation and Frontier* (J. R. Commons et al., eds., *A Documentary History of American Industrial Society,* New York, 1910-11, I), 283-89.
506. Flint, *History and Geography of the Mississippi Valley,* II, 217; T. P. Abernethy, *The Formative Period in Alabama, 1815-28* (Montgomery, 1922), 24-32.
507. Hodgson, *Letters,* I, 186; [Ingraham], *Southwest,* II, 204-208.
508. The reports are abstracted in *Niles' Weekly Register,* IX, supplement, 149-50, 165-66.
509. Turner, *Rise of the New West,* 30-31, citing Virginia Constitutional Convention, *Debates* (1829-30), 405.
510. Gray, *History of Agriculture in the Southern United States,* II, chap. xxxvii.
511. W. A. Schaper, "Sectionalism and Representation in South Carolina," Am. Hist. Assoc., *Ann. Rep. for 1900,* I, 433-38.
512. E. L. Fox, *The American Colonization Society, 1817-1840* (Johns Hopkins Univ., *Studies,* XXXVII, no. 3), 46-124.
513. Jefferson, *Writings,* X, 157.
514. John Quincy Adams, *Memoirs,* IV, 526, 530-31.
515. Abraham Lincoln, *Early Speeches, 1832-1856* (W. C. Whitney, ed., New York, 1907), 1.

BOOK VI   The Rise of the Common Man, 1830-50

1. J. D. Richardson, ed., *A Compilation of the Messages and Papers of the Presidents, 1789-1908* (Washington, 1908), II, 449.
2. W. T. Sherman and John Sherman, *Letters* (Rachel Sherman Thorndike, ed., New York, 1894), 6-7, 10-12.
3. Andrew Johnson, *Life and Speeches* (Frank Moore, ed., Boston, 1865), 56.
4. E. L. Bogart, *Economic History of American Agriculture* (New York, 1923), 17-29, 32-50, 61-100; L. B. Schmidt and E. D. Ross, eds., *Readings in the Economic History of American Agriculture* (New York, 1923), chaps. xii-xiv.
5. W. V. Pooley, *The Settlement of Illinois, 1830-1850* (Univ. of Wis., *Bull.,* no. 220, I, 1908), 335-46.
6. M. B. Hammond, *The Cotton Industry* (Am. Econ. Assoc., *Publs.,* new ser. 1, pt. 1); U. B. Phillips, "The Economic Cost of Slaveholding in the Cotton Belt," *Pol. Sci. Quart.,* XX, 257-75; same author, "Plantations as a Civilizing Factor," *Sewanee Rev.,* XII, 257-67; same author, "Origin and Growth of the Southern Black Belts," *Am. Hist. Rev.,* XI, 798-816; same author, *American Negro Slavery* (New York, 1918), chaps. xiii, xvi-xvii.
7. There are histories of the American merchant marine which cover these years by W. W. Bates, *American Marine* (Boston, 1897), 127-49, 166-73; W. L. Marvin, *The American Merchant Marine from 1620 to 1920* (New York, 1902), chaps. xi-xii; J. R. Spears, *The Story of the American Merchant Marine* (New York, 1910), 173-76, 201-68, 277-84.
8. A. B. Hulbert, *Historic Highways of America* (Cleveland, 1902-15), I, VIII-XI; H. M. Chittenden, *History of Early Steamboat Navigation on the Missouri River* (New York, 1903), and other studies; G. B. Merrick, *Genesis of Steamboating on Western Rivers* (Madison, Wis., 1912); and same author, *Old Times on the Upper Mississippi* (Cleveland, 1909).
9. Raymond MacFarland, *New England Fisheries* (New York, 1911), chaps. ix-x.
10. Obed Macy, *The History of Nantucket... Rise and Progress of the Whale Fishery* (Boston, 1835), I, 210-14; Alexander Starbuck, *History of American Whale Fishery* (Waltham, 1878), 95-104, 110; J. R. Spears, *The Story of the New England Whalers* (New York, 1910), chaps. xi-xii; A. H. Verrill, *The Real Story of the Whaler* (New York, 1916), a popular treatment.

11. A. B. Hulbert, *The Cumberland Road* (*Historic Highways,* X, Cleveland, 1904), chaps. ii–iii, v, appendix A.

12. Note Lincoln's attempt. J. G. Nicolay and John Hay, *Abraham Lincoln* (New York, 1890), I, 70–71.

13. Lewis Collins, *History of Kentucky* (Covington, 1874), 542–53; anon., *History of the Ohio Falls Cities* (Cleveland, 1882), 42–56.

14. See this volume Book V, 409.

15. Charles Dickens, *American Notes* (Philadelphia, 1859), 61–71, describes a journey on this canal in 1842.

16. The *Report* of the Philadelphia & Reading Railroad for 1857 showed four locomotives constructed in 1838 still in use without rebuilding.

17. Phila. & Reading Railroad, *Report for 1857.*

18. Anon., "Baird's Spark Arrester," *Scientific American,* VI (1850), 9.

19. H. G. Richey, *Railroad Improvements, 1845–1857* (unpublished thesis, Univ. of Wis.).

20. A good account of the situation in 1850 is to be found in Dionysius Lardner, *Railway Economy* (New York, 1850), 387–414.

21. This controversy may be followed through the period in Edward Stanwood, *American Tariff Controversies in the Nineteenth Century* (Boston, 1903), I, chaps. viii–x, and F. W. Taussig. *Tariff History of the United States* (New York, 1914), chap. iii.

22. These twenty years are most important in the industrial revolution in the United States, but the movement has not been adequately studied. See, however, R. M. Tryon, *Household Manufactures in the United States, 1640–1860* (Chicago, 1917).

23. This subject has been admirably presented in J. R. Commons, "Labor Organization and Labor Politics, 1827–1837," *Quart. Journ. of Econ.,* XXI, 323–29, and J. R. Commons and Associates, *History of Labour in the United States* (New York, 1918), I, 71–88, 153–84, 215, 322.

24. The condition of women is discussed somewhat unfavorably by Edith Abbott, *Women in Industry* (New York, 1910), chaps. vii–viii, x–xi. The universally favorable comments of travelers capable of making contemporary comparisons seem more important, as Harriet Martineau, *Society in America* (London, 1837), II, 242–55. See also G. S. White, *Memoir of Samuel Slater . . . History of Cotton Manufacture* (Philadelphia, 1836), 125–40, 165–69.

25. V. S. Clark, *History of Manufactures in the United States, 1607 to 1860* (Carnegie Inst., *Contribs. to Am. Econ. Hist.,* Washington, 1916), 245, 262, 314, 401–92, 509–76; C. S. Boucher, "The Ante-Bellum Attitude of South Carolina towards Manufacturing and Agriculture," Washington Univ., *Studies,* III, 243–70.

26. E. W. Byrn, *The Progress of Invention in the Nineteenth Century* (New York, 1900), chap. ii.

27. S. F. B. Morse, *Letters and Journals* (E. L. Morse, ed., New York, 1914), II, chaps. xxix, xxx–xxxiii.

28. H. N. Casson, *Cyrus Hall McCormick* (Chicago, 1909), chaps. iii–v.

29. B. H. Hibbard, *History of Agriculture in Dane County, Wisconsin* (Univ. of Wis., *Bull.* no. 101), 67–214.

30. On heating, see Fredrika Bremer, *Homes of the New World* (New York, 1853), I, 66, 71–72, and passim.

31. In 1850 the United States imported tin plate and bars valued at $2,868,190.

32. See such books as *Laws of Etiquette by a Gentleman* (Philadelphia, 1839), and Mrs. Kate C. Maberly, *Art of Conversation* (New York, 1846).

33. A. J. Downing, *Cottage Residences* (New York, 1847); J. R. Ritch, *The American Architect* (New York, 1852); Samuel Sloan, *The Model Architect* (Philadelphia, 1852); Gervase Wheeler, *Rural Homes* (New York, 1852).

34. G. M. Davison, *The Traveller's Guide* (8th ed., Saratoga, 1840), gives a good

account of all public buildings existing and in process of construction. See also Sir Charles Lyell, *Travels in North America* (New York, 1845), I, 88–92.

35. On the leading hotels, see Hiram Hitchcock, "The Hotels of America," in C. M. Depew, ed., *One Hundred Years of American Commerce* (New York, 1895), I, 151–52.

36. See John Finch, *Travels in the United States of America* (London, 1833), 17, 42–43, 126, and passim, on local building material.

37. S. C. Johnson, *History of Emigration from the United Kingdom to North America, 1763–1912* (London, 1913), 39–67, 80–81, 158–59, 176–96, 316; S. H. Collins, *The Emigrant Guide to and Description of the United States of America* (Hull, Eng., 1830).

38. Stephen Byrne, *Irish Emigration to the United States* (New York, 1874), chaps. iii–v, x; J. F. Maguire, *The Irish in America* (London, 1868), chaps. xi–xiii, xvii.

39. G. R. Curtis, *Documents Relating to the Ursuline Convent in Charlestown, Mass.* (Boston, 1842); same author, *The Rights of Conscience and of Property . . . The Ursuline Convent Question* (Boston, 1842); Patrick Donahue, comp., *The Charlestown Convent: Its Destruction by a Mob on the Night of August 11, 1834* (Boston, 1870).

40. S. F. B. Morse, *Foreign Conspiracy against the Liberties of the United States* (New York, 1835), first published in the *New York Observer* for 1834.

41. Joseph Schafer, "Know-Nothingism in Wisconsin," *Wis. Mag. of Hist.,* VII, 3–21.

42. A. B. Faust, *The German Element in the United States* (Boston, 1909), I, 581–88, II, 59–74; Gustave Koerner, *Memoirs* (J. T. McCormack, ed., Cedar Rapids, Iowa, 1909), I, chaps., xiii–xiv, xvi–xvii. Frederick von Raumer, *America and the American People* (New York, 1846), says in his preface, "If we are forced to despair of the future progress of the Germanic race in America whither could we turn our eyes for deliverance, except to a new and direct creation from the hand of God."

43. F. A. von Gerstner, *Berichte aus den Vereinigten Staaten von Nord Amerika* (Leipzig, 1839); T. Bromme, *Gemälde von Nord Amerika* (Stuttgart, 1842).

44. Report of Consul General Adam Løvenskjold, October 15, 1847, *Wis. Mag. of Hist.,* VIII, 77–88.

45. R. B. Anderson, *The First Chapter of Norwegian Immigration (1821–1840)* (Madison, Wis., 1895); G. T. Flom, *A History of Norwegian Immigration to the United States . . . to 1848* (Iowa City, 1909).

46. Mrs. Susan Dabney Smedes, *Memorials of a Southern Planter* (Baltimore, 1887), chaps. v, vi–viii.

47. The best presentation of the case for homesteads is in the speech of Andrew Johnson delivered in the Senate of the United States, May 20, 1858. Johnson, *Life and Speeches,* 12–76.

48. J. S. Bassett, *The Life of Andrew Jackson* (Garden City, N.Y., 1911), II, 684–92.

49. Edwin Bottomley, *An English Settler in Pioneer Wisconsin* (M. M. Quaife, ed., Wis., Hist. Soc., *Colls.,* XXV), passim.

50. Compare J. B. McMaster, *History of the People of the United States* (New York, 1883–1927), with J. R. Green, *History of the English People* (London, 1877–78). The former seems generally throughout this period a much more confusing picture than any part of the latter.

51. C. W. Brewster, *National Standard of Costume* (Portsmouth, 1837); see particularly *Godey's Lady's Book and Magazine* (Philadelphia, 1830, and throughout the period).

52. G. W. Docine, *Manners Maketh Man* (Philadelphia, 1852); Eliza W. R. Farrar, *The Young Lady's Friend* (Boston, 1836); *The Laws of Etiquette* (Philadelphia, 1839); *The Young Man's Own Book* (Boston, 1832).

53. Robert Hoe, *A Short History of the Printing Press* (New York, 1902), 31–32, and passim.

54. Horace Greeley, *Recollections of a Busy Life* (New York, 1868), 136–43, 167, 261.

55. Lawrence Barrett, *Edwin Forrest* (Laurence Hutton, ed., *Am. Actor Series,* Boston, 1881), chaps. iv–vi; N. M. Ludlow, *Dramatic Life as I Found It* (St. Louis, 1880), chaps. xxxviii, xli, xlv–xlvii, l–lxv; Anna C. R. Mowatt [Mrs. A. C. Ritchie], *Autobiography of an Actress, or Eight Years on the Stage* (Boston, 1853), chaps. ii, xii–xxi, xxv–xxvii; A. H. Quinn, *A History of the American Drama to the Civil War* (New York, 1923), chaps. vii–xi; *Charlotte Cushman, Her Letters and Memories of Her Life* (Emma Stebbins, ed., Boston, 1878), chaps. ii–vi, viii–x.

56. *N.Y. Tribune,* December 1, 1847; *N.Y. Herald,* February 23, March 1, 20, 23, 1848.

57. I. J. Greenwood, *The Circus: Its Origin and Grown Prior to 1835* (New York, 1898).

58. M. R. Werner, *Barnum* (New York, 1923), 118–19, 153–57.

59. For baseball see Thurlow Weed, *Autobiography* (Harriet A. Weed, ed., Boston, 1884), 202. Agricultural fairs and horseracing need scientific treatment. Consult *History of Delaware County* [Ohio] (Chicago, 1880), 259–76, and Robert Peter, *History of Fayette County* [Kentucky] (Chicago, 1882), 106–79.

60. Andrew Dickson White, *Autobiography* (New York, 1905), II, 468–85.

61. Margaret Fuller Ossoli, *Woman in the Nineteenth Century* (A. B. Fuller, ed., Boston, 1855), 217–227.

62. Anthony Comstock, *Frauds Exposed* (New York, 1880), 388.

63. See this volume, Book II, 95.

64. Rupert Hughes, *The Golden Ladder* (New York, 1924); Frances Anne Kemble, *Journal of a Residence on a Georgian Plantation in 1838–1839* (New York, 1863), 14–15, 23 and passim; Meade Minnigerode, *The Fabulous Forties* (New York, 1924), chaps. iv, ix; Herbert Quick, *Vandemark's Folly* (Indianapolis, 1922), a novel which gives an admirable picture of frontier opinion; George Ticknor, *Life, Letters, and Journals* (G. S. Hilliard et al., eds., Boston, 1876), II, 240.

65. Allan Nevins, ed., *American Social History as Recorded by British Travellers* (New York, 1923), 245.

66. See for example, Bouck White, *The Book of Daniel Drew* (New York, 1911); Daniel Webster, "Speech on a Uniform System of Bankruptcy, June 5, 1840," *Writings and Speeches* (Nat'l ed., Boston, 1903), IX, 26–39.

67. *House Documents,* 25 Cong., 2 sess. IX, no. 297, 241–58.

68. Hermann von Holst, *The Constitutional and Political History of the United States* (8 vols., Chicago, 1889–92), II, 355n.

69. Edward Stanwood, *A History of the Presidency* (Boston, 1898), 163, 185, 203, 223, 243.

70. [Seba Smith], *The Life and Writings of Major Jack Downing, of Downingville, away down East in the State of Maine. Written by Himself* (Boston, 1833); same author, *Letters of J. Downing, Major, Downingville Militia* (New York, 1834).

71. Charles Ogle, *Speech on the Regal Splendor of the President's Palace* (Boston, 1840); same author, *Rede über die Königliche Pracht und die Verschwendung im Präsidenten-Palast* (Philadelphia, 1840).

72. Consult C. B. Going, *David Wilmot, Free-Soiler* (New York, 1924), 80–84, for an example of the currents in Pennsylvania.

73. Emerson Davis, *The Half Century* (Boston, 1851), 183–88.

74. The *Census of 1850,* however, reported accommodations for 14,234,825 in a population of 23,191,876; the value of church property was $89,983,028. J. D. De Bow, comp., *Statistical View of the United States . . . Compendium . . . Seventh Census* (Washington, 1854), 39, 138.

75. *Constitution of the Commonwealth of Massachusetts* (Boston, 1873), art. xi, 35–36, 44; S. H. Cobb, *Rise of Religious Liberty* (New York, 1902), 51ff.

76. For example, see Rev. Richard Fuller, *Domestic Slavery Considered as a Scriptural Institution* (New York, 1847), and S. B. Howe, *Slaveholding Not Sinful* (New York, 1855).

77. E. H. Anderson, *A Brief History of the Church of Jesus Christ of Latter Day Saints*

(Salt Lake City, 1902), pts. ii–iv; William Berriam, *Catalogue of Books, Early Newspapers and Pamphlets on Mormonism* (New York, 1898); William Clayton, *Journal* (Salt Lake City, 1921).

78. H. H. Bancroft, *History of Utah, 1540–1886* (*Works,* San Francisco, 1883–90, XXVI), chaps. iv–xiii.

79. J. R. G. Hassard, *Life of the Most Reverend John Hughes* (New York, 1866), chaps. vii–xx; Thomas O'Gorman, *A History of the Roman Catholic Church in the United States* (Philip Schaff et al., eds., *The American Church History Series,* New York, 1893–97, IX), chaps. xxii–xxv.

80. Hiram Bingham, *A Residence of Twenty-one Years in the Sandwich Islands* (Hartford, 1849): H. H. Jessup, *Fifty-three Years in Syria* (New York, 1910), passim; Francis Wayland, *Memoir of the Life and Labors of the Reverend Adoniram Judson* (Boston, 1853), I, chaps. xii–xiii; II, chaps. i, iii–v, vii.

81. Rev. and Mrs. O. H. Gulick, *The Pilgrims of Hawaii* (New York, 1918), chaps. xiv–xxi.

82. W. H. Lamon, *The Life of Abraham Lincoln* (Boston, 1872), 157–58, 486–504.

83. Horace Bushnell, *Life and Letters* (Mrs. Mary B. Cheney, ed., New York, 1880), chaps. iv–xii.

84. J. W. Chadwick, *William Ellery Channing* (Boston, 1903), chaps. viii, x–xi.

85. Woodbridge Riley, *American Thought* (New York, 1913), chap. vi; see also R. W. Emerson, *Complete Works* (Boston, 1903–12), passim; same author, *Journals* (E. W. Emerson and W. E. Forbes, eds., Boston, 1909–14), passim.

86. J. E. Cabot, *A Memoir of Ralph Waldo Emerson,* (Cambridge, Mass., 1887) I, chap. vii; H. C. Stoddard, "Transcendentalism" (W. P. Trent et al., eds., *Cambridge History of American Literature,* New York, 1917–21), I, 333–34.

87. O. B. Frothingham, *Transcendentalism in New England* (New York, 1876), chaps. vi–ix, xi–xiii.

88. E. P. Cubberley, *Public Education in the United States* (Boston, 1919), 174, 216–17.

89. A. V. G. Allen, *Life and Letters of Phillips Brooks* (New York, 1900), I, 53–67, 100–143.

90. Cubberley, *Public Education in the United States,* 190–94.

91. E. E. Brown, *The Making of Our Middle Schools* (New York, 1903), chaps. ix–xii.

92. A. C. Tilton, "Literary and Debating Societies in New Hampshire Towns and Academies," *Granite Monthly,* LI, 306–18.

93. W. M. Meigs, *The Life of John Caldwell Calhoun* (New York, 1917), 49–66.

94. Transylvania is a good example of the local interest in colleges. Robert and Johanna Peter, "Transylvania University, Its Origin, Rise, Decline, and Fall" (Filson Club, *Publs.,* no. 11, Louisville, 1896), passim; Robert Peter, "The History of the Medical Department of Transylvania University" (Johanna Peter, ed., Filson Club, *Publs.,* no. 20, Louisville, 1905), passim.

95. Josiah Quincy, *The History of Harvard University* (Boston, 1860), II, 290–91.

96. R. C. Alexander, "History of the College," *Union College Centennial Anniversary, 1795–1895* (New York, 1897), 65–66.

97. A. C. Tilton, "The Dartmouth Literary or Debating Societies," *Granite Monthly,* LII, 157–69, 202–13, 249–63.

98. Josiah Quincy, *History of Harvard University,* II, 374–380, 404, 586; Thomas Jefferson and J. C. Cabell, *Early History of the University of Virginia* (J. W. Randolph, ed., Richmond, 1856), 387–90, 424, 520–22.

99. P. H. Douglas, *American Apprenticeship and Industrial Education* (Columbia Univ., *Studies,* XCI), chap. iii.

100. See G. M. Tucker, *American Agricultural Periodicals* (Albany, 1909), 72–76.

101. J. R. Commons, ed., *A Documentary History of American Industrial Society* (Cleveland, 1909–11), V, 94–107, esp. 99–100.

102. Educational statistics are very unsatisfactory, but it is significant that between 1840

and 1850, the number of colleges and universities was reported as increasing from 173 to 239, while academies and such schools increased from 3,242 to 6,085. *Seventh Census, 1850. . . . Compendium,* 141–43, 151.

103. W. C. Brown, *The History of Brown University, 1764–1914* (Providence, 1914), chap. vi; C. E. Hughes, "Historical Address," *The Sesquicentennial of Brown University, 1764–1914* (Boston, 1915), 179–86.

104. L. W. Spring, *A History of Williams College* (Boston, 1917), 155, 214–26; Calvin Durfee, *A History of Williams College* (Boston, 1860), chap. xiii.

105. Cubberley, *Public Education in the United States,* 203–4.

106. For the influence of a revival on the mind of Salmon P. Chase, then (1826) a Dartmouth undergraduate, see A. M. Schlesinger, ed., *Salmon Portland Chase, Undergraduate and Pedagogue* (Columbus, 1919), 130–32.

107. W. G. Ballantine, ed., *The Oberlin Jubilee, 1833–1883* (Oberlin, 1883), 141–46, 153–79, 322, and passim; C. G. Finney, *Memoirs* (New York, 1876), chap. xxiv.

108. H. W. Arey, *The Girard College and its Founder* (Philadelphia, 1853), 30–44; C. A. Herrick, *Stephen Girard* (Philadelphia, 1923), 135–41, 155–58.

109. As late as 1840 only one half of the children of New England were given free education, one seventh of those of the Middle states and one sixth of those of the West. *Seventh Census, 1850, . . . Compendium,* 150–151.

110. J. P. Wickersham, *A History of Education in Pennsylvania* (Lancaster, 1886), chaps. xv–xvi; J. A. Woodburn, *Life of Thaddeus Stevens,* (Indianapolis, 1915), 41–54.

111. Thaddeus Stevens, "Speech in Defense of the Pennsylvania Free School System," U.S. Commissioner of Educ., *Rep. for 1898–1899.* I, 516–24.

112. Mrs. Mary P. Mann, *Life of Horace Mann* (Boston, 1865), chaps. iii–iv; A. D. Mayo, "Horace Mann and the Great Revival of the American School, 1830–1850," U.S. Commissioner of Educ., *Rep. for 1896–1897,* I, 715–67.

113. See A. O. Norton, ed., *The First State Normal School in America, The Journals of Cyrus Peirce and Mary Swift* (Cambridge, 1926).

114. Charles Hammond, *New England Academies and Classical Schools* (Boston, 1877); G. F. Mills, *The Academy System of the State of New York* (Albany, 1922); E. E. Brown, "History of Secondary Education in the United States" [bibliography], *School Rev.,* V, 84–94. 139–47.

115. Brown, *Making of Our Middle Schools,* chaps. xiii–xiv.

116. H. B. Adams, "Educational Extension in the United States," U. S. Commissioner of Educ., *Rep. for 1899–1900,* I, 284–99; *The American Lyceum* (*Old South Leaflets,* no. 139, Boston, n.d.).

117. H. A. Bridgeman, *New England in the Life of the World* (Boston, 1920); L. K. Mathews, *The Expansion of New England* (Boston, 1909).

118. The income of the elementary schools, amounting in all to $9,529,542, was derived as follows: $182,594 from endowments, $4,653,096 from taxes, $2,552,402 from public funds, and $2,141,450 from other sources. The secondary schools were supported by $288,855 from endowments, $14,202 from taxes, $115,724 from public funds, and $4,225,433 from other sources. *Seventh Census, 1850, . . . Compendium,* 142–43.

119. P. A. Barba, "Cooper in Germany," *German-Am. Annals,* new ser., XII, 3–60.

120. Lea Brothers and Company, *One Hundred Years of Publishing, 1785–1885* (Philadelphia, 1885), passim; A. H. Smyth, *The Philadelphia Magazine and Periodical Contributors, 1741–1850* (Philadelphia, 1892), 204–44.

121. B. B. Minor, *The Southern Literary Messenger, 1834–1864* (New York, 1905); M. J. Moses, *The Literature of the South* (New York, 1910), chaps. vii–xii.

122. G. A. Wanchope, *The Writers of South Carolina* (Columbia, S.C., 1910), 7–84 and passim.

123. U.S. Supreme Court, *Rep. on Wheaton v. Peters* (New York, 1834); R. R. Bowker, *Copyright, Its History and Its Law* (Boston, 1912), 35–36; Francis Lieber, *On*

International Copyright (New York, 1840); P. H. Nicklin, *Remarks on Literary Property* (Philadelphia, 1838).

124. M. A. DeW. Howe, *Life and Letters of George Bancroft* (New York, 1908), I, chap. xx and passim; II, chaps. vi-vii.

125. George Ticknor, *Life of William Hickling Prescott* (Boston, 1864), chap. vii and passim.

126. T. W. Higginson, *Cheerful Yesterdays* (Boston,, 1901), 167-95.

127. Lindsay Swift, *Brook Farm* (New York, 1900).

128. J. D. Wade, *Augustus Baldwin Longstreet* (New York, 1924), chaps. v-xii.

129. Laura E. Richards and Maud H. Elliott, *Julia Ward Howe, 1819-1910* (Boston, 1915), I, chaps. iv-vi; S. G. Howe, *Letters and Journals* (Laura E. Richards, ed., Boston, 1906-9), I, 389-419; II, 96-166, 237-72.

130. O. B. Frothingham, *Gerrit Smith* (New York, 1879), 137-44; Lewis Tappan, *The Life of Arthur Tappan* (New York, 1870), chaps. ix-x, xii, xv-xvi.

131. Francis Tiffany, *Life of Dorothea Lynde Dix* (Boston, 1890), chaps. viii-xv.

132. H. E. Barnes, *The Repression of Crime* (New York, 1926), 203-5.

133. O. F. Lewis, *Development of American Prisons and Prison Customs, 1776-1845* (New York, 1922), chap. xxv; Gustave de Beaumont and Alexis de Tocqueville, *On the Penitentiary System in the United States* (Francis Lieber, tr., Philadelphia, 1833); Dorothea L. Dix, *Remarks on Prisons and Prison Discipline in the United States* (Philadelphia, 1845); F. C. Gray, *Prison Discipline in America* (Boston, 1847); G. W. Smith, *Defence of the System of Solitary Confinement* (Philadelphia, 1833).

134. The following account of the temperance movement is based largely upon J. A. Krout, *Origins of Prohibition* (New York, 1925), 119-86, 208-52; but see also H. W. Blair, *The Temperance Movement* (Boston, 1888), chaps. xx-xxiv, and John Marsh, *Temperance Recollections* (New York, 1866), chap. ii.

135. *Journal of the American Temperance Union, Tenth Rep.* (Boston, March, 1837), 39.

136. Neal Dow, *Reminiscences* (Portland, Me., 1898), chaps. vi, viii-xi, xiv-xvii; Krout, *Origins of Prohibition,* chap. xi; Gallus Thomann, *Liquor Laws of the United States* (New York, 1885), chaps. viii-ix.

137. F. P. Robinson, *Reform Movements of the Thirties and Forties* (unpublished thesis, Univ. of Wis., 1925).

138. Nevins, *American Social History,* 58-60.

139. A. W. Calhoun, *A Social History of the American Family* (Cleveland, 1917-19), II, chaps. iv-v; M. J. McIntosh, *Women in America* (New York, 1850).

140. Sarah M. Grimké, *Letters on the Equality of the Sexes* (Boston,, 1838); Anna D. Hallowell, *Life and Letters of James and Lucretia Mott* (Boston,, 1884), chaps. vi-xiii; Elizabeth C. Stanton, Susan B. Anthony, and Matilda J. Gage, eds., *History of Woman Suffrage* (New York, 1881-1922), I, chaps. iv, v-vii, and passim; Theodore Stanton and Harriet S. Blatch, *Elizabeth Cady Stanton* (New York, 1922), I, 125-50.

141. Augusta G. Violette, *Economic Feminism in American Literature Prior to 1848* (Univ. of Maine, *Studies,* ser. 2, XXVII, no. 2), chaps. v-ix.

142. A. M. Schlesinger, *New Viewpoints in American History* (New York, 1922), 137-40.

143. Edith Abbott, *Women in Industry* (New York, 1919), 158-66, 192, 248-53.

144. This account is based very largely on Mary R. Beard, *A Short History of the American Labor Movement* (New York, 1920), chaps. iv-vii; J. R. Commons et al., *History of Labour in the United States* (New York, 1918), I, pts. iii-iv; Selig Perlman, *History of Trade Unionism in the United States* (New York, 1922), 18-39.

145. F. J. Garrison and W. P. Garrison, *William Lloyd Garrison, 1805-1879: The Story of His Life Told by His Children* (New York, 1885-89), I, chaps. vii-xii; II, chaps. i, iii-v; III, chaps. ii, ix.

146. W. H. Siebert, *The Underground Railroad* (New York, 1898), chaps. iv–viii, x–xi; B. T. Washington, *Frederick Douglass* (E. P. Oberholtzer, ed., *American Crisis Biographies,* Philadelphia, 1906), chaps. iii–viii.
147. Carlos Martyn, *Wendell Phillips: the Agitator* (Carlos Martyn, ed., *American Reformers,* New York, 1890), I, chap. v; II, chaps. i, vi–viii, x, xiv; Wendell Phillips, *Speeches, Lectures and Letters* (Boston, 1891), 1–39.
148. Emil Olbrich, *The Development of Sentiment on Negro Suffrage to 1860* (Univ. of Wis., *Bull.,* no. 477), chaps. ii–iv; C. G. Woodson, *The Education of the Negro Prior to 1861* (New York, 1915), 162–228, 232–95; D. R. Fox, "The Negro Vote in New York," *Pol. Sci. Quar.,* XXXII, 252–75.
149. A. C. Cole, *The Whig Party in the South* (Washington, 1913), chaps. ii–v.
150. J. R. Lowell, *Writings* (Boston, 1848), VIII, 76; see also the *Anti-Slavery Papers* of James Russell Lowell (Boston, 1902).
151. C. H. Ambler, *Sectionalism in Virginia from 1776 to 1861* (Chicago, 1910), chap. ix; J. N. Norwood, *The Schism in the Methodist Episcopal Church, 1844* (Alfred Univ., *Studies,* I).
152. Between 1830 and 1850 the population of the Atlantic seaboard increased from 8,633,632 to 12,729,859; that of the Mississippi Valley and Gulf from 4,232,388 to 10,344,746. The trans-Missouri region to the Rocky Mountains remained Indian country. *Compendium, . . . Seventh Census,* 41.
153. A graphic history of the improvements in transportation is given in J. L. Ringwalt, *Development of the Transportation System in the United States* (Philadelphia, 1888), 73–91, 103–106, 115–19.
154. In 1850 there were in the entire country 38,183 churches with property valued at $87,983,028. *Compendium, . . . Seventh Census,* 133.
155. Ibid., 153.
156. The annual circulation of newspapers alone increased from an average, in 1828, of about six to the individual to about twenty-two to the individual in 1850. Ibid., 158.
157. Ibid., 184.
158. Gustavus Myers, *History of the Great American Fortunes* (Chicago, 1910), esp. II, passim.
159. In 1850 about one half of the national area was organized into states. Of the state area, a total of 851,508 square miles was slaveholding, and 612,597 free soil with slavery forbidden or in course of extinction.
160. The mileage of railroads in use increased from 32 in 1830 to 9,021 in 1850. U. S. Bureau of Census, *Statistical Abstract* (Washington, 1921), 376.
161. A. H. Clark, *The Clipper Ship Era* (New York, 1911), chaps. iv, ix.
162. J. B. McMaster, *A History of the People of the United States* (New York, 1884–1927), VIII, 106–20; Otis Clapp, "The Post-Office as It Has Been, Is, and Should Be; as a Means of Modern Civilization," *Hunt's Merchants' Mag.,* XXXV (1856), 680–97.
163. See, for example, Minnigerode, *Fabulous Forties,* chap. ix; Eliza Ripley, *Social Life in Old New Orleans* (New York, 1912), chap. viii; and any of the women's fashion magazines during these years.
164. W. L. Marvin, *The American Merchant Marine* New York, 1902), chap. xii.

BOOK VII The Irrepressible Conflict, 1850–65

1. *Agriculture of the United States in 1860 (U. S. Eighth Census),* 247.
2. Hairston, who personally owned nearly 2,000 blacks, had control of 1,000 more slaves, the property of his mother-in-law. The annual increase of 100 a year made it necessary to purchase a large plantation annually on which to settle them. His wealth was estimated at from $3 to $5 million. He resided in a beautiful mansion

on a magnificent estate. He had a brother in Henry County, Virginia, who owned 700 blacks, and two brothers in Mississippi who owned, respectively, 1,000 and 600 slaves. Another brother in Henry County who had distributed most of his property among his children still owned 150. *Richmond Whig,* cited in *Belleville (Ill.), Advocate,* June 21, 1854. See also William Chambers, *American Slavery and Colour* (London, 1857), 194-95.

3. Goulden is not even mentioned in the works of Ulrich B. Phillips, a native of Georgia and a writer on black slavery.

4. D. R. Hundley, *Social Relations in Our Southern States* (New York, 1860), 95.

5. *Savannah Republican,* June 27, July 10, 1851.

6. In 1859 a skilled mechanic of Columbia, South Carolina, was tarred and feathered and expelled from the community because he had made the remark that slaves should be confined to work on plantations. *N.Y. Tribune,* January 2, 1860.

7. W. K. Boyd, "North Carolina on the Eve of Secession," Am. Hist. Assoc., *Ann. Rep. for 1910,* 174-75; Julia A. Flisch, "Common People of the Old South," Am. Hist. Assoc., *Ann. Rep. for 1908,* I, 140-41.

8. J. S. C. Abbott, *South and North* (New York, 1860), 146-47. See also F. L. Olmsted, *The Cotton Kingdom* (New York, 1862), II, 44; C. G. Parsons, *Inside View of Slavery* (Cleveland, 1855), 113-14.

9. F. L. Olmsted, *A Journey in the Back Country* (New York, 1863), 395, also 259.

10. H. R. Helper, *The Impending Crisis of the South* (New York, 1857), 43-44. James D. B. De Bow replied in a pamphlet entitled *The Interest in Slavery of the Southern Non-Slaveholder* (New Orleans, 1860).

11. P. H. Buck, "The Poor White in the Ante-bellum South," *Am. Hist. Rev.,* XXXI, 41-55.

12. John Cummings, ed., *Negro Population in the United States, 1790-1915* (Washington, 1918), 55.

13. Commissioner of Patents, *Report for 1860,* 226; D. R. Goodloe, cited in C. D. Wright, *The Industrial Evolution of the United States* (Meadville, Pa., 1895), 151. See also D. R. Goodloe, "Resources and Industrial Condition of the South," Comnr. of Agr., *Rep. for 1865,* 119. Of course, part of the profits of Southern agriculture under slave labor was to be found in the normal slave increase by birth; it was nothing for the number on a plantation to double in less than a dozen years. U. B. Phillips. *Plantation and Frontier* (J. R. Commons, ed., *Documentary History of American Industrial Society,* Cleveland, 1910-11, I-II), I, 179.

14. [Catherine C. Hopley], *Life in the South* (London, 1863), II, 46, 47; Olmsted, *Cotton Kingdom,* II, 350ff. See also *De Bow's Rev.,* VIII (1850), 22-23, 182-85. 294-96; U. B. Phillips, *American Negro Slavery* (New York, 1918), 488, 510; H. M. Henry, *Police Control of the Slave in South Carolina* (Emory, Va., 1914).

15. See the case of Harriet Hall, *Richmond Enquirer,* February 3, cited in *N.Y. Herald,* February 5, 1859.

16. F. L. Olmsted, *Journey in the Seaboard Slave States* (New York, 1859), 125.

17. C. G. Woodson, *The Education of the Negro prior to 1861* (New York, 1915), 236-37.

18. The Placide's Varieties Theatre reserved its third tier of boxes for blacks. *New Orleans Commercial Bulletin,* January 1, 1851. See also Olmsted, *Journey in the Seaboard Slave States,* 14, and Dicey, *Six Months in the Federal States,* II, 114.

19. Phillips, *American Negro Slavery,* 434.

20. *Belleville Advocate,* January 3, 1868. See also Mitchell, *Ten Years Residence in the United States,* 235, and J. A. C. Chandler et al., *The South in the Building of the Nation* (Richmond, 1909-10), X, 180.

21. C. O. Wilson, "Negroes Who Owned Slaves," *Pop. Sci. Mo.,* LXXXI (1912), 492-93. See also Mitchell, *Ten Years Residence in the United States,* 160.

22. *National Intelligencer* (Washington), November 1, 1859, January 7, 27, March 13, 18, 27, August 25, September 1, 4, October 31, November 9, December 14, 1860.

See also [Hopley], *Life in the South,* I, 156, and Thomas Ellison, *Slavery and Secession in America* (London, 1861), 42, 26.

23. *Baltimore Sun,* January 7, 1860; Richardson, *Beyond the Mississippi,* 217.

24. *National Intelligencer,* January 27, 1860; *N.Y. Times,* January 21, 1860. See also J. B. McMaster, *History of the People of the United States* (New York, 1883–1913), VIII, 430.

25. Anon., "A Fresh Catalogue of Southern Outrages upon Northern Citizens," Am. Anti-Slavery Soc., *Publs.,* n. s., no. 14 (1860). See also *Savannah Republican,* April 19, 1859; *National Intelligencer,* September 8, 1860; *Mobile Advertiser,* December 23, 1859.

26. *Southern Intelligencer,* cited in *De Bow's Rev.,* XXVI (1859), 236.

27. See anon., "Common Schools and Universities," *De Bow's Rev.,* XVIII (1855), 545–55; Olmsted, *Journey in the Back Country,* 25; Chandler, *South in the Building of the Nation,* X, 227–28, and passim.

28. T. D. Ozanne, *The South as It Is* (London, 1863), 193–215; J. W. Du Bose, *The Life and Times of William Lowndes Yancey* (Birmingham, 1892), 318; *N.Y. Tribune,* February 10, 1860; *Baltimore Sun,* February 15, 1860.

29. *National Intelligencer,* March 3, 1857; *Belleville Advocate,* March 4, 1857.

30. *Washington Republic,* September 25, 1851.

31. "Southern Convention at Savannah," *De Bow's Rev.,* XXII (1857), 100; *Belleville Advocate,* May 20, 1857; *Hunt's Merchants' Mag.,* XXXIV (1856), 392. The great improvement in Northern school textbooks is noted in *Harper's Wkly.,* VI, 692 (November 1, 1862).

32. Ozanne, *The South as It Is,* 214–15.

33. See *De Bow's Rev.,* XXIII (1857), 102.

34. See this volume, Book VI, 517.

35. "The Education, Labor, and Wealth of the South," *De Bow's Rev.,* XXVII (1859), 278. The article continued: "Some parishes will not receive any of it. Tensas, for instance, which is taxed $16,000 for the support of public schools, has 'not a single public school,' says the Report, 'in it, yet nearly every planter has a school in his own house.' "

36. *Richmond Examiner,* cited in *Belleville Advocate,* November 6, 1857.

37. J. H. Van Evrie, *Negroes and Negro "Slavery"* (New York, 1861).

38. Jennette R. Tandy, "Pro-Slavery Propaganda in American Fiction of the Fifties," *South Atlantic Quar.,* XXI (1922), 41–50, 170–78.

39. Published in New York in 1859.

40. George Fitzhugh, *Cannibals All!* (Richmond, 1857), 368. See also his *Sociology for the South* (Richmond, 1854), and A. C. Cole, *Lincoln's "House Divided" Speech* (Chicago, 1923).

41. *Belleville Advocate,* March 15, 1854.

42. Thornton Stringfellow's *Scriptural and Statistical Views in Defense of Slavery* reached its fourth edition in 1856; in the same year Howell Cobb issued his *Scriptural Examination of the Institution of Slavery,* and other less notable exponents, like the Reverend N. L. Rice, the Reverend W. S. Brown, and Davis Ewart, made their contributions.

43. B. M. Palmer, *The South: Her Peril and Her Duty* (New Orleans, 1860). See also W. C. Johnston, *Life and Letters of Benjamin Morgan Palmer* (Richmond, 1906).

44. W. G. Brownlow and Abram Pryne, *Ought American Slavery to Be Perpetuated* (Philadelphia, 1858).

45. Robert Toombs, "Slavery: Its Constitutional Status, and Its Influence on Society and the Colored Race," *De Bow's Rev.,* XX (1856), 602; U. B. Phillips, *The Life of Robert Toombs* (New York, 1913), 164.

46. It became noticeable, however, that through trains carried back to the East a heavy passenger traffic, only exceeded by the flood tide of colonists that moved in the opposite direction. *Cleveland Herald,* cited in *Baltimore Sun,* April 25, 1860.

47. See F. L. Paxson, *History of the American Frontier, 1763-1893* (Boston, 1924), 424-25; W. W. Folwell, *A History of Minnesota* (St. Paul, 1921-31), II, chap. i; G. B. Merrick, *Old Times on the Upper Mississippi* (Cleveland, 1909), 162ff.

48. J. C. Malin, *Indian Poicy and Westward Expansion* (Univ. of Kansas, *Bull.*, XXII, no. 17), 91-94; Stephen Bonsal, *Edward Fitzgerald Beale, a Pioneer in the Path of Empire, 1822-1903* (New York, 1912).

49. On the Kansas-Nebraska act, see F. H. Hodder, "The Genesis of the Kansas-Nebraska Act," Wis. Hist. Soc., *Proceeds.*, LX, 69-86, and same author, "The Railroad Background of the Kansas-Nebraska Act," *Miss. Valley Hist. Rev.*, XXII, 3-22. Cf. P. O. Ray, *The Repeal of the Missouri Compromise* (Cleveland, 1909).

50. See speech of Bernhart Henn, Iowa member of Congress, in *Congressional Globe*, 33 Cong., 1 sess., app., 888.

51. *National Intelligencer* (Washington), March 21, 23, 31, 1861. See also W. E. Miller, *The Peopling of Kansas* (Columbus, 1906).

52. Eli Thayer, *A History of the Kansas Crusade* (New York, 1889), 18, 23-25, 58-59; E. E. Hale, *Kansas and Nebraska* (Boston, 1854), 222; S. A. Johnson, "The Genesis of the New England Emigrant Aid Company," *New England Quar.*, III, 95-122.

53. For activities in Washington, see testimony of Daniel Mace, 34 Cong., 1 sess., *House Rep.*, II, 829.

54. W. L. Fleming, "The Buford Expedition to Kansas," *Am. Hist. Rev.*, VI, 38-48.

55. *N.Y. Tribune*, April 4, 1856.

56. J. C. Malin, "Colonel Harvey and His Forty Thieves," *Miss. Valley Hist. Rev.*, XIX, 57-76.

57. Erastus Beadle, *To Nebraska in '57* (New York, 1923).

58. Richardson, *Beyond the Mississippi*, 564.

59. M. K. Armstrong, *History and Resources of Dakota, Montana, and Idaho* (Yankton, S.D., 1866), 34-35.

60. H. V. Huntley, *California: Its Gold and Its Inhabitants* (London, 1856); Ernest Seyd, *California and Its Resources* (London, 1858); L. B. Patterson, *Twelve Years in the Mines of California* (Cambridge, Mass., 1862).

61. F. B. Goddard, *Where to Emigrate, and Why* (Philadelphia, 1869), 40; R. G. Cleland and Osgood Hardy, *March of Industry* (J. R. McCarthy, ed., *California;* Los Angeles, 1929), 40, 42ff.

62. *N.Y. Herald*, Jan. 31, 1854.

63. Samuel Bowles, *Across the Continent* (Springfield, Mass., 1865), iv. See also same vol., chaps. xxvi, xxviii, and Richardson, *Beyond the Mississippi*, chaps. xxvi-xxvii.

64. W. L. Hill, cited in Goddard, *Where to Emigrate, and Why*, 67.

65. George Thomas, *The Development of Institutions under Irrigation* (L. H. Bailey, ed., *The Rural Science Series;* New York, 1920), chaps. ii-iv; L. E. Young, *The Founding of Utah* (New York, 1923).

66. M. R. Werner, *Brigham Young* (New York, 1925), chaps. vi-xii.

67. Bowles, *Across the Continent*, 103. See also B. G. Ferris, *Utah and the Mormons* (New York, 1854); Jules Remy, *Journey to Great Salt Lake City with Sketches of the History, Religion and Customs of the Mormons* (London, 1861); R. F. Burton, *The City of the Saints, and across the Rocky Mountains to California* (New York, 1862).

68. William Gilpin, *The Central Gold Region* (Philadelphia, 1860); H. H. Bancroft, *History of Nevada, Colorado, and Wyoming* (same author, *Works,* San Francisco, 1883-90, XXV), v-viiff.

69. Bancroft, *History of Nevada, Colorado, and Wyoming*, 363-420.

70. S. L. Clemens (Mark Twain, pseud.), *Roughing It* (Hartford, 1872).

71. See this volume, Book I, 29.

72. See poem in *Boston Post*, clipped in *Belleville (Ill.) Advocate*, April 25, 1850. He was, of course, doubtless unwittingly, misquoting Bishop Berkeley's poem of a century earlier.

73. Douai, *Land und Leute,* 245, 247.

74. Auguste Laugel, *The United States during the War* (New York, 1866), 177. See also A. C. Cole, *The Era of the Civil War* (C. W. Alvord, ed., *The Centennial History of Illinois,* Springfield, 1918-20, III), 14.

75. *Cincinnati Daily Enquirer,* January 8, 1861.

76. J. R. Commons, ed., *A Documentary History of American Industrial Society* (Cleveland, 1909-11), VIII, 151ff.; S. P. Orth, *The Armies of Labor* (Allen Johnson, ed., *The Chronicles of America Series,* New Haven, 1918-21, XL), 53-54.

77. *Statistical View of the United States (U. S. Seventh Census,* 1850), 164; *Hunt's Merchants' Mag.,* XXVI (1852), 120-21; Mass. Bureau of Statistics of Labor, *Annual Report for 1872,* 522.

78. J. R. Commons et al., *History of Labour in the United States* (New York, 1918), I, 607-10.

79. *N.Y. Tribune,* February 28, March 7, 8, 1860; *Baltimore Sun,* February 21, 29, March 1, 19, 1860; Mass. Bur. of Labor Stat., *Ann. Rep. for 1880,* 16-19.

80. McMaster, *A History of the People of the United States,* VIII, 287-88.

81. Ibid., VIII, 297-302; Orth, *Armies of Labor,* 61-62.

82. *N.Y. Herald,* March 7, 1853, April 5, 9, May 2, 1858; *Cleveland Leader,* August 17, 1860; Charles Mackay, *Life and Liberty in America,* (New York, 1859), I, 35-36; Mitchell, *Ten Years Residence in the United States,* 143-44.

83. Mackay, *Life and Liberty in America,* I, 164; Theodor Griesinger, *Lebende Bilder aus Amerika* (Stuttgart, 1858), 225-29; *Atlantische Studien,* I (1853), 161-69, 220-45; Russell, *My Diary,* 252; Trollope, *North America,* 447; Woods, *The Prince of Wales in the United States,* 364. See also Herbert Asbury, *The Gangs of New York* (New York, 1928), and C. L. Bran, *The Dangerous Classes of New York and Twenty Years among Them* (New York, 1872).

84. Mitchell, *Ten Years Residence in the United States,* 165-67; L. F. Schmeckebier, *History of the Know Nothing Party in Maryland* (Johns Hopkins Univ., *Studies,* XVII, nos. 4-5), 43-44.

85. Dicey, *Six Months in the Federal States,* I, 17; Griesinger, *Lebende Bilder,* 73-80, 148-56, 322-28. See also W. W. Sanger, *History of Prostitution* (New York, 1858).

86. McMaster, *History of the People of the United States,* VIII, 69-70.

87. Russell, *My Diary,* 244; James Stirling, *Letters from the Slave States* (London, 1857), 142, 165. See also Murray, *Letters from the United States,* II, 152-53, and Douai, *Land und Leute,* 68-69.

88. Carl Sandburg, *Abraham Lincoln: The Prairie Years* (New York, 1926), II, 116.

89. Robert Everest, *Journal through the United States and Part of Canada* (London, 1855), 150; W. E. Baxter, *America and the Americans* (London, 1855), 118-21.

90. J. B. Gough, *Autobiography and Personal Recollections* (Springfield, 1870), 261, 514.

91. William H. Russell to J. C. B. Davis, June 22, 1861, *Historical Outlook,* XVI (1925), 253.

92. *North State Whig,* December 11, 1850, February 12, 1851.

93. Ernest Gordon, *The Maine Law* (New York, 1919); J. A. Krout, *The Origins of Prohibition* (New York, 1925), 283-95.

94. McMaster, *History of the People of the United States,* VIII, 127-32.

95. Griesinger, *Lebende Bilder,* 86.

96. *N.Y. Herald,* February 5, 1858; *National Intelligencer* (Washington), February 8, March 26, 1858. See also later cases, *N.Y. Herald,* January 1, 1859; *N.Y. Tribune,* June 2, 1860.

97. "Summer Fashions," *Harper's Mo.,* III (1851), 288.

98. Elizabeth C. Stanton, *Elizabeth Cady Stanton as Revealed in Her Letters, Diary and Reminiscences* (Theodore Stanton and Harriot S. Blatch, eds., New York, 1922), II, 27-31.

99. *Ohio Statesman* (Columbus), July 2, 1851.

100. Ibid., July 5, 1851.

101. A. C. Cole, "Illinois Women of the Middle Period," Ill. State Hist. Soc., *Trans. for 1920*, 91.

102. In 1858 there was a sudden revival of the bloomer which was advocated as a costume in keeping with physiological laws that would aid the wearer "in attaining that position side by side with man, . . . his co-worker in life and its duties, . . . and give a more correct idea of the natural proportions of the human form." *Aurora (Ill.) Beacon*, April 8, 1858. At the third annual convention of the National Dress Reform Association at Cortlandville, New York, in July, 150 women delegates appeared in various types of bloomer costume. *Harper's Wkly.*, II, 470 (July 24, 1858).

103. No critics accomplished the results of Addison of the *Spectator* when he belabored the hoops of Queen Anne's day. See *Ohio State Journal* (Columbus), May 2, 1856.

104. Mackay, *Life and Liberty in America*, I, 21. See also Beste, *The Wabash*, II, 214–15; Dicey, *Six Months in the Federal States*, I, 305; Trollope, *North America*, 191–93; Russell, *My Diary*, 12; [Bishop], *Englishwoman in America*, 341, 361; Elizabeth McClellan, *Historic Dress in America, 1800–1870* (Philadelphia, 1910), 253.

105. *N.Y. World*, October 2, 1863.

106. *Vanity Fair*, III, 126 (March 16, 1861). See reproduction in Sandburg, *Abraham Lincoln*, II, 421, and W. E. Barton, *The Life of Abraham Lincoln* (Indianapolis, 1925), I, 515–17.

107. *N.Y. Herald*, April 14, 1858.

108. *Dollar Newspaper* (Philadelphia), May 25, 1859; *Toledo Blade*, April 10, 1860.

109. A. W. Calhoun, *A Social History of the American Family* (Cleveland, 1917–19), II, 67.

110. *Presbyterian Mag.*, cited in Calhoun, *Social History of the American Family*, II, 69; *Baltimore Sun*, January 4, 1858.

111. Walt Whitman, *I Sit and Look Out* (Emory Holloway and Vernolian Schwarz, eds., New York, 1932), 115. See also Griesinger, *Lebende Bilder*, 265–66, which cites specific contraceptives and abortive medicines; G. W. Sala, *My Diary in America in the Midst of War* (London, 1865), II, 161; *Round Table*, I, 178, 242 (March 5, April 2, 1864).

112. See this volume, Book VIII, p. 721.

113. Richardson, *Beyond the Mississippi*, 147–48; *Baltimore Sun*, January 28, 1860.

114. Stanton, *Elizabeth Cady Stanton*, II, 49.

115. Alice Stone Blackwell, *Lucy Stone* (Boston, 1930), chap. xi.

116. Calhoun, *Social History of the American Family*, II, 73, 83, 89.

117. J. M. Taylor, *Before Vassar Opened* (Boston, 1914).

118. Caroline H. Dall, *The College, the Market, and the Court* (Boston, 1867), 381.

119. Annie N. Meyer, ed., *Woman's Work in America* (New York, 1891), chaps. ii–iv.

120. T. W. Higginson, *Atlantic Essays* (Boston, 1871), 96.

121. Sallie Holley, *A Life for Liberty* (J. W. Chadwick, ed., New York, 1864), 120.

122. See constitution in its *Second Annual Report* (1854), 3–4.

123. Anon., "Progress of Womanhood," *Harper's Mo.*, XVI (1858), 492–94; H. T. Tuckerman, *America and Her Commentators* (New York, 1864), 333, citing Philip Schaff, *Sketch of the Political, Social and Religious Character of the United States of America* (New York, 1855).

124. J. T. Morse, Jr., *Life and Letters of Oliver Wendell Holmes* (Boston, 1897), I, 186.

125. Dall, *College, Market, and Court*, 185n. See also articles by F. C. Waite in *New England Journ. of Medicine*, CCV (1931), 1053–55, 1195–98.

126. *N.Y. Herald*, February 12, 1858.

127. *N.Y. Herald*, April 4, 1858. See also anon., "Woman and the 'Woman's Movement,'" *Putnam's Mo.*, I (1853), 279–88.

128. *Alabama Journal* (Montgomery), January 2, 16, 1851.

129. Whitman, *I Sit and Look Out,* 46.

130. Cole, *Era of the Civil War,* 4.

131. *N.Y. Tribune,* April 25, 27, 28, 1860. Cf. issue of January 9, 1860.

132. E. D. Fite, *Social and Industrial Conditions in the North during the Civil War* (New York, 1910), 217.

133. *Chicago Weekly Democrat,* June 4, 1859.

134. *N.Y. Herald,* June 7, 1858. See also issues of March 30, 1853, May 28, 31, 1858, and April 3, 1861.

135. C. E. Norton, "Dwellings and Schools for the Poor," *N. Am. Rev.,* LXXIV (1852), 469.

136. Andrew D. White, *Autobiography* (New York, 1905), I, 107-10; J. C. Dalton, "Disease in Cities," *N. Am. Rev.,* CVI (1868), 355-62; Council of Hygiene and Public Health of the Citizens' Association of New York, *Report upon the Sanitary Condition of the City* (New York, 1865); *Am. Medical Times,* IV (1862), 98-99; *Hunt's Merchants' Mag.,* XLVIII (1863), 120-24; Mitchell, *Ten Years Residence in the United States,* 146, 150.

137. W. T. Howard, *Public Health and Administration and the Natural History of Disease in Baltimore, 1797-1920* (Washington, 1924), 65, 70, 507; D. F. Wilcox, *Great Cities in America* (R. T. Ely, ed., *The Citizen's Library of Economics, Politics, and Sociology;* New York, 1910), 6, 25, 222.

138. H. W. Bellows, "Cities and Parks, with Special Reference to the New York Central Park," *Atlantic Mo.,* VII (1861), 416.

139. *N.Y. Tribune,* July 1, 1861.

140. H. P. Batcheler, *Jonathan at Home* (London, 1864), 223.

141. *N.Y. Tribune* and *N.Y. Herald,* August 1-November 15, 1855. See also R. C. Holcomb, *A Century with Norfolk Naval Hospital, 1830-1930* (Portsmouth, Va., 1930), 251-73, and W. S. Forest, *The Great Pestilence in Virginia* (New York, 1856).

142. See contemporary newspapers. See also Cole, *Era of the Civil War,* 216-17; Emmeline S. Wortley, *Travels in the United States, etc., during 1849 and 1850* (New York, 1855), 42, 111; Edmund Patten, *A Glimpse at the United States* (London, 1853), 97, 98; Dalton, "Disease in Cities," 352, 358.

143. See this volume, Book VIII, p. 721.

144. Griesinger, *Lebende Bilder,* 41; Kohl, *Travels,* I, 36-37.

145. Oliver Wendell Holmes, *Medical Essays, 1842-1882* (Boston, 1893), 203; *Ohio State Journal* (Columbus), June 7, 1860; review in *Am. Journ. of the Medical Sciences,* XL (1860), 462-74.

146. T. W. Higginson, *Letters and Journals* (Mary T. Thacher, ed., Boston, 1921), 37, 38, 56. See also J. T. Trowbridge, *My Own Story with Recollections of Noted Persons* (Boston, 1903), 181, 197, 199, and *Ohio State Journal,* September 23, 30, 1851, October 1, 6, 1856, June 21, 1860.

147. Nichols, *Forty Years of American Life,* II, 363. See also J. G. Jones and William Sherwood, *American Eclectic Practice of Medicine* (Cincinnati, 1857), and Griesinger, *Lebende Bilder,* 41-49.

148. N. S. Davis, *History of the American Medical Association* (Philadelphia, 1855).

149. Released from its connection with the university in 1863, this medical faculty continued for six years as an independent institution under the name of the Chicago Medical College and then became the medical department of Northwestern University. N. S. Davis, "The Earlier History of the Medical School," A. H. Wilde, ed., *Northwestern University: A History, 1855-1905* (New York, 1905), III, 291-312; W. H. Welch, *Papers and Addresses* (Baltimore, 1920), III, 121.

150. Charles Warren, "Medical Education in the United States," U. S. Comnr. of Educ., *Rep. for 1870,* 384-96; Abraham Flexner, *Medical Education in the United States* (New York, 1910), 8-10.

151. M. M. Davis, *Clinics, Hospitals, and Health Centres* (New York, 1927), 4-5; W. G. Wylie, *Hospitals: Their History, Organization, and Construction* (New York, 1877).

152. Anon., "Why We Get Sick," *Harper's Mo.*, XIII (1856), 642, 646. See also anon., "Our Sons," same mag., XVII (1858), 58; Harriet B. Stowe, "Sermon on Your Health," *Atlantic Mo.*, XVIII (1865), 85; Elizabeth Blackwell, *The Laws of Life, with Special Reference to the Physical Education of Girls* (New York, 1852), 29.

153. Baxter, *America and the Americans*, 99; Murray, *Letters from the United States*, II, 250; Grattan, *Civilized America*, II, 313-314.

154. T. W. Higginson, *Old Cambridge* (G. E. Woodberry, ed., *National Studies in American Letters;* New York, 1899), 92-93; O. W. Holmes, *The Autocrat of the Breakfast Table* (same author, *Writings*, Boston, 1893-95, I), 170-73. See also this volume, Book VIII, p. 721.

155. Edward Everett, *Orations and Speeches on Various Occasions* (Boston, 1865-72), III, 407.

156. T. W. Higginson, "Saints and Their Bodies," *Atlantic Mo.*, I (1857-58), 582-95; same author, "Physical Courage," same mag., II (1858), 728-37; Holley, *A Life for Liberty*, 166-67. See also A. C. Cole, "Our Sporting Grandfathers, the Cult of Athletics at Its Source," *Atlantic Mo.*, CL (1932), 88-96.

157. *N.Y. Herald*, July 12, 1858. Cf., however, anon., "How to Keep Well," *Harper's Mo.*, XIV (1856), 59-60.

158. J. D. J. Kelley, *American Yachts: Their Clubs and Races* (New York, 1884), 9.

159. William Elliott, *Carolina Sports by Land and Water* (New York, 1859); Captain Flack, *A Hunter's Experiences in the Southern States of America* (London, 1866).

160. Woods, *The Prince of Wales in the United States*, 305-306. See also G. F. Berkeley, *The English Sportsman in the Western Prairies* (London, 1861); Parker Gillmore (Ubique, pseud.), *Accessible Field Sports* (London, 1869); B. H. Revoil, *Shooting and Fishing in the Rivers, Prairies and Backwoods of North America* (London, 1865).

161. *Cleveland Leader*, August 18, 1860.

162. Edit., *Harper's Mo.*, XVIII (1858), 127-28.

163. Bohun Lynch, *Knuckles and Gloves* (New York, 1923), chap. xx.

164. E. P. Weston, *"The Pedestrian"* (New York, 1862).

165. *Boston Eve. Transcript*, May 31, 1855; A. G. Spalding, *America's National Game* (New York, 1911), 57ff.

166. *N.Y. Tribune*, July 25, 1862.

167. *N.Y. Herald*, September 17, 1855; Mitchell, *Ten Years Residence in the United States*, 329. See also Francis Brinley, *Life of William T. Porter* (New York, 1860); Nichols, *Forty Years of American Life*, II, 393; Hiram Woodruff, *The Trotting Horse of America* (C. J. Foster, ed., Philadelphia, 1868).

168. F. E. Leonard, *A Guide to the History of Physical Education* (R. T. McKenzie, ed., *Physical Education Series;* Philadelphia, 1927), 259.

169. Frances E. Willard, *Glimpses of Fifty Years* (Chicago, 1889), 105.

170. *Baltimore Sun*, April 4, 1860.

171. See this volume, Book X, p. 873.

172. *Western Citizen* (Chicago), October 1, 1850.

173. Trollope, *North America*, 98. See also Russell, *My Diary*, 365; Pisani, *Lettres sur les États-Unis d'Amérique*, 389-90; Auguste Laugel, *The United States during the War* (London, 1866), 133-37; [Bishop], *Englishwoman in America*, 222.

174. Whitman, *I Sit and Look Out*, 104. See also anon., "Are We a Polite People?," *Harper's Mo.*, XV (1857), 390, and edit., same mag., XVII (1858), 122.

175. *New Orleans Commercial Bulletin*, January 18, 1851.

176. *Cairo Democrat*, October 1, 1863.

177. Robert Everest, *Journey through the United States and Part of Canada* (London, 1855), 51.

178. Murray, *Letters from the United States,* I, 37.

179. "Domestic Intelligence," *Harper's Wkly.,* II, 470 (July 24, 1858).

180. J. R. Dix, *A Hand-Book of Newport, and Rhode-Island* (Newport, 1852), 72–75; Mackay, *Life and Liberty in America,* I, 103; Fuller, *Belle Brittan on a Tour,* 159.

181. *Richmond Whig,* July 23, cited in *N.Y. Herald,* July 28, 1858.

182. *N.Y. Herald,* August 20, 1855.

183. Ozanne, *The South as It Is,* 231–33.

184. B. A. Hinsdale, *Horace Mann and the Common School Revival in the United States* (N. M. Butler, ed., *The Great Educators,* New York, 1898), 247.

185. Cole, *Era of the Civil War,* 234–35; anon., "Board of National Popular Education," *Am. Journ. of Educ.,* XV (1865), 271–74; Mae E. Harveson, *Catherine Esther Beecher* (Philadelphia, 1932).

186. Anon., "American Normal Schools," *N.Y. Teacher,* n.s., II (1861), 337–44; R. G. Boone, *Education in the United States* (New York, 1889), 132–33; E. G. Dexter, *History of Education in the United States* (New York, 1904), 376; E. P. Cubberley, *Public Education in the United States* (Boston, 1919), 290–93.

187. Fite, *Social and Industrial Conditions,* 247n.

188. S. S. Randall, *History of the Common School System of the State of New York* (New York, 1871), 220–28, 312–13; Francis Adams, *The Free School System of the United States* (London, 1875), 47, 78; J. M. Wightman, comp., *Annals of the Boston Primary School Committee* (Boston, 1860); W. O. Bourne, *History of the Public School Society of the City of New York* (New York, 1870), 579–90; Boone, *Education in the United States,* 330; Hinsdale, *Horace Mann,* 296.

189. E. D. Grizzell, *Origin and Development of the High School in New England before 1865* (New York, 1923), esp. 272–79; John Swett, *American Public Schools, History and Pedagogics* (New York, 1900), 74–75; Baxter, *America and the Americans,* 162–63; Cubberley, *Public Education in United States,* 196–98; State Commissioner of Public Schools of Ohio, *Seventh Annual Report* (1860), 45–52; *Baltimore Sun,* February 15, 1858.

190. C. F. Thwing, *The American and the German University* (New York, 1928), 42–43.

191. Henry James, *Charles W. Eliot* (Boston, 1930), I, 72, 94; F. A. P. Barnard, "On Improvements Practicable in American Colleges," *Am. Journ. of Educ.,* I (1855), 174–85; J. D. Dana, "Science and Scientific Schools," same mag., II (1856), 350; C. A. Bristed, "Five Years in an English University," *N. Am. Rev.,* LXXV (1852), 79–80.

192. Elizabeth M. Farrand, *History of the University of Michigan* (Ann Arbor, 1885), 112–13.

193. Andrew D. White, *Autobiography* (New York, 1905), I, 42.

194. E. H. Hedge, "University Reform," *Atlantic Mo.,* XVIII (1866), 299. See also *Michigan Alumnus,* XXXIII (1926), 104. Of his own college Dr. Hedge remarked: "Harvard College is simply a more advanced school for boys, not differing essentially in principle and theory from the public schools in all our towns. In this, as in those, the principle is coercion. Hold your subject fast with one hand, and pour knowledge into him with the other. The professors are task-masters and police officers, the President is chief of the College police."

195. "Professor Agassiz on the Origin of Species," *Am. Journ. of Science and Arts,* XXX (1860), 154. See also Asa Gray's review in same mag., XXIX (1860), 153; B. J. Loewenberg, "The Reaction of American Scientists to Darwinism," *Am. Hist. Rev.,* XXXVIII, 687–701.

196. *N.Y. Herald,* January 12, 13, 1859; *Dollar Newspaper* (Philadelphia), April 20, 1859; H. H. Ballard, "History of the Agassiz Association," *Science,* IX, 93.

197. Laugel, *United States during the War,* 139.

198. Hinsdale, *Horace Mann,* 242–264; Mary Mann, *Life of Horace Mann* (Boston, 1865), 402ff.

199. Fite, *Social and Industrial Conditions,* 253 n.

200. F. W. Shearman, *The System of Instruction and Primary School Laws of Michigan* (Lansing, 1852), 420.

201. R. U. Johnson, *Remembered Yesterdays* (Boston, 1923), 26. Dr. Henry B. Blackwell, husband of Lucy Stone, in a single year established 1,500 "Farmers' Libraries," consisting largely of the publications of Augustus Moore, in the school districts of Illinois. Blackwell, *Lucy Stone,* 194, 196–97.

202. Laugel, *United States during the War,* 139, 161. See also *Boston Eve. Transcript,* October 6, 1860; U. S. Bureau of Education, *Public Libraries in the United States of America (Special Rep.,* Washington, 1876), 893.

203. Kohl, *Travels,* I, 4–6, 36; II, 196–201; Trollope, *North America,* 270, 271. Cf. Higginson, *Atlantic Essays,* 12–13.

204. Trollope, *North America,* 128, 144; Gasparin, *Uprising of a Great People,* 60–61; Baxter, *America and the Americans,* 84–85.

205. See also *Chicago Gem of the Prairie,* February 26, 1848; Dorothy A. Dondore, *The Prairie and the Making of Middle America* (Cedar Rapids, Iowa, 1926), 194–209, 239–87; W. T. Coggeshall, *Poets and Poetry of the West* (Columbus, 1860); H. E. Fleming, "The Literary Interests of Chicago," *Am. Journ. of Sociology,* XI, 377–408, 499–531, 784–816; XII, 68–118; W. H. Venable, *Beginnings of Literary Culture in the Ohio Valley* (Cincinnati, 1891); R. L. Rusk, *Literature of the Middle Western Frontier* (New York, 1925).

206. Coggeshall, *Poets and Poetry of the West,* cited in Venable, *Beginnings of Literary Culture,* 123.

207. B. P. Shillaber, *Knitting Work: Web of Many Textures by Ruth Partington* (Boston, 1859).

208. Edmund Pearson, *Queer Books* (New York, 1928), 166–81.

209. Venable, *Beginnings of Literary Culture,* 293–95. Judson had a notable Civil War career as chief of scouts; he later rambled through the West with Buffalo Bill and Wild Bill Hickok, whom he then introduced to a rapidly growing circle of admirers. Gilbert Patten, "Dime Novel Days," *Saturday Eve. Post,* CCIV, 33, 36 (March 7, 1931).

210. Review by William Everett in *N. Am. Rev.,* XCIX (1864), 303–309; Edmund Pearson, *Dime Novels* (Boston, 1929), 50–52; H. M. Robinson, "The Dime Novel," *Century,* CXVI (1928), 62–63. The 1859 song book was published by Irwin P. Beadle.

211. Baxter, *America and the Americans,* 85.

212. Horace Greeley, *Recollections of a Busy Life* (New York, 1868), 205–206.

213. *Atlantische Studien,* I (1853), 136; *N.Y. Herald,* March 2, 1853, July 8, 1858; edit., *Harper's Mo.,* XXVI (1863), 564. See also Reverend F. Wilson, *Popular Amusements, or How Far May a Christian Indulge in Popular Amusements* (Charleston, 1856), 30–38.

214. See comments in Douai, *Land und Leute,* 239; Griesinger, *Lebende Bilder,* 179–89; *Atlantische Studien,* I (1853), 106–109.

215. W. A. Weaver, *Lithographs of N. Currier and Currier & Ives* (New York, 1925–26); Russel Crouse, *Mr. Currier and Mr. Ives: A Note on Their Lives and Times* (New York, 1931).

216. Bishop Fraser, cited in Adams, *Free School System of the United States,* 238.

217. Carl Schurz, *Reminiscences* (New York, 1907-8), II, 79.

218. Cole, *Era of the Civil War,* 249; Peter Cartwright, *Autobiography* (W. P. Strickland, ed., New York, 1857), 470ff.

219. Robert Richardson, *Memoirs of Alexander J. Campbell* (Philadelphia, 1870), II, 601–602; W. W. Jennings, *Origin and Early History of the Disciples of Christ* (Cincinnati, 1919), 325.

220. J. L. Neve, *A Brief History of the Lutheran Church in America* (Burlington, Iowa, 1916), 388–91, 437–38; J. M. Rohne, *Norwegian American Lutheranism up to*

1872 (New York, 1926), 136–79; G. M. Stephenson, *The Religious Aspects of Swedish Immigration* (Minneapolis, 1932), chap. xiii.

221. Williston Walker, *A History of the Congregational Churches in the United States* (Philip Schaff et al., eds., *The American Church History Series,* New York, 1893–97, III), 382–83; A. E. Dunning, *Congregationalists in America* (New York, 1894), 337.

222. Dunning, *Congregationalists in America,* 423ff.; T. O. Douglass, *The Pilgrims of Iowa* (Boston, 1911), 143–44; Warren Upham, ed., *Congregational Work of Minnesota, 1832–1890* (Minneapolis, 1921), 47–51.

223. Cole, *Era of the Civil War,* 247.

224. *N.Y. Herald,* May 18, June 30, 1858; Georges Fisch, *Nine Months in the United States during the Crisis* (London, 1863), 55.

225. Laura C. Smith, *Life of Philander Chase* (New York, 1903), 339–40; *Aurora Beacon,* October 25, 1860; *Church Record,* January 1, September 15, October 1, 1859, August 15, November 1, 1860.

226. Fredrika Bremer, *America of the Fifties* (A. B. Benson, ed., New York, 1924), 191–92; Beste, *The Wabash,* II, 99, 222, 332; *Ohio State Journal* (Columbus), May 16, 1856; Sister Monica, *The Cross in the Wilderness* (New York, 1930).

227. Patrick Kearney, "The Fountain of Spiritualism," *Am. Mercury,* IV (1925), 331–36.

228. Grattan, *Civilized America,* II, 355–72; Francis Pulszky and Theresa Pulszky, *White, Red, Black* (New York, 1853), I, 298–308; Bremer, *America of the Fifties,* 203, 334–36; W. J. Stillman, *The Autobiography of a Journalist* (Boston, 1901), 179–97, 236; *Atlantische Studien,* I (1853), 67–70, 134, 145–49, 216–18.

229. *Ann Arbor Local News,* November 3, 1857, March 16, 1858.

230. *N.Y. Herald,* March 14, 1858.

231. *N.Y. Herald,* January 1, 1859.

232. Gasparin, *Uprising of a Great People,* 67, 86; A. P. Marvin, "Three Eras of Revivals in the United States," *Bibliotheca Sacra,* XVI (1859), 291; "Monthly Record of Current Events," *Harper's Mo.,* XVI (1858), 833. The Methodists gained in 1858 more than 100,000 members above the normal annual increase. Addie G. Wardle, *History of Sunday School Movement in the Methodist Episcopal Church* (New York, 1918), 93.

233. *Chicago Daily Times,* cited in *Mound City (Ill.) Emporium,* November 12, 1857; cf. *Chicago Democrat,* May 13, 1858.

234. *N.Y. Herald,* May 31, June 6, 21, 1858.

235. Edit., *Harper's Mo.,* XVII (1858), 262.

236. *Liberator* (Boston), March 23, 1860; Gasparin, *Uprising of a Great People,* 76. See also J. H. Hopkins, *A Scriptural, Ecclesiastical, and Historical View of Slavery* (New York, 1864).

237. William Jay, *An Examination of the Mosaic Laws of Servitude* (New York, 1854).

238. For the split in Methodist and Baptist churches, see this volume, Book VI, p. 517.

239. As a matter of fact many of the Catholic clergy and laity seemed to be opposed to the war when the crisis came. They detected signs that the war crusaders had marked popery as the next victim to follow slavery. John M'Keon, a New York lawyer, collected and published evidence that satisfied him that "when the knife is taken from the throats of the Southern people, it will be turned to the throat of every Catholic in the North." See *Cincinnati Enquirer,* January 2, 16, 1864; *Harper's Wkly.,* VIII, 2 (Jan. 2, 1864). Surviving anti-Catholic sentiment made for grave suspicion that this fear reflected a Roman Catholic complicity in the rebellion. See extraordinary charges in Charles Chiniquy, *Fifty Years in the Church of Rome* (New York, 1886), 686–87, 691, 695, 700–702, 706, 714–15.

240. When the war came, however, the Southern dioceses seceded with their states. S. D. McConnell, *History of the American Episcopal Church* (New York, 1891), 361.

241. *Ohio State Journal,* May 28, 1860, May 7–10, 1860; Methodist Episcopal Church,

Journal of the General Conference for 1860, 425-26; J. M. Buckley, *A History of Methodists of the United States* (Schaff et al., eds., *American Church History Series,* V), 501; W. W. Sweet, *The Methodist Episcopal Church and the Civil War* (Cincinnati, 1912), 38-40.

242. R. E. Thompson, *A History of the Presbyterian Churches in the United States* (Schaff et al., eds., *American Church History Series,* VI), 133-35.

243. L. G. Vander Velde, *The Presbyterian Churches and the Federal Union, 1861-1869 (Harvard Historical Studies,* XXXIII), pt. ii, chaps. i-iii.

244. Cole, *Era of the Civil War,* 223-24.

245. *Congressional Globe,* 33 Cong., 1 sess., app., 654.

246. *Joliet (Ill.) Signal,* June 17, 1856.

247. J. C. Stiles, *Modern Reform Examined* (Philadelphia, 1857), 274-75.

248. W. C. Beecher and Samuel Scoville, *A Biography of Henry Ward Beecher* (New York, 1888), 283-300.

249. Abraham Lincoln, *Complete Works* (J. G. Nicolay and John Hay, eds., New York, 1905), II, 282.

250. Theodore Parker, *Speeches, Addresses, and Occasional Sermons* (Boston, 1861), III, 154.

251. *Liberator* (Boston), September 27, 1850.

252. Cole, *Era of the Civil War,* 72.

253. For this and other estimates, see W. H. Siebert, *The Underground Railroad* (New York, 1898), 235-37.

254. John Cummings, ed., *Negro Population in the United States, 1790-1915* (Washington, 1918), 55.

255. *Ottawa (Ill.) Free Trader,* February 26, 1853; Cole, *Era of the Civil War,* 225-26.

256. Cole, *Era of the Civil War,* 226; Gustave Koerner, *Memoirs, 1809-1896* (T. J. McCormack, ed., Cedar Rapids, Iowa, 1909), II, 30-31; N. D. Harris, *The History of Negro Servitude in Illinois and of the Slavery Agitation in That State, 1719-1864* (Chicago, 1904), 188.

257. *National Intelligencer* (Washington), February 14, 1860.

258. Dicey, *Six Months in the Federal States,* I, 65-81.

259. Griesinger, *Lebende Bilder,* 150.

260. Kohl, *Travels,* I, 34-35.

261. *Frederick Douglass' Paper* (Rochester, N.Y.), March, 1854; B. C. Bacon, *Statistics of the Colored People of Philadelphia* (Philadelphia, 1856), 15.

262. Dicey, *Six Months in the Federal States,* II, 35; Mackay, *Life and Liberty in America,* II, 137-38; Mitchell, *Ten Years Residence in the United States,* 158-61; *Atlantische Studien,* I (1853), 192-94.

263. Gasparin, *The Uprising of a Great People,* 57; Fisch, *Nine Months in the United States during the Crisis,* 126.

264. Cole, *Era of the Civil War,* 227; F. U. Quillan, *The Color Line in Ohio* (Ann Arbor, 1913), 61.

265. *Cleveland Leader,* July 24, 25, 31, August 1, 1860; J. W. Massie, *America: The Origin of Her Present Conflict* (London, 1864), 185-87.

266. Frederick Douglass, *My Bondage and My Freedom* (New York, 1855); Austin Steward, *Twenty-Two Years a Slave and Forty Years a Freeman* (Rochester, 1857); Solomon Northup, *Twelve Years a Slave* (New York, 1855); anon., *The Experience of Thomas Jones, Who Was a Slave for Forty-Three Years* (Boston, 1850).

267. C. G. Woodson, *The Education of the Negro prior to 1861* (New York, 1915), 319, 325, 329; Bourne, *History of the Public School Society of the City of New York,* 594-95, 665ff.; Holley, *A Life for Liberty,* 168.

268. *National Intelligencer,* October 29, 1858.

269. Cole, *Era of the Civil War,* 228.

270. *Ann Arbor Local News,* August 21, 1860.

271. Siebert, *Underground Railroad,* 284, 327-33.

272. W. P. Garrison and F. J. Garrison, *William Lloyd Garrison, 1805-1879* (New York, 1885-87), III, 412. See also copies of the *Liberator,* and Higginson, *Letters and Journals,* 77-79. John Jay declared the Union "at present a most grievous curse to the American people." Bayard Tuckerman, *William Jay and the Constitutional Movement for the Abolition of Slavery* (New York, 1894), 154.

273. *Liberator,* June 22, 1860.

274. Fitzhugh, *Cannibals All!,* 154.

275. Speech at Cincinnati, September 17, 1859, Lincoln, *Complete Works,* V, 214-15; New Haven Speech, March 6, 1860, same vol., 358; J. E. Cairnes, *The Slave Power* (New York, 1862), 163 n.; Cole, *Lincoln's "House Divided" Speech,* 5-10.

276. Lincoln, *Complete Works,* V, 360.

277. Gasparin, *Uprising of a Great People,* 76-77, 162.

278. *Newark Mercury,* February 11, 1861, cited in C. M. Knapp, *New Jersey Politics during the Civil War and Reconstruction* (Geneva, N.Y., 1924), 52.

279. [Catherine C. Hopley], *Life in the South* (London, 1863), I, 140.

280. *Boston Post,* December 21, 1859.

281. *N.Y. Tribune,* January 23, 1860; [Hopley], *Life in the South,* I, 122.

282. [Hopley], *Life in the South,* I, 127.

283. *N.Y. Tribune,* November 6, 1860.

284. J. G. Nicolay and John Hay, *Abraham Lincoln* (New York, 1890), III, 280.

285. *N.Y. Herald,* November 29, December 10, 1860; *Springfield (Mass.) Republican,* November 17, 24, 1860; L. T. Lowrey, *Northern Opinion of Approaching Secession* (Smith College, *Studies,* III, no. 4).

286. Anon., "The Commercial Revulsion," *De Bow's Rev.,* XXXI (1861), 93. See also *New Orleans True Delta,* November 20, 1860.

287. *Clayton Banner,* cited in *N.Y. Tribune,* December 28, 1860; William Watson, *Life in the Confederate Army* (New York, 1888), 70, 71. Cf., however, W. C. Corsan (An English Merchant, pseud.), *Two Months in the Confederate States* (London, 1863), 111, 133.

288. *Boston Eve. Transcript,* July 28, 1862; *Southern Literary Messenger,* cited in *Belleville (Ill.) Advocate,* February 5, 1864; William Alexander, "Elements of Discord in Secessia," Loyal Publication Soc., *Pamphlets,* no. 15 (1863), 1-7, 11-12.

289. Russell, *My Diary,* 179.

290. [Hopley], *Life in the South,* I, 283, 284.

291. *Richmond Enquirer,* April 13, 1861, cited in A. B. Moore, *Conscription and Conflict in the Confederacy* (New York, 1924), 4-5.

292. R. S. Tharin, *Arbitrary Arrests in the South* (New York, 1863), 81.

293. A number of exiles hurled their printed broadsides at the Southern disunionists and appealed to the people upon whom they declared the political leaders had forced secession and civil war. See W. G. Brownlow, *Sketches of the Rise, Progress, and Decline of Secession* (Philadelphia, 1862); Tharin, *Arbitrary Arrests in the South;* J. W. Hunnicutt, *The Conspiracy Unveiled* (Philadelphia, 1863); R. J. Walker, *American Slavery and Finances* (London, 1864).

294. J. W. Taylor, *Alleghania* (St. Paul, 1862); H. T. Tuckerman, *America and Her Commentators* (New York, 1864), 277-78. Jones County, Mississippi, was a hotbed of Union sentiment.

295. E. g., anon., "The Terror at the South," *Harper's Wkly.,* VII, 802 (Dec. 19, 1863); anon., "Union Refugees in the Louisiana Swamps," same mag., VIII, 310 (May 14, 1864); Western Sanitary Commission, *Report on the White Union Refugees of the South* (St. Louis, 1864), 3-39; Loyal Publication Society, *Pamphlets,* no. 73.

296. F. A. Shannon, *The Organization and Administration of the Union Army* (Cleveland, 1928), II, 76, 77. See also Lincoln, *Complete Works,* X, 166, 167.

297. Cf. J. C. Schwab, *The Confederate States of America* (New Haven, 1913), 198;

Moore, *Conscription and Conflict in the Confederacy,* esp. 108; Bela Estvàn, *War Pictures from the South* (New York, 1863), 162–63.

298. *Columbus (Ga.) Weekly Sun,* September 2, 1862, cited in Moore, *Conscription and Conflict in the Confederacy,* 55, 56.

299. J. B. Jones, *A Rebel War Clerk's Diary* (Philadelphia, 1866), II, 281.

300. T. L. Livermore, *Numbers and Losses in the Civil War in America, 1861-1865* (Boston, 1901), 63. See also C. B. Hite, "The Size of the Confederate Army," *Current History,* XVIII (1923), 251–53; A. B. Casselman, "Numerical Strength of the Confederate Army," *Century,* XLIII (1892), 795, and "How Large Was the Confederate Army," *Current History,* XVII (1923), 653–57; R. H. McKim, *The Numerical Strength of the Confederate Army* (New York, 1912).

301. Randolph Abbott Shotwell, *Papers* (J. G. deR. Hamilton, ed., Raleigh, 1929–31), I, 128–29, 169–70, 187–88, 444; J. H. Browne, *Four Years in Secessia* (Hartford, 1865), 42, 43; William Watson, *Life in the Confederate Army* (New York, 1888), 339.

302. Shotwell, *Papers,* II, 73.

303. A. B. Moore, *History of Alabama and Her People* (New York, 1927), I, 542–43.

304. See *North Carolinan Times,* cited in *N.Y. Tribune,* August 3, 1864.

305. J. A. Wyeth, *With Sabre and Scalpel* (New York, 1914), 202; A. L. Long, *Memoirs of Robert E. Lee* (New York, 1886), 637.

306. Corsan, *Two Months in the Confederate States,* 70–71.

307. J. S. Wise, *The End of an Era* (Boston, 1899), 394.

308. Ella Lonn, *Desertion during the Civil War* (New York, 1928), 21–36; Moore, *Conscription and Conflict in the Confederacy,* 129–30.

309. W. H. Russell to J. C. B. Davis, September 25, 1861, *Historical Outlook,* XVI, 255; Russell, *My Diary,* 358. These foreign-born had constituted a fair share of the peacetime regular army. Russell, *My Diary,* 4; Kohl, *Travels,* I, 16.

310. Russell, *My Diary,* 334, 341, 483, 580, 583; Schurz, *Reminiscences,* II, 338–340; Dicey, *Six Months in the Federal States,* II, 47, 48; John Bigelow, *Retrospections of an Active Life* (New York, 1909–13), II, 276, 341–42.

311. Dicey, *Six Months in the Federal States,* II, 21; Higginson, *Letters and Journals,* 199.

312. Edits., *Harper's Wkly.,* V, 802 (December 21, 1861); VI, 530–31 (Aug. 23, 1862); *N.Y. Tribune,* July 11, August 5, 1862. This was the cause of the bitter antipathy revealed in the New York draft riots of 1863.

313. See handbill appeal anent Corcoran's capture, etc., *N.Y. Daily News,* July 26, 1861.

314. *Cleveland Leader,* September 9, 18, 1861.

315. F. A. Shannon, *The Organization and Administration of the Union Army* (Cleveland, 1928), I, 295–323; II, 11–174.

316. Ibid., II, 247–60.

317. E. N. Wright, *Conscientious Objectors in the Civil War* (Philadelphia, 1931), 62ff.; Lincoln, *Complete Works,* X, 216.

318. *Congressional Globe,* 37 Cong., 3 sess., 995.

319. J. W. Bowyer and C. H. Thurman, *The Annals of Elder Horn* (New York, 1930), 46.

320. Ella Lonn, *Desertion during the Civil War* (New York, 1928), 62–76, 181–82; Shannon, *Organization and Administration of the Union Army,* I, 177–80, and passim.

321. The horrors of the battlefield may be glimpsed in G. A. Townsend, *Campaigns of a Non-Combatant* (New York, 1866), 207, 270–72; Browne, *Four Years in Secessia,* 47, 53–54, 75, 76–77; M. W. Tyler, *Recollections of the Civil War* (New York, 1912), 195–96; Shotwell, *Papers,* I, 227, 289, 295–300, 430–31; Mary A. Livermore, *My Story of the War* (Hartford, 1889), 223–24; Wyeth, *With Sabre and Scalpel,* 247–48; W. W. Orme to Wife, December 9, 1862, Ill. State Hist. Soc., *Journ.,* XXIII, 266–67.

322. F. T. Miller, ed., *The Photographic History of the Civil War* (New York, 1912), esp. II, III, IX, passim.

323. A. T. Volwiler, ed., "Letters from a Civil War Officer," *Miss. Valley Hist. Rev.,* XIV, 528-29.

324. Livermore, *My Story of the War,* 659-60. For a case of similar "vandalism" by General W. T. Sherman, see his *Memoirs* (New York, 1875), II, 256.

325. George H. Hepworth, *Whip, Hoe, and Sword* (Boston, 1864), 99-100, 272.

326. Sherman, *Memoirs,* II, 182; Townsend, *Campaigns of a Non-Combatant,* 80; Hepworth, *Whip, Hoe, and Sword,* 278-80.

327. Shotwell, *Papers,* I, 319; II, 47, 75, 81. For other scruples against confiscation, see E. H. Frank to Catherine Varner, April 20, 1863, *N. D. Hist. Quar.,* IV, 191-92, and Higginson, *Letters and Journals,* 207.

328. W. W. Orme to Wife, October 20, 1862, 256, 304-5.

329. Russell, *My Diary,* 414; H. V. Boynton, *Sherman's Historical Raid* (Cincinnati, 1875), 23; Horace Greeley, *The American Conflict* (Hartford, 1866), II, 248; H. H. McGuire and G. L. Christian, *The Confederate Cause and Conduct in the War between the States* (Richmond, 1907), 74; Frank Moore, ed., *The Rebellion Record* (New York, 1861-68), III, "Documents," 2-3.

330. J. D. Richardson, comp., *Messages and Papers of the Presidents, 1789-1897* (Washington, 1897), VI, 117-18. The Confederate retaliatory order did not include confiscation. See *Official Records of Armies,* ser. 2, IV, 836-37; Southern Hist. Soc., *Papers,* I (1876), 300-302.

331. Volwiler, "Letters from a Civil War Officer," 524. See also Sherman, *Memoirs,* II, 185-86, 207-8, 213, 227; J. D. Cox, *The March to the Sea (Campaigns of the Civil War,* X, New York, 1913), 24, 36; G. W. Pepper, *Personal Recollections of Sherman's Campaigns in Georgia and the Carolinas* (Zanesville, Ohio, 1866), 246-47, 275-76, 279, 306-20, 331; G. W. Nichols, *The Story of the Great March* (New York, 1865), 240.

332. Sherman, *Memoirs,* II, 227-28, 254, 286-87.

333. *Official Records of Armies,* ser. 1, XLIII, pt. i, 37, 43; "Domestic Intelligence," *Harper's Wkly.,* VIII, 675 (October 22, 1864); Richard Taylor, *Destruction and Reconstruction* (New York, 1879), 46-47; E. A. Pollard, *Life of Jefferson Davis* (Philadelphia, 1869), 401-2.

334. Shotwell, *Papers,* I, 318-21, 348, 372-73, 493, 496; G. E. Pickett, *Soldier of the South: War Letters to His Wife* (A. C. Inman, ed., Boston, 1928), 50.

335. Pickett, *Soldier of the South,* 10, 104-5; J. W. Thomason, Jr., *Jeb Stuart* (New York, 1930), 266.

336. Taylor, *Destruction and Reconstruction,* 60; R. N. Early, ed., *Lieutenant General Jubal Anderson Early, C. S. A.* (Philadelphia, 1912), 401-4.

337. Walt Whitman, *Complete Prose Works* (Philadelphia, 1892), 79-80.

338. Townsend, *Campaigns of a Non-Combatant,* 145-46; Regis de Trobriand, *Four Years with the Army of the Potomac* (Boston, 1889), 221 ff.

339. Bigelow, *Retrospections of an Active Life,* I, 504, 521.

340. Charles Smart, *The Medical and Surgical History of the War of the Republic* (Washington, 1888), pt. iii, I, 1ff.

341. Townsend, *Campaigns of a Non-Combatant,* 108, 229; Trobriand, *Four Years with the Army of the Potomac,* 208. On work of the ambulance corps, see esp. T. L. Livermore, *Days and Events, 1860-1866* (Boston, 1920), 226, and passim.

342. See advertisement for four such "praying men" in *N.Y. Tribune,* September 5, 1863.

343. Tiffany, *Life of Dorothea Lynde Dix,* 336-41; Livermore, *My Story of the War,* 246.

344. C. J. Stillé, *History of the United States Sanitary Commission* (Philadelphia, 1866); J. S. Newberry, *United States Sanitary Commission in the Valley of the Mississippi* (Cleveland, 1871); F. L. Olmsted, *Books and Papers Relating to Con-*

cerns of the United States Sanitary Commission in the War of the Rebellion (n. p., 1890); Livermore, *My Story of the War,* 133ff; Trobriand, *Four Years with the Army of the Potomac,* 244ff.

345. W. W. Malet, *An Errand to the South in the Summer of 1862* (London, 1863), 46–47, 56, 177, 213–14. Many a free black demonstrated in practice his loyalty to the Confederacy and his desire to share in its defense. L. P. Jackson, "Free Negroes of Petersburg, Virginia," *Journ. of Negro History,* XII, 387–88.

346. A. J. Fremantle, *Three Months in the Confederate States* (New York, 1864), 179, 191; Malet, *Errand to the South,* 116–17, 292.

347. *N.Y. Times,* October 23, 1862.

348. Cf. Joseph Segar, *Letter to a Friend in Virginia* (Washington, 1862), 29; *N.Y. Tribune,* July 21, 1862; *N.Y. Times,* October 17, 1862.

349. *N.Y. Tribune,* May 5, 16, 1862; *Independent,* May 22, 1862.

350. Nearly 4,000 reached Kansas by March, 1862. *Independent,* March 13, 27, 1862.

351. C. G. Woodson, *A Century of Negro Migration* (Washington, 1918), 104ff.; Livermore, *My Story of the War,* 257ff.; [E. L. Pierce], "The Contrabands of Fortress Monroe," *Atlantic Mo.,* VIII (1861), 628, 630, 632.

352. *Congressional Globe,* 37 Cong., 2 sess., app., 84, 244–47; House of Representatives of Ohio, *Journal for 1862,* 106, 170, 213, 251, 253, 263, 278, 298, 333–35, 358; C. M. Knapp, *New Jersey Politics during the Period of the Civil War and Reconstruction* (Geneva, N.Y., 1924), 69, 92; "The Lounger," *Harper's Wkly.,* V, 802 (Dec. 21, 1861); VI, 530–31 (Aug. 23, 1862); *N.Y. Tribune,* July 11, 1862.

353. *Cairo Gazette,* August 19, 1862.

354. Cole, *Era of the Civil War,* 333–35.

355. *Boston Recorder,* cited in *National Intelligencer* (Washington), January 8, 1865.

356. *Independent,* October 1, 1863; Dicey, *Six Months in the Federal States,* I, 233.

357. House of Representatives of Ohio, *Journal for 1864,* app., 56–62.

358. *Liberator,* September 12, 1862. See also *Independent,* April 16, 1863.

359. A. B. Hart, *Salmon Portland Chase* (J. T. Morse, Jr., ed., *American Statesmen;* Boston, 1899), 259; Lincoln, *Complete Works,* VIII, 1–9, 97–98; W. L. Fleming, "Deportation and Colonization: An Attempted Solution of the Race Problem," J. W. Garner, ed., *Studies in Southern History and Politics* (N.Y., 1914), 8–30.

360. T. W. Higginson, *Army Life in a Black Regiment* (Boston, 1870), 1; B. F. Butler, *Private and Official Correspondence during the Civil War Period* (Boston, 1917), II, 192, 209–11, 270–71; same author, *Autobiography and Reminiscences* (Boston, 1892), 491–93.

361. Higginson, *Army Life in a Black Regiment,* 1–45, 269–72. See illustration in *Leslie's Illustrated Newspaper,* XV, 200–201 (December 20, 1862).

362. *Official Records of Armies,* ser. 3, V, 661; G. W. Williams, *A History of the Negro Troops in the War of the Rebellion, 1861–1865* (New York, 1888); Shannon, *Organization and Administration of the Union Army,* II, 160.

363. Higginson, *Army Life in a Black Regiment,* 278–92; B. T. Washington, *Frederick Douglass* (Philadelphia, 1906), 223, 232.

364. Higginson, *Army Life in a Black Regiment,* 57.

365. *Official Records of Armies,* ser. 1, XXIV, pt. i, 96, 106, 547. General Andrew J. Smith, "a former slaveholder," thanked the black troops for their "conspicuous gallantry" at Tupelo. *Wisconsin State Journal* (Madison), October 17, 1864. See also Bigelow, *Retrospections of an Active Life,* II, 278.

366. Lincoln, *Complete Works,* VIII, 233.

367. The number of failures in 1861 exceeded those of 1857 although less money was involved. *American Annual Cyclopedia,* V (1865), 349.

368. *N.Y. World,* October 10, 1861. See also *N.Y. Times,* March 22, 1863.

369. Trollope, *North America,* 148, 152; Dicey, *Six Months in the Federal States,* II, 164; *Boston Eve. Transcript,* July 5, 1861.

370. Anon., "Wall Street in War Time," *Harper's Mo.,* XXX (1865), 615.

371. *Cleveland Leader,* September 3, 6, 1861; *Am. Ann. Cyc.,* I (1861), 307.

372. *N.Y. Wkly. Tribune,* February 15, 1862. During the preceding eighteen months real property had depreciated one third in New York, if not generally in the North. *Independent,* April 10, 1862. See also issue of March 27, 1862.

373. *N.Y. Herald,* January 1, 1863; *N.Y. Times,* May 22, 1863; *N.Y. Tribune,* September 25, 1863; Bigelow, *Retrospections of an Active Life,* II, 43–44.

374. *National Intelligencer* (Washington), January 5, 1865. Contrast this to the depression of his business in 1860–61 with resulting discharge of large numbers of his clerks. *N.Y. Tribune,* January 9, 1860.

375. Failures in 1861 more than doubled those of 1860 and involved nearly three times the liabilities. *Am. Ann. Cyc.,* V (1865), 349; *N.Y. Herald,* January 1, 1862.

376. *Am. Ann. Cyc.,* III (1863), 410.

377. Robert Tomes, "The Fortunes of War," *Harper's Mo.,* XXIX (1864), 229.

378. Jeremiah Best, "Wall Street in War Time," *Harper's Mo.,* XXX (1865), 615, 621.

379. Bigelow, *Retrospections of an Active Life,* II, 229–30.

380. *N.Y. Tribune,* May 9, 24, 1864; G. A. Sala, *My Diary in America in the Midst of War* (London, 1865), II, 189–94; *Leslie's Illustrated Newspaper* (New York), XVIII, 162, 163 (June 4, 1864).

381. Fite, *Social and Industrial Conditions in the North during the Civil War,* chap. iv.

382. *N.Y. Tribune,* December 14, 1864.

383. *Ohio Farmer* (Cleveland), X (1861), 142, 150.

384. U. S. Commissioner of Agriculture, *Report for 1865,* 83, 87.

385. Anon., "Times in Iowa," *Home Missionary,* XXXIV (1862), 295.

386. Bigelow, *Retrospections of an Active Life,* II, 256–59. A native-born Southerner and slaveholder pointed out that the grain and flour receipts of Chicago for 1861 were nearly double in weight the total cotton crop of the South. See also Russell, *My Diary,* 358; Lorin Blodget, *The Commercial and Financial Strength of the United States* (Philadelphia, 1864), 37; Fite, *Social and Industrial Conditions in the North during the Civil War,* 19–21; L. B. Schmidt, "The Influence of Wheat and Cotton on Anglo-American Relations during the Civil War," *Iowa Journ. of History and Politics,* XVI, 400–439.

387. U. S. Comnr. of Agr., *Rep. for 1865,* 70ff.; *Hunt's Merchants' Mag.,* XLVIII (1863), 400–403; LIV (1866), 382–83.

388. *N.Y. Times,* March 28, 1863; Auguste-Laugel, *Les États-Unis pendant la Guerre* (Paris, 1866), 152–55; H. C. Hill, "The Development of Chicago as a Center of the Meat Packing Industry," *Miss. Valley Hist. Rev.,* X, 262–63.

389. Cole, *Era of the Civil War,* 378–79; *Chicago Tribune,* March 4, 10, 1863; *Ohio Farmer,* XI (1862), 26, 46, 118.

390. *N.Y. World,* January 26, 1863; *N.Y. Tribune,* January 12, 1864.

391. *Carthage (Ill.) Republican,* June 9, 1864.

392. *Scientific American,* IX (1863), 9; Livermore, *My Story of the War,* 145–46; Frederick Merk, *Economic History of the Civil War Decade* (Hist. Soc. of Wis., *Studies,* I), 52–56, 145–46.

393. *Chicago Tribune,* March 2, 1863; *Ohio Farmer,* XII (1863), 136; Laugel, *United States during the War,* 146–47.

394. G. T. Barrett, *Out West* (London, 1866), I, 154. See also E. D. Fite, "Industrial Development of the West," *Quar. Journ. of Econ.,* XX, 274–75.

395. *Wisconsin State Journal* (Madison), October 14, 1864.

396. *N.Y. Tribune,* September 14, 1863.

397. See Aldrich report, 52 Cong., 2 sess., *Senate Rep.,* III, 176. See also U. S. Commissioner of Labor, *Annual Report for 1886,* 74; Mass. Bureau of Statistics of Labor, *Annual Report for 1872,* 516–20; F. W. Taussig, "Results of Recent Investigations on Prices in the United States," *Yale Rev.,* II (1893), 231–47.

398. Under acts of December 21, 1861, and July 16, 1862, salaries of government

employees were to be regulated according to the rates paid in other establishments.

399. *London Morning Herald,* cited in *N.Y. Times,* May 23, 1863; Bigelow, *Retrospections of an Active Life,* II, 95; P. H. Bagenal, *The American Irish and Their Influence on Irish Politics* (London, 1882), 139–40n.; J. B. McMaster, *A History of the People of the United States during Lincoln's Administration* (New York, 1927), 372–76. See Seward's explanation in 38 Cong., 1 sess., *Senate Exec. Doc.,* I, no. 54.

400. H. T. Tuckerman, "A Village in Massachusetts," *Harper's Mo.,* XXXII (1865), 114.

401. B. A. Gould, *Investigations in the Military and Anthropological Statistics of American Soldiers* (New York, 1869), 27.

402. *National Intelligencer,* January 15, 1861; *Philadelphia Inquirer,* February 25, 1861; T. V. Powderly, *Thirty Years of Labor* (Columbus, 1890), 44–46; J. R. Commons et al., *History of Labour in the United States* (New York, 1918), 10–12.

403. *Columbus (Ohio) Crisis,* April 8, 1863; Mass. Bur. of Stat. of Labor, *Ann. Rep. for 1870,* 100; Bur. of Labor Stat. of Ohio, *Ann. Rep. for 1877,* 31; Mary R. Beard, *A Short History of the American Labor Movement* (New York, 1920), 62–79.

404. Commons et al., *History of Labour,* II, 23–26.

405. J. R. Commons et al., eds., *A Documentary History of American Industrial Society* (Cleveland, 1910–11), IX, 118–25.

406. *The War of the Rebellion: A Compilation of the Official Records of the Union and Confederate Armies* (Washington, 1880–1901), ser. 3, III, 1008, 1009.

407. *N.Y. Tribune,* July 11, 1862; Fite, *Social and Industrial Conditions in the North during the Civil War,* 189, 203ff.

408. Wendell Phillips, *Speeches, Lectures, and Letters* (2d ser., Boston, 1905), 139; Carlos Martyn, *Wendell Phillips: The Agitator* (New York, 1890), 378ff.

409. Anon., "War as a Schoolmaster," *Harper's Wkly.,* V, 658 (October 19, 1861). Religious leaders could look to war as "the restorer of national life," and this war as "destined to educate the nation to a loftier patriotism." Anon., "War as an Educator," *Independent,* April 18, 1861. See also *Monthly Religious Magazine,* XXV (1861), 378; XXVII (1862), 198ff.; *Christian Examiner,* LXXI (1861), 114–15; *Boston Review,* I (1861), 252ff.

410. Commissioner of Statistics of Ohio, *Eighth Annual Report* (1864), 54; *N.Y. Times,* January 5, 1865. See also issues of August 23, 1861, May 11, 1862, June 29, July 15, 1865; *Rockford (Ill.) Register,* August 12, 1865; *Nation,* II, 802 (June 26, 1866).

411. The number of convictions and commitments is not an adequate gauge of the situation since offenders were often allowed to enlist to avoid the penalty of their offense. Even the pardoning power was often exercised with amazing generosity. *N.Y. Times,* March 3, 1862; Gideon Haynes, *Pictures from Prison Life* (Boston, 1869), 107. Cf., however, Fite, *Social and Industrial Conditions in the North during the Civil War,* 304–305.

412. *Cleveland Herald,* January 9, 1863; John B. Gough, *Autobiography and Personal Recollections* (Springfield, Mass., 1869), 526–28.

413. Sala, *My Diary in America,* I, 288. See also F. A. Shannon, "The Life of the Common Soldier in the Union Army, 1861–1865," *Miss. Valley Hist. Rev.,* XIII, 481; *Norfolk Day Book,* March 21, 1862, cited in Frank Moore, ed., *The Rebellion Record* (New York, 1861–68), IV, "Diary," 65.

414. *Cincinnati Enquirer,* January 2, 4, 8, 11, 15, 1864; *Springfield (Mass.) Republican,* May 7, 1864.

415. *Am. Ann. Cyc.,* IV (1864), 769–70; *Leslie's Illustrated Newspaper,* XVII, 67 (October 24, 1863).

416. Cole, *Era of the Civil War,* 420–21. On Cincinnati, see *Cincinnati Enquirer,* January 2, 1864; on Chicago, *Columbus Crisis,* March 2, 1864, and *Chicago Trib-*

une, July 22, 24, 1865; on New York, Dicey, *Six Months in the Federal States,* II, 17; Herbert Asbury, *Gangs of New York* (New York, 1928), 175; *N.Y. Times,* March 3, 1862; *Philadelphia Press,* April 4, 1863, January 21, 1864; *Leslie's Illustrated Newspaper,* XX, 227 (July 1, 1865); on Boston, Sala, *My Diary in America,* II, 162.

417. Commissioner of Common Schools of Ohio, *Eighth Annual Report* (1862), 6.

418. *Cincinnati Enquirer,* January 29, 1864.

419. *Acts of Kentucky for 1861-1863,* 265; *N.Y. Times,* September 1, 1862; Bessie L. Pierce, *Public Opinion and the Teaching of History* (New York, 1926), 29-34.

420. Anson Smyth in Comnr. of Common Schools of Ohio, *Eighth Ann. Rep.,* 18. A later commissioner, E. E. White, concluded: "I am fully satisfied that, so far as our common schools are concerned, it is neither necessary, practicable nor desirable to attempt to include in them the school of the soldier." Comnr. of Common Schools of Ohio, *Twelfth Ann. Rep.,* 69-70.

421. *Independent,* August 7, 1862. See also *Round Table,* I, 148 (February 20, 1864).

422. During the first year of the war five Northern governors made favorable mention of this proposal in their messages. *N.Y. Tribune,* December 31, 1861, July 3, 1862; *N.Y. Times,* March 8, 1862.

423. Stanton, *Elizabeth Cady Stanton,* II, 88-89, 91.

424. Fite, *Social and Industrial Conditions in the North during the Civil War,* 237.

425. M. W. Tyler, *Recollections of the Civil War* (New York, 1912), 8, 18; Henry James, *Charles W. Eliot* (Boston, 1930), I, 89; Andrew D. White, *Autobiography* (New York, 1905), I, 91.

426. Auditor of State of Ohio, *Report for 1862,* 18.

427. Caroline Ticknor, ed., *Dr. Holmes's Boston* (Boston, 1915), 58.

428. Dicey, *Six Months in the Federal States,* II, 222.

429. *Columbus Crisis,* July 15, 1863. See also Cole, *Era of the Civil War,* 431, and *N.Y. World,* October 14, 1863. On October 15, 1863, Prof. Richard S. McCulloh was expelled from the faculty of Columbia College "for having abandoned his post and joined the rebels." He had meantime made discoveries concerning gunpowder which enabled him to secure a commission from the Confederate government to undertake the destruction of Northern war materials. *Independent,* November 12, 1863; *Official Records of Armies,* ser. 4, III, 37-38, 1097; ser. 2, VIII, 567.

430. *Independent,* January 21, 1864. There was noted in "all colleges" a tendency "toward weakening the public force in favor of individual rights." W. H. Dixon, *New America* (London, 1867), 450.

431. G. R. Carpenter, *Walt Whitman* (New York, 1909), 89-96; Walt Whitman, *Autobiographia* (New York, 1892), 48ff.; Bliss Perry, *Walt Whitman, His Life and Work* (Boston, 1906), 132-57.

432. Perry, *Walt Whitman,* 150-51.

433. *N.Y. Tribune,* February 3, 1862; S. T. Pickard, ed., *Life and Letters of John Greenleaf Whittier* (Boston, 1894), II, 467-68.

434. H. H. Brownell, *War Lyrics and Other Poems* (Boston, 1866); E. W. Emerson, *Early Years of the Saturday Club, 1855-1870* (Boston, 1918), 399.

435. *N.Y. World,* October 8, 1863.

436. *N.Y. Tribune,* February 1, 1862. Not only did the German troops continue the traditions of the *Männerchor,* but the Yankee choirmaster and singing teacher helped the New England troops beguile many an otherwise tedious evening. Moore, *Rebellion Record,* IV, "Incidents," 49. See also J. T. Howard, *Our American Music* (New York, 1931), chap. ix.

437. "The Lounger," *Harper's Wkly.,* V, 722-23 (November 16, 1861); R. G. White, *National Hymns* (New York, 1861).

438. *Cleveland Leader,* May 9, 1861; [Hopley], *Life in the South,* I, 352.

439. "The Lounger," *Harper's Wkly.,* VI, 787 (December 13, 1862). See also *U. S.*

Service Mag., I (1864), 48; Townsend, *Campaigns of a Non-Combatant,* 249; *Independent,* August 29, 1861; *N.Y. Tribune,* February 10, 1862; *Leslie's Illustrated Newspaper,* XX, 163 (June 3, 1865).

440. F. L. Owsley, "The Confederacy and King Cotton," *N. C. Hist. Rev.,* VI, 371–79. See also Corsan, *Two Months in the Confederate States,* 113–14, 130–31.

441. Robert Toombs, Alexander H. Stephens, and Howell Cobb, *Correspondence* (U. B. Phillips, ed., Am. Hist. Assoc., *Ann. Rep. for 1911,* II), 595; U. B. Phillips, *The Life of Robert Toombs* (New York, 1913), 247.

442. J. F. Rhodes, *History of the United States* (New York, 1892-1919), V, 372, 428–29.

443. Rhodes, *History of the United States,* V, 368–71.

444. *Illinois State Journal* (Springfield), February 14, March 20, 1861.

445. Shotwell, *Papers,* I, 468; J. L. M. Curry, *Civil History of the Government of the Confederate States* (Richmond, 1901), 159–60, 165; Corsan, *Two Months in the Confederate States,* 68; Rhodes, *History of the United States,* V. 363–66. See also J. D. Richardson, comp., *A Compilation of the Messages and Papers of the Confederacy* (Nashville, 1906), I, 331–35.

446. Corsan, *Two Months in the Confederate States,* 66, 67.

447. J. L. Sellers, "The Co-Relation of the Salt and Flood Supplies of the Confederacy" (unpublished article).

448. Rhodes, *History of the United States,* V, 449–52.

449. A. B. Moore, *History of Alabama and Her People* (Chicago, 1927), I, 559; edit., *De Bow's Rev.,* XXXII (1862), 164.

450. Anon., "Education of Southern Women," *De Bow's Rev.,* XXXI (1861), 381–90.

451. *Charleston Courier,* September 17, 1864; G. C. Eggleston, *A Rebel's Recollections* (New York, 1875), 106.

452. E. W. Knight, *Public School Education in North Carolina* (Boston, 1916), 184.

453. C. E. Jones, *Education in Georgia* (H. B. Adams, ed., *Contribs. to Am. Educational History,* no. 5, Washington, 1889), 65–66; Rhodes, *History of the United States,* V, 469.

454. *Catholic Standard* (New Orleans), cited in Edward McPherson, *The Political History of the United States of America during the Great Rebellion* (Washington, 1865), 516–17.

455. *N.Y. World,* March 23, 1864; W. L. Fleming, "The Churches of Alabama during the Civil War," *Gulf States Hist. Mag.,* I (1902), 110; McPherson, *Political History of United States,* 523–24.

456. McPherson, *Political History of United States,* 515n.

457. Frank Moore, *The Rebellion Record,* III, "Incidents," 13.

458. A. B. Moore, *Conscription and Conflict in the Confederacy* (New York, 1924), 58n., 59.

459. J. B. Jones, *A Rebel War Clerk's Diary* (Philadelphia, 1866), II, 64.

460. Lincoln, *Complete Works,* VIII, 29–30.

461. Curry, *Civil History of the Confederate States,* 177, 178; J. A. C. Chandler et al., *The South in the Building of the Nation* (Richmond, 1909-10), X, 513; J. W. Jones, *Christ in the Camp* (Richmond, 1887); Shotwell, *Papers,* I, 275–76, 385. An interdenominational Evangelical Tract Society distributed religious literature among the soldiers to the point that, after the second battle of Bull Run, the ground was "covered with leaves of tracts and bibles." Dicey, *Six Months in the Federal States,* II, 27.

462. [Hopley], *Life in the South,* I, 172, 194, 351, 405; II, 104; Pickett, *Soldier of the South: War Letters to His Wife,* 48, 100. See also W. L. Fagan, *Southern War Songs* (New York, 1890), and Frank Moore, ed., *Songs and Ballads of the Southern People, 1861-1865* (New York, 1886).

463. Fitzgerald Ross, *A Visit to the Cities and Camps of the Confederate States* (London, 1865), 40.

464. [Hopley], *Life in the South,* I, 137, 139, 273; Thomason, *Jeb Stuart,* 45.
465. Belle Boyd, *Belle Boyd in Camp and Prison* (London, 1865).
466. A collection of letters to prisoners in Camp Chase, Columbus, Ohio, formerly on file in the Ohio State Library, revealed a lack of feminine enthusiasm for the Southern cause; wives not only deplored this "awful war" but even indulged in elaborate denunciation of the alleged right of secession.
467. *The War of the Rebellion: A Compilation of the Official Records of the Union and Confederate Armies* (Washington, 1880-1901), ser. 4, III, 1013.
468. *Official Records of Armies,* ser. 4, III, 1009.
469. *Am. Ann. Cyc.,* V (1865), 198.
470. J. L. Sellers, "Civil War Finance," *Am. Hist. Rev.,* XXX, 287-97.
471. *Cairo (Ill.) News,* April 20, 1865.
472. Charles W. Eliot to his mother. Henry James, *Charles W. Eliot, President of Harvard University, 1869-1909* (Boston, 1930), I, 140.

BOOK VIII   The Emergence of Modern America, 1865–78

1. J. F. Rhodes, *History of the United States from the Compromise of 1850* (New York, 1893-1919), V. 187; E. P. Oberholtzer, *History of the United States since the Civil War* (New York, 1917-26), I, 51; T. L. Livermore, *Numbers and Losses in the Civil War* (Boston 1900), 1-65.
2. "Report of the Joint Committee on Reconstruction," *House Rep.,* 39 Cong., 1 sess., no. 30, pt. ii, 68ff.
3. M. P. Andrews, *Women of the South in War Times* (Baltimore, 1920); Susan D. Smedes, *Memorials of a Southern Planter* (Baltimore, 1887), 225; Myrta L. Avary, *Dixie after the War* (New York, 1906), 158ff.
4. G. W. Nichols, *The Story of the Great March* (New York, 1865), chaps. xxviii-xxix.
5. Sidney Andrews, *The South since the War* (Boston, 1886), chaps. i-ii; Whitelaw Reid, *After the War: a Southern Tour* (Cincinnati, 1866), 57ff.
6. *American Annual Cyclopedia* (New York, 1861-1903), V (1865), 391ff.; W. L. Fleming, *Civil War and Reconstruction in Alabama* (New York, 1905), chap. v., sec. 1.
7. *Nation* (New York), II (1866), 270.
8. For speculation, profiteers, and the newly enriched Southerners, see C. Mildred Thompson, *Reconstruction in Georgia* (Columbia Univ., *Studies,* LXIV), chap. v.
9. Reid, *After the War,* 360.
10. W. K. Boyd, *Story of Durham* (Durham, 1925), 80-93. For another instance, see M. G. Fulton, *Southern Life in Southern Literature* (Boston, 1917), 373. Robert E. Lee turned heroically to education.
11. See Charles Seymour, ed., *The Intimate Papers of Colonel House* (Boston, 1926), I, chap. ii, for Texas disorders; H. H. Bancroft, *Pacific States of North America* (San Francisco, 1882-90), XI, 480ff.
12. Fleming, *Reconstruction in Alabama,* chaps. v-vi; *House Rep.,* 39 Cong., 2 sess., no. 16, 12ff.
13. *Commercial and Financial Chronicle* (New York), September 16, 23; October 14, 1865; *N.Y. Eve. Post,* September 29, 1865.
14. *Richmond Inquirer,* November 13, 1865.
15. Andrews, *South Since the War,* chap. xxxviii. The *N.Y. Herald,* December 27, 1865, reported that Texas was full of traders and that goods were being rapidly shipped in.
16. *Am. Ann. Cyclop.,* VI (1866), 8ff.
17. For outrages against the blacks by the "poor whites" of the Appalachian belt, and for the friction between former Unionists and former Confederates in these dis-

tricts, see J. T. Trowbridge, *The South* (Hartford, 1866), 240; "Report of the Joint Committee on Reconstruction," *House Rep.,* 39 Cong., 1 sess., pt. 1, 109ff. On the labor question, see O. O. Howard, *Autobiography* (New York, 1907), II, 245-65; Carl Schurz, "Report," *Senate Exec. Doc.,* 39 Cong., 2 sess., no. 6, 144, 156ff. The sufferings of the South from seizures of Confederate cotton and the subsequent cotton tax are described in W. L. Fleming, ed., *Documentary History of Reconstruction* (Cleveland, 1906-7), I, 25.

18. Fleming, *Reconstruction in Alabama,* 200ff.; *Am. Ann. Cyclop.,* V (1865), 6, 788ff.

19. *Am. Ann. Cyclop.,* VII (1867), 518ff.; *Com. and Fin. Chron.,* October 12, 1867; September 19, 1868.

20. Secretary of War, *Annual Reports,* 1866-68, passim; Howard, *Autobiography,* II, 163-445; P. S. Pierce, *The Freedmen's Bureau* (Univ. of Iowa, *Studies,* III, no. 1), 1-191.

21. *N.Y. Eve. Post,* November 14, 1865: *Am. Ann. Cyclop.,* VI (1866), 12ff; Fleming, *Reconstruction in Alabama,* 200ff.

22. *Am. Ann. Cyclop.,* V (1865), 29, 392; VI (1866), 521.

23. George Petrie, "William F. Samford," Alabama Hist. Soc., *Trans.,* IV, 465-85; *Nation,* XV, August 15, 1872.

24. *Nation,* ibid.

25. J. W. Garner, *Reconstruction in Mississippi* (New York, 1901), chap. iv; Fleming, *Reconstruction in Alabama,* 273ff.

26. Holland Thompson, *The New South* (Allen Johnson, ed., *The Chronicles of America Series,* New Haven, 1918-21, XLII), 167ff.; Fleming, *Documentary History,* II, chaps. lviii-lix.

27. Pierce Butler, *Judah P. Benjamin* (*American Crisis Biographies,* Philadelphia, 1907), chaps, xiii-xiv.

28. B. C. Truman, "Report," *Senate Exec. Doc.,* 39 Cong., 1 sess., no. 43, 15ff.; *Am. Ann. Cyclop.,* X (1870), 683. For Southern laws to encourage immigration, see, for example, *Laws* of Virginia, 1872-73, 272; of Texas, 1871, 127; of Georgia, 1869, 26.

29. Howard, *Autobiography,* II, 248ff.

30. Trowbridge, *The South,* 239; J. S. Kiddoo, "Report," *Senate Exec. Doc.,* 39 Cong., 2 sess., no. 6, 144ff.

31. Robert Somers, *The Southern States since the War, 1870-1871* (New York, 1871), 84ff.; Sir George Campbell, *White and Black* (London, 1879), 359ff.

32. Somers, *Southern States,* chap. xviii. One marked social result of emancipation was the tendency of many black women to refuse work in the fields.

33. Fleming, *Reconstruction in Alabama,* chap. v.

34. The decline in land values was greatest in Louisiana, Alabama, Mississippi, Arkansas, and South Carolina; it was least in Tennessee, Texas, and Virginia. For exact statistics see Commissioner of Agriculture, *Report for 1879,* 147ff. See also Garner, *Reconstruction in Mississippi,* chap. iv; Fleming, *Reconstruction in Alabama,* chap. v, sec. 1; and *Am. Ann. Cyclop.,* IX (1869), 12.

35. J. S. Pike, *The Prostrate State, South Carolina under Negro Government* (New York, 1874), 117ff.; Campbell, *White and Black,* 327.

36. Thompson, *Reconstruction in Georgia,* chap. v.

37. Improved land could be had at from $3 to $5 an acre. Garner, *Reconstruction in Mississippi,* chap. iv.

38. Bliss Perry, *Life and Letters of Henry Lee Higginson* (Boston, 1921), 247ff.; Royal Cortissoz, *Life of Whitelaw Reid* (New York, 1921), I, 123ff.

39. C. W. Ramsdell, *Reconstruction in Texas* (Columbia Univ., *Studies,* XXXVI, no. 1), 44ff.; Bancroft, *Pacific States,* XI, 480ff.

40. *Com. and Fin. Chron.,* February 6, 1869; *Am. Ann. Cyclop.,* IX (1869), 256ff.

41. *Com. and Fin. Chron.,* April 24, 1869.

42. *Am. Ann. Cyclop.,* IX (1869), 206.

43. Commissioner of Agriculture, *Report for 1876,* 128-32.

44. Somers, *Southern States,* 64-65.

45. *Com. and Fin. Chron.,* October 23, 1869.

46. C. W. Burkett and C. H. Poe, *Cotton, its Cultivation . . . and the Problems of the Cotton World* (New York, 1906), 72. For the gouging by loan sharks, see Somers, *Southern States,* chap. vii.

47. But for the vicious one-crop system see Charles Nordhoff, *The Cotton States in the Spring and Summer of 1875* (New York, 1876), 108.

48. Somers, *Southern States,* 64.

49. See *Scientific American,* October 1, 1870, on cotton; *Com. and Fin. Chron.,* January 1, 1876, on cotton mills.

50. Edward King, "The Great South," *Scribner's Monthly,* VI-IX (1873-74), passim.

51. D. A. Wells, *Recent Economic Changes* (New York, 1889), 65.

52. Special Commissioner of Revenue, *Report* (December 1869). See also *Scientific American,* September 15, 1866: "There are more men in New York today whose annual incomes reach $100,000 than there were twenty-five years ago of those whose entire possessions amounted to as much."

53. Special Commissioner of Revenue, *Report* (January 1869).

54. John and W. T. Sherman, *Letters* (Rachel S. Thorndike, ed., New York, 1894), 258.

55. *Abstract of the Census of Manufactures,* 1919 (Washington, 1923), 13, table 3.

56. C. D. Wright, *The Industrial Evolution of the United States* (New York, 1901), chap. xiv; H. U. Faulkner, *American Economic History* (New York, 1924), 574.

57. Waldemar Kaempffert, ed., *A Popular History of American Invention* (New York, 1924), II, 83.

58. V. S. Clark, *History of Manufactures in the United States, 1607-1860* (Carnegie Inst., Contribs. to Am. Econ. Hist., Washington, 1916), 415, 456.

59. See *Statistical Abstract of the United States, 1921* (Washington, 1922), 868.

60. W. O. Scroggs, *Century of Banking Progress* (Garden City, N.Y., 1924), 203.

61. *Com. and Fin. Chron.,* April 25, 1874.

62. *Com. and Fin. Chron.,* August 3, 1878; H. W. Lanier, *A Century of Banking in New York, 1822-1922* (New York, 1922), chap. x.

63. Philip Davis, *Immigration and Americanization* (Boston, 1920), 66, presents the figures by years. See *Com. and Fin. Chron.,* September 1, 1866, for comment.

64. R. E. Park, *The Immigrant Press and Its Control* (New York. 1922), 320; Hester M. Pollock, *Our Minnesota* (New York, 1917), 333.

65. See *Am. Ann. Cyclop.,* XVII (1877), 386, for general review.

66. *N.Y. Eve. Post,* July 13, 1865; *Am. Ann. Cyclop.,* IX (1869), 260ff.

67. Special Commissioner of Revenue, *Report for December, 1866,* 14ff.; *N.Y. Eve. Post* and *N.Y. Herald,* January 4, 1867, for comment.

68. Special Commissioner of Revenue, *Report for December, 1868; Nation,* IX, July 15, 1869.

69. *N.Y. Eve. Post,* July 13, 1865.

70. J. R. Commons et al., *History of Labour in the United States* (New York, 1921), II, 87ff., 124ff., 138-39; F. T. Carlton, *The History and Problems of Organized Labor* (New York, 1921), 63; J. R. Commons et al., *Documentary History of American Industrial Society* (Cleveland, 1910-11), IX, 26.

71. J. C. Sylvis, *The Life, Speeches, Labors and Essays of William H. Sylvis* (Philadelphia, 1872); Commons et al., *Labour in the United States,* II, 111.

72. Mary Beard, *A Short History of the American Labor Movement* (New York, 1920), 72ff.; Commons et al., *Labour in the United States,* II, chap. iv.

73. D. D. Lescohier. *The Knights of St. Crispin, 1867-1874* (Univ. of Wis., Econ. and Pol. Sci. Series, VII, 1910, no. 1).

74. *United States Statistical Abstract, 1910* (Washington 1911), table 23.

75. W. D. Howells, *The Rise of Silas Lapham* (Boston, 1884), 75.

76. J. H. Jallings, *Elevators* (Chicago, 1915), 7ff.

77. H. C. Brown, *The Last Fifty Years in Old New York* (New York, 1926), 100.

78. Moses King, ed., *Handbook of New York City* (Boston, 1892).
79. *Nation*, V, July 25, 1867.
80. *Scientific American*, April 3, 1870.
81. *Com. and Fin. Chron.*, May 31, 1879; *U.S. Tenth Census* (1880), XVIII, 557.
82. *U.S. Tenth Census* (1880), XVIII, 812.
83. *Popular Science Monthly*, VII (1875), 80ff.
84. *Harper's Weekly*, March 17, 1866.
85. *Nation*, III, July 12, 1866.
86. *Nation*, XIII, October 19, 1871.
87. *Nation*, XIII, November 9, 1871; *Am. Ann. Cyclop.*, XI (1871), 393ff.
88. *Nation*, XV, November 14, 1872.
89. *Scientific American*, September 25; October 23, 1869.
90. Postmaster General, *Report of 1868*, 24ff.; same author, *Report of 1869*, 18; same author, *Report of 1870*, 16; same author, *Report of 1872*, 36. The government at the same time was establishing a national weather service, of great value to farmers, mariners, and the general public. *Am. Ann. Cyclop.*, X (1870), 797ff.
91. Kaempffert, *History of American Invention*. For the history of the typewriter, see I, 264–85; for the telephone, I, 286–317.
92. Herkimer County Historical Society, *The Story of the Typewriter, 1873-1923* (Herkimer, N.Y., 1923), 30ff.
93. A. B. Paine, *Mark Twain, A Biography* (New York, 1912), I, 537.
94. H. N. Casson, *The History of the Telephone* (Chicago, 1910), 26.
95. G. M. Towle, *American Society* (London, 1870), II, 175ff.
96. Joseph Husband, *The Story of the Pullman Car* (Chicago, 1917), 32.
97. Husband, *Pullman Car*, 42ff.
98. *Detroit Commerical Advertiser,* June 1, 1867, quoted by Husband, 49.
99. See W. F. Rae, *Westward by Rail* (London, 1870), 28, for transcontinental accommodations. He is enthusiastic about the splendor of the cars; but, actually, most of the early Pullmans, with carved wood, heavy upholstery, and silver plate, were vulgarly ornate.
100. H. G. Prout, *A Life of George Westinghouse* (New York, 1921), 26ff.; F. E. Leupp, *George Westinghouse, His Life and Achievements* (Boston, 1918), 18ff.
101. Prout, *George Westinghouse*, 32.
102. E. H. Mott, *Between the Ocean and the Lakes: the Story of Erie* (New York, 1899), 140.
103. *Am. Ann. Cyclop.*, XVI (1876), 516.
104. C. F. Adams, Jr., "The Revere Catastrophe," *Atlantic Monthly*, XXXVII (1876), 92–103.
105. Secretary of the Interior, *Report for 1872*, 402ff.
106. *Am. Ann. Cyclop.*, VII (1867), 403.
107. The Secretary of the Interior in 1872 classified all the Indians of the United States as follows: civilized, 97,000; semicivilized, 125,000; utterly barbarous, 78,000. He reported that about 180,000 had treaties with the government, 40,000 more were without reservations but more or less under the control of agents, and 55,000 were totally uncontrolled. Secretary of the Interior, *Report for 1872*, 402ff.
108. Livingston Farrand, *Basis of American History* (A. B. Hart, ed., *American Nation, a History*, New York, 1904-18, II), chap. ix.
109. F. L. Paxson, *The Last American Frontier* (New York, 1910), chap. xxii.
110. See General Halleck in 1866 on the Apache: "They must be hunted and exterminated." Secretary of War, *Report for 1866*, 31ff.
111. H. H. Jackson, *A Century of Dishonor* (New York, 1881), chap. iii.
112. P. E. Byrne, *Soldiers of the Plains* (New York, 1926), 140.
113. *Senate Reps.*, 39 Cong., 2 sess., no. 156.
114. Committee on the Conduct of the War, *Report*, III (massacre of the Cheyenne Indians).
115. Commissioner of Indian Affairs, *Report for 1866*.

116. *Nation,* II, January 11, 1866.
117. Sherman testified that hunting Indians was like hunting the Confederate cruiser *Alabama.* Secretary of War, *Report for 1867,* 31ff.
118. Commissioner of Indian Affairs, *Report for 1865,* 699ff.
119. W. T. Hornaday, "Extermination of the American Bison," Smithsonian Museum, *Report for 1887,* 367ff.
120. F. A. Root and W. E. Connelley, *The Overland Stage to California* (Topeka, 1901), chap. ii.
121. See unsigned article on the "Destruction of the Buffalo," *Popular Science Monthly,* IX (1876), 377.
122. R. I. Dodge, *The Plains of the Great West and their Inhabitants* (New York, 1877), 134ff.
123. See G. A. Sala, *America Revisited* (London, 1883), II, 174, and W. A. Bell, *New Tracks in North America* (London, 1869), II, 233, for foreign views of conditions.
124. Colonel Dodge computed that 5.5 million bison were shot in the three years 1872–74. *Plains of the Great West,* 142–44.
125. Bitter winters slew many buffalo. J. H. Beadle, *The Undeveloped West* (Philadelphia, 1873), 436.
126. For Indian dependence on the buffalo, see G. B. Grinnell, "The Last of the Buffalo," *Scribner's Mag.,* XII (1892), 267–86.
127. *Senate Exec. Docs.,* 48 Cong., 2 sess., no. 95.
128. U.S. Commissioner of Indian Affairs, *Report for 1872.* Extracts from this report are reprinted in H. H. Jackson, *A Century of Dishonor* (rev. ed., 1886), 411.
129. J. F. Meline, *Two Thousand Miles on Horseback* (New York, 1867), 8–10.
130. *Am. Ann. Cyclop.,* IX (1869), 447ff.
131. W. E. Miller, *The Peopling of Kansas* (Columbus, Ohio, 1906), passim; *Am. Ann. Cyclop.,* X (1870), 421.
132. For an excellent contemporary answer, see L. P. Brockett, *Our Western Empire* (Philadelphia, 1880), chap. iii.
133. Between 1860 and 1880 almost 470,000 applications for homesteads were filed. Thomas Donaldson, *The Public Domain* (Washington, 1884), 208.
134. B. H. Hibbard, *A History of the Public Land Policies* (New York, 1924), chap. xiii.
135. Ibid., 254–55; *Com. and Fin. Chron.,* December 14, 1872.
136. Hibbard, *Public Land Policies,* 261.
137. W. B. Hazen, "The Great Middle Region of the United States," *Northern American Rev.,* CCXLVI (1875), 1–34.
138. *Scientific American,* June 30, 1866.
139. W. G. Moody, *Land and Labor in the United States* (New York, 1883), 63ff.
140. For the increase of foreign-born in the Northwest, see *U.S. Tenth Census* (1880), I, xl.
141. See *Lincoln Illustrated* (1887); J. S. Morton, Albert Watkins et al., eds., *Illustrated History of Nebraska* (Lincoln, 1905–6).
142. *Am. Ann. Cyclop.,* XIV (1874), 586; XV (1875), 412.
143. *Nation,* XVII, July 31, 1873.
144. *Am. Ann. Cyclop.,* VI (1866), 442.
145. F. L. Paxson, "The Cow Country," *Am. Hist. Rev.,* XXII, 65–86.
146. Emerson Hough, *The Story of the Cowboy* (New York, 1897), 30ff.
147. J. G. McCoy, *Historic Sketches of the Cattle Trade of the West and Southwest* (Kansas City, 1874).
148. R. A. Clemen, *The American Livestock and Meat Industry* (New York, 1923), 192ff.
149. J. S. Gould, "Texas Cattle Disease," *Journ. of Social Sci.,* I, 56–71; J. M. Hunter, ed., *The Trail Drivers of Texas* (2 ed., rev., Nashville, 1925), I, 20ff.
150. Hough, *Story of the Cowboy,* 6ff.; Clemen, *American Livestock and Meat Industry,* 177ff.

151. Bancroft, *Pacific States,* XXVI, 720ff.
152. J. H. Cook, *Fifty Years on the Old Frontier* (New Haven, 1923), 106, gives a vivid firsthand description of a cattle stampede during a thunderstorm at night.
153. P. A. Rollins, *The Cowboy . . . His Part in the Development of the West* (New York, 1922).
154. James McIntyre, *Early Days in Texas* (Kansas City, 1902), 45ff.; Mary J. Jaques, *Texan Ranch Life* (London, 1894).
155. Theodore Roosevelt, *Hunting Trips of a Ranchman* (Sagamore ed., New York, 1886), chap. i.
156. Hough, *Story of the Cowboy,* chap. iii.
157. Ibid., chap. ix.
158. Clark Stanley, *Life and Adventures of the American Cowboy* (Providence, n.d.), 82ff.
159. Rollins, *The Cowboy,* 55.
160. Competition among manufacturers reduced barbed-wire prices by 1874 to twenty cents a pound. H. U. Faulkner, *American Economic History* (New York, 1924), 409.
161. See President Hayes's proclamation, J. D. Richardson, ed., *Messages and Papers of the Presidents* (Washington, 1896–99), VIII, 489.
162. F. R. Bechdolt, *Tales of the Oldtimers* (New York, 1924), 61ff.; C. A. Siringo, *A Texas Cowboy* (Chicago, 1885), chap. xxvii.
163. See R. M. Wright, *Dodge City, the Cowboy Capital* (Wichita, 1913), chap. viii, for a vivid picture of a border town where twenty-five men were killed the first year. Railway corporations and other interests which needed gunmen used to recruit them in Dodge City. Wild cowboys, buffalo hunters, "bullwhackers," and "mule-skinners" (freighters) made the town a hotbed of violence till the decent element chose a city marshal ready to use his buffalo rifle with effect. See G. D. Bradley, *The Story of the Santa Fé* (Boston, 1920), for the towns filled with saloons, brothels, and gambling dens. Notorious outlaws became so well known by nicknames that their real appellations were forgotten—Scarface Ike, Bullwhack Jones, Coach Joe. For the wickedness of Newton, Kansas, see T. A. McNeal, *When Kansas Was Young* (New York, 1922), 37.
164. F. W. Rolt-Wheeler, *The Book of Cowboys* (Boston, 1921), 364; Hunter, *Trail Drivers of Texas,* II, 25.
165. Theodore Roosevelt, *An Autobiography* (New York, 1914), 95.
166. J. A. Lomax, *Cowboy Songs* (New York, 1910).
167. Bancroft, *Pacific States,* XXV, chaps. v-vi.
168. C. H. Shinn, *Story of the Mine as Illustrated by the Great Comstock Lode of Nevada* (New York, 1896), 101–3, 118ff.
169. Adolph Sutro, *The Mineral Resources of the United States . . . with Special Reference to the Comstock Lode and the Sutro Tunnel* (Baltimore, 1868), describes the project. See also Bancroft, *Pacific States,* XX, 141ff.
170. See Mary McV. Mathews, *Ten Years in Nevada* (Buffalo, 1880), for a picture of life in Virginia City.
171. Shinn, *Story of the Mine,* passim.
172. Bancroft, *Pacific States,* XX, chap. x.
173. For the Austin camp, see Samuel Bowles, *Across the Continent* (Springfield, Mass., 1866), 141ff.; for White Pine, Rae, *Westward by Rail,* 203ff.; anon., "Up in the Po-Go-Nip," *Overland Monthly,* II (1869), 273–80; *Am. Ann. Cyclop.,* VIII (1868), 534ff.
174. L. E. Young, *The Founding of Utah* (New York, 1923), chap. xiv.
175. A. D. Richardson, *Beyond the Mississippi* (Hartford, 1867), 338ff.
176. Bowles, *Across the Continent,* 98ff.; Justin McCarthy, "Brigham Young," *Galaxy,* IX (1870), 178–87; Mrs. T. B. H. Stenhouse, *The Rocky Mountain Saints* (London, 1882).

177. M. R. Werner, *Brigham Young* (New York, 1925), 437; Rae, *Westward by Rail,* 110ff.

178. Young, *Founding of Utah,* 435ff. Pages 295-372 deal in detail with cultural institutions.

179. Werner, *Brigham Young,* 418ff. Woodbridge Riley, *The Founder of Mormonism* (New York, 1902), is a psychological portrait of Young.

180. Josiah Royce, *California from the Conquest of 1848 to the Second Vigilance Committee in San Francisco* (*American Commonwealth Series,* Boston, 1886), is an admirable short history of California to the Civil War.

181. For a description of San Francisco in this period see B. E. Lloyd, *Lights and Shades of San Francisco* (San Francisco, 1876).

182. A. B. Paine, *Mark Twain, A Biography,* I, chaps. xlvi-xlvii; H. H. Bancroft, *Retrospection Political and Personal* (New York, 1912), 203ff.

183. *Am. Ann. Cyclop.,* VI (1866), 64; VIII (1868), 86.

184. During the decade 1860-70 a heavy surplus of wheat was produced for export. E. J. Wickson, *Rural California* (New York, 1923), 75.

185. *N.Y. Tribune,* May 4, 1866.

186. Wickson, *Rural California,* 162ff., 282.

187. Rae, *Westward by Rail,* 266ff.

188. *Am. Ann. Cyclop.,* XIII (1873), 82.

189. Wickson, *Rural California,* 304ff.

190. J. S. Hittell, *Resources of California* (San Francisco, 1863), is full upon this subject. See also Bancroft, *Pacific States,* XIX, 70.

191. G. F. Seward, *Chinese Immigration in Its Social and Economical Aspects* (New York, 1881), 10ff.; Richardson, *Beyond the Mississippi,* 389.

192. *Senate Rep.,* 49 Cong., 2 sess., no. 689.

193. George McNeill et al., *Labor Movement in America* (Boston, 1887), 454.

194. Mary R. Coolidge, *Chinese Immigration* (New York, 1909), 80.

195. Charles Nordhoff, *Northern California, Oregon, and the Sandwich Islands* (London, 1874), chap. v.

196. For the paucity of women in the Far Northwest see *Harper's Weekly,* X, January 6, 1866.

197. For economic development, see Joseph Schafer, *A History of the Pacific Northwest* (New York, 1905), chaps. xviii, xix; E. S. Meany, *History of the State of Washington* (New York, 1909), chap. xxviii.

198. U. S. Commissioner of Agriculture, *Report for 1870,* 308; *Am. Ann. Cyclop.,* X (1870), 710ff.; Meline, *Two Thousand Miles on Horseback,* chap. xvii.

199. "Who knows how to be rich in America?" demanded Godkin. "Plenty of people know how to get money; but not very many know what best to do with it. To be rich properly is indeed a fine art. It requires culture, imagination, and character." *Nation, II,* March 8, 1866.

200. Described in E. P. Oberholtzer, *Jay Cooke* (Philadelpia, 1907), II, 33, 447. *Sloan's Homestead Architecture* (Philadelphia, 1866), an architectural guide compiled by Samuel Sloan, highly recommended architectural monstrosities of the kind described in the text; its popularity is evidenced by the fact that it was already in its second edition in 1867.

201. *Art Journal,* III (1877), 260ff.

202. *Art Journal,* II (1876), 45, 247.

203. *N. Y. Times,* March 6, 1876. The *Times* noted a growing protest against mansard roofs, a new interest in simplicity, and an increasing taste for Oriental rugs. See also *Appleton's Annual Cyclopedia* (New York, 1861-1903), XV (1876), 262ff.

204. Towle, *American Society,* I, chap. xviii.

205. M. F. Egan, *Recollections of a Happy Life* (New York, 1924), 66-67.

206. *Nation,* XII, March 2, 1871.

207. Helen Nicolay, *Our Capital on the Potomac* (New York, 1924), 403-404.

208. S. L. Clemens (Mark Twain, pseud.), *Life on the Mississippi* (Hartford, 1883), 295–99.

209. For an excellent picture of a well-to-do Indiana home in the seventies, see the first pages of Booth Tarkington's *The Magnificent Ambersons* (New York, 1922).

210. Henry Holt, *The Garrulities of an Octogenarian Editor* (Boston, 1923), 125, 170.

211. Allan Nevins, *The Evening Post* (New York, 1922), 368–69.

212. *N.Y. World,* December 18, 1875; January 24, 1876.

213. See the files of *Godey's* and *Demorest's,* 1865–66.

214. *Valentine's Manual of Old New York* (new ser., New York, 1923), 4ff.

215. G. C. Eggleston, *A Rebel's Recollections* (New York, 1875), 177.

216. Towle, *American Society,* I, chap. xviii.

217. C. D. Wright, *Industrial Evolution of the United States* (New York, 1901), chap. xiv.

218. But for the more convivial, artistic, and literary circle of New York, see Egan, *Recollections,* 107ff.

219. Frederick Merk, *Economic History of Wisconsin during the Civil War Decade* (State Hist. Soc. of Wis., *Studies,* I, 1916), 152ff.

220. Sala, *America Revisited,* II, 58ff.

221. Egan, *Recollections,* 65.

222. J. H. Ward, "The New Sunday," *Atlantic Monthly,* XLVII (1881), 526–37.

223. James Huneker, *Steeplejack* (New York, 1920), I, 92.

224. Clara Barrus, *The Life and Letters of John Burroughs* (Boston, 1925), I, 133, 182. The *Atlantic* would have nothing to do with Whitman, and *Scribner's* returned his poems with insulting notes.

225. C. L. Brace, *Gesta Christi* (New York, 1888), 307ff. Cf. Don C. Seitz, *The Dreadful Decade* (Indianapolis, 1926), 213ff.

226. *Nation,* VII, December 3, 1868, 453.

227. Towle, quoted by A. W. Calhoun, *Social History of the American Family* (Cleveland, 1917), III, 183.

228. Campbell, *White and Black,* 283.

229. *Nation,* VI, March 5, 1868.

230. U.S. Commissioner of Labor, *Rep. on Marriage and Divorce in the United States, 1867–1886* (Washington, 1889).

231. See Jennie L. Wilson, *The Legal and Political Status of Women in the United States* (Cedar Rapids, Iowa, 1912).

232. W. D. Howells, *A Modern Instance* (Boston, 1881), chap. xxxi, passim.

233. *N.Y. Eve. Post,* July 12, 1865.

234. Hamlin Garland, *Ulysses S. Grant, His Life and Character* (New York, 1898), 398. Ocean Grove and Asbury Park were founded soon after the war, primarily for Methodist visitors.

235. *N.Y. Times,* editorial, October 7, 1876.

236. E. King, "The Great South," *Scribner's Monthly,* IX (1874), 1–31.

237. *Nation,* XVII, August 7, 1873.

238. *N.Y. Eve. Post,* August 31, September 8, 18, 1865.

239. Towle, *American Society,* I, chap. xix, gives a good description of a fashionable evening party in New York.

240. *N.Y. Eve. Post,* May 7, 1867.

241. See A. G. Spalding, *America's National Game* (New York, 1911), chap. viii.

242. F. L. Paxson, "The Rise of Sport," *Miss. Valley Hist. Rev.,* IX, 143–68.

243. The first college league for baseball was formed in 1879. See R. H. Barbour, *The Book of School and College Sports* (R. D. Paine et al., eds., New York, 1904).

244. *N.Y. Eve. Post,* July 1, 1865, describes it extent.

245. Walter Camp and L. F. Deland, *Football* (Boston, 1896); A. A. Stagg, "Touchdown," *Sat. Eve. Post,* September 18, 1926.

246. Paxson, "The Rise of Sport," 143–68.

247. R. F. Coffin, "The History of American Yachting," in F. S. Cozzens, ed., *Yachts and Yachting* (n.p., 1887). 11–100.
248. *Nation,* III, August 9, 1866.
249. *Scientific American,* January 9, 1869.
250. Towle, *American Society,* II, 30ff.
251. See P. T. Barnum, *Struggles and Triumphs: or Forty Years Recollections of P. T. Barnum, Written by Himself* (Buffalo, 1882), for a remarkable self-revelation.
252. M. R. Werner, *Barnum* (New York, 1923), 309–11.
253. Egan, *Recollections,* 68.
254. *Nation,* VI, January 30, 1868.
255. See J. R. Lowell on Europe and America in his *Letters* (C. E. Norton, ed., New York, 1893), II, 112–13.
256. See *Nation,* XIX, October 22, 1874, on frontier and other influences.
257. See *Nation,* XX, May 20, 1875, for the rapid spread of advertising.
258. See *Nation,* XX, February 4, 1875, on the Beecher trial; and XXII, June 29, 1876, on Blaine.
259. James Bryce, *The American Commonwealth* (London, 1888), III, chaps. xcv, cvii, cviii.
260. See A. D. White, *Autobiography* (New York, 1905), I, 266–87.
261. W. P. Trent et al., eds., *Cambridge History of American Literature* (New York, 1917), III, chaps. xi–xiii.
262. Paine, *Mark Twain; a Biography,* I, chap. lxxxi.
263. Rebecca Harding Davis, *Bits of Gossip* (Boston, 1904), 47ff.
264. Hamlin Garland, *A Son of the Middle Border* (New York, 1917), 273.
265. John Forster, *Life of Charles Dickens* (London, 1872–74), bk. x. See *Nation,* XVII, March 12, 1874.
266. *Nation,* IV, May 16, 1867; *Am. Ann. Cyclop.,* VII (1867), 430ff.
267. J. H. Harper, *The House of Harper* (New York, 1912), 114, 393, 446.
268. Holt, *Garrulities of an Octogenarian Editor,* 46.
269. C. F. Adams, Jr., *An Autobiography* (Boston, 1916), 179.
270. *Nation,* II, June 15, 1866.
271. J. S. Bassett, *The Middle Group of American Historians* (New York, 1917), 314.
272. See this volume, Book VI, 517.
273. *Nation,* XIX, July 2, 1874. The really excellent juvenile stories of Louisa M. Alcott and J. T. Trowbridge should be mentioned on the credit side of the ledger.
274. *Nation,* XIV, May 23, 1872.
275. *Publishers' Weekly,* May 20, 1876.
276. *Nation,* XXVIII, March 5, 1879.
277. *Am. Ann. Cyclop.,* XIII (1873), 523.
278. N.Y. Public Library, *The Beadle Collection of Dime Novels* (New York, 1922), 3–17.
279. See Washington Gladden, *Recollections* (Boston, 1909), 182ff., for the *Independent.*
280. *Am. Ann. Cyclop.,* VIII (1868), 408ff.; Paine, *Mark Twain,* I, lxxxiv.
281. J. R. Howard, *Remembrance of Things Past* (New York, 1925), 215–41.
282. See J. B. Pond, *Eccentricities of Genius* (New York, 1900), for Redpath and his work; *Nation,* VIII, April 8, 1869.
283. A. B. Paine, *Life of Th. Nast* (New York, 1904), 367. See Charles Francis Horner, *Life of James Redpath and the Development of the Modern Lyceum* (New York, 1926).
284. Pond, *Eccentricities of Genius,* 533ff.
285. J. L. Hurlbut, *The Story of Chautauqua* (New York, 1921), chaps. iv–vi.
286. D. C. Seitz, *Life of Joseph Pulitzer* (New York, 1924); J. H. Wilson, *Life of Charles A. Dana* (New York, 1907); Cortissoz, *Life of Whitelaw Reid;* Henry Watterson, *"Marse Henry," an Autobiography* (New York, 1919).

287. Wilson, *Life of Charles A. Dana,* 381.

288. It should be noted that several newspapers—the *N.Y. Evening Post, Springfield Republican,* and others—showed striking political independence in 1872 and afterwards. See Allan Nevins, *The Evening Post: a Century of Journalism* (New York, 1922), chap. xvii; Richard Hooker, *The Story of an Independent Newspaper* (New York, 1924), chap. xvi.

289. A. R. Spofford, "Public Libraries of the United States," *Journ. of Social Sci.,* II, 92–114.

290. U.S. Commissioner of Education, *Report 1899–1900,* I, xxxi.

291. Algernon Tassin, *The Magazine in America* (New York, 1916). For the *Overland Monthly* see Rae, *Westward by Rail,* 320ff.

292. Horace Scudder, *James Russell Lowell* (Boston, 1901), II, 361.

293. W. D. Howells, *Literary Friends and Acquaintances* (New York, 1911), 70.

294. Clara Barrus, *Life and Letters of John Burroughs* (Boston, 1925), I, 139ff.

295. Gustav Pollak, *Fifty Years of American Idealism* (Boston, 1915), 5ff.; W. P. Garrison, *Letters and Memorials* (Boston, 1908), 142ff.

296. Brander Matthews, *These Many Years* (New York, 1917), 170ff.

297. See Rollo Ogden, ed., *E. L. Godkin, Life and Letters* (New York, 1907), II, 66–67. "You always say what I would have said—if I had only thought of it." J. R. Lowell, *Letters* (C. E. Norton, ed., N. Y., 1893), II, 76. W. P. Garrison as literary editor was an invaluable aid to Godkin and a force of original power.

298. M. J. Moses, *The American Dramatist* (Boston, 1911), 52.

299. C. F. Thwing, "President Eliot's Administration," *Harvard Grad. Mag.,* XVII (1909), 376.

300. H. E. Starr, *William Graham Sumner* (New York, 1925), 80.

301. J. F. A. Pyre, *Wisconsin* (New York, 1920), 159ff. In comparison with the total population, the number of American college students was yet very small; in 1873 it was (exclusive of professional schools) only 23,000.

302. H. C. Lodge, *Early Memories* (New York, 1913), 186–87.

303. Matthews, *These Many Years,* 101ff.; G. S. Hall, *Life and Confessions of a Psychologist* (New York, 1923), 158ff.

304. This was Charles Murray Nairne. See F. P. Keppel, *Columbia* (New York, 1914), 146.

305. Keppel, *Columbia,* 118–20.

306. See J. M. Taylor, *Before Vassar Opened* (Boston, 1914).

307. Starr, *Sumner,* 161.

308. J. H. Gardiner, *Harvard* (New York, 1914), 50.

309. M. A. De W. Howe, *Letters of Charles Eliot Nortion* (Boston, 1913), II, 3ff.

310. See Hall, *Life and Confessions of a Psychologist,* 183.

311. Fabian Franklin, *The Life of Daniel Coit Gilman* (New York, 1910), 182ff.; D. C. Gilman, *The Launching of a University* (New York, 1906), passim. See the *Nation,* XX, January 28, 1875, for penetrating comment on Gilman's plans.

312. Allan Nevins, *Illinois* (New York, 1917), 30.

313. For a study of the founder, see A. B. Cornell, *True and Firm: A Biography of Ezra Cornell* (New York, 1884).

314. A. D. White tells the story of Cornell's early years with great literary charm in his *Autobiography,* I, 330–427.

315. See the answer to this volume: Anna C. Brackett et al., *The Education of American Girls* (New York, 1874).

316. B. J. Lossing, *Vassar College and Its Founder* (New York, 1867), 20ff.; J. M. Taylor and Elizabeth H. Haight, *Vassar* (New York, 1915), 61–84.

317. L. C. Seelye, *Early History of Smith College* (Boston, 1923), chaps. i–ii.

318. Florence Morse Kingsley, *The Life of Henry Durant* (New York, 1924), 235ff.

319. Horace White, "The Financial Crisis in America," *Fortnightly Rev.,* XXV (1876), 820.

320. D. A. Wells, *Recent Economic Changes* (New York, 1889), chap. 1.
321. Special Commissioner of Revenue, *Report for 1869; Am. Ann. Cyclop.*, IX (1869), 260.
322. *Com. and Fin. Chron.*, January 24, 1873.
323. *Com. and Fin. Chron.*, October 14, 1872; January 4, 1973.
324. *Com. and Fin. Chron.*, September 7, 21, 1872. The *N.Y. Times,* September 16, 1873, editorially denounced the wildcat railway investing.
325. *Com. and Fin. Chron.*, July 15, 1876.
326. Oberholtzer, *Jay Cooke*, II, 400.
327. *Com. and Fin. Chron.*, April 11, 1873.
328. *N.Y. Tribune,* September 9, 10, 14, 15, 1873; *N.Y. Herald,* September 14, 1873.
329. Oberholtzer, *Jay Cooke*, 422ff.
330. *N.Y. Tribune,* September 19, 1873; *N.Y. Eve. Post,* September 18-20, 1873.
331. Oberholtzer, *Jay Cooke*, II, 424.
332. Horace White, "The Financial Crisis in America," *Fortnightly Rev.*, XXV (1876), 810ff.
333. *N.Y. Tribune,* September 19, 20, 22, 1873.
334. A. D. Noyes, *Thirty Years of American Finance* (New York, 1909), 18; Dewey, *Financial History,* 372.
335. Oberholtzer, *Jay Cooke,* II, 437.
336. The failures in these years may be summarized as follows: 1871—2,915 concerns for $85,252,000; 1872—4,069 for $121,056,000; 1873—5,183 for $228,499,000. *Com. and Fin. Chron.*, January 24, 1874.
337. White, "Financial Crisis in America," *Fortnightly Rev.*, XXV, 810ff.
338. *Nation,* XXI, July 1, 1875.
339. *Com. and Fin. Chron.* August 7, 1875.
340. Edith A. Abbott, *Wages of Unskilled Labor in the United States* (Chicago, 1905), 363. See also F. W. Smith, *The Hard Times* (Boston, 1877).
341. C. D. Wright, "Comparative Wages, Prices and Cost of Living," Massachusetts Bureau of Labor, *Sixteenth Ann. Rep. for 1885.*
342. Moody, *Land and Labor,* chap. xii. Statistics of pauperism may be found in the *U.S. Tenth Census* (1880), XXI, xix.
343. See *Nation,* XXVI, January 24, 1878, on "the tramp evil."
344. Aldrich Committee, *Senate Report,* 52 Cong., 2 sess., III, pt. i.
345. See "Report on the Necessities of Life," *U.S. Tenth Census* (1880), XX. However, large swings in pig-iron prices are not rare.
346. *Com. and Fin. Chron.*, January 15, 1876.
347. *Com. and Fin. Chron.*, January 5, 19, 1878.
348. Horace White, "The Tariff Question," *Journ. of Social Science,* IX (1878), 117-31.
349. Moody, *Land and Labor,* 191.
350. Am. Iron and Steel Assoc., *Report for July, 1878.*
351. *N.Y. World, N.Y. Herald, N.Y. Tribune,* May 11-12, 1876.
352. *Appletons' Ann. Cyclop.*, VI (1876), 262ff., has a comprehensive description of the Exhibition. See also *Report* of the Exhibition and numerous handbooks and guides.
353. *Nation,* XXII, May 11, 1876.
354. *Nation,* XXII, May 1, 1876.
355. *Senate Exec. Docs.*, 48 Cong., 3 sess., no. 74.
356. *Appletons' Ann. Cyclop.* VI (1876), 272.
357. J. R. Lowell, "The World's Fair, 1876," *Nation,* XXI, August 5, 1875. See the *N.Y. Tribune*'s editorial of May 8 on the ironic reminders of the Centennial, also the *Nation*'s editorial, XXII, January 27, 1876.
358. *N.Y. Herald,* October 22, November 24, 1876.
359. See *N.Y. World*'s summary of press opinions, February 26, 1876.

360. *N.Y. Tribune*, June 6, 1876.
361. See the *N.Y. Tribune*'s caustic arraignment, May 12, 1876, and also the *N.Y. Herald*, May 8, 1876.
362. T.P. Cook, *Life and Public Services of Hon. S. J. Tilden* (New York, 1876), 189; *N.Y. Tribune*, May 8, 1876.
363. *N.Y. Tribune*, May 16, 1876.
364. For the condemnatory report of a congressional investigating committee on Shepherd's grandoise $18 million scheme, see *Senate Rep.*, 49 Cong., 1 sess., no 453.
365. *N.Y. Tribune*, January 4, 1876; S. P. Orth, *The Boss and the Machine* (Allen Johnson, ed., *Chronicles of America Series*, New Haven, 1918-21, XLIII), chap. vi.
366. For the fall of Beecher in public esteem, see the *Nation*, XVIII, June 3, 1874; XXI, July 8, 1875.
367. This condemnation extended to the business corruption of the period; and the reckless financial methods of the Lackawanna, the Delaware & Hudson, the New Jersey Central, and the Lehigh railroads, which invested greedily in anthracite lands and attempted to establish a monopoly, were bitterly excoriated. See *N.Y. Tribune*, September 8, 14, 1876.
368. Goldwin Smith, *The Moral Crusader: William Lloyd Garrison* (New York, 1892), 176.
369. *N.Y. Eve. Post*, August 31, 1865.
370. See Jacob Riis, *How the Other Half Lives* (New York, 1890), chaps. i-iv; also N.Y. Metropolitan Bd. of Health, *First Ann. Rep.* (1871).
371. Boston Bd. of Health, *Report for 1873*.
372. F. W. Draper, "The Homes of the Poor in Our Cities," Mass. State Bd. of Health, *Fourth Ann. Rep. for 1872* (*Mass. Pub. Docs.*, IV, no. 31), 396-441.
373. N.Y. Metropolitan Bd. of Health, *Report for 1869*.
374. Philadelphia Bd. of Health, *Reports for 1868* and *1869*.
375. The Philadelphia Bd. of Health complained of malodorous half-open sewers. See *Report for 1870*.
376. N.Y. Metropolitan and Philadelphia Bds. of Health, *Reports for 1866-1872*.
377. One half of New York City's population furnished three fourths of the total sickness and mortality. See N.Y. Metropolitan Bd. of Health, *Report for 1871;* also *N.Y. Eve. Post*, August 31, 1865.
378. Elisha Harris, "Health Laws and their Administration," *Journ. of Social Science*, II (1870), 176-87.
379. *U.S. Tenth Census* (1880), XVIII, 571.
380. G. C. Whipple, *State Sanitation* (Cambridge, Mass., 1917), I, 39ff. The other state health boards established were those of Louisiana (1867), California (1870), Virginia (1872), Minnesota (1872), Michigan (1874), Maryland (1874), Alabama (1875), Georgia (1875), Colorado, (1876), Wisconsin (1876), Mississippi (1877), New Jersey (1877), Tennessee (1877), Illinois (1877). N. S. Shaler, ed., *The United States of America* (New York, 1894), III, 1227-28.
381. Boston Bd. of Health, *Report for 1878*.
382. *U.S. Tenth Census* (1880), XXIX, 276.
383. *N.Y. Eve. Post,* July 13, 1865.
384. *Nation*, IV, February 21, 1867.
385. Commons et al., *History of Labour in the United States*, II, 133.
386. R. T. Ely, *Labor Movement in America* (rev. ed., New York, 1905), 82.
387. *Appletons' Ann. Cyclop.*, XVI (1876), 735.
388. G. B. Bartlett, "The Recreation of the People," *Journ. of Social Science*, XII (1880), 141.
389. Philadelphia reported the largest number, 517; New Orleans reported 365. Baltimore roughly estimated hers at 300; Chicago hers at 200, and New York menda-

ciously declared there were only 183 within her precincts. *U.S. Tenth Census* (1880), XXI, liv ff.

390. *Nation,* IV, February 21, 1867. Professional abortionists flourished in many cities; their advertisements were common in the press; one, Mme. Restelle, was notorious in New York City. She was actively prosecuted by Anthony Comstock, then starting his career.

391. N.Y. Bd. of State Charities, *Report for 1867.*

392. "Simply brutal," was the phrase used by the Ohio board. Ohio Bd. of State Charities, *Report for 1867,* 12.

393. F. B. Sanborn, "Poverty and Public Charity," *North Am. Rev.,* CX (1870), 347ff.

394. Ill. Bd. of State Charities, *Report for 1870;* A. G. Warner, *American Charities* (3d ed., New York, 1919), 435ff., for state work.

395. *Nation,* V, August 22, 1867.

396. E. C. Wines and T. W. Dwight, *Report on the Prisons and Reformatories of the United States and Canada*—made to the New York legislature, January 1867.

397. Campbell, *White and Black,* 384.

398. *Appletons' Ann. Cyclop.,* XIX (1879), 600.

399. Tenn. State Bd. of Health, *Report for 1878.* See *Appleton's Ann. Cyclop.,* XIX (1879), 539, for equally shocking data upon Kentucky prisons.

400. F. H. Wines, *Punishment and Reformation* (rev. ed., New York, 1919), chap. x.

401. The *Proceedings* of this body are a valuable source of information.

402. S. H. Coleman, *Humane Society Leaders in America* (Albany, 1924), chap. iii.

403. On the heavy postwar drinking in the South, see Somers, *Southern States,* 245.

404. See *Appletons' Ann. Cyclop.,* XIX (1879), 579, for a long historical article on prohibition in Maine. For Massachusetts, see *Am. Ann. Cyclop.,* VII (1867), 480; *Nation,* VIII, April 1, 1869. See *Nation,* XIII, April 4, 1872, for comment on the situation in the Middle West.

405. E. H. Cherrington, *Evolution of Prohibition in the United States* (Westerville, Ohio, 1920), chap. vi.

406. *Nation,* XVIII, March 19, 1874; A. M. Schlesinger, *New Viewpoints in American History* (New York, 1922), 151–52.

407. Ida M. Harper, *Life and Work of Susan B. Anthony* (Indianapolis, 1898–1908), I, chap. xv; Schlesinger, *New Viewpoints,* 146–48.

408. Harper, *Susan B. Anthony,* I, chap. xvii.

409. Ibid., I, chap. xviii.

410. "His support was of course invaluable," said the *Nation,* XVII, May 17, 1874.

411. Elizabeth Cady Stanton, Susan B. Anthony, et al., *History of Woman Suffrage* (New York, 1882–1922), II, chap. xxvi. There was a sharp difference in the temper of the two associations, the National being decidedly the more radical. See M. A. De Wolfe Howe, *Causes and Their Champions* (Boston, 1926), 194ff.

412. *Nation,* VII, November 26, 1868.

413. *U.S. Twelfth Census* (1900), volume on *Occupations,* xlix ff.

414. *Appletons' Ann. Cyclop.,* XIX (1879), 2ff.

415. See tables in the *Nation,* XIV (1872), 198ff.

416. For the struggle in Arkansas preceding the Democratic victory, see J. M. Harrell, *The Brooks and Baxter War* (St. Louis, 1893); Powell Clayton, *The Aftermath of the Civil War in Arkansas* (New York, 1915).

417. Garner, *Reconstruction in Mississippi,* 196–200.

418. P. L. Haworth, *The Hayes-Tilden Disputed Presidential Election* (Cleveland, 1906), 92ff., treats both state contests in detail.

419. See *Com. and Fin. Chron.,* September 13, 1879, for summary.

420. U.S. Commissioner of Agriculture, *Report for 1874,* 215ff.

421. *Compendium, U.S. Tenth Census* (1880), 333.

422. A South Carolinian (pseud.), "South Carolina Society," *Atlantic Monthly,* XXXIX (1877), 682.

423. A. W. Calhoun, *A Social History of the American Family* (Cleveland, 1917), III, 11ff.

424. J. L. Underwood, *Women of the Confederacy* (New York, 1906), 65; see also W. F. Tillett, "Southern Womanhood as Affected by the War," *Century Mag.,* XLIII (1891–92), 9–16.

425. E. W. Knight, *The Influence of Reconstruction on Education in the South* (Teachers College, Columbia Univ., *Contribs. to Education,* no. 60), 88ff.

426. Finlay Dun, *American Farming and Foods* (London, 1881), 421ff.; *Appletons' Ann. Cyclop.,* XIX (1879), 165.

427. Deseret News Steam Printing Establishment, *Death of President Young* (Salt Lake City, 1877).

428. Young, *Founding of Utah,* chap. xl.

429. Bancroft, *Pacific States,* XXI, 750ff.

430. *U.S. Tenth Census* (1880), volume on *Population,* xix–xx.

431. Charles Nordhoff, *California for Health, Pleasure, and Residence* (New York, 1883), chap. xiv.

432. J. S. Hittell, *Resources of California* (San Francisco, 7th ed., 1879), chap. viii.

433. W. M. Raine, *Wyoming, A Story of the Outdoor West* (New York, 1908), 163ff.

434. For Colorado's varied development, see Secretary of the Interior, *Report for 1875,* 122ff.

435. For the unemployment figures in Massachusetts from 1875 to 1878, see Moody, *Land and Labor,* 160.

436. G. E. McNeill, ed., *Labor Movement* (Boston, 1887), 398.

437. Mary R. Beard, *A Short History of the American Labor Movement* (New York, 1920), 81.

438. T. V. Powderly, *Thirty Years of Labor* (Columbus, Ohio, 1890), 134.

439. J. D. McCabe (pseud. E. W. Martin), *History of the Great Riots, together with a Full History of the Molly Maguires* (Philadelphia, 1877); F. W. Dewees, *The Molly Maguires* (Philadelphia, 1877), 160ff.; J. F. Rhodes, *A History of the United States* (New York, 1893–1919), VIII, 52–87; Allan Pinkerton, *The Molly Maguires and the Detectives* (New York, 1878), 522.

440. Pennsylvania Secretary of Internal Affairs, *Annual Report for 1876–1877,* pt iii; R. P. Porter, "The Truth about the Strike," *Galaxy,* XXIV (1877), 725; Andrew Roy, *History of the Coal Miners of the United States* (Columbus, Ohio, 1907), 99; Arthur Suffern, *Conciliation and Arbitration in the Coal Industry* (Boston, 1915), 213.

441. *N.Y. Herald,* January 19, 1876; McNeill, *Labor Movement,* 221ff. French-Canadian immigrants began coming in to take the place of the strikers.

442. For his proclamation, see Richardson, *Messages and Papers of the Presidents,* VII, 447.

443. Adjutant-General of Maryland, *Report for 1877.*

444. Secretary of War, *Report for 1877;* J. A. Dacus, "The Great Strike," *Harper's Weekly,* (August 11, 1877).

445. Rhodes, *History of the United States,* VIII, 23.

446. Pennsylvania Legislative Committee on the Pittsburgh Riots, *Report for 1878,* I, 79, 176ff., 485; *N.Y. Tribune* and *N.Y. Herald,* July 23–25, 1877.

447. *Iowa City Daily Press,* July 30, 1877.

448. A. R. Leeds, "State Geological Surveys," *Pop. Sci. Mo.,* XIV (1873), 226–29; C. F. Chandler, "Report on the Quality of the Kerosene Oil Sold in the Metropolitan District," N.Y. City Bd. of Health, *Annual Report for 1870,* 3ff.

449. J. G. Pyle, *Life of James J. Hill* (Garden City, N.Y., 1917), I, 63ff.; Henry Villard, *Memoirs* (Boston, 1904), II, 131ff.; *Com. and Fin. Chron.,* January 10, 1880.

BOOK IX   The Nationalizing of Business, 1878–98

1. Bureau of the Census, *Abstract of the Twelfth Census* (1900), 32.
2. Message of December 9, 1885, J. D. Richardson, comp., *A Compilation of the Messages and Papers of the Presidents* (Washington, 1896–99), VIII, 359.
3. This volume, Book X, 873.
4. *Appletons' Annual Cyclopaedia,* n.s., IV (1879), 641–42.
5. M. F. Bernard in *Journal des Économistes,* quoted by D. A. Wells, *Recent Economic Changes* (New York, 1889), 176.
6. Richmond Mayo-Smith, *Emigration and Immigration* (New York, 1890), 46, 186. See also this volume, Book X, 873, and J. B. Hedges, *Henry Villard and the Railways of the Northwest* (New Haven, 1930), chap. vi.
7. Mayo-Smith, *Emigration and Immigration,* 28, 51.
8. Andrew Carnegie, *Triumphant Democracy* (New York, 1886), 34–35.
9. H. P. Fairchild, *Immigration* (New York, 1913), chap. vii.
10. Ibid., chap. vi; R. L. Garis, *Immigration Restriction* (New York, 1927), 87–102.
11. Richardson, *Messages and Papers,* IX, 757–61.
12. James Bryce, *The American Commonwealth* (London, 1888), II, 386, 394; Mary R. Coolidge, *Chinese Immigration* (New York, 1909), chap. viii.
13. E. P. Oberholtzer, *A History of the United States since the Civil War* (New York, 1917), IV, 283–88.
14. W. M. Malloy, comp., *Treaties, Conventions, International Pacts . . . between the United States of America and Other Powers* (Washington, 1910), I, 237–39.
15. Oberholtzer, *History of United States,* IV, 298–305.
16. *U.S. Statutes at Large,* XXXII, pt. i, 176.
17. Pick Overturf's opinion of the Red River Valley. Ramsey Benson, *Hill Country* (New York, 1928), 3.
18. W. Z. Ripley, ed., *Railway Problems* (Boston, 1907), 417; L. H. Haney, *A Congressional History of Railways in the United States, 1850-1887* (Univ. of Wis., *Bull.,* no. 342), chap. ix.
19. Thomas Donaldson, comp., *The Public Domain* (Washington, 1884), 415.
20. J. W. Powell, *Report on the Lands of the Arid Region of the United States* (2d ed., Washington, 1879).
21. F. H. Newell, *Report on Agriculture by Irrigation in the Western Part of the United States, at the Eleventh Census: 1890* (Washington, 1894), 91.
22. Ibid., 12.
23. F. L. Paxson, *History of the American Frontier* (Boston, 1924), chap. lviii.
24. Bureau of the Census, *Abstract of the Twelfth Census* (1900), 217.
25. Professional and personal services accounted for 4,074,238; trade and transportation for 1,810,256; and manufacturing, mechanical, and mining industries for 3,837,112. *U.S. Compendium of Tenth Census* (1880), pt. ii, 1343.
26. The exact amount was $2,213,402,564. *U.S. Compendium of Tenth Census,* pt. i, 685.
27. W. W. Folwell, *A History of Minnesota* (St. Paul, 1921–30), III, 68–69.
28. *Appletons' Annual Cyclopaedia,* n.s., VI (1881), 350.
29. U.S. Industrial Commission. *Report* (Washington, 1900–1902), I, 114.
30. *Appletons' Annual Cyclopaedia,* n.s., V (1880), 126.
31. *U.S. Compendium of Tenth Census,* pt. ii, 926–27.
32. Horace Bushnell, "Work and Play," C. D. Warner, ed., *Library of the World's Best Literature* (New York, 1896–98), V, 2921.
33. J. D. Hicks, *The Populist Revolt* (Minneapolis, 1931), 55–60.
34. Editorial digest of the report on farm mortgages made by the Eleventh Census, *N.Y. Evening Post,* September 6, 1893.
35. S. J. Buck, *The Granger Movement (Harvard Hist. Studies,* XIX), 302–4.
36. N. B. Ashby, *The Riddle of the Sphinx* (Des Moines, 1890), 439–40.

37. Ibid., 441–42.
38. Hicks, *Populist Revolt,* 98–104.
39. Ashby, *Riddle of the Sphinx,* 407–8.
40. Edward Wiest, *Agricultural Organization in the United States* (Univ. of Kentucky, *Studies,* II), 464.
41. Ibid., 465.
42. Ibid., 466–467; Hicks, *Populist Revolt,* 134–37.
43. W. S. Morgan, *History of the Wheel and Alliance, and the Impending Revolution* (St. Louis, 1891), 97, 204, 246.
44. Hicks, *Populist Revolt,* 137–40.
45. Ibid., 30–31.
46. Ibid., 113–27.
47. *Chicago, Milwaukee and St. Paul Railway Co.* v. *Minnesota,* 134, *U.S. Reports,* 418.
48. F. M. Drew, "The Present Farmers' Movement," *Polit. Sci. Quar.,* VI, 300.
49. The so-called Ocala demands, adopted in December 1890. Hicks, *Populist Revolt,* 430–31.
50. See table in Drew, "Present Farmers' Movement," 295.
51. F. E. Haynes, *Third Party Movements since the Civil War* (Iowa City, 1916), 246–47.
52. F. E. Haynes, *James Baird Weaver* (Iowa City, 1919), chaps. vi–xiv.
53. Edward Stanwood, *A History of the Presidency from 1788 to 1897* (Boston, 1898), 509–13.
54. Ibid., 494–504.
55. Haynes, *James Baird Weaver,* 335–38.
56. Haynes, *Third Party Movements,* 270.
57. J. R. Commons et al., *History of Labour in the United States* (New York, 1918), II, 245n.
58. G. E. McNeill, ed., *The Labor Movement: the Problem of To-day* (Boston, 1887), chap. xix; Independent Order of the Knights of Labor, *Constitution of the General Assembly Adopted at Columbus, Ohio, February 14, 1895* (n.p., n.d.), 3–6.
59. Leo Wolman, *The Growth of American Trade Unions, 1880–1923* (Natl. Bur. of Econ. Research, *Publs.,* no. 6), 32.
60. McNeill, *Labor Movement,* 411.
61. E. W. Bemis, *Co-operation in the Middle States* (Johns Hopkins Univ., *Studies,* VI), 162.
62. Commons et al., *History of Labour,* II, 433.
63. Ibid., II, 437–38.
64. See 873.
65. U.S. Immigration Commission, *Reports* (Washington, 1911), XXXIX, 29–50.
66. Commons et al., *History of Labour,* II, 381.
67. The figure for 1885 does not include 41 anti-Chinese boycotts on the Pacific Coast. Nearly all the boycotts began with, or were taken up by, the Knights of Labor. Commons et al., *History of Labour,* II, 365–66.
68. U.S. Commissioner of Labor, *Third Annual Report* (1887), 30–33.
69. Selig Perlman, *A History of Trade Unionism in the United States* (New York, 1922), 86–87.
70. Commons et al., *History of Labour,* II, 383–84.
71. *St. Louis Republican,* March 11, 1886.
72. F. W. Taussig, "The South-Western Strike of 1886," *Quar. Journ. of Economics,* I, 184–222.
73. L. L. Lorwin, *The American Federation of Labor* (Brookings Inst., *Publs.,* no. 50), 16–19, 113–14.
74. Samuel Gompers, *Seventy Years of Life and Labor* (New York, 1925), I, 225.
75. Commons et al., *History of Labour,* II, 376–77.

76. Illinois Bureau of Labor Statistics, *Fourth Biennial Report* (1886), 466.
77. D. A. Wells, *Recent Economic Changes* (New York, 1889), 415.
78. Gompers, *Seventy Years of Life and Labor,* I, 291.
79. Of writers on economics, George Gunton, *Wealth and Progress* (New York, 1887), chaps. iii–iv, supported this contention; Wells, *Recent Economic Changes,* 439–44, argued against it.
80. Gunton, *Wealth and Progress,* 254–56.
81. E. L. Bogart and C. M. Thompson, *The Industrial State, 1870–1893* (C. W. Alvord, ed., *The Centennial History of Illinois,* IV, Springfield, 1920), 163n.
82. Commons et al., *History of Labour,* II, 384–85.
83. Gompers's opinion, U.S. Industrial Commission, *Report* (Washington, 1900–1902), VII, 623.
84. Bogart and Thompson, *Industrial State,* 168. See also the *Arbeiter-Zeitung,* November 28, 1884, quoted by Commons et al., *History of Labour,* II, 389–90.
85. Bogart and Thompson, *Industrial State,* 166. W. T. Hutchinson, *Cyrus Hall McCormick: Harvest, 1856–1884* (New York, 1935), 615–17, sheds light on the family background of the younger McCormick's attitude toward labor.
86. C. E. Russell, *These Shifting Scenes* (New York, 1914), 85.
87. Morris Hillquit, *History of Socialism in the United States* (New York, 1903), 245.
88. Bogart and Thompson, *Industrial State,* 169–70.
89. Hillquit, *History of Socialism,* 246–47.
90. Russell, *Shifting Scenes,* 106.
91. *Chicago Inter Ocean,* May 10, 1886.
92. Russell, *Shifting Scenes,* 88.
93. Rudolph Schnaubelt and William Seliger were also arrested, but Schnaubelt, released by the police for reasons not clear, escaped from the country, and Seliger was granted immunity for turning state's evidence. In the judgment of those observers closest to the affair as well as of later students, Lingg had manufactured the bomb and Schnaubelt threw it. Through the European anarchist press, however, Schnaubelt repeatedly denied any connection with the deed. Bogart and Thompson, *Industrial State,* 172 n.; Hillquit, *History of Socialism,* 247.
94. J. E. Gary, "The Chicago Anarchists of 1886," *Century Mag.,* n.s., XXIII (1892–93), 835.
95. W. D. Howells, *Life in Letters of William Dean Howells* (Mildred Howells, ed., Garden City, 1928), I, 393.
96. Russell, *Shifting Scenes,* 102.
97. Hillquit, *History of Socialism,* 252.
98. W. R. Browne, *Altgeld of Illinois* (New York, 1924), 95–105; J. P. Altgeld, *Reasons for Pardoning Fielden, Neebe and Schwab* (Chicago, 1893).
99. Bogart and Thompson, *Industrial State,* 187n.
100. T. V. Powderly, *Thirty Years of Labor* (Columbus, 1889), 540.
101. Commons et al., *History of Labour,* II, 423.
102. Ibid., II, 482.
103. Lorwin, *American Federation of Labor,* 21–23.
104. Perlman, *History of Trade Unionism,* 131–33.
105. Commons et al., *History of Labour,* II, 410n.; Lorwin, *American Federation of Labor,* 484.
106. R. R. Doane, *The Measurement of American Wealth* (New York, 1933), II.
107. Ibid., 13, 44.
108. W. Z. Ripley, ed., *Trusts, Pools and Corporations* (Boston, 1905), 79.
109. Andrew Carnegie, *Autobiography* (Boston, 1920), 246–47.
110. J. H. Bridge, *The Inside History of the Carnegie Steel Company* (New York, 1903), 206–8.
111. *Appletons' Annual Cyclopaedia,* n.s., XVII (1892), 626–27. Other sources for the Homestead strike are Secretary of Internal Affairs of the Commonwealth of

Pennsylvania, *Annual Report for 1892,* pt. iii; C. D. Wright, *The Industrial Evolution of the United States* (New York, 1897), chap xxv; Bridge, *Inside History of Carnegie Company,* 209-23; and contemporary newspapers.

112. B. J. Hendrick, *The Life of Andrew Carnegie* (Garden City, 1932), I, 410-11. For a somewhat different representation of Carnegie's attitude, with supporting documents, see Bridge, *Inside History of Carnegie Company,* 203-6.

113. For contemporary explanations of the Panic, see Felix Flügel and H. U. Faulkner, eds., *Readings in the Economic and Social History of the United States* (New York, 1929), 710-17.

114. *N.Y. Evening Post,* September 5, 1893.

115. "Retrospect of 1893," *Commercial and Financial Chronicle,* LVIII, 9-19 (January 6, 1894). A general complaint of brokers and investors in railroad securities was that the information furnished the public was so meager that no intelligent appraisal could be made of their value. See a study called *The Anatomy of a Railroad* (New York, 1895), published by Thomas Woodlock of the *Wall Street Journal.* His conclusion as to the Erie was that its fixed charges were too heavy to be earned even in average years.

116. Commons et al., *History of Labour,* 501.

117. Pullman claimed that he built, in 1893, 300 passenger cars each at $300 less than cost. Cattle cars and refrigerator cars were built at a corresponding loss.

118. U.S. Strike Commission, *Report on the Chicago Strike* (53 Cong., 3 sess., *Senate Exec. Doc.,* no. 7), xxxv-xxxvi.

119. "The Pullman Boycott," *Nation,* LIX, 5-6 (July 5, 1894).

120. Browne, *Altgeld of Illinois,* 117-120.

121. *N.Y. World,* July 2, 1894.

122. U.S. Strike Commission, *Report,* xxviii-xxxi.

123. U.S. Strike Commission, *Report,* xxxi.

124. Editorial, *Public Opinion,* XVII, 305 (July 5, 1894).

125. Editorial, *Nation,* LIX, 19 (July 12, 1894).

126. In an official report the Chicago superintendent of police referred to these deputies as, "thugs, thieves and ex-convicts," a characterization amply supported by the testimony of many witnesses before the U.S. Strike Commission.

127. Robert McElroy, *Grover Cleveland* (New York, 1923), II, 150-56.

128. Ibid., II, 146-49.

129. U.S. Strike Commission, *Report,* 143.

130. Henry Vincent, *The Story of the Commonweal* (Chicago, 1894), 49.

131. Ibid., 51-53.

132. Speech at Williamsport, Md., April 18, 1894, quoted in Ibid., 53-54.

133. D. L. McMurry, *Coxey's Army* (Boston, 1929), 113-18.

134. Ibid., 120.

135. Ibid., chaps. viii-ix. Nineteen-year-old Jack London was a member of Kelly's army. He kept a diary of the journey from San Francisco until he left the army at Hannibal, Mo. See J. E. Briggs, ed., "A Jack London Diary," *Palimpsest,* VII (1926), 129-58.

136. McMurry, *Coxey's Army,* 199-205.

137. "The Progress of the World," *Am. Rev. of Revs.,* IX (1894), 650.

138. W. T. Stead, "Coxeyism," *Am. Rev. of Revs.,* X (1894), 52.

139. M. J. Savage, "The Present Conflict for a Larger Life," *Arena,* X (1894), 303.

140. Doane, *Measurement of American Wealth,* 11.

141. John Moody, *The Truth about the Trusts* (New York, 1904), 453-67.

142. President of the Western Union Telegraph Company, *Annual Report for 1898,* 6.

143. *U.S. Twelfth Census* (1900), I, xxii.

144. President of the Western Union Telegraph Company, *Annual Report for 1898,* 6.

145. Bureau of the Census, *Abstract of Twelfth Census,* 320.

146. Ibid., 217.

147. Wolman, *Growth of American Trade Unions,* 32; Commons et al., *History of Labour,* II, 482.
148. Lorwin, *American Federation of Labor,* 484.
149. Perlman, *History of Trade Unionism,* 152-53.
150. U.S. Industrial Commission, *Report,* XIX, 864-70.
151. H. D. Lloyd, *Wealth against Commonwealth* (New York, 1894), 497.
152. C. R. Henderson, *The Social Spirit in America* (Chicago, 1901), chap. viii.

BOOK X   The Rise of the City, 1878–98

1. R. H. Edmonds, *Facts about the South* (Baltimore, 1902), 14-33, gives a good summary of Southern economic progress, 1880-1900. See also P. A. Bruce, *The Rise of the New South* (G. C. Lee and F. N. Thorpe, eds., *The History of North America,* Philadelphia, 1903-1907, XVII), 17-306, and J. A. C. Chandler et al., *The South in the Building of the Nation* (Richmond, 1909), VI, passim.
2. A. K. McClure, *The South: Its Industrial, Financial, and Political Condition* (Philadelphia, 1886), 149-62.
3. From 1880 to 1900 over a million new farms were added. See *U.S. Twelfth Census* (1900), V, 688-89, 692-93, for these and later statistics. The census definition of farm refers to operation, not ownership; thus a tract of 1,000 acres divided among a dozen tenants is reported as twelve farms.
4. See this volume, Book VIII, 721.
5. Anon., "A Georgia Plantation," *Scribner's Mo.,* XXI (1880-81), 830-36.
6. L. C. Gray et al., "Farm Ownership and Tenancy," U.S. Dept. of Agr., *Yearbook for 1923,* esp. 529-32; Bureau of the Census, *Plantation Farming in the United States (Special Rep.,* 1916), 7, 13; R. P. Brooks, *The Agrarian Revolution in Georgia, 1865-1912* (Univ. of Wis., *Bull.,* no. 639), 48-49, 65-68.
7. G. K. Holmes, "The Peons of the South," Am. Acad. of Polit. and Social Sci., *Annals,* IV (1893-94), 265-74; C. H. Otken, *The Ills of the South* (New York, 1894); M. B. Hammond, *The Cotton Industry* (Am. Econ. Assoc., *Publs.,* n.s., no. 1), chap. v; B. B. Kendrick, "Agrarian Discontent in the South, 1880-1900," Am. Hist. Assoc., *Rep. for 1920,* 270-72.
8. A. M. Arnett, *The Populist Movement in Georgia* (Columbia Univ., *Studies,* CIV, no. 1), 57-58. *Cf.* Hammond. *Cotton Industry,* 155.
9. The figures for the years 1880-1900 are given in *U.S. Twelfth Census,* V, 688-89; the two races are not separated. See also Brooks, *Agrarian Revolution,* chap. iv.
10. Quoted in the *Charleston News and Courier,* March 18, 1881, and cited by Broadus Mitchell, *The Rise of Cotton Mills in the South* (Johns Hopkins Univ., *Studies,* XXXIX, no. 2), 90.
11. W. K. Boyd, *The Story of Durham* (Duke Univ., *Publs.;* Durham, 1925), chaps. iv-v; Meyer Jacobstein, *The Tobacco Industry in the United States* (Columbia Univ., *Studies,* XXVI, no. 3), pt. ii, chap. iii.
12. If Maryland and Missouri be included as part of the Upper South the totals would be $30,765,441 and $54,372,568. Florida also became important in tobacco manufacturing, producing over $8 million worth of cigars and cigarettes by 1890. *U.S. Tenth Census,* (1880), II, 78, 79; *U.S. Twelfth Census,* IX, 647, 649, 661.
13. Mitchell, *Rise of Cotton Mills,* 112-115.
14. Edward Atkinson, *Address Given in Atlanta* (Boston, 1881).
15. Mitchell, *Rise of Cotton Mills,* chap. iv; Holland Thompson, *From the Cotton Field to the Cotton Mill* (New York, 1906), 59ff., 81; Edmonds, *Facts about the South,* 25.
16. The population of the principal cities in 1890 was: New Orleans, 242,039; Louisville, 161,129; Richmond, 81,388; Atlanta, 65,533; and Memphis, 64,495. Chatta-

nooga, like Birmingham an iron center, grew from 12,892 in 1880 to 29,100 in 1890. *U.S. Twelfth Census,* I, 430–33.

17. Edmonds, *South's Redemption,* 5–6, 14.

18. R. H. Edmonds in issue of December 21, 1889, and in his *South's Redemption,* 47. See also F. W. Moore, "The Condition of the Southern Farmer," *Yale Rev.,* III (1894–95), 63.

19. This generalization is based on a manuscript study of the background of 300 postwar industrialists of Virginia, North and South Carolina, Georgia, Alabama, and Tennessee, made in 1928 by G. W. Adams of the Harvard Graduate School. Of a total of 254, about 80 percent came of nonslaveholding parentage; of the entire 300, only 13 percent were born in the North, about half of them having gone south before the war.

20. *American Annual Cyclopedia,* X (1870), 749. Of course, the South sought farmers as well as factory hands. See 61 Cong., 3 sess., *Senate Docs.,* XXI, passim, for abstracts of Southern laws relating to immigration. Coolie labor was envisaged as a solution of the Southern economic problem in A. P. Merrill, "Southern Labor," *De Bow's Rev.,* VI (1869), 586–92; in refutation, see W. M. Burwell, "Science and the Mechanic Arts against Coolies," same issue, 557–71. An English visitor reported having seen 600 or 700 Chinese digging ditches alongside blacks on the Alabama & Chattanooga Railway in 1870, but this was exceptional. Robert Somers, *The Southern States since the War* (London, 1871), 163–64, 225.

21. Southern Immigration Association *Proceedings* (Nashville, 1884). See also W. M. Barrows, *The New South* (New York, 1884), 4–5, and U.S. Industrial Commission, *Reports* (Washington, 1900–1902), XV, 550–75.

22. D. A. Tompkins, "The Mountain Whites as an Industrial Labor Factor," Chandler et al., *South in Building of Nation,* VI, 58–61; W. G. Frost, "Our Contemporary Ancestors in the Southern Mountains," *Atlantic Mo.,* LXXXIII (1899), 311–19. For a discussion of the various mountaineer groups, see S. T. Wilson, *The Southern Mountaineers* (New York, 1906), chaps. ii, iv–vi.

23. The census definition of child laborer is a boy of sixteen or under and a girl of fifteen or under. E. G. Murphy, *Problems of the Present South* (New York, 1904), 96–125; *U.S. Eleventh Census* (1890), IV, 89.

24. A. D. Mayo, "The Third Estate of the South," *Journ. of Social Sci.,* XXVII (1890), xx–xlii; F. B. Simkins, *The Tillman Movement in South Carolina* (Duke Univ., *Publs.;* Durham, 1926), 176–77. See also a speech by E. A. Alderman before the National Congress of Education, October 25, 1895. U.S. Commissioner of Education, *Report for 1894–95,* II, 1748.

25. J. W. Johnston, *The Emancipation of the Southern Whites and Its Effects on Both Races* (Baltimore, 1887), argued that the whites had derived greater benefit from emancipation than the blacks.

26. For population data, see *U.S. Eleventh Census,* I, xcviii, 560–63; *U.S. Tenth Census,* I, 480–83; *U.S. Twelfth Census,* I, 485.

27. None of the mob was ever indicted or brought to trial. *U.S. Foreign Relations for 1891,* 665–67, 671–72, 674–86, 712–13; J. B. Moore, *A Digest of International Law* (Washington, 1906), VI, 837–41. Later mob outbreaks occurred against the Italians elsewhere in Louisiana: at Hahnville in 1896 when three held on a charge of homicide met violent death; and at Tallulah in 1899 when five others were taken from jail and lynched. Moore, *Digest,* VI, 843–45.

28. W. B. Bizzell, *Rural Texas* (L. H. Bailey, ed., *Rural State and Province Series;* New York, 1924), 123–36, 155–232; W. C. Holden, "West Texas Drouths," *Southwestern Hist. Quar.,* XXXII, 103–23.

29. By the Great West is meant that section of the country lying between the Pacific and the first tier of states west of the Mississippi River, exclusive of Texas.

30. *U.S. Eleventh Census* (1890), I, 914.

31. For the data in this paragraph, see *U.S. Eleventh Census,* I, cxii–cxv, cxxiv.

32. Mrs. Lucy A. Ide's diary of this journey has been edited by J. O. Oliphant under the title, "In a Prairie Schooner, 1878," *Wash. Hist. Quar.,* XVIII, 122–31, 191–98, 277–88.

33. J. B. Hedges, "The Colonization Work of the Northern Pacific Railroad," *Miss. Valley Hist. Rev.,* XIII, 320–21, 327, 332–33; same author, "Promotion of Immigration to the Pacific Northwest by the Railroads," same mag., XV, 183–203; G. D. Bradley, *The Story of the Santa Fé* (Boston, 1920), chap. v. The emigrant guidebooks of the 1880s ignored the possibility of traveling by wagon.

34. Briggs, "Great Dakota Boom," 80.

35. But travelers must complain however they ride! See Helen Hunt Jackson's amusing account of her trip by Pullman from Chicago to San Francisco in 1878 in H. H. (pseud.), *Bits of Travel at Home* (Boston, 1878), 3–40.

36. Briggs, "Great Dakota Boom," 86.

37. R. L. Stevenson, *Across the Plains* (New York, 1892), esp. 26–39. See also Rosaline Masson, *The Life of Robert Louis Stevenson* (New York, 1923), 147–53, 168–69, 178–81.

38. Described in R. L. Stevenson, *The Amateur Emigrant* (Chicago, 1895). For a detailed account of a steerage passage made by a Swedish immigrant in 1891, see A. G. Carlson, *En Emigrants Resa* (Chicago, 1894).

39. For accounts of such activities, see Hedges, "Northern Pacific Railroad," 315–19, 322–25, 329–30, and Bradley, *Santa Fé,* 113ff. The state governments also carried on similar work. See, for example, Briggs, "Great Dakota Boom," 105–108.

40. *U.S. Eleventh Census,* I, lxxxii, lxxxvii, 395.

41. L. P. Brockett, *Our Western Empire* (Philadelphia, 1884), 71.

42. James Bryce, *The American Commonwealth* (London, 1888), III, 86.

43. Brockett, *Western Empire,* 671–73.

44. Ibid., 118.

45. L. P. Brockett, *Handbook of the United States of America* (New York, 1883), 120–27; F. V. Hayden, *The Great West* (Bloomington, Ill., 1880), 221–24, 247, 283–91.

46. Brockett, *Handbook,* 116.

47. F. L. Paxson, "The Cow Country," *Am. Hist. Rev.,* XXII, 71–82; W. P. Webb, *The Great Plains* (Boston, 1931), 227–44; E. E. Dale, *The Range Cattle Industry* (Norman, Okla., 1930), chap. v; E. S. Osgood, *The Day of the Cattleman* (Minneapolis, 1929), chaps. iv–vii.

48. Overstocking of the ranges and a succession of severe winters hastened the end. Twelve great companies which in 1883 had been in a flourishing condition passed their dividends in 1887. R. A. Clemen, *The American Livestock and Meat Industry* (New York, 1923), 186.

49. C. C. Davis, *Olden Times in Colorado* (Los Angeles, 1916), 114–304.

50. R. M. Wright, *Dodge City, the Cowboy Capital* (n.p., n.d.), chaps. vii–xvii.

51. He died at the age of twenty-one with the reputation of having killed one man for each of his years. Emerson Hough, *The Story of the Outlaw* (New York, 1907), 196–226, 256–73, 300–312; W. N. Burns, *The Saga of Billy the Kid* (Garden City, 1926), 53–289.

52. Hough, *Story of the Outlaw,* chap. xvi.

53. Robertus Love, *The Rise and Fall of Jesse James* (New York, 1926), 300–399.

54. A recrudescence of brigandage, inspired by the example of the James Boys, occurred in Oklahoma territory in 1891–92 when the Dalton Brothers' gang ran their swift and bloody course as train and bank robbers. Hough, *Story of the Outlaw,* 375–91.

55. In every case the rate of growth exceeded that of the population in general. *U.S. Eleventh Census,* I, 398.

56. "The Last Longhorn," J. A. Lomax, comp., *Cowboy Songs and Other Frontier Ballads* (New York, 1910), 198.

57. Three excellent accounts are Finlay Dun, *American Farming and Food* (London, 1881), 199-212; W. G. Moody, *Land and Labor in the United States* (New York, 1883), chaps. ii-iii; and H. E. Briggs, "Early Bonanza Farming in the Red River Valley of the North," *Agricultural History*, VI, 26-37. See also Brockett, *Western Empire*, 78-79, 740-45 n., and Paul de Rousiers, *American Life* (A. J. Herbertson, tr., Paris, 1892), chap. iv.

58. [W. G. Moody], "The Bonanza Farms of the West," *Atlantic Mo.*, XLV (1880), 42-44.

59. U.S. Dept. of Agr., *Yearbook for 1899*, 323; *U.S. Twelfth Census*, V, xxi, xliv-xlvi, cxxv, 688; C. D. Warner, *Studies in the South and West* (New York, 1889), 124-25.

60. D. S. Jordan, "California and the Californians," *Atlantic Mo.*, LXXXII (1898), 793-801; E. J. Wickson, *Rural California* in L. H. Bailey, ed., *Rural State and Province Series;* (New York, 1923), 79-82, 169-76, 292-97; Osgood Hardy, "Agricultural Changes in California, 1860-1900," Pacific Coast Branch, Am. Hist. Assoc., *Proceeds. for 1929*, 216-230.

61. *Appletons' Annual Cyclopaedia*, XXI (1881), 860; D. L. Leonard, "Six Years in Utah," *Missionary Rev.*, IX (1896), 807-13; Sala, *America Revisited*, II, 316n.

62. R. T. Ely, "Economic Aspects of Mormonism," *Harper's Mag.*, CVI (1903), 667-78, is an unusually discriminating account.

63. H. H. Bancroft, *History of the Pacific States* (San Francisco, 1882-90), XXI, 686-87. Cf. E. H. Murray, "The Crisis in Utah, *N. Am. Rev.*, CXXXIV (1882), 340-42; Sala, *America Revisited*, II, 291-92.

64. Compare, for example, C. W. Penrose, "Church Rule in Utah," *Forum*, V (1888), 673, with the charges of anti-Mormon critics: G. E. Edmunds, "Political Aspects of Mormonism," *Harper's Mag.*, LXIV (1882), 286, and Theodore Schroeder, "Polygamy and the Constitution," *Arena*, XXXVI (1906), 493-95.

65. *U.S. Statutes at Large*, XXII, 30-32.

66. According to the "Report" of the Utah Commission, 50 Cong., 1 sess., *House Exec. Doc.*, no. 447. See also *Deseret News*, July 8, 1888; *Latter-day Saints' Millennial Star*, L (1888), 568-70; W. A. Linn, *The Story of the Mormons* (New York, 1902), 599-600.

67. *U.S. Statutes at Large*, XXIV, 635-41.

68. For example, see *Latter-day Saints' Millennial Star*, XLIV (1882), 267-69, 284-86; XLIX (1887), 648-49, 809-11.

69. Such periodicals as the *Democrat* and the *Republican* of St. Louis, *Harper's Magazine*, and territorial newspapers were to be found in many Cherokee homes in the eighties. Commissioner of Indian Affairs, *Report for 1886*, 148. See also W. P. Adair, "The Indian Territory in 1878," and V. A. Travis, "Life in the Cherokee Nation," *Chronicles of Oklahoma*, IV, 255-74, and 16-30; and Brockett, *Western Empire*, 797-813.

70. Dale, *Range Cattle Industry*, chap. vii.

71. M. B. Leavitt, *Fifty Years of Theatrical Management* (New York, 1911), chap. xi; F. J. Wilstach, *Wild Bill Hickok* (Garden City, 1926), chap. xiii. When Wild Bill took to the stage, he had behind him a record of perhaps eighty-one homicides, not all of them performed in the interests of public justice though all his victims fell in fair fight. Hough, *Story of the Outlaw*, 182-85.

72. J. D. Hicks, *The Populist Revolt* (Minneapolis, 1931), 153-70, 179-81.

73. J. D. Hicks, *The Constitutions of the Northwest States* (Univ. of Neb., *Studies*, XXIII, nos. 1-2).

74. Stevenson, *Across the Plains*, 15-17.

75. Babcock, *Scandinavian Element in the United States* (Urbana, Ill, 1897), 136-37.

76. For example, see F. S. Laing, "German-Russian Settlements in Ellis county, Kansas," Kan. State Hist. Soc., *Colls.*, XI, 518-22.

77. For such pleasures in Iowa and Dakota, see Hamlin Garland, *Boy Life on the*

Prairie (New York, 1899); in Kansas, J. E. House, "A Boy's Job in the Eighties," *Sat. Eve. Post,* CXCVII, 10ff. (May 16, 1925); in Wisconsin, Grant Showerman, *A Country Chronicle* (New York, 1916)—fictional autobiography—and Joseph Schafer, *A History of Agriculture in Wisconsin* (Wis. *Domesday Book, General Studies,* I), 172-78.

78. Garland, *Boy Life,* 273. For further expressions of this lyric mood, see his *Prairie Songs* (Cambridge, Mass., 1893) and Herbert Quick, *One Man's Life* (Indianapolis, 1925), chaps. ix-x.

79. Hamlin Garland, *A Son of the Middle Border* (New York, 1917), 204-206; Quick, *One Man's Life,* 240-41; Showerman, *Country Chronicle,* 148-49.

80. "The 'drift to the cities,' " Quick added, "has been largely a woman movement." "Women on the Farms," *Good Housekeeping,* LVII (1913), 426-36.

81. Eugene Davenport, "The Exodus from the Farm," U.S. Dept. of Agr., *Experiment Station Bull.,* no. 41 (1897), 84-86.

82. H. J. Fletcher, "The Drift of Population to Cities," *Forum,* XIX (1895), 737-45.

83. There were 1,028 towns ranging in population from 1,000 to 8,000 in the year 1890, 102 cities of from 8,000 to 25,000, and 32 of 25,000 or over. *U.S. Twelfth Census,* I, lxvi.

84. Ade recalls his childhood in "The Dark Ages," *Hearst's International and Cosmopolitan,* LXXXI (1926), 80ff.

85. *U.S. Eleventh Census,* I, lxvii.

86. *U.S. Eleventh Census,* I, lxxxiii, lxxxvii-lxxxviii, xc, cxxxviii-cxxxix.

87. J. F. Willard (Josiah Flynt, pseud.), "The German and the German-American," *Atlantic Mo.,* LXXVIII (1896), 655-64.

88. Quoted by Turner, "Dominant Forces in American Life," 438. See also G. W. Steevens, *The Land of the Dollar* (New York, 1897), 144, and J. C. Ridpath, "The Mixed Populations of Chicago," *Chautauquan,* XII (1891), 483-93.

89. *U.S. Eleventh Census,* I, clxii-clxiii.

90. For this purpose the Census Bureau classifies as urban any compact community of 1,000 or more. *U.S. Eleventh Census,* I, lxix-lxxi. See also E. W. Miller, "The Abandoned Farms of Michigan," *Nation* (New York), XLIX (1889), 498; H. J. Fletcher, "The Doom of the Small Town," *Forum,* XIX (1895), 214-23; anon., "The City in Modern Life," *Atlantic Mo.,* LXXV (1895), 552-56.

91. *U.S. Twelfth Census,* I, lxxxiv-lxxxv. In terms of cities of 8,000 or more inhabitants the urban percentages for the two years were 43.1 and 51.8. *U.S. Eleventh Census,* I, lxviii.

92. Rousiers, *American Life,* 189.

93. *U.S. Eleventh Census,* I, lxviii-lxxi. See also M. A. Veeder, "Deserted Farms in New York," *Nation,* XLIX (1889), 431; Clarence Gordon, "The Revival of Agriculture," same vol., 498-99; J. R. Elliott, *American Farms* (*Questions of the Day Series,* LXII, 2d ed., New York, 1890), 46.

94. Thus, in 1857, Professor J. W. Patterson estimated that that very season had seen an exodus to the West of 300,000 "from the impoverished hillsides and valleys of New England." *Address before the Grafton County Agricultural Society* (Hanover, N.H., 1857), 7.

95. Josiah Strong, *The New Era* (New York, 1893), 167. See also J. D. Long et al., "The Future of the New England Country," *New England Mag.,* n.s., III (1890-91), 661-73.

96. F. H. Fowler, "Abandoned Farms," L. H. Bailey, ed., *Cyclopedia of American Agriculture* (New York, 1909), IV, 102-106; W. L. Anderson, *The Country Town* (New York, 1906), 66-69; Elliott, *American Farms,* 42-43, 60-64.

97. G. F. Wells, "The Status of Rural Vermont," *Twenty-Third Ann. Vt. Agricultural Rep.,* 621.

98. C. C. Nott, "A Good Farm for Nothing," *Nation,* XLIX (1889), 406. A. F. Sanborn, "The Future of Rural New England," *Atlantic Mo.,* LXXX (1897), 74-83, also

presents a striking picture of a decayed town—its outward dilapidation and the emptiness of its inner life. Even more lugubrious is R. L. Hartt. "A New England Hill Town," *Atlantic Mo.*, LXXXIII (1899), 561-74, 712-20.

99. Comments quoted in R. L. Hartt, "Our Rural Degeneracy," *Boston Transcript*, May 17, 1899. On this subject, see also R. L. Hartt, "The Regeneration of Rural New England: Social," *Outlook*, LXIV (1900), 577-83; Sanborn, "Rural New England; Anderson, *Country Town*, chaps. v-vi; and Strong, *New Era*, chap. viii.

100. *U.S. Eleventh Census*, I, cxviii-cxix, clv, 606-609.

101. Compared with Chicago, Greater New York in 1890 possessed more Irish, English, Germans, Russians, and Italians, but Chicago had a larger number of Scandinavians, Bohemians, Poles, and Canadians. Thirty-nine percent of the population of New York-Brooklyn was foreign-born in 1890.

102. Kate H. Claghorn, "The Foreign Immigrant in New York City," U.S. Industrial Comn., *Reports*, XV, 465-92. See also J. A. Riis, *How the Other Half Lives* (New York, 1890), chap. iii.

103. The specialized character of Italian clannishness is shown by the fact that Neapolitans and Calabrians clung to the Mulberry Bend district, a colony of Genoese lived in Baxter Street, a Sicilian colony in Elizabeth Street between Houston and Spring, while north Italians predominated in the eighth and fifteenth wards west of Broadway, and south Italians in "Little Italy" between 110th and 115th Streets in Harlem.

104. D. M. A. Magnan, *Histoire de la Race Française aux États-Unis* (Paris, 1912), 250; Alexandre Beslisle, *Histoire de la Presse Franco-Américaine* (Worcester, 1911), 4-9.

105. Before 1890, when the federal enumerators (*Eleventh Census*, I, clxxiii-clxxv) first took cognizance of French Canadians as distinguished from Anglo-Canadians, statistics of settlement must be based on state census reports.

106. C. E. Amaron, *Your Heritage; or New England Threatened* (Springfield, Mass., 1891), 116.

107. Édouard Hamon, *Les Canadiens-Français de la Nouvelle-Angleterre* (Quebec, 1891), 57, 60, 175; Magnan, *Histoire*, 255-61, 266, 273-74, 296-97; Prosper Bender, "A New France in New England, *Mag. of Am. History*, XX (1888), 391.

108. *U.S. Eleventh Census*, I, 698-701; *U.S. Twelfth Census*, I, 850-53; *Mass. Census of 1895*, III, 152-54.

109. Adélard Desrosiers and P. A. Fournet, *La Race Française en Amérique* (Montreal, 1910), 240.

110. *U.S. Twelfth Census*, I, lxxxiv-lxxxv.

111. *U.S. Eleventh Census*, I, lxvii.

112. The data for the above discussion are derived from C. B. Spahr, *An Essay on the Present Distribution of Wealth in the United States* (New York, 1896), 46-49, which concludes the passage with the observation: "When American political parties shall again divide upon issues vitally affecting the distribution of wealth, the clearly marked line of division will not be between East and West, but between city and country."

113. See the authorities cited by A. F. Weber, *The Growth of Cities in the Nineteenth Century* (Columbia Univ., *Studies*, XI), 210-11n.

114. Ibid., 46, 68, 73, 82, 84.

115. For a contemporary appreciation of the dynamic role of the city, see F. J. Kingsbury, "The Tendency of Men to Live in Cities," *Journ. of Social Sci.*, XXXIII (1895), 1-19.

116. U.S. Commissioner of Education, *Report for 1894-95*, I, 3-8.

117. Bryce, *American Commonwealth*, III, 621. See also E. Catherine Bates, *A Year in the Great Republic* (London, 1887), I, 248, and Paul Blouët (Max O'Rell, pseud.), *A Frenchman in America* (New York, 1891), 244-45.

118. Willard Glazier, *Peculiarities of American Cities* (Philadelphia, 1883), 290. On New York, see also Rousiers, *American Life*, chap. xiii; W. G. Marshall, *Through*

America (London, 1881), chap. i: G. J. Holyoake, *Among the Americans* (Chicago, 1881), chap. ii; Sala, *America Revisited,* I, chaps. ii–vi; S. R. Hole, *A Little Tour in America* (New York, 1895), chaps. iv–vi.

119. Glazier, *Peculiarities of American Cities,* 301; J. F. Muirhead, *The Land of Contrasts* (New York, 1898), 193–97; H. C. Brown, *In the Golden Nineties (Valentine's Manual of Old New York,* XII, Hastings-on-Hudson, 1927), 25–48.

120. Raymond Westbrook, "Open Letters from New York," *Atlantic Mo.,* XLI (1878), 92.

121. Muirhead, *Land of Contrasts,* 193.

122. H. C. Brown, *New York in the Elegant Eighties (Valentine's Manual of Old New York,* XI, Hastings-on-Hudson, 1926), 11–16; anon., "Along the Bowery, When Vice Stalked Openly," *Police Gazette,* November 29, 1930.

123. This attitude was one of the certain symptoms of *Newyorkitis,* a malady amusingly described by J. H. Girdner in a small volume so titled (New York, 1901).

124. Rousiers, *American Life,* 242.

125. See Emily Faithfull, *Three Visits to America* (Edinburgh, 1884), chap. viii; Steevens, *Land of the Dollar,* 50–53; O'Rell, *Frenchman in America,* chaps. xvi–xvii.

126. Steevens, *Land of the Dollar,* 115–16. See also Rousiers, *American Life,* 209–214, and Ephraim Turland, *Notes on a Visit to America* (Manchester, 1877), 21.

127. Muirhead, *Land of Contrasts,* 218. See also H. L. Nelson, "Social Washington," *Atlantic Mo.,* LII (1883), 818–25; Hole, *Tour in America,* chap. xxi; Paul Blouët (Max O'Rell, pseud.) and Jack Allyn, *Jonathan and His Continent* (Madame Paul Blouët, tr., New York, 1889), 39–42; A. M. Low, "Washington: the City of Leisure," *Atlantic Mo.,* LXXXVI (1900), 767–78.

128. Hole, *Tour in America,* 246.

129. Steevens, *Land of the Dollar,* 144–45. See also Dun, *American Farming and Food,* chap. xii; William Archer, *America To-day* (New York, 1899), chap. ix; Hole, *Tour in America,* chap. xviii; Marshall, *Through America,* chap. iv; Sala, *America Revisited,* II, chap. ix; C. D. Warner, *Studies in the South and West* (New York, 1889), 184–86, 200–201; Glazier, *Peculiarities of American Cities,* chap. ix.

130. Rudyard Kipling, *American Notes* (Boston, 1899), esp. 91.

131. A Chicagoan of these times, being asked his opinion of New York, which he had just visited, replied, "Wal, I guess it's too far away from Chicago to do any partic'lar amount of business!" Marshall, *Through America,* 103.

132. J. W. Buel, *Metropolitan Life Unveiled* (St. Louis, 1882), 26. For similar reactions, see Rousiers, *American Life,* 240; Hole, *Tour in America,* 43–45; Marshall, *Through America,* 7.

133. G. W. Tillson, *Street Pavements and Paving Materials* (New York, 1900), chaps. ix–x; N. P. Lewis, "Modern City Roadways," *Pop. Sci. Mo.,* LVI (1899–1900), 524–39.

134. Marshall, *Through America,* 26. At the formal opening the trip from Trinity Church to Central Park took twenty-two minutes. *N.Y. Tribune,* May 1, 1878.

135. Bureau of the Census, *Street and Electric Railways, 1902 (Special Rep.),* 36.

136. *Appletons' Annual Cyclopaedia,* XXVI (1886), 122–25, gives a technical description.

137. H. H. Vreeland, "The Street Railways of America," C. M. Depew, ed., *One Hundred Years of American Commerce* (New York, 1895), I, 141–43.

138. By T. A. Edison at Menlo Park, C. J. Van Depoele in Chicago and elsewhere, Leo Daft in Boston and elsewhere, E. M. Bentley and W. H. Knight in Cleveland, J. C. Henry in Kansas City (where the term "trolley" probably originated), S. H. Short in Denver, and by others. Germany really led the way, Berlin having constructed a line in 1867 on the third-rail principle. T. C. Martin, "History and Development of Electric Traction," *Street and Electric Railways, 1902,* 160–67.

139. Anon., "A Retrospect of the Year 1895," *Scientific Am.*, LXXIV (1896), 2; Vreeland, "Street Railways," 144. Steps were also taken to electrify the elevated systems, though New York did not do so until 1901-1903. For an explanation, see Brown, *New York in Elegant Eighties*, 16-17.

140. A. Fairlie, *Municipal Administration* (New York, 1901), 296.

141. G. M. Shaw, "The Telephone and How It Works," *Pop. Sci. Mo.*, XII (1877-78), 559-69.

142. A. B. Paine, *In One Man's Life* (New York, 1921), chap. xxiii; Bureau of the Census, *Telephones and Telegraphs, 1902 (Special Rep.)*, 66-67; J. W. Stehman, *The Financial History of the American Telephone and Telegraph Company* (Boston, 1925), 13-18.

143. H. N. Casson, *The History of the Telephone* (Chicago, 1910), 118-25; E. W. Byrn, *The Progress of Invention in the Nineteenth Century* (N.Y., 1900), 82-85; Paine, *One Man's Life*, 161-62.

144. Other exchanges, established the same year, were Meriden, Connecticut; San Francisco, Albany, Chicago, Wilmington, Delaware, St. Louis, Detroit, and Philadelphia. Casson, *History of the Telephone*, 143-47; anon., *Things Worth Knowing about the Telephone* (New York, 1929), 43.

145. Casson, *History of the Telephone*, 153-55; Katherine M. Schmitt, "I Was Your Old 'Hello' Girl," *Sat. Eve. Post*, CCV, 18ff. (July 12, 1930).

146. Anon., "The Telephonic Exchange in the United Sates," *Nature*, XXIV (1880), 495; *Telephones and Telegraphs, 1902*, 5.

147. Anon., "Progress of the Bell Telephone," *Scientific Am.*, LXX (1894), 250.

148. K. B. Miller, "Merits of Independent and Industrial Telephone Systems," *Engineering Mag.*, XVIII (1900), 550-57; *Telephones and Telegraphs, 1902*, 9-11, 67.

149. Azel Ames, "Removal of Domestic Excreta," Am. Public Health Assoc., *Public Health*, IV (1877), 74.

150. G. E. Waring, "Recent Modifications in Sanitary Drainage," *Atlantic Mo.*, XLIV (1879), 62.

151. G. E. Waring, *Modern Methods of Sewage Disposal* (New York, 1894); G. W. Rafter and M. N. Baker, *Sewage Disposal in the United States* (New York, 1894).

152. Charles Zueblin, *American Municipal Progress* (New York, 1902), 120-26; Fairlie, *Municipal Administration*, 250-51.

153. N. S. Shaler, ed., *The United States of America* (New York, 1894), III, 1235-37; M. N. Baker, *Municipal Engineering and Sanitation* (R. T. Ely, ed., *The Citizen's Library of Economics, Politics, and Sociology;* (New York, 1901), chap. xx.

154. About ninety cities had installed furnaces by the end of 1898. W. F. Morse, *The Collection and Disposal of Municipal Waste* (New York, 1908), 99-116.

155. Zueblin, *American Municipal Progress*, chap. iv.

156. W. T. Sedgwick, "Notable Sanitary Experiments in Massachusetts," *Forum*, XX (1895-96), 752-56; G. C. Whipple, *State Sanitation* (Cambridge, Mass., 1917), I, 125-28.

157. C. V. Chapin, *Municipal Sanitation in the United States* (Providence, 1901), 298.

158. The death rate per 10,000 inhabitants was: New York 3.36; Boston 3.5; Chicago 6.25; Philadelphia 6.8. Shaler, *United States*, III, 1230.

159. Hiram Hitchcock, "The Hotels of America," Depew, *American Commerce*, I, 153-55; Alexander Craib, *America and the Americans* (London, 1892), chap. xxvii; Brown, *Golden Nineties*, 311-23.

160. Muirhead, *Land of Contrasts*, 255-57. See also [J. F. Muirhead]. *The United States* (Karl Baedeker, ed., *Handbook for Travellers;* 2d rev. edn., Leipsic, 1899), xxvi-xxvii.

161. Over 4.5 million cheap lodgings were provided in such houses in the single year 1888 in New York. H. L. Myrick, *The Importance of the Scientific and Practical Study of Crime* (New York, 1895), 25; Riis, *How the Other Half Lives*, chap. viii.

162. *U.S. Thirteenth Census* (1910), I, 73-75; *Street and Electric Railways, 1902,*

26-29; Brown, *New York in Elegant Eighties,* 69-73; A. F. Weber, "Suburban Annexations," *N. Am. Rev.,* CLXVI (1898), 612-17.

163. R. W. De Forest and Lawrence Veiller, eds., *The Tenement House Problem* (New York, 1903), I, 57, 131-70.

164. A New York invention, the dumb-bell tenement was unknown in any European city. Ibid., I, 8-14, 100-102; Riis, *How the Other Half Lives,* 18-19.

165. For various estimates, see Riis, *How the Other Half Lives,* 275, 300; De Forest and Veiller, *Tenement House Problem,* I, 5, 37; II, 78.

166. Theodore Roosevelt, *An Autobiography* (New York, 1919), 169. Riis's *The Battle with the Slum* (New York, 1902) is autobiographical.

167. De Forest and Veiller, *Tenement House Problem,* I, 5, 95-116; II, 207-345.

168. W. F. Howe and A. H. Hummel, *Danger!* (Buffalo, 1886), chap. iii; Helen Campbell et al., *Darkness and Daylight* (Hartford, 1891), chap. vi; Herbert Asbury, *The Gangs of New York* (New York, 1927), 238-46.

169. W. M. F. Round, "Immigration and Crime," *Forum,* VIII (1889-90), 428-40; S. G. Fisher, "Immigration and Crime," *Pop. Sci. Mo.,* XLIX (1896), 625-30; F. H. Wines, *Report on Crime, Pauperism, and Benevolence in the United States* (*U.S. Eleventh Census,* 1890, XXII), I, 23-43, 131-33.

170. J. F. Willard (Josiah Flynt, pseud.), *Notes of an Itinerant Policeman* (Boston, 1900), 10.

171. Wines, *Report,* I, II, 124. In general, crime statistics need to be used with considerable caution because of lack of registration in most states, divergent legal definitions of crime in the United States and abroad, differences in law enforcement as between states and from time to time within the same state, and other similar circumstances.

172. Figures cited in S. S. McClure, "The Increase of Lawlessness in the United States," *McClure's,* XXIV (1904), 168. For the same years suicides numbered 605, 2,640, and 5,920.

173. See, for example, H. M. Boies, *Prisoners and Paupers* (New York, 1893), chaps. i, vi-xi; I. C. Parker, "How to Arrest the Increase of Homicides in America," *N. Am. Rev.,* CLXII (1896), 667-73; W. D. Morrison, *Juvenile Offenders* (New York, 1897), esp. chap. ii; Cesare Lombroso, "Why Homicide Has Increased in the United States," *N. Am. Rev.,* CLXV (1897), 641-48; CLXVI (1898), 1-11; James O'Meara, "Concealed Weapons and Crimes," *Overland Mo.,* XVI (1890), 11-16.

174. G. C. Holt, "Lynching and Mobs," *Journ. of Social Sci.,* XXXII (1894), 76-81.

175. See this volume, Book VIII, 721.

176. For the marching columns of the jobless in 1894, see D. L. McMurry, *Coxey's Army* (Boston, 1929).

177. J. J. McCook, "A Tramp Census and Its Revelations," *Forum,* XV (1893), 753-66. Thirteen hundred forty-nine tramps were interviewed. Their ages averaged younger than those of tramps in England and Germany. Nearly half of them said they had taken to the road within a week of losing their last real job. Of immigrant elements the Irish were the most prominent, accounting for one fifth of all the tramps.

178. E. L. Bailey (an ex-tramp), "Tramps and Hoboes," *Forum,* XXVI (1898-99), 217-21; Flynt, *Notes,* 49-53, 118-40; Jack London, *The Road* (New York, 1907).

179. J. F. Willard (Josiah Flynt, pseud.), *Tramping with Tramps* (New York, 1899), 381-98, contains a glossary with comments. This student of trampdom estimated that at least 3,000 distinctive expressions had been in vogue in the previous twenty years. Cf. the glossary in J. F. Willard (Josiah Flynt, pseud.) *The World of Graft* (New York, 1901), 219-21.

180. Jacques Offenbach, *America and the Americans* (London, 1876), 43-44; S. C. de Soissons, *A Parisian in America* (Boston, 1896), 8.

181. Matthew Arnold, *Civilization in the United States* (Boston, 1888), 168-69.

182. William Saunders, *Through the Light Continent* (London, 1879), 401. See also

Faithfull, *Three Visits to America,* 323, and E. Catherine Bates, *A Year in the Great Republic* (London, 1887), II, 281–83.

183. Mrs. John Sherwood, *Manners and Social Usages* (New York, 1884), 147.

184. Florence H. Hall, *Social Customs* (Boston, 1887), 177; Mrs. Burton Harrison, *The Well-Bred Girl in Society* (New York, 1898), 39. See also Mrs. Burton Kingsland, "A Daughter at Sixteen," *Ladies' Home Journ.,* XI (1894), no. 10, 10.

185. Sherwood, *Manners and Social Usages,* 147 (rev. ed., 1900, 196).

186. Ibid., 153–54 (rev. ed., 1900, 202–203).

187. *Supplementary Analysis and Derivative Tables (U.S. Twelfth Census, Special Rep.),* 86, 89.

188. Mary G. Humphreys, "Women Bachelors in New York," *Scribner's Mag.,* XX (1896), 626–36. See also anon., "The Old Maid," *Harper's Bazar,* XII (1879), 251; anon., "Old Maids," *Harper's Bazar,* XV (1882), 434. Mrs. Burton Harrison's novel, *A Bachelor Maid* (New York, 1894), is a gentle satire on the "new woman."

189. *Supplementary Analysis and Derivative Tables,* 386, 395–402.

190. Milicent W. Shinn, "The Marriage Rate of College Women," *Century,* L (1895), 946–48; Horace Davis, "Collegiate Education of Women," *Overland Mo.,* XVI (1890), 337–44; Mary R. Smith, "Statistics of College and Non-College Women," Am. Stat. Assoc., *Publs.,* n.s., VII, 1–26.

191. J. S. Billings, "The Diminishing Birth Rate in the United States," *Forum,* XV (1893), esp. 475–77. Contraceptive information and devices had been excluded from the mails under heavy penalties by a federal act of 1873. Anthony Comstock, *Frauds Exposed* (New York, 1880), 401.

192. Bryce, *The American Commonwealth,* III, 676; *Supplementary Analysis and Derivative Tables,* 376, 379, 408–409.

193. Clara S. J. Moore (Mrs. H. O. Ward, pseud.), *Sensible Etiquette* (16th rev. ed., Philadelphia, 1878), 353.

194. That a husband with a slatternly wife "stays at home as little as possible is no wonder," he added. "It is a wonder that such a man does not go on a whaling voyage of three years, and in a leaky ship." Reprinted in T. DeW. Talmage, *The Wedding Ring* (New York, 1896), 80–81, 83.

195. See this volume, Book VI, 517.

196. Annie N. Meyer, ed., *Woman's Work in America* (New York, 1891), 271–74, 446–48; H. C. Whitney, *Marriage and Divorce, the Effect of Each on Personal Status and Property Rights* (Philadelphia, 1894); G. J. Bayles, *Woman and the Law* (New York, 1901).

197. Anon., *America and the Americans* (New York, 1897), 222. See also Bates, *Year in Great Republic,* I, 52; Hugo Münsterberg, *American Traits from the Point of View of a German* (Boston, 1902), 129; 254–60; edit., *Ladies' Home Journ.,* IX (1892), no. 7, 12.

198. Martha B. Mosher, *Child Culture in the Home* (New York, 1898), 168; Kate Douglas Wiggin, *Children's Rights* (Boston, 1892), 3. See also Hall, *Social Customs,* chap. xi; Mary V. Terhune (Marian Harland, pseud.), *The Secret of a Happy Home* (New York, 1896), chaps. xxi, xxiii; anon., "The Next Generation," *Harper's Bazar,* XV (1882), 754; E. W. Bok, "The Blot on Our American Life," *Ladies' Home Journ.,* XII (1895), no. 8, 14.

199. Edit., *Ladies' Home Journ.,* X (1893), no. 8, 12.

200. Muirhead, *Land of Contrasts,* 70.

201. G. S. Hall, "The Contents of Children's Minds on Entering School," *Pedagogical Seminary,* I (1891), 139–73. See also C. D. Kellogg, "Child-Life in City and Country," *Journ. of Social Sci.,* XXI (1885), 207–23; Stewart Culin, "Street Games of Boys in Brooklyn, N.Y.," *Journ. of Am. Folk-Lore,* IV (1891), 221–37; R. A. Woods, ed., *The City Wilderness* (Boston, 1898), 198.

202. U.S. Commissioner of Education, *Report for 1879,* ccxi–ccxii; for *1882–83,* ccvi; Campbell et al., *Darkness and Daylight,* 398–400.

203. Bureau of the Census, *Occupations at the Twelfth Census (Special Rep.)*, lxvi–lxviii; U.S. Industrial Commission, *Reports* (Washington, 1900–1902), XIX, 917, 922; Campbell et al., *Darkness and Daylight*, chaps. iv–v.

204. C. E. Rainwater, *The Play Movement in the United States* (Chicago, 1921), chap. ii.

205. Campbell et al., *Darkness and Daylight*, 313–17; R. A. Woods et al., *The Poor in Great Cities* (New York, 1895), 131–50.

206. Porter Sargent, *A Handbook of Summer Camps* (Boston, 1925), 17–31; Louis Rouillon, "Summer Camps for Boys," *Am. Rev. of Revs.*, XXI (1900), 697–703.

207. "No other people existing, or that ever did exist, could command such a variety of edible products for daily consumption as the mass of the American people habitually use to-day." C. D. Warner, *The Relation of Literature to Life* (New York, 1897), 264. See also Shaler, *United States of America*, III, 1243.

208. W. A. Taylor, "The Influence of Refrigeration on the Fruit Industry," U.S. Dept. of Agr., *Yearbook for 1900*, 561–80.

209. Depew, *American Commerce*, II, 390, 393; D. A. Wells, *Recent Economic Changes* (New York, 1889), 340.

210. For instance, from 1880 to 1887 the importation of bananas into the United States grew fortyfold. Wells, *Recent Economic Changes*, 339; anon., "Bananas," *Good Housekeeping*, VIII (1889), 112. See also Depew, *American Commerce*, II, 603–605, and Arnold, *Civilization in United States*, 165.

211. Depew, *American Commerce*, II, 398–99; J. H. Collins, *The Story of Canned Goods* (New York, 1924), esp. 38, 80–82, 126–27, 155, 166, 187; anon., "Canned Goods," *Good Housekeeping*, X (1890), 105ff.

212. Anon., "Ready-made Housekeeping," *Good Housekeeping*, V (1887), 266.

213. H. C. Nixon, "The Cleavage within the Farmer's Alliance Movement," *Miss. Valley Hist. Rev.*, XV, esp. 25–26. For the similar strife over compound lard and vegetable shortening, see 26–31.

214. R. A. Clemen, *By-Products in the Packing Industry* (Chicago, 1927), 170–80.

215. Wells, *Recent Economic Changes*, 384–85.

216. U.S. Comr. of Educ., *Rep. for 1878*, cxcv.

217. See A. P. Bryant, "Some Results of Dietary Studies in the United States," U.S. Dept. of Agr., *Yearbook for 1898*, 439–52, and A. C. True and R. D. Milner, "Development of the Nutrition Investigations of the Department of Agriculture," U.S. Dept. of Agr., *Yearbook for 1899*, 403–14. Fannie Merritt Farmer's *The Boston Cooking-School Cook Book*, which quickly became standard, was first published in 1896.

218. In *As We Were Saying* (New York, 1891), 80–85, C. D. Warner amusingly deplores the wasted energy resulting from the "gum habit" of "the last ten years."

219. Ice-making plants first appeared in the South in the 1870s and, after the failure of the natural-ice crop in the two mild winters of 1888–90, spread rapidly through the North. T. M. Prudden, "Our Ice supply," *Pop. Sci. Mo.*, XXXII (1888), 668–82; F. A. Fernald, "Ice-Making and Machine Refrigeration," *Pop. Sci. Mo.*, XXXIX (1891), 19–20.

220. Depew, *American Commerce*, II, 470–74.

221. Mosher, *Child Culture*, 202–203; Depew, *American Commerce*, II, 420–21; Meyer Jacobstein, *The Tobacco Industry in the United States* (Columbia Univ., *Studies*, XXVI, no. 3), 45–52.

222. Hall, *Social Customs*, 290–91.

223. See this volume, Book VIII, 721.

224. W. D. Howells, *A Hazard of New Fortunes* (New York, 1889), I, 58–60. For other descriptions, see anon., "Forty Years Ago, and Now," *Harper's Bazar*, XIII (1880), 514, and anon., "N.Y. Fashions: House-Furnishing," *Harper's Bazar*, XV (1882), 323.

225. Mrs. J. A. Logan, *The Home Manual* (Boston, 1889), 267–68; Rose E. Cleveland, ed., *The Social Mirror* (St. Louis, 1888), 345, 348.

226. See, for example, J. L. Ford, *Forty-Odd Years in the Literary Shop* (New York, 1921), 75-77; C. D. Warner, *Studies in the South and West* (New York, 1889), 153; F. A. Fernald, "Household Arts at the World's Fair," *Pop. Sci. Mo.*, XLIII (1893), 803-12.

227. M. E. W. Sherwood, *The Art of Entertaining* (New York, 1892), 206-20. See also Julia M. Wright, *The Complete Home* (Philadelphia, 1879), chap. xviii; Helen Campbell, *Household Economics* (New York, 1897), chap. xi; Lucy M. Salmon, *Domestic Service* (New York, 1897), esp. chaps. vi-ix.

228. Among the Cleveland Papers in the Library of Congress are protests against the proposed literacy test of 1897 on the ground that thereby the incoming stream of domestic servants would be seriously reduced. Mr. J. L. Norton has called my attention especially to letters of J. H. Semmes to J. G. Carlisle, February 18, 1897, and C. S. Hamlin to H. T. Thurber, February 23, 1897.

229. Robert Grant, "The Art of Living," *Scribner's Mag.*, XVII (1895), esp. 308 (later printed in book form under the same title). See also Florence R. Simmons, "Superannuated Trash," *Good Housekeeping*, XII (1891), 41.

230. Campbell, *Household Economics*, 113-14.

231. Mrs. M. J. Plumstead, "Sweeping Day," *Good Housekeeping*, III (1886), 51; Sarah B. Thayer, "A Reconstructed Household," same mag., XII (1891), 11.

232. Clarence Cook, "Beds and Tables, Stools and Candlesticks," *Scribner's Mo.*, XIII (1876-77), 86; C. F. Wingate, "The Unsanitary Homes of the Rich," *N. Am. Rev.*, CXXXVII (1883), 172; Campbell, *Household Economics*, 75-77.

233. G. E. Waring, Jr., "Recent Modifications in Sanitary Drainage," *Atlantic Mo.*, XLIV (1879), 56-62; W. P. Trowbridge, "Modern Sanitary Engineering," *Harper's Mag.*, LXVIII (1884), 761; W. T. (pseud.), "Some Common Facts about Plumbing," *Architectural Record*, I (1891), 97-108.

234. J. W. Richards, "Recent Progress in the Aluminum Industry," Franklin Inst., *Journ.*, CSLIX, 451, 454.

235. Edith Minister, "Ironing Day," *Good Housekeeping*, XVII (1893), 20.

236. Anon., "The Promise of the Dawn," *Harper's Bazar*, XVI (1883), 18. See also Robert Burdette, "Woman Yesterday and Today," *Ladies' Home Journ.*, IX (1892), no. 2, 11.

237. Anon., "Women as Inventors," *Good Housekeeping*, VIII (1889), 119.

238. Faithfull, *Three Visits to America*, 275. See also Mary P. Jacobi, *"Common Sense" Applied to Woman Suffrage* (New York, 1894), 16, 118-19, 201.

239. *Occupations at the Twelfth Census*, lxxxvi; Bayles, *Woman and the Law*, 257-60; F. J. Stimson, *Handbook to the Labor Law of the United States* (New York, 1896), 55, 71, 79-80.

240. W. F. Tillett, "Southern Womanhood as Affected by the War," *Century*, XLIII (1891-92), 9-16.

241. "Contributors' Club," *Atlantic Mo.*, XLVI (1880), 724-25.

242. Thérèse Blanc, *The Condition of Woman in the United States* (Abby L. Alger, tr., Boston, 1895), 107.

243. By 1896 the membership consisted of 495 individual clubs and 20 state federations. Ellen M. Henrotin, "The General Federation of Women's Clubs," *Outlook*, LX (1897), 443-44.

244. Kate G. Wells, "The Transitional American Woman," *Atlantic Mo.*, XLVI (1880), 817-18 (reprinted in her *About People*, Boston, 1885).

245. Ruth Ashmore, "Side-Talks with Girls," *Ladies' Home Journ.*, VII (1890), no. 4, 10. See also her "The Restlessness of the Age" same mag.; XII (1895), no. 2, 16; and editorials in VII (1890), no. 11, 10; X (1893), no. 5, 18.

246. Francis Parkman, "The Woman Question," *N. Am. Rev.*, CXXIX (1879), 303-21. See also his reply to his critics, "The Woman Question Again," in same mag., CXXX (1880), 16-30.

247. Anon., "The Other Side of the Woman Question," *N. Am. Rev.*, CXXIX (1879), 413-46.

248. T. W. Higginson, *Common Sense about Women* (Boston, 1881), 329.

249. Susan B. Anthony et al., *History of Woman Suffrage* (Rochester and N.Y., 1881–1926), V, 623.

250. Ida H. Harper, *The Life and Work of Susan B. Anthony* (Indianapolis, 1898–1908), II, passim.

251. Montana, Iowa, and Louisiana established a form of taxation suffrage, respectively in 1887, 1894, and 1898; Kansas municipal suffrage in 1887 and Michigan in 1893 (declared unconstitutional). E. A. Hecker, *A Short History of Women's Rights* (New York, 1910), 167.

252. Mary A. Greene, "Results of the Woman-Suffrage Movement," *Forum*, XVII (1894), esp. 414–16.

253. Anon., "Clothed and in Her Right Mind," *Harper's Bazar*, XIV (1881), 562.

254. See, for example, anon., "Childish Children," *Harper's Bazar*, XIV (1881), 663; Isabel A. Mallon, "Dressing a Growing Girl," *Ladies' Home Journ.*, X (1893), no. 9, 21.

255. Modish skirts in 1890 were from four and a half to five yards wide at the bottom. *Ladies' Home Journ.*, VII (1890), no. 7, 15.

256. One well-known pulpiteer, calling attention to the fact that "Arnold of the Revolution proposed to sell his country in order to get money to support his home wardrobe," announced that a similar cause had "sent prominent business men to the watering of stocks, and life insurance presidents to perjured statements about their assets, and some of them to the penitentiary, and has completely upset our American finances." Talmage, *Wedding Ring*, 103–104.

257. Dr. R. L. Dickinson of Brooklyn estimated the pressure exerted by corsets as varying, in given cases, from twenty-one to eighty-eight pounds. Helen G. Ecob, *The Well-Dressed Woman* (New York, 1892), 27–29, 34–35. See also B. W. Richardson, "Dress in Relation to Health," *Pop. Sci. Mo.* XVII (1880), 182–99. But Mrs. Terhune declared: "Women will wear corsets; they always have and they always will. We may as well consider this a settled fact." Mary V. Terhune (Marion Harland, pseud.), *Talks upon Practical Subjects* (New York, 1895), 119.

258. Julia A. Sprague, *History of the New England Women's Club* (New York, 1894), 19–20; Julia Ward Howe, "Dress and Undress," *Forum*, III (1887), esp. 315; Ecob, *Well-Dressed Woman*, 130–32.

259. Ecob, *Well-Dressed Woman*, 143–46. A series of articles favorable to the movement appeared in the *Arena*, VI–VIII (1892–93).

260. May R. Kern, "Dressing without the Corset," *Ladies' Home Journ.*, X (1893), no. 8, 17; C. H. Crandall, "What Men Think of Women's Dress," *N. Am. Rev.*, CLXI (1895), 251–54.

261. The divorce rate in Switzerland, which was the highest of any European country, was about three sevenths that of the United States at the close of the century. Bureau of the Census, *Marriage and Divorce, 1867–1906 (Special Rep.)*, pt. i, 12–13, 19, 54–55, 62–64.

262. E. H. Bennett, "National Divorce Legislation," *Forum*, II (1886–87), 429–38; same author, "Marriage Laws," *Forum*, III (1887), 219–29; E. J. Phelps, "Divorce in the United States," *Forum*, VIII (1889–90), 349–64; Duncan Convers, *Marriage and Divorce in the United States* (Philadelphia, 1889); Bayles, *Woman and the Law*, 55–119; *Marriage and Divorce, 1867–1906*, pt. i, chaps. ii–iii.

263. Whitney, *Marriage and Divorce*, 10–12; S. G. Fisher, *The Cause of the Increase of Divorce* (Philadelphia, 1890), esp. 19–20.

264. *Marriage and Divorce, 1867–1906*, pt. i, 19.

265. In the South, where cities were fewer and women less accustomed to the idea of earning their own living, wives were less active in seeking to sever the marriage tie. In four Southern states, indeed, more divorces were granted to husbands than to wives. *Marriage and Divorce, 1867–1906*, pt. i, 24–25, 94–95.

266. S. E. Dike, *A Review of Fifteen Years* (Natl. Divorce Reform League, *Rep. for 1895*), esp. 11–12.

267. Howe and Hummel, *Danger!,* chap. xii. See also Asbury, *Gangs of New York,* chap. ix.

268. See frontispiece map and first appendix of W. T. Stead, *If Christ Came to Chicago!* (Chicago, 1894). For Boston, see Woods, *City Wilderness,* 159-73, and F. A. Bushee, *Ethnic Factors in the Population of Boston* (Am. Econ. Assoc., *Publs.,* IV, no. 2), 107-16.

269. Police Inspector Thomas Byrnes in 1893 believed there were 40,000 prostitutes in New York City. National Purity Congress, *Papers* (New York, 1896), 113. Stead's estimate for Chicago about the same time was 10,000. *If Christ Came to Chicago,* 35. The census figures possess even less reliability; thus, in 1890, Indianapolis was credited with nearly as many brothels as New York, and Baltimore with three times as many as either Philadelphia or Washington. *U.S. Eleventh Census* (1890), XXIII, 1024-35. For the 1880 figures, see *U.S. Tenth Census* (1880), XXI, 566.

270. Stead, *If Christ Came to Chicago,* 252. Cf. W. F. Garrison, "The Relation of Poverty to Purity," Natl. Purity Congress, *Papers,* 398-405.

271. D. F. Wilcox, *The American City* (New York, 1904), 127-33; Stead, *If Christ Came to Chicago,* 37, 382; G. W. Hale, ed., *Police and Prison Cyclopaedia* (rev. ed., Boston, 1893), 189ff. See also a series of articles on "Official Complicity with Vice" in six different cities, in *Christian Union,* XLVI (1892).

272. Theodore Roosevelt, *An Autobiography* (New York, 1919), esp. 196.

273. See this volume, Book VI, 517.

274. E. P. Cubberley, *Public Education in the United States* (Boston, 1919), 252-53; E. W. Knight, *The Influence of Reconstruction on Education in the South* (Teachers College, *Contribs. to Educ.,* no. 60), esp. 99.

275. Though such laws were to be found in Massachusetts (enacted in 1852), Vermont, and the District of Columbia before 1870, they were of a crude and unsatisfactory character. For their spread after 1870, see *Reports* of the U.S. Commissioner of Education: for *1882-83,* xxx-xxxvi; *1886-87,* 56; *1888-89,* I, 15-16, 475-531; *1894-95,* I, 1118-21; *1896-97,* II, 1525.

276. U.S. Comr. of Educ., *Rep. for 1888-89,* I, 501.

277. U.S. Comr. of Educ., *Rep. for 1897-98,* II, 1695.

278. U.S. Comr. of Educ., *Rep. for 1897-98,* II, 2537; E. G. Dexter, *A History of Education in the United States* (New York, 1904), 166-69.

279. U.S. Comr. of Educ., *Rep. for 1898-99,* II, 1842, 1844.

280. U.S. Comr. of Educ., *Rep. for 1890-91,* I, x. "The increase in urban population is accompanied by increase in the length of the school year," remarked the commissioner, *Rep. for 1898-99,* I, x.

281. U.S. Comr. of Educ., *Rep. for 1883-84,* xxxiv; *1899-1900,* I, x-xi.

282. In 1880 the eighteen Northern states had 909 minors for every 1,000 adults; the sixteen ex-slave states 1,242. The net wealth per capita of minors in the North was $2,225, in the South $851. U.S. Comr. of Educ., *Rep. for 1887-88,* 22-29.

283. U.S. Comr. of Educ., *Rep. for 1889-90,* I, xviii, 11-12. This statement needs to be read in light of the fact that, though enrolling a larger proportion of the whole population, the South did not enroll a larger proportion of the population of school age. Also, the school term was much shorter. *Rep. for 1886-87,* 89.

284. U.S. Comr. of Educ., *Rep. for 1898-99,* I, xiv.

285. Cited from report of the North Carolina superintendent of education, by U.S. Comr. of Educ., *Rep. for 1887-88,* 161. In a somewhat similar spirit Governor F. W. M. Holliday of Virginia declared to the legislature in 1878, "Public free schools are not a necessity. The world, for hundreds of years, grew in wealth, culture, and refinement, without them." E. W. Knight, *Public Education in the South* (Boston, 1922), 347-48.

286. U.S. Comr. of Educ., *Rep. for 1882-83,* xxix.

287. The wide variation among sections is indicated by the average monthly salary of $136.23 paid in 1898-99 to men teachers in Massachusetts as contrasted with $50.00 in Ohio and $25.07 in North Carolina. In these same states women were

paid $51.41, $40.00, and $22.24, respectively. U.S. Comr. of Educ., *Rep. for 1888-89*, I, 8; *1898-99*, I, lxxix-lxxx.

288. U.S. Comr. of Educ., *Rep. for 1888-89*, I, 23, 319, 327-28; *1891-92*, II, 669; *1898-99*, I, lxxviii.

289. The state superintendents were Grace E. Patton in Colorado and Estelle Reel in Wyoming. U.S. Comr. of Educ., *Rep. for 1896-97*, II, 1528-33.

290. In the Midwest the changes ran as high as sixty-five. J. T. Prince, "American and German Schools," *Atlantic Mo.*, LXVI (1890), esp. 415.

291. G. S. Hall, "The Case of the Public Schools," *Atlantic Mo.*, LXXVII (1896), esp. 405-407; anon., "Confessions of Public School Teachers," *Atlantic Mo.*, LXXVIII (1896), 97-110. The extent of the corrupt activities of schoolbook publishers will never be known, but the fact was generally admitted. In the case of Washington in 1890 a member of the state board of education exposed a prominent book concern (which he named) which had paid him $5,000 in the expectation of receiving help in securing statewide adoptions. *Publishers' Wkly.*, XXXVII, 793 (June 14, 1890).

292. S. C. Parker, *History of Modern Elementary Education* (Boston, 1912), chap. xvii.

293. Bryce, *American Commonwealth*, III, 52. See also Faithfull, *Three Visits to America*, 219-20.

294. The corresponding figures for native-born whites were: 8.7 percent, 6.2 percent, and 4.6 percent; for foreign-born whites: 11.9 percent, 13 percent, and 12.8 percent. J. A. Hill, "Illiteracy," *Supplementary Analysis and Derivative Tables*, 328-75.

295. All kinds of schooling, whether in public or private schools or colleges, are included. These statistical years consist of ten months of twenty school days each. U.S. Comr. of Educ., *Rep. for 1899-1900*, I, xvi.

296. H. B. Adams, "Chautauqua: a Social and Educational Study," U.S. Comr. of Educ., *Rep. for 1894-95*, I, 977-1077; J. H. Vincent, *The Chautauqua Movement* (Boston, 1886); Ellwood Hendrick, *Lewis Miller* (New York, 1925), chaps. xxi-xxiii; L. H. Vincent, *John Heyl Vincent* (New York, 1925), chaps. xi-xiii; J. L. Hurlbut, *The Story of Chatauqua* (New York, 1921).

297. G. H. Palmer, "Doubts about University Extension," *Atlantic Mo.*, LXIX (1892), esp. 369-70.

298. Melvil Dewey, "The American Library Association," *Library Journ.* (New York), I (1876-77), 247.

299. Sixteen states already had permissive laws before 1878, most of them enacted after 1871. Dexter, *History of Education*, 484-85.

300. T. W. Koch, *A Book of Carnegie Libraries* (White Plains, 1917).

301. W. S. Rossiter, "Printing and Publishing," *U.S. Twelfth Census* (1900), IX, 1045, gives these and other data cited.

302. Though the *Atlantic* had three editors—W. D. Howells (1871-81), T. B. Aldrich (1881-90), and H. E. Scudder (1890-98)—an examination of its files reveals no change in editorial policy or standards.

303. E. W. Bok, *The Americanization of Edward Bok* (New York, 1920), chaps. xv-xviii.

304. S. S. McClure, *My Autobiography* (New York, 1914), chap. vii; same author, "An Open Letter," *Haldeman-Julius Wkly.*, no. 1475, 4 (March 8, 1924). *Cosmopolitan* had been founded by John Brisben Walker in 1886, *Munsey's* by Frank A. Munsey in 1891.

305. F. A. Munsey, "Advertising in Some of Its Phases," *Munsey's*, XX (1898-99), 480.

306. In 1880 there were two copies of a newspaper issued for every three persons; twenty years later there were two copies for each individual. For these and other data cited in the text, see Rossiter, "Printing and Publishing," 1037-1119.

307. The figures for 1880 were 16.5 million for weeklies and semiweeklies and 3.5 million for dailies. Rossiter, "Printing and Publishing," 1046.

308. Based on the census of 1890. See D. F. Wilcox, "The American Newspaper," Am. Acad. of Polit. and Social Sci., *Annals,* XVI (1900), 59-61.

309. Bryce, *American Commonwealth,* III, 571. See also anon., "The American College," *Atlantic Mo.,* LXXV (1895), esp. 703.

310. This was a more rapid growth of enrollment than of total population. U.S. Comr. of Educ., *Rep. for 1887-88,* 632, and later *Reports,* passim.

311. C. F. Smith, "Southern Colleges and Schools," *Atlantic Mo.,* LIV (1884), 544-47. Ohio was not the only sinner: Illinois had twenty-five colleges, Iowa eighteen, Indiana sixteen, Michigan ten. U.S. Comr. of Educ., *Rep. for 1887-88,* 1040-41.

312. F. W. Kelsey, "State Universities and Church Colleges," *Atlantic Mo.,* LXXX (1897), 826-32. See also A. A. Johnson, "The State Universities and Denominational Colleges," *Educ.,* XVI (1895-96), 435-37.

313. South Dakota, 1882; North Dakota and Texas, 1883; Nevada and Wyoming, 1886; Idaho, 1889; Arizona and New Mexico, 1891; Oklahoma, 1892; and Montana, 1895.

314. G. E. Howard, "The State University in America," *Atlantic Mo.,* LXVII (1891), esp. 340; Sara A. Burstall, *The Education of Girls in the United States* (London, 1894), chap. vi.

315. Faithfull, *Three Visits to America,* 56-58. Thomas Woody, *A History of Women's Education in the United States* (J. M. Cattell, ed., *Science and Education,* IV, New York, 1929), bk. ii, chaps. iv-vi, is the fullest treatment of the subject.

316. Only the state universities of Virginia, Georgia, and Louisiana declined to change. Dexter, *History of Education in the United States,* 446-47.

317. In calculating the proportions, separate women's colleges were not included. U.S. Comr. of Educ., *Rep. for 1889-90,* II, 764; for *1900-1901,* I, xlix.

318. U.S. Comr. of Educ., *Rep. for 1883-84,* clviii; D. R. Phillips, "The Elective System in American Education," *Pedagogical Seminary,* VIII (1901), 206-30.

319. The elective system took the curse off coeducation for many parents who would hae been unwilling to let their daughters take the traditional prescribed course for men. Annie N. Meyer, ed., *Woman's Work in America* (New York, 1891), 76-77. A synoptic view of courses of study in over a hundred colleges is given in U.S. Comr. of Educ., *Rep. for 1888-89,* II, 1224-1361.

320. C. F. Thwing, *A History of Higher Education in America* (New York, 1906), 439-45; same author, *A History of Education in the United States since the Civil War* (Boston, 1910), chap. v.

321. President and Treasurer of Harvard College, *Annual Report for 1899-1900,* esp. 120.

322. H. D. Sheldon, *Student Life and Customs* (W. T. Harris, ed., *International Education Series,* LI, New York, 1901), chap. v.

323. The average age at Harvard rose from eighteen years nine months in 1878 to nineteen years six months in 1889; during the years 1856-60 it had been seventeen years eleven months. See U.S. Comr. of Educ., *Rep. for 1889-90,* II, 799-803, for various colleges.

324. W. R. Baird, *American College Fraternities* (New York, 1879), 160-61; (5th ed., 1898), 424-31. See also J. A. Porter, "College Fraternities," *Century,* XXXVI (1888), 749-60; E. H. L. Randolph, "Greek-Letter Societies in American Colleges," *New England Mag.,* n.s., XVII (1897), 70-82; P. F. Piper, "College Fraternities," *Cosmopolitan,* XXII, (1897), 641-48.

325. A. D. White, "College Fraternities," *Forum,* III (1887), 243-53.

326. According to Baird, writing in 1898, within the past twenty years "the Universities of California, Missouri, Alabama, North Carolina, Georgia, Iowa, Harvard, and Vanderbilt have either repealed their antifraternity laws or allowed them to drop into disuse." In 1897, however, the South Carolina legislature succeeded in driving fraternities from the state university. Baird, *American College Fraternities* (5th ed.), 410, 415.

327. C. F. Thwing, *The American and the German University* (New York, 1928), 42. Much smaller numbers of students were to be found in Austria, Switzerland, and the University of Paris. U.S. Comr. of Educ., *Rep. for 1897-98,* II. 1702-1703; *1902,* I, 617. See also Samuel Sheldon, "Why Our Science Students Go to Germany," *Atlantic Mo.,* LXIII (1889), 463-66.

328. Even college presidents received only from $2,000 to $6,000. Bryce, *American Commonwealth,* III, 437; W. R. Harper, "The Pay of American College Professors," *Forum,* XVI (1893-94), 96-109; One of Them (pseud.), "The Status of the American Professor," *Educational Rev.,* XVI (1898), 417-34.

329. In some instances, Germans themselves were translated to American faculties, notably in the case of the historian Hermann von Holst and the neurologist Adolf Meyer at the new University of Chicago and of Kuno Francke at Harvard.

330. Of the first holders of fellowships at Hopkins, one became professor of political economy at Michigan, another of natural history at Williams, a third of physics in New York University, a fourth of Greek at the University of Virginia, a fifth of political science at Middlebury College; two were called to chairs at Harvard; and three were retained on the Hopkins faculty. Other American graduate centers were, of course, performing a similar service. Between 1870 and 1890, the Cornell graduate school furnished fourteen college professors and twenty-four college presidents.

331. In recognition of its transformed character, Yale College assumed the name of Yale University in 1887, Columbia did likewise in 1896, and in the same year the College of New Jersey changed to Princeton University.

332. Other significant contributors to medical bacteriology were Roux, Strauss, Metchnikoff, and Bouchard of Paris; Fränkel, Behring, and Klebs in Germany; and Kitasato of Japan.

333. D. E. Salmon, "Some Examples of the Development of Knowledge Concerning Animal Diseases," U.S. Dept. of Agr., *Yearbook for 1899,* esp. 124-34; Paul de Kruif, *Microbe Hunters* (New York, 1926), chap. viii.

334. G. F. Shrady, "Recent Triumphs in Medicine and Surgery," *Forum,* XXIII (1897), 33-41. Dr. Henry Gradle of Chicago, a former student of Koch, published in 1883 *Bacteria and the Germ Theory of Disease,* the first book in the English language on the subject.

335. See his readable volume, *American Nervousness* (New York, 1881), with its provocative sociological explanation of the disorder.

336. J. R. Parsons, "Professional Education," N. M. Butler, ed., *Education in the United States* (Albany, 1900), II, 513-15.

337. Anthony Comstock, *Frauds Exposed* (New York, 1880), chap. xix; G. P. Rowell, *Forty Years an Advertising Agent* (New York, 1906), chaps. xlv-xlvi.

338. The Kickapoo Indian Medicine Company, organized in 1881, for a time hired about 1,000 Indians as "atmosphere" for its wagon shows. N. T. Oliver (Nevada Ned) and Wesley Stout, "Med Show," *Sat. Eve. Post,* CCII, 12ff. (September 14, 1929). T. J. Le Blanc, "The Medicine Show," *Am. Mercury,* V (1925), 232-37, is a veracious sketch. Both James Whitcomb Riley and Paul Dresser, future composer of "On the Banks of the Wabash," traveled with such shows in the 1870s. Marcus Dickey, *The Youth of James Whitcomb Riley* (Indianapolis, 1919), chap. v, and Theodore Dreiser, *The Songs of Paul Dresser* (New York, 1927), v.

339. Shrady, "Recent Triumphs in Medicine and Surgery," 28-33; same author, "American Achievements in Surgery," *Forum,* XVII (1894), 167-78; Frederick Peterson, "Recent Progress in Medicine and Surgery," *Journ. of Social Sci.,* XXXI (1894), 1-lx.

340. In his classic paper, "Perforating Inflammation of the Vermiform Appendix; with Special Reference to Its Early Diagnosis and Treatment," published in the first volume of the *Transactions* of the Association of American Physicians in 1886, he named the disease appendicitis, traced its origin to the appendix, and, in defiance of existing practice, advocated radical surgical intervention for its cure.

341. See this volume, Book VIII, 721.

342. *Appletons' Annual Cyclopaedia*, XVIII (1878), 315–22; XIX (1879), 359–64.

343. A national board was also created in 1879, but unfortunately was allowed to lapse four years later. In addition, the new interest led to the holding of an international sanitary conference at Washington in 1881. S. W. Abbott, *The Past and Present Condition of Public Hygiene and State Medicine in the United States* (H. B. Adams, ed., *Monographs on American Social Economics*, XIX, Boston, 1900), 11, 14–16.

344. F. P. Gorham, "Bacteriology and Its Relation to Public Health Work," M. P. Ravenel, ed., *A Half Century of Public Health* (New York, 1921), 76–90.

345. In the absence of reliable vital statistics for most of the country, these figures, strictly interpreted, apply only to the registration area. See *U.S. Twelfth Census* (1900), III, lvii, lxxxvi–lxxxvii, and *Supplementary Analysis and Derivative Tables*, 495, 504–507.

346. Hurlbut, *Story of Chautauqua*, 184.

347. Bryce's phrase in *American Commonwealth*, III, 559.

348. For a contemporaneous appreciation of this fact, see C. D. Warner, "Aspects of American Life," *Atlantic Mo.*, XLIII (1879), 1–9.

349. Quoted by W. G. Moody, *Land and Labor in the United States* (New York, 1883), 279.

350. Such as the Freemasons (1730) and the Odd Fellows (1819), introduced from England; the Ancient Order of Hibernians (1836) from Ireland; the German Turnerbund (1850); and the Bohemian Sokol (1865).

351. H. C. Merwin, "A National Vice," *Atlantic Mo.*, LXXI (1893), esp. 769; W. B. Hill, "The Great American Safety-Valve," *Century*, XLIV (1892), 383–84.

352. Walter Basye, *History and Operation of Fraternal Insurance* (Rochester, 1919), chaps. i, iv–v.

353. These data are taken from H. B. Meyer, "Fraternal Beneficiary Societies in the United States," *Am. Journ. of Sociology*, VI, 655–56. According to this enumeration, which seems more reliable than the somewhat different estimates in A. C. Stevens, comp., *Cyclopaedia of Fraternities* (New York, 1899), only seventy-eight fraternal orders antedated 1880.

354. Stevens, *Cyclopaedia*, v, 114; W. S. Harwood, "Secret Societies in the United States," *N. Am. Rev.*, CLXIV (1897), 617–24; J. M. Foster, "Secret Societies and the State," *Arena*, XIX (1898), 229–39.

355. Josiah Strong, *The New Era* (New York, 1893), 128 *n*.

356. Anon., "New York Theatres," *Atlantic Mo.*, XLIII (1879), 452–55. For general treatments of the drama during the period, see L. C. Strang, *Players and Plays of the Last Quarter Century* (Boston, 1902), II; M. J. Moses, *The American Dramatist* (Boston, 1926), chaps. v–xi; Arthur Hornblow, *A History of the Theatre in America* (Philadelphia, 1919), chaps. xxiii–xxix; Mary C. Crawford, *The Romance of the American Theatre* (Boston, 1913), chaps. xii–xiv; A. H. Quinn, *A History of the American Drama from the Civil War* (New York, 1927), I.

357. The *N.Y. Dramatic Mirror* in 1879 listed the routes of forty-nine traveling companies; twenty years later the list was nearly ten times as great.

358. Difficulties of booking also increased, leading by gradual stages to the formation of a theatrical syndicate or trust in 1896. See M. B. Leavitt, *Fifty Years in Theatrical Management* (New York, 1912), 265–72; Ford, *Forty-Odd Years*, chap. xii; Norman Hapgood, *The Stage in America, 1897–1900* (New York, 1901), chap. i.

359. Cited by W. W. Stout, "Little Eva Is Seventy-Five," *Sat. Eve. Post.*, CC, 10ff. (October 8, 1927).

360. These figures include performers in musical plays as well as the legitimate drama. *U.S. Tenth Census* (1880), I, 744; *U.S. Twelfth Census* (1900), II, cxliv.

361. Strang, *Players and Plays*, II, chap. vii. The lack of an international copyright provision until 1891 was a discouragement to the native playwright as well as to the native *littérateur*.

362. His more important play "Margaret Fleming," produced in 1890, proved quite too bold in its realism, according to the standards of the time, to win public favor. Herne's confession of faith, "Art for Truth's Sake in the Drama," *Arena,* XVII (1897), 361-70, is a significant document in the history of the American drama.

363. Among Harrigan's chief comedies were *The Mulligan Guard Ball* (1879), *The Mulligan Guard Nominee* (1880) and *Cordelia's Aspirations* (1883). Harrigan also acted in the plays; and the team name of Harrigan and Hart was considered by theatergoers a guarantee of an evening of unmitigated fun.

364. J. F. Davis, "Tom Shows," *Scribner's Mag.,* LXXVII (1925), 350-60.

365. *N.Y. Dramatic Mirror,* XLI, no. 1043, 40 (December 24, 1898).

366. See 721.

367. Quinn, *American Drama from the Civil War,* I, 118-24.

368. Leavitt, *Fifty Years,* chaps. x-xi; M. R. Werner, *Barnum* (New York, 1923), chap. xiii.

369. In the second season Sitting Bull and other Sioux who had participated in the Custer massacre joined the company. W. F. Cody (Buffalo Bill, pseud.), *Story of the Wild West and Camp Fire Chats* (Chicago, 1902), 693-700, and Leavitt, *Fifty Years,* esp. 143.

370. The staid *Philadelphia Public Ledger* editorially gave *Pinafore* a clean bill of health and invited the attendance of the pure-minded. J. P. Sousa, *Marching Along* (Boston, 1928), 62.

371. T. A. Brown, *A History of the New York Stage* (New York, 1903), III, 485-506; Rudolph Aronson, *Theatrical and Musical Memoirs* (N.Y., 1913), chaps. iv-viii; same author, "Most Successful Operetta Ever Heard Here," *Theatre,* XVIII (1913), 17ff.

372. U.S. Twelfth Census, X, 181-84; P. G. Hubert, "The New Talking Machines," *Atlantic Mo.,* LXIII (1889), 256-61.

373. In every case above the composer's name is given. Many popular songs of the period have been reprinted by Sigmund Spaeth in *Read 'Em and Weep* (Garden City, N.Y., 1926) and *Weep Some More, My Lady* (Garden City, N.Y., 1927). See also E. C. May, "Words with Music," *Sat. Eve. Post,* CXCVII, 11ff. (October 18, 1924), and Isaac Goldberg, *Tin Pan Alley* (New York, 1930), chaps. v-vi.

374. U.S. Bureau of Education, *Circular of Information for 1886,* no. 1.

375. Soissons, *Parisian in America,* 186. From 1880 to 1900 the number of establishments making pianos and materials increased from 174 to 263, their products from more than $12 million to well over $35 million. While before 1866 nearly all the pianos made were square pianos, by 1900 nearly all of them were uprights, an indication perhaps of the more crowded conditions of living. *U.S. Twelfth Census,* X, 448, 454.

376. L. P. Brockett, *Our Western Empire* (Philadelphia, 1882), 198-99.

377. For the composers mentioned in the text and others, see J. T. Howard, *Our American Music* (New York, 1931), 315-403, and Rupert Hughes, *Contemporary American Composers* (Boston, 1900), chaps. ii-v.

378. I. N. Hollis, "Intercollegiate Athletics," *Atlantic Mo.,* XC (1902), esp. 543. See also D. A. Sargent, "The Physical State of the American People," Shaler, *United States of America,* III, 1135-36.

379. By 1894 it had encircled the globe and had ardent advocates in such extremes as Paris and Melbourne. J. P. Paret, "Basketball," *Outing,* XXXI (1897), 224.

380. S. C. Hildreth and J. R. Crowell, *The Spell of the Turf* (Philadelphia, 1926), chaps. ii-vii. On all phases of sport, J. A. Krout, *Annals of American Sport* (R. H. Gabriel, ed., *The Pageant of America,* New Haven, 1926-29, XIV), is valuable.

381. This was the last bare-knuckle championship fight. The quotation is from Vachel Lindsay's rhythmic commemoration of the event in *Collected Poems* (New York, 1925), 93-95. For pugilistic development in general, see Alexander Johnston, *Ten —and Out* (New York, 1927), chaps. vi-xi.

382. R. F. Dibble, "Robert Prometheus Fitzsimmons," *Dict. of Am. Biog.*, VI, 443.
383. A. G. Spalding, *America's National Game* (New York, 1911), chaps. xiv-xx, xxxiv; G. L. Moreland, *Balldom* (New York, 1914), 16-133; Bozeman Bulger, "What Made Great Ball Players Great," *Des Moines Register*, March 14-April 11, 1924, passim.
384. The World Series was revived in 1903 between the winner of the National League and the newly formed American League.
385. Thomas Stevens, *Around the World on a Bicycle* (New York, 1887-88).
386. Anon., "Skirt Protecting Screen for Bicycles," *Scientific Am.*, LXXIV (1896), 261.
387. In the single year 1895, over half a million were manufactured; in 1900, well over a million. A. A. Pope, "The Bicycle Industry," Depew, *One Hundred Years of American Commerce*, II, 551; *U.S. Twelfth Census*, X, 328.
388. Not only skirts of short walking length, but even bloomers, it was urged, might be worn without offense to "feminine dignity and modesty." L. H. Porter, *Cycling for Health and Pleasure* (New York, 1895), 3-22, 106-17, 177-95.
389. G. B. Bartlett, "The Recreations of the People," *Journ. of Social Sci.*, XII (1880), 141.
390. J. H. Mandigo, "Outdoor Sports," *Chautauquan*, XIX (1894), 393.
391. *Daily Eagle* (Red Wing. Minn.), February 2, 1928.
392. *Puck*, XXI, 236 (June 1, 1887).
393. Muirhead, *Land of Contrasts*, 158.
394. Bryce, *American Commonwealth*, III, 483.
395. [J. B. Harrison], *Certain Dangerous Tendencies in American Life* (Boston, 1880), 10-11.
396. See comments of the French psychologist Gabriel Compayré, quoted in U.S. Comr. of Educ. *Report for 1895-96*, II, 1165.
397. See this volume, Book VIII, 721.
398. The antievolutionists made the most of the internal strife among naturalists, which, however, did not question the fact of evolution but rather the particular mode set forth by Darwin. See *Nation* (New York), XLIV, 121-23 (February 10, 1887), and LX, 31 (January 10, 1895).
399. Henry Calderwood, *The Relations of Science and Religion* (New York, 1881), esp. 298, 308; C. B. Warring, *Miracle, Law and Evolution* (New York, 1887), esp. 8; review of Arnold Guyot's *Creation, Am. Catholic Quar.*, IX (1884), 374.
400. S. B. Goodenow, "Primeval Man," *Bibliotheca Sacra*, LI (1894), esp. 159.
401. T. T. Munger, "Religion's Gain from Science," *Forum*, VI (1888), 45-54.
402. E. J. Goodspeed, *A Full History of the Wonderful Career of Moody and Sankey in Great Britain and America* (Ashland, Ohio, 1877), 315.
403. Washington Gladden, *Recollections* (Boston, 1909), 320-21.
404. Lyman Abbott, *Reminiscences* (Boston, 1915), 460-62; C. W. Shields, "Does the Bible Contain Scientific Errors?," *Century*, XLV (1892-93), 126-34; C. A. Briggs, "Works of the Imagination in the Old Testament," *N. Am. Rev.*, CLXIV (1897), 356-73.
405. White, *Warfare of Science with Theology*, I, 313-16. Winchell's views are set forth in *The Doctrine of Evolution* (New York, 1874) and *Adamites and Pre-Adamites* (Syracuse, 1878).
406. G. F. Moore, "An Appreciation of Professor Toy," *Am. Journ. of Semitic Languages and Literatures*, XXXVI, 3-5; White, *Warfare of Science with Theology*, I, 316-18; Simkins, *Tillman Movement in South Carolina*, 142, 144.
407. The professors were J. W. Churchill, George Harris, E. Y. Hincks, W. J. Tucker, and E. C. Smyth, the last for some reason being the only one adjudged guilty. The case was taken before the state supreme court and in 1893 a decision handed down against the board. W. J. Tucker, *My Generation* (Boston, 1919), chap. vii.
408. His work *Creed and Deed* (New York, 1877) sets forth his view that the essence of religion is "fervent devotion to the highest moral ends."

409. For her exposition of the tenets of Theosophy, see *Isis Unveiled* (New York, 1877) and *The Secret Doctrine* (London, 1888).

410. [Harrison], *Certain Dangerous Tendencies,* 206-13; F. H. Hedge, *The Church in Modern Society* (n.p., 1882), 266-67; C. F. Thwing, "Young Men and the Preaching They Want," *Century,* XLIX (1894-95), 637-39.

411. Awareness of this failure is expressed in books like Washington Gladden, *Applied Christianity* (Boston, 1886), 146-79; S. L. Loomis, *Modern Cities and Their Religious Problems* (New York, 1887), esp. chap. iii; Strong, *New Era,* chap. x; and Stead, *If Christ Came to Chicago!,* 389-405; as well as in an abundant periodical literature, including O. F. Adams, "Aristocratic Drift of American Protestantism," *N. Am. Rev.,* CXLII (1886), 194-99; C. M. Morse, "The Church and the Working Man," *Forum,* VI (1888), 653-61; T. B. Wakeman, "Our Unchurched Millions," *Arena,* II (1890), 604-13; and C. A. Briggs, "The Alienation of Church and People," *Forum,* XVI (1893-94), esp. 375-77.

412. Data in regard to the distribution of churches in urban centers are summarized in Loomis, *Modern Cities,* 7-9, 88-89, and Strong, *New Era,* 197-201.

413. R. T. Ely, *Social Aspects of Christianity* (rev. ed., New York, 1889), 44-45. In at least one case on record, that of a Lutheran congregation in Oshkosh, Wis., in February, 1894, trade unionists were excluded from the church on the ground that membership in a labor organization violated the law of God. Stead, *If Christ Came to Chicago,* 394-95n.

414. R. H. Johnson, "American Baptists in the Age of Big Business," *Journ. of Religion,* XI, esp. 72.

415. H. F. Perry, "The Workingman's Alienation from the Church," *Am. Journ. of Sociology,* IV (1898-99), esp. 622.

416. W. R. Crafts, "Impressions of a Transcontinental Tour," *Our Day* (Boston), IV (1889), 543; Bryce, *American Commonwealth,* III, 488; B. J. Ramage, "Sunday Legislation," *Sewanee Rev.,* IV (1895), 121.

417. J. H. Ward, "The New Sunday," *Atlantic Mo.,* XLVII (1881), 526-38; C. W. Clark, "The Day of Rest," *Atlantic Mo.,* LXIV (1889), 366-75. For the Catholic attitude, see anon., "The Catholic Sunday and the Puritan Sabbath," *Catholic World,* XXIII (1876), 550-65.

418. Loomis, *Modern Cities,* 104.

419. See, for example, W. R. Crafts, "Valid Grounds for Sabbath Observance," *Our Day,* II (1888), 262-75.

420. F. W. Farrar, "The Salvation Army," *Harper's Mag.,* LXXXII (1891), 897-906; C. A. Briggs, "The Salvation Army," *N. Am. Rev.,* CLIX (1894), 697-710.

421. A schism within the ranks led in 1896 to the establishment of the Volunteers of America, which had less military autocracy in its form of organization but was otherwise devoted to a similar mission. Anon., "Ballington Booth and the Salvation Army," *Public Opinion,* XX (1896), 304-305.

422. Two recent biographies are E. F. Dakin, *Mrs. Eddy* (rev. ed., New York, 1930), a critical study, and L. P. Powell, *Mary Baker Eddy* (New York, 1930), a work commended by Mrs. Eddy's followers.

423. There were many later editions and revisions. Though in retrospect Mrs. Eddy denied any indebtedness to Quimby, Powell in *Mary Baker Eddy,* 103, admits he played an important role in shaping her thinking. Incidentally, the exact term, "Christian Science" had occasionally been used by Quimby. P. P. Quimby, *The Quimby Manuscripts* (H. W. Dresser, ed., 2d ed., New York, 1921), 388. Unadulterated Quimbyism became the basis of the New Thought movement which began to emerge toward the end of the century.

424. Moreover, "Healing the sick through mind instead of matter, enables us to heal the absent as well as the present." Ed. of 1875, 334, 348, 398. Conversely, vindictive persons, through malicious animal magnetism ("M.A.M."), can produce disease or misfortune in others—a doctrine which first appeared in the edition of 1878.

425. Sibyl Wilbur (O'Brien), *The Life of Mary Baker Eddy* (New York, 1907), 198.

426. *U.S. Eleventh Census* (1890), XVI, 297–98; *Christian Science Journal,* XVIII (1900), 202. From a scrutiny of the advertisements in the *Journal* it appears that the number of practitioners rose from 14 in April 1883, to 200 in April 1890, and to 963 in April 1896.

427. *Christian Science Journal,* XII (1894), 90–93, 451–54; *Boston Herald,* January 7, 1895. Edward Eggleston's novel *The Faith Doctor* (New York, 1891) satirized the growing enthusiasm for Christian Science among the socially ambitious of New York.

428. Professor R. T. Ely, though not a cleric, also wielded great influence, especially through his volume *Social Aspects of Christianity.*

429. Gladden, *Recollections,* 291–93, 300–305; same author, *Applied Christianity,* 1–37, 102–45.

430. The religious statistics of the period, unhappily, have to be used with great caution. The statements in the text must therefore be regarded as only rough approximations. The principal sources of information are Philip Schaff, "Progress of Christianity in the United States," *Princeton Rev.,* LV (1879), esp. 217–19; Bryce, *American Commonwealth,* III, 476, giving figures for 1887; H. K. Carroll, *Report on Statistics of Churches (U.S. Eleventh Census,* XVI); same author, *The Religious Forces of the United States* (Philip Schaff et al., eds., *The American Church History Series,* I, New York, 1893); Daniel Dorchester, *Christianity in the United States* (rev. ed., New York, 1895), pt. iii; David Sulzberger, "Growth of Jewish Population in the United States," Am. Jewish Hist. Soc., *Publs.,* no. 6 (1897), 144–45, 149; Daniel Dorchester, "The Evangelical Churches at the Close of the Nineteenth Century," *Christian Advocate,* LXXVI, 52–53 (January 10, 1901).

431. Gerald Shaughnessy, *Has the Immigrant Kept the Faith?* (New York, 1925). 162–72.

432. The first American cardinal, John McCloskey, was appointed in 1875; James Gibbons, his successor, was elevated in 1886.

433. H. J. Desmond, *The A. P. A. Movement* (Washington, 1912). For the earlier anti-Catholic movement, see this volume, Book VI, 517.

434. In Chicago in 1894 the mayor, chief of police, fire chief, city attorney, a number of judges, forty-five aldermen, nine out of ten policemen, four fifths of the fire department and two thirds of the schoolteachers were said to be Catholics. Stead, *If Christ Came to Chicago,* 265. It was alleged that the municipal offices of New York, St. Louis, New Orleans, San Francisco, and other important cities were also largely under Catholic control. W. H. J. Traynor, "The Aims and Methods of the A.P.A.," *N. Am. Rev.,* CLIX (1894), 69. Traynor, the national president, claimed a membership of 2.5 million for the A.P.A.

435. Washington Gladden, "The Anti-Catholic Crusade," *Century,* XLVII (1893–94), 789–95; T. J. Jenkins, "The A.P.A. Conspirators," *Catholic World,* LVII (1893), 685–93.

436. Anon., "The Purchase of Guns by the A.P.A.," *Public Opinion,* XVI (1893–94), 621.

437. The movement also possessed strength in Massachusetts and Rhode Island and in parts of the remoter West. Desmond, *A.P.A. Movement,* chaps. iii, vii.

438. McKinley kept his peace while his Democratic opponent denounced the A.P.A. As late as October 1894, Governor McKinley, when asked by a heckler, "What is the matter with the A.P.A.?" replied blandly, "The question with us is: What is the matter with the country?" "The A.P.A. in Politics," *Public Opinion,* XVII (1894–95), 615; Desmond, *A.P.A. Movement,* 34.

439. Gladden, *Recollections,* 359–65; Theodore Roosevelt, "What Americanism Means," *Forum,* XVII (1894), 196; G. F. Hoar, *Autobiography of Seventy Years* (New York, 1903), II, 278–93.

440. H. D. Sedgwick, Jr., "The United States and Rome," *Atlantic Mo.,* LXXXIV (1899), 445–58.

441. W. G. Sumner, *What Social Classes Owe to Each Other* (New York, 1883), 112; Bryce, *American Commonwealth,* III, 498.

442. Annie N. Meyer, ed., *Woman's Work in America* (New York, 1891), chaps. xii-xv, xvii-xviii.

443. Among the more noted settlement workers who visited for a time at Toynbee Hall, besides Jane Addams, were Stanton Coit, Ellen G. Starr, Charles Zueblin, and Robert A. Woods.

444. Jane Addams, *Twenty Years at Hull House* (New York, 1910), chaps. iv-xi; Dorothea Moore, "A Day at Hull House," *Am. Journ. of Sociology,* II (1897), 629-42; Thérèse Blanc, *The Condition of Woman in the United States* (Abby L. Alger, tr., Boston, 1895), 67-87; Jane Addams et al., *Philanthropy and Social Progress* (New York, 1893), chap. ii.

445. A chronological table of the more important ones is given in C. R. Henderson, *Social Settlements* (New York, 1899), 43-46; a complete list in R. A. Woods and A. J. Kennedy, eds., *Handbook of Settlements* (New York, 1911).

446. See, for example, Addams, *Twenty Years,* chaps. vii, ix-x, xiii-xiv; Eleanor H. Woods, *Robert A. Woods* (Boston, 1929), chaps. xi, xiii; R. A. Woods and A. J. Kennedy, *The Settlement Horizon* (New York, 1922), chaps. xvi-xvii; Julia C. Lathrop and others, "Social Settlements and the Labor Question," Natl. Conf. of Charities and Correction, *Proceeds. for 1896,* pt. iii.

447. On this point, see J. R. Elliott, *American Farms (Questions of the Day Series,* LXII, 2d ed., New York, 1890), 236-39.

448. Frances E. Willard, *Glimpses of Fifty Years* (Boston, 1889), 368-478.

449. Loomis, *Modern Cities,* 101-102; Raymond Calkins, *Substitutes for the Saloon* (Boston, 1901), chap. i; John Koren, *Economic Aspects of the Liquor Problem* (Boston, 1899), chap. viii.

450. J. S. Billings, comp., *Report on the Social Statistics of Cities (U.S. Eleventh Census,* 1890), 109-17.

451. Koren, *Economic Aspects of Liquor Problem,* 35-37; Calkins, *Substitutes for Saloon,* 303-13; T. V. Powderly, *Thirty Years of Labor* (Columbus, 1889), 580-626; *Cyclopaedia of Temperance and Prohibition* (New York, 1891), 264-66.

452. Koren, *Economic Aspects of Liquor Problem,* 37-38; *Economic Aspects of the Liquor Problem* (U.S. Comr. of Labor, *Ann. Rep. for 1897),* chap. vii.

453. Rhode Island from 1886 to 1889, and South Dakota from 1889 to 1896, had prohibition by constitutional amendment. Kansas in 1880, Maine in 1884, and North Dakota in 1889 made prohibition a constitutional requirement. E. H. Cherrington, *The Evolution of Prohibition in the United States* (Westerville, 1920), 202-66; D. L. Colvin, *Prohibition in the United States* (New York, 1926), 137-44, 177-83, 202-16.

454. E. L. Fanshawe, *Liquor Legislation in the United States and Canada* (London, 1893), chap. iv. As a variant from the usual methods of dealing with the liquor problem, South Carolina in 1893, under prod of Governor Tillman, set up exclusive government dispensaries, a system which remained in force until 1907. Its dual purpose was to garner larger revenues for the state and reduce the private-profit motive in the sale of drinks. Though modeled upon a municipal system in Athens, Georgia, the plan gained no favor elsewhere; for once prohibitionists and private saloonists saw eye to eye. F. H. Wines and John Koren, *The Liquor Problem in Its Legislative Aspects* (2d ed., Boston, 1898), 141-80*b;* Simkins, *Tillman Movement,* chap. viii; Gallus Thomann, *The South Carolina Dispensary* (New York, 1905).

455. This view of the situation is based upon evidence presented in Wines and Koren, *Liquor Problem,* 22-95, and Fanshawe, *Liquor Legislation,* chap. vii. These authors also review enforcement difficulties in Massachusetts, New York, Pennsylvania, Ohio, Indiana, Iowa, Missouri, South Carolina, and elsewhere.

456. If 10 percent reduction be allowed for use in manufactures and the arts, the

increase in personal consumption still remains startling. The capital investment in liquor grew from $118 million to $458 million. *U.S. Statistical Abstract for 1906,* 687; *U.S. Twelfth Census* (1900), IX, 599, 612, 624.

457. Meyer, *Woman's Work in America,* 404.

458. See this volume, Book VIII, 721.

459. *Appletons' Annual Cyclopaedia,* XIX (1879), 539-40. As for lesser prisons, according to a leading penal authority, "the American jails of today are, with here and there an exception, substantially what Howard in the eighteenth century found jails to be." Z. R. Brockway, "Needed Reforms in Prison Management," *N. Am. Rev.,* CXXXVII (1883), esp. 40.

460. G. W. Cable gives a harrowing account of the system in *The Silent South* (New York, 1885), 111-80. In *The American Siberia* (Philadelphia, 1891) J. C. Powell describes vividly his fourteen years as manager of a Florida convict camp.

461. The Elmira plan was drawn very largely from the Irish prison system established by Sir Walter Crofton in the middle of the century. For the Elmira system in operation, see Alexander Winter, *The New York State Reformatory at Elmira* (London, 1891); F. H. Wines, *Punishment and Reformation (Crowell's Library of Economics and Politics,* VI, New York, 1895), chap. x; Z. R. Brockway, *Fifty Years of Prison Service* (New York, 1912), pt. ii; and F. B. Sanborn, "The Elmira Reformatory," S. J. Barrows, ed., *The Reformatory System in the United States* (Washington, 1900), 28-47.

462. *Appletons' Annual Cyclopaedia,* XXVII (1887), 703; Brockway, *Fifty Years,* 325.

463. Flora W. Seymour, *The Story of the Red Man* (New York, 1929), chap. xvii; L. H. Roddis, "The Last Indian Uprising in the United States," *Minn. History,* III, 273-90.

464. "The Report of the Senate Committee on the Removal of the Northern Cheyennes to Indian Territory," 46 Cong., 2 sess., *Senate Rep.,* no. 708 (June 8, 1880).

465. The Ponca episode is described in "The Report of the Senate Committee on the Removal of the Poncas to Indian Territory," 46 Cong., 2 sess., *Senate Rep.,* no. 670 (May 31, 1880).

466. Women's National Indian Association, *Report for 1885,* 26. This body, formed in 1879 under Protestant auspices, had seventy branches in leading centers in 1886.

467. G. F. Parker, "Grover Cleveland's First Administration," *Sat. Eve. Post,* CLXCV, esp. 52, 54 (April 7, 1923). Cleveland's private papers reveal that he also received much unsolicited advice from the spirit world through the Indian "controls" of self-avowed mediums. Robert McElroy, *Grover Cleveland* (New York, 1923), I, 226.

468. Secretary of Interior, *Rep. for 1879,* 4; *1884,* xi; Mohonk Conference, *Proceeds. for 1886,* 34; *1887,* 68.

469. One hundred and sixty acres for each head of family, smaller allotments for others, the amounts to be doubled in the case of grazing lands. *U.S. Statues at Large,* XXIV, 388-91. Because of the discrimination against the younger and more educable tribesmen a supplementary act of 1891 provided for tracts of eighty acres share and share alike. *U.S. Statutes at Large,* XXVI, 794-96. Eleven tribes were, for various reasons, exempted from the operation of these laws.

470. *U.S. Statutes at Large,* XXX, 495-519. This antagonistic attitude was due to many causes, chiefly perhaps to the position of power and profit held in the semiautonomous Indian states by mixed bloods and to the influence of cattle magnates who were benefiting from a cheap rental of the rich pasture lands. In 1901 the Five Tribes were brought specifically under the terms of the Dawes law. *U.S. Statutes at Large,* XXXI, 848, 861.

471. Comr. of Indian Affairs, *Rep. for 1892,* 185-95.

472. W. N. Hailmann, "Education of the Indian," N. M. Butler, ed., *Education in the United States* (Albany, 1900), II, 941-72; H. L. Dawes, "Have We Failed with the Indian?," *Atlantic Mo.,* LXXXIV (1899), 280-83.

473. The government reserved relatively small tracts for religious and educational purposes and as timber preserves. Detailed figures as regards allotments may be found
in Esther F. Cooper, The Genesis and Application of the Dawes Act (M.A. thesis,
Univ. of Iowa, 1924), 111-12, and app. C. See also Dawes, "Have We Failed with
the Indian?," 283.

474. The original statute was amended from time to time to permit leasing but under
strict conditions. *U.S. Statutes at Large,* XXVI, 794; XXVIII, 305; XXX, 85.

475. Comr. of Indian Affairs, *Rep. for 1892,* 139, 186, 192; *1893,* 335.

476. See, for example, edit., "Political Rights of Negroes," *Andover Rev.,* XIII (1890),
305; R. P. Hollowell, *The Southern Question Past and Present* (Boston, 1890),
21-26. The policy of noninterference was facilitated by the fact that until 1889
the Republicans were at no time in effective control of both the presidency and
the two houses of Congress.

477. J. F. Rhodes, *History of the United States from Hayes to McKinley* (New York,
1919), 358-64.

478. W. L. Fleming, " 'Pap' Singleton, the Moses of the Colored Exodus," *Am. Journ.
of Sociology,* XV, 61-82; J. C. Hartzell, "The Negro Exodus," *Methodist Quar.
Rev.,* LXI (1879), 722-48; F. R. Guernsey, "The Negro Exodus," *International
Rev.,* VII (1879), 373-90; J. B. Runnion, "The Negro Exodus," *Atlantic Mo.,* XLIV
(1879), 222-30; *Appletons' Annual Cyclopaedia,* XIX (1879), 354-58; XX (1880),
417.

479. Successful examples of black colonies were Nicodemus, Baxter Springs, Morton
City, and Singleton. F. H. Fletcher, *Negro Exodus* (n.p., 1879); Henry King, "A
Year of the Exodus in Kansas," *Scribner's Mo.,* XX (1880), 211-18; anon., "The
Administration of Governor John P. St. John," Kan. Hist. Soc., *Colls.,* IX, 378-95.

480. "The Proceedings of a Migration Convention and Congressional Action Respecting
the Exodus of 1879," *Journ. of Negro History,* IV, 41-92.

481. *Negroes in the United States* (Bur. of the Census, *Bull.,* no. 129, 1915), 12-13,
57-58.

482. *Appletons' Annual Cyclopaedia,* XX (1880), 585. See also Frederick Douglass,
"The Negro Exodus," *Journ. of Social Sci.,* IX (1880), esp. 12-21.

483. B. T. Washington, "The Awakening of the Negro," *Atlantic Mo.,* LXXVIII (1896),
esp. 322. See also same author, *Up from Slavery* (New York, 1901), chaps. vii-
xii, and M. B. Thrasher, *Tuskegee* (Boston, 1900).

484. The quotations are taken from his noted speech in 1895 at the opening of the
Atlanta Exposition, reprinted in *Up from Slavery,* 218-25, and elsewhere.

485. U.S. Comr. of Educ., *Reps.,* 1878-1901, passim; esp. J. L. M. Curry, "The Slater
Fund and the Education of the Negro," *Rep. for 1894-95,* II, 1367-1424; Kelley
Miller, "The Education of the Negro," *Rep. for 1900-01,* I, 731-859; and A. D.
Mayo, "The Work of Certain Northern Churches in the Education of the Freedmen,
1861-1900," *Rep. for 1901-02,* I, 285-314.

486. See earlier, 721.

487. Miller estimates that the per capita school expenditure in the ex-slave states was
in 1878-79 $2.60 for whites and $1.00 for blacks, the comparable figures for
1897-98 being $4.25 and $2.27. "Education of the Negro," 753. If his estimates
are accurate, it is probable that the disparity may be, in considerable degree,
accounted for by the difference in the per capita expenditure on education in the
cities, where blacks were few, and in the rural districts where the vast bulk of
them dwelt.

488. U.S. Comr. of Educ., *Rep. for 1898-99,* II, 2202. The rural school term usually
lasted about two months, and black parents were not able to lengthen it by
voluntary contributions as was often done by the whites for their own schools.

489. S. J. Barrows, "What the Southern Negro Is Doing for Himself," *Atlantic Mo.,* LXVII
(1891), 805-15; P. A. Bruce, *The Plantation Negro as a Freemen (Questions of
the Day Series,* LVII; New York, 1889), chaps. xiii-xiv; L. J. Greene and C. J.
Woodson, *The Negro Wage Earner* (Washington, 1930), chap. ii.

490. Barrows, "What the Southern Negro Is Doing," 807, 810; C. H. Wesley, *Negro Labor in the United States* (New York, 1927), 226-35; Greene and Woodson, *Negro Wage Earner,* chap. iii.

491. Wesley, *Negro Labor,* 236-37, 254-63.

492. Bruce, *Plantation Negro,* 48-53; G. W. Cable, *The Negro Question* (New York, 1890), 21-24.

493. Bruce, *Plantation Negro,* 53-55, 243. See also same author, "The Negro Population of the South," *Conservative Rev.,* II (1899), 276.

494. 109 U.S. (1883), 1; Franklin Johnson, *The Development of State Legislation Concerning the Negro* (New York, 1919), 14-19, and passim.

495. Nearly four fifths of the victims were blacks. J. E. Cutler, *Lynch-Law* (New York, 1905), chap. vi; Ida B. Wells, *A Red Record* (Chicago, ca. 1895); Walter White, *Rope and Faggot* (New York, 1929), app.

496. S. B. Weeks, "History of Negro Suffrage," *Polit. Sci. Quar.,* IX, 671-703; W. A. Dunning, *Essays on the Civil War and Reconstruction* (New York, 1904), 363-85; W. C. Hamm, "The Three Phases of Colored Suffrage," *N. Am. Rev.,* CLXVIII (1899), 285-96; Paul Lewinson, *Race, Class, & Party* (London, 1932), chaps. iv-v.

497. Cable, *Negro Question,* 66.

498. *Negroes in United States,* 29, 158-60.

499. W. E. B. Du Bois, "Strivings of the Negro People," *Atlantic Mo.,* LXXX (1897), 196.

500. Henry Adams, *The Education of Henry Adams* (Boston, 1918), 331. After accounting for the origin of the phrase a contemporary writer says: "Everywhere we are treated to dissertations on fin-de-siècle literature, fin-de-siècle statesmanship, fin-de-siècle morality." "Contributors' Club," *Atlantic Mo.,* LXVII (1891), 859-60.

501. The philosophy of fashionable boredom is amusingly depicted in Edmund Vance Cooke's poem "Fin de Siècle," which was set to music and introduced into Hoyt's farce, *A Night in New York,* E. V. Cooke, *Rimes to Be Read* (rev. ed., New York, 1905), 67-69.

502. Josiah Strong, *Expansion under New World Conditions* (New York, 1900), 72-73.

503. H. D. Lloyd, *Wealth against Commonwealth* (New York, 1894), 7, 494.

504. Woodrow Wilson, "On Being Human," *Atlantic Mo.,* LXXX (1897), 322.

505. J. J. Greenough, "The Basis of Our Educational System," *Atlantic Mo.,* LXXV (1895), 530.

506. Wilson, "On Being Human," 321.

507. Quoted by D. A. Wells, *Recent Economic Changes* (New York, 1889), 325.

508. F. J. Turner, *The Frontier in American History* (New York, 1920), 38.

509. See earlier, 721.

510. *Latter-day Saints' Millennial Star,* LII (1890), 648, 721-25, 737-41, 744-45, 753-57.

511. *Supplementary Analysis and Derivative Tables,* 44-45, 277.

512. *U.S. Twelfth Census* (1900), I, lxxxiv-lxxxv.

513. Luna E. Kellie, "Vote for Me," *Farmers' Alliance* (Lincoln, Neb.), September 6, 1890, quoted by J. D. Barnhart, History of the Farmers' Alliance and of the People's Party in Nebraska (unpublished Ph.D. thesis, Harvard Univ., 1930), 124.

514. McMurry, *Coxey's Army.*

515. Such societies in the number of 163 were active in 1891 from coast to coast. *Nationalist* (Boston), III (1891), 505.

516. W. D. Howells, *Life in Letters* (Mildred Howells, ed., Garden City, 1928), II, 26.

517. Ferris Greenslet, *Life of Thomas Bailey Aldrich* (Boston, 1908), 168-69.

518. Margaret S. Sibley, "A 'Fin-de-Siècle' Vision," *Arena,* XI (1894-95), 99.

519. Platform of 1892, quoted in T. H. McKee, *The National Conventions and Platforms of All Political Parties* (Baltimore, 1900), 281.

520. W. D. Howells, *A Traveller from Altruria* (New York, 1894), 50.

521. Anon., "The Relief of the Unemployed during the Winter of 1893-94," *Journ. of Social Sci.,* XXXII (1894), 1-51; C. C. Closson, Jr., "The Unemployed in American Cities," *Quar. Journ. of Econ.,* VIII (1894), 168-217; F. D. Watson, *The Charity Organization Movement in the United States* (New York, 1922), 248-65.

522. C. B. Spahr, *An Essay on the Present Distribution of Wealth in the United States* (R. T. Ely, ed., *Library of Economics and Politics,* XII, New York, 1896), esp. 69.

523. C. D. Wright, "Are the Rich Growing Richer and the Poor Poorer?," *Atlantic Mo.,* LXXX (1897), 300-309.

524. F. J. Kingsbury, "The Tendency of Men to Live in Cities," *Journ. of Social Sci.,* XXXIII (1895), 15. See also C. D. Warner, *The Relation of Literature to Life* (New York, 1897), 263-64, and S. Weir Mitchell, *Wear and Tear* (5th ed., Philadelphia, 1887), 3-4.

525. In the case of the Southern trade the increase was fully one inch around the chest and waist. Edward Atkinson, "The American Physique," *Science,* X (1887), 239-40, 276.

526. G. M. Beard, *American Nervousness* (New York, 1881), chaps. ii-v; Mitchell, *Wear and Tear,* 7-10, 22-30; Grace Peckham, "The Nervousness of Americans," *Journ. of Social Sci.,* XXII (1887), 37-49; W. B. Platt, "Certain Injurious Influences of City Life," *Journ. of Social Sci.,* XXIV (1888), 24-30; Edward Wakefield, "Nervousness: The National Disease of America," *McClure's,* II (1894), 302-307.

527. A. F. Weber, *The Growth of Cities in the Nineteenth Century* (Columbia Univ., *Studies,* XI), 392.

528. Mitchell, *Wear and Tear,* 30-55; edit., *Ladies' Home Journ.,* X (1893), no. 9, 14.

529. W. E. Smythe, "Real Utopias in the Arid West," *Atlantic Mo.,* LXXIX (1897), 609; Bryce, *American Commonwealth* III, 54.

530. See this volume, Book IX.

BOOK XI   The Quest for Social Justice, 1898–1914

1. Thomas Beer, *The Mauve Decade* (New York, 1926).

2. F. J. Turner, *The Frontier in American History* (New York, 1921); F. L. Paxson, *History of the American Frontier* (Boston, 1924).

3. C. W. Wright, "The Significance of the Disappearance of Free Land in Our Economic Development," *Am. Econ. Rev.,* XVI, sup., 264-71.

4. C. B. Spahr, *The Present Distribution of Wealth in the United States* (New York, 1896), 65.

5. W. I. King, *The Wealth and Income of the People of the United States* (New York, 1915), 72-87, 90-105.

6. Bureau of the Census, *Employees and Wages (Special Rep, for 1900),* ci-civ.

7. Interstate Commerce Commission, *Thirteenth Annual Report* (1899), 34, 40.

8. J. A. Ryan, *A Living Wage* (New York, 1906), 162; W. E. Walling, "The New Unionism the Problem of the Unskilled Worker," Am. Acad. of Polit. and Social Sci., *Annals,* XXIV, 300.

9. Bureau of the Census, *Census of Manufactures for 1905,* pt. iv, 645.

10. These figures are for Massachusetts for 1902, a state in which foodstuffs and coal are comparatively high, and represent the annual average prices. Commision on the Cost of Living, *Report* (Boston, 1910), 64.

11. Ryan, *Living Wage,* chap, vii; R. C. Chapin, *The Standard of Living in New York City* (New York, 1909), 246; F. H. Streightoff, *The Standard of Living among the Industrial People of America* (Boston, 1911), 162. See also the *Monthly Labor Review,* I, no.4, 18-21.

12. Robert Hunter, *Poverty* (New York, 1904), 60ff.

13. J. L. Gillin, *Poverty and Dependency* (New York, 1921), 36.

14. J. A. Riis, *A Ten Years' War* (Boston, 1900), chap. ii; Hunter, *Poverty,* 73ff.

15. Mark Sullivan, *Our Times* (New York, 1926-35), I, 299.

16. Massachusetts Commission on the Cost of Living, *Report* (Boston, 1910), 194ff.

17. The commission also pointed out that the wage-earners' share of the net product of industry in the case of manufactures had declined from 44.9 percent in 1889 to 40.2 in 1909. Commission on Industrial Relations, *Final Report* (Washington, 1916), I, 21.

18. I. M. Rubinow, "The Recent Trend of Real Wages," *Am. Econ. Rev.,* IV, 194ff.

19. E. B. Woods, "Have Wages Kept Pace with the Cost of Living?," Am. Acad. of Polit. and Social Sci., *Annals,* LXXXIX, 135-47.

20. Bureau of the Census, *Abstract of the Thirteenth Census,* 239.

21. Hunter, *Poverty,* 244, 356-57.

22. The Dingley tariff of 1897 raised the average level to 57 percent, the highest up to that time since the Civil War. It maintained in general the lower rates of 1894 on metals, but high duties were reimposed on raw wool and hides, while the rates on linens, silks, woolens, pottery, and sugar were raised.

23. *U.S. Statutes at Large,* XXXI, 45.

24. Of these 318 industrial trusts, 236 had been incorporated since January 1, 1898 (170 of them organized under New Jersey laws), five sixths of the capital being held by those dating since the beginning of 1898. John Moody, *The Truth about the Trusts* (New York, 1904), 486. For another contemporary tabulation of combinations, see Luther Conant, Jr., "Industrial Consolidations in the United States," Am. Statistical Assoc., *Publs.,* VII, 208-17.

25. This list, it will be noted, does not include transportation companies or other public utilities where the same movement toward consolidation was evident.

26. Bureau of the Census, *Abstract of the Census of Manufactures for 1919,* 354.

27. A. D. Noyes, *Forty Years of American Finance* (New York, 1909), 309ff.

28. *Commercial and Financial Chronicle,* LXXXIV, 1514 (June 29, 1907); LXXXV, 371 (August 17, 1907).

29. Committee on Banking and Currency of the House of Representatives, *Money Trust Investigation* (3 vols., Washington, 1913).

30. Committee to Investigate Concentration of Control of Money and Credit, *Report* (62 Cong., 3 sess., *House Rep.,* no. 1593), 131.

31. Committee to Investigate Money and Credit, *Report,* 130.

32. Committee on Banking and Currency, *Money Trust Investigation,* II, 1568.

33. Selig Perlman, *Growth of American Trade Unionism* (New York, 1924), 33.

34. G. E. Barnett, "Growth of Labor Organizations" *Quar. Journ. of Econ.,* XXX, 780.

35. J. R. Commons et al., *History of Labour in the United States* (New York, 1918), II, 521ff.

36. *American Labor Yearbook for 1916,* 20. See also Selig Perlman, *A History of Trade Unionism in the United States* (New York, 1922), 163ff.

37. Samuel Gompers, *Seventy Years of Life and Labor* (New York, 1925), II, 104ff. Help came also from the National Consumers' League, organized in 1898, an effective agency in combating the sweatshop evil; from the National Child Labor Committee, formed in 1904 to agitate for the abolition of child labor; and from the American Association of Labor Legislation (1906), which was interested in both better labor legislation and the stricter enforcement of existing laws.

38. Commons et al., *History of Labour,* II, 524.

39. John Mitchell, *Organized Labor* (Philadelphia, 1903), 347.

40. U. S. Commissioner of Labor, *Twenty-First Annual Report* (1907), 32.

41. Ibid., 15; and analysis in G. G. Groat, *Organized Labor in America* (New York, 1919), chap. x. The number of strikes had increased from 471 in 1881 to 1,056 in 1898, 3,494 in 1903, and 2,077 in 1905. Of the 36,757 strikes taking place in the quarter century 1881-1905, over half (18,596) had occurred in the last eight years.

42. In 1903 it founded the Citizens' Industrial Association to oppose the demands of labor, and four years later fathered the National Council for Industrial Defense in order to lobby against labor bills in the state and federal legislatures.

43. 1,676,000 in 1904, and 1,562,000 in 1910.

44. American Federationist, XIII (1906), 529-31.

45. In the election of 1912 the Socialist popular vote was about eight times the enrolled party membership.

46. Morris Hillquit, *History of Socialism in the United States* (New York, 1903), pt. ii, chap. iv.

47. R. F. Hoxie, "The Socialist Party in the November Elections," *Journ, of Polit. Economy,* XX, no. 3, 205-23; C. E. Merriam, *The American Party System* (New York, 1922), 93ff.

48. Groat, *Organized Labor in America,* 372.

49. Vincent St. John, *The I.W.W., Its History, Structure and Methods* (3d ed., Cleveland, 1913), 5; P. F. Brissenden, *The I.W.W.; a Study of American Syndicalism* (Columbia Univ., *Studies,* LXXXIII), app. ii.

50. St. John, *The I.W.W.,* 9.

51. Brissenden, *The I.W.W.,* 87.

52. Ibid., app. iv, table D.

53. Carleton Parker, *The Casual Laborer* (New York, 1920), 108.

54. "Gompers and Burns on Unionism and Dynamite," *McClure's,* XXXVIII (1912), 363ff.

55. Gompers, *Seventy Years of Life and Labor,* II, 183ff.; *American Year Book for 1911,* 352-54; *American Federationist,* XVIII (1911), 433-50, 606, 611; XIX (1912), 17-23, 44-48, 132-35, 201-206; American Federation of Labor, *Rep. of the Proceeds of the Thirty-First Ann. Conv.* (1911), 41-45.

56. W. T. Davis, "The Strike War in Colorado," *Outlook,* CVII, 70 (May 9, 1914).

57. Subcommittee of the Committee on Mines and Mining, *Conditions in the Coal Mines of Colorado* (Washington, 1914), II, pt. x, 2880.

58. Davis, "Strike War in Colorado," 73.

59. *American Year Book for 1914,* 416-17.

60. Subcommittee of the Committee on Mines, *Coal Mines of Colorado,* II, pt. x, 2841ff.; testimony of J. D. Rockefeller, Jr., in American Federation of Labor, *Rep. of Proceeds, of the Thirty-Fifth Ann. Conv.* (1915), 70-73.

61. Barnett, "Growth of Labor Organizations" 780ff., puts the wage-earners as 3.5 percent organized in 1900 and 7 percent in 1910. Leo Wolman's estimate of 7.7 is in approximate agreement. See his "The Extent of Trade Unionism," Am. Acad. of Polit, and Social Sci., *Annals,* LXIX, 118ff.

62. Earlier laws of 1868 and 1892 had been so restricted as to be of little value. J. R. Commons and J. B. Andrews, *Principles of Labor Legislation* (New York, 1916), 226ff.

63. Commission on Industrial Relations, *Final Report* (Washington, 1916), I, 48.

64. *Ritchie* v. *People,* 155 Ill., 98 (1895).

65. In re Morgan, 26 Colo., 415; 58 Pacific, 1071 (1899).

66. *Lochner* v. *New York,* 198 U.S., 45 (1905).

67. *People* v. *Williams,* 189 N.Y., 131; 80 N. E., 778 (1907).

68. *Holden* v. *Hardy,* 169 U.S., 366; *Muller* v. *Oregon,* 208 U.S., 412; *Miller* v. *Wilson,* 236 U.S., 373.

69. *Ritchie* v. *Wayman,* 244 Ill., 509; *People* v. *Charles Schweinler Press,* 214 N.Y., 395.

70. Quoted by Lincoln Steffens, *The Struggle for Self-Government* (New York, 1906), 16.

71. Quoted by F. C. Howe, "Joseph W. Folk," *Cosmopolitan,* XXXV (1903), 555. On Folk, who was circuit attorney of Missouri from 1900 until 1904, when he was elected governor, see also W. A. White, "Folk: the Story of a Little Leaven in a Great Commonwealth," *Cosmopolitan,* XXXV (1903), 545-60.

72. Quoted by Lincoln Seteffens, "Rhode Island: a State for Sale," *McClure's,* XXIV (1905), 340; "A Short View of Bribery," *Nation,* LXXVII, 45 (July 16, 1903).

73. Steffens, *Struggle for Self-Government,* 133-34.

74. Alabama (1901), Virginia (1902), Michigan (1908), New Hampshire (1912), Louisiana (1913).
75. W. F. Dodd, *State Government* (2d ed., New York, 1928), 107.
76. J. B. Phillips, *Recent State Constitution-Making* (Univ. of Colo., *Studies,* II, no. 2), 79–80.
77. J. Q. Dealey, "General Tendencies in State Constitutions," *Am. Polit. Sci. Rev.,* I, 211; H. G. James, "Reorganization of State Government," *Am. Polit. Sci. Rev.,* IX, 297–98.
78. F. C. Howe, *The City the Hope of Democracy* (New York, 1905).
79. Sullivan, *Our Times,* II, 445–446, explains the origin of this term.
80. R. M. La Follette, *Autobiography* (Madison, 1913), chap. xiii.
81. Eugene Thwing, *Life and Meaning of Theodore Roosevelt* (New York, 1919), 154ff.
82. This included the Mann-Elkins act, a bill establishing a commerce court, one authorizing the interstate commerce commission to undertake a valuation of the railroads, acts establishing postal-savings banks and a parcels-post system, an expense-publicity act, an employers' liability law and an act making an appropriation for a scientific study of the tariff.
83. Theodore Roosevelt, "The Progressives, Past and Present," and E. H. Abbott, "Mr. Roosevelt in the West," *Outlook,* XCVI, 19–30, 64–67 (September 3, 1910).
84. On the Roosevelt–La Follette controversy, see La Follette, *Autobiography,* chaps. xii–xiii; and B. P. DeWitt, *The Progressive Movement* (New York, 1915), 76ff.
85. With the exception of North Dakota and Wisconsin which went for La Follette and Massachusetts which Taft won by a small majority, Roosevelt carried all of the presidential-primary states.
86. It called for direct primaries including presidential primaries, the initiative, referendum, recall, short ballot, direct election of U.S. senators, woman suffrage, recall of judicial decisions, an easier method of amending the federal Constitution, an inclusive program of social legislation, downward revision of the tariff, income and inheritance taxes, and better control over corporations by means of a federal commission.
87. W. F. McCombs, *Making Woodrow Wilson President* (New York, 1921), tells the story of the convention and nomination of Wilson, but his account in certain details must be accepted with caution.
88. Roosevelt's introduction to S. J. Duncan-Clark, *The Progressive Movement* (Boston, 1913), chap. xvi.
89. See this volume, Book VI, 517.
90. J. E. Homans, *Self-Propelled Vehicles* (6th ed., New York, 1907), 1.
91. R. S. Epstein, *Automobile Industry* (Chicago, 1928), 316–17.
92. T. W. Allen et al., *Highways and Highway Transportation* (U.S. Dept. of Agr., *Bull.,* no. 914), 178–81.
93. Aero Club of America, *Navigating the Air* (New York, 1907), xiii.
94. S. P. Langley, "Experiments with the Langley Aerodrome," Smithsonian Institution, *Ann. Rep. for 1904,* 113–25; Sullivan, *Our Times,* II, 557–68; newspaper reports for October 8 and December 9, 1903.
95. *Chicago Tribune,* December 10, 1903, 6; *Boston Herald,* December 10, 1903, 6.
96. Orville Wright, "How We Made the First Flight," *Flying,* II (1913), 36. See also Aero Club of America, *Navigating the Air,* 6–12, and Henry Wodehouse, "History of the Conquest of the Air," *Flying,* V (1916), 229–42.
97. Bureau of the Census, *Central Electric Light and Power Stations, 1902,* 106; C. D. Thompson, *Public Ownership* (New York, 1925), 269. Condensed statistics on the increased use of electric power in manufacturing are given in Bureau of the Census, *Abstract of the Fourteenth Census, 1920,* 1034–50. See also C. O. Ruggles, "Problems in the Development of a Super-Power System," *Harvard Business Rev.,* II (1924), 161.

98. Born in Austria, he was a Serb by nationality. T. C. Martin and S. L. Coles, *The Story of Electricity* (New York, 1919), I, 420.

99. *New International Year Book for 1913*, 230.

100. Federal Trade Commission, *Supply of Electrical Equipment and Competitive Conditions* (70 Cong., 1 sess., *Sen. Doc.*, no. 46), 4-13, 159ff.

101. Bureau of the Census, *Electric Railways, 1922 (Census of Electrical Industries*, Washington, 1925), 5-6. See also E. P. Burch, *Electric Traction* (New York, 1911), and F. J. Sprague, "The Electric Railway," *Century*, LXX (1905), 434-51, 512-27.

102. See this volume, Book X, 873.

103. Herbert Croly, "The New York Rapid Transit System," *Am. Rev. of Revs.*, XXX (1904), 306-11.

104. J. B. Walker, *Fifty Years of Rapid Transit* (New York, 1918), 289. Even more remarkable from an engineering point of view was the tunnel under the Detroit River at Detroit, built by the Michigan Central and opened for regular service October 16, 1910, after four years of construction

105. Burch, *Electric Traction*, 13ff.

106. The New York, New Haven and Hartford had acquired by 1909 about 1,500 miles of trolley line in New England, and the New York Central about half as much in the Mohawk Valley. Ibid., 21.

107. Most of these plans were, however, delayed for years because of the precarious financial condition which confronted many of the companies. Ibid., chap. xv.

108. The independent companies operated 1,053,866 telephones in 1902 and 3,644,565 in 1912. "Telephone Systems," *Encyclopedia Americana*, XXVI, 384.

109. See this volume, Book VIII, 721.

110. *Yearbook of Wireless Telegraphy and Telephony for 1914*, 17-34; O. E. Dunlap, Jr., *The Story of the Radio* (New York, 1927), chaps. i-iii; Waldemar Kaempffert, ed., *A Popular History of American Invention*, (New York, 1924), 351-78.

111. Of the female population ten years of age and over, which numbered 28,246,000 in 1900, 5,317,000 are given as breadwinners, and of the 34,553,000 in 1910, 8,076,000 are so listed, a relative increase of 3.8 percent. See *U.S. Thirteenth Census* (1910), IV, 30, 41.

112. Economists generally agreed in 1914 that for women under American conditions $7 a week provided a bare subsistence and that more than $8 was necessary for a "living wage." C. E. Persons, "Women's Work and Wages in the United States," *Quar. Journ. of Econ.*, XXIX, 207, 209.

113. U. S. Department of Labor, *Summary of the Report on Condition of Women and Child Wage Earners in the United States* (U.S. Bur. of Labor Statistics, *Bull.*, no. 5), 21.

114. Persons, "Women's Work and Wages," 212ff.

115. Alice Henry, *The Trade Union Woman* (New York, 1915), 62ff.

116. Croly, "New York Rapid Transit System," 310.

117. Charlotte P. Gilman, "The Passing of the Home in Great American Cities," *Cosmopolitan*, XXXVIII (1904), 139.

118. In 1900 there were 1.33 telephones per hundred population in the United States; in 1905, 4.02, and by 1915, 10.09.

119. See this volume, Book X, 873.

120. "Breakfast Foods," *Independent*, LX, 1577-78 (December 26, 1906).

121. For many years the black chef accompanied advertisements for Cream of Wheat.

122. "Vigor, Vim, Perfect Trim, Force Made Him Sunny Jim."

123. R. W. De Forest and Lawrence Veiller, *The Tenement House Problem* (New York, 1903), I, 3-4. Of course a tenement house is not necessarily a slum.

124. See this volume, Book X, 873.

125. De Forest and Veiller, *Tenement House Problem*, II, app. v.

126. *Tenement House Department* v. *Katie Moeschen*, 179 N.Y., 325.

127. Committee of Fifteen, *The Social Evil* (New York, 1902).

128. Ibid., app., 159. Under the Raines law only hotels having at least ten rooms to rent above the basement could sell liquor on Sunday, with the result that thousands of saloons were turned into assignation houses and loitering places for prostitutes.

129. Committee of Fifteen, *The Social Evil* (2d ed., New York, 1912), chap. iii.

130. Ibid., 216, 231ff.; see also Committee of Fourteen, *Annual Report for 1914.*

131. G. K. Turner, "The City of Chicago," *McClure's,* XXXVIII (1907), 575-92; also "Tammany's Control of New York by Professional Politicians," *McClure's,* XXXIII (1909), 117-34.

132. Vice Commission of Chicago, *The Social Evil in Chicago* (Chicago, 1911); Minneapolis Vice Commission, *Report* (Minneapolis, 1911); Portland Vice Commission, *Report* (Portland, 1913); and Hartford Vice Commission, *Report* (Hartford, 1913).

133. Vice Commission of Chicago, *Social Evil,* 70.

134. P. U. Kellogg, ed., *Wage-Earning Pittsburgh* (same ed., *The Pittsburgh Survey,* Russell Sage Found., New York, 1909-14, VI), 350.

135. American Society of Sanitary and Moral Prophylaxis, *Transactions,* I (1906); II (1908); III (1910).

136. *U.S. Statutes at Large,* XXXVI,pt. i, 825; C. G. Roe, *Panders and Their White Slaves* (New York, 1910).

137. Committee of Fifteen, *Social Evil* (2d ed.), 207ff.; Commission for the Investigation of the White Slave Traffic, So Called, *Report* (*Mass. House Doc.,* no. 2281).

138. Bureau of the Census, *Abstract of the Thirteenth Census, 1910,* 22. The rate of population increase was 26 percent from 1870 to 1880; 24.9 from 1880 to 1890; 20.7 from 1890 to 1900; 21 from 1900 to 1910; and 15 from 1910 to 1920.

139. Bureau of the Census, *Abstract of the Thirteenth Census,* 260. In this census the term "family" means a household or group of persons, whether related by blood or not, who share a common abode and usually the same table.

140. E. A. Ross, *Principles of Sociology* (New York, 1923), 35.

141. R. E. Baber and E. A. Ross, *Changes in the Size of American Families in One Generation* (Univ. of Wis., *Studies,* no. 10), 3.

142. Ross, *Principles of Sociology,* 392.

143. Lydia K. Commander, "Has the Small Family Become an American Ideal?," *Independent,* LVI, 836-40 (April 14, 1904).

144. Theodore Roosevelt, *Autobiography* (New York, 1913), 176-84; Lydia K. Commander, "Why Do Americans Prefer Small Families?," *Independent,* LVII, 847-50 (October 13, 1904).

145. H. H. Laughlin, *Eugenical Sterilization: 1926, Historical, Legal, and Statistical Review of Eugenical Sterilization in the United States* (New Haven, 1926), passim.

146. Mary W. Dennett, *Birth Control Laws* (New York, 1926), 7ff., app. i.

147. For a statement of the position of the Catholic Church, see P. J. Ward, "The Catholics and Birth Control," *New Republic,* LIX, 35-38 (May 29, 1929).

148. Dennett, *Birth Control Laws,* chaps. ii-iii; Theodore Shroeder, *List of References on Birth Control* (New York, 1918); Julia E. Johnson, *Selected Articles on Birth Control* (New York, 1915); F. H. Hankins, "Birth Control," *Encyclopaedia of the Social Sciences,* II, 561-64.

149. Charlotte P. Gilman, "The Passing of the Home in Great American Cities." *Cosmopolitan,* XXXVIII (1904), 139.

150. Ella W. Wilcox, "The Restlessness of the Modern Woman, *Cosmopolitan,* XXXI (1901), 314-17.

151. Mrs. Burton Harrison, *The Well-Bred Girl in Society* (Philadelphia, 1898), 86; One of the Four Hundred (pseud.), *Bad Breaks* (New York, 1897), 41.

152. Mrs. Frank Learned, *The Etiquette of New York Today* (New York, 1906), 286.

153. J. D. Richardson, comp., *Messages and Papers of the Presidents* (Washington, 1910), X, 7072; Bureau of the Census, *Marriage and Divorce, 1887-1906.* See also Bureau of the Census, *Marriage and Divorce, 1916.*

154. See this volume, Book VIII, 721 and Book X, 873.

155. Colorado, South Dakota, West Virginia, Maine, Mississippi, Alabama, and North Dakota.

156. Julia E. Johnson, ed., *Selected Articles on Marriage and Divorce* (New York, 1925); R. L. Hartt, "The Habit of Getting Divorces," *World's Work,* XLVIII (1924), 402-409, 519-24; W. E. Carson, *The Marriage Revolt* (New York, 1915), 157ff.

157. F. S. Hall and E. W. Brooke, *American Marriage Laws in Their Social Aspect* (New York, 1919).

158. *Proceedings* of the National Congress on Uniform Divorce Laws held at Washington on February 19, 1906, and *Proceedings* of the Adjourned National Congress on Uniform Divorce Laws held at Philadelphia on November 13, 1906; E. W. Huffcut, "The National Congress on Uniform Divorce Laws," *Independent,* LXI, 1265 (November 9, 1906).

159. Frances A. Allen, "Fig Leaves," *Am. Mercury,* XIII (1928), 59-66; Mary Blossom, "The Well Gowned Woman," *Cosmopolitan,* XXXI (1901), 135-44.

160. Rheta C. Dorr, *What Eight Million Women Want* (Boston, 1910), 42.

161. Mary I. Wood, *The History of the General Federation of Women's Clubs* (New York, 1912), 249-50.

162. Mary R. Beard, *Women's Work in Municipalities* (New York, 1915).

163. E. A. Hecker, *A Short History of Woman's Rights* (2d ed., New York, 1914), 196-97; G. J. Bayles, *Women and the Law* (New York, 1901), 172-73.

164. Summarized by Hecker, *History of Woman's Rights,* 174-225.

165. Dorr, *What Eight Million Women Want,* chap. iv.

166. See this volume, Book X, 873.

167. Carrie C. Catt and Nettie R. Shuler, *Woman Suffrage and Politics* (New York, 1923), chaps. ix-xi.

168. P. H. B. d'Estournelles de Constant, *America and Her Problems* (New York, 1915), 61.

169. Catt and Shuler, *Woman Suffrage,* 174, 176; Abigail S. Duniway, *Path Breaking* (Portland, Ore., 1914); Ida H. Harper et al., eds., *The History of Woman Suffrage* (New York, 1881-1922), IV, 27-58.

170. Harper et al., *Woman Suffrage,* VI, 14.

171. Catt and Shuler, *Woman Suffrage,* chap. xiv.

172. Montana, Nevada, North Dakota, South Dakota, Nebraska, Missouri, and Ohio.

173. Catt and Shuler, *Woman Suffrage,* 195.

174. Ibid., 235.

175. Harper et al., *Woman Suffrage,* VI, 44; Catt and Shuler, *Woman Suffrage,* 237ff.

176. Doris Stevens, *Jailed for Freedom* (New York, 1920), chap. ii. "Where are the people?" Wilson is reported to have asked on his arrival in Washington. "On the Avenue watching the suffragists parade," was the answer. Stevens, *Jailed for Freedom,* 21.

177. *N.Y. Times,* March 4, 5, 1913.

178. Ida H. Harper, *Life of Susan B. Anthony* (Indianapolis, 1908), III.

179. See this volume, Book XII, 1055.

180. Lavinia Hart, "Women as College Presidents," *Cosmopolitan,* XXXIII (1902), 72-79.

181. Bureau of the Census, *Mortality Statistics for 1911,* 23-25; G. B. Mangold, *Problems of Child Welfare* (New York, 1914), chaps. i-iii.

182. Bureau of the Census, *Mortality Statistics for 1911,* 74.

183. Mangold, *Child Welfare,* 84ff.

184. Ibid., 87.

185. C. E. Rainwater, *The Play Movement in the United States* (Chicago, 1922), 19, 31; E. B. Mero, *American Playgrounds* (Boston, 1918), 20; E. A. Rice, *A Brief History of Physical Education* (New York, 1926), 259-61; L. F. Hammer and C. A. Perry, *Recreation in Springfield, Illinois* (Russell Sage Found., New York, 1914).

186. *Acts and Resolves of Massachusetts for 1908,* chap. dxiii, 464.

187. Third Annual Playground Congress, *Proceedings* (New York, 1910), 56.

188. L. W. Barclay, *Education Work of the Boy Scouts* (U.S. Bur. of Educ., *Bull. for 1919,* no. 24).

189. John Spargo, *The Bitter Cry of the Children* (New York, 1906), 145.

190. O. R. Lovejoy, "Some Unsettled Questions about Child Labor," Fifth Ann. Conf. on Child Labor, *Proceeds.* (New York, 1909), 59.

191. Spargo, *Bitter Cry,* 146, 150, 154ff., 163ff.; "Child Labor in Canneries," *Child Labor Bull.,* I, no. 4, 28, 40. See also Mrs. John Van Vorst, *The Cry of the Children* (New York, 1908), passim.

192. Spargo, *Bitter Cry,* 141.

193. Helen L. Sumner and Ella A. Merritt, *Child Labor Legislation in the United States* (Children's Bur., *Industrial Ser.,* no. 1, 1915).

194. John Dewey, *The School and Society* (Chicago, 1899), and *Democracy and Education* (New York, 1916); John Dewey and Evelyn Dewey, *Schools of Tomorrow* (New York, 1915).

195. D. B. Leary, "Development of Educational Psychology," I. L. Kandel, ed., *Twenty-Five Years of American Education* (New York, 1924), 104.

196. Henry Adams, *The Education of Henry Adams* (Boston, 1918), 55.

197. U.S. Commissioner of Education, *Report for 1898–1899,* I, xi; *Rep. for 1916,* II, 1.

198. These estimates are for both private and public schools. U.S. Comr. of Educ., *Rep. for 1917,* II, 511; U.S. Bur. of Educ., *Bull. for 1919,* no. 91, 127–28, 310. Discussed by A. J. Inglis in Kandel, *Twenty-Five Years of American Education,* 251ff. See also this volume, Book XII, "America at School," 1055.

199. E. P. Cubberley, *Public Education in the United States* (Boston, 1919), 361. See also E. W. Knight, *Public Education in the South* (Boston, 1922), chaps. xii–xiii; and U.S. Comr. of Educ., *Rep. for 1916,* II, 586.

200. The average for 1900 was 5.23. U.S. Comr. of Educ., *Rep. for 1916,* II, 6.

201. C. L. Robbins, "Elementary Education," Kandel, *Twenty-Five Years of American Education,* 228.

202. U. S. Comr. of Educ., *Rep. for 1898–1899.* I, lxxv, lxxix.

203. U. S. Comr. of Educ., *Rep. for 1914,* I, chap. xxiv.

204. "An Educational Study of Alabama," U.S. Bur. of Educ., *Bull. for 1919,* no. 41, 349; "The Rural Teacher of Nebraska," *Bull. for 1919, no. 20, 31;* "Status of the Rural Teacher in Pennsylvania," *Bull. for 1921,* no. 34, 31.

205. *Biennial Survey of Education for 1916–1918* (U.S. Bur. of Educ., *Bull. for 1919,* nos. 88–91), IV, 9–121.

206. Dewey and Dewey, *Schools of Tomorrow,* 175–204, 251ff.

207. A. J. Inglis, "Secondary Education," Kandel, *Twenty-five Years of American Education,* 252; U.S. Comr. of Educ., *Rep. for 1898–1899,* 1843ff.; *Rep. for 1916,* chap. viii.

208. *Biennial Survey of Education for 1916–1918,* I, 7, 56.

209. H. R. Bonner, comp., "Statistics of Universities, Colleges and Professional Schools, 1917–1918," U.S. Bur. of Educ., *Bull. for 1920,* no. 34, 19.

210. See this volume, Book XII, 1055.

211. E. E. Slosson, *Great American Universities* (New York, 1910), 75ff.; R. S. Baker, *Woodrow Wilson* (Garden City, N.Y., 1927), II, chaps. xv, xvii.

212. Slosson, *Great American Universities,* 452.

213. Thorstein Veblen, *The Higher Learning in America* (New York, 1918), 64. See also Upton Sinclair, *The Goose Step* (Pasadena, 1923), a book crammed with facts generally accurate but giving an exaggerated picture of the situation. For a contemporary view of the situation, see H. C. Warren, "Academic Freedom," *Atlantic Mo.,* CXIV (1914), 689–99.

214. American Association of University Professors, *Bull.,* II, no. 3, 27.

215. Professor Fisher was twice mayor of Middletown, Connecticut, and in 1914 candi-

date on the Progressive ticket for governor of the state. Am. Assoc. of Univ. Profs., *Bull.*, II, no. 2, pt. ii, 75-76. See also case of Joseph H. Brewster at the University of Colorado in the same *Bull.*, 3-71.

216. Am. Assoc. of Univ. Profs., *Bull.*, II, no. 1, 11.

217. 61 Cong., 2 sess., *Sen. Rep.*, no. 405.

218. *The General Education Board, an Account of Its Activities, 1902-1914* (New York, 1915), passim.

219. P. H. B. d'Estournelles de Constant, *America and Her Problems* (New York, 1915), 267. See also Sir Philip Burne-Jones, *Dollars and Democracy* (New York, 1903), 33ff.

220. H. K. Carroll, *The Religious Forces of the United States* (rev. ed., New York, 1912), lxix.

221. *N.Y. Times Book Rev.*, November 28, 1920, 3.

222. Membership as given by the *World Almanac for 1900*, 334, estimates the Protestants at 27,710,004 and the Catholics at 8,447,801, while the estimates of H. K. Carroll as given in the *Bulletins of Church Statistics*, published by the Federal Council (1914), give the Protestants at 38,059,428 and the Catholics at 13,673,787. The Bureau of the Census, *Religious Bodies, 1916*, pt. I, 526-27, gives total church membership as 21,699,000 in 1890, 35,068,000 in 1906, and 41,927,000 in 1916.

223. Gerald Shaughnessy, *Has the Immigrant Kept the Faith?* (New York, 1925), chap. x.

224. John Farley, an Irish immigrant; William O'Connell, a son of Irish immigrants; and Monsignor Diomede Falconio, a naturalized American citizen then serving as apostolic delegate at Washington.

225. James Cardinal Gibbons, *A Retrospect of Fifty Years* (Baltimore, 1916), 210-34; A. S. Will, *Life of Cardinal Gibbons* (New York, 1922), I, 508.

226. Carroll, *Religious Forces*, lxxi, puts the denominations showing the largest absolute increase during the period 1890-1910 as follows: Roman Catholic 6,183,680 or 99 percent; Southern Baptist 1,003,000 or 78 percent; Methodist Episcopal, 946,508 or 42 percent; Disciples of Christ (older branch) 667, 065 or 104 percent; Methodist Episcopal Church, South, 641,173 or 53 percent; Presbyterian (Northern) 540,490 or 69 percent; Colored Baptist 441,176 or 33 percent; Northern Baptist 410,263 or 51 percent; Lutheran Synodical Conference 409,128 or 115 percent; Protestant Episcopal 396,726 or 75 percent; and Congregational 222,629 or 43 percent.

227. Elizabeth R. Hooker, *United Churches* (New York, 1926), 23-25.

228. See this volume, Book X, "The Changing Church," 873.

229. E.g, W. N. Rice, *Christian Faith in an Age of Science* (New York, 1903).

230. J. A. Faulkner, "The Tragic Fate of a Famous Seminary," *Bibliotheca Sacra*, LXXX, 449-64.

231. One of the most interesting and most widely discussed series of muckraking articles was that by Harold Bolce, starting with one entitled "Blasting at the Rock of Ages," *Cosmopolitan*, XLVI (1909), 665-76, which purported to tell how ruthlessly college professors in the leading institutions of learning dealt with age-old religious and moral beliefs. Although these articles confirmed the opinion of many that the colleges were hotbeds of infidelity and radicalism, they helped to awaken the church to a realization that a new day had come.

232. See this volume, Book VIII, 721.

233. Lindsay Denison, "The Rev. Billy Sunday and His War on the Devil," *American*, LXIV (1907), 451-68.

234. Charles Stelzle, *The Workingman and Social Problems* (New York, 1903); C. B. Thompson, *The Churches and the Wage Earners* (New York, 1909), 108; H. F. Perry, "The Workingmen's Alienation from the Church," *Am. Journ. of Sociology*, IV, 622ff.

235. *Encyclopedia of Social Reform,* 211-12.
236. National Council of the Congregational Churches, *Minutes of 1901,* 37; *Minutes of 1904,* 414-29.
237. Charles Stelzle, *A Son of the Bowery* (New York, 1926), chap. vii.
238. "Report on the Church and Social Problems," Methodist Episcopal Church, *Journal of the Twenty-Fifth Delegated General Conference* (1908), 121-50, 545-49.
239. Federal Council of the Churches of Christ in America, *Report of the First Meeting* (Philadelphia, 1908), 239.
240. Though certain English Catholics, basing their policy on the great Encyclical of Leo XIII, and believing that the time was ripe to take an active part in the great social movements of the day, organized in England in 1909 the Catholic Social Guild; it was not until the World War that American Catholics, through the National Catholic War Council (1917) and its successor, the National Catholic Welfare Council (1919), formulated a definite social program. Henry Parkinson, "Catholic Social Guild," *Cath. Encyc.,* XVII (sup. 1), 168; National Catholic War Council, *Social Reconstruction* (Washington 1919).
241. American Federation of Labor, *Report of the Proceedings of the Twenty-Fifth Annual Convention* (1905), 155; Stelzle, *Son of the Bowery,* 88.
242. Shailer Mathews, "The Development of Social Christianity in America," G. B. Smith, ed., *Religious Thought in the Last Quarter Century* (Chicago, 1927), 228-39.
243. Stelzle, *Son of the Bowery,* chap. xi.
244. *American,* LXVIII (1909), passim.
245. C. E. Russell, "The Tenements of Trinity Church," *Everybody's,* XIX (1908), 54.
246. Georgine Milmine, "Mary Baker G. Eddy: the Story of Her Life and the History of Christian Science," *McClure's,* XXVIII-XXXI (1907-1908), later published in book form.
247. J. C. Welliver, "The Mormon Church and the Sugar Trust," *Hampton's,* XXIV (1910), 82-93; A. H. Lewis, "The Viper on the Hearth," *Cosmopolitan,* LX (1910), 439-50, "The Trail of the Viper," 683-703. "The Viper's Trail of Gold," 823-33; Richard Barry, "The Political Menace of the Mormon Church," *Pearson's,* XXIV (1910), 312-30. "The Mormon Evasion of Anti-Polygamy Laws," 443-51. "The Mormon Method in Business," 571-78; B. J. Hendrick, "The Mormon Revival of Polygamy," *McClure's,* XXXVI (1911), 245-61, 449-84.
248. J. M. Barker, *The Saloon Problem and Social Reform* (Everett, Mass., 1905), 32.
249. Raymond Calkins, *Substitutes for the Saloon* (Boston, 1901), 25.
250. *Literary Digest,* XXV, 338 (September 20, 1902).
251. Many of these are listed in the *Anti-Saloon League Yearbook for 1913,* 280-81. In 1908 a National Interchurch Temperance Federation was organized to secure the cooperation of the various temperance boards of the church.
252. Its Committee on Temperance was first appointed in 1892.
253. M. E. Church, *Journ. of the Twenty-Sixth Del. Gen. Conf.* (1912), 654-63.
254. *Bonfort's Wine and Spirit Circular,* October 25, 1914. According to the president of the Brewers' Association, E. A. Schmidt, the strongest forces arrayed on the side of the bills for a constitutional amendment were the members of the Methodist and Baptist churches, the W.C.T.U., the Epworth League, and the Anti-Saloon League. U. S. Brewers Association, *Yearbook for 1914,* 9.
255. *The Pocket Cyclopedia of Temperance,* 241-42.
256. "All of the states in the Republic except two have laws requiring the study of scientific temperance in the schools, and all these laws were secured by the W.C.T.U.," exulted Frances E. Willard in 1898. These two were soon to be added. *World Almanac for 1898,* 302; F. C. Inglehart, *King Alcohol Dethroned* (New York, 1917), 339; Sullivan, *Our Times,* II, 192.
257. In the summer of 1904 a number of New York reformers opened a saloon at the

junction of Bleeker and Mulberry Streets, known as the "subway tavern," which hoped to promote temperance by providing a clean and wholesome place where men would "feel impelled to drink little rather than much, where the beverages will be the best of their kind at moderate price, and where every influence will discourage rather than induce drunkenness." This saloon was formally dedicated by Bishop Henry C. Potter of the Episcopal Church, but his action was denounced with equal virulence by the Anti-Saloon League and the liquor dealers. *Literary Digest,* XXIX, 185–86, 233–34 (August 13, 20, 1904); *Independent,* LVII, 339, 465 (August 11, 25, 1904).

258. P. H. Odegard, *Pressure Politics* (New York, 1928), chap. i, 107–13, 228–40. See also Justin Steuart, *Wayne Wheeler, Dry Boss* (New York, 1928).

259. Odegard, *Pressure Politics,* 29–34, 36ff.

260. *Anti-Saloon League Yearbook for 1908,* 15; Odegard, *Pressure Politics,* chaps. iv–v.

261. In spite of these legislative victories for prohibition, the total consumption of wines and liquors was greater in 1913 than in any previous year and the per-capita consumption greater than in all years but two. *Anti-Saloon League Yearbook for 1915,* 47.

262. See maps in Odegard, *Pressure Politics,* 164–65, showing progress, 1904–17, and in the *Anti-Saloon League Yearbook for 1915,* 105ff.

263. *U.S. Statutes at Large,* XXXVII, pt. i, 699; *Anti-Saloon League Yearbook for 1913,* 20–21; Odegard, *Pressure Politics,* 144–47.

264. F. P. Dunne, "Mr. Dooley on the Power of the Press," *American,* LXII (1906), 613.

265. W. G. Bleyer, *Main Currents in the History of American Journalism* (Boston, 1927), 339. The statistics for the *New York American* and the *New York Times* were obtained from the circulation departments of these papers.

266. J. M. Lee, *History of American Journalism* (Boston, 1917), 392.

267. See this volume, Book X, 873.

268. R. L. McCardell, "Opper, Outcault and Company," *Everybody's,* XII (1905), 763–72.

269. S. S. McClure, *My Autobiography* (New York, 1914), 179; Lee, *American Journalism,* 389.

270. Will Irwin, "The American Newspaper," *Collier's,* XLVI, 15–18 (January 21, 1911), and succeeding numbers.

271. Lee, *American Journalism,* 390.

272. M. A. McRae, *Forty Years in Newspaperdom* (New York, 1924), 123.

273. *Editor and Publisher,* XIV, 54–72 (June 8, 1914); *N.Y. Tribune,* November 17, 1914.

274. These laws, passed in 1912, required that all editorials or reading matter for which a consideration was received be plainly marked "advertisement" and provided that magazines and other publications file with the post-office department and publish semiannually a list of their officers and of the principal stock- and bond-holders. *U. S. Statutes at Large,* XXXVII, pt. i, 553–54.

275. W. B. Cairns, "Later Magazines," W. P. Trent et al., eds., *The Cambridge History of American Literature* (New York, 1917–21), III, chap. xix; Algernon Tassin, *The Magazine in America* (New York, 1910), chap. xiv.

276. Leon Whipple, "SatEvePost," *Survey Graphic,* XII (1928), 699ff.

277. Talcott Williams, "The Change in Current Fiction," *Am. Rev. of Revs.,* XXII (1900), 754ff.; same author, "Fiction Read and Written in 1901," *Am. Rev. of Revs.,* XXIV (1901), 586ff.

278. P. L. Ford, "The American Historical Novel," *Atlantic Mo.,* LXXX (1897), 721–28.

279. The proportion of fiction to the whole reached 27.4 percent in 1901, but was only 12.2 percent in 1907 and 8.77 in 1914. F. E. Woodward, "A Graphic Survey of Book Publication, 1890–1916," *U. S. Bur. of Educ., Bull. for 1917,* no. 14.

280. These estimates as to the popularity of books are based upon the *Bookman,* which in 1901 formulated a point system which probably comes as close to the truth as anything except the actual sales statistics of publishing houses.

281. The *Bookman* lists the best sellers as follows: 1905, Katherine Cecil Thurston's *The Masquerader;* 1906, Edith Wharton's *The House of Mirth;* 1907, Frances Little's *The Lady of the Decoration;* 1908, Frances Hodgson Burnett's *The Shuttle;* 1909, John Fox's *The Trail of the Lonesome Pine;* 1910, Florence Barclay's *The Rosary;* 1911, *The Rosary* sharing honors with Jeffrey Farnol's *The Broad Highway.* Mary Johnston's *The Long Roll* and others; 1912, Gene Stratton Porter's *The Harvester,* Harold Bell Wright's *The Winning of Barbara Worth* and Basil King's *The Street Called Straight;* 1913 and 1914, Winston Churchill's *The Inside of the Cup.*

282. Charmian London, *Jack London* (London, 1921).

283. H. L. Mencken, *A Book of Prefaces* (New York, 1917), 67ff.

284. See this volume, Book XII, 1055.

285. T. W. Koch, *A Book of Carnegie Libraries* (New York, 1917), vii–viii, 15.

286. Theodore Roosevelt, *The Strenuous Life* (New York, 1900), 1, 7.

287. W. H. Nugent, "The Sports Section," *Am. Mercury,* XVI (1929), 328–38.

288. C. M. Robinson, *The Improvement of Towns and Cities* (New York, 1901), 154–55.

289. *Public Recreation Facilities* (Am. Acad. of Polit. and Social Sci., *Annals,* XXXV, no. 2). See also A. W. Crawford, "The Development of Park Systems in American Cities," Am. Acad. of Polit. and Social Sci., *Annals,* XXV, 218ff.

290. F. W. Kelsey, *The First County Park System* (New York, 1905); Alonzo Church, *The Essex County Park Commission* (New York, 1913).

291. D. A. Willey, "The Trolley-Park," *Cosmopolitan,* XXXIII (1902), 265–72.

292. *International Year Book for 1899,* 254.

293. See earlier, 1055.

294. During the first part of the period many villages as well as cities had professional or semiprofessional teams and local leagues.

295. A. G. Spalding, *America's National Game* (New York, 1911), chap. xxiii. See also G. W. Axelson, *"Commy," the Life Story of Charles A. Comiskey* (Chicago, 1919).

296. McGraw has replied to those who criticized this deal in *My Thirty Years in Baseball* (New York, 1923), chap. xxiv.

297. See F. C. Richter, *History and Records of Baseball* (Philadelphia, 1914), 213ff.; Spalding, *America's National Game.* chap. xxxiii.

298. New York won in 1904, 1905, 1911, 1912, 1913; Pittsburgh in 1909; and Boston in 1914.

299. McGraw, *Thirty Years in Baseball,* 205.

300. Other victors were Boston, 1903, 1904, 1912, and Chicago, 1906.

301. In the remaining years the world championship was won by Boston (A.L.) 1903, New York (N.L.) 1905, Chicago (A.L.) 1906, Chicago (N.L.) 1907 and 1908, Pittsburgh, (N.L.) 1909, Boston (A.L.) 1912, and Boston (N.L.) 1914. There was no series in 1904.

302. Alexander Johnston, *Ten—and Out* (New York, 1927), 187–92; Jack Johnson, *Jack Johnson in the Ring—and Out* (Chicago, 1927), 169ff.

303. *N.Y. Tribune,* March 18, 1897, and July 5, 1910.

304. *Outlook,* LXXXIX, 48, 354 (May 9 and June 20, 1908); *New International Year Book for 1911,* 595.

305. S. C. Hildreth and J. R. Crowell, *The Spell of the Turf* (Philadelphia, 1926), 186.

306. J. D. Travis and J. R. Crowell, *The Fifth Estate* (New York, 1926), chap. i.

307. *International Year Book for 1898,* 722; *for 1899,* 768.

308. *Literary Digest,* XXXI, 566, 861 (October 21, and December 9, 1905).

309. *Independent,* LIX, 1184, 1294 (November 16, 30, 1905).

310. See *World Almanac for 1915,* 865, for records; also A. B. Reeve, "Football Safe and Sane," *Independent,* LXI, 1220–24 (November 22, 1906).

311. J. C. Riley, *How to Coach and Play Basketball* (Champaign, Ill., 1926), 2; E. J. Mather and E. D. Mitchell, *Basketball* (Ann Arbor, Mich., 1922).

312. *Nation,* XCIV, 482 (May 16, 1912).

313. New York City saw its first motion-picture show at Koster and Bial's Theater on Twenty-Third Street on April 27, 1896. Homer Croy, *How Motion Pictures Are Made* (New York, 1917), 55.

314. B. J. Lubschez, *The Story of the Motion Picture 65 B. C. to 1920 A. D.* (New York, 1920), 43.

315. G. E. Walsh, "Moving Picture Drama for the Multitude," *Independent,* LXIV, 306-10 (February 6, 1908).

316. Lubschez, *The Motion Picture,* 52ff.

317. L. C. Strang, *Celebrated Comedians* (Boston, 1901), 102-107.

318. *The Theatre,* X (1909), no. 105, xiii.

319. Israel Zangwill, "The Future of Vaudeville in America," *Cosmopolitan,* XXXVIII (1905), 639-46.

320. The term "photoplay" came as the result of prize competitions conducted by the Essanay Company in 1910.

321. The Freemasons and Odd Fellows boasted over 1.6 million members in the United States and Canada, while ten others claimed over 400,000—the Modern Woodmen of America, Knights of Pythias, Independent Order of Rechabites, Order of the Eastern Star, Woodmen of the World, International Order of Good Templars. Red Men, and the famous "animal orders" of Moose, Elks, Owls, and Eagles. In the case of the Rechabites and Templars, the membership was not entirely in the United States. *World Almanac for 1915,* 563.

322. "Notes on the Pan-American Exposition," *Cosmopolitan,* XXXI (1901), 451. In the same number (476-82) F. P. Dunne, "Mr. Dooley on the Midway," is an excellent example of current humor.

323. Adams, *Education of Henry Adams,* 466-467.

BOOK XII   The Great Crusade and After, 1914–28

1. See this volume, Book XI.

2. See Leonard Wood, "Plattsburg and Citizenship," *Century,* XCIV (1917), 49-54.

3. F. A. Ogg, *National Progress,* A. B. Hart, ed., *The American Nation: A History* (New York, 1905-17), XXVII, 297-300.

4. *American Year Book for 1916,* 97-99.

5. Woodrow Wilson, *The New Democracy* (New York, 1926), II, 407-14.

6. *St. Louis Globe-Democrat,* February 27, 1917.

7. E. H. Crowder, *The Spirit of Selective Service* (New York, 1920), is a useful study of the operation of the draft.

8. Charles Seymour, *Woodrow Wilson and the World War,* Allen Johnson, ed., *The Chronicles of America Series* (New Haven, 1918-21), XLVIII, 122-23.

9. T. G. Frothingham, *The American Reinforcement in the World War* (Garden City, 1927), 118.

10. John Ihlder, "Our New Cities," *Survey,* XXXIX (October 27, 1917), 88-93.

11. Frothingham, *The American Reinforcement,* 119.

12. L. P. Ayres, *The War with Germany* (Washington, 1919), 22, 101.

13. "The evidence available indicates fifty to sixty percent of the men between 31 and 46 years of age could not have passed for general military service if the physical requirements had remained unchanged." J. H. Beard. "Physical Rejection for Military Service," *Scientific Mo.,* IX (1919), 5.

14. D. W. La Rue, "The Rationale of Testing Intelligence, with Special Reference to Testing in the Army," *Scientific Mo.,* VII (1918), 411.

15. See F. P. Stockbridge, "The Khaki University," *World's Work,* XXXVII (1919), 332-39, for a description of technical training of army men in the trades of peace.

16. Isaac Marcosson, *S.O.S.* (New York, 1919), ably describes the multiform tasks performed by the Services of Supply.

17. Ayres. *War with Germany,* 123-30.

18. *Survey,* XLI (November 16, 1918), 194. See also G. M. Price, "Mobilizing Social Forces against Influenza," and J. P. Murphy, "Meeting the Scourge," *Survey,* XLI (October 26, 1918), 95-96, 97-100.

19. F. M. Surface, *The Stabilization of the Price of Wheat during the War and Its Effect upon the Returns to the Producer* (Washington 1925), 13-15, 43-48.

20. Ibid., 17.

21. For example, the tons of raw garbage collected in Chicago declined from 12,862 during the month of June 1916 to 8,386 for the same month a year later. In some cities, persons who had contracted to collect garbage for feeding purposes were forced to go out of business. Ivan Pollock, *The Food Administration in Iowa,* B. F. Shambaugh, ed., *Iowa Chronicles of the World War* (Iowa City, 1923), I, 181; II, 12.

22. Norma B. Kastl. "Wartime, the Place and the Girl," *Independent,* XCVI (October 12, 1918), 56.

23. Blackman-Ross Company, *The Effect of the War on Business Conditions* (New York, 1918), 6-7. See also Harriet S. Blatch, *Mobilizing Woman Power* (New York, 1918); Ida C. Clarke, *American Women and the World War* (New York, 1918); and Mrs. Nevada D. Hitchcock, "The Mobilization of Women," Am. Acad. of Polit. and Social Sci., *Annals,* LXXVIII, 24-31.

24. The habit prevailed of carrying propaganda into the names of wartime institutions, thus "liberty bonds," the "liberty motor" of the airplane, and the "liberty cabbage" to take the alien taint from sauerkraut. Humorists proposed to rename dachshunds "liberty pups."

25. *American Labor Year Book for 1917-1918,* 11-21.

26. Bing, *War-Time Strikes,* 255-69.

27. Cited from J. B. Scherer, *The Nation at War* (New York, 1918), 121.

28. Two excellent studies survey the field and classify the types of conscientious objectors in the war: C. M. Case, *Non-Violent Coercion* (New York, 1923), and N. M. Thomas, *The Conscientious Objector in America* (New York, 1923).

29. Thomas, *The Conscientious Objector,* 27.

30. *N.Y. World,* January 16, 1919.

31. E. H. Bierstadt, *Aspects of Americanization* (Cincinnati, 1922), 74.

32. For the Reconstruction scandals after the Civil War, see this volume, Book VII, 616.

33. See "The Cult of Nationalism," 616.

34. A. G. Gardiner, *Portraits and Portents* (New York, 1926), 13. See also Will Irwin, *How Red Is America?* (New York, 1927).

35. "In June, 1920, forty-three delegates met in Chicago and organized the American branch of the O.B.U. They asserted that they represented 40,000 members, but in 1922 one of the organizers claimed only 30,000 members in this country." James O'Neal. "The Passing of the I.W.W.," *Current History,* XXI (1925), 531-32.

36. Labor disputes in 1919 numbered 2,665; employees involved, 4,160,348, D. J. Saposs, "Labor," *Am. Journ. of Sociology,* XXXIV, 79.

37. Commission of Inquiry, Interchurch World Movement, *Report on the Steel Strike of 1919* (New York, 1920).

38. *The Steel Strike of 1919,* 11-12.

39. Dated October 2, 1919. *The Steel Strike of 1919,* 230.

40. Selig Perlman. *A History of Trade Unionism in the United States* (New York, 1923), chaps. xi-xv.

41. Except in 1919, the number of strikers from 1916 to 1922 was annually between 1 and 2 million; after 1923 it decreased rapidly to between 300,000 and 400,000 in 1926 and 1927. Saposs, "Labor," 79. The decreasing extent of strikes reflected mainly the prosperity and comparative stability of prices which prevailed during

the period 1924–28, but in part also a decline in the strength of trade unionism during the immediately preceding period of depression. See Leo Wolman, "Labor," *Recent Economic Changes,* II, chap. vi.

42. "The Kansas Strike Cure," *Literary Digest,* LXIV (February 7, 1920), 17.

43. "A Blow to Compulsory Arbitration," *Literary Digest,* LXXXV (April 25, 1925), 11.

44. Wolman, "Labor," 481–85; E. T. Devine, "American Labor's Improved Status since 1914," *Current History,* XXVIII (1928), 804–809. Some constructive aspects of American trade unionism are discussed in "The Ways of Prosperity," 831.

45. Such Socialist dailies as the *New York Call,* and such periodicals as *Wiltshire's* and the *Appeal to Reason,* passed out of existence without leaving successors. The ever-lively *Masses* (and its successors the *Liberator* and the *New Masses*) preached an esoteric and "Greenwich-Villagey" Bolshevism that appealed much more to college sophomores than to workingmen.

46. James O'Neal. "Changing Fortunes of American Socialism," *Current History,* XX (1924), 95.

47. The Socialist party membership declined from 1912 to 1920 from 118,000 to 26,000; its vote increased only from 897,000 to 915,000 in spite of the enlargement of the electorate by the grant of equal suffrage to women. Ibid., 92.

48. See A. G. Hays, *Let Freedom Ring* (New York, 1928), for a breezy account of the activities of the Civil Liberties Union by one of the leading participants.

49. Some of the deported radicals on the "Soviet Ark," as the newspapers called the *Buford,* were anarchists who found in Russia a far more stringent "police state" than America. Other emigrants, such as William D. Haywood, the I.W.W. leader who had "skipped bail" and fled abroad on his own account, started with more sympathy for Bolshevism, but they also seem to have suffered some disillusionment.

50. Chafee, *Freedom of Speech,* 107.

51. "Albany's Ousted Socialists," *Literary Digest,* LXIV (January 24, 1920) 19–20; "The Socialists' Hour at Albany," *Literary Digest,* LXVII, (October 2, 1920), 11.

52. For the Ku Klux Klan and other manifestations of hypersensitive nationalism, see "The Cult of Nationalism," 616.

53. Felix Frankfurter, *The Case of Sacco and Vanzetti* (Boston, 1927), is an acute analysis by a legal scholar. Upton Sinclair, *Boston* (New York, 1928), is a fictionized version.

54. Jeannette Marks, *Thirteen Days* (New York, 1929), gives a sympathetic account of the last frantic efforts in Boston to stay the execution.

55. The present writer witnessed the Plymouth gathering from the consulate. The crowd of about 200 dock laborers and unemployed seemed moved by no special excitement, but merely to be "demonstrating" according to a prearranged program. After the execution these demonstrations ceased, though the still open question of the guilt or innocence of the accused continued to be debated by the periodical press of both continents. Friends of the men founded a monthly magazine, The *Lantern,* in Boston in 1928 to keep the issues presented by the case before the public.

56. Andrew W. Mellon, secretary of the treasury; Charles G. Dawes, vice president during President Coolidge's elective term; Frank O. Lowden, governor of Illinois, aspirant for the presidency and leader of the farm-relief movement, were typical examples of the successful businessman in politics.

57. In 1928, owing to the agitation of the prohibition question and the outstanding personal popularity of both candidates, there was a temporary increase in the vote.

58. An excellent analysis may be found in "The Vanishing Voter," by A. M. Schlesinger and E. M. Eriksson, *New Republic,* XL (October 15, 1924), 162–67.

59. "A dynamic history of the period might give a volume or two to the automobile and a footnote to affairs of state." R. L. Duffus, "1900–1925," *Century,* CIX (1925), 488.

60. "There are no reliable records of the number of crimes, murders or otherwise, committed in the United States. The National Crime Commission is now working on a plan for the gathering of simple statistics throughout the country." Letter of Mr. Louis Howe of the National Crime Commission to the writer, July 23, 1928. See also F. L. Hoffman, "Murder and the Death Penalty," *Current History,* XXVIII (1928), 408-10.

61. Average homicide rate for the registration area of the census: 1914-18, 7.2 per 100,000; 1919-23, 7.92 per 100,000. If the white population alone be considered, the increase is less marked and would be eliminated if the low rate of 1918 (when so much of the nation was under military discipline) be omitted. The census bureau estimates of relatively little change are confirmed from other sources. Figures compiled by the Metropolitan Life Insurance Company for the year 1926 showed a decreased homicide rate as compared with 1923, 1924, and 1925 but "a slightly upward tendency" for the whole period 1911-26 apart from slight annual fluctuations. See Metropolitan Life Insurance Company, *Statistical Bull.,* VII, no. 12, 1.

62. *N.Y. Times,* November 28, 1925. For a detailed comparison of American and European conditions, very little flattering to American vanity, see R. B. Fosdick, *American Police Systems* (New York, 1920).

63. Fosdick, *American Police Systems,* 17.

64. Lawrence Veiller, "The Rising Tide of Crime," *World's Work,* LI (1925), 134.

65. C. E. Gehlke, "Crime," *Am. Journ. of Sociology,* XXXIV, 164.

66. Kirchwey, "What Makes Criminals," *Current History,* XXVII (1927), 318.

67. John Knight, "Difficulties in Enforcing Criminal Law," *Current History,* XXVII (1927), 325. In 1929, President Hoover appointed a commission to study the whole problem of law enforcement.

68. H. E. Barnes, *The Repression of Crime* (New York, 1926), chap. v; T. M. Osborne, *Prisons and Common Sense* (Philadelphia, 1924).

69. S. S. Glueck, *Mental Disorder and the Criminal Law* (Boston, 1925), analyzes the existing legislation, legal practice, and court decisions with respect to the question of irresponsibility in criminal cases because of alleged insanity.

70. Watson Davis, "The Nation-Wide Campaign to Reduce Crime," *Current History,* XXVII (1927), 304. Colorado adopted a similar law in 1927. See also Malcolm Logan, "Demobilizing the Alienists," *North Am. Rev.,* CCXXVII (1929), 117-21.

71. See "Race Relations in the South," 1055.

72. Metropolitan Life Insurance Company, *Statistical Bull.,* VIII, no. 8, 1.

73. For the beginnings of the prohibitory movement, see this volume, Book VII, 616.

74. W. E. Lanphear, "Progress toward Ending the Saloon," *Independent,* LXXX (December 7, 1914), 349.

75. Arkansas, Idaho, Iowa, South Carolina, Alabama (1915); Michigan, Montana, Nebraska, South Dakota (1916); Indiana, New Hampshire, New Mexico, Utah (1917); Wyoming, Florida, Ohio, Nevada, Texas (1918). The Webb-Kenyon act of 1913 had protected statewide prohibition by not permitting the shipment of liquor into states which forbade its sale.

76. *U.S. Statutes at Large,* XL, pt. i, 282, 1046-47. This was to go into effect July 1, 1919.

77. See Justin Steuart, *Wayne Wheeler, Dry Boss* (New York, 1928), chap. vii.

78. 68.3 percent of the population and 95.4 percent of the area of the nation were dry by state law or local regulation. See T. N. Carver, "The Greatest Social Experiment of Modern Times," F. H. Hooper, ed., *These Eventful Years* (New York, 1924), II, 584-85.

79. Ordinarily a constitutional amendment approved by Congress is before the country indefinitely and may be ratified by the legislatures at any subsequent time. Many people desired to limit the period of agitation for the prohibition amendment.

80. *U.S. Statues at Large,* XLI, pt. i, 305-23. The .5 percent standard was older than

the Volstead act, being the definition line, for revenue purposes, of the Bureau of Internal Revenue for fermented liquor.

81. No compensation was granted to saloon keepers for their loss of business. This was the rule in American laws as distinguished from British local-option laws. When the present writer questioned Wayne B. Wheeler, general counsel for the Anti-Saloon League, on this point, Mr. Wheeler explained that in England a license was considered part of the property of the public-house keeper; in the United States it's merely a permit to trade, granting legal "immunity from prosecution" for a limited term and under whatever restrictions the public authorities might impose. Perhaps there is a remote analogy in the fact that Great Britain granted, and the United States refused to grant, compensation to slave owners when slavery was abolished within their respective dominions.

82. Irving Fisher, *Prohibition at Its Worst* (New York, 1926), 42, 44.

83. For an account of the homebrewing industry at its height, see J. T. Flynn, "Home, Sweet Home-Brew," *Collier's,* LXXXII, no. 9 (September 1, 1928).

84. The writer has seen this advertisement in Washington, D.C.; and in Detroit the shop sign, "Malt and Hops. Try Ours for Better Results." Though the desired "results" could not be legally stated, every passerby knew what was meant.

85. A policeman in a Virginia city said, "White men used to get rich selling whisky to Negroes, but in these days the Negroes are getting rich selling whisky to white men." R. L. Hartt, "Prohibition as It Is," *World's Work,* XLIX (1925), 511–12.

86. These tables were reprinted in *Annals* of the American Academy of Political and Social Science, CIX, 153.

87. J. B. Kennedy, "—And Mix with Fresh Water," *Collier's,* LXXXII (October 27, 1928), 9.

88. Said to be derived from the hailing cry of the holdup man, "Hi! Jack."

89. Martha B. Bruère, *Does Prohibition Work?* (New York, 1927), 181.

90. See the editorial, "For better Bootleggers," *N.Y. Times,* October 15, 1928.

91. "It may be safely admitted by the opponent of prohibition that the consumption of drink now is not so great as before the adoption of the Eighteenth Amendment; though no one really knows what it amounts to." Senator William C. Bruce (Maryland), *Current History,* XXII (1925), 697. The printed debate, "Is Prohibition a Success?," in this number of *Current History* between Senator Bruce and Wayne B. Wheeler is a good summary of the experience of the first years of prohibition as viewed by the wets and drys.

92. Albert Levitt, "Prohibition after Eight Years," *Current History,* XXVIII (1928), 15. It should be remembered that many states were already under prohibition by 1918.

93. For an extended argument on this point see Fisher, *Prohibition at Its Worst,* and for attacks on Professor Fisher's statistical estimates, see Clarence Darrow and Victor Yarros, *The Prohibition Mania* (New York, 1927).

94. Herman Feldman, *Prohibition, Its Economic and Industrial Aspects* (New York, 1927), 367. The table for 626 towns and cities given by Professor Fisher, *Prohibition at Its Worst,* 43, shows the same fall to 1920, rise to 1923, and then plateau.

95. Feldman, *Prohibition,* 397.

96. *Washington Post,* May 22, 1927.

97. To quote a New York physician on these poisoning cases, "Instead of cut liquor, the working man who wants an alcoholic beverage is turning to raw alcohol. . . . This stuff is not poisonous in the ordinary sense of the term, but an ounce or two of it has an effect on the heart equal to that of a whole bottle of hard liquor that has been properly aged in wood." *N.Y. Times,* October 8, 1928.

98. *Collier's,* LXXIII (January 26, 1924), 5; *Literary Digest,* LXXX (February 23, 1924), 17.

99. Hence the saying: "The rich are of two classes: those who still have a little and those who have a little—still!"

100. Bruère, *Does Prohibition Work?*, 286–87.
101. *Literary Digest*, LXXV (October 28, 1922), 8.
102. Feldman, *Prohibition*, 66–67.
103. As the saying went, "The man who called that near-bear was a poor judge of distance!"
104. Feldman, *Prohibition*, 80, 82–84.
105. Ibid., 75, 77.
106. Ibid., 89, 92.
107. *Yearbook of Agriculture for 1927*, 324.
108. Feldman, *Prohibition*, 99. Of course other possible causes suggest themselves, such as the aftereffect of war restrictions, health teaching, the desire to reduce weight, and the greater number of women whose duties forced them to lunch "downtown" instead of at home.
109. See "The Ways of Prosperity," 831, on general economic trends.
110. Fisher, *Prohibition at Its Worst*, chap. xi. His estimate is based on the transfer of labor from the liquor industry to other forms of production, and on the presumed increased efficiency of sober workmen.
111. Federal Council of Churches, *Prohibition Situation*, 14–16.
112. Ibid., 38.
113. Hermann Keyserling, "Caste in America," *Forum*, LXXX (1928), 106.
114. For example, see this volume, Book VI, 517, and Book VIII, 721.
115. *U.S. Fourteenth Census*, (1920), IV, 34. The census bureau believes that the 1910 figures were "an overenumeration," especially for women farm laborers. Same vol., 23–24. If this be true, the increase in the number of women gainfully employed was much greater than the face of the returns would indicate.
116. *U.S. Fourteenth Census*, IV, 34–43.
117. Ibid, IV, 693.
118. "The report for thirty-three industries in the State of Illinois showed that the average weekly wages for women during the month of May 1924, was $17. 15. In the cotton industry throughout the country the statistics showed that in 1922 the female employees received a wage ranging from about $12 to $19 a week. In the report of the women wage earners employed in the five- and ten-cent stores of New York State (1921) it is shown that of the total group of full-time women workers exactly one-half received less than $13.49 a week." B. P. Chass, "American Women Who Are Earning Wages," *Current History* (1925), 256.
119. Ibid., 254–55.
120. Edna Kenton, "The Ladies' Next Step," *Harper's Mag.*, CLII (1926), 366–74.
121. Dorothy Canfield (Fisher), *The Home Maker* (New York, 1924).
122. *U.S. Fourteenth Census* (1920), IV, 43.
123. For a discussion of the problem, see Ethel M. Smith, "America's Domestic Servant Shortage," *Current History*, XXVI (1927), 213–18.
124. Julius Klein, "Servicing Our 260 American Wage," *Mag. of Business*, LIV (1928), 37.
125. *Commerce Yearbook for 1928*, I, 275.
126. *Commerce Yearbook for 1926*, I, 270.
127. C. T. Crowell, "Is Coal Committing Suicide?" *Outlook*, CXLVIII (March 14, 1928), 417.
128. Of course, the farmhouse had fewer such conveniences than the city or suburban home.
129. "The most radical revision of that relation [landlord and tenant] ever attempted in this country." "Moving day," *Survey*, XLV (October 9, 1920), 54. This editorial summarizes the rental laws.
130. *U.S. Daily* (Washington), May 7, 1929.
131. Ibid., November 7 and 9, 1928.
132. J. M. Gillette, "Family Life," *American Year Book for 1925*, 665.

133. B. B. Lindsey and Wainwright Evans, *The Companionate Marriage* (New York, 1927). See also the same authors' *The Revolt of Modern Youth* (New York, 1925).

134. W. F. Ogburn, "Divorce: A Menace that Grows," *N.Y. Times*, December 18, 1927.

135. W. S. Rossiter, *Increase of Population in the United States, 1910–1920* (*Census Monographs*, I, 1922), 28.

136. Ibid., 101.

137. L. I. Dublin, *Health and Wealth* (New York, 1928), 219.

138. See this volume, Book XI, "Women, Home, and Family Life," 981.

139. See this volume, Book XI, "Children's Rights," 981.

140. R. S. Lynd and Helen M. Lynd, *Middletown* (New York, 1929). The community in question, Muncie, Indiana, was studied by a corps of investigators after the manner of social anthropology. Its typical character was perhaps vitiated by its homogeneity: Blacks and foreign-born were relatively few. The field work was conducted in 1924–25.

141. Ibid., 16–17.

142. Ibid., 135.

143. Ibid., 146–47.

144. Ibid., 155, 174. Curiously enough, the authors regard this particular countercurrent as reactionary and retrogressive (175, 498), as though science has less "right" to bring industries back into the home than to take them out!

145. "The fact that out of a hundred white children ninety-six or ninety-seven are born in wedlock indicates that our society has attained a fair degree of success in the control of the sex relation." E. A. Ross, *What Is America?* (New York, 1919), 41.

146. Bruère, *Does Prohibition Work?*, 301.

147. We had nearly said that there were no statistics on twentieth-century lovemaking, but that would have done injustice to the tabulating epoch. "Marriage and Love Affairs," by G. V. Hamilton and Kenneth Macgowan, *Harper's Mag.*, CLVII (1928), 277–87, solemnly tabulates with the proper graphs, the 1,358 love affairs of 200 young married persons of the educated classes; about seven cases of love apiece. It is a pity that we have no comparable figures for earlier generations.

148. H. G. Wells, *Joan and Peter* (New York, 1918), 293.

149. "The Passing Corset," *Collier's*, LXXXII (July 21, 1928), 50.

150. Percival White, "Figuring Us Out," *North Am. Rev.*, CCXXVII (1929), 69.

151. *N.Y. Times*, November 11, 1928.

152. Devere Allen, "Personal Decoration," *The World Tomorrow*, VIII (1925), 77.

153. White, "Figuring Us Out," 69.

154. C. J. McGuirk, "A Subtle Something," *Sat. Eve. Post*, CXCIX (December 4, 1926), 72.

155. Rose Feld, "The Cosmetic Urge," *Collier's*, LXXIX (March 12, 1927), 22.

156. Dept. of Commerce, *Statistical Abstract of the United States for 1925*, tables 757–59.

157. *U.S. Daily*, March 23, 1929.

158. "The Suffrage Conquest of Illinois," *Literary Digest*, XLVI (June 28, 1913), 1409–10.

159. "Suffragists Take New York," *Literary Digest*, LV (November 17, 1917), 14–15; *American Year Book for 1917*, 180–81.

160. Doris Stevens, *Jailed for Freedom* (New York, 1920), pts. ii–iii.

161. *N.Y. Times*, December 31, 1928.

162. See H. L. Keenleyside, "The American Political Revolution of 1924," *Current History*, XXI (1925), 838.

163. "Ten Years of Woman Suffrage," *Literary Digest*, CV (April 26, 1930), 11.

164. T. N. Carver, *The Present Economic Revolution in the United States* (Boston, 1925), foreword.

165. Among the very numerous studies of American economic life by foreign observers the following may be mentioned as typical: J. E. Barker, *America's Secret; the*

Causes of Her Economic Success (London, 1927); A. Demangeon, *America and the Race for World Dominion* (New York, 1921); Kurt Hassert, *Die Vereinigten Staaten von Amerika als Politische und Wirtschaftliche Weltmacht* (Tübingen, 1922); Julius Hirsch, *Das Amerikanische Wirtchaftswunder* (Berlin, 1926); Hermann Levy, *Die Vereinigten Staaten von Amerika als Wirtschaftsmacht* (Leipzig, 1923). See review by H. D. Hill, "European Books on America," *Sat. Rev. of Literature,* V (May 11, 1929), 1002. For an able summary, see E. F. Gay's "Introduction" to Committee on Recent Economic Changes, *Recent Economic Changes* (New York, 1929), I, 1–12.

166. National Industrial Conference Board, *Bull.,* no. 5 (1927), 34.

167. Federal Trade Commission, *National Wealth and Income* (69 Cong. 1 sess., *Senate Doc.,* no. 126, 1926). The latest study is M. A. Copeland, "The National Income and Its Distribution," *Recent Economic Changes,* II, 756–839.

168. Natl. Indus. Conf. Board, *Bull.,* no. 5, 36.

169. Ibid., 40.

170. Using the estimate of the world's aggregate wealth given by Stuart Chase in the *N.Y. Times,* August 22, 1926.

171. "At the beginning of the World War we owed $4,500,000,000 abroad whereas now we are creditors to the extent of about $16,000,000,000." J. W. O'Leary, president of the Chamber of Commerce of the United States. "Twenty-Five Years of American Prosperity," *Current History,* XXIII (1926), 699.

172. American Bankers' Assoc., *Journ.,* XIX (1926), 179.

173. Federal Trade Commission, *National Wealth and Income,* 3.

174. E. T. Devine, "American Labor's Improved Status since 1914," *Current History,* XXVIII (1928), 807.

175. Ibid., 807–808.

176. Julius Klein, director of the bureau of foreign and domestic commerce, estimated the increase in money wage in the United States for the period 1914 to 1927 at 160 percent, and the British for the same period at 80 percent, the cost of living in the two nations having gone up in the meantime by 45 and 42 percent respectively. Klein, "Servicing Our 260 American Wage," 35.

177. Data taken from "Cost of Living in the United States," U.S. Bur. of Labor Statistics, *Bull.,* no. 357. The survey included ninety-two industrial towns and cities.

178. J. C. Laue, "Cost of Living Shown for a New York Family," *N.Y. Times,* February 13, 1927.

179. J. E. Barker, *America's Secret* (London, 1927), 104–105.

180. F. V. Willey and Guy Locock, "America's Economic Supremacy," *Current History,* XXIII (1926), 504.

181. Leo Wolman, "Labor," *Recent Economic Changes,* II, 479–81.

182. Some believe this to be an underestimate since the census of 1920 was taken in the winter when fewer children are employed on farms, while the census of 1910 was taken in the spring.

183. B. P. Chass, "American Children in Bondage," *Current History,* XXI (1925), 855.

184. See R. G. Fuller, *Child Labor and the Constitution* (New York, 1923), 238–42.

185. W. C. Mitchell, "A Review," *Recent Economic Changes,* II, 879.

186. For an excellent discussion of employee ownership, see Carver, *Present Economic Revolution.*

187. Ibid., 99.

188. Ibid., 107.

189. W. Z. Ripley, *Main Street and Wall Street* (Boston, 1927), 116.

190. J. G. Frederick, "The Steel Corporation's 25-Year Record," *Current History,* XXIV (1926), 928.

191. D. F. Houston, "Every Worker a Capitalist," *World's Work,* XLIX (1925), 274.

192. A typical instance was the Pacific Gas and Electric Company with 4,128 stockholders in 1914 and 26,294 in 1923, or the Southern California Edison with 2,000

holders in 1917 and 65,636 in 1923. One hundred and eighty-five companies reported to the National Electric Light Association 652,900 stockholders obtained through customer-ownership campaigns from 1914 through 1923. Hundreds of thousands of customers held some stake in either telephone or telegraph industries. Houston, "Every Worker a Capitalist," 275.

193. "I told him I was the lady from the bank who had come to talk thrift to the workers. Immediately he raised an admonishing finger. 'Now, look ahere, lady, don't you come 'round here pullin' any of that Benjamin Franklin stuff on us. I know all about that guy. I've looked him up. He overdone it, he did.' " Experience related by Margaret Dodge in *Commerce, Finance and Industry,* May 1926, 15.

194. *Commerce Yearbook for 1928,* I, 653.

195. S. S. Fontaine in *World Almanac for 1930,* 146.

196. W. C. Plummer, "Social and Economic Consequences of Buying on the Installment Plan," Am. Acad. of Polit. and Social Sci., *Annals,* CXXIX, supplement, 2.

197. Ibid., 3.

198. The domestic-commerce division of the department of commerce prepared a *Chain Store Bibliography* (Washington, 1928) covering the books, reports, magazine articles, and trade periodicals dealing with the question.

199. W. S. Hayward, *Chain Stores* (New York, 1922), 332.

200. Evans Clark, "Big Business Now Sweeps Retail Trade," *N.Y. Times,* July 8, 1928.

201. "The Challenge of the Chains," an interview of the United Grocers in the *Mag. of Business,* LIV (1928), 28.

202. *N.Y. Times,* July 8, 1928.

203. Read the first chapter of S. H. Adams's novel *Success* (Boston, 1921).

204. V. E. Pratt, *Selling by Mail* (New York, 1924), 394. "About 25 percent of its business is done through the mails, and the annual volume of the store reaches as high as $1,500,000 . . . over 25 percent of the sales are made beyond the hundred-mile limit."

205. Willey and Locock, "America's Economic Supremacy."

206. H. L. Barber, *Story of the Automobile* (Chicago, 1927), 74.

207. For statistics of production, see *Facts and Figures of the Automobile Industry,* issued annually by the National Automobile Chamber of Commerce, N.Y.; also such historical surveys as R. C. Epstein, *The Automobile Industry* (Chicago, 1928). The contrast between the humble beginnings and the mighty growth of the industry is well brought out in the series of articles by Chris Batchelder, *Nation's Business,* XV (1927), no. 10, 20–22, and no. 13, 40–42.

208. *N.Y. Times,* April 12, 1929.

209. Epstein, *Automobile Industry,* 4, 6.

210. In 1926, Canada and New Zealand, with one passenger car to about ten persons, came nearest the record of the United States. Great Britain and Ireland had 43, France 44, Germany 196, Italy 325, Russia over 7,000 and China over 21,000 persons to each automobile. *Facts and Figures of the Automobile Industry for 1927,* 44. In 1927 nine tenths of all passenger cars and four fifths of all buses and trucks were of American manufacture.

211. E. G. Fuller, "The Automobile Industry in Michigan," *Mich. History Mag.,* XII (1928), 281.

212. Waldemar Kaempffert, "The Dramatic Story behind Ford's New Car," *N.Y. Times,* December 18, 1927.

213. Fuller, "Automobile Industry in Michigan," 288.

214. There were few magazines of general circulation which did not have one or more articles on the Ford factories after 1914, when his sudden increase of wages first attracted universal attention to his industrial methods. Probably the fullest summary of his ideas is in his autobiography, *My Life and Work* (Garden City, 1922), written in collaboration with Samuel Crowther.

215. Waldemar Kaempffert, "The Mussolini of Highland Park," *N.Y. Times,* January 8, 1928.

216. "Probably the most monotonous task in the whole factory is one in which a man picks up a gear with a steel hook, shakes it in a vat of oil, then turns it into a basket. . . . Yet the man on that job has been doing it for eight solid years . . . and he stubbornly resists every attempt to force him into a better job!" Ford, *My Life and Work,* 106.

217. Evans Clark in the *N.Y. Times,* April 15, 1928.

218. In 1917 only one car in five was of the six-cylinder type, by 1926 two in every five. Epstein, *Automobile Industry,* 122.

219. Barber, *Story of the Automobile,* 174.

220. W. F. Sturm, "The Motor Outlook for 1927," *Liberty,* IV (May 27, 1927), 93.

221. J. T. Flynn, "Riders of the Whirlwind," *Collier's,* LXXXIII (January 19, 1929), 8ff, tells the story of William C. Durant, the Fisher brothers, and the General Motors Corporation.

222. Epstein, *Automobile Industry,* 9.

223. Ford, *My Life and Work,* 201–204.

224. T. H. Reed, *The Vanishing Township* (Univ. of Michigan, *Official Publs.,* XXIX, no. 43), 17.

225. C. S. Johnson, "The Changing Economic Status of the Negro," Am. Acad. of Polit. and Social Sci., *Annals,* CXL, 131; C. H. Wesley, *Negro Labor in the United States, 1850–1925* (New York, 1927), 291–98.

226. W. S. Rossiter, *Increase of Population in the United States, 1910–1920 (Census Monographs,* I, 1922), 127.

227. Wesley, *Negro Labor,* 291–93.

228. R. L. Hartt, "When the Negro Comes North," *World's Work,* XLVIII (1924), 84.

229. Ibid., 86.

230. Ibid., 84.

231. See H. H. Donald's careful study, "The Negro Migration of 1916–1918," *Journ. of Negro History,* VI (1921), 415–16.

232. For statistical evidence on this point, see J. T. Sellin, "The Negro Criminal," Am. Acad. of Polit. and Social Sci., *Annals,* CXL, 52–64.

233. *Myers* v. *Anderson,* 238 U.S. 368; *Nixon* v. *Herndon,* 273 U.S. 536; J. W. Johnson and H. J. Seligmann, "Legal Aspects of the Negro Problem," Am. Acad. of Polit. and Social Sci., *Annals,* CXL, 91–92.

234. "Peonage and Murder," *Independent,* CV (April 16, 1921), 407.

235. Cited from E. J. Scott, *Negro Migration during the War* (New York, 1920), 154, 155, which gives many other newspaper comments to the same effect.

236. Donald, "The Negro Migration," 438–39.

237. These statistics are mainly from the record kept by the Tuskegee Institute. The annual figures vary slightly according to their source but not enough to make an appreciable difference.

238. Thomas Randolph, "The Governor and the Mob," *Independent,* LXXXIX (February 26, 1917), 347–48.

239. J. W. Johnson, "The Practice of Lynching," *Century,* CXV (1927), 68.

240. In the period 1914–28, as in previous periods, only from a fifth to a fourth of all lynchings were for rape or attempted rape. The usual accusation was murder. One interesting phenomenon of the period was that in all years the number of white persons lynched was small, and in three or four years none. During the nineteenth century the lynchings of white persons were only a little less numerous than the lynchings of blacks. So the passing of frontier conditions, as well as improvement in racial relationships, helps explain the remarkable decline of what many criminologists have termed *"the* American crime."

241. For an expression of the radical viewpoint, see especially W. E. B. Du Bois, *Darkwater* (New York, 1920); for the conservative view, prevalent at Tuskegee, see R. R. Moton, *What the Negro Thinks* (New York, 1929).

242. R. L. Hartt, "The New Negro," *Independent,* CV (January 15, 1921), 76.

243. For Garveyism, see T. H. Talley, "Marcus Garvey—The Negro Moses?" and "Gar-

vey's Empire of Ethiopia," *World's Work,* XLI (1920–21), 153–66, 264–70; and R. L. Hartt, "The Negro Moses, *Independent,* CV (February 26, 1921), 205.

244. *U.S. Daily,* September 15, 1928.
245. Ibid., September 16, 1928.
246. N. C. Newbold, "Common Schools for Negroes in the South," Am. Acad. of Polit. and Social Sci., *Annals,* CXL, 213–14.
247. W. S. Scarborough, "The Negro Farmer in the South," *Current History,* XXI (1925), 569.
248. *N.Y. Times,* December 10, 1928. Estimate by the New York Urban League.
249. R. L. Hartt, "I'd Like to Show You Harlem," *Independent,* CV (April 2, 1921), 335.
250. Ibid., 357.
251. E. F. Frazier, "The American Negro's New Leaders," *Current History,* XXVIII (1928), 56–59.
252. That is, including the border states of Kentucky, Maryland, Missouri, Oklahoma, West Virginia, and the District of Columbia as well as the eleven ex-Confederate states.
253. *Blue Book of Southern Progress for 1928* (published by the *Manufacturers' Record*), 202–204.
254. Ibid., 203–204.
255. T. W. Martin, "Hydro-Electric Development in the South," *The South's Development* (Baltimore, 1924), 241.
256. Marjorie A. Potwin, *Cotton Mill People of the Piedmont* (New York, 1927), 58. This careful and interesting study, mainly of South Carolina mills, stresses the philanthropic work of the mill owners, is favorable to the expansion of industry, and conservative on the child-labor question. Frank Tannenbaum, *Darker Phases of the South* (New York, 1924), chap. ii, "The South Buries its Anglo-Saxons," points out the drawbacks of mill life under the benevolent feudalism of the manufacturers. In 1929 serious labor riots took place at Gastonia and Marion, North Carolina.
257. Potwin, *Cotton Mill People of the Piedmont,* 64.
258. P. M. Wilson, *Southern Exposure* (Chapel Hill, N.C., 1927), 188.
259. W. J. Robertson, *The Changing South* (New York, 1927), 269.
260. *World Almanac for 1929,* 895.
261. Stuart Chase, "Play," C. A. Beard, ed., *Whither Mankind* (New York, 1928), 338. The whole article is valuable in giving evidence of the magnitude, standardization, and mechanization of American amusements.
262. W. S. Hiatt, "Billions—Just for Fun," *Collier's,* LXXIV (October 25, 1924), 31.
263. *Science News-Letter,* February 12, 1927.
264. Hiatt, "Billions—Just for Fun," 19.
265. *N.Y. Times,* October 5, 1928.
266. Grantland Rice, "The Real All-America," *Collier's,* LXXVIII (November 20, 1926), 16.
267. *New International Year Book for 1927,* 302.
268. See *Literary Digest,* LXXXIX (May 15, 1926), 31. See also Carnegie Foundation for the Advancement of Teaching, *Bull.,* 23 (1929), a critical survey of collegiate athletics.
269. *Liberty,* III (July 17, 1926).
270. *Columbia Alumni News,* XX (January 11, 1929), 16.
271. William Cunningham, "No Wonder They Want to Fight," *Collier's,* LXXIV (September 18, 1924), 14.
272. Grantland Rice, "The National Rash," *Colliers,* LXXXII (October 20, 1928), 10.
273. R. L. Duffus, "The Age of Play," *Independent,* CXIII (December 20, 1924), 540.
274. Hiatt, "Billions—Just for Fun," 31.
275. Paul Whiteman, "In Defense of Jazz," *N.Y. Times,* March 13, 1927.
276. "The soprano saxophone has been blamed for the sins of the secondary rag. In fact, that silvery screecher merely releases impulses which the constant tickling of

one, two, three upon one, two, three, four [the underlying rhythm] has brought clamoring to the surface." Don Knowlton, "The Anatomy of Jazz," *Harper's Mag.,* CLII (1926), 581.

277. Charles Merz, "Tom-Tom," *Golden Book,* IX (1929), 60.

278. Knowlton, "Anatomy of Jazz," 584.

279. Beatrice Barmby, "What It Means to Be a Book Publisher at 29." *McClure's,* LIX (1927), 63.

280. Kathleen Norris, "I Know a New Game," *Ladies Home Journ.,* XLV (1928), 14.

281. Dorothy Canfield (Fisher), address before Kansas University in 1928, Univ. of Kansas, *Graduate Mag.,* XXVI, 8-9.

282. A questionnaire investigation covering the period 1923-26 showed that the most frequent form of amusement mentioned by children and young people of all ages was the newspaper, especially the comic section. Next in order, among eighteen-year-old boys, stood automobiling, moving pictures, and "watching sports," Chase, "Play," 341.

283. H. E. Stearns, ed., *Civilization in the United States, an Inquiry by Thirty Americans* (New York, 1922).

284. See "The Mind of a Nation," 1055.

285. Agnes Repplier, "On a Certain Condescension in Americans," *Atlantic Mo.,* CXXXVII (1926), 577-84, is perhaps the best account of American assertions of superiority as regards Europe, and Struthers Burt, "Furor Britannicus," *Sat. Eve. Post,* CC (August 20, 1927), 6ff, is a typical example of American resentment at similar European assertions of superiority to the United States.

286. The number of immigrants in the fiscal year 1914 was more than 1.2 million; in the following year only 326,700, and it remained low until the close of the war.

287. There were very few true Russians (Muscovites); most of the Russian-born were of non-Russian nationality, such as the Jews, Poles, and Lithuanians.

288. See this volume, Book VI, 517.

289. For newspaper comment, pro and con, on Dr. Flexner's statement, see *Literary Digest,* XCIX (October 13, 1928), 32.

290. R. DeC. Ward, "Our New Immigration Policy," *Foreign Affairs,* III (1924), 104. This article (99-111) is a good summary of the restrictionist argument.

291. *U.S. Statutes at Large,* XLII, pt. i, 540. On the quota laws, see R. L. Garis, *Immigration Restriction* (New York, 1927), chaps. vi-viii.

292. Garis, *Immigration Restriction,* chap. x; R. L. Buell, "Japanese Immigration," World Peace Found., *Pamphlets,* VIII (1924), nos. 5-6.

293. "Americanism, to the Klansman, is the thing of the spirit, a purpose and a point of view, that can only come through instinctive racial understanding . . . he believes also that few aliens can understand that spirit." Imperial Wizard H. W. Evans, "The Klan's Fight for Americanism," *North Am. Rev.,* CCXXIII (1926), 53.

294. "Fired by war talk from across the seas, and visualizing our own entry into the fray, at some later time, the idea of '100 percent Americanism' seized him. Nativism caught his fancy. Perhaps the German represented the arch-opponent to American nativism as he envisioned it, but all foreigners, more or less, must be foes." Robertson, *The Changing South,* 245.

295. Ibid., 250-51.

296. Frank Bohn, "The Ku Klux Klan Interpreted," *Am. Journ. of Sociology,* XXX, 385.

297. "The textbooks have been so perverted that Americanism is falsified, distorted and betrayed." Evans, "The Klan's Fight for Americanism," 58.

298. See J. M. Mecklin, *The Ku Klux Klan: A Study of the American Mind* (New York, 1924).

299. "The Negro is not a menace to Americanism in the sense that the Jew or the Roman Catholic is a menace. He is not actually hostile to it. He is simply racially incapable of understanding, sharing in or contributing to Americanism." Imperial Wizard H. W. Evans, *The Klan of Tomorrow* (pamphlet, n.p., 1924).

300. Note the debate between Charles C. Marshall and Alfred E. Smith on this subject, *Atlantic Mo.*, CXXXIX (1927), 540–49, 721–28.

301. From an anonymous pamphlet, *The Foreign Language Press, America's Greatest Menace* (n.p. 1923), 20.

302. Reported in the *Fellowship Forum*, June 2, 1928.

303. "By 1921 the Wizard [Colonel Simmons] resembled the hen which had hatched out a mixed brood of goslings and turkeys. . . . To go into a county of 25,000 inhabitants and organize a thousand healthy, sturdy, adventure-loving young men . . . to fire their hearts with the thought that their beloved country was in imminent danger of destruction; and then to expect them to be satiated by repeating the Klan ritual twice a month and waiting for election day, surely that was expecting to pluck figs from thistles." Bohn, "The Ku Klux Klan Interpreted," 397–98.

304. Robertson, *The Changing South*, 253.

305. W. G. Shepherd, "The Fiery Double Cross," *Collier's*, LXXXII (July 28, 1928), 8. His series of articles: "How I Put over the Klan" (an interview with Colonel Simmons), *Collier's* LXXXII, no. 2; "Ku Klux Koin," LXXXII, no. 3; and "The Fiery Double Cross," together tell the story of the change in ownership of the Klan mainly from the standpoint of the Simmons faction.

306. Norman Hapgood, "Henry Ford's Jew Mania," *Hearst's International*, XLII (1922), 39.

307. Bessie L. Pierce, *Public Opinion and the Teaching of History in the United States* (New York, 1926), chap. vii, contains the best account of the war on the textbooks.

308. A. M. Schlesinger, "Points of View in Historical Writing," *Publishers' Wkly.*, CXIII (1928), 147, lists the supporting organizations.

309. Pierce, *Public Opinion and the Teaching of History*, 312–16, gives the text of this report.

310. Including such important biographies as those by Albert J. Beveridge, N. W. Stephenson, William E. Barton, and Carl Sandburg. England, too, awoke to the American Civil War period, and as a result of this interest we had Lord Charnwood's interpretation of Lincoln, John Drinkwater's historical plays on Lincoln and Lee, and Sir Frederick Maurice's military studies of the war. Stephen Vincent Benet's *John Brown's Body*, an epic of the Civil War, attained popularity with both public and critics. It was awarded the Pulizer prize for American verse in 1929.

311. Samuel Crowther, "Henry Ford's Village of Yesterday," *Ladies' Home Journ.*, XLV, no. 9 (1928), 10. See also Henry A. Haigh, "Henry Ford's Typical Early American Village at Dearborn," *Mich. History Mag.*, XIII (1929), 506–43.

312. Bur. of Educ., *Bull.*, no. 21, 2.

313. Ibid., no. 33, 10.

314. Ibid., no. 31, gives statistics for private schools.

315. E. A. Ross, *What Is America?* (New York, 1919), 63.

316. *U.S. Daily*, May 5, 1928, 3.

317. Ibid., May 1, 1929.

318. *N.Y. Times*, December 8, 1928.

319. G. S. Counts, "Education," *Am. Journ. of Sociology*, XXXIV, 185. Thus the evidence from expenditure on schools agrees with the evidence from so many other indices of prosperity that the real economic advance of the American people was entirely an affair of the middle and later 1920s, the war and reconstruction period being one of inflated prices but not of enhanced prosperity, except for a few fortunate individuals or classes.

320. Bur. of Educ., *Bull.*, no. 13, 3.

321. B. P. Chass, "America's Poorly Paid School Teachers," *Current History*, XXIV (1926), 68.

322. Ibid., 69.

323. W. S. Deffenbaugh, "Recent Movements in City School Systems," Bur. of Educ., *Bull.,* no. 8, 11.

324. *N.Y. Times,* December 8, 1928.

325. In general, the highest salaries were in the great cities and on the Pacific Coast and the lowest in the cotton belt, but as this was true of wages and salaries generally it still left the teacher everywhere at a disadvantage by the standards of his own locality.

326. Bur. of Educ., *Bull,* no. 13, 12.

327. Ibid., no. 13, 3-4.

328. Ibid., no. 13, 2.

329. Ibid., no. 21.

330. See 981.

331. See this volume, Book XI, 981.

332. The General Education Board, a Rockefeller philanthropic enterprise, was offering financial aid to popularize the system.

333. There were other factors in the Tammany victory. Mayor Mitchel, though a Catholic, had made enemies by exposing the maladministration of some church charitable institutions which received public money; the Republican vote was split by an independent candidate, and the pacifists of all parties voted for Morris Hillquit, the Socialist, who polled an enormous vote, greater than that of any other Socialist candidate for any office in the history of the city. Hylan's second election was secured by his struggle with the private transportation companies on the five-cent-fare issue. Under Mayor Walker, Tammany continued to rule New York for the remainder of the period.

334. Deffenbaugh, "Recent Movements in City School Systems," 6.

335. Lynd and Lynd, *Middletown,* 194-95.

336. J. H. Butler, "Our Spendthrift Schools," *Current History,* XXVI (1927), 49.

337. Ibid., 51.

338. Lynd and Lynd, *Middletown,* 193. Only English, mathematics, history, and vocational courses exceeded Latin.

339. H. W. Holmes, "Chaos or Cosmos in American Education," *Atlantic Mo.,* CXL (1927), 493.

340. A. F. Macdonald, *Federal Aid* (New York, 1928), chap. vii.

341. *U.S. Daily,* January 24, 1929.

342. Counting all departments, there were 822,895 students enrolled (509,732 men and 313,163 women). Bur. of Educ., *Bull.,* no. 40, 1, 3.

343. One editor ventured the estimate that there would be no final halt until the ratio increased to one in five. *Boston Transcript,* January 12, 1927.

344. Bur. of Educ., *Bull.,* no. 40, 1.

345. Sometimes several institutions would join forces in a common publicity campaign, perhaps the most notable instance being the collective appeal by the presidents of the best-known women's colleges, Barnard, Bryn Mawr, Mount Holyoke, Radcliffe, Smith, Vassar, and Wellesley. "The Question of the Women's Colleges," *Atlantic Mo.,* CXL (1927), 577-84. For a criticism of incompetent financial management by the colleges, see W. B. Munro "Are Our Colleges Playing Poor?," *Atlantic Mo.,* CXLII (1928), 433-40, and also the rejoinder by W. A. Neilson, 'Women's Colleges Reply," *Atlantic Mo.,* CXLIII (1929), 111-15.

346. J. M. Cattell, "Academic Slavery," *School and Society,* VI (October 13, 1917), 421-26; T. B. Veblen, *The Higher Learning in America* (New York, 1918); J. E. Kirkpatrick, *The American College and its Rulers* (New York, 1926).

347. *School and Society,* XXIII (June 26, 1926), 810.

348. A detailed account of the honors work offered by more than a hundred American universities and colleges was prepared by President Frank Aydelotte of Swarthmore. "Honors Courses in American Colleges and Universities," Natl. Research Council, *Bull.,* X, no. 52, 1-96, supplementing his first *Bull.,* VII, no. 40.

349. Alexander Meiklejohn, *The Experimental College* (Univ. of Wis., *Bull.*, 1928), and *The First Year of the Experimental College* published by its "pioneer class" (Madison, 1928). See also R. M. Lovett, "Meiklejohn at Madison," *New Republic*, LV (July 11, 1928), 193–95.

350. *Atlantic Mo.*, CXXXIX (1927), 593–604.

351. M. J. Moses, "The Cost of College," *Good Housekeeping*, LXXXV, no. 5 (1927), 247–48, circularized 600 college presidents on Mr. Rubinow's contentions and summaraized their findings.

352. This conclusion was based on data collected from 763 colleges and universities. *U.S. Daily*, January 18, 1929.

353. D. A. Robertson, ed., *American Universities and Colleges* (New York, 1928), 865.

354. Ibid., 49.

355. E. E. Calkins, "Beauty and the Booster," *Atlantic Mo.*, CXLV (1930), 291.

356. *U.S. Daily*, April 11, 1929.

357. *N.Y. Times*, September 5, 1926.

358. C. H. Walker, "America's Titanic Strength Expressed in Architecture," *Current History*, XXI (1925), 555. See also T. E. Tallmadge, *The Story of Architecture in America* (New York, 1927), 288–89, for the effect on style of the New York and Chicago building codes.

359. Tallmadge, *Story of Architecture*, 290.

360. Ibid., 291.

361. S. P. Sherman, *Points of View* (New York, 1924), 191.

362. *N.Y. Times*, March 17, 1929.

363. "Let the reader as an exercise begin, say, with *Main Street* and *These United States*, and . . . count his way out to the newest collection of *Americana, The Great American Band-Wagon*, or such later contributions as may by this time have appeared. Let him by no means forget the historical and biographical works of the 'debunkers.' . . . we Americans have rolled up a literature of self-depreciation of absolutely staggering proportions." H. S. Harrison, "Last Days of the Devastators," *Yale Rev.*, XVIII (1928), 88–103.

364. *Harper's Mag.*, CLVII (1928), 395.

365. For one example from hundreds, see Struthers Burt, "These Standardized United States," *Sat. Eve. Post*, CCI (May 11, 1929), 10.

366. F. L. Bullard in the *N.Y. Times*, April 28, 1929.

367. Note his dialect studies on *The American Language* (New York, 1919; rev., 1921, 1923).

368. Similar organizations included the Literary Guild, the American Bookseller's Association, the Religous Book Club, the Book League of America, the Catholic Book Club, the Detective Story Club, the Poetry Clan, and the Freethought Book Club.

369. W. B. Pressey in the *New International Year Book for 1927*, 470. For attacks on the book-of-the-month clubs by publishers, see *Lit. Digest*, CI (June 1, 1929), 27.

370. Tables of annual production are given in *Publishers' Wkly.*, CXV (January 19, 1929), 275–78.

371. Ibid., CXV, 278.

372. E. W. Burgess, "Communication," *Am. Journ. of Sociology*, XXXIV, 125.

373. *Publishers' Wkly.*, LXXXV (February 7, 1914), 404–405.

374. J. C. Powys, "The Crime Wave in Fiction," *World's Work*, LVIII (1929), 66–69. From a brief examination of the most popular books of this sort, however, the conclusion arises that the taste for mystery tales is not a perverse taste for the morbid or even a romantic craving for excitement, but merely a liking for puzzles similar to that which created the crossword puzzle fad a few years earlier.

375. *Publishers' Wkly.*, CXV (January 19, 1929), 267–68. The 1927 fiction list started with Sinclair Lewis's *Elmer Gantry* and Booth Tarkington's *Plutocrat*, followed by two books by Warwick Deeping, while Will Durant's *Story of Philosophy*, the best of the myriad "outline-of-everything" books, led the nonfiction. In library demand

Theodore Dreiser's *An American Tragedy* held first place, though it did not do so well on the bookstands, *Publishers' Wkly.,* CXIII (January 21, 1928), 232-33.

376. See R. L. Hartt, "The Church in Politics," *World's Work,* L (1925), 299-304.

377. *Chicago Daily Tribune,* March 27, 1927.

378. *U.S. Daily,* September 28, 1928; *N.Y. Times,* same date. In what other country would the collection of religious data be done by the department of commerce?

379. John Richelsen, "What's Happening in Protestantism," *Scribner's Mo.,* LXXXIV (1928), 93, 95.

380. *Literary Digest,* XCIII (April 30, 1927), 28.

381. Homer Croy, "Atheism Beckons to Our Youth," *World's Work,* LIV (1927), 18-26.

382. Lynd and Lynd, *Middletown,* 321.

383. Ibid., 342.

384. Ibid., 399.

385. P. M. Mazur, *American Prosperity* (New York, 1928), 267.

Index

Ballou, Hosea, 443
Baltimore, Md., 261, 413, 443, 491, 493, 497,
    499, 500, 529, 530, 537, 585, 642, 643,
    654, 774, 808, 907
  British occupation of, 360
  labor riot in, 826
  population of, 299, 424, 894–95
  slum reform in, 1006
Bancroft, Elizabeth, 11
Bancroft, George, 489, 493, 573, 587, 670
Bancroft, H. H., 790
banking, 366, 451–52, 456, 608, 613
  national system of, 735
Bank of North America, 366
Banks, N. P., 694
Bannon, John Francis, 1166
Baptists, 311, 313, 315, 318, 370, 388, 390,
    393, 404, 445, 459–60, 571, 605, 672,
    677, 958, 961, 1029, 1161
Barber, Jedediah, 457
Barbour, Philip, 473
Bard, John, 306
Bard, Samuel, 477
Barlow, Joel, 423
Barnard, Charles, 946
Barnard, Henry, 928
Barnes, Anthony, 147
Barnes, Elmer, 1192
Barnes, Harry Elmer, 15, 17, 19
Barnes, Mary, 150
Barnum, P. T., 556, 614, 781, 947
Barnum, William H., 804
Barras, Charles M., 948
Barriers Burned Away (Roe), 785
Barrow, James, 168–69
Barry, Jack, 1045
Barry, John, 362
barter system, 457–58
Barton, Benjamin Smith, 475
Barton, Bruce, 1158
Barton, Clara, 806
Barton, Mary, 83
baseball, 502, 557, 660, 1125
  popularity of, 952–53
  professionalization of, 778–80, 1044–
    1045
basketball, 951, 1128
Bassit, Goody, 150

Bates, Benjamin, 122
Bates, Thomas, 168
bathing, recreational, 662–63
"Battle Hymn of the Republic" (Howe), 711,
    924
"Battle of Bunker's Hill" (Trumbull), 400
Baxter, Richard, 324, 490
Beach, Alfred, 745
Beach, Rex, 1040
Beadle, Erastus F., 669, 787
Beadle, Irwin P., 669
Beadle's Dime Song Book, 711
Beal, Hannah, 162
Beal, Jeremiah, 119
Beal, John, 121, 161
Beal, Joshua, 122
Beard, Charles A., 11, 18, 19, 20, 24, 892,
    1188, 1192, 1198, 1199
Beard, Dan C., 1019
Beard, George M., 940
beard vogue, 647–48, 773
Beaumont, William, 482
Beaux Stratagem, The, 277
Beccaria (criminologist), 383
Beck, Charles, 503
Becker, Carl, 12, 14, 15, 17, 20, 25, 1176
Beecher, Charles, 677
Beecher, Henry Ward, 566, 631, 669, 673,
    678, 783, 786, 787, 788, 804, 816, 1159
Beecher, Lyman, 463
Beefsteak Club, 270, 271
Belasco, David, 945, 946
Belknap, Jeremy, 319, 399, 493
Bell, Alexander Graham, 744, 745, 1003
Bell, C. A., 948
Bellamy, Edward, 976
Bellingham, Richard, 123
Bellini, Charles, 374, 395
Bellomont, Earl of, 213
Belmont, August, 777
Benavides, Alonso de, 36
Bender, Charles, 1045
Bender, Thomas, 23
Benezet, Anthony, 291, 313, 318, 384
Benjamin, Asher, 485
Benjamin, Judah P., 726
Bennet, Richard, 255
Bennett, Arnold, 1158